An International Approach to the Interpretation of the United Nations Convention on Contracts for the International Sale of Goods (1980) as Uniform Sales Law

In 1980, the United Nations Convention for the International Sale of Goods (CISG) came into being as an attempt to create a uniform commercial sales law. This book compares two major restatements – the UNIDROIT Principles and the Principles of European Contract Law (PECL) – with CISG articles. In this work scholars and legal practitioners from twenty countries contribute analysis on the various issues covered in the articles of the CISG, comparing them with how each issue is treated in the UNIDROIT and PECL restatements. The introductory section of the book addresses theoretical and practical issues of the appropriate interpretive methodology as mandated in CISG Article 7, and it is followed by individual analyses of the Convention's provisions.

John Felemegas is a Senior Lecturer in Law at the Faculty of Law, University of Technology, Sydney, where he teaches International Sale of Goods and Equity & Trusts. He also conducts legal research and writing as Fellow of the Institute of International Commercial Law, Pace University School of Law in New York. His main research interest is the interpretation of the CISG, and he has published his work in the Review of the Convention on Contracts for the *International Sale of Goods*, the *Pace International Law Review*, and the *Vindobona Journal of International Commercial Law and Arbitration*.

An International Approach to the Interpretation of the United Nations Convention on Contracts for the International Sale of Goods (1980) as Uniform Sales Law

Edited by

JOHN FELEMEGAS

B.A., LL.B., LL.M., Ph.D

Senior Lecturer in Law

University of Technology, Sydney

This work was produced under the auspices of the Pace Institute of International Commercial Law

CAMBRIDGE
UNIVERSITY PRESS

CAMBRIDGE UNIVERSITY PRESS
Cambridge, New York, Melbourne, Madrid, Cape Town, Singapore, São Paulo

Cambridge University Press
32 Avenue of the Americas, New York, NY 10013-2473, USA

www.cambridge.org
Information on this title: www.cambridge.org/9780521868723

First published 2007

Printed in the United States of America

A catalog record for this publication is available from the British Library.

Library of Congress Cataloging in Publication Data

Interpretation of the United Nations Convention on Contracts for the International
Sale of Goods (1980) as Uniform Sales Law / edited by John Felemegas.
p. cm.
Includes bibliographical references and index.
ISBN-13 978-0-521-86872-3 (hardback)
ISBN-10 0-521-86872-6 (hardback)
1. United Nations Convention on Contracts for the International
Sale of Goods (1980) 2. Export sales contracts. I. Felemegas, John, 1970–
K1028.3198.159 2006
343′.0878–dc22 2006008749

ISBN 978-0-521-86872-3 hardback

Contents

Foreword

Eric E. Bergsten
Professor of Law, Emeritus, Pace University;
Secretary, United Nations Commission on International Trade Law, Retired.

"Over recent years, discussion has intensified on possible harmonization of substantive private law, in particular contract law."[1]

The dream of unifying, or harmonizing, the law is an old one. For some, especially in Europe, it is a dream of a return to the golden age of a *jus commun*. For others a unified law is an important symbol of a unified nation.[2] A more immediately pragmatic dream is that the unification of commercial law will reduce the cost of transborder transactions and thereby increase international trade. Although pragmatic, such a dream is still idealistic. As stated in the Preamble to the United Nations Convention on Contracts for the International Sale of Goods (CISG),

> The States Parties to this Convention,
> * * *
> Considering that the development of international trade on the basis of equality and mutual benefit is an important element in promoting friendly relations among States, ...

The quotation that opens this foreword is from a Communication of the European Commission and was meant to apply primarily to developments in the European Union. However, it applies equally well to developments with a universal application and particularly to the CISG. To date 67 States that conduct more than two-thirds of international trade have made the CISG positive law by becoming party to it. The CISG is directly applicable to international sales of goods in those States, unless the parties to the contract exclude its application. The Convention must be considered to be a major success in the efforts to unify an important aspect of contract law. There is, however, a significant concern. Will the courts interpret the CISG in a consistent way? Will the unification of text be undermined by a dis-unification of interpretation?

The drafters of the CISG were acutely aware of the problem. They provided in Article 7(1) that

> In the interpretation of this Convention, regard is to be had to its international character and to the need to promote uniformity in its application and the observance of good faith in international trade.

Upon adoption of the CISG by a State, Article 7 becomes part of the law of that State and constitutes a direction to the courts as to how to interpret the Convention. Nevertheless, it is understandable that the judges, trained in the law of their own domestic legal system, will have a home-State bias when faced with the need to interpret and apply the

[1] Communication from the Commission to the Council and the European Parliament on European Contract Law, para. 1, COM(2001) 398 Final, 11 July 2001.

[2] The examples of the Civil Code in France and the BGB in Germany come quickly to mind. A unified/harmonized substantive private law in Europe would have the same effect for a broader geographical area.

Convention. Furthermore, to promote uniformity in its application the judge must know how the Convention has been interpreted in the other States that have adopted it. That is not easy for obvious reasons. UNCITRAL itself has undertaken to make the interpretations of the CISG by the courts available through its CLOUT abstracts (Case Law On Uncitral Texts) and through its recently published UNCITRAL Digest of Case Law on the United Nations Convention on the International Sale of Goods.[3] A further major resource is the CISG Web site maintained at Pace Law School with its unsurpassed collection of court decisions and bibliography of books and articles on the CISG.[4] Not to be forgotten are the other Web sites that collect and publish decisions in non-English languages.[5]

Although these resources are of immense importance to help satisfy "the need to promote uniformity in its application," they do not necessarily help the interpreter "regard... its international character." The international character of the CISG calls for the interpreter to go beyond the need for uniformity in its application. It calls for an appreciation of the differences between the appropriate legal solutions to the problems arising in domestic sales of goods and international sales of goods. But where is the interpreter to look for help in fulfilling the obligation? One potential source is this book, which compares the CISG and two recently adopted texts on international contract law. One is the UNIDROIT Principles of International Contract Law. The other is the Principles of European Contract Law.

To understand the significance of these two texts for their potential help in interpreting the CISG, it is necessary to be aware that they have taken entirely different approaches to the unification/harmonization of international contract law. The UNIDROIT Principles of International Commercial Contracts are an "international restatement of general principles of contract law."[6] It should be noted that, like the CISG, the UNIDROIT Principles are restricted to commercial contracts. According to the Introduction to the Principles, "[n]aturally, to the extent that the UNIDROIT Principles address issues also covered by CISG, they follow the solutions found in that Convention, with such adaptations as were considered appropriate to reflect the particular nature and scope of the Principles."[7] The UNIDROIT Principles are, therefore, in many respects a further development of the CISG itself. It is clear that when the Preamble provides that "[t]hey may be used to interpret or supplement international uniform law instruments," it is primarily the CISG that was considered.[8] Although they have no binding force unless the parties themselves refer to them in their contract, they have taken on something of a positive law nature by the number of courts and arbitral tribunals that have cited them.[9]

The Principles of European Contract Law have an entirely different purpose. "The main purpose of the Principles is to serve as a first draft of a European Civil Code,"[10] although it was also hoped that they would be referred to by arbitrators. It is certainly far from clear whether there will ever be a European Civil Code, but the Principles have

[3] Both the CLOUT abstracts and the Digest are available on the UNCITRAL Web site, http://www.uncitral.org

[4] http://cisgw3.law.pace.edu

[5] Links to these Web sites are to be found on the Pace Web site.

[6] Introduction, UNIDROIT Principles of International Commercial Contracts (1994). Reference to the UNIDROIT Principles throughout this book are to the 1994 edition. In 2004 UNIDROIT published a new edition of the Principles. The primary change was an addition of six chapters to the earlier text. Chapter 2 of the 1994 text was re-numbered and there were a few minor changes to the provisions.

[7] *Ibid.*

[8] *See* comment 6 to the Preamble.

[9] The cases can be found at http://www.unilex.info/

[10] Lando, "Principles of European Contract Law in the Third Millennium" in *Transnational Law in Commercial Legal Practice* (Center for Transnational Law (ed.) 1998), p. 76.

indeed served as the starting point for preliminary work in that direction.[11] This means that the European Principles do not purport to have universal significance. Nevertheless, because the European Union comprises States with both civil law and common law legal systems, the solutions found at a pan-European level for common contract problems would also have suggestive value for interpretation of the CISG. However, two caveats must be kept in mind. First, a European Civil Code, and therefore the Principles, would apply to consumer contracts, as well as to commercial contracts. Because consumer contracts raise certain policy concerns not present in commercial contracts, the Principles must always be scrutinized carefully to see whether those concerns have affected the particular provision being considered. Second, the European Principles stand somewhere between being a self-sufficient set of contract principles for current application and a first draft of a European Civil Code. Being a first draft means that there will be changes. Indeed, the preliminary work on a European Civil Code has already produced drafts that differ in some respects from the Principles.

The authors of the various chapters in this book comprise an outstanding list of scholars from all over the world. Many are leading authorities in their countries. Others are younger entrants into international legal scholarship. The fact that this is a collaborative effort by so many authors with widely varying legal backgrounds and experience leads to the natural fear that their contributions will suffer from an inconsistency of approach. It is to the credit of the editor and the authors that this fear is not realized. The quality of the work is consistently very high. There is little doubt that this is a book that will occupy a proud place in the growing library on the CISG. More importantly, this is a work that will serve to help lawyers, judges, and other scholars approach the interpretation of the CISG with a more international outlook than they might otherwise have had.

[11] The current developments in the Study Group on a European Civil Code are available at http://www.sgecc.net/. See also the European Commission Web site, http://europa.eu.int/comm/consumers

Contributors

Orkun Akseli has an LL.B., Dokuz Eylul University School of Law Turkey; LL.M., University of Georgia School of Law, USA; M.A., Istanbul Bilgi University School of Law, Turkey; Ph.D., University of Manchester School of Law and is an attorney-at-law and member of the Izmir and Turkish Bar Associations and a Lecturer in Law, University of Newcastle, England.

Jorge Oviedo Albán, a Lawyer (J.D.), Javeriana University (Bogotá D.C. – Colombia), is a specialist in Commercial Law at Javeriana University and a Professor of Contracts and Commercial Law at La Sabana University (Bogotá D.C. – Colombia). Professor Oviedo Albán has lectured in Colombian and other international universities and is author of publications on International Commercial Law in Argentina, Spain, Colombia, Peru, Mexico, and the United States.

Camilla Baasch Andersen is a lecturer at University of Leicester, visiting lecturer at University of London at SOAS and Queen Mary's Centre for Commercial Law Studies, Fellow of the Institute of Commercial Law at Pace University School of Law, and assistant editor of the database at CISGW3.

Dr. Friedrich Blasé is Rechtsanwalt and Counsel at MPK – Michaelis Pfeifer König Rechtsanwälte, Frankfurt, Germany.

Bojidara Borisova received her law degree from Sofia University "St.Kl.Ohridsky," Bulgaria, and is currently a Ph.D. candidate at the same university, working on her research project on international investment law, more particularly the right of protection of foreign investments in cases of expropriation. Since July 2003 she has been working as a part-time legal advisor at the Bulgarian Investment Agency.

Allison E. Butler received her J.D. from Loyola University School of Law, New Orleans, Louisiana, USA (Common Law Program) and her B.A. in International Relations, with honors, from the University of South Florida, Tampa, Florida, USA. She is a published author and a private practitioner in Martin County, Florida, USA.

Anja Carlsen is an attorney-at-law in Denmark.

Avv. Cecilia Carrara is a Research Fellow at the CERADI – Luiss Guido Carli University in Rome and an Italian attorney, and is counsel to the law firm Macchi Cellere Gangemi.

Andrea L. Charters is an Adjunct Professor at the Washington University School of Law, St. Louis, Missouri, USA, with a J.D. from Harvard Law School, an M.S.W. from Washington University, and an A.B. from Yale University.

Predrag N. Cvetkovic is on the Faculty of Law, Department for Trade Law at the University of Nis, Serbia. He received his LL.B. and LL.M. from the University of Nis [Dissertation title: Formation of Contracts for the International Sale of Goods]. His Ph.D. dissertation is on International Protection of Foreign Investments.

Sieg Eiselen is a Professor of Private Law on the Faculty of Law at the University of South Africa and an Advocate of the High Court of South Africa.

Hossam El-Saghir is a Professor of Law on the Faculty of Law, Menoufia University, Egypt.

John Felemegas has a Doctorate in Law, is a Fellow at the Pace Law School Institute of International Commercial Law, and is a Senior Lecturer on the Faculty of Law at the University of Technology, Sydney.

Dionysios P. Flambouras, LL.B. (Athens), LL.M. (Bristol), M. Stud. (Oxon), and Advocate of the Athens Bar, is a Solicitor in England and Wales.

Alejandro M. Garro is a Professor of Law at the Parker School of Foreign and Comparative Law, Columbia Law School, New York.

René Franz Henschel is an Assistant Professor (Law of Obligations) at the Aarhus School of Business. He expresses his sincere thanks to Associate Professor Hans Henrik Edlund, Aarhus School of Business, for reviewing an earlier version of his chapter.

Philipp Höttler, LL.M. (Queensland), is a Ph.D. candidate at the University of Cologne, Germany.

Christopher Kee is an Associate Lecturer in Law at Deakin University and a Partner with Keelins, Melbourne Australia (ckee@keelins.com).

Bertram Keller studied law and philosophy in Heidelberg, Cambridge (UK), Paris, and Vienna and is now writing a Ph.D. thesis on the theoretical foundations of contract law at Munich University.

Robert Koch is a Professor in Commercial Law, Corporate Law, and International Trade Law, Institute of Business Law at Nürtingen University (Germany).

Joachim A. Kuckenburg, FCIArb, is a German attorney in the Paris law firm De Busschère Kuckenburg.

Chengwei Liu, is LL.M. from Renmin University of China and Attorney-at-Law at Global Law Office, Beijing.

Ulrich Magnus is a Professor of Law at the University of Hamburg and Judge on the Court of Appeal of Hamburg.

Francesco G. Mazzotta is Dottore in Giurisprudenza, University of Naples "Federico II" (Italy), 1993; has his LL.M. in International and Comparative Law, University of Pittsburgh School of Law (USA), 2000; and is an Associate of the Institute of International Commercial Law of the Pace University School of Law.

Florian Mohs Dr. iur. (University of Basel); LL.M. (Victoria University of Wellington) and Postdoctoral researcher at the University of Basel, Switzerland.

Chantal Niggemann is Legal Counsel at Techem Energy Services GmbH&KG, Frankfurt and Main, Germany.

Elisabeth Opie, B.A., LL.B. (Hons), LL.M., GAICD, Senior Legal Counsel, Commonwealth Scientific and Industrial Research Organisation (Australia).

Joseph M. Perillo is Alpin J. Cameron Professor of Law, Fordham University School of Law, New York.

Jumpita Ruangvichathorn has a Doctorate in Law; is a lawyer for the Electricity Generating Authority of Thailand (EGAT); and is an Adjunct Law Lecturer, Faculty of Law, Thammasat University, Thailand.

Friederike Schäfer is a Research Assistant at the European Legal Studies Institute, University of Osnabrück, Germany.

Ulrich G. Schroeter has a Dr. iur. (Freie Universität Berlin) and is Assistant Professor at the Institute for Foreign and International Private Law, University of Freiburg (Germany).

Stephen E. Smith, Esquire, is a Senior Lecturer at Northwestern University School of Law (Chicago, Ill., USA) and the faculty advisor for their Willem C. Vis International Commercial Arbitration Moot team. Mr. Smith thanks David Tahan and Peng Zhao for their research assistance and Jennifer A. Woyan for her patient revisions and useful suggestions as to the format for his chapter.

Maja Stanivukovic is Professor of Private International Law, Novi Sad Faculty of Law, Serbia.

Jarno J. Vanto has a Master of Laws degree from the University of Turku, Finland, and an LL.M. degree from the New York University School of Law, USA. He is an attorney at the law firm of Covington & Burling, Brussels.

Dr. Andrea Vincze is a Fellow of the Institute of International Commercial Law of the Pace University School of Law and Assistant Professor at University of Miskolc Law School, Hungary. His main areas of research are International Trade Law, International Commercial Arbitration, ICSID Arbitration, and Conflict of Laws.

Pilar Perales Viscasillas has a Doctorate in Law, is a Professor of Commercial Law, University Carlos III of Madrid, and is a Spanish representative at UNCITRAL.

Colin Ying is an Associate Professor on the Faculty of Law at the University of Technology, Sydney. He has a B.A. (Manit.) and an LL.M. (London), and is a Barrister at Law of Lincoln's Inn and the Supreme Court of New South Wales.

Jonathan Yovel has his S.J.D. (1997, Northwestern University, Chicago, Ill., USA); LL.M. with honors (1995, Northwestern University, Chicago Ill., USA); and LL.B., and B.A. (Philosophy) magna cum laude (Tel-Aviv, 1992). He is a Senior Lecturer in Law and Jurisprudence on the Faculty of Law, University of Haifa, Israel.

Bruno Zeller has a Doctorate in Law; is Senior Lecturer in Law, Victoria University Law School, Melbourne, Australia; and is Adjunct Professor of Law, Murdoch University, Perth.

Introduction

John Felemegas

I. UNIFORM LAW FOR THE INTERNATIONAL SALE OF GOODS

International trade historically has been subject to numerous domestic legal systems, mainly by virtue of the rules of private international law. The disputes arising out of international sales contracts have been settled at times according to the *lex loci contractus*, or the *lex loci solutionis*, or the *lex fori*. This diversity of the various legal systems applied has hindered the evolution of a strong, distinct, and uniform modern *lex mercatoria*. Such legal diversity creates legal uncertainty and imposes additional transactional costs on the contracting parties.

The idea of a unified international trade law represents the revival of an ancient[1] trend toward unification that can be traced to the Middle Ages and that had given rise to

[1] *See* Ronald Harry Graveson, "The International Unification of Law," 16 *Am. J. Comp. L.* 4 (1968), where the author states "the international process of assimilating the diverse legal systems of various countries goes back into ancient history." The need for uniform laws has been widely acknowledged; *see* e.g., René David, "The International Unification of Private Law," in 2 *International Encyclopedia of Comparative Law* (Mogr, Tübingen 1971) [hereinafter David, *Unification of Private Law*] Ch. 5; *see* also John O. Honnold, *Uniform Law for International Sales under the United Nations Convention* 1–8 (2nd ed. 1991) [hereinafter Honnold, *Uniform Law for Int'l Sales*]. However, there has also been some criticism of this trend; *see* Graveson (1968),

the "law merchant."[2] Historically, international trade law has developed in three stages[3]: the old "law merchant,"[4] its integration into municipal[5] systems of law, and finally, the emergence of the new "law merchant."[6]

op. cit., at 5–6, stating that "it may be necessary to correct the assumption that uniform law is good in itself and that the process of unification is one to be encouraged in principle."

[2] Filip de Ly, *International Business Law and Lex Mercatoria* 15 (1992), notes that "the medieval law merchant is also referred to as *lex mercatoria, ius mercatorum, ius mercatorium, ius mercati, ius fori, ius forense, ius negotiatorum, ius negotiale, stilus mercatorum* or *ius nundinarum*."

[3] On the history of the law merchant, *see* Theodore F. T. Plucknett, *A Concise History of the Common Law* 657 (5th ed. 1956); Wyndham Anstis Bewes, *The Romance of the Law Merchant* 12–13 (1986); René A.Wormser, *The Law* 500 (1949); Harold J. Berman & Colin Kaufmann, "The Law of International Commercial Transactions (*Lex mercatoria*)," 19 *Harv. Int'l. L.J.* 221. 225 (1978); Rudolph B. Schlesinger, *Comparative Law* 185 (Found. Press 2nd ed. 1960).

[4] In the Middle Ages, commercial law appeared in the form of the "law merchant" – "a body of truly international customary rules governing the cosmopolitan community of international merchants who traveled through the civilized world, from port to port and fair to fair." Clive M. Schmitthoff, "The Unification of the Law of International Trade," *J. Bus. L.* 105 (1968). *See* also Tuula Ammala, "The International *Lex mercatoria*," in *Juhlajulkaisu Juha Tolenen: Oikeustieteen rajoja etsimässä, Kirjapaino Grafia: Turku* 295–311 (2001) [What is the *Lex mercatoria*; Choice of law; Customary law; The UNIDROIT Principles, Principles of European Contract Law, The *lex mercatoria* in arbitration]; Filip De Ly, De *Lex mercatoria*. Inleiding op de studie van het transnationaal handelsrecht [The *lex mercatoria*. Introduction to the study of transnational trade law – *in Dutch*] (1989) (Thesis, Ghent) (Antwerpen/Apeldoorn: Maklu, 1989). The discussion of the existence and precise role of a *lex mercatoria* has not reached consensus. Regarding the debate as to the very existence of a *lex mercatoria, see* Thomas E. Carbonneau, "A Definition and Perspective on the *Lex mercatoria* Debate," in *Lex mercatoria and Arbitration: A Discussion of the New Law Merchant* 11–21 (Thomas Carbonneau ed., The Hague, 1998). The skeptics' point of view is perhaps best encapsulated in the statements of M. J. Mustill and S. Boyd, *The Law and Practice of Commercial Arbitration in England* (Butterworths 2nd ed. 1989) at p. 81 where the authors write, "Indeed we doubt whether a *lex mercatoria* even exists, in the sense of an international commercial law divorced from any State law: or, at least, that it exists in any sense useful for the solving of commercial disputes."

For a similar approach, *see* Georges R. Delaume, "Comparative Analysis as a Basis of Law in State Contracts: The Myth of the *Lex mercatoria,*" 575 *Tulane Law Review* (1989). *See* also some more recent articles seeking to debunk the "myth" of a universal *lex mercatoria*: Emmanuel Gaillard, "Transnational Law: A Legal System or a Method of Decision-Making?," in *The Practice of Transnational Law* 53–65 (Klaus Peter Berger ed., Kluwer Law International, 2001) [The Renewed Debate on *Lex mercatoria* (Is *Lex mercatoria* Defined by its Content or by its Sources?, Is *Lex mercatoria* a List or a Method?), The Issue of *Lex mercatoria* as a Distinct Legal System Revisited (Completeness, Structured Character, Evolving Character, Predictability)]; Albrecht Cordes, "Auf der Suche nach der Rechtswirklichkeit der mittelalterlichen *Lex mercatoria*" [In search of the legal reality of the medieval *lex mercatoria – in German*], Zeitschrift der Savigny-Stiftung für Rechtsgeschichte 168 (2001); Albrecht Cordes, "The Search for a Medieval *Lex mercatoria,*" *Oxford University Comparative Law Forum* 5 (2003), also at <http://ouclf.iuscomp.org/articles/cordes.shtml>; Albrecht Cordes, " À la recherche d'une *Lex mercatoria* au Moyen Âge" [An inquiry into the *lex mercatoria* of the Middle Ages – *in French*], in Stadt und Recht im Mittelalter / La ville et le droit au Moyen Âge 118 (Monnet / Oexle eds., Göttingen 2003); Felix Dasser, *Lex mercatoria*: Werkzeug der Praktiker oder Spielzeug der Lehre? [*Lex mercatoria*: Practitioner's tool or theoretical game – *in German*], Schweizerische Zeitschrift für internationales und europäisches Recht 299 (1991); Georges R. Delaume, "The Myth of the *Lex mercatoria* and State Contracts," in *Lex mercatoria and Arbitration* 11 (Thomas Carbonneau ed., The Hague 2nd ed. 1998).

[5] The second stage of the development of international trade law is marked by the incorporation of the "law merchant" into municipal systems of law in the eighteenth and nineteenth centuries, as the idea of national sovereignty acquired prominence. It is interesting to note, however, that this process of incorporation differed in motives and methods of implementation. *See Clive M. Schmitthoff's Select Essays on International Trade Law* 25–26 (Chia-Jui Cheng ed., 1988) [hereinafter: *Schmitthoff's Select Essays*].

On the effect of the enactment of the first codes in Europe, *see* René David & John E. C. Brierley, *Major Legal Systems in the World Today* 66 (3rd ed. 1985), where the authors state that "codes were treated, not as new expositions of the 'common law of Europe' but as mere generalisations... of 'particular customs' raised to a national level... [T]hey were regarded as instruments of a 'nationalisation of law.'" Since the beginning of the twentieth century efforts had been made to overcome the nationality of commercial law, which originated from the emergence of national States in Europe and from the enactment of the first codes. *See* Rudolf B. Schlesinger et al., *Comparative Law* 31 (Found. Press 5th ed. 1987).

[6] *See* Clive M. Schmitthoff, "International Business Law: A New Law Merchant," *in* 2 *Current Law and Social Problems* 129 (1961). The third stage of the evolution is characterized by the increased involvement

The 1980 United Nations Convention on Contracts for the International Sale of Goods (CISG)[7] represents the most recent attempt to unify or harmonize international sales law. The Convention creates a uniform law for the international sale of goods.[8]

of the United Nations and the activities of specialized international organizations (such as UNCITRAL, UNIDROIT, and the International Chamber of Commerce), which signal a return to a universal concept of trade law that characterized the old "law merchant." The new general trend of commercial law is to move away from the restrictions of national law and toward the creation of an autonomous body of "international conception of commercial law which represents a common platform for the jurists of the East and West . . . [thus] facilitating co-operation between capitalist and socialist countries" (*Schmitthoff's Select Essays*, *supra* note 5, at 28). This development has been welcomed and hailed as "the emergence of a new *lex mercatoria* . . . a law of universal character that, though applied by authority of the national sovereign, attempts to shed the national peculiarities of municipal laws" (*Schmitthoff's Select Essays*, *supra* note v, at 22).

At the end of the 1920s, Ernst Rabel suggested to the Governing Council of the International Institute for the Unification of Private Law (UNIDROIT) that it start the work necessary for the unification of the law of international sales of goods. Ernst Rabel's involvement in the effort has been widely acknowledged: *see* Michael Joachim Bonell, "Introduction to the Convention," in *Commentary on the International Sales Law: The 1980 Vienna Convention* 3 (Cesare Massimo Bianca & Michael Joachim Bonell eds., Giuffrè, Milan 1987) [hereinafter Bonell, *Introduction*]. It has to be noted, however, that although the old "law merchant" had developed from usage and practice, the new "law merchant" is the result of careful and, at times, political deliberations and compromises by large international organizations and diplomats. The repercussions of such action are not always benign.

For conflicting views as to the existence of the new *lex mercatoria* and its essence *see* Klaus Peter Berger, "The CENTRAL-List of Principles, Rules and Standards of the *Lex mercatoria*: Developed and Maintained by the Center for Transnational Law (CENTRAL) Münster, Germany," in *Transnational Law in Commercial Legal Practice* 121–164 (Münster: Quadis, 1999).

Cf. Michael J. Mustill, "The New *Lex mercatoria*: The First Twenty-five Years," 4 *Arbitration International* 86–119 (1988). *See* also Lisa E. Bernstein, "The Questionable Empirical Basis of Article 2's Incorporation Strategy: A Preliminary Study," 66 *U. Chi. L. Rev.* 710–780 (1999), Berkeley Olin Program in Law & Economics, Working Paper Series, Paper 26 (January 20, 1999) <http://repositories.cdlib.org/blewp/26>, with the following lead sentence: "The UCC, the CISG and the modern *Lex mercatoria* are based on the premise that unwritten customs and usages of trade exist and that in commercial disputes they can, and should, be discovered and applied by courts." The author proceeds to offer commentary on the "incorporation principle" expressed in UCC sections dealing with course of dealing, usage of trade, and course of performance, in which she concludes that, although some industry-wide usages of trade do exist, the pervasive existence of usages of trade and commercial standards is a legal fiction rather than a merchant reality.

7 United Nations Conference on Contracts for the International Sale of Goods, *Official Records*, U.N. Document No. A/CONF. 97/19 (E.81.IV.3) (1980). The popular acronym of the Convention is CISG. The Convention entered into force on January 1, 1988.

8 Adopted by a diplomatic conference on April 11, 1980, the Convention establishes a comprehensive code of legal rules governing the formation of contracts for the international sale of goods, the obligations of the buyer and seller, remedies for breach of contract, and other aspects of the contract. The uniform rules in existence prior to the CISG were provided in the 1964 Hague Conventions, sponsored by the International Institute for the Unification of Private Law (UNIDROIT): one Convention dealing with formation of contracts for international sale (ULF) and the other one with obligations of parties to such contracts (ULIS). The CISG combines the subject matter of the two 1964 Hague Conventions that had failed to receive substantial acceptance outside Western Europe and had received widespread criticism as reflecting primarily the legal traditions and economic realities of continental Western Europe, the region that had most actively contributed to their preparation. *See* John Honnold, *Documentary History of the Uniform Law for International Sales* 5–6 (1989) [hereinafter: Honnold, *Documentary History*].

For commentary on the CISG's membership of the new *"lex mercatoria," see* Bernard Audit, "The Vienna Sales Convention and the *Lex mercatoria,*" in 173–194 *Lex Mercatoria and Arbitration* (Thomas E. Carbonneau ed., rev. ed.) [reprint of a chapter of the 1990 edition of this text], (Juris Publishing, 1998), at 175 [hereinafter Audit, *Lex Mercatoria*], also available online at <http://cisgw3.law.pace.edu/cisg/biblio/audit.html>:

> The Convention's self-effacing character is one of its most striking features. Article 6 allows parties to stipulate out of the Convention or any of its provisions; article 9 gives superior weight to trade usages, regardless of whether the parties specifically designated an applicable law. These two provisions, perhaps the Convention's most significant, clearly demonstrate that the Convention does not compete with the *lex mercatoria*, but rather that the two bodies of law are complementary. Moreover, the Convention itself can be regarded as the expression of international mercantile customs.

This is clearly stated in the Preamble[9] that introduces the Articles of the Convention:

> THE STATES PARTIES TO THIS CONVENTION,
>
> BEARING IN MIND the broad objectives in the resolutions adopted by the sixth special session of the General Assembly of the United Nations on the establishment of a New International Economic Order,
>
> CONSIDERING that the development of international trade on the basis of equality and mutual benefit is an important element in promoting friendly relations among States,
>
> BEING OF THE OPINION that the adoption of uniform rules which govern contracts for the international sale of goods and take into account the different social, economic and legal systems would contribute to the removal of legal barriers in international trade and promote the development of international trade,
>
> HAVE DECREED as follows . . .

The Preamble to the CISG introduces the legal text that binds the signatory States of the Convention.[10] Thus, the CISG attempts to unify the law governing international commerce, seeking to substitute one sales law for the many and diverse national legal systems that exist in the field of sales.

The benefits of a uniform law for the international sale of goods are indeed many and substantial, and not merely of a pecuniary nature.[11] A uniform law would provide parties with greater certainty as to their potential rights and obligations. This is to be compared with the results brought about by the amorphous principles of private international law and the possible application of an unfamiliar system of foreign domestic law.[12]

Another advantage of a uniform law of international sales of goods is that it would serve to simplify international sales transactions and thus, as envisaged in the Preamble,

[9] The Preamble was drafted at the 1980 Conference, and it was adopted without significant debate. *See Report of the Drafting Committee*, U.N. Doc. A/CONF.97/17, reprinted in U.N. Conference on Contracts for the International Sale of Goods, *Official Records* 154 (1981); *Summary Records of the 10th Plenary Meeting*, U.N. Doc. A/CONF.97/SR.10, paras. 4–10, reprinted in U.N. *Official Records*, at 219–220.

For commentary on the CISG Preamble, *see* editorial comments by Albert H. Kritzer available at <http://cisgw3.law.pace.edu/cisg/text/cross/crosspreamble.html>.

[10] The United Nations Treaty Section <http://untreaty.un.org/English/treaty.asp> reports that sixty-seven States have adopted the Convention (December 2005). *See* also the UNCITRAL Web site, which also offers information about the status of the Convention, at <http://www.uncitral.org/uncitral/en/uncitral_texts.html>.

[11] Lord Justice Kennedy wrote extrajudicially in "The Unification of Law," 10 *J. Soc'y Comp. Legis.* 214–215 (1909):

> The certainty of enormous gain to civilised mankind from the unification of law needs no exposition. Conceive the security and the peace of mind of the ship-owner, the banker, or the merchant who knows that in regard to his transactions in a foreign country the law of contract, of movable property, and of civil wrongs is practically identical with that of his own country. . . . But I do not think that the advocate of the unification of law is obligated to rely solely upon such material considerations, important as they are. The resulting moral gain would be considerable. A common forum is an instrument for the peaceful settlement of disputes which might otherwise breed animosity and violence . . . [i]f the individuals who compose each civilised nation were by the unification of law provided, in regard to their private differences or disputes abroad with individuals of any other nation, not indeed with a common forum (for that is an impossibility), but with a common system of justice in every forum, administered upon practically identical principles, a neighbourly feeling, a sincere sentiment of human solidarity (if I may be allowed the phrase) would thereby gradually be engendered amongst us all – a step onward to the far-off fulfilment of the divine message, "On earth peace, goodwill toward men.

[12] *See* Audit, *Lex Mercatoria, supra* note 8, at 173–175; also available online at <http://cisgw3.law.pace.edu/cisg/biblio/audit.html>:

> Municipal laws are ill-adapted to the regulatory needs of international trade and, in particular, to those of international sales. These laws, by and large, are antiquated and their applicability to international transactions is determined by a choice of law process that varies from country to country. [. . .] Devising uniform rules specifically for international trade, therefore, appears to be the optimal solution.

"contribute to the removal of legal barriers in international trade and promote the development of international trade."[13] The CISG seeks to achieve such uniformity.[14] Whether or not the uniform law is successful will largely depend on two things: first, whether domestic tribunals interpret its provisions in a uniform manner, and second, whether those same tribunals adopt a uniform approach to the filling of gaps in the law.

The unification or harmonization of international commercial law is generally desirable because it can act as a "total conflict avoidance device"[15] that, from a trader's point of view, is far better than conflict solution devices, such as the choice of law clauses.[16] Textual uniformity is, however, a necessary but insufficient step toward achieving substantive legal uniformity, because the formulation and enactment of a uniform legal text provide no guarantee of its subsequent uniform application in practice. The main question regarding the success or failure of the Convention as truly uniform sales law relates to the proper interpretation and uniform application of its provisions as the international sales law of contracts governed by it. Several commentaries have evaluated the CISG from this perspective, and the authors have disagreed on how successful CISG will be in reaching this unifying goal.[17]

[13] Lower transactional costs and more speedy resolution of disputes are the main tangible benefits of a uniform international legal regime. *See* also V. Susanne Cook, "The Need for Uniform Interpretation of the 1980 United Nations Convention on Contracts for the International Sale of Goods," 50 *U. Pitt. L. Rev.* 197–226 (1988), also available online at <http://cisgw3.law.pace.edu/cisg/biblio/cook2.html>.

[14] *See* Francis A. Gabor, "Stepchild of the New *Lex Mercatoria*: Private International Law from the United States Perspective," 8 *NW. J. Int'l L. & Bus.* 538–560 (1988), also available online at <http://cisgw3.law.pace.edu/cisg/biblio/gabor.html>: V. Proposal for Implementation of International Uniform Laws:

> Revitalization of the ancient *lex mercatoria* is one of the major achievements of our century. The creation of a uniform substantive law applicable to the international sale of goods eliminates a major non-tariff barrier to the free flow of goods and services across national boundaries.

Cf. Willis L. M. Reese, Commentary on Professor Gabor's Stepchild of the New *Lex mercatoria* (Symposium Reflections)," 8 *Nw. J. Int'l L. & Bus.* 570–573 (1988), also available online at <http://cisgw3.law.pace.edu/cisg/biblio/reese.html>.

[15] Professor Schmitthoff long ago declared that only a uniform law could act as "total conflict avoidance device." Clive M. Schmitthoff, "Conflict Avoidance in Practice and Theory in the Preventative Law of Conflicts," 21 *Law & Contemp. Probs*. 432 (1956). However, it is arguable that no code can ever truly act as a total conflict avoidance device without a law making it a crime to interpret it in a different way. A jurisdiction with such a law is Brobdingnag, as reported by Lemuell Gulliver (Jonathan Swift, *Travels into Several Remote Nations of the World: Part II. A Voyage to Brobdingnag*, 1726):

> No Law of that Country must exceed in Words the Number of Letters in their Alphabet, which consists only of two and twenty. But, indeed, few of them extend even to that Length. They are expressed in the most plain and simple Terms, wherein those People are not mercurial enough to discover above one Interpretation: And to write a Comment upon any Law is a capital Crime. As to the Decision of civil Causes, or Proceedings against Criminals, their Precedents are so few, that they have little Reason to boast of any extraordinary Skill in either.

[16] Choice of law clauses are usually inserted in most contracts, but they can only act as a "partial conflict avoidance device." Clive M. Schmitthoff, *supra* note 15, at 454.

Cf. Andreas Kappus, "Conflict avoidance" durch *"lex mercatoria"* und UN-Kaufrecht ["Conflict avoidance" through *"lex mercatoria"* and Cisg – *in German*], 36 *Recht der Internationalen Wirtschaft, Heidelberg* 788–794 (1990); Andreas Kappus, *"Lex mercatoria"* in Europa und Wiener UN-Kaufrechtskonvention 1980 – "Conflict avoidance" in Theorie und Praxis schiedsrichterliche und ordentliche Rechtsprechung in Konkurrenz zum Einheitskaufrecht der Vereinten Nationen [*"Lex mercatoria"* in Europe and Vienna Sales Convention – "Conflict avoidance" in theory and practice of arbitral and court jurisdiction in competition to the CISG – *in German*] (1990) (Thesis Innsbruck, Frankfurt a.M); Bernardo M. Cremades & Steven L. Plehn, "The New *"Lex mercatoria"* and the Harmonization of the Laws of International Commercial Transactions," *B .U. Int'l L.J.* 317 (1984).

[17] For example, compare Arthur Rosett, "Critical Reflections on the United Nations Convention on Contracts for the International Sale of Goods," 45 *Ohio St. L. J.* 265 (1984), concluding that the *CISG* will not be successful in harmonizing the law of international trade, with Jan Hellner, "The UN Convention on International Sales of Goods – An Outsider's View," in *Ius Inter Nationes: Festschrift fur S. Riesenfeld* 71 (Erik Jayme et al. eds., 1983), concluding that even with its shortcomings, the CISG will provide a basis for unification of the law of international commerce. *See* also Peter H. Schlechtriem, "25 Years CISG – An International Lingua Franca for Drafting Uniform Laws, Legal Principles, Domestic Legislation and Transnational

II. PROBLEMS OF INTERPRETATION OF UNIFORM LAW

Uniform law, by definition, calls for its common interpretation in different legal systems that have adopted it.[18] The CISG is an important legal document, because it establishes a uniform code of legal rules governing the formation of contracts for the international sale of goods, the obligations of the buyer and seller, remedies for breach of contract, and other aspects of the contract. As stated in its Preamble,[19] the CISG was created "to remove legal barriers in international trade and promote the development of international trade." For the Convention to accomplish its objectives, it is essential that its provisions are interpreted properly.

The CISG is uniform law binding buyers and sellers from different legal cultures to its set of rules and principles. Uniformity in the Convention's application, however, is not guaranteed by the mere adoption or ratification of the CISG. The political act of adoption of the Convention by different sovereign States is merely the necessary preliminary step toward the ultimate goal of unification of the law governing contracts for the international sale of goods. The long process of unification of international sales law can be completed only in practice – if the CISG is interpreted in a consistent manner in all legal systems

Contracts," 2 *Cile Studies. The CISG and the Business Lawyer: The UNCITRAL Digest as a Contract Drafting Tool* (forthcoming 2006), offering a strong argument in favor of the CISG as a *lingua franca* of international commercial law.

[18] *See* R. J. C. Munday, "The Uniform Interpretation of International Conventions," 27 *Int'l. & Comp. L. Q.* 450 (1978), stating "[t]he principal objective of an international convention is to achieve uniformity of legal rules within the various States party to it. However, even when outward uniformity is achieved following the adoption of a single authoritative text, uniform application of the agreed rules is by no means guaranteed, as in practice different countries almost inevitably come to put different interpretations upon the same enacted words."

[19] The importance of the wording of the CISG's Preamble and the weight to be placed on it cannot be fixed precisely. We can get some guidance from Article 31(2) of the United Nations Convention on the Law of Treaties (1969), which specifically mentions the Preamble of a treaty as being part of the context for the purpose of the interpretation of the treaty; that is, the Preamble can be relevant to the interpretation of a treaty. Academic opinions, however, differ as to the legal importance of this Preamble. Some commentators believe that the language of the Preamble, for various reasons, counts for virtually nought, whereas others argue that the Preamble "informs" other provisions of the Convention, most particularly Article 7. Support for the first view, that the Preamble may not be used for the interpretation and gap-filling of the substantive legal provisions, can be found in: Peter Schlechtriem, *The U.N. Convention on Contracts for the International Sale of Goods* (Manzsche 1986) [hereinafter: Schlechtriem, *Uniform Sales Law*], at 38 n.111; *see* also Bonell, *Introduction*, *supra* note 6, at 25, stating "[T]he scope for interpretation in the light of the Preamble may not be very wide and it will be of interest to see how far the case law may accord its provisions the status of something more than general declarations of political principle." *See* also Honnold, *Uniform Law for Int'l Sales*, *supra* note 1, at 541, where Honnold argues that the short preparation and consideration of its provisions deprive the Preamble of its "weight" as an aid to the interpretation of CISG's provisions (including Art. 7) that were discussed at length in UNCITRAL and at the Diplomatic Conference.

For the exactly opposite view, *see* Amy H. Kastely, "Unification and Community: A Rhetorical Analysis of the United Nations Sales Convention," 8 *Nw. J. Int'l L. & Bus.* (1988) [hereinafter Kastely, *Rhetorical Analysis*], at 572; Joseph M. Lookofsky, "The 1980 United Nations Convention on Contracts for the International Sale of Goods," in *1 International Encyclopaedia of Laws* – Contracts 18, para. 4 (Blainpain ed., 1993). *See* also Fritz Enderlein & Dietrich Maskow, *International Sales Law* (Oceana 1992) [hereinafter Enderlein & Maskow, *International Sales Law*], at 19–20, who state, "It would ... be inappropriate to dismiss the preamble from the start as insignificant from a legal point of view. The principles it contains can be referred to in interpreting terms or rules of the Convention, such as the terms of 'good faith' (Article 7(1)) or the rather frequent and vague term 'reasonable.' It could also be used to fill gaps because those principles can be counted among, or have an influence on, the basic rules underlying the Convention Article 7(2)). The spirit of the preamble should also be taken account of when agreed texts of sales contracts are to be interpreted." For a similar view, *see* Horacio A. Grigera Naón, "The UN Convention on Contracts for the International Sale of Goods," *in The Transnational Law of International Commercial Transactions: Studies in Transnational Economic Law* 92 (Horn & Schmittoff eds., 1982). Most of the above citations can be found in a thorough report on the legal importance of the CISG Preamble, *Report on different opinions as to legal importance of Preamble* in Annotated Text of the Cisg (Albert H. Kritzer, ed.) at <http://cisgw3.law.pace.edu/cisg/text/reportpre.html>.

that have adopted it. In contrast, if domestic courts and tribunals introduce divergent textual interpretations of the CISG, this uniform law will be short-lived.

The practical success of the Convention depends on whether its provisions are interpreted and applied similarly by different national courts and arbitral tribunals. Furthermore, as the uniform law must remain responsive to the contemporary needs of the community it serves in a dynamic global marketplace, despite the lack of machinery for legislative amendment in the CISG, it is vital that the CISG be interpreted in a manner that allows the uniform law to develop in a uniform fashion, consistent with its general principles, so as to continue to "promote the development of international trade" well into the future.

As has been persuasively stated elsewhere, the success of a uniform law code that intends to bind parties transacting worldwide depends on the creation of "an international community of people who perceive themselves as bound together and governed by a common legal system and who have some way to deliberate together over matters of continuing verification and development."[20] It is this achievement of establishing an "international community," a kind of international legal consensus, that is regarded by some as the true underlying purpose of CISG and as the key to its eventual triumph or demise.[21] It is also the focus of the most forceful criticism of CISG, as it has been argued that achieving international consensus on significant legal issues is impossible.[22]

III. ISSUES OF INTERPRETATION IN THE CISG

It is natural that disputes will arise as to the meaning and application of the CISG's provisions. The CISG, however, comes with its own, in-built interpretation rules, which are set forth in Article 7.[23] Article 7 is the provision that sets forth the Convention's interpretive standards. The provision in Art. 7(1) expressly prescribes the *international* character of the Convention and *uniform* direction that should be adopted in the interpretation and application of its provisions. Owing to its unique nature as an autonomous and self-contained body of law,[24] it is necessary that CISG exist on top of a legal order that can provide doctrinal support and solutions to practical problems – such as resolving issues that are *governed but not expressly settled by* the Convention, as per the gap-filling provisions in Art. 7(2). This doctrinal support guarantees CISG's functional continuity and development without offending its values of internationality and uniformity mandated in Art. 7(1).

[20] Kastely, *Rhetorical Analysis*, *supra* note 19, at 577.

[21] *See* generally Kastely, *Rhetorical Analysis*, *supra* note 19; *see* also Camilla Baasch Andersen, "The Uniform International Sales Law and the Global Jurisconsultorium" (2005), available online at <http://cisg-online.ch/cisg/The_Uniform_International_Sales_Law_and_the_Global_Jurisconsultorium.pdf> [hereinafter Andersen, *Global Jurisconsultarium*].

[22] *See* Arthur Rosett, *supra* note 17, at 282–286. *See* also Rosett, "Note: Unification and Certainty: The United Nations Convention on Contracts for the International Sale of Goods," 97 *Harv. L. Rev.* (1984). *Cf.* It has been argued that this criticism by Rosett dismisses the possibility of genuine discourse within the international community too easily. *See* Kastely, *Rhetorical Analysis*, *supra* note 19, at 577, n. 9.

[23] Article 7 of the CISG provides the following:

(1) In the interpretation of this Convention, regard is to be had to its international character and to the need to promote uniformity in its application and the observance of good faith in international trade.

(2) Questions concerning matters governed by this Convention which are not expressly settled in it are to be settled in conformity with the general principles on which it is based or, in the absence of such principles, in conformity with the law applicable by virtue of the rules of private international law.

[24] For a thesis in support of the statement that the CISG is an autonomous, self-contained body of law, *see* John Felemegas, "The United Nations Convention on Contracts for the International Sale of Goods: Article 7 and Uniform Interpretation," *Pace Review of the Convention on Contracts for the International Sale of Goods (CISG)* 115–379 (Kluwer Law International, 2000–2001), also available online at <http://cisgw3.law.pace.edu/cisg/biblio/felemegas.html>[hereinafter Felemegas, *Uniform Interpretation*].

To avoid divergent interpretations of the CISG some commentators had hoped for the establishment of an international court with jurisdiction over disputes arising under the CISG. The main advantage of such a court would probably be the uniformity that a centralized judicial system can produce on disputes arising within its jurisdiction. Although the internal correlation of decisions handed down by a central judicial authority has a superficial attraction, the idea has never been a realistic possibility for the CISG.[25]

The risk that inconsistent interpretation could frustrate the goal of uniformity in the law was well understood by those working on the CISG.[26] This problem is not, however, exclusive to the present structures administering justice under the CISG. All centralized judicial systems are also prone to this danger (although there is ultimately a final appellate level to provide redress). The nature of the CISG's subject matter (i.e., trade) is in itself unsuitable to the time-consuming, delay-laden mechanism of a single judicial authority. As such, the implicit assumption is that the CISG will be applied by domestic courts and arbitral tribunals.[27]

The essence of the problem of the CISG's divergent interpretation lies with the interpreters themselves; its nature is substantive and not structural. All the attention has been focused on the necessity, for the various courts and arbiters applying the CISG, to understand and respect the commitment to uniformity and to interpret the text in light of its international character. It has been suggested that a feasible solution to the problems associated with decision making under the CISG is the "development of a jurisprudence of international trade."[28] Arguably, the success of the Convention depends on the achievement of this goal.

The dynamic for developing a jurisprudence of international trade is established in Articles 7(1) and 7(2).[29] These are arguably the most important articles in the CISG, not

[25] *See* David, *Unification of Private Law*, *supra* note 1, at 4. The enormity of the financial task and the administrative structures necessary for the establishment of such a closed-circuit judicial system are prohibitive for the creation of an international commercial court.

A significant development took place in 2001 when the CISG Advisory Council was established as a private initiative to respond to the emerging need to address some controversial, unresolved issues relating to the CISG that would merit interpretative guidance. The Advisory Council is a private initiative that aims at *promoting a uniform interpretation* of the CISG. The Council is guided by the mandate of Article 7 of the Convention as far its interpretation and application are concerned: the paramount regard to international character of the Convention and the need to promote uniformity. In practical terms, the primary purpose of the Advisory Council is to issue opinions relating to the interpretation and application of the Convention on request or on its own initiative. Requests may be submitted to the Council, in particular, by international organizations, professional associations, and adjudication bodies. It publicizes all its opinions widely through printed and electronic media and welcomes comments from the readership. Further information on the Council's membership and work is available online at <http://cisgw3.law.pace.edu/cisg/CISG-AC.html>.

[26] *See* Michael J. Bonell, "Some Critical Reflections on the New UNCITRAL Draft Convention on International Sales," 2 *Uniform L. Rev.* 5–9 (1978); E. Allen Farnsworth, "Problems of the Unification of Sales from the Standpoint of the Common Law Countries: Problems of Unification of International Sales Law," in 7 *Digest of Commercial Laws of the World* (Dobbs Ferry 1980) [hereinafter Farnsworth, *Problems of Unification*]. The effort to ensure uniform interpretation of the Sales Convention and to inspire international discourse on issues raised by it has been discussed elsewhere. *See, e.g.*, John Honnold, "Methodology to Achieve Uniformity in Applying International Agreements, Examined in the Setting of the Uniform Law for International Sales under the 1980 U.N. Convention," in *Report to the Twelfth Congress of the International Academy of Comparative Law* (Sydney/Melbourne 1986).

[27] *See Progressive Development of the Law of International Trade: Report of the Secretary-General*, 21 U.N. GAOR Annex 3, Agenda Item 88, U.N. Doc. A/6396, reprinted in [1970] 1 *Y.B.U.N. Comm'n on Int'l Trade L.* 18, at 39–40, U.N. Doc. A/CN.9/SER.A/1970.

[28] *See, e.g.*, Kastely, *Rhetorical Analysis*, *supra* note 19, at 601. *See* also Andersen, *Global Jurisconsultarium*, *supra* note 21.

[29] *See, e.g.*, Audit, *Lex Mercatoria*, *supra* note 8, at 187 commenting on the ability of the Convention to generate new rules:

> The Convention is meant to adapt to changing circumstances. Amending it is practically impossible. A conference of the magnitude of the one held in Vienna is difficult to organize. Achieving the unanimity of the participating

only because their central location and stated purpose demand detailed treatment but also because their success or failure will determine the CISG's eventual fate as uniform law. The debate regarding the application of the CISG generally, as well as in individual cases, necessarily involves Article 7.

Article 7 expressly directs that in the interpretation of CISG "regard is to be had to its international character and to the need to promote uniformity in its application and the observance of good faith in international trade."[30] Interpreters of the CISG are further instructed that questions concerning matters governed by the CISG that are not expressly settled in it "are to be settled in conformity with the general principles" on which the CISG is based or, in the absence of such principles, "in conformity with the law applicable by virtue of the rules of private international law."[31]

Matters *governed by the CISG which are not expressly settled in it* are issues to which CISG applies but which it does not expressly resolve; that is, gaps *praeter legem*.[32] It is only with this type of gap that Art. 7(2) CISG is concerned, as opposed to questions regarding matters that are excluded from the scope of CISG, such as the matters mentioned in CISG Arts. 2, 3, 4 and 5; that is, gaps *intra legem*.

Article 7(1) directs tribunals to discuss and interpret the detailed provisions of the text with regard to its international character and the need for uniformity in its application. If domestic courts and tribunals pay heed to the drafters' directions in Article 7 and to the spirit of equality and loyalty with which the CISG is imbued, then Article 7 will have contributed to the coherence of the precariously fragile international community. Article 7(2) provides the important mechanism for filling in any gaps *praeter legem* in the CISG and thus complements Article 7(1) by laying the course for the text's deliberation and future development. In this way, the CISG acquires the flexibility necessary for any instrument that attempts to deal with a subject matter as fluid and dynamic as international trade.

The spirit of international cooperation extends to the treatment that tribunals will afford to decisions of other national courts that are as significant as their own interpretation of the Convention.[33] Article 7(1), by directing an interpreter's attention to the CISG's international character and stressing the goal of uniformity, emphasizes the need for an international discussion among different national courts. Although the CISG, once ratified, becomes part of the domestic law of each Member State, it does not lose its international and independent character.

The recourse to rules of private international law in interpreting [Art. 7(1)] or gap-filling [Art. 7(2)] the provisions of the Convention arguably hinders and undermines the search for the elusive goal of uniformity by producing divergent interpretive

states on proposed changes also would present substantial obstacles. The provisions of the Convention must be flexible enough to be workable without formal amendment for a long period of time. The Convention, therefore, must be regarded as an autonomous system, capable of generating new rules. This feature of the Convention is reflected in article 7, dealing with interpretation and gap-filling.

[30] CISG Art. 7(1).

[31] CISG Art. 7(2).

[32] *See* Franco Ferrari, *Interprétation uniforme de la Convention de Vienna de 1980 sur la vente internationale*, 48 *Revue internationale de droit comparé* 813, 842 (1996), as well as Ferrari, "General Principles and International Uniform Law Commercial Law Conventions: A Study of the 1980 Vienna Sales Convention and the 1988 UNIDROIT Conventions," 2 *Uniform Law Review* 451–473 (1997), at 454, where Ferrari uses the expression *lacunae praeter legem* for issues not expressly regulated by the law although governed by it and *lacunae intra legem* for issues not governed by the law.

[33] *See* Working Group on International Sale of Goods, *Report on the Work of the Second Session*, U.N. GAOR, 24th Sess., Supp. No. 18, U.N. Doc. A/7618, (1968), *reprinted in* [1971] 2 *Y.B.U.N. Comm'n on Int'l Trade L.* 50, U.N. Doc. A/CN.9/SER.A/197, *also reprinted in* Honnold, *Documentary History*, *supra* note 8, at 62: "It was also suggested that the provision would contribute to uniformity by encouraging use of foreign materials, in the form of studies and court decisions, in construing the Law." *See* also Andersen, *Global Jurisconsultarium*, *supra* note 21.

results.[34] An interpretive approach that has been suggested as suitable to the proper application of the CISG as truly global uniform sales law is based on the concept of internationality and on generally acknowledged principles of commercial law, such as the UNIDROIT Principles and the Principles of European Contract Law (PECL).[35]

It is arguable that the legal backdrop for CISG's existence and application can be provided by general principles of international commercial law, such as those exemplified by the *UNIDROIT Principles of International Commercial Contracts* (1994) and the *Principles of European Contract Law* (1998) would in many instances aid in rendering unnecessary the textual reference in Article 7(2) CISG to private international law, a positive step toward substantive legal uniformity.

IV. INTERPRETATION OF THE CONVENTION: ARTICLE 7(1)

Paragraph (1) of Article 7 mandates that in the interpretation of the Convention one must pay close attention to three points: (a) the "international character" of the CISG, (b) "the need to promote uniformity in its application," and (c) "the observance of good faith in international trade."

It is the opinion of many scholars that the first two of these points are not independent of each other,[36] but that, in fact, the second "is a logical consequence of the first."[37] The third point is of a rather special nature, and its placement in the main interpretation provision of the CISG has caused a lot of argument as to its precise meaning and scope.[38]

1. The International Character of the Convention

Every legislative instrument raises issues of interpretation as to the precise meaning of its provisions, even within the confines of a national legal system. Such problems are more prevalent when the subject has been drafted at an international level. In the interpretation of domestic legislation, reliance can be placed on methods of interpretation and established principles within a particular legal system – the legal culture or infrastructure upon which the particular legislation is seated. However, when dealing with a piece of legislation, such as the CISG, that has been prepared and agreed upon at the international level and has been incorporated into many diverse national legal systems, interpretation becomes far more uncertain and problematic because there is no equivalent international legal infrastructure. Does that mean that the CISG is seated on a legal vacuum? The answer is yes and no. The CISG was given an autonomous, free-standing nature by its drafters, and it is true that there are no clearly defined international foundations (equivalent to those in a domestic legal setting) upon which the CISG is placed.[39]

Principles of interpretation could be borrowed from the law of the forum or the law that according to the rules of private international law would have been applicable in

[34] *See* Audit, *Lex Mercatoria*, *supra* note 8, at 187, commenting on the ability of the Convention to generate new rules: "The express reference to national law represents a failure in an instrument meant to unify law for international transactions."

[35] *See* Felemegas, *Uniform Interpretation*, *supra* note 24, at chapter 5.

[36] *See, e.g.*, Honnold, *Uniform Law for Int'l Sales*, *supra* note i, at 135; Michael Joachim Bonell, "General Provisions: Article 7," in *Commentary on the International Sales Law: The 1980 Vienna Sales Convention* (C. M. Bianca & M. J. Bonell eds., Giuffrè 1987), at 72 [hereinafter Bonell, *General Provisions*].

[37] Bonell, *General Provisions*, *supra* note 36, at 72.

[38] For a discussion of the competing arguments, *see* Felemegas, *Uniform Interpretation*, *supra* note 24, at chapter 3.

[39] As is argued in this Introduction, there are, however, general principles of international commercial law (e.g., the UNIDROIT Principles and the PECL) that can provide a part of the platform upon which the CISG, like any other piece of domestic or international piece of legislation, must be based.

the absence of the uniform law. Either approach would result in a diverse construction and implementation of the same piece of legislation by different Contracting States. According to some commentators, the result would be not only a lack of uniformity but also the promotion of forum shopping.[40] Such a result would undermine the purpose of the uniform legislation and defeat the reasons for its existence.

On the other hand, an autonomous and uniform interpretation, if it could be achieved in practice, would go a long way toward completing the process of unification and achieving the aims of the drafters of the uniform international instrument. Article 7(1) declares that such an autonomous approach must be followed in interpretation, befitting the special character and purpose of the Convention. To have regard to the international character of the Convention means that its interpreter must understand that, although the CISG has been formally incorporated into many different national legal systems, the special nature of the CISG as a piece of legislation prepared and agreed upon at an international level helps it retain its independence from any domestic legal system.

Arguably it is essential for the long-term success of the CISG that the rules and techniques traditionally followed in interpreting ordinary domestic legislation are avoided.[41] The CISG is uniform law intended to cover the field of international contracts of sale and, in doing so, to replace all national statutes and case law previously governing matters within that field. The autonomy of this international sales law depends not only on the drafting of the respective rules into a separate body of rules but also on the emancipation of this body of rules from other branches of the law in the international and domestic legal systems.[42]

Even though the CISG is incorporated into municipal law, international sales law should not be regarded as a part of various national legal systems because doing so would inhibit its development as an autonomous branch of law and distort its interpretation and application. Instead, it is suggested that international sales law rules should be seen as part of international law in the broad sense and should be entitled to an international, rather than national, interpretation. The consequence of realizing the essence of the Convention's international character and autonomy is that there should be no reason to adopt a narrow interpretation of the CISG.[43]

[40] *See* Honnold, *Uniform Law for Int'l Sales*, *supra* note 1, at 142, stating, "The settlement of disputes would be complicated and litigants would be encouraged to engage in forum shopping if the courts of different countries persist in divergent interpretations of the Convention."

Contra Fritz Enderlein, "Uniform Law and its Application by Judges and Arbitrators," in *International Uniform Law* in *Practice: Acts and Proceedings of the 3rd Congress on Private Law*, UNIDROIT (Rome, September 7–10, 1987), at 340–341, who thinks that the lack of uniformity in the interpretation of uniform laws has no influence on the choice of forum, so the danger of forum shopping is not real in these circumstances.

[41] The tendency of national tribunals to apply law in accordance with ingrained national patterns was discussed at the Twelfth International Congress of Comparative Law (Sydney 1986).

[42] *See* Jerzy Jakubowski, "The Autonomy of International Trade Law and its Influence on the Interpretation and Application of its Rules," in *Law and International Trade, Recht und Internationaler Handel* 209 (Clive M. Schmitthoff ed., 1973). *Cf.* Bonell, *General Provisions*, *supra* note 36, at 92–93, although recognizing the necessity to interpret uniform laws "autonomously" in general, is of the opinion that an exception must be made if an insuperable divergence of interpretation of a particular provision of the CISG exists between Contracting States. Bonell offers a supporting citation of Jan Kropholler, *Internationales Einheitsrecht*, Allgemeine Lehren 204 (1975). *See* also Van der Velden, *Netherlands Reports to the Twelfth International Congress of Comparative Law* – Sydney/Melbourne 1986, (P. H. M. Gerver et al. eds., Frans J. A. Van der Velden trans., 1987).

[43] Expressing support for this point is Bonell, *General Provisions*, *supra* note 36, at 73: "Instead of sticking to its literal and grammatical meaning, courts are expected to take a much more liberal and flexible attitude and to look, wherever appropriate, to the underlying purposes and policies of individual provisions as well as of the Convention as a whole." *See* also Bruno Zeller, "The UN Convention on Contracts for the International Sale of Goods (Cisg) – A Leap Forward towards Unified International Sales Laws," 12 *Pace Int'l L. Rev.* 79, 105–106 (2000), *also* available at <http://cisgw3.law.pace.edu/cisg/biblio/zeller3.html>.

It is submitted that Article 7 represents an implied provision in the Convention for undertaking such a liberal approach to the interpretation of the body of law in question. It must be acknowledged, however, that the danger with adopting a broad view of the CISG is that it might open the way to diverse national interpretations, if "broad" and "liberal" were equated with notions of theoretical diversity and practical relaxation of the rules of the CISG's interpretation. Thus, a paradox may possibly exist: that internationalism might be better served by a narrow interpretation of the CISG. However, this is merely an aberration, or rather an illusion, because both the nature of the CISG and the intentions of its drafters point unequivocally to its broad and liberal interpretation. If its interpreters realize the true spirit of the CISG and enforce it in practice, then a liberal approach, far from diversifying the results, will achieve uniform results. This is so because the broad and liberal approach, in this case, does not mean the endorsement of many different national views, but the adoption of a single, uniform, *a-national* approach. Such an approach is broad and liberal by definition, because it operates outside and above the restrictions, limitations, and narrowness of established national approaches to interpretation. The broad global scope of the CISG requires that its interpretation be of a similar nature. For the "legal barriers in international trade" to be removed successfully, a broad and liberal approach to the interpretation of the CISG is required. Only such an approach can successfully "take into account the different social, economic, and legal systems"[44] that the CISG is aiming to unite, at least in the field of sale of goods. The proper interpretation of the CISG must be broad and liberal, but not lax or abstract.

2. Uniformity of Application

At this point, the interrelation between the first two parts of Article 7(1) becomes more apparent. The autonomous interpretation of the CISG is not simply a consequence of the "international" characterization of the CISG, but also a necessity, if "the need to promote uniformity in its application" is to be taken seriously. In the CISG, the elements of "internationality" and "uniformity" are interrelated thematically and structurally because of their position in the same Part and Article of the Convention; they are interrelated functionally because an autonomous approach to interpretation is necessary for the functioning of both, and they are interdependent because the existence of one is a necessary prerequisite for the existence of the other. The international, rather than national, interpretation is necessary for uniformity in the application of the CISG to be achieved, and uniformity of application is vital if the CISG is to maintain its international character.

The biggest danger concerning the interpretation of the CISG has been attributed to "a natural tendency to read the international text through the lenses of domestic law."[45] This reading can be the result of a conscious, or unconscious, inclination of judges to place the uniform law against the background of their own municipal law (*lex fori*) and to interpret the uniform law on the basis of principles with which they are already familiar, thus threatening the goal of international uniformity in interpretation.[46]

[44] CISG Preamble.

[45] John Honnold, "The Sales Convention in Action – Uniform International Words: Uniform Application?," 8 *J.L. & Com.* 207, 208 (1988).

[46] Among other causes that can give rise to diverging interpretations of a uniform law are problems that are "internal" to the uniform law because they have their source in the uniform law itself. Such divergences in interpretation are "normal" results of defects in the drafting of the uniform rules. These include mistakes in grammar and translation, lack of clarity, or gaps in the law. *See* Michael F. Sturley, "International Uniform Laws in National Courts: The Influence of Domestic Law in Conflicts of Interpretation," 27 *Va. J. Int'l. L.* 729, 731 (1986). Other reasons that can lead to divergent interpretations are "external" because they are independent from the uniform law itself. On this aspect, it has been said that some interpretative differences can result from various national interests that the different interpreters want to prevail over the national interests of other States. In relation to the CISG, it has been asserted that "the disparity of economic, political,

It is submitted that this goal of international uniformity cannot be achieved if national principles or concepts, taken from the law of the forum or from the law that in the absence of the CISG would have been applicable according to the rules of private international law, are allowed to be used in the interpretation of the CISG. In fact, a "nationalistic" approach to the interpretation of the CISG would achieve results that are contrary to what was intended by the creation of the uniform law and would foster the emergence of divergent national interpretations.[47] The nationalization of the uniform rules deprives the instrument of its unifying effect.

3. The Observance of Good Faith in International Trade

According to the third element of Article 7(1), in interpreting the provisions of the Convention one must have regard to the need to promote the "observance of good faith in international trade." The legislative history of this provision shows that the final inclusion of the good faith principle represented a compromise. This solution was worked out between those delegates to the Vienna Convention who supported its inclusion, stating that, at least in the formation of the contract, the parties should observe the principles of "fair dealing" and act in "good faith," and those who were opposed to any explicit reference to the principle in the Convention, on the ground that it had no fixed meaning and would lead to uncertainty and nonconformity.[48]

a. Good Faith as a Mere Instrument of Interpretation

The placement of the good faith principle in the context of an operative provision dealing with the interpretation of the CISG creates uncertainties as to the principle's exact nature, scope, and function within the CISG.[49] Scholarly opinion on the issue is divided. Some commentators insist on the literal meaning of the provision and conclude that the principle of good faith is nothing more than an additional criterion to be used by judges and arbitrators in the interpretation of the CISG.[50] Under this approach, good faith is merely a tool of interpretation at the disposal of the judges to neutralize the danger of reaching inequitable results.

However, even if included in the CISG as a mere instrument of interpretation, the good faith principle can pose problems in achieving the ultimate goal of the CISG – that is, uniformity in its application – because the concept of good faith has not only different meanings among different legal systems but also multiple connotations within legal systems.

and legal structure of the countries represented at the Vienna Conference suggests the difficulty of achieving legal uniformity." *See* Alejandro M. Garro, "Reconciliation of Legal Traditions in the U.N. Convention on Contracts for the International Sale of Goods," 23 *Int'l Law.* 443, 450 (1989).

[47] The negative consequences of a "nationalistic" interpretation have also been pointed out by courts. The House of Lords, in *Scruttons Ltd. v. Midland Silicones Ltd.* 1962 A.C. 446, at 471, stated that "it would be deplorable if the nations, after protracted negotiations, reach agreement . . . and that their several courts should then disagree as to the meaning of what they appeared to agree upon."

[48] *See* Honnold, *Uniform Law for Int'l Sales*, *supra* note 1, at 146. *See* also Bonell, *General Provisions*, *supra* note 36, at 83–84.

[49] *See* Gyula Eörsi, "A Propos the 1980 Vienna Convention on Contracts for the International Sale of Goods," 31 *Am. J. Comp. L.* 333, 349 (1983), who is of the opinion that the provision as it now stands represents "a strange compromise, in fact burying the principle of good faith."

[50] *See* E. Allen Farnsworth, "The Convention on the International Sale of Goods from the Perspective of the Common Law Countries," in La *Vendita Internazionale, La Convenzione di Vienna dell' 11 Aprile 1980* 5 (Dott. A. Giuffrè ed., 1981), at 18, where the author speaks of "seemingly harmless words." *See also* Peter Winship, "International Sales Contracts Under the 1980 Vienna Convention," 17 *UCC L. J.* (1984) 55, 67 n. 40. *Cf.* Bruno Zeller, *Good Faith – The Scarlet Pimpernel of the Cisg* (2000), available *online* at the Pace Web site: <http://cisgw3.law.pace.edu/cisg/biblio/zeller2.html>.

b. Good Faith in the Relations between the Parties

However, there is academic opinion favoring a broader interpretation of the reference to good faith as contained in Article 7(1), pointing out that the duty to observe "good faith in international trade is also necessarily directed to the parties to each individual contract of sale."[51]

The main theoretical difficulty with the above suggestion is that, in effect, it implies that the interpreters of the CISG are not only the judges or arbitrators but the contracting parties as well.[52] This point is controversial, and there are practical and theoretical objections to it. If Article 7 is addressed to the parties, then that provision might be excluded by them under Article 6. This would be an unwelcome result because, in practice, it would hinder the uniformity of interpretation. The theoretical objection is that the statement seems to obliterate the distinction between interpretation by the court and performance of the contract by the parties. One of the main practical objections to the inclusion in the CISG of a provision imposing on the parties a general obligation to act in good faith was that this concept was too vague and would inevitably lead to divergent interpretations of the CISG by national courts.

The possibility of imposing additional obligations on the parties is clearly not supported by the legislative history of the CISG. Article 7(1), as it now stands in the CISG's text, is the result of a drafting compromise between two diverging views; it reflects the political and diplomatic maneuvering necessary for the creation of an international Convention. It cannot now be given the meaning originally suggested by those advocating the imposition of a positive duty of good faith on the parties, as doing so would reverse the intent of the compromise. On the other hand, this does not mean that the opposite view (i.e., that good faith represents merely an instrument of interpretation) should be adopted instead. That interpretation would unnecessarily deny the value of good faith and its potential function within the CISG.

It is submitted that "good faith," like all the other terms in the CISG, must be approached afresh and be given a new definition that will describe its scope and meaning within the CISG, separate from the peculiar loads that it carries in different, and often within, legal systems. It may take some time for the principle of good faith to develop naturally and to crystallize in the case law, in the spirit of continuing deliberation and discourse that characterizes the community of the CISG members.

V. REMEDIES AGAINST DIVERGENT INTERPRETATIONS

It has been eloquently – and accurately – stated elsewhere that international trade law is subject to the tension between two forces: "the divisive impact of nationalism and our

[51] Bonell, *General Provisions*, *supra* note 36, at 84. *See also* Gyula Eörsi, "General Provisions," in *International Sales: The United Nations Convention on Contracts for the International Sale of Goods* 8–9 (Nina M. Galston & Hans Smit eds., 1984) [hereinafter: Eörsi, *General Provisions in International Sales*], stating, "[i]t might be argued that [in cases in which interpretation of the Convention leads to application of the good faith clause] it was not the Convention which was interpreted but the contract.... [H]owever, interpretation of the two cannot be separated since the Convention is necessarily interpreted by the parties also; after all, the Convention constitutes the law of the parties insofar as they do not make use of Article 6 on freedom of contract." For similar statements, *see* Schlechtriem, *Uniform Sales Law*, at 39; Fritz Enderlein & Dietrich Maskow, *supra* note 19, at 55; Dietrich Maskow, "The Convention on the International Sale of Goods from the Perspective of the Socialist Countries," in *La Vendita Internazionale, La Convenzione di Vienna dell' 11 Aprile 1980* 45–47 (1981). *Cf.* the opinion offered in Arthur Rosett, "Critical Reflections on the United Nations Convention on Contracts for the International Sale of Goods," 45 *Ohio St. L.J.* 265, 290 (1984).

[52] *See* Enderlein & Maskow, *International Sales Law*, *supra* note 19, at 55.

unwillingness to confine our activities within national borders."[53] The CISG attempts to establish uniform international rules for the international sale of goods to minimize the uncertainties and misunderstandings in commercial relationships that result from the uncertainty over the correct identification – and the subsequent proper application – of the relevant applicable law in case of a dispute.

Uniformity does not result automatically from an agreement on the wording of the uniform rules. The objectives of that agreement can be undermined by different domestic approaches to interpreting and applying the uniform international rules in practice. For a uniform application of the CISG to be attained, it does not suffice that the CISG be considered as an autonomous body of law, because it could still be interpreted in different autonomous ways in various States. If such an unfortunate scenario were to develop, uniformity would be attained only as a "very unlikely coincidence."[54] In theory there exists a wide range of remedies against such a risk,[55] but in practice it will be up to the national judges and arbitrators interpreting the CISG to attain, and then maintain, its uniform application to the highest degree possible.

There are some interpretative aids at the disposal of the interpreters of the CISG that may facilitate its uniform application and may act as a hindrance to the development of divergent interpretations. For example, in cases of ambiguities or obscurities in language, the existence of several equally authentic language versions of the Convention permits the interpreter to consult another official version of the CISG for assistance.[56] What follows is an examination of different means that can be used in the battle against divergent interpretations of the CISG.

1. Jurisprudence (Case Law)

Arguably the most effective means of achieving uniformity in the application of the CISG is to have regard to the way it is interpreted in other countries. The development of a body of case law based on the provisions of the CISG and the careful consideration of this jurisprudence by later courts are very important steps in the process of interpretation of the CISG. A judge, or arbitrator, faced with a particular question of interpretation of the CISG's provisions, which may have already been brought to the attention of a court in another Contracting State, should take into consideration the solutions so far elaborated in the foreign courts.[57] Given also the lack of machinery for legislative amendment in the CISG, the importance of case law in understanding international sales law will be

[53] John Honnold, "Uniform Words and Uniform Application. The 1980 Sales Convention and International Juridical Practice," in *Einheitliches Kaufrecht und Nationales Obligationrecht* 119 (Peter Schlechtriem ed., 1987) [hereinafter Honnold, *Uniform Words and Application*].

[54] *See* Franco Ferrari, "Uniform Interpretation of the 1980 Uniform Sales Law," 24 *Ga. J. Int'l & Comp. L.* 183 (1994) [hereinafter: Ferrari, *Uniform Interpretation*], at 204, where the author uses the following numerical example to illustrate this point: Supposing that there are three equally plausible autonomous interpretations of the same provision, the chance that two interpreters construing the same provision independently will arrive at a uniform result amounts only to 33 percent, whereas the probability of diverging interpretations is 67 percent.

[55] *See* David, *Unification of Private Law, supra* note 1, at 107–122.

[56] *See* Bonell, *General Provisions, supra* note 36, at 90, who is of the opinion that such comparison "becomes obligatory, if the text actually applied is only a translation into a national language which is not one of the official languages of the United Nations."

[57] *See* Audit, *Lex Mercatoria, supra* note 8, at 188–189:

> The Convention must be interpreted with a view to maintaining its uniformity. Divergent interpretations by national courts should not be allowed to undermine the uniform law. A lack of harmony in interpretation would have the unfortunate consequence of reintroducing the conflicts methodology that the Convention was meant to eliminate.
>
> Courts, therefore, should consider foreign decisional law and scholarly commentary on the Convention in reaching their determinations [references omitted].

all the greater. Thus, it is arguable that, as a matter of principle and common sense, courts should at least consider the jurisprudence developed by foreign courts applying the CISG.[58] The difficulty lies in the importance (e.g., binding force or merely persuasive value) that a court should place on a decision of a foreign court and the reasoning behind that decision, as well as the degree to which any such "precedent" may be followed and adopted by other foreign courts.

In terms of how the evaluation of existing case law should affect interpretation of the CISG's provisions, the basic question that needs answering concerns the reaction of a judge or arbitrator, who, when faced with an issue of interpretation in the CISG, discovers that divergent solutions have been adopted in regard to that same issue by different national courts. The prevailing view is that, as long as the divergences are rather isolated and rendered by lower courts or are to be found even within the same jurisdiction, "it is still possible either to choose the most appropriate solution among the different ones so far proposed or to disregard them altogether and attempt to find a new solution."[59]

Even though no mention is made in Article 7 of the authority of decided cases, the exhortation in Article 7(1) to treat the CISG as an international text and to promote *uniformity* in its interpretation will require deference to judicial opinions from other countries. This body of opinions may not quite develop as a system of precedent, in the common law sense, but in a new and unique jurisprudential system like the CISG's, in which case law will be at a premium, courts have an obligation to expand their reasoning process if they are to transmit relevant persuasion to courts of other legal systems.[60]

[58] For the necessity of having regard to other countries' decisions, *see* Albert H. Kritzer, *Guide to Practical Applications of the United Nations Convention on Contracts for the International Sale of Goods* 108–109 (1989) [hereinafter Kritzer, *Guide to Practical Applications*]. The domestic legislative instruments in most common law countries are traditionally interpreted narrowly so as to limit their interference with the law developed by the courts. *See* generally Cook, "The Need for Uniform Interpretation of the 1980 United Nations Convention on Contracts for the International Sale of Goods," 50 *U. Pitt. L. Rev.* 197–226 (1988). Progress on this issue – that is, the development of a body of case law citing rulings of courts of foreign jurisdictions – is slower than desired but nonetheless evident. *See, e.g.*, the following case law:

- Italy January 31, 1996 District Court Cuneo (*Sport d'Hiver di Genevieve Culet v. Ets. Louys et Fils*), case presentation including English translation available at <http://cisgw3.law.pace.edu/cases/960131i3.html>
- France October 23, 1996 Appellate Court Grenoble (*Gaec des Beauches v. Teso Ten Elsen*), case presentation including English translation available at <http://cisgw3.law.pace.edu/cases/961023f1.html>
- Switzerland January 8, 1997 Appellate Court Luzern, case presentation including English translation available at <http://cisgw3.law.pace.edu/cases/970108s1.html>
- United States June 29,1998 Federal Appellate Court [11th Circuit] (*MCC-Marble Ceramic Center v. Ceramica Nuova D'Agostino*), case presentation available at <http://cisgw3.law.pace.edu/cases/980629u1.html> (a case that, although not citing foreign precedents, as there was none on the issue considered, did point out the need to consider such precedents
- United States May 17, 1999 Federal District Court [Louisiana] (*Medical Marketing v. Internazionale Medico Scientifica*), case presentation available at <http://cisgw3.law.pace.edu/cases/990517u1.html> (a case citing the ruling of a court of a foreign jurisdiction)
- Italy December 29, 1999 District Court Pavia (*Tessile v. Ixela*), case presentation including English translation available at <http://cisgw3.law.pace.edu/cases/991229i3.html> (a case that cites the ruling of a court of a foreign jurisdiction)
- Italy July 12, 2000 District Court Vigevano (*Rheinland Versicherungen v. Atlarex*), case presentation including English translation available at <http://cisgw3.law.pace.edu/cases/000712i3.html> (a case that cites and comments on forty rulings of courts of foreign jurisdictions)
- United States May 21, 2004 Federal District Court [Illinois] (*Chicago Prime Packers v. Northam Food Trading Co.*), case presentation available at <http://cisgw3.law.pace.edu/cases/040521u1.html> (citing rulings by courts of Germany, Italy, and Netherlands)

[59] Bonell, *General Provisions*, *supra* note 36, at 92.

[60] *See* Philip T. Hackney, "Is the United Nations Convention on the International Sale of Goods Achieving Uniformity," 61 *LA. L. Rev.* 473–486 (2001) at 479, available online at <http://cisgw3.law.pace.edu/cisg/biblio/hackney.html>:

> It cannot be argued that the Convention itself requires the courts to apply the principle of *stare decisis* and make prior case law binding. [. . .] Therefore, a reasonable reading of this Convention directive would be that it

Interpretations of an international Convention by sister signatories should be taken into account in a comparative manner and with the "integrative force of a judgment... based on the persuasive reasoning which the decisions of the Court bring to bear on the problem at hand."[61] A judge ought to be "obliged to search for and to take into consideration foreign judgments... at least the judgments from other Contracting States, when he is faced with a problem of interpretation of an international convention."[62]

Access to foreign decisions has become a lot easier than it used to be. UNCITRAL has taken many steps to ameliorate any practical difficulties relating to access, including the establishment of CLOUT, through which the original texts of decisions and other materials may be obtained from the UNCITRAL Secretariat.[63]

In recognition of the importance of foreign decisions to the uniform interpretation of the CISG, many international organizations and law schools have made efforts to collect, translate, and provide commentary to relevant decisions.[64] An updated and growing collection of CISG jurisprudence, including English translation and relevant commentary, can be found on the CISG database maintained by the Pace Law School.[65]

2. Doctrine (Scholarly Writings; Commentaries)

Another "antidote"[66] to the danger of divergent interpretations of the CISG is the use of doctrine (i.e., academic writings). The literature on the CISG is voluminous and still growing. The value of scholarly writings and international commentaries in the promotion

requires a principle similar to *jurisprudence constante*, a principle from Civil-Law legal systems. This principle holds that case law is not a binding source of law, but a persuasive source of law. This would mean that when interpreting the Convention, a court should look to other court's interpretations of the Convention, including the interpretations of courts from other countries. These interpretations, however, would not be binding, but only persuasive.

[61] Jürgen Schwarze, "The Role of the European Court of Justice (ECJ) in the Interpretation of Uniform Law among the Member States of the European Communities (EC)," in *International Uniform Law in Practice: Acts and Proceedings of the 3rd Congress on Private Law* 221 (UNIDROIT, Rome, September 7–10, 1987) (1988). *See* also Harry M. Flechtner, "Several Texts of the CISG in a Decentralized System: Observations on Translations, Reservations and Other Challenges in the Uniformity Principle in Article 7(1)," *17 J. L. & Com.* 187–217 (1998), also available online at <http://cisgw3.law.pace.edu/cisg/biblio/flecht1.html> (where the author explores the theme of uniformity in the Convention arguing that the uniformity principle "requires a process or methodology involving awareness of and respect for, but not necessarily blind obedience to, interpretations of the CISG from outside one's own legal culture – an approach not unlike the treatment U.S. courts accord decisions of other jurisdictions when applying our Uniform Commercial Code"). *See* also Philip T. Hackney, *supra* note 60, at 479, available online at <http://cisgw3.law.pace.edu/cisg/biblio/hackney.html> (also suggesting that U.S. Uniform Commercial Code case law could be used as a model for tribunals to interpret the Convention by evaluating relevant international case law).

[62] Schwarze, *id. See* also Andersen, *Global Jurisconsultarium, supra* note 21.

[63] The system for reporting and distributing decisions is described in the *UNCITRAL* document, *Case Law on UNCITRAL Texts (CLOUT)*, U.N. Doc. A/CN.9/SER.C/GUIDE/1 (May 19, 1993).

[64] *E.g.*, the Centre for Comparative and Foreign Law Studies in Rome maintains the Unilex database, which provides a collection of case law and an international bibliography on the CISG. For a comment on Unilex as a tool to promote the CISG's uniform application, *see* Fabio Liguori, "'Unilex': A Means to Promote Uniformity in the Application of CISG," in *Zeitschrift für Europäisches Privatrecht* 600 (1996).

[65] The Pace Law School Institute of International Commercial Law <http://cisgw3.law.pace.edu/cisg/text/institute.html> offers an Electronic Library on Uniform International Commercial Law <http://cisgw3.law.pace.edu>, which provides case annotations for each Article of the CISG; as of December 2005, there were 1,700 cases and 5,000 case annotations reported. For a description on how this, as well as other Internet sites dealing with the CISG, are to be used, *see* Claire M. Germain, "The United Nations Convention on Contracts for the International Sale of Goods: Guide to Research and Literature," in *Review of the Convention on Contracts for the International Sale of Goods* 117 (*Cornell Int'l L. J.* eds., 1995) [hereinafter *Cornell Review*]; *see* also Albert H. Kritzer, "The Convention on Contracts for the International Sale of Goods: Scope, Interpretation and Resources," in *Cornell Rev.*, at 147.

[66] This expression is used by Honnold, "The Sales Convention in Action – Uniform International Words: Uniform Application?," 8 *J.L. & Com.* 207, 208 (1988).

of an autonomous, international interpretation of the CISG and its uniform application cannot be overstated.[67]

The role played by doctrine in the interpretation of legislation varies in different legal systems. In civil law countries, recourse to doctrine as an instrument of interpretation for domestic and foreign law has never been doubted. On the other hand, common law jurisdictions have traditionally given little effect to scholarly writings. But even in common law countries, such as England, where judges traditionally have been reluctant to have recourse to scholarly writing, the need for uniformity in interpreting international Conventions has led to a more liberal approach and the use of doctrine has become increasingly common.[68]

In considering the interpretation given to the CISG by foreign courts, all national courts should consider the doctrinal writings that influenced such interpretation in those foreign courts. This practice gains its legitimacy by the recognition of the vital role that doctrine can play in avoiding interpretative diversity in the CISG. It is achieved by the introduction, through the use of doctrine, of international, rather than domestic lenses to view the CISG.

3. *Travaux Préparatoires* (Legislative History)

Another useful guide for resolving doubts about the exact meaning, scope, and effect of the CISG's provisions is the legislative history of the CISG (i.e., the study of the *travaux préparatoires*, which include not only the acts and proceedings of the Vienna Conference but also the summary records of the previous deliberations within UNCITRAL).

The CISG directs interpreters to have regard to the "international character" of its provisions and requires, in addition to the international experience that will be developed through jurisprudence and doctrine, that the Convention be placed in the proper international setting of its legislative history.[69]

During the formative stages of the Convention, numerous difficulties arose and were resolved through debate and compromise among the diplomatic delegates to the Vienna

[67] *See* Edgar Bodenheimer, "Doctrine as a Source of the International Unification of Law," 34 *Am. J. Comp. L.* 67 (1986 Supplement), at 71, where the author examines from a comparative point of view and in detail the question of "whether doctrinal writings may be considered primary authorities of law on par with legislation and (in some legal systems) court decisions, or whether they must be relegated to the status of secondary sources."

[68] In the United States, academic writing is cited freely in judicial opinions, and there was similar reliance in England, in *Fothergill v. Monarch Airlines Ltd.*, 1981 A.C. 251 (House of Lords).The sharpest divergence from traditional common law practice is reported in Canada, where courts long ago shed their reluctance to use scholarly writing and regularly cite textbooks, law reviews, and other scholarly literature. According to one commentator, this development is explained "by the wide geographical dispersal of Canadian courts, a less cohesive bar, less specialization among judges and the greater influence exercised by Canadian law schools." *See* Honnold, *Uniform Words and Application*, *supra* note 53, at 126. It is interesting to note that some of the factors responsible for the Canadian development could also be true, structurally at least, in the context of the CISG and its worldwide application.

[69] *See* Honnold, *Uniform Law for Int'l Sales*, *supra* note 1, at 136–137. *See* also Audit, *Lex Mercatoria*, *supra* note 8, at 187–188:

> The international character of the Convention should encourage courts to refer to the Convention's legislative history and prior instruments (*i.e.*, the ULIS and ULF) in order to ascertain the most likely intent underlying the wording of a given provision. Reference should also be made to the various official texts of the Convention to resolve ambiguities in one of the texts. For example, article 39 states that the buyer must notify the seller of a lack of conformity within a reasonable time after discovery. On this score, the English text refers to the "[lack of] conformity *of the goods*." Does this restriction mean that article 39 is inapplicable if the non-conformity appears in the documents instead of in the goods – although delivery of documents is closely associated in the Convention with delivery of the goods themselves? The French text is not as restrictive and speaks of *défaut de conformité* in general terms.

Convention.[70] The adoption of the CISG being essentially a political act by the governments of member States made it inevitable that the final version of CISG contains several textual compromises, which, in fact, are unresolved substantive difficulties. The most significant of these difficulties relates to the CISG's gap-filling procedures and its use of Western legal concepts.

The legislative history of the CISG is of great importance, not merely as the starting point of reference to the law it promotes but also as a crucial tool of understanding the meaning of that law.[71] In determining the meaning of an international treaty, one of the rules of the *U.N. Convention on the Law of Treaties* 1969 is that recourse may be had to supplementary means of interpretation, including the preparatory work of the treaty.[72] The principal commentator of the CISG has correctly observed that "[w]hen important and difficult issues of interpretation are at stake, diligent counsel and courts will need to consult the [CISG's] legislative history. In some cases this can be decisive."[73]

Reference to the legislative history of the Convention is generally advocated by most commentators.[74] The relationship between the old and the new law can often be found in the "*travaux préparatoires.*" The same commentators have, however, also stressed that the value of the legislative history should not be overestimated.[75] There are a few reasons for this caution. First, it should not be forgotten that the CISG, once adopted by the Contracting States, acquires a "life of its own,"[76] and its meaning can change with time and use. It becomes apparent that the original intention of the drafters, documented in the *travaux préparatoires*, is only one of the elements to be taken into account for the purpose of the CISG's current interpretation. Another reason for a cautious treatment of the legislative history of the CISG is that the *travaux préparatoires* sometimes reveal a difference of opinion among the drafters themselves. Also, even when the arguments put forward in favor of the adoption of a given provision were not controversial, they are not always, or necessarily, decisive for the final product. In other instances, the difference in opinion documented is of a political rather than legal nature. It should always be kept in mind that the provisions of the CISG were adopted in a diplomatic conference, in what is a political act by representatives of different sovereign States.

[70] Honnold has stressed the importance of discussion to the work of UNCITRAL, leading to consensus without the need for formal votes. *See* Honnold, "The United Nations Commission on International Trade Law: Mission and Methods," 27 *Am. J. Comp. L.* 201, 210–211 (1979). For general comments on UNCITRAL's history, structure, mission, and methods, *see* E. Allen Farnsworth, "UNCITRAL – Why? What? How? When?," 20 *Am. J. Comp. L.* 314 (1972); for one participant's wry view of this process, *see* Gyula Eörsi, "Unifying the Law (A Play in One Act, with a Song)," 25 *Am. J. Comp. L.* 658 (1977).

[71] The material found in the CISG's legislative history adds depth to the international understanding that underlies the Convention's text. Honnold's *Documentary History of the Uniform Law for International Sales* (Kluwer, 1989) reproduces the relevant documents and provides references, thereby making it easier to trace the legislative history and development of the CISG's provisions.

[72] Vienna Convention on the Law of Treaties, May 23, 1969, 1155 U.N.T.S. Art. 32, at 331 (entered into force January 27, 1988).

[73] John Honnold, "Uniform Laws for International Trade," *Int'l Trade & Bus. L. J.* 5 (1995).

[74] *See* Honnold, *Uniform Law for Int'l Sales*, *supra* note 1, at 136; Bonell, *General Provisions*, *supra* note 36, at 90. Among civil law commentators, it is widely accepted that the legislative history of the uniform law must be taken into account when interpreting the uniform law. *See, e.g.*, Bernard Audit, *La Vente Internationale de Marchandises: Convention des Nations Unies du 11 Avril 1980* [The International Sales of Goods, UN Convention of 11 April 1980 – *in French*] (Paris: Librairie Générale de Droit et de Jurisprudence, 1990), at 48 [hereinafter Audit, *International Sales*]; Fritz Enderlein et al., Internationales Kaufrecht [International Sales Law – *in German*] 61 (1991).

[75] Honnold, *Uniform Law for Int'l Sales*, *supra* note 1, at 141–142; Bonell, *General Provisions*, *supra* note 36, at 90.

[76] Bonell, *General Provisions*, *supra* note 36, at 90.

4. Neutral Language – A New *Lingua Franca*[77]

The quality of the international character attributed to the CISG has yet a further dimension. Such a characterization denotes that the terms and concepts of the CISG must be interpreted autonomously of meanings that might traditionally be attached to them within national legal systems. To have regard to CISG's international character must mean that the interpreter should not apply domestic law to solve the interpretative problems raised in the CISG. The reading of the CISG in light of the concepts of the interpreter's domestic legal system would be a violation of the requirement that it be interpreted with regard to its international character.[78] The terms of the CISG must be interpreted "in the context of the Convention itself."[79] Such a conclusion becomes necessary when one looks at the background of the CISG.

The CISG is a code that contains a defined set of topics (formation of contract, rights and obligations of parties, remedies), and its provisions regulate issues relating to those topics using rules that are underpinned by a coherent set of general principles on which the Convention is based. The Convention has adopted a new common language to express those rules and general principles that operate throughout the CISG, frequently using plain words that refer to specific events that are typical of international commercial transactions. The rules on risk of loss provide good examples of the use of event-oriented words. CISG Art. 67(1) provides that "the risk passes to the buyer when the goods are *handed over* to the first carrier for transmission to the buyer in accordance with the contract of sale." In a similar tone, Art. 69(1) states that in contracts that do not involve carriage, "...the risk passes to the buyer when he *takes over* the goods." The drafters of the Convention opted for the use of plain language when referring to things and events for which there are words of neutral content devoid of domestic legal nuances. Such words as "delivery" and such concepts as "property" and "title," which are loaded with peculiar domestic importance, have been intentionally avoided.

The form and content of the CISG are the outcome of prolonged deliberations among lawyers representing a multitude of diverse legal and social systems and cultural backgrounds. The provisions of the CISG had to be formulated in sufficiently neutral language to reach a consensus that would not be vitiated by misunderstanding among its drafters. An important decision that the drafters of the CISG had to make regarding this issue was whether to include in the CISG detailed definitions of significant terms.[80] The eventual choice was to include some definitions as needed within the text of particular provisions,[81] but not to have definitions of key terms as a separate part of the CISG.[82] This decision

[77] *See* Peter H. Schlechtriem, "25 Years CISG – An International Lingua Franca for Drafting Uniform Law, Legal Principles, Domestic Legislation and Transnational Contracts," 2 *CILE Studies. The* CISG *and the Business Lawyer: The UNCITRAL Digest as a Contract Drafting Tool* (forthcoming 2006), offering a strong argument in favor of the CISG as a *lingua franca* of international commercial law.

[78] *See* Honnold, *Uniform Law for Int'l Sales, supra* note 1, at 136, where the author also states, "[t]o read the words of the Convention with regard for their 'international character' requires that they be projected against an international background."

[79] *Id.*

[80] *See* generally Farnsworth, *Problems of Unification, supra* note 26.

[81] *See* CISG Art. 14, stating "[a] proposal for concluding a contract addressed to one or more specific persons constitutes an offer..."; CISG Art. 18, stating "[a] statement made by or other conduct of the offeree indicating assent to an offer is an acceptance"; CISG Art. 25, stating "[a] breach of contract committed by one of the parties is fundamental..."

[82] This style is more reflective of civil code drafting style than common law statutory practice. *See* generally Farnsworth, *Problems of Unification, supra* note 26. This style contrasts with the detailed definitional system in the American Uniform Commercial Code.

on drafting style is a further indication of the wishes of the drafters to produce a law that promotes international cooperation in its application.[83]

It has to be conceded that, despite the diverse composition of the drafting team and the attention given to all official language versions of the CISG, the drafting debate tended to focus on legal concepts drawn from either the civil law or common law traditions.[84] As a result, most of the words and concepts used in the CISG are Anglo-American or Western European in origin, but the ramifications of this origin must not be overestimated. It may be that, in creating this modern uniform legal regime for the international sale of goods, certain concepts[85] or words were borrowed from developed legal systems, but such words or concepts do not (and should not) bring with them to the CISG the special depth of meaning that they have in their original context. The choice of one word rather than another represents the process of a compromise, rather than the acceptance of a concept peculiar to a specific domestic legal system. The drafters attempted to avoid terms that have been endorsed and shaped by diverse historical, social, economic, and cultural structures in the various legal systems. They employed neutral, "a-national" language to avoid such distortions. The neutrality of the words chosen for the CISG promotes the CISG's autonomy and advances UNCITRAL's objectives of internationality and uniformity of interpretation and application.

Any interpretation of the CISG's terms that relies on specific national connotations will be calamitous because what is required is an interpretation of the CISG that is not only uniform but truly international as well. Interpreters of the text must not violate the spirit of the law that is embodied in the Preamble and the interpretation provisions of the Convention. The meaning of any words imported from domestic legal systems must be circumscribed by their new legal context.

The Preamble expressly acknowledges the cultural, social, and legal diversity that characterizes its member States. The remedial provisions of the CISG are also structured to reflect the commitment to equality in the formal parallelism between buyer and seller.[86] The commitment to equal treatment and respect for the different cultural, social, and legal backgrounds of its international members is consistent with other important values underlying the CISG, such as commitment to keeping the contract alive, forthright communication between parties, reasonableness, etc. The interpretation of the text of the Convention must be guided by these enunciated principles.

[83] Kastely argues that this choice of drafting style has rhetorical significance because detailed definitional sections "... encourage the reader to understand the words in a technical and limited way, and to perceive the text as self-contained. The reader is led to interpret such a text as limited to its specifically defined terms and to disregard its broader implications or implicit significance." On the other hand, Kastely notes that "informal, contextual definitions ... encourage a broad and conversational interpretation of the words of the text, leading to greater depth and complexity in the interpretation of individual provisions." Kastely, *Rhetorical Analysis*, *supra* note 19, at 593–594.

[84] *See* Gyula Eörsi, "Problems of Unifying the Law on Formation of Contracts for the International Sale of Goods," 27 *Am. J. Comp. L.* 315–323 (1979).

[85] For example, a party may, by notice fixing an additional final period for performance of the other party's obligations, make time of the essence, where it is not clear from the contract itself or from the surrounding circumstances whether failure to make timely performance amounts to a fundamental breach; *see* CISG Art. 47(1) and Art. 63(1). It has been commented that "Art. 47(1) is based on the German concept of '*Nachfrist*' but it has a well-known counterpart in equity in contracts for the sale of land [references omitted]." Jacob S. Ziegel, *Report to the Uniform Law Conference of Canada on Convention on Contracts for the International Sale of Goods* (July 1981), University of Toronto, excerpt available at <http://cisgw3.law.pace.edu/cisg/text/ziegel47.html>.

[86] Hellner has observed that "the symmetry in the rules on the remedies for the seller's and the buyer's breach of contract is probably prompted by a desire of being impartial to the seller's and the buyer's sides." Jan Hellner, "The UN Convention on International Sales of Goods – An Outsider's View," in *Ius Inter Nationes: Festschrift fur S. Riesenfeld* 85 (Erik Jayme et al. eds., 1983).

Individual terms or problematic provisions can and must be construed with regard to the CISG's underlying values if the overall linguistic and thematic structure is to be reinforced and enriched. This is the mandate expressed in Articles 7(1) and 7(2) of the CISG. The direction taken on this issue will determine whether the members of the CISG's community form a true community of entities that abide by a uniform law or simply a collective of independent entities that, at times, cooperate with each other via a harmonization of sorts on specific topics. Simply put, uniformity in international sales law cannot be achieved merely by the universal adoption of uniform rules, but only by the establishment of a uniform interpretation of these rules universally.

VI. GAP-FILLING IN THE CONVENTION: ARTICLE 7(2)

The CISG does not constitute an exhaustive body of rules and thus does not provide solutions for all the problems that can originate from an international sale transaction.

Indeed, the issues governed by the Convention are limited to the formation of the contract and the rights and obligations of the parties resulting from such a contract.[87] This limitation gives rise to problems relating to the need to fill gaps that exist in any type of incomplete body of rules.[88]

It is to comply with such a need that Article 7(2), designating the rules for filling any gaps in the CISG, was drafted. The justification for such a provision lies in the fact that "it is hardly possible for an international group to draft a voluminous and complicated piece of legislation without leaving gaps behind,"[89] especially in the field of contract, as contracts have infinite variety.

The legislative history of this provision is informative because it reveals the drafting compromise that is Art. 7(2)[90]:

> Questions concerning matters governed by this Convention which are not expressly settled in it are to be settled in conformity with the general principles on which it is based or, in the absence of such principles, in conformity with the law applicable by virtue of the rules of private international law.

[87] *See* CISG Art. 4, stating "[t]his Convention governs only the formation of the contract of sale and the rights and obligations of the seller and the buyer arising from such a contract. In particular, except as otherwise expressly provided in this Convention, it is not concerned with: (a) the validity of the contract or of any of its provisions or of any usage; (b) the effect which the contract may have on the property in the goods sold."
For further exclusions to the applicability of CISG, *see* CISG, *supra* note 1, art. 2 (sale of certain goods), art. 3 (supply and manufacture contracts and labor contracts), and art. 5 (liability for death or personal injury). In addition, the Convention does not govern rights based on fraud or agency law; *see* Honnold, *Uniform Law for Int'l Sales*, *supra* note 1, at 114–116.

[88] Note that for the purposes of this text, any reference to "gaps" is a reference to gaps *praeter legem* (i.e., matters "governed by the CISG which are not expressly settled in it"); in other words, issues to which CISG applies but which it does not expressly resolve. Matters that are excluded from the scope of CISG (such as the matters discussed in CISG Arts. 2, 3, 4 and 5) are gaps *intra legem* and do not concern Art. 7(2).

[89] Eörsi, *General Provisions in International Sales*, *supra* note 51, at 2–11. *See* also Audit, *Lex Mercatoria*, *supra* note 8, at 190, commenting on issues of gap-filling in the CISG:

> Although the Convention is intended to be an all-encompassing framework, unprovided-for circumstances perforce will surface. Article 7(2) deals with these circumstances. Where a gap is found in the Convention, it is not to be filled immediately by reference to an applicable domestic law; the reference to such a domestic law is only subsidiary. Initial reference must be made to the Convention's "general principles." The Convention constitutes an autonomous system; it is not to be regarded as one statute among others.

[90] There were arguments in favor of a gap-filling provision excluding the use of the rules of private international law (i.e., in terms similar to those in Article 17 ULIS). The opposing view was that the uniform law could not be considered as totally separated from the various national laws – as the uniform law did not deal with a number of important questions related to contracts of sale – and that it would be unrealistic and impractical to construe many undefined terms contained in the Cisg without having recourse to national law. *See* "Legislative History of Art. 7(2)" in Felemegas, *Uniform Interpretation*, *supra* note 24, ch. 4.

In the manner that Article 7(2) is drafted, the risk of diversity in the Convention's gap-filling from one jurisdiction to another is minimized, because recourse to domestic laws is to be had only when it is not possible to fill a gap by applying the general principles on which the Convention is based.[91]

The aim of this provision is not very different from that of the interpretation rules found in Article 7(1); that is, uniformity in the CISG's interpretation and application. Article 7(2) and gap-filling are directly connected to Article 7(1) and interpretation, not only due to the proximity of their location in the text but, more importantly, because of their substantive relationship with each other.[92] Gaps in the law constitute a danger to the uniformity and autonomy of the CISG's interpretation, because "one way to follow the homeward trend is to find gaps in the law."[93] Further, interpretation must be the means whereby gaps in the CISG are filled, because when a gap *praeter legem* is detected the problem arising thereby should be solved through interpretation of the CISG.

However, the relevant textual reference in Article 7(2) leaves the CISG prone to divergent gap-filling (i.e., in conformity with the relevant law applicable according to the rules of private international law). It is arguable that the use of the rules of private international law to resolve questions concerning matters governed but unresolved by the CISG will harm the Convention's uniform application by producing divergent results. An alternative approach to gap-filling – one based on the concept of internationality and on generally acknowledged principles upon which the CISG is based – would serve and promote the purpose of the new law (i.e., uniformity in its application), rather than hinder it.

In accordance with the basic criteria established in Article 7(1) and discussed earlier, uniformity in the CISG's application is the ultimate goal. It follows that for the interpretation of the CISG in general – not only in the case of ambiguities or obscurities in the text but also in the case of gaps *praeter legem* – "courts should to the largest possible extent refrain from resorting to the different domestic laws and try to find a solution within the Convention itself."[94]

[91] *See, e.g.*, Audit, *Lex Mercatoria, supra* note 8, at 193–94, where the author writes, "The relationship between the Convention and the *lex mercatoria* can be summarized by outlining the hierarchy of norms that may apply to an international sales contract under the Convention:

(1) The "mandatory norms" of domestic law, which prevail over the rules of the Convention (art. 4[a]);
(2) Trade usages, either expressly referred to by the parties (art. 9[l]) or found applicable by a court or arbitrator (art. 9[2]);
(3) Contract provisions (art. 6);
(4) The rules of the Convention;
(5) The "general principles" on which the Convention is based (art. 7[l]);
(6) If no such principles are identified, the non-mandatory norms of the law applicable under the conflict rules of the forum (art. 7[2]).

Although domestic laws appear at the top of the hierarchy, their application should be the exception. Under the Convention, the *lex mercatoria* is the chief source of the applicable law for international transactions either directly as trade usages (the second heading) or indirectly through the application of the principle of party autonomy in contract (the third heading). The Convention elaborates the common law and practices of international sales and the common core of domestic commercial rules. The Convention itself purports to formulate the most common practice and therefore qualifies as an expression of *lex mercatoria*. But, as its place in the hierarchy indicates, the Convention is above all a recognition by states of the paramount importance of existing and more specific commercial practices, to which the Convention gives the force of law.

[92] The line between implied terms and interpretation is a difficult one to draw – indeed it is not clearly drawn in some jurisdictions – which supports my view of the connection between Cisg Article 7(1) and 7(2). *See C Itoh & Co. Ltd. v. Companhia de Navegacao Lloyd Brasilieiro*, 1 Lloyd's Rep. 201 (Eng. Comm. Ct. 1998, Clarke J), affirmed by the English Court of Appeal at 1 Lloyd's Rep 115 (Eng. C.A. 1999) (use of the officious bystander test when interpreting a contract).

[93] Eörsi, *General Provisions in International Sales*, *supra* note 51, at 2–9.

[94] Bonell, *General Provisions*, *supra* note 36, at 75.

1. Gaps *Praeter Legem*

Before the gap-filling rule in Article 7(2) can be put into operation, the matters to which the rule applies must first be identified. The starting point of the gap-filling analysis is the observation that the gaps to which the rule refers are not gaps *"intra legem"* (i.e., matters that are excluded from the scope or the application of the Convention – such as the matters discussed in CISG Articles 2,[95] 3,[96] 4[97] and 5[98]); rather, they must be gaps *"praeter legem"* [99](i.e., matters that are governed but are not expressly resolved by the CISG). The absence of a uniform law provision dealing with such issues cannot be regarded as a lacuna.

2. Gap-Filling Methodology

Three different approaches exist to fill gaps *praeter legem*. The first approach is based on the application of the general principles of the statute and is known as the "true Code" approach.[100] The drafters of the 1964 Hague Conventions chose that approach.[101] ULIS's pursuit of absolute independence from domestic law failed the test of acceptance.

[95] CISG Art. 2, states that CISG does not apply to consumer sales, to auctions, or to sales of shares, vessels, and electricity.

[96] CISG Art. 3 excludes the application of the Convention in cases of "supply and manufacture" contracts and labor contracts.

[97] CISG Art. 4 sets out the scope of the Convention and, except as otherwise expressly provided in the Convention, excludes from it the issue of validity of the contract and the effect of the contract on the property in the goods.

[98] CISG Art. 5 excludes from the scope of the Convention the issue of the liability of the seller for death or personal injury caused by the goods to any person.

[99] The terms *"intra legem"* and *"praeter legem"* are discussed in Ferrari, *Uniform Interpretation, supra* note 54, at 217. For the distinction between gaps *"intra legem"* and gaps *"praeter legem," see* Ferrari,*Uniform Interpretation, id.* at n. 186, referring to H. Deschenaux, *Der Einleitungstitel*, in 2 *Schweizerisches Privatrecht* 95 (Max Gutzwiller et al. eds., 1967).

[100] *See* William D. Hawkland, "Uniform Commercial 'Code' Methodology," *U. Ill. L. Rev.* 291. 292 (1962). *See* also, Ferrari, *Uniform Interpretation, supra* note 54, at 218, fn.189, stating that the "true code" approach corresponds to what Kritzer calls the "internal analogy approach," in Kritzer, *Guide to Practical Applications, supra* note 58, at 117. According to the "true Code" approach, a court, when faced with a gap in a Code, should only look at the Code itself, including the purposes of the Code and the policies underlying the Code, but no further. It follows that, for the solution of questions governed by a Code, the answer can be found within the framework of that Code. The justification of this approach lies in the belief that a "true Code" is comprehensive, and as such, "it is sufficiently inclusive and independent to enable it to be administered in accordance with its own basic policies." Hawkland, *op. cit.*, at 292.

This approach had been discussed during the 1951 Hague Conference (January 1–10). For a discussion of the 1951 Conference, *see* Ernst Rabel, "The Hague Conference on the Unification of Sales Law," 1 *Am. J. Comp. L.* 88 (1952). Rabel said this about this gap-filling approach: "... within its concerns ... the text must be self sufficient. Where a case is not expressly covered the text is not to be supplemented by the national laws – which would at once destroy unity – but be construed according to principles consonant with its spirit". *Id.* In effect, the Code is approached as a source of law itself.

[101] *See, e.g.*, E.Wahl, "Article 17," in *Kommentar Zum Einheitlichen Kaufrecht* 126b (Hans Dölle ed., 1976), where the commentator, after having listed the three different approaches to filling gaps *praeter legem*, states that "ULIS has adopted the first method. The text of Article 17, its legislative history as well as the provision contemplated in Article 2 show that the application of the rules of international private law had to be limited." See Convention Relating to a Uniform Law on the International Sale of Goods [ULIS], July 1, 1964, 834 U.N.T.S. 107, reprinted in 13 *Am. J. Comp. L.* 453 (1964).

ULIS Art. 2 excludes the application of rules of private international law, except in a few instances; *see, e.g.*, Harold J. Berman, "The Uniform Law on International Sale of Goods: A Constructive Critique", 30 *L. & Cont. Probs.* 354, 359 (1965).

ULIS Art. 17 provides that the general principles underlying the 1964 Uniform Law are to be used to fill any gaps. It has been correctly concluded that "[t]his has the intended negative implication that courts may not refer to the domestic law of the country whose law would otherwise apply under the rules of private international law." Peter Winship, "Private International Law and the U.N. Sales Convention," 21 *Cornell Int'l L. J.* 487, 492 (1988).

The solution adopted in ULIS has been criticized and has been considered by some commentators as one of the reasons for its failure to win wide acceptance.[102]

The second approach relies on the use of external legal principles to fill gaps found in the Code and is known as the "meta-Code approach."[103]

The third approach to gap-filling is a combination of the foregoing approaches.[104] According to this approach, one is supposed to first apply the general principles of the Code. In the absence of any such principles, however, one should resort to the rules of private international law. It is this approach that was adopted by the drafters of the CISG. Therefore, in practice, when a matter is governed by the CISG but is not expressly settled in it, Article 7(2) offers a solution by (i) internal analogy, when the CISG's other provisions contain an applicable general principle or (ii) reference to external legal principles (the rules of private international law) when the CISG does not contain an applicable general principle.[105]

Pursuant to Art. 7(2) any gaps must be filled, whenever possible, within the Convention itself; a solution that complies with the aim of Article 7(1); that is, the promotion of the Convention's uniform application.[106] As has been noted above, there are various types of logical reasoning that can be employed to find a solution to a gap within the CISG itself, and recourse to the CISG's general principles constitutes only one method of gap-filling. This observation leads to a further interpretation issue, the interpretation of Article 7(2) itself. One must determine whether Article 7(2) should be interpreted broadly; that is, whether it includes other methods of legal reasoning as well, such as analogical application,[107] or whether it is to be interpreted restrictively.

It is submitted that Art. 7(2) must be interpreted broadly and that there are two complementary methods of gap-filling allowed under this provision: (a) an analogical application of specific provisions of the CISG and (b) a consideration of the general

[102] *See, e.g.*, Isaak I. Dore & James E. DeFranco, "A Comparison of the Non-Substantive Provisions of the UNCITRAL Convention on the International Sale of Goods and the Uniform Commercial Code," 23 *Harv. Int'l. L.J.* 49, 63 (1982).

[103] For the expression "meta-Code," *see* Steve H. Nickles, "Problems of Sources of Law Relationships under the Uniform Commercial Code – Part I: The Methodological Problem and the Civil Law Approach," 31 *Ark. L. Rev.* 1 (1977). This approach is based on the idea that external legal principles should supplement the provisions of a Code, unless this is expressly disallowed by that Code. *See, e.g.*, U.C.C. §1–103, which states "that unless displaced by the particular provisions of the Act, the principles of law and equity . . . shall supplement its provisions." *Id.* This approach seems to be favored in common law, *see* Dore & DeFranco, *op. cit.* In regards with the U.C.C., however, note the tension that is created within the U.C.C. due to the wording of §1–102(1), which states that "this Act shall be liberally construed and applied to promote its underlying purposes and policies". *Id.* at §1–201(1). For an approach more closely associated with civil law, *see* Mitchell Franklin, "On the Legal Method of the Uniform Commercial Code," 16 *L. & Contemp. Probs.* 330, 333 (1951).

[104] For further references to the three approaches, *see* generally Kritzer, *Guide to Practical Applications, supra* note 58.

[105] For a similar appraisal of the Convention's gap-filling measures, *see* Kritzer, *Guide to Practical Applications, supra* note 58, at 117.

[106] *See* Enderlein & Maskow, *International Sales Law, supra* note 19, at 58, where the authors state that Article 7(2) indicates that gaps must be "closed . . . from within the Convention. This is in line with the aspiration to unify the law which . . . is established in the Convention itself."

[107] The difference between the two gap-filling methods is explained well by Bonell, *General Provisions, supra* note 36, at 80 as follows:

> Recourse to "general principles" as a means of gap-filling differs from reasoning by analogy insofar as it constitutes an attempt to find a solution for the case at hand not by mere extension of specific provisions dealing with analogous cases, but on the basis of principles and rules which because of their general character may be applied on a much wider scale.

For further discussion of the distinction between analogical application and the recourse to general principles in the context of a uniform law, *see* Jan Kropholler, *Internationales Einheitsrecht, Allgemeine Lehren* 292 (1975).

principles underlying the CISG as a whole, when the gap cannot be filled by analogical application of specific provisions.

Analogical application has also been accepted as a method of gap-filling by many other scholars in this area.[108] An explanation of this method is provided by Enderlein and Maskow, who, in endorsing a broad interpretation of Article 7(2), state that "gap-filling can be done, as we believe, by applying such interpretation methods as extensive interpretation and analogy. The admissibility of analogy is directly addressed in the wording contained in the CISG because it is aimed at obtaining, from several comparable rules, one rule for a not expressly covered fact and/or a general rule under which the fact can be subsumed."[109]

3. Gap-Filling by Analogy

The method of analogical application requires examination of the provisions of the CISG, because the rule laid down in an analogous provision may be restricted to its particular context, and thus, its extension to other situations would be arbitrary and contrary to the intention of the drafters or the purpose of the rule itself.[110]

There is some diversity in academic opinion on the exact test to be applied in such cases. Ferrari,[111] using a criterion similar to that offered by Bonell,[112] states that when the matters expressly settled in the Convention and the matters in question are related so closely that it would be "unjustified to adopt a different solution," one can fill the gap by analogy. Honnold offers a different test, placing the focus of the inquiry on whether the cases were so analogous that the drafters "would not have deliberately chosen discordant results." Only in such circumstances, according to Honnold, would it be reasonable to conclude that the rule embracing the analogous situation is authorized by Article 7(2) CISG.[113]

It is important to note that gap-filling by analogy is concerned with the application of certain rules, or solutions, taken from specific CISG provisions to be applied in analogous cases to resolve legislative gaps. This method should not be confused with the application of general principles that are expressed in the CISG or upon which the CISG is founded. It is my contention that gap-filling by analogy is *primary* gap-filling. Only when no analogous solutions can be found in the CISG's provisions should the interpreter resort to the application of the CISG's general principles – internal and external – which is *secondary* gap-filling. This is a fine, but clear, distinction. It deserves to be maintained, although there may ultimately not be a lot of practical importance attached to maintaining it because of the tendency of commentators to blur the distinction by focusing on the use of general principles in gap-filling and the potential of general principles to dominate the CISG's gap-filling function. However, the value of recognizing its existence lies in the

[108] There is strong academic opinion in favor of the view that not only does the CISG permit both methods of gap-filling but also that, in the case of a gap in the CISG, "the first attempt to be made is to settle the unsolved question by means of an analogical application of specific provisions." Bonell, *General Provisions*, *supra* note 36, at 78.

[109] Enderlein & Maskow, *International Sales Law*, *supra* note 19, at 58.

[110] Bonell, *General Provisions*, *supra* note 36, at 78.

[111] *See* Ferrari, *Uniform Interpretation*, *supra* note 54, at 222.

[112] Bonell opines that where there are no special reasons for limiting the analogical application of a specific rule to another CISG provision, the interpreter must consider whether the case regulated by this rule and the gap at hand are so analogous "that it would be inherently unjust not to adopt the same solution." Bonell, *General Provisions*, *supra* note 36, at 79.

[113] *See* Honnold, *Uniform Law for Int'l Sales*, *supra* note 1, at 156. *See* also Siegfried Eiselen, *Electronic Commerce and the UN Convention on Contracts for the International Sale of Goods (CISG) 1980*, 6 EDI L. Rev. 21–46 (1999) (fax, e-mail and EDI communications also encompassed by the definition of "writing" in CISG Article 13).

theoretical clarity and legitimacy that this distinction adds to the consistent and systematic examination of the interpretative structure embedded in the CISG.

4. General Principles and the CISG

When the solution to a gap-filling problem cannot be achieved by analogical application of a rule that might be found in a specific CISG provision dealing with issues similar to those present in the gap, gap-filling can be performed by the application of the "general principles" on which the CISG is based.[114]

As explained above, this procedure differs from the analogical application method, in that it does not solve the case in question solely by extending specific provisions dealing with analogous cases; rather it solves the case on the basis of rules that, because of their general character, may be applied on a much wider scale. At this point it is appropriate to note another fine but valid distinction in the types of general principles that concern the CISG and its interpretation. The distinction must be drawn between principles extrapolated from specific CISG provisions and general principles of comparative law – namely, those rules of private law that command broad adherence throughout various countries, or general principles of law of civilized nations – on which the CISG is generally based.

a. Principles in CISG's Provisions

Despite the clear provision for the use of the CISG principles in gap-filling by Article 7(2), there is no other textual reference to the identification of such principles and the manner of their application, once identified, to fill a gap in the CISG.

General principles that are capable of being applied to matters governed by, but not expressly regulated by the CISG, may be inferred from specific rules established by specific CISG provisions dealing with specific issues.[115] A general principle stands at a higher level of abstraction than a rule or might be said to underpin more than one such rule.

Some general principles can be identified easily because they are expressly stated in the provisions of the CISG itself. One such principle is the principle of good faith.[116] The principle of autonomy[117] is another general principle expressly outlined in the CISG. Most

[114] CISG Art. 7(2).

[115] For academic support on this point, *see* Schlechtriem, *Uniform Sales Law*, *supra* note 19, at 38, stating "[t]he authoritative principles can be inferred from the individual rules themselves and their systematic context"; Honnold, *Uniform Law for Int'l Sales*, *supra* note 1, at 155, stating "[g]eneral principles [must] be moored to premises that underlie specific provisions of the Convention"; Bonell, *General Provisions*, *supra* note 36, at 80.

[116] CISG Art. 7(1). The good faith principle has been recognized as one of the general principles expressly laid down by the Convention. *See, e.g.*, Audit, *International Sales*, *supra* note 74, at 51, where the author states that good faith is one of the general principles, even though it must be considered a mere instrument of interpretation; Enderlein & Maskow, *International Sales Law*, *supra* note 19, at 59, where the authors list the good faith principle among those principles "which do not necessarily have to be reflected in individual rules"; Rolf Herber & Beate Czerwenka, *Internationales Kaufrecht. Kommentar zu dem Übereinkommen der Vereinten Nationen vom 11 April 1980 über Vertrage über den Internationalen Warenkauf* [International Sales Law, Commentary on the United Nations Convention on Contracts for the International Sale of Goods] 49 (1991), where it is stated that the good faith principle is the only general principle expressly provided for by the Convention.

[117] CISG Art. 6. *See, e.g.*, Honnold, *Uniform Law For Int'l Sales*, *supra* note 1, at 47, who in his introduction of the Convention states that "[t]he dominant theme of the Convention is the role of the contract construed in the light of commercial practice and usage – a theme of deeper significance than may be evident at first glance." Party autonomy has been described as the most important principle of the CISG; *see* Kritzer, *Guide to Practical Applications*, *supra* note 58, at 114. Some commentators have inferred from this principle that the CISG plays solely a subsidiary role as it provides only for those cases that the parties neither contemplated, nor foresaw. For this thesis, *see* Honnold, *Uniform Law for Int'l Sales*, *supra* note 1, at 48, stating that "the Convention's rules play a supporting role, supplying answers to problems that the parties have failed to solve by contract." *Id.* For a similar conclusion, *see* K. Sono, "The Vienna Sales Convention: History and

general principles, however, have not been expressly provided by the CISG. Therefore, they must be deduced from its specific provisions by analyzing the contents of such provisions. If it can be concluded that they express a more general principle, capable of being applied also to cases different from those specifically regulated, then they could also be used for the purposes of Article 7(2).

There is a notable divergence of opinion as to the exact nature of such an analysis of specific CISG provisions. Bonell states that

> just as in interpreting specific terms and concepts adopted in the text of the Convention, also in specifying "general principles" courts should, in accordance with the basic criteria of Article 7(1), avoid resorting to standards developed under their own domestic law and try to find the particular solution "autonomously", *i.e.*, within the Convention itself, or, should this not be possible, by using standards which are generally accepted at a comparative level.[118]

Bonell's argument relies on the premise that, although there are principles, such as that of party autonomy and the dispatch rule, which can be applied directly, others, such as the principle of "good faith" and the concept of "reasonableness," need further specification to offer a solution for a particular case. The question that arises here relates to the standards to be used to identify the principles that belong to the latter category. For example, how could a judge of a highly industrialized country apply the "reasonableness" test to determine which party in a particular circumstance has been acting with due diligence? Arguably, the judge should not automatically refer to the standards of care and professional skill normally required from his country's business people when conducting domestic affairs. Bonell is of the opinion that the answer should be found "either in the Convention itself or at least on the basis of standards which are currently adopted in other legal systems."[119]

On the other hand, there is strong academic opinion that comparative law should not be used to identify such general principles. Enderlein and Maskow are of the opinion that it is

> not possible to obtain the Convention's general principles from an *analysis prepared by comparison of the laws* of the most important legal systems of the Contracting States ... as it was supported, in some cases, in regard to Article 17 [of] ULIS.... The wording of the Convention does in no way support the application of this method.[120]

In addressing this issue, interpreters of the CISG must be conscious of the mandate in Art. 7(1) to have regard to the Convention's international character and to promote uniformity in its application. Although Bonell's model is not the same as resorting to rules of private international law, the temptation to adopt a domestic law analysis of the problem should be resisted. Tribunals must recognize the uniquely international

Perspective," in *International Sale of Goods: Dubrovnik Lectures* 14 (P. Sarcevic & P. Volken eds., 1986), affirming that "the rules contained in the Convention are only supplementary for those cases where parties did not provide otherwise in their contracts." *Id.*

According to this premise, it is logical to conclude that in case of conflict between the parties' autonomy and any other general principle of the CISG, the former always prevails. *See* E. Allen Farnsworth, "Rights and Obligations of the Seller," in *Wiener Ubereinkommen von 1980 über den Internationalen Warenkauf* (Lausanner Kolloquium 1984) (Schweizerisches Institut für Rechtsvergleichung ed., 1985) at 83, 84 where the author draws the same conclusion: "in case of a conflict between the contract and the Convention, it is the contract – not the Convention – that controls." *Id.* Note that this result is "contrary to the Uniform Commercial Code where principles of 'good faith, diligence, reasonableness and care' prevail over party autonomy". U.C.C. §1-102(3). *See* also Kritzer, *Guide to Practical Applications*, *supra* note 58, at 115.

[118] Bonell, *General Provisions*, *supra* note 36, at 81.

[119] *Id.*, at 82.

[120] Enderlein & Maskow, *International Sales Law*, *supra* note 19, at 60. *See also See* Ferrari, *Uniform Interpretation*, *supra* note 54, at 224.

nature of the CISG and its proper function as uniform law. Bearing in mind what has already been written about the potential threats to the autonomy and uniformity of the CISG's interpretation and application posed by the use of different domestic concepts and laws, it seems that the latter, rather than the former, opinion is better. It is hoped that the difficulties that can arise, let us say, in a dispute between a German seller and a Zambian buyer relating to a notice of nonconformity "within a reasonable time" under CISG Art. 39, can be solved in a way that respects the CISG's (international) character and (uniformity) objective – bearing in mind the different perceptions that may exist in these two countries as to time.[121]

Irrespective of the result in the debate as to the theoretical justification of the method of extracting general principles by analyzing the contents of specific provisions of the CISG, in practice, several general principles can be deduced by this method and then applied to cases not specifically regulated by any of the CISG's provisions.[122] For instance, it is commonly understood[123] that the concept of "reasonableness" constitutes a general principle of the Convention.[124]

[121] My suggestion regarding this hypothetical dispute is that the concept of *reasonableness* might be allied with the Art. 8(2) reference to "the understanding that a reasonable person of the same kind as the other party would have had in the same circumstances" or even with the provision on usage (under CISG Art. 9) to permit regional variation of due diligence.

[122] The following is a list of such general principles of the Convention, although one should not be dogmatic in such classifications as sometimes it is not sufficiently clear whether something is a "general principle" underpinning certain rules or merely a rule:

- the principle of mitigation, which provides that the parties relying on a breach of contract must take reasonable measures to limit damages resulting from the breach of the contract; *see* CISG Arts. 77, 85–88
- the principle of cooperation, according to which the parties must cooperate "in carrying out the interlocking steps of an international sales transaction": Kritzer, *Guide to Practical Applications*, *supra* note 58, at 115. This duty is closely related to the duty to communicate "information that is obviously needed by a trading partner": Honnold, *Uniform Law for Int'l Sales*, *supra* note 1, at 155; *see* CISG Arts. 32(3), 48(2), 60(a), 65
- the principle that a party cannot contradict a representation on which the other party has reasonably relied (i.e., that the parties must not act *venire contra factum proprium*); *see* CISG Arts. 16(2)(b), 29(2)
- the principle of *favor contractus*, which means that "whenever possible, a solution should be adopted in favor of the valid existence of the contract and against its premature termination on the initiative of one of the parties": Bonell *General Provisions*, *supra* note 36, at 81; *see* CISG Arts. 19(2), 25, 26, 34, 37, 48, 49, 59, 51(1), 64, 71 and 72.

[123] *See, e.g.*, Audit, *International Sales*, *supra* note 74, at 51; Rolf Herber, "Article 7," in *Commentary on the UN Convention on the International Sale of Goods* 94 (Peter Schlechtriem ed., 1998).

[124] Citing the numerous references to reasonableness in the CISG, Schlechtriem states that "the rule that the parties must conduct themselves according to the standard of the 'reasonable person'... must be regarded as a general principle of the Convention": Schlechtriem, *Uniform Sales Law*, at 39 and 22 n.41. For confirming citations, *see* views of several commentators on references to *reasonableness* in the CISG available online at <http://cisgw3.law.pace.edu/cisg/text/reason.html#view>. *See* also Albert H. Kritzer, "Overview Comments on 'Reasonableness' – A General Principle of the CISG," available online at <http://cisgw3.law.pace.edu/cisg/text/reason.html#over>:

> Although not specifically defined in the CISG, reasonableness is so defined in the Principles of European Contract Law. Moreover, the PECL definition of reasonableness also fits the manner in which this concept is used in the CISG. This definition can help researchers apply reasonableness to the CISG provisions in which it is specifically mentioned and as a general principle of the CISG. As a general principle of the CISG, reasonableness has a strong bearing on the proper interpretation of all provisions of the CISG. No provision of any law can purport to expressly settle all questions concerning matters governed by it. The CISG recognizes this and provides in its Article 7(2):
>
> *Part One*: Such matters are to be settled in conformity with the general principles on which the CISG is based. *Part Two*: In the absence of general principles on which the CISG is based, such matters are to be settled in conformity with the law applicable by virtue of the rules of private international law. There is much doctrine in support of the good-faith and uniform-law logic of seeking to apply Part One of Article 7(2) in lieu of its Part Two, wherever it is reasonable to do so [...] We submit that regarding reasonableness as a fundamental principle of the CISG and reading reasonableness into every article of the CISG; whether specifically mentioned in the article or not, helps tilt the scales in favor of Part One rather than Part Two applications of Article 7(2) – a tilting of scales that we submit is required by virtue of the good-faith and uniform-law mandate recited in Article 7(1) of the CISG [citations omitted]. *Id.*

b. General Principles of Comparative Law on Which the CISG Is Based

As was noted earlier, an important distinction must be drawn between those principles extrapolated from within specific CISG provisions and the general principles of comparative law on which the CISG as a whole is founded. This distinction provides the theoretical framework for the introduction of elements of the *UNIDROIT Principles of International Commercial Contracts* and the *Principles of European Contract Law* – as part of the "general principles" on which the CISG is based – into the gap-filling function of Article 7(2).

The CISG is the world's uniform international sales law. Two more recent documents can be regarded as companions to the CISG: the *UNIDROIT Principles of International Commercial Contracts* (promulgated in 1994)[125] and the *Principles of European Contract Law* (PECL) (revised version 1998).[126]

Unlike the CISG, which is a uniform sales law the PECL are a set of principles whose objective is to provide general rules of contract law in the European Union that will apply when the parties have agreed to incorporate them into their contract or that their contract is to be governed by them.[127] Similarly to the PECL, a stated purpose of the UNIDROIT Principles is that "[t]hey may be used to interpret or supplement international uniform law instruments."[128]

What follows is a discussion of the nature of the UNIDROIT Principles and the PECL as general principles of comparative law on which the CISG is based, and the proposed important function those Principles (both UNIDROIT and PECL) have as aids in the proper interpretation of the CISG as uniform sales law.[129]

[125] *UNIDROIT Principles of International Commercial Contracts* (UNIDROIT ed., 1994).

[126] *Principles of European Contract Law*, Parts I and II (Ole Lando and Hugh Beale eds., 2000).

[127] PECL Art. 1:101(1)(2).

[128] Preamble to the UNIDROIT Principles.

[129] The weight of academic opinion is that the UNIDROIT Principles form part of the new *lex mercatoria, see*: Michael Joachim Bonell, "The UNIDROIT Principles in Transnational Law," in *The Practice of Transnational Law* 23–41(Klaus Peter Berger ed., Kluwer Law International, 2001) [The Parties' Express Choice of the UNIDROIT Principles as the Law Governing Their Contract (Application of the UNIDROIT Principles by Domestic Courts, Application of the UNIDROIT Principles by Arbital Tribunals), Application of the UNIDROIT Principles in the Absence of an Express Reference by the Parties (The UNIDROIT Principles as a Source of "General Principles of Law," "*Lex mercatoria*" or the Like, The UNIDROIT Principles as a Means of Interpreting and Supplementing International Uniform Law, The UNIDROIT Principles as a Means of Interpreting and Supplementing Domestic Law)]; Philippe Kahn, "Vers l'institutionnalisation de la *lex mercatoria*: a propos des principes d'UNIDROIT relatifs aux contrats du commerce international" [Towards Institutionalization of the *Lex mercatoria*: The UNIDROIT Principles on International Commercial Contracts – *in French*], in *Liber amicorum commission droit et vie des affaires* 125 (1988) 125; Klaus Peter Berger, *The Creeping Codification of the Lex mercatoria*, (Kluwer Law International, 1999) [includes discussion on UNIDROIT Principles and PECL, at 143–206 and elsewhere; contains annotated "List of Principles, Rules and Standards of the *Lex mercatoria*," 278–311]; Klaus Peter Berger, "The Relationship between the UNIDROIT Principles of International Commercial Contracts and the new *lex mercatoria*" [*International Uniform Law Conventions, Lex mercatoria and UNIDROIT Principles*: Symposium held at Verona University (Italy), Faculty of Law, November 4–6,1999] in *Unif. L. Rev.* 152–170 (2000); Klaus Peter Berger, "The New Law Merchant and the Global Market Place – A 21st Century View of Transnational Law," in *The Practice of Transnational Law* 1–22 (Klaus Peter Berger ed., Kluwer Law International, 2001) [The "Milestones" of the *Lex mercatoria* Doctrine (Malynes and Blackstone: "From the Ancient Law Merchant to the Codification Wave," Zitelmann: "The Vision of a "World Law," Goldman, Fouchard and Kahn: "The Rebirth of the *Lex mercatoria* by the French School," Clive Schmitthoff: "The Power of International Arbitrators and International Formulating Agencies," UNIDROIT: "The Report on the 'Progressive' Codification of the Law of International Trade," Dezalay, Garth and Teubner: "The Sociological Approach," UNIDROIT, Lando-Commission, Central: "The New Phenomenon of the 'Creeping Codification' of Transnational Law"), "The Present State of the Doctrine of Transnational Law" ("The Evolution of a 'Global Market Place' and a 'Global Civil Society,'" "The Decreasing Significance of State Sovereignty in the Traditional Theory of Legal Sources," "The Modern Law Merchant in the Global Market Place")]; Fabrizio Marrella, "*Lex mercatoria* e Principi UNIDROIT. Per una recostruzione sistematica del diritto del commercio internazionale" [*Lex mercatoria* and UNIDROIT Principles: Toward a Systematic Rebuilding of International Commercial Law – *in*

VII. UNIDROIT PRINCIPLES AND PECL

The UNIDROIT Principles and the PECL were drafted by legal experts, many of whom had been associated with the drafting of the CISG. Although both Principles are broader than the CISG in scope, each in different ways, these are "Restatements" that include provisions derived from the CISG (as well as other sources). Both "Restatements" take cognizance of insights derived from the text of the CISG, from scholarly commentaries on the CISG, from cases that have interpreted the CISG, and from other sources.[130]

Italian], Contratto e Impresa / Europa, 5 (2000) 29–79; Jorge Oviedo Alban, "Transformaciones de la Contratación mercantil: la conformación de la *lex mercatoria* a partir de los Principios de UNIDROIT para los contratos mercantiles imternacionales y la Convención de Viena para la Compraventa internacional de mercaderias" [Changes in commercial contracting: The formation of the *lex mercatoria* after the UNIDROIT Principles of International Commercial Contracts and the Vienna Convention on Contracts for the International Sale of Goods – *in Spanish*], Conferencia presentada en el seminario "Código de comercio: 30 años", Facultad de Derecho de la Universidad de La Sabana, Forum Legis (Octubre 1 de 2001), Publicación en CD ROM, Legis: Bogatá, Colombia.

See also Gesa Baron, "Do the UNIDROIT *Principles of International Commercial Contracts* Form a New *Lex mercatoria*?," 15 *Arbitration Int'l.* 115–130 (1999), also available online at <http://cisgw3.law.pace.edu/cisg/biblio/baron.html>, where the author pursues the question of whether the UNIDROIT Principles can really be considered as a new *lex mercatoria* [Starting with a historical description of the ancient *lex mercatoria*, the commentary turns to the theory of a modern *lex mercatoria* and outlines the debate concerning the *lex mercatoria* as being an autonomous body of law. The commentary then examines the UNIDROIT Principles in light of the specific characteristics of a *lex mercatoria* and the criticism put forward against it. The commentary concludes that the Principles with their autonomous and yet nonbinding character meet not only the substantive requirements of a true law merchant but that they also counter some of the main points of criticism against the modern *lex mercatoria*: "As such, the Principles constitute a cornerstone in the *lex mercatoria* debate and may become the heart of the new *lex mercatoria*"]. *Id.*

See also Institute of International Business Law and Practice ed., *UNIDROIT Principles for International Commercial Contracts: A New Lex mercatoria*, Paris: ICC Publication No. 490/1 (1995); Jürgen Basedow, "National Report: Germany," in *A New Approach to International Commercial Contracts: The UNIDROIT Principles of International Commercial Contracts*, XVth International Congress of Comparative Law, Bristol, 26 July–1 August 1998 125–150 (Kluwer Law International, 1999) [General characterization of the UNIDROIT Principles; The UNIDROIT Principles and German contract law compared; The use of the UNIDROIT Principles and German law (Survey; The Principles as "General principles of law" or *lex mercatoria*; Filling the gaps of the applicable national law; Interpretation and supplementation of international conventions on uniform private law)]; Mª del Pilar Perales Viscasillas, "UNIDROIT Principles of International Commercial Contracts: Sphere of Application and General Provisions," 13 *Ariz. J. Int'l & Comp. L.* 380–441 (1996) [Primary issues analyzed: whether or not the Principles may be applied as *lex mercatoria*, whether or not they are part of the general principles referred to in CISG Article 7; the mutual relationship of the UNIDROIT Principles and the CISG is discussed throughout this work, especially in the discussion of the general provisions of the Principles, which show the strong influence of the general provisions of the CISG].

Cf. A. Leduc, "L'emergence d'une nouvelle *lex mercatoria* à l'enseigne des principles d'UNIDROIT relatives aux contracts du commerce international: thèse et antithèse" [The emergence of a new *lex mercatoria* under the standard of the UNIDROIT Principles of International Commercial Contracts: pros and cons – *in French*], *Revue Juridique Thèmis* 429–451 (2001); Ulrich Drobnig, "The Use of the UNIDROIT Principles by National and Supra-national courts," in *UNIDROIT Principles for International Commercial Contracts: A New Lex mercatoria?*, ICC Publication No. 490/1 223–232 (1995).

130 *See* Michael Joachim Bonell, "The UNIDROIT Principles of International Contracts and CISG: Alternative or Complementary Instruments?," *Uniform Law Review* (1996) at 26–39, also available online at <http://cisgw3.law.pace.edu/cisg/biblio/ulr96.html> [hereinafter: Bonell, *Alternative or Complementary Instruments*]: "In view of its intrinsic merits and world-wide acceptance, CISG was of course an obligatory point of reference in the preparation of the UNIDROIT Principles. To the extent that the two instruments address the same issues, the rules laid down in the UNIDROIT Principles are normally taken either literally or at least in substance from the corresponding provisions of CISG; cases where the former depart from the latter are exceptional."

See also Pilar Perales Viscasillas, "UNIDROIT Principles of International Commercial Contracts: Sphere of Application and General Provisions," 13 *Ariz. J. Int'l. & Comp. L.* 385 (1996): "[T]he Principles have been deeply influenced by the Convention." *See* also Ulrich Magnus, "Die allgemeinen Grundsätze im UN-Kaufrecht," 59 *Rabels Zeitschrift* 492–493 (1995). Magnus points out that the harmony between the Convention and the UNIDROIT Principles comes as no surprise, because the Convention could be considered the "godfather" of the UNIDROIT Principles.

The main issue here is whether – and to what degree – the UNIDROIT Principles and the PECL can aid in the interpretation of the CISG's provisions.[131] There are instances where Restatements can be regarded as "fleshing out bones already present in the skeletal structure of the uniform law,"[132] and where the Restatements have bones and accompanying flesh that cannot be readily affixed to the uniform law they accompany. For example, a recent survey of the PECL has revealed the following[133]:

(1) PECL provisions that are *identical* to counterpart CISG provisions and either (a) go no further than their CISG counterparts or (b) embellish, add to, or make more explicit that which is implicit in the CISG provisions. Just as one regards the UCC as more detailed than the CISG, the latter categories of PECL material are more detailed than their CISG analogs.
(2) PECL provisions that are *substantially the same* as or similar to the CISG provisions
(3) PECL provisions that are *somewhat similar* to the CISG provisions
(4) PECL provisions that are *substantively different* from the CISG counterparts

Where provisions of the CISG are skeletal and those of the PECL more full-bodied, for the CISG researcher the utility of PECL comparatives ranges from most relevant to least relevant. It is arguable that where either set of the Principles (UNIDROIT or PECL) can be regarded as *fleshing out bones* already present in the skeletal structure of the uniform law, they can be utilized in interpreting problematic CISG provisions. It is doubtful whether the same can happen where the Restatements have "bones and accompanying flesh" that cannot be readily affixed to the uniform law they accompany. Where, as is often the case, the PECL dovetails with or approximates the CISG, PECL comparatives can be helpful to the CISG researchers and interpreters. For example, the PECL offers enlightenment (a) with comments that explain provisions and illustrations

See also Peter Schlechtriem, "25 Years CISG – An International Lingua Franca for Drafting Uniform Law, Legal Principles, Domestic Legislation and Transnational Contracts," 2 *CILE Studies. The CISG and the Business Lawyer: The UNCITRAL Digest as a Contract Drafting Tool* (forthcoming 2006): "[B]oth the UNIDROIT Principles and the Uniform Sales Law came from the same well, and there was also some identity of drafters, for a number of experts who had worked on the CISG later joined UNIDROIT's working teams. Thus, it is small wonder that key solutions and central concepts of the CISG and the UNIDROIT Principles are closely related . . . " In his footnote to the above, Schlechtriem states, "It could well be assumed that the founding fathers of the UNIDROIT Principles were . . . motivated by the desire to preserve the great treasure of comparative law solutions that went into the Sales project."

[131] Restatements can help interpret a law. For instance, the Uniform Commercial Code is the U.S. uniform domestic law and a Restatement has served as its companion. The U.S. Restatement of Contracts (Second) has a broader scope than the U.C.C.; it takes cognizance of insights derived from the text of the U.C.C., from scholarly commentaries on the U.C.C., from cases that have interpreted the U.C.C., and from other sources. In the United States, when a tribunal is ruling on sales provisions of the U.S. Uniform Commercial Code, references to the Restatement of Contracts are frequently encountered. Its examples and explanations of the meaning of terms and concepts are useful. In U.C.C. proceedings, courts and arbitrators refer to the Restatement of Contracts as it helps them reason through the applicable law. *See Observations on the use of the PECL as an aid to CISG research*, on the Pace Law Web site, *at* <http://cisgw3.law.pace.edu/cisg/text/peclcomp.html>.

Similar observations can be made on the use of the UNIDROIT Principles as an aid to CISG comparative research: <http://cisgw3.law.pace.edu/cisg/text/matchup/general-observations.html>. For a commentary on similarities and differences between the UNIDROIT Principles and the CISG, *see* A. S. Hartkamp, "The UNIDROIT Principles for International Commercial Contracts and the United Nations Convention on Contracts for the International Sale of Approval," in *Essays on Comparative Law, Private International Law and International Commercial Arbitration in honour of Dimitra Kokkina-Intridou* 85–98 (Boeli-Woelki/Grosheide/Hondius/Steenhof eds., Martinus Nijhoff 1994). *See also* Joseph M. Perillo, "UNIDROIT Principles of International Commercial Contracts: The Black Letter Text and a Review," 63 *Fordham L. Rev.* 281–316 (1994).

[132] This metaphor, along with the "skeletal" theory that is used here, belongs to Albert H. Kritzer.

[133] *See Observations on the use of the PECL as an aid to CISG research*, on the Pace Law Web site at <http://cisgw3.law.pace.edu/cisg/text/peclcomp.html>.

that apply them to case law environments and (b) with notes that identify domestic antecedents and analogs that match provisions with continental and common law doctrine and jurisprudence.

Several examples of cases exist in which tribunals have referred to the UNIDROIT Principles as it helped them reason through the CISG.[134] One can anticipate many such references to the UNIDROIT Principles in the CISG proceedings. The general affinity of the CISG to its companion Restatements demands such a comparative approach, especially where it can be shown that their respective provisions share a common intent.[135] Thus, the UNIDROIT Principles and the PECL could and should help reduce the need to resort to rules of private international law for gap-filling, thus helping maintain the integrity of the CISG's uniform and international application and interpretation.

Although the CISG chronologically preceded the PECL and the UNIDROIT Principles, it is arguable that there is significant affinity between the three instruments as the latter two also form part of the new international legal order to which the CISG belongs. The temporal discordance of the instruments should not be used to hide their similarities in origin and substance or to impede their common purpose, which is the unification or harmonization of international commercial law. In essence, it is arguable the word "based," in Article 7(2), should be given a substantive and thematic nuance, which is broader than the one merely signifying a strict temporal correlation. Where it can be shown that a relevant Restatement provision shares a common intent with a CISG provision under examination, then the former can help interpret the latter by being utilized as an expression of the "general principles" upon which the CISG is based.[136] This

[134] *See* relevant case law and arbitral awards:

- Austria June 15, 1994 Vienna Arbitration proceeding SCH-4318; case presentation including English translation available at <http://cisgw3.law.pace.edu/cases/940615a4.html>
- Austria June 15, 1994 Vienna Arbitration proceeding SCH-4366; case presentation including English translation available at <http://cisgw3.law.pace.edu/cases/940615a3.html>
- ICC Arbitration Case No. 8128 of 1995; case presentation including English translation available at <http://cisgw3.law.pace.edu/cases/958128i1.html>
- France October 23, 1996 Appellate Court Grenoble (*Gaec des Beauches v. Teso Ten Elsen*) case presentation including English translation available at <http://cisgw3.law.pace.edu/cases/961023f1.html>
- Belarus May 20, 2003 Supreme Economic Court (*Holzimpex Inc. v. State Farm-Combine Sozh*), cases 7–5/2003 and 8–5/2003, case presentations available at <http://cisgw3.law.pace.edu/cases/0305020b5.html> and <http://cisgw3.law.pace.edu/cases/o305020b6.html>
- Russian Federation June 6,2003 Tribunal of International Commercial Arbitration at the Russian Federation Chamber of Commerce and Industry, Proceeding No. 97/2002; case presentation including English translation available at <http://cisgw3.law.pace.edu/cases/030606r1.html>

For further remarks on this subject, *see generally* Michael Joachim Bonell, "The UNIDROIT Principles in Practice – The Experience of the First Two Years," *Unif. L. Rev.* (1997) at 34–45, also available online at <http://cisgw3.law.pace.edu/cisg/biblio/pr-exper.html>. *See* also Bonell, *Alternative or Complementary Instruments, supra* note 130; Bonell, "The UNIDROIT Principles of European Contract Law: Similar Rules for Same Purposes?," *Unif. L. Rev.*(1996) at 229–246, also available online at <http://cisgw3.law.pace.edu/cisg/biblio/bonell96.html>.

[135] An important caveat to recourse to the Principles to fill gaps in the CISG is pointed out by Bonell: "So far it has been each judge's or arbitrator's task case by case both to determine those general principles and from the general principles to derive the solution for the specific question to be settled. This latter task could be facilitated by resorting to the UNIDROIT Principles. The only condition which needs to be satisfied is to show that the relevant provisions of the UNIDROIT Principles are the expression of a general principle underlying CISG." Bonell, *Alternative or Complementary Instruments, supra* note 130.

[136] When either the PECL or the UNIDROIT Principles are used in this Introduction to aid CISG research as "general principles," they illustrate a concept that can apply to either.

Ulrich Magnus provides the conceptual framework for resort to the UNIDROIT Principles as expressions of general principles underlying the CISG. He states

> Art. 7(2) CISG allows utilization of the general principles, on which the Convention is based and which merely haven't been expressed directly, for the purpose of filling gaps. In general, any general principles existing outside of the CISG are not to be considered. Is that also true for the "Principles"? As seen above, their authors, among other things, have designed the "Principles" for the purpose of providing a guideline for interpretation and for

would reduce, if not eliminate, the need for recourse to conflict of laws rules in that context.[137]

The wide recognition of the Principles as a clear expression of "general principles" of private law[138] adds legitimacy to the argument for their inclusion in the gap-filling

filling gaps in international Conventions regarding commercial contracts. . . . To be sure, this intention alone cannot suffice. However, in my opinion the "Principles" are nevertheless to be considered as additional general principles in the context of the CISG. The most important reason for this is that they vastly correspond both to the respective provisions of the CISG as well as to the general principles which have been derived from the CISG . . . In light of the fact that the CISG basically was the force behind the "Principles," this correspondence is not surprising.

Further, the approach in developing the "Principles" appears appropriate with respect to the current state of attempts to unify law. The CISG provides a basic set of rules which has resulted from an intensive comparison of legal systems and politically supported compromises between these legal systems. Therefore, the CISG can and should constitute the basis for the creation of a general law of contracts. Its provisions are to be generalized only to supplement new issues and solutions and align these issues and solutions with the needs of the industry. The UNIDROIT working group has proceeded with this concept in mind. Thus, its results, to the extent that they formulate general principles which cannot be derived directly from the CISG, can be utilized for filling gaps in the Convention. . . . " Ulrich Magnus, "Die allgemeinen Grundsätze im UN-Kaufrecht," 59 *Rabels Zeitschrift* 492–493 (1995); English translation of the Magnus article available at <http://cisgw3.law.pace.edu/cisg/text/magnus.html>.

[137] *Cf.* U. Drobnig, "The Use of the UNIDROIT Principles by National and Supra-national courts," in *UNIDROIT Principles for International Commercial Contracts: A New Lex Mercatoria?*, ICC Publication No. 490/1 (1995) 223–232: "Article 7 para 2 refers for matters governed by the Convention to the general principles on which the Convention is based . . . And if there are no such principles, the provision refers to the law applicable by virtue of the rules of private international law . . . Thus there does not seem to be any room for recourse to the UNIDROIT Principles [in interpreting and supplementing CISG]."

It seems that Drobnig is treating the UNIDROIT Principles as a formal source of law that, because it is not listed in Article 7(2), may not be invoked. The Principles are actually more like a useful summary of what might be obtained via a comparative legal survey. The balance of academic opinion, however, seems to be that Article 7(2) legitimizes resorting to the UNIDROIT Principles as a means of interpreting and supplementing the CISG, as long as there is a gap on a matter governed by the CISG and the relevant provisions of the UNIDROIT Principles are the expression of a general principle underlying the CISG and not inconsistent with the CISG provision in question; *see, e.g.*, Bonell, *Alternatives or Complementary Instruments*, *supra* note 130, at 33. For evidence of favorable opinion on the possible use of the UNIDROIT Principles in interpreting and supplementing CISG, *see* also *id.* the references to: S.N. Martinez Cazon, "A Practitioner's View of the Applicability of the UNIDROIT Principles of International Commercial Contracts in Interpreting International Uniform Laws" 3 (paper presented at the 25th *IBA Biennial Conference*, Melbourne, Oct. 9–14, 1994); F. Enderlein, "The UNIDROIT Principles as a Means for Interpreting International Uniform Laws" 12 (paper presented at the 25th *IBA Biennial Conference*, Melbourne, Oct. 9–14, 1994). *See* also Ulrich Magnus, "Die allgemeinen Grundsätze im UN-Kaufrecht," 59 *Rabels Zeitschrift* 492–493 (1995); English translation of the Magnus article available at <http://cisgw3.law.pace.edu/cisg/text/magnus.html>.

[138] Evidence of the wide acknowledgment that the UNIDROIT Principles reflect general principles of private law is provided by

- a survey of arbitral awards rendered by the Court of Arbitration of Berlin in 1992, the Court of Arbitration of the International Chamber of Commerce in 1995 and 1996: *see* the references in Dietrich Maskow, "Hardship and *Force Majeure*," 40 *Am. J. Com. L.* 657, 665 (1992)
- and an *unpublished* decision of the Court of Appeal of Grenoble January 24, 1996. *Cf.* the summary published in *Uniform Law Review* (1997) 1.

In those instances, the UNIDROIT Principles were applied as a means of interpreting the applicable domestic law to demonstrate that a particular solution provided by the applicable domestic law corresponds to the general principles of law as reflected in the UNIDROIT Principles. Of course, for the UNIDROIT Principles to be of assistance in the proper interpretation of CISG, the relevant UNIDROIT provision must be linked (explicitly or implicitly) to a general principle underlying CISG and must not be inconsistent with the CISG provision in question.

There are also awards in which the UNIDROIT Principles were chosen as the law governing the contract, implicitly considering the UNIDROIT Principles as a source of the *lex mercatoria* and a reflection of wide international consensus:

- Three of these awards have been rendered by the Court of Arbitration of the International Chamber of Commerce. For extensive references, *see* P. Lalive, "*L'arbitrage international et les Principes UNIDROIT*" [*International arbitration and the UNIDROIT Principles*], *in* Contratti Commerciali Internazionali e Principi UNIDROIT 77–89 (Bonell ed. 1997). *See also* Katharina Boele-Woelki, "Principles and Private International Law – The UNIDROIT Principles of International Commercial Contracts and the Principles of European Contract Law: How to Apply Them to International Contracts," *Uniform Law Review* (1996)

mechanism laid out in CISG Art. 7(2). From such a position, and assuming that they satisfy the formal requirements for their use in conjunction with the CISG, the Principles could offer considerable assistance in enabling the uniform interpretation and application of the Convention that the drafters of the CISG had intended.[139]

It is submitted that the CISG is, and must remain, a self-contained body of rules independent of, and distinct from, the different domestic laws. The nature of the effort that created the Convention indicates, indeed it demands, that the CISG should stand on its own feet, supported by the general principles that underlie it. Because of its unique nature and limitations, it is necessary that the CISG exist on top of a legal order that can provide doctrinal support and solutions to practical problems – such as gap-filling – in order to guarantee the CISG's functional continuity and development without offending its values of internationality and uniformity. The necessary legal backdrop for the CISG's existence and application can be provided by general principles of international commercial law consistent with the intent of the CISG legislators, such as those exemplified by many of the provisions of the UNIDROIT Principles and the PECL.

Against that background, the recourse to rules of private international law represents regression into doctrinal fragmentation and practical uncertainty. The relevant reference to such a method in Article 7(2) is unfortunate, as it does not assist the goal of uniformity. By producing divergent results in the application of the Convention, recourse to the rules of private international law impedes and frustrates the unification movement and can reverse the progress achieved by the worldwide adoption of the CISG as a uniform body of international sales law.

On the other hand, minimizing the need to invoke the rules of private international law in the context of Article 7(2) goes a long way toward strengthening the unification effort. This approach requires reliance upon and an aggressive search for general principles that underlie the Convention. Such principles can (often) be found in international Restatements, such as the UNIDROIT Principles and the PECL. These two instruments belong, together with the CISG, to a new international legal order that their respective drafters had envisaged. The interpretative and supplementary functions of these instruments concerning the proper application of the CISG best reflect the objectives of the United Nations, as these are were stated in CISG's Preamble – to remove "legal barriers in international trade and promote the development of international trade". Providing answers to unresolved matters governed by the CISG affects the uniformity of the Convention's application. It is arguable that in such cases international uniformity is promoted if the answer can be given by reference to any of the CISG's general principles that may be provided elsewhere (e.g., in the UNIDROIT Principles or the PECL answers to such unresolved matters). Conversely, recourse to the rules of private international law for the same purpose hinders and harms uniformity.

I have argued elsewhere,[140] as did many delegates present at the 1980 Vienna Diplomatic Conference, that recourse to rules of private international law should not have been made a part of Article 7(2). Nonetheless, the text is there for all to peruse. The various academic and theoretical objections to this inclusion have been recorded and

652, at 661, who points out that "[t]his significant award may be regarded as the official entrée of the Principles into international arbitration." *Id.*

- Another award of this kind was rendered by the National and International Court of Arbitration of Milan, Award No. 1795 of December 1, 1996.

[139] *See, e.g.*, Netherlands October 16, 2002 Appellate Court's-Hertogenbosch, case presentation, including English translation available at <http://cisgw3.law.pace.edu/cases/021016n1.html>: that court decision draws on the UNIDROIT Principles (see para. 2.7) and the PECL (see para 2.8) to help interpret the CISG.

[140] *See* generally Felemegas, *Uniform Interpretation*, *supra* note 24, at chapters 4 and 5.

have been themselves discussed further, but the main question remains essentially the same: ultimately, can the CISG unify the law of international sales?

The answer to that question is twofold. The CISG indeed has the potential to achieve the vision of its drafters and satisfy the needs of international buyers and sellers for certainty and uniformity. But its potential is endangered by the specific reference to conflict of laws for purposes of gap-filling in Article 7(2). The overwhelming preponderance of the evidence (i.e., the text and its legislative history) points to a strong, common desire in favor of uniformity, despite evidence of compromise in the final form of the CISG, as found in the relevant compromise in Art. 7(2). The traces of the political differences that remain in the text are, however, important ones in terms of the CISG's goal of achieving uniformity in the law of international sales. This is because they are arguably capable of turning the CISG into little more than an improved – but ultimately disappointing – revision of its predecessors, the 1964 Hague Conventions that failed to achieve the same goal.

The interpreter called upon to apply the CISG now (and in the future) has a clearly defined, albeit difficult task – to apply the provisions of the Convention according to the specific rules of interpretation contained in Article 7. The relevant textual reference in Article 7(2) to domestic law leaves the CISG prone to divergent gap-filling; that is, in the absence of general principles, the solution is to be provided in conformity with the relevant law applicable according to the rules of private international law – a development that endangers the uniformity of the Convention's interpretation and application. The Convention's fundamental general principle of "reasonableness" has a strong bearing on the proper interpretation of all provisions of the CISG, as per Article 7(2). Kritzer[141] argues in support of gap-filling in the CISG with reference to general principles in lieu of the recourse to the rules of private international law, wherever it is *reasonable* to do so:

> ... regarding reasonableness as a fundamental principle of the CISG and reading reasonableness into every article of the CISG, whether specifically mentioned in the article or not, helps tilt the scales in favor of Part One rather than Part Two applications of Article 7(2) – a tilting of scales that... is required by virtue of the good-faith and uniform-law mandate recited in Article 7(1) of the CISG.[142]

Thus, it is submitted that the proper interpretation of the Convention must be based on general principles, rather than on the rules of private international law, where it is reasonable to do so. Because it is also reasonable to read into Article 7(2) the good faith and uniform law mandates recited in Article 7(1), it would also be reasonable to make such election (i.e., to rely on general principles, rather than on the rules of private international law) in the operation of Article 7(2) when these mandates (i.e., the promotion of uniformity in the Convention's application and the observance of good faith in international trade) are at stake.

From what has been written so far, one main conclusion can be drawn: ultimately, it is the interpreter's task to decide whether the CISG can really become a uniform law; that is, whether universalism prevails over nationalism and whether any progress has been made since the enactment of the national codes that overturned what could have been a basis for a new *ius commune*. Unlike the 1964 Hague Conventions, the 1980 Vienna Convention provides an ideal framework that should permit a positive answer to that question.

141 *See* Kritzer's editorial remarks on "reasonableness," which include further citations and references, available online on the Pace Web site at <http://cisgw3.law.pace.edu/cisg/text/reason.html>.

142 *Id.*

Article 7 provides that the CISG's provisions should be interpreted and any gaps *praeter legem* in the CISG be filled in accordance with the general principles that bind the individual member States into a community. As a result of either a political reality (see the debates in the legislative history of Article 7) or a legal reality (i.e., the acknowledgement that no provision of any law can purport to expressly settle all questions concerning matters governed by it) or both, however, the rules of private international law have been placed in the gap-filling mechanism of the Convention. It is made clear in the text of Article 7(2) that, in the absence of any relevant general principles, a court applying the CISG is obliged to turn to domestic law. Obviously, such a development would hinder the search for the CISG's elusive goal of uniformity.

In the proper construction and application of the CISG as uniform international sales law, the necessary legal backdrop could be provided by general principles of international commercial law, such as those exemplified by the UNIDROIT Principles and the PECL. The UNIDROIT Principles, the PECL, and the CISG belong to the new legal order that the United Nations has envisaged, and working in tandem, they best reflect the objectives of that body to remove "legal barriers in international trade and promote the development of international trade" in the spirit of equality and friendly cooperation among its member States. This substantive affinity among the three distinct instruments legitimizes resorting to the Principles as a means of interpreting and supplementing the CISG – so long as there is a gap *praeter legem* in the CISG and the relevant provisions of the Principles are the expression of a general principle underlying the CISG and are not inconsistent with the CISG provision in question.

As far as the reference to the rules of private international law in Article 7(2) is concerned, two things must be said. First, this reference is incorporated into the text of the CISG. Second, the strength of this textual reference is clearly undermined by an examination of its legislative history and an analysis of its effect on the overall scheme of the Convention. There is strong academic support for the view that in interpreting the CISG, in the absence of general principles of the Convention (i.e., as *ultima ratio*),[143] one not only is allowed to make recourse to the rules of private international law but one is also obliged to do so.[144] This conclusion is strictly valid, and it stems from the text of Article 7(2). Fulfilling this obligation, however, not only offers nothing to "the development of international trade on the basis of equality and mutual benefit" but it also fosters the creation of divergent interpretations of the CISG as well, thus endangering the CISG's long-term success and survival. Courts, especially in countries without an established tradition in extrapolating general principles from a codified instrument, can fatally injure the CISG's credibility as uniform transnational law by abusing the "last resort" option.

Any court applying the CISG should not miss the importance of the mandate in Article 7(1) that, in interpreting the provisions of the Convention (including Art. 7(2) itself), "regard is to be had to its international character and to the need to promote uniformity in its application and the observance of good faith in international trade." Such an interpretative approach not only respects the mandate of the new law as expressed in Art. 7(1) but it also helps in many instances to render the reference to the rules of private international law superfluous. Thus, it is a positive step toward the realization of substantive legal uniformity.

On the other hand, the recourse to rules of private international law, in the context of the CISG's gap-filling, represents regression into doctrinal fragmentation and practical

[143] *See* M. J. Bonell, "Article 7," in *Convezione di Vienna sui Contratti di Vendita Internazionale di Beni Mobili* 25 (Cesare Massimo Bianca ed., 1991); Rolf Herber, "Article 7," in *Kommentar zum Einheitlichen UN-Kaufrecht* 91–100 (Ernst Caemmerer & Peter Schlechtriem eds., 2d ed. 1995), at 93.

[144] *See* Ferrari, *Uniform Interpretation*, *supra* note 54, at 228, stating that "recourse to domestic law for the purpose of filling gaps under certain circumstances is not only admissible, but even obligatory."

uncertainty. The relevant textual reference in Article 7(2) leaves the CISG prone to divergent gap-filling (i.e., in conformity with the relevant domestic law applicable according to the rules of private international law). In resolving gaps *praeter legem*, the proper interpretation of the Convention requires preference to be given to a comprehensive search for a solution provided by the general principles underlying the CISG, rather than the ready application of a domestic law applicable by virtue of the rules of private international law. Only such an approach pays proper regard to the international character of the CISG and can promote uniformity in the Convention's application.

VIII. CISG – UNIDROIT PRINCIPLES – PECL COMPARATIVE ANALYSIS

The following chapters examine in more detail the nature of this proposed role of the UNIDROIT Principles and the PECL. To assist in efforts to utilize the Principles to fill gaps in the CISG or otherwise help interpret the Convention, we present counterpart provisions of the CISG and the UNIDROIT Principles, as well as the PECL. The corresponding matchups of CISG provisions with counterpart provisions of the UNIDROIT Principles and the PECL are presented with our analyses of the individual articles of the CISG.

In some instances, the counterpart provisions are virtually identical. In such instances, the typical commentary to the Principles (UNIDROIT and PECL) acknowledges its CISG antecedents and provides helpful illustrations. In other instances, although the Principles are more expansive than their CISG counterparts, the intent of the counterpart provisions appears to be the same. In still other cases, the comparative matchups only partially track one another.

The team of scholars, thirty-nine in number, who participated in this comparative research project, comprises academics and practitioners who represent civil law and common law jurisdictions in twenty-one countries. The participating scholars who have authored the comparative editorials have done their best to enable the reader to draw his or her own conclusions as to the extent to which the matched Principles can properly be used to help interpret the CISG. It is hoped that the results of this truly international collaborative research effort will provide further stimulus for the CISG researcher to investigate and arrive at the proper interpretation of the Convention as uniform sales law.

Freedom of contract: Remarks on the manner in which the UNIDROIT Principles may be used to interpret or supplement Article 6 of the CISG

Bojidara Borisova

I. INTRODUCTION

The principle of party autonomy entrenched in CISG Article 6 represents an important guarantee for the effective functioning of international trade and accommodates the fulfillment of the principle of freedom of contract, which is a basic tenet of international commercial relations.[1] The inclusion of this principle in the provisions of the CISG reflects the strong conviction of the international community that specific warranties must be created for the establishment of a freely operating, market-oriented international economy within which the contracting parties have the freedom to act in conformity with their business interests. Similar provisions were also incorporated in other international uniform laws adopted before the CISG.[2]

The UNIDROIT Principles, which were promulgated almost fifteen years after the adoption of the CISG, contain two articles that correspond in substance with CISG Art. 6. UNIDROIT Principles Arts 1.1 and 1.5, though similar in essence to CISG Art. 6, better illustrate the concept of party autonomy and can be used for the interpretation and application of CISG Art. 6.[3] This concept was regulated in two other important conventions on international commercial relations – one adopted the same year as the CISG and the other a few years later.[4] The solid interest that the international community has shown in the importance of party autonomy once again underlines its significance. Although today it seems unthinkable to have a uniform act that regulates international commercial relations without explicitly emphasizing party autonomy, there was strong opposition to the inclusion of this concept during the draft process of the Convention.[5]

[1] *See* the Official Comments on Art. 1.1 of the UNIDROIT Principles, available online at <http://cisgw3.law.pace.edu/cisg/principles/uni6.html#official>.

[2] *See* the Uniform Law on the International Sale of Goods and the Uniform Law on the Formation of Contracts for the International Sale of Goods. For detailed historical analysis of the party autonomy concept *see* Murphy, "United Nations Convention for the International Sale of Goods: Creating Uniformity in International Sales Law," 12 *Fordham Int'l. L.J.* 727–750 (1998), also available online <http://cisgw3.law.pace.edu/cisg/biblio/murphy.html>.

[3] *See* "General Observations on Use of the UNIDROIT Principles to Help Interpret the CISG," available online at <http://cisgw3.law.pace.edu/cisg/text/matchup/general-observations.html>.

[4] *See* The Convention on the Law Applicable to Contractual Obligations (the so-called Rome Convention of 1980) and The 1986 Hague Convention on the Law Applicable to Contracts for the International Sale of Goods (the so-called 1986 Choice of Law Convention).

[5] For the positions of the different CISG Contracting States, see Murphy, *supra* note 2.

When discussing the provisions of CISG Art. 6, one must take into consideration the following basic problems.

- First, what is the major prerequisite that allows the contracting parties to choose freely the law applicable to their contractual relations? In this connection, the dispositive character of the CISG provisions must be examined.
- Second, does CISG Art. 6 and its counterpart UNIDROIT Principles Arts. 1.1 and 1.5 provide the obligatory manner in which the choice of law must be made?
- Third, what is the scope of the party autonomy?
- Fourth, might party autonomy be limited and in what manner? With respect to this question, special attention must be drawn to the so-called mandatory provisions of the CISG.

II. CISG'S DISPOSITIVE CHARACTER

Although the principle of freedom of contract is generally recognized as one of the basic principles that ensures the establishment and application of fair and competitive international economic rules, it might not be automatically enforced. Hence, as far as the prescriptions of one particular international act are concerned, an explicit text providing the possibility for the contracting parties to choose the applicable law and thus to define the exact terms of their contract must be included.[6] An additional requirement that makes the principle of party autonomy workable is the character of the Convention's prescriptions. If the Convention contains mandatory rules (i.e., rules from which the parties may not deviate), party autonomy cannot be applied, and the contracting parties must define the exact terms of their contract in conformity with the corresponding provisions of the Convention.

This is for the most part not the case with the CISG and the UNIDROIT Principles. Both international instruments are of a primarily non-mandatory character, as stated unambiguously both in scholarly writing[7] and in the Official Comments on the UNIDROIT Principles.

III. MANNER IN WHICH PARTY AUTONOMY MIGHT BE EXERCISED

Both CISG Art. 6 and its counterpart UNIDROIT Principles Arts. 1.1 and 1.5 do not explicitly stipulate the manner in which the contracting parties may define the law

[6] For confirmation that CISG Art. 6 provides the opportunity for the exclusion of the Convention, *see* the following illustrative case decisions:

- Italy 10 March 2000 *Suprema Corte di Cassazione* [Supreme Court], case presentation including English translation available at <http://cisgw3.law.pace.edu/cases/000310i3.html>
- Germany 12 October 2000 *Landgericht* [District Court] Stendal, case presentation including English translation available at <http://cisgw3.law.pace.edu/cases/001012g1.html>
- France 6 November 2001 *Cour d'appel* [Appellate Court] Paris, <http://cisgw3.law.pace.edu/cases/011106f1.html>
- United States 29 January 2003 Federal District Court [Illinois], *Ajax Tool Works, Inc. v. Can-Eng Manufacturing Ltd.*, <http://cisgw3.law.pace.edu/cases/030129u1.html>

[7] *See* Leete, "Contract Formation under the United Nations Convention on Contracts for the International Sale of Goods and the Uniform Commercial Code: Pitfall for the Unwary," 6 *Temp. Int'l. Comp. L.J.* 193–215 (1992), also available online at <http://cisgw3.law.pace.edu/cisg/text/leete6.html>; Ferrari, "Specific Topics of the CISG in the Light of Judicial Application and Scholarly Writing," 15 *J.L. & Com.* 1–126 (1995), also available online at <http://cisgw3.law.pace.edu/cisg/text/franco6.html>; Schlechtriem, *Uniform Sales Law in the Decisions of the Bundesgerichtshof* [Federal Supreme Court of Germany], available online at <http://cisgw3.law.pace.edu/cisg/biblio/schlechtriem3.html>.

applicable to their contractual relations. The decision not to be explicit was long debated during the drafting period of the CISG, which attempts to balance the concept of party autonomy with the need for protection of the weaker party to the contract.[8]

Because of the unclear wording of CISG Art. 6, a controversy exists whether the application of the CISG might be explicitly or implicitly excluded. In general, there are two contrary opinions.

According to one school of thought, the CISG as a uniform set of rules allows only express exclusion.[9] The first argument made by the proponents of this opinion is that only express exclusion can guarantee the uniform application of the CISG and, consequently, can ensure the success of the Convention.

The second argument in favor of express exclusion is derived from the provision of the CISG under Art. 7, which includes the interpretation and gap-filling mechanism that the Convention must apply; it provides that both operations must be fulfilled in conformity with the general principles underlying the Convention. One of the general principles of the international trade practice that the CISG has been said to proclaim is the principle of fairness, which protects the weaker party from the dominant's party behavior and thus guarantees the equality of both contracting parties.[10] There are authors who support only the express exclusion for purely pragmatic reasons.[11] According to them, requiring only express exclusion of the Convention will give more contractual certainty to the contracting parties and will overcome the scholarly discrepancies.

Over the years of the CISG's application, the opinion stating that Art. 6 provides also for the implied opting-out of the Convention has received increasing support not only in commentary[12] but also in the case law.[13] This option is clearly stated also in the Official Comments as regards the interpretation and application of the UNIDROIT Principles.

Two basic arguments in favor of implied exclusion of the CISG can be stated.[14] The first is derived from the strict interpretation of the prescription of CISG Art. 6 and is based on the inference that if the drafters of the Convention wanted to allow only the express exclusion they would have formulated the text of this article differently, including in it an indisputable indication about the manner in which the exemption and the choice of law must be made. In view of the fact that such specification was not made, it is argued that implied exclusion is possible.

In this respect, it might be arguable that the Official Comments to the UNIDROIT Principles contribute to the assertion that CISG Art. 6 provides the possibility that both an

[8] For the legislative history of the CISG Art. 6, *see* Murphy, *supra* note 2.

[9] *See* Murphy, *supra* note 2; Winship, "Changing Contract Practices in the Light of the United Nations Convention: A Guide for Practitioners," 29 *Int'l. Law* 525–554 (1995), also available online at <http://cisgw3.law.pace.edu/cisg/text/winship6.html>.

[10] *See* Murphy, *supra* note 2.

[11] *See* Winship, *supra* note 9.

[12] *See* Enderlein & Maskow, *International Sales Law* (Oceana Publications 1992), also available online at <http://cisgw3.law.pace.edu/cisg/biblio/enderlein-art06.html>; Schlechtriem, "Uniform Sales Law-The Experience with Uniform Sales Laws in the Federal Republic of Germany," *Juridikrift Tidskrift* 1–28 (1991/92), also available online at <http://cisgw3.law.pace.edu/cisg/biblio/schlechtriem3.html>; Ferrari, *supra* note 7.

[13] *See* the following case decisions:

- Italy 12 July 2000 *Tribunale* [District Court] Vigevano, *Rheinland Versicherungen v. Atlarex*, case presentation including English translation available at <http://cisgw3.law.pace.edu/cases/000712i3.html>
- Austria 22 October 2001 *Oberster Gerichtshof* [Supreme Court], case presentation including English translation available at <http://cisgw3.law.pace.edu/cases/011022a3.html>
- Switzerland 3 December 2002 *Handelsgericht* [Commercial Court] St. Gallen, case presentation including English translation available at <http://cisgw3.law.pace.edu/cases/021203s1.html>

[14] *See* Murphy, *supra* note 2.

express and an implied exclusion of the Convention are to be achieved by the contracting parties. Consequently, because CISG Art. 6 and its counterpart UNIDROIT Principles Arts. 1.1 and 1.5 do not stipulate the exact manner for the opting-out of the uniform law, both methods are possible.

The second argument in favor of implied exclusion is based on the currently existing practice of international trade, which also confirms the possibility of excluding the application of the uniform law expressly or implicitly.[15]

When discussing party autonomy, the next important question that needs to be clarified is how to determine whether there is or is not an implied exclusion. In this respect, the UNIDROIT Principles Official Comment on Art. 1.5 provides certain indications of what circumstances would cause one to conclude that the contracting parties have implicitly excluded the application of the uniform law.

The first and probably most obvious occasion, which can also be applicable to the exclusion of the CISG, is when the contracting parties have negotiated contract terms that are totally inconsistent with the regulations of the uniform law. Thus, the contracting parties, with one action, have managed to achieve the exclusion of the Convention and also to determine the applicable law. The Official Comments to the UNIDROIT Principles do not differentiate between contract terms that are individually negotiated or those that form part of standard terms.[16]

In scholarly writings, it is unanimously accepted that the choice of the law of a non-Contracting State constitutes an implied exclusion.[17] However, such a definite conclusion cannot be made when the contracting parties have chosen the law of a Contracting State without explicitly referring to the domestic law of that State.[18] When a State adopts the CISG, the Convention becomes part of its law, and only a direct indication that the contracting parties have chosen the domestic rules of a Contracting State may lead to the conclusion that an implied opting-out of the Convention is made.

Finally, some authors[19] support the opinion that the choice of a forum or of an arbitral tribunal can be regarded as an implied exclusion if two requirements are met. The first condition is to deduce from the contracting parties' choice their intention to subject the contractual relation to the domestic law of the State where the forum or the arbitral tribunal is located. The second requirement is that the forum or the arbitral tribunal be located in a non-Contracting State. Both conditions concurrently are said to amount to an implied exclusion of the CISG.

[15] *Id.*

[16] For confirmation that the use of standard terms can exclude the Convention's application *see* Ferrari, *supra* note 7; Schlechtriem, *Uniform Sales Law – The UN Convention on Contracts for the International Sale of Goods* (Manz 1986), also available online at <http://cisgw3.law.pace.edu/cisg/biblio/schlechtriem-06.html>.

[17] *See* Ferrari, *supra* note 7; Bonell & Liguori, "The UN Convention on the International Sale of Goods: A Critical Analysis of Current International Case Law," *Uniform Law Review* 385–395 (1997), also available online at <http://cisgw3.law.pace.edu/cisg/text/libo6.html>.

[18] *See* Leete, *supra* note 7; Ferrari, *supra* note 7; Bonell & Liguori, *supra* note 17; Enderlein & Maskow, *supra* note 12. *See* also the following case decisions:

- United States 27 July 2001 Federal District Court [California], *Asante Technologies v. PMC-Sierra*, at <http://cisgw3.law.pace.edu/cases/010727u1.html>
- Austria 22 October 2001 *Oberster Gerichtshof* [Supreme Court], case presentation including English translation available at <http://cisgw3.law.pace.edu/cases/011022a3.html>
- Belgium 15 January 2002 *Tribunal de commerce* [District Court] Namur, case presentation including English translation available at <http://cisgw3.law.pace.edu/cases/020115b1.html>
- United States 11 June 2003 Federal Appellate Court [5th Circuit], *BP Oil International v. Empresa Estatal Petroleos de Ecuador*, case presentation available at <http://cisgw3.law.pace.edu/cases/030611u1.html>

[19] *See* Ferrari, *supra* note 7.

IV. SCOPE OF PARTY AUTONOMY

The basic objective of party autonomy is not the exclusion of the uniform law, but the exercise of the freedom of the contracting parties to choose the law applicable to their contractual relationship. In this connection, what is important is the extent of the contracting parties' freedom of choice.

Both CISG Art. 6 and its counterpart UNIDROIT Principles Art. 1.5 indicate in similar manner the scope of party autonomy. Both generally stipulate that contracting parties may exclude the application of the Uniform Law in whole, or they may choose to derogate only from the effect of any of its provisions.[20] Such an inference can be easily drawn from the interpretation of CISG Art. 6 and is confirmed also in the Official Comments to the UNIDROIT Principles and in scholarly writings.[21]

Regarding the operation of party autonomy, several issues must be discussed. What must be considered first is the effect of the full or partial exclusion of the Convention when the contracting parties have chosen the applicable law. Second, both full and partial exclusion of the Convention must be discussed in the context of the lack of designation of applicable law.

When contracting parties opt-out of the Convention entirely when choosing the applicable law, it must be noted once again that if the choice refers to the law of a Contracting State it is best to specifically state that the domestic law of that State is chosen. In cases of total exclusion without indication of the applicable law, both legal scholars and international case practice unanimously state that the rules of private international law should determine the applicable law.[22]

Basically, that also applies in the same manner when the contracting parties derogate only part of the CISG's provisions. With respect to the scope of a partial derogation of the CISG's articles, the following question arises. Is it necessary to apply the General Provisions of the Convention (Part I, Chapter II) along with the prescriptions of the law chosen by the contracting parties or the law determined by the rules of the private international law? That is, can we use the approach stated in the Official Comments on UNIDROIT Principles Art. 1.5? [23] The answer to this question is in the negative and requires that the different nature of the two sets of rules – CISG and UNIDROIT Principles – be taken into consideration. The former is part of the substantive law

[20] CISG Art. 6 states, "The parties may exclude the application of this Convention or, subject to article 12, derogate from or vary the effect of any of its provisions." UNIDROIT Principles Art. 1.5 states, "The parties may exclude the application of these Principles or derogate from or vary the effect of any of their provisions, except as otherwise provided in the Principles."

[21] *See* Schlechtriem, *supra* note 16. *See* also the following case decisions:

- Spain 16 November 2000 *Audiencia Provincial* [Appellate Court] Alicante, case presentation including English translation available at <http://cisgw3.law.pace.edu/cases/001116s4.html>
- Austria 14 January 2002 *Oberster Gerichtshof* [Supreme Court], case presentation including English translation available at <http://cisgw3.law.pace.edu/cases/020114a3.html>
- Belgium 15 January 2002 *Tribunal de commerce* [District Court], case presentation including English translation available at <http://cisgw3.law.pace.edu/cases/020115b1.html>
- Switzerland 3 December 2002 *Handelsgericht* [Commercial Court] St. Gallen, case presentation including English translation available at <http://cisgw3.law.pace.edu/cases/021203s1.html>
- Austria 15 June 1994 Vienna Arbitration proceeding SCH-4318, case presentation including English translation available at <http://cisgw3.law.pace.edu/cases/940615a4.html>

[22] *See* Ferrari, *supra* note 7.

[23] *See* Official Comments of the UNIDROIT Principles on Art. 1.5, available online at <http://cisgw3.law.pace.edu/cisg/principles/uni6.html#official>. Comment 2: Exclusion or modification may be express or implied. *Id.*

regulating the international sale of goods and is automatically applicable if the conditions of CISG Art. 1(1) are fulfilled, whereas the latter requires the parties' consent.[24]

On the other hand, the Final Provisions of the CISG also regulate some general questions concerning the ratification and acceptance process of the Convention, its entrance into force and its denouncement,[25] the rights of the Contracting States to make reservations,[26] and some other technical issues regarding the application of the Convention.[27] The opinion that the contracting parties cannot modify these provisions of the CISG, being the Contracting States' obligations under public international law, is accepted more or less unanimously. However, some authors accept the possibility that the contracting parties in their contract may modify even the effect of the CISG Final Provisions.[28]

V. PARTY AUTONOMY LIMITATIONS

Party autonomy is not unlimited. Both CISG Art. 6 and its counterpart UNIDROIT Principles Art. 1.5 impose certain restrictions on the contracting parties' freedom of choice.

In the case of partial exclusion of the Convention, the contracting parties may not derogate the application of two groups of prescriptions: (1) the mandatory provisions of the CISG itself and (2) the mandatory provisions of the law that should regulate the contractual relation in cases when the party autonomy concept was not applied.[29] CISG Art. 6 indicates only one prescription of the Convention that has a mandatory character – CISG Article 12 – and therefore the contracting parties may not derogate from its application.[30] The mandatory prescriptions in the second group of prescriptions should be determined in each separate case.

The limitation of CISG Art. 12 does not apply in the case of total exclusion of the Convention.[31] In that case the contracting parties should act only in conformity with the mandatory provisions of the domestic law that normally would regulate the contractual relation.[32]

Finally, some scholars express the opinion that in addition to CISG Art. 12 there are other mandatory provisions of the Convention that impose a limitation on the contracting parties' freedom of choice under the provision of CISG Art. 6.[33] To this effect the UNIDROIT Principles Official Comment provides little assistance toward the clarification of this problem, because it uses a more general and definition-type approach. Still the issue is very controversial and must be approached carefully by the contracting parties.

[24] *See* UNIDROIT Principles, Preamble, second sentence.

[25] *See* CISG Arts. 89, 91, and 99–101.

[26] *See* CISG Arts. 92 and 95–98.

[27] *See CISG* Arts. 90, 93, and 94.

[28] *See* Ulrich G. Schroeter, *Freedom of Contract: Comparison between Provisions of the CISG (Article 6) and Counterpart Provisions of the Principle of European Contract Law*, note 14, also available online at <http://cisgw3.law.pace.edu/cisg/text/peclcomp6.html>.

[29] *See* Schlechtriem, *supra* note 16.

[30] *See* Enderlein & Maskow, *supra* note 12, citing and discussing the opinion of Bonell that CISG in addition to Art. 12 contains other prescriptions that may not be derogated by the contracting parties.

[31] *See* Ferrari, *supra* note 7.

[32] *See* Schlechtriem, *supra* note 16.

[33] For example, CISG Arts. 4, 7, 28, etc. See also Ulrich G. Schroeter, *supra* note 28, notes 10–14.

Comparative editorial remarks on the provisions regarding good faith in CISG Article 7(1) and the UNIDROIT Principles Article 1.7

Ulrich Magnus

I. GOOD FAITH IN THE CISG AND THE UNIDROIT PRINCIPLES

The CISG mentions the good faith principle in Art. 7(1), which rules on the interpretation of the Convention as a uniform international law text. According to that provision, the CISG is to be interpreted and applied in a way that "the observance of good faith in international trade" is promoted. The CISG, however, does not contain an express provision that the individual contract has to obey the maxim of good faith as well.

In contrast, the UNIDROIT Principles address good faith as a principle directed to the parties of international contracts: "Each party must act in accordance with good faith and fair dealing in international trade" (Art. 1.7(1) Principles). Even more specifically Art. 4.8(2)(c) of the Principles refers to good faith and fair dealing as a determining element when and which omitted contract term has to be implied. On the other hand, the provision on the interpretation of the Principles (Art. 1.6) does not mention the maxim of good faith.

But despite these obvious differences of wording, both texts accord in their essence. For, it is commonly held that under the CISG the good faith principle also applies to the interpretation of the individual contract and to the parties' contractual relationship as such.[1] On the other hand the UNIDROIT Commentary to the Principles acknowledges that the good faith principle "may also be seen as an expression of the underlying purpose of the Principles" and may be used in interpreting the Principles.[2]

Thus the interpretation of the unified law texts themselves, of individual contracts, and also of the whole contractual relationship of the parties has to be guided by the maxim of good faith. Under both CISG and the UNIDROIT Principles, the maxim therefore fulfills a twofold function: it governs as one of the decisive factors the meaning of both the

[1] Compare Bianca/Bonell (-Bonell), "Commentary on the International Sales Law," (1987) Art. 7 no. 2.4.1.; von Caemmerer/Schlechtriem (-Herber), *Kommentar zum Einheitlichen UN-Kaufrecht* (2nd ed. 1995) Art. 7 no. 7; Staudinger (-Magnus), *Kommentar zum Bürgerlichen Gesetzbuch (Cisg)* (13th ed. 1994) Art. 7, no. 10.
[2] UNIDROIT (ed.) *Principles of International Commercial Contracts* (1994) 15.

abstract law rules and the individual contract. There is only a slight difference in weight that the CISG and the Principles grant to good faith.

II. THE CONTENTS OF THE GOOD FAITH PRINCIPLE

1. International Good Faith

Under the CISG and under the Principles it is clear that no specific national good faith concept can be applied but rather only one that fits for international trade relations. Both texts expressly stress this idea.[3]

In some areas of trade, an international standard of good faith may already exist and may be revealed and defined clearly – at least in businesses with a long-standing tradition. In other areas, that standard may not exist, but remains to be developed by business circles, arbitrators, and courts; for instance in areas using evolving technology like telesales.

2. The Object of Good Faith

Evidently under the Principles the object of the good faith and fair dealing maxim is the behavior of the contract parties. The parties shall act in accordance with the maxim; their conduct is regulated.

Under the CISG the object of the principle is less clear. But the Convention also intends to secure that (sales) contracts between parties from different countries are governed by the good faith principle.[4]

Thus, the Principles can help clarify the actual object of the good faith principle contained in the CISG.

3. Specific Good Faith Rules

Both the CISG and the Principles provide a number of rules specifying what good faith is designated to mean in certain situations. The CISG constitutes the more specific regulation, concentrating on a single type of contract only. It is the Principles that because of their general character contain a larger number of and more detailed provisions on good – and bad – faith.

a. Precontractual Obligations in the Negotiation Process

The CISG addresses the precontractual phase only indirectly by Art. 16(2)(b). The provision makes an offer irrevocable once the offeror has created a situation in which the offeree reasonably relied on the offer as irrevocable and acted in reliance on the offer. The same rule in identical wording is also adopted by the Principles Art. 2.4(2)(b).

The binding effect of some particular conduct and reliance on it emanate from the good faith principle that no one should take advantage of acts or situations that are irreconcilable with one's prior conduct (prohibition of *venire contra factum proprium*).

But in contrast to the CISG, the Principles establish a further duty not to continue or break off precontractual negotiations in bad faith (Art. 2.15(2)). And according to Art. 2.5(3), it is bad faith when a party starts or continues negotiations while "intending not to reach an agreement with the other party." The good faith principle thus demands fair negotiations with a clear view to reaching agreement. Misuse of the negotiation process to the detriment of the other party offends the standard of good faith in the Principles.[5]

Although the CISG does not govern the precontractual phase, the regulation in the Principles will be helpful in cases in which the parties negotiate a modification or

[3] *See* also UNIDROIT Principles 18; Bonell, "An International Restatement of Contract Law" 81 (1994).
[4] Bianca/Bonell (-Bonell) Art. 7 no. 2.4.2; von Caemmerer/Schlechtriem (-Herber) Art. 7, no.15.
[5] For further examples of bad faith *see* UNIDROIT Principles 51 *et seq*.

termination of an existing CISG contract. The solution envisaged by Principles Art. 2.15 is suitable also under the CISG.

b. Formation and Modification of Contract

Under both the CISG and the Principles a contract and its alteration need not be in written form to be valid.[6] Only if a written contract contains a no oral modification clause must any modification also be in writing or in the form on which the parties agreed.[7] But to this exception, the CISG as well as the Principles allow an identical sub-exception grounded on the good faith principle: "a party may be precluded by its conduct from asserting such a clause to the extent that the other party has acted in reliance on that conduct."[8] Again conduct that creates a situation of reliance and acting on it override rules of strict formality.

c. Material Validity

Unparalleled in the CISG are those provisions of the Principles that deal with questions of material validity of contracts (UNIDROIT PRINCIPLES Arts. 3.1–3.20) because the CISG does not govern these questions (CISG Art. 4(a)). The Principles also here apply the good faith principle.[9]

d. Interpretation of Contracts

As already mentioned, only the Principles provide more or less clearly that contract interpretation must be guided by good faith and fair dealing (Principles Arts. 1.7 and 4.8). Under the CISG, however, the same solution should prevail. Application of the Principles could and should help one interpret the CISG.

e. Express Contractual Obligations

Under the CISG a few provisions on the parties' statutory obligations contain good faith elements: thus, for instance, CISG Art. 35(2)(b) obliges the seller to supply goods that are fit for a particular purpose indicated to the seller except where the buyer could not reasonably rely on the seller's skill. Or, under CISG Art. 42(2)(b) a seller is not in breach of his obligations if he delivers goods not free from third-party rights when these rights resulted from the seller's compliance with the buyer's particular wishes as to the manufacture, design, etc. of the goods.

No wonder, the Principles as a general regulation for all kinds of contracts contain no comparable specific obligations.

f. Implied Obligations

The Principles expressly state that contractual obligations may be implied under the maxim of good faith (Principles Art. 5.2).[10] The CISG does not contain a comparable rule. Nevertheless, it is widely accepted that under the CISG additional obligations can be implied; in particular, a general duty to cooperate.[11] Just that same rule is now expressly provided for by Principles Art. 5.3: "Each party shall cooperate with the other party when such cooperation may reasonably be expected for the performance of that party's obligations." The rule can be understood as an expression of the general principle – based on good faith – that neither party must hinder performance of the other nor otherwise

[6] Art. 11 CISG; Art. 1.9(1) Principles.

[7] Art. 29(2) and (1) CISG; Art. 2.18(1) Principles.

[8] Art. 29(2) and (2) CISG and – in identical terms – Art. 2.18(2) Principles.

[9] *See* Art. 3.5(1)(a): if "it was contrary to reasonable commercial standards of fair dealing to leave the mistaken party in error"; similar Art. 3.8; 3.10(2).

[10] For examples of implied duties *see* UNIDROIT Principles 102.

[11] *See* Bianca/Bonell (-Bonell) Art. 7 no. 2.3.2.2; Honnold, *Uniform Law for International Sales under the 1980 United Nations Convention* (2nd 1991).

militate against the contractual purpose.[12] The Principles' rule prominently assists the CISG interpretation.

g. Non-Performance Caused by Creditor

Both the CISG and the Principles state that a "party may not rely on the non-performance of the other party to the extent that such non-performance was caused by the first party's act or omission" or – as only the Principles add – "by another event as to which the first party bears the risk."[13] This provision again can be traced back to the sub-principle of good faith that no one should profit from one's own unlawful or otherwise forbidden acts. The addition in the Principles seems to be a helpful rule for a situation not explicitly regulated by the CISG.

h. Mitigation of Damage

A principle very similar to the one just mentioned explains the well-known mitigation rule. An aggrieved party cannot claim damages for losses that she herself could have avoided. The aggrieved party should not profit from her own omissions. Both the CISG and the Principles contain mitigation rules, although they are worded differently.[14] The Principles' mitigation rule seems to reduce the aggrieved party's claim in any case when that party's failure to mitigate was causally connected with the loss, whereas the CISG formulation gives some discretion in that respect ("may claim a reduction in the damages in the amount by which the loss should have been mitigated").

III. FINAL REMARKS

The differences between the CISG and the Principles can be nearly ignored as far as the general concept of good faith in international contracts is concerned. Some textual differences do not matter in essence.

Both the CISG and the Principles acknowledge that good faith plays an important role in international contracts. Furthermore, both texts do not exclusively rely on one abstract and general rule of good faith but try to specify the concept in more specific rules that elaborate the principle in some detail. In a number of situations the Principles prove to be of assistance in interpreting the good faith principle in the CISG. By combining the CISG and the Principles, one gets a good impression of what good faith in international commercial relations should and could mean.

[12] Magnus, *Int'l. Trade & Bus. L. Ann.* III (1997) 46.
[13] Art. 80 CISG; Art. 7.1.2 Principles.
[14] Art. 77 CISG Art. 7.4.8. Principles.

Interpretation of the contract: Editorial remarks on the manner in which the UNIDROIT Principles may be used to interpret or supplement CISG Article 8

Joseph M. Perillo

a. Article 8 of the CISG is entitled "Interpretation of Statement or Other Conduct of a Party." Surprisingly, the CISG makes no explicit statement concerning the interpretation of a contract that is the joint product of the parties' negotiations resulting in the adoption of common language. As Professor Honnold has noted, the provisions of Article 8 have "special significance for agreements that have not resulted from detailed negotiations."[1] Uncomplicated sales of goods, in which no formalized contractual documents are produced, are quite common, but more complex transactions that interweave sales with support services are also very important.[2] The UNIDROIT Principles' focus is broader than simple sales and provides explicit guidance for the interpretation of contracts and not merely for the interpretation of individual communications. It thus fills a wide gap in the CISG text.

b. Article 4.1 of the Principles talks in terms of the interpretation of "contracts". It starts with a subjective notion. If the parties have a common intention, the common intention will prevail. This, on the face of it, is the same rule that has been adopted by the American Restatement,[3] but the common law objectifies intention by erecting barriers to evidence of what the parties really intended as opposed to what they said or wrote.[4] The Principles, however, disclaim any limitation on evidence of the parties' intentions.[5]

c. If the common intention of the parties cannot be determined, the Principles would apply an objective test to determine the meaning of the contract. Once again the Principles fill in a gap as the CISG is silent on the question of interpreting the joint intention of the parties. The objective test is that the interpretation should be the "meaning that reasonable persons of the same kind as the parties would give to it in the same circumstances."[6]

d. The CISG has rules concerning the interpretation of the statements and other conduct of individual parties. Article 4.2 of the Principles, except for stylistic changes, is identical to CISG Articles 8(1), and 8(2). The primary standard is the subjective intention of the party whose statement or conduct is in issue, provided, however, that the other party knows or should know of that intent. If that standard cannot be attained – for example, the other party had no reason to know the first party's intent – then the standard is that of the reasonable person in the position of the other party.

e. Article 8(3) of the CISG requires that "due consideration is to be given to all relevant circumstances of the case including the negotiations . . . "[7] The Principles echo this rule. According to the Principles, the interpretation process must take into account "the preliminary negotiations between the parties."[8]

f. Can a merger clause change this result? According to CISG Article 6, the parties are free by agreement to vary (with one minor exception) the effect of any provision of the Convention.[9] Thus, a merger clause that explicitly barred evidence of negotiations would be effective by virtue of Article 6. Although the Principles recognize the validity of a merger clause that indicates that the writing is totally integrated, they state that a merger clause does not bar evidence of prior statements of agreements for purposes of

[1] John Honnold, Uniform *Law for International Sales under the 1980 United Nations Convention* (2d ed. 1991) at ¶105 p. 163.

[2] *See, e.g., Advent Systems Ltd. v. Unisys Corp.*, 925 F.2d 670 (3d Cir.1991).

[3] Restatement (Second) Contracts §201(1) & Illus. 1, 3 (1979).

[4] *See* John D. Calamari & Joseph M. Perillo, *The Law of Contracts* (3d ed. 1987), ch. 3.

[5] *See* Principles Arts. 1.2, 2.17, and 4.3.

[6] Principles Article 4.1(2). However, the commentary advises the court that the actual subjective common intention of the parties and their reasonable understanding may be subordinated to the understanding of average users of "standard terms," as defined in Article 2.19. Principles Art. 4.1, comment 4.

[7] *See* Honnold, *supra* note 1, at 111.

[8] Principles Art. 4.3(a).

[9] The exception is Article 12, which provides that if a Contracting State makes a reservation under Article 96 and imposes writing or other form requirements on contracts, the parties cannot derogate from those requirements.

interpreting the writing.[10] This statement appears to conflict with the CISG. Yet, because of the principle of party autonomy that underlies the Principles, it certainly leaves open the possibility of effectively drafting a clause that expressly prohibits the parties from introducing such evidence for any purpose, including for interpretation.[11] However, the standard merger clause that states that there are no other understandings between the parties is unlikely to bar evidence of parol evidence for purposes of interpretation. Drafters of contracts should be aware of the narrow effect that a court is likely to give to a merger clause if the CISG applies to the case,[12] particularly in light of the hostility toward barriers to the introduction of evidence of the negotiations shown by its companion, the Principles.

g. One aspect of the parol evidence rule concerns the admissibility of supplementary or inconsistent terms in the face of an integrated writing. Absent a merger clause, do the CISG or the Principles permit the admission of such terms in contexts where the common law would exclude them? Although this question goes more to the issue of the content of the contract rather than its meaning, it is usually analyzed in the same framework as issues of interpretation. The answer is that both documents are parol-evidence-friendly. Neither the CISG nor the Principles contain any rule that bars evidence of additional or conflicting terms akin to the common law's parol evidence rule.[13] Under the CISG, all relevant evidence is admissible[14], and the same is true under the Principles. Although the CISG states this mostly in general terms, the Principles flesh this out in detail.

h. Article 4.3 of the Principles agrees with the CISG and directs that the court consider "all the circumstances." However, it goes beyond the CISG and itemizes six non-exclusive kinds of relevant circumstance: (1) preliminary negotiations, (2) course of dealing, (3) course of performance, (4) the nature and purpose of the contract, (5) trade terms, and (6) usages. These are familiar kinds of evidence offered in common law cases. The main difference is that there is no preliminary hurdle of ambiguity that many jurisdictions impose (in non-UCC cases) prior to the admission of evidence, such as evidence of preliminary negotiations,[15] or course of performance.[16] The latter is freely admissible under the UCC as is evidence of trade usage and course of dealing.[17]

i. Article 8 of the CISG does not contain what the U.S. Restatement calls "rules in aid of interpretation and standards of preference." The Principles, however, lay down several such rules and thus provide a basis for the fleshing out of the CISG. One rule is that words should be interpreted in the context of the whole contract or other document in which they appear.[18] Another is that specific provisions prevail over more general

[10] Principles Art. 2.17, final sentence.

[11] Principles Arts. 1.1 & 1.5.

[12] In an earlier article, I wrote, "As an apparent exception to the general rule of contractual freedom adopted by Principles, a merger clause cannot effectively bar parol evidence for the purpose of interpreting a writing." For this proposition, I cited Principles Article 2.17 and comment 3 to Article 4.3. Joseph M. Perillo, "UNIDROIT Principles of International Commercial Contracts: The Black Letter Text and a Review," 63 *Fordham L. Rev.* 281, 291 (1994). This may have been the intent of the drafters of those provisions, but I have since reconsidered. That intent, if it exists, is overridden by Articles 1.1 & 1.5.

[13] For an explanation of the absence of a reference to the parol evidence rule, *see* Honnold, *supra* note 1, at ¶ 110. Of course, the parol evidence rule is a rule of substantive law that has incidental evidentiary effects.

[14] Cisg Art. 8(3). It is unfortunate that an American court that was faced with this issue stumbled. In *Beijing Metals & Minerals Import Corp. v. American Business Center, Inc.*, 993 F.2d 1178, 1182 n.8 (5th Cir.1993), the court without discussion or analysis applied the Texas parol evidence rule to bar evidence of an alleged additional oral term to a written contract governed by the CISG. An earlier case had recognized the absence of a parol evidence rule in the CISG. *Filanto, S.p.A. v. Chilewich Intern. Corp.*, 789 F.Supp. 1229, 1238 n.7 (S.D.N.Y. 1992).

[15] *W.W.W. Assocs. v. Giancontieri*, 77 N.Y.2d 157, 566 N.E.2d 639, 565 N.Y.S.2d 440 (1990).

[16] *Continental Cas. Co. v. Rapid-American Corp.*, 80 N.Y.2d 640, 609 N.E.2d 506, 593 N.Y.S.2d 966 (1993) (evidence of practical construction not admissible if the contract is unambiguous).

[17] UCC §2–202(a).

[18] Principles Art. 4.4.

ones.[19] The contract, of course, can contain rules of interpretation (e.g., subordinating the terms of one document to that of another document that is part of one complex contract).[20] All terms of the contract are to be given effect.[21] Also, the Principles adopt the principle of *contra proferentem* – interpretation against the party who supplied the language.[22] All of these rules are consistent with traditional approaches.

j. One rule that the Principles promulgate deals with a problem seldom encountered in purely domestic contracts – conflicts among versions of the contract in different languages. In the event of discrepancies, the Principles generally favor the version that was originally drawn up. The CISG is silent on this important issue, and the Principles advance the cause of certainty in international trade by providing a definite and logical rule.

k. The Principles announce a rule with respect to the vexing problem of the omitted term. Where no term of the contract covers an event that has occurred, the tribunal is faced with an omitted term.[23] Perhaps the event was unforeseen or perhaps it was foreseen as a possibility, but was too thorny an issue to be resolved by negotiation. Strictly, the supplying of a term is not interpretation of the parties' agreement. The court must create rather than interpret. However, some gap-fillers are routine, and many are found in the CISG (e.g., the buyer must notify the seller of any nonconformity of the goods within a reasonable time).[24] If the gap does not concern this kind of routine event, the Principles provide criteria for filling it.[25] Once again, the Principles identify raw material with which to fill the gap in the CISG.

[19] Principles Art. 4.4, comment 2.
[20] *Id.*
[21] Principles Art. 4.5.
[22] Principles Art. 4.6.
[23] Restatement (Second) of Contracts §204 (1979).
[24] CISG Art. 39.
[25] Principles Art. 4.8.

Usages and practices: Editorial remarks on the manner in which the UNIDROIT Principles may be used to interpret or supplement CISG Article 9

Jorge Oviedo Albán

I. INTRODUCTION

Article 9 CISG is located in Chapter II, entitled "General Provisions," of the Convention. The other provisions of the Convention included in that chapter deal with general matters, such as the interpretation of the Convention (Art. 7) and the conduct of the parties (Art. 8)

Similarly, in the UNIDROIT Principles of International Commercial Contracts, Art. 1.8, which has a similar structure to that of Art. 9 CISG, is located in Chapter 1, entitled "General Provisions." Included in that chapter are similar references to rules of interpretation sources.

Thus, it may be said that the recognition of the normative value of international usages and practices in contracts of international trade is a characteristic common to these two instruments of international commercial law.

II. NORMATIVE VALUE OF USAGES AND PRACTICES

Art. 9, paragraph (1), of the Convention recognizes the normative value of usages by pointing out that "[t]he parties to a contract are bound by any usage to which they have agreed and by any practices which they have established between themselves."

Furthermore, Art. 9, paragraph (2), provides that "[t]he parties are considered, unless otherwise agreed, to have impliedly made applicable to their contract or its formation a usage of which the parties knew or ought to have known and which in international trade is widely known to, and regularly observed by, parties to contracts of the type involved in the particular trade concerned."[1]

Art. 1.8 of the UNIDROIT Principles also refers to the normative value of usages and practices:

> (1) The parties are bound by any usage to which they have agreed and by any practices which they have established between themselves.
>
> (2) The parties are bound by a usage that is widely known to and regularly observed in international trade by parties in the particular trade concerned except where the application of such a usage would be unreasonable.

At first, it can be considered that the counterpart provisions acknowledge the normative value of usages and practices[2]; that is, the parties to the contract are bound by any relevant usages and established practices. It would be convenient to clarify those respective provisions, because other provisions of the CISG (Art. 8(3)),[3] as well as provisions of the

[1] Art. 9(1) and 9(2) CISG. For relevant commentary in Spanish and in English, *see* the following selection: OVIEDO ALBÁN, J., "El sistema de fuentes del contrato de compraventa internacional de mercaderías," in *Estudios de Contratación Internacional. Régimen uniforme e internacional privado.* Pontificia Universidad Javeriana, Facultad de Ciencias Jurídicas, Bogotá D.C. – Colombia, 2004, pp. 221–304; SCHLECHTRIEM, P., *Uniform Sales Law – the U.N. Convention on Contracts for the International Sale of Goods*, Manz, Vienna, 1986, pp. 39–42; PENDON MELENDEZ, M. A., "Comentario al artículo 1.8," in *Comentario a los Principios de UNIDROITpara los Contratos del Comercio Internacional*; MORÁN BOVIO, D., (Coordinator), Thomson Aranzadi, segunda edición, Elcano Navarra, 2003, pp. 86–93; OVIEDO ALBÁN, J., "La costumbre en la compraventa internacional de mercaderías (comentarios a los artículos 8(3) y 9 de la Convención de Viena de 1980" [Custom in the International Sale of Goods (Commentary on Arts. 8.3 and 9 of the Vienna Convention of 1980)], *Revista de Derecho Internacional y del;* MERCOSUR. La Ley, Buenos Aires – Argentina, año 7 n° 3, 2003, pp. 17–37; GOLDSTAJN, A., "Usages of Trade and Other Autonomous Rules of International Trade According to the UN (1980) Sales Convention," in SARCEVIC P. & VOLKEN P., eds., *International Sales of Goods: Dubrovnik Lectures*, Oceana (1986) Ch. 3, 55–110.

[2] "The so called 'normative' usages were extremely controversial. According to the German understanding, their validity is not based on the parties' agreement": SCHLECHTRIEM, P., *supra* note 1, at p. 39. *See* GARRO, A. and ZUPPI, A., *Compraventa Internacional de Mercaderías*, Ediciones La Rocca, Buenos Aires, Argentina, p. 61.

[3] Art. 8(3) CISG provides, "In determining the intent of a party or the understanding a reasonable person would have had, due consideration is to be given to all relevant circumstances of the case including the negotiations, any practices which the parties have established between themselves, usages and any subsequent conduct of the parties."

UNIDROIT Principles (Art. 4.3 (b), (e), and (f)),[4] refer to usages and practices in an interpretive function.

Although the counterpart articles in the CISG and the UNIDROIT Principles, to which those other provisions make reference, are apparently similar – structurally as well as linguistically – reference must be made to some possible difficulties in the interpretation of Art. 9 CISG, and to the manner in which the provision in Art. 1.8 UNIDROIT Principles may be used to assist that interpretation.

III. DISTINCTION AMONG USAGES, PRACTICES, AND CUSTOM

Both Art. 9 of the Convention and Art. 1.8 of the UNIDROIT Principles require the interpreter to establish a distinction among usages, contractual practices, and custom.

The Convention's provision makes reference, on the one hand, to *established practices* between the parties to the contract, and, on the other hand, to *trade usages*, which acquire a sense of generality. The counterpart provision in Art. 1.8 of the UNIDROIT Principles adopts an identical way to refer to practices and usages agreed upon by the parties to the contract.

Custom can be conceived as a general and obligatory behavior for a community, confirmed by public facts, uniform in substance, and reiterated in a certain place. The Italian author, Domenico Barbero, affirms, "Custom is a form of production of juridical norms that consists on the general, constant repetition and uniform of a certain behavior in certain circumstances."[5]

On the contrary, in usages, the characteristics of publicity and uniformity are not present as they are in custom. Usages are constituted as behaviors observed by people in their contracts or in the conduct of their own business in general.

The Convention, in Art. 9, and the UNIDROIT Principles, in Art. 1.8, make reference to contractual practices and conventional usages,[6] pointing out that the parties will be bound by any usage to which they have agreed and by any practices that they have established between themselves. In other words, it is a series or a sequence of previous behaviors of the parties, related in particular to transactions carried out previously between the parties, that can be always considered obligatory for the parties in future negotiations and transactions, so that they become a rule common of behavior.

In Art. 9(1) CISG and Art. 1.8(1) UNIDROIT Principles, a distinction must be maintained between conventional usages and contractual practices.[7] The usages and practices

[4] Art. 4.3 of the UNIDROIT Principles, located in Chapter 5 and entitled "Interpretation" provides

> In applying Article 4.1 [interpretation of the intention of the parties] and 4.2 [interpretation of the conduct of the parties], regard shall be had to all the circumstances, including [...] (b) practices which the parties have established between themselves; [...] (e) the meaning commonly given to terms and expressions in the trade concerned; (f) usages.

[5] Barbero, D., "Sistema del derecho privado," *I. Ediciones Jurídicas Europa América*, Buenos Aires, 1967, p. 92.

[6] Illescas Ortiz, R. and Perales Viscasillas, M. del P., *Derecho Mercantil International, El derecho uniforme*, Universidad Carlos III de Madrid, Editorial Centro de Estudios Ramón Areces S.A., Madrid, 2003, p. 125. *See* ICC Arbitration Award 8611/HV/JK of 23 January 1997: "Nevertheless, regarding the relationship between the parties, a prompt delivery of replacement parts had become normal practice as defined by Art. 9(1) of the CISG by which the [seller] was bound." Abstract available at Unilex Database. Case presentation and English translation available at <http://cisgw3.law.pace.edu/cases/978611i1.html>.

[7] *See* Illescas Ortiz, R. and Perales Viscasillas, *supra* note 7. *See* Official Comment on Art. 1.8 of the UNIDROIT Principles, available at <http://www.cisg.law.pace.edu/cisg/principles/uni9.html>. It is helpful to consider the explanation contained in the Official Comment on Art. 1.8 of the UNIDROIT Principles:

> 2. Practices established between the parties
> A practice established between the parties to a particular contract is automatically binding, except where the parties have expressly excluded its application. Whether a particular practice can be deemed to be "established" between the parties will naturally depend on the circumstances of the case, but behaviour on the occasion of only one previous transaction between the parties will not normally suffice.

that the parties have established between themselves can be agreed upon expressly or tacitly.[8] Consequently, it is the series of previous behaviors of the parties, related in particular to transactions carried out previously, that, if carried out regularly, can be always considered obligatory between themselves in future negotiations.[9]

On the other hand, Art. 9(2) CISG refers to a different category that is neither the practices nor the conventional usages mentioned in Art. 9(1). The same observation may be made in relation to Art. 1.8(2) UNIDROIT Principles. Based on the analysis provided below, it is submitted that where the respective provisions make reference to a usage that the parties *knew or ought to have known* and that in *international trade is widely known* to, and regularly observed by, parties to contracts of the type involved in the particular trade concerned, such reference is to the *general customs of international trade*.

IV. INTERNATIONAL CUSTOM

In Art. 9(2), the Convention refers to international customs – that is, objective and international usages whose validity has not been made a pact by the parties in an expressed or tacit way.[10]

Next, reference must be made to the requirements mentioned in Art. 9(2) CISG that highlight the differences between that provision and those established in Art. 1.8 of

3. Agreed usages
By stating that the parties are bound by usages to which they have agreed, para. (1) of this article merely applies the general principle of freedom of contract laid down in Art. 1.1. Indeed, the parties may either negotiate all the terms of their contract, or for certain questions simply refer to other sources including usages. The parties may stipulate the application of any usage, including a usage developed within a trade sector to which neither party belongs, or a usage relating to a different type of contract. It is even conceivable that the parties will agree on the application of what are sometimes misleadingly called usages, i.e. a set of rules issued by a particular trade association under the title of "Usages," but which only in part reflects established general lines of conduct.

[8] Carlsen, A. "Remarks on the Manner in which the PECL May Be Used to Interpret or Supplement Art. 9 Cisg," available online at <http://cisgw3.law.pace.edu/cisg/text/peclcomp9.html#er>. *See* China post-1989 Cietac Arbitration proceedings (*Contract #QFD890011*), translation available online at <http://cisgw3.law.pace.edu/cases/900000c1.html>; Austria 21 March 2000 *Oberster Gerichtsfhof* [Supreme Court], presentation available online at <http://cisgw3.law.pace.edu/cases/000321a3.html>, Case Law on UNCITRAL Texts (CLOUT) abstract no. 425.

[9] Perales Viscasillas, M. del P., *La formación del contrato en la compraventa internacional de mercaderías*, Tirant Lo Blanch, Valencia, 1996, p. 81. "The Convention does not state when it is possible to speak of 'practices established between the parties.' According to some courts, for these practices to be binding on the parties pursuant to article 9(1), it is necessary that the parties' relationship lasts for some time and that it has led to the conclusion of various contracts. One court expressly emphasized this requirement, as it stated that the practice it had to decide upon 'does not establish usage in the meaning of [article 9(1)], which would require a conduct regularly observed between the parties and thus requiring a certain duration and frequency [. . .]. Such duration and frequency does not exist where only two previous deliveries have been handled in that manner. The absolute number is too low." The UNCITRAL Digest of Case Law on the United Nations Convention on the International Sale of Goods. A/CN.9/SER.C/DIGEST/CISG/9 [8 June 2004], available online at <http://cisgw3.law.pace.edu/cisg/text/anno-art-09.html#udfn6>. See relevant case law:

- Germany 13 April 2000 *Amtsgericht* [Lower Court], case presentation and English translation available online at <http://cisgw3.law.pace.edu/cases/000413g1.html>, CLOUT abstract no. 360
- Austria 6 February 1996 *Oberster Gerichtshof* [Supreme Court], case presentation and English translation at <http://cisgw3.law.pace.edu/cases/960206a3.html>, CLOUT abstract no. 176: "The parties had initially intended to enter into a 'basic agreement,' which would contain the general conditions of the seller and would constitute the trade usages that would govern the transactions between the parties, but could not reach an agreement. The draft of the 'basic agreement' stated that all orders should be in writing. However, the seller could not prove that the 'basic agreement' nor the general conditions had been made known to the buyer." In this case the Court considered that preliminary business conversations can become practices according with Article 9 Cisg. The court found that the parties could be bound by any trade practices or usage established between themselves (Article 9(1) Cisg). In such instances, Article 9(1) Cisg must be interpreted in the light of Article 8(1) Cisg to the effect that a party must have known of the intent of the other party.

[10] *See* Calvo Caravaca, A. L., "Comentario, Artículo 9," in DÍEZ PICAZA Y PONCE DE LEON, L., *La compraventa internacional de mercaderías. Comentario de la Convención de Viena. Civitas*, Madrid, 1998, p. 138.

the UNIDROIT Principles. The initial conclusion is that the provisions in Art. 9 CISG can be used for different conceptions, whereas Art. 1.8 of the UNIDROIT Principles provides a wider formula, to which one may turn for assistance in interpreting and applying Art. 9(2) CISG.

In consequence, there are two requirements laid down in Art. 9(2) of the Convention.

1. A Usage of Which the Parties Knew or Ought to Have Known

The provisions in Art. 9(2) require that the parties to the contract indeed know and understand usages that are incorporated into the contract as custom, because the obligation such usages impose is derived from the generality of such usages. Such usages constitute a custom, thus maintaining the distinction between usages that are particular (to the parties) and conventional usages. In many fields of international trade – such as maritime sales, insurance, financial transactions, etc. – there exist certain accepted usages that are observed and applied to contracts of the type involved in the particular trade, despite possible ignorance of the particular merchants or of their inclusion of such usages in like contracts.[11]

It has been pointed out that Art. 9(2) of the Convention is based on two theories that recognize custom or usages in commercial contracts in the particular trade concerned.[12]

The first theory, known as a "subjective theory," comprises usages that are applicable only when the parties have had knowledge of them; in consequence, if the usages are not known by the parties, they are not applicable to the contract.[13]

In a contrary way, pursuant to the "objective theory," certain usages that might be unknown to the parties may yet be applicable to the contract.[14]

In that sense, Art. 9(2) of the Convention, through its incorporation of the two theories *of influence of trade usages* in commercial contracts,[15] provides that usages of which the parties *had* or *ought to have had* knowledge prevail and are, thus, applicable to the contract.

Tribunals and courts have recognized the normative value of usages of international trade. For example, the U.S. Court of Appeals, Fifth Circuit has ruled, "The CISG incorporates Incoterms through article 9(2), [. . .] Even if the usage of Incoterms is not global, the fact that they are well known in international trade means that they are incorporated through article 9(2)."[16]

[11] *See* United States 10 May 2002 Federal District Court [New York] (*Geneva Pharmaceuticals Tech. Corp. v. Barr Labs. Inc.*), case presentation available at <http://cisgw3.law.pace.edu/cases/020510u1.html>, where the court stated, in para 25, "The usages and practices of the parties or the industry are automatically incorporated into any agreement governed by the Convention, unless expressly excluded by the parties. CISG Art. 9."

[12] *See* CARLSEN, A., *supra* note 11.

[13] *Id.*

[14] "According to the subjective theory, usages unknown to either party are not applicable. Contrary hereto is the objective theory, whereby usages are applicable if they represent a legal norm. According to the objective theory, usages unknown to both parties may be applicable to an agreement. Both theories agree that the usage must be so widespread and widely recognized that businesspersons knew or ought to have known of it." *Id.*

[15] See CARLSEN, *supra* note 11; GARRO, A., *supra* note 2,; ZUPPI, A. L., op. cit., pp. 61–62.

[16] United States 11 June 2003 Federal Appellate Court [5th Circuit] (*BP Oil International v. Empresa Estatal Petroleos de Ecuador*) available online at <http://cisgw3.law.pace.edu/cases/030611u1.html>, where the court held, at III. B. that "[t]he CISG incorporates Incoterms through article 9(2) [. . .]. Even if the usage of Incoterms is not global, the fact that they are well known in international trade means that they are incorporated through article 9(2)." The judgment, at footnote 9, also cites FOLSOM, R. et al.: "Incoterms could be made an implicit term of the contract as part of international custom. Courts in France and Germany have done so, and both treaties and the UNCITRAL Secretariat describe Incoterms as a widely-observed usage for commercial terms." FOLSOM, R. GORDON, M., SPANOGLE, J. *International Business Transactions* (2d ed., West Group 2001), p. 72.

The wording of the counterpart provision in Art. 1.8 of the UNIDROIT Principles provides that "[t]he parties are bound by a usage that is widely known to a regularly observed in international trade by parties in the particular trade [. . .]."

It is apparent that the UNIDROIT Principles do not require that the *parties to the contract* knew or ought to have known the applicable usage. That is because the UNIDROIT Principles adopt an approach in which usages that are widely known and observed in trade acquire juridical value independently of the degree of knowledge of the parties to the contract; because of the widespread observance of such usages, the participants in international trade are assumed to know of them. The objective parameter used to determine the existence of such custom or widely observed usages in the particular trade is the fact that they are observed widely and regularly by the participants in international trade. Note, however, the important qualification contained in Art. 1.8(2) of the UNIDROIT Principles that the application of such usage must not be unreasonable.[17]

As such, the UNIDROIT Principles, like the Convention, refer to the requirement of *generality* attributed to the custom in terms of doctrine and jurisprudence, not different national regulations.

2. A Usage That in International Trade is Widely Known to and Regularly Observed by Parties to Contracts of the Type Involved in the Particular Trade Concerned

In this respect, it is the requirements of generality, publicity, uniformity, and reiteration that are operative in international trade. As for the requirement for usages to be *widely known*, it is not required that they are so known in all the commercial places; rather, they may be widely known in regional or parochial operations,[18] provided they arise from transactions in international trade. That is to say, the application of usages developed or emanating from transactions in *domestic* trade should be rejected as irrelevant for the purposes of international trade. In principle, only usages that are observed in international trade, not domestic, should form the source of the legal effects envisaged in Art. 9 CISG.[19]

It must be noted, however, that a local usage *might* perhaps be applicable in some instances, provided it is linked directly to transactions in *international* trade.[20]

See also United States 26 March 2002 Federal District Court [New York] (*St. Paul Guardian Insurance Company et al. v. Neuromed Medical Systems & Support et al.*), available online at <http://cisgw3.law.pace.edu/cases/020326u1.html>, where the court concluded that the risk of loss passed to the buyer upon delivery to the port of shipment by virtue of the CIF delivery term. The court found that the International Chamber of Commerce's 1990 CIF Incoterm governed by virtue of Article 9(2) CISG. The court also noted that German courts apply the Incoterm as a commercial practice with the force of law (CLOUT abstract no. 447, prepared by WINSHIP, P.

[17] Art. 1.8(2) of the UNIDROIT Principles. *See* also text accompanying notes 24 and 25, *infra*.

[18] See PERALES VISCASILLAS, M. del P., *supra* note 10, at p. 84.

[19] See FOLSOM, R.; GORDON, M. W., SPANOGLE, J. A., *International Business Transactions in a Nut Shell* (West Group 2000), p. 62.

[20] *See* Austria 21 March 2000 *Oberster Gerichtshof* [Supreme Court], case presentation available at <http://cisgw3.law.pace.edu/cases/000321a3.html>, CLOUT abstract no. 425, prepared by NIEDERBERGER, S.: "In the sense of article 9(2) a usage is widely known and regularly observed when it is recognized by the majority of persons doing business in the same field. To be applicable such usages must be known or at least should have been known by the parties having their place of business in the area of the usages. The Supreme Court affirmed the findings of the court of first instance, noting that since the plaintiff in its acceptance of the order expressly stated the applicability of the 'Tegernseer Gebräuche' and had delivered wood to the defendant before, the defendant must have known these usages." *See* also "Editorial remarks," excerpt from analysis of Austrian case law by Willibald Posch & Thomas Petz, "Austrian Cases on the UN Convention on Contracts for the International Sale of Goods," 6 *Vindobona J. Int'l Com. L. & Arbitration* 1–24 (2002), at 10: *Usages and practices*. "In [this] decision on the relationship of trade usages and CISG, the Austrian Supreme Court had the opportunity to decide on the merits of the case. [G]enuine domestic usages for the trade of timber, the 'Tegernsee Usages,' were at stake. The Austrian Supreme Court held that these Bavarian usages prevailed over the provisions of CISG, since it had been established by

Such extension of applicable usages is, for example, contemplated in the Official Comment on Art. 1.8 of the UNIDROIT Principles.[21]

Further support for that proposition can be found in the case law. The Court of Appeal [OLG] of Graz, Austria, 9 November 1995, held that

> Art. 9(2) CISG, save a limited number of exceptions, could not be interpreted as barring the application of national or local usage in interpreting a contract even though no mention of such usage was made in the contract itself. Accordingly, a seller who has been engaging in business in a country for many years and has repeatedly concluded contracts of the type involved in the particular trade concerned is obliged to take national usage into consideration.[22]

In conclusion, regarding the interpretation of Art. 9(2) of the Convention, much doctrine and jurisprudence point to the possible applicability of *local* usages, but with the provisos that have been stated above. That does not, however, mean that local usages may always be applicable to contracts for the sale of goods governed by the Convention, as it will be required that the parties to the contract had or ought to have had knowledge of usages that are widely known and regularly observed in the particular trade concerned. That last characteristic can also be given to a local usage if the parties knew of it or it is widely known and observed.

Support for that proposition can be found in the decision of the Appellate Court of Frankfurt, 5 July 1995, which held that

> no contract had been concluded by means of a letter of confirmation followed by silence. Although there is an established trade usage which recognizes such a conclusion of contract by silence in the jurisdiction of the recipient's place of business, due to the international character of the CISG, regard is to be given only to trade usages that are known to the law both in the jurisdiction of the offeror and in the jurisdiction of the recipient (Art. 9(2) CISG). Moreover, the legal effects of the trade usage have to be known to both parties.[23]

In the counterpart provisions of the UNIDROIT Principles, in Art. 1.8, the wording used is wider than that of Art. 9 CISG, and it does not define what is a "usage" nor does it require – as the Convention does – that the usage is either known or ought to be known to the contracting parties.

It is submitted that the UNIDROIT Principles concentrate in a broader way than the CISG does on the requirement of "generality" of the custom, whereas it seems that Art. 9(2) of the Convention restricts its approach to usages *known to both parties* to the contract.

As for the requirement that the usage is obligatory on the parties unless the application of this use is not *reasonable*, it is helpful to consider the explanation and

the Court of First Instance that these usages were widely known to and regularly observed by parties in cross-border timber trade between Austria and Germany."

[21] *See* Official Comment on Art. 1.8 of the UNIDROIT Principles, available online at <http://cisgw3.law.pace.edu/cisg/principles/uni9.html#official>.

[22] Austria 9 November 1995 *Oberlandesgericht* [Appellate Court] Graz, case presentation and English translation available at <http://cisgw3.law.pace.edu/cases/951109a3.html>: "In remanding the case to the court of first instance, the Court of Appeal held that article 9(2) CISG, save a limited number of exceptions, could not be interpreted as barring the application of national or local usage in interpreting a contract even though no mention of such usage was made in the contract itself. Accordingly, a seller who has been engaging in business in a county for many years and has repeatedly concluded contracts of the type involved in the particular trade concerned is obliged to take national usage into consideration." CLOUT abstract no. 175.

[23] Germany 5 July 1995 *Oberlandesgericht* [Appellate Court] Frankfurt, case presentation and English translation available at <http://cisgw3.law.pace.edu/cases/950705g1.html>.

See also PERALES VISCASILLAS, M. del P., "Tratamiento jurídico de las cartas de confirmación en la Convención de Viena de 1980 sobre Compraventa Internacional de Mercaderías," available online at <http://cisgw3.law.pace.edu/cisg/biblio/confirma.html>.

illustration contained in the Official Comment on Art. 1.8(2) of the UNIDROIT Principles[24]:

> A usage may be regularly observed by the generality of businesspeople in a particular trade sector but its application in a given case may nevertheless be unreasonable. Reasons for this may be found in the particular conditions in which one or both parties operate and/or the atypical nature of the transaction. In such cases the usage will not be applied.

Reasonableness is an important concept in the Convention and it is regarded as a general principle of the CISG. As a general principle of the Convention, reasonableness has a strong bearing on the proper interpretation of all provisions of the CISG.[25]

On the validity and proof of usages, the Convention does not contain any special disposition. Pursuant to Art. 4 of the Convention,[26] the matter of validity must be generally left to the norms of international private law. Therefore, reliance must be placed on private international law, the opinions of the Chamber of Commerce of the relevant place, or the summaries of such usages made by specialized institutions.[27] If a party to the contract alleged the existence and applicability of a usage, he should bear the onus of proving it.[28]

Finally, applicable usages, practices, and custom will prevail over the provisions of the Convention[29] and over the UNIDROIT Principles[30] as implied terms of the contract, although they will be superseded by any contrary express contractual terms.

V. CONCLUSIONS

The counterpart provisions in the Convention and in the UNIDROIT Principles dealing with conventional usages and practices established between the parties to the contract

[24] *See* Official Comment on Art. 1.8(2) of the UNIDROIT Principles, available online at <http://cisgw3.law.pace.edu/cisg/principles/uni9.html#official>. Comment 5. The following illustration of the comment is offered. *Id.*

> A usage exists in a commodity trade sector according to which the purchaser may not rely on defects in the goods if they are not duly certified by an internationally recognized inspection agency. When A, a buyer, takes over the goods at the port of destination, the only internationally recognized inspection agency operating in that port is on strike and to call another from the nearest port would be excessively costly. The application of the usage in this case would be unreasonable and A may rely on the defects it has discovered even though they have not been certified by an internationally recognized inspection agency.

[25] "Reasonableness" is an important concept in the Convention; "reasonableness" is specifically mentioned in numerous provisions of the CISG and it is regarded a general principle of the CISG; *see* KRITZER, A. H., "Overview Comments on Reasonableness – A General Principle of the CISG," available online at <http://cisgw3.law.pace.edu/cisg/text/reason.html#overv>. *See* Art. 7(2) CISG, which contains the built-in interpretation mechanism of the Convention; *see* also relevant scholarly writing on the proper interpretation of Art. 7 CISG, presentation available online at <http://cisgw3.law.pace.edu/cisg/text/e-text-07.html>.

[26] See Article 4 CISG, which states: "[. . .] *except as otherwise expressly provided* in this Convention, [the CISG] is not concerned with: (a) the validity of the contract or of any of this provisions or of any usage [. . .]" (emphasis added).

[27] See FERNÁNDEZ DE LA GÁNDARA, L., CALVO CARAVACA, A.-L., "El contrato de compraventa internacional de mercaderías," in *Contratos Internacionales*, CALVO CARAVACA, A. L.; FERNANDEZ DE LA GÁNDARA, L. (Directors), BLANCO MORALES LIMONES, P., (Coordinator) (Tecnos, Madrid, 1999), pp. 187–188.

[28] Germany 9 July 1998 *Oberlandesgericht* [Appellate Court] Dresden, case presentation and English translation available at <http://cisgw3.law.pace.edu/cases/980709g1.html>, where the court held that the buyer did not prove that there was a usage known in international trade whereupon silence to a commercial letter of confirmation amounted to consent (Article 9 CISG)." CLOUT abstract no. 347.

[29] See FOLSOM, GORDON, SPANOGLE, *supra* note 20, at pp. 13–14, where the authors state: "[I]t should be noted that, although CISG gives wide recognition to "party autonomy" (the ability of the parties to determine the terms of their deal), in Article 6 it only recognizes the ability of the parties to exclude the Convention."

[30] See Official Comment on Art. 1.8(2) of the UNIDROIT Principles, available online at <http://cisgw3.law.pace.edu/cisg/principles/uni9.html#official>. Comment 6:

> Both courses of dealing and usages, once they are applicable in a given case, prevail over conflicting provisions contained in the Principles. The reason for this is that they bind the parties as implied terms of the contract as a whole or of single statements or other conduct on the part of one of the parties. As such, they are superseded by any express term stipulated by the parties but, in the same way as the latter, they prevail over the Principles, the only exception being those provisions which are specifically declared to be of a mandatory character.

recognize the obligatory value of such norms on the parties, and unless the parties agree otherwise, such norms are presumed to have been incorporated by the parties into the contract.

Usages or customs are applied to contracts of sale, provided they fulfill these requirements: they are widely known in international trade and regularly observed by parties to contracts of the type involved in the particular trade concerned.

This chapter's comparative analysis of the counterpart provisions on usages identified several similarities in structure and application but also some distinctions in the wording and approach adopted in the respective instruments.

"Place of business": Comparison between the provisions of CISG Article 10 and the counterpart provisions of UNIDROIT Principles Article 1.10

Allison E. Butler

I. General Interpretation and Application in the CISG and UNIDROIT Principles
II. Scope of the Term "Place of Business"
III. Definition of "Place of Business"
IV. Party with More Than One Place of Business
  1. General
  2. Habitual
V. Conclusion

I. GENERAL INTERPRETATION AND APPLICATION IN THE CISG AND UNIDROIT PRINCIPLES

UNIDROIT Principles Art. 1.10 is similar in substance and form to its counterpart provision contained in Art. 10 CISG. Both provisions exemplify the drafters' intent to adopt the "closest connection" principle in contract interpretation and supplementation when determining the relevant "place of business."[1] Additionally, each has application beyond the scope of its respective provision.[2] Case law under Article 10 CISG provides judicial application of this principle, thereby giving it additional supplemental authority.

[1] See Art. 10 CISG; Art. 1.10 UNIDROIT. The "closest relationship theory" is the place of business having the closest relationship with the contract. In contrast, there is the "theory of the principal place of business," which holds that the relevant place of business is where the main seat is located. *See* generally Franco Ferrari, "Specific Topics of the CISG in the Light of Judicial Application and Scholarly Writing," 15 *J.L. & Com.* (1995), Section II. 4. "The 'Place of Business' under CISG," available at <http://cisgw3.law.pace.edu/cisg/biblio/2ferrari.html>. The original intent of the drafters of the CISG when adopting the theory of "principal place of business" as evidenced by the proposal reprinted in UNCITRAL Yearbook, vol. II (1971) 52, available at <http://www.uncitral.org/english/yearbooks/yearbook-index-e.htm>; however, this was later rejected.

[2] There are numerous applications of the place of business in particular provisions of both documents; *see* the examples offered in the Secretariat Commentary to the Draft Convention as manifestations of the concept CISG Articles 12, 20(2), 24, 31(c), 42(1)(b), 57(1)(a), and 96; Text of Secretariat Commentary on Article 9 of the 1978 Draft [*draft counterpart of Article 10 CISG*], available at <http://cisgw3.law.pace.edu/cisg/text/secomm/secomm-10.html>; *See also* UNIDROIT Articles 1.9(3), 2.8(2); 6.1.6, and 6.1.14(a). *See* Official Comments on Articles of the UNIDROIT Principles, available at <http://cisgw3.law.pace.edu/cisg/principles/un10.html>.

II. SCOPE OF THE TERM "PLACE OF BUSINESS"

Application of Article 1.10 illustrates that a party's place of business is of relevance in a number of contexts throughout the UNIDROIT Principles. For example, place of business is relevant for the place for the delivery of notices (Art. 1.9(3)); a possible extension of the time of acceptance because of a holiday falling on the last day (Art. 2.8(2)); the place of performance (Art. 6.1.6); and the determination of the party who should apply for a public permission (Art. 6.1.14(a)). Hence, the term has applicability outside the realm of Article 1.10.

Similarly, the issue of determining the relevant place of business of a party frequently arises in several provisions under the CISG.[3] However, the primary and most common usage of "place of business" as facilitated under Article 10 CISG is its interpretive part in the unilateral conflict rule contained in Article 1(1)(a) CISG.[4]

III. DEFINITION OF "PLACE OF BUSINESS"

The concept of "place of business" is not defined under the UNIDROIT Principles. The relevant place of business is, however, that which has the closest relationship to the contract and to its performance.[5] Under Article 10 CISG, there is an overwhelming cognizance that the place of business is where "the center of the business activity directed to the participation is located," which links the contracting party to the State where the business is conducted, provided the party has autonomous power.[6] Notably, a business's "autonomous power" appears to be the key component when courts have scrutinized this term.[7] Consequently, this assumption has led many commentators and courts to conclude that a place of business, such as the location of an agent, representative, or

[3] *See* CISG discussion, *supra* note 2.

[4] When both articles are read in conjunction they "form the *lex specialis* of conflicts of laws in contract applicable to contracts of sale of goods between parties whose places of business are in different Contracting States to the Convention." Carolina Saf, "A Study of Interplay between the Conventions Governing International Contracts of Sale," available at <http://cisgw3.law.pace.edu/cisg/biblio/saf.html>. *See* illustrative case, Germany 13 April 2000 Amtsgericht [Lower Court] Duisburg, English translation available online at <http://cisgw3.law.pace.edu/cases/000413g1.html>.

[5] *See* Official Comments on Articles of the UNIDROIT, Article 1.10, Comment 2, available at <http://cisgw3.law.pace.edu.cisg/principles/uni 10.html>.

[6] *See* Ferrari, *supra* note 1, referencing BGH, 2 June 1982, VIII ZR 43/81, *Neue Juristische Wochenschrift (NJW)* 1982, 2730–2732 (German Federal Supreme Court's interpretation of "place of business" in ULIS Article 1).

[7] *See* the relevant case law:

- Germany 28 February 2000, *Oberlandesgerticht* [Appellate Court] Stuttgart, English translation available at <http://cisgw3.law.pace.edu/cases/000228g1.html> (holding that the location of a Spanish representative of a German manufacturer-seller in Spain was not a place of business absent legal authority to bind the German manufacturer to the Spanish buyer);
- Germany 13 November 2000, *Landgericht* [District Court] Köln, available at <http://cisgw3.law.pace.edu/cases/001113g1.html> (holding that an Italian agent in Germany did not have the authority to bind an Italian company in a German-Italian contract dispute)
- United States 27 July 2001, Federal District Court, *Asante Technologies, Inc. v. MC-Sierra, Inc.*, available at <http://cisgw3.law.pace.edu/cases/010727u1.html> (holding that a U.S. nonexclusive distributor not acting as an agent did not have authority to bind a U.S. company in contract with a Canadian company)
- France 4 January 1995, *Cour de Cassation* [Supreme Court], *Fauba France FDIS GC Electronique v. Fujitsu Mikroelectronik GmbH*, English translation available at <http://cisgw3.law.pace.edu/cases/950104f1.html> (holding that a liaison office of a German company in France was not its principal place of business absent corporate status in action against a French buyer)
- ICC Arbitration Case No. 7531 of 1994, available at <http://cisgw3.law.pace.edu/cases/947531i1.html> (holding an Austrian-buyer liaison located in China was not the place of business in a Chinese-Austrian dispute, notwithstanding that the liaison office in China may have been involved in the negotiating process)

distributor[8]; liaison office[9]; conference center or exhibition or a rented office(s) at an exhibition, *fails* to constitute a place of business for the purposes of Article 10 CISG, absent facts to the contrary. At least one court did find that a corporate branch was the place of business under Article 10 CISG and not the company's headquarters located in a different country. This finding was based on the fact that the branch had the closest relationship to the contract and its performance.[10]

IV. SEVERAL PLACES OF BUSINESS UNDER THE CISG AND THE UNIDROIT PRINCIPLES

1. General

Article 1.10 of the UNIDROIT Principles provides that when a party has multiple places of business (normally a central office and various branch offices), the relevant place of business should be considered to be that which has the closest relationship to the contract and to its performance.[11] Absent from this provision is what place of business controls when the place of the conclusion of the contract and that of performance differ. The Official Comments to the UNIDROIT Principles provide that the place of performance would be more relevant.[12] However, in determining the place of business that has the closest relationship to a given contract and to its performance, attention should be given to the circumstances known to or contemplated by both parties at any time before or at the conclusion of the contract.[13] Consequently, facts that are known only to one of the parties or of which the parties became aware only after the conclusion of the contract cannot be taken into consideration.

Article 10(a) CISG also establishes similar criteria to resolve this issue. Notably, when reference is made to the performance of the contract, it is referring to the performance that the parties knew or contemplated when they were entering into the contract. For example, if it was contemplated by a party that performance of the contract would be in State A, a determination that the party's place of business was in State A would not be altered by the party's subsequent decision to perform the contract at the party's place of business in State B.

In judicial application of Article 10 CISG, however, the courts have routinely looked not only to the intent of the parties but also to the "totality of the contract."

This term is used to mean an examination of the contract as a whole. Hence, the fact that a third party negotiated a contract has had little significance to the courts when determining the place of business. Certain factors that are not known or contemplated by both parties at the time of entering into the contract may not be taken into consideration. Such factors include, but are not limited to, supervision over the making of the contract by a head office located in another State or the foreign origin or final destination of the

[8] *See* Germany 28 February 2000, *Oberlandesgericht* [Appellate Court] Stuttgart, *supra* note 7; Germany 13 November 2000, District Court Köln, available at <http://cisgw3.law.pace.edu/cases/001113g1.html>; U.S. 27 July 2001, Federal District Court, *Asante Technologies, Inc. v. MC-Sierra, Inc.*, *supra* note 7.

[9] *See* France 4 January 1995, *Cour de Cassation* [Supreme Court], *Fauba France FDIS GC Electronique v. Fujitsu Mikroelectronik GmbH*, *supra* note 7; ICC Arbitration Case No. 7531 of 1994, *supra* note 7.

[10] Switzerland 20 February 1997, *Zivilgericht* [District Court] Saane, available at <http://cisgw3.law.pace.edu/cases/970220s1.html>. This is a very interesting case as it illustrates the flexibility and subjectivity in the judicial application of Article 10 CISG. In this case, an Austrian company entered into a contract with the Swiss branch of a company with headquarters in Liechtenstein for the purchase and transport of spirits to Russia. Notably, Liechtenstein is not a Contracting State to the CISG. A contractual dispute arose between the parties and the contract was never performed. The court found that the CISG was applicable because the Swiss branch, not the Liechtenstein headquarters, was the place of business that had the closest relationship to the contract and its performance (Articles 1(1)(a) and 10(a) CISG).

[11] *See* UNIDROIT Comments, *supra*, note 5. [12] *Id.*

[13] *Id.*

goods.[14] As with Article 1.10 of the UNIDROIT Principles, these matters are reviewed subjectively.

2. Habitual Residence

UNIDROIT Principles Article 1.10 fails to specifically deal with the case where one of the parties does not have a place of business but is still subject to the Principles. However, logic concludes that the test used for the place of business would be applicable. In contrast, Article 10(b) CISG specifically sets forth that a factual determination is to be made as to the party's habitual residence. Upon such finding, performance is to be effected there. "Habitual residence" is where the party actually lives. Notably, it is irrelevant whether he or she has a permit to live in the country or whether the party frequents another country, provided he or she normally returns to the first place. This holds true provided that the contract is for sale of goods intended for commercial purposes and not simply for "personal, family or household use" within the meaning of Article 2(a) CISG.[15]

V. CONCLUSION

A comparison of the two provisions illustrates that both the respective articles of the CISG and the UNIDROIT adopt the "closest relationship" theory to determine the relevant place of business. Moreover, in application, it is apparent that both provisions extend beyond the scope of their provisions by having further application and reference throughout their respective documents. Judicial review under the CISG has further refined the definition by expressly excluding those places that do not contribute to the totality of the sale, which the parties had intended. Therefore, CISG case law provides a valuable insight into the terms and application of the "closest connection" principle. This is also evident in the CISG's inclusion of the habitual residence provision.

[14] Secretariat Commentary, *supra*, note 2, Comment 8.

[15] *Id.*, Comment 9. *See also, e.g.*, Austria 10 November 1994 *Oberster Gerichtshof* [Supreme Court], English translation available at <http://cisgw3.law.pace.edu/cases/941110a3.html> (finding that an international sale occurred under CISG in a contract of sale of Chinchilla furs between breeder and buyer).

Formal requirements: Editorial remarks on the manner in which the UNIDROIT Principles of International Commercial Contracts may be used to interpret or supplement Article 11 of the CISG

Chantal Niggemann

a. Parties to international contracts need to be able to rely on their agreement. Therefore, they need to know whether there are any formal requirements that have to be met for their agreement or its amendment to be valid. Some jurisdictions ask for specific form or comparable requirements to be met for the validity of commercial sales contracts, whereas most legal systems opt for the rule of consensualism (i.e., freedom of form).

During the deliberations of UNCITRAL on the elaboration of the CISG, one of the most controversial issues at the Vienna Conference was whether or not the principle of freedom of form of Article 15 ULIS should be incorporated into the text of the CISG. Finally, a compromise was adopted with freedom of form as a basic rule and the reservation clause of Articles 12 and 96 CISG.[1] Where at least one of the parties to the contract has its place of business in a reservation State and a court of that State hears the case, the court must determine the law applicable to form according to its conflict of law rules, just as a court of another State, which did not adopt the CISG, would have done.[2]

Although the issue of freedom of form might as well have been regulated in Part II of the CISG dealing with the formation of the contract, it has been integrated as a general provision. Therefore, it also applies when a party has its place of business in a State that declared a reservation under Article 92 CISG.[3]

The UNIDROIT Principles opted for unconditional freedom of form, which is expressed in Articles 1.2 and 3.2.[4]

b. Article 1.2 of the UNIDROIT Principles merely refers to the writing requirement of contracts, whereas Article 11 CISG, sentence one, states that the contract is not subject to "any other requirement as to form" (i.e., not only writing requirements). However, this difference is only in appearance because although Article 1.2 of the UNIDROIT Principles mentions only the requirement of writing, it has to be extended to other requirements as to form.[5] Moreover, Article 1.2 of the UNIDROIT Principles is to be seen in conjunction with Article 3.2 of the UNIDROIT Principles, stating that a contract is concluded "without any further requirement." Article 3.2 of the UNIDROIT Principles seems to go even beyond the scope of Article 11 CISG; in comparison to Article 11 CISG, which names requirements "as to form," Article 3.2 of the UNIDROIT Principles does not contain such a restriction. It is, however, undisputed that Article 11 CISG also includes quasi-formal requirements, such as consideration as is to be found in common law systems.[6] The commentary to Article 3.2 of the UNIDROIT Principles makes it clear that also excluded is the requirement of cause that exists in some civil law systems, as well as rules regarding so-called real contracts, which require the handing over of goods for their conclusion.[7] Although the exclusion of the cause requirement and the real-contract rules is not discussed under the Convention, the same exclusion should apply, and they should be displaced by the principle of freedom of form in Article 11 CISG.

c. Both the UNIDROIT Principles in Article 1.2, second sentence, and the CISG in Article 11, second sentence, make clear that the principle of freedom of form implies the admissibility of oral evidence in judicial proceedings. The language of both clauses is perfectly identical, as is their understanding in the commentaries.[8] Article 1.2 UNIDROIT Principles, second sentence may, therefore, merely support the interpretation of Article 11 CISG, sentence two.

[1] Schlechtriem, *Uniform Sales Law – The UN-Convention on Contracts for the International Sale of Goods* (1986) at p. 43, available at <http://cisgw3.law.pace.edu/cisg/biblio/schlechtriem.html>.

[2] Schlechtriem in v. Caemmerer/Schlechtriem, *Kommentar zum Einheitlichen UN-Kaufrecht – CISG –* (3d ed. 2000), Art. 12 at marginal note 2 with further citations; Melis in Honsell, *Kommentar zum UN-Kaufrecht* (1997), Art. 12 at marginal note 4.

[3] Magnus in Staudinger, *Kommentar zum BGB – Wiener UN-Kaufrecht (CISG)* (1999), Art. 11 at marginal note 6; Witz in Witz/Salger/Lorenz, *International Einheitliches Kaufrecht*, 2000, Art. 11–12 at marginal note 2; Heuzé, La *vente internationale de marchandises*, 1992, at note 196; see also Honnold, *Uniform Law for International Sales under the 1980 United Nations Convention* (3d ed. 1999), Art. 11 at note 127.1.

[4] This principle of freedom of form may, however, be overridden by mandatory rules of the applicable law; *see* Article 1.4 of the UNIDROIT Principles and note 2 of the Official Comments of Article 1.2.

[5] Official Comments on articles of the UNIDROIT Principles, Article 1.2 at note 1.

[6] Witz, *supra* note 3, Art. 11–12 at marginal note 5; Schlechtriem, *supra* note 2, Art. 11 at marginal note 11; Magnus, *supra* note 3, Art. 11 at marginal note 9; *see* also Secretariat's Commentary Art. 27 note. 2 referring to Article 29 CISG.

[7] Official Comments on articles of the UNIDROIT Principles, Article 3.2 at notes 2 and 3. With regard to the requirement of *cause*, other effects that may derive from it, such as its illegality, are not concerned.

[8] Schlechtriem, *supra* note 2, Art. 11 at marginal notes 12 and 13 with further reference; Official Comments on Articles of the UNIDROIT Principles, Article 1.2 at note 1.

d. According to Article 6 CISG, the parties are of course also free to agree, orally or in writing, on specific form requirements to be met for the validity of the contract, and that might also to be applied to modifications and/or termination.[9] This is also expressed in Article 2.13 of the UNIDROIT Principles, and the illustrations contained in the Official Comments to Article 2.13 of the UNIDROIT Principles may be helpful in the interpretation of Article 11 CISG.[10] In this regard and concerning written modification clauses, please refer to the Editorial remarks regarding Article 29 CISG.

e. In case one of the parties confirms the content of a contract, whereby such confirmation contains additional or different terms, the question arises whether such terms may become part of the contract in case the confirmation is not in writing; that is, whether Article 11 CISG and the concept of freedom of form also apply to such confirmation. The CISG does not explicitly deal with this issue. Where the rules for commercial letters of confirmation (*kaufmännisches Bestätigungsschreiben*) apply (e.g., as usages by which the parties are bound; see Article 9 CISG), scholars and tribunals tend to ask for a written confirmation.[11] In contrast, Article 2.12 of the UNIDROIT Principles deals with such a confirmation and explicitly requires it to be in writing.

f. Article 11 CISG only applies to the formation of the contract, not to its modification or termination as does Article 3.2 of the UNIDROIT Principles. With regard to the manner in which the UNIDROIT Principles may be used to interpret or supplement Article 29 CISG for modifications and termination, please see the Editorial remarks regarding Article 29 CISG.

g. As a result it can be said that the intent of Article 11 CISG is reproduced in Article 1.2 read in conjunction with Article 3.2 of the UNIDROIT Principles. Thereby, the Official Comments of Articles 1.2 and 3.2 of the UNIDROIT Principles support the interpretation of Article 11 CISG. In addition, Articles 2.12 and 2.13 of the UNIDROIT Principles assist the further interpretation of freedom of form under Article 11 CISG.

[9] Honnold, *supra* note 3, Art. 11 at note 127; Schlechtriem, *supra* note 2, Art. 11 at marginal note 16; Melis, *supra* note 2, Art. 11 at marginal note 3; Rajski in Bianca/Bonell, *Commentary on the International Sales Law* (1987), Art. 11 at note 3.1.

[10] Official Comments on Articles of the UNIDROIT Principles, Article 2.13 at note 2.

[11] Schlechtriem, *supra* note 2, Art. 11 at marginal note 6; Civil Court Basel, judgment dated 21 December 1992, in application of Austrian and Swiss legal rules regarding writings in confirmation, in BJM (1993), p. 310 subs.

Growth of the CISG with changing contract technology: "Writing" in light of the UNIDROIT Principles and CISG-Advisory Council Opinion no. 1

Andrea L. Charters

I. INTRODUCTION

Article 13 of the CISG,[1] defining a writing, raises particular questions of interpretation given the technological advances that have occurred since its drafting in 1980. CISG Article 13 states that

> For the purpose of this Convention "writing" *includes telegram and telex.*[2]

From both a common-sense and a syntactical approach, this provision must be interpreted flexibly because of the use of "includes" and the omission of paper and ink.[3]

Because of this demand for flexibility, there are many reasons for looking at the application of the UNIDROIT Principles of International Commercial Contracts[4] to the interpretation of Article 13 CISG. Principles Article 1.10 uses a functional approach to define writing:

> Writing means any mode of communication that preserves a record of the information contained therein and is capable of being reproduced in tangible form.[5]

These stark differences in definitional style reflect not a different philosophy of drafting, but different technological environments at the time of drafting. The Principles, after all, define "court" not as an organization that "means" something, but as it "*includes* an arbitral tribunal."[6] By 1994, however, electronic commerce had grown in types of media and significance and was becoming a growth area in the law.[7] Thus, listing examples

[1] United Nations Convention, adopted 1980, available at <http://cisgw3.law.pace.edu/cisg/text/treaty.html>.
[2] CISG Article 13 (emphasis added).
[3] On the generally held view that "includes" requires an expansive reading, see Ulrich G. Schroeter, "Interpretation of "writing": Comparison between provisions of CISG (Article 13) and counterpart provisions of the Principles of European Contract Law," 6 *Vindobona J. Int'l Com. L. and Arbitration* (2002–1) 267–274, at Section 1, also available at <http://cisgw3.law.pace.edu/cisg/biblio/schroeter3.html>.
[4] Adopted 1994 by UNIDROIT, available at <http://cisgw3.law.pace.edu/cisg/principles.html>.
[5] *Id.* at Article 1.10 (emphasis added).
[6] Principles Article 1.10, first definition (emphasis added). Other definitions include "place of business," "obligor," and "oblige" and use forms of the verb "to be" or "to refer" in simple declarative statements.
[7] *See generally*, Benjamin Wright, *The Law of Electronic Commerce*, 2d ed. (1995) (a loose-leaf service, the second volume of which became available not long after the Principles were adopted, this treatise discusses the types of electronic commerce, their function, needed business cautions in working with them, and developing law in the area).

of "writing" or even of electronic commerce could only have been doomed to obsolescence by the time of drafting of the Principles.[8] Not only had facsimile, electronic data interchange, the Internet, and e-mail come into common use but also combinations of services were appearing; the development of new products was inevitable.[9] Thus, a functional approach was a logical choice for an international provision, the aim of which was to maintain flexibility for the future by being open-ended.[10]

The Principles have in turn prompted a new CISG commentary, as discussed in Section VI below, CISG-Advisory Council Opinion no. 1,[11] which adopts a functional approach similar to that of the Principles:

> The term "writing" in CISG also includes any electronic communication retrievable in perceivable form.[12]

Thus, the provisions in the Principles of "preserve a record" and "retrievable in perceivable form" are condensed in the more detailed provision "retrievable in perceivable form," adding the requirement that the information must be "perceivable."

Several detailed reasons to consider the interpretation of the CISG writing definition in light of that in the Principles are discussed in this chapter.

II. CONTEXT FOR INTERPRETING ARTICLE 13 IN LIGHT OF UNIDROIT PRINCIPLES ARTICLE 1.10

The context for interpreting Article 13 CISG in light of UNIDROIT Principles Article 1.10 has several aspects: the historical changes in interpretations of Article 13 CISG, the evolving electronic environment, and the need to avoid an anomalous result with an UNCITRAL model law.

1. Interpretations Contemporary to Adoption of the CISG Are Silent or Raise Questions about Article 13

The interpretations of Article 13 that were contemporary to adoption of the CISG were silent or raised no questions with regard to this now problematic provision, reflecting the unproblematic nature of its provisions at the time. There is no Secretariat Commentary on Article 13 nor any pre-UNCITRAL legislative history.[13] The UNCITRAL legislative history is sparse[14] and reflects little debate.[15] Examples of restricting the view of electronic

[8] *See* John O. Honnold regarding the CISG in *Uniform Law for International Sales under the 1980 United Nations Convention* (3d ed. 1999) [hereafter "Honnold, 1999 Treatise"] at 222, where the author states, "Consequently, courts and codifiers have had to describe, in general terms, those understandings that would have been written into the contract if the parties had drafted a contract provision to deal specifically with the question that led to dispute." (Citations omitted.)

[9] *See* Wright, *supra* note 7 at Chapters 2–3 (describing products, interactions of products, and players, such as lawyers and accountants); *see also infra* note 43 and sources cited therein for further indication of movement in the e-mail field.

[10] *Cf.* Principles of European Contract Law (PECL) Article 1:301(6), which lists four examples, telegram, telex, telefax and electronic mail, and also "other means of communication capable of providing a readable record of the statement on both sides," available at <http://cisg3.law.pace.edu/cisg/text/peclcomp13.html>. *See* also Schroeter, *supra* note 3 at Section 4 (describing the current-day use of facsimile, electronic mail, electronic data interchange, and the Internet and World Wide Web).

[11] CISG-AC Opinion no. 1, Electronic Communications under CISG, 15 August 2003. Rapporteur: Professor Christina Ramberg, Gothenburg, Sweden [hereafter "CISG-AC Opinion no. 1"], available at <http://cisgw3.law.pace.edu/cisg/CISG-AC-op1.html>.

[12] *Id.*, at CISG Art. 13 Opinion no. 1 (emphasis added).

[13] Legislative History, Data on the Secretariat Commentary, and Data on the pre-UNCITRAL legislative history of the CISG, available at <http://cisgw3.law.pace.edu/cisg/text/roadmap/intro-13.html>.

[14] *See* Legislative History, 1980 Vienna Diplomatic Conference, Chronological Record of Proceedings, CISG article 13, development of, available at <http://cisgw3.law.pace.edu/cisg/chronology/chrono13.html>.

[15] *See infra* Section IIIa (discussing addition of telegram and telex and emphasis on placement as a definition).

communication to telegram and telex abound. Gyula Eörsi summed up Article 13 in 1984, shortly after the 1980 adoption of the Convention, in a major commentary: "This Article needs no comment."[16] In 1986, Kazuaki Sono wrote that an Article 96 reservation in favor of requiring writing, which was sought mainly by Socialist countries, "would in most cases not result in much practical difference" from having no writing requirement, because telegram and telex are included as examples in Article 13.[17] J. Rajski, in a Bianca and Bonell 1987 treatise, reviewed some then-recent East European statutes on what constituted "writing."[18] Jacob S. Ziegel raised two questions about Article 13 in 1981: (1) whether electronic means would be included or whether a paper record would be required and (2) whether the requirements of Articles 12 and 96 would have been met "where the domestic law of the declarant state has a narrower definition of writing." The answer to the second question was "presumably no" because Article 12 was designed to enable States to retain their own writing requirements.[19] Commenting on the legislative history, Peter Schlechtriem praised the initiative by the Federal Republic of Germany of adding the telegram and telex provisions to facilitate quick decisions in commerce, and he further argued the conclusion reached by Professor Ziegel with regard to Article 96 reservations.[20]

As is shown Section IIc, within five years, scholarship had shifted to arguing for the inclusion of other electronic means within the definition of writing in response to the growing practical need to accommodate the use of other electronic means of communication.

2. Practical Needs of Traders Using Electronic Media

The practical need to accommodate the growing use of other electronic means of communication has affected both the lives of traders and the growth of the CISG. The day-to-day life of a lawyer or legal scholar attests to the prevalence and growth of these means of communication.[21] The prevalence of electronic forms as contract media is also reflected in the growth of laws and legal literature about these forms.[22] The development of CISG law also requires that the CISG accommodate these forms to avoid being "petrified" and "unable to change or be changed as needed." Thus, in fact, electronic communications are an "assay" for whether the CISG can grow.[23]

[16] *See* Chapter 2.9, General Provisions, in N. M. Galston & H. Smit, *International Sales: The United Nations Convention on Contracts for the International Sale of Goods* (1984). (This was perhaps a reference for the CISG scholar to the legislative history, which tailored the introduction of these two forms to prior Soviet legislation. *See infra* note 35).

[17] *Formation of International Contracts Under the Vienna Convention: A Shift above the Comparative Law*, in P. Sarcevic and P. Volken, eds., *International Sale of Goods, Dubrovnik Lectures* (1986), at 129–130 (Professor Sono stated the importance of written contracts for some States that "consider the requirement that contracts for the international sale of goods be in writing to be a matter of important public policy even in the context of the relation between the parties", at 129).

[18] C. Bianca and M. J. Bonell, *Commentary on the International Sales Law* (CISG) (1987) at 128.

[19] *Report to the Uniform Law Conference of Canada on Convention on Contracts for the International Sale of Goods* (July 1981), at Article 13 Comment, available at <http://cisgw3.law.pace.edu/cisg/text/ziegel13.html>; *see infra* Section IIIa (legislative history).

[20] *Uniform Sales Law – The UN-Convention on Contracts for the International Sale of Goods*, at 46 (1986) (citations omitted), available at <http://cisgw3.law.pace.edu/cisg/biblio/schlechtriem-13.html>.

[21] As a participant observer in both fields, much information retrieval, as well as communication, has been obtained via these forms. Even five years ago, e-mail and the Internet were in their infancy. The growth rate of the electronic forms is staggering.

[22] *See generally*, Wright, *supra* note 7 (compound forms and technological development); D. Reiter, E. Blumenfeld and M. Boulding, eds., *Internet Law for the Business Lawyer* (Section of Business Law, American Bar Association) (2001) (discussing regulation, taxation, and jurisdiction, among other matters).

[23] Siegfried Eiselen, "Electronic Commerce and the UN Convention on Contracts for the International Sale of Goods (CISG) 1980," 6 *EDI L. Rev.* (1999) at 21, also available at <http://cisgw3.law.pace.edu/cisg/biblio/eiselen1.html>.

3. Recent Scholarship on the CISG Endorses the Use of Electronic Communication

The recent scholarship on the CISG endorses the use of electronic communication. Just five years after his 1986 comments regarding the Article 96 reservation and the necessity of telegraph and telex, in 1991/92, Peter Schlechtriem further argued that fax should be included as "writing."[24] An internal gap in the CISG should be filled pursuant to Article 7(2), because fax "was unknown when the Convention was drafted."[25] Fritz Enderlein and Dietrich Maskow in 1992 focused on the 1988 Factoring Convention approach to "telecommunication capable of being reproduced in tangible form,"[26] another functional approach. The PECL approach, adopted six years later, was to look to four examples of electronic communication – telegram, telex, telefax, and electronic mail – and "other means of communication capable of providing a readable record of the statement on both sides." This provision is thus a liberalization of the "reproduction" language and also, in part, a functional approach.[27] In his comparative analysis of CISG Article 13 and the counterpart provisions in the PECL, Ulrich Schroeter analyzes four means of contemporary communication, two of which are PECL examples:[28] telefax, electronic data interchange, electronic mail, and the Internet and World Wide Web.[29] John Honnold in the 1999 edition of his treatise, *Uniform Law for International Sales under the 1980 United Nations Convention*, identified facsimiles and electronic data interchange as major means of electronic communication, along with telegram and telex.[30]

4. UNCITRAL Model Law – Avoid Anomaly

It would be anomalous for an UNCITRAL Convention, the CISG, to include provisions inconsistent with an UNCITRAL Model Law. The UNCITRAL Model Law on Electronic Commerce (1996) provides in Article 6 that the requirement of writing is met "by a data message if the information contained therein is accessible so as to be usable for subsequent reference."[31] The "subsequent reference" language is parallel to the "readable record" of the PECL[32] and to the "retriev[al] in perceivable form" of the CISG-AC Opinion no. 1.[33] "Data message" is defined as "information generated, sent, received or stored by electronic, optical or similar means including, but not limited to, electronic data

[24] *See Uniform Sales Law – The Experience with Uniform Sales Laws in the Federal Republic of Germany*, [at Article 13] reprinted with permission from *Juridisk Tidskrift* 1991/92, available at <http://cisgw3.law.pace.edu/cisg/text/schlechtriem13.html>; *see also* Peter Schlechtriem, "Article 13," in Peter Schlechtriem, ed., *Commentary on the UN Convention on the International Sale of Goods* (CISG) 94–95 (1998) (trans. Geoffrey Thomas) [hereafter Schlechtriem, Article 13]

[25] *Id.* and *infra*, subsection d. "Internal gaps" are to be filled with reference to the CISG and its sources, rather than with regard to domestic law, as discussed in Franco Ferrari, *Interpretation of the Convention and Gap-filling: Article 7*, in Franco Ferrari, Harry Flechtner and Ronald A. Brand, ed., *The Draft UNCITRAL Digest and Beyond: Cases, Analyses and Unresolved Issues in the U.N. Sales Convention*, at 138–171 (2004) [hereafter *Draft UNCITRAL Digest*].

[26] *International Sales Law*, at Article 13 Commentary (1992), available at <http://cisg3.law.pace.edu/cisg/biblio/enderlein-art13.html>; *see also* UNIDROIT Convention on International Factoring (Ottawa, 28 May 1988), available at <www.unidroit.org/english/conventions/c-fact.htm>.

[27] *See* PECL, *supra* note 10. Enumerating certain examples has the advantage of clarity but the disadvantage of creating a bias against any new technology.

[28] *See supra*, note 3 (discussing these forms of contemporary contract media).

[29] *Supra* note 10.

[30] Honnold, 1999 Treatise, *supra* note 8 at 141; see also E. Allen Farnsworth, *Farnsworth on Contracts*, 3d ed., at Sections 1.7, 1.8a and 1.9 (2004) (reviewing electronic communications forms and laws, CISG, and Principles).

[31] Article 6, available at <www.uncitral.org/english/texts/electcom/ml-ecomm.htm>.

[32] *See* PECL, *supra* note 10.

[33] *See supra* Section I for comparison of CISG-AC Opinion no. 1 and Principles.

interchange (EDI), electronic mail, telegram, telex or telecopy."[34] Thus, the Model Law definition is consistent with the interpretations advanced in the recent era of scholarship on the CISG, and it would be anomalous for it to be otherwise.

Given this context, it is important to turn to the characteristics of the definition of writing. The first major feature of the definition of is just that; it is a definition. How this feature affects the need for interpretation is presented below.

III. ARTICLE 13 PRESENTS A MONOLITHIC DEFINITION OF WRITING THAT MAY NOT BE SUFFICIENTLY FLEXIBLE FOR ALL USES

Writing is defined in both the CISG and the Principles in a monolithic manner that may not be sufficient for all purposes, as seen in Subsection b and Section VI below. As a definition, "writing" applies to all uses of the term.

1. Legislative History Introduced Examples of Electronic Communication and Made "Writing" a Definition

The legislative history reflects introduction of the two then-prevalent means of electronic communication, telegraph and telex,[35] and the assurance that "writing" remained a definition.[36]

2. Article 13 Does Not Address Burden of Proof or Presumptions; Sparse Case Law

As a definition that specifies the inclusion of telegram and telex, the definition of writing does not address burdens of proof or presumptions; this tends to create a bias against the inclusion of modern electronic communication in the definition of writing. From a litigation perspective, a party favoring exclusion of modern means of communication from the definition of writing could argue post-transaction that the specific reference to "telegraph" and "telex" indicated a preference for these means over other electronic means. This would be a textual argument, simple to make and concise to argue. This point could be raised to advance litigation strategy, not out of a genuine preference for these dated media. Similar arguments have long plagued the Common Law Statute of Frauds.[37]

The party arguing for inclusion of modern media would face a much more fact-based argument in favor of practicality and common sense, absent scholarship and comparison to the Principles. How this burden of proof and presumption problem is treated in the CISG-AC Opinion no. 1 is addressed in Section VI.

The sparse case law and arbitral decisions regarding the definition of writing under the CISG do not resolve this litigation dilemma. One case merely recited the CISG

[34] *See supra* note 31, Article 2.

[35] Summary Records of Meetings of the First Committee, 7th meeting, Friday, 14 March 1980, paras 71–77, available at <http://cisgw3.law.pace.edu/cisg/firstcommittee/Meeting7.html> (in response to Soviet legislation that made these forms qualify as "writing"). The Draft UNCITRAL Digest notes the parallel in this provision to a provision in the 1974 UNCITRAL Convention on the Limitation Period in the International Sale of Goods. *Draft* UNCITRAL *Digest*, *supra* note 25 at 571. Peter Schlechtriem notes that the presence of such a provision in the Convention on Limitation facilitated the incorporation of telegram and telex into CISG Article 13. *See* Schlechtriem, Article 13, *supra* note 24.

[36] Summary Records of Meetings of the First Committee, 35th meeting, Friday, 4 April 1980, para 63–67, available at <http://cisgw3.law.pace.edu/cisg/firstcommittee/Meeting7.html>.

[37] *See* Michael Bridge, *A Commentary on Articles 1–13 and 78*, in *Draft* UNCITRAL *Digest*, *supra* note 25 at 256 ("It is well-known in those countries that have Statute of Frauds provisions that the objection raised by a party to the lack of formality is usually made, not for purist reasons, but rather to shroud the true, often, but by no means always, unmeritorious, reason for escaping from the contract.")

definition.[38] Another two cases are reported in English to have ruled out application of the CISG definition to leases, which are not sale of goods transactions.[39] Two Russian arbitrations provide some direction as to how an arbitral tribunal, at least in Russia, might look at Article 13. The first tribunal ruled on a case involving telex messages, noted the Article 13 provision, and bolstered the reference with a citation of the New York Convention on Recognition and Enforcement of Foreign Arbitral Awards 1958.[40] The second tribunal looked to domestic law to accept facsimile changes to an agreement.[41] One scholar has noted that this last arbitration apparently accepted looking to domestic law under Article 13.[42]

Before turning to the comparative law answer to this litigation dilemma in Section VI, let us compound the problem.

IV. CURRENT ELECTRONIC MEANS OF COMMUNICATION POSE TECHNOLOGICAL DILEMMAS

Many security, retrieval, and storage concerns plague electronic communications media and raise the specter of exotic, hard-to-trace fraud and mistakes. In addition, modern e-mail may be tampered with, and messages may be lost through confusion with Spam.[43]

"Writing" in the UNCITRAL Model Law or in scholarship about the CISG is designed to permit perceiving and storing information[44] and is a limited means of preventing fraud.[45]

This new purpose is grounded in a reasonable[46] approach to communications in general. No one has quantified how easy it is to commit fraud with paper and ink versus

[38] *See* Finland 26 October 2000 Helsinki Court of Appeals [Helsingin hoviokeus], Case presentation and English translation available at <http://cisgw3.law.pace.edu/cases/001026f5.html> (5th paragraph under "Law" heading) (also addressed the "principle of loyalty" to the contractual relationship, "widely recognized in scholarly writings" – a principle that was also addressed in a Pace case commentary excerpt from Larry A. DiMatteo et al., 34 *Nw. J. Int'l L. & Bus.* (Winter 2004) 299–440 at 316–317 and 326).

[39] *See Draft* UNCITRAL *Digest*, *supra* note 25 at 571–572, citing two decisions of the Austrian Supreme Court [Oberster Gerichtshof]:

- Austria 2 July 1993 Supreme Court, case presentation available at <http://cisgw3.law.pace.edu/cases/930702a3.html> and
- Austria 26 April 1997 Supreme Court, case presentation available at <http://cisgw3.law.pace.edu/cases/970426a3.html>.

[40] *See* Russia 28 April 1995 Arbitration proceeding 400/1993, case presentation and English translation available at <http://cisgw3.law.pace.edu/cases/950428r1.html>, at 3.4 (buyer lost claim of lack of authority of its representative; interest was applied).

[41] *See* Russia 10 June 1999 Arbitration proceeding 55/1998, case presentation and English translation available at <http://cisgw3.law.pace.edu/cases990610r1.html>, at 3.5 (another claim by a buyer of failures by its representative; buyer lost the claim).

[42] *See* Djakhongir Saidov, "Cases on CISG Decided in the Russian Federation," 7 *Vindobona J. Int'l Comm. L. & Arbitration* 1 at 11–12 (2003) (citations omitted) (canvassing Russian arbitrations), available at <http://cisgw3.law.pace.edu/cisg/biblio/saidov1.html>.

[43] See, *e.g.*, the colorful advertisements on the Internet that humorously describe the common problems most of us have experienced. The titles capture the themes of the advertisements. *Postal Service Offers Certified E-mail*, May 18, 2000 ("Fact is, the e-mail simply does not always go through. The recent 'Love Bug' virus resulted in the loss of untold thousands of email messages around the world."), available at <http://usgovinfo.about.com/library/egov/aa051800a.htm> [last visited 10/12/2004]; *Combatting Spam using Certificates of Approval – Draft v1.0 of 03/14/03*, available at <www.madoverlord.com/Projects/SPAMIDEA.t> [last visited 10/12/2004]; *Email tracing basic seminar*, <www.pimall.com/nais/emailtracing.html> [last visited 10/12/2004]; *IzyDelivers Certified eMail[TM]*, available at <http://izymail.com/id_default.aspx?> [last visited 10/12/2004].

[44] *See supra* Sections I and II.d.

[45] *Cf.* E. Allen Farnsworth, *Farnsworth on Contracts*, 3rd ed., at Section 6.1 (2004) (history and functions of the Statute of Frauds).

[46] *See* Albert H. Kritzer, ed., "Reasonableness," January 23, 2001, available at <http://cisgw3.law.pace.edu/cisg/text/reason.html> ("reasonableness" specifically mentioned in thirty-seven CISG provisions and clearly alluded to in others).

telegram, telex, facsimile, e-mail, electronic data interchange, or other mechanisms.[47] Even telex has been subject to serious fraud, partly through human policy and procedure error.[48]

Given the extent of these problems, our answer is to turn, initially, to the deal lawyer's approach.

V. PRACTITIONERS' APPROACH AS A SPRINGBOARD INTO DEFAULT RULES

The reality of all these means of communication is that from a prospective position, where a lawyer is advising a client, particularly on a large transaction or on a series of transactions, the counseling interaction between the lawyer and client is the critical determinant for security and retrieval of data and record storage. All of these issues are neither purely business nor purely legal issues. New products are available all the time to make electronic communications more secure.[49] A practitioner thus has to work with clients on appropriate choices of communications media for contracts,[50] retrieval systems, record storage, and security.[51] It does no good to have sent that notice timely and not be able to find the Postal System's certified mail receipt and copy of the letter. Business, information technology, and legal knowledge all need to be integrated to achieve the best approach. The client needs a team that can satisfy its needs.

What follows from this is that prospectively, in drafting a contract, a definition of a writing requirement, such as for amendments of the contract and for notice, must be crafted by the attorney and client in negotiation with their counterparts. Relying on default rules will not do the job for the lawyered contract. For example, would a certain brand of "certified e-mail" be an acceptable means of communication, whereas perhaps fax and other brands of "certified e-mail"[52] would not be? A facsimile is subject to loss in the office system, after all, whereas a "certified e-mail" could be sent to multiple company officers, with an opportunity for the sender to receive a confirmation when any of them had opened the message.

Model contracts for use in CISG transactions already include model provisions for choosing among media to fulfill the "writing" requirement.[53] Under Article 6 of the CISG, the parties may derogate from the provisions of the CISG in their contract to adopt the means of communication they choose.[54] CISG jurisprudence has demonstrated that the agreement of the parties will be honored, even if it is contrary to expected norms of commercial behavior, as demonstrated in *MCC-Marble Ceramic Center v. Ceramica Nuova D'Agostino*.[55]

[47] *Cf.* Wright, *supra* note 7, at Section 4.7 (people have long tolerated imperfect controls and recordkeeping with paper and telexes).

[48] *See Id.* at Section 4.2 (citations omitted) (policy control omissions contributed to $13.5 million fraud on Chase Manhattan Bank).

[49] *See supra* note 43 citations as examples of products claiming superior e-mail performance, including "certified" e-mail, which provides a receipt indicating whether e-mail has been "opened."

[50] *Cf.* William F. Fox, Jr., *International Commercial Agreements: A Primer on Drafting, Negotiating and Resolving Disputes*, 2d ed. at 48 (1992) ("In international trade, parties to an agreement almost always execute a writing of some sort to establish a contract enforceable at law to remove uncertainty and to reduce risk.")

[51] *See* Wright, *supra* note 7 at Section 4.7 (not just the contract itself, but these other business systems are critical for securing electronic information or any other information).

[52] *See supra* note 43 and accompanying text.

[53] *See* John P. McMahon, "Guide for Managers and Counsel: Drafting CISG Contracts and Documents and Compliance Tips for Traders," January 2004, available at <http://cisgw3.law.pace.edu/cisg/contracts.html> and sources cited therein.

[54] CISG, *supra* note 1, at Article 6 ("the parties may... derogate from or vary the effect of any of [the Convention's] provisions.").

[55] United States 29 June 1998 Federal Appellate Court [11th Circuit] (*MCC-Marble Ceramic Center v. Ceramica Nuova D'Agostino*), case presentation available at <http://cisgw3.law.pace.edu/cases/980629u1.html>

MCC-Marble is a second springboard, however, into the jurisprudence of default rules. For the CISG is ultimately a law for the trader who does not always have time or a large enough transaction to go to a lawyer, such as in the *MCC-Marble* transaction at a trade show.[56] When faced with another party's invoice, the trader experiences the default rules as the critical issue for fairness under the CISG.

It is then the scholar's job to guide court decisions that will protect the trader in the unlawyered transaction. A major purpose of the CISG, without a traditional parol evidence rule or traditional writing requirement,[57] is to handle these true agreements by merchants at the trade show and in quick meetings. Today, these are often agreements over the e-mail circuits.[58] A great advantage of e-mail is that potential trading partners can find each other over the Internet and build a relationship through e-mails about very small transactions until their relationship warrants investing in travel and personal meetings. They may also wish to attend international trade shows and work with introducing parties, but there is no substitute for the Internet and e-mail.[59]

The importance of these means of contracting is indicated by the efforts of the International Chamber of Commerce Electronic Commerce Project to bolster the ability of traders to rely on electronic means of contracting.[60] The Project is focusing on the ability of traders to undertake the following tasks: "conducting their negotiations, making contracts, arranging for finance, transport or insurance on-line" for the reasons that "most of the rules that apply to international trade still presume the use of paper. Given that paper has certain inherent weaknesses as an information carrier, these rules create barriers that are unnecessary in the digital environment."[61]

Interpretation of the CISG, which applies to trade between nations that account for over two-thirds of world trade,[62] is thus essential to paving the way for traders to accomplish their trade goals along the lines just outlined. The CISG, as an international law, can be interpreted along the lines of both common law and civil law and a combination of the two that allows an autonomous interpretation of the CISG. Such an autonomous interpretation allows CISG Article 7(1)'s goal of an "international character"[63] to be fulfilled.[64] By

(holding that traditional notions of parol evidence did not apply under the CISG per its terms, even where an American businessperson signed a document claiming not to have read the reverse side terms, which were in a language he did not understand, and affidavits stated that there had never been any contractual intent on either side to abide by the reverse side terms).

56 *See id.*

57 In contrast to the model Uniform Commercial Code $500 limit for transactions without a statute of frauds, the CISG provides in Article 11, "A contract of sale need not be concluded in or evidenced by writing and is not subject to any other requirement as to form. It may be proved by any means, including witnesses." The UCC provision is found at Section 2–201(1) of the American Bar Association, *The Portable UCC*, 3d ed. (2000): "Except as otherwise provided in this Section a contract for the sale of goods for the price of $500 or more is not enforceable by way of action or defense unless there is some writing sufficient to indicate that a contract for sale has been made. . . ."

58 I take myself as a participant observer on this point.

59 *Id.*

60 International Chamber of Commerce, The ICC Electronic Commerce Project (ECP), available at <www.iccwbo.org/home/electronic_commerce/electronic_commerce_project.asp>, [last visited 10/17/2004].

61 *Id.*

62 Pace Law School Institute, *CISG by State*, CISG *Database*, (2002) at <http://cisgw3.law.pace.edu/cisg/cisgintro.html>.

63 CISG, *supra* note 1, Article 7(1): "In the interpretation of this Convention, regard is to be had to its international character and to the need to promote uniformity in its application and the observance of good faith in international trade."

64 Pace CISG Database, "Taming the Dragons of Uniform Law Case Law: Sharing the reasoning of courts and arbitral tribunals," available at <http://cisgw3.law.pace.edu/cisg/text/schedule.html>. (The editor invites translators to "tame the dragons" of disparate languages in the world's cases, in addition to making a theoretical and practical argument. Contacts are Albert H. Kritzer, Executive Secretary of the Pace CISG Database, and Loukas A. Mistelis, Secretary of the CISG-AC, at e-mail addresses listed on this Web page.)

looking to both of these interpretive techniques, scholars can facilitate the development of the law. This development may lead, rather than follow, case law. Traders, through a reliance on lawyers and on such international bodies as the International Chamber of Commerce that in turn rely on international bodies of scholarship,[65] look to the default rules elaborated by scholars for fairness where the code or statute leaves gaps.

When fairness is considered, having a default rule that encourages parties to plan, by taking the rule into account, is also important. Thus, the rule chosen should not only be fair but also efficient.[66] Whether fairness and efficiency are in sync or at odds is a question for the next section.

Given the problematic nature of contemporary electronic communications, fairness, and efficiency, should the CISG default rule be interpreted in light of the broad UNIDROIT standard, which would make essentially all electronic communications that could be reduced to a tangible form into CISG "writing" or should some middle ground be struck?

VI. INTERPRETATION IN LIGHT OF UNIDROIT PRINCIPLES, BY CISG-ADVISORY COUNCIL OPINION NO. 1, ADDRESSES THE CHALLENGES OF FLEXIBILITY, FAIRNESS, AND EFFICIENCY

It is not necessary to characterize the influence of the Principles on interpretation of the CISG as a blunt instrument.

1. Private Organization, Interpretive, Not Authoritative

A private, collaborative, scholarly initiative has produced an interpretive commentary on just what constitutes writing and related issues under the CISG. The CISG-Advisory Council, a private group of CISG scholars from around the world, has produced Opinion no. 1 regarding Electronic Communications.[67] The CISG-AC "is a private initiative supported by the Institute of International Commercial Law at Pace University School of Law and the Centre for Commercial Law Studies, Queen Mary, University of London."[68]

Although the text was prepared as a private initiative for partly pragmatic reasons,[69] a theoretical argument underpins the work. As a commentary that is not authoritative, it is ultimately flexible. It has the freedom of providing detailed interpretation that can be

[65] The International Chamber of Commerce website cries out for the CISG-AC development of law on electronic commerce: "Today, buyers and [sic] sellers in different parts of the world have no legal framework. . . . " *Supra* note 60.

[66] *See* David Charny, "Hypothetical Bargains: The Normative Structure of Contract Interpretation", 89 *Mich. L. Rev.* 1815, 1820–1821 (1991) (setting forth a four-space matrix for determining what forms of market analysis should be used for various types of cases); Clayton P. Gillette, "The Law Merchant in the Modern Age: Institutional Design and International Usages under the CISG," 5 *Chi. J. Int'l L.* 157 (2004) (putting a premium on efficient adjudication); and Avery Wiener Katz, "The Relative Costs of Incorporating Trade Usage into Domestic Versus International Sales Contracts: Comments on Clayton Gillette 'Institutional Design and International usages under the CISG,'" 5 *Chi. J. Int'l L.* 181 (2004) (Commenting on the former).

[67] *Supra*, note 11. Members conferring on Opinion no. 1 were Peter Schlechtriem, Chair; Eric E. Bergsten; Michael Joachim Bonell; Alejandro M. Garro; Roy M. Goode; Sergei N. Lebedev; Pilar Perales Viscasillas; Jan Ramberg; Ingeborg Schwenzer; Hiroo Sono; Claude Witz; Loukas A. Mistelis, Secretary; and Christina Ramberg, Rapporteur. Albert H. Kritzer, Executive Secretary of the Pace CISG Database, was also present. Loukas Mistelis, "CISG-AC Publishes First Opinions" (2004), available at <http://cisgw3.law.pace.edu/cisg/CISG-AC.html> [last visited 10/17/04].

[68] *Id.* at note 1.

[69] E-mail exchange between myself and the Secretary of the CISG-AC, Dr. Loukas Mistelis, 10/13/04–10/15/04 (perhaps ironically, paper copy on file with the author).

relied on without becoming ossified.[70] There is no governmental body of any type that must acknowledge change if a new interpretation is needed.

Thus, the benefit of detailed default rules can be had without the drawbacks of either having to spawn ever more detailed rules in order to change the law or having to rely on great discretion in the hands of judges, with a lack of predictability for parties and the potential for manipulability.[71]

Some have called for an authoritative commentary and body like the U.S. Permanent Editorial Board of the Uniform Commercial Code, but sponsored by UNCITRAL for the CISG.[72] Given the pragmatic issues of international agreements and the theoretically sound reasons for having a private commentary, the CISG-AC work is of great benefit to the CISG community. The CISG-AC is profound evidence of an international community of scholars. Communication among such a group is greatly facilitated by e-mail, one of the very subjects of Opinion no. 1.[73]

The choice of writing as a topic for the Advisory Council's Opinion no. 1 shows the benefit of a private, scholarly undertaking. There is little case law and little scholarship on Article 13 of the CISG,[74] yet there is a huge need to advance the law, given the rapid advance of technology beyond what was contemplated at the adoption of the CISG, as acknowledged by the International Chamber of Commerce.[75] The Advisory Council has thus filled a vacuum in the development of the law. This type of forward movement in the law can best be achieved by an independent group, free from the types of constituencies that surround a governmental or quasi-governmental body.

2. The Commentary Builds on the Principles' Approach to "Writing"

The commentary builds on the Principles' approach to the definition of writing and consists of two types of remarks, Opinions and Commentaries, regarding each affected section.[76] The Opinion on Article 13 is built around the language of "retrievable in perceivable form," and thus uses the Principles' approach to interpreting the CISG, where the Principles use the language "preserves a record" and is "capable of being reproduced in tangible form."[77]

The Opinion is not limited to this language. Two other features of the Opinion are critically important. There are three Comments to Article 13 and additional Opinions and Comments on related sections of the CISG text.[78] The related sections are treated in other chapters of this book. Thus, the monolithic definition of writing has been separated into terms better suited for the particular uses to which the term is put.

[70] Harold J. Berman has written in favor of common customary practices for international trade, and the avoidance of codification. *See, e.g.*, Harold J. Berman, "The Law of International Commercial Transactions (*Lex Mercatoria*)," 2 *Emory J. Int'l Disp. Resol.* 235, 235 (1988) (such practices are widespread); Peter B. Maggs, "International Trade and Commerce, A Conference on the Work of Harold J. Berman," *Essay*, 42 *Emory L.J.* 449, 466 (1993) (codification can freeze the law); James E. Bailey, "Facing the Truth: Seeing the Convention on Contracts for the International Sale of Goods as an Obstacle to a Uniform Law of International Sales," 32 *Cornell Int'l L.J.* 273, 275 (1999) (the title conveys the conclusion of the argument).

[71] The points made in this paragraph are both subjects of vast bodies of literatures in the United States and also to common conversation. For a look into this literature and more detailed analyses of these issues, see generally a classic article, Duncan Kennedy, "Form and Substance in Private Law Adjudication," 89 *Harv. L. Rev.* 1685 (1976).

[72] John E. Murray, Jr., "The Neglect of CISG: A Workable Solution", 17 *J. L. & Com.* 365, 375 (1998) (calling for such a body, following the suggestion of Michael Joachim Bonell in 1987, and extending the work of the body to interpretations and illustrations of the CISG, with nonbinding comments).

[73] One can e-mail the Secretary of the CISG-AC, Loukas A. Mistelis, or Albert H. Kritzer, the Executive Secretary of the Pace Law School CISG Database, at the addresses given on the Cisg Web pages, for example.

[74] *See supra* Sections II and IIIa.

[75] *See supra* notes 60 to 61 and accompanying text.

[76] Opinion no. 1, *supra* note 11.

[77] *See supra* notes 4 to 12 and accompanying text.

[78] Opinion no. 1, Article 13, *supra* note 11.

The three Comments on Article 13 refer to the uses of the term "writing" and exclude the issue of Article 96 reservations by States that wish to require writings under Article 12 for policy reasons.[79] Finally, the second Comment introduces the middle ground of a presumption into the interpretation of Article 13 writing, another means of tailoring the monolith to the particular transaction.

3. A Presumption, Related to Article 9 Trade Usages

The middle ground traced by Comment 13.2, the second Comment under Article 13, is a presumption:

> Unless the parties have limited the notion of writing, there should be a presumption that electronic communications are included in the term "writing." This presumption could be strengthened or weakened in accordance to the parties' prior conduct or common usages (CISG Art. 9(1) and (2).[80]

Thus, the presumption builds on trade usages[81] for flexibility.

A default rule that has the flexibility of a presumption and the benefit of trade usages is thus an efficient default rule, one that requires a minimum of "planning around" the rule and a minimum of results contrary to what the parties would have agreed.[82]

This efficiency is not gained at the expense of fairness, as a court or arbitral tribunal is free to decide against the presumption as well, if that is warranted, particularly based on the history of dealings between the parties. Having a presumption in favor of the contemporary means of electronic communication allows deciding tribunals to avoid the pitfalls of prior litigation over the Statute of Frauds, where the writing requirement became used for deleterious purposes.[83]

Having a presumption allows a default rule that is not overly rigid and does not create the problem of "ossification" of a trade statute.[84] Referring to Article 9 on trade usages further draws the tradition of agreed-upon trade norms into the growing law of electronic commerce.

VII. CONCLUSION

CISG-AC Opinion no. 1 regarding Article 13 is thus an example of the CISG and trade norms closing circle in the hands of an institutional system of scholars, in a manner that tailors the writing definition to the transaction and achieves legal and policy objectives by preventing the definition from appearing monolithic.

The definition of writing has become a comparative law project. Not only has the definition from the Principles been used to interpret the older definition from the CISG but scholarship has also amplified it and generated more functional default rules through the use of presumption and trade usage. This process has allowed filling a gap by reference within the CISG, for flexible rules, related to the trade history of the parties. Fairness and efficiency are not at odds, but operating consistently through the use of the presumption in favor of electronic commerce. Where parties have not contracted with each other regarding written terms, a presumption informed by Article 9 is the default rule they would want to achieve flexibility and fit to their transaction.

[79] *See supra* notes 35–36 and accompanying text. (Such reasons apply primarily to Socialist states in which economic actors have strong government ties.).

[80] Comment 13.2, Opinion no. 1, *supra* note 11.

[81] See generally Gillette, *supra* note 66 and Katz, *supra* note 66 for discussions of the literature and theory behind Article 9 and to the sources in note 70 for a discussion of the norms of international trade custom.

[82] *See generally* Charny, *supra* note 66 and accompanying text.

[83] *See supra* note 37 and accompanying text.

[84] *See supra* note 70 and accompanying text.

This presumption should be in favor of electronic commerce, both based on the history of writing definitions across multiple laws and interpretations and on the prevalence of electronic commerce. It is not necessary to select examples of electronic commerce, which would inevitably create a presumption against those forms not listed. The details of these results thus again show how the scholarship has filled an internal gap in the CISG, using communication facilitated by the very media that are subject to the analysis of Article 13.

Providing a pathway for the traders the International Chamber of Commerce is serving thus advances scholarship in a practical, as well as theoretical, way that is aimed at allowing international trade to flourish, taking advantage of contemporary electronic communications media.

Criteria for an offer: Editorial remarks on the manner in which the UNIDROIT Principles may be used to interpret or supplement CISG Article 14

Jorge Oviedo Albán

I. INTRODUCTION

In Part II of the CISG, entitled "Formation of the Contract," the Convention provides the rules on contract formation, making reference to the model of offer and acceptance, provided in CISG Arts. 14 to 24. In the UNIDROIT Principles of International Commercial Contracts, the counterpart provisions on formation, also adopting the model of offer and acceptance, are located in Chapter 2, Arts. 2.1. to 2.22.

In both instruments the offer is defined and the relevant requirements are listed. In the Convention, the definition of and the requirements of an offer are contemplated in Art. 14. In the UNIDROIT Principles, it is Art. 2.2 that provides the definition of an offer.[1]

II. DEFINITION OF OFFER

Article 14(1) of the CISG commences:

"A proposal for concluding a contract [. . .] constitutes an offer [. . .]"

[1] Art. 2.14 of the UNIDROIT Principles deals with contracts with "open terms"; in the Convention, it is Art. 55 CISG that deals with open-price contracts.

Similarly, Article 2.2 of the UNIDROIT Principles provides a definition of offer, commencing:

"A proposal for concluding a contract constitutes an offer [. . .]"

The concept of "offer" is the same in the two instruments, in the sense that both instruments conceive it as the invitation by one of the parties to conclude a contract; this invitation is accompanied by other requirements to which I refer in this comparative analysis.[2]

The following difference between the counterpart provisions must, however, be noted: the regime of contract formation under the UNIDROIT Principles can be applicable to any type of commercial contract, whereas the Convention's regime is, in principle, limited to the formation of contracts of the international sale of goods (i.e., only contracts to which the Convention is directly applicable).[3]

The international doctrine on contract formation has provided various analyses of what constitutes an offer. Its characteristic element, as several authors highlight, is the declared will of the offeror to be bound, in case of acceptance, to a contract.[4]

III. REQUIREMENTS

Both the Convention and the UNIDROIT Principles provide the following requirements that an invitation must meet to conclude a contract to produce a legal effect.

1. Sufficiently Definite

The CISG regulates the matter in the following way in Art. 14 [emphasis added below]:

> (1) A proposal for concluding a contract addressed to one or more specific persons constitutes an offer if it is *sufficiently definite* and indicates the intention of the offeror to *be bound* in case of acceptance. A proposal is sufficiently definite if it indicates the goods and expressly or implicitly fixes or makes provision for determining the quantity and the *price*.

Art. 14(1) provides two indispensable requirements for an offer to be sufficiently definite: that the proposal (1) indicates or describes the goods and (2) expressly or implicitly fixes or makes provision for determining the quantity and the price of the goods.

The first thing to be noted in that provision is that Art. 14 CISG does not expressly require that the offeror identify precisely the goods that are to be the object of the contract; it will be enough to merely indicate the nature and the characteristics that would allow the offeree to identify the goods that are of interest to the offeror, as well as the quantity of the goods or parameters of an objective order to determine the quantity.

In determining the qualities and characteristic of the goods, except for any expressed stipulation by the parties, important relevant matters to bear in mind are the concept of reasonableness, the intention of the contracting parties, and good faith – which are provided in the content of Arts. 7(1), 8(1), and 8(2) of the Convention.

It is, furthermore, equally important to consider that it is the obligation of the seller to deliver "goods which are of the quantity, quality and description required by the contract and which are contained or packaged in the manner required by the contract."[5] Those

[2] For a comparative analysis of CISG Art. 14 and the counterpart provisions of another Restatement of Contract law, *see* CVETKOVIK, P., "Remarks on the manner in which the PECL may be used to interpret or supplement CISG Art. 14," available online at <http://cisgw3.law.pace.edu/cisg/text/peclcomp14.html#er>.

[3] CISG Arts. 1 to 6.

[4] See FARNSWORTH, E. A., *Contracts* (Aspen Law & Business 1999), pp. 112–132; LEVY, D.A., "Contract formation under the UNIDROIT Principles of International Commercial Contracts: UCC, Restatement, and CISG", 30 *UCC L.J.* 249–332 (1998, at 277; PERALES VISCASILLAS, M. del P., *La formación del Contrato de Compraventa Internacional de Mercaderías* (Tirant Lo Blanch 1996), p. 69.

[5] Art. 35 CISG.

specified elements (i.e., the quantity, quality, description, and appropriate packaging of the goods) would perhaps have to be indicated in the proposal made to the offeree in order for him to indicate effectively his assent to the offer.

The quantity of the goods, based on the inference drawn from the related provision in Art. 35 CISG, should be fixed in the proposal, or at least, the parties must have agreed on the manner of determining the quantity according to objective parameters – quantity is a matter that has to be resolved in the same sense in the offer. However, and in view of the prescription contained in Art. 14 CISG, it would be advisable to include in the offer a certain quantity of the goods or to fix *maxima*, or *minima*, of quantity to ensure the observance of the aforementioned requirement.[6] Several relevant factors may end up determining the quantity of the goods; they are present as much in the offer as at the moment of conclusion of the contract, following any practice established previously between the parties or according to the approaches of good faith and reasonableness.[7]

It must be noted, however, that Art. 55 CISG, dealing with "open-price" terms,[8] provides a regime different from that in Art. 14 CISG regarding the determination of the price of the goods. Pursuant to Art. 55 CISG, parties to validly concluded contracts are considered, in the absence of any contrary indication, to have implicitly agreed on the price generally paid under comparable circumstances in the trade concerned.[9]

The apparent contradiction[10] between those two provisions of the Convention can be traced to the different drafting solutions debated in the sessions held by UNCITRAL

[6] FOLSOM, R. H., GORDON, M. W., SPANOGLE, J. A., *International Business Transactions* (2d. ed., West Group 2001), p. 30.

[7] VÁZQUEZ LAPINETTE, T., *Compraventa Internacional de Mercaderías. Una Visión Jurisprudencial*, Aranzadi Editorial, Elcano (Navarra), 2000, p. 114.

"Reasonableness" is an important concept in the Convention; "reasonableness" is specifically mentioned in numerous provisions of the CISG, and it is regarded a general principle of the CISG, *see* KRITZER, A. H., "Overview Comments on Reasonableness – A General Principle of the CISG," available online at <http://cisgw3.law.pace.edu/cisg/text/reason.html#overv>.

See also Art. 7(1) and (2) of the CISG, which contains the in-built interpretation mechanism of the Convention, with references to the concept of good faith; *see* also relevant scholarly writing on the proper interpretation of Art. 7 CISG, presentation available online at <http://cisgw3.law.pace.edu/cisg/text/e-text-07.html>.

[8] Some jurisdictions do not allow "open-price" terms; *see* Colombian Civil Code Arts. 1591 and 592; Chilean Civil Code Arts. 1808 and 1809. Some other jurisdictions allow "open-price" terms; *see* BGB §315 and §453, Italian Civil Code Art. 1474, and UCC §2–305.

[9] Art. 55 CISG:

> Where a contract has been validly concluded but does not expressly or implicitly fix or make provision for determining the price, the parties are considered, in the absence of any indication to the contrary, to have impliedly made reference to the price generally charged at the time of the conclusion of the contract for such goods sold under comparable circumstances in the trade concerned.

[10] *See* ENDERLEIN F. and MASKOW D., *International Sales Law* (Oceana Publications 1992), p. 85, Article 14 "Offer," Comment 10, also available online at <http://cisgw3.law.pace.edu/cisg/biblio/enderlein-art14.html>, where the authors state the following:

> While the price belongs here to the minimum content of an offer, Article 55 concedes that a contract may also be validly concluded if the price has not been fixed expressly or implicitly and nothing has been agreed that would make provision for its determination. Thus there is a contradiction between Articles 14 and 55, which has been duly reflected in various sources [. . .]. Article 55 presupposes the existence of a valid contract which pursuant to Article 14 simply cannot exist. It seems to us that the price problem has been over-emphasized in the discussion because Article 14, in the extreme, permits that nothing be said about the price but that the possibility of determining it is implied [references omitted].

See also KHOO W. L. H. in BIANCA-BONELL, *Commentary on the International Sales Law* (Guiffrè 1987), p. 46:

> Article 55 deals with cases in which a contract has apparently been concluded but without any agreement on provision as to price. In these instances, Article 55 makes it clear that its provision takes effect subject to the contract having been validly concluded by the criteria of the applicable domestic law." The pre-Vienna Diplomatic Conference legislative history of the CISG is in accord. *See* UNCITRAL Yearbook VIII, A/CN.9/SER.A/1977, at pp. 48–49, paras. 323–330, 336–340; *see also* HONNOLD J., *Uniform Law for International Sales under the 1980 United Nations Convention* (2d ed. 1991), p. 201.

and reflect the different solutions given to that matter in different national juridical classifications.[11]

Scholarly opinion is divided on the manner in which the two provisions interact with one another[12]; some commentators analyze the application of CISG Art. 14 in an isolated way,[13] whereas others prefer the application of CISG Art. 55.[14]

The different approaches in the available doctrine are also reflected in the relevant international case law. As an example of the divergent approaches, mention may be made of the decision of the Hungarian Supreme Court in the case of *Pratt & Whitney vs. Malev Hungarian Airlines*,[15] as well as the subsequent scholarly critiques of that decision.[16]

Following the criticism of that decision in the commentary offered by Perales, it is clear that the court did not consider the interplay between Art. 14 and Art. 55 of the Convention. In that critique, it is furthermore noted that that there is another important element to consider – the use of the rules of interpretation of the conduct of the parties (CISG Art. 8) according to which, even in a case where the price has not been determined in the offer and there is no market price for the particular goods, it might still be possible to deduce the price of the goods based on all the relevant circumstances of the case and, thus, to conclude that a price has been implied in the agreement of the parties.[17]

Support for that proffered approach can be found in the case law, where tribunals have dealt with the matter of determination of the price according to objective parameters agreed to by the parties previously or tacitly, as well as in situations where the parties have not agreed on the price but have concluded contracts with "open-price" terms. Such an interpretive approach would provide much desired uniformity on the issue under examination.[18]

[11] PERALES VISCASILLAS, (1996), *supra* note 4, at p. 318; HONNOLD, J. *Derecho uniforme sobre compraventas internacionales (Convención de las Naciones Unidas de 1980)*, Madrid (Editorial Revista de Derecho Privado, Editoriales de Derecho Reunidas S.A. 1987), p. 189.

[12] See *Transcript of a Workshop on the Sales Convention*, where leading CISG scholars discuss *inter alia* contract formation using a hypothetical case involving the interplay between Arts. 14(1) and 55 CISG, 18 *J.L. & Com.* 191–258 (1999), excerpt also available online at <http://cisgw3.law.pace.edu/cisg/biblio/workshop-14,55,18.html>.

[13] PERALES VISCASILLAS, *supra* note 4, at p. 336.

[14] HONNOLD, *supra* note 1, at n 137, pp. 187–188. DÍEZ PICAZO, "Comentario al artículo 14," in *La Compraventa Internacional de Mercaderías. Comentario de La Convención de Viena.* DÍEZ PICAZO and PONCE DE LEÓN, L., eds. (Civitas1998), p. 168. FERNÁNDEZ DE LA GÁNDARA, L., CALVO CARAVACA, A. L., "El Contrato de Compraventa Internacional de Mercancías," in *Contratos Internacionales*, CALVO CARAVACA, A.L. and FERNÁNDEZ DE LA GÁNDARA, LUIS. (Directors) (Tecnos, Madrid, 1997), p. 220.

[15] Hungary 25 September 1992 Supreme Court (*Pratt & Whitney v. Malev*), English translation at 13 *J.L. & Com.* 31–47 (1993); case presentation also available online at <http://cisgw3.law.pace.edu/cases/920925h1.html>. Case law on UNCITRAL texts (CLOUT) abstract no. 53. At issue was whether a valid contract was concluded for the supply of jet engines. The Hungarian Supreme Court held that no valid contract had been concluded because the alleged offer and acceptance were vague and did not satisfy the requirements of CISG Art. 14(1). The reasoning of the Hungarian Supreme Court was based *inter alia* on the following grounds:
- The description, quantity, and price of goods are all essential elements of an offer [CISG Art. 14(1)].
- CISG Art. 55 cannot be used to determine the price term of an offer for goods that have no market price.

[16] The reasoning of the decision of the Hungarian Supreme Court has been much criticized; a selection of relevant commentaries is available at <http://cisgw3.law.pace.edu/cases/920925h1.html#cabc>.

[17] PERALES VISCASILLAS, *supra* note 4, at p. 368.

[18] *See* the following case law:
- Hungary 24 March 1992 *Fovárosi Bíróság* [Metropolitan Court] (*Adamfi Video v. Alkotók Studiósa Kisszövetkezet*), CLOUT abstract no. 52, case presentation and commentary available online at <http://cisgw3.law.pace.edu/cases/920324h1.html>
- Germany 8 March 1995 *Oberlandesgericht* [Appellate Court] München, CLOUT abstract no. 134, case presentation available at <http://cisgw3.law.pace.edu/cases/950308g1.html>

It is also worthwhile to examine the treatment afforded by the counterpart provisions of the UNIDROIT Principles of this issue. The UNIDROIT Principles, in Art. 2.2, stipulate as relevant requirements that the proposal should be sufficiently definite and indicate the intention of the offeror to be bound in case of acceptance by the offeree.[19]

The Principles further require that the parties understand one another in terms of the precision of the offer, which should indicate with sufficient clarity the elements incorporated into the contract. That clarity would be achieved even if some elements are not precisely determined in the proposal but are at least determinable by means of the practices established by the parties or by reference to internationally accepted usages[20]; in that way the Principles provide for filling gaps in some of the other related provisions. Thus, under the UNIDROIT Principles, the essential elements of an offer might be uncertain, without that uncertainty resulting in fatal inexactness of the offer, because the vital element is the intention of the parties to be bound by the offer and its subsequent acceptance.[21]

Furthermore, contract formation under the Principles is regulated with stipulations about terms that have been left open deliberately. In that sense, Art. 2.14 of the Principles expressly provides the following:

> (1) If the parties intend to conclude a contract, the fact that they intentionally leave a term to be agreed upon in further negotiations or to be determined by a third person does not prevent a contract from coming into existence.
>
> (2) The existence of the contract is not affected by the fact that subsequently
>
> (a) the parties reach no agreement on the term; or
>
> (b) the third person does not determine the term, provided that there is an alternative means of rendering the term definite that is reasonable in the circumstances, having regard to the intention of the parties.

- Russia 3 March 1995 Arbitration proceeding 304/1993, case presentation and English translation available at <http://cisgw3.law.pace.edu/cases/950303r2.html>
- Switzerland 3 July 1997 *Bezirksgericht* [District Court] St. Gallen, CLOUT abstract no. 215, case presentation available at <http://cisgw3.law.pace.edu/cases/970703s1.html>

See also the following commentaries GABUARDI, C.A., "Open Price Terms in the CISG, the UCC and Mexican Commercial Law", available online at <http://cisgw3.law.pace.edu/cisg/biblio/gabuardi.html>; AMATO, P., "U.N. Convention on Contracts for the International Sale of Goods – The Open Price Term and Uniform Application: An Early Interpretation by the Hungarian Courts," 13 *J.L. & Com.* 1–29 (1993), also available online at <http://cisgw3.law.pace.edu/cisg/biblio/amato.html>.

[19] UNIDROIT Principles Art. 2.2. – Definition of Offer:

> A proposal for concluding a contract constitutes an offer if it is sufficiently definite and indicates the intention of the offer or to be bound in case of acceptance.

[20] *See* Official Comments on Art. 2.2 of the UNIDROIT Principles, available at <http://cisgw3.law.pace.edu/cisg/principles/uni14.html#official>. Comment 1, *Definiteness of an offer*:

> [...]. Even essential terms, such as the precise description of the goods or the services to be delivered or rendered, the price to be paid for them, the time or place of performance, etc., may be left undetermined in the offer without necessarily rendering it insufficiently definite: all depends on whether or not the offeror by making the offer, and the offeree by accepting it, intends to enter into a binding agreement, and whether or not the missing terms can be determined by interpreting the language of the agreement in accordance with Arts. 4.1 *et seq.*, or supplied in accordance with Arts. 4.8 or 5.2. Indefiniteness may moreover be overcome by reference to practices established between the parties or to usages (see Art. 1.8), as well as by reference to specific provisions to be found elsewhere in the Principles (e.g. Arts. 5.6 (Determination of quality of performance), 5.7 (Price determination), 6.1.1 (Time of performance), 6.1.6 (Place of performance), and 6.1.10 (Currency not expressed)).

[21] *See* Official Comment on Art. 2.2. UNIDROIT Principles, where the following illustrative example on point is provided:

> A has for a number of years annually renewed a contract with B for technical assistance for A's computers. A opens a second office with the same type of computers and asks B to provide assistance also for the new computers. B accepts and, despite the fact that A's offer does not specify all the terms of the agreement, a contract has been concluded since the missing terms can be taken from the previous contracts as constituting a practice established between the parties.

Under that regime of the Principles, the parties may decide to leave undetermined some contractual matters that are essential elements of the contract, provided there is an agreement between the parties on the manner in which those matters will be determined subsequently. That approach can be adopted if the parties themselves resolve the pending matters at a later stage (i.e., subsequent to the conclusion of the contract) or if this function is assigned to a third party – this function and, in any event, the existence of the contract are not affected even if the parties themselves subsequently do not reach agreement on the terms left open or the third party does not determine them, so long as there exists another way of determining the open terms in a reasonable fashion according to the circumstances of the case and the intention of the parties.

Therefore, according to the Principles, the absence of final determination of certain essential elements of the contract would not prevent formation of the contract or undermine its existence, because what determines the existence or nonexistence of the contract is the intention of the parties to conclude the contract.

2. Intention to Be Bound in Case of Acceptance

The available doctrine distinguishes between the offer, in a strict sense, and a preliminary invitation to conclude a contract, holding that in the first case the offeror has the intention to be bound in case his proposal is accepted by the offeree, whereas such an intention does not exist in an invitation to consider entering into a contract.

In practice it can be very difficult to determine the exact moment when the offeror is bound, having crossed the dividing line between preliminary invitation to the other party (to consider entering into a contract) and the actual offer made to the offeree.

The Convention expressly specifies in CISG Art. 14(1), first sentence, that

> [a] proposal for concluding a contract addressed to one or more specific persons constitutes an offer if it is *sufficiently definite* and indicates the intention of the offeror *to be bound* in case of acceptance [emphasis added].

It is clear that under the Convention an offer must include, in principle, the intention on the part of the offeror to be bound in the event of acceptance of his proposal.

The UNIDROIT Principles in Art. 2.2 include the same requirement and in similar wording to that found in the counterpart provision in the Convention.[22]

It is submitted that in the context of the Convention as well as the UNIDROIT Principles, the intention to be bound need not be specifically declared immediately or in the document that contains the proposal. It will be enough that in an unequivocal way such an intention is deduced, having regard to the type of the contract (see 3.3, *infra*) or the circumstances that surround the offer.[23]

Equally, the existence of the requisite intention to be bound by the proposal in case of its acceptance by the offeree will depend on the interpretation of the parties' statements or conduct,[24] based on the content of some positive dispositions expressed in the Convention, such as the observance of good faith in interpretation,[25] the subjective intent of the party making the statement or engaging in conduct (if the other party knew or could

[22] *See* Art. 2.2 UNIDROIT Principles: "A proposal for concluding a contract constitutes an offer if it is sufficiently definite and indicates the intention of the offeror to be bound in case of acceptance."

[23] DÍEZ PICAZO L., *supra* note 14, at pp. 165–166. PERALES VISCASILLAS, M. del P., *El Contrato de Compraventa Internacional de Mercancías* (2001), available online at <http://cisgw3.law.pace.edu/cisg/biblio/perales1--14.html>; PERALES VISCASILLAS, *supra* note 4, at p. 270.

[24] VÁZQUEZ LAPINETTE, *supra* note 7, at p. 111.

[25] CISG Art. 7(1).

not have been unaware what was that intent),[26] or, if the former is not applicable, the understanding of a reasonable person of the same kind as the offeree would have had in the same circumstances, including the negotiations between the parties, any established practices, usages, and any subsequent conduct of the parties (i.e., objective standard) to determine that intent.[27] Further relevant factors are the content of any previous conduct or practices established previously between the parties in negotiations, as well as any trade usages applicable to contracts of the type involved in the particular trade concerned.[28]

3. Communication to the Offeree

In order for the statements or conduct of the party to lead toward the production of the desired legal effects, it is required that the relevant intent transcends the party's internal domain; that is, it must be externalized and manifested.

However, in not all cases does the manifested conduct impose a binding force upon the actor when it transcends his internal domain. In some cases, the law (domestic law) or the parties might require that the manifestation of intent be channeled through some established means that comprises a general formality. Without it, there might not be a legal effect, unless what the parties want is that the relevant conduct or the contract that might have already been concluded is evidenced in writing. In other cases, it might be required that the manifestation of relevant intent reaches the offeree, either by being properly dispatched to him, or even that the offeree has indeed taken cognizance of the content of the communication. Such requirements might be found in regimes used in different domestic jurisdictions to establish the specific moment when the offer becomes binding and capable of leading to conclusion of a contract based on the conduct or statement communicated to the offeree. Such approaches are not, however, generally favored in most jurisdictions and the international doctrine.

The conclusion of a sales contract by electronic means, if the Convention is applicable to the contract,[29] will be held to the norms of offer and acceptance contained in CISG Arts. 18(2) and 15(1); this occurs when the sale is international, as the provisions of the Convention regarding formation have sufficient scope of application to regulate such transactions. For example, CISG Art. 13 arguably provides a suitable extension of the term "writing" to include messages of data in general, and not only to telegram or the telex. It is submitted that the textual reference in that provision is not limiting or restrictive, but rather on the contrary, by analogy, it can be understood as including electronic means.[30]

Under the regime of the Convention, like the UNIDROIT Principles, the offer becomes effective from the moment that it *reaches* the offeree,[31] adopting the "system of the reception".[32]

[26] CISG Art. 8(1) provides the following:

> For the purposes of this Convention statements made by and other conduct of a party are to be interpreted according to his intent where the other party knew or could not have been unaware what that intent was.

[27] CISG Art. 8(3) provides

> In determining the intent of a party or the understanding a reasonable person would have had, due consideration is to be given to all relevant circumstances of the case including the negotiations, any practices which the parties have established between themselves, usages and any subsequent conduct of the parties.

[28] CISG Art. 9.

[29] ILLESCAS ORTIZ, R., *Derecho de la Contratación Electrónica* (Civitas 2001), p. 257.

[30] *See* SCHROETER, U., "Editorial Remarks on Art. 13 CISG – PECL Comparative Provisions," available online at <http://cisgw3.law.pace.edu/cisg/text/peclcomp13.html>.

[31] The counterpart provisions in CISG Art. 15(1) and UNIDROIT Principles Art. 2.3(1) contain identical wording: "An offer becomes effective when it reaches the offeree."

[32] DÍEZ PICAZO Y PONCE DE LEÓN, L., *supra* note 14, at pp. 171–172. The system of the reception requires that the offer is *received by the addressee* when it reaches its destination. It does not matter under that system that the offer *arrives* but rather that the possibility exists that it is *received* by the offeree.

Art. 2.3(1) and Art. 1.9 of the UNIDROIT Principles may be read together. The latter provides

> (1) Where notice is required it may be given by any means appropriate to the circumstances.
>
> (2) A notice is effective when it reaches the person to whom it is given.
>
> (3) For the purpose of paragraph (2) a notice "reaches" a person when given to that person orally or delivered at that person's place of business or mailing address.
>
> (4) For the purpose of this article "notice" includes a declaration, demand, request or any other communication of intention.[33]

Equally, in the Convention, CISG Art. 24 provides the following:

> For the purposes of this Part of the Convention, an offer, declaration of acceptance or any other indication of intention "reaches" the addressee when it is made orally to him or delivered by any other means to him personally, to his place of business or mailing address or, if he does not have a place of business or mailing address, to his habitual residence.

Thus, it is submitted that counterpart provisions in the Convention and in the Principles correspond to one another[34] by establishing that the offer *reaches* the offeree:

> a) when it is communicated to him orally (i.e., system of knowledge or information); or
>
> b) if the offer is in writing,[35] when it is delivered to him in his place of business or postal address, or if he has no place of business to his habitual residence[36] (i.e., receipt theory).[37]

This principle of receipt may, however, be modified by means of an expressed pact of the parties that can adopt any other system; for example, that of the expedition.[38]

[33] *See* Official Comments on Art. 1.9 of the UNIDROIT Principles, available online at <http://cisgw3.law.pace.edu/cisg/principles/uni24.html#official>.
Comment 2 reads

> With respect to all kinds of notices the Principles adopt the so-called 'receipt' principle, *i.e.* they are not effective unless and until they reach the person to whom they are given.

Comment 4 explains

> It is important in relation to the receipt principle to determine precisely when the communications in question "reach" the addressee. In an attempt to define the concept, para. (3) of this article draws a distinction between oral and other communications. The former 'reach' the addressee if they are made personally to it or to another person authorized by it to receive them. The latter "reach" the addressee as soon as they are delivered either to the addressee personally or to its place of business or mailing address. The particular communication in question need not come into the hands of the addressee. It is sufficient that it be handed over to an employee of the addressee authorized to accept it, or that it be placed in the addressee's mailbox, or received by the addressee's fax, telex or computer.

[34] *See* also FELEMEGAS, J., "Comparison between Provisions of the CISG (Article 24) and the Counterpart Provisions of the UNIDROIT Principles (Art. 1.9)," available online at <http://cisgw3.law.pace.edu/cisg/principles/uni24.html#ed>.

[35] Art. 1.10 of the UNIDROIT Principles provides that "writing" means any mode of communication that preserves a record of the information contained therein and is capable of being reproduced in tangible form." *See* also Official Comment on Art. 1.10 of the UNIDROIT Principles, available online at <http://cisgw3.law.pace.edu/cisg/principles/uni13.html#official>. Comment 4:

> The Principles define this formal requirement in functional terms. Thus, a writing includes not only a telegram and a telex, but also any other mode of communication that preserves a record and can be reproduced in tangible form. This formal requirement should be compared with the more flexible form of a "notice."

[36] GARRO, A., "La Convención de las Naciones Unidas sobre los Contratos de Compraventa Internacional de Mercaderías: su Incorporación al Orden Jurídico Argentino," La Ley, p. 6. FERRARI, F., La Compraventa International. Aplicabilidad y aplicaciones de la Convención de Viena de 1980) Tirant Lo Blanch 1999, p. 66.

[37] *See* the Official Commentary on Art. 1.9 UNIDROIT Principles, Comment 4, *supra* note 33.

[38] *See* Official UNIDROIT Commentary, Comment 3:

> Dispatch principle to be expressly stipulated. The parties are of course always free expressly to stipulate the application of the dispatch principle. This may be appropriate in particular with respect to the notice a party has to give in order to preserve its rights in cases of the other party's actual or anticipated non-performance when it would not be fair to place the risk of loss, mistake or delay in the transmission of the message on the former. This is all the more true if the difficulties which may arise at international level in proving effective receipt of a notice are borne in mind.

IV. INVITATION TO MAKE OFFERS

In a literal interpretation of CISG Art. 14, which states that "[a] proposal *other than one addressed to one or more specific persons* is [. . .]" [emphasis added], it is arguable that the Convention's provisions do not apply to offers made to the public, unless the contrary is clearly indicated by the person making the proposal.

The UNIDROIT Principles make no reference to offers made to the public. This omission might be used to make an even stronger argument that a similar approach also fits the Convention, unless the offeror indicates the opposite.[39]

V. CONCLUSIONS

The counterpart provisions of the Convention and the UNIDROIT Principles define the offer in similar terms, as a proposal made by one party to another to conclude a contract.

Both instruments refer to the same essential requirements for such a proposal to constitute an offer: (a) the proposal is sufficiently definite, (b) the offeror indicates the intention to be bound in case of acceptance, and (c) the proposal is communicated to the offeree.

The basic requirement of sufficient definition of the proposal can give rise to misunderstandings and divergent interpretations of the Convention's provisions. It is submitted that, based on the preceding comparative analysis, which found substantial similarities in the policy, structure, and wording of the counterpart provisions, the UNIDROIT Principles may be of assistance in understanding and applying the Convention's requirement that a proposal be "sufficiently definite" to constitute an "offer" under the CISG.

[39] Pursuant to the principle of party autonomy embedded in Art. 6 CISG: "The parties may [. . .] *derogate from or vary* the effect of any of its provisions" [emphasis added].

Revocability of offer: Remarks on whether and the extent to which the UNIDROIT Principles may be used to help interpret Article 16 of the CISG

Andrea Vincze

I. INTRODUCTION TO THE ISSUE OF IRREVOCABILITY OF OFFERS

a. Article 16 CISG dealing with the revocation of an offer is a rather controversial provision of the Convention. Most of the difficulties derive from the different interpretative approaches of civil law and common law regarding the revocability of offers. Although the drafters of the CISG provision were determined to create a compromise solution reflecting the approaches of the two systems, the practical application of Article 16 CISG still reflects several ambiguities of interpretation.[1]

b. Before examining whether the Official Comments to Article 2.4 of the UNIDROIT Principles may be used to help interpret Article 16 CISG, this chapter examines different approaches of civil and common law in interpreting revocation of the offer.

c. In civil law systems a contract is concluded only if the acceptance reaches the offeror. Before that, the offeror impliedly gives the offeree a reasonable time to consider the offer, during which time the offer is irrevocable unless otherwise indicated by the offeror. If the offer states a time limit for acceptance, the offer is usually irrevocable, and if it does not, the offer is irrevocable for a reasonable period.[2]

d. In common law systems, however, the contract is concluded as soon as the offeree dispatches the acceptance. Prior to that point in time, the offer is revocable at any time, even if it must be accepted within a time period. This may sometimes also be the case even if the offeror expressly states that the offer is irrevocable.[3]

e. The structure of Article 16 CISG mixes the two competing approaches. Delegates from civil law countries approved of incorporating the general rule of revocability in Article 16(1) CISG. In turn, the civil law idea of irrevocability in situations where there is a fixed time for acceptance or irrevocability is otherwise indicated was embodied in Article 16(2)(a).[4] The second exception from the general rule of revocability (i.e., Article 16(2)(b), which is very similar to the principle of promissory estoppel[5]) is also of a common law nature. Although civil law systems similarly do not allow for revocation in bad faith (*venire contra factum proprium*), the wording of the CISG seemed unfamiliar to civil law lawyers.[6] Some civil law characteristics are also recognizable in the application of the second exception to the revocability of offers, by the fact that it is applicable only if the offeree needs time to investigate whether or not he should accept the offer.[7]

[1] Burt A. *Leete*, "Contract Formation under the United Nations Convention on Contracts for the International Sale of Goods and the Uniform Commercial Code: Pitfalls for the Unwary," at 'B', at <http://cisgw3.law.pace.edu/cisg/text/leete16.html#bl94>.

[2] See Alejandro M. *Garro*, "Reconciliation of Legal Traditions in the U.N. Convention on Contracts for the International Sale of Goods, II. 2.," at <http://cisgw3.law.pace.edu/cisg/biblio/garro1.html>; Gyula *Eörsi*, "Problems of Unifying Law on the Formation of Contracts for the International Sale of Goods," at <http://cisgw3.law.pace.edu/cisg/text/eorsi16.html>; Leete, *supra* note 1; Kazuaki Sono, "Formation of International Contracts under the Vienna Convention: A Shift above the Comparative Law," Ch. 1., at <http://cisgw3.law.pace.edu/cisg/biblio/sono2.html>.

[3] Garro, *supra* note 2; Leete, *supra* note 1; Kazuaki Sono, *supra* note 2.

[4] Garro, supra note 2; Shahdeen Malik, "Offer: Revocable or Irrevocable. Will Art. 16 of the Convention on Contracts for the International Sale Ensure Uniformity?," Ch. III. 2., at <http://cisgw3.law.pace.edu/cisg/biblio/malik.html>.

[5] For a commentary on the equitable principle of estoppel as a general principle of the CISG, citing Art. 16 (2) (b) as an example – Art. 29 also – see Colin King, "The CISG – Another One of Equity's Darlings?", 8 *Vindobona J. Int'l Coml L. & Arbitration* (2004), 264–267.

[6] Eörsi, *supra* note 2; Maria del Pilar Perales Viscasillas, "The Formation of Contracts and the Principles of European Contract Law," Ch. VII, at <http://cisgw3.law.pace.edu/cisg/biblio/perales3.html>.

[7] Leete, *supra* note 1, at "B."

f. The wording of Article 2.4 of the UNIDROIT Principles is exactly the same as that of Article 16 CISG,[8] yet each provision must be examined in its own context.[9] In addition, the UNIDROIT Principles may not be the most appropriate auxiliary rules to help interpret a provision of the CISG because there are many obstacles to overcome concerning the interpretation of both of these instruments. Yet, the applicability of the UNIDROIT provisions to Article 16 CISG cannot be excluded, but should be handled with special care.

II. THE GENERAL RULE OF REVOCABILITY OF OFFERS IN THE CISG AND THE UNDROIT PRINCIPLES

g. The general rule of revocability of offers is set out in the provisions contained in Article 16(1) CISG and Article 2.4(1) UNIDROIT Principles; the latter was literally taken from the former.[10] The provisions specify two conditions for revoking an offer: (1) the revocation must be made before the contract is concluded, and (2) it must reach the offeree before he has dispatched an acceptance. Seemingly, these conditions must be applied concurrently, but in practice doing so could cause several ambiguities.

h. Let us see what happens if the offeror sends a letter of revocation to the offeree that the latter receives only shortly after he dispatched his letter of acceptance. The first condition (i.e., a revocation can be made only prior to the conclusion of the contract) is fulfilled because, pursuant to Articles 23 and 18(2) CISG and Articles 2.1 and 2.6(2) UNIDROIT Principles,[11] the letter of acceptance has not reached the offeror by the time the letter of revocation was received by the offeree. However, we come to a different conclusion if we examine the second condition (i.e., the letter of revocation is only effective if it reaches the offeree before he dispatches the letter of acceptance). In this case, it is evident that revocation would not be effective, either with regard to the CISG provision or to that of the UNIDROIT Principles.

i. Assuming the same situation with the difference that the offeree performs an act indicating assent instead of sending a letter of acceptance, pursuant to Articles 18(3)

[8] The PECL, by way of contrast, took a different approach. Although a real balance between civil and common law principles could not be reached in either the Convention or the UNIDROIT Principles, the PECL managed to achieve this goal. Perales Viscasillas, *supra* note 6, at Ch. 1. Perales Viscasillas explains here that the Principles of European Contract Law "achieved a set of rules balanced between the different principles that inspire both common law and civil law systems" not by selecting the "most appropriate rules" of the two different legal systems and not by summarizing the rules common to both of them. The PECL created a system of its own, built on the basis of enabling commercial exchange between the EU Member States and providing an autonomous interpretation of the rules of international trade and also influenced by trade practices.

[9] "Caveat" in "Data on the pre-UNCITRAL legislative history of the CISG," at <http://cisgw3.law.pace.edu/cisg/text/roadmap/RoadmapL-16.html>.

[10] Official Comments to Article 2.4. UNIDROIT Principles, Comment 1, op. cit.

[11] These provisions are nearly the same, the CISG being a bit more specific in places.

See Article 23 CISG: "A contract is concluded at the moment when an acceptance of an offer becomes effective in accordance with the provisions of this Convention."

Cf. Article 2.1. UNIDROIT Principles: "A contract may be concluded either by the acceptance of an offer or by conduct of the parties that is sufficient to show agreement."

See also *Article 18(2) CISG*: "An acceptance of an offer becomes effective at the moment the indication of assent reaches the offeror. An acceptance is not effective if the indication of assent does not reach the offeror within the time he has fixed or, if no time is fixed, within a reasonable time, due account being taken of the circumstances of the transaction, including the rapidity of the means of communication employed by the offeror. An oral offer must be accepted immediately unless the circumstances indicate otherwise."

Cf. Article 2.6. (2) UNIDROIT Principles: "An acceptance of an offer becomes effective when the indication of assent reaches the offeror."

CISG and 2.6(3) UNIDROIT Principles, the contract is concluded upon the latter act and before the letter of revocation arrives.[12] Therefore, the revocation is not effective even if the offeror is not yet aware of the act indicating assent. As the time period for revocation is restricted by the performance of an act, only the "contract-conclusion" condition is applicable in such cases.

j. To avoid such misunderstandings, scholars[13] suggest and the Official Comments on the UNIDROIT Principles [hereinafter UNIDROIT Comments] equally express that the "contract-conclusion" condition should only be applied in the case of oral negotiations or acceptance by conduct without giving notice to the offeror. If the offer is accepted in writing, the latter condition is not applicable and the time limit for revocation is restricted until the offeree dispatches the acceptance, whereas the contract itself is concluded only when the acceptance reaches the offeror. Commentaries to Article 16 CISG acknowledge that the latter method of interpretation might be disadvantageous to the offeror who can never be sure about whether revocation can be made in time or whether the offeree has already sent his acceptance or indicated his assent by performing an act.[14]

k. Responding to this problem, Eörsi suggests that a higher level of good faith should be applied with regard to the rules of revocation by including in the wording of Article 16 CISG that "the offeree is bound to give notice if the revocation has reached him late."[15] Until this might happen, the approach taken by the UNIDROIT Comments might be applied to the CISG but not by all means and not restrictively: "It is, however, justified in the view of the legitimate interest of the offeree in the time available for revocation being shortened."[16] This view can be supported by the fact that it is the offeror who unilaterally gives the offeree the right to conclude the contract and that, unlike the offeree, the offeror has sufficient time before making an offer to weigh and asses the situation, possible risks, and consequences. Of course, there might be situations where the offeror is forced to revoke an offer because of unexpected events, perhaps even independent of him, but those cases represent only a rather small part of all offers-acceptances. For instance, in such a case, following the approach of the UNIDROIT Comments might not be appropriate because the legitimate interest of the offeror might collide with and actually prevail over that of the offeree. Thus, in such cases it is in the legitimate interest of the offeror who will obviously be unable to perform a prospective contract not to be forced to conclude such a contract because the offeree might have no chance to enforce performance. Of course, such subsequent impossibility of performance should be handled with care so as not to develop a malpractice where offerors can freely revoke an offer by referring to unexpected events or *force majeure* if they simply want to cancel the legal relationship with the offeree. Therefore, if we accept the approach set in the UNIDROIT Comments,

[12] *See Article 18(3) CISG*: "However, if, by virtue of the offer or as a result of practices which the parties have established between themselves or of usage, the offeree may indicate assent by performing an act, such as one relating to the dispatch of the goods or payment of the price, without notice to the offeror, the acceptance is effective at the moment the act is performed, provided that the act is performed within the period of time laid down in the preceding paragraph."

Cf. Article 2.6. (3) UNIDROIT Principles: "However, if, by virtue of the offer or as a result of practices which the parties have established between themselves or of usage, the offeree may indicate assent by performing an act without notice to the offeror, the acceptance is effective when the act is performed."

[13] Malik, *supra* note 3, at Ch. III. 1; Fritz Enderlein & Dietrich Maskow, "International Sales Law – United Nations Convention on Contracts for the International Sale of Goods, Commentary," at <http://cisgw3.law.pace.edu/cisg/biblio/enderlein-art16.html>.

[14] *Id.*; Eörsi, *supra* note 2.

[15] Eörsi, *supra* note 2.

[16] Comments to Article 2.4. UNIDROIT Principles, para 1 at <http://cisgw3.law.pace.edu/cisg/principles/uni16.html>.

each case must be examined separately and very carefully, and consistent trade and court practices must be developed.

In conclusion, it must be noted that in spite of the general principle of revocability, recent trends in national and international practice are toward strengthening irrevocability of offers.[17]

III. EXCEPTIONS TO THE GENERAL RULE OF REVOCABILITY

l. Articles 16(2)(a)&(b) CISG and 2.4(2)(a)&(b) UNIDROIT Principles provide for one civil law and one common law exception from the general common-law-rooted principle of revocability of offers.

1. Indication of Irrevocability Contained in the Offer (Article 16(2)(a) CISG and Article 2.4(2) (a) UNIDROIT Principles)

m. A practical interpretation of this provision is not easy. The wording of the provision derives from the civil law countries' wish to incorporate a rule following their legal traditions, but the wording is not unambiguous, which raises several questions.

n. The first problem is that for a common law attorney, indication of a fixed time for acceptance would only mean that the offer, which is still revocable, will lapse after that time, whereas for a civil law attorney, the offer is also irrevocable up until then. Furthermore, as wording of the CISG does not balance the two opposing views – this contradiction is enhanced even further when a legal relationship is exclusively between parties from a common law country or a civil law country – it allows revocation of offers in relationships between parties from common law countries.[18] If the parties are from countries belonging to different legal systems, the communications and intentions of the parties and the exact circumstances of the particular case in the light of their dealing and usage of trade shall be taken into account to determine the status of the offer.[19]

At this point it might be useful to supplement the CISG provisions on interpretation with the more detailed rules set out in Chapter 4 of the UNIDROIT Principles, dealing with interpretation of the contract. For example, by the interpretation of the intent, statements, and conduct of the parties, in addition to their negotiations, practices, usages, and subsequent conduct, the nature and purpose of the contract and the meaning commonly given to terms and expressions in the trade concerned should also be taken into account.[20] Such reference could perhaps assist in determining whether a particular offer was meant to be revocable or irrevocable.

o. Another problem concerning the indication of irrevocability contained in the offer relates to the wording used by the parties. Undoubtedly, if an offer expressly states that it is irrevocable, then, pursuant to Article 16(2)(a), the offeror cannot revoke it. The question is, however, how should a statement of a time fixed for acceptance be interpreted, whether it by itself means that such an offer is irrevocable, and what "other ways" are appropriate for expressing irrevocability of an offer?

[17] See Malik, *supra* note 4, at Ch. II referring to recent trends in England, the United States (U.C.C., New York General Obligations Law), or Canada. In Chapter V, Malik also points out that for the CISG to become the law of the future, a more liberal irrevocability approach should be taken. This would also serve the interest of developing countries that, in selling their raw materials, are very much dependent on faraway commodity markets that determine the prices of raw materials.

[18] Eörsi, *supra* note 2; Leete, *supra* note 1, at "B."

[19] Garro, *supra* note 2; Eörsi, *supra* note 2.

[20] Article 4.3. UNIDROIT Principles.

Expressing irrevocability in other ways can be inferred by determining the intent of the parties with regard to their statements and conduct.[21] As suggested by the UNIDROIT Comments, this should be done case by case.[22]

p. Concerning the indication of a fixed time for acceptance, some scholars believe that it makes the offer irrevocable[23]; others like Honnold[24] deny such an effect. Not even the UNCITRAL deliberations were unanimous because at one place automatic irrevocability in "fixed-time" cases is declared and it is denied at another place.[25] Malik suggests that "para (2) [of Article 16] is to be taken in the spirit of civil law whose rule it embodies" (i.e., stating a fixed time should mean irrevocability). Yet, this should not be automatic, and the Comments to the UNIDROIT Principles on Article 2.4(2)(a) serve as useful guidelines to interpret Article 16(2)(a) CISG[26]: "the indication of a fixed time for acceptance may, but not necessarily, amount by itself to an implicit indication of an irrevocable offer. The answer must be found in each case through a proper interpretation of the terms of the offer in accordance with the various criteria laid down in the general rules of interpretation in Chapter 4 [UNIDROIT Principles]."[27]

q. Here, again, in addition to Article 8 CISG, one could pay attention to the rules of interpretation of the UNIDROIT Principles to determine whether an offer, under Article 16(2)(a) CISG, shall be treated as revocable or irrevocable. Furthermore, distinction shall be made between stating a fixed date for acceptance as a simple expiration date, in which case the offer is not irrevocable during that time, and limiting the time for acceptance, meaning that such an offer is irrevocable.[28]

r. Last but not least, even the UNIDROIT Comments repeat the above-mentioned problematic interpretation dichotomy that, beyond all other details, when interpreting the parties' intent concerning the revocability issue, one must pay attention to the legal traditions of the respective legal systems. In other words, if the offeror comes from a country where fixing a time for acceptance indicates irrevocability then "it may be assumed" that the offer is considered to be irrevocable, and also the other way round with revocability. Although this suggestion does not serve the mandate of uniform interpretation of the CISG[29] very well, it is undeniable that in practice making an offer frequently relies upon domestic legal traditions. In this meaning, that last remark of the UNIDROIT Comments might not be helpful to interpret Article 16(2)(a) CISG.

2. Reliance by the Offeree on Irrevocability of the Offer (Articles 16(2)(b) CISG; Article 2.4(2)(b) UNIDROIT Principles)

s. The reliance provisions do not raise as many questions as do the previus ones. Pursuant to these provisions, an offer is also irrevocable if "it was reasonable for the offeree to rely on the offer as being irrevocable and the offeree has acted in reliance on the offer."

[21] *See* Article 8 CISG dealing with the interpretation of statements or other conduct of the parties.

[22] Official Comments to Article 2.4. UNIDROIT Principles, Comment 2, op. cit.: "The answer must be found in each case through a proper interpretation of the terms of the offer in accordance with the various criteria laid down in the general rules on interpretation in Chapter 4."

[23] J. D. Feltham, "UN Convention on Contracts for International Sale of Goods," *J. Bus. L.* (1981), p. 339, 346; and S.K. Date Bah, "UN Convention for Contracts for Sale of Goods: Overview," *Rev. Ghana L.*, vol. 11 (1979), p. 50 at pp. 57–58, both cited by Malik, *supra* note 4, at Ch. III.2.

[24] J. *Honnold, Uniform Law for International Sales under the 1980 United Nations Convention,* Kluwer Academic, Netherlands, 1982, n. 34, p. 171.

[25] *See* Malik, *supra* note 4, at Ch. III.2.

[26] *See* also Henry Mather, "Firm Offers under the UCC and the CISG," at <http://cisgw3.law.pace.edu/cisg/biblio/mather2.html>.

[27] *Supra* note 20.

[28] Mather, *supra* note 26.

[29] *See* Article 7(1) CISG .

These are two concurrent conditions upon which reasonable reliance on the offer is substantiated if, for example, the offeree had a good reason to believe that the offer was irrevocable (e.g., as a result of the circumstances in the case of urgent orders)[30] or if the offeror was aware that the offer was in connection with the fulfilment of another obligation on the offeree's side, and by performing acts like examining the offer, carrying out a costly investigation, or preparing an offer to a third person.[31]

t. The UNIDROIT Comments do not go any further than that, except for providing further examples of acts as a result of reliance. Among them the following are listed: making preparations for production, buying or hiring materials or equipment, and incurring expenses; they can be useful in interpreting unclear CISG cases as well. Furthermore, the UNIDROIT Comments determine the general conditions of justifying such acts by stating that they must be regarded as normal in the trade concerned or should otherwise have been foreseen by, or known to, the offeror.[32] These conditions are also very useful in interpreting whether a certain act is justifiable under Article 16(2)(b).

The CISG provision is similar to the common law principle of promissory estoppel, but it also has some civil law characteristics because it is applicable only if the offeree needs time to investigate whether or not he should accept the offer.[33]

IV. CONCLUSIONS

As already mentioned above, using the UNIDROIT Principles in the interpretation of the Convention's provisions is not the most appropriate method because the UNIDROIT Principles were not successful in eliminating difficulties appearing in the CISG. In spite of this, its applicability to the interpretation of the CISG cannot be fully excluded.

[30] Mather, *supra* note 26, II. F, Enderlein & Maskow, *supra* note 13, at [8].

[31] Mather, *supra* note 26, II. F; Malik, *supra* note 4, at Ch. III.3.

[32] Official Comments to Article 2.4. UNIDROIT Principles, Comment 2.

[33] *Leete*, *supra* note 1, at "B". Furthermore, in *Geneva Pharmaceuticals Tech. Corp. v. Barr Inc.* the U.S. District Court expressed that promissory estoppel is actually different from what is written in Article 16(2)(b) CISG becaue the latter would preempt domestic law only if a plaintiff were to bring a promissory estoppel claim to avoid the need to prove the existence of a firm offer. The Court argued that "the latter did not expressly require that the offeree's reliance must have been foreseeable to the offeror and does not expressly require that the offeree's reliance be detrimental"; as a result, the court dismissed the claim that was originally based on the promissory estoppel. The court also stated that the CISG, by establishing a modified version of promissory estoppel, would contradict the CISG and stymie its goal of uniformity. *See* case presentation available online at <http://cisgw3.law.pace.edu/cases/020510u1.html>. Pilar Perales Viscasillas opines that the Court failed to analyze the problem based on the core provisions of the CISG itself. She explains that the CISG governs contract formation either in a traditional offer-acceptance form or in other ways where sufficient agreement of the parties is present, and protection of the party relying on the other party's statements or conduct is an inherent requirement of the CISG. Therefore, this latter principle is applicable to cases where "the promise and the acts done in reliance on the promise (statements or conduct made by the other party) are enough to show an indication of assent to a contract, i.e. an intention to be bound." It is also important to mention that such reliance cases do not equal precontractual liability, which is not governed by the CISG. (*See The Draft UNCITRAL Digest and Beyond: Cases, Analysis and Unresolved Issues in the U.N. Sales Convention – Papers of the Pittsburgh Conference Organized by the Center for International Legal Education (CILE)*, Franco Ferrari, Harry Flechtner & Ronald A. Brand eds., Sweet & Maxwell, Thomson, Sellier, 2004, p. 262–264.

A contrary decision was made in *Vienna Arbitration proceeding SCH-4318* (Austria, 15 June 1994) where the tribunal held that although estoppel is not expressly settled by the CISG, it forms a general principle underlying the CISG (being "*venire contra factum proprium*"). *See* case presentation available online at <http://cisgw3.law.pace.edu/cases/940615a4.html>.

1. Applicability of Article 2.4(1) UNIDROIT Principles to Article 16(1) CISG

Article 16(1) CISG and Article 2.4(1) UNIDROIT Principles and the Comments on these Principles are in accord on most questions. The notion in the UNIDROIT Principles, suggesting that performing an act indicating acceptance can be disadvantageous to the offeror but it is justified in view of the legitimate interest of the offeree, might be applied to interpreting the CISG.

2. Applicability of Article 2.4(2)(a) UNIDROIT Principles to Article 16(2)(a) CISG

In interpreting what is the fixed time for acceptance or another indication of irrevocability, it might be useful to supplement the provisions of Article 8 CISG with the application of Chapter 4 UNIDROIT Principles. On the other hand, the interpretation method suggested in the Official UNIDROIT Comments – that in determining whether an offer was meant to be revocable or irrevocable, special regard shall be paid to the legal traditions of the respective countries – if applied to the CISG could, in one sense, be said to undermine the mandate of uniform interpretation of the CISG. Yet, this is only one way of looking at the issue. Another way is to accept that autonomy of the parties[34] is one of the most fundamental principles of the CISG and that the parties' intent[35] trumps the provisions of the Convention. In cases where the offeror and the offeree are both from common law countries or both from civil law countries (meaning similar legal traditions), the presumed intent of the parties should therefore play a role in the impact of Article 16(2)(b) CISG on Article 16(1). Rather than regarding this as an undermining of the mandate of uniform interpretation, a special kind of uniform interpretation will be present for parties from specific, and similar, legal backgrounds – an interpretation that pays special heed to principles of party autonomy and presumed intent. Accordingly, it will be useful to pay attention to whether both parties are either from common law or civil law countries. Bearing in mind that uniform interpretation of the CISG is required, it should be carried out separately in cases where both parties are from the same legal background (i.e., both common law or both civil law).

3. Applicability of Article 2.4(2)(b) UNIDROIT Principles to Article 16(2)(b) CISG

The Comments to Article 2.4(2)(b) UNIDROIT Principles, providing for the exact meaning and conditions of reliance, are useful in the interpretation of the counterpart CISG article as well.

[34] Art. 6 CISG: "The parties may exclude the application of the Convention or [. . .] derogate from or vary the effect of any of its provisions." The principle of party autonomy ensconced in Art. 6 is arguably the most important general principle of the Convention. *See* <http://cisgw3.law.pace.edu/cisg/text/e-text-06.html> for a presentation including legislative history as well as relevant doctrine and jurisprudence on that provision.

[35] The intent of the parties can be derived by reference to the provisions in Art. 8 CISG, which deals with the intepretation of statements and other conduct of the parties, and Art. 9 CISG, which deals with usages and established practices applicable to the contract.

Rejection of offer followed by acceptance: Comparison between the provisions of CISG Article 17 and the counterpart provisions of UNIDROIT Principles Article 2.5

Stephen E. Smith

I. INTRODUCTION

This chapter addresses the powerful effects of CISG Article 17, perhaps the shortest Article of the CISG, and puts its utility into perspective. This utility is informed by other CISG Articles and UNIDROIT Principles, as described and referenced here.

CISG Article 17 provides the following: "[a]n offer, even if irrevocable, is terminated when a rejection reaches the offeror." Accordingly, it is seemingly misplaced in its setting within Articles that benefit the offeror in the formation of the contract. Those Articles, CISG Articles 15 through 18, provide grounds upon which the offeror, after having dispatched his offer, may be freed from the binding effects of his offer and therefore reallocate the resources committed. Before the offer has reached the offeree, the offeror may withdraw the offer (CISG Article 15(2)). CISG Articles 16 and 18 contemplate actions that can be taken after the offer has reached the offeree: the offeror may revoke the offer unless it is irrevocable (CISG Article 16).[1] The offeror is also freed from his offer upon the expiration of the time for its acceptance (CISG Article 18(2)).

CISG Article 17, however, foresees as a cause of termination of the offer an initiative emanating from the offeree (i.e., the rejection of the offer) and as such is an obvious offeree benefit. Further, even though irrevocable, the offeree may still reject the offer, an option not allowed the offeror regarding an irrevocable offer (CISG Article 16). Herein lies much of CISG Article 17's power.

UNIDROIT Article 2.5, in virtually the same words as CISG Article 17, explicates the same issue. There is, though, one minor difference in wording. CISG Article 17 contains the clarification that the offer terminates when the rejection reaches the offeror, even if the offer is *irrevocable*. It may be observed that the clarification contained in CISG

[1] *See* Shahdeen Malik's insightful work regarding CISG Article 16, "Offer: Revocable or Irrevocable. Will Article 16 of the Convention on Contracts for the International Sale Ensure Uniformity?," 25 *Indian J. Int'l L.* 26–49 (1985); also available at <http://cisgw3.law.pace.edu/cisg/biblio/malik.html>.

Article 17 – "even if irrevocable" – was inserted because this rule is not accepted in all legal systems.[2]

II. SCOPE OF APPLICATION

Both CISG Articles 17 and UNIDROIT Principles Article 2.5 deal only with the issue of the termination of the offer by the offeree. Other causes for termination of the offer, such as death, incapacity, or insolvency of the offeror, are by intent not covered under the CISG.[3]

III. IRREVOCABILITY

The comment of UNIDROIT Principles Article 2.5 specifies that it applies to both revocable and irrevocable offers.[4] Accordingly, it is no longer necessary to distinguish between the two types of offers. An offer can be irrevocable not only by its own nature or the description but also because of the reliance of the offeree on its irrevocability.[5]

IV. TERMINATION

Although CISG lacks a specific definition and explanation of what is the effect of a termination, UNIDROIT Principles Article 7.3.5 provides that "termination of the contract releases both parties from their obligation to demand and receive future performance." Termination occurring by rejection of the offer by the offeree then extinguishes future obligations of the offeror.

V. NOTICE

Both CISG Articles 17 and UNIDROIT Principles Article 2.5 make it clear that the rejection must *reach* the offeror; mere *dispatch* of the rejection is not sufficient.[6] In the case of contradicting declarations by the offeree (acceptance sent after rejection or vice versa), the declaration that first reaches the offeror is effective. Where the contradicting declarations reach the offeror at the same time, the offeror may only rely on the declaration that has been sent last, as it corresponds to the real intent of the offeree.[7] There are

[2] *Cf* Honnold, J. O., *Uniform Law for International Sales under the 1980 United Nations Convention* (Deventer Kluwer, 3d ed. 1999) p. 154, no. 3 . *See* also Text of Secretariat Commentary on Article 15 of the 1978 Draft [*draft counterpart of* CISG Article 17], Comment 2, <http://cisgw3.law.pace.edu/cisg/text/secomm/secomm-17.html>. *See* "The Legislative History of CISG Article 17: Match-up with 1978 Draft to Assess Relevance of Secretariat Commentary," available at <http://cisgw3.law.pace.edu/cisg/text/matchup/matchup-d-17.html>. "CISG Article 17 and 1978 Draft Article 15 are identical. The Secretariat Commentary on 1978 Draft CISG Article 15 should therefore be relevant to the interpretation of CISG Article 17." *Id.*

[3] Report of the Working Group on the International Sale of the Movable Objects on Work of its 9th Session (Geneva, September 19–30, 1977, Doc. A/CN.9/142 N. 283). [*trans.*]

[4] Official Comment on UNIDROIT Principles Article 2.5, Comment 1, available at <http://cisgw3.law.pace.edu/cisg/principles/uni17.html#official>.

[5] "However, an offer cannot be revoked (a) if it indicates, whether by stating a fixed time for acceptance or otherwise, that it is irrevocable; or (b) if it was reasonable for the offeree to rely on the offer as being irrevocable and the offeree has acted in reliance on the offer." CISG Article 16.2.

[6] *Cf.* Enderlein F. and Maskow D., *International Sales Law* (Oceana Publications-1992), Article 18, no. 15, p. 91.

[7] According to Heuzé, in: *The International Sales of Merchandise* (Paris 2000), p. 162: "From Articles 15 and 22, it appears to be able to be deduced without temerity that the Vienna Convention intended to set up a general rule whereby the author of an expression of will can validly rescind the offer, since it puts its correspondent on notice to know his change of intention, or be placed in his initial position." [*trans.*]

sufficient and consistent definitions and explanations as to when a certain communication "reaches" the addressee.[8] Here in the clause at issue, we should apply the same rules as universally applied.[9] Most important of these, of course, is the language of CISG Article 17 itself.

VI. REJECTION

1. Explicit

What kind of information in what form constitutes a valid rejection has long been an unsettled matter. CISG Article 19 provides,

> A reply to an offer which purports to be an acceptance but contains material additions, limitations or other modifications is a rejection of the offer and constitutes a counteroffer.

On the other hand, it provides that

> ... [a] reply to an offer which purports to be an acceptance but contains additional or different terms which do not materially alter the terms of the offer constitutes an acceptance, unless the offeror, without undue delay, objects orally to the discrepancy or dispatches a notice to that effect ...

Given that it is a commonly accepted rule that acceptance with modification is considered a counter-offer,[10] both the CISG and the UNIDROIT Principles are careful in their approaches to the subject. The CISG names the items that can be taken as immaterial

[8] CISG-Ac Opinion No 1, Electronic Communications under CISG, 15 August 2003. Rapporteur: Professor Christina Ramberg, Gothenburg, Sweden. The opinion is available online at <http://cisgw3.law.pace.edu/cisg/CISG-AC-op1.html>. Regarding the impact of electronic communications in the context of CISG Article 17, the Opinion states

> OPINION
> The term "reaches" corresponds to the point in time when an electronic message has entered the offeror's server. An offer is terminated when a rejection enters the offeror's server. A prerequisite is that the offeror has consented expressly or impliedly to receiving electronic communications of that type, in that format, and to that address.
> COMMENT
> 17.1. An offer is terminated when rejection reaches the offeror. In electronic environments the exact time of "reaches the offeror" can be determined. The offeree can no longer create a contract by dispatching an indication of assent. If the offeree changes his mind after having dispatched a rejection of the offer and wishes to conclude a contract, the indication of assent must enter the offeror's server before the rejection enters the offeror's server.

[9] A rejection "reaches" the addressee when it is made orally to him or delivered by any other means to him personally, to his place of business or mailing address or, if he does not have a place of business or mailing address, to his habitual residence. CISG Article 24. According to the UNIDROIT Principles, an oral rejection reaches the addressee when it is made personally to the personal qualified as the addressee, whereas other communications reach the addressee when they are delivered personally to the addressee or his working place. In the latter situation, the addressee does not need to be personally handed the rejection, but it will also become effective once it is in the addressee's mailbox, fax, computer, etc. UNIDROIT Principles Article 1.9.4. Both Article 1.9 of the UNIDROIT Principles and Article 24 of the Convention define the point of time at which a communication *reaches* the addressee. The counterpart provisions adopt the same "receipt" principle, make the same distinction between oral and other communications, and provide similar definitions of the relevant concepts. *See* Felemegas J., "Comparison between Provisions of the CISG (Article 24) and the Counterpart Provisions of the UNIDROIT Principles (Article 1.9)," available at <http://cisgw3.law.pace.edu/cisg/principles/uni24.html#ed>.

[10] "Acceptance with modifications normally to be considered a counter-offer. In commercial dealings it often happens that the offeree, while signifying to the offeror its intention to accept the offer ("acknowledgement of order"), nevertheless includes in its declaration terms additional to or different from those of the offer. Para. (1) of this article provides that such a purported acceptance is as a rule to be considered a rejection of the offer and that it amounts to a counter-offer by the offeree, which the offeror may or may not accept either expressly or impliedly, e.g. by an act of performance." *See* Official Comment to UNIDROIT Principles Article 2.11. <http://www.unilex.info/instrument.cfm?pid=2&do=Comment&pos=1>.

modifications,[11] whereas the UNIDROIT Principles describe what are modifications that do not change the nature of the acceptance.[12] Accordingly, a certain degree of vagueness remains. The comment to UNIDROIT Principles Article 2.5, allows that "[a]n offer may be rejected either expressly or impliedly." This enlarges the scope of the means of acceptance and is consistent with the modes of acceptance described in UNIDROIT Principles Article 2.6.

2. Implicit

Moreover, both commentaries to the texts specify that the offeree's rejection need not be express, but may be implicit, including through conduct.[13] Of course, the determination of whether a certain statement or conduct amounts to a rejection is a question of interpretation (CISG Article 8; see also the discussion of CISG Article 19 above).

3. Implied Terms

Perhaps the clearest of the non-explicit rejections is this "material/immaterial" variant. CISG Article 19, by providing that an acceptance in terms that materially alter the offer "is a rejection of the offer" and "constitutes a counter-offer," takes care of most situations. According to the clear wording of CISG Article 19, an acceptance that must be considered as a counter-offer terminates the initial offer. By contrast, an acceptance that does not materially alter the terms of the offer only amounts to a rejection if the offeror thereto objects (CISG Article 19(2)). There is then generally no room for considering that the initial offer may survive a negotiating process conducted on the basis of such initial offer without the offeree losing the benefit thereof.[14]

4. Conduct

Perhaps more difficult is this non-verbal approach, whether directed to the offeror or another. This creation of a tri-party paradigm leads to market inefficiency and unfairness, which are not usually seen in either the CISG or the UNIDROIT Principles.

Further, neither the CISG nor the UNIDROIT Principles and their respective commentaries address the issue of whether the offeree's conduct implying rejection of the offer may be directed toward a third person rather than toward the offeror, and yet free the latter. The answer depends on whether the offeree has a legitimate interest in relying upon the irrevocable offer and in being bound by it for its entire duration.

[11] "Additional or different terms relating, among other things, to the price, payment, quality and quantity of the goods, place and time of delivery, extent of one party's liability to the other or the settlement of disputes are considered to alter the terms of the offer materially." CISG Article 19(3).

[12] "What amounts to a 'material' modification cannot be determined in the abstract but will depend on the circumstances of each case. Additional or different terms relating to the price or mode of payment, place and time of performance of a non-monetary obligation, the extent of one party's liability to the other or the settlement of disputes, will normally, but need not necessarily, constitute a material modification of the offer. An important factor to be taken into account in this respect is whether the additional or different terms are commonly used in the trade sector concerned and therefore do not come as a surprise to the offeror." See Official Comment to UNIDROIT Principles Article 2.11. <http://www.unilex.info/instrument.cfm?pid=2&do=Comment&pos=1>.

[13] Text of Secretariat Commentary on CISG Article 15 of the 1978 Draft [*draft counterpart of* CISG *Article 17*], Comment 2, <http://cisgw3.law.pace.edu/cisg/text/secomm/secomm-17.html>; Official Comment on UNIDROIT Principles Article 2.5, Comment 1, <http://cisgw3.law.pace.edu/cisg/principles/uni17.html#official>.

[14] This rigidity is criticized by Heuzé, *supra* note 7, at p. 163: "this solution is undoubtedly not very convenient, insofar as it discourages negotiation, since it exposes the recipient of the offer to accept the offer, without a modification of the conditions." [*trans.*]

VII. ILLUSTRATIONS

1. Irrevocability versus Rejection

One inconsistency arising from CISG Article 17 is that because of the irrevocability of the offer, the offeree may claim that even if it has issued a rejection that has reached the offeror, the offeree should still have the right to keep the offeror obligated to perform on the original offer. This may seem incongruous because the provision clearly rules out such claims, but query: do situations like the following one justify clarification?

> Illustration: B receives an offer from A, which includes the following sentence: "A cannot withdraw or revoke this offer in any situation within one month and B can accept this offer at any time during the period." B rejects the offer in the next week but decides to accept it soon afterward. Does A not need to keep the offer open because B's rejection has trumped his right to accept the offer; in this case the offer was terminated by B's rejection. A need not keep open, withdraw, or revoke his offer.

2. Counter-Offer as Rejection

Where the offeree replies to the offer by raising some material alterations, even if the parties do not call the communication a rejection, it will be regarded as a rejection because such a communication constitutes a counter-offer (see discussion of Notice, §5 above)

> Illustration: In response to A's offer, B asks for a lower price. A does not accept the new price. Even if there is still time before the expiration of A's offer, A does not need to carry out the original offer even if now B agrees to the original price offered by A, as B's counteroffer has terminated A's obligation.

3. Is Silence an Acceptance or a Rejection?

Both the UNIDROIT Principles and the CISG make distinctions between the situations where the offeree sends out a counter-offer and where the offeree's communication is regarded as acceptance. However, it is not always easy to distinguish a counter-offer from an acceptance, even if both documents try to define what are material modifications. As if this is not troublesome enough, what if, no response is made?

> Illustration: In response to A's offer, B agrees with all the material conditions that A offers, but asked A to put a sticker on each box of the commodity with B's contact information on it. A makes no response to this request within a reasonable time. Accordingly, A is bound to carry out the offer with the obligation to put these stickers on each box as A has failed to establish that this additional request was material. Without timely communication from A after B's response, B's response has been taken as an acceptance of the original offer with this nonmaterial addition.

VIII. CONCLUSION

As can be seen from the above discussion, the most nettlesome issue addressed by a comparison of CISG Article 17 and UNIDROIT Principles Article 2.5, with the inclusion of those ancillary articles of both necessary for such a comparison, is the termination of an irrevocable offer by the offeree. It is hoped that this short chapter has shed some light on this issue and its resolution. The counterpart provisions adopt a similar approach and are also worded in almost identical terms.

Acceptance of an offer: Commentary on the manner in which the UNIDROIT Principles Arts. 2.6 and 2.7 may be used to interpret or supplement CISG Art. 18

Jorge Oviedo Albán

I. ACCEPTANCE OF AN OFFER

Under the Convention and also under the UNIDROIT Principles, the contract is concluded when an offer is accepted.[1] Art. 18(1) of the Convention defines acceptance in the following terms:

> A statement made by or other conduct of the offeree indicating assent to an offer is an acceptance. Silence or inactivity does not in itself amount to acceptance.

Thus, the acceptance must be in the form of an active assent to an offer.[2] Art. 2.6(1) of the UNIDROIT Principles defines acceptance in an identically worded provision:

> A statement made by or other conduct of the offeree indicating assent to an offer is an acceptance. Silence or inactivity does not in itself amount to acceptance.

In general, it is accepted that under both instruments the contract is perfected when the offer and the acceptance coincide. The acceptance may be given in several ways, and it does not necessarily have to consist of an expressed act of declaration of will. Both the Convention and the Principles establish that the acceptance can consist of a declaration or an act of the offeree that indicates assent.[3]

[1] CISG Art. 23 provides, "A contract is concluded at the moment when an acceptance of an offer becomes effective in accordance with the provisions of this Convention." UNIDROIT Principles Art. 2.1 provides, "A contract may be concluded either *by the acceptance of the offer* or by conduct of the parties that is sufficient to show agreement" [emphasis added].

For a comparative analysis of CISG Art. 18 and the counterpart provisions of another Restatement of Contract law, the Principles of European Contract Law 1998, *see* CARRARA, C. and KUCKENBURG, J., "Remarks on the manner in which the Principles of European Contract Law may be used to interpret or supplement Article 18 of the CISG," available online at <http://cisgw3.law.pace.edu/cisg/text/peclcomp18.html#er>.

[2] *See* SONO, K.: "Formation of International Contracts under the Vienna Convention: A Shift above the Comparative Law," in SARCEVIC P. and VOLKEN P. (eds.): *International Sale of Goods: Dubrovnik Lectures*, Oceana (1986) 111–131; also available at <http://cisgw3.law.pace.edu/cisg/biblio/sono2.html>.

[3] *See* ENDERLEIN, F. and MASKOW, D.: "Article 18," *International Sales Law*, Oceana publications, (1992), also available online at <http://cisgw3.law.pace.edu/cisg/biblio/enderlein.html#art18-1a>:

> The statement of acceptance does not expressly have to declare acceptance of the offer; it is necessary that assent to the offer be expressed by the offeree. The statement or conduct is interpreted pursuant to [CISG]

II. MODE OF ACCEPTANCE

1. Express Acceptance

The acceptance of an offer can be express or tacit. The first is expressly presented as the assent of the offeree. The second, when it is an act that constitutes acceptance, is expressed by means of acts that denote such an assent (*i.e.*, acts of contractual execution). This form of acceptance has been called "acceptance by conduct or an act of dominion."[4]

2. Tacit Acceptance by Conduct and Acceptance by Silence

In some cases, and especially in business transactions, it is not unusual to conclude a contract without the acceptance having been manifested in an express way, but rather tacitly by conduct. In such cases it might be difficult to precisely determine the moment and place of acceptance. However, based on other factors or elements present in previous orders or dealings between the parties, the legal effect of acceptance can be deduced from the surrounding circumstances to arrive at the desired effect, which is the formation of the contract.[5]

Some legal systems are not clear as to the validity of the acceptance by silence, and neither is the doctrine unanimously accepted or recognized as a likely or effective way of acceptance. As a general rule, silence is not effective to denote the acceptance of the offer.[6] To be effective as an acceptance, silence must be accompanied by acts that allow the inference or deduction of the offeree's acceptance of the offered contract, adding as a requirement that the offeree has knowledge of the offer in the terms provided by the applicable in the law. It is also necessary to mention that tacit acquiescence must be manifested in unequivocal facts of contractual execution; it cannot consist of simple manifestations of the offeree's general intention in the sense of having received the offer or merely agreeing to it. As with a proposal that constitutes an offer, the acceptance must be characterized by the presence of the intention of the relevant party to bind himself to a contractual obligation when manifesting such assent to an offer.

The above remarks point to a difference between silence, on the one hand, and acceptance by conduct,[7] on the other hand: the *mere* silence or inactivity of the parties is not sufficient to conclude a contract, but when it is accompanied by what are denominated unequivocal acts of contractual execution, all those acts that entail execution of the contractual benefits or preparation of the same, it is effective.[8]

Article 8. The *statement must express assent to the offer*. The mere *acknowledgment of receipt* of the offer is *thus not sufficient*, neither is an expression of interest in it.

[4] CALAMARI, J.; PERILLO, J.: *The Law of Contract* (1998), Hornbook Series, West Group, St. Paul Minn., p. 85.

[5] *See* CISG Art. 9 [Usages and practices applicable to the contract].

[6] SCHLECHTRIEM, P.: "Acceptance of an Offer (Articles 18–22)," *in Uniform Sales Law – The UN-Convention on Contracts for the International Sale of Goods,* Manz, Vienna: 1986, also available online at <http://cisgw3.law.pace.edu/cisg/biblio/schlechtriem.html#a29>.

[7] *See* Germany 13 January 1993 *Oberlandesgericht* [Appellate Court], case presentation available at <http://cisgw3.law.pace.edu/cases/930113g1.html> (the court held that a contract had been validly concluded between the parties, noting that the buyer's taking delivery of the goods constituted conduct indicating assent to the offer and amounted therefore to an *implied* acceptance of the standard terms contained in the letter of confirmation sent by the seller (Art. 18(1) CISG)).

[8] *See* relevant case law:

- Argentina 14 October 1993 *Cámara Nacional de Apelaciones en lo Comercial* [Appellate Court] *Inta v. Officina Meccanica*), case presentation available at <http://cisgw3.law.pace.edu/cases/931014a1.html> (the court remarked that there was an implicit acceptance of the offer in that case: by countersigning the invoice forms and sending them to a financial institution, the buyer performed an act relating to the payment of price, amounting to acceptance according to Art. 18(3) CISG)
- France 10 September 2003 *Cour d'appel* [Appellate Court] Paris (*Société H. H... GmbH & Co. v. SARL MG...*), case presentation including English translation available at <http://cisgw3.law.pace.edu/cases/030910f1.html> (the court held that even though acceptance may result from the behavior of the offeree, silence or inactivity does not *in itself* amount to acceptance)

The Convention requires that the acceptance of the offer be express, but it also permits acceptance by conduct. CISG Art. 18(1), first sentence, reads:

> A statement made by or *other conduct* of the offeree indicating assent to an offer is an acceptance [emphasis added].

Art. 2.6(1) of the UNIDROIT Principles, first sentence, is conceived and worded in an identical manner:

> A statement made by or *other conduct* of the offeree indicating assent to an offer is an acceptance [emphasis added].

CISG Art. 18(1), second sentence, points out that silence alone does not constitute acceptance:

> Silence or inactivity does not *in itself* amount to acceptance[9] [emphasis added].

Article 2.6(1) of the Principles, second sentence, reads identically:

> Silence or inactivity does not *in itself* amount to acceptance [emphasis added].

It is thus clear that both under the Convention and the UNIDROIT Principles, mere silence or inaction, which is not accompanied by acts of contractual execution, does not have the legal effect of concluding a contract. In the first part of the counterpart provisions, it is clearly indicated that assent can be shown either by means of an express declaration of assent or by means of other conduct of the offeree indicating such (*i.e.*, acts that can be understood as unequivocal acts of execution of the contract).[10] In the second part, however, both provisions also instruct that *mere silence* or inaction does not have any legal effect to conclude a contract.[11]

Under the Convention, acceptance by conduct has a contractual legal effect provided it is accompanied by acts that indicate assent. The text of CISG Art.18(3) provides by way of example two instances that can be assumed to be effective acts of contractual

[9] *See* relevant case law:
- Switzerland 10 July 1996 *Handelsgericht* [Commercial Court] Zürich, case presentation available at <http://cisgw3.law.pace.edu/cases/960710s1.html> (the court stated that mere silence or inactivity does not amount to acceptance (CISG Art. 18(1) and (2)), *unless* other conduct of the offeree exists indicating consent or the offeree performs an act (CISG Arts 18(1) and (3))
- Belgium 2 December 1998 *Rechtbank van Koophandel* [District Court] Hasselt, case presentation available at <http://cisgw3.law.pace.edu/cases/981202b1.html> (the court remarked that CISG Art. 18 excludes acceptance of contract terms by mere silence)

[10] *See* Official Comments on Art. 2.6 of the UNIDROIT Principles, available online at <http://cisgw3.law.pace.edu/cisg/principles/uni18.html#official>.

> Comment 1. *Indication of assent to an offer*. For there to be an acceptance the offeree must in one way or another indicate 'assent' to the offer. The mere acknowledgement of receipt of the offer, or an expression of interest in it, is not sufficient. Furthermore, the assent must be unconditional, i.e. it cannot be made dependent on some further step to be taken by either the offeror [. . .] or the offeree [. . .]. Finally, the purported acceptance must contain no variation of the terms of the offer or at least none which materially alters them (*see* Art. 2.11).
> Comment 2. *Acceptance by conduct*. Provided that the offer does not impose any particular mode of acceptance, the indication of assent may either be made by an express statement or be inferred from the conduct of the offeree. Para. (1) of this article does not specify the form such conduct should assume: most often it will consist in acts of performance, such as the payment of an advance on the price, the shipment of goods or the beginning of work at the site, etc.

[11] *See* Official Comments on Art. 2.6 of the UNIDROIT Principles.

> Comment 3. *Silence or inactivity*. By stating that "[s]ilence or inactivity does not in itself amount to acceptance," para. (1) makes it clear that as a rule mere silence or inactivity on the part of the offeree does not allow the inference that the offeree assents to the offer. The situation is different if the parties themselves agree that silence shall amount to acceptance, or if there exists a course of dealing or usage to that effect. In no event, however, is it sufficient for the offeror to state unilaterally in its offer that the offer will be deemed to have been accepted in the absence of any reply from the offeree. Since it is the offeror who takes the initiative by proposing the conclusion of the contract, the offeree is free not only to accept or not to accept the offer, but also simply to ignore it.

execution – one relating to the dispatch of the goods by the seller and one relating to the payment of the price by the buyer. That provision may, however, fit many other instances and that can be appreciated further in other concrete cases. Díez Picazo mentions, for example, other such acts, such as the parties' acts *toward the preparation* of the dispatch of the goods or for the payment of the price, (e.g., the opening of a documentary letter of credit).[12]

CISG Art. 18(3) clearly permits the possibility of acceptance in a tacit way: an acceptance is effective if "by virtue of the offer or as a result of practices which the parties have established between themselves or of usage[[13]] the offeree [indicates] assent by performing an act, such as one relating to the dispatch of the goods or payment of the price, without notice to the offeror." In other words, the Convention recognizes cases in which the presence of execution acts will point out the acceptance of the offer.

The available doctrine that is relevant to those provisions of the Convention supports equally the proposition that mere silence does not constitute an acceptance. However, as pointed out above, there exist some factors in combination with which silence may constitute an effective acceptance as understood between the parties. Such factors include legal dispositions (e.g., as set out in CISG Arts. 19(2) and 21), usages and practices,[14] and

[12] See DIEZ PICAZO, L.: La Compraventa Internacional de Mercaderías. Comentario de la Convención de Viena, Civitas, Madrid, 1998, p. 182. *See* also relevant case law:

- Spain 26 May 1998 *Tribunal Supremo* [Supreme Court] (*Nordgemüse Wilhelm Krogmann v. Javier Vierto*), case presentation available at <http://cisgw3.law.pace.edu/cases/980526s4.html> (the court noted in obiter, making reference to Arts. 18 and 19 CISG, that the existence of certain documents presented was enough to prove the existence of the contracts because it provided evidence of the existence of typical acts of contractual execution between the parties);
- Spain 17 February 1998 Supreme Court, case presentation available at <http://cisgw3.law.pace.edu/cases/980217s4.html> (the court held that the documents presented in that case were proof enough of the existence of commercial relations between the parties and even of the conclusion of a contract by performing customary contractual acts (pursuant to CISG Arts. 18 and 19));
- United States 7 December 1999 Federal District Court [Illinois] (*Magellan International v.* Salzgitter Handel GmbH), case presentation available at <http://cisgw3.law.pace.edu/cases/991207u1.html> (the court held that a contract had been concluded with the buyer's acceptance of the seller's counter-offer, which could reasonably be inferred from the buyer's issuing of the letter of credit (CISG Art.18(1));
- United States 10 May 2002 Federal District Court [New York] (*Geneva Pharmaceuticals Tech. Corp. v. Barr Labs. Inc.*), case presentation available at <http://cisgw3.law.pace.edu/cases/020510u1.html> (the seller, a Canadian manufacturer of a chemical ingredient (clathrate) for use in the production of an anticoagulant medication (warfarin sodium), in 1994 supplied the buyer, a U.S. company, with samples of the ingredient and confirmed that it would support the buyer's application for approval by the Food and Drug Administration (FDA) as the supplier of the ingredient for the manufacture of the drug. In 1995, the seller issued a letter to the FDA confirming it would serve as a supplier of clathrate to the buyer. The court held that pursuant to CISG Art. 18(3) the provision of the reference letter to the FDA *could* qualify as an act indicating assent to a contract. Whether the seller's acts actually indicated assent to a contract would be analyzed at trial on the basis of industry custom).

[13] *See* relevant case law:

- France 21 October 1999 *Cour d'appel* [Appellate Court] Grenoble (*Calzados Magnanni v. Shoes General International*), CLOUT abstract number 313:

  Although the seller denied the very existence of a contract of sale and relied on article 18(1) CISG, according to which silence or inactivity does not in itself amount to acceptance, the Court held that the contract had indeed been concluded, even in the absence of any express acceptance on the part of the seller. The Court referred to the practice of previous years, the seller having always fulfilled the French company's orders without expressing its acceptance. Moreover, the seller did not produce, in reply to the many letters of claim from the buyer, any document stating that it had not received any order. In addition, the seller was aware of the buyer's intention to penetrate the footwear market by the summer of 1995 and, even if it had not received any order, it should, after manufacturing samples and being left with the original material in its possession, have questioned the buyer as to how the absence of an order should be interpreted. *See* also comprehensive case presentation including English translation also available at <http://cisgw3.law.pace.edu/cases/991021f1.html>;

- France 27 January 1998 *Cour de Cassation* [Supreme Court] (*Hughes v. Société Technocontact*), case presentation including English translation available at <http://cisgw3.law.pace.edu/cases/980127f1.html>.

[14] *See* United States 14 April 1992 Federal District Court [New York] (*Filanto v. Chilewich*), case presentation available at <http://cisgw3.law.pace.edu/cases/920414u1.html>. For identification of pivotal issues and

the existence of a duty upon the parties to communicate (reply/answer to communications).[15] We would add to such a list of factors/circumstances certain cases in which the parties have agreed to a certain mode of acceptance, either in previous dealings between themselves or in the particular contract in question – keeping in mind that CISG Art. 6 permits the parties to "derogate from or vary the effect of any of [the Convention's] provisions,"[16] thus entrenching in the Convention the principle of party autonomy and its ultimate power over (almost) any of the Convention's provisions.[17]

In a similar way to the Convention, the UNIDROIT Principles have recognized the value of acceptance *by conduct*, in almost identically worded counterpart provisions; see Arts. 2.6(1) and (3) of the Principles.

Art. 2.6(3) of the Principles is almost identical to its counterpart Art. 18(3) of the Convention; however, the latter includes additional wording (a) to illustrate the type of acts contemplated in both counterpart provisions ("such as one relating to the dispatch of the goods or payment of the price") and (b) to clarify the timing of such an acceptance by directly linking that issue to the provisions contained in CISG Art. 18(2).

The latter additional content of CISG Art. 18(3), compared to Art. 2.6(3) of the Principles, does not, however, weaken or undermine the thematic and substantive similarities between the counterpart instruments and their respective provisions, because Art. 2.7 of the Principles ("Time of Acceptance")[18] is substantively identical to CISG Art. 18(2).

miscellaneous observations of the court, *see* analysis offered by KRITZER, A., "*Editorial Remarks*," available at <http://cisgw3.law.pace.edu/cisg/wais/db/editorial/920414u1editorial.ht>, *see* relevant excerpt:

> *Conclusion of contract/Acceptance of offer/Silence or inactivity as acceptance/Practices of the parties*. The pivotal holding of the court is as stated in UNCITRAL's abstract of the case: 'Although under Article 18(1) silence is not usually acceptance, the court finds that under Article 8(3) the course of dealing between the parties created a duty on the part of the [offeree] to object promptly and that its delay in objecting constituted acceptance of the ... offer.'
>
> *General principles (duty to communicate)/Good faith*. Winship puts a key ruling of the court as follows: '[T]he opinion may ... be read as saying that parties in a long-term relationship owe to each other a duty to communicate, a duty which ultimately may be derived from a duty to act in good faith' (Peter Winship, "The UN Sales Convention and the Emerging Case law," in *Emptio-Venditio Internationales*, Neumayer ed. (Basel 1997) 228).

See also ENDERLEIN and MASKOW, *op. cit.*:

> Silence could express acceptance if usages and practices that exist between the parties (Article 9) called for expressly rejecting an offer. In the case of longstanding business relations, silence for reason of good faith (c. Article 7) may mean acceptance [...]. Through an inquiry or an invitation to submit an offer it may be communicated that one's own silence should be interpreted as acceptance [...]. The parties may also agree that for future contracts silence would amount to acceptance, e.g. in the case of continuous orders [...]. It is not clear, however, at which moment the contract is concluded in the event of agreed silence [...] probably not when the offer is received but rather after a reasonable time [references omitted].

[15] FOLSOM, R.; GORDON, M. W.; SANOGLE, J. JR.: *International Business Transactions* (Second edition), West Group, St. Paul, Minn. United States, (2001), p. 32. *See* also KRITZER, and ENDERLEIN & MASKOW, *supra* note 14.

[16] ADAME GODDARD, J.: *El contrato de compraventa internacional*, McGraw Hill, Mexico, (1994), p. 108.

[17] CISG Art. 6 reads: "The parties may exclude the application of this Convention or, subject to article 12, derogate from or vary the effect of any of its provisions."

[18] *See* Official Comment on Art. 2.7 of the UNIDROIT Principles, available online at <http://cisgw3.law.pace.edu/cisg/principles/uni18.html#official>:

> With respect to the time within which an offer must be accepted, this article, which corresponds to the second part of para. (2) of Art. 18 CISG, distinguishes between oral and written offers. Oral offers must be accepted immediately unless the circumstances indicate otherwise. As to written offers, all depends upon whether or not the offer indicated a fixed time for acceptance: if it did, the offer must be accepted within that time, while in all other cases the indication of assent must reach the offeror 'within a reasonable time having regard to the circumstances, including the rapidity of the means of communication employed by the offeror.'
>
> It is important to note that the rules laid down in this article also apply to situations where, in accordance with Art. 2.6(3) [see above], the offeree may indicate assent by performing an act without notice to the offeror: in these cases it is the act of performance which has to be accomplished within the respective periods of time.
>
> For the determination of the precise starting point of the period of time fixed by the offeror, and the calculation of holidays occurring during that period of time, see Art. 2.8; as to cases of late acceptance and of delay in transmission, see Art. 2.9.

Furthermore, the Official Comment on UNIDROIT Principles Art. 2.6(3) expressly highlights the similarity in policy and content of the counterpart provisions: "This article corresponds to para. (1), (2) first part and (3) of Art.18 CISG."[19]

Thus, it can be concluded that, as in the Convention, under the Principles silence *alone* cannot constitute acceptance. It should be made clear that, when the offeror unilaterally determines, as he may, the mode of acceptance, the offeree cannot argue that an effective acceptance has taken place through the latter's silence. The official commentary on Art. 2.6 of the Principles clearly supports this interpretation.

Furthermore, in accordance with the opinion expressed by Perales, I concur that for silence to constitute an acceptance, such a result could only be derived from (a) an express agreement of the parties (Art. 1.1 of the Principles), (b) usages or practices established between the parties (Art. 1.8 of the Principles), or (c) when other applicable law/principles recognize an acceptance in that form (Arts. 2.9 and 2.22 of the Principles).[20]

3. Necessity of Communicating Acceptance

An acceptance can be communicated by different means, unless the offeror has demanded a specific formality. In cases where the offeror has used a specific medium to communicate his offer but did not request obligatory observance of the same means for the communication of the offeree's acceptance, nothing prevents the offeree from communicating an acceptance by different means.

An express acceptance can be made orally. Oral conclusion of a sales contract can be proved by a letter of confirmation sent afterward by one party to the other.[21]

Under the Convention's regime, applying the principle of freedom from formalities in ways contemplated in CISG Art. 11,[22] a contract can be accepted by many different means suitable to the offeree to communicate or prove his assent to the offer. Under the Convention, an acceptance can also be given in writing, and for such mode this expression ("writing") includes telegram and the telex, in accordance with CISG Art. 13.

The UNIDROIT Principles equally establish the principle of freedom from formalities, in Art. 1.2. [*No form required*]:

> Nothing in these Principles requires a contract to be concluded in or evidenced by writing. It may be proved by any means, including witnesses.

Art. 1.10 of the UNIDROIT Principles defines the word "writing" in the following way:

> "writing" means any mode of communication that preserves a record of the information contained therein and is capable of being reproduced in tangible form.

Art. 1.10 of the Principles may be used to aid the interpretation of CISG Art. 13 in a broad manner to include modern means of communication, so that the reference to "telegram" and "telex" in the test of the Convention is not understood in a restrictive way

[19] *See* Official Comments on Art. 2.6 of the Principles, *op. cit.*, Comment 4.

[20] PERALES VISCASILLAS, M.: Comentario a los principios de UNIDROIT para los contratos del comercio internacional. p. 118.

[21] Germany 22 February 1994 *Oberlandesgericht* [Appellate Court] Köln, case presentation including English translation available at <http://cisgw3.law.pace.edu/cases/940222g1.html> (the court held that according to CISG Art. 18(1) silence does not in itself amount to acceptance; however silence may amount to acceptance when it is linked to other circumstances – the court also noted that importance of commercial letters of confirmation as evidence of the formation of contract).

[22] CISG art. 11: "A contract of sale need not be concluded in or evidenced by writing and is not subject to any other requirement as to form. It may be proved by any means, including witnesses."

that might exclude other modern media by which a party may dispatch a communication (e.g., messages of electronic data and in general electronic communications).[23]

4. Moment When Acceptance Becomes Effective

As with an offer, it is equally important to determine the exact moment when the acceptance becomes effective to conclude the contract. That moment will depend on the provisions/rules of the applicable legal system, which might conceivably endorse a system/theory based (a) on the offeree's *dispatch* of his assent, (b) on the *receipt* by the offeror of the offeree's assent, or (c) the mere *communication* of the offeree's assent to the offeror.

The Convention regulates acceptance by distinguishing among several suppositions in the following way: pursuant to CISG Art. 18(2), first sentence, acceptance of the offer becomes effective "at the moment when the indication of the offeree's assent *reaches* the offeror" [emphasis added]. The theory of *receipt* is, thus, adopted under the Convention's regime for contract formation.[24]

CISG Art. 18(2), in sentence two, further provides that an acceptance "is not effective if the indication of assent does not reach the offeror within the time he has fixed or, if no time is fixed, within a reasonable time, due account being taken of the *circumstances* of the transaction, *including* the rapidity of the means of communication employed by the offeror" [emphasis added].

As for offers made orally by the offeror, Art. 18(2), sentence three, provides that such offers "must be accepted *immediately* unless the circumstances indicate otherwise" [emphasis added].

As for the exact moment when a tacit acceptance produces the desired legal effect (*i.e.*, to conclude a contract), it should be kept in mind that CISG Art. 18(3) is partly based on the principle that the offeror must have knowledge of the offeree's acceptance by conduct, except – and it is the exception introduced by this chapter – in cases where the acceptance becomes effective either pursuant to practices established between the parties or is based on usages under which the offeree may manifest his acceptance without communicating it to the offeror. In the latter cases, it is assumed that the offeror has knowledge of the acceptance at the moment of execution of the offerees' act that configures the requisite – and, in all respects, effective to conclude the contract – acceptance by conduct. That is to say, the Convention permits, by virtue of established practices or usages, the possibility that the offeree may indicate his assent executing an act "... such as one relating to the dispatch of the goods or payment of the price, *without notice to the offeror*, the acceptance is effective at the moment the act is performed, provided that the act is performed within the period of time laid down in the preceding paragraph" [CISG Art. 18(3), emphasis added]. In this case it is not necessary that the offeror receive a notification of such an executed act.

[23] For a comparative analysis of CISG Art. 13 and UNIDROIT Principles Art.1.10, *see* CHARTERS, A.: *Editorial remarks*, available online at <http://cisgw3.law.pace.edu/cisg/principles/uni13.html#er>.

[24] *See* the CISG-*AC Opinion no 1*, "Electronic Communications under CISG," 15 August 2003. Rapporteur: Professor Christina Ramberg, Gothenburg, Sweden. The CISG-*AC*'s Opinion regarding CISG Art. 18(2) is available online at <http://www.cisg.law.pace.edu/cisg/CISG-AC-op1.html#art18-2>:

> An acceptance becomes effective when an electronic indication of assent has entered the offeror's server, provided that the offeror has consented, expressly or impliedly, to receiving electronic communications of that type, in that format, and to that address.
>
> The term "oral" includes electronically transmitted sound in real time and electronic communications in real time. An offer that is transmitted electronically in real time communication must be accepted immediately unless the circumstances indicate otherwise provided that the addressee consented expressly or impliedly to receiving communications of that type, in that format, and to that address.

In cases, however, where the above suppositions do not apply, the offeree must communicate to the offeror the execution of the requisite act to conclude the contract; otherwise the offeror can revoke the offer pursuant to the provision in CISG Art. 16(1).

For an offer to become effective the UNIDROIT Principles, like the Convention, adopt the system of *receipt*, pursuant to Art. 2.6(2): "An acceptance of an offer becomes effective when the indication of assent *reaches* the offeror" [emphasis added]. The drafters of the Principles considered it more sensible to place on the offeree the risk of the transmission, because the offeree is the one who chooses the means of communicating his assent, and it is the offeror who is more able or better equipped to adopt the necessary measures in ensuring that the acceptance arrives at its destination.[25]

Art. 2.6(3) of the Principles, however, like the Convention, also permits the possibility that, by virtue of the offer or as a result of the practices established between the parties or pursuant to applicable usages, the offeree manifest his assent by executing an act *without* communicating it to the offeror. In such cases, the act of acceptance produces the desired legal effect (*i.e.*, conclusion of the contract) at the moment when the requisite act is executed,[26] without any necessity to make that known to the offeror; that is to say, bypassing the method of the declaration of assent by the offeree.

Nevertheless the above-mentioned possibility would also fit the system/theory of *information*, in cases where a third party informs the offeror of the acts that constitute acceptance of the proposal.[27]

CISG Art. 24 provides that the communication of offer and acceptance (i.e., any indication of the intention of the parties in the context of contract formation under the Convention) *reaches* the addressee "when it is delivered to him, not when it is dispatched."[28]

The UNIDROIT Principles, in Art. 1.9(2), also adopt the *receipt* principle to validate the effect of a notice or other communication when "it reaches the person to whom it is given." The Official Commentary on Article 1.9 explains that a "notice *reaches* a person when given to that person orally or delivered at that person's place of business or mailing address."[29]

[25] *See* Official Comments on Art. 2.6(3) of the UNIDROIT Principles, *op. cit.*

> Comment 4. *When acceptance becomes effective*: According to para. (2) an acceptance becomes effective at the moment the indication of assent reaches the offeror (see Art. 1.9(2)). For the definition of "reaches" see Art. 1.9(3). The reason for the adoption of the "receipt" principle in preference to the "dispatch" principle is that the risk of transmission is better placed on the offeree than on the offeror, since it is the former who chooses the means of communication, who knows whether the chosen means of communication is subject to special risks or delay, and who is consequently best able to take measures to ensure that the acceptance reaches its destination. As a rule, an acceptance by means of mere conduct likewise becomes effective only when notice thereof reaches the offeror. It should be noted, however, that special notice to this effect by the offeree will be necessary only in cases where the conduct will not of itself give notice of acceptance to the offeror within a reasonable period of time.[...].
>
> An exception to the general rule of para. (2) is to be found in the cases envisaged in para. (3), i.e. where "by virtue of the offer or as a result of practices which the parties have established between themselves or of usage, the offeree may indicate assent by performing an act without notice to the offeror." In such cases the acceptance is effective at the moment the act is performed, irrespective of whether or not the offeror is promptly informed thereof [illustrations provided therein are omitted].

[26] See: VÁSQUEZ LÉPINETTE, T.: *Compraventa Internacional de Mercaderías, una visión jurisprudencial*. Aranzadi editorial, Elcano Navarra, 2000, pp. 131.

[27] *See* Official Comments on Art. 2.6(3) of the UNIDROIT Principles, *op. cit.* Comment 4.

> [...] In all other cases, e.g. where the conduct consists in the payment of the price, or the shipment of the goods by air or by some other rapid mode of transportation, the same effect may well be achieved simply by the bank or the carrier informing the offeror of the funds transfer or of the consignment of the goods.

[28] *See* the Text of the Secretariat Commentary on Article 22 of the 1978 Draft [*draft counterpart of CISG Article 20*], Comment 1, available online at <http://cisgw3.law.pace.edu/cisg/text/secomm/secomm-24.html>.

[29] *See* the Official UNIDROIT Commentary on Article 1.9, available online at <http://cisgw3.law.pace.edu/cisg/principles/uni24.html#official>, Comment 2 states:

> With respect to all kinds of notices the Principles adopt the so-called '*receipt*' principle, i.e. they are not effective unless and until they reach the person to whom they are given. For some communications this is expressly stated in the provisions dealing with them: see Arts. 2.3(1), 2.3(2), 2.5, 2.6(2), 2.8(1) and 2.10. The purpose of para. (2)

Thus, it is concluded that Art. 1.9 of the UNIDROIT Principles and Art. 24 of the Convention – the counterpart provisions that define the point of time when a communication *reaches* the addressee – adopt the same *receipt* principle, make the same distinction between oral and other communications, and provide similar definitions of the relevant concepts.[30]

III. TIME OF ACCEPTANCE

Article 18(2) of the Convention provides that "[a]n acceptance of an offer becomes effective at the moment the indication of assent *reaches* the offeror. An acceptance is not effective if the indication of assent does not reach the offeror. An acceptance is not effective if the indication of assent does not reach the offeror *within the time he has fixed* [. . .]."

Art. 2.7 of the Principles corresponds directly to part of Art. 18(2) CISG, and it is worded in an almost identical manner:

> An offer must be accepted within the time the offeror has fixed or, if no time is fixed, within a reasonable time having regard to the circumstances, including the rapidity of the means of communication employed by the offeror. An oral offer must be accepted immediately unless the circumstances indicate otherwise

The two counterpart provisions make reference to the following situations:[31]

1. The Offeror Has Fixed a Time for Acceptance

Where the offeror has fixed a time for acceptance, both the CISG (Art. 18(2)) and the UNIDROIT Principles (Art. 2.7) require that the offer is accepted within the set time.[32] Otherwise, the purported acceptance will not produce the legal effect of contract conclusion, subject to exceptions contemplated in CISG Art. 21 and its counterpart Art. 2.9 of the UNIDROIT Principles.[33]

2. The Offeror Has Not Fixed a Time for Acceptance

Where the offeror has not fixed a time for acceptance, both the Convention and the Principles provide that the acceptance must arrive *within a reasonable time*, taking into account the circumstances of the transaction, "*including* the rapidity of the means of communication employed by the offeror."[34]

of the present article is to indicate that the same will also be true in the absence of an express statement to this effect: see Arts. 2.9, 2.11, 3.13, 3.14, 6.1.16, 6.2.3, 7.1.5, 7.1.7, 7.2.1, 7.2.2, 7.3.2 and 7.3.4.

[30] For a comparison between CISG Art. 24 and the counterpart provisions of the UNIDROIT Principles Art. 1.9, *see* FELEMEGAS, J.: *Editorial remarks*, available online at <http://cisgw3.law.pace.edu/cisg/biblio/felemegas11.html>.

[31] CISG Art. 20 deals with the interpretation of the offeror's time limits for acceptance of an offer to conclude a contract, and it provides a mechanism for calculating when that period begins to run in cases where the commencement of the period of time during which an offer can be accepted by the offeree has not been expressly fixed by the offeror. Art. 2.8 of the Principles is a similar provision dealing with the calculation of the time for acceptance of an offer. For a comparison between CISG Art. 20 and the counterpart provisions of Art. 2.8 of the Principles, *see* FELEMEGAS, J.: *Editorial remarks*, available online at <http://cisgw3.law.pace.edu/cisg/biblio/felemegas9.html>.

[32] *See* ICC Arbitration Case No. 7844 of 1994, case presentation available at <http://cisgw3.law.pace.edu/cases/947844i1.html> (the arbitral tribunal held that pursuant to CISG Art. 18(2) an offer cannot be accepted after the time for acceptance has expired, unless the offeror orally informs the offeree without delay that it considers the late acceptance as effective (CISG Art. 21(2)).

[33] For a comparison between CISG Art. 21 and the counterpart provisions of Art. 2.9 of the UNIDROIT Principles, *see* FELEMEGAS, J.: *Editorial remarks*, available online at <http://cisgw3.law.pace.edu/cisg/biblio/felemegas12.html>.

[34] CISG Art. 18(2); UNIDROIT Principles Art. 2.7.

Other circumstances that ought to be kept in mind when determining the reasonable term would be the object of the contract, the complexity of the transaction, geographical circumstances, etc.[35]

3. Oral Offers

In the case of oral offers, the counterpart provisions of the Convention (CISG Art. 18(2)) and the Principles (Art. 2.7) require that they are accepted immediately.

It is also obvious that both instruments adopt the same differentiating approach to determine the duration of the offer, depending on whether the offer is in writing or is oral.

IV. CONCLUSIONS

Both the Convention and the UNIDROIT Principles adopt the same policy – which is expressed in similar wording in the counterpart provisions of the two instruments – to deal with the issue of the time and manner for indicating assent to an offer.

The counterpart provisions provide that an offer can be accepted expressly or tacitly.

Both instruments deny that silence *in itself* is capable of producing the legal effect of an acceptance to an offer.

An acceptance becomes effective when it *reaches* the offeror. Equally, an acceptance becomes effective when by virtue of usages or established practices between the parties, the offeree performs a relative act of execution of the contract.

If the offeror has fixed a time for acceptance of the offer, both the Convention and the Principles provide that the acceptance must take place within that time – and where there is not a time fixed for acceptance, within a reasonable time.

Both instruments also expressly provide that oral offers must be accepted immediately.

Furthermore the official commentaries on UNIDROIT Principles Arts. 2.6 and 2.7 state that these provisions correspond to CISG Art. 18.

Based on the preceding comparative analysis of the two instruments, it is submitted that the counterpart provisions and the contexts in which they are set are substantively identical. As such, the provisions of the Principles and the corresponding official comments on these provisions may arguably be used to interpret or supplement the counterpart provisions of the CISG.

[35] "What is reasonable always depends on the circumstances of each case." ENDERLEIN & MASKOW, *op. cit.*, at <http://www.cisg.law.pace.edu/cisg/biblio/enderlein.html#art18-1a>.

Interpretation of offeror's time limit for acceptance: Comparison between the provisions of CISG Art. 20 and the counterpart provisions of the UNIDROIT Principles of International Commercial Contracts (Art. 2.8)

John Felemegas

I. Introduction
II. Calculating the Period for Acceptance Fixed by Offeror
III. Commencement of the Period
  1. CISG Art. 20(1)
    a. Non-Instantaneous Means of Communication
    b. Instantaneous Means of Communication

I. INTRODUCTION

Article 18 of the Convention provides that "[a]n acceptance of an offer becomes effective at the moment the indication of assent reaches the offeror. An acceptance is not effective if the indication of assent does not reach the offeror *within the time he has fixed* [. . .]."

It is an important element of certainty for parties who contemplate entering into a contract that there is a clear point of time at which the period fixed by the offeror for acceptance of the offer commences. In the case where the offeror fixes a precise date by which the offeree must accept the offer (e.g., "no later than August 31"), there are no special problems regarding the period allowed for acceptance of the offer by the offeree. However, in the case where the offeror merely indicates a period of time for acceptance (e.g., "ten days"), problems may arise as to when exactly that period begins, due to possible ambiguity and uncertainty whether the period starts from the time the communication was prepared by the offeror, the time it was sent, or the time it was received by the other party.

II. CALCULATING THE PERIOD FOR ACCEPTANCE FIXED BY THE OFFEROR

In Part II of the Convention, entitled "Formation of the Contract," Article 20 deals with the interpretation of the offeror's time limits for acceptance of an offer to conclude a contract.[1] CISG Article 20 provides a mechanism[2] for calculating when that period begins to run in cases where the commencement of the period of time during which an offer can be accepted by the offeree has not been expressly fixed by the offeror.[3]

The UNIDROIT Principles in Chapter 2, entitled "Formation," include Article 2.8, entitled "Acceptance within a Fixed Period of Time." It is a similar provision dealing with the calculation of the time for acceptance of an offer.[4]

[1] CISG Art. 20 is situated among the eleven provisions of the Convention dealing with contract formation; *see* CISG Part II, Arts. 14–24.

[2] Honnold J. O., *Uniform Law for International Sales* (Kluwer Law International, 3rd ed. 1999), at 193-4 notes, "Article 20 is merely a guide to interpreting the offeror's statements. [. . .] Article 20 [. . .] plays the modest role of answering questions concerning the meaning of the offer when no answer is provided by the usual rules for interpreting the statements of the parties." For the Convention's rules on the interpretation of statements or other conduct of the parties, *see* Art. 8 of the CISG.

[3] *See* the Text of the Secretariat Commentary on article 18 of the 1978 Draft [*draft counterpart of CISG article 20*], available online at <http://cisgw3.law.pace.edu/cisg/text/secomm/secomm-20.html>. Art. 18 of the 1978 Draft and Art. 20 of the CISG are worded in almost identical terms, except for some inconsequential rewording. *See* the "Legislative History of CISG Article 20: Match-up with 1978 Draft to Assess Relevance of Secretariat Commentary," available at <http://cisgw3.law.pace.edu/cisg/text/matchup/matchup-d-20.html>: "The Secretariat Commentary on 1978 Draft article 18 remains relevant to CISG article 20. An 'an' was replaced by a 'the' in paragraph (1) and paragraph (2) contains various word changes and a re-positioning. However, all are drafting modifications and none effect changes in the substantive contents of the text."

See also Enderlein and Maskow *International Sales Law* (Oceana Publications1992) 102; also available online at <http://cisgw3.law.pace.edu/cisg/biblio/enderlein.html>, Art. 20, Comment 1: "The objective of this rule is for the two parties to find identical bases for the calculation of that period."

[4] UP Art. 2.8 is situated in Chapter 2 of the UNIDROIT Principles dealing with the rules of contractual formation; *see* UP Arts. 2.1–2.22.

III. COMMENCEMENT OF THE PERIOD

1. CISG Art. 20(1)

CISG Art. 20 makes a distinction in the rules for calculating the period of time available for acceptance,[5] depending on the means of communication used by the offeror to communicate the offer to the offeree.

a. Non-Instantaneous Means of Communication

CISG Art. 20(1), sentence 1, provides that the period of time for acceptance fixed by the offeror in a telegram "begins to run from the moment the telegram is handed in for dispatch."

If the period of time for acceptance is communicated to the offeree by letter, the time runs "from the date shown on the letter, or if no such date is shown, from the date shown on the envelope."[6]

In other words, the CISG adopts the moment of dispatch of the communication as being effective.[7]

b. Instantaneous Means of Communication

CISG Art. 20(1), sentence 2, provides that if the period of time for acceptance is communicated by "telephone, telex or other means of instantaneous communication," the period "begins to run from the moment that the offer *reaches* the offeree."[8]

In such instances where instantaneous means of communication are used, the moments of dispatch and receipt of the communication occur almost simultaneously.[9]

[5] *See* Ziegel J., "Report to the Uniform Law Conference of Canada on Convention on Contracts for the International Sale of Goods" (1981), available at <http://cisgw3.law.pace.edu/cisg/text/ziegel21.html>, where the learned author opines, "[CISG Art. 20] Paragraph (1) provides some sensible rules to determine the commencement of the period of time during which an offer can be accepted and appears to be unobjectionable from a common law point of view."

[6] The Secretariat Commentary on Article 18 of the 1978 Draft *[draft counterpart of CISG Article 20], supra* note 3, explains that "[t]his order of preference was chosen for two reasons: first, the offeree may discard the envelope but he will have the letter available as the basis for calculating the end of the period during which the offer can be accepted and second, the offeror will have a copy of the letter with its date but will generally have no record of the date on the envelope. Therefore, if the date on the envelope had not been checked, the offeror could not know the termination date of the period during which the offer could be accepted." Comment 3, *id.*

[7] *See* Enderlein and Maskow, *supra* note 3, Comment 1, where the learned authors also note that "the moment of dispatch is generally easier to prove than the moment of receipt."

[8] *Cf.* CISG Art. 24: "For the purpose of this Part of the Convention, an offer, declaration of acceptance or any other indication of intention 'reaches' the addressee when it is made orally to him or delivered by any other means to him personally, to his place of business or mailing address or, if he does not have a place of business or mailing address, to his habitual residence." CISG-AC Opinion no 1, Electronic Communications under CISG, 15 August 2003. Rapporteur: Professor Christina Ramberg, Gothenburg, Sweden. The opinion is available online at <http://cisgw3.law.pace.edu/cisg/CISG-AC-op1.html>. Regarding the impact of electronic communications in the context of Art. 20(1), the Opinion states, "A period of time for acceptance fixed by the offeror in electronic real time communication begins to run from the moment the offer enters the offeree's server. A period of time for acceptance fixed by the offeror in e-mail communication begins to run from the time of dispatch of the e-mail communication. 'Means of instantaneous communications' includes electronic real time communication. The term 'reaches' is to be interpreted to correspond to the point in time when an electronic communication has entered the offeree's server."

[9] It is considered that an offer could be made by electronic means of three different types: (1) offers in e-mail, (2) offers at passive Web sites, and (3) offers at chat sites where communication occurs in real time. CISG-AC Opinion no 1, op. cit., Comment 20.2.

Note, however, that not all electronic means are regarded as "instantaneous" means of communication. Regarding offers in e-mail, *see* CISG-AC Opinion no 1, Comment 20.3: "E-mail is not instantaneous communication and, with respect to dating, it is not wholly equivalent to letters sent in envelopes. CISG does not provide any interpretative help with respect to e-mails and uncertain situations must be solved by ordinary

2. UNIDROIT Principles Art. 2.8(1)

UP Art. 2.8(1), like its counterpart provision in the CISG, makes a distinction depending on the means of communication used by the offeror to communicate the offer to the offeree. Furthermore, the Principles adopt the same rules used in the Convention.

a. Non-Instantaneous Means of Communication

The wording in UP Art. 2.8(1), sentence 1, is identical to that used in CISG Art. 20(1), sentence 1.

As does the rule contained in CISG Art. 20(1) regarding non-instantaneous means of communication, UP Art. 2.8(1) provides,

> A period of time for acceptance fixed by the offeror in a telegram or a letter begins to run from the moment the telegram is handed in for dispatch or from the date shown on the letter or, if no such date is shown, from the date shown on the envelope.

b. Instantaneous Means of Communication

The wording in UP Art. 2.8(1), sentence 2, is substantively identical to that used in CISG Art. 20(1), sentence 2.[10]

As does the rule contained in CISG Art. 20(1) regarding non-instantaneous means of communication, UP Art. 2.8(1) provides that

> A period of time for acceptance fixed by the offeror by means of instantaneous communication begins to run from the moment that offer reaches the offeree.

means of interpretation taking into account that the party being unilaterally bound (the offeror) normally deserves more protection. E-mails normally produce information about when they were sent and when they were received. CISG provides no direct guidance as to whether the time span starts to run from the time of sending or receiving. A period of time for acceptance fixed by the offeror in e-mail communication begins to run from the time of dispatch of the e-mail communication. This is so because this time can be easily ascertained and e-mails can be seen as functional equivalents of letters." *Id.*

Regarding offers in passive Web sites, *see* Comment 20.4: "When offers are contained in web sites it is often uncertain whether they constitute offers in the legal sense. However, the web site holder may explicitly state that his offer is binding during a certain period of time. No guidance can be found in CISG where the web site holder has provided a time limit of three days without specifying from when the time limit starts to run. Uncertain situations must be solved by ordinary means of interpretation taking into account that the party being unilaterally bound (the offeror) normally deserves more protection. This opinion does not cover non-real time communication over passive websites." *Id.*

Regarding offers in real-time chat sites, see Comment 20.5: "Parties may communicate over the Internet by real-time communication (this is common for chat-programs). The technique is such that if the sender writes an 'a' the letter 'a' immediately appears on the addressee's screen. The parties are both present at the same time and they may talk orally or write to each other just as if they were present in the same room or were talking over the phone. This type of communication qualifies as 'instantaneous.'" CISG Art. 20(1) applies also to electronic communication in real time. If the sender sends an offer and stipulates that it is binding for two hours, the period starts to run from the point in time when the message reaches the addressee (i.e., immediately). For real-time communication it is assumed that the addressee has indicated his willingness to receive electronic messages of the relevant type." *Id.*

For further comments on the impact of electronic communications on Art. 20(1) and other provisions of the Convention, *see* Siegfried Eiselen, "Electronic Commerce and the UN Convention on Contracts for the International Sale of Goods (Cisg) 1980," 6 *EDI L. Rev.* (1999) 21–46, also available online at <http://cisgw3.law.pace.edu/cisg/biblio/eiselen1.html>.

[10] The only difference in the wording of the counterpart provisions is that CISG Art. 20(1), sentence 2, reads, "A period of acceptance fixed by the offeror by *telephone, telex or other* means of instantaneous communication [. . .]" (emphasis added); whereas UP Art. 2.8(1), sentence 2, reads, "A period of acceptance fixed by the offeror by means of instantaneous communication [. . .]". It is arguable that the additional words "*telephone, telex or other* . . ." used in CISG Art. 20(1) do not add anything of substance to the interpretation or the application of the CISG provision that is not already covered by the more economical phraseology used in its UP counterpart.

IV. EFFECT OF HOLIDAYS AND NON-BUSINESS DAYS: CISG ART. 20(2) AND UP ART. 2.8(2)

The counterpart provisions in CISG Art. 20(2) and in UP Art. 2.8(2) dealing with the effect of holidays and non-business days contain identical rules and are phrased in identical wording.

The basic rule adopted in both the Convention and the Principles provides that official holidays and non-business days occurring during the period fixed for acceptance are included in calculating the period.[11]

Where the notice or acceptance cannot be delivered on the last day of the period fixed for acceptance-reply because it falls on a holiday or non-business day at the place of delivery (i.e., at the place of the offeror-addressee, as the case may be),[12] both counterpart provisions grant an extension of the period until the first business day that follows.[13]

V. CONCLUSION

The provisions dealing with the calculation of the time fixed by the offeror for acceptance of an offer under the Convention and the UNIDROIT Principles share the same rationale (i.e., the creation of certainty for the parties contemplating entering into a contract), adopt the same solutions to the problem they address (i.e., by providing rules based first on objective evidence of *dispatch*, whenever such evidence is available), and are worded in almost completely identical terms.

It is concluded that the counterpart provisions are substantively identical.[14]

[11] *See* Enderlein and Maskow, *supra* note 3, Comment 5, where the authors state that "[o]nly holidays or non-business days at the place of business of the *offeror* are being taken into consideration because those may not be known to the offeree."

[12] *See* Enderlein and Maskow, *id.*: "If, however, the last day of the period falls on a holiday at the place of business of the *offeree* and the offeree is prevented from dispatching an acceptance, he has to take this into account and hand in his acceptance for dispatch earlier."

[13] *See* Schlechtriem P., *Uniform Sales Law – The UN-Convention on Contracts for the International Sale of Goods* (Manz, Vienna 1986) 55, also available at <http://cisgw3.law.pace.edu/cisg/biblio/schlechtriem-21.html>, where the learned author states, "Legal holidays or non-business days generally have no influence on the calculation of the deadline (Article 20(2) sentence 1). Parties in international trade cannot be expected to adjust to the various national, regional, or local holidays [. . .] For the offeree's reply, however, when the acceptance could not be delivered to the offeror because of a holiday, sentence 2 allows an extension of the deadline for acceptance until the first following business day. This should not make the offeror uncertain because he must reasonably take into account the possibility that the other party would not know of a holiday which prevents delivery and, therefore, would take advantage of the entire period." *See* also Ziegel, *supra* note 5, who states that this rule in CISG Art. 20(2) "is a logical corollary to the reception rule for acceptances adopted in art. 18(2). Since the acceptance is not effective until it reaches the offeror some provision is necessary where the last day for acceptance is a non-business day or an official holiday at the offeror's place of business. The practical effect of art. 20(2) appears to be to extend the period for acceptance by at least one day where the notice of acceptance cannot be delivered. It may of course be longer depending on the circumstances."

Cf. CISG Article 9 on the issue of international trade usages applicable to the contract.

[14] *See* also the Official UNIDROIT Commentary, also available online at <http://cisgw3.law.pace.edu/cisg/principles/uni20.html#official>, which states that UP Art. 2.8 "corresponds to CISG Article 20. For a comparison between CISG Art. 20 and the counterpart provisions of the Principles of European Contract Law, *see* Felemegas J., at <http://cisgw3.law.pace.edu/cisg/biblio/felemegas3.html>.

Late acceptances: Comparison between the provisions of CISG Art. 21 and the counterpart provisions of the UNIDROIT Principles of International Commercial Contracts (Art. 2.9)

John Felemegas

I. INTRODUCTION

In Part II of the Convention, entitled "Formation of the Contract," Article 21 deals with the issue of *late acceptance*[1] by an offeree, the response to that by the offeror, and the effect that a late acceptance has in the context of contract formation.[2]

The UNIDROIT Principles, Chapter 2, entitled "Formation," includes Article 2.9, entitled "Late Acceptance. Delay in Transmission," which regulates the same issues concerning late acceptance in contract formation.[3]

The Convention provides that a late acceptance can nonetheless be effective as an acceptance, and so do the UNIDROIT Principles. Both the Convention and the Principles deal with the issue of late acceptance – whether the offeree accepted the offer late or the acceptance was late merely because of a delay in its transmission – in almost identical terms.

II. LATE ACCEPTANCE OF OFFER TO CONCLUDE CONTRACT

Art. 21 of the Convention "deals with acceptances that arrive after the expiration of the time for acceptance."[4] Therefore, Art. 21 must be viewed in the context of the basic rule of the Convention that a late acceptance is ineffective.[5]

[1] For an acceptance that has not reached the offeror in *due time*; *see* CISG Art. 18(2).
[2] CISG Art. 21 is situated among the eleven provisions of the Convention dealing with contract formation; *see* CISG Part II, Arts. 14–24.
[3] UP Art. 2.9 is situated in Chapter 2 of the UNIDROIT Principles dealing with the rules of contractual formation; *see* UP Arts. 2.1–2.22.
[4] *See* the Text of the Secretariat Commentary on Art. 19 of the 1978 Draft [*draft counterpart of CISG Art. 21*], available online at <http://cisgw3.law.pace.edu/cisg/text/secomm/secomm-21.html>: "If the acceptance is late, the offer lapses and no contract is concluded by the arrival of the acceptance." Art. 19 of the 1978 Draft and Art. 21 of the CISG are identical, except for some inconsequential rewording that does not affect the substance of the provision; *see* <http://cisgw3.law.pace.edu/cisg/text/matchup/matchup-d-21.html>. The Secretariat Commentary on this article is, therefore, very relevant.
[5] CISG Art. 18(2).

Honnold states that CISG Art. 21, "like Article 20, extends and elaborates the basic rule"[6] for late acceptances by providing the answer to some related, important questions that can arise when an acceptance does not reach the offeror within the time he has fixed for acceptance.[7]

CISG Art. 21 makes a distinction in the rules applicable to a late acceptance depending on whether the acceptance was sent late by the offeree or the lateness of the acceptance was caused by delays in its transmission. The counterpart provision of the UNIDROIT Principles, Article 2.9, makes the same distinction.

III. NOTICE BY OFFEROR GIVING EFFECT TO LATE ACCEPTANCE

1. CISG Art. 21(1)

In the case of a belated dispatch of acceptance by the offeree, an affirmative subsequent response by the offeror can make the late acceptance nevertheless effective to conclude the contract.[8]

Where the offeree has dispatched belatedly an acceptance – either after the period for acceptance set by the offeror has expired or before the expiration of the fixed period but using a mode of communication that would not ensure that acceptance reaches the offeror in due time – it must be presumed that the offeree is aware that his acceptance is (or is going to be) late for the purposes of contract formation. In that case, it is argued that the offeree "knows that his acceptance is actually a counter-offer and needs to be confirmed through an acceptance. Silence by the offeror cannot be inferred by him to be an acceptance (CISG Art. 18, paragraph 1)."[9]

From the basic rule of the Convention that an acceptance of an offer becomes effective at the moment *it reaches the offeror* (pursuant to Art. 18(2)), it follows that the risk of transmission is borne by the offeree.[10] Furthermore, pursuant to Art. 21(1) the offeror has the power to consider a late acceptance as having arrived in due time. If the offeror so elects to be bound by the late acceptance, he must inform *without delay* the offeree "orally or by dispatch of a notice that he considers the acceptance to be effective."[11] It must be stressed that the subsequent – and *without delay* – response by the offeror to a late acceptance acts only as validation of the contractually binding effect of what was a late acceptance by the offeree, and it does not constitute a counter-offer.[12]

[6] Honnold J. O., *Uniform Law for International Sales* (Kluwer Law International, 3rd ed. 1999), 195.

[7] For a relevant discussion regarding computation of time for acceptance of offer, *see* Felemegas J., "Comparison between Provisions of the CISG (Art. 20) and the Counterpart Provisions of the UNIDROIT Principles of International Commercial Contracts (Art. 2.8)," available online at <http://cisgw3.law.pace.edu/cisg/biblio/felemegas9.html>.

[8] CISG Art. 21(1); *see* also ULF Article 9(1).

[9] Enderlein F. and Maskow D., *International Sales Law* (Oceana Publications 1992) 103; also available at <http://cisgw3.law.pace.edu/cisg/biblio/enderlein-art21.html>. The authors also consider the case where the offeror has not fixed a time for acceptance – the indication of the offeree's assent must reach the offeror within a reasonable time (Art. 18(2)): "In that case, the offeror and the offeree may well consider different periods as being reasonable. Objectively, a reasonable time may have expired already, even though the offeree assumes that the acceptance was made in due time." *Id.*

[10] *See Id*, at 104.

[11] Text of the Secretariat Commentary on article 19 of the 1978 Draft, *supra* note 4. *Cf.* Enderlein and Maskow, *supra* note 9, at 104–105, where the authors (a) describe the wording "without delay" as being "not quite comprehensible" because the offeror probably needs time to reflect on whether to accept the late acceptance, and (b) state that this rule is "questionable, in particular when the acceptance is declared very late and the circumstances as a whole have changed in the meantime" (further references provided therein are omitted).

[12] Text of the Secretariat Commentary on Art. 19 of the 1978 Draft, *supra* note 4:

> [U]nder this paragraph [CISG 21(1)] it is the *late acceptance* which becomes the effective acceptance as of the *moment of its receipt*, even though it requires a *subsequent* notice to validate it [emphasis added].

See also Schlechtriem P., *Uniform Sales Law – The UN-Convention on Contracts for the International Sale of Goods* (Manz Vienna 1986) 55:

It follows that the offeror need not respond to the offeree regarding the late acceptance, in which case no contract is concluded.[13]

If the offeror wishes to assent to the contract he may do so by informing the offeree either orally[14] or by dispatching a notice[15] that the late acceptance is effective. The information can also be given to the offeree in an electronic message.[16]

2. UNIDROIT Principles Art. 2.9(1)

According to the UNIDROIT Principles, a late acceptance is ineffective (i.e., in order for an acceptance to be effective it must reach the offeror within the time fixed for acceptance).[17] That same basic rule on late acceptance is also found in the Convention.

The Principles, like the Convention, make a distinction between an acceptance that was sent late by the offeree[18] and an acceptance that was late because of transmission delays.[19] Like the Convention, the Principles provide a different rule for each of those two cases.[20]

The wording in UP Art. 2.9(1) is almost completely identical to that used in its counterpart provision of the CISG. In cases of late dispatch of the offeree's acceptance, notwithstanding the rule in UP Art. 2.7, UP Art. 2.9(1) provides that the offeror may validate the effectiveness of the acceptance by treating it as valid. The offeror may do

> This notice [by offeror], however, does not constitute the acceptance of a counter-offer; the date of the contract depends on when the acceptance was received, even though it was received late; also available online at <http://cisgw3.law.pace.edu/cisg/biblio/schlechtriem-21.html>.

See also Ziegel J., "Report to the Uniform Law Conference of Canada on Convention on Contracts for the International Sale of Goods," (1981), available at <http://cisgw3.law.pace.edu/cisg/text/ziegel21.html>, who states "[t]he late acceptance takes effect from the date of its receipt and not from the time when the offeror communicates with the offeree."

Cf. Enderlein and Maskow, *supra* note 9, at 105, where the authors state:

> It is not clear whether the late acceptance becomes effective at the moment when the offeror informs the offeree or dispatches the relevant communication or whether it becomes effective retroactively from the moment it is received. (Since the offeror needs to inform the offeree without delay, there will only be a slight difference in time [. . .]) (further references provided therein are omitted).

For the Convention's rules regarding counter-offers, *see* CISG Art. 19.

[13] *See* Enderlein and Maskow, *supra* note 9, at 104: "[I]t is *up to the offeror whether or not he considers the acceptance to be valid*. If he wants a contract [...] he must inform the offeree accordingly [...]. Should the offeror keep silent [...] there will be no contract.The same policy is adopted in UNIDROIT Principles Art. 2.9; *see* Official Comments on UP Art. 2.9, available online at <http://cisgw3.law.pace.edu/cisg/principles/uni21.html#official>, Comment 1:

> *Late acceptance normally ineffective*: According to the principle laid down in Art. 2.7 for an acceptance to be effective it must reach the offeror within the time fixed by the latter or, if no time is fixed, within a reasonable time. This means that as a rule an acceptance which reaches the offeror thereafter *is without effect and may be disregarded by the offeror* [emphasis added].

[14] *See* CISG-AC Opinion no 1, Electronic Communications under CISG, 15 August 2003. Rapporteur: Professor Christina Ramberg, Gothenburg, Sweden. The opinion is available online at <http://cisgw3.law.pace.edu/cisg/CISG-AC-op1.html>. Regarding Electronic Communications in the context of Art. 21(1), the Opinion states

> The term "oral" includes electronically transmitted sound provided that the offeree expressly or impliedly has consented to receiving electronic communication of that type, in that format, and to that address.

[15] CISG-AC Opinion no 1, *op. cit.* The Opinion states

> The term "notice" includes electronic communications provided that the offeree expressly or impliedly has consented to receiving electronic messages of that type, in that format, and to that address.

[16] *Id.*, Comment 21.1:

> The important factor is that the information be conveyed to the offeree, not in what *form* it was conveyed [emphasis added].

[17] UP Art. 2.7 – *Time for Acceptance*; UP Art. 2.8 – *Acceptance within a Fixed Period of Time*.

[18] UP Art. 2.9(1).

[19] UP. Art. 2.9(2).

[20] Official Comments on UP Art. 2.9, *op .cit.*, Comment 3:

> As long as the acceptance is late because the offeree did not send it in time, it is natural to consider it as having no effect unless the offeror expressly indicates otherwise. The situation is *different* when the offeree has replied in time, but the acceptance reaches the offeror late because of an unexpected delay in transmission ... [emphasis added].

so if he informs the offeree without *delay*[21] that he assents to the late acceptance. Such response by the offeror has the effect of binding him to the acceptance and concluding the contract, effective from the moment the late acceptance reached him.[22]

Like the Convention, the UNIDROIT Principles do not treat the late acceptance as a *new offer* that the offeror may accept within the time set for acceptance.[23]

IV. LATE ARRIVAL OF ACCEPTANCE BECAUSE OF TRANSMISSION DELAYS

1. Cause of Delay Evident to Offeror: Duty to Inform Offeree

According to the Convention, if the late arrival of the acceptance was evidently caused by a delay in transmission, the acceptance is effective *unless* the offeror informs the offeree that the offer has indeed lapsed.[24]

a. CISG Art. 21(2)

Art. 21(2) provides that, if "a letter or other writing[25] containing the late acceptance shows that it was sent in such circumstances that if its transmission had been normal it would have reached the offeror in due time," the offeror has an obligation to notify – either orally or by dispatching[26] a relevant notice[27] – without delay, the offeree in order to prevent a contract from being concluded.[28]

[21] UP Art. 2.9(1) reads: "... if without *undue* delay ..." [emphasis added]. CISG Art. 21(1) reads: "... if without delay ...". *See* also note 11, *supra*.

[22] Official Comments on UP Art. 2.9, *op.cit.*, Comment 2:

> Para. (1) of this article, which corresponds to Art. 21 CISG, states that the offeror may nevertheless consider a late acceptance as having arrived in time and thus render it effective, provided that the offeror 'without undue delay [...] so informs the offeree or gives notice to that effect.' If the offeror takes advantage of this possibility, the contract is to be considered as having been concluded as soon as the late acceptance reaches the offeror and not when the offeror informs the offeree of its intention to consider the late acceptance effective.

See also *supra* note 12.

[23] Official Comments on UP Art. 2.9, *op.cit.*, Comment 2 is entitled "Offeror may nevertheless 'accept' *late acceptance*" [emphasis added]. *See* also note 12, *supra*.

[24] CISG Art. 21(2); *see* also ULF Art. 9(2). *See* also the Text of the Secretariat Commentary on article 19 of the 1978 Draft [*draft counterpart of CISG article 21*], *supra* note 4:

> [I]f the letter or document which contains the late acceptance shows that it was sent in such circumstances that if its transmission had been normal, it would have been communicated in due time [...] the late acceptance is considered to have arrived in due time, and the contract is concluded as of the moment the acceptance reaches the offeror, unless the offeror without delay notifies the offeree that he considers the offer as having lapsed.

[25] CISG-AC Opinion no 1, *op. cit.* Regarding Electronic Communications in the context of Art. 21(2), the Opinion states

> The term "writing" covers any type of electronic communication that is retrievable in perceivable form. A late acceptance in electronic form may thus be effective according to this article.

[26] CISG-AC Opinion no 1, *op. cit.* states

> The term "dispatch" corresponds to the point in time when the notice has left the offeree's server. A prerequisite is that the offeree has consented expressly or impliedly to receiving electronic messages of that type, in that format, and to that address.

See also Comment 21.5, *id.*:

> It is enough that the notice has been dispatched; it does not have to reach the addressee. However, it must have been dispatched correctly. This means that the address must be correctly stated and that the sender uses a computer program that the addressee has indicated he is willing to accept.

[27] CISG-AC Opinion no 1, *op. cit.* Comment 21.6:

> The offeror should inform the offeree about a late acceptance by dispatching a notice. Dispatch occurs when the notice leaves the offeror's server. If, however, the offeree does not use the kind of electronic communication that the notice is sent in, the offeror is not considered to have dispatched the notice. The offeree must have indicated that he is willing to receive electronic acceptances of the type and format used by the offeror. CISG Arts. 8 and 9 may be of assistance in determining whether the offeree has impliedly indicated his willingness to receive such messages.

[28] CISG-AC Opinion no 1, *op. cit.* Comment 21.4:

> When the offeror provides a quick notice that that the acceptance has arrived too late, the acceptance is not effective. Information to the offeree about the late acceptance can be given in an electronic message. The important factor is that the information be conveyed to the offeree, not in what form it is conveyed. According to this Article such notice shall be communicated orally or by a [written] notice. The offeror may provide the

It is said that the provision in Art. 21(2) mitigates the rigor of the Convention's rule that an acceptance must *reach the offeror* to be effective (Art. 18(2)), and thus it "protects the offeree's reasonable reliance interests where he has no reason to anticipate that his acceptance will not reach the offeror on time."[29]

It must be noted, however, that the offeror is not obliged to be bound by the late acceptance.[30] Furthermore, if it is shown that the relevant communication of acceptance was sent out on time and the offeror does not want to conclude a contract, he should be under no duty to do anything and can simply disregard the late acceptance. Conversely, if the offeror nonetheless wishes to conclude the contract, he must notify, *without delay*,[31] the offeree that he considers the late acceptance to be effective pursuant to Art. 21(1).[32]

b. UNIDROIT Principles Art. 2.9(2)

The wording in UP Art. 2.9(2) is also almost completely identical to that used in its counterpart provision of the Convention.

The Official Comment on UP Art. 2.9 explains that where the offeree sent his acceptance in a timely fashion but only a delay in its transmission caused its late arrival at the offeror, the offeror must notify the offeree if he does not assent to the contract.[33]

2. Failure So to Inform Offeree: Acceptance Is Effective

a. CISG Art. 21(2)

It follows from what was written earlier that if the offeror does not inform the offeree – either orally or by dispatching a relevant notice – that he considers his offer as having lapsed, the acceptance is effective and concludes the contract pursuant to Art. 21(2).[34] In

information by electronically conveyed sound or by an electronic message under the precondition that the sender of the late acceptance has indicated that he is willing to receive such electronic messages.

[29] Ziegel, *supra* note 12. *See* also note 33, *infra*.

[30] Enderlein and Maskow, *supra* note 9, at 105, where the authors point out that "[t]he offeror could not foresee that an acceptance would arrive even after the period for acceptance had expired" and he "may have made other arrangements or have lost his interest in the transaction."

[31] Kritzer A. H., *Guide to Practical Applications of the United Nations Convention on Contracts for the International Sale of Goods* (Kluwer 1988) 190, stresses that

> [I]f the offeror wants to treat such an acceptance as invalid, he may if he proceeds without delay. A concern is that where an acceptance is late under these circumstances, Article 21 may give the offeror an opportunity to speculate and decide whether to honor the late acceptance on the basis of a rise or fall of prices in the interim period.

Regarding the potential for opportunistic speculation by the offeror at the expense of the offeree, in the application of Art. 21, Honnold, *op. cit.*, at 197, opines

> This opportunity will be avoided [...] by construing Article 21(1) in relation to the basic rule in Article 18(1) that a statement is an acceptance only if it indicates "assent" to the offer in the light of the objective facts available to both parties when (Art. 18(2)) the reply "reaches the offeror." This result would also respond to the rule of Article 7(1) that "in the interpretation of this Convention, regard is to be had ... to the need to promote ... the observance of good faith in international trade."

[32] *See* the Text of the Secretariat Commentary, *supra* note 4.

[33] Official Comments on UP Art. 2.9(2), *op.cit.*, Comment 3: *Acceptance late because delay in transmission* reads:

> [W]hen the offeree has replied in time, but the acceptance reaches the offeror late because of an unexpected delay in transmission [...] the *reliance* of the offeree on the acceptance having arrived in time *deserves protection*, with the consequence that the late acceptance is considered to be effective *unless* the offeror objects without undue delay. The only condition required by para. (2) is that the letter or other writing containing the late acceptance shows that it has been sent in such circumstances that, had its transmission been normal, it would have reached the offeror in due time [emphasis added].

[34] CISG-AC Opinion no 1, *op. cit.*, Comment 21.3:

> The purpose of this Article is to make a delayed acceptance effective when the offeror does not inform the other party that the acceptance has been delayed and the acceptance has reached the offeror too late. A typical situation is when an electronic acceptance is delayed and does not reach the offeror within the normal time-span. The article is only applicable if the acceptance is sent in a letter or other writing. The article applies also when the acceptance is sent by an electronic message as long as this electronic message fulfils the two functions of writing, *i.e.* that it can be understood and saved.

that case, the late acceptance is considered to have arrived in due time, and the contract is concluded as of the moment the acceptance reaches the offeror.[35]

b. UNIDROIT Principles Art. 2.9(2)

It is clear also in UNIDROIT Principles Art. 2.9(2) that where the offeree sent his acceptance in a timely manner but its arrival was late because of transmission delays,[36] the acceptance should be considered effective unless the offeror without delay informs the offeree that it considers its offer as having lapsed or gives notice to that effect.

V. CONCLUSION

The wording used in the counterpart provisions of the CISG and the UNIDROIT Principles dealing with the effect of a late acceptance is almost completely identical. Furthermore, based on the striking similarity in policy and structure of the approach adopted in the CISG and the UNIDROIT Principles to deal with the issue of late acceptance, it can be concluded that these counterpart provisions are substantively identical.[37]

[35] Schlechtriem, *supra* note 12, states, "[T]he acceptance becomes effective on arrival and thus concludes the contract, unless the offeror protests orally or in writing." *See* also note 14, *supra*.

[36] *Supra* note 33.

[37] *See* also Official Comments on UP Art. 2.9, *op. cit.*, Comment 2, which declares that Art. 2.9 "corresponds to Art. 21 CISG." For a related comparative analysis of CISG Art. 21and another Restatement of Contract Law, *see* Felemegas J., "Comparison between Provisions of the CISG Regarding Late Acceptance (Article 21) and the Counterpart Provisions of the PECL (Art. 2:207)," available online at <http://cisgw3.law.pace.edu/cisg/biblio/felemegas8.html>.

Withdrawal of acceptance: Comparison between provisions of the CISG (Art. 22) and the counterpart provisions of the UNIDROIT Principles of International Commercial Contracts (Art. 2.10)

John Felemegas

I. INTRODUCTION

Article 18(2) of the Convention provides that "[a]n acceptance of an offer becomes effective at the moment the indication of assent *reaches the offeror* [. . .]." Article 22 of the Convention, however, allows the possibility that an offeree may withdraw an acceptance "if the withdrawal reaches the offeror *before or at the same time* as the acceptance would have become effective." In other words, CISG Art. 22 provides a final time for withdrawal of an acceptance.

The UNIDROIT Principles, Article 2.10, provide a similar regime for the effective withdrawal of an acceptance.

II. PERMISSIBILITY OF WITHDRAWAL

In Part II of the Convention, entitled "Formation of the Contract," Article 22 deals with the withdrawal of an acceptance by an offeree.[1] As such, the Convention provides to an offeree the opportunity to permissibly withdraw an acceptance of an offer to conclude a contract.

CISG Art. 22 provides the rule on the timing for an effective withdrawal of an acceptance.[2] This provision must be analyzed in the context of the basic rule of the Convention that an acceptance cannot be withdrawn after it has become effective. Further, it complements the rule in CISG Art. 23 that a contract is concluded "at the moment *when an acceptance of an offer becomes effective*."[3]

The UNIDROIT Principles in Chapter 2, entitled "Formation," include Article 2.10, entitled "Withdrawal of an Acceptance,"[4] which is a similar provision dealing with the timing for an effective withdrawal of an acceptance by an offeree.

III. WITHDRAWAL MUST REACH OFFEROR BEFORE OR AT DATE OF EFFECTIVENESS

1. CISG Art. 22

CISG Art. 22 provides that an offer may be withdrawn if the withdrawal *reaches*[5] "the offeror *before or at least at the same time* as the notice of acceptance."[6]

[1] CISG Art. 22 is situated among the eleven provisions of the Convention dealing with contract formation; *see* CISG Part II, Arts. 14–24.

[2] *See* the Text of the Secretariat Commentary on Article 20 of the 1978 Draft [*draft counterpart of CISG article 22*], available online at <http://cisgw3.law.pace.edu/cisg/text/secomm/secomm-22.html>. Art. 20 of the 1978 Draft and Art. 22 of the CISG are worded in identical terms. *See* the "Legislative History of CISG Article 20: Match-up with 1978 Draft to Assess Relevance of Secretariat Commentary," available at <http://cisgw3.law.pace.edu/cisg/text/matchup/matchup-d-22.html>: "CISG article 22 and 1978 Draft article 20 are identical. The Secretariat Commentary on 1978 Draft article 20 should therefore be relevant to the interpretation of CISG article 22." *Id.*

[3] Text of the Secretariat Commentary, *supra* note 2. *See* CISG Art. 23, which deals with the effect of an acceptance and the time of the conclusion of the contract. *See* also CISG Arts. 18(2) and 18(3) that state when an acceptance becomes effective.

CISG Art. 20 deals with the computation of time for acceptance of an offer; for a relevant discussion of that provision; *see* Felemegas J., Editorial remarks, "Comparison between Provisions of the CISG (Article 20) and the Counterpart Provisions of the UNIDROIT Principles of International Commercial Contracts (Art. 2.8)," available online, at <http://cisgw3.law.pace.edu/cisg/principles/uni20.html#ed>.

CISG Art. 21 deals with the effect of acceptances that arrive after the expiration of the time for acceptance; for a discussion of the comparison between provisions of the CISG regarding late acceptance (Article 21) and the counterpart provisions of the PECL (Art. 2:207), see Felemegas J., "Editorial Remarks," available online at <http://cisgw3.law.pace.edu/cisg/text/peclcomp21.html#er>.

[4] UP Art. 2.10 is situated in Chapter 2 of the UNIDROIT Principles dealing with the rules of contractual formation; *see* UP Arts. 2.1–2.22.

[5] *See* CISG-AC Opinion no. 1, Electronic Communications under CISG, 15 August 2003. Rapporteur: Professor Christina Ramberg, Gothenburg, Sweden. The opinion is available online at <http://cisgw3.law.pace.edu/cisg/CISG-AC-op1.html>. Regarding the impact of electronic communications in the context of Art. 22, the Opinion states, "The term 'reaches' corresponds to the point in time when an electronic communication has entered the offeror's server, provided that the offeror expressly or impliedly has consented to receiving electronic messages of that type, in that format, and to that address."

[6] Schlechtriem P., *Uniform Sales Law – The UN-Convention on Contracts for the International Sale of Goods*, Manz, Vienna (1986) 54. *See* also CISG-AC Opinion no. 1, *supra* note 5, Comment 22.2: "The underlying purpose of this article is to ensure that the offeror has an opportunity to read the withdrawal if he so chooses. It is not required that the offeror actually read the withdrawal, but rather that the withdrawal becomes accessible for reading (the distinction between 'reach the mind' and 'reach the desk' or 'reach the legal

That provision reflects exactly the parallel approach adopted in the Convention, Art. 15, regarding the effectiveness of an offer.[7] Art. 15(2) provides that "[a]n offer, even if it is irrevocable, may be withdrawn if the withdrawal reaches the offeree *before or at the same time* as the offer."

Regarding the application of the rule in Art. 22, it has been noted that, by permitting an effective withdrawal of an acceptance, it creates an opportunity for an offeree to perhaps speculate at the expense of the offeror.[8]

That problem is likely to arise mainly where traditional means of communication have been used by the parties. For instance, an offeree who may have sent an acceptance by ordinary paper mail may later withdraw it by sending a notice of withdrawal using a faster method of transmission (e.g., fax or other electronic methods) that reaches the offeror before the ordinary mail.[9]

2. UNIDROIT Principles (UP) Art. 2.10

The wording in Article 2.10 is completely identical to that used in its counterpart provision of the Convention. The UNIDROIT Principles Official Comment on Art. 2.10 explains that the offeree may withdraw the acceptance provided that the withdrawal reaches the offeror *before or at the same time* as the acceptance.[10]

entity'). Therefore, when a withdrawal of assent has entered the offeror's sphere of control, it must be assumed to have reached the offeror."

See also Comment 22.3: "The proposition that a withdrawal only needs to be accessible and not actually read is designed to facilitate evidence. It is possible (more or less easily, but at least conceptually) to prove when a message becomes accessible; it is very difficult to prove when someone actually addressed his mind to it." *Id.*

[7] *See* CISG Art. 15.

See also Honnold J. O., *Uniform Law for International Sales*, Kluwer Law International, 3rd ed. (1999), 199, where the author notes that Art. 22 applies to acceptances the same approach that the Convention provides for offers. Honnold states, "Indeed, these articles may constitute specific applications of a general principle that a party may withdraw or modify a communication by a second communication that overtakes the first" (further references provided therein are omitted). *Id.*

See also Ziegel J., "Report to the Uniform Law Conference of Canada on Convention on Contracts for the International Sale of Goods," (1981), available at <http://cisgw3.law.pace.edu/cisg/text/ziegel22.html>.

[8] Farnsworth E. Allan, "Withdrawal of Acceptance (Art. 22)," in Bianca C. M. and Bonell M. J. eds. *Commentary on the International Sales Law*, Milan: Giuffrè (1987) 196. Farnsworth contemplates that the application of Art. 22 "may result in a period during which the offeror is bound but the offeree is not, giving the offeree an opportunity to speculate on a fluctuating market. By sending an acceptance, the offeree binds the offeror, who can no longer revoke his offer under Article 16. But the offeree can still withdraw his acceptance by sending an overtaking withdrawal. Therefore he might speculate during the period when he is not bound by watching the market to see if it is to his advantage to withdraw his acceptance." For a response to that potential problem with Art. 22, see Kritzer A. H., *Guide to Practical Applications of the United Nations Convention on Contracts for the International Sale of Goods*, Kluwer, (1988) 191–192, where it is suggested that problem might be overcome by application of the Convention's good faith proviso (CISG Art. 7(1)).

See also Enderlein F. and Maskow D., *International Sales Law*, Oceana Publications (1992) 106, also available online at <http://cisgw3.law.pace.edu/cisg/biblio/enderlein-art22.html>, where the authors also acknowledge the prevailing opinion that the potential problem might be overcome by the application of the rule of good faith (Art. 7(1)), but state, "It is not clear to us why the revoking of an acceptance which has not been received by the offeror constitutes a misuse which has to be fought with good faith. Unclear is also how such a misuse could be proved. Since our law is based on the assumption that an offer is generally binding, the unilateral binding of the offeror is not a problem."

[9] *See* CISG-AC Opinion no. 1, *supra* note 5, Comment 22.1, where it is noted, "The problem in relation to electronic means of communication is that there are rarely any practical means of faster communication than electronic messages sent by e-mail or communicated over websites or other EDI-arrangements. However, the question becomes of practical importance in situations where the acceptance is sent by traditional paper mail and the withdrawal is sent electronically." *Id.*

[10] Official UNIDROIT Commentary to Principles 2.10, available online at <http://cisgw3.law.pace.edu/cisg/principles/uni22.html#official>, where it is also noted that Art. 2.10 "lays down the same principle as that contained in Art. 2.3 concerning the withdrawal of an offer."

Furthermore, the Official UNIDROIT Comment makes clear that "while the offeror is bound by the offer and may no longer change its mind once the offeree has dispatched the acceptance (see Art. 2.4(1)), the offeree loses its freedom of choice only at a later stage (i.e., when the notice of acceptance reaches the offeror)."

IV. CONCLUSION

The wording used in the counterpart provisions of the CISG and the UNDROIT Principles is completely identical. Furthermore, based on the similar regime for offers and acceptances and the same policy adopted in the CISG and the UNDROIT Principles to permit an effective withdrawal of an acceptance (and identical counterpart provisions dealing with the withdrawal of an offer), it can be concluded that the counterpart provisions regarding withdrawal of an acceptance are substantively identical.[11]

Thus, it is arguable that the UNIDROIT Official Comments on UP Art. 2.10, which recognize that the offeree enjoys his freedom of choice to enter a contract longer than the offeror, help interpret the meaning of the provision contained in CISG Art. 22.

[11] *See* also the Official UNIDROIT Commentary to Principles 2.10, available online at <http://cisgw3.law.pace.edu/cisg/principles/uni22.html#official>: "This article corresponds to Art. 22 CISG."

When communication "reaches" addressee: Comparison between the provisions of CISG Article 24 and the counterpart provisions in Article 1.9 of the UNIDROIT Principles

John Felemegas

I. INTRODUCTION

The CISG provisions dealing with contract formation can be found in Part II of the Convention.[1] For the purposes of contract formation, during the exchange of communications of offer and acceptance between the parties, many of the applicable CISG Articles provide that a communication becomes effective when it "reaches" the other party (i.e., the addressee).[2]

[1] There are eleven provisions of the Convention dealing with contract formation; *see* CISG Part II, Arts. 14–24.

[2] *See* CISG Art. 15(1) (offer), Art. 15(2) (withdrawal of offer), Art. 16(1) (revocation of offer), Art. 17 (rejection of offer), Art. 18(2) (acceptance), Art. 20(1) (fixed time limit for acceptance), Art. 21 (late acceptance), and Art. 22 (withdrawal of acceptance).

It has been correctly identified that "[p]ractical problems of proof would arise if the applicability of [those] provisions depended on evidence that a communication came to the personal attention of the addressee."[3]

To address such problems, CISG Art. 24 provides the elements of what constitutes an effective communication to an addressee under Part II of the Convention.[4]

The UNIDROIT Principles (UP), like the Convention, adopt the offer and acceptance model of contract formation,[5] which contemplates the exchange of notices and other communications between the parties. In Chapter 1, entitled "General Provisions," the UP include Article 1.9, entitled "Notice," which is a provision similar to its CISG counterpart regarding the effectiveness of a notice or other communication of intention between the parties.

II. TIME WHEN A COMMUNICATION "REACHES" THE ADDRESSEE: CISG ART. 24 AND UP ART. 1.9

Article 24 of the Convention provides that the communication of offer and acceptance – any indication of the intention of the parties in the context of contract formation under the CISG – *reaches*[6] the addressee "when it is delivered to him, not when it is dispatched."[7]

Consequently, an offer (Art. 15) or an acceptance (Art. 20) may be withdrawn if the withdrawal reaches the other party before or at the same time as the respective offer or acceptance that is being withdrawn.[8]

The UNIDROIT Principles, in Art. 1.9(2), also adopt the "receipt" principle to validate the effect of a notice or other communication as when "it reaches the person to whom it is given." The Official Comment on UP Article 1.9 explains that a "notice 'reaches' a person when given to that person orally or delivered at that person's place of business or mailing address."[9]

[3] Honnold J. O., *Uniform Law for International Sales*, Kluwer Law International, 3rd ed. (1999), at 201.

[4] *See* Ziegel J., "Report to the Uniform Law Conference of Canada on Convention on Contracts for the International Sale of Goods," (1981), available at <http://cisgw3.law.pace.edu/cisg/text/ziegel24.html>, Comment 1: "Art. 24 is a definition section and is a necessary complement to the Convention's adoption of the reception rule to determine the time of effectiveness of acceptances and other communications."

[5] *See* Chapter 2 of the UNIDROIT Principles dealing with the rules of contract formation: Arts. 2.1–2.22.

[6] *See* CISG-AC Opinion no 1, Electronic Communications under CISG, 15 August 2003. Rapporteur: Professor Christina Ramberg, Gothenburg, Sweden. The opinion is available online at <http://cisgw3.law.pace.edu/cisg/CISG-AC-op1.html>. Regarding the impact of electronic communications on the interpretation of Art. 24, the Opinion states, "The term 'reaches' corresponds to the point in time when an electronic communication has entered the addressee's server, provided that the addressee expressly or impliedly has consented to receiving electronic communications of that type, in that format, and to that address."

[7] *See* the Text of the Secretariat Commentary on Article 22 of the 1978 Draft [*draft counterpart of CISG Article 20*], Comment 1, available online at <http://cisgw3.law.pace.edu/cisg/text/secomm/secomm-24.html>. Art. 22 of the 1978 Draft and Art. 24 of the CISG are worded in almost identical terms, except for some inconsequential rewording. See the "Legislative history of CISG Article 22: Match-up with 1978 Draft to Assess Relevance of Secretariat Commentary," available at <http://cisgw3.law.pace.edu/cisg/text/matchup/matchup-d-24.html>: "The Secretariat Commentary on 1978 Draft article 22 remains relevant to CISG article 24. There is a drafting change (a reference to 'this Part of the Convention' rather than 'Part II of this Convention') and an added emphasis ('delivered . . . to him' has become 'delivered . . . to him personally')."

[8] Secretariat Commentary, *supra* note 7, Comment 2. "Furthermore, an offeree who learns of an offer from a third person prior to the moment it reaches him may not accept the offer until it has reached him. Of course, a person authorized by the offeror to transmit the offer is not a third person in this context." *Id.*

[9] *See* the Official UNIDROIT Commentary on Article 1.9, available online at <http://cisgw3.law.pace.edu/cisg/principles/uni24.html#official>, Comment 2 states, "With respect to all kinds of notices the Principles adopt the so-called '*receipt*' principle, i.e. they are not effective unless and until they reach the person to whom they are given. For some communications this is expressly stated in the provisions dealing with them: see Arts. 2.3(1), 2.3(2), 2.5, 2.6(2), 2.8(1), and 2.10. The purpose of para. (2) of the present article is to

It must be noted that the Principles apply this rule[10] to all notices,[11] whereas the wording of CISG Art. 24 apparently limits the application of the latter provision to Part II of the Convention.[12] However, this difference may not be significant (see "IV. Relevance to Other Provisions of the Convention," *infra*).

III. DELIVERY TO ADDRESSEE'S PLACE OF BUSINESS OR MAILING ADDRESS

Article 24 of the Convention makes clear that the point of time at which a communication *reaches* the addressee is when it is delivered "to him personally, to his place of business or mailing address."[13,14] This would require that a *delivery*[15] of the communication is made – orally[16] or by other means[17] – either to an *appropriate place* or to an *authorized employee* of the addressee.[18] There are no apparent problems regarding either the

indicate that the same will also be true in the absence of an express statement to this effect: see Arts. 2.9, 2.11, 3.13, 3.14, 6.1.16, 6.2.3, 7.1.5, 7.1.7, 7.2.1, 7.2.2, 7.3.2, and 7.3.4."

[10] *Cf.* Official UNIDROIT Commentary, *supra* note 9., Comment 3: "Dispatch principle to be expressly stipulated. The parties are of course always free expressly to stipulate the application of the dispatch principle. This may be appropriate in particular with respect to the notice a party has to give in order to preserve its rights in cases of the other party's actual or anticipated non-performance when it would not be fair to place the risk of loss, mistake or delay in the transmission of the message on the former. This is all the more true if the difficulties which may arise at international level in proving effective receipt of a notice are borne in mind."

[11] UP Art. 1.9(4): "For the purpose of this article 'notice' includes a declaration, demand, request or any other communication of intention." *Cf.* CISG Art. 24: "For the purposes of this Part of the Convention, an offer, declaration or any other indication of intention . . . "

[12] *Cf.* CISG Art. 24: "For the purposes of *this Part* of the Convention . . . " (emphasis added).

Cf. Ziegel, *supra* note 4, Comment 2: "Where an offeror has evinced an intention that an offer must be accepted in a given way presumably, that will be *sufficient to override* the presumptive effect of art. 24. See [CISG] art. 6" (emphasis added). *Id.*

[13] Secretariat Commentary, *supra* note 7, Comment 3. "In such a case it will have legal effect even though some time may pass *before* the addressee, if the addressee is an individual, or the person responsible, if the addressee is an organization, knows of it" (emphasis added). *Id.*

[14] *See* Schlechtriem P., *Uniform Sales Law – The UN-Convention on Contracts for the International Sale of Goods*, Manz, Vienna (1986) 49 n. 156, available online at <http://cisgw3.law.pace.edu/cisg/biblio/schlechtriem.html>: "'Mailing address' means the place where mail is received, such as a mail box, but not an address that has been changed – such as by a move – and not yet corrected."

[15] Enderlein F. and Maskow D., *International Sales Law*, Oceana Publications (1992) 108, Article 24, Comment 4, available online at <http://cisgw3.law.pace.edu/cisg/biblio/enderlein.html>: "*Delivery does not mean* that the addressee has *taken cognizance* of the statement. The communication, however, needs to have reached his area of receipt or disposal, and it needs to have been 'recognizable.' It would not be sufficient if it were left in an unattended place or on the door steps" (references omitted).

[16] *See* Schlechtriem, *supra* note 14, at 50: "For oral declarations, however, the theory of cognizance should apply under Article 24, *i.e.*, the declaration must have been perceived by the addressee."

See also CISG-AC Opinion no 1, *supra* note 6: "The term 'orally' includes electronically transmitted sound and other communications in real time provided that the addressee expressly or impliedly has consented to receive electronic communications of that type, in that format, and to that address."

[17] *See* Schlechtriem, *supra* note 14, at 49: "Article 24, like ULF Article 12(1) and the German Civil Code, provides that a 'materialized' expression of intent has reached the addressee when it reaches his sphere of control – or, in more concrete terms, when it is delivered to him. Delivery should occur preferably in person, alternatively to the place of business or mailing address, and finally to the habitual residence. Even though the Convention, unlike ULF Article 12(2), does not specify that the declaration must have been 'intelligible' for the delivery to be effective, the requirement presumably applies to the Convention as well" (references contained therein are omitted). *Cf.* CISG Art. 27.

Cf. UP Art. 1.9(1): "Where a notice is required it may be given by any means *appropriate to the circumstances*" (emphasis added).

[18] *See* Honnold, op. cit., at 201, where the author states: "Leaving a letter or telegram on the door-step or in some other unattended place would not constitute 'delivery' to the addressee's 'place of business'; one relying on such a communication would need to show that the letter or telegram reached the addressee or an authorized employee."

geographical location[19] of such an appropriate place or an appropriately authorized agent[20] of the addressee.

As an exception applicable only in cases where the addressee has neither a place of business nor a mailing address, a communication *reaches* the addressee on delivery to his habitual residence.[21]

Article 1.9(3) of the Principles, like its CISG counterpart, provides that a notice "reaches" a person "when given to that person orally or delivered at that person's place of business or mailing address."

Furthermore, the Principles, like the CISG, make a distinction between oral and other communications.[22]

IV. RELEVANCE TO OTHER PROVISIONS OF THE CONVENTION

Based on a literal interpretation of the wording in Art. 24, it seems that the provision is applicable only to indications of the respective parties' intention in the context of contract formation governed by Part II of the Convention.[23] In that respect, the relevant provision may be contrasted with and distinguished from the general rule in Part III of the Convention that provides that notices and other communications are effective when they are dispatched.[24]

Several commentators have, however, observed that the provision in Art. 24 may be applied more broadly and by analogy to other communications between the parties, outside the narrow context of Part II of the Convention.

A principal commentator on the CISG, Professor Honnold states

> The definition in Article 24 [...] of when a communication "*reaches*"' the addressee applies only to Part II, but there is no indication of a legislative intent to reject the approach of Article 24 in construing [...] references to the "*receipt*" of communications. Indeed, the

[19] Secretariat Commentary, *supra* note 7, Comment 5: "There are no geographical limitations on the place at which personal delivery can be made... In fact such delivery is often made directly to the addressee at some place other than his place of business. Such delivery may take place at the place of business of the other party, at the addressee's hotel, or at any other place at which the addressee may be located."

[20] *Id.*, Comment 6: "Personal delivery to an addressee which has legal personality includes personal delivery to an agent who has the requisite authority. The question as to who would be an authorized agent is left to the applicable national law." *See* also Enderlein and Maskow, *supra* note 15, at 108, Comment 6: "Delivery to the addressee and deliveries to his statutory representative or agent have equal status."

[21] *Cf.* CISG Art. 10(b) (definition of "place of business"). See also Secretariat Commentary, *supra* note 7, Comment 4: "As with an indication of intention delivered to the addressee's place of business or mailing address, it will produce its legal effect even though the addressee may not know of its delivery."

[22] See the Official Commentary on UP Art. 1.9, op. cit., Comment 4, which explains, "It is important in relation to the receipt principle to determine precisely when the communications in question 'reach' the addressee. In an attempt to define the concept, para. (3) of this article draws a distinction between oral and other communications. The former 'reach' the addressee if they are made personally to it or to another person authorized by it to receive them. The latter 'reach' the addressee as soon as they are delivered either to the addressee personally or to its place of business or mailing address. The particular communication in question need not come into the hands of the addressee. It is sufficient that it be handed over to an employee of the addressee authorized to accept it, or that it be placed in the addressee's mailbox, or received by the addressee's fax, telex or computer."

[23] CISG Art. 24: "For the purposes of *this Part* of the Convention..." (emphasis added).

[24] Part III of the Convention, entitled "Sale of Goods," comprises CISG Arts. 25–88. In Part III, the general rule is that a communication is effective from the time of its dispatch and the risk of non-arrival or late arrival lies with the recipient; *see* CISG Art. 27. Note, however, the exceptions to the dispatch rule: CISG Art. 47(2) (Buyer's receipt of notice from seller that he will not perform within the additional period fixed); Art. 48(4) (Buyer's receipt of notice from seller requesting that buyer make known whether he will accept cure after date of delivery), Art. 63(2) (Seller's receipt of notice from buyer that he will not perform within the additional period fixed), Art. 65 (Buyer's receipt of notice from seller supplying missing specifications), Art. 79(4) (Receipt of notice of impediment affecting a party's ability to perform).

normal meaning of "*receipt*" is close to that expressed in Article 24; the widespread use of the approach of Article 24 [. . .] seems to justify the use of this article by analogy (references omitted).[25]

Furthermore, the case law provides some support for such an analogical application of Art. 24 to other provisions of the Convention in CISG Part III. Examining the effectiveness of communications exchanged between parties to a contract governed by the CISG, a Dutch court adopted an analogous approach to determine whether a letter – dispatched by the German seller to the address previously provided by the Dutch buyer – demanding payment for the goods did "reach" the addressee, even though the buyer never actually received the letter because he had moved to another address.[26]

V. CONCLUSION

Both Art. 1.9 of the UNIDROIT Principles and Art. 24 of the Convention define the point of time at which a communication *reaches* the addressee.

The counterpart provisions adopt the same "receipt" principle, make the same distinction between oral and other communications, and provide similar definitions of the relevant concepts.

Neither instrument, however, provides any further guidance on the *precise* time that a communication reaches the addressee effectively.[27]

[25] Honnold, *supra* note 3, at 202. *See* also Farnsworth E. Allan, in Bianca C. M. and Bonell M. J. eds. *Commentary on the International Sales Law*, Milan: Giuffrè (1987) pp. 203–204.: ". . . Since Article 24 is expressly limited to 'the purposes of this Part of the Convention," it does not literally apply to [cited articles in Part III]. However, the reasoning that underlies Article 24 is equally applicable to those articles. Furthermore, the analogy between the time when a communication 'reaches' an addressee under Part II and the time when there is 'receipt' of a communication under Part III is striking. These reasons justify extension of the principle of Article 24 to Part III" (further references omitted). For a similar conclusion on point, see Enderlein and Maskow, *supra* note 15, at 108, Art. 24, Comment 1: "The definition of '*reaches*' may be applied analogously in those cases. *See* also Kritzer A. H., *Guide to Practical Applications of the United Nations Convention on Contracts for the International Sale of Goods*, Kluwer, (1988) 196, where the author recognized that particular issue and suggested the following: "Because a communication that '*reaches*' the addressee when it is delivered to his place of business or mailing address . . . will have legal effect even though some time may pass before the addressee . . . knows of it . . . even though the addressee may not know of its delivery . . . a prudent response to application of Article 24 concepts to Part III of the Convention is the use of a contract clause which identifies by position title, parties to whom notices or other communications must be addressed" (references omitted).

[26] *See* Netherlands 5 October 1994 District Court Amsterdam (*Tuzzi Trend Tex Fashion v. Keijer-Somers*), available online at <http://cisgw3.law.pace.edu/cases/941005n1.html>. German law was applicable to the contract between the parties. Germany was a CISG Contracting State in 1991; therefore, the Convention applied pursuant to CISG Art. 1(1)(b). Under German law a declaration of one party is effective only when it *reaches the addressee* (German Civil Code, Section 130). Pursuant to Art. 24 CISG, a declaration "reaches" the addressee when it has been delivered to his place of business or mailing address. The court held that the relevant communication in question (i.e., seller's letter demanding payment for the goods) had *reached* the buyer.

For an editorial comment on that case, see Kritzer A. H., available online at <http://cisgw3.law.pace.edu/cases/941005n1.html#ce>: "Commenting on the effectiveness of a communication [i.e., a letter from seller to buyer, demanding payment for the goods] that was mailed to an address previously provided by the buyer but not received by the buyer because the buyer had moved to another address; the court stated: 'It is indeed decisive that the statement is received by the other party (according to German and Dutch law). But following article 24 of the CISG . . . a statement is received by a party if it is delivered to his place of business or mailing address. Therefore the [communication] has reached [the buyer].'"

[27] The precise time that a communication reaches the addressee can be relevant; *see* Farnsworth, *supra* note 25. In that respect it has been suggested that the counterpart provisions of the United States Uniform Commercial Code provide a certain type of guidance on the precise time that a communication *reaches* the addressee under the CISG; *see* Kritzer, *supra* note 25, at 197, where reference is made to UCC Section 1–201:

> (26) A person "notifies" or "gives" a notice or notification to another by taking such steps as may be reasonably required to inform the other in ordinary course whether or not such other actually comes to know of it. A person

The only perceptible distinction of significance between the counterpart provisions is that the Principles apply the rule in Art. 1.9 to all notices exchanged between the parties, whereas Art. 24 of the Convention appears to be limited only to communications for the purposes of CISG Part II.

There is, however, CISG jurisprudence and doctrine in support of extending by analogy the definition of when a communication "reaches" the addressee under CISG Part II to other communications between the parties, observing that the reasoning that underlies Art. 24 is equally applicable to provisions in Part III of the Convention.

"receives" notice or notification when
(a) it comes to his attention; or
(b) it is duly delivered at the place of business through which the contract was made or at any other place held out by him as the place for receipt of such communication.
(27) Notice, knowledge or a notice or notification received by an organization is effective for a particular transaction from the time when it is brought to the attention of the individual conducting the transaction, and in any event from the time that it would have been brought to his attention if the organization had exercised due diligence. An organization exercises due diligence if it maintains reasonable routines for communicating significant information to the person conducting the transaction and there is reasonable compliance with the routines. Due diligence does not require an individual acting for the organization to communicate information unless such communication is part of his regular duties or unless he has reason to know of the transaction and the transaction would be materially affected by the information.

"Fundamental breach": Commentary on whether the UNIDROIT Principles of International Commercial Contracts may be used to interpret or supplement Article 25 CISG

Robert Koch

3. Curability of the Breach
   a. Relationship between Cure and Avoidance for Fundamental Breach
   b. Wording of Article 50 CISG
   c. Doctrinal Reasons against Consideration of Curability
   d. Overriding Purpose of the Fundamental Breach Requirement

I. INTRODUCTION

The concept of *fundamental breach* under Article 25 CISG plays a crucial role within the remedial system of the CISG because it determines the availability of the avoidance remedy in respect of any breach other than late performance (Articles 49(1)(a), 64(1)(a), 72(1), and 73(1) CISG) and of the substitute delivery remedy (Article 46(2) CISG). Fundamental breach is also important for the transfer of risk (Article 70 CISG). Its UNIDROIT Principles counterpart, *fundamental non-performance*, is defined in Article 7.3.1(2) of the UNIDROIT Principles. Unlike Article 25 CISG, its scope is limited to the termination of a contract. Before addressing the issue of whether or not Article 7.3.1(2) of the UNIDROIT Principles may be used to interpret or supplement Article 25 CISG, it is necessary to first take a closer look at the elements constituting fundamental breach, because recourse to the UNIDROIT Principles is only admissible where the language of the CISG provision gives rise to doubts as to the precise meaning of its content.[1]

II. ELEMENTS CONSTITUTING FUNDAMENTAL BREACH

Article 25 provides that a breach is fundamental if

> . . . it results in such detriment to the other party as substantially to deprive him of what he is entitled to expect under the contract, unless the party in breach did not foresee and a reasonable person of the same kind in the same circumstances would not have foreseen such result.

Article 25 CISG attempts to define fundamental breach in terms of "detriment," "substantial deprivation," and "foreseeability." There is no reference to examples of events that transform a simple breach of contract into a fundamental breach.[2]

1. Detriment

The CISG does not contain any definition for the term "detriment." It is thus unclear whether the detriment requires actual injury, damage, or loss and whether it refers only to material losses or to intangible losses as well. It is also unclear whether a legal detriment, as distinguished from a detriment in fact, is required.[3] Neither the French, Spanish,

[1] *See infra* Section IV.

[2] *See* Graffi, "Case Law on the Concept of 'Fundamental Breach' in the Vienna Sales Convention," *Int'l. Bus. L.J.* (2003) No. 3, at 338 (stating that the CISG simply provides general interpretive guidelines); available online at <http://cisgw3.law.pace.edu/cisg/biblio/graffi.html>; Bonell, "The UNIDROIT Principles of International Commercial Contracts and the Vienna Sales Convention (CISG) – Alternatives of Complementary Instruments?," *Unif. L. Rev.* (1996) 26, at 28 (stating that the language of Article 25 CISG is "vague and ambiguous"); available online at <http://cisgw3.law.pace.edu/cisg/biblio/ulr96.html>.

[3] *See* van der Velden, "The Law of International Sales: The Hague Conventions 1964 and the UNCITRAL Uniform Sales Code 1980 – Some Main Items Compared," in Voskuil & Wade eds., *Hague-Zagreb Essays* 4 (The Hague: Asser Instituut/Martinus Nijhoff, 1983), at 64–65 (suggesting the employment of the detriment definition given by the *Corpus Iuris Secundum*, according to which "the detriment need not be real and involve actual loss, nor does it necessarily refer to material disadvantage to the party suffering it, but means a legal detriment as distinguished from a detriment in fact. It has also been defined as giving up something which one had the right to keep, or doing something which one had the right to do.")

or Russian versions of detriment[4] nor the Secretariat Commentary on the 1978 Draft Convention provides any greater assistance in this respect. The latter states, "The determination whether the injury is substantial must be made in the light of the circumstances of each case, *e.g.*, the monetary value of the contract, the monetary harm caused by the breach, or the extent to which the breach interferes with other activities of the injured party."[5] It seems that the detriment element serves as a mere *filter* for those cases in which breach of a fundamental obligation occurred but has caused no injury. For example, where the seller fails in his duty to package or insure the goods but they arrive safely, there is no detriment. If, on the other hand, the buyer lost a customer or the opportunity to resell the goods, there would be a detriment.[6]

2. Substantial Deprivation

A breach must cause a detriment that "substantially deprives" the aggrieved party of what he is "entitled to expect under the contract" for it to be fundamental. The reference to the expectation *under the contract* makes clear that the yardstick for breach of contract is first and foremost to be found in the express and implied terms of the contract itself. This reference leaves open the question of whether other circumstances of the case, including the negotiations, trade practices established between the parties, usages, and any subsequent conduct of the parties, should also be taken into account. Moreover, it is unclear when a breach substantially deprives the aggrieved party of his expectations. Is a party, for instance, substantially deprived when he has completely lost his interest in the performance? Or does substantial deprivation require that the aggrieved party's purpose in entering the contract be "frustrated" or the benefit of the bargain be lost due to the breach? Is the monetary injury or harm suffered by the non-breaching party decisive? Literal interpretation does not provide answers to any of these questions.[7]

3. Foreseeability

a. Function of this Requirement

From the wording of the conditional clause, "unless the party in breach did not foresee and a reasonable person of the same kind in the same circumstances would not have foreseen such result," one may infer that there is a requirement of foreseeability of the consequences of the breach. It thus confirms the opinion of many scholars that

[4] The French version uses the word "*préjudice*," the Spanish "*perjuicio*," and the Russian "*bpeg*." The English, French, Russian, and Spanish versions are available online at <http://www.uncitral.org/en-index.htm>.

[5] *See* Commentary on the Draft Convention on Contracts for the International Sale of Goods prepared by the Secretariat, Document A/Conf.97/5 (Secretariat Commentary), at Comment 3, Art. 23 of the 1978 Draft Convention [which became CISG Article 25]. Available online at <http://cisgw3.law.pace.edu/cisg/text/secomm/secomm-25.html>.

[6] *See* Will, "Art. 25," Comment 2.1.1.2, in Bianca & Bonell eds., *Commentary on the International Sales Law, The 1980 Vienna Sales Convention* (Milan: Giuffrè 1987); for a similar notion, *see* Liu, "Remedies for Non-Performance: Perspectives from CISG, UNIDROIT & PECL, at 7.2 and 8.2.2.1," available online at <http://cisgw3.law.pace.edu/cisg/biblio/chengwei.html#07–2> and <http://cisgw3.law.pace.edu/cisg/biblio/chengwei.html#08–1>; Gonzalez, "Remedies under the U.N. Convention for the International Sale of Goods," 2 *Int'l Tax & Bus. L.* (1984) 79, at 86 (stating that the "Convention's definition of fundamental breach makes it possible to reconcile the interests of the parties in cases where an insignificant deviation from the contract produces surprising and serious consequences"); Mark L. Ziontz, "A New Uniform Law for the International Sale of Goods: Is It Compatible with American Interests?," *Nw. J. Int'l. L. & Bus.* (1980) 129, at 173 (stating that "[a]voidance of an international sales contract is a remedy reserved for serious breaches by one of the parties").

[7] *See* Koch, "The Concept of Fundamental Breach of Contract under the United Nations Convention on Contracts for the International Sale of Goods (CISG)", *Pace Review of the Convention on Contracts for the International Sale of Goods* (Cisg) 1998, Kluwer Law International (1999), at 263–264; also available online at <http://cisgw3.law.pace.edu/cisg/biblio/koch.html>.

foreseeability is not only a burden of proof rule but also requires taking into account the breaching party's knowledge or foreseeability of the harsh consequences of the breach in determining whether or not it is fundamental.[8] On the other hand, the foreseeability requirement under Article 25 CISG has a similar effect as the foreseeability requirement under the general rule for calculation of damages in Article 74 CISG, because it limits the rights of the aggrieved party in the event the other party did not foresee the far-reaching consequences and helps determine the severity of the breach.[9] It therefore seems plausible to conclude that only the detriment/substantial deprivation component is what makes a breach "fundamental" and that the foreseeability element serves solely to exempt the breaching party from his liability for breach of the contract.[10]

b. Reasonable Person Test

Another ambiguity results from the phrase "*and* a reasonable person of the same kind in the same circumstances."[11] To determine foreseeability, the subjective and objective perspective of the party in breach must be considered. Additionally, the objective perspective of the reasonable merchant in the breaching party's position is relevant.[12] In other words, the party in breach is considered to have been able to foresee the consequences of the breach if, when objectively viewed, it is determined that he could or should have known them. But what happens when the breaching party had special knowledge and thus could have foreseen more than the average merchant? The conjunction "and" makes it possible to conclude that such special knowledge cannot be taken into account, allowing the breaching party to escape a finding of fundamental breach by hiding behind the paradigm of the reasonable person of the same kind in the same circumstances.[13]

c. Relevant Point in Time

Finally, the text of Article 25 CISG does not expressly address the point in time at which the foreseeability standard is to be applied. The use of the present tense "[a] breach of contract committed . . . is fundamental if it results" in depriving the other party "of what he is entitled to expect under the contract" makes it possible to conclude that a judge should place himself at the time the breach of contract occurred.[14] Likewise, where Article 25 CISG states "unless the party in breach did not foresee . . . such a result" it would appear

[8] *See, e.g.*, Schlechtriem, "Art. 25," Comment 11, in: Schlechtriem ed., *Commentary on the U.N. Convention on the International Sale of Goods* (Clarendon Press: Oxford 1998), (stating that knowledge or foreseeability of the aggrieved party's expectations is relevant for interpreting and assessing the importance of the obligation breached and its significance for the aggrieved party); *see* also Enderlein & Maskow, *International Sales Law* (New York: Oceana 1992), "Art. 25," Comment 4.1.

[9] *See* Enderlein & Maskow, *supra* note 8, at 4.1 (emphasizing that the special circumstances make up the severity of the breach).

[10] For this conclusion, see Babiak, "Defining 'Fundamental Breach' under the United Nations Convention on Contracts for the International Sale of Goods," 6 *Temple Int'l & Comp. L.J.* (1992) 113, at 118; Graffi, *supra* note 2, at 340; for a different conclusion, see Liu, *supra* note 5, at 8.2.3.1.

[11] Emphasis added.

[12] For the same conclusion *see* Babiak, *supra* note 10, at 118; Grigera Naón, "The U.N. Convention on Contracts for the International Sale of Goods," in Horn/Schmitthoff eds., *The Transnational Law of International Commercial Transactions: Studies in Transnational Economic Law* (Deventer: Kluwer 1982), 89, at 105 (stating that the decisive test can only be an objective one and that the judge will therefore have to analyze objectively the position of the non-performing party); Will, *supra* note 6, Art. 25, Comment 2.2.2.2.4; Enderlein & Maskow, *supra* note 8, Art. 25, Comment 4.2.

[13] For a similar conclusion, *see* Chengwei Liu, *supra* note 6, at 8.2.3.2; for a different conclusion, *see* Enderlein & Maskow, *supra* note 8, Art. 25, Comment 4.2; Will, *supra* note 6, Art. 25, Comment 2.2.2.2.4 (stating that "an overly astute merchant [who] in fact knew and foresaw more than his peers should not be allowed to hide behind the reasonable person of the same kind in the same circumstances").

[14] This point has been emphasized by Levasseur, "The Civil Code of Quebec and the Vienna Convention on International Contracts for the Sale of Goods: Some Comments," in Canadian Institute for Advanced Legal Studies ed., *Nouveau Code Civile* (Cowansville, Québec: Yvon Blais 1992), 269, at 282.

that one should be placed at the time of the breach.[15] The French, Spanish, and Russian texts of Article 25 CISG, however, give rise to a different conclusion. The use of the past tense *"était"* instead of *"est," "tenia"* instead of *"tiene,"* and *"byla"* instead of *"yest"* in the French, Spanish, and Russian texts, respectively, conveys the impression that the formation of the contract is the relevant point in time to determine foreseeability.[16] This view is confirmed by the reference to the rights that the aggrieved party was entitled to expect *under the contract*.[17]

III. CONCEPT OF FUNDAMENTAL NON-PERFORMANCE UNDER UNIDROIT PRINCIPLES

1. Article 7.3.1(2) of the UNIDROIT Principles

The concept of fundamental non-performance is laid down in Article 7.3.1(2) of the UNIDROIT Principles. According to this provision "[a] party may terminate the contract where the failure of the other party to perform an obligation under the contract amounts to a fundamental non-performance." With regard to the *detriment/substantial deprivation* requirement, the UNIDROIT Principles provide a more express guideline than does Article 25 CISG as to which factors are relevant in determining fundamental non-performance. In addition to the general criterion laid down in Article 25 CISG (i.e., the fact that the non-performance must substantially deprive the aggrieved party of what it was entitled to expect under the contract, provided the other party could not reasonably have foreseen such a result), paragraph (2) of Article 7.3.1 of the UNIDROIT Principles indicates further factors to be taken into account in each single case:

> [...] (b) strict compliance with the obligation which has not been performed is of essence under the contract;
>
> (c) the non-performance is intentional or reckless;
>
> (d) the non-performance gives the aggrieved party reason to believe that it cannot rely on the other party's future performance;
>
> (e) the non-performing party will suffer disproportionate loss as a result of the preparation or performance if the contract is terminated.[18]

2. Article 7.1.4 of the UNIDROIT Principles

Another relevant factor results from Article 7.1.4(1) of the UNIDROIT Principles. According to this provision, the buyer's right to terminate is suspended provided that (a) the seller, without undue delay, gives notice indicating the proposed manner and timing of the cure; (b) cure is appropriate in the circumstances; (c) the aggrieved party has no legitimate interest in refusing cure; and (d) cure is effected promptly.

Moreover, according to Article 7.1.4(2) of the UNIDROIT Principles, the seller's right to cure is not precluded by notice of termination. In other words, the buyer cannot

[15] *Id.*, at 282.

[16] With regard to the French text of Article 25, this point has been emphasized by Levasseur, *id.*, at 282.

[17] For the same conclusion, *see, e.g.*, Schlechtriem, *Uniform Sales Law: The UN Convention on Contracts for the International Sale of Goods* (Vienna: Manz 1986), at 60. For a different conclusion, *see* Flechtner, "Remedies under the New International Sales Convention: The Perspective from Article 2 of the U.C.C.", 8 *J.L. & Com.*, pp. 53–108, fn. 114 (1988), also available online at <http://cisgw3.law.pace.edu/cisg/biblio/flecht.html>. He argues that if, after the formation of the contract, it becomes clear that a failure to perform will cause substantial detriment, nothing in the text of Art. 25 CISG prevents such failure to perform up to this expectation from being a fundamental breach. *See* also Graffi, *supra* note 2, at 340 (relying on the general principle of good faith); Liu, *supra* note 6, at 8.2.3.3.

[18] To date no cases have been reported in which tribunals have applied Article 7.1.3(2) of the UNIDROIT Principles.

exercise his right of termination for the purpose of denying the seller an opportunity to cure. Under the UNIDROIT Principles, therefore, curability is, *de facto*, a relevant criterion in determining whether or not non-performance is fundamental.[19]

IV. PERMISSIBILITY OF USING THE CRITERIA EMPLOYED BY ARTICLES 7.3.1(2) AND 7.1.4(1) OF THE UNIDROIT PRINCIPLES IN DETERMINING FUNDAMENTAL BREACH

According to Article 7(1) CISG, "[i]n the interpretation of this Convention regard is to be had to its international character and to the need to promote uniformity in its application [. . .]". Because the UNIDROIT Principles are also of an international character, it seems permissible to make use of them as a means of interpreting the CISG, provided that the relevant provisions of the UNIDROIT Principles serve the same purpose as their corresponding provisions in the CISG and that they are in conformity with the rules of interpretation under the CISG.[20] These rules, which can also be regarded as general principles in terms of Article 7(2) CISG, require first and foremost taking account of the plain text of a provision.[21] If the wording is vague, as with Article 25 CISG, the literal interpretation must be supported by other methods of interpretation, namely looking at the provision's legislative history, its context within the CISG's remedial system, its objectives, and underlying policies.[22]

1. Identical Underlying Purpose of Article 25 CISG and Article 7.3.1 of the UNIDROIT Principles

By allowing avoidance/termination of the contract only when the breach/non-performance qualifies as "fundamental," Article 25 CISG and Article 7.3.1 of the UNIDROIT Principles follow the same policy, namely to preserve the enforceability of the contract whenever feasible.[23] The first condition for making use of the criteria set forth by the UNIDROIT Principles is thus fulfilled.

[19] *See* Koch, *supra* note 7, at 232.

[20] *See* Felemegas, "The United Nations Convention on Contracts for the International Sale of Goods: Article 7 and Uniform Interpretation," in *Pace Review of the Convention on Contracts for the International Sale of Goods (CISG)*, Kluwer Law International (2000–2001) 115–265, at Chapter 4, 6(b), also available online at <http://cisgw3.law.pace.edu/cisg/biblio/felemegas.html#ch4>; Garro, "The Gap Filling Role of the UNIDROIT Principles in International Sales Law: Some Comments on the Interplay between the Principles and the CISG," 69 *Tul. L .Rev.* (1995) 1149, at 1157 and 1185 (stating that "the UNIDROIT principles may be resorted to in order to determine whether or not there has been a fundamental breach of contract"); Perillo, "UNIDROIT Principles of International Commercial Contracts: The Black Letter Text and a Review," 63 *Fordham L. Rev.* (1994) 281, at 308–309; Bonell, *supra* note 2 (suggesting that the criteria laid down in article 7.3.1 of the UNIDROIT Principles may be used for a better understanding of Art. 25).

[21] *See* Koch, *supra* note 7, at 194; Enderlein, "Uniform Law and Its Application by Judges and Arbitrators," in UNIDROIT ed., *International Uniform Law Practice* (New York: Oceana 1988) 329–353, at 331; van der Velden, *supra* note 3, at 24; and Diedrich, "Maintaining Uniformity in International Uniform Law via Autonomous Interpretation: Software Contracts and the CISG," 8 *Pace Int'l L.Rev.* (1996) 303, at 328, also available at <http://cisgw3.law.pace.edu/cisg/biblio/Diedrich.html>.

[22] *See* Honnold, *Uniform Law for International Sales under the 1980 United Nations Convention* (3rd ed., Kluwer 1999), at § 103.2; Koch, *supra* note 7, at 192 *et seq*.

[23] *See* Koch, supra note 7, at 334; Hillman, "Applying the United Nations Convention on Contracts for the International Sale of Goods: The Elusive Goal of Uniformity," in *Review of the CISG, Cornell Law Review* (1995) 21–49 C.1 (stating that the Convention's goal of saving deals promotes important international values pertinent to the contracting process), online available at <http://cisgw3.law.pace.edu/cisg/biblio/hillman1.html>; Audit, "The Vienna Sales Convention and the *Lex Mercatoria*," in *Lex Mercatoria and Arbitration* (Carbonneau ed., 1990), 173, at 183; the reprint of the 1990 edition of this text is also available online at <http://cisgw3.law.pace.edu/cisg/biblio/audit.html>; Dubé, "The Civil Code of Quebe and the Vienna Convention on International Contracts for the Sale of Goods," in Canadian Institute for Advanced Legal Studies ed., *Nouveau Code Civile* (Cowansville, Québec: Yvon Blais 1992) 205, at 219; and Magnus, "The General Principles of the CISG," 3 *Int'l Trade & Bus. L.A.* (1997) 33–56, at Comment 9 (concluding from the fact that the Convention allows contract avoidance only under narrow conditions and as a last resort, that the *favor*

2. Conformity of the Criteria with the CISG's Rules on Interpretation?

With regard to the second condition, a differentiation between the various factors to be considered in determining the fundamental nature of a non-performance is necessary.

a. Strict Compliance and No-Reliance

The reference in Article 25 CISG to the expectations under the contract allows resorting to the criteria focusing on the *nature of the contractual obligation* (Art. 7.3.1(2)(b) of the UNIDROIT Principles)[24] and the *reliance* on one party's future performance (Art. 7.3.1(2)(d) of the UNIDROIT Principles)[25] in determining fundamental breach.[26]

b. Intentional or Reckless Non-Performance

No use can be made of the factor focusing on whether the breach was committed *intentionally* or *recklessly* (Art. 7.3.1(2)(d) of the UNIDROIT Principles). Although it is true that the wording of Article 25 CISG does not prevent the determination of the fundamental nature of a breach by taking into account the breaching party's intent or conduct, it should be noted that under the CISG, "fault" is not generally a prerequisite to a finding of contractual liability. In addition, this principle is as true with respect to the right to avoid the contract as it is to the right to require substitute delivery or to claim damages. Neither remedy depends on "fault" in the sense of deliberate or negligent wrongdoing. In light of the CISG's remedial system, it therefore seems to be more plausible not to automatically qualify any intentional or reckless breach as fundamental in terms of Article 25 CISG.[27] The intention of the breach can be only taken into account where the willful or reckless conduct creates uncertainty as to the breaching party's future performance.[28]

c. Disproportionate Loss for the Party in Breach as Negative Requirement

The approach that focuses on whether the breaching party will suffer disproportionate loss as a result of the preparation for performance if the contract is avoided (Art. 7.3.1(2)(e) of the UNIDROIT Principles) is not applicable under the CISG. First, the language of Article 25 CISG does not allow consideration of the consequences for the breaching party when the breach is treated as fundamental. Second, it is not clear under which circumstances a breaching party's loss becomes significant. Any determination of fundamental breach would therefore be arbitrary and cause uncertainty. Third, the UNIDROIT factor is aimed at limiting the exercise of the right of avoidance, not at determining fundamental breach. In other words, it limits the availability of the avoidance remedy in spite of the existence of a fundamental breach, but it does not prevent a breach from being fundamental.[29]

contractus rule is one of the Convention's general principle), also available online at <http://cisgw3.law.pace.edu/cisg/biblio/magnus.html>.

[24] For further references to cases where the courts found for fundamental breach where strict performance was of the essence of the contract, *see* Koch, *supra* note 7, at 236 *et seq*.

[25] For further references to cases where the courts found for fundamental breach because a party legitimately lost his faith and confidence in the other party's future performance *see* Koch, *supra* note 7, at 246–247.

[26] *See* Koch, *supra* note 7, at 266–267; for a similar conclusion, *see* Liu, *supra* note 6, at 8.3.1. and 8.3.3.

[27] *See* Koch, *supra* note 7, at 298; for a similar conclusion, *see* Liu, *supra* note 6, at 8.3.2.

[28] *See* Koch, *supra* note 7, at 267; for a similar conclusion, *see* Liu, *supra* note 6, at 8.3.2.; for a comparative analysis of Art. 25 CISG and the counterpart provisions in the Principles of European Contract Law, *see* Hossam El-Saghir, "Fundamental Breach: Remarks on the Manner in which the Principles of European Contract Law May Be Used to Interpret Or Supplement Article 25 CISG" (2000); available online at <http://cisgw3.law.pace.edu/cisg/text/peclcomp25.html#er>.

[29] *See* Koch, *supra* note 7, at 266; for a similar conclusion, *see* Liu, *supra* note 6, at 8.3.4.

3. Curability of the Breach

With regard to this factor, it is to be noted that in *industry practices* and the various *manufacturing, export and importing, retailing trades*, the right to cure defective goods is almost invariably reserved by the seller in the case of manufactured goods of substantial value (e.g., machinery, motor vehicles, and other hard goods).[30] In these cases, no recourse to the UNIDROIT principles is necessary. In the absence of such clauses, consideration of curability as a limiting factor in determining fundamental breach, in view of its present definition, is only permissible if one argues that, where cure of a breach is feasible and the breaching party is willing to cure, the aggrieved party is not substantially deprived of his expectations under the contract. Recent case law confirms that view.[31] With regard to the buyer's right to avoidance, such an interpretation, though plausible, seems hard to reconcile with the CISG's remedial provisions, in particular with the text of Article 48(1).

a. Relationship between Cure and Avoidance for Fundamental Breach

The opening words of Article 48(1) make the seller's right to cure "[s]ubject to Article 49." Giving these words their ordinary and plain meaning, it appears that the buyer's right to declare the contract avoided in accordance with Article 49(1)(a) prevails over the seller's right to cure.[32] The determination of fundamental breach in the light of any offer to cure, however, would enable the seller to prevent the buyer from avoiding the contract and would, therefore, actually allow the seller's right to cure to prevail over the buyer's right to avoid. Even if one argues that the opening words do not clarify their exact relationship, the position that the right to cure is paramount ignores the fact that the majority of the delegations at the Vienna Diplomatic Conference took the exact opposite view.[33]

[30] *See* Ziegel, "Commentary on 'Party Autonomy and Statutory Regulation: Sale of Goods," 6 *J. Cont. L.* North Ryde NSW, Australia (1993) 123, at 125–126 (referring to a Report on Sale of Goods, conducted by the Ontario Law Reform Commission that examined several dozen standard forms supplied by members of the Canadian Manufacturers' Association), available online at <http://www.cisg.law.pace.edu/cisg/biblio/ziegel4.html>.

[31] *See* relevant case law:

- Germany 14 October 2002 *Oberlandesgericht* [Appellate Court] Köln, case presentation including English translation available online at <http://cisgw3.law.pace.edu/cases/021014g1.html> (stating that "not only the weight of the defect, but also the preparedness of the seller to cure the defect without unacceptable delay and burden to the buyer is of importance")
- Switzerland 5 November 2002 *Handelsgericht* [Commercial Court] des Kantons Aargau, case presentation including English translation available online at <http://cisgw3.law.pace.edu/cases/021105s1.html> (stating with regard to the preservation of contract objective of the fundamental breach requirement that "as long as and so far as (even) a fundamental defect can still be removed by remedy or replacement, the fulfillment of the contract by the seller is still possible and the buyer's essential interest in the performance is not yet definitively at risk")
- Germany 27 February 2002 *Landgericht* [District Court] München, case presentation including English translation available online at <http://cisgw3.law.pace.edu/cases/020227g1.html> (denying fundamental breach because "this kind of defect and lack of compliance is in principle remediable through the removal of the defective motors")

[32] For a similar conclusion, *see* Ziegel, "The Remedial Provisions in the Vienna Sales Convention: Some Common Law Prespectives," in Galston/Smit eds., *International Sales* (New York: Matthew Bender 1984) ch. 9, at 22; Schnyder & Straub, in: Honsell ed., *Kommentar zum UN-Kaufrecht* [CISG commentary] (Berlin/Heidelberg/New York: Springer 1997), Art. 48, Comment 29; Graffi, *supra* note 2, at 343; Williams, "Forecasting the Potential Impact of the Vienna Sales Convention on International Sales Law in the United Kingdom," *Pace Review of the Convention on Contracts for the International Sale of Goods (CISG)*, Kluwer Law International (2000–2001), 9, at IV.C.3, also available online at <http://cisgw3.law.pace.edu/cisg/biblio/williams.html>.

Honnold, *supra* note 22, at § 296, takes a very different position. He argues, with reference to the legislative history, that the amendment to art 48(1) "leaves little room for doubt" that the right to cure is the paramount provision and that the cure provision of Art. 48(1) could be frustrated "by an unqualified application of article 49(1)."

[33] *See* United Nations Conference on Contracts for the International Sale of Goods, Official Records, U.N. Document No. A/Conf.97/19, (Vienna, 10 March–11 April 1980), at 341–43; Honnold, "The Studies,

b. Wording of Article 50 CISG

Another argument against the determination of fundamental breach in light of an offer to cure can be found in the text of Article 50 CISG, where it is expressly stated that the seller's right to cure prevails over the buyer's right to reduce the price. In view of such clear wording, it is plausible to conclude that if the delegates to the Diplomatic Conference had really wanted the right to cure to prevail over the right to declare the contract avoided, they would have used similar words either in Article 48 or 49 CISG.[34]

c. Doctrinal Reasons against Consideration of Curability

Furthermore, the employment of an offer to cure as a relevant factor in determining fundamental breach would cause both theoretical and practical problems.[35] The notion of an offer retrospectively frustrating the buyer's existing right of avoidance is difficult to justify in theory. As a practical matter, this approach gives rise to the question of whether the seller must make his offer to cure before the buyer makes his notice of avoidance. If priority were decisive, one would provoke a competition between buyer and seller and produce purely arbitrary results.[36] Ignoring that such competition in exercising a remedy should not be a consideration under law, it would also leave the seller in limbo as long as he does not know of the defect.[37]

d. Overriding Purpose of the Fundamental Breach Requirement

Notwithstanding such doctrinal concerns, it cannot be disputed that the *ratio legis* of Article 25 CISG clearly supports the consideration of curability for determining fundamental breach.[38] The concerns, expressed in my earlier writings against giving the teological interpretation overriding effect where other interpretive techniques lead to

Deliberations and Decisions That Led to the 1980 United Nations Convention with Introductions and Explanations," in *Documentary History of the Uniform Law for International Sales* (Deventer: Kluwer Law International 1989), at 562–64.

[34] *See* Koch, *supra* note 7, at 323.

[35] See Karollus, *UN-Kaufrecht: Vertragsaufhebung und Nacherfüllungsrecht bei Lieferung mangelhafter Ware*, ZIP 1993, 490, at 495; and Huber, in Schlechtriem (ed.), *supra* note 8, Art. 46, Comment 18 (both Karollus and Huber criticize the curability approach on the grounds that it enables the seller retrospectively to frustrate the buyer's right of avoidance); *see also* the critical comments by Will, *supra* note 6, Art. 48, Comment 3.2.2, where the author asks the question of whether there is any "need to resort to so unconvincing a construction" to protect the seller's right to cure by giving the following illustration: "Suppose that yesterday [the buyer] concluded that a certain breach was fundamental; today he is awaiting the seller's offer to cure – the very breach has changed its nature and become a non-fundamental one; and if tomorrow all hope vanishes – the breach is automatically re-converted into a fundamental breach. Fundamental – non-fundamental – from day to day does not allow for any legal certainty in international transactions."

[36] This point is rightly emphasized by Schnyder & Straub, *supra* note 32, Art. 49 Comment 26; and Karollus, *supra* note 35, at 495; for a different view, *see* Mullis, "Avoidance for Breach under the Vienna Convention; A Critical Analysis of Some of the Early Cases," in *Anglo-Swedish Studies in Law* (Andreas & Jarborg eds.), Lustus Forlag (1998), pp. 326–355, at 343, also available online at <http://cisgw3.law.pace.edu/cisg/biblio/mullis1.html>.

[37] For the same criticism, *see* Karollus, *supra* note 35, at 495.

[38] *See* supporting case law:

- Switzerland 5 November 2002 *Handelsgericht* [Commercial Court] des Kantons Aargau, case presentation including English translation available at <http://cisgw3.law.pace.edu/cases/021105s1.html> (stating that "an objective fundamental defect does not mean a fundamental breach of contract when the defect is removable and the seller agrees to remedy this defect without creating unreasonable delay or burden on the buyer")
- Germany 14 October 2002 *Oberlandesgericht* [Appellate Court] Köln, case presentation including English translation available online at <http://cisgw3.law.pace.edu/cases/021014g1.html> (stating that "[t]he remedy of avoidance shall only be available to the seller as the last resort to react to a breach of contract by the other party, which is so fundamental that it essentially deprives him of his positive interest")
- Germany 31 January 1997 Oberlandesgericht [Appellate Court] Koblenz; case presentation available at <http://cisgw3.law.pace.edu/cases/970131g1.html>

different results, still apply.[39] It seems to be contrary to the principle of uniform application to disregard the plain wording to give effect to what it deems the overriding purpose of a single provision.[40] In the context of the seller's right to cure a defect and the buyer's right to avoid the contract, however, it is to be noted that giving account for curability is not excluded by the wording of Article 25 CISG. It would therefore seem reasonable to make use of the criteria recited in Article 7.1.4(1) of the UNIDROIT Principles to deny fundamental breach where the requirements of this provision are met. To avoid the aforementioned theoretical and practical problems for the seller, the right to cure should be precluded by the notice of avoidance, as is the case with Article 7.1.4(2) of the UNIDROIT Principles.

[39] *See* Koch, *supra* note 7, at 204–205.

[40] For a similar reasoning and conclusion, *see* Magnus, "UN-Kaufrecht" [UN-Sales Law, article by article commentary – *in German*], in Staudinger, Julius von Staudingers *Kommentar zum Bürgerlichen Gesetzbuch mit Einführungsgesetz und Nebengesetzen* (13th ed., Berlin: Sellier/de Gruyter 1995), Art. 7, Comment 32; for a somewhat different conclusion, *see* Bonell in Bianca & Bonell, *supra* note 6, Art. 7, Comment 2.2.1 (stating that courts are expected to look whenever it is possible to the underlying purposes and policies of individual provisions as well as the Convention as a whole instead of sticking to their grammatical meaning).

Comparative analysis between the provisions of the CISG regarding notice requirements (Arts. 39 & 26) and the counterpart provisions of the UNIDROIT Principles and the PECL

Camilla Baasch Andersen

I. INTRODUCTION

Doctrinal writing and case law on the problems of giving notice abound where the CISG is concerned, whereas there are few reported problems with the PECL or UNIDROIT. It is one of the most popular areas of dispute as a proper notification is central to *any* remedial relief. The second opinion from the CISG Advisory Council[1] focuses on the requirements of examination and notification and contains an overview of the relevant case law on point.

CAVEAT on terminology: Any comparison of notice requirements under the PECL, UNIDROIT, and CISG will unearth a significant difference in terminology. The CISG

[1] CISG-AC Opinion no 2, "Examination of the Goods and Notice of Non-Conformity: Articles 38 and 39," 7 June 2004. Rapporteur: Professor Eric E. Bergsten, Emeritus, Pace University School of Law, New York; available online at <http://cisgw3.law.pace.edu/cisg/CISG-AC-op2.html>.

solely encompasses selected formalities concerning validity of contract (such as form of communication, form of contract: Art. 12), but sets most validity issues outside the sphere of application by way of Article 4(a). It thus does not concern itself with most cases in which the contract is not valid due to misrepresentation, threat, fraud, or a similar formality. It also uses the term "avoid" for termination and revocation as the only language of contract cancellation. In contrast, both the UNIDROIT Principles and the PECL refer to rescission by the term "avoid" and use "termination" for the equivalent of the CISG term "avoidance." This chapter uses CISG terminology and indicates where it is not used in the same manner in the UNIDROIT Principles and the PECL.

II. CISG VANTAGE POINT: *ALL* NON-CONFORMITIES REQUIRE SPECIFIC AND TIMELY NOTICE

Article 39 CISG requires notice for ALL non-conformities, and *in addition,* Article 26 CISG requires notice in case of avoidance specifying this remedy. Both must be given within a "reasonable time." A single notice can satisfy both requirements. The consequence of not giving a notice within a reasonable time is for Art. 26 that the contract cannot be avoided; for Art. 39 it is the complete loss of all remedies under the CISG, excepting the existence of a reasonable excuse under Art. 44 or the seller's bad faith or negligence under Art. 40 – the latter will only apply if notice is given within the two-year cut-off period in Article 39(2).

Both notices pose two problems. First, what is "reasonable time" (CISG Arts. 39 and 26? Second, what degree of particularity is required in "specifying the nature of the non-conformity" (CISG Art. 39) and/or providing a proper "declaration of avoidance" (CISG Art. 26)?

III. PECL AND UNIDROIT: *ONLY* AVOIDANCE ("TERMINATION") REQUIRES NOTICE

In the PECL and the UNIDROIT Principles, there are two immediate contrasts to the CISG approach.

First, because these two sets of principles also deal with the validity of contracts, they include notification requirements for rescission of contract in case of invalidity, which they both term "avoidance" (UNIDROIT Principles Art. 3.14 and PECL Art. 4.112).

Second, in contrast to CISG Art. 39, not all remedies in effect of breach require a formal notification under the PECL or UNIDROIT. However, the two counterpart instruments do contain requirements for notification of avoidance (CISG terminology) like CISG Art. 26 does, namely in PECL 9.303 and UNIDROIT 7.3.2.

The CISG equivalent to the notification requirements in the UNIDROIT Principles and the PECL is thus *not* Art. 39, but Art. 26. However, the notice provision in Art. 26 also requires that the conditions of Art. 39 be met, as no remedy can be exercised without a CISG Art. 39 notice. Note, however, that in the CISG regime a notice can serve as both Art. 26 and Art. 39 notice if it adequately meets the requirements for each provision; therefore, separate notices are not required. Thus, where a buyer wishes to avoid a contract based on a non-conformity of the goods, the situation is very similar under all three regulatory frameworks.

Interestingly, both sets of Principles do set out the timeliness of notification as "reasonable time" in line with the CISG time frames, but do not assist in the determination of how this reasonable time period is to be measured. Reasonableness, although understandably palatable and thus popular in modern drafting, is a very broad and flexible term that can be understood very differently. It permeates both sets of principles as well as the CISG, but it does not specifically define anything, leaving the practitioner with little by way of a yardstick with which to measure a time period (*see* Section VI, *infra*, on the issue of timeliness).

The official UNIDROIT commentary[2] contributes the following with regard to the reasoning behind Art. 7.3.2:

> Para. (1) of this article reaffirms the principle that the right of a party to terminate the contract is exercised by notice to the other party. The notice requirement will permit the non-performing party to avoid any loss due to uncertainty as to whether the aggrieved party will accept the performance. At the same time it prevents the aggrieved party from speculating on a rise or fall in the value of the performance to the detriment of the non-performing party.[3]

Although this commentary can be helpful in determining the need for a notification requirement and thus help indicate the necessity for speediness, it does not help define the concept of "reasonable time."

IV. FORM OF NOTICE

Extensions or embellishments of notice requirements are found in both UNIDROIT Principles Art. 1.9. and PECL Art. 1.303. These two provisions are remarkably similar in content, both providing that notice may be given by any "appropriate" means and that it is effective when reaching the addressee, with "reaches" defined as delivered to his business or mailing address or habitual residence. They also both define notice as a communication or declaration ("... of intention," according to UNIDROIT).

It seems unnecessary to restate these basic principles of offer and acceptance, common to all three regimes, especially for notice giving, and the fact that the CISG is commonly accepted to have the same rules for notices without such special codification would seem to render this regulating superfluous.

PECL Art. 1.303 contains a further embellishment of the distribution of risk for notices for non-performance that are delayed or altered in transit. Subsection (4) provides that such notices (including anticipatory non-performance), if dispatched properly, shall have effect as if they had arrived under normal circumstances. This curious special rule also seems superfluous, imposing a "mailbox rule" that is seen to apply to notices in other regulatory frameworks even without the inclusion of such a provision.

Although these provisions do embellish the concept of a notice to some extent, they *do not* help as guidelines for any further determination of the two main problems of notification, namely timeliness and specificity. There is – as of yet – very little case law available on the application of the corresponding PECL and UNIDROIT provisions to assist with a determination of these issues.

An overview of CISG case law on the form of notice can be found in Section 2 of the CISG Case Law annexed to the CISG Advisory Opinion 2.[4] Although there is no form requirement in the CISG for notice giving, one main problem is that oral/telephone notices are difficult to prove, and many cases concern notices that the buyer claims were given over the telephone. The burden of evidence of notice giving is clearly on the buyer, and if this cannot be proven, the judge will not allow the buyer to rely on the notice, which will result in the loss of a remedy (notwithstanding CISG Arts. 44 and 40).[5] It is worth noting that the no form requirement in the CISG prevents the requirements of

[2] Available online at <http://cisgw3.law.pace.edu/cisg/principles/uni26.html#official>.
[3] *Id.* Comment 1.
[4] Available online at <http://cisgw3.law.pace.edu/cisg/CISG-AC-op2.html>.
[5] *See* for examples of such cases:
- Germany 6 October 1995 *Amtsgericht* [Lower Court] Kehl, case presentation including English translation available online at <http://cisgw3.law.pace.edu/cisg/cases/951006g1.html>
- Germany 22 June 1995 *Landgericht* [District Court] Kassel; case presentation available at <http://cisgw3.law.pace.edu/cisg/cases/950622g1.html>
- Germany 23 May 1995 *Oberlandesgericht* [Appellate Court] Frankfurt case presentation including English translation available online at <http://cisgw3.law.pace.edu/cisg/cases/950523g1.html>

Arts. 39 and 26 from being met in a single notice if it specifies both the nature of the non-conformity and the intention to avoid (see Section VI, *infra*).

V. CASE LAW AND ISSUES OF NOTIFICATION

Because of the lack of cases involving the UNIDROIT and PECL, an analysis of these issues is solely based on the case law of the CISG.

1. Timeliness

Much has been written on the timeliness of notification under Art. 39 (which also includes Art. 26) of the CISG.[6] The immediate problem is that the time frame is so flexible and subject to different guidelines in its interpretation of "reasonable time." The time frame was meant to be flexible, determinable by the facts of the case in each instance, but this poses a problem for numerous systems of law that wish to form and apply a more tangible/rigid concept of time (primarily civil law systems). In Germany and Switzerland, attempts to introduce a generous "*grosszugige Monat*" guideline of an outside period of one month, determinable by the facts of the case to reduce it, have found some support.[7] In Austria, similar attempts to determine a more objective and rigid time frame of fourteen days have surfaced in case law.[8] The Swiss Courts have followed the German evolution of a one-month time frame in some cases.[9]

- Switzerland 9 September 1993 *Handelsgericht* [Commercial Court] Zürich, case presentation available at <http://cisgw3.law.pace.edu/cases/930909s1.html>

the latter clearly prescribes that the burden of proof for notice giving rests on the buyer.

[6] *See*, among many other sources, the CISG Advisory Council's second opinion, available at <http://cisgw3.law.pace.edu/cisg/CISG-AC-op2.html>. *See* also Camilla Baasch Andersen, "Reasonable Time in Article 39(1) of the CISG," in *Review of the Convention on Contracts for the International Sale of Goods* (Kluwer 1998) 66–176, available online at <http://cisgw3.law.pace.edu/cisg/biblio/andersen.html> and Peter Schlechtriem, "Commentary on Issues Associated with Article 39(1): Lack of Conformity Notice, Timeliness," January 2000 (commentary provided with online case presentation at <http://cisgw3.law.pace.edu/cisg/cases/991103g1.html>). A bibliography of scholarly writing on CISG Art. 39 is available at <http://cisgw3.law.pace.edu/cisg/text/e-text-39.html>.

[7] Introduced in the case

- Germany 8 March 1995 *Bundesgerichtshof* [Supreme Court], case presentation including English translation available online at <http://cisgw3.law.pace.edu/cisg/cases/950308g3.html>. The German Supreme Court's judgment also includes a reference to Swiss scholar Schwenzer's writing *in* von Caemmerer/Schlechtriem, *Kommentar zum Einheitlichen UN-Kaufrecht* (Commentary on the Uniform U.N. Law of Sales) 2nd ed., (in German).

Restated in many German cases since then, the latest reference in the *Bundesgerichtshof* [German Supreme Court] is

- Germany 3 November 1999 Supreme Court, case presentation including English translation available at <http://cisgw3.law.pace.edu/cisg/cases/991103g1.html>.

But restatements of this principle abound in German law at all instances; *see* for example:

- Germany 29 January 1996 *Amtsgericht* [Lower Court] Augsburg, case presentation available online at <http://cisgw3.law.pace.edu/cisg/cases/960129g1.html>
- Germany 2 July 2002 *Landgericht* [District Court] Saarbrücken, case presentation including English translation available at <http://cisgw3.law.pace.edu/cisg/cases/020702g1.html>
- Germany 26 May 1998 *Oberlandesgericht* [Appellate Court] Thüringer [Jena], case presentation including English translation available at <http://cisgw3.law.pace.edu/cisg/cases/980526g1.html>

[8] The "fourteen-day" principle was first introduced in

- Austria 15 October 1998 *Oberster Gerichtshof* [Supreme Court], case presentation including English translation available at <http://cisgw3.law.pace.edu/cisg/cases/981015a3.html>

and was recently restated in

- Austria 14 January 2002 *Oberster Gerichtshof* [Supreme Court], case presentation including English translation available at <http://cisgw3.law.pace.edu/cisg/cases/020114a3.html>

[9] *See* for instance Switzerland 30 November 1998 *Handelsgericht* [Commercial Court] Zürich case presentation available at <http://cisgw3.law.pace.edu/cisg/cases/981130s1.html>.

There is no clear way to define this time frame or the criteria that influence it. This definition is – although it ideally would not be – subject to the jurisdiction in question and its influences. Most scholars and jurisdictions are in favor of retaining the inherent flexibility of the provision to suit it to each case, with the determination of certain criteria for shortening/lengthening it. Some criteria for reducing the time frame in most circumstances include rapid deterioration of the goods (economic or physical),[10] or another reason why time would be of the essence between the parties (see also CISG Art. 9). If more rigid standards for the determination of reasonable time were to become universally accepted across the different jurisdictions, then it might be possible to look for guidelines in the PECL or the UNIDROIT Principles, but no such standards exist here.

There is, in the official UNIDROIT commentary, a not very helpful definition of "reasonable time":

> Reasonable time
> An aggrieved party who intends to terminate the contract must give notice to the other party within a reasonable time after it becomes or ought to have become aware of the non-performance (para. (2)).
> What is "reasonable" depends upon the circumstances. In situations where the aggrieved party may easily obtain a substitute performance and may thus speculate on a rise or fall in the price, notice must be given without delay. When it must make enquiries as to whether it can obtain substitute performance from other sources the reasonable period of time will be longer.[11]

And in Art. 1:302 of the PECL, "reasonable" is defined as follows:

> Under these Principles reasonableness is to be judged by what persons acting in good faith and in the same situation as the parties would consider to be reasonable. In particular, in assessing what is reasonable the nature and purpose of the contract, the circumstances of the case and the usages and practices of the trades or professions involved should be taken into account.[12]

The overall conclusion on timeliness of notification would seem to be that it is flexible, based on circumstances of the case, for the CISG as well as for the UNIDROIT time frames, with the exception of those CISG jurisdictions that have attempted to introduce

[10] Scholars emphasized this before the Convention even entered into force, *cf.* John Honnold, *Uniform Law for International Sales under the 1980 UN Convention* (Kluwer, 1982): "Considerations indicating the need for speed include the perishable nature of the goods . . . " The reality of this consideration is extended to economic perishability; *see* Germany 6 October 1995 Lower Court Kehl, (where the court emphasized the need for speed as the goods were seasonal); case presentation including English translation available at <http://cisgw3.law.pace.edu/cisg/cases/951006g1.html>.

[11] Comment 3, available online at <http://cisgw3.law.pace.edu/cisg/principles/uni26.html#official>.

[12] For the definition of reasonableness recited in the Principles of European Contract Law and references to reasonableness in continental and common law domestic rules, doctrine, and jurisprudence, go to <http://cisgw3.law.pace.edu/cisg/text/reason.html#def>, with further references, and PECL Article 1:302. Ole Lando & Hugh Beale eds., *Principles of European Contract Law: Parts I and II*, Kluwer Law International (2000) 126–128. To drive home the correlation between the PECL's definition of reasonableness and the evident same meaning of this term to CISG legislators when they used the concept either specifically or as a general principle of the uniform law they drafted, *see* <http://cisgw3.law.pace.edu/cisg/text/reason.html#over>.

Reasonableness is also regarded as a general principle of the CISG. *See* Albert *Kritzer*, "Overview Comments on Reasonableness," available online at :<http://cisgw3.law.pace.edu/cisg/text/reason.html> "Reasonableness is specifically mentioned in thirty-seven provisions of the CISG and clearly alluded to elsewhere in the Uniform Sales Law. Reasonableness is a general principle of the CISG." *See* also comments by Jelena Vilus, available online at <http://cisgw3.law.pace.edu/cisg/text/reason.html#vilus>.

more rigid guidelines. It is clear that such a jurisdictionally independent evolution of guidelines is an obstacle to applied uniformity of the CISG, but a reality nonetheless.

2. Specificity

The degree of specificity required under CISG Art. 26 is not overly controversial. It must be evident to a reasonable person (using the criteria of CISG Art. 8) that the notice in question must clearly express the aggrieved party's wish to avoid the contract as a remedy in consequence of a particular breach. Implied intentions to avoid can be permitted, but the implication must be very strong.

The specificity required under CISG Art. 39, however, is a different and far more controversial matter. The notice must sufficiently specify the nature of the non-conformity, meaning exactly what is wrong with the goods, thereby enabling the seller to determine a choice of action based on the notification and any request for relief. Some cases have applied this doctrine of specificity very harshly, cutting the buyer off from all relief where details of the non-conformity were lacking in the notice, even in a (strongly criticized) case where the language used to describe the non-conformity was an established phrase in the specific trade ("soft truffles" = worm ridden).[13]

Note that Art. 44 CISG may help provide an excuse for why no properly specific notice is given, but a successful excuse has yet to surface in the case law.

VI. CONCLUSION

In conclusion, a comparison of the texts of the notice requirements under the three regulatory frameworks discloses that, although structured differently, and with the major discrepancy of the CISG notice requirement for *all* exercising of remedies in Art. 39, the three sets of rules are very similar to one other.

Nevertheless, with the exception of the official commentaries, there is no aid to be found in either set of Principles that may be applied in interpreting the two issues of timeliness and specificity of notice under the Convention. These two major issues are not addressed in a helpful way, nor is there at the time of this writing any reported case law from these two regimes that could plausibly be used as an inspirational guideline for resolving the problems in other regimes.

[13] *See* Germany 24 January 1996 *Landgericht* [District Court] Bochum, case presentation including English translation available at <http://cisgw3.law.pace.edu/cisg/cases/960124g1.html>.

Delay or error in communications: Comparison between the provisions of CISG Article 27 and counterpart provisions of the UNIDROIT Principles and the PECL

Chengwei Liu

I. FORM OF NOTICE

For the purpose of this comparative editorial, the "notices" discussed below cover the whole range of notices, declarations and other communications.[1]

a. As for the form of the notice, the CISG is silent on whether the notice must be in writing or can be presented orally. Although one may submit that Art. 27 does not include a rule for oral declarations,[2] it seems more appropriate to conclude from the Convention's "informality principle," as contemplated in Art. 11,[3] that generally there are no formal requirements for the notice under the Convention and it can be oral or written. This "informality principle" regarding the notice is clearly adopted under each of the two sets of Principles: in Art. 1.9(1) of the UNIDROIT Principles of International Commercial Contracts and PECL Art. 1:303(1), respectively. In other words, it is the principle that notices or any other kinds of communication of intention (declarations, demands, requests, etc.) required by individual provisions of the two sets of Principles are not subject to any particular requirement as to form, but may be given by any means appropriate in the circumstances.[4] However, this informality principle does not apply if the contract, usages, or practices provide otherwise.[5]

b. On the other hand, it would not be consistent with good faith and fair dealing for a party to rely on, for instance, a purely casual remark made to the other party. The comments to the PECL provide,"For notices of major importance written form may be appropriate."[6] As an example, although notice by telephone may suffice, it can be harder to prove than written notice. Particular care will have to be taken when choosing the means for communication of such an important decision like avoidance. All the three texts require that the notice be given by means *appropriate in/to the circumstances*. Which means are appropriate will depend on the actual circumstances of the case, in particular on the availability and the reliability of the various modes of communication and the importance and/or urgency of the message to be delivered. Thus, if the postal service is unreliable, it

[1] The "notices" include under the Convention Part II declarations *any notice, request, or other communication* given or made by a party in accordance with Part III (CISG Art. 27); under the UNIDROIT Principles *a declaration, demand, request or any other communication of intention* (UPICC Art. 1.9(4)); under the PECL, *the communication of a promise, statement, offer, acceptance, demand, request or other declaration* (PECL Art. 1:303(6)).

[2] For instance, Schlechtriem states in this respect: "Unfortunately, Article 27 does not include a rule for oral declarations. The wording – 'transmission of the communication' and 'failure to arrive' – makes it clear, however, that the Article refers only to messages transmitted by means similar to correspondence. On the basis of Article 7, it can be assumed that an oral declaration must be intelligible to those present or on the telephone; a statement that is not intelligible or not perceptible to the addressee has not been communicated by appropriate means." Peter Schlechtriem, *Uniform Sales Law – The UN-Convention on Contracts for the International Sale of Goods*, Manz: Vienna (1987) fn. 14, p. 62. Available online at <http://cisgw3.law.pace.edu/cisg/biblio/schlechtriem-27.html>.

[3] CISG Art. 11 reads: "A contract of sale need not be concluded in or evidenced by writing and is not subject to any other requirement as to form. It may be proved by any means, including witnesses."

[4] *See* Comment 1 on Art. 1.9 UNIDROIT Principles.

[5] Furthermore, it is to be noted that eight States, including China, made declarations under CISG Art. 96 rejecting provisions of CISG that allowed effective notification in form other than in writing (e.g., Arts. 11, 12, and 96). For online identification of declarations, *see* <http://www.uncitral.org/english/status-e.htm>. It is also to be noted that the "informality principle" has been clearly adopted by the new China Contract Law (e.g., Art. 10).) Nonetheless, even when Contracting States make use of the reservation in Art. 96, domestic requirements on form are only to be regarded as far as they relate to the formation of the contract, its modification, or consensual termination. The precise formulation contained in Arts. 12, 29, and 96 – "its modification or termination by agreement" – makes it clear that a one-sided declaration to terminate a contract does not fall within the scope of the reservation and the corresponding domestic regulations on form. Schlechtriem, *supra* note 5, at 45.

[6] *See* Comment and Notes to the PECL Art. 1:303. Comment B. Available online at <http://cisgw3.law.pace.edu/cisg/text/peclcomp27.html>.

might be more appropriate to use fax, telex, or other forms of electronic communication for a communication that has to be made in writing or to use the telephone if an oral communication is sufficient. In choosing the means of communication, the sender must as a rule take into account the situation that exists both in his own and in the addressee's country.[7]

c. In short, notices may be made in any form – orally, in writing, by telex, by fax, or by e-mail, for example – provided that the form of notice used is appropriate to the circumstances.[8] A communication is appropriate in the circumstances if it is appropriate to the situation of the parties. However, a means of communication that is appropriate in one set of circumstances may not be appropriate in another set of circumstances.[9] On the other hand, more than one means of communication may be appropriate in the circumstances. In such a case, the sender may use the one that is the most convenient for him.[10]

II. THE CISG APPROACH

d. A number of scholars interpret the rule in Art. 27 CISG as an acceptance of the dispatch theory. Without reference to the veracity of such a proposition, it can never be concluded that Art. 27 establishes the general dispatch principle for the whole CISG. First, Art. 27 only applies to Part III of the CISG. Unlike the declarations covered in Part III, Part II declarations are, for the most part, expressly regulated under the receipt theory.[11] Second, Part III of the Convention contains exceptions to this rule in cases where it was considered that communication ought to be received to be effective (Official Records [O.R.], 27).[12] As clarified by the Secretariat Commentary, the general rule in Art. 27 that the risk of delay, error, or loss of a communication is to be borne by the addressee arises out of the consideration that it is desirable to have, as far as possible, one rule governing the hazards

[7] Comment 1 on Art. 1.9 UNIDROIT Principles [8] Comment and Notes to the PECL Art. 1:303.

[9] For example, even though a particular form of notice may normally be sent by airmail, in a given case the need for speed may make only electronic communication, telegram, telex, or telephone a means appropriate "in the circumstances." *Infra.* note. 10, Comment 2. For guidance on Electronic Communications under CISG, *see* CISG-AC Opinion no. 1. Available online at <http://cisgw3.law.pace.edu/cisg/CISG-AC-op1.html>.

[10] *See* Secretariat Commentary on Art. 25 of the 1978 Draft *[counterpart of* CISG *Art. 27]*, Comment 3. Available online at <http://cisgw3.law.pace.edu/cisg/text/secomm/secomm-27.html>.

[11] In Part II of the CISG, the legal effectiveness of an offer under Article 15(1) and the legal effectiveness of an acceptance under Article 18(2) are tied to the moment of receipt as defined in Article 24. The same rule applies to the withdrawal of an offer (Article 15(2)), the rejection of an offer (Article 17), a declaration fixing a period of time for acceptance of an offer (Article 20(1)), and the withdrawal of an acceptance (Article 22). *Infra* note 15. Article 16(1) is an exception; it turns on the common law "mailbox rule": an offeror may not revoke an offer once the offeree has dispatched his acceptance.

[12] Such exceptions to Art. 27 in Part III are contained in Article 47, paragraph 2, and Article 63, paragraph 2, in which receipt of a notice is actually already a condition for the activities of the other party caused by it; Article 48, paragraph 2, Article 65, paragraphs 1 and 2, and Article 79, paragraph 4. *See* Fritz Enderlein & Dietrich Maskow, *International Sales Law: United Nations Convention on Contracts for the International Sale of Goods*, Oceana Publication (1992), p. 119. Available online at <http://cisgw3.law.pace.edu/cisg/biblio/enderlein.html>. Schlechtriem also states similarly but in more detail as the following: "Part III of the CISG contains five articles which tie the legal effectiveness of a contract to the receipt of a buyer's or seller's notice. Under Article 47(2), a seller's notice that he will not perform within the period fixed by the buyer becomes effective upon receipt of this notice. Similarly under Article 63(2), the legal effectiveness of a buyer's notice that he will not perform within the period fixed by the seller also becomes effective upon such receipt. The same rule applies to (1) the seller's request for clarification or notice that the buyer will perform within a specified timed; (2) the seller's request that the buyer supply missing specifications and the seller's notice to the buyer that he will supply such specifications if buyer fails to do so; and (3) the notice of an impediment and its effect upon a party's ability to perform." *Infra* note. 15.

of transmission.[13] One advantage of the rule is that at least a clear and unequivocal solution has been found for this question, which was generally left open by ULF and ULIS.[14]

e. The theory of dispatch would be useful where a party fulfilled an obligation or required remedy for a loss and not, however, where it served to substantiate an obligation for the other party (O.R., 303). Thus, under the Convention, as with most Part II declarations on offer and acceptance, the legal effectiveness of Part III declarations regulated under Articles 47(2), 48(4), 63(2), 65(1), 65(2), and 79(4) is tied to the moment of receipt. One way to treat these declarations is to rule not only that the declaring party is bound from the moment that his declaration is received but also to allow him to withdraw or change his declaration up until this moment.[15] However, on the other hand, it was believed that acceptance of a generalized receipt theory would have required that the Convention contain supporting procedural rules to establish whether a notice had in fact been received by the addressee; this is because legal systems that operated on the theory that notices were effective on dispatch often did not contain such supporting rules.[16] As a result, it is not very clear whether a general dispatch or a general receipt has been established under the Convention.

III. THE *RECEIPT* PRINCIPLE AS A GENERAL RULE

f. By contrast with the CISG's ambiguity with regard to the general principle, both the UNIDROIT Principles (UP) and the PECL adopt the receipt principle as a general rule. UP Art. 1.9(2) stipulates that "*[a] notice is effective when it reaches the person to whom it is given.*" Similarly, Art. 1:303(2) PECL states pertinently that "*any notice becomes effective when it reaches the addressee.*" It is important in relation to the receipt principle to determine precisely when the communications in question "reach" the addressee. In this respect, both Art. 1.9(3) of the UNIDROIT Principles and PECL Art. 1:303(3) follow in substance the rule in CISG Art. 24.[17] In an attempt to define the concept, UNIDROIT Principles Art. 1.9(3) draws a distinction between oral and other communications. Oral communications "reach" the addressee if they are made personally to it or to another person authorized by it to receive them. Other types of communications "reach" the addressee as soon as they are delivered either to the addressee personally or to its place of business or mailing address. The particular communication in question need not come into the hands of the addressee. It is sufficient that it be handed over to an employee of the addressee authorized to accept it, be placed in the addressee's mailbox, or received by the addressee's fax, telex, or computer.[18] In other words, as confirmed by PECL Art. 1:303(3), it is not necessary that the notice should actually have come to the addressee's attention provided that it has been delivered to him in the normal way (e.g., a letter placed in his letter box or a message sent to his telex or fax machine).[19]

[13] *See* Secretariat Commentary on Art. 25 of the 1978 Draft *[counterpart of* CISG *Art. 27]*, Comment 4.
[14] Schlechtriem, *supra* note 5, at 61.
[15] *See* Peter Schlechtriem, "Effectiveness and Binding Nature of Declarations (Notices, Requests or Other Communications) under Part II and Part III of the CISG," in *Cornell Review of the Convention on Contracts for the International Sale of Goods* (1995), pp. 95–114. Available online at <http://cisgw3.law.pace.edu/cisg/biblio/schlecht.html>.
[16] Secretariat Commentary, *supra* note 13.
[17] CISG Art. 24 reads: "For the purpose of this Part [Part II] of the Convention, an offer, declaration of acceptance or any other indication of intention "reaches" the addressee when it is made orally to him or delivered by any other means to him personally, to his place of business or mailing address or, if he does not have a place of business or mailing address, to his habitual residence."
[18] *See* Comment 4 on Art. 1.9 UNIDROIT Principles. [19] *Supra.* fn. 6, Comment C.

g. A plain understanding of the receipt principle is that a party cannot rely on a notice sent to the other party unless and until the notice reaches that party.[20] The most practical importance of this receipt concept is the ability of the declaring party to withdraw or change his declaration at any time prior to the time of receipt. Accordingly, PECL Art. 1:303(5) expressly sets out, "*A notice has no effect if a withdrawal of it reaches the addressee before or at the same time as the notice.*" Without a similar counterpart, such a rule seems to be implied by the general receipt principle established in UNIDROIT Principles Art. 1.9(2). Similarly the risk of errors in the notice is normally placed upon the sender. However, the principle of good faith and fair dealing means that a party cannot complain that it has not received a notice or has not received it in time if it has deliberately evaded receiving it.[21] On the other hand, as the result of practices or usages, the dispatch rule can apply. Moreover, the parties are of course always free expressly to stipulate the application of the dispatch principle. This may be appropriate with respect to the notice a party has to give to preserve its rights in cases of the other party's actual or anticipated non-performance when it would not be fair to place the risk of loss, mistake, or delay in the transmission of the message on the former. This is all the more true if one bears in mind the difficulties that may arise at an international level in proving effective receipt of a notice.[22]

IV. THE *DISPATCH* PRINCIPLE FOR CASES OF DEFAULT

h. However, this rigid solution of UNIDROIT Principles Art. 1.9 might lead to some unreasonable situations. Particularly, many of the situations in which one party gives a notice to the other are ones in which the party to be notified is in default or it appears that a default is likely. Here it seems appropriate to put the risk of loss, mistake, or delay in the transmission of the message on the defaulting party, rather than on the aggrieved party.[23] It is to be mentioned that UNIDROIT Principles Art. 1.9 is optional and does not eliminate the application of party autonomy. The parties are therefore at liberty to set other requirements, such as dispatch for communications to be effective.[24] Nonetheless, such a solution is not sufficient, particularly in consideration of the complexity of international contracts. In this respect, CISG Art. 27 demonstrates merit and is persuasive, for example, in the case of a notice of defects, because the seller is responsible for ensuring that the quality of goods conforms to the contract. Such a persuasive solution as adopted in CISG Art. 27 is also followed by PECL Art. 1:303(4).[25] As mentioned above, the PECL adopts the receipt principle as a general rule. At the same time PECL Art. 1:303 links this general rule to two qualifications for the operative effect of communications, one of which is set out in PECL Art. 1:303(4).[26]

[20] *Id.*

[21] *Supra* note 19.

[22] *See* Comment 3 on Art. 1.9 UNIDROIT Principles.

[23] Comment and Notes to the PECL Art. 1:303, Comment. D.

[24] *See* Comment 3 on Art. 1.9 UNIDROIT Principles.

[25] It is to be mentioned again: either CISG Art. 27 or PECL Art. 1:303(4) is optional, and the parties are also at liberty to set other requirements, such as receipt for communications to be effective. Even absent explicit agreement, usages or practices established between the parties can modify the principle stated in CISG Art. 27 or PECL Art. 1:303(4).

[26] The dispatch principle thus applies to notices given under the following articles of the PECL 7:109 Property not accepted; 7:110 Money not accepted; 8:105 Assurance of performance; 8:106 Notice fixing additional time for performance; 9:102(3) Nonmonetary obligation (loss of right to specific performance); 9:301 Right to terminate the contract; 9:303 Notice of termination; and 9:304 Anticipatory non-performance. The dispatch rule does not apply to a notice that is to be given by the defaulting party (e.g., under Article 8:108(3)) or by a party that wishes to invoke hardship; *see* Article 6:111, or to an assurance of performance under 8:105(2). (*Supra* note 23.)

i. A notice subject to the general receipt principle takes effect when it is received. A notice subject to the dispatch principle may be effective even though it never arrives or is delayed, but it is not effective the moment it is dispatched. It would not be fair that even a non-performing party should be affected by a notice from a time at which it could not have known about it. Accordingly the notice takes effect only from the time at which it would normally have been received.[27] In other words, in the event of loss of the communication, effectiveness occurs at the hypothetical moment of receipt under normal circumstances.[28] Finally, it is to be noted that the dispatch principle will not apply if the means of notice was not appropriate in the circumstances. For instance, for the dispatch principle to apply, the means chosen must be fast enough. If great speed is needed, a letter sent by airmail may not be appropriate, and the sender may not rely on the fact that it was dispatched. It will be able to rely on it only if and when it arrives.[29]

[27] *Supra.* note. 6, Comment F.

[28] In a CISG case in which Schlechtriem participated as an expert witness on uniform sales law, the buyer declared avoidance of the contract, claiming that the machines he purchased produced an unacceptable amount of waste because of a malfunctioning electronic control system. The seller denied any non-conformity and rejected the buyer's declaration of avoidance (and his demand for repayment of the purchase price). More than three years of litigation followed. Taking into account the uncertainties of the lawsuit, the buyer mitigated his losses by repairing the machines himself. During the litigation, the court determined that the machines had not conformed to the contract when they were delivered and that this non-conformity amounted to a fundamental breach. The court also realized that the seller was in serious financial straits and would not be able to refund the purchase price or pay the damages caused by the breach of contract. To avoid having to return the machines and account to the seller for the benefits the buyer had derived from them in the meantime, the buyer revoked his declaration of avoidances. The buyer instead declared a reduction of the purchase price under Article 50, claiming restitution of only a part of the purchase price and additional damages. He was well aware that even this reduced demand would not be satisfied by the seller, but cut his overall losses by keeping the machines, which were now functioning more or less properly. The seller objected to the revocation of the declaration of avoidance. He agreed with a termination of the contract and asked for the machines to be returned to him. This case illustrates some of the practical reasons supporting a rule that permits the revocation of a declaration governed by Article 27 after the declaration has been dispatched. Although not relevant to this buyer, the theory that such declarations should at least remain ineffective prior to receipt makes sense. A declaration that avoids the contract or reduces the price should not occur before the other party has a chance to know the declaration and the change in the legal situation brought about thereby. Such a declaration is characterized as a "unilaterally shaping declaration" (*einseitige Gestaltungserklärung*). *Supra* note 15.

[29] *Supra* note 6, Comment E.

The right to require specific performance: Comparison between the provisions of the CISG (Arts. 28, 46, and 62) and counterpart provisions of the UNIDROIT Principles (Arts. 7.2.1–7.2.5)

John Felemegas

I. INTRODUCTION

In Part III entitled "Sale of Goods," the Convention provides and regulates the respective obligations and rights of the parties to an international sales contract governed by the CISG, including the remedies available to a party for breach by the other party of the latter's corresponding obligations (duties) arising under the Convention.[1]

In Chapter II, "Obligations of the Seller" (Art. 30), Sections I,"Delivery of the Goods and Handing over of Documents" (Arts. 31–34), and II, "Conformity of the Goods and Third Part Claims" (Arts. 35–44), the Convention sets forth the seller's obligations to the buyer. The buyer's remedies for the seller's breach of these obligations are set forth in Section III, "Remedies for Breach of Contract by the Seller" (Arts. 45–52).

In an exercise of structural, as well as substantive, equality between the parties to the contract, in Chapter III, "Obligations of the Buyer" (Art. 53), Sections I, "Payment of the Price" (Arts. 54–59), and II, "Taking Delivery" (Art. 60), the Convention sets forth the buyer's obligations to the seller. The seller's remedies for the buyer's breach of the corresponding obligations are set forth in Section III, "Remedies for Breach of Contract by Buyer" (Arts. 61–65).

The present analysis focuses on the right of a party to *require the other party to perform* his obligations to the former pursuant to the Convention's provisions (CISG Arts. 28, 46, and 62).

Under the regime of the UNIDROIT Principles, the counterpart provisions regarding the right of a party to require performance by the other party are set forth in Chapter 7, "Non-Performance," Section 2, "Right to Performance" (Arts. 7.2.1–7.2.5).

II. CISG ART. 28: SPECIFIC PERFORMANCE AND THE RULES OF THE FORUM

The legislative history of and subsequent commentary on CISG Art. 28 reveal the purpose of the provision, its scope, and the reason for its inclusion in the Convention as well as the compromises (semantic, substantive, and political) that it contains.[2]

The practical effect of CISG Art. 28 is to restrict in some cases an aggrieved party's general right,[3] which is granted pursuant to CISG Arts. 46 (buyer's

[1] The Convention further provides in Part III supplementary rules on remedies that are applicable to both parties, *see* Chapter V, "Provisions Common to the Obligations of the Seller and of the Buyer," Sections I, "Anticipatory Breach and Installment Contracts" (Arts. 71–73); II, "Damages" (Arts. 74–77); III, "Interest" (Art. 78); IV, "Exemptions" (Arts. 79–80); V, "Effects of Avoidance" (Arts. 81–84); and VI, "Preservation of the Goods" (Arts. 85–88).

[2] In preparing the Vienna Convention, the drafters of CISG Art. 28 generally followed its predecessor [Art. VII (1) of the 1964 Hague Convention, and Art. 16 of the Uniform Law on the International Sale of Goods (Ulis)]. *See* the Text of Secretariat Commentary on Art. 26 of the 1978 Draft [*draft counterpart of CISG Art. 28*], available online at <http://cisgw3.law.pace.edu/cisg/text/secomm/secomm-28.html#sec>. *See* also Bergsten E. E., "Subsequent Commentary on CISG Art. 28," *Les Ventes Internationales de Marchandises (Problèmes juridiques d' actualité)," Paris Economica* 1981, pp. 11–14; available online at <http://cisgw3.law.pace.edu/cisg/text/secomm/secomm-28.html#sub>.

[3] *See* Enderlein F. & Maskow D., *International Sales Law*, Oceana (1992), p. 122; also available online at <http://cisgw3.law.pace.edu/cisg/biblio/enderlein.html>:

> The CISG grants the obligee a *right to specific performance*. In the event of a breach of contract such right persists as long as there is no right to avoidance or it can be asserted alternatively instead of the latter

right)[4] and Art. 62 (seller's right)[5] to require *specific performance*[6] of the other party's obligation after a breach of contract by the latter.[7]

Although the regime of the Convention's remedies includes the general rules (CISG Arts. 46 and 62) that a party in breach may be compelled to perform his obligations, thus establishing the primacy of the remedy of specific performance under the Convention, it does not specify and instead leaves to the *domestic law of the forum* any *procedural* measures necessary to enforce the remedies available under the Convention.

The inclusion of CISG Art. 28 in the text of the Convention, carving out an exception from the general right of an obligee to require specific performance by a defaulting obligor,[8] is seen as a necessary compromise[9] that recognizes the historically divergent approaches in doctrine and civil procedure to *requiring performance*[10]

> (Art. 46, paragraph 1; Art. 62): The rights to delivery of substitute goods and to repair, respectively under certain restrictive conditions (Art. 46, paragraphs 2 and 3), constitute specific forms of the right to performance.

Enderlein & Maskow also note that there possibly exist in the Convention further, albeit indirect, *restrictions* of the right to specific performance, relating to the application of CISG Arts. 88(2) and 77.

Honnold J. O., *Uniform Law for International Sales*, Kluwer Law International, 3rd ed. (1999), at 225, also available online at <http://cisgw3.law.pace.edu/cisg/biblio/honnold.html>, notes that CISG Art. 28 permits deviation *only* from the rules of the Convention that *require performance* of a party's obligations and does not affect the Convention's *restrictions* on specific performance.

[4] CISG Art. 46(1) reads, "The buyer may *require performance* by the seller of his obligations [. . .]." *See* further analysis, Section III, *infra*.

[5] CISG Art. 62 reads, "The seller may *require* the buyer to pay the price, take delivery or perform his other obligations [. . .]." *See* further analysis, Section IV, *infra*.

[6] CISG Art. 28 may in certain cases restrict the obligee's right to *require specific performance* from the obligor, but it does not affect other remedies available under the Convention (e.g., avoidance (CISG Arts. 49 and 64), damages (Arts. 74–76), etc.). The *UNCITRAL Digest of Case Law* on CISG Art. 28, (A/CN.9/SER.C/DIGEST/CISG/28 [8 June 2004]), available online at <http://cisgw3.law.pace.edu/cisg/text/anno-art-28.html#ucd>, provides the following definition of *specific performance*:

> Para 2. "Specific performance" means that a party may require the other party to perform its obligations under the contract (and seek enforcement through court action).

[7] *See* Honnold (1999), *supra* note 3, at 218, where the author commences his analysis of the right *to require performance* in the following terms:

> [A] judicial "requirement" of performance [. . .], a type of remedy that in "common law" may be implemented by a judicial decree ordering "specific" performance. The scope of the remedy "requiring" (specific) performance was one of the most stubborn issues encountered in the preparation of the uniform rules. Article 28 [. . .] relaxes general rules on coerced performance that appear later in the Convention [*see* Arts. 46 and 62].

[8] The right of an obligee to require specific performance by the defaulting obligor of his contractual obligations is said to reflect a principle that has emanated from civil law theory. *See* Dawson J. P., "Specific Performance in France and Germany," 57 *Mich. L. Rev.* (1959) 495; Treitel G. H., *Remedies for Breach of Contract – A Comparative Account*, Oxford: Clarendon (1988), Ch. III. Note, however, that although the principle of specific performance is embedded in civil law theory, the frequency of invocation and enforcement of the remedy of specific performance in practice must not be overestimated. *See* Henrik Lando, "The Myth of Specific Performance in Civil Law Countries" (April 2004), *American Law & Economics Association Annual Meetings. American Law & Economics Association 14th Annual Meeting*. Working Paper 15; available online at <http://law.bepress.com/alea/14th/art15>. In that paper, the author argues that when breach involves the non-performance of an action (i.e., when performance cannot be ensured by the handing over of an existing good), specific performance is largely a myth in the three civil law countries of Denmark, France, and Germany. The paper provides evidence that suggests that a claim for specific performance of an action is, roughly speaking, not enforced in Denmark, weakly enforced in France, and though enforced in Germany, only rarely sought. According to the evidence presented in that paper, it is concluded that specific performance is largely irrelevant as a remedy for the non-performance of an action in civil law countries. Furthermore, the paper argues that the non-use of specific performance can be ascribed to the costs and difficulties of forcing the breaching party to perform an action.

[9] *See UNCITRAL Digest* on CISG Art. 28, *supra* note 6:

> Para 1. The article constitutes a compromise between legal systems that deal differently with the contractual right of a party to claim specific performance of the contract. According to article 28, a court is not obliged to grant specific performance under the Convention if it would not do so for similar sales contracts under domestic law.

[10] "Specific performance" in common law parlance. In common law systems, specific performance is granted only when alternative remedies (e.g., damages) are not adequate. *See, e.g.*, Piliounis P., "The Remedies of Specific Performance, Price Reduction and Additional Time (*Nachfrist*) under the CISG: Are These

under different legal systems – this view is shared by many commentators of the CISG.[11]

Thus, CISG Art. 28 provides that, if one party is entitled to require performance of an obligation by the other party (i.e., in accordance with CISG Arts. 46 and 62):

> [A] court is not bound to enter a judgment for specific performance unless the court would do so under its own law in respect of similar contracts of sale not governed by this Convention.

Essentially, CISG Art. 28 may be applied to determine whether an obligee can obtain the aid of a court to enforce the obligation of a defaulting obligor to perform the contract. Generally speaking, courts in legal systems that as a matter of doctrine and judicial procedure grant orders of specific performance should not be affected by the application of CISG Art. 28. On the other hand, the provision has more practical significance in jurisdictions that do not grant certain forms of specific performance.[12]

Thus, pursuant to CISG Art. 28, a court belonging to the latter category (e.g., common law system) is not bound[13] to require specific performance of the breaching party's

Worthwhile Changes or Additions to English Sales Law?," Cambridge University (September 1999), Section 4, available online at <http://cisgw3.law.pace.edu/cisg/biblio/piliounis.html>, where the author summarizes the traditional English law approach in the following succinct manner: "Under English law, granting specific performance of the terms of a contract is an extraordinary remedy, granted in very limited circumstances."

[11] For relevant commentary on point, *see* Honnold (1999), *supra* note 3, at pp. 219–220, and further references provided therein. *See* also Enderlein & Maskow, *supra* note 3, at 120–121:

> This provision [Art. 28] contains a *compromise* between the legal systems of the continental European countries and those countries which are influenced by their law, which generally provide for the right to performance, on the one hand, and the legal systems which are based on the common law, on the other [. . .]. The right to specific performance is granted in the common law countries only under particular conditions [references omitted].

[12] To illustrate the point, commentators usually refer to the divergences between common law and civil law doctrine and procedure: the enforcement of specific performance is extensive in civil law systems in order to uphold the *pacta sunt servanda* principle, whereas in common law systems it is more limited because damages are seen as the primary remedy for breach of contract; *see* Huber U., in Schlechtriem (ed.) *Commentary on the UN Convention on the International Sale of Goods*, Clarendon Press, Oxford, 1998, p. 199. *See* also Schlechtriem P., *Uniform Sales Law – The UN-Convention on Contracts for the International Sale of Goods*, Manz: Vienna (1986), at 62; also available online at <http://cisgw3.law.pace.edu/cisg/biblio/schlechtriem.html>, where the author states "Article 28 provides a procedural exception primarily tailored to suit the peculiarities of Anglo-American law, which does not generally provide the remedy of specific performance in the context of most sales contracts."

For a detailed examination of the remedy of specific performance under the CISG, accompanied by a comparative analysis of the remedy in the French Civil Code (representative of civil law systems) and the U.S. Uniform Commercial Code (representative of common law systems), *see* Boghossian N., "A Comparative Study of Specific Performance Provisions in the United Nations Convention on Contracts for the International Sale of Goods," *Pace Review of the Convention on Contracts for the International Sale of Goods*, Kluwer (1999–2000) 3–78; also available online at <http://cisgw3.law.pace.edu/cisg/biblio/boghossian.html>. *See* also Honnold (1999), *supra* note 3, at 225–228; Enderlein & Maskow, *supra* note 3.

[13] The expression "not bound" does not limit any rights to specific performance that may ensue from the proper application of the Convention's provisions. *See* Enderlein & Maskow, *supra* note 3, at 122, where the authors states that a court "*can* grant a right to specific performance in such events where it would *normally not do so*" [emphasis added]. "*See* also Honnold (1999), *supra* note 3, at 224–225, where the author states that the expression in question [I]ndicates that a court that would not "require" performance under its own law is free either to "require" performance or to apply other remedies provided by the Convention such as awarding damages under Article 74."

It has been further suggested that the proper application of CISG Art. 28 has an impact on *many* legal systems (civil law as well as common law systems) by generally ameliorating the effect of the Convention's rules requiring specific performance. *See* Honnold (1999), *supra* note 3, at 228, where the author concludes his analysis of CISG Art. 28 with the following remarks:

> Article 28, properly understood in the setting of domestic procedural systems, can mitigate the appearance of rigidity of the Convention's general rules on "requiring performance." Certainly it would be wrong to assume that there are only two rules: (1) Rigid rules of the civil law world, embodied in Articles 46(1) and 62, that call for coerced performance; (2) A more flexible approach under Article 28 applicable only to actions before "common-law" courts. The flexibility permitted under Article 28 is not confined to the procedural approach of one legal system. As Professor Treitel has shown, remedial law in many legal systems is less rigid than the "require performance" rule of the Convention [Treitel G. H., *Remedies for Breach of Contract – A Comparative Account*,

obligations under a contract governed by the Convention unless it *would*[14] do so under its *own* law[15] in respect of domestic contracts of sale.[16] Effectively, if the law of the forum would not grant specific performance in a domestic contract of sale (i.e., in accordance with domestic law of contract), the court is not bound to enter a judgment of specific performance in respect of the particular international contract of sale under the Convention.[17]

Oxford: Clarendon (1988), Ch. III, at 47 *et seq.*]. In sum, domestic rules mitigating the harshness and dangers of abuse from demands of coerced performance are available in any *forum* where the Convention is in force.

See also Bergsten, *Subsequent Commentary* on CISG Art. 28, *supra* note 2:

> By [the] combination of [CISG Arts. 28, 46 and 62], the principle is preserved that as a matter of the law of sales a party has the right to require performance by the other party, but the Convention itself recognizes that there may be limitations on the enforcement of the right.
>
> [...]
>
> The balance between Article 28 on the one hand and Articles 46 and 62 on the other is not, therefore, a compromise only between the civil law recognition of the principle that a party has the right to require the other party to perform the contract and the common law restriction on that right. It is also a recognition that in many legal systems the courts will use discretion in enforcing the right and that such discretion is to be preserved by the Convention.

[14] At the Vienna Diplomatic Conference, a single but significant change was made to the text of the provision restricting the right to require performance. CISG Art. 28 reads "unless the court *would* do so under its own law..." rather than "unless the court *could* do so" that was written in the 1978 UNCITRAL Draft Text of the Convention. The purpose and political nature of the drafting compromise in the text of the provision have been documented and discussed widely. *See* Enderlein & Maskow, *supra* note 3, at 123:

> In a Soviet-American compromise in the lobby, [...], "could" was changed into "*would*" at the conference following a British and an American proposal which, in regard to the substance, were identical. Hence, American and British concerns were met, noting that their courts had a large scope of operation, but did not exhaust it. The projected rule, however, could force them to do so [references omitted].

See also Schlechtriem (1986), *supra* note 12, at 62, where the author has commented that the effect of the particular change in the wording of CISG Art. 28 was to restrict "the possibilities of a judgment compelling specific performance."

[15] The reference by the rule in CISG Art. 28 to a national court's "own law" leads to the important question whether the language of the provision invokes the domestic *lex fori* on specific performance or instead *the proper law of the contract* applicable by virtue of the rules of private international law. The answer to that question, however, has created little controversy; *see* Honnold (1999), *supra* note 3, at 223–225. *See* also Enderlein & Maskow, *supra* note 3, at 122:

> This rule positively determines the applicable national law. It does not refer to the norms of the international private law of the forum [...]. The rule itself rather has the character of a conflict-of-law rule, to put it more concretely, of a *horizontal conflict-of-*law *rule*, [...] even if only a very specific legal issue is connected. The law of the courts is to be invoked even when another law is the statute of the contract [...]. It is also not relevant whether what matters is material or procedural law.

For supporting commentary, *see* Schlechtriem (1986), *supra* note 12, at 62–63, who cautions, however, against resorting too readily to the *lex fori* outside the particular remedial context created in CISG Art. 28 regarding specific performance:

> Even where absolute obstacles in performance would release a party from its obligations under domestic law, the remedy of specific performance remains intact under the Convention. Nevertheless, a court may not compel an impossible performance; Article 28 allows consideration to be given to the more extensive release that domestic law provides. But this interpretation should not open the road to domestic law whenever CISG gives a remedy unknown to the local law of the forum, such as the claim for repair in Article 46(3). "Its own law," however, does not refer to the conflict rules of the forum, which would invoke perhaps a foreign law allowing enforcement of specific performance. A contrary interpretation would be contrary to the purpose of Article 28 [references omitted].

[16] *See* Kritzer A. H., *Guide to Practical Applications of the United Nations Convention on Contracts for the International Sale of Goods*, Kluwer, (1988), pp. 217–218, where the author offers the following comparison of the buyer's right to require performance by the seller under the Convention to the counterpart provisions granting buyer the right to compel performance under the U.S. Uniform Commercial Code:

> Like UCC 2–716(2), [CISG] Article 45(2) permits appropriate damages in addition to performance. Under [CISG] Article 28, a court is not bound to require performance under the Convention unless it would do so under the domestic rules of the forum. Therefore, if a buyer seeks to require performance pursuant to [CISG] Article 46 and the forum is a U.S. state which has enacted the uniform Commercial Code, the seller is permitted to assert applicable UCC 2–716(1) defenses to an action for specific performance.

Regarding the seller's right to require performance by the buyer, under the Convention and the UCC, *see* Kritzer, *id.*, at 218–219.

[17] For relevant case law, *see*

- Argentina 21 July 2002 Appellate Court (*Cervecería y Malteria Paysandú S.A. v. Cervecería Argentina S.A.*); case presentation including English translation available at <http://cisgw3.law.pace.edu/

It has been said that CISG Art. 28 has a potential for mischief because "parties will be encouraged to forum-shop for a national court system that will or will not grant specific performance."[18] However, the practical importance of this provision has been questioned by several other commentators, mainly because the right to require specific performance is rarely asserted in international trade.[19] It also

cases/020721a1.html>. In this case a Uruguayan seller commenced proceedings against an Argentinian buyer for payment of the purchase price of the goods (malted barley). The appellate court, confirming the lower court's decision, found that CISG was applicable as the Argentinian rules of private international law led to the application of Argentinian law as the governing law of the contract and then to the Convention by virtue of CISG Art. 1(1)(b). The court found that as the goods had been correctly delivered, the seller had complied with his obligations and that the buyer was therefore obliged to pay the agreed price. The court also held that according to Argentinian law, which was applicable in the case at hand, the alleged lack of conformity could only be ascertained according to a specific procedure of arbitration and expertise. As the buyer had not initiated such a procedure, its defenses based on the alleged lack of conformity had to be rejected. Thus, the court concluded that the seller was entitled to *require* payment of the purchase price, pursuant to CISG Arts. 28, 53, 59, 61, and 62 (as well as interest, pursuant to CISG Art. 78).

- United States 7 December 1999 Federal District Court [Illinois] (*Magellan International v. Salzgitter Handel*), presentation available at <http://cisgw3.law.pace.edu/cases/991207u1.html>. This court stated that the remedy of specific performance sought by the buyer in this case is generally available under the Convention (CISG Art. 46(1)), with the exception that a court is not bound to enter judgment for specific performance unless it would do so under its own law of contracts (CISG Art. 28). In this case, it was held that the U.S. Uniform Commercial Code was applicable and in accordance with Ucc 2–716(1) (pursuant to which, specific performance may be granted when the buyer proves the difficulty of obtaining similar goods on the market), the court upheld the buyer's claim for specific performance.
- Switzerland 31 May 1996 Zürich Arbitration proceeding, presentation available online at <http://cisgw3.law.pace.edu/cases/960531s1.html>. This case concerned multi-party litigation and the CISG: the buyer was a group of companies operating aluminum casting works in Argentina and Hungary, and the seller was a Russian firm that produced raw aluminium (the "goods"). When the seller's new owners stopped all deliveries of raw aluminum to buyers, the buyers commenced proceedings in various forums, including this arbitral tribunal. The tribunal, dealing with the buyers' request for specific performance, stated,

  > 348. The Arbitral Tribunal believes that this is primarily a question of the applicable law. It sees no basis for claims for specific performance under Russian law. The Vienna Convention does not provide for this. If the law applicable to the procedure (Swiss law? - again the Vienna Convention) applied, the Arbitral Tribunal sees no basis for specific performance either.
  > 349. Apart from that the Arbitral Tribunal fails to see how specific performance could be an appropriate remedy for [buyers] in this case. They can hardly expect to be able, under the New York Convention or otherwise, to have an award enforced in Russia providing the [seller] must specifically perform its obligations under the various contracts for the next eight or ten years, producing the aluminum and delivering it to [buyers].
  > 350. The Arbitral Tribunal will accordingly grant [buyers'] "alternative" request for relief in the form of damages.

  [The Tribunal ultimately awarded buyers damages in an amount in excess of US $19 million.]

[18] Kastely A. H., "Unification and Community: A Rhetorical Analysis of the Convention," 8 *Nw. J. Int'l. L. & Bus.* (1988) 574–622, at 615, including supporting references to Gonzalez O., "Remedies under the U.N. Convention for the International Sale of Goods," 2 *Int'l Tax & Bus. Law* (1984) 79–100 at 96–97 (1984) and Grigera Naón H., "The U.N. Convention on Contracts for the International Sale of Goods," in Horn/Schmitthoff ed., *The Transnational Law of International Commercial Transactions: Studies in Transnational Economic Law*, Deventer: Kluwer (1982) vol. 2, 89–124, at 107.

[19] *See* Schlechtriem (1986), *supra* note 12, at 62:

> Although legal systems differ in the enforcement of claims for specific performance, [. . .] this regulation will not have much impact in actual practice, since parties in international trade normally shun such time-consuming procedures as judicial enforcement of specific performance and, therefore, promptly liquidate their unsuccessful transactions. On the other hand, where the goods are unique, such as art objects or specially made machines and installations, the remedy of specific performance should be enforceable in Anglo-American courts as well [references omitted].

See also Enderlein & Maskow, *supra* note 3, at 121:

> [T]the *right to specific performance of the contract* in international trade *in many instances is not practicable* because assertion of that right, even if it exists without any doubt, is much more complicated than in the case of financial claims and of the right to avoid the contract. But this depends on the state of performance. In general, the realization of a transaction cannot be halted until there is a decision on the right to specific performance. The enforcement of a relevant decision entails additional problems. The authors of this commentary, therefore, agree in that the right to performance is rarely asserted.

seems that the legislative history of the Convention supports the latter body of opinion.[20]

The UNIDROIT Principles contain no counterpart provision to CISG Art. 28. In their Definitions section, Art. 1.10, the Principles, however, provide a definition of a word also contained in CISG Article 28: "court."[21] The Official Commentary on the Principles also states that the term "court" covers arbitral tribunals as well as courts and it explains the reasons why it is so defined.[22]

The definition of "court" contained in the Principles may serve to answer a relevant question regarding the interpretation of the same word (i.e., "court") contained in CISG Art. 28, so that the reference to that word in the Convention may be interpreted similarly as being *inclusive* of arbitral tribunals.[23]

See also Bergsten, *supra* note 2, where the author explains:

> In principle, the right to require performance is the natural remedy in all continental legal systems. In practice, in the Western market economy legal systems if one party does not perform, the other party will not insist that he do so when it would be cheaper, easier and faster to procure the goods or services from some other party. If there are consequent additional costs, they can eventually be recovered as damages. The right to require performance is of practical importance where the party in breach is the only supplier, or the only supplier who can deliver in the requisite period of time. What is in principle the natural remedy in the continental Western market economy countries is the most important remedy in the planned economies of the socialist States of Eastern Europe. [...] Nevertheless, Article 28 may not have been of importance to a proper integration of the Convention into the domestic law in the civil law countries whereas it was of vital importance to the common law. This arises from the fact that in the civil law legal systems the statement as to the rights of the parties, including remedies for breach of contract, tends to be set forth in the Civil Code as a statement of the relationship between the parties themselves. The means of enforcing those rights in the courts is set forth in the law of civil procedure. The fact that the right to require performance by the other party may be absolute as a matter of civil law does not necessarily mean that the obligation of the court to enforce that right would be absolute as a matter of civil law procedure.

See also Henrik Lando, *supra* note 8, where the author argues that specific performance is largely irrelevant as a remedy for the non-performance of an action in civil law countries and, furthermore, that the non-use of specific performance can be ascribed to the costs and difficulties of forcing the breaching party to perform an action.

[20] *See* the legislative history of the Convention, which contains a 1972 Secretary-General report stating the following:

> Finding a generally acceptable provision on the right to require performance has been difficult. However, it would be easy to exaggerate the practical importance of this "right." Enforcing this right is subject to the delays of litigation. Since a seller who is resisting performance will usually claim some justification, such as a dispute over required quality or breach by buyer in providing for payment, the buyer can seldom anticipate a final decision by the trial and appellate courts – and eventual coerced performance – within the period required by his business needs. Instead, he will supply his needs elsewhere; if damage results he can pursue this claim without interrupting his business activity. Hence, even in legal systems where specific performance is theoretically available in the normal cases, this remedy is seldom invoked in legal proceedings. In practical operation, the threat of a damage claim (and the loss of confidence by the buyer and others in the trade) seem to be more effective sanctions than the threat of an action compelling specific performance. UNCITRAL, Yearbook V, A/CN.9/SER.A/1974, p. 53, para. 127; Honnold J.O., *Documentary History of the Uniform Law for International Sales*, Kluwer (1989), p. 130.

[21] Art. 1.10 – *Definitions* of the UNIDROIT Principles reads

> In these Principles – "court" includes an arbitral tribunal.

[22] *See* Official Comments on Art. 1.10 of the UNIDROIT Principles, available online at <http://cisgw3.law.pace.edu/cisg/principles/uni28.html#official>:

> Comment 1. *Courts and arbitral tribunals*: The importance of the Principles for the purpose of the settlement of disputes by means of arbitration has already been stressed (see ... the comments on the Preamble). In order however to avoid undue heaviness of language, only the term "court" is used in the text of the Principles, on the understanding that it covers arbitral tribunals as well as courts.

[23] Further support for such inclusive interpretation of the word "court" is found in the Text of Secretariat Commentary on the Articles of the 1978 Draft. *See* Secretariat Commentary on Art. 42 of the 1978 Draft *[draft counterpart of CISG Art. 46]*, available at <http://cisgw3.law.pace.edu/cisg/text/secomm/secomm-46.html>:

> Comment 9: Although the buyer has a right to the assistance of a court *or arbitral tribunal* to enforce the seller's obligation to perform the contract, article 26 *[draft counterpart of CISG Art. 28]* limits that right to a certain degree [...] [emphasis added].

See also Secretariat Commentary on Art. 58 of the 1978 Draft *[draft counterpart of CISG Art. 62]*, available at <http://cisgw3.law.pace.edu/cisg/text/secomm/secomm-62.html>:

> Comment 6. Although the seller has a right to the assistance of a court *or arbitral tribunal* to enforce the buyer's obligations to pay the price, take delivery and perform any of his other obligations, article 26 *[draft counterpart of CISG Art. 28]* limits that right to a certain degree [...]"[emphasis added].

III. CISG ART. 46: BUYER'S RIGHT TO REQUIRE SPECIFIC PERFORMANCE

CISG Art. 46 provides the general rule on the buyer's right to require performance by the seller of his contractual obligations. The buyer may invoke this rule when the seller has failed to perform *any*[24] of his obligations[25] under the Convention[26] and the contract.[27]

CISG Art. 46 also provides, however, specific restrictions[28] on the invocation of the right to compel specific performance.

[24] *See* the Text of Secretariat Commentary on Art. 42 of the 1978 Draft *[draft counterpart of CISG Art. 46]*. Paragraphs (1) and (2) of Art. 42 of the 1978 Draft and CISG Art. 46 are virtually identical. A paragraph (3) was added to CISG Art. 46 at the 1980 Vienna Diplomatic Conference to make express reference to the buyer's right to repair of nonconforming goods. *See* match-up of CISG Art. 46 with Art. 42 of the 1978 Draft, available at <http://cisgw3.law.pace.edu/cisg/text/matchup/matchup-d-46.html>, which validates the relevancy of the Secretariat Commentary on CISG Art. 46.

> Secretariat Comment 11: Subject to the rule in paragraph (2) relating to the delivery of substitute goods, *[and the rules on repair contained in paragraph (3) that was added to article 46 of the Official Text]*, this article does not allow the seller to refuse to perform on the grounds that the non-conformity was not substantial or that performance of the contract would cost the seller more than it would benefit the buyer. The choice is that of the buyer.

For case law holding that pursuant to CISG Art. 46(1) the buyer may require performance of *any* due obligation, *see* the following cases (NB. in these cases the buyers, however, resorted to other remedies, such as damages and avoidance):

- ICC Arbitration Case No. 8786 of January 1997; case presentation available at <http://cisgw3.law.pace.edu/cases/978786i1.html> (case concerned late delivery)
- Egypt Arbitration Award of 3 October 1995 (Cairo Chamber of Commerce and Industry); case presentation including English translation available at <http://cisgw3.law.pace.edu/cases/951003e1.html> (case concerned the extension of a bank guarantee; making express reference to Art. 45 CISG, the arbitrator held that the seller had breached its contractual duties by refusing to extend the bank guarantee in favor of the buyer)
- Germany 17 September 1991 *Oberlandesgericht* [Appellate Court] Frankfurt case presentation including English translation available at <http://cisgw3.law.pace.edu/cases/910917g1.html> (case concerned seller's breach of an exclusive sales agreement with the buyer)

The legislative history of the Convention reveals that Professor Farnsworth (U.S. delegate at the Vienna Diplomatic Conference) proposed that the *seller* should "be permitted to determine the manner in which he intended to remedy his failure to perform." This proposal was rejected. *See* OR 352, paras. 31–35 [OR = Official Records of the United Nations Conference on Contracts for the International Sale of Goods, Vienna 10 March 1980, A/CONF. 97/19].

[25] For a detailed analysis of the seller's obligations under the Convention, *see* Schlechtriem P., "The Seller's Obligations under the United Nations Convention on Contracts for the International Sale of Goods," in Galston & Smit ed., *International Sales: The United Nations Convention on Contracts for the International Sale of Goods*, Matthew Bender (1984), Ch. 6, pp. 6–1 to 6–35; also available online at <http://cisgw3.law.pace.edu/cisg/biblio/schlechtriem10.html>.

[26] Regarding the obligations of the seller under the Convention, *see* the text of the Convention, Chapter II, "Obligations of the Seller" (Art. 30), Sections I, "Delivery of the Goods and Handing over of Documents" (Arts. 31–34) and II, "Conformity of the Goods and Third Part Claims" (Arts. 35–44). The buyer's remedies for seller's breach of these obligations are set forth in Section III, "Remedies for Breach of Contract by the Seller" (Arts. 45–52).

[27] *See* CISG Art. 6 [The contract and the Convention (primacy of the contract)]:

> The parties may exclude the application of this Convention or, subject to article 12, derogate from or vary the effect of any of its provisions.

See also the Text of Secretariat Commentary on Art. 5 of the 1978 Draft *[draft counterpart of CISG Art. 6]*, available online at <http://cisgw3.law.pace.edu/cisg/text/secomm/secomm-06.html>:

> Comment 1: The non-mandatory character of the Convention is explicitly stated in article 5 *[draft counterpart of CISG Art. 6]*. The parties may exclude its application entirely by choosing a law other than this Convention to govern their contract. They may also exclude its application in part or derogate from or vary the effect of any of its provisions by adopting provisions in their contract providing solutions different from those in the Convention.
> The text of CISG article 6 and Art. 5 of the 1978 Draft are identical. The Secretariat Commentary on Art. 5 of the 1978 Draft should therefore be relevant to the interpretation of CISG Art. 6; *see* match-up of CISG Art. 6 with Art. 5 of the 1978 Draft, at <http://cisgw3.law.pace.edu/cisg/text/matchup/matchup-d-06.html>.

[28] Note that CISG Art. 46 must be read in conjunction with CISG Art. 28; *see* Section II, *supra* note 26. *See* also Secretariat Commentary on Art. 58 of the 1978 Draft *[draft counterpart of CISG Art. 62]*, available at <http://cisgw3.law.pace.edu/cisg/text/secomm/secomm-62.html>, Comment 6, *supra*. In addition to such limitations as may be present under the *lex fori* (CISG Art. 28) and that are contained in CISG Art. 46, the buyer's right to require specific performance may be subject to additional restrictions that ensue from the application of CISG Arts. 7, 9(1), 77, 85, 86, and 88(2). *See* Kritzer, *supra* note 16, at 351–352, and accompanying references therein.

The first restriction is in CISG Art. 46(1), which provides that the buyer's right to specific performance is subject to the buyer not having resorted to another remedy that is inconsistent with the requirement that the seller in breach perform his obligations (e.g., declaring the contract avoided pursuant to CISG Art. 49(1)).[29]

Furthermore, in the case where the seller has delivered goods that do not conform with the contract, thus breaching his obligations under CISG Arts. 35, 41, or 42,[30] the Convention provides the buyer with the right to require substitute goods (Art. 46(2)) or the repair[31] of non-conforming goods (Art. 46(3)). The exercise of this right is circumscribed in the following manner:

> Art. 46(2) provides that the buyer's right to require the seller to deliver substitute goods that conform with the contract is available only[32] if the lack of conformity[33] constitutes a *fundamental breach*[34] of contract[35];

[29] The remedies of specific performance and avoidance are inconsistent with each other. *See* CISG Art. 81(1) [Effect of avoidance], which provides the following:

> Avoidance of the contract *releases* both parties from their obligations under it, subject to any damages which may be due [. . .]"[emphasis added].

Similarly, a buyer's declaration of a reduction of the price under CISG Art. 50 is inconsistent with the remedy of specific performance. *See* the Text of Secretariat Commentary on Art. 42 of the 1978 Draft *[draft counterpart of* CISG *Art. 46]*, Comment 7.

On the contrary, an action for damages for breach of contract (CISG Art. 74) is not inconsistent with a request for specific performance. *See* the Secretariat Commentary:

> Comment 4: In addition to the right to require performance of the contract, article 41(2) *[draft counterpart of* CISG *Art .45(2)]* ensures that the buyer can recover any damages he may have suffered as a result of the delay in the seller's performance.

[30] *See* Enderlein and Maskow, *supra* note 3, at 178:

[31] The reference to "repair" in paragraph (3) of Article 46 was added at the Diplomatic Conference. *See* Kritzer, *supra* note 16, at 347, where the author comments

> This paragraph was added to specifically set forth the buyer's right to require repair if the goods do not conform to the contract (this was in response to concerns that under certain legal systems [the UCC for example], this is not expressly provided for in the applicable sales code in situations in which the contract is silent on the subject.

See also Conference relevant colloquy: OR 335–337, paras. 11–45[OR = Official Records of the United Nations Conference on Contracts for the International Sale of Goods, Vienna 10 March–11 April 1980, A/CONF. 97/19].

Cf. Under the U.S. Uniform Commercial Code substitute goods or repair are not normally available to an aggrieved buyer unless volunteered by the seller (e.g., in an attempt to cure non-conforming goods under UCC 2–508). *See* Flechtner H., "Remedies under the New International Sales Convention," 8 *J.L. & Com.* (1988) 58, n. 27, available online at <http://cisgw3.law.pace.edu/cisg/biblio/flecht.html> where the author comments that, under the UCC

> A court's power [. . .] to order specific performance may also include the power to require delivery of substitute goods if, for instance, seller was the sole source of supply and the goods it had delivered could not be repaired. Unlike the remedies provided in Articles 46(2) and (3) of the Convention, however, an order requiring repair or delivery of substitute goods [. . .] is presumably limited to situations falling within UCC 2–716(1) [. . .] that is, where the goods are unique or in the proper circumstances.

[32] Note that the buyer who requires substitute goods under this provision must comply with CISG Art. 82 regarding restitution of the goods he received. *See* the Secretariat Commentary on CISG Art. 46:

> Comment 13. If the buyer does require the seller to deliver substitute goods, he must be prepared to return the unsatisfactory goods to the seller. Therefore, article 67(1) *[draft counterpart of* CISG *article 82(1)]* provides that, subject to three exceptions set forth in article 67(2) *[draft counterpart of* CISG *article 82(2)]*, "the buyer loses his *[the]* right. . . to require the seller to deliver substitute goods if it is impossible for him to make restitution of the goods substantially in the condition in which he received them.

Cf. Enderlein & Maskow, *supra* note 3, at 179, where the authors make the following comment:

> Even if the buyer is not allowed to require delivery of substitute goods, the seller may deliver such goods if this is more favourable to him (unless such substitution of goods is an unreasonable inconvenience to the buyer).

[33] The reason for such restriction to specific performance is made clear in the Secretariat Commentary:

> Comment 12. If the goods which have been delivered do not conform to the contract, the buyer may want the seller to deliver substitute goods which do conform. However, it could be expected that the costs to the seller of shipping a second lot of goods to the buyer and of disposing of the non-conforming goods already delivered might be considerably greater than the buyer's loss from having non-conforming goods.

[34] For commentary and case law on the concept of *fundamental breach, see* note 34a in Addendum at the end of this section.

[35] In that case, the buyer must request substitute goods either in conjunction with a notice of non-conformity (CISG Arts. 39 and 43) or within a *reasonable* time thereafter (CISG Art. 46(2)). In other words, the buyer

Art. 46(3) provides that the buyer may require[36] the seller to remedy the lack of conformity (which does not need to constitute fundamental breach) by repair[37] unless this is *unreasonable*[38] having regard to all the circumstances.[39]

IV. CISG ART. 62: SELLER'S RIGHT TO REQUIRE SPECIFIC PERFORMANCE

CISG Art. 62 sets forth the general rule on the seller's right to require the buyer to perform his obligations under the Convention[40] and the contract[41] – a parallel rule to the one set forth in CISG Art. 46, which was discussed in Section III, *supra*.

forfeits his right by failure to give the required notice. The buyer is also entitled to set an additional period of time for performance in accordance with CISG Art. 47.

See also Enderlein & Maskow, *supra* note 3, at 180, where the authors note:

> If the buyer does not through immediate notice request a delivery of substitute goods or repair, he has to do so *within a reasonable time*. The CISG is based on the assumption that this rule serves the interests of both parties. Usually the buyer is interested in receiving conform[ing] goods as quickly as possible, and the seller wants to know the claims of the buyer. It should be avoided in any case that the buyer can speculate on rising market prices. What is appropriate here is therefore to fix a short time and by no means another two-year period as allowed for under Article 39, paragraph 2.

[36] Also in that case, the buyer must make the request for repair either in conjunction with a notice of non-conformity (CISG Arts. 39 and 43) or within a *reasonable* time thereafter (CISG Art. 46(3)). In other words, the buyer forfeits his right by failure to give the required notice. The buyer is also entitled to set an additional period of time for performance in accordance with CISG Art. 47.

[37] In the case where the non-conformity of the goods is insubstantial, a request to repair is less onerous and more efficient than delivery of substitute goods. Note that the buyer's right to remedy the lack of conformity of the goods may be exercised in various ways. *See* the Secretariat Commentary on CISG Art. 46, *op. cit.*:

> Comment 14: In place of requesting the seller to perform pursuant to this article, the buyer may find it more advantageous to remedy the defective performance himself or to have it remedied by a third party. Article 73 *[draft counterpart of CISG article 77]*, which requires the party who relies on a breach of contract to mitigate the loss, authorizes such measures to the extent that they are reasonable in the circumstances.

See also Enderlein & Maskow, *supra* note 3, at 180, where the authors opine that the seller has an obligation to bear all costs involved in the repair of non-conforming goods: "Cure includes delivery of spare parts, and substitution of parts as well as repair itself." The authors further note, "If there is a third party right or claim in respect of the goods, the cure may be such that the seller buys a patent or a license, or redeems a pledge or other right in title."

[38] *See* Honnold (1999), *supra* note 3, at 309, where the author writes that at the Diplomatic Conference it was noted that "some minor repairs could be made more readily by the buyer, particularly when the seller's facilities for repair are in a foreign country. The statutory language was designed to encourage a reasonable and flexible approach to such cases."

See also Kritzer, *supra* note 16, at 348, where the author explains that the proviso of reasonableness in CISG Art. 46(3) was "so phrased to allow the courts to take into account the *relative practicality* of repairs for *both* buyer and seller" [references omitted and emphasis added].

See also Enderlein & Maskow, *supra* note 3, at 180–181, where the authors comment,

> A claim for repair may be unreasonable if there is no reasonable *ratio between the costs* involved *and the price* of the goods or if the seller is a dealer who does not have the means for repair [. . .], or if the buyer himself can repair the goods at lesser cost. *Repair* may not only be unreasonable; it may be *technically impossible* (this could, however, constitute a fundamental breach of contract). The nature of some goods is such as to exclude repair at all, e.g. in the case of agricultural products. A repair can also be impractical, e.g. as with throw-away goods. In such cases the buyer nevertheless retains the right to a reduction in price and compensation for damages [references omitted].

It must also be noted that, in addition to being specifically mentioned in CISG Art. 46(3), *reasonableness* is a general principle of the Convention. For further views of commentators (Vilus, Schlechtriem, van der Velden, Maskow, Bonell, and Honnold) on references to *reasonableness* in the CISG, go to <http://cisgw3.law.pace.edu/cisg/text/reason.html#view>.

[39] For commentary and relevant case law on the buyer's right to require repair of non-conforming goods, *see* note 39a in Addendum at the end of this section.

[40] Regarding the obligations of the buyer under the Convention, *see* the text of the Convention, Chapter III, "Obligations of the Buyer" (Art. 53), Sections I, "Payment of the Price" (Arts. 54–59) and II, "Taking Delivery" (Art. 60). The seller's remedies for the buyer's breach of the latter's corresponding obligations are set forth in the Convention Section III, "Remedies for Breach of Contract by Buyer" (Arts. 61–65).

[41] *See* CISG Art. 6, which establishes the primacy of the contractual provisions over the Convention.

CISG Art. 62 provides that the seller may require[42] the buyer to pay the price[43] for the goods,[44] take delivery of the goods,[45] and perform his *other obligations*.[46]

The buyer may conceivably default in his obligations either after he has received and retains the goods[47] or by refusing to receive the goods.[48] In any case, a proviso, similar to

[42] The seller's right to require performance of the other party's obligations is subject to the concession to domestic law provided by CISG Art. 28; *see* Section II, *supra*. *See* also Secretariat Commentary on Art. 58 of the 1978 Draft [*draft counterpart of* CISG *Art.* 62], Comment 6. The same restriction applies to the corresponding remedy available to the buyer; *see* Sections II and III, *supra*.

[43] Regarding the limitation imposed by CISG Art. 28 on CISG Art. 62, Farnsworth opines that the former does not compel payment of the price under the latter. *See* Farnsworth E. A., "Damages and Specific Relief," 27 *Am. J. Comp. L.* (1979) 247–253; also available online at <http://cisgw3.law.pace.edu/cisg/biblio/farns.html>. *Id.*, at 249–250:

> [T]he words "judgement for specific performance" suggest that the provision does not apply to a suit in which the seller tenders the goods to the recalcitrant buyer and claims the price. Such a suit, traditionally one at law rather than in equity, is not commonly thought of as one for "specific performance," even though it gives the seller relief that might accurately be described as "specific."

Cf. Honnold (1999), *supra* note 3, at 381–382:

> [J]urists of common law persuasion do not think of an action to recover the price as comparable to an action to require delivery of the goods. But one cannot be tied to local terminology in construing the Convention.

See also Schlechtriem (1986), *supra* note 12, at p. 84, n. 333a:

> Whether an action by the seller for the price is a form of specific performance is controversial. In the end, it is merely a problem of denomination, because no one doubts that the action is enforceable against the buyer [references omitted].

For a detailed analysis of the issue, *see* Ziegel J. S., "The Remedial Provisions in the Vienna Sales Convention: Some Common Law Perspectives," in Galston & Smit ed., *International Sales: The United Nations Convention on Contracts for the International Sale of Goods*, Matthew Bender (1984), Ch. 9, pp. 9–1 to 9–43; also available at <http://cisgw3.law.pace.edu/cisg/biblio/ziegel6.html>.

[44] For relevant case law regarding the requirement to pay the price, *see* note 44a in Addendum at the end of this section.

[45] There is hardly any case law on the seller's right to require buyer to take delivery of the goods. For a general statement regarding *inter alia* buyer's refusal to take delivery, *see* Germany 8 February 1995 *Oberlandesgericht* [Appellate Court] München; CLOUT case No. 133; case presentation including English translation available at <http://cisgw3.law.pace.edu/cases/950208g1.html> (case concerned contract for the sale of eleven cars).

[46] For an explanatory note on the expression "[buyer's] *other* obligations," *see* the Text of the Secretariat Commentary on Art. 58 of the 1978 Draft [*draft counterpart of* CISG *Art.* 62]:

> Comment 9. In some cases the seller may be authorized or required to substitute his own performance for that which the buyer has failed to do. Article 61 [*draft counterpart of* CISG *Art.* 65] provides that in a sale by specification, if the buyer fails to make the specifications required on the date requested or within a reasonable time after receipt of a request from the seller, the seller may make the specifications himself. Similarly, if the buyer is required by the contract to name a vessel on which the goods are to be shipped and fails to do so by the appropriate time article 73 [*draft counterpart of* CISG *Art.* 77], which requires the party who relies on a breach of contract to mitigate losses, may authorize the seller to name the vessel so as to minimize the buyer's losses.

[47] In that case, Art. 62 should apply in a straightforward manner. *See* the Text of the Secretariat Commentary on Art. 58 of the 1978 Draft [*draft counterpart of* CISG *Art.* 62], available at <http://cisgw3.law.pace.edu/cisg/text/secomm/secomm-62.html>:

> Comment 2. This article recognizes that the seller's primary concern is that the buyer pay the price at the time it is due. Therefore, if the price is due under the terms of [CISG Art. 58 and 59] and the buyer does not pay it, this article authorizes the seller to require the buyer to pay it.

CISG article 62 and 1978 Draft Art. 58 are identical except for the reference to "this requirement" rather than "such requirement"; *see* match-up of CISG Art. 62 with Art. 58 of the 1978 Draft, available at <http://cisgw3.law.pace.edu/cisg/text/matchup/matchup-d-62.html>. The Secretariat Commentary on Art. 58 of the 1978 Draft should therefore be relevant to the interpretation of CISG Art. 62.

Enforcing the buyer's obligation to pay the price resembles an action to collect a debt, and it may give seller the right to recover the goods under CISG Art. 81(2). *See* Honnold, (1999), *supra* note 3, 378–379.

Cf. U.S.A. *Uniform Commercial Code* 2–709 *Action for the Price*. Section 2–709(1)(a), which provides for recovery of the price when goods have been accepted by buyer.

[48] In that case, the seller's right to compel the consummation of the transaction including receipt of the goods may not be so straightforward. When the seller remains in possession of the goods other provisions of the Convention (CISG Arts. 85–88, provisions regarding preservation of the goods) may further restrict his right to compel the buyer to take delivery and pay the price. *See* Honnold, (1999), *supra* note 3, 379–383.

the one contained in CISG Art. 46(1),[49] is also incorporated in and limits[50] the application of CISG Art. 62; that is, the party's right to specific performance by the other party of his obligations is subject to the *obligee* not having resorted to another remedy (e.g., declaration of avoidance) that is inconsistent[51] with the requirement that the *obligor* in default perform.[52]

V. UNIDROIT PRINCIPLES ARTS. 7.2.1–7.2.5: RIGHT TO PERFORMANCE

Under the regime of the UNIDROIT Principles (UP) the provisions regarding the right of a party to require performance by the other party are set forth in Chapter 7, "Non-Performance," Section 2, "Right to Performance" (Arts. 7.2.1–7.2.5).

The rules regarding the right of the obligee to require performance by the obligor under the UNIDROIT Principles, unlike the rules of the Convention, make a clear distinction between performance of monetary and of non-monetary obligations.

1. UP Art. 7.2.1: Performance of Monetary Obligation

UP Art. 7.2.1 provides the general rule of the UNIDROIT Principles that where a party who is obliged to pay money under a contractual obligation does not do so, the other

Cf. U.S.A. *Uniform Commercial Code* Section 2–709(1)(b), which provides that a seller in possession of the goods may recover the price from the buyer when the seller is unable after reasonable efforts to resell the goods at a reasonable price.

[49] *See* Section III, *supra*.

[50] Further possible limitations on the remedy that CISG Art. 62 provides the seller to require performance of the buyer's obligations have been identified in relation to other provisions of her Convention (Arts. 7, 77, 78 and 79); *see* Kritzer, *supra* note 16, at 422.

Regarding the application of *CISG* Art. 79 [Impediment excusing a party from damages] and Art. 78 [Interest on sum in arrears], *see* Sevón L., "Obligations of the Buyer under the UN Convention on Contracts for the International Sale of Goods," in Sarcevic P. & Voken P. eds., *International Sale of Goods: Dubrovnik Lectures*, Oceana (1986), Ch. 6, 203–238, also available at <http://cisgw3.law.pace.edu/cisg/biblio/sevon1.html>, at 224, where the author states

> Under Article 79(1) a party is not liable for failure to perform any of his obligations if he proves that the failure was due to an impediment beyond his control. According to Article 79(5), nothing in that Article prevents either party from exercising any right other than to claim damages. It would seem that the seller is entitled to require payment even if the buyer is exempted from damages. The implications of this are not all that clear. Presenting such a requirement may affect the seller's right to interest on the price if under national law such a demand is necessary. Since interest, according to the Convention [Article 78], does not fall under the heading of damages, the provision in Article 79(5) would also apply to interest.

Regarding CISG Art. 77 [Mitigation of damages], which provides that "a party who relies on a breach of contract must take such measures as are reasonable in the circumstances to mitigate the loss," *see* Secretariat Commentary on Art. 73 of the 1978 Draft *[draft counterpart of CISG Art. 77]*, available at <http://cisgw3.law.pace.edu/cisg/text/secomm/secomm-77.html>.

> Comment 3. The sanction provided by article 73 *[draft counterpart of CISG Art. 77]* against a party who fails to mitigate his loss only enables the other party to claim a reduction in the damages. It does not affect a claim for the price by the seller pursuant to article 58 *[draft counterpart of CISG Art. 62]* or a reduction in the price by the buyer pursuant to article 46 *[draft counterpart of CISG Art. 50]*.

Nor are principles of mitigation said to apply to an action by the buyer for specific performance under CISG Art. 46. The Secretariat Commentary on Article 42 [*draft counterpart of CISG Article 46(1) and (2)*], states

> Comment 11: [T]his article does not allow the seller to refuse to perform on the grounds that the non-conformity was not substantial or that performance of the contract would cost the seller more than it would benefit the buyer. The choice is that of the *buyer* [emphasis added].

Also, mitigation principles do not appear to require the injured party to choose the remedy that would be least expensive to the party in breach. A qualification to this conclusion could, however, apply to choice of damages remedies (i.e., as between Art. 75 and Art. 76 [provisions regarding the measurement of damages when contract has been avoided]). Language contained in the 1976 Draft of these articles that permitted the injured party to choose the damages remedy most beneficial to himself was changed. UNCITRAL Yearbook VIII, A/CN.9/SER.A/1977, pp. 161 and 59–60, paras. 472 and 489. Prior to that change, there was a Secretariat Commentary that stated that this was permissible. UNCITRAL Yearbook VII, A/CN.9/SER.A/1976, p. 137. However, with that change, this portion of that Secretariat Commentary was deleted.

[51] For the remedies of specific performance and avoidance are inconsistent with each other, *see* note 51a in Addendum at the end of this section.

[52] For the purposes of CISG Art. 62, *obligee* denotes seller and *obligor* denotes buyer.

party may require payment.[53] This rule, which gives an aggrieved party the right to require the party in default to perform his monetary obligations under the contract, should be applicable, for instance, to the payment of the price for the goods under a sales contract.

The principle of contractual performance of the parties' (monetary) obligations, on which this rule is based, is also *generally* recognized in the Convention[54] as well as *specifically* embodied in CISG Art. 62, which sets forth the seller's right to require the buyer to pay the price for the goods.[55]

2. UP Art. 7.2.2: Performance of Non-Monetary Obligation

UP Art. 7.2.2 provides the general rule of the Principles that where a party who owes a non-monetary obligation does not perform, the obligee may require performance of that obligation.[56] This rule again reflects the general approach of the counterpart provisions of the Convention.

In stark contrast to the Convention (CISG Art. 28), however, the Principles do not treat specific performance as a discretionary remedy that is dependent on domestic law and the rules of the forum.[57] Under UP Art. 7.2.2, specific performance of a non-monetary obligation must be granted to an aggrieved obligee, unless one of the specific exceptions enumerated in paras. (a)–(e) of the said article applies:

(a) performance is impossible in law or in fact[58]

[53] This rule is said to "reflect a generally accepted principle that payment of money which is due under a contractual obligation can always be demanded and, if the demand is not met, enforced by legal action before a court." *See* Official Comment on UP Art. 7.2.1. The Official Commentary on UNIDROIT Principles, available online both at <http://cisgw3.law.pace.edu/cisg/principles/uni46.html#official> and <http://cisgw3.law.pace.edu/cisg/principles/uni62.html#official>. The Official Commentary also makes clear that, in exceptional circumstances, "the right to require payment of the price of the goods or services to be delivered or rendered may be *excluded*. This is in particular the case where a usage [UP. Art. 1.8] requires a seller to resell goods which are *neither accepted nor paid for* by the buyer" [emphasis added]. *Id.*

[54] *See* Section III, *supra*.

[55] *See* Section IV, *supra*.

[56] *See* Official Comments on UP Art. 7.2.2.

Comment 1. Right to require performance of non-monetary obligations

In accordance with the general principle of the binding character of the contract (see Art. 1.3), each party should as a rule be entitled to require performance by the other party not only of monetary, but also of non-monetary obligations, assumed by that party. While this is not controversial in civil law countries, common law systems allow enforcement of non-monetary obligations only in special circumstances.

Following the basic approach of CISG (Art. 46) this article adopts the principle of specific performance, subject to certain qualifications.

The principle is particularly important with respect to contracts other than sales contracts. Unlike the obligation to deliver something, contractual obligations to do something or to abstain from doing something can often be performed only by the other contracting party itself. In such cases the only way of obtaining performance from a party who is unwilling to perform is by enforcement.

[57] *See* Official Comments on UP Art. 7.2.2.

Comment 2. Remedy not discretionary

While CISG provides that 'a court is not bound to enter a judgement for specific performance unless the court would do so under its own law in respect of similar contracts of sale not governed by [the] Convention' (Art. 28), under the Principles specific performance is not a discretionary remedy, i.e. a court must order performance, unless one of the exceptions laid down in the present article applies.

[58] *See* Official Comments on UP Art. 7.2.2.

Comment 3. Exceptions to the right to require performance

a. Impossibility. A performance which is impossible in law or in fact, cannot be required (sub-para. (a)). However, impossibility does not nullify a contract: other remedies may be available to the aggrieved party. See Arts. 3.3 and 7.1.7(4).

The refusal of a public permission which is required under the applicable domestic law and which affects the validity of the contract renders the contract void (see Art. 6.1.17(1)), with the consequence that the problem of enforceability of the performance cannot arise. When however the refusal merely renders the performance impossible without affecting the validity of the contract (see Art. 6.1.17(2)), sub-para. (a) of this article applies and performance cannot be required.

Cf. CISG Art. 4(a), which provides that, except as otherwise expressly provided in the Convention, the CISG is "not concerned with the validity of the contract or of any of its provisions or of any usage."

(b) performance or, where relevant, enforcement is unreasonably burdensome or expensive[59]
(c) the party entitled to performance may reasonably obtain performance from another source[60]
(d) performance is of an exclusively personal character[61]
(e) the party entitled to performance does not require performance within a reasonable time after it has, or ought to have, become aware of the non-performance[62]

It is arguable that the basis of the stated exceptions is provided by the application of the general principle – also recognized in the Convention – of *reasonableness* to the various contexts in which UP Art. 7.2.2 (a)–(e) is applicable.

3. UP Art. 7.2.5: Change of Remedy

UP Art. 7.2.5 provides that the aggrieved party may abandon the remedy of requiring performance of a non-monetary obligation and opt instead for another remedy or remedies.[63]

[59] *See* Official Comments on UP Art. 7.2.2.
Comment 3. Exceptions to the right to require performance
b. Unreasonable burden. In exceptional cases, particularly when there has been a drastic change of circumstances after the conclusion of a contract, performance, although still possible, may have become so onerous that it would run counter to the general principle of good faith and fair dealing (Art. 1.7) to require it. See also Illustration 1, *id.*

[60] *See* Official Comments on UP Art. 7.2.2.
Comment 3. Exceptions to the right to require performance
c. Replacement transaction. Many goods and services are of a standard kind, i.e. the same goods or services are offered by many suppliers. If a contract for such staple goods or standard services is not performed, most customers will not wish to waste time and effort extracting the contractual performance from the other party. Instead, they will go into the market, obtain substitute goods or services and claim damages for non-performance. In view of this economic reality sub-para. (c) excludes specific performance whenever the party entitled to performance may reasonably obtain performance from another source. That party may terminate the contract and conclude a replacement transaction. See Art. 7.4.5. The word "reasonably" indicates that the mere fact that the same performance can be obtained from another source is not in itself sufficient, since the aggrieved party could not in certain circumstances reasonably be expected to have recourse to an alternative supplier. See also Illustration 2, *id.*

[61] *See* Official Comments on UP Art. 7.2.2.
Comment 3. Exceptions to the right to require performance
d. Performance of an exclusively personal character. Where a performance has an exclusively personal character, enforcement would interfere with the personal freedom of the obligor. Moreover, enforcement of a performance often impairs its quality. The supervision of a very personal performance may also give rise to insuperable practical difficulties, as is shown by the experience of countries that have saddled their courts with this kind of responsibility. For all these reasons, sub-para. (d) excludes enforcement of performance of an exclusively personal character. The precise scope of this exception depends essentially upon the meaning of the phrase "exclusively personal character." The modern tendency is to confine this concept to performances of a unique character. The exception does not apply to obligations undertaken by a company. Nor are ordinary activities of a lawyer, a surgeon or an engineer covered by the phrase for they can be performed by other persons with the same training and experience. A performance is of an exclusively personal character if it is not delegable and requires individual skills of an artistic or scientific nature or if it involves a confidential and personal relationship. The performance of obligations to abstain from doing something does not fall under sub-para. (d). See also Illustrations 3 and 4, *id.*

[62] *See* Official Comments on UP Art. 7.2.2.
Comment 3. Exceptions to the right to require performance
e. Request within reasonable time. Performance of a contract often requires special preparation and efforts by the obligor. If the time for performance has passed but the obligee has failed to demand performance within a reasonable time, the obligor may be entitled to assume that the obligee will not insist upon performance. If the obligee were to be allowed to leave the obligor in a state of uncertainty as to whether performance will be required, the risk might arise of the obligee's speculating unfairly, to the detriment of the obligor, upon a favourable development of the market. For these reasons sub-para. (e) excludes the right to performance if it is not required within a reasonable time after the obligee has become, or ought to have become, aware of the non-performance. For a similar rule concerning the loss of the right to terminate the contract, see Art. 7.3.2(2).

[63] *See* Official Comments on UP Art. 7.2.5.
Comment 1. *Aggrieved party entitled to change of remedy.* This article addresses a problem which is peculiar to the right to require performance. The aggrieved party may abandon the remedy of requiring performance of a

UP Art. 7.2.5(1) provides that an aggrieved obligee who has required and who has not received performance within a period fixed (or otherwise within a reasonable) period of time[64] may invoke any other remedy.[65]

UP Art. 7.2.5(2) further provides that the aggrieved obligee may invoke any other remedy where the decision of a court for performance of a non-monetary obligation cannot be enforced.[66]

4. UP Art. 7.2.3: Repair and Replacement of Defective Performance

UP Art. 7.2.3, similarly to CISG Art. 46(3), expressly provides that the obligee's right to require the obligor to remedy his defective performance includes, in appropriate cases,[67] the right to require repair, replacement,[68] or other cure.[69]

non-monetary obligation and opt instead for another remedy or remedies. This choice is permitted on account of the difficulties usually involved in the enforcement of non-monetary obligations. Even if the aggrieved party first decides to invoke its right to require performance, it would not be fair to confine that party to this single option. The non-performing party may subsequently become unable to perform, or its inability may only become evident during the proceedings.

[64] *See* Official Comments on UP Art. 7.2.5.

Comment 4. *Time limits*. In the event of a subsequent change of remedy the time limit provided for a notice of termination under Art. 7.3.2(2) must, of course, be extended accordingly. The reasonable time for giving notice begins to run, in the case of a voluntary change of remedy, after the aggrieved party has or ought to have become aware of the non-performance at the expiry of the additional period of time available to the non-performing party to perform; and in the case of para. (2) of this article, it will begin to run after the aggrieved party has or ought to have become aware of the unenforceability of the decision or award requiring performance.

[65] *See* Official Comments on UP Art. 7.2.5.

Comment 2. *Voluntary change of remedy*. Two situations must be addressed. In the first case, the aggrieved party has required performance but changes its mind before execution of a judgment in its favour, perhaps because it has discovered the non-performing party's inability to perform. The aggrieved party now wishes to invoke one or more other remedies. Such a voluntary change of remedy can only be admitted if the interests of the non-performing party are duly protected. It may have prepared for performance, invested effort and incurred expense. For this reason para. (1) of this article makes it clear that the aggrieved party is entitled to invoke another remedy only if it has not received performance within a fixed period or otherwise within a reasonable period of time. How much additional time must be made available to the non-performing party for performance depends upon the difficulty which the performance involves. The non-performing party has the right to perform provided it does so before the expiry of the additional period.

[66] *See* Official Comments on UP Art. 7.2.5.

Comment 3. *Unenforceable decision*. Para. (2) addresses the second and less difficult case in which the aggrieved party has attempted without success to enforce a judicial decision or arbitral award directing the non-performing party to perform. In this situation it is obvious that the aggrieved party may immediately pursue other remedies.

[67] For limitations, which are based on the concept of *reasonableness* and are placed on the right to require cure of defective performance, *see* Official Comments on UP Art. 7.2.3.

Comment 3. *Restrictions*. The right to require cure of a defective performance is subject to the same limitations as the right to performance in general. Most of the exceptions to the right to require performance that are set out in Art. 7.2.2 are easily applicable to the various forms of cure of a defective performance. Only the application of sub-para. (b) calls for specific comment. In many cases involving small, insignificant defects, both replacement and repair may involve 'unreasonable effort or expense' and are therefore excluded. *See* also Illustration, *id*.

[68] *See* Official Comments on UP Art. 7.2.3.

Comment 1. *Right to performance in case of defective performance*. This article applies the general principles of Arts. 7.2.1 and 7.2.2 to a special, yet very frequent, case of non-performance, i.e. defective performance. For the sake of clarity the article specifies that the right to require performance includes the right of the party who has received a defective performance to require cure of the defect.

Comment 2. *Cure of defective performance*. Under the Principles cure denotes the right both of the non-performing party to correct its performance (Art. 7.1.4) and of the aggrieved party to require such correction by the non-performing party. The present article deals with the latter right. The article expressly mentions two specific examples of cure, namely repair and replacement. Repairing defective goods (or making good an insufficient service) is the most common case and replacement of a defective performance is also frequent. The right to require repair or replacement may also exist with respect to the payment of money, for instance in case of an insufficient payment or of a payment in the wrong currency or to an account different from that agreed upon by the parties.

[69] For an explanation of other forms of cure, *see* Official Comments on UP Art. 7.2.3.

Comment 2. Apart from repair and replacement there are other forms of cure, such as the removal of the rights of third persons over goods or the obtaining of a necessary public permission.

5. UP Art. 7.2.4: Judicial Penalty

UP Art. 7.2.4 sets forth a provision to which there is no counterpart in the Convention: a judicially imposed sanction to ensure compliance with judgments ordering the performance of contractual obligations.[70]

UP Art. 7.2.4(1), in contradistinction to the provisions of the Convention, provides that a court[71] that orders a party to perform may[72] also direct that party to pay a penalty if it does not comply with the order.[73]

UP Art. 7.2.4(2) makes clear that payment[74] of the judicial penalty to the aggrieved party[75] does not exclude any claim for damages,[76] but it is subject to the mandatory rules of the *lex fori*.[77]

[70] For the Convention does not provide penalties for noncompliance, nor does it make provision for *judicial* penalties, *see* note 70a in Addendum at the end of this section.

[71] *See* Official Comments on UP Art. 7.2.4.

Comment 6. *Penalties imposed by arbitrators*. Since according to Art. 1.10 "court" includes an arbitral tribunal, the question arises of whether arbitrators might also be allowed to impose a penalty. While a majority of legal systems seems to deny such a power to arbitrators, some modern legislation and recent court practice have recognised it. This solution, which is in keeping with the increasingly important role of arbitration as an alternative means of dispute resolution, especially in international commerce, is endorsed by the Principles. Since the execution of a penalty imposed by arbitrators can only be effected by, or with the assistance of, a court, appropriate supervision is available to prevent any possible abuse of the arbitrators' power.

[72] *See* Official Comments on UP Art. 7.2.4.

Comment 2. *Imposition of penalty at discretion of the court*. The use of the word "may" in para. (1) of this article makes it clear that the imposition of a penalty is a matter of discretion for the court. Its exercise depends upon the kind of obligation to be performed. In the case of money judgments, a penalty should be imposed only in exceptional situations, especially where speedy payment is essential for the aggrieved party. The same is true for obligations to deliver goods. Obligations to pay money or to deliver goods can normally be easily enforced by ordinary means of execution. By contrast, in the case of obligations to do or to abstain from doing something, which moreover cannot easily be performed by a third person, enforcement by means of judicial penalties is often the most appropriate solution.

[73] *See* Official Comments on UP Art. 7.2.4.

Comment 1. *Judicially imposed penalty*. Experience in some legal systems has shown that the threat of a judicially imposed penalty for disobedience is a most effective means of ensuring compliance with judgments ordering the performance of contractual obligations. Other systems, on the contrary, do not provide for such sanctions because they are considered to constitute an inadmissible encroachment upon personal freedom. The present article takes a middle course by providing for monetary but not for other forms of penalties, applicable to all kinds of orders for performance including those for payment of money.

[74] *See* Official Comments on UP Art. 7.2.4.

Comment 5. Form *[and Procedure]*. A judicial penalty may be imposed in the form of a lump sum payment or of a payment by installments.

[75] *See* Official Comments on UP Art. 7.2.4.

Comment 3. *Beneficiary*. Legal systems differ as to the question of whether judicial penalties should be paid to the aggrieved party, to the State, or to both. Some systems regard payment to the aggrieved party as constituting an unjustified windfall benefit which is contrary to public policy. While rejecting this latter view and indicating the aggrieved party as the beneficiary of the penalty, the first sentence of para. (2) of this article expressly mentions the possibility of mandatory provisions of the law of the forum not permitting such a solution and indicating other possible beneficiaries of judicial penalties.

[76] *See* Official Comments on UP Art. 7.2.4.

Comment 4. Judicial *penalties distinguished from damages and from agreed payment for non-performance*. The second sentence of para. (2) makes it clear that a judicial penalty paid to the aggrieved party does not affect its claim for damages. Payment of the penalty is regarded as compensating the aggrieved party for those disadvantages which cannot be taken into account under the ordinary rules for the recovery of damages. Moreover, since payment of damages will usually occur substantially later than payment of a judicial penalty, courts may to some degree be able, in measuring the damages, to take the payment of the penalty into account. Judicial penalties are moreover to be distinguished from agreed payments for non-performance which are dealt with in Art. 7.4.13, although the latter fulfill a function similar to that of the former. If the court considers that the contractual stipulation of the payment of a sum in case of non-performance already provides a sufficient incentive for performance, it may refuse to impose a judicial penalty.

[77] *See* Official Comments on UP Art. 7.2.4.

Comment 5. *[Form and] Procedure*. The procedure relating to the imposition of a judicial penalty is governed by the *lex fori*.

Comment 7. Recognition *and enforcement of decisions imposing penalties*. Attention must be drawn to the problems of recognition and enforcement, in countries other than the forum State, of judicial decisions and of arbitral awards imposing penalties. Special rules on this matter are sometimes to be found in national law and to some extent in international treaties.

VI. CONCLUSIONS

The comparison between provisions of the Convention regarding the right to specific performance and the counterpart provisions of the UNIDROIT Principles has revealed similarities and differences between the two instruments.

As a starting point, both the Convention and the UNIDROIT Principles adopt the principle of contractual performance of the parties' obligations, which is embodied in counterpart rules regarding the right of the obligee to require specific performance by the obligor.

There are, however, several distinctions, structural and substantive, between the counterpart provisions of the two instruments.

Under the regime of the UNIDROIT Principles, the provisions regulating the right of a party to require performance by the other party do not follow the distinctive structure adopted in the Convention's counterpart provisions – the latter instrument makes separate, albeit similarly balanced, provisions for a seller and a buyer in an international sales contract governed by the Convention.

On the other hand, the rules regarding the right of the obligee to require performance by the obligor under the UNIDROIT Principles, unlike the rules of the Convention, form what is arguably a more detailed and coherent set of regulations, and they make a clear distinction between performance of monetary and non-monetary obligations.

In stark contrast to the Convention, the Principles do not treat specific performance as a discretionary remedy that is dependent on domestic law and the rules of the forum. Rather, the Principles expressly provide several exceptions to the general rule on the obligee's right to require performance of non-monetary obligations. These exceptions are based on specific manifestations of the general principle of *unreasonableness* – which is also a general principle on which the Convention is based.

Furthermore, the Principles include a provision to which there is no counterpart in the Convention: a judicially imposed sanction (*judicial penalty*) to ensure compliance with judgments ordering the performance of contractual obligations.

VII. ADDENDUM[34a,39a,44a,51a,70a]

[34a]For the definition of *fundamental breach*, *see* CISG Art. 25: A fundamental breach with regard to non-conformity of the goods occurs when the delivery of the defective goods substantially deprives the buyer of what the buyer is entitled to expect under the contract. For an analysis of the concept of fundamental breach and its application under the Convention, *see* Koch R., "The Concept of Fundamental Breach of Contract under the United Nations Convention on Contracts for the International Sale of Goods," in *Pace Review of the Convention on Contracts for the International Sale of Goods*, 1998, Kluwer Law International (1999) 177–354; also available online at <http://cisgw3.law.pace.edu/cisg/biblio/koch.html>.

A fundamental breach under CISG Art. 46(2) has to be determined in the same way as under Article 49 and in accordance with the general definition given in CISG Art. 25.

See the *UNCITRAL Digest* of case law on CISG Art. 46 (A/CN.9/SER.C/DIGEST/CISG/46 [8 June 2004]), available online at <http://cisgw3.law.pace.edu/cisg/text/anno-art-46.html#ucd>, which makes the remarks quoted below (with accompanying references to corresponding case law):

Para 13. "Leading court decisions on the point (although rendered in respect of art. 49) have held that a non-conformity concerning quality remains a non-fundamental breach of contract as long as the buyer can – without unreasonable inconvenience – use the goods or resell them even with a rebate"; *see* the following:

- Germany 3 April 1996 *Bundesgerichtshof* [Supreme Court]; CLOUT case No. 171; case presentation including English translation available at <http://cisgw3.law.pace.edu/cases/960403g1.html> (case concerned the sale of cobalt sulphate with specific technical qualities; the delivered cobalt was of a lower quality than that agreed to under the contracts; in determining whether the non-conformity was fundamental (CISG Art. 25), the court held that it is decisive whether the buyer can still make use of the goods or resell them in the usual commercial relationships without incurring any unreasonable difficulties; the fact that the buyer might be forced to resell the goods at a lower price is not to be considered in itself an unreasonable difficulty).

- Switzerland 28 October 1998 *Bundesgericht* [Supreme Court]; CLOUT case No. 248; case presentation including English translation available at <http://cisgw3.law.pace.edu/cases/981028s1.html> (in this case, the delivery of frozen meat that was too fat and too wet and therefore according to expert opinion worth 25 percent less than meat of the contracted quality was considered not to constitute a fundamental breach of contract because the buyer had the opportunity to resell the meat at a lower price or to process it otherwise)

Para 13, *ibid.*: "On the contrary, if the non-conforming goods cannot be used or resold with reasonable effort this constitutes a fundamental breach"; *see*

- France 23 January 1996 *Cour de Cassation* [Supreme Court] (*Sacovini/M Marrazza v. Les fils de Henri Ramel*); CLOUT case No. 150; case presentation including English translation available at <http://cisgw3.law.pace.edu/cases/960123f1.html> (case concerned artificially sweetened wine)
- Germany 18 January 1994 *Oberlandesgericht* [Appellate Court] Frankfurt; CLOUT case No. 79; case presentation including English translation available at <http://cisgw3.law.pace.edu/cases/940118g1.html> (case concerned shoes with fissures in the leather)
- Germany 5 April 1995 *Landgericht* [District Court] Landshut; case presentation including English translation available at <http://cisgw3.law.pace.edu/cases/950405g1> (case concerned T-shirts that shrank by about 10 to 15 percent (two sizes) after the first washing)

Para 13, *ibid.*: "The same is true where the goods suffer from a serious defect – although they may still be used to some extent"; *see*

- Austria 1 July 1994 *Oberlandesgericht* [Appellate Court] Innsbruck; CLOUT case No. 107; case presentation including English translation available at <http://cisgw3.law.pace.edu/cases/940701a3.html> (case concerned garden flowers (daisies) that should flourish the whole summer but did so only for a minor part of it)

Para 13, *id.*: "[O]r where the goods have major defects and the buyer needs the goods for manufacture"; *see*

- United States 6 December 1995 Federal Appellate Court [2nd Circuit] (*Delchi Carrier v. Rotorex*); CLOUT case No. 138; case presentation available at <http://cisgw3.law.pace.edu/cases/951206u1.html> (case concerned lower cooling capacity and higher power consumption than contracted for compressors delivered for the manufacture of air conditioners)
- France 23 January 1996 *Cour de Cassation* [Supreme Court] (*Sacovini/M Marrazza v. Les fils de Henri Ramel*); CLOUT case No. 150; case presentation including English translation available at <http://cisgw3.law.pace.edu/cases/960123f1.html> (case concerned artificially sweetened wine)
- France 26 May 1999 *Cour de Cassation* [Supreme Court] (*Schreiber v. Thermo* Dynamique); CLOUT case No. 315; case presentation including English translation available at <http://cisgw3.law.pace.edu/cases/990526f1.html> (case concerned metal sheets absolutely unfit for the foreseen kind of manufacture by the buyer's sub-buyer)

Para 13, *ibid.*: "The same solution has been reached where the non-conformity of the goods resulted from added substances the addition of which was illegal both in the country of the seller and the buyer"; *see*

- France 23 January 1996 *Cour de Cassation* [Supreme Court] (*Sacovini/M Marrazza v. Les* fils *de Henri Ramel*) (case concerned artificially sweetened wine that is forbidden under European Union law and national laws);
- Germany 12 October 1995 *Landgericht* [District Court] Trier; CLOUT case No. 170; case presentation including English translation available at <http://cisgw3.law.pace.edu/cases/951012g1.html> (case concerned bottles of artificially sweetened wine that were seized and destroyed by German authorities in the buyer's country)

See also UNCITRAL *Digest* of case law on CISG Art. 46, *op. cit.*:

Para 14: "Special problems arise when the *goods are* – even seriously – *defective but reparable*. Several courts have found that easy reparability of defects excludes any fundamentality of the breach"; *see*

- Switzerland 26 April 1995 *Handelsgericht* [Commercial Court] Zürich; CLOUT case No. 196; case presentation including English translation available at <http://cisgw3.law.pace.edu/cases/950426s1.html> (case concerned leak in a saltwater isolation tank; the court held that the buyer had lost its right to declare the contract avoided under CISG Art. 49 because the buyer had failed to notify the seller about the lack of conformity of the goods in a timely fashion (CISG Art. 39 and 49(2)(b)(i)); the court also mentioned that the seller's failure to perform its obligation was probably not a fundamental breach as the damage concerned was easily repairable; however, because the buyer had lost its right under CISG Art. 49(2)(b)(i), the court did not address this question fully)

Para 14, *id.*: "At least when the seller offers and effects speedy repair without any inconvenience to the buyer courts will not find that a breach is fundamental. This is in line with seller right to cure as provided for in article 48 of the Convention"; *see*

- France 26 April 1995 *Cour d'appel* [Appellate Court] Grenoble (*Marques Roque Joachim v. Manin Rivière*); CLOUT case No. 152; case presentation including English translation available at <http://cisgw3.law.pace.edu/cases/950426f2.html> (case concerned the sale of a second-hand portable warehouse shed; a certain quantity of the goods were not fit for the particular purpose of reassembly; because that defect related to only part of the warehouse and concerned metal elements that could be repaired, it did not constitute a fundamental breach such as to deprive the buyer of what he was entitled to expect under the contract)

- Germany 31 January 1997 *Oberlandesgericht* [Appellate Court] Koblenz; CLOUT case No. 282; case presentation available at <http://cisgw3.law.pace.edu/cases/970131g1.html> (case concerned the quantity of the goods (acrylic blankets); because the seller had made an offer to deliver new goods, which was refused by the buyer, the lack of quality did not amount to a fundamental breach of contract (CISG Art. 25); in considering a breach to be fundamental, account has to be taken not only of the gravity of the defect but also of the willingness of the party in breach to provide substitute goods without causing unreasonable inconvenience to the other party (CISG Art. 48(1)); thus, in this case, even a serious lack of quality was said not to constitute a fundamental breach as the seller had offered to furnish additional blankets (CISG Art. 49(1)); therefore, not only was the buyer not entitled to damages as it had rejected the seller's offer for new delivery without justification (CISG Art. 80) but the buyer had also lost its right to reduce the price (CISG Art. 50))

[39a]For commentary and relevant case law on the buyer's right to require repair of non-conforming goods, *see UNCITRAL Digest* of case law on CISG Art. 46, *op. cit.*: Para 17. "Article 46(3) provides for a right to repair if the delivered goods do not conform to the contract in the sense of article 35. Moreover, repair must be reasonable in the light of all the circumstances. Finally, the buyer must give timely notice of its request for repair"; *see* the following:

- France 29 January 1998 *Cour d'appel* [Appellate Court] Versailles (*Giustina International v. Perfect Circle Europe*); CLOUT case No. 225; case presentation including English translation available at <http://cisgw3.law.pace.edu/cases/980129f1.html> (case concerned defects in high-tech equipment; the court noted that the buyer, when reporting the defects, had requested their rectification and had thus complied with the requirements set out in CISG Art. 46; with regard to the reasonable time for exercising the right of avoidance (CISG Art. 49), the court noted that the buyer had not failed to comply with that provision by suing the seller after giving notice of its intention to have the contract avoided, because the buyer had reasonably endeavored to maintain the contract in force and the seller had requested additional periods of time, which were granted by the buyer (CISG Art. 47))

Para 18. "It is necessary that the goods are reparable so that the defect can be cured by repair. A request for repair would, however, be unreasonable if, e.g., the buyer could easily repair the goods himself. But the seller remains liable for any costs of such repair"; *see*

- Germany 9 June 1995 Oberlandesgericht [Appellate Court] Hamm; CLOUT case No. 125; case presentation including English translation available at <http://cisgw3.law.pace.edu/cases/950609g1.html> (the court held that the seller had to bear the costs incurred by the buyer in installing the substitute window panes delivered by the seller)

Para 19. "Repair is effectively executed when after repair the goods can be used as agreed"; *see*

- France 26 April 1995 *Cour d'appel* [Appellate Court] Grenoble (*Marques Roque Joachim v. Manin Rivière*); CLOUT case No. 152; case presentation including English translation available at <http://cisgw3.law.pace.edu/cases/950426f2.html> (case concerned the sale of a second-hand portable warehouse shed)

Para 19, *id.*: "If the repaired goods subsequently become defective the buyer must give notice of the defects"; *see*

- Germany 9 November 1994 *Landgericht* [District Court] Oldenburg; case presentation including English translation available at <http://cisgw3.law.pace.edu/cases/941109g1.html> (the court opined that a failed repair represents another non-performance of the contract, so that the exercise of remedies of the buyer for breach of contract by the seller requires another notice)

Para 19, *id.*: "It has been held that as to this notice the period of time of article 39 applies"; *see*:

- Germany 9 November 1994 *Landgericht* [District Court] Oldenburg

Para 19, *id.*: "However, the request for repair can be notified within a reasonable time thereafter"; *see*

- France 29 January 1998 *Cour d'appel* [Appellate Court] Versailles (*Giustina International v. Perfect Circle Europe*); CLOUT case No. 225; case presentation including English translation available at <http://cisgw3.law.pace.edu/cases/980129f1.html> (case concerned defects in high-tech equipment; the buyer, in conjunction with the notices of non-conformity, had required the seller to remedy the defects, in compliance with CISG Art. 46(3); the buyer granted to the seller an additional period of time for performance of its obligations as a result of the seller's announcement that it intended to repair the machines; in the opinion of the Court, having regard to the difficulties involved in the repairs, the additional period of time was of reasonable length and therefore satisfied the requirements of CISG Art. 47(1))

Para 19, *id.*: "A first notice within two weeks, a second notice after a month and further notices after six and eleven months have been regarded as notices within a reasonable time"; *see*

- France 29 January 1998 *Cour d'appel* [Appellate Court] Versailles (*Giustina International v. Perfect Circle Europe*) *supra*

[44a]For relevant case law regarding the requirement to pay the price, *see* the UNCITRAL *Digest* of case law on CISG Art. 62 (A/CN.9/SER.C/DIGEST/CISG/62 [8 June 2004]); also available at <http://cisgw3.law.pace.edu/cisg/text/anno-art-62.html#ucd>. There are numerous cases on point, *see e.g.*:

- Germany 21 April 2004 *Oberlandesgericht* [Appellate Court] Düsseldorf; case presentation available at <http://cisgw3.law.pace.edu/cases/040421g2.html> (court upheld seller's claim for the payment of the price in accordance with CISG Arts. 53 and 62)
- Switzerland 19 February 2004 *Bundesgericht* [Supreme Court]; case presentation available at <http://cisgw3.law.pace.edu/cases/040219s1.html> (court held that buyer was thus obliged to pay in

accordance with CISG Art. 53, and the seller was entitled to seek payment in accordance with CISG Art. 62)

- Germany 27 October 2003 *Oberlandesgericht* [Appellate Court] Rostock; case presentation including English translation available at <http://cisgw3.law.pace.edu/cases/031027g1.html> (court held that, under CISG Art.53, the buyer must pay the price for the goods as required by the contract and the Convention, and, accordingly, the seller may require the buyer to pay the price under CISG Art. 62)
- Russia 17 September 2003 Arbitration proceeding 24/2003; case presentation including English translation available at <http://cisgw3.law.pace.edu/cases/030917r1.html> (the tribunal granted the seller's claim for payment for goods delivered, in accordance with CISG Arts. 53, 54, 61, and 62, as well as annual interest for the delay in payment, pursuant to CISG Art. 78)
- Germany 15 July 2003 *Landgericht* [District Court] Mönchengladbach; case presentation including English translation available at <http://cisgw3.law.pace.edu/cases/030715g1.html> (case concerned buyer's refusal to pay the purchase price, but court awarded the seller the purchase price in accordance with CISG Arts. 53 and 62)
- Belgium 2 December 2002 *Hof van Beroep* [Appellate Court] Gent; case presentation available at <http://cisgw3.law.pace.edu/cases/021202b1.html> (court ruled on the obligations of the buyer to take receipt of goods and pay the price pursuant to CISG Arts. 53 and 62)
- Argentina 21 July 2002 Cámara Nacional de Apelaciones en lo Comercial [Appellate Court] Buenos Aires (*Cervecería y Malteria Paysandú S.A. v. Cervecería Argentina S.A.*); case presentation including English translation available at <http://cisgw3.law.pace.edu/cases/020721a1.html> (court concluded that the seller was entitled to payment of the price plus interest, according to CISG Arts. 28, 53, 59, 61, 62, and 78)
- Germany 27 February 2002 *Landgericht* [District Court] München; case presentation including English translation available at <http://cisgw3.law.pace.edu/cases/020227g1.html> (court upheld the seller's claim for payment of the price pursuant to CISG Arts. 53 and 62, but also allowed a reduction of 30 percent in the purchase price for defects in the goods)
- Germany 29 July 1998 *Landgericht* [District Court] Erfurt; CLOUT case No. 344; case presentation including English translation available at <http://cisgw3.law.pace.edu/cases/980729g1.html> (court held that the seller was entitled to recover the price under CISG Art. 62, plus interest under CISG Art. 78)
- Germany 9 July 1997 *Oberlandesgericht* [Appellate Court] München; CLOUT case No. 273; case presentation including English translation available at <http://cisgw3.law.pace.edu/cases/970709g1.html> (court found that the seller's claim for the full purchase price was justified in accordance with CISG Arts. 53 and 62)
- Germany 2 August 1996 *Landgericht* [District Court] Bielefeld; CLOUT case No. 376; case presentation including English translation available at <http://cisgw3.law.pace.edu/cases/960802g1.html> (court ordered buyer (i) to fulfil his obligation under the contract, which was considered duly formed, and pay seller, in accordance with CISG Art. 62, the remainder of the purchase price; (ii) to reimburse seller for costs incurred due to bounced checks in accordance with Cisg Art. 61; and (iii) to pay interest on the purchase price in accordance with CISG Art. 78)
- Germany 8 March 1995 *Oberlandesgericht* [Appellate Court] München; CLOUT case No. 134; case presentation including English translation available at <http://cisgw3.law.pace.edu/cases/950308g1.html> (it was held that a contract for 3,000 tons of electrolyte nickel/copper cathodes for approximately US $17 million had been effectively concluded between the parties and that the seller's claim for payment was justified under CISG Arts. 53 and 62)
- Icc Arbitration Case No. 7197 of 1992; CLOUT case No. 104; case presentation available at <http://cisgw3.law.pace.edu/cases/927197i1.html> (in this case the tribunal
  - observed that in accordance with CISG Art. 54 the obligation of the buyer to pay the price involves the obligation to take all measures and comply with all contractual and legal formalities required for payment of the price, such as the opening of a documentary credit or a bank guarantee or even the authorization to transfer currency
  - found that the buyer committed a breach of contract in that it failed to open the irrevocable and divisible letter of credit provided for in the contract, despite the additional period of time allowed by the seller (CISG Arts. 54, 62, and 63(1))
  - also found that the seller was entitled to demand performance (CISG Art. 62), without losing its right to request damages (CISG Art. 74) because no *force majeure* was involved (CISG Arts. 61(1)(a), 61(2), and 79(1))
  - in accordance with CISG Art. 74, awarded to the seller the expenses it had incurred in the deposit of the goods
  - nevertheless, held that the buyer was not liable for the damages to the goods due to the prolonged deposit period because the risk in respect of the goods had not passed to the buyer as the seller neither delivered the goods nor placed them at the disposal of the buyer (Art. 69 CISG)
  - also awarded the seller interest on the amount due (CISG Art. 78))

[51a]The remedies of specific performance and avoidance are inconsistent with each other. *See* CISG Art. 81(1) [Effect of avoidance], which provides the following:

> Avoidance of the contract *releases* both parties from their obligations under it, subject to any damages which may be due [. . .] [emphasis added].

See also the Text of Secretariat Commentary on CISG Art. 62, *op. cit.*:

> Comment 11[Inconsistent Acts by the Seller] Article 58 *[draft counterpart of* CISG *Art. 62]* also provides that in order for the seller to exercise the right to require performance of the contract he must not have acted inconsistently with that right, e.g. by avoiding the contract under article 60 *[draft counterpart of CISG Art. 64]*.

The seller is also deprived of the right to specific performance if he has fixed an additional period of time for performance (CISG Art. 63). *See* the *UNCITRAL Digest* of case law on CISG Art. 62, *op. cit.*, para 3.

Cf. Sevón, *supra* note 50, at 223, where the author states

> If the seller has fixed an additional period of time for payment, during this period he may not, under Article 63(2), resort to any remedy for breach of contract. It may be asked whether he still may require the price to be paid during this period. It seems that fixing an additional period of time for payment of the price is one way of requiring payment. It is difficult to see any reason why such a requirement may not be repeated during the fixed period.

On the contrary, an action for damages for breach of contract (CISG Art. 74) is not inconsistent with a request for specific performance. *See* the Secretariat Commentary:

> Comment 7: The seller can require performance under this article and also sue for damages. Where the buyer's non-performance of one of his obligations consists in the delay in the payment of the price, the seller's damages would normally include interest. [*See* also CISG Art. 78, a provision that was added to the Official Text after the Secretariat Commentary was written. Art. 78 states: "If a party fails to pay the price or any other sum that is in arrears, the other party is entitled to interest on it, without prejudice to any claim for damages recoverable under article 74.]

[70a]The Convention does not provide penalties for noncompliance, nor does it make provision for *judicial* penalties. *See* relevant case law regarding *contractual* penalties, the validity and enforcement of which is left to the gap-filling performed by the applicable domestic law (in accordance with CISG Art. 7(2)):

- ICC Arbitration Case No. 7197 of 1992; CLOUT case No. 104; case presentation available at <http://cisgw3.law.pace.edu/cases/927197i1.html> (in this case the tribunal, applying Austrian law pursuant to CISG Art. 7(2), ruled that the exercise of the seller's right to demand compensation was not contrary to the penalty clause contained in the contract)
- Russia 5 June 2003 Arbitration proceeding 2/2002; case presentation including English translation available at <http://cisgw3.law.pace.edu/cases/030605r1.html> (the tribunal found that pursuant to CISG Art. 53 the buyer must pay the sum in arrears sought by the seller for the goods delivered; the tribunal also stated that as any issues not settled in the CISG had to be governed by Russian domestic law (CISG Art. 7(2)), the seller could recover the payment of *contractual* penalties for the delay by buyer in payment of the price, in accordance with the Russian Federation Civil Code)
- Russia 4 April 1997 Arbitration proceeding 387/1995; case presentation including English translation available at <http://cisgw3.law.pace.edu/cases/970404r1.html> (in this case, there existed a contractual provision that a fine shall be paid for any delay in payment; however, the tribunal took into account a confidential agreement signed by the parties, in accordance with which the period of time within which the payment was to be made was extended to 120 days, and thus it ruled that the seller's claim of penalties for the delay in payment buyer could not sustained)

Modification or termination of contract and formalities: Remarks on the manner in which the UNIDROIT Principles of International Commercial Contracts may be used to interpret or supplement Article 29 of the CISG

Sieg Eiselen

a. Article 29 of the CISG deals with the requirements for the modification and termination of contracts. It further entrenches the principles of party autonomy, freedom of contract, and freedom from formalities contained in Article 11 of the CISG.[1] These principles also form the foundation of the UNIDROIT Principles of International Commercial

[1] Ferrari F., in Schlechtriem P. H. & Bacher K., *Kommentar zum einheitlichen UN Kaufrecht* 3rd ed (2000 München) Art 7 Rn 48; Magnus U., in Martinek M. (ed) *J. von Staudingers Kommentar zum Bürgerlichen Gesetzbuch mit Einführungsgesetz und Nebengesetze: Wiener UN-Kaufrecht* (1999 Berlin) Art 7 Rn 42, Art 29 Rn 1, 2 & 9; Burkhart F *Interpretatives Zusammenwirken von CISG und UNIDROIT Principles* (2000 Baden-Baden) 194; Karollus M., in Honsell H., *Kommentar zum UN Kaufrecht* (1997 Berlin) Art 29 Rn 9; Witz W., Salger in Salger H. C. & Lorenz M., *Internationales Einheitliches Kaufrecht* (2000 Heidelberg)

Contracts as expressed in Articles 1.1, 1.5, and 2.18 and should therefore form the governing principles in the interpretation of any contract as well as its modification or termination.[2]

b. Article 2.18 of the UNIDROIT Principles in itself sheds little light on the interpretation or augmentation of Article 29 of the CISG as both Articles are formulated in almost exactly the same words, with one insignificant exception. Where Article 2.18 of the UNIDROIT Principles deals with the abuse of the written modification clause, it refers to the prohibition to rely on such clause to the extent that the other party has "acted in reliance" on that conduct. The CISG merely refers to the extent that the other party has "relied on that conduct." It is submitted that nothing turns on this divergence as reliance in itself implies some action or failure to act on the part of that party.

c. In interpreting the scope of Article 2.18 of the UNIDROIT Principles, regard should also be had to the provisions of Article 3.2, which deals with freedom of form and formalities. In the Comments it is stated that mere agreement between the parties is sufficient for the valid conclusion, modification, and termination of agreements without any further requirements to be found in domestic law. Specific reference is made to the fact that the requirement of consideration, which may be applicable in common law legal systems, is excluded. This is in conformity with the approach taken in the CISG.[3]

d. The first object of both Article 29 CISG and Article 2.18 of the UNIDROIT Principles is to reinforce the principle that any agreed modification or termination will be valid in whatever form it is made or contained.[4] Its second object is also to eliminate an important difference in approach between civil and common law; namely, clearly establishing that no consideration is necessary for any amendment to be valid.[5] However, it also entrenches the time-honored principle that where parties have by agreement voluntarily restricted their ability to modify or terminate a contract by requiring formalities for such actions, that agreement will be valid and enforceable.[6]

Art 29 Rn 8; Kritzer A. H., *Guide to the Practical Applications of the United Nations Convention on Contracts for the International Sale of Goods* (1989 Deventer) 115.

[2] UNIDROIT Principles Art 2.18 Comment 1; Petz T., *Die UNIDROIT Prinzipien für internationale Handelsverträge* (2000 Wien) 56–57; Bonell M. J., 1995 *Tul. L. Rev.* 1134–1135.

[3] *See* paragraph **d.**, *infra*.

[4] Enderlein F. & Maskow D., *International Sales Law – United Nations Convention on Contracts for the International Sale of Goods* (1992 New York) par 1.1 at p. 123 <http://cisgw3.law.pace.edu/cisg/biblio/enderlein.html>; Salger Art 29 Rn 13; Honsell/Karollus Art 29 Rn 1 & 8; Schlechtriem Art 29 Rn 3; Magnus Art Rn 7 & 9; and United States 22 September 1994 Federal District Court [New York] (*Graves v. Chilewich*) <http://cisgw3.law.pace.edu/cases/940922u1.html>. In the case Germany 22 February 1994 *Oberlandesgericht* [Appellate Court] Köln <http://cisgw3.law.pace.edu/cases/940222g1.html>, the court held that although a termination could not be construed from silence or inaction in itself, silence or inaction in conjunction with other factors may provide sufficient evidence of an acceptance of an offer of termination. It is suggested that this also holds true for modifications. *See* Switzerland 5 October 1999 *Obergericht* [Appellate Court] Basel <http://cisgw3.law.pace.edu/cases/991005s1.html> where the principle was discussed but the court found that on the facts an amendment had not been proven; and Belgium 17 May 2002 *Hof van Beroep* [Appellate Court] Gent <http://cisgw3.law.pace.edu/cases/991005s1.html> where the failure of the one party to respond to the letter of another was interpreted as constituting an acceptance of the amendment offered by the other party. On this issue, *see* also Enderlein & Maskow para 6.1 at p. 125.

[5] Commentary of the UNCITRAL Secretariat on Article 27 of the 1978 Draft, Document A/CONF.97/5 pp. 27–28 as reprinted in Honnold J., *Documentary History of the Uniform Law for International Sales* (1989 Deventer) and at <http://cisgw3.law.pace.edu/cisg/text/secomm/secomm-29.html>. *See* also John E. Murray, Jr., excerpt from 8 *J.L. & Com.* (1988) 11–51 "An Essay on the Formation of Contracts and Related Matters under the United Nations Convention on Contracts for the International Sale of Goods" <http://cisgw3.law.pace.edu/cisg/text/murray29.html>. This has been confirmed in the following decisions: United States 17 December 2001 Federal District Court [Michigan] (*Shuttle Packaging v. Tsonakis*) <http://cisgw3.law.pace.edu/cases/011217u1.html>; ICC Arbitration Case No. 7331 of 1994 <http://cisgw3.law.pace.edu/cases/947331i1.html>.

[6] Honsell/Karollus Art 29 Rn 1,9 & 11; Salger Art 29 Rn 13 & 14; Magnus Art 29 Rn 7 & 9.

e. The commentary to Article 2.18 of the UNIDROIT Principles makes it clear that the second object of the Article is to generally render oral modifications or terminations void where parties have prescribed formalities, thereby rejecting the idea that such modification or termination may be viewed as an implied abrogation of the written modification or termination clause. This approach confirms the same interpretative conclusion reached by Schlechtriem in respect of Article 29 CISG.[7]

f. Both Article 29 CISG and Article 2.18 of the UNIDROIT Principles seem to apply only where the modification or restriction clause is contained in a "written agreement."[8] In interpreting what constitutes a written agreement, the UNIDROIT Principles may be helpful as Article 13 CISG only extends the concept of writing to telegrams and telexes. Article 1.10 of the UNIDROIT Principles extends the meaning of written to "any mode of communication that preserves a record of the information contained therein and is capable of being reproduced in tangible form." It is generally recognized that Article 13 CISG contains a gap in that it only refers to older forms of technology and does not provide for more modern forms of electronic communications, such as e-mail, fax, or Internet communications.[9] It is suggested that the meaning of "written" should be extended to include these forms of communications in accordance with the definition contained in Article 1.10 of the UNIDROIT Principles.[10] That definition has the advantage of being clear, practical, and technologically neutral without losing sight of the object of the written formality; namely, preserving an objective reproducible record of the communication between the parties.

g. The issue of merger clauses is not dealt with in this chapter as it is covered more appropriately under Article 8 CISG, which deals with the interpretation and proof of agreements.[11]

h. The exception created in Article 29(2) CISG is one area in which the application of Article 29 may lead to interpretational difficulties.[12] The rule is based on principles contained in the so-called *Mißbrauchseinwand* of German law, the "*nemo suum venire contra factum proprium*" principle of Roman law, or the doctrine of waiver and estoppel of Anglo-American law.[13]

[7] Schlechtriem Art 29 Rn 5. *See* also Salger Art 29 Rn 5; Honsell/Karollus Art 29 Rn 15; Magnus Art 29 Rn 12.

[8] Schlechtriem Art 29 Rn 9; Honsell/Karollus Art 29 Rn 12.

[9] Eiselen S., "Electronic Commerce and the UN CISG," 1996 *EDI L. Rev.* 21 <http://cisgw3.law.pace.edu/cisg/biblio/eiselen1.html>; Schlechtriem Art 13 Rn 2; Magnus Art 29 Rn 13.

[10] *See* Honnold, *Uniform Law for International Sales under the 1980 United Nations Convention* 3rd ed. (1999 Deventer) Rn 130; Eiselen 21. For a contrary view on electronic communications, *see* Schlechtriem Art 13 Rn 2.

For a further relevant discussion of CISG Art. 13, *see* Ulrich G. Schroeter, "Editorial Remarks on the Manner in which the Principles of European Contract Law May Be Used to Interpret or Supplement CISG Article 13," available at <http://cisgw3.law.pace.edu/cisg/text/peclcomp13.html#er>.

[11] *See* the Editorial Remarks by Perillo J. M. on Article 8 CISG, at <http://cisgw3.law.pace.edu/cisg/principles/uni8.html#edrem>.

[12] *See* the discussion in Honsell/Karollus Rn 17–23; Robert A. Hillman, "Article 29(2) of the United Nations Convention on Contracts for the International Sale of Goods: A New Effort at Clarifying the Legal Effect of 'No Oral Modification' Clauses," 21 *Cornell Int'l. L. J.* (1988) 449–466 at <http://cisgw3.law.pace.edu/cisg/biblio/hillman2.html> p. 458, 460 and 465. In the case law, the exception has been mentioned but denied in cases where there was a lack of any evidence showing reliance. *See* Belgium 2 May 1995 *Rechtbank van* [District Court] *van koophandel* Hasselt (*Vital Berry Marketing v. Dira-Frost*) <http://cisgw3.law.pace.edu/cases/950502b1.html>. However, in Austria 15 June 1994 Vienna Arbitration proceeding SCH-4318 <http://cisgw3.law.pace.edu/cases/940615a4.html>, the arbitrator did apply the exception relying on the principle of estoppel.

[13] Schlechtriem Art 29 Rn 10; Honnold Rn 204 footnote 8; Salger Art 29 Rn 16; Kritzer 235; Honsell/Karollus Art 29 Rn 18 & 19; Enderlein & Maskow para 5.1 at p 125. *See* also Austria 15 June 1994 Vienna Arbitration proceeding Sch-4318 <http://cisgw3.law.pace.edu/cases/940615a4.html> para 5.4. These principles

i. The illustrations contained in the Comments to Article 2.18 of the UNIDROIT Principles may be helpful in the interpretation of Article 29 CISG in this regard. See also the examples mentioned by Schlechtriem.[14] It may be asked, however, whether the Comments call for a further requirement not specifically contained in Article 2.18 of the UNIDROIT Principles; namely, that the reliance must have been *reasonable* under the circumstances.[15] It would seem that this requirement is justifiable when viewed in light of the principle of good faith. Where reliance was not reasonable under the circumstances, a party ought not to be allowed to use the defense contained in Article 29(2).[16]

j. Neither the CISG nor the UNIDROIT Principles make provision for the case where the parties have agreed to further formalities, such as signature or witnesses for an amendment or termination.[17] It is submitted that it would be in accordance with the provisions of Articles 29 CISG and 2.18 of the UNIDROIT Principles that the parties be held bound to such formalities and that non-complying modifications or terminations would be void, unless the abuse exception contained in Articles 29(2) CISG and 2.18 of the UNIDROIT Principles should apply.[18]

are also underpinned by the principle of *bona fides* contained in Art 7 CISG. In this regard, *see* the comments in Mexico 30 November 1998 Compromex Arbitration (*Dulces Luisi v. Seoul International*) <http://cisgw3.law.pace.edu/cases/981130m1.html>; and Austria 15 June 1994 Vienna Arbitration proceeding Sch-4318 <http://cisgw3.law.pace.edu/cases/940615a4.html>.

[14] Art 29 Rn 10. *See* also the discussion and examples mentioned in Honnold Rn 204; Salger Art 29 Rn 16 & 18; Honsell/Karollus Art 29 Rn 18 & 19.

[15] This would seem to be the scope of the decision in Germany 22 May 1992 *Landgericht* [District Court] Mönchengladbach <http://cisgw3.law.pace.edu/cases/920522g1.html> where the court states that when receiving a document such as an expert's opinion rendered on behalf of the other party, the latter should be held bound to that document as a declaration of will if the party receiving it should have understood it as such and in fact understood it as such, looking at it objectively.

[16] Magnus Art 29 Rn 17; Honsell/Karollus Art 29 Rn 20. *See* also the discussion of the necessity to apply this exception with *flexibility* in Salger Art 29 Rn 17. *See* also the concept of reasonableness as a general principle of the CISG <http://cisgw3.law.pace.edu/cisg/text/reason.html>.

[17] Honsell/Karollus Art 29 Rn 14.

[18] Enderlein & Maskow para 3.2 at p 124; Honnold Rn 202. Note the contrary view of Honsell/Karollus Art 29 Rn 14 who argues that, unless there is a clear indication that the parties indeed insisted on stricter formalities, there should be no presumption that the parties required such strict compliance.

Conformity of the goods: Interpreting or supplementing Article 35 of the CISG by using the UNIDROIT Principles of International Commercial Contracts and the Principles of European Contract Law

René Franz Henschel

a. The provisions in the CISG on the conformity of goods to the sales contract are included in Article 35.[1] This article is in three sections, of which the first, the conformity

[1] See Henschel, R. F., *Conformity of Goods in International Sales. An Analysis of Article 35 in the United Nations Convention on the International Sale of Goods (CISG)* (forthcoming, Copenhagen, 2005); Kruisinga, S., *(Non-) Conformity in the 1980 UN Convention on Contracts for the International Sale of Goods: A Uniform Concept?* (2004); Schwenzer, I. in Schlechtriem, P. & Bacher, K.(eds.), *Kommentar zum Einheitlichen UN-Kaufrecht* 3rd ed. (München, 2000), Art. 35; Schlechtriem, P., *Einheitliches Kaufrecht und nationales Obligationenrecht* (Baden-Baden, 1987), Art. 35; Bianca, C. M. & Bonell, M. J., *Commentary on the International Sales Law* (Milan, 1987), Art. 35; Honnold, J. O., *Uniform Law for International*

of the goods to the terms of the contract, consists of the *primary rule* for assessing lack of conformity. Only where the parties have not agreed otherwise will the *secondary* rule in Article 35(2) apply, which provides a number of positively expressed assumptions about the contractual requirements for the goods. Finally, Article 35(3) contains an exception to the seller's liability for some lack of conformity of goods, where the buyer knew or could not have been unaware of the lack of conformity.

b. Unlike the CISG, the UNIDROIT Principles and the PECL cover not only sales contracts but also other types of contracts (e.g., contracts of service). To provide maximum flexibility and to facilitate future development of the two sets of principles, the fundamental rules regarding the conformity of performance have been described in more general terms. In Article 7.1.1. of the UNIDROIT Principles, non-performance is defined as a failure by a party to perform any of its obligations under the contract, including defective performance or late performance. The same approach is taken in PECL; see Article 8:101(1)[2] with Comment A.[3] Although the UNIDROIT Principles and the PECL do not have any rules that directly resemble CISG Article 35, several articles may be used to interpret or supplement it. The following paragraphs analyze the

Sales under the 1980 United Nations Convention (The Hague, 1999); Kritzer, A., *Guide to the Practical Application of the 1980 United Nations Convention on Contracts for the International Sale of Goods* (Deventer, 1994); Bernstein, H. & Lookofsky, J., *Understanding the* CISG *Europe*, 2nd ed. (The Hague, 2003), p. 74 *et seq.*; von Staudinger, J., *Kommentar zum Bürgerlichen Gesetzbuch mit Einführungsgesetz und Nebengesetzen: Wiener UN-Kaufrecht (Cisg)* (Berlin, 2000), Art. 35; Ramberg, J. & Herre, J., *Internationella köplagen (*CISG*)* (Stockholm, 2001), Art. 35; Bridge, M., *The International Sale of Goods. Law and Practice* (Oxford, 2000); Achilles, W., *Kommentar zum UN-Kaufrechtsübereinkommen* (CISG) (Neuwied, 2000), Art. 35; Enderlein, F. & Maskow, D., *International Sales Law* (New York, 1994), Art. 35, also available online at <http://cisgw3.law.pace.edu/cisg/biblio/enderlein.html#art35>; Audit, B., *La vente internationale de marchandises* (Paris, 1990), Article 35; Heuzé, V., *La vente internationale de marchandises* (Paris, 2000), Article 35; Bergem, J. & Rognlien, R., *Kjøpsloven 1988 og FN-konvensjonen 1980 om internasjonale løsørekjøp* (Oslo, 1995), Art. 35; Gomard, B. & Rechnagel, H., *International Købelov* (Copenhagen, 1990), Art. 35; Piltz, B., *Internationales UN-Kaufrecht* (München, 1993), Art. 35; Galston, N. M. & Smit, H., *International Sales. The United Nations Convention on Contracts for the International Sale of Goods* (New York, 1984), Art. 35; Herber, R. & Czerwenka, B., *Internationales Kaufrecht* (München, 1991), Art. 35; Bucher, E., *Wiener Kaufrecht* (Bern, 1991), Art. 35; Karollus, M., *UN-Kaufrecht* (Wien, 1991), Art. 35; Heilmann, S., *Mängelgewährleistung im UN-Kaufrecht* (Berlin, 1994); Veneziano, A., "Non Conformity of Goods in International Sales. A Survey of Current Caselaw on CISG," *Int'l. Bus. L. J.* no. 1 (1997), p. 39–65; Poikela, T., "Conformity of Goods in the 1980 United Nations Convention on the International Sale of Goods", Nordic *J. Com. L*, No. 1, 2003, available at <http://www.njcl.fi/1_2003/article5.htm>; Henschel, R. F., "Conformity of Goods Governed by CISG Article 35: Caveat Venditor, Caveat Emptor and Contract Law as Background Law and as a Competing Set of Rules," *Nordic J. Com. L*, No. 1, 2004, available at: <http://www.njcl.fi/1_2004/article2.htm>; Aue, J., *Mängelgewährleistung im UN-Kaufrecht unter besonderer Berücksichtigung Stillschweigender Zusicherungen* (Frankfurt A.M., 1989); Krüger, U., *Modificierte Erfolgshaftung im UN-Kaufrecht* (Frankfurt A.M., 1989); Su, X., *Die vertragsgemäße Beschaffenheit der Ware im UNCITRAL-Kaufrecht im vergelich zum deutschen und chinesischen Recht* (Münster, 1996); Ziegler, U., *Leistungsstüringsrecht nach dem UN-Kaufrecht* (Baden-Baden, 1995); Flesch, K., *Mängelhaftung und Beschaffenheitsirrtum beim Kauf* (Baden-Baden, 1994); Zeller, B., *Methodology for the Interpretation and Application of the United Nations Convention for the International Sale of Goods* (Melbourne, 2003) available at <http://cisgw3.law.pace.edu/cisg/biblio/4corners.html>; Felemegas, J., "The United Nations Convention for the International Sale of Goods: Article 7 and Uniform Interpretation," *Pace Review of the Convention on Contracts for the International Sale of Goods (*CISG*)*, Kluwer Law International (2000–2001) 115–265 (New York, 2001), also available online at <http://cisgw3.law.pace.edu/cisg/biblio/felemegas.html>.

[2] Article 8.101(1) states, "Whenever a party does not perform an obligation under the contract and the non-performance is not excused under Article 8:108, the aggrieved party may resort to any of the remedies set out in chapter 9." See Lando, O. & Beale, H., *The Principles of European Contract Law. Parts I and II. Combined and Revised* (Hague, 2000), Article 8:101.

[3] Id., in comment A: "Under the system adopted by the Principles there is non-performance whenever a party does not perform any obligation under the contract. The non-performance may consist in a defective performance or in a failure to perform at the time performance is due, be it a performance which is effected to early, too late or never" (the second sentence is omitted by this author).

manner in which Articles in the UNIDROIT Principles and the PECL may be used to interpret or supplement the different parts of CISG Article 35, in particular Article 35(1), Article 35(2)(a), and Article 35(2)(b).

c. According to Article 35(1) of the Convention, the seller must deliver goods that are of the quantity, quality, and description required by the contract and that are contained or packaged in the manner required by the contract. This provision is the primary rule on the assessment of the conformity of goods to the contract, and it covers all kinds of defects except defects of title, which are dealt with under CISG Article 41, and defects in intellectual property rights, *cf.* CISG Article 42. The rule establishes that the assessment of conformity depends primarily on what the parties have *agreed*. This is also emphasized by the Commentary prepared by the UNCITRAL Secretariat, which states that the agreement between the parties is the *primary* source for assessing conformity.[4] As mentioned above, the primary role of the contract is also emphasized in the UNIDROIT Principles Article 7.1.1 and the PECL Article 8:101 with Comment A.

d. Under the CISG, the establishment of the specific content of a contract is based on the interpretation of the agreement between the parties (*cf.* CISG Article 8 and Article 9). Here, the Articles on interpretation in the UNIDROIT Principles Chapter 4 and the PECL Chapter 5 are of relevance to interpret or supplement CISG Article 8 and Article 9 and therefore also for the interpretation of the conformity of the goods to the contract in CISG Article 35.[5]

e. If the parties have not agreed otherwise, the *secondary* rule in Article 35(2) applies. According to Article 35(2)(a) of the Convention (*cf.* Article 35(2)), except where otherwise agreed, goods do not conform with the contract unless they are fit for the purposes for which goods of the same description would ordinarily be used. With these default rules, the parties do not need to specify the purpose, as long as the goods are to be used for their ordinary purposes. Some consider this rule to be the most important rule in practice in Article 35(2),[6] expressing one of the clearest and most fundamental rules about the seller's implied obligation to provide goods that conform to the contract.[7] This rule is so widely accepted[8] that Article 35(2)(a) can probably be considered as a codification of a basic principle of international sales law.

f. In relation to Article 35(2)(a), the general assumption is that, among the ordinary purposes of goods, they should be capable of being resold.[9] In connection with this purpose, there is a dispute about whether, to be fit for this purpose, they should be of *average* quality or merely of *merchantable* quality, so that goods of below average quality but still merchantable may also be said to conform to the contract.[10] During the drafting

[4] *See* Honnold, J. O., *supra* note 1; Secretariat Commentary to Article 35(1) (Section 33(1) of the Commentary): "Paragraph (1) states the standards by which the seller's obligation to deliver goods which conform to the contract is measured. The first sentence emphasizes that the goods must conform to the quantity, quality and description required by the contract and must be contained or packaged in the manner required by the contract. This provision recognizes that the overriding source for the standard of conformity is the contract between the parties. The remainder of paragraph (1) describes specific aspects of the seller's obligations as to conformity which apply except where otherwise agreed." Comment 4. The Secretariat Commentary is also available online at <http://cisgw3.law.pace.edu/cisg/text/secomm/secomm-35.html>.

[5] For an analysis of the connection between Article 35 and Articles 8 and 9, *see* Henschel, *supra* note 1, at chapter 3.

[6] *Cf.* Lookofsky, J., *Understanding the* CISG *in Scandinavia*, 2nd ed. (Copenhagen, 2002), p. 88.

[7] *Cf.* Honnold, *supra* note 1, at 255.

[8] *Cf.* Schwenzer, I., in Schlechtriem, P., *supra* note 1, at 377, note 38.

[9] *Id.*, p. 377, pt. 14; Veneziano, A, *supra* note 1, at 44.

[10] Those in favor of the average quality standard include: Herber, R. in Herber, R. & Czerwenka, B., *op. cit.*, p. 164, pt. 4; Ziegler: *supra* note 1, at 70; Su, *supra* note 1, at 28. Those who are undecided or leave the question open include Schwenzer, I. in Schlechtriem, P., *supra* note 1, at 378, pt. 15; Bianca, C. M, *supra*

negotiations of the CISG, a Canadian proposal that goods should be of average quality was withdrawn, because several common law countries did not support it.[11] The practice in English law was of particular importance, as under English law goods that were of below average quality could be considered as conforming to the contract as long as they were merchantable.[12] As suggested by Schwenzer,[13] this argument, which is rooted in the practice of the English courts, has been somewhat weakened because the English Sale of Goods Act has been amended so it now requires goods to be of "satisfactory quality," which is decided on the basis of the expectations of a reasonable buyer.[14] In Schwenzer's opinion, this means that the two viewpoints will become closer to one another, which seems probable.

g. In the famous *Mussels* case,[15] the German Federal Supreme Court declined to decide this question on practical grounds, because no evidence had been given as to whether the cadmium levels in the mussels were higher than in corresponding mussels from New Zealand.[16] However, the court did say that, even if it was assumed that the goods should be merchantable, this did not mean that the mussels did not conform to the contract, as the seller could not be expected to know the special public law regulations on product safety, public health, etc., in the destination State.

h. In this connection, it should be relevant to consult both the UNIDROIT Principles and the PECL. Article 5.1.6 of the UNIDROIT Principles provides, "Where the quality of performance is neither fixed by, nor determinable from, the contract a party is bound to render a performance of a quality that is reasonable and not less than average in the circumstances." The relevance of this Article in the interpretation of CISG Article 35(2)(a) is supported by the illustration used in the Comment to performance of average quality, which involves the sale of goods.[17] According to the Comment to performance of a quality that is reasonable, the purpose of a reasonableness test is that a party should not be able to perform what would be an average quality in the buyer's market, if this quality is most unsatisfactory in the market of the seller.[18] There is still no available case law that makes use of Article 5.1.6.[19]

note 1, at 281; Honnold, J. O., *Uniform Law, supra* note 1, at 255 *et seq.*, pt. 225; Ramberg, J. in Ramberg, J. & Herre, J., *supra* note 1, at 233 *et seq.*, pt. 4; Achilles, *supra* note 1, at 95, pt. 6; Lookofsky, J., *supra* note 9, at 83 *et seq.*

[11] *Cf.* Honnold, J. O., *supra* note 1, at 120 *et seq.*; Bianca, C.M, *supra* note 1, at 271, pt. 1.5., p. 274, pt. 2.5.1, and p. 280 *et seq.*, pt. 3.1.

[12] For a general discussion of this, *see* Hyland, T., in Schlechtriem, P., *Einheitliches Kaufrecht und nationales Obligationenrecht*, p. 316 *et seq.*

[13] Schwenzer, I. in Schlechtriem, P., *supra* note 1, at 378, pt. 15.

[14] *Cf.* Bridge, M, *supra* note 1, at 81.

[15] Germany 8 March 1995 Bundesgerichtshof [Supreme Court], case presentation including English translation available at <http://cisgw3.law.pace.edu/cisg/cases/950308g3.html>; *see* also the Unilex database at <http://www.unilex.info/case.cfm?pid=1&id=108&do=case>.

[16] In one instance, the average quality test has been adopted in favor of the merchantability test; *see* Germany 15 September 1994 Landgericht [District Court] Berlin, case presentation including English translation available at <http://cisgw3.law.pace.edu/cisg/cases/940915g1.html>; *see* also Unilex at <http://www.unilex.info/case.cfm?pid=1&id=218&do=casehttp://www.unilex.info/case.cfm?pid=1&id=218&do=case>.

[17] In the Commentary to UNIDROIT Principles 2004 the following example is given at p. 136: "A buys 500 kgs. of oranges from B. If the contract says nothing more precise, and no other circumstances call for a different solution, those oranges may not be of less than average quality. Average quality will however suffice unless it is unreasonable defective."

[18] *Cf.* the Commentary to Article 5.1.6 of the UNIDROIT Principles 2004, at p. 137: "A company based in country X organizes a banquet to celebrate its 50th anniversary. Since the cuisine in country X is mediocre, the company orders the meal from a renowned restaurant in Paris. In these circumstances the quality of the food provided must not be less than the average standards of the Parisian restaurant; it would clearly not be sufficient simply to meet the average standards of country X." One may assume that in such cases the price will often be decisive.

[19] *Cf.* <www.unilex.info> as of 1 November 2004.

i. Similar provisions apply under PECL Article 6:108: "If the contract does not specify the quality, a party must tender performance of at least average quality." In the Comments to this Article it is stressed that the various factors mentioned in the Article on reasonableness (Article 1:302) should be taken into account when applying Article 6:108. Therefore, such factors as the normal price for the same performance as the performance in question, the contract itself, previous dealings between the parties, and trade usages should be taken into consideration.

j. In connection to the quality of goods, the view of Bianca on Article 35(2)(a) can also be given[20]: "In the absence of an express Convention provision it is not possible to determine once and for all the precise degree of quality to which the buyer is entitled. It must be said, however, that the quality can be more or less good within a tolerable degree, at least not conspicuously below the standard reasonable expected according to the price and other circumstances." Whether goods shall be of average quality or of higher or lower quality will therefore usually be decided on the basis of other factors; for example, the price of the goods.[21]

k. This view is supported by a recent arbitral award on the CISG, in which the arbitrators refused to use either the "average quality test" or the "merchantability test."[22] Instead, the test of a reasonable quality was used, as this was considered to be a truly uniform solution to the problem.[23] In my opinion, this solution is in conformity with the UNIDROIT Principles Article 5.1.6., which explicitly refers to a *reasonable quality* that is not less than average *in the circumstances*. In this way, a rigid, mathematical average level is avoided, and instead such factors as the price and expectations of the parties should be taken into consideration. The same solution could be reached using PECL Article 6:108 with Comments, although the wording of the Article seems a bit more inflexible.

l. The conclusion is that the arbitral tribunal could have supported its findings by a reference to the UNIDROIT Principles Article 5.1.6. However, the solution in the PECL seems to favor more the average quality test, although the corresponding Comment to that provision softens this approach considerably. At the same time, it should not be forgotten that if both parties to a sales contract come from the same legal culture, this might indicate that the parties' reasonable expectations[24] point toward either the "average quality test"

[20] Bianca, C. M., in Bianca, C. M. & Bonell, M. J., *supra* note 1, at 281, pt. 3.1.

[21] *Cf.* Achilles, W., *supra* note 1, at 95.

[22] *See* Netherlands 15 October 2002 Netherlands Arbitration Institute, Case no. 2319, case presentation including English translation available at <http://cisgw3.law.pace.edu/cisg/cases/021015n1.html>; *see* also Unilex at <http://www.unilex.info/case.cfm?pid=1&id=836&do=case>.

[23] *Cf.* the award, paragraphs 117 and 118:

[117] "On the basis of the arguments above, the Tribunal holds that neither the merchantability test nor the average quality test are to be used in CISG cases and that the reasonable quality standard referred to above (see No. 71) is to be preferred."

[118] "The choice in favour of a test of reasonable quality is supported by the authors and the case cited above in No. 71 as well as by those scholarly writings that have rejected the average quality test. It is compatible with the *travaux préparatoires* since the Canadian amendment does not exclude an interpretation in favour of reasonable quality since it provided that under article 35(2)(a) CISG goods are fit for their ordinary use if it is reasonable to expect a certain quality having regard to price and all other relevant circumstances. Also, any such interpretation complies with article 7(1) CISG imposing to take into account the international character of CISG and its reluctance to rely immediately on notions based on domestic law. Furthermore, the interpretation preferred by the Arbitral Tribunal is consistent with article 7(2) CISG, which primarily refers to the general principles of CISG as possible gap fillers. In this respect, it may be noted that CISG often uses open-textured provisions referring to reasonableness (e.g., articles 8, 18, 25, 33, 34, 37, 38, 39, 43, 44, 46, 48, 49, 65, 72, 75, 77, 79, 86, 87 and 88). Finally, even if one were to rely on domestic law by virtue of article 7(2) CISG, Dutch law would be applicable and would also impose a standard of reasonable quality."

[24] *Cf.* CISG Article 8.

or the "merchantable quality test"; however, the supporters of the last mentioned test seem to have decreased in number.

m. As stated in Article 35(2)(*cf.* Article 35(2)(b)), unless otherwise agreed by the parties, goods do not conform with the contract unless they are fit for any particular purpose expressly or implicitly made known to the seller at the time of the conclusion of the contract. The rule in Article 35(2)(b) can be derogated from if the circumstances show that the buyer did not rely on, or that it was unreasonable for him to rely on, the seller's skill and judgment. Reasonableness is a general principle of the CISG,[25] and as mentioned above, it should be relevant to consult the concepts of reasonableness in both the UNIDROIT Principles and the PECL[26] in this connection.

n. As mentioned above, in the *Mussels* case, the court did say that, even if it was assumed that the goods should be merchantable, this did not mean that the mussels did not conform to the contract, as the seller could not be expected to know the special public law regulations on product safety, public health, etc., in the destination State. In general, the seller should not be obliged to deliver goods that conform with special law requirements in the buyer's country, unless other circumstances indicate otherwise.[27] This has been confirmed in other cases, including decisions from common law jurisdictions.[28] Furthermore, the UNIDROIT Principles Article 6.2.14(a) seems to support this view. It follows from the said Article that, where the law of a State requires a public permission affecting

[25] *Cf.* Albert Kritzer: *Reasonableness* (Editorial remarks on reasonableness), available at <http://cisgw3.law.pace.edu/cisg/text/reason.html#def> with further references, and PECL Article 1:302 with comments in Lando & Beale: *PECL*, p. 126 *et seq*. *See* also Guillaume Weiszberg: *Le "Raisonnable en Droit du Commerce International* (Paris, 2003), available at the <http://cisgw3.law.pace.edu/cisg/biblio/Reasonableness.html>, and the reasoning in the award from the Netherlands Arbitration Institute, Case no. 2319, above note 23.

[26] *Cf.* PECL Article 1:302, with comments in Lando & Beale: *Id.*

[27] Whether the decision would have been different if, for example, the seller knew of the public health regulations in the buyer's State, or if the buyer could have assumed that the seller either knew or ought to have known of these regulations, perhaps because

(1) the seller had a branch in the buyer's State
(2) the parties had had a long-term trading arrangement
(3) the seller had regularly exported to the buyer's State or
(4) the seller had marketed his goods in the buyer's State

was according to the German Supreme Court irrelevant in this case, as the buyer had not asserted any of these circumstances. Compare with CISG Article 42 on industrial property or other intellectual property.

[28] See relevant case law:

- United States 17 May 1999 Federal District Court [Louisiana] (*Medical Marketing v. Internazionale Medico Scientifica*), case presentation available at <http://cisgw3.law.pace.edu/cisg/cases/990517u1.html>; *see* also Unilex at <http://www.unilex.info/case.cfm?pid=1&id=360&do=case>
- Spain 3 October 2002 Audiencia Provincial [Appellate Court] Pontevedra, case presentation available at <http://cisgw3.law.pace.edu/cisg/cases/021003s4.html>; *see* also Unilex at <http://www.unilex.info/case.cfm?pid=1&id=895&do=case>
- Spain 2 March 2000 Audiencia Provincial [Appellate Court] Granada, case presentation including English translation available at <http://cisgw3.law.pace.edu/cisg//cases/000302s4.html>; *see* also Unilex at <http://www.unilex.info/case.cfm?pid=1&do=case&id=889&step=Keywords>
- Germany 21 August 1995 Landgericht [District Court] Ellwangen, case presentation including English translation available at <http://cisgw3.law.pace.edu/cisg/cases/950821g2.html>; *see* also Unilex at <http://www.unilex.info/case.cfm?pid=1&id=164&do=case>
- Germany 29 January 2004 Oberlandesgericht [Appellate Court] Frankfurt am Main, case presentation including English translation available at <http://cisgw3.law.pace.edu/cisg/cases/040129g1.html>; *see* also Unilex at <http://www.unilex.info/case.cfm?pid=1&id=970&do=case>
- Australia 17 January 2003 Supreme Court of Western Australia (*Ginza Pte Ltd v Vista Corporation Pty Ltd*), case presentation available at <http://cisgw3.law.pace.edu/cisg/cases/030117a2.html>; *see* also Unilex at <http://www.unilex.info/case.cfm?pid=1&id=961&do=case>
- Austria 13 April 2000 Oberster Gerichtshof [Supreme Court]; case presentation including English translation available at <http://cisgw3.law.pace.edu/cases/000413a3.html>; *see* also Unilex at <http://www.unilex.info/case.cfm?pid=1&id=687&do=case>

the validity of the contract or its performance and neither that law nor the circumstances indicate otherwise, if only one party has its place of business in that State, that party shall take the measures necessary to obtain the permission. The Comment to this Article holds that the term "public permission" should be given a broad interpretation and that it includes all permission requirements established pursuant to a concern of a public nature, such as health, safety, or particular trade policies. Thus, the findings of the German Supreme Court and later decisions could be supported by a reference to the principle in the UNIDROIT Principles Article 6.2.14(a) too.

o. The question of mistake and of mistaken assumptions is closely linked to the issue of conformity of goods to the contract. According to ULIS Article 34, a buyer could not make claims on the basis of other legal remedies in connection with the conformity of goods that were primarily directed against objections to validity on the basis of mistake. The prevailing view on Article 35, in theory, is that it ought to displace or exhaust national rules on validity (*cf.* also the principle of the functionally adequate solution).[29] This means that the buyer will not be able to get around CISG Article 39 and the rules on making complaints.[30] However, this does not apply if there is a mistake on matters other than the conformity of the goods to the contract, because then the matter will likely be dealt with under national law.[31]

p. However, this view is resisted in some jurisdictions, where a buyer is not regarded as being prevented from relying on the rules on validity when there is a mistake in the characteristics of the goods, etc. This is the prevailing view in France, Belgium, Italy, Spain, Austria, and Switzerland.[32] For example, in France and in Austria the same period is allowed for making complaints about lack of conformity of goods to the contract under sale of goods law as for objections under the rules on validity of contracts; having the same period is an attempt to prevent a buyer from making objections to the validity of the contract several years later when some mistake is identified.[33] In Portugal, each case of complaint about lack of conformity of the goods is treated as a complaint about a mistake, so the doctrine of lack of conformity is wholly subordinate to the doctrine of contractual validity.[34]

q. In other jurisdictions the rules on lack of conformity must be regarded as exhaustive special regulations, so that claims of invalidity due to mistake must be considered as excluded. For example, this is the prevailing view in Germany,[35] whereas in Denmark

[29] *Cf.* Ferrari, F., in Schlechtriem, P., *Kommentar zum Einheitlichen UN-Kaufrecht (CISG)*, p. 97, pt. 4; Honnold, J. O., *supra* note 1, at 261 *et seq.*; Ramberg, R. in Ramberg, R. & Herre, J., *supra* note 1, at 112; Achilles, W., *supra* note 1, at 19; Flesch, K., *op. cit.*, p. 140 *et seq.*, especially at pp. 156–159; Heilmann, J., *op. cit.*, p. 146, though here the view is that only the buyer's mistake is covered, not the seller's; Zeller, B., *op. cit.*, p. 194 *et seq.*; but opposed to this, *see* Gomard, B. & Rechnagel, H., *op. cit.*, p. 38, where it is argued that national law should apply, and correspondingly Gstoehl, M., *Das Verhältnis von Gewährleistung nach UN-Kaufrecht und Irrtumsanfechtung nach nationalem Recht* (Zeitschrift für Rechtsvergleichung, Internationales Privatrecht und Europarecht, 1998/1, p. 1 *et seq.*).

[30] Compare with Flesch, K., *op. cit.*, p. 151 *et seq.*, where, by referring to the two-year rule in Article 39 as a general principle (*cf.* Article 7(2)), it is argued that there is no scope for national rules on validity of contracts that obviate this Convention principle. This is indeed a dynamic interpretation of the Convention that not everybody (including the present writer) will support.

[31] *Cf.* Switzerland 24 August 1995 Handelsgericht [Commercial Court] St. Gallen, where a buyer was unsure whether the agreement concerned the purchase of samples to a value of DM 500 or a full delivery to a value of *SFr* 90,000; case presentation is available at <http://cisgw3.law.pace.edu/cisg/cases/950824s1.html>; *see* also Unilex at <http://www.unilex.info/case.cfm?pid=1&do=case&id=162&step=Abstract>

[32] *Cf.* Schwartze, A., *Europäische Sachmängelgewährleistung beim Warenkauf* (Tübingen, 2000), p. 47 *et seq.*; Gstoehl, M., *op. cit.*, p. 1 *et seq.*; Flesch, K., *op. cit.*, p. 23 *et seq.*

[33] *Cf.* Schwartze, A., *supra* note 32, at 50.

[34] *Id.*, 51 *et seq.*

[35] With certain qualifications, *cf.* Schwartze, A., *id.*, 50 *et seq.* In relation to CISG Article 35, *cf.* Germany 14 May 1993 Landgericht [District Court] Aachen, case presentation available at <http://www.cisg.law.

there is *de facto* disagreement,[36] and the new European Directive on consumer sales does not take a view on the question.[37] The practice of the courts when interpreting CISG Article 35 seems to be split, depending on which tradition is followed in national law and the factual circumstances of the case.[38]

r. Altogether, the conclusion must be that courts may be expected to reach divergent decisions, depending on the legal tradition of the jurisdiction in question and the extent to which a dynamic or a restrictive approach is used. However, there seems to be a development toward acknowledging the primacy of Article 35, even in jurisdictions that have traditionally used a restrictive interpretation (*cf.* the decision of the *Austrian Supreme Court* of 13 April 2000).[39]

s. This development could be supported by a reference to the UNIDROIT Principles Article 3.7, which maintains the principle of the exhaustion of rights: "A party is not entitled to avoid the contract on the ground of mistake if the circumstances on which that party relies afford, or could have afforded, a remedy for non-performance." In the Commentary on this article,[40] the following example (mutual mistake)[41] is given of the application of this rule:

> A, a farmer, who finds a rusty cup on the land sells it to B, an art dealer, for 100,000 Austrian schillings. The high price is based on the assumption of both parties that the cup is made of silver (other silver objects had previously been found on the land). It subsequently turns out that the object in question is an ordinary iron cup worth only 1,000 schillings. B refuses to accept and to pay for it on the ground that it lacks the assumed quality. B also avoids the contract on the ground of mistake as to the quality of the cup. B is entitled only to the remedies for non-performance.

pace.edu/cisg/cases/930514g1.html>, *see* also Unilex <http://www.unilex.info/case.cfm?pid=1&do=case&id=23&step=Keywords>.

[36] *Cf.* Andersen, M. B. & Lookofsky, J., *Lærebog i Obligationsret*, p. 185 *et seq.*; *see* also Werlauff, E., "Review of *Lrebog i Obligationsret* by Andersen, M. B. & Lookofsky, J." (*Juristen* October 2002, p. 307 *et seq.*) with reference to the decision of the Danish Supreme Court in the case against Dansk Eternit (*Ugeskrift for Retsvsen* 2002, p. 249 *et seq.*), but refer also to Gomard, B., *Obligationsret*, Vol. 1, p. 133.

[37] *Cf.* Schwartze, A, *supra* note 32, at 53 *et seq.*

[38] *See* Germany 14 May 1993 Landgericht [District Court] Aachen, *supra* note 33, but compare that decision with the following decisions:

- Austria 20 March 1997 Supreme Court, case presentation available at <http://cisgw3.law.pace.edu/cisg/cases/970320a3.html>; *see* also Unilex at <http://www.unilex.info/case.cfm?pid=1&do=case&id=254&step=Keywords>
- Hungary 1 July 1997 Fovárosi Biróság [Metropolitan Court] Budapest, case presentation available at <http://cisgw3.law.pace.edu/cisg/cases/970701h1.html>; *see* also Unilex at <http://www.unilex.info/case.cfm?pid=1&do=case&id=270&step=Keywords>
- Switzerland 11 December 2000 Federal Supreme Court (*Rhomberg GmbH v. Ruth & Walter Ott*), case presentation including English translation available at <http://cisgw3.law.pace.edu/cisg/cases/001211s1.html>; *see* also Unilex at <http://www.unilex.info/case.cfm?pid=1&id=750&do=case> (although the case was about mutual mistake, and not unilateral mistake)
- Switzerland 22 December 2000 Federal Supreme Court (*Roland Schmidt GmbH v. Textil-Werke Blumenegg AG*), case presentation including English translation available at <http://cisgw3.law.pace.edu/cisg/cases/001222s1.html>; *see* also Unilex at <http://www.unilex.info/case.cfm?pid=1&do=case&id=729&step=Keywords>
- Austria 13 April 2000 Supreme Court, case presentation including English translation available at <http://cisgw3.law.pace.edu/cisg/cases/000413a3.html>, referred to below.

[39] Austria 13 April 2000 Supreme Court, case presentation including English translation available at <http://cisgw3.law.pace.edu/cisg/cases/000413a3.html>; *see* also Unilex at <http://www.unilex.info/case.cfm?pid=1&id=687&do=case>.

[40] *Cf.* p. 103 *et seq.*

[41] Compare this with the decision from the Swiss Federal Supreme Court of 22 December 2000, referred to above, note 36.

t. However, according to PECL Article 4:119, a party that is entitled to a remedy under the validity chapter in circumstances that afford that party a remedy for non-performance may pursue either remedy. This reveals a striking difference between the solutions given in the UNIDROIT Principles and the PECL.

u. Neither the UNIDROIT Principles nor the PECL seems to contain any provisions that might help in interpreting or that supplement the rest of CISG Article 35, (Art. 35(2)(b)–(d) (the conformity of goods according to special purpose, sample, or model, and the packaging of the goods) or CISG Article 35(3) (the buyer's knowledge of the non-conformity)), although the general rules on the interpretation of the contract in the UNIDROIT Principles and the PECL still have to be taken into consideration (*cf.* para **d.** above).

Early delivery and the seller's right to cure lack of conformity: Comparison between the provisions of Article 37 CISG and the counterpart provisions of the UNIDROIT Principles

Bertram Keller

a. In the words of Art. 37 CISG, the seller may cure a "lack of conformity . . . before the date for delivery." Once the date of delivery has passed, the limitations of Art. 48 CISG apply. For documents, Art. 34 CISG applies as *lex specialis*. Unlike the CISG, the UNIDROIT Principles (UP) stipulate one general right to cure in Art. 7.1.4 regardless of object or time.[1] Any interpretation of Art. 37 CISG in light of Art. 7.1.4 UP must take into consideration that the norm is only one part of the curing constructions provided by the CISG.

b. The legal history of Art. 37 CISG stretches from the nearly equivalent Art. 37 ULIS to the first codified right to cure in Sec. 2–508 UCC.[2] In particular the civil law tradition is less familiar with the seller's right to "tender a second time" as the seller gave the goods autonomously outside his disposal power.[3] However, the stated aim of CISG and UNIDROIT Principles is to find concepts that transcend legal traditions. As part of an "International Restatement of Contract Law"[4] Art. 7.1.4 UP encourages the worldwide acceptance of a general right to cure.[5]

[1] UNIDROIT, Principles of International Commercial Contracts (1994), Comment to Art. 7.1.4, no. 1, available online at <http://cisgw3.law.pace.edu/cisg/principles/uni37.html#official>.

[2] Ulrich Magnus in Heinrich Honsell (ed.) *Kommentar zum UN-Kaufrecht* (1997), Art. 37, no. 1; Jakob S. Ziegel, "Report to the Uniform Law Conference of Canada on CISG," available online at <http://cisgw3.law.pace.edu/cisg/text/ziegel37.html>.

[3] Herbert Stumpf in Hans Dölle (ed.), *Kommentar zum Einheitlichen Kaufrecht*. (1976); C. M. Bianca in C. M. Bianca/M. J. Bonell (eds.), *Commentary on the International Sales Law* (1987), Art. 37, no. 1.3; Karl H. Neumayer/Catharine Ming, *Convention de Vienne sur les contrats de vente internationale de marchandise* (1993) Art. 37, p. 292. Cf. also Ingeborg H. Schwenzer in Peter Schlechtriem (ed.), *Commentary on the UN Convention on the International Sale of Goods*. English Translation (1998), Art. 37, no.2. (the right to cure was unknown in Roman law).

[4] *M. J. Bonell, An International Restatement of Contract Law. The UNIDROIT Principles of International Commercial Contracts* (1997); *E. A. Farnsworth*, "An International Restatement: The UNIDROIT Principles of International Commercial Contracts" (1997) 26 *Univ. Balt. L. Rev.* 1–7.

[5] *E.g.*, the recent German reform of contract law newly introduced a right to cure after delivery for Sale Contracts in §§ 437, 439 BGB.

c. Comparing the legal context of Art. 37, the provisions in Art. 52(1) and Art. 72 CISG are relevant for the system of early performance. Whereas under Art. 52(1) CISG the buyer may deliberately refuse to take any early delivery, Art. 6.1.5 UP restricts this right if he "has no legitimate interest in so doing." However, the difference between the two Articles decreases if one considers that the option to refuse early delivery under the CISG is limited by "the observance of good faith" under Art. 7(1) and the obligation "to preserve" the goods under Art. 86.[6] The provision of anticipatory non-performance in Art. 72 CISG is very similar to the corresponding Arts. 7.3.3 and 7.3.4 UP.[7]

d. Even more common ground is offered by the *ratio legis* of the cure provisions. The CISG and the UNIDROIT Principles support the principle of maintaining contracts (*favor contractus*).[8] The possibility of cure in Art. 37 CISG and Art. 7.1.4 UP stabilizes the relations between the parties even after a defect has occurred and has the effect of preserving their deal.[9] A second common principle underlying the cure provisions is the mitigation of damages, which is reflected in Art. 77 CISG and Art. 7.4.8 UP.[10] Curing a defect minimizes economic waste. Notwithstanding the slight systematic differences, these two principles offer a solid normative basis for cross-interpretation and gap-filling.[11]

e. The phrase "before the date for delivery" in Art. 37 CISG raises the question whether the seller may cure up to the beginning or to the end of an agreed period of time (Art. 33(b),(c) CISG). Considering the leading idea is to maintain the contract and the justified expectations of the other party, most scholars are in favor of the latter alternative.[12]

[6] Fritz Enderlein/Dietrich Maskow, *International Sales Law* (1992), Art. 52, no.2; Secretariat Commentary on Art. 48, no. 3 and 4; available online at <http://cisgw3.law.pace.edu/cisg/text/secomm/secomm-48.html>; M. Will in Bianca/Bonell, Art. 52, no. 2.1.3; Ulrich Huber in Schlechtriem, Art. 52, no. 3; Neumayer/Ming, Art. 52, no. 1. But critized by Vincent Heuzé, *La vente internationale de marchandises* (2000), no. 244; John O. Honnold, *Uniform Law for International Sales under the 1980 United Nations Convention* (1999), Art. 52, no. 319 ("the buyer could gain little by an unreasonable refusal to take an early delivery").

[7] *Cf.* Sieg Eiselen, "Editorial Remarks on the Manner in Which the UNIDROIT Principles of International Commercial Contracts May Be Used to Interpret or Supplement Articles 71 and 72 of the CISG"; available online at <http://cisgw3.law.edu/cisg/principles/uni71,72.html#er>.

[8] *Cisg:* M. J. Bonell in Bianca/Bonell, Art. 7, 2.3.2.2; Ulrich Magnus, "Die allgemeinen Grundsätze im UN-Kaufrechts," 59 *Rabels Zeitung* (1995) 469 (477), in English: "General Principles of UN-Sales Law"; available online at <http://cisgw3.law.pace.edu/cisg/biblio/magnus.html>; Bernard Audit, *La vente internationale de marchandise* (1990) 51; Schlechtriem/Huber, Art. 45; reflected also in German Bundesgerichtshof (3.4.1996), *Zeitschrift für Wirtschaftsrecht* 1996, 1044. UNIDROIT *Principles:* UNIDROIT Comment to Art. 1.3 and Art. 6.2.1.; M. J. Bonell, "The UNIDROIT Principles of International Commercial Contracts, Nature, Purposes and First Experiences in Practice," available online at <http://www.unidroit.org/english/principles/pr-exper.htm>; *cf.* also Klaus-Peter Berger, *The Creeping Codification of the Lex Mercatoria* (1999).

[9] *Art. 37 CISG:* A. E. Farnsworth in Swiss Institute of Comparative Law," The 1980 Vienna Convention on the International Sale of Goods," Lausanne Colloquium (1985) 84 *et seq.*; Hans van Houtte/ Patrick Wautelet, "The Duties of Parties and the Sanctions for Non-Performance under the CISG," 3–4 *Int'l. Bus. L. J.* (2001) 293 (302); Schlechtriem/Schwenzer, Art. 37; Ulrich Magnus in M. Martinek (ed.), J. von Staudingers *Kommentar zum Bürgerlichen Gesetzbuch*: Wiener UN-Kaufrecht (1999 Berlin), Art. 37, no. 3. *Art. 7.1.4 UP:* UNIDROIT Comment to Art. 7.1.4, no. 1.

[10] UNIDROIT Comment to Art. 7.1.4, no. 1; Honnold, no. 244 and 245.1; Rex J. Ahdar, "Seller Cure in the Sale of Goods," *Lloyd's Marit. Com. L. Q.* (1990), 370.

[11] Alejandro M. Garro, "The Gap-Filling Role of the UNIDROIT Principles in Internationational Sales Law: Some Comments on the Interplay between the Principles and the CISG," 69 *Tul. L. Rev.* (1995) 1149 (1185).

[12] For a right to cure under Art. 37 CISG up to the end of the period of time, *cf.* Fritz Enderlein, "Rights and Obligations of the Seller under the UN Convention on Contracts for the International Sale of Goods," in Petar Sarcevic/ Paul Volken (eds.), *International Sale of Goods*, Dubrovnik Lectures (1996) 163; also available online at <http://cisgw3.law.pace.edu/cisg/biblio/enderlein1.html>; Honnold, no. 245; Schlechtriem/Schwenzer, Art. 37, no. 5; Heuzé (2000) 263. Different Rolf Herber/Beate Czerwenka, *Internationales Kaufrecht* (1991) Art. 37, no. 3; *cf.* also Uta Gutknecht, "Das Nacherfüllungsrecht des Verkäufers bei Kauf- und Werklieferungsverträgen. Rechtsvergleichende Untersuchung zum Cisg, zum

Unfortunately, Art. 7.1.4 UP is of no help in the interpretation as it enables cure before and after the time of performance.

f. The wording "lack of conformity" in Art. 37 CISG seems to exclude the legal defects set forth by Arts. 41 and 42 CISG. Despite the different structure of the right to cure in the CISG, the wording "any non-performance" in Art. 7.1.4(1) UP supports a wider interpretation.[13] The literal evaluation from Art. 37 ULIS, "any defect in the goods," to Art. 37 CISG, "any lack of conformity," supports this view. Considering the existence of a more general right to cure, the next question that arises is whether the seller should then also be allowed to effect a cure of higher quality (i.e., change the delivered goods).[14] Even if the wording of Art. 7.1.4 UP ("any non-performance") allows such an extensive interpretation, this issue is systematically closer to the excess in quantity under Art. 52(2) CISG.[15]

g. Whereas under Arts. 37 and 48 CISG only the "seller" is allowed to cure, Art. 7.1.4 UP neutrally refers to the "non-performing party." The restrictive wording of Arts. 37 and 48 CISG is a function of their systematic place under Chapter II, "Obligations of the Seller." In corresponding constellations where the buyer breaches the contract before the date of performance (e.g., opening a wrong letter of credit), the occurring gap might be filled by analogy to Art. 37 CISG in light of Art. 7.1.4 UP.[16]

h. Under Art. 37 CISG, the right to cure is limited by the "unreasonable inconvenience or unreasonable expense" of the buyer. The identical formula is only used in Arts. 34 and 86(2). The objective standard of reasonableness, however, is the general and therefore most indefinite weighing tool of the CISG.[17] In contrary, the UNIDROIT Principles provide a set of differentiated limits in Art. 7.1.4(1)(a)-(d). The key formula of "legitimate interest" in subparagraph (c) sets a subjective standard, which is presumed[18] and limited by the objective elements of a notice (a), appropriateness (b), and prompt effect (d). The objective of reasonableness aims to protect the buyer if the right to cure unduly tilts the balance in favor of the seller. Nonetheless, reasonableness always includes an intersubjective element when it is applied to a special case. This personal "appropriateness" can only be determined by examining the concrete circumstances of the individual case.[19] The subjective element of "legitimate interest" in Art. 7.1.4(1)(c) UP might therefore offer a helpful additional formula.

US-amerikanischen Uniform Commercial Code, zum deutschen Recht und zu dem Vorschlag der Kommission zur Überarbeitung des deutschen Schuldrechts" (1997) 44 *et seq.*

[13] For a broad interpretation cf. Staudinger/Magnus, Art. 37, no. 13; H. Ercüment Erdem, *La livraison des marchandises selon la convention de Vienne* (1990) 161; for a corresponding "global concept of conformity" *cf.* Houtte/Wautelet (2001) 306. *Cf.* also Honnold, no. 245.1; Schlechtriem/Schwenzer, Art. 37, no. 6; Enderlein (1996) 164.

[14] Heiko Lehmkuhl, *Das Nacherfüllungsrecht des Verkäufers im UN-Kaufrecht* (2001) 115 *et seq.* favors a solution under the right to cure (Arts. 37and 48 CISG).

[15] For an analogy to Art. 52(2) CISG in case of "higher quality," *cf.* Staudinger/Magnus, Art. 48, no. 9 and Art. 52, no. 27 et seq; Herber/Czerwenka, Art. 39, no. 15; Amin Dawwas, *Die Gültigkeit des Vertrages und das UN-Kaufrecht* (1998) 83 *et seq.* Different Schlechtriem/Huber (1998) Art. 52, no. 11 (CISG not applicable).

[16] *Cf.* Lehmkuhl (2001) 81 for Art. 48 Cisg in light of Art. 7.1.4 UP. For general reflections on the right to cure for the buyer based on English law, *cf.* Antonia Apps, "The Right to Cure Defective Performance," *Lloyd's Marit. Com. L. Q.* (1994) 525 (527); cf. also *Enrico Frust & Co v. W. E. Fischer Ltd.* (1960) 2 *Lloyd's List L. Rep.* 340; *Kronman & Co v. Steinberger* (1922) 10 *Lloyd's List L. Rep.* 39.

[17] For a general definition of the standard, *cf.* Albert H. Kritzer, "Reasonableness," available online at <http://cisgw3.law.pace.edu/cisg/text/reason.html#over>.

[18] UNIDROIT Comment to Art. 7.1.4, no. 4.

[19] For the determination in the individual case *cf.* Schlechtriem/Schwenzer, Art. 37, no. 13; Staudinger/Magnus, Art. 37, no. 16. *Cf.* also Bianca/Bonell, Art. 37, 2.5 ("Unreasonable is an inconvenience exceeding in an intolerable way the normal prejudice brought about to the buyer by the replacement or repair of the goods.").

i. Even if not specifically required by Art. 37 CISG, an attempt to cure without notice is likely to cause unreasonable inconvenience.[20] In Art. 7.1.4(1)(a) UP, the notice is an essential prerequisite for cure regardless of the time of performance. As cure is inherently uncertain,[21] the buyer needs a clue on which to rely. Also if delivery is too early, he has to adjust his dispositions to the situation. To enable reasonable business transactions, the seller has to "seasonably" (Sec. 2-508 UCC) notify the buyer of his intent to cure.[22] It is therefore considered unreasonable under Art. 37 CISG, if the seller "surprises" the buyer by curing the defect without notice.[23] Bearing in mind the adjusted dispositions of the buyer, the cure must additionally be effected promptly as provided in Art. 7.1.4(1)(d) UP, even before the agreed date of delivery.

j. Considering the forms of cure available under Art. 37 CISG, the seller is free to choose any method of cure regardless of the buyer's consent.[24] However, replacement or repair might be inadequate if the goods are already in the buyer's possession.[25] The corresponding Art. 7.1.4(1)(b) UP requires the cure to be "appropriate in the circumstances." Appropriateness depends on the nature of the contract and takes into account whether or not the proposed cure promises to be successful.[26] These elements also provide for a more distinct formula to determine the possible number of attempts to cure. Even though each new attempt increases the inconvenience,[27] the reasonable number may vary with the prospect of success.

k. Closely connected is the question of a slightly imperfect cure. The seller has to restore the goods to a fully sound condition.[28] Under Art. 7.1.4(1)(b) UP, repairing constitutes "appropriate" cure only when it leaves no evidence of the prior non-preformance.[29] Nevertheless, the language and idea of Art. 37 CISG indicate that perfection is not required, unless "unreasonable inconvenience" is caused.[30] In this context, the subjective standard of the buyer's "legitimate interest" as provided in Art. 7.1.4(1)(c) UP might help. The buyer has a legitimate interest in refusing, "if it is likely that, when attempting cure, the non-performing party will cause damage to person or property."[31] In light of the buyer's "legitimate interest," immaterial impacts might also cast doubt on the

[20] Henry Gabriel, *Practitioner's Guide to the CISG and UCC* (1994) 113; Olga Gonzalez, "Remedies under the UN Convention for the International Sale of Goods," 2 *Int'l. Tax & Bus. Law.*(1984) 89; Enderlein/Maskow, Art. 37, no. 6. Different Neumayer/Ming, Convention de Vienne, Art. 37, 292.

[21] Michael Bridge, "The International Sale of Goods," *L. & Pract.* (1999) no. 3.32 and 3.34.

[22] Eric C. Schneider, "The Seller's Right to Cure," 7 *Ariz. J. Int'l. & Comp. L.* (1989) 76 (under reference to Sec. 2–508(1) UCC); William A. Hancock (ed.), *Guide to the International Sale of Goods Convention, UCC/CISG Case Comparisons on the Right to Cure: A Comparison of CISG Articles 37 and 48 with UCC § 2–508* (1999) 103.503, analyzing *E.L.E.S.C.O. v. Northern States Power Co.* (Minnesota Court of Appeal, 1985) in light of Art. 37 CISG; *cf.* also James M. Klotz/John A. Barrett, *International Sales Agreements. An Annotated Drafting and Negotiating Guide* (1998) 169 *et seq.*

[23] Schlechtriem/Schwenzer, Art. 37, no. 13; Staudinger/Magnus, Art. 37, no. 16.

[24] Dölle/Stumpf, Art. 37 ULIS, no. 5; Staudinger/Magnus, Art. 37, no. 12; Schlechtriem/Huber, Art. 48, no. 9 and Schlechtriem/Schwenzer, Art. 37, no. 11; Ahdar (1990) 375; Neumayer/Ming Convention de Vienne, Art. 37, p. 291. *Cf.* Hancock (1999) 103.502, analyzing *Allied Semi-Conductors International Limited v. Pulsar Components International, Inc* (E.D.N.Y., 1993) in light of Art. 37 Cisg.

[25] Bianca/Bonell, Art. 37, 2.6 and 2.1; Enderlein/Maskow, Art. 37, no. 5.

[26] UNIDROIT Comment to Art. 7.1.4, no. 3.

[27] Schlechtriem/Schwenzer, Art. 37, no. 11. *Cf.* also Hancock (1999) 103.501, analyzing *Traynor v. Walters* (M.D.Pa., 1972) in light of Art. 37 CISG.

[28] Binaca/Bonell, Art. 37, 2.6. For corresponding comments on the "perfect tender rule" (Sec. 2–601 UCC) cf. James J. White/ Robert S. Summers, "Uniform Commercial Code (2000) §8–3b"; William H. Lawrence, "Cure under Article 2 of the Uniform Commercial Code: Practices and Prescriptions," 21 *U.C.C. L. J.* (1988) 138 (167).

[29] UNIDROIT Comment to Art. 7.1.4, no. 6.

[30] Honnold, no. 247.

[31] UNIDROIT Comment to Art. 7.1.4, no. 4.

reasonableness of cure.[32] However, every such indication is limited by the basic principles of Art. 37 CISG. Where the seller is seriously seeking to maintain the contract and minimize the damage, the buyer may have to accept a cure that is even more than slightly imperfect.[33]

l. A separate issue is whether partial delivery causes "unreasonable inconvenience" under Art. 37 CISG. As fractioned delivery always constitutes an inconvenience for the buyer, his approval might generally be considered necessary.[34] However, the buyer has no remedies for fractioned early performance because both Art. 51 CISG (reference to Arts. 46 to 50) and Art. 6.1.3 UP presuppose that the time for performance is due. As a result at this systematic structure, the seller may complete partial delivery before the consigned date of delivery without the permission of the buyer.[35] Once again the subjective standard of the buyer's "legitimate interest" provided not only in Art. 7.1.4(1)(c) but also in Art. 6.1.3(1) UP may serve as an adequate limit.

m. The seller has to cure the non-performance at his own expense. His corresponding obligation under Art. 48 CISG is *a fortiori* effective under Art. 37 CISG and stipulated in Art. 7.1.4 (1) UP. The limit of "unreasonable expense" addresses further financial disadvantages for the buyer arising out of the cure (e.g., storage costs). Although the buyer may claim these expenses as damages under Art. 37 CISG, he has to pre-finance the costs and thus bears the risk of insolvency. The cure might be unreasonable if the seller offers no safety or pre-payment of the costs.[36] A possible solution is a "right of retention"[37] that fits the concept of "legitimate interest" in Art. 7.1.4(1)(c) UP.

n. In general, early delivery very seldom amounts to a fundamental breach as the buyer may refuse it.[38] Nevertheless, as a consequence of the pending cure, remedies under Art. 45 *et seq*. are excluded.[39] In line with Art. 7.1.4(3) UP, the rights under Art. 72 CISG are also suspended upon an effective notice of cure. However, there might be some rare cases where a right of the buyer to withhold his own performance as provided in Art. 7.1.4 (4) UP is helpful even before the consigned time of performance is due. Corresponding to Art. 7.1.4 (5) UP, Art. 37 CISG covers not only unreasonable but also reasonable expenses caused by the cure[40] in line with the principle of full compensation underlying Art. 74 CISG and stipulated in Art. 7.4.2 UP.

o. If the buyer refuses cure under Art. 37 or Art. 48 CISG, only the right to price reduction is expressly excluded in Art. 50. The duty of cooperation in Art. 5.3 UP requires the buyer

[32] Schlechtriem/Huber, Art. 48, no. 8. *Cf.* also the "shaken-faith" doctrine under the UCC: White/Summers (2000) 323; Ahdar (1990) 375 with reference to the leading case *Zabriskie Chevrolet Inc. v. Alfred J. Smith* (Superior Court of New Jersey, 1968). Lehmkuhl (2001) 44 *et seq*. applies the "shaken-faith" doctrine directly to the CISG.

[33] *Cf.* Bridge (1999) no. 3.37.

[34] Enderlein/Maskow, Art. 37, no. 3.

[35] Enderlein (1996) 164; similar Staudinger/Magnus, Art. 37, no. 16.

[36] Audit (1990) no. 132; Erdem (1990) 164.

[37] Schlechtriem/Schwenzer, Art. 37, no. 10; Bianca/Bonell, Art. 37, 3.1 ("right to refuse the handing back"); Herber/Czerwenka, Art. 37, no. 7 (idea of Art. 86(1) CISG). Different Staudinger/Magnus, Art. 37, no. 17; Ahdar (1990) 378.

[38] *Cf.* Tribunal of International Commercial Arbitration at the Russian Federation Chamber of Commerce and Industry (25 April 1995) CLOUT abstract no. 141, available online at <http://cisgw3.law.pace.edu/cases/950425r1.html>.

[39] Schlechtriem/Schwenzer, Art. 37, no. 15; Staudinger/Magnus, Art. 37, no. 19; Enderlein (1996) 163; Herbert Bernstein/Joseph Lookofsky, *Understanding the CISG in Europe* (1997) § 6–9; Heuzé (2000) 263. Different but without any reasons Gonzalez (1984) 89.

[40] Ahmad H. Al-Rushoud, "The Right to Cure Defects in Goods and Documents," *Lloyd's Marit. Com. L. Q.* 1999, 458; Enderlein (1996) 165. *Cf.* also UNIDROIT Comment to Art. 7.1.4, no. 9.

to cooperate and permit cure under Art. 7.1.4 UP.[41] Consequently, the buyer loses his remedies for non-performance if he refuses groundlessly to accept cure under Art. 37 CISG.[42] Moreover, the buyer is obliged to examine the goods under Art. 38 CISG and to give notice under Art. 39 specifying the nature of the lack of conformity to enable cure.[43] However, it is not clear whether the duty of examination under Art. 38 CISG arises only at the date of delivery. Without knowledge of the non-conformity, the seller would be deprived of his right to repair. In line with the general principle of cooperation in Art. 5.3 UP, the obligation of the buyer in Arts. 38 and 39 CISG is therefore not dependent on the date of delivery.[44]

[41] UNIDROIT Comment to Art. 7.1.4, no. 10; *cf.* also M. Darin Hammond, "When a Buyer Refuses the Seller's Right to Cure," 27 *Idaho L. Rev.* (1990/91) 562.

[42] Bianca/Bonell, Art. 37, 3.2; Schlechtriem/Schwenzer, Art. 37, no, 17 (general principle underlying Art. 80 CISG); Heuzé (2000) 264 (also recurring on Art. 80 CISG); Neumayer/Ming, Art. 37, 294. *Cf.* also Hancock (1999) 103.503, analyzing *Uchitel v. F. R. Trippler & Co* (New York Supreme Court, 1980) in light of Art. 37 CISG.

[43] Secretariat Commentary, Art. 35 (draft counterpart of CISGArticle 37), footnote 2, available online at <http://cisgw3.law.pace.edu/cisg/text/secomm/secomm-37.html>; Neumayer/Ming, Art. 37, 292; Bridge (1999) no. 3.38. *Cf.* also Arbitration Court of the Chamber of Commerce and Industry of Budapest, Hungary (5 December 1995), CLOUT no. 164, available online at <http://cisgw3.law.pace.edu/cases/951205h1.html>.

[44] Houtte/Wautelet (2001) 293 (302); Enderlein (1996) 163. Different Staudinger/Magnus, Art. 38, no. 21, 37; Herber/Czerwenka, Art. 38, no. 8; Gutknecht (1997) 46.

Buyer's right to declare avoidance based on non-compliance with a *Nachfrist*: Commentary on whether the UNIDROIT Principles of International Commercial Contracts may be used to interpret or supplement Articles 47 and 49(1)(b) of the CISG

Robert Koch

I. INTRODUCTION

Article 49 CISG regulates a buyer's right of avoidance in case of breach of contract by the seller. Although paragraph (1) lays down the conditions under which the buyer is entitled to declare the contract avoided, paragraph (2) provides for situations where he loses the remedy of avoidance. Because the consequences of this remedy are harsh for the seller,[1] the remedy is limited to two situations. Subparagraph (1)(a) gives the buyer the right to avoid the contract where the seller's breach amounts to a *fundamental breach of the contract* in terms of Article 25 CISG. Subparagraph (1)(b) deals with *late delivery* and cases where the seller does not deliver the goods at all. Even if late delivery or non-delivery does not *per se* qualify for fundamental breach but only if timely delivery is of the essence of the contract,[2] the buyer can declare the contract avoided where the seller fails to deliver the goods within an additional period (*Nachfrist*) set by the buyer in accordance with Article 47(1) CISG.[3] The avoidance regime under the UNIDROIT Principles also distinguishes between termination based on fundamental non-performance (Article 7.3.1 of the UNIDROIT Principles, the UNIDROIT Principles counterpart to fundamental breach) and a termination in case of late delivery due to non-compliance with a *Nachfrist* (Article 7.1.5 of the UNIDROIT Principles). In this chapter, only the second of the two grounds for avoidance/termination under both instruments is analyzed. This is because the concept of fundamental breach, including the relationship between the seller's right to cure under Article 48 CISG and the avoidance remedy, has been discussed in detail in

[1] *See, e.g.*, Schlechtriem, "Uniform Sales Law in the Decisions of the Bundesgerichtshof," in *50 Years of the Bundesgerichtshof [Federal Supreme Court of Germany], A Celebration Anthology from the Academic Community* [English translation of this text] (2001), at III.1, available online at <http://cisgw3.law.pace.edu/cisg/biblio/schlechtriem3.html> (emphasizing that avoidance of the contract, with the necessary return shipment of the goods, regularly entails storage and transport costs in addition to the associated risks for the goods).

[2] *See* relevant case law:
- Germany 20 February 2002 Landgericht [District Court] München, case presentation including English translation available online at <http://cisgw3.law.pace.edu/cases/020220g1.html> (stating that "[t]he failure to meet a delivery deadline cannot, as a rule, be regarded as a fundamental breach of contract within the meaning of Art. 25 CISG; reasons for an exception such as the stipulation of a transaction for which time is of the essence were not put forward");
- Germany 24 April 1997 Oberlandesgericht [Appellate Court] Düsseldorf, case presentation including English translation available online at <http://cisgw3.law.pace.edu/cases/970424g1.html> (stating that "[t]he particular importance of the date of delivery can result from the contract itself, as for example in the case of a transaction where time is of the essence, as well as from the circumstances, e.g., in the case of delivery of seasonal items").

[3] This requirement is inspired by the German concept of *Nachfrist* although similar results are obtained by different conceptual means in other legal systems. *See* Treitel, "Remedies for Breach of Contract," in *International Encyclopedia of Comparative Law*, Chapter 16 (Tübingen, Mouton, The Hague, Paris: J.C.B. Mohr, 1976) §§ 149–151 (discusses the *Nachfrist* provision in German law and similar provisions in other legal systems).

my remarks on the manner in which the UNIDROIT Principles may be used to interpret or supplement Article 25 CISG.[4]

II. AVOIDANCE BASED ON NON-COMPLIANCE WITH A *NACHFRIST*

1. Scope of Article 47 and 49(1)(b) CISG/Article 7.1.5 of the UNIDROIT Principles

a. Restriction to Non-Delivery

aa. Article 47 and 49(1)(b) CISG. Article 47(1) CISG provides that

> [t]he buyer may fix an additional period of time of reasonable length for performance by the seller of his obligations.

By its terms, Article 47(1) CISG is not limited to non-delivery but also applies to cases of non-conforming delivery, when the buyer notifies the seller of the defect and of the demands for repair within the *Nachfrist* pursuant to Articles 46(3) CISG. In the context of Article 49(1)(b) CISG, however, it becomes clear that fixing of a *Nachfrist* is only of relevance in cases of *non-delivery* and where the buyer wants to provide the basis for avoidance without proof that the delay constitutes a fundamental breach should the seller fail to comply with a *Nachfrist*. Non-delivery thus needs to be distinguished from the delivery of non-conforming goods. Although delivery is not defined under the Convention, it follows from Articles 30–34 CISG that delivery is the act that the seller is obliged to perform to give the buyer possession of the goods.[5] Therefore, not only the seller's failure to hand over the goods in question but also his failure to deliver documents are to be considered as non-delivery if *documents of title* are concerned, such as bills of lading or warehouse receipts.[6] On the other hand, the delivery of a faulty Certificate of Origin or of Quality cannot be regarded as non-delivery. If the documents are faulty, the same principles apply that apply to the goods themselves: once the documents have been handed over to the buyer, they are "delivered" with the consequence that neither Article 47(1) nor Article 49(1)(b) CISG applies.[7]

bb. Article 7.1.5 of the UNIDROIT Principles. Article 7.1.5(1) of the UNIDROIT Principles, the counterpart to Article 47(1) CISG, provides that

> [i]n a case of non-performance the aggrieved party may by notice to the other party allow an additional period of time for performance.

[4] *See* Koch, "Commentary on Whether the UNIDROIT Principles of International Commercial Contracts May Be Used to Interpret or Supplement Article 25 CISG," available online at <http://cisgw3.law.pace.edu/cisg/text/>.

[5] For a similar statement *see* Huber, U., in: Schlechtriem ed., *Commentary on the U.N. Convention on the International Sale of Goods* (Oxford: Clarendon Press: 1998), Art. 30 Comment 5; Plate, "The Buyer's Remedy of Avoidance under the CISG: Acceptable from a Common Law Perspective?," 6 *Vindobona J. Int'l. Com. L. & Arbitration* (2002) 57, at 67, available online at <http://cisgw3.law.pace.edu/cisg/biblio/plate.html>.

[6] *See* Schlechtriem, *Uniform Sales Law: the UN Convention on Contracts for the International Sale of Goods* (Vienna: Manz 1986), at 77 (stating that "by analogy, the provision [Art. 49(1)(b) CISG) also applies to the failure to transfer documents of title"), available online at <http://cisgw3.law.pace.edu/cisg/biblio/schlechtriem.html>; Schnyder/Straub, in Honsell ed., *Kommentar zum UN-Kaufrecht* [CISG article-by-article commentary] (Berlin/Heidelberg/New York: Springer 1997), Art. 49, Comment 100; Jafarzadeh, *Buyer's Right to Withhold Performance and Termination of Contract: A Comparative Study under English Law, Vienna Convention on Contracts for the International Sale of Goods 1980, Iranian and Shi'ah Law*, at Part Two, 2.2.2.2, available online at <http://cisgw3.law.pace.edu/cases/960403g1.html>.

[7] For such a statement, *see* Germany 3 April 1996 Bundesgerichtshof [German Supreme Court); case presentation including English translation available online at <http://cisgw3.law.pace.edu/cases/960403g1.html>.

Article 7.1.1 of the UNIDROIT Principles defines non-performance as a "failure by a party to perform any of its obligations under the contract, including defective performance or late performance." It follows from the reference to "a case of delay" in the opening phrase of sentence 1 of Article 7.1.5(3) of the UNIDROIT Principles (UP)[8] that the UP *Nachfrist* too is only of relevance in situations where the seller performs late or not at all.

b. No Extension to Cases of Non-Conformity by Analogy

There has been some scholarly discussion of whether Article 49(1)(b) CISG could or should be applied by analogy to cases of lack of conformity of the goods where the seller did not fulfill the buyer's request to repair the goods under Article 46(3) CISG within the *Nachfrist*.[9] It has been argued that the buyer should have some recourse when the seller does not fulfill his obligation to repair the goods in question.[10] Leaving aside the question of whether such an interpretative technique is admitted under the CISG, from my civil law perspective, to apply a rule of law by analogy there must be a gap to be filled. Legislative history shows, however, that it was the conscious decision of the drafters not to broaden the scope of Article 49(1)(b) CISG to defective performance.[11] There is thus no room under the CISG for an analogy.[12] In such cases, the remedies of the buyer are limited to reducing the price or to using the non-conforming goods as well as possibly liquidating the resulting damages.

c. Qualification of *Aliud*-Delivery

From a *factual* perspective, the delivery of an *aliud* (delivery of the wrong goods) is to be distinguished from the delivery of a *peius* (delivery of non-conforming goods). This distinction gives rise to the question of whether the *aliud*-delivery can be qualified as non-delivery. The Convention does not specifically address this problem. The very fact, however, that the relevant CISG provisions dealing with the seller's obligations do not differentiate between the delivery of an *aliud* or *peius* allows the conclusion that both have to be treated equally. Consequently, scholars take the view that the delivery of an *aliud* cannot be qualified as non-delivery but rather as delivery of defective goods.[13] Recent German[14]

[8] *See infra* II.4.b.

[9] *See* "Transcript of a Workshop on the Sales Convention: Leading CISG Scholars Discuss Contract Formation, Validity, Excuse for Hardship, Avoidance, *Nachfrist*, Contract Interpretation, Parol Evidence, Analogical Application, and Much More," 18 *J. L. & Com.* (1999) 191, at 201 *et seq.*; available at <http://cisgw3.law.pace.edu/cisg/biblio/workshop.html>.

[10] *See* Yoshino, in *Transcript of a Workshop on the Sales Convention, supra* note 9, at 213.

[11] For an overview *see* Jafarzadeh, *supra* note 6, at Part Two, 2.2.2.

[12] *See* Schlechtriem and Flechtner, in *Transcript of a Workshop on the Sales Convention, supra* note 9, at 251 (the former stressing that there was a conscious decision by the drafters of the CISG to limit the availability of avoidance using the so-called *Nachfrist* procedure and emphasizing that in the predecessor Hague Sales Convention, the additional-period-of-time procedure for avoidance was allowed in cases of non-conformity).

[13] *See* Honnold, *Uniform Law for International Sales under the 1980 United Nations Convention* (3rd ed., The Hague: Kluwer 1999), at § 256.1; Karollus, "Judicial Interpretation and Application of the CISG in Germany 1988–1994," *Cornell Review of the Convention on Contracts for the International Sale of Goods* (1995) 51–94, at Article 49, available online at <http://cisgw3.law.pace.edu/cisg/biblio/karollus.html>; Schlechtriem, *supra* note 1; Plate, *supra* note 5, at 67.

[14] *See* relevant case law:

- Germany 3 April 1996 Bundesgerichtshof [Federal Supreme Court], case presentation including English translation available online at <http://cisgw3.law.pace.edu/cases/960403g1.html> (stating an *aliud*-delivery, at least generally, does not constitute a nondelivery);
- Germany 12 March 2001 Oberlandesgericht [Appellate Court] Stuttgart, case presentation including English translation available online at <http://cisgw3.law.pace.edu/cases/010312g1.html> (stating that an *aliud*-delivery in any case does not constitute a non-delivery in the meaning of Art. 49(1)(b) CISG);
- Germany 11 April 2002 Amtsgericht [Lower Court] Viechtach, case presentation including English translation available online at <http://cisgw3.law.pace.edu/cases/020411g1.html> (stating that Art. 35(1) CISG intentionally affords parity treatment to a defect and an *aliud*-delivery to avoid difficulties in distinguishing

and Austrian[15] case law confirms this view. According to the German Supreme Court, non-delivery could only be assumed in very blatant and obvious cases of divergence between the goods agreed upon and the goods delivered.[16] In such situations, however, in my view, no distinction would be necessary because they qualify for fundamental breach.[17] It is further to be noted that Article 49(1)(b) CSIG is applicable to cases of late delivery of substitute goods requested by the buyer under Article 46(2) CISG, because the substitute delivery is to be regarded as delivery under Articles 30–34 CISG.[18]

2. Requirements for an Effective *Nachfrist* Notice

a. Content of the Notice

The *Nachfrist* notice does not have to meet any formal requirements. Although in theory, even an oral notice suffices,[19] from the practitioner's viewpoint a written notice is more than advisable because in case of a dispute it is up to the buyer to prove that the seller has received the notice.[20] The notice must contain a specific demand for performance[21] and a fixed (given date) or determinable (e.g., four weeks from today) deadline when performance will be accepted at the latest.[22] A general demand by the buyer that the seller perform or that he perform "promptly" or the like is not a fixing of a period of time under Article 47(1) CISG.[23]

b. Determination of *Nachfrist*'s Reasonable Length

The *Nachfrist* must be "of reasonable length." In the absence of an express agreement between the parties, the determination of whether the *Nachfrist* is reasonable must be

between the two and that this aim would be foiled if one chose to extend the sphere of non-delivery if the sphere was extended, the difficulty in distinguishing between *aliud*-delivery and defect would be shifted to the distinction between delivery and non-delivery).

For a different view, *see*

- Germany 10 February 1994 Oberlandesgericht [Appellate Court] Düsseldorf, case presentation including English translation available online at <http://cisgw3.law.pace.edu/cases/940210g2.html> (stating that [i]nsofar as the [seller] delivered textiles in a color not ordered by the [buyer], [seller] effected the delivery of an *aliud*, which led to a partial non-performance).

[15] *See* Austria 29 June 1999 Oberster Gerichtshof [Supreme Court], case presentation including English translation available online at <http://cisgw3.law.pace.edu/cases/990629a3.html>.

[16] *See* Germany 3 April 1996 *Bundesgerichtshof* [German Supreme Court), case presentation including English translation available online at <http://cisgw3.law.pace.edu/cases/960403g1.html> (stating an *aliud*-delivery does, at least generally, not constitute a non-delivery, leaving the question open for the case of an especially blatant deviation of the goods from the qualities required by the contract).

[17] For a similar view *see* Schlechtriem, *supra* note 1 (emphasizing that "[t]he more extreme the deviation, the easier it will be to classify it as a fundamental breach of contract").

[18] *See* Karollus, *supra* note 13. In contrast, *see* Jafarzadeh, *supra* note 6 (overlooking that Art. 46(2) CISG is a request for substitute delivery).

[19] *See, e.g.*, Müller-Chen, in Schlechtriem/Schwentzer eds., *Kommentar zum Einheitlichen UN-Kaufrecht*, (4th ed., München: Beck 2004), Art. 47, Comment 13.

[20] *See* Plate, *supra note* 5, at 67.

[21] This requirement has been stressed, for example, by Honnold, *supra* note 13, at § 289.

[22] *See* relevant case law:

- Germany 24 April 1997 Oberlandesgericht [Appellate Court] Düsseldorf, case presentation including English translation available online at <http://cisgw3.law.pace.edu/cases/970424g1.html> (stating that a *Nachfrist* notice "must contain a precise request for performance that is combined with the fixing of a specific deadline")
- Germany 11 October 1995 Landgericht [District Court] Düsseldorf, case presentation including English translation available online at <http://cisgw3.law.pace.edu/cases/951011g1.html> (stating that "[i]nsofar as the [buyer] has contended that [buyer] had reminded the [seller] several times about the delivery, it cannot be gathered from this general statement that the [buyer] has also fixed a deadline for the [seller]")

[23] *See* Secretariat Commentary on Article 43(1) of the 1978 Draft [*draft counterpart of Article 47(1)*], Comment 7, available online at <http://cisgw3.law.pace.edu/cisg/text/secomm/secomm-47.html>.

made in light of the circumstances of the case at hand. Special consideration may be given to the period of time originally set for delivery, the buyer's need for quick delivery of the goods, the nature of the goods to be delivered, and the event that caused the delay.[24]

c. Consequences in Case of Unreasonable Length

aa. Article 47(1) and 49(1)(b) CISG. Court practice shows that the *Nachfrist* fixed by the buyer often is not of reasonable length; namely, it is too short. Fixing a period that is too short triggers the question about the consequences stemming from the *Nachfrist* notice. The prevailing opinion among scholars is that Article 47(1) and 49(1)(b) CISG should be interpreted so that a *Nachfrist* of unreasonable length does not make the notice ineffective but initiates a period of reasonable length.[25] This view is confirmed by case law.[26] Some commentators take a different view. They argue that Article 47(1) and 49(1)(b) CISG (by reference to Article 47(1) CISG) require a period of reasonable length and conclude from that language that an unreasonable period – either too short or too long – makes the notice ineffective. Consequently, the buyer would not be entitled to declare the contract avoided after the *Nachfrist* had expired, but would have to serve a new notice and to fix a new *Nachfrist* of reasonable length.[27] The latter view is not persuasive because it cannot be supported by the rules of interpretation under Article 7(1) CISG. Neither the language of Article 47(1) and 49(1)(b) CISG nor their legislative history, their context within the CISG's remedial system, or their objectives preclude the extension of an unreasonable *Nachfrist*.[28]

[24] *See e.g.*, Will in Bianca & Bonell eds., *Commentary on the International Sales Law, The 1980 Vienna Sales Convention* (Milan: Giuffrè 1987), Art. 47, Comment 2.1.3.2.

[25] For this view *see* Plate, *supra* note 5, at 68. Müller-Chen, *supra* note 19, Art. 47, Comment 9; Herber/Czerwenka, *Internationales Kaufrecht* [*International Sales Law, Article-by-Article Commentary on the CISG – in German*] (München: Beck 1991), Art. 47, Comment 4; Magnus, "UN-Kaufrecht" [UN-Sales Law, article-by-article commentary – *in German*], in Staudinger, Julius von Staudingers *Kommentar zum Bürgerlichen Gesetzbuch mit Einführungsgesetz und Nebengesetzen* (13th ed., Berlin: Sellier/de Gruyter 1995), Article 47, Comment 20; Huber, P., in *Münchener Kommentar zum Bürgerlichen Gesetzbuch*, Vol. 3, Chapter on CISG [article-by-article commentary – *in German*] (4th ed., München: Beck 2004), Art. 47, Comment 11.

[26] *See* relevant case law:

- Germany 27 April 1999 Oberlandesgericht [Appellate Court] Naumburg, case presentation including English translation available online at <http://cisgw3.law.pace.edu/cases/990427g1.html> (stating that the Court does not need to decide whether the additional period of time set by the buyer was too short, as in that instance a reasonable period of time would have started to run).
- Germany 24 May 1995 Oberlandesgericht [Appellate Court] Celle, case presentation including English translation available online at <http://cisgw3.law.pace.edu/cases/950524g1.html> (stating that a possibly too short *Nachfrist* does not make the notice ineffective where the notice has merely extended a period of time).
- Icc Arbitration Case No. 7645 of March 1995, case presentation available online at <http://cisgw3.law.pace.edu/cases/957645i1.html> (stating in *obiter dictum* that "irrespectively of these circumstances and of the delay of shipment of five days [buyer] could not have declared avoided the contract based on the delay of shipment alone, because the shipment occurred within the *hypothetical additional period of time for performance* which [buyer] would have had to fix to [seller]) [emphasis added]."

[27] *See, e.g.*, Schnyder/Straub, in Honsell ed., *Kommentar zum UN-Kaufrecht* [CISG Commentary] (Berlin/Heidelberg/New York: Springer, 1997), Art. 47, Comment 24, and Art. 49 Comment 102).

[28] For an overview of the CISG's rules on interpretation with further references to scholarly writings, *see, e.g.*, Koch, "The Concept of Fundamental Breach of Contract under the United Nations Convention on Contracts for the International Sale of Goods (CISG)," *Pace Review of the Convention on Contracts for the International Sale of Goods* (Cisg) 1998, Kluwer Law International (1999), at 189 *et seq.*; also available online at <http://cisgw3.law.pace.edu/cisg/biblio/koch.html>.

Moreover, this view does not seem to give appropriate account to the "observance of good faith in international trade" as an aid to statutory interpretation.[29] In this regard, reasonableness is to be considered not only as a general principle in terms of Article 7(2) CISG but also as a *concretization* of the good faith requirement under Article 7(1) CISG.[30] In light of the negative consequences of an ineffective notice for both parties, a narrow interpretation of Article 47(1) and 49(1)(b) CISG seems unreasonable. An ineffective notice would not only impose on the buyer the extra burden of fixing a new *Nachfrist* but would also allow him to resort to other remedies because the restriction of Article 47(2) CISG would not apply. Such a consequence is not in the interests of the seller because it would frustrate his efforts to effect delivery. His expenses incurred in attempting to perform would be wasted, and even if one qualified the declaration of avoidance upon the expiration of a too short *Nachfrist* as breach of contract,[31] those expenses would not necessarily be (fully) recoverable under Article 74 CISG.

bb. Article 7.1.5(3) of the UNIDROIT Principles. Sentence 2 of Article 7.1.5(3) of the UNIDROIT Principles expressly states that

> [i]f the additional period allowed is not of reasonable length it shall be extended to a reasonable length.

The UNIDROIT Principles, therefore, follow a slightly different approach than the CISG. Unlike Article 47(1) CISG, they do not require that the buyer fix a *Nachfrist of reasonable* length, but they limit his right to exercise the avoidance remedy if the *Nachfrist* is of *unreasonable* length. Despite that difference, the approach taken by the UNIDROIT Principles confirms my view that only an extension of a reasonable length is in itself reasonable. Sentence 2 of Article 7.1.5(3) of the UNIDROIT Principles thus can be seen as an *exemplification* of the principle of reasonableness in international trade. As pointed out before, reasonableness is also a general principle under the CISG. Even if one is not willing to follow my conclusion that the observance of good faith requires an interpretation of Article 47(1) and 49(1)(b) CISG in the sense of sentence 2 of Article 7.1.5(3) of the UNIDROIT Principles, such an interpretation would therefore follow from Article 7(2) CISG. According to that provision "[q]uestions concerning matters

[29] For a concise and thorough analysis of the meaning of "good faith" as an instrument of interpretation, *see* Felemegas, "The United Nations Convention on Contracts for the International Sale of Goods: Article 7 and Uniform Interpretation," in *Pace Review of the Convention on Contracts for the International Sale of Goods* (CISG), Kluwer Law International (2000–2001) 115–265, at Chapter 3, 5(a), also available online at <http://cisgw3.law.pace.edu/cisg/biblio/felemegas.html#ch3>.

[30] For the relationship between reasonableness and good faith, *see* Schlechtriem, *supra* note 6, at 39; Honnold, *supra* note 13, at § 95; for the relevance of the standard of reasonableness in determining good faith, *see* Kritzer's editorial remarks on "reasonableness," which include further citations and references, at <http://cisgw3.law.pace.edu/cisg/text/reason.html> (stating that "... regarding reasonableness as a fundamental principle of the CISG and reading reasonableness into every article of the CISG, whether specifically mentioned in the article or not ... is required by virtue of the good-faith and uniform-law mandate recited in Article 7(1) of the CISG."); Bonell, in: Bianca & Bonell eds., *supra* note 24, Art. 7, Comment 2.3.2.2 (stating that "just as in interpreting specific terms and concepts adopted in the text of the Convention, also in specifying 'general principles' courts should, in accordance with the basic criteria of Article 7(1) ...") and Felemegas, *supra* note 29, at chapter 4, 5(a) (thoroughly and accurately analyzing Bonell's statement in that Bonell relies on the premise that, although there are principles, such as party autonomy and the dispatch rule, which can be directly applied, others, such as the principle of good faith and the concept of reasonableness, need further specification to offer a solution for a particular case).

[31] *See* Plate, *supra* note 5, at 68–69; Müller-Chen, *supra* note 19, Art. 47, Comment 9 (both stating that if the buyer has fixed too short a period and accordingly declares the avoidance of the contract upon the expiration of that period, this constitutes a breach of contract itself).

governed by this Convention which are not expressly settled in it are to be settled in conformity with the *general principles* on which is based ...".[32]

3. Effects of a *Nachfrist*

a. Article 47(2) CISG

The effects of a *Nachfrist* are described in Article 47(2) CISG. It provides that

> [u]nless the buyer has received notice from the seller that he will not perform within the period so fixed, the buyer may not, during that period, resort to any remedy for breach of contract. However, the buyer is not deprived thereby of any right he may have to claim damages for delay in performance.

According to Article 47(2) CISG, during the *Nachfrist* the buyer may not resort to any remedy for breach of contract (except for damages for delay in performance). As a consequence, even if the late delivery qualifies for fundamental breach under Article 49(1)(a) CISG, the buyer cannot avoid the contract if he fixed a *Nachfrist*.[33] The purpose of Article 47(2) CISG is to protect the seller, who is relying on the buyer's declaration when trying to cure the defect, possibly at considerable expense.[34] The only situation in which avoidance is possible before the expiration of the *Nachfrist* is where the seller declares an ultimate refusal to perform within the period fixed.[35]

b. Article 7.1.5(2) UNIDROIT Principles

Article 7.1.5(2) UNIDROIT Principles states that

> [d]uring the additional period the aggrieved party may withhold performance of its own reciprocal obligations and may claim damages but may not resort to any other remedy. If it receives notice from the other party that the latter will not perform within that period, or if upon expiry of that period due performance has not been made, the aggrieved party may resort to any of the remedies that may be available under this Chapter.

Except for the right to withhold performance, Article 7.1.5(2) UNIDROIT Principles is substantively identical to Article 47(2) CISG. The right to withhold performance of its own reciprocal obligations during the *Nachfrist*, however, follows under the Convention from Article 58 CISG. According to Article 58(1) CISG, the buyer, in the absence of any stipulation to the contrary, is not obliged to pay the price until the seller places the goods at the buyer's disposal.[36] Moreover, according to Article 58(3) CISG, the buyer in general is not bound to pay the price until he has had an opportunity to examine the goods. If the buyer has agreed to pay before receiving the goods but, prior to the time for payment,

[32] Emphasis added.

[33] *See* Plate, *supra* note 5, at 69; Müller-Chen, *supra* note 19, Article 47, Comment 14.

[34] *See* Secretariat Commentary on Article 43(1) of the 1978 Draft [*draft counterpart of Article 47(1)*], *supra* note 22, Comment 9.

[35] *Id.*, Comment 9.

[36] *See* relevant case law:

- Bundesgerichtshof [German Supreme Court), 3 April 1996, case presentation including English translation available online at <http://cisgw3.law.pace.edu/cases/960403g1.html> (denying buyer's right of retention according to Art. 58(1) CISG because the scope of this provision is limited to "so-called true transfer documents"; in addition, similar documents grant the buyer a right of disposition to the goods)
- ICC Arbitration Case No. 7645 of March 1995, case presentation including English translation available online at <http://cisgw3.law.pace.edu/cases/957645i1.html> (stating with regard to Article 58(1) CISG that the purchaser is not bound to pay the purchase price as long as the seller has not performed or at least adequately tendered correct performance)

See also Jafarzadeh, *supra* note 6, at Part Two, 1.2.2.

it becomes apparent that the seller will not deliver the goods, the buyer is entitled to suspend payment pursuant to Article 71(1) CISG.[37]

4. Seller's Non-Compliance with the Buyer's *Nachfrist* Ultimatum

a. Article 49(1)(b) CISG

Article 49(1)(b) CISG provides that if the seller fails to perform within the *Nachfrist*, the buyer may declare the contract avoided. Article 49(1)(b) CISG also provides an alternative condition under which the buyer may avoid the contract, which is a declaration or indication by the seller that he will ignore the *Nachfrist* notice. The buyer may already in its notice provide that if the other party fails to perform within the period allowed by the notice the contract will automatically be avoided.[38]

b. Article 7.1.5(3) of the UNIDROIT Principles

Sentence 1 of Article 7.1.5(3) of the UNIDROIT Principles is substantively identical to Article 49(1)(b) CISG.[39] Sentence 3 expressly states that "[t]he aggrieved party may in its notice provide that if the other party fails to perform within the period allowed by the notice the contract shall automatically terminate."

III. TIME LIMITATIONS ON THE RIGHT OF AVOIDANCE

1. Article 49(2) CISG

Article 49(2) CISG provides for certain circumstances under which the buyer may lose his right to avoid the contract. Subparagraph (a) deals with late delivery, whereas subparagraph (b) applies to other cases of breach of contract.

a. Late Delivery

In the case of late delivery, Article 49(2)(a) CISG states that

> [w]here the seller has delivered the goods, the buyer loses the right to declare the contract avoided unless he does so: (a) in respect of late delivery, within a reasonable time after he has become aware that delivery has been made [. . .]

It is to be noted that Article 49(2)(a) CISG is only applicable to late delivery (even if late delivery qualifies for fundamental breach[40]) but not to non-delivery. Before delivery has been effected the buyer may, without limits on time, avoid the contract. Once the

[37] *See, e.g.*, Germany 6 April 2000 Landgericht [District Court] München, case presentation including English translation available online at <http://cisgw3.law.pace.edu/cases/000406g1.html> (stating that buyer "had the right to stop payment of her cheque and to temporarily refuse the payment of the purchase price (Art. 71(1)(b) CISG), because [seller] did not deliver furniture in a material mix and combination in compliance with the terms set out in their sales contract"); *see* also Kimbel, "*Nachfrist* Notice and Avoidance under the CISG," 18 *J. L. & Com.* (1999) 301–331, at fn. 31 (stating that the failure to deliver satisfies the substantial part requirement under Article 71(1) CISG, and a party may suspend its performance during the *Nachfrist* period), available at <http://cisgw3.law.pace.edu/cisg/biblio/kimbel.html>; Jafarzadeh, *supra* note 6, at Part Two, 1.2.1.

[38] *See* Müller-Chen, *supra* note 19, Art. 49, Comment 22; Plate, *supra* note 5, at 72; Herber/Czerwenka, *supra* note 25, Article 49, Comment 11; Magnus, *supra* note 25, Article 49, Comment 26; *see* also Austria 28 April 2000 Oberster Gerichtshof [Austrian Supreme Court], case presentation including English translation available online at <http://cisgw3.law.pace.edu/cases/000428a3.html> (stating that it is a question of interpretation of the seller's *Nachfrist* notice [under Article 63(1) CISG] if the contract will be terminated upon expiration of the *Nachfrist* without further notice).

[39] Sentence 1 of Article 7.1.5(3) of the UNIDROIT Principles reads as follows:

> Where in a case of delay in performance which is not fundamental the aggrieved party has given notice allowing an additional period of time of reasonable length, it may terminate the contract at the end of that period.

[40] *See* Plate, *supra* note 5, at 69; Müller-Chen, *supra* note 19, Art. 49, Comment 27.

goods have been delivered he must avoid the contract within a reasonable time. What is reasonable depends upon the circumstances. If the buyer has already obtained substitute goods from another source, in my view, he must declare the avoidance of the contract without unnecessary delay. If the goods are perishable or subject to price fluctuations (e.g., oil), notice must be given almost instantaneously. Where the buyer has not made a substitute purchase and must make inquiries as to whether he can obtain substitute performance from other sources, the reasonable period of time will be longer.[41]

b. Other Types of Breach

In cases of fundamental breach of any of the seller's obligations other than delivery, Article 49(2)(b) CISG provides that the buyer loses the right to avoid the contract if he fails to do so

> within a reasonable time
> (i) after he knew or ought to have known of the breach
> (ii) after the expiration of any additional period of time fixed by the buyer in accordance with paragraph (1) of article 47, or after the seller has declared that he will not perform his obligations within such an additional period
> (iii) after the expiration of any additional period of time indicated by the seller in accordance with paragraph (2) of article 48, or after the buyer has declared that he will not accept performance

aa. Article 49(2)(b)(i) CISG. Generally, the buyer must declare the avoidance of the contract in accordance with Article 49(2)(b)(i) CISG; that is, within a reasonable time after he knew of the breach or could have been aware of it. In case of the delivery of non-conforming goods, the time limits begin to run at the moment when the buyer discovered or ought to have discovered the lack of conformity on examination of the goods in accordance with Article 38 CISG.[42] As with Article 49(2)(a) CISG, the length of reasonable time under Article 49(2)(b)(i) CISG in particular depends on the nature of the goods. In cases of delivery of non-conforming goods, however, the reasonable period of time, in general, will be longer than in case of late delivery because determining whether a given defect qualifies for fundamental breach requires extra time (e.g., for seeking legal advice).[43] For that reason, the time limits for notice of avoidance and notice of the defect under Article 39(1) CISG begin to run simultaneously, but only in exceptional cases do they coincide in length.[44]

bb. Article 49(2)(b)(ii) CISG. Article 49(2)(b)(ii) CISG deals with the situation where the buyer fixed a *Nachfrist* for remedying the defective performance in accordance with Article 47(1) CISG. The time for avoidance starts to run when the seller does not perform within the *Nachfrist* (including a second and any further *Nachfrist*[45]) or when the buyer has received the seller's declaration that he will not perform within that period.

[41] *See* Plate, *supra* note 5, at 69; Müller-Chen, *supra* note 19, Art. 49, Comment 29.

[42] For a similar statement *see* Honnold, *supra* note 13, § 308; Will, *supra* note 24, Art. 49, Comment 2.2.2.1.

[43] For a similar statement *see* Germany Oberlandesgericht [Appellate Court] Koblenz 31 January 1997, text of the decision [in German] available online at <http://www.cisg-online.ch/cisg/urteile/256.htm>; Plate, *supra* note 5, at 70; Huber, P., *supra* note 25, Art. 49, Comment 65.

[44] For a similar statement *see* Will, *supra* note 24, Art. 49, Comment 2.2.2.1. There is a controversial discussion among scholars about whether or not the seller's knowledge of a defect in the goods removes the "reasonable time" limit on avoidance. For the different views *see* Honnold, *supra* note 13, § 308.1 (*contra*), and Will, *supra* note 24, Art. 49, Comment 2.2.2.2 (*pro*).

[45] For a similar statement *see* Will, *supra* note 24, Art. 49, Comment 2.2.1.2.

cc. Article 49(2)(b)(iii) CISG. Article 49(2)(b)(iii) CISG deals with the situation where an additional period of time has not been fixed by the buyer, but has instead been proposed by the seller under Article 48(2) CISG. The time for avoidance starts to run when the seller has not remedied his defective performance within that period or when the buyer has declared that he will not accept performance.

2. Article 7.3.2(2) of the UNIDROIT Principles

The counterpart to Article 49(2) CISG can be found in Article 7.3.2(2) of the UNIDROIT Principles. The latter states that

> [i]f performance has been offered late or otherwise does not conform to the contract the aggrieved party will lose its right to terminate the contract unless it gives notice to the other party within a reasonable time after it has or ought to have become aware of the offer or of the non-conforming performance.

Article 7.3.2 of the UNIDROIT Principles covers late delivery as well as defective performance. It is substantively identical to Article 49(2)(a) and Article 49(2)(b)(i) CISG.

IV. CONCLUSIONS

The requirements for avoidance for non-delivery or late delivery under the CISG and the UNIDROIT Principles do not differ in substance. With regard to the effect of a *Nachfrist* of unreasonable length, the solution provided in sentence 2 of Article 7.1.5(3) of the UNIDROIT Principles may be used to supplement Article 47(1) and 49(1)(b) CISG.

Cure after date for delivery: Remarks on the manner in which the UNIDROIT Principles may be used to interpret or supplement Article 48 of the CISG

Christopher Kee

I. INTRODUCTION

Article 48 is the middle of a trinity of articles that are arguably among the most significant provisions in the Convention. The other two provisions are Articles 47 and 49.

Article 48 is in many ways an unremarkable article. The basic premise of the provision is simple – a seller can remedy any of its obligations even after the time of delivery provided he does so without unreasonable delay or inconvenience to the buyer. The philosophy of this article fits neatly within the broader intentions of the CISG to keep contracts "on-foot."

Article 7.1.4 of the UNIDROIT Principles (UNIDROIT) is grounded in the same philosophy. As Bertram Keller notes in his editorial remarks to CISG Article 37, the civil law tradition has been generally less familiar with the notion of a right to cure,[1] and its inclusion in UNIDROIT does indeed "encourage the world wide acceptance of a general right to cure."[2]

However, there are some critical differences in the approach and effect of CISG Article 48 and UNIDROIT Article 7.1.4. This chapter focuses principally on the literal and structural differences between CISG Article 48 and UNIDROIT Article 7.1.4.

II. LITERAL AND STRUCTURAL DIFFERENCES

As mentioned in the introduction, CISG Article 48 is a simply worded article.[3] There are very few form requirements with which a seller must comply before exercising the right provided to the seller by this article. Under Article 48(1) a seller can rectify any defect in its performance, provided the contract has not been avoided by the buyer pursuant to Article 49[4] and that it is not unreasonable to do so – that is, there will not be an unreasonable delay in performing the remedy and it will not impose on the buyer unreasonable inconvenience or any uncertainty of reimbursement. The seller does not need to provide notice to the buyer of its intention to cure subject to the conditions just mentioned. The seller has a right to cure *per se* and does not need to activate this right in any way. However, the seller is left in a position of uncertainty because that right can be overridden if the buyer avoids the contract pursuant to Article 49. Therefore Articles 48(2) and 48(3) allow the seller to send a request or notice, respectively, requiring the buyer to indicate whether it intends to terminate the contract. If the buyer indicates that it is prepared to allow the time requested by a seller to cure its breach, then the buyer is precluded from taking advantage of any remedy inconsistent with that allowance – principally the buyer cannot avoid the contract. Similarly, if the buyer fails to respond to the request or notice within a reasonable time, the buyer is deemed to be allowing the seller an opportunity to cure in accordance with the terms of the request or notice. Conceptually, therefore, Articles 48(2) and 48(3) can be likened or viewed as a mechanism to force a *Nachfirst* notice from a buyer.[5]

Article 7.1.4 UNIDROIT adopts a very different approach. An immediate difference is that it operates for the benefit of any non-performing party, whereas CISG Article 48 is for the benefit of the seller only. This difference has more to do with the overall structure

[1] *See* Keller, B. "Editorial Remarks," in guide to CISG Article 37, available online at <http://cisgw3.law.pace.edu/cisg/principles/uni37.html#er> at para. (b).

[2] *Id.*

[3] Although not strictly part of the structure of Article 48, it should also be noted that both CISG Article 49(2)(b)(iii) and Article 50 specifically refer to Article 48.

[4] On the priority issue between Articles 48 and 49, *see* X. GmbH v. Y. e.V., Switzerland 5 November 2002 Commercial Court des Kantons Aargau [available at <http://cisgw3.law.pace.edu/cases/021105s1.html>], which suggests that "when the seller notifies the buyer of his readiness for performance, the buyer may not within a reasonable period of time 'resort to any remedy which is inconsistent with performance by the seller.' For this reason, the buyer does not have the right to avoid the contract even in case of an objective fundamental defect as long as and as far as the seller comes up with a remedy (subsequent cure of the defect) and such is still possible," at 4(b)(aa). This case in turn refers to Germany 31 January 1997 Appellate Court [Oberlandesgericht] Koblenz, 2 U 31/96 = Cisg Online 256 [available at <http://cisgw3.law.pace.edu/cases/970131g1.html>]. The rationale of these cases is that if the potential exists for the seller to cure then the breach itself cannot be a fundamental one, and therefore the buyer cannot avail itself of Article 49 in any event. Contrast this view with Koch, R. *The Concept of Fundamental Breach of Contract under the United Nations Convention on Contracts for the International Sale of Goods (CISG)*, 1998, Kluwer Law International (1999) 177–354 at p. 322.

[5] It is particularly interesting to use this conceptualization when debating the priority between CISG Article 47 and CISG Article 48, see the "Commentary" section below. For an explanation of a *Nachfrist* notice and commentary on CISG Article 47 generally, *see* the Annotated Text of CISG Article 47 and associated links available at <http://www.cisg.law.pace.edu/cisg/text/e-text-47.html>.

of the UNIDROIT Principles rather than being a reflection on the CISG. With this in mind, this chapter continues to use the language of buyer and seller, as it enables a more meaningful comparison.

There are two other differences that are significant and deserve comment. The first is that under Article 7.1.4(1)(a) a seller must give the buyer a notice of cure before the right to cure arises. The second difference is that, even if the buyer might have issued a notice of termination, the effects of that purported termination are suspended if the seller issues a valid notice of cure.

In most other respects the counterpart articles are the same. Although expressed differently, the principal effect and purpose of the remaining parts of Article 7.1.4 are that it must be reasonable for the seller to cure.[6]

III. COMMENTARY

As noted above, in the CISG the right to cure exists *per se*, whereas under UNIDROIT it must be invoked by a valid notice to the buyer. In both instruments the purpose of the request or notice is to eliminate any uncertainty. Although at one level it might be simply said that the failure of UNIDROIT to recognize the right to cure as a right *per se* is merely a reflection of the civil law not fully embracing this concept, a notice requirement would serve to avoid another tension that exists in the CISG. Reference was made in the introduction to a trinity of CISG articles. Article 48 is clearly expressed to be subject to Article 49, but what is its relationship to Article 47? There is undoubtedly a potential conflict between these two articles as both refer to reasonableness. The concept of reasonableness is one that appears frequently throughout the CISG. Much has been written on this concept.[7] Anything that is not unreasonable must be reasonable. So although it might be reasonable for a seller to offer to cure within eight weeks under Article 48, it may also be reasonable for the buyer to require the cure within six weeks. The buyer's right in Article 47, like the seller's right in Article 48, is a *per se* right. Although this is perhaps an unlikely tension, it is one that has on occasion been decided judicially.[8] The UNIDROIT position prevents this potential confusion; the first to send an effective notice prevails.

The second difference referred to above is the consequence that a notice to cure has on a buyer's attempt to avoid the contract. The "rights of the [buyer] that are inconsistent with the [seller's] performance are suspended until the time for cure has expired," including the effects of any notice of termination. This can only be interpreted to mean that if the breach is capable of cure it cannot be a "fundamental non-performance";[9] to be

[6] Although the drafters of the UNIDROIT provisions choose to avoid the use of the word "reasonable" in the provisions themselves, they do imbue that word into the meaning of Article 7.1.4 through the Official Comments where it is used frequently. "[T]he comments on the articles are to be seen as an integral part of the Principles" (UNIDROIT).]

[7] *See* in particular Anderson, C.B. "Reasonable Time in Article 39(1) of the CISG – Is Article 39(1) Truly a Uniform Provision," Part I, para. 2.3, at <http://cisgw3.law.pace.edu/cisg/biblio/andersen.html>. Reasonableness is regarded as one of the general principles of the Convention; *see* Albert H. Kritzer, "Overview Comments on Reasonableness," at <http://cisgw3.law.pace.edu/cisg/text/reason.html#over>.

[8] *See* for example Germany 24 September 1998 District Court Regensburg, available online at <http://cisgw3.law.pace.edu/cases/980924g1.html> where it was found that a buyer's purported avoidance following the allowance of a further fourteen-day period for delivery was considered to "thwart" the seller's right to cure under Article 48. To simply extract and refer to an issue such as this does run the risk of decontextualizing the decision; however, it would certainly seem that the Court held the view that the seller's right to cure took precedence to the buyer's right to set an additional period for performance. A better interpretation of the facts in that case may have been that the period allowed by the seller was unreasonable and therefore the declaration of avoidance was premature.

[9] UNIDROIT Article 7.3.1; *see* general discussion of this point in note 3 earlier.

otherwise would mean that it was possible to do the impossible and breathe new life into a terminated contract.[10] As a result, the UNIDROIT provision has been rightly criticized for the uncertain position in which it places the buyer,[11] and implicit in that criticism is a preference for the CISG Article 48 approach.

The final issue to be noted by way of commentary is the similarity between the articles. Both CISG Article 48 and UNIDROIT Article 7.1.4 require the buyer to receive the relevant communication (request or notice) before the provision becomes effective. Although UNIDROIT does generally require receipt,[12] the CISG on the other hand generally prefers to refer to dispatch pursuant to Article 27.[13]

IV. CONCLUSION

A comparative analysis between CISG Article 48 and UNIDROIT Article 7.1.4 is a useful exercise in the task of understanding each provision more fully. Often one learns more from understanding what something is not than from simply trying to interpret what it is. In this instance, though they share some common features, it cannot be said that the counterpart provisions in the CISG and the UNIDROIT Principles are "on all fours" because there contain some important structural differences, which have been identified in this chapter and are worthy of further debate.

[10] However, *see* Janse van Vuuren, E. "Termination of International Commercial Contracts for Breach of Contract: The Provisions of the UNIDROIT Principles of International Commercial Contracts," 15 *Ariz. J. Int'l & Comp. Law* 583 at 633, who takes the view that the non-performing party may be able to suspend the effects of termination notwithstanding a valid termination by the aggrieved party.

[11] Koch, R., *supra* note 4, at 324.

[12] *See* UNIDROIT Article 1.9

[13] "Th[e] general rule [of the CISG] making notices effective on dispatch is subject to specific exceptions in Articles 47(2), 48(4), 63(2), 65(1)&(2), and 79(4). Nearly all of these provisions involve a communication by a party who is in breach of contract; the 'receipt' principle was used so that a mishap in transmission would not add to the burdens of the aggrieved party." John O. Honnold, *Uniform Law for International Sales*, 3d ed., Kluwer Law International (1999) at p. 217, citing the legislative history of CISG Article 27 at the 1980 Vienna Diplomatic Conference. On this issue generally *see* Chengwei Liu, "Remedies for Non-Performance: Perspectives from CISG, UNIDROIT Principles & PECL," available online at <http://cisgw3.law.pace.edu/cisg/biblio/chengwei.html#fulltext>.

Open-price contracts: Commentary on whether the UNIDROIT Principles of International Commercial Contracts may be used to interpret or supplement Article 55 of the CISG

Jumpita Ruangvichathorn

I. INTRODUCTION

Article 55 of the Convention provides a mechanism for the determination of the price in an international sales contract that has been validly concluded; however, it does not state a price or expressly or implicitly make provision for determining the price. In other words, CISG Art. 55 deals with the uneasy question concerning open-price contracts, and it becomes a controversial provision in light of CISG Article 14(1), which provides that determination of price is one of the criteria for an offer. The two provisions seemingly contradict each other.[1]

Counterpart provisions regulating the same issues, but in a more detailed manner, are also found in the UNIDROIT Principles of International Commercial Contracts (the Principles) Articles 5.7, "Price Determination," and 2.2, "Definition of Offer".

This chapter examines whether and the extent to which the provisions of the Principles may be used to aid the interpretation of Art. 55 of the Convention.

II. RELATIONSHIP BETWEEN CISG ARTS. 14(1) AND 55

CISG Art. 14 generally deals with the criteria for an offer, and Art. 14(1) expressly provides that for an offer to be *sufficiently definite*, the price must be expressly or implicitly fixed or a provision must be made to determine the price.

> A proposal for concluding a contract addressed to one or more specific persons constitutes an offer if it is sufficiently definite and indicates the intention of the offeror to be bound in case of acceptance. A proposal is sufficiently definite if it indicates the goods and expressly or implicitly fixes or makes provision for determining the quantity and *the price*.[2]

On the other hand, CISG Art. 55 permits the possibility that a contract may be validly[3] concluded even *without* expressly or implicitly fixing the price.

> Where a contract has been validly concluded but does not expressly or implicitly fix or make provision for determining the price, the parties are considered, in the absence of any indication to the contrary, to have impliedly made reference to the *price generally charged at the time of the conclusion of the contract for such goods* sold under comparable circumstances in the trade concerned.[4]

The legislative history of the Convention offers no clear or convincing explanation of the interrelationship between CISG Arts. 14(1) and 55.[5] However, two distinct interpretations

[1] *See*, for example, Ziegel J., "Report to the Uniform Law Conference of Canada on Convention on Contracts for the International Sale of Goods," (1981), available online at <http://cisgw3.law.pace.edu/cisg/text/ziegel55.html>. Comment 1, *id.*, reads Art. 55 must be read in conjunction with art. 14 which deals with the essential constituents of an offer. Art. 55 was substantially amended at Vienna. The adopted version attempts to reconcile the price requirements of Art. 14 with the need to provide for a case where the contract contains no reference to the price, and does so by deeming the parties to have impliedly agreed to adopt the price generally charged for such goods at the time of the conclusion of the contract. It is not clear whether this formula is sufficient to overcome the limitations of Art. 14, although it was clearly meant to. Difficulties may still be encountered because Art. 55 does not come into play unless a contract has been validly concluded. [. . .]

[2] CISG Art. 14 (1). Emphasis added. For an online presentation of basic information and further links to the relevant legislative history, case law, and scholarly commentary on CISG Art. 14, go to <http://cisgw3.law.pace.edu/cisg/text/e-text-14.html>.

[3] CISG Art. 4 reads [emphasis added]

> This Convention governs only the formation of the contract of sale and the rights and obligations of the seller and the buyer arising from such a contract. In particular, *except as otherwise expressly provided in this Convention*, it is not concerned with:
> (a) the *validity* of the contract or of any of its provisions or of any usage;
> (b) the effect which the contract may have on the property in the goods sold.

[4] CISG Art. 55. Emphasis added. For an online presentation of basic information and further links to the relevant legislative history, case law, and scholarly commentary on CISG Art. 55, go to <http://cisgw3.law.pace.edu/cisg/text/e-text-55.html>.

[5] *See*, generally, Amato, P. "U.N. Convention on Contracts for the International Sales of Goods – The Open Price Term and Uniform Application: An Early Interpretation by the Hungarian Courts," 13 *J.L. & Com.* (1993), p. 6; also available online at <http://cisgw3.law.pace.edu/cisg/biblio/amato.html>.

of the relationship between those two provisions are drawn from the views of two leading CISG commentators, Professors Honnold and Farnsworth.[6]

The main divergence between those two interpretative approaches is that, according to the approach propounded by Prof. Honnold, CISG Art. 14(1) should be read together with Article 55. Doing so results in an interpretation that a contract "*may* be validly concluded" – not that a contract "*must already have been* concluded" in the first place, either under a domestic sales law or a declaration under CISG Art. 92(1)[7] – before the Convention's mechanism to determining the price under Article 55 can be activated, as per the approach of Prof. Farnsworth.

The former approach, the chief proponent of which is Prof. Honnold, seems to have gained most support in academic circles.[8]

III. RELATIONSHIP BETWEEN UNIDROIT PRINCIPLES ARTS. 2.2 AND 5.7

The counterpart to CISG Art. 14(1) in the Principles is found in Art. 2.2, which reads,

> A proposal for concluding a contract constitutes an offer if it is sufficiently definite and indicates the intention of the offeror to be bound in case of acceptance.

In defining an offer, the Principles specify the same two requirements as are embedded in the Convention: the proposal must (i) be sufficiently definite to permit the conclusion of the contract by mere acceptance and (ii) indicate the intention of the offeror to be bound in case of acceptance.

Furthermore, the wording of the Principles is, to a degree, similar to CISG Art. 14(1). However, it is not similarly detailed, because, unlike the Convention, it does not make reference to the matters of "quantity" and "price" to determine whether the proposal is sufficiently definite to constitute an offer.

The Principles merely focus on the matter of "the intention of the offeror to be bound in case of acceptance."[9] In this regard, and based on the Official Commentary on the Principles, no apparent contradiction exists similar to the one that exists in the CISG. As such, it is easier to read Arts. 2.2 and 5.7 together.[10] In that regard, it is submitted that

[6] *Id.*, at 4–6.

[7] CISG Art. 92(1) reads,

> A Contracting State may declare at the time of signature, ratification, acceptance, approval or accession that it will not be bound by Part II of this Convention or that it will not be bound by Part III of this Convention.

[8] Other approaches to this issue also exist; *see*, for example, Enderlein F and Maskow D., *International Sales Law*, Oceana Publications (1992), at pp. 209–210, also available online at <http://cisgw3.law.pace.edu/cisg/biblio/enderlein-art55.html> (stating that the validity of the contract in the case of an open-price term shall be determined solely under national law):

> Herewith reference can be made to the *prerequisites for validity* as contained in the CISG and to national validity conditions [. . .]. Some authors, therefore, proceed on the assumption that without having fixed a price there is no offer under Article 14, paragraph 1, sentence 2 and, therefore, no delivery can be taken. Hence, there will be no contract so that the rules governing the substance of the contract including Article 55 are irrelevant where there are no exceptions [. . .]. Others suppose, and the text speaks in favour of this assumption, that the validity of a contract in this case is to be judged only according to national law [references omitted].

[9] *See* the Official UNIDROIT Commentary on Article 2.2, available online at <http://cisgw3.law.pace.edu/cisg/principles/uni14.html#official>, Comment 2, "Intention to be bound":

> The second criterion for determining whether a party makes an offer for the conclusion of a contract, or merely opens negotiations, is that party's intention to be bound in the event of acceptance. Since such an intention will rarely be declared expressly, it often has to be inferred from the circumstances of each individual case. The way in which the proponent presents the proposal (e.g. by expressly defining it as an "offer" or as a mere "declaration of intent") provides a first, although not a decisive, indication of possible intention. Of even greater importance are the content and the addressees of the proposal. Generally speaking, the more detailed and definite the proposal, the more likely it is to be construed as an offer. A proposal addressed to one or more specific persons is more likely to be intended as an offer than is one made to the public at large.

[10] *Id.*, Comment 1, "Definiteness of an offer":

> Even essential terms, such as the precise description of the goods or the services to be delivered or rendered, the price to be paid for them, the time or place of performance, etc., *may be left undetermined* in the offer without necessarily rendering it insufficiently definite: all depends on whether or not the offeror by making the offer, and

the Principles offer a similar but simpler regime when compared to the Convention and might arguably be used to aid the interpretation of the particular textual controversy in the Convention, discussed above.

IV. MECHANISM TO DETERMINE AN OPEN-PRICE TERM: CISG ART. 55 AND UNIDROIT PRINCIPLES ART. 5.7

Regarding a sales contract that neither fixes the price to be paid for the goods nor makes provision for determining the price, the Principles provide a presumption that the parties "have made reference to the price *generally charged at the time of the conclusion of the contract* for such performance in comparable circumstances in the trade concerned, or, if no such price is available, to a *reasonable* price" [emphasis added]. The applicable provision (Principles Art. 5.7) also permits the rebuttal of the presumption if there is any indication to the contrary.[11]

The Official UNIDROIT Commentary on Article 5.7 sheds illuminating light on the origins of this general rule governing price determination by revealing that the provision "is inspired by Art. 55 CISG."[12]

Furthermore, the notion of "reasonableness," which prevails in that article of the Principles, is also a general principle on which the Convention is based.[13]

Thus, it is submitted that the two instruments adopt the same general policy to determine open-price terms.

There are, however, three noteworthy differences between the counterpart provisions.

First, the words "[w]here a contract has been validly concluded [. . .]" that appear in CISG Art. 55 are not included in Principles Art. 5.7(1). Thus, and considering the interrelationship of Art. 5.7 to Art. 2.2 of the Principles (see Section 3, above), it may be argued that the Principles have in that manner attempted,[14] successfully it seems,

the offeree by accepting it, intends to enter into a binding agreement, and whether or not the missing terms can be determined by interpreting the language of the agreement in accordance with Arts. 4.1 *et seq.*, or supplied in accordance with Arts. 4.8 or 5.2. Indefiniteness may moreover be overcome by reference to practices established between the parties or to usages (see Art. 1.8), as well as by reference to specific provisions to be found elsewhere in the Principles (e.g. Arts. 5.6 (Determination of quality of performance), 5.7 (Price determination), 6.1.1 (Time of performance), 6.1.6 (Place of performance), and 6.1.10 (Currency not expressed)).

[11] UNIDROIT Principles Art. 5.7 reads [emphasis added]:

> (1) Where a contract does not fix or make provision for determining the price, the parties are considered, in the absence of any indication to the contrary, to have made reference to the price generally charged at the time of the conclusion of the contract for such performance in comparable circumstances in the trade concerned or, if no such price is available, to a *reasonable* price.
> (2) Where the price is to be determined by one party and that determination is manifestly *unreasonable*, a *reasonable* price shall be substituted notwithstanding any contract term to the contrary.
> (3) Where the price is to be fixed by a third person, and that person cannot or will not do so, the price shall be a *reasonable* price.
> (4) Where the price is to be fixed by reference to factors which do not exist or have ceased to exist or to be accessible, the nearest equivalent factor shall be treated as a substitute.

[12] *See* the Official UNIDROIT Commentary on Article 5.7, available online at <http://cisgw3.law.pace.edu/cisg/principles/uni55.html#official>. Comment 1 reads,

> This article is inspired by Art. 55 CISG. The rule has the necessary flexibility to meet the needs of international trade. It is true that in some cases the price usually charged on the market may not satisfy the reasonableness test which prevails elsewhere in this article. Recourse would then have to be made to the general provision on good faith and fair dealing (Art. 1.7), or possibly to some of the provisions on mistake, fraud and gross disparity (Chapter 3). Some international contracts relate to operations which are unique or at least very specific, in respect of which it is not possible to refer to the price charged for similar performance in comparable circumstances. According to para. (1) the parties are then deemed to have made reference to a reasonable price and the party in question will fix the price at a reasonable level, subject to the possible review by courts or arbitral tribunals.

[13] *See* "Overview Comments on Reasonableness," Kritzer A., available online at <http://cisgw3.law.pace.edu/cisg/text/reason.html>:

> Reasonableness is specifically mentioned in thirty-seven provisions of the CISG and clearly alluded to elsewhere in the Uniform Sales Law. Reasonableness is a general principle of the CISG.

[14] There is, however, no mention of any such motivation in the Official Commentary on the Principles.

to solve the apparent textual contradiction found in the corresponding provisions of the Convention (see Sections 1 and 2, above).

Second, in cases where a contract does not fix or make provision for determining the price, Principles Art. 5.7(1) has employed the concept of "reasonable price" in addition to the "market price" that is found in CISG Art. 55.

Third, the Principles, compared to CISG Art. 55, have adopted a more refined and detailed mechanism for determining the price in a contract

(i) in the case where the price is to be determined by one party,[15]
(ii) in the case where the price is to be fixed by a third person,[16] and
(iii) in the case where the price is to be fixed by reference to factors that do not exist or have ceased to exist or to be accessible.[17]

V. CONCLUSION

Following an analysis of the counterpart provisions dealing with open-price contracts under the CISG and UNIDROIT Principles, it is submitted that whereas the two instruments adopt the same general policy and also establish similar regimes to regulate the issue, the Principles offer more expansive provisions than the CISG to deal with the issue.

It is thus submitted that Principles Art. 5.7 could be properly and efficiently used to interpret and supplement CISG Art. 55.[18]

[15] If that determination is "manifestly unreasonable," Principles Art. 5.7(2) provides that "a reasonable price shall be substituted notwithstanding any contract term to the contrary." *See* also Official Commentary, Comment 2, which elaborates as follows:

> In those cases where the parties have made such a provision for determining the price, it will be enforced. To avoid possible abuses however, para. (2) enables judges or arbitrators to replace a manifestly unreasonable price by a reasonable one. This provision is mandatory.

[16] If the designated third party cannot or will not do so, Principles Art. 5.7(3) provides that "the price shall be a reasonable price."

See also Official Commentary, Comment 3, which explains

> [I]f that third person is unable to accomplish the mission (not being the expert he or she was thought to be) or refuses to do so. Para. (3) provides that the price, possibly determined by judges or arbitrators, shall be reasonable.

[17] If reference cannot be made to the specific external factor, Principles Art. 5.7(4) provides that the "nearest equivalent factor shall be treated as a substitute."

See also the Official Commentary, Comment 4, which explains and illustrates the point:

> In some situations the price is to be fixed by reference to external factors, typically a published index, or quotations on a commodity exchange. In cases where the reference factor ceases to exist or to be accessible, para. (4) provides that the nearest equivalent factor shall be treated as a substitute.

Illustration

> The price of a construction contract is linked to several indexes, including the "official index of charges in the construction sector," regularly published by the local Government. Several installments of the price still have to be calculated when that index ceases to be published. The Construction Federation, a private trade association, decides however to start publishing a similar index to replace the former one and in these circumstances the new index will serve as a substitute.

[18] For an analysis of CISG Art. 55 compared to another Restatement of Contract Law, the Principles of European Contract Law, *see* Vincze A., "Remarks on Whether and the Extent to which the Principles of European Contract Law (PECL) May Be Used to Help Interpret Article 55 of the CISG," available online at <http://cisgw3.law.pace.edu/cisg/text/peclcomp55.html#er>.

For selective references of relevant case law interpreting CISG Art. 55, please *see* the following cases:

- Russia 30 May 2001 Arbitration proceeding 185/2000, case presentation including English translation available online at <http://cisgw3.law.pace.edu/cases/010530r2.html> (the Tribunal found the parties' contract was "valid although it did not specify the price, since CISG Art. 55 contains provisions for determination of the price for contracts that are validly concluded")
- ICC Arbitration Case No. 9819 of September 1999, case presentation available online at <http://cisgw3.law.pace.edu/cases/999819i1.html> (in *dicta* reference to CISG, the Tribunal stated, "Sale without prior fixing of a price is common in international trade, as is shown by the Vienna Convention of 11 April 1980 on the international sale of goods (art. 55) . . . ")

(*Continued*)

(*Continued footnote*)

- Switzerland 3 July 1997 *Bezirksgericht* [District Court] St. Gallen, CLOUT abstract no. 215, case presentation available at <http://cisgw3.law.pace.edu/cases/970703s1.html> (the purchase price had not been fixed by the parties and was determined by the court in application of CISG Art. 55);
- Russia 3 March 1995 Arbitration proceeding 309/1993, CLOUT abstract no. 139, case presentation available online at <http://cisgw3.law.pace.edu/cases/950303r1.html> (the tribunal held that CISG Art. 55 was not applicable because the parties had implicitly indicated the need to reach agreement on the price in future)
- Austria 10 November 1994 *Oberster Gerichtshof* [Supreme Court], CLOUT abstract no. 106, case presentation including English translation available online at <http://cisgw3.law.pace.edu/cases/941110a3.html> (the Austrian Supreme Court found that the proposal in that case was sufficiently definite to constitute an offer under CISG Art. 14, because it could be perceived as such by a reasonable person in the same circumstances as the seller (CISG Art. 8(2) and (3)). In determining that the order was sufficiently definite, the Court took into consideration the behavior of the buyer who accepted the delivered goods and sold them further without questioning their price, quality, or quantity. As the price was found to be sufficiently definite, the Court held that the application of Article 55 CISG was unnecessary in that case)
- Hungary 10 January 1992 *Fovárosi Bíróság* [Metropolitan Court] (*Pratt & Whitney v. Malev*) case presentation including English translation available online at <http://cisgw3.law.pace.edu/cases/920110h1.html> (the court held that, in accordance with CISG Art. 14(1), the offers in question were sufficiently definite, even though they granted the buyer the unilateral power in respect to the choice of the aircraft engines and relative quantity and they indicated the price of only some of the engines offered)
- Hungary 25 September 1992 *Legfelsobb Bíróság* [Supreme Court] (*Pratt & Whitney v. Malev*), CLOUT abstract no. 53, case presentation including English translation available online at <http://cisgw3.law.pace.edu/cases/920925h1.html> (the Supreme Court of Hungary held, *inter alia*, (i) an offer must indicate the product, the quantity, and the price or contain directions as to how these terms can be identified; (ii) the description of the goods, quantity, and the price are all essential elements of an offer; (iii) CISG Art. 55 cannot be used to determine the price term of an offer for a product, such as a jet engine, which has no market price; (iv) a party's declaration merely that it intends to conclude a contract is insufficient for the conclusion of a contract. On the facts, the Court found that the offer was vague and, therefore, ineffective because it failed to explicitly or implicitly fix or make provision for determining the price of the engines ordered; thus, the Court overturned the decision of the first instance and held that there was no valid contract concluded);
- France 26 April 1995 *Cour d'appel* [Appellate Court] Grenoble (*Alain Veyron v. Ambrosio*), CLOUT abstract no. 151, case presentation including English translation available online at <http://cisgw3.law.pace.edu/cases/950426f1.html> (the court found that "the reference made by Article 55 CISG to a market price, in as much as this Article is applicable to the case, is overridden by a contrary agreement between the parties, such as the provisions of CISG in their entirety, with the exception of Article 12 (Art. 6)")
- Hungary 24 March 1992 *Fovárosi Bíróság* [Metropolitan Court] (*Adamfi Video v. Alkotók Studiósa Kisszövetkezet*), CLOUT abstract no. 52, case presentation available online at <http://cisgw3.law.pace.edu/cases/920324h1.html> (the court held that an offer was sufficiently definite, as the quality, quantity, and price of the goods were fixed by the practices established between the parties (Art. 9(1) CISG), whereby the seller had repeatedly delivered the same type of goods ordered by the buyer who had paid the price after delivery)
- Russia 22 November 1995 Arbitration proceeding 99/1994, case presentation including English translation available online at <http://cisgw3.law.pace.edu/cases/951122r1.html> (the tribunal held that CISG Art. 55 was applicable to a contract between the parties that had provided for the basic price for the goods having a minimum content of a certain indicator. There was no provision as to the price for the goods in which a content of the indicator was below the minimum level. In such a situation, pursuant to the contract, the price was to be agreed upon by the parties. In some of the delivered goods the level of content of the indicator was below the minimum. In this situation, the ICAC deemed it possible to apply Article 55 to determine the price.
- For criticism of the tribunal's judgment, *see* Saidov D., "Cases on CISG Decided in the Russian Federation," 7 *Vindobona J. Int'l. Com. L. & Arbitration* (2003) 1–62, at 37– 38:

  It is not clear why the Tribunal deemed it possible to apply Article 55. Such a decision seems to run counter to the provision of the contract according to which in the situation that took place in the case, a price was to be agreed upon by the parties. It is submitted that Article 55 could only be applied where the parties intended to regard an open price contract as valid. Therefore, a price could be determined according to Article 55 only if such a determination of a price stemmed from interpretation of the contract. The decision does not make it clear whether the Tribunal interpreted the agreement. On the basis of the information available, it seems that the parties' intention was not to leave the price open, but to come to an agreement to this effect. In such a case, Article 55 could not be applied. This decision appears to be inconsistent with the decision taken in a case No 304/1993 [of 3 March 1995] where Article 55 was held to be inapplicable in the situation where the parties have agreed to negotiate the price in future and failed to do so [citations omitted]).

Seller's right to declare avoidance based on non-compliance with *Nachfrist*: Commentary on whether the UNIDROIT Principles of International Commercial Contracts may be used to interpret or supplement Articles 63 and 64 of the CISG

Robert Koch

I. INTRODUCTION

Article 64 CISG deals with a seller's right of avoidance in case of breach of contract by the buyer. It is the counterpart provision to the buyer's right to avoid the contract under Article 49 CISG. Although paragraph (1) lays down the conditions under which the seller is entitled to declare the contract avoided, paragraph (2) provides for situations where he loses the right to the remedy of avoidance. The avoidance remedy is limited to two situations. Subparagraph (1)(a) gives the seller the right to avoid the contract where the buyer's breach amounts to a *fundamental breach of the contract* in terms of Article 25 CISG. Subparagraph (1)(b) deals with *non-payment* or *not taking delivery of the goods*. Non-payment or not taking delivery does not *per se* qualify for a fundamental breach but only if timely payment or timely taking of delivery is of the essence of the contract.[1] However, the seller can declare the contract avoided, where the buyer fails to pay and/or take delivery of the goods within an additional period (*Nachfrist*) set by the seller in accordance with Article 63(1) CISG.[2] The avoidance regime under the UNIDROIT Principles similarly distinguishes between termination based on fundamental non-performance (Article 7.3.1 of the UNIDROIT Principles, the UNIDROIT Principles counterpart to fundamental breach) and a termination in case of late payment or late taking delivery due to non-compliance with a *Nachfrist* (Article 7.1.5 of the UNIDROIT Principles). In this chapter, only the second grounds for avoidance/termination under both instruments are compared because the concept of fundamental breach has been discussed in detail in my remarks on the manner in which the UNIDROIT Principles may be used to interpret or supplement Article 25 CISG.[3]

II. AVOIDANCE BASED ON NON-COMPLIANCE WITH A *NACHFIRST*

1. Scope of Articles 63 and 64(1)(b) CISG/Article 7.1.5 of the UNIDROIT Principles

a. Articles 63 and 64(1)(b) CISG

Article 63(1) CISG provides that

> [t]he seller may fix an additional period of time of reasonable length for performance by the buyer of his obligations.

By its terms, Article 63(1) CISG is not limited to non-payment or not taking delivery, but is also applicable, for example, to the buyer's failure to specify goods in accordance with Art. 65 CISG[4] or his noncompliance with the obligation not to re-export the goods[5] when the seller notifies the buyer of the nonperformance and demands performance within the *Nachfrist*. In considering Article 64(1)(b) CISG, however, it becomes clear that fixing of a *Nachfrist* is only of relevance in cases of *nonpayment* or *not taking delivery* and where

[1] *See* relevant case law:
- France 4 February 1999 *Cour d'appel* [Appellate Court] Grenoble, case presentation including English translation available online at <http://cisgw3.law.pace.edu/cases/990204f1.html> (stating that "in order to determine whether the breach of not taking delivery at the end of August is fundamental, [the court] must look at the context in which this timing was agreed to")
- ICC Arbitration Case No. 7585 of 1992, CLOUT abstract no. 301, with editorial remarks by Kritzer, both available online at <http://cisgw3.law.pace.edu/cases/927585i1.html> (the tribunal stated that delay in payment [failure to obtain the required letter of credit] is not always in itself a fundamental breach)
- Switzerland 12 December 2002 *Kantongericht* [District Court] Zug, case presentation including English translation available online at <http://cisgw3.law.pace.edu/cases/021212s1.html> (finding for fundamental breach after the buyer failed to take delivery of the goods within an additional period fixed by the seller)

[2] This requirement is inspired by the German concept of *Nachfrist*, although similar results are obtained by different conceptual means in other legal systems. *See* Treitel, "Remedies for Breach of Contract," in *International Encyclopedia of Comparative Law*, Chapter 16 (Tübingen, Mouton, The Hague, Paris: J.C.B. Mohr, 1976) §§ 149–151 (discusses the *Nachfrist* provision in German law and similar provisions in other legal systems).

[3] *See* Koch, "Commentary on Whether the UNIDROIT Principles of International Commercial Contracts May Be Used to Interpret or Supplement Article 25 CISG," available online at <http://cisgw3.law.pace.edu/cisg/biblio/koch1.html>.

[4] *See* Honnold, *Uniform Law for International Sales under the 1980 United Nations Convention* (3rd ed., The Hague: Kluwer 1999), at § 351.

[5] *See* France 22 February 1995 *Cour d'appel* [Appellate Court] Grenoble (*BRI Production "Bonaventure" v. Pan African Export*), case presentation including English translation available online at <http://cisgw3.law.pace.edu/cases/950222f1.html> (the court did not have to decide the applicability of Article 64(1)(b) CISG because it considered the buyer's disregard of the seller's destination requirement as a fundamental breach).

the seller wants to provide the basis for avoidance without proof that the delay constitutes a fundamental breach should the seller fail to comply with a *Nachfrist*. [6]

aa. Nonpayment. The buyer's obligation to pay the price is set forth in Article 53 CISG. Article 54 CISG identifies enabling steps that are a part of this obligation. According to the latter provision, the buyer's obligation to pay includes all of the measures agreed upon in the contract "to enable payment to be made," such as registering the contract with a government office or with a bank, procuring the necessary foreign exchange, as well as applying for a letter of credit or a bank guarantee to facilitate the payment of the price.[7] The buyer's failure to take any of these steps within an additional period of time fixed by the seller in accordance with Article 63 would authorize the seller to declare the contract avoided under Article 64(1)(b) CISG.

bb. Not taking delivery. The buyer's obligation to take delivery is subject to Article 60 CISG. First, he must perform all the acts that could reasonably be expected of him to enable the seller to make delivery. For example, if under the contract of sale the buyer is to arrange for the carriage of the goods, he must make the necessary contracts of carriage so as to permit the seller to hand the goods over to the first carrier for transmission to the buyer.[8] Second, the buyer must take over the goods. The latter obligation is of importance where the contract calls for the seller to make delivery by placing the goods at the buyer's disposal at a particular place or at the seller's place of business.[9] In such a case the buyer must physically remove the goods from that place in order to fulfill his obligation to take delivery.[10]

b. Article 7.1.5 of the UNIDROIT Principles

Article 7.1.5(1) of the UNIDROIT Principles, the counterpart to Article 63(1) CISG, provides that

> [i]n a case of non-performance the aggrieved party may by notice to the other party allow an additional period of time for performance.

Although Article 7.1.1 of the UNIDROIT Principles defines nonperformance as a "failure by a party to perform *any* of its obligations under the contract, including defective performance or late performance," it follows from the reference to "a case of delay" in the opening phrase of sentence 1 of Article 7.1.5(3) of the UNIDROIT Principles

[6] For the same conclusion, *see* Honnold, *supra* note 4, at § 351; Hager, in Schlechtriem/Schwenzer eds., *Kommentar zum Einheitlichen UN-Kaufrecht* (4th ed., München: Beck 2004), Art. 64, Comment 8; P. Huber, in *Münchener Kommentar zum Bürgerlichen Gesetzbuch*, Vol. 3, Chapter on CISG [article-by-article commentary – *in German*] (4th ed., München: Beck 2004), Art. 63, Comment 2; Liu, "Remedies for Non-Performance: Perspectives from CISG, UNIDROIT & PECL," at 4.4.3.2, available online at <http://cisgw3.law.pace.edu/cisg/biblio/chengwei-47.html#04-3>.

[7] *See* Secretariat Commentary on article 50 of the 1978 Draft [*draft counterpart of CISG article 54*], Comment 2, available online at <http://cisgw3.law.pace.edu/cisg/text/secomm/secomm-54.html>.
For a similar statement *see* case law:
- Switzerland 20 February 1997 *Bezirksgericht* [District Court] Saane, case presentation including English translation available online at <http://cisgw3.law.pace.edu/cases/970220s1.html>
- ICC Arbitration Case No. 7197 of 1992, CLOUT abstract no. 104, available online at <http://www.unilex.info/case.cfm?pid=1&do=case&id=37&step=Abstract> (stating that the obligation to pay the price under Article 54 CISG involves the obligation to take all measures and comply with all contractual and legal formalities required for payment of the price, such as the opening of a documentary credit or a bank guarantee or even the authorization to transfer currency)

[8] *See* Secretariat Commentary on article 56 of the 1978 Draft [*draft counterpart of CISG Article 60*], Comment 2, available online at <http://cisgw3.law.pace.edu/cisg/text/secomm/secomm-60.html>.

[9] *See* Article 31(b)(c) CISG.

[10] *See* Secretariat Commentary, *supra* note 8. Comment 4.

that, according to the UNIDROIT Principles, the *Nachfrist* too is only of relevance in situations where the buyer performs late or not at all.

2. Requirements for an Effective *Nachfrist* Notice

a. Content of the Notice

The *Nachfrist* notice does not have to meet any formal requirements. Although in theory, even an oral notice suffices,[11] from the practitioner's viewpoint a written notice is more than advisable because in case of a dispute it is up to the seller to prove that the buyer has received the notice.[12] The notice must contain a specific demand for performance[13] and a fixed (given date) or determinable (e.g., "one week from today") deadline when performance will be accepted at the latest.[14] A general demand by the seller that the buyer performs or that he performs "promptly" or the like is not a fixing of a period of time under Article 63(1) CISG.[15]

b. Determination of a *Nachfrist*'s Reasonable Length

The *Nachfrist* must be "of reasonable length." In the absence of an express agreement between the parties, the determination of whether the *Nachfrist* is reasonable must be made in light of the circumstances of the case at hand. Special consideration may be given to the period of time originally set for payment, the seller's need for quick payment of the goods, currency and market price fluctuations, the nature of the goods, the event that caused the delay, and, with regard to the buyer's obligation to take delivery, the seller's need to clear his warehouse.[16]

c. Consequences in Case of Unreasonable Length

aa. Articles 63(1) and 64(1)(b) CISG. Fixing a *Nachfrist* of unreasonable length triggers the question regarding the consequences to the *Nachfrist* notice. The prevailing opinion among scholars is that Articles 63(1) and 64(1)(b) CISG should be interpreted so that a *Nachfrist* of unreasonable length does not make the notice ineffective, but rather initiates a period of reasonable length.[17] This view is confirmed by case

[11] *See, e.g.*, P. Huber, *supra* note 6, Art. 63, Comment 7.

[12] *See e.g.*, Müller-Chen, in: Schlechtriem/Schwenzer eds., *supra* note 6, Art. 47 Comment 13 (regarding the counterpart provision on the buyer's right to avoidance in Article 47(2) CISG).

[13] This requirement has been stressed, for example, by Honnold, *supra* note 4, at § 289 (regarding the counterpart provision on the buyer's right to avoidance in Article 47(2) CISG).

[14] *See* relevant case law (regarding the counterpart provision on the buyer's right to avoidance in Article 47(2) CISG):

- Germany 24 April 1997 *Oberlandesgericht* [Appellate Court] Düsseldorf, case presentation including English translation available online at <http://cisgw3.law.pace.edu/cases/970424g1.html> (stating that a *Nachfrist* notice "must contain a precise request for performance that is combined with the fixing of a specific deadline")
- Germany 11 October 1995 *Landgericht* [District Court] Düsseldorf, case presentation including English translation available online at <http://cisgw3.law.pace.edu/cases/951011g1.html> (stating that "[i]nsofar as the [buyer] has contended that [buyer] had reminded the [seller] several times about the delivery, it cannot be gathered from this general statement that the [buyer] has also fixed a deadline for the [seller]")

[15] *See, e.g.*, Knapp in: Bianca & Bonell eds., *Commentary on the International Sales Law, The 1980 Vienna Sales Convention* (Milan: Giuffrè 1987), Art. 63, Comment 2.10.

[16] *See, e.g.*, Hager, *supra* note 6, Art. 63, Comment 13; Enderlein/Maskow/Strohbach, *Internationales Kaufrecht* [article-by-article commentary – *in German*] (Berlin: Haufe 1991), Art. 63, comment 3.

[17] For this view *see* Hager, *supra* note 6, Art. 63, Comment 3; Magnus, "UN-Kaufrecht" [UN-Sales Law, article-by-article commentary – *in German*], in Staudinger, Julius von Staudingers *Kommentar zum Bürgerlichen Gesetzbuch mit Einführungsgesetz und Nebengesetzen* (13th ed., Berlin: Sellier/de Gruyter 1995), Art. 63, Comment 16; P. Huber, *supra* note 6, Art. 63, Comment 10.

law.[18] Some commentators take a different view. They argue that Articles 63(1) and 64(1)(b) CISG (by reference to Article 63(1) CISG) require a period of reasonable length and conclude from that language that an unreasonable period – either too short or too long – makes the notice ineffective. Consequently, the seller would not be entitled to declare the contract avoided after the *Nachfrist* had expired but would have to serve a new notice and to fix a new *Nachfrist* of reasonable length.[19] The latter view is not persuasive because it cannot be supported by the rules of interpretation under Article 7(1) CISG. Neither the language of Article 63(1) and Article 64(1)(b) CISG nor their legislative history, their context within the CISG's remedial system, or their objectives preclude the extension of an unreasonable *Nachfrist*.[20]

Moreover, this view does not seem to give appropriate account to the "observance of good faith in international trade" as an aid to statutory interpretation.[21] In this regard, it is to be noted that the concept of "reasonableness" is to be considered not only as a general principle in terms of Article 7(2) CISG but also as a *concretization* of the good faith requirement under Article 7(1) CISG.[22] In light of the negative consequences of an

[18] *See* relevant case law on Article 64(1)(b):

- Germany 21 September 1995 *Landgericht* [District Court] Kassel, text of the decision [in German] available online at <http://www.cisg-online.ch/cisg/urteile/192.htm> (stating in *obiter* – with regard to Article 64(1)(b) – that even if the additional period of time set by the buyer was too short, a reasonable period of time would have started to run)

See relevant case law on Article 49(1)(b), the counterpart provision on buyer's right to avoidance:

- Germany 27 April 1999 *Oberlandesgericht* [Appellate Court] Naumburg, case presentation including English translation available online at <http://cisgw3.law.pace.edu/cases/990427g1.html> (stating that the court does not need to decide whether the additional period of time set by the buyer was too short, as in that instance a reasonable period of time would have started to run)
- Germany 24 May 1995 *Oberlandesgericht* [Appellate Court] Celle, case presentation including English translation available online at <http://cisgw3.law.pace.edu/cases/950524g1.html> (stating that a possibly too short *Nachfrist* does not make the notice ineffective where the notice has merely extended a period of time)
- Icc Arbitration Case No. 7645 of March 1995, case presentation available online at <http://cisgw3.law.pace.edu/cases/957645i1.html> (stating in *obiter dictum* that "irrespectively of these circumstances and of the delay of shipment of five days [buyer] could not have declared avoided the contract based on the delay of shipment alone, because the shipment occurred within the *hypothetical additional period of time for performance* which [buyer] would have had to fix to [seller]") [emphasis added]

[19] *See, e.g.*, Schnyder/Straub, in: Honsell ed., *Kommentar zum UN-Kaufrecht* [Cisg commentary] (Berlin/Heidelberg/New York: Springer, 1997), Art. 63, Comment 19, and Art. 64, Comment 73.

[20] For an overview of the Cisg's rules on interpretation with further references to scholarly writings, *see, e.g.*, Koch, "The Concept of Fundamental Breach of Contract under the United Nations Convention on Contracts for the International Sale of Goods (Cisg)," *Pace Review of the Convention on Contracts for the International Sale of Goods* (Cisg) 1998, Kluwer Law International (1999), at 189 *et seq.*; also available online at <http://cisgw3.law.pace.edu/cisg/biblio/koch.html>.

[21] For a concise and thorough analysis of the meaning of "good faith" as an instrument of interpretation, *see* Felemegas, "The United Nations Convention on Contracts for the International Sale of Goods: Article 7 and Uniform Interpretation," *Pace Review of the Convention on Contracts for the International Sale of Goods* (Cisg), Kluwer Law International (2000–2001) 115–265, at Chapter 3, 5(a), also available online at <http://cisgw3.law.pace.edu/cisg/biblio/felemegas.html#ch3>.

[22] For the relationship between reasonableness and good faith, *see* Schlechtriem, *Uniform Sales Law: The UN Convention on Contracts for the International Sale of Goods* (Vienna: Manz 1986), at 39; Honnold, *supra* note 4, at § 95; for the relevance of the standard of reasonableness in determining good faith, *see* Kritzer's editorial remarks on "reasonableness," which include further citations and references, at <http://cisgw3.law.pace.edu/cisg/text/reason.html> (stating that "... regarding reasonableness as a fundamental principle of the Cisg and reading reasonableness into every article of the Cisg, whether specifically mentioned in the article or not ... is required by virtue of the good-faith and uniform-law mandate recited in Article 7(1) of the Cisg"); Bonell, in: Bianca & Bonell eds., *supra* note 15, Art. 7, Comment 2.3.2.2 (stating that "just as in interpreting specific terms and concepts adopted in the text of the Convention, also in specifying 'general principles' courts should, in accordance with the basic criteria of Article 7(1) ... ") and Felemegas, *supra* note 21, at chapter 4, 5(a) (thoroughly and accurately analyzing Bonell's statement in that Bonell relies on the premise that, although there are principles, such as that of party autonomy and the dispatch rule, which can be directly applied, others, such as the principle of good faith and the concept of "reasonableness," need further specification in order to offer a solution for a particular case).

ineffective notice for both parties, a narrow interpretation of Articles 63(1) and 64(1)(b) CISG seems unreasonable. An ineffective notice would not only impose on the seller the extra burden of fixing a new *Nachfrist* but would also allow him to resort to other remedies because the restriction of Article 63(2) CISG would not apply. Such a consequence is not in the interest of the buyer because it would frustrate his efforts to effect payment or take delivery. His expenses incurred in attempting to perform would be wasted, and even if one qualified the declaration of avoidance upon the expiration of a too short *Nachfrist* as breach of contract,[23] those expenses would not necessarily be (fully) recoverable under Article 74 CISG.

bb. Article 7.1.5(3) of the UNIDROIT Principles. Sentence 2 of Article 7.1.5(3) of the UNIDROIT Principles expressly states that

> [i]f the additional period allowed is not of reasonable length it shall be extended to a reasonable length.

The UNIDROIT Principles, therefore, follow a slightly different approach than the CISG. Unlike Article 63(1) CISG, they do not require that the buyer fix a *Nachfrist* of *reasonable* length, but they limit his right to exercise the avoidance remedy if the *Nachfrist* is of *unreasonable* length. Notwithstanding that difference, the approach taken by the UNIDROIT Principles confirms my view that only an extension of a reasonable length is in itself reasonable. Sentence 2 of Article 7.1.5(3) of the UNIDROIT Principles thus can be seen as an *exemplification* of the principle of reasonableness in international trade. As pointed out before, reasonableness is also a general principle under the CISG. Even if one is not willing to follow my conclusion that the observance of good faith requires one to interpret Articles 63(1) and 64(1)(b) CISG in the sense of sentence 2 of Article 7.1.5(3) of the UNIDROIT Principles, such an interpretation would therefore follow from Article 7(2) CISG. According to that provision "[q]uestions concerning matters governed by this Convention which are not expressly settled in it are to be settled in conformity with the *general principles* on which is based . . . "[24]

3. Effects of a *Nachfrist*

a. Article 63(2) CISG

The effects of a *Nachfrist* are described in Article 63(2) CISG. It provides that

> [u]nless the seller has received notice from the buyer that he will not perform within the period so fixed, the seller may not, during that period, resort to any remedy for breach of contract. However, the seller is not deprived thereby of any right he may have to claim damages for delay in performance.

According to Article 63(2) CISG, during the *Nachfrist* period the seller may not resort to any remedy for breach of contract (except for damages for delay in performance). As a consequence, even if the nonpayment of late payment and/or not taking or late taking delivery qualifies for fundamental breach under Article 64(1)(a) CISG, the seller cannot avoid the contract if he fixed a *Nachfrist*.[25] The purpose of Article 63(2) CISG is to protect

[23] *See* Plate, "The Buyer's Remedy of Avoidance under the CISG: Acceptable from a Common Law Perspective?," 6 *Vindobona J. Int'l Com. L. & Arbitration* (2002) 57, at 68–69, available online at <http://cisgw3.law.pace.edu/cisg/biblio/plate.html>; Müller-Chen, *supra* note 6, Art. 47, Comment 9 (both stating with regard to the counterpart provision on buyer's right of fixing a *Nachfrist* that if the buyer has fixed too short a period and accordingly declares the avoidance of the contract upon the expiration of that period, this constitutes a breach of contract itself).

[24] Emphasis added.

[25] For the same conclusion, *see* Hager, *supra* note 6, Art. 63, Comment 4.

the buyer, who is relying on the seller's declaration when he is trying to effect payment or to make necessary preparations for taking delivery, possibly at considerable expense.[26] The only situation in which avoidance is possible before the expiration of the *Nachfrist* is where the buyer declares an ultimate refusal to perform within the period fixed.[27] With regard to the latter situation, it is to be noted that the seller is entitled to declare the contract avoided without fixing of a *Nachfrist* when the buyer unequivocally declares his unwillingness to perform before seller has fixed a *Nachfrist*.[28]

b. Article 7.1.5(2) UNIDROIT Principles

Article 7.1.5(2) UNIDROIT Principles states that

> [d]uring the additional period the aggrieved party may withhold performance of its own reciprocal obligations and may claim damages but may not resort to any other remedy. If it receives notice from the other party that the latter will not perform within that period, or if upon expiry of that period due performance has not been made, the aggrieved party may resort to any of the remedies that may be available under this Chapter.

Except for the right to withhold performance, Article 7.1.5(2) UNIDROIT Principles is substantively identical to Article 63(2) CISG. The aggrieved party's right to withhold performance of its own reciprocal obligations during the *Nachfrist*, however, follows under the Convention from Article 58 CISG. According to Article 58(1) in sentence 2, and Article 58(2) of the CISG, the seller, in the absent of any stipulation to the contrary, may make payment a condition for handing over the goods or documents.[29] If the seller has agreed to deliver the goods before being paid but, prior to the time of taking delivery, it becomes apparent that the buyer will not pay for the goods, the seller is entitled to prevent the handing over of the goods to the buyer pursuant to Article 71(2) CISG.[30]

4. Buyer's Noncompliance with the Seller's *Nachfrist* Ultimatum

a. Article 64(1)(b) CISG

Article 64(1)(b) CISG provides that if the buyer fails to perform within the *Nachfrist*, the seller may declare the contract avoided. Article 64(1)(b) CISG also provides an alternative condition under which the seller may avoid the contract, which is a declaration or indication by the buyer that he will not perform within the *Nachfrist*. The seller may already in its notice provide that if the other party fails to perform within the period allowed by the notice the contract shall be automatically avoided.[31]

[26] *See* Secretariat Commentary on article 59 of the 1978 Draft [*draft counterpart of* CISG *article* 63], Comment 9, available online at <http://cisgw3.law.pace.edu/cisg/text/secomm/secomm-63.html>.

[27] *See* Secretariat Commentary, *supra* note 26.

[28] *See* Austria 10 December 1997 Vienna Arbitration proceeding S 2/97, case presentation including English translation available online at <http://cisgw3.law.pace.edu/cases/971210a3.html> (stating that the seller does not have to fix an additional time for the buyer, if the buyer had declared that she did not want to perform the contract any more because the fixing of an additional period would make no sense in such a case).

For the same conclusion with regard to the counterpart provisions on buyer's right of avoidance *see* Huber, in Schlechtriem ed., *Commentary on the U.N. Convention on the International Sale of Goods* (Clarendon Press: Oxford 1998), Art. 49 Comment 22; *see also* Treitel, *supra* note 2, § 150 (stating with regard to the *Nachfrist* requirement under German, Austrian, and Swiss law that the main purpose of the requirement of a *Nachfrist* is to protect the promiser by giving him a further period of grace within which to perform, but that in case of the seller's refusal, "no useful purpose would be served by the *Nachfrist*").

[29] *See, e.g.*, Schlechtriem, *supra* note 22, at 81 (stating that "as long as the contract does not obligate the seller to perform first, the seller can make payment a condition precedent to a transfer of the goods or documents controlling their disposition (Article 58(1) sentence 2 and 58(2)"), available online at <http://cisgw3.law.pace.edu/cisg/biblio/schlechtriem.html>.

[30] For further details on stoppage of goods in transit *see, e.g.*, Honnold, *supra* note 4, at 390.

[31] *See* relevant case law:

- Austria 28 April 2000 *Oberster Gerichtshof* [Austrian Supreme Court], case presentation including English translation available online at <http://cisgw3.law.pace.edu/cases/000428a3.html> (stating that it is

b. Article 7.1.5(3) of the UNIDROIT Principles

Sentence 1 of Article 7.1.5(3) of the UNIDROIT Principles is substantively identical to Article 64(1)(b) CISG.[32] Sentence 3 expressly states that "[t]he aggrieved party may in its notice provide that if the other party fails to perform within the period allowed by the notice the contract shall automatically terminate."

III. TIME LIMITATIONS ON THE RIGHT OF AVOIDANCE

1. Article 64(2) CISG

a. Scope of Article 64(2) CISG

Article 64(2) CISG sets time-limits on the seller's right to avoid the contract in cases where the buyer has paid the price. Subparagraph (a) deals with late performance, whereas subparagraph (b) applies to other cases of breach of contract. In the case of late performance, according to Article 64(2)(a) CISG

> the seller loses the right to declare the contract avoided unless he does so [. . .] before the seller has become aware the performance has been rendered [. . .]

It is to be noted that before the price has been *fully* paid the seller may, without limits on time, avoid the contract.[33]

b. Relationship between Article 64(2)(a) and Article 64(2)(b) CISG

There is ongoing debate regarding the scope of Article 64(2)(a) CISG and its relationship to Article 64(2)(b) CISG. By its terms, Article 64(2)(a) CISG is not limited to late payment or late taking delivery, but is also applicable to other obligations, such as the obligation not to re-export the goods. Such a reading, however, would leave Article 64(2)(b) CISG meaningless according to which, in cases other than late performance, the seller loses the right to avoid the contract if he fails to do so

> within a reasonable time
> (i) after [he] knew or ought to have known of the breach; or
> (ii) after the expiration of any additional period of time fixed by [him] in accordance with paragraph (1) of article 63, or after the buyer has declared that he will not perform his obligations within such an additional period.

In my view, it follows from Article 64(2)(b)(ii) CISG that Article 64(2)(a) CISG applies only to late payment and late taking delivery (even if it qualifies for fundamental breach[34]).[35] With regard to these obligations of the buyer, Article 64(2)(a) CISG

a question of interpretation of the seller's *Nachfrist* notice under Article 63(1) CISG if the contract will be terminated upon expiration of the *Nachfrist* without further notice)

- Switzerland 20 February 1997 *Bezirksgericht* [District Court] Saane case presentation including English translation available online at <http://cisgw3.law.pace.edu/cases/970220s1.html> (stating that the seller expressly declared the avoidance of the sales contract by denying any further performance and acceptance under the sales contract, if the buyer did not meet the requirements as set out in the final request to the buyer to perform)

[32] Sentence 1 of Article 7.1.5(3) of the UNIDROIT Principles reads as follows:

> Where in a case of delay in performance which is not fundamental the aggrieved party has given notice allowing an additional period of time of reasonable length, it may terminate the contract at the end of that period.

[33] For a similar view *see* Secretariat Commentary on article 60 of the 1978 Draft [*draft counterpart of CISG article 64*], Comment 9, online available at <http://cisgw3.law.pace.edu/cisg/text/secomm/secomm-64.html>; Enderlein/Maskow, *International Sales Law [Commentary on the CISG*] (New York: Oceana Publications 1992), Art. 64, Comment 6, also available online at <http://cisgw3.law.pace.edu/cisg/biblio/enderlein.html#art64–4a>; Knapp, *supra* note 15, Art. 64, Comment 3.7.

[34] *See* Hager, *supra* note 6, Art. 64, Comment 19.

[35] For a different view *see* Magnus, *supra* note 17, Art. 64 Comment 41–43; P. Huber, *supra* note 6, Art. 64, Comment 23.

determines the *latest point in time* when the seller loses his right to avoidance. For example, if the buyer delays payment and the seller has fixed a *Nachfrist* that has expired, the seller loses the right to avoid the contract within a reasonable time – or even earlier, if the buyer effects payment and informs the seller accordingly. The same is true with regard to delivery taken late by the buyer.[36] If the buyer delays taking over the goods but has duly paid the price for them, the seller loses his right to avoid the contract if the buyer takes over the goods and informs the seller accordingly. The seller cannot argue that Article 64(2)(b)(ii) CISG allows a declaration of avoidance simply "within a reasonable time." Where the buyer is in breach of an obligation other than late performance and this breach amounts to a fundamental one(e.g., buyer's non-compliance with the obligation not to re-export the goods[37]) seller's right of avoidance is subject to Article 64(2)(b)(i) CISG.

c. Determination of Reasonable Time

What is reasonable in terms of Article 64(2)(b) CISG depends upon the circumstances of each case. Where avoidance is based on late payment and/or late taking delivery (Article 64(2)(b)(ii) CISG), the length of reasonable time in particular depends on the nature of the goods. If the goods are perishable or subject to price fluctuations (e.g., oil), notice must be given almost instantaneously. In other situations (Article 64(2)(b)(i) CISG), the reasonable period of time, in general, will be longer because the determination of whether a given breach qualifies for fundamental breach requires extra time (e.g., for seeking legal advice).

2. Article 7.3.2(2) of the UNIDROIT Principles

The counterpart to Article 64(2) CISG can be found in Article 7.3.2(2) of the UNIDROIT Principles. The latter states that

> [i]f performance has been offered late or otherwise does not conform to the contract the aggrieved party will lose its right to terminate the contract unless it gives notice to the other party within a reasonable time after it has or ought to have become aware of the offer or of the non-conforming performance.

Article 7.3.2 of the UNIDROIT Principles covers late payment as well as late taking delivery. It is substantively identical to Article 64(2)(a) and Article 64(2)(b)(i) CISG.

IV. CONCLUSIONS

The requirements for avoidance for nonpayment or not taking delivery under the CISG and the UNIDROIT Principles do not differ in substance. With regard to the effect of a *Nachfrist* of unreasonable length, it makes sense to use the solution provided in sentence 2 of Article 7.1.5(3) of the UNIDROIT Principles to supplement Article 63(1) and 64(1)(b) CISG.

[36] For a similar view *see* Hager, *supra* note 6, Art. 64, Comment 16; P. Huber, *supra* note 6, Art. 64 Comment 22; Neumayer/Ming, *Convention de Vienne sur les contrats de vente internationale de marchandises*. Commentaire [Commentary on the CISG – *in French*] (Lausanne: CEDIDAC, Vol. 24, 1993), Art. 64, Comment 7.

[37] *See* case law cited *supra* note 5.

Anticipatory breach: Remarks on the manner in which the UNIDROIT Principles of International Commercial Contracts may be used to interpret or supplement Articles 71 and 72 of the CISG

Sieg Eiselen

a. Articles 71–73 of the CISG deal with the situation where it becomes apparent or clear that one of the parties to an agreement will or may not perform a substantial part of its obligations in terms of the agreement.[1] The object of Article 72 is to provide the innocent party with a remedy in cases where it is clear that the other party will not perform at all or will commit another fundamental breach.[2] This remedy based on the Anglo-American doctrine of anticipatory breach allows the innocent party to avoid the contract when the breach occurs without having to wait until performance becomes due.[3] Whereas Article 72 is aimed at the phenomenon of anticipatory breach of contract (i.e., a breach of contract that takes place before the performance is due by the party in breach), Article 71 has a wider scope in that it deals with anticipatory breach as well as incomplete performance.[4] The remedies provided in Article 71 are aimed at keeping the contract intact, whereas the remedies in Article 72 are aimed at avoiding the contract.[5] Article 73 provides for anticipatory breach installment contracts. It is for that reason that these articles contain different requirements for the exercising of the respective remedies.[6]

b. The UNIDROIT Principles is similarly structured in Articles 7.3.3 and 7.3.4. Article 7.3.3 makes provision for a party to terminate the agreement where it is clear that there will be a fundamental non-performance by the other party. There is no requirement to give notice as is the case with Article 72 of the CISG. If a party is uncertain as to whether there will be a fundamental breach or not, but has a reasonable suspicion that it may occur, that party is, in terms of Article 7.3.4, entitled to demand an adequate assurance from the other party that the latter will perform. Failure to provide an adequate assurance is a ground in terms of Article 7.3.4 to terminate the agreement. There is therefore,

[1] Leser H. G., & Hornung R., in Schlechtriem P. H. & Bacher K., *Kommentar zum Einheitlichen UN Kaufrecht* 3rd ed (2000 München) Art 71 Rn 1; Art 72 Rn 1, Art 73 Rn 1; Magnus U., in Martinek M. (ed) *J von Staudingers Kommentar zum Bürgerlichen Gesetzbuch mit Einführungsgesetz und Nebengesetze: Wiener UN-Kaufrecht* (1999 Berlin) Art 71 Rn 1, Art 72 Rn 1, Art 73 Rn 1; Burkhart F., *Interpretatives Zusammenwirken von CISG und UNIDROIT Principles* (2000 Baden-Baden) 194; Schnyder A. K. and Straub R. M., in Honsell H., *Kommentar zum UN Kaufrecht* (1997 Berlin) Art 71 Rn 1, Art 72 Rn 1, Art 73 Rn 1; Witz W., Salger H. C. & Lorenz M., *Internationales Einheitliches Kaufrecht* (2000 Heidelberg) Art 71 Rn 1, Art 72 Rn 1 & 2, Art 73 Rn 1; Kritzer A. H., *Guide to the Practical Applications of the United Nations Convention on Contracts for the International Sale of Goods* (1989 Deventer) 465–467; Honnold J. O., *Uniform Law for International Sales* 3rd ed (1999 The Hague), also available online at <http://cisgw3.law.pace.edu/cisg/biblio/honnold.html>, para 395 at p. 437.

[2] Enderlein F. & Maskow D., *International Sales Law – United Nations Convention on Contracts for the International Sale of Goods* (1992 New York), also at <http://cisgw3.law.pace.edu/cisg/biblio/enderlein.html> para. 1 at p. 291.

[3] Witz/Salger/Lorenz Art 72 Rn 2.

[4] Staudinger/Magnus Art 71 Rn 34.

[5] Staudinger/Magnus Art 71 Rn 1; Art 72 Rn 1.

[6] *See* Schlechtriem P., *Uniform Sales Law – The UN-Convention on Contracts for the International Sale of Goods* (Vienna 1986) 389 *et seq*., also available at <http://cisgw3.law.pace.edu/cisg/biblio/schlechtriem-72.html>; Staudinger/Magnus Art 72 Rn 8 & 9; Flechtner H. M., 8 *J. L. & Com.* (1988) 53–108, also at <http://cisgw3.law.pace.edu/cisg/text/flecht71,72.html>. Initial efforts to combine the articles during the drafting process were intentionally rejected. *See* Enderlein/Maskow p. 284 Note 1 & 2, p. 291 N 1; Honsell/Schnyder/Straub Art 72 Rn 10. *See* also Kee C., "Comparative Editorial Remarks to Articles 51 & 73" at <http://cisgw3.law.pace.edu/cisg/text/peclcomp51.html>.

quite a close connection between the provisions of Article 7.3.3 and 7.3.4. As is shown below, this is not necessarily the case with the very similar Article 72 and Article 71 of the CISG.

c. There are a number of interpretational issues regarding Article 72 on which there is a divergence of opinion. Commentators differ on the exact interpretation and meaning of the meaning of the words "it is clear" (Article 72(1)) and "it becomes apparent" (Article 71(1))[7] and whether there is any difference in the meaning or the standards to be applied.[8] They also differ on whether the giving of notice of termination is an essential requirement to become entitled to the remedy or whether it is only necessary in circumstances where objectively speaking the other party would have been able to give an adequate assurance.[9] Lastly there is also a difference of opinion on whether a failure to give an adequate assurance on demand under Article 71(1) automatically entitles a party to avoid the contract under Article 72.[10] The construction and provisions of Article 7.3.3 and 7.3.4 of the UNIDROIT Principles may be helpful in solving these issues.

d. In certain circumstances, a party may be entitled to rely on either Article 71 or 72.[11] If an anticipatory breach occurs, the innocent party may want to enforce specific performance, in which case it would make use of its right to suspend performance under Article 71, rather than to avoid the contract under Article 72 even if it is entitled to do so. However, in the case of part performance a party may apparently only rely on Article 51 in conjunction with Article 45 where Article 51 applies or on Article 71 (if it wants to enforce full performance) or Article 49 (if it wants to avoid the contract), but not on Article 72. Article 72 is therefore a remedy that is only to be used in true circumstances of anticipatory breach and not where an actual breach has already taken place.[12] However where the contract consists of a series of performances (installments, for instance, or delivery of a certain number of goods on a monthly basis), a serious deficiency in quality of the first installment entitles the innocent party to exercise its rights under Article73 and avoid the contract.[13]

e. At first blush there seems to be a slight difference between the provisions of Article 72(1) of the CISG and Article 7.3.3 of the UNIDROIT Principles. In Article 72(1), it is required that it must be clear that the counter party *will commit* a fundamental breach. Article 7.3.3 of the UNIDROIT Principles is apparently formulated more broadly in that it only requires that it must be clear that a fundamental non-performance will take place. This difference is more apparent than real. Under the CISG, any fundamental non-performance is regarded as a breach of contract, whether the performance was possible or not.[14] Thus, where substantial performance becomes impossible,

[7] Enderlein/Maskow p. 286 Note 2; Honsell/Schnyder/Straub Art 71 Rn 24–26, Art 72 Rn 25; Staudinger/Magnus Art 71 Rn 18. Honnold p. 429 para. 388 remarks that these provisions were consciously so drafted and that this difference in terminology is also found in the French and Spanish versions of the CISG.

[8] Enderlein p. 286 Note 2; Honnold para. 388 at p. 429.

[9] Enderlein p. 293 Note 6; Honsell/Schnyder/Straub Art 72 Rn 35 & 36.

[10] Enderlein/Maskow p. 290 Note 1.

[11] Enderlein/Maskow p. 286 Note 3; Schlechtriem Art 72 Rn 9.

[12] Honsell/Schnyder/Straub Art 72 Rn 15; Germany 18 November 1993 *Oberlandesgericht* [Appellate Court] Düsseldorf <http://cisgw3.law.pace.edu/cases/931118g1.html>; Germany 15 February 1995 *Bundesgerichtshof* [Federal Supreme Court] <http://cisgw3.law.pace.edu/cases/950215g1.html]>.

[13] This is to be distinguished from the situation where only 1,000 pairs of shoes have been delivered instead of 2,000 on the date of performance. In this instance, the correct remedies are either Article 51 and Article 45 or Article 71 and not Article 72. *See* Witz/Salger/Lorenz Art 71 Rn 1; Art 73 Rn 1; Honsell/Schnyder/Straub Art 72 Rn 15; Austria 10 December 1997 Vienna Arbitration proceeding S 2/97 <http://cisgw3.law.pace.edu/cases/971210a3.html>; Germany 18 November 1993 *Oberlandesgericht* [Appellate Court] Düsseldorf <http://cisgw3.law.pace.edu/cases/931118g1.html>; Germany 15 February 1995 *Bundesgerichtshof* [Federal Supreme Court] <http://cisgw3.law.pace.edu/cases/950215g1.html>.

[14] Schlechtriem/Stoll Art 79 Rn 6; Honsell/Schnyder/Straub Art 71 Rn 29, Art 72 Rn 19.

even if such impossibility results from circumstances beyond the control of the obligor, non-performance or mal-performance is still regarded as a breach.[15] This is also the approach followed in the UNIDROIT Principles.

f. The most difficult aspect of interpreting Article 72 (and Article 71 for that matter) is to establish what measure of certainty is required that a fundamental breach will occur.[16] Article 7.3.3 of the UNIDROIT Principles is, unfortunately, of no assistance in this regard as it uses exactly the same terminology as Article 72. In a 1992 German decision, the *Landgericht* [District Court] Berlin[17] has given the best judicial exposition of the standards required under Article 72. It defined the words "it is clear" ("*offensichtlich*") in terms of the probabilities that a fundamental breach will be committed. It stated that a very high degree of probability is required,[18] but that this did not mean a probability almost reaching certainty.[19]

g. Both the CISG and the UNIDROIT Principles require a clear indication of a fundamental non-performance (i.e., that it must be clear that there will be a fundamental non-performance).[20] Because the terminology used is very similar, the UNIDROIT Principles therefore shed little light on what measure should be used to determine whether "it is clear." Commentators offer different interpretations on whether "it is clear" (in Article 72) has the same meaning as "it becomes apparent" (in Article 71).[21] The majority opinion seems to be that Article 72 requires a higher standard of prospective certainty than Article 71, mainly because of the more drastic nature of the remedy under Article 72, namely avoidance.[22] Suspension as provided for in Article 71 is less drastic in that it is only a temporary remedy, especially if the contract is to be avoided without giving notice to the counter party.[23]

h. This approach also seems to be supported by the case law[24] and by the provisions of Articles 7.3.3 and 7.3.4 of the UNIDROIT Principles, where there is a clearly formulated

[15] Honsell/Schnyder/Straub Art 72 Rn 18.

[16] Staudinger/Magnus Art 72 Rn 7; Honnold p. 439 para. 397; Honsell/Schnyder/Straub Art 72 Rn 26–28; Australia 17 November 2000 Supreme Court of Queensland (*Downs Investments v. Perwaja Steel*) <http://cisgw3.law.pace.edu/cases/001117a2.html>.

[17] Germany 30 September 1992 *Landgericht* [District Court] Berlin, at <http://cisgw3.law.pace.edu/cases/920930g1.html>.

[18] In the words of the court, *"einer sehr hohen naheliegender Wahrscheinlichkeit."*

[19] In the words of the court, *"eine an Sicherheit grenzende Wahrscheinlichkeit." See also* Germany 18 November 1993 *Oberlandesgericht* [Appellate Court] Düsseldorf <http://cisgw3.law.pace.edu/cases/931118g1.html>; Germany 28 April 1993 *Landgericht* [District Court] Krefeld <http://cisgw3.law.pace.edu/cases/930428g1.html>; Australia 17 November 2000 Supreme Court of Queensland (*Downs Investments v. Perwaja Steel*) <http://cisgw3.law.pace.edu/cases/001117a2.html>.

[20] *See* Schlechtriem P., *Uniform Sales Law – The UN-Convention on Contracts for the International Sale of Goods* (Vienna 1986) 389 *et seq.*, also available at <http://cisgw3.law.pace.edu/cisg/biblio/schlechtriem-72.html>; Staudinger/Magnus Art 72 Rn 8, 9 & 18; Flechtner H. M. 8 *J.L. & Com.* (1988) 53–108 at <http://cisgw3.law.pace.edu/cisg/text/flecht71,72.html>.

[21] Enderlein/Maskow p. 291 Note 1; Honsell/Schnyder/Straub Art 72 Rn 20–24; Witz/Salger/Lorenz Art 72 Rn 7; Staudinger/Magnus Art 72 Rn 8 & 9.

[22] Honsell/Schnyder/Straub Art 72 Rn 23–25 indicates that this is the proper interpretation when due regard is had to the history and drafting of these articles. *See* also Staudinger/Magnus Art 72 Rn 9; Salger/Lorenz Art 72 Rn 8.

[23] Staudinger/Magnus Art 72 Rn 9–11.

[24] The clearest example where this has been applied has been ICC Arbitration Case No. 8786 of January 1997 <http://cisgw3.law.pace.edu/cases/978786i1.html> where one party declared that it would not perform by the date agreed due to a delay. Under the circumstances the delay was a fundamental breach, and it was held that it was not necessary to give notice to the other party. *See* also Austria 10 December 1997 Vienna Arbitration proceeding S 2/97 <http://cisgw3.law.pace.edu/cases/971210a3.html>. In Switzerland 20 February 1997 *Zivilgericht* [District Court] Saane <http://cisgw3.law.pace.edu/cases/970220s1.html> and Switzerland 31 May 1996 Zürich Arbitration proceeding <http://cisgw3.law.pace.edu/cases/960531s1.html> reliance on Article 72 was rejected due to a lack of evidence that there was an intention to repudiate; it was not clear.

difference in the requirements. In terms of Article 7.3.3 it is required that it must be clear that there will be a fundamental non-performance, whereas in terms of Article 7.3.4 there need only be a reasonable belief on the part of the innocent party that there will be a fundamental non-performance.

i. If there is any doubt on whether, due to the conduct of the other party or the prevailing circumstances, there is an anticipatory breach objectively speaking, a party should exercise the right to suspend performance under Article 71 CISG and require an adequate assurance from the other party, rather than issue a notice of avoidance under Article 72(2).[25] It is the safer option because the giving of a notice of avoidance in terms of Article 72(2) under circumstances where it is not warranted may in itself constitute an anticipatory breach entitling the other party to avoid the contract.[26]

j. There is a difference of opinion among commentators on whether a failure or a refusal to produce adequate security where it has been demanded is in itself a fundamental breach or whether it may only be a clear indication that the other party will commit a fundamental breach.[27] Article 7.3.4 UNIDROIT Principles may be of assistance in interpreting the interplay between Articles 72 and 71. Article 7.3.4 UNIDROIT Principles makes express provision for the innocent party to demand an adequate assurance where it reasonably suspects that there will be a fundamental non-performance. In terms of Article 7.3.4 it is clearly stipulated that a failure to provide this assurance within a reasonable period of time entitles the other party to terminate (avoid) the agreement. Whether this is possible in light of the drafting history of the CISG is debatable.[28]

k. The CISG takes a more lenient approach to anticipatory breach than the UNIDROIT Principles in that it obliges the innocent party, when time allows, to notify the other party if it intends avoiding the contract, except where the other party has clearly declared its intention not to perform.[29] The object of the notification is to enable the other party to provide adequate assurance that it will perform. There are different opinions on whether the obligation to give notice is a condition precedent for the valid exercising of the right to avoid.[30] It is submitted that in interpreting the duty to inform, a court should follow a stricter approach toward the necessity to inform if regard is to be had to the approach followed under the UNIDROIT Principles.[31] If there is doubt on whether the innocent party should have informed or not, the court ought to rule in favor of the innocent party (i.e., that there was no duty to inform). In terms of Article 7.3.3 of the UNIDROIT Principles, a party is not obliged to inform the other party, but may as a precaution require an adequate assurance of due performance, failing which that party is entitled to terminate the agreement.

l. Where it is apparent that notice will be totally ineffective in that it is impossible for the obligor to prevent the eventual breach, is there still a formal obligation to notify? It is submitted that this is a situation where the innocent party is not required to notify

[25] Enderlein/Maskow p. 292 Note 3.

[26] Commentary of the Secretariat Comment 2, *Document A/CONF.975* p. 53 as reprinted in Honnold J., *Documentary History of the Uniform Law for International Sales* (Deventer 1989) and at <http://cisgw3.law.pace.edu/cisg/text/secomm/secomm-72.html>; Enderlein/Maskow p. 291 Note 1; Germany 21 September 1995 *Landgericht* [District Court] Kassel <http://cisgw3.law.pace.edu/cases/950921g1.html>.

[27] Secretariat Commentary 2 p. 53; Enderlein/Maskow p. 290 Note 10; Honsell/Schnyder/Straub Art 71 Rn 51; Staudinger/Magnus Art 71 Rn 52; Honnold Art 71 Rn 394.

[28] *See* the Secretariat Commentary 2 p. 53.

[29] Honsell/Schnyder/Straub Art 72 Rn 34 & 35.

[30] Honsell/Schnyder/Straub Art 72 Rn 35 & 36. Witz/Salger/Lorenz is of the opinion that the failure to give notice does not affect the effectiveness of the avoidance. However, *see* the decision to the contrary in ICC Arbitration Case No. 8574 of September 1996 <http://cisgw3.law.pace.edu/cases/968574i1.html>.

[31] For a contrary opinion, *see* Honsell/Schnyder/Straub Art 72 Rn 41 & 42.

the other party.[32] The object of the notice requirement is to enable the other party to provide adequate assurance of his performance. If that has become impossible, then the necessity to give notice must surely fall away. There is, however, also a strong contrary view on this issue.[33]

m. In the literature there is a controversy on whether the requirement of "reasonableness" only refers to the notice or whether it also has a reference to the duty to give notice. The controversy, however, is mainly among German writers and is caused by an inaccurate translation into the (unofficial) German text.[34]

[32] Enderlein/Maskow p. 293 Note 6; Witz/Salger/Lorenz Art 72 Rn 15; Staudinger/Magnus Art 72 Rn 22; Schlechtriem Art 72 Rn 16 & 17; Honsell/Schnyder/Straub Art 72 Rn 45; ICC Arbitration Case No. 8574 of September 1996 <http://cisgw3.law.pace.edu/cases/968574i1.html>.

[33] *See* Honsell/Schnyder/Straub Art 72 Rn 36; Schlechtriem /Leser/Hornung Art 72 Rn 13 et seq.; Germany 9 July 1992 *Landgericht* [District Court] Düsseldorf <http://cisgw3.law.pace.edu/cases/920709g1.html>.

[34] *See* Honsell/Schnyder/Straub Art 72 Rn 45; Staudinger/Magnus Art 72 Rn 21.

Measuring damages for breach of contract: Remarks on the manner in which the UNIDROIT Principles of International Commercial Contracts may be used to interpret or supplement Article 74 of the CISG

Sieg Eiselen

a. The right to claim damages as a result of a breach of contract is probably the single most important remedy available to the aggrieved party.[1] The law of damages is a complex set of rules and principles hiding behind fairly simple-looking formulas, such as those found in CISG Articles 74 to 76. The interpretation of Article 74 CISG is therefore fraught with all kinds of difficulties of which the interpreter should be aware. Not the least of these difficulties could be the different notions and understanding of damages in the particular legal system of the interpreter.

b. Although the CISG deals with damages in some detail, several vexing practical issues, which are dealt with in most legal systems and also in the UNIDROIT Principles, have been left open or unresolved. These issues include the time at which damages are to be calculated, the liability and calculation of future damages, contributory conduct of the claimant that increases the amount of damages, saved expenses, loss of an opportunity

[1] Honnold J. O., *Uniform Law for International Sales under the 1980 United Nations Convention* 3rd ed. (1999 Deventer), also available online at <http://cisgw3.law.pace.edu/cisg/biblio/honnold.html>, para. 403–404, at pp. 445–446; Enderlein F. & Maskow D., *International Sales Law – United Nations Convention on Contracts for the International Sale of Goods* (1992 New York) 297–302, also available online at <http://cisgw3.law.pace.edu/cisg/biblio/enderlein.html>; Magnus U., in Martinek M. (ed) *J. von Staudingers Kommentar zum Bürgerlichen Gesetzbuch mit Einführungsgesetz und Nebengesetze: Wiener UN-Kaufrecht* (1999 Berlin) Art 74, Rn 2 & 3; Bernstein H & Lookofsky J., *Understanding the CISG in Europe* (1997 The Hague) 96; Schönle in Honsell 1 & 10; Witz W., Salger H. C. & Lorenz M., *Internationales Einheitliches Kaufrecht* (2000 Heidelberg) Art 74, Rn 1 & 2; Kritzer A. H., *Guide to the Practical Applications of the United Nations Convention on Contracts for the International Sale of Goods* (1989 Deventer) 474–482; Stoll H in Schlechtriem P. H. & Bacher K. (eds) *Kommentar zum einheitlichen UN Kaufrecht* 3rd ed (2000 München) Art 74, Rn 1 & 2.

or chance, penalty clauses, and proof of damages. The provisions of Articles 7.4.1 and 7.4.2 of the UNIDROIT Principles may be helpful in interpreting and applying Article 74 CISG.

c. The basic premise underlying both the provisions of Article 74 CISG and Articles 7.4.1 and 7.4.2 of the UNIDROIT Principles is that the breaching party is liable to compensate the aggrieved party in full for all pecuniary damages suffered by the aggrieved party, including the loss of profit.[2] The second shared premise in the CISG and the UNIDROIT Principles is that the claim for damages is available over and above any other remedies that the aggrieved party may have or exercise.[3] The third shared premise is that the breaching party is only liable for damages that were either actually foreseen or foreseeable by the breaching party at the time of the conclusion of the contract – that is, according to the so-called contemplation principle.[4] The UNIDROIT Principles, however, contain more detailed provisions than the CISG in respect of what is to be understood under full compensation. These provisions and their applicability in the interpretation of Article 74 CISG are discussed below.

d. There is one radical difference between the damages provisions in the CISG and those in the UNIDROIT Principles; namely, regarding non-pecuniary damages or damages resulting from personal injury or death. Article 5 CISG excludes the claim for such damages from the scope of the Convention.[5] Therefore, whether a party will be entitled to such damages will depend on the provisions of the applicable national legal system. However, Article 7.4.2 of the UNIDROIT Principles specifically includes liability for such damages. This does not so much reflect a difference in the basic approach between the CISG and UNIDROIT Principles as the fact that the drafters of the CISG wished to remove the complex area of product liability from the sphere of the CISG.[6] The fact that such a provision is included in the UNIDROIT Principles provides good grounds for arguing that the provisions of Article 5 CISG should be restrictively interpreted and only the liability for personal injury or death should be excluded, but not other personal damages, such as damage to reputation.[7]

[2] Honsell/Schönle Art 74 Rn 10; Honnold para 417 at 456; Enderlein/Maskow (1992) Notes 1 & 4, at pp. 297–298; Witz/Salger/Lorenz Art 74, Rn 12 & 19; Staudinger/Magnus, Art 74, Rn 12, 16 & 19; Liu C., "Remedies for Non-Performance: Perspectives from CISG, UNIDROIT PRINCIPLES & PECL," September 2003 at 13.2 available at <http://cisgw3.law.pace.edu/cisg/biblio/chengwei-74.html>. For relevant case law, *see* ICC Arbitration Case No. 8574 of September 1996, available online at <http://cisgw3.law.pace.edu/cases/968574i1.html>; Germany 21 September 1995 *Landgericht* [District Court] Kassel, available online at <http://cisgw3.law.pace.edu/cases/950921g1.html>; Austria 9 March 2000 *Oberster Gerichtshof* [Supreme Court], available online at <http://cisgw3.law.pace.edu/cases/000309a3.html>; United States 9 September 1994 Federal District Court [New York] (*Delchi Carrier v. Rotorex*), available online at <http://cisgw3.law.pace.edu/cases/940909u1.html>; Austria 14 January 2002 Supreme Court, available online at <http://cisgw3.law.pace.edu/cases/020114a3.html>.

[3] Staudinger/Magnus, Art 74, Rn 8.

[4] *See* para g, *infra*.

[5] Staudinger/Magnus, Art 5, Rn 1; Enderlein/Maskow (1992), Note 1 at p. 46; Liu at 13.4. *Cf.* Germany 2 July 1993 *Oberlandesgericht* [Appellate Court] Düsseldorf, available online at <http://cisgw3.law.pace.edu/cases/930702g1.html>. This case involved a claim for indemnification for an obligation stemming from a personal injury related to defects in the goods. The court erroneously regarded indemnification of such an obligation as an allowable element of damages under the CISG. For criticism of the court for overlooking Article 5 CISG in so ruling, *see* commentary by Schlechtriem, P. at the above URL.

[6] *See* legislative history of Article 5 CISG at the 1980 Vienna Diplomatic Conference, available online at <http://cisgw3.law.pace.edu/cisg/chronology/chrono05.html>; *see* also Staudinger/Magnus, Art 74, Rn Art 5 Rn 3; Bianca C. M. & Bonell J. M., *Commentary on the International Sales Law – the 1980 Vienna Sales Convention* (1987 Milan), Art. 5, Note 2.1.

[7] Liability for a loss of reputation seems to be generally recognized as one such instance; *see* relevant case law: Russia 24 January 2000 Arbitration proceeding 54/1999, available online at <http://cisgw3.law.pace.edu/cases/000124r1.html>; Switzerland 28 October 1998 *Bundesgericht* [Supreme Court], available

e. The provisions of Article 74 CISG are reflected in Articles 7.4.1 and 7.4.2 of the UNIDROIT Principles. In Article 7.4.2 of the UNIDROIT Principles the emphasis is on *full compensation* for harm sustained as a result of breach.[8] The wording "harm sustained" in the UNIDROIT Principles is probably broader than the words "a sum equal to the loss suffered" in the CISG, reflecting the difference in approach to personal injuries discussed above. In case of doubt the interpretation of Article 74 CISG should also lean toward full compensation for *harm* as far as harm has not been excluded from the scope of the CISG by Article 5.

f. Article 7.4.2 of the UNIDROIT Principles further requires that any gain received by the aggrieved party should be taken into account when calculating the loss.[9] This issue is not pertinently dealt with in the CISG, and therefore Article 7.4.2 of the UNIDROIT Principles might be useful in interpreting Article 74 of the CISG with reference to such gain. This interpretation is further strengthened when the principles underlying CISG Articles 77 (duty to mitigate) and 80 (prevention or causation by the creditor) are also taken into account.[10]

g. The extent of the liability of a party for breach of contract is restricted in both instruments by the so-called contemplation principle.[11] The test of foreseeability is worded differently in the two instruments. In Article 74 CISG, the emphasis is on loss that was actually foreseen or that the party ought to have foreseen in light of circumstances known to him or of which he should have known as a possible consequence of the breach.[12] The

online at <http://cisgw3.law.pace.edu/cases/981028s1.html>; Germany 21 September 1995 *Landgericht* [District Court] Kassel, available online at <http://cisgw3.law.pace.edu/cases/950921g1.html>. *See* also Staudinger/Magnus, Art 74, Rn 27, 45 & 50; Witz/Salger/Lorenz, Art 74, Rn 14; Honsell/Schönle, Art 74, Rn 2 & 7. However, for a contrary decision, *see* France 21 October 1999 *Cour d'appel* [Appellate Court] Grenoble (*Calzados Magnanni v. Shoes General International*), available online at <http://cisgw3.law.pace.edu/cases/991021f1.html>.

8 Honsell/Schönle, Art 74, Rn 9–17; Witz/Salger/Lorenz, Art 74, Rn 15–20; Austria 9 March 2000 *Oberster Gerichtshof* [Supreme Court], available online at <http://cisgw3.law.pace.edu/cases/000309a3.html>.

9 Schlechtriem/Stoll 32; Honsell/Schönle, Art 74, Rn 11.

10 Liu at 13.5.

11 Kritzer 479; Witz/Salger/Lorenz, Art 74, Rn 2 & 27; Honnold, para. 406 at p. 447; Staudinger/Magnus, Art 74, Rn 5; Vékás L., "The Foreseeability Doctrine in Contractual Damage Cases," (2002) 43 *Acta Juridica Hungarica* 145–174, available at <http://cisgw3.law.pace.edu/cisg/biblio/vekas.html>; Saidov D., 2001, "Methods of Limiting Damages under the Vienna Convention on Contracts for the International Sale of Goods" <http://cisgw3.law.pace.edu/cisg/biblio/saidov.html>; Liu at 14.2.2; Austria 14 January 2002 Supreme Court, available online at <http://cisgw3.law.pace.edu/cases/020114a3.html>. In United States 6 December 1995 Federal Appellate Court [2d Circuit] (*Delchi Carrier v. Rotorex*), available online at <http://cisgw3.law.pace.edu/cases/951206u1.html>, the American court dealt with a number of issues reflecting on damages and foreseeability. Unfortunately, the court relied on domestic interpretations of foreseeability rather than an approach free of domestic legal influence; *see* the editorial discussion of Kritzer A. H. on the case at <http://cisgw3.law.pace.edu/cisg/wais/db/editorial/951206u1editorial.html>. Cook S. V., "The UN Convention on Contracts for the International Sale of Goods: A Mandate to Abandon Legal Ethnocentricity," (1997) 16 *J.L. & Com* 257–263, available online at <http://cisgw3.law.pace.edu/cisg/biblio/1cook.html>, correctly points out at 258–259 that the court made use of the *Hadley v. Baxendale* approach and jurisprudence, which is not supported by the wording of the CISG. *See* also Schneider E. C., "Consequential Damages in the International Sale of Goods: Analysis of Two Decisions," (1995) 16 *J. Int'l. Bus. L.* 615–668, available online at <http://cisgw3.law.pace.edu/cisg/Articles/schnedr2.html>.

See also relevant case law, Germany 21 September 1995 *Landgericht* [District Court] Kassel, available online at <http://cisgw3.law.pace.edu/cases/950921g1.html> where it was held that it was foreseeable that a failure to perform to a wholesaler would negatively influence its trade relationships with retailers; Switzerland 28 October 1998 *Bundesgericht* [Supreme Court], available online at <http://cisgw3.law.pace.edu/cases/981028s1.html>.

12 Germany 24 October 1979 *Bundesgerichshof* [Federal Supreme Court] [ULIS precedent], available online at <http://cisgw3.law.pace.edu/cases/791024g1.html>; United States 6 December 1995 Federal Appellate Court [2d Circuit] (*Delchi Carrier v. Rotorex*), available online at <http://cisgw3.law.pace.edu/cases/951206u1.html>; Stockholm Chamber of Commerce Arbitration Award of 1998, available online at

test is therefore either subjective (where there is actual knowledge) or objective (where there is no subjective knowledge).[13] This accords with the provisions of Article 7.4.4 of the UNIDROIT Principles.

h. In Article 7.4.4 of the UNIDROIT Principles, however, emphasis is placed on the "foreseeability of harm being *likely* to result from its non-performance."[14] The CISG standard as formulated in Article 74, however, is "foresaw or ought to have foreseen . . . as a *possible* consequence of the breach of contract." This standard seems to be much broader than that in the UNIDROIT Principles. Ziegel[15] explains the difference between "likely to result" and "a possible consequence" with reference to the following example: "if one takes a well-shuffled pack of cards it is quite possible, though not likely, that the top card will prove to be the nine of diamonds even though the odds are 51 to 1 against." Farnsworth,[16] however, in comparing Article 74 with the American Restatement provision, remarks quite correctly that the wide ambit of the word "possible" is cut back by the preceding requirement of "in the light of the facts."

In the Official Comments[17] on Article 7.4.4, the test of foreseeability is also linked to the requirement in Article 7.4.3 of the UNIDROIT Principles that the harm must be certain. Therefore, it must have been foreseeable that harm will with certainty (is likely to) flow from such a breach. The Comment further makes it clear that the breaching party is not liable for harm that was not foreseeable even if the breach was willful, as is the case in some legal systems.[18] Foreseeability must therefore be interpreted narrowly. This narrow interpretation is also important for the restrictive interpretation of Article 74 CISG in light of the broad phrasing of Article 74. The Comment to Article 7.4.4 further makes it clear that the emphasis is on the conduct of a "normally diligent person" in foreseeing the consequences of non-performance. This should also be the approach in the interpretation and application of Article 74 of the CISG.[19] Finally the Comment also makes it clear that the foreseeability relates to "the nature or type of." This should also be the approach under Article 74 of the CISG.[20]

i. The liability for damages is further limited in both the CISG and the UNIDROIT Principles by the causality requirement. In the CISG, this requirement is found in the words "as a consequence of" and in the UNIDROIT Principles in the words "as a result of."[21] Stoll argues that there is only a need for factual causation (*conditio sine qua non*)

<http://cisgw3.law.pace.edu/cases/980107s5.html>; Finland 5 November 1996 District Court of Kuopio, available online at <http://cisgw3.law.pace.edu/cases/961105f5.html; ICC Arbitration Case No. 8769 of December 1996, available online at <http://cisgw3.law.pace.edu/cases/968769i1.html>; Germany 2 October 1996 *Landgericht* [District Court] Heidelberg, available online at <http://cisgw3.law.pace.edu/cases/961002g1.html>.

[13] Enderlein/Maskow, Note 7–10 at pp. 300–301; Honsell/Schönle, Art 74, Rn 23–27; Witz/Salger/Lorenz, Art 74, Rn 2; Bernstein & Lookofsky 100–101.

[14] Germany 23 March 1978 *Oberlandesgericht* [Appellate Court] Hamm [ULIS precedent], available online at <http://cisgw3.law.pace.edu/cases/780323g1.html>.

[15] Ziegel J., "Parker School Text" as quoted in Kritzer H. *Guide to Practical Applications of the United Nations Convention on Contracts for the International Sale of Goods* (Kluwer 1994) 587–588.

[16] "Damages and Specific Relief," 27 *Am. J. Comp. L.* 253.

[17] The Official Comments on the UNIDROIT Principles cited are available online at <http://cisgw3.law.pace.edu/cisg/principles/uni74.html#official>.

[18] This is also the case with the CISG; *see* Enderlein/Maskow, Note 8 at p. 301.

[19] *See* Staudinger/Magnus Art 74, Rn 35; Honsell/Schönle, Art 74, Rn 24.

[20] *See*, however, Germany 15 September 1997 *Landgericht* [District Court] Heilbronn, available online at <http://cisgw3.law.pace.edu/cases/970915g1.html> where the court seems to have taken the opposite view. *See also* Staudinger/Magnus, Art 74, Rn 34; Witz/Salger/Lorenz, Art 74, Rn 31; Austria 14 January 2002 Supreme Court, available online at <http://cisgw3.law.pace.edu/cases/020114a3.html>.

[21] Saidov D., "Causation in Damages: The Convention on Contracts for the International Sale of Goods, the UNIDROIT Principles of International Commercial Contracts, the Principles of European Contract

inquiry as the foreseeability rule is employed in the place of the legal causation requirement.[22] The UNIDROIT Principles shed no further light on this issue as the Comments to Article 7.4.2 simply refer to causation without further elaboration.

j. Neither Article 74 CISG nor the UNIDROIT Principles contain an express provision about the time at which damages are to be calculated.[23] However, the underlying principle is suggested by the provisions in Article 76 CISG and Article 7.4.6 of the UNIDROIT Principles that deal with the current price of goods as a presumptive measure for the calculation of damages. These provisions would suggest that damages are to be calculated at the time that the action is lodged and not at the time of the breach.

k. Article 74 CISG contains an apparent gap in that it does not deal with the issue of future damages.[24] The UNIDROIT Principles may be helpful because this issue is fully dealt with in Article 7.4.3 under the heading "Certainty of Harm." The principle that the party is not liable for harm that has not occurred and that also is not likely to occur can be assumed. Such an interpretation of Article 74 CISG is strengthened by the interpretation of Article 7.4.3 of the UNIDROIT Principles. In calculating the harm, there are two approaches that a court may follow: where the amount of harm, including future harm, can be established with certainty, the court will award that amount. However, where it is certain that harm has resulted or will result, but where the amount cannot be established with sufficient certainty, the court has discretion in assessing the amount.

l. It is submitted that Article 7.4.3 of the UNIDROIT Principles may be helpful in interpreting Article 74 CISG and filling the apparent gap that exists. The UNIDROIT Principles clearly accept the principle that the defaulting party is liable for future damages and provide a practical, reasonable, and equitable approach for the determination of such damages.

m. A specific application of the liability for future damages is the liability for the loss of a chance or opportunity. Article 7.4.3 of the UNIDROIT Principles makes express provision for liability in such a case. It establishes two principles: (1) the defaulting party is liable and (2) the calculation of the loss is in proportion to the probability of its occurrence.

It is submitted that Article 7.4.3 of the UNIDROIT Principles can be used to fill the gap in Article 74 CISG by establishing liability for loss of a chance as well as the manner of calculating the amount of damages. Loss of profit, which is included specifically in Article 74 CISG, may further indicate that liability for future damages and loss of a chance should be accounted for in terms of the CISG.

n. The CISG contains no indication of the currency in which the loss is to be calculated[25] or where it is to be paid.[26] Article 7.4.12 of the UNIDROIT Principles, by stipulating that

Law," at fn 1–3; Schlechtriem/Stoll Art 74 Rn 12. *See also* Staudinger/Magnus, Art 74, Rn 28. Saidov, "Limiting Damages" at fn 22–25, however, expresses doubt whether the combination of factual causality and foreseeability is adequate to deal with complex situations of causality.

[22] Schlechtriem/Stoll art 74 Rn 12.

[23] Staudinger/Magnus, Art 74, Rn 55; Schlechtriem/Stoll 33.

[24] Enderlein/Maskow, Note 5 at pp. 299–300. Liu at 14.3. In Switzerland 5 February 1997 *Handelsgericht* [Commercial Court] Zürich, available online at <http://cisgw3.law.pace.edu/cases/970205s1.html>, the issue was raised but not pertinently decided. The court in its exposition apparently relied on the principles of Swiss law.

[25] In Switzerland 3 December 2002 Commercial Court St. Gallen, available online at <http://cisgw3.law.pace.edu/cases/021203s1.html>, the court dealt with this matter according to Swiss law without any reference to the CISG and any possible gap. This recourse to domestic law should be rejected as the issue is clearly one that falls within the scope of the CISG. The gap needs to be filled in accordance with Article 7.

[26] In Germany 2 July 1993 *Oberlandesgericht* [Appellate Court] Düsseldorf, available online at <http://cisgw3.law.pace.edu/cases/930702g1.html>, it was decided that damages had to be paid at the place of

loss can be calculated either in the currency in which the monetary obligation (price) was expressed in the contract or in the currency in which the harm was suffered, whichever is more appropriate, allows the court to exercise discretion For instance, where replacement goods were bought or where the current market price presumption is used to calculate damages, those currencies would *prima facie* seem most appropriate. It is suggested that this approach should be used in the interpretation and application of CISG Articles 74 *et. seq.*[27] The CISG also does not deal with losses due to a devaluation of a currency or a drop in the exchange rate in the cases of late payment. There are conflicting decisions in the case law on this issue.[28] In principle, such damages ought to be awarded.

o. The CISG consciously does not deal with so-called liquidated damages and penalty clauses. The framers of the Convention agreed that the validity and application of such clauses were to be dealt with in terms of the applicable legal system because of the widely divergent approaches in the different legal systems.[29] Article 7.4.13 of the UNIDROIT Principles, however, is based on the validity of such clauses subject to judicial discretion to reduce the amount where it is grossly excessive. The vagaries of private international law will therefore decide this issue, and the UNIDROIT Principles cannot provide any interpretative assistance to the CISG.[30]

p. Except indirectly, the CISG does not deal with the issue of contributory conduct of the aggrieved party that adds to the loss of harm suffered.[31] Article 77 CISG deals with the duty of the aggrieved party to mitigate damages, which covers only one aspect of the issue

business of the creditor. In United States 6 December 1995 Federal Appellate Court [2d Circuit] (*Delchi Carrier v. Rotorex*), available online at <http://cisgw3.law.pace.edu/cases/951206u1.html>, the court employed the American "breach day rule" without proper justification or reference to any other possible approaches – *see* Kritzer's editorial comment at <http://cisgw3.law.pace.edu/cisg/wais/db/editorial/951206u1editorial.html>. *See* also Darkey J. M., "A U.S. Court's Interpretation of Damage Provisions under the U.N. Convention on Contracts for the International Sale of Goods: A Preliminary Step towards an International Jurisprudence of CISG or a Missed Opportunity?," (1995) 15 *J.L. & Com.* 139–152 at 138–139, also available online at <http://cisgw3.law.pace.edu/cisg/biblio/darkey2.html>; Murray J. E. Jr., "The Neglect of CISG: A Workable Solution," *J.L. & Com.* (1998) 17 365–379, also available on line at <http://cisgw3.law.pace.edu/cisg/biblio/murray1.html>.

[27] In Germany 28 February 1997 *Oberlandesgericht* [Appellate Court] Hamburg, available online at <http://cisgw3.law.pace.edu/cases/970228g1.html>, it was decided that the damages had to be calculated in the currency in which they were suffered. *See also* Staudinger/Magnus, Art 74, Rn 56.

[28] *See* Germany 27 January 1981 *Landgericht* [District Court] Heidelberg, available online at <http://cisgw3.law.pace.edu/cases/810127g1.html> [ULIS case]; Germany 14 January 1994 *Oberlandesgericht* [Appellate Court] Düsseldorf, available online at <http://cisgw3.law.pace.edu/cases/940114g1.html> where such claims were rejected. *See also* Enderlein Maskow 302.

Cf. the following case law: Netherlands 6 May 1993 *Arrondissementsrechtbank* [District Court] Roermond (*Gruppo IMAR v. Protech Horst*), available online at <http://cisgw3.law.pace.edu/cases/930506n1.html>; Germany 28 April 1993 *Landgericht* [District Court] Krefeld, available online at <http://cisgw3.law.pace.edu/cases/930428g1.html>; Netherlands 15 April 1997 *Gerechtshof* [Appellate Court] Arnhem (*Celli v. Agrolang*), available online at <http://cisgw3.law.pace.edu/cases/970415n1.html>; Switzerland 5 February 1997 *Handelsgericht* [Commercial Court] Zürich, available online at <http://cisgw3.law.pace.edu/cases/970205s1.html> where such a claim was recognized.

This is also the practical effect of the "day of breach rule" applied in United States 9 September 1994 Federal District Court [New York] (*Delchi Carrier v. Rotorex*), available online at <http://cisgw3.law.pace.edu/cases/940909u1.html>. *See also* Honnold 446 fn 4; Staudinger/Magnus, Art 74, Rn 48; Witz/Salger/Lorenz, Art 74, Rn 21.

[29] Staudinger/Magnus, Art 74, Rn 59 & 60; Honsell/Schönle Art 74, Rn 32; Witz/Salger/Lorenz, Art 74, Rn 42.

[30] Russia 23 November 1994 Arbitration proceeding 251/1993, available online at <http://cisgw3.law.pace.edu/cases/941123r1.html>, restricting the damages to the extent of the penalty clause.

[31] Enderlein/Maskow, Note 1 at p. 308 & Note 5 at p. 309; Bernstein & Lookofsky 103–104; Honnold. para 417 at p. 456; Saidov at fn 77078, 84–86; Liu at 14.4. In respect of the issue of causality, *see* Austria 9 March 2000 *Oberster Gerichtshof* [Supreme Court], available online at <http://cisgw3.law.pace.edu/cases/000309a3.html> and the editorial comment by A. H. Kritzer.

at stake here. This is clear from the fact that the issue of contributory conduct is dealt with separately in the UNIDROIT Principles in Article 7.4.7, whereas the mitigation duty is dealt with in Article 7.4.8 of the UNIDROIT Principles. If it is a separate issue, there is a gap in the CISG that can be filled by interpretation of either Article 74 or Article 77. In a German case[32] it seems that the court simply assumed, without further reference to authority, that contributory conduct could play a role.[33]

q. The principle that damages are to be reduced to the extent that they were caused by the aggrieved party or by circumstances for which it bore the risk is found in the general principle established in Article 7.1.2 of the UNIDROIT Principles; this restricts its remedies where non-performance is partly caused by the conduct of the aggrieved party.

r. The principle contained in Article 7.1.2 of the UNIDROIT Principles is reflected in the similar provisions found in CISG Articles 77 and 80. Article 7.4.7 of the UNIDROIT Principles can therefore be helpful in the interpretation of Article 74 of the CISG, when read together with Articles 77 and 80, in establishing the extent to which the defaulting party is excused from liability for damages due to the conduct of the aggrieved party.[34] The formulation of Article 7.4.7 of the UNIDROIT Principles and the Official Comments are helpful in this process. It is clear that in such a case the amount of damages ought to be reduced proportionally. Such apportionment of damages will often involve judicial discretion in weighing the different facts contributing to the eventual damages suffered.

s. As far as the burden of proof is concerned, it is generally accepted that the burden of proving the extent of damages lies on the aggrieved party.[35] However, where parties have failed to prove the exact extent of their loss, there is a divergence in the case law about the consequences. Belgian and Swiss courts seem to award an estimated amount *ex aequo et bono* where it is clear that damages have been suffered, but not clear what the extent thereof was.[36] German and American courts seem to dismiss the claim for

[32] Germany 23 March 1978 *Oberlandesgericht* [Appellate Court] Hamm [ULIS precedent], available online at <http://cisgw3.law.pace.edu/cases/780323g1.html>.

[33] In the Israeli case of 22 August 1993 Supreme Court (*Eximin v. Textile and Footwear*), available online at <http://cisgw3.law.pace.edu/cases/930822i5.html>, the court relied on Israeli law to deal with apportionment without reference to CISG authority. *See also* the critical comments of Reich A. at the above reference. In Germany 25 June 1996 *Landgericht* [District Court] Paderborn, available online at <http://cisgw3.law.pace.edu/cases/960625g1.html> reliance on contributory causation was rejected.

[34] *See* generally Enderlein/Maskow, Art 80, Note 1 at p. 335 and Note 6 at p. 339. Liu at 14.4.1.

[35] Enderlein/Maskow, Art 74, Note 6 at p. 300; Witz/Salger/Lorenz, Art 74, Rn 40; Honsell/Schönle, Art 74, Rn 33; Staudinger/Magnus, Art 74, Rn 61; Australia 17 January 2003 Supreme Court of Western Australia (*Ginza Pte Ltd v Vista Corporation Pty Ltd*), available online at <http://cisgw3.law.pace.edu/cases/030117a2.html>; Switzerland 10 March 2003 District Court Appenzell Auserrhoden, available online at <http://cisgw3.law.pace.edu/cases/030310s1.html>; Germany 2 February 2004 Appellate Cout Zweibrücken, available online at <http://cisgw3.law.pace.edu/cases/040202g1.html>

For other relevant case law, *see* Switzerland 26 April 1995 *Handelsgericht* [Commercial Court] Zürich, available online at <http://cisgw3.law.pace.edu/cases/950426s1.html>; Spain 20 June 1997 *Audiencia Provincial* [Appellate Court] Barcelona, available online at <http://cisgw3.law.pace.edu/cases/970620s4.html>; Germany 15 February 1996 *Landgericht* [District Court] Kassel, available online at <http://cisgw3.law.pace.edu/cases/960215g1.html>; Italy 11 December 1998 *Corte di Appello* [Appellate Court] Milano (*Bielloni Castello v. EGO*), available online at <http://cisgw3.law.pace.edu/cases/981211i3.html>.

[36] Belgium 18 May 1999 *Hof van Beroep* [Appellate Court] Antwerp (*Vandermaesen Viswaren v. Euromar Seafood*), available online at <http://cisgw3.law.pace.edu/cases/990518b1.html>; Belgium 8 October 1996 *Rechtbank van Koophandel* [District Court] Hasselt (*Vandermaesen Viswaren v. Euromar Seafood*), available online at <http://cisgw3.law.pace.edu/cases/961008b1.html>; Netherlands 15 April 1997 *Gerechtshof* [Appellate Court] Arnhem (*Celli v. Agrolang*), available online at <http://cisgw3.law.pace.edu/cases/970415n1.html>; Belgium 2 May 1995 *Rechtbank van Koophandel* [District Court] Hasselt (*Vital Berry*

damages under similar circumstances.[37] On the available doctrine, Lookofsky is of the opinion that problems of proof and certainty of loss are procedural matters that remain within the province of national law.[38]

t. Neither the CISG nor the UNIDROIT Principles devote explicit attention to the issue of legal fees or litigation costs. It is therefore unlikely that the UNIDROIT Principles can come to the aid in solving the controversy that has erupted after the decision in the *Zapata Hermanos* case[39] where the court on appeal overturned an earlier decision.[40] The court held that attorneys' fees are not covered by Article 74 of the CISG, but that this is a procedural matter falling outside the scope of the CISG and that it must therefore be dealt with in terms of the domestic law of the forum.[41] This is in contrast to certain German decisions where legal fees have been awarded as part of the damages recoverable under Article 74.[42]

Marketing v. Dira-Frost), available online at <http://cisgw3.law.pace.edu/cases/950502b1.html>; Switzerland 26 September 1997 *Handelsgericht* [Commercial Court] Aargau, available online at <http://cisgw3.law.pace.edu/cases/970926s1.html>. *Cf.* Switzerland 10 March 2003 *Kantonsgericht* [Cantonal Court] Appenzell Auserrhoden, available online at <http://cisgw3.law.pace.edu/cases/030310s1.html>.

[37] Germany 5 March 1996 *Landgericht* [District Court] Düsseldorf, available online at <http://cisgw3.law.pace.edu/cases/960305g1.html>; Germany 17 June 1996 *Landgericht* [District Court] Hamburg, available online at <http://cisgw3.law.pace.edu/cases/960617g1.html>. In Germany 2 February 2004 Appellate Court Zweibrücken, available online at <http://cisgw3.law.pace.edu/cases/040202g1.html>, the court held that it was entitled to decide damages cases in two stages in appropriate circumstances. In the first stage, it is established whether a breach has occurred entitling a party to damages. In the second stage, the quantum of the damages is established.

[38] Bernstein & Lookofsky 101. *See* also Honsell/Schönle, Art 74, Rn 35; Staudinger/Magnus Art 74 Rn 61; Giovannucci Orlandi, C., "Procedural Law Issues and Uniform Law Conventions," 2000–2001 *Unif. L. Rev.* 23–41, available online at <http://cisgw3.law.pace.edu/cisg/biblio/orlandi.html>. In Germany 9 January 2002 *Bundesgerichtshof* [Federal Supreme Court], available online at <http://cisgw3.law.pace.edu/cases/020109g1.html> the court held that *"however, [...] the burden of proof rules of the CISG cannot go farther than the scope of its substantive applicability,"* thereby indicating clearly and quite correctly that the application of the CISG to issues of burden of proof is limited to those instances where those issues are regulated by the CISG expressly or by necessary implication. For a discussion of this case *see* Perales, "Battle of the Forms and the Burden of Proof: An Analysis of BGH 9 January 2002," 2002 (6) *Vindobona J. Int'l. L. & Arbitration* 217, available online at <http://cisgw3.law.pace.edu/cisg/biblio/perales2.html>. A distinction must be drawn between general issues of proof and procedure that are governed by the *lex fori* unless the CISG contains a clear provision on that aspect and issues of burden of proof where the express or implied provisions of the CISG will take precedence over the *lex fori*. In the latter instance the *lex fori* will only be applied if the issue to be determined falls outside the general scope of the CISG.

[39] United States, 19 November 2002 Federal Appellate Court [7th Circuit] (*Zapata Hermanos v. Hearthside Baking*), available online at <http://cisgw3.law.pace.edu/cases/021119a1.html>.

[40] United States, 28 August 2001 Federal District Court [Illinois] (*Zapata Hermanos v. Hearthside Baking*), available online at <http://cisgw3.law.pace.edu/cases/010828u1.html>.

[41] Schlechtriem P., "Attorneys' Fees as Part of Damages," (2002) 14 *Pace Int'l. L. Rev.* 205–209, available online at <http://cisgw3.law.pace.edu/cisg/biblio/schlechtriem4.html>; Felemegas J., "An Interpretation of Article 74 by the U.S. Circuit Court of Appeals" (2003) 15 *Pace Int'l. L. Rev.* 91–147, available online at <http://cisgw3.law.pace.biblio/felemegas4.html>; Vanto J., "Attorneys' Fees as Damages in International Commercial Litigation" (2003) 5 *Turku L. J.* 89 and 15 *Pace Int'l. L. Rev.* (2003) 203–222, also available at <http://cisgw3.law.pace.biblio/vanto1.html>; Flechtner H. & Lookofsky J., "Viva Zapata! American Procedure and CISG Substance in a U.S. Circuit Court of Appeal," (2003) 7 *Vindobona J. Int'l. Com. L. & Arbitration* 93–104, also available at <http://cisgw3.law.pace.biblio/flechtner5.html>; Keily T., "How Does the Cookie Crumble? Legal Costs under a Uniform Interpretation of the United Nations Convention on Contracts for the International Sale of Goods," (2003) *Nordic J. Com. L.*, available online at <http://www.njcl.utu.fi> and at <http://cisgw3.law.pace.edu/biblio/keily2.html>; Zeller B., "Interpretation of Article 74 – *Zapata Hermanos v. Hearthside Baking* – Where Next?, (2004) *Nordic J. Com. L.*, available online at <http://www.njcl.fi/1_2004/commentary1.pdf>.

[42] Germany 11 April 2002 Lower Court Viechtach, available online at <http://cisgw3.law.pace.edu/cases/020411g1.html>; Germany 14 January 1994 Appellate Court Düsseldorf, available online at <http://cisgw3.law.pace.edu/cases/940114g1.html>; Vanto at II; Felemegas at 4(c).

Measurement of damages when contract avoided: Remarks on the manner in which the UNIDROIT Principles may be used to interpret or supplement Article 75 of the CISG

Bojidara Borisova

I. INTRODUCTION

CISG Article 75 and its counterpart UNIDROIT Principles Article 7.4.5. regulate substitute transaction in a similar manner. Both articles correspond to each other in substance; hence the Official Comments on this Article of the UNIDROIT Principles can arguably be used for the interpretation and gap-filling of the CISG.[1]

The basic premises that must be taken into consideration when interpreting the text of CISG Article 75 are the characteristics of the substitute transaction, the time and manner in which the substitute transaction should be made, the nature of recoverable damages, and any further damages recoverable for additional harm.

Starting with the prerequisite included in both articles – avoidance of the contract (termination of the contract in the terminology of the Principles) by the injured party – it must be noted that this particular element in CISG Article 75 and UNIDROIT Principles Article 7.4.5 provides for a special application of the general rule that is applicable to the proof of the existence and the amount of the harm caused to one of the contracting parties by the other.[2]

The new element that both counterpart Articles introduce is the facilitated mechanism for measuring damages that does not require proof of market price. However, instead it provides for the comparison between the contractual price and the price of the substitute transaction, and it is that difference that defines the amount of the damages.[3]

II. SUBSTITUTE TRANSACTION

The Official Comments to the UNIDROIT Principles contain several instructions on the particularity of the substitute transaction. The replacement transaction must be performed with the intention to be a substitute for the original transaction, which means that its purpose, basic terms, and characteristics must be identical to the original transaction

[1] *See* Kritzer, "General Observations on Use of the UNIDROIT Principles to Help Interpret the CISG," available online <http://cisgw3.law.pace.edu/cisg/text/matchup/general-observations.html> and Liu, "Remedies for Non-Performance: Perspectives from CISG, UNIDROIT Principles and PECL," available online <http://cisg3.law.pace.edu/cisg/biblio/chengwei-75.html>.

[2] *See* Sutton, "Measuring Damages under the United Nations Convention on the International Sale of Goods," 50 *Ohio St. L.J.* (1989), 737–752, also available online at <http://cisgw3.law.pace.edu/cisg/biblio/sutton.html>.

[3] *See* Text of Secretariat Commentary on Article 71 of the 1978 Draft Convention, available online at <http://cisgw3.law.pace.edu/cisg/text/secomm/secomm-75.html>.

to the extent of reasonableness.[4] Consequently both transactions need not be absolutely identical.[5]

According to the Principles, no substitute transaction is performed if the aggrieved party has itself fulfilled the obligation that lay upon the non-performing party. The substitute transaction must be concluded with a different contracting party, because the comparison between the price of the two contracts yields the amount of the remedy. In cases of self-performance, the objective method for measuring damages pursuant to CISG Article 75 cannot be applied; therefore, the other CISG provisions regulating the law for damages will be applicable.[6]

The Principles stipulate that there is no replacement if an aggrieved party, after the termination of the initial contract, uses its equipment for the performance of another contract, which it could have performed at the same time as the first. Hence the substitute transaction rule does not regulate the so-called lost volume sales, where the seller has a sufficient supply and insufficient demand.[7]

In the classic lost volume situation, the remedy is provided only to the seller, whereas CISG Article 75 and its counterpart UNIDROIT Principles Article 7.4.5 provide a remedy to both contracting parties. CISG Article 75 explicitly states that the damages recoverable under this Article are provided to the buyer who has bought goods in replacement or to the seller who has resold the goods.[8]

The remedy that both Articles regulate is given for the performance of the substitute transaction and not for any other action undertaken by the injured party. That is why the definition of the substitute transaction is essential for the application of the specific method for measuring damages that CISG Article 75 provides.[9]

The UNIDROIT Principles Comments, together with the descriptive methods for defining the replacement transaction found in CISG Article 75, provide a comprehensive description of this term, which facilitates the complete interpretation of CISG Article 75 and its proper application.

III. REASONABLENESS

The UNIDROIT Principles, similar to the Convention, do not contain a specific definition of the term "reasonableness."[10] However, bearing in mind that reasonableness is a general

[4] *See* Flechtner, "Remedies under the New International Sales Convention: The Perspective from Article 2 of the U.C.C.," 8 *J.L. & Com.* (1988) 53–108, also available online at <http://cisgw3.law.pace.edu/cisg/biblio/flecht.html>.

[5] See Sutton, *supra* note 2; see also Text of Secretariat Commentary on Article 71 of the 1978 Draft Convention *supra* note 3.

[6] See Official Comments on Articles of the UNIDROIT Principles.

[7] *Id.*; Sutton, *supra* note 2; Saidov, "Methods of Limiting Damages under the Vienna Convention on Contract for the International Sale of Goods," 2001, available online at <http://cisgw3.law.pace.edu/cisg/biblio/saidov.html>.

[8] *See* Sutton, *supra* note 2.

[9] For the characteristics of the substitute transaction, *see* the following case decisions:
- Italy 11 December 1998 Appellate Court Milan, case presentation available at <http://cisgw3.law.pace.edu/cases/981211i3.html>
- Icc Arbitration Case No. 8786 of January 1997, case presentation available at <http://cisgw3.law.pace.edu/cases/978786i1.html>
- Switzerland 20 February 1997 District Court Saane, case presentation available at <http://cisgw3.law.pace.edu/cases/970220sl.html>
- China 30 October 1991 Cietac Arbitration Proceeding, case presentation available at <http://cisgw3.law.pace.edu/cases/911030c1.html>

[10] *See* Liu, *supra* note 1 and the following case decisions for the determination of the term "reasonableness":
- Germany 14 January 1994 Appellate Court Düsseldorf, case presentation available at <http://cisgw3.law.pace.edu/cases/940114gl.html>
- Switzerland 15 September 2000 Supreme Court, case presentation available at <http://cisgw3.law.pace.edu/cases/000915s1.html>

principle of the CISG and as such is mentioned in many of the Convention's provisions,[11] including Article 75, a careful consideration of that term is warranted.

The Official Comments to the UNIDROIT Principles do not contain a thorough examination of the term "reasonableness." The Principles only provide brief and general guidelines of the basic idea carried by this term. According to the Principles, the expressions "reasonable time" and "reasonable manner" are meant to avoid the prejudice of the non-performing party by "hasty or malicious conduct."[12]

Consequently, the Principles do not directly indicate the meaning of the term "reasonableness" and the measures that should be applied for its definition; they only point out the results that must be accomplished following the fulfillment of this condition. Each case will require separate consideration and interpretation of the term "reasonableness." The aggrieved party in each case may calculate which is the most appropriate moment for the conclusion of and what are the most appropriate conditions of the substitute transaction and, thus, act within the boundaries of reasonableness.[13]

No particular criterion exists for the determination of reasonableness. The aggrieved party must take into consideration and act as the reasonable person would (i.e., follow the behavior of a hypothetical person acting in a similar situation, having the same quality and engaged in the same branch of business or in the same trade).[14]

The Official Comments to the UNIDROIT Principles prescribe that the aggrieved party should not react in a "hasty"manner (i.e., must consider thoroughly the situation, the characteristics of the original contract that was breached, and the terms and conditions of the substitute transaction). The aggrieved party must also judge the consequences of its behavior (the replacement transaction).[15]

If the substitute transaction is not to the detriment of the non-performing party and it only restores the situation to the way it should be if the original contract was diligently performed, then it can be concluded that the reasonableness criterion is fulfilled. In contrast, if the injured party concludes a substitute transaction that maliciously harms the non-performing party, the requirement to act in a "reasonable manner" will not be fulfilled and Article 75 will not be applicable.

From the Official Comments to the UNIDROIT Principles still another peculiarity can be drawn. CISG Article 75 and its counterpart Principles Article 7.4.5 are designed to provide a remedy for the injured contracting party and must restore it into the position that it would have been if the initial contract had been performed properly. However, this does not mean that the non-performing party should be excessively damaged. As already mentioned, the performance of the substitute transaction must not prejudice the non-performing party. The purpose of the remedy provided in CISG Article 75 and its UNIDROIT Principles counterpart is to mitigate the damages, not to punish the non-performing party.[16]

- Netherlands 15 October 2002 Netherlands Arbitration Institute, Case No. 2319, case presentation available at <http://cisgw3.law.pace.edu/cases/021015nl.html>

[11] *See* A. H. Kritzer, "Comments on the Concept of "Reasonableness" in the CISG," <http://cisgw3.law.pace.edu/cisg/text/reason.html#over>.

[12] Official Comments on Articles of the UNIDROIT Principles, op.cit.

[13] *See* Honnold, *Uniform Law for International Sales under the 1980 United Nations Convention*, 3d ed. Kluwer Law International (1999).

[14] *See* Vilus, *Commentary on Common Law Institutions in the United Nations Sales Convention*, Estudios en Homenaje a Jorge Barrera Graf, Bd. 2, Mexico: Universidad Nacional Autónoma de Mexico (1989) 1431–1457.

[15] *See* Tunc, *Commentary of the Hague Convention on International Sale of Goods*, Records and Documents of Conference, Vo. 1 – Records, The Hague (1966) 355–391.

[16] *See* Farnsworth, "Damages and Specific Relief," 27 *Am. J. Comp. L.* 247 (1979), also available at <http://cisgw3.law.pace.edu/cisg/biblio/farns.html>. See also Article 77 CISG, providing for mitigation of damages under the Convention.

IV. DAMAGES

Both counterpart provisions use the same method for measuring damages in case of a replacement transaction. The rule is that the aggrieved party may recover the difference between the two contract prices. According to the UNIDROIT Principles Official Comments, Article 7.4.5 only established a minimum right of recovery.[17] This conclusion is based on the fact that the aggrieved party may recover further damages under the other provisions in the Principles that regulate the law on damages.[18] Bearing in mind that CISG Article 75 and UNIDROIT Principles Article 7.4.5. correspond in substance, the same inference is also true for CISG Article 75.[19]

Concerning the method for measuring damages, there is little room for interpretation, because both articles use very clear wording. The amount of the remedy required under CISG Article 75 and its counterpart UNIDROIT Principles Article 7.4.5 is the difference between the prices of the original transaction and the substitute transaction concluded by the aggrieved party.[20]

Both articles apply the so-called concrete method, which uses objective and rather practical criteria for measuring damages caused by a party's breach of contract.[21]

V. CONCLUSION

In conclusion, it must be underlined that both counterpart Articles represent a specific hypothesis of the general rule regulating the corresponding remedy in case of breach of contract. The remedy provided in CISG Article 75 – and its counterpart UNIDROIT Principles Article 7.4.5 – applies to both contracting parties and consequently gives a general guarantee of the proper performance of the contractual obligations of both the buyer and the seller under an international contract for the sale of goods.

More important, both Articles, along with the possibility of the innocent party declaring the contract avoided, stipulate an additional method of protection for the injured party by providing the possibility to claim damages.[22]

[17] *See* the following case decisions, which confirm the statement that as far as it concerns the method for measuring damages the text of Article 75 of the CISG does not provide any difficulty for the national courts or the arbitral tribunals:

- ICC Arbitration Case No. 8740 of October 1996, case presentation available at <http://cisgw3.law.pace.edu/cases/968740i1.html>
- ICC Arbitration Case No. 8574 of September 1996, case presentation available at <http://cisgw3.law.pace.edu/cases/968574.html>
- Spain 28 January 2000 Supreme Court, case presentation available at <http://cisgw3.law.pace.edu/cases/000128s4.html>
- Germany 30 July 2001 District Court Braunschweig, case presentation available at <http://cisgw3.law.pace.edu/cases/01730g1.html>

[18] *See* Text of Secretariat Commentary on Article 71 of the 1978 Draft Convention, *supra* note 3; Flechtner, *supra* note 4.

[19] *See* Saidov, *supra* note 7.

[20] *See* Schlechtriem, "Extent and Measure of Damages (CISG Arts. 74–76)," in *Uniform Sales Law – The UN-Convention for the International Sale of Goods*, Vienna: Manz (1986), also available online at <http://cisgw3.law.pace.edu/cisg/biblio/schlechtriem.html>, and Liu, *supra* note 1.

[21] *See* Sutton, *supra* note 2; Saidov, *supra* note 7; case decision Russia 22 October 1998 Arbitration Proceeding 196/1997, case presentation available at <http://cisgw3.law.pace.edu/cases/981022r1.html>.

[22] *See* Vilus, "Provisions Common to the Seller and the Buyer," Petar Sarcevic & Paul Volken eds., *International Sale of Goods: Dubrovnik Lectures*, Oceana (1986), also available online at <http://cisgw3.law.pace.edu/cisg/biblio/vilus.html>; and Schlechtriem, *supra* note 20.

Therefore, this right might be executed only after the moment of avoidance of the contract is finally defined and the strict requirements outlined in CISG Article 75 and its counterpart UNIDROIT Principles Article 7.4.5 are fulfilled.[23]

[23] *See* for this inference the following case decisions:
- Austria 6 February 1996 Supreme Court, case presentation available at <http://cisgw3.law.pace.edu/cases/960206a3.html>
- Russia 24 January 2000 Arbitration Proceeding 54/1999, case presentation available at <http://cisgw3.law.pace.edu/cases/000124r1.html>
- Austria 9 March 2000 Supreme Court, case presentation available at <http://cisgw3.law.pace.edu/cases/000309a3.html>
- Germany 6 April 2000 District Court München, case presentation available at <http://cisgw3.law.pace.edu/cases/000406g1.html>
- Germany 13 January 1999 Appellate Court Bamberg, case presentation available at <http://cisgw3.law.pace.edu/cases/990113g1.html>

Measurement of damages when contract avoided: Remarks on the manner in which the UNIDROIT Principles may be used to interpret or supplement Article 76 of the CISG

Bruno Zeller

I. INTRODUCTION

It is true that both the UNIDROIT Principles and the Convention are instruments that can be used to assist in the interpretation of contracts if they address the same issues. Indeed the Preamble to the Principles states that they may be used to interpret or supplement international uniform law instruments.[1] The ICC Court of Arbitration in Paris took advantage of this possibility in a case where no express choice of law clause was included in the contract. It referred to both Article 76 CISG and Article 7.4.6 of the UNIDROIT Principles as being relevant to assist in their deliberations.[2] Arguably the tribunal was guided by the Official Comments on the UNIDROIT Principles, which included a direct reference to CISG Article 76:

> The purpose of this Article, which corresponds in substance to Art. 76 CISG, is to facilitate proof of harm where no replacement transaction has been made . . . [3]

However, it must also be remembered that the CISG is part of municipal law; that is, courts are obliged to use it when applicable. At best, the UNIDROIT Principles can be used by courts to assist where the provisions of the CISG are not clear. Furthermore, such

[1] *See* Kritzer, A. "General Observations on Use of the UNIDROIT Principles to Help Interpret the CISG," available at <http://cisgw3.law.pace.edu/cisg/text/matchup/general-observations.html>.
[2] ICC Court of Arbitration, Case No. 8502, November 1996, available at <http://cisgw3.law.pace.edu/cases/968502i1.html>.
[3] *See* the Official Comments on Article 7.4.6 of the UNIDROIT Principles, Comment 1, available online at <http://cisgw3.law.pace.edu/cisg/principles/uni76.html#official>.

assistance can only be considered if CISG Articles 7 or 8 have not produced a solution. It can be argued that if there is a gap in the CISG, then the UNIDROIT Principles should be consulted if possible to fill it before recourse to domestic law is taken.[4]

A set of rules and principles is placed in a fairly simple-looking formula.[5] The drafters of the Convention purposefully used earthy words devoid of municipal meaning, and it must also be understood that Articles within the CISG cannot be read in isolation. CISG Articles 7 and 8 clearly demand that all interpretation and application of any principle contained in the Convention must be undertaken within the four corners of the CISG.[6] All principles and therefore all Articles are an interlocking construct regulating the interactions of international contracting parties with the aims of maintaining business relations as long as possible and affording compensation to parties without unduly disadvantaging the breaching party.

II. AVOIDANCE

CISG Article 76 is no exception. The first criterion is that this Article only applies if the contract has been avoided pursuant to CISG Article 25 and hence CISG Articles 49 or 64. This is confirmed by the District Court of München, where the court indicated that compensation of damages for non-performance cannot be claimed if the contract has not been avoided.[7] The court added that otherwise the rules pertaining to the avoidance of contract would be superfluous.[8]

The UNIDROIT Principles do not use the word "avoidance," but instead use "termination" when referring to such a situation. Arguably the different terminology of "avoidance" or "termination" is of little significance. In either case the parties do not intend to fulfil their contractual obligations. It can also be further argued that CISG Article 76 and the counterpart UNIDROIT Principle are merely additions to CISG Article 74; namely, fully compensating[9] the innocent party for a loss suffered due to a breach of contract. Article 76 attempts to clarify situations where despite the avoidance of the contract the party seeks to demand damages if they purchased goods from another source.

III. CALCULATION OF DAMAGES

CISG Article 76 and the counterpart UNIDROIT Principle in essence establish a formula whereby the injured party can calculate damages where the contract has been avoided and no substitute transaction has been entered into.[10] It is established that CISG Article 76 and hence UNIDROIT Article 7.4.6 are only to be used if a concrete calculation of damages pursuant to CISG Article 75 is not possible.[11]

The formula allows calculating damages "abstractly"; that is, without having made a clearly definable cover transaction. The purpose of both instruments is to prescribe a

[4] For further elaboration *see* Kritzer, A., *supra* note 1.

[5] *See* Eiselen. S, "Remarks on the Manner in which the UNIDROIT Principles of International Commercial Contracts May Be Used to Interpret or Supplement Article 74 of the CISG," para. a.; available online at <http://cisgw3.law.pace.edu/cisg/principles/uni74.html#editorial>.

[6] *See* Zeller, B., "Four Corners – The Methodology for Interpretation and Application of the UN Convention on Contracts for the International Sale of Goods," available online at <http://cisgw3.law.pace.edu/cisg/biblio/4corners.html>.

[7] Germany, *Landgericht* [District Court] München 12 HKO 4174/99; case presentation including English translation available online at <http://cisg3.law.pace.edu/cases/000406g1.html>.

[8] *Id.*

[9] For a treatment of Article 74 and the concept of full compensation *see* also Sieg Eiselen on <http://cisgw3.law.pace.edu/cisg/text/anno-art-74.html>.

[10] The Secretarial Commentary is the closest counterpart to an Official Commentary on the CISG; *see* <http://cisgw3.law.pace.edu/cisg/text/secomm/secomm-76.html>.

[11] Germany 22 September 1992 *Oberlandesgericht* [Appellate Court] Hamm, case presentation available at <http://cisgw3.law.pace.edu/cases/920922g1.html>.

method by which the market price can be calculated. The ICC Court of Arbitration reached its conclusion by analyzing both instruments. As they yielded the same result, it can be argued that there is no significant difference between CISG Article 76 and UNIDROIT Article 7.4.6.

Nevertheless, differences between the two provisions are observable. The CISG distinguishes between situations where there was no substitute purchase or resale and situations where goods have been taken over. The Principles, on the other hand, merely point to the fact that no replacement transaction has taken place. It is true that the situation in which goods have been taken over only applies to the buyer.[12] There are really only two situations that could reasonably be contemplated; namely, either the buyer avoided the contract after taking over the goods, or in relation to Subsection (2) of CISG Article 76, by fixing an earlier time to prevent the buyer from speculating.[13] The Principles arguably may be lacking in failing to take these situations into consideration, and the CISG would need to be used to clarify and help interpret the Principles.

IV. CURRENT PRICE

CISG Article 76(2) and UNIDROIT Principle 7.4.6 (2) attempt to clarify the current price by tying it to the prevailing place where delivery of the goods should have been made. In general, UNIDROIT Article 7.4.6 uses simpler language and condenses parts of CISG Article 76 into a more readable form. It can be argued therefore that it would be advantageous if the Principle were read before the counterpart provision of the CISG is applied. Doing so would allow the court or arbitral tribunal to get a "feeling" of what the CISG attempts to achieve.

CISG Article 76 and UNIDROIT Article 7.4.6 attempt to give solutions to two problems: determining the date when the contract has been declared avoided and the place where the current price has to be determined.

The problem of timing has been addressed and clarified at the tenth plenary meeting of the Diplomatic Conference at which the CISG was promulgated.[14] The meeting minutes clearly state that the time is not the time when the party who "declared the contract avoided had for the first time the right to do so."[15] Instead the crucial time is the "time of avoidance." This phrase is found in both the CISG and the UNIDROIT Principles. Both instruments use the same phraseology, and therefore the time is definitely not when a *Nachfrist* was granted pursuant to CISG Articles 49 or 64.

V. TIMING OF CALCULATION OF DAMAGES

CISG Article 76 also adds to the timing the "taking over of goods," whereas UNIDROIT Article 7.4.6 does not, as mentioned above. Arguably the promoters of the Principles took note of Schlechtriem, who argues that the "taking over of goods" as a trigger point is difficult to justify. Schlechtriem notes,

> In the event of a delayed or non-conforming performance, the buyer who can neither undertake nor prove a definite cover transaction under Article 75 uses the reasonable[16] time period

[12] Enderlein, F., and Maskow, D., *International Sales Law*, Oceana 1992, at 307, also available online at <http://cisgw3.law.pace.edu/cisg/biblio/enderlein.html>.

[13] *Id.*, at 307.

[14] Legislative History, 1980 Vienna Diplomatic Conference, Summary Records of Meetings of the Plenary Meetings, para. 38 et seq. (A/Conf.97/C.L.245).

[15] *Id.*, para. 40.

[16] Reasonableness is a general principle of the CISG and is directly mentioned in thirty-seven provisions of the Convention. For further comments on the definition and operation of this concept *see* A. H. Kritzer, "Reasonableness: Overview Comments," available at <http://cisgw3.law.pace.edu/cisg/text/reason>.

> permitted by Article 49(2) at his own risk. In the case of Article 49(2)(b)(i), the reference point actually precedes the moment when the buyer could avoid the contract because the buyer, at the that time, still did not know of the breach.[17]

In this situation, as pointed out above, the UNIDROIT Principles are of little help to overcome this problem. It appears though that Schlechtriem foresaw a problem that technically can cause problems. However, jurisprudence on this point has not revealed any disputes.

VI. CONCLUSION

The question of how to determine the "current price" does not appear to pose any problems. That is the case as CISG Article 76 and UNIDROIT Principles Article 7.4.6 are essentially identical, and the ICC Court also in its determination did not distinguish between the two counterpart provisions. The court's decision simply confirmed that the market price is to be determined pursuant to the place of delivery of goods.[18] Arguably, if the promoters of the Principles had seen or anticipated problems in the application of CISG Article 76 they would have worded UNIDROIT Article 7.4.5 differently to overcome the perceived problem. This has been done on other occasions, such as in UNIDROIT Article 7.3.1, which can be used for a better understanding of CISG Article 25.

The time of avoidance or the time the contract is terminated is not always an uncontroversial point of reference. The problem still remains that a party can delay avoidance to gain an advantage, However, the problem is that the party may be held to have violated the duty to mitigate as well as being in breach of CISG Article 7; namely, disregarding the principle of good faith. [19]

[17] Schlechtriem, P. *Uniform Sales Law – The UN-Convention on Contracts for the International Sale of Goods* (1986), at 98, also available online at <http://cisgw3.law.pace.edu/cisg/biblio/schlechtriem.html>.

[18] ICC Court of Arbitration, Case No. 8502, *supra* note 2.

[19] The concept of good faith has generated a lively debate. Felemegas in his editorial on CISG Art. 7, available online at <http://cisgw3.law.pace.edu/cisg/text/peclcomp7.html#er>, states that it is "circumscribed to the interpretation of the law and should not be allowed to impose additional duties of a positive nature to the parties." It is my opinion that good faith in addition also imposes a duty on the behavior or the parties (*see* "Four Corners," *supra* note 6). *See* also the remarks by Ulrich Magnus, available online at <http://cisgw3.law.pace.edu/cisg/principles/uni7.html#um>.

Mitigation of losses: Remarks on the manner in which the UNIDROIT Principles may be used to interpret or supplement Article 77 of the CISG

Elisabeth Opie

I. INTRODUCTION

If the underlying principle of the United Nations Convention on the International Sale of Goods (CISG or Convention) is reasonableness,[1] Art. 77 CISG could certainly require a plaintiff or respondent to rise to the challenge of being reasonable during what is likely a difficult situation – when he or she is already losing money (or is about to[2]) because of the other party to the international sales contract.

This chapter examines the obligations imposed on parties pursuant to Art. 77 CISG by comparing this Article with Art. 7.4.8 UNIDROIT Principles ("Mitigation of Harm").[3]

Article 77, appearing in Section II of the Convention ("Damages"),[4] applies only when a party is claiming damages for breach of contract[5] and not in relation to any other remedy sought (such as specific performance).[6] Article 77 states,

> A party who relies on a breach of contract must take such measures as are reasonable in the circumstances to mitigate the loss, including loss of profit, resulting from the breach. If he fails to take such measures, the party in breach may claim a reduction in the damages in the amount by which the loss should have been mitigated.

Article 7.4.8 of the UNIDROIT Principles (UNIDROIT), entitled "Mitigation of Harm" and also appearing in a section entitled "Damages" provides,

> (1) The non-performing party is not liable for harm suffered by the aggrieved party to the extent that the harm could have been reduced by the latter party's taking reasonable steps.

[1] *See* generally, Kritzer, A., "Reasonableness," at <http://cisgw3.law.pace.edu/cisg/text/reason.html#view>.

[2] It is noted that the United Kingdom disagreed with the Commentary that the principle of mitigation applies to anticipatory breach: *Legislative History*, 1980 Vienna Diplomatic Conference, "Analysis of Comments and Proposals by Governments and International Organizations on the Draft Convention on Contracts for the International Sale of Goods, and on Draft Provisions Concerning Implementation, Reservations and Other Final Clauses" prepared by the Secretary-General, Document A/CONF.97/9 ('*Legislative History*'), original in English, 21 February 1980; available at <http://cisgw3.law.pace.edu/cisg/Fdraft.html>. Article 73 in the Text of [1978] Draft Convention on Contracts for the International Sale of Goods approved by the United Nations Commission on International Trade (*see* Official Records of the General Assembly, Thirty-third Session, Supplement No. 17 (A/33/17) chap. II, para. 28) was the precursor to Art. 77 and is substantively similar to Art. 77. For a general discussion on the principle of mitigation and anticipatory breach, *see* Saidov, D., "Methods of Limiting Damages under the Vienna Convention on Contracts for the International Sale of Goods," December 2001, at Part 4(c); available at <http://cisgw3.law.pace.edu/cisg/biblio/saidov.html#icv>.

[3] For use of the UNIDROIT Principles to assist in the interpretation on CISG, *see* Kritzer, A, "General Observations on Use of the UNIDROIT Principles to Help Interpret the CISG," available at <http://cisgw3.law.pace.edu/cisg/text/matchup/general-observations.htm>. It is noted that other UNIDROIT Principles may be relevant to the interpretation of Art. 77 CISG, including Art. 7.4.1. This paper does not include a discussion of these articles, but does note that the use of the term "harm" in the UNIDROIT Principles is given the same meaning as "damages" under the CISG. Nor does this chapter deal with other relevant provisions in the CISG, such as Art. 74 that requires that any damages sought under the CISG must be foreseeable and arise as a consequence of the breach for which damages are sought.

[4] Sutton notes that "[a] subspecies of the many remedial provisions found in the Convention, the measurement of damages rules are located in articles 74–78. These sections address the following issues: (1) a general rule for the measurement of damages [Article 74] (2) the measurement of damages in contract avoidance situations by substitute transactions [Article 75] or by current price [Article 76], (3) the mitigation of damages [Article 77], (4) and the interest on money damages [Article 78]." *See* Sutton, J. S., "Measuring Damages under the United Nations Convention on the International Sale of Goods," 50 *Ohio St. L. J.* (1989) 737–752, at Section IIIA; also available online at <http://cisgw3.law.pace.edu/cisg/biblio/sutton.html>.

[5] *See* Kritzer, A. H., extract from *Guide to Practical Applications of the United Nations Convention on Contracts for the International Sale of Goods*, Kluwer Law International (1994); also available at <http://cisg3.law.pace.edu/cisg/biblio/kritzer2.html#loss>.

[6] During the drafting of the Convention, the proposal by the United States in respect of Art. 58 of the draft Convention (which became CISG article 62) that the mitigation principle be extended to a corresponding modification or adjustment of other remedies than damages was rejected. See *Legislative History*, *fn* 3. Domestic doctrines of mitigation may, however, come into play in the case of specific performance by virtue of Art. 28 CISG.

(2) The aggrieved party is entitled to recover any expenses reasonably incurred in attempting to reduce the harm.

II. MITIGATION OF LOSS

Commentators have variously described the obligation imposed by Art. 77 as a statement of "public policy against waste,"[7] a duty to mitigate,[8] a duty to cooperate,[9] and "an obligation for oneself."[10,11] A literal interpretation of this Article does place a requirement on the party relying on the breach to do something – provided that it is reasonable in the circumstances – to reduce loss or damage.[12] If the party relying on the breach fails to do so (again on a literal interpretation), the non-performing party[13] has the option to seek a reduction in any damages that are otherwise payable. The difference between Art. 77 CISG and Art. 7.4.8 UNIDROIT Principles is not that one appears to impose an obligation on a party and the other does not. The point of difference is that Art. 7.4.8(1) expressly provides that a reduction of damages (harm suffered by the aggrieved party) is automatic if the aggrieved party could have taken reasonable steps to reduce the harm (but fails to do so[14]). On this reading, the difference between the option and the right to have damages reduced would appear minimal – in practice, the non-performing party would most likely seek to reduce any damages payable for a breach of contract.[15]

III. REASONABLENESS

"The obligation stated in Art. 77 CISG is to be interpreted taking into account the competing interests of the parties,[16] as well as commercial customs and the principle of

[7] McMahon, J. P., "Guide for Managers and Counsel: Drafting CISG Contracts and Documents and Compliance Tips for Traders," <http://cisgw3.law.pace.edu/cisg/contracts.html#a77>.

[8] *See* Sutton, *supra* note 4, at 737–752, at Part B, Section 5; also available at <http://cisgw3.law.pace.edu/cisg/biblio/sutton.html>.

[9] *See* Vilus, J., "Provisions Common to the Obligations of the Seller and the Buyer," in Sarcevic, P & Volken P (eds.), *International Sale of Goods: Dubrovnik Lectures*, Oceana (1986) at p. 250; also available at <http://cisgw3.law.pace.edu/cisg/biblio/vilus.html>.

[10] *See* Austria 24 January 2002 *Oberlandesgericht* [Appellate Court] Graz, case presentation including English translation available at <http://cisgw3.law.pace.edu/cases/020124a3.html>, citing Karollus, *UN-Kaufrecht*, at p. 225.

[11] *Cf.* Saidov, D., *supra* note 2, at Part 4(a); available at <http://cisgw3.law.pace.edu/cisg/biblio/saidov.html#iv>.

[12] The requirement is imposed on a party relying on the breach by the words "must take such measures [. . .] to mitigate the loss [. . .]."

[13] The second sentence of Art. 77 states that "the party in breach *may* claim a reduction in the damages in the amount by which the loss should have been mitigated."

[14] Although these words are not contained in Art. 7.4.8(1) UNIDROIT Principles, the author considers that this Principle only makes sense if the harm has not been reduced when it could have been.

[15] This comment is based on a literal interpretation of Art. 77; see *infra fn* 13. *Cf.* Arbitration (ICC) June 1999, Case 9187, where it was held that

> [t]he party claiming damages has an obligation to mitigate the loss (Art. 77 CISG), else it loses its right to damages. Whether the claiming party has complied with this duty has to be considered by the Arbitral Tribunal *ex officio*, whereby the burden of proof for the fact that a loss could have been avoided lies with the party owing damages (Stoll in V Caemmerer/Schlechtriem, *op. cit.*, N 12 to Art. 77 CISG)[citations included in decision]. Available at <http://www.cisg-online.ch/cisg/urteile/705.htm>.

[16] For this reason, it would appear contrary to the underlying principles of the Art. 77 to permit a party relying on a breach to fail to take into account the cost of the mitigating measures to the party in breach. "[M]itigation principles do not appear to require the injured party to choose the remedy which would be least expensive to the party in breach," but the measures taken must be reasonable in the circumstances; (*see* Text of Secretariat Commentary on Art. 73 of the 1978 Draft [*draft counterpart of CISG article 77*], presentation available at <http://www.cisg.law.pace.edu/cisg/text/secomm/secomm-77.html>). Arguably, the duty to mitigate does apply to the cost of measures employed to mitigate the loss: *see* "IV. Reimbursement of Expenses" below.

good faith."[17] The obligation imposed by Art. 77 is also to be interpreted in light of the words "reasonable in the circumstances."[18] There is no definition of reasonable in the CISG or the UNIDROIT Principles.[19]

The assessment of reasonableness is a question of fact and takes into account such circumstances as the time within which action was undertaken to diminish an avoidable loss[20] and whether a substitute transaction was conducted on an arm's length basis.[21] Conversely, "loss caused by a breach of contract is not recoverable if it could have been reduced by taking reasonable measures. A potential measure to mitigate damages is reasonable, if in good faith it could be expected under the circumstances. This is to be determined according to the actions of a reasonable person in the same circumstances."[22]

Given the case-by-case assessment that is necessarily undertaken for a reduction of damages pursuant to Art. 77, the types of factors to be considered (such as the perishability of goods, fluctuation in market price, availability of a market, and third-party obligations) and the measures taken by the party not in breach are not exhaustive.[23] However, in determining the reasonableness of action in a particular set of circumstances, guidance may be sought from the commentary accompanying Art. 7.4.8(1) UNIDROIT Principles.[24] It states,[25]

> The purpose of this article is to avoid the aggrieved party passively sitting back and waiting to be compensated for harm which it could have avoided or reduced. Any harm which the aggrieved party could have avoided by taking reasonable steps will not be compensated.
>
> Evidently, a party who has already suffered the consequences of non-performance of the contract cannot be required in addition to take time-consuming and costly measures. On the

[17] *See* Austria 24 January 2002 Appellate Court Graz, citing Karollus, *UN-Kaufrecht*, at p. 225; supra note 10.

[18] Secretariat Commentary, Comment 1. Article 7(1) CISG also "suggests that the international character of the Convention and the need to promote uniformity in its application and the observance of good faith in international trade are to be taken into account in the interpretation process": Netherlands 15 October 2002 Netherlands Arbitration Institute, Case No. 2319 at paragraph 104; available at <http://cisgw3.law.pace.edu/cases/021015n1.html>. For an online presentation of Art. 7 CISG, which provides the Convention's in-built interpretative mechanism, *see* <http://cisgw3.law.pace.edu/cisg/text/e-text-07.html>.

[19] *See* Kritzer, A. H., "Reasonableness," *supra* note 1 and Borisova, B., "Remarks on the Manner in which the UNIDROIT Principles May Be Used to Interpret or Supplement Article 75 of the CISG," May 2004, (including commentary and cases cited at fn 10); available at <http://www.cisg.law.pace.edu/cisg/biblio/borisova1.html#10>.

[20] *See* Switzerland 12 December 2002 *Kantonsgericht* [District Court] Zug, case presentation including English translation available at <http://cisgw3.law.pace.edu/cases/021212s1.html>, where the seller sold goods to an alternate buyer two days after the seller knew with certainty that the original buyer would not take delivery of the goods that were the subject of the agreement. The court held that two days was not too long a period for the seller to enter into a substitute transaction, despite the fact that the market price of the goods had fallen in the meantime. The calculation of damages was therefore calculated by taking into account the benefit received from the substitute transaction, with the difference in price being payable by the original buyer (including interest from the date of payment under the contract). *See* also Denmark 31 January 2002 *Sø og Handelsretten* [Maritime Commercial Court] (*Dr. S. Sergueev Handelsagentur v. DAT-SCHAUB A/S*), case presentation including English translation available at <http://cisgw3.law.pace.edu/cases/020131d1.html>.

[21] Netherlands 15 October 2002 Netherlands Arbitration Institute, Case No. 2319 at paragraph 151; case presentation and English text available at <http://cisgw3.law.pace.edu/cases/021015n1.html>; Austria 24 January 2002 *Oberlandesgericht* [Appellate Court] Graz, case presentation including English translation available at <http://cisgw3.law.pace.edu/cases/020124a3.html>.

[22] *See* Austria 14 January 2002 *Oberster Gerichtshof* [Supreme Court], case presentation including English translation available at <http://cisgw3.law.pace.edu/cases/020114a3.html>.

[23] Saidov notes that there are a wide range of measures that might be undertaken to mitigate damages under Art. 77: *see* Saidov, D., *supra* note 2, at Part 4(b).

[24] It is noted that the words "in the circumstances" do not appear in Art. 7.4.8 UNIDROIT Principles. Nonetheless, the assessment of reasonableness will still be done on a case-by-case basis under that Article.

[25] UNIDROIT Principles of International Commercial Contracts [1994], full text in English available online at <http://www.unidroit.org/english/principles/contracts/principles1994/fulltext.pdf>.

other hand, it would be unreasonable from the economic standpoint to permit an increase in harm which could have been reduced by the taking of reasonable steps.

One commentator writes, "The creditor should attempt to undertake everything possible in order to diminish the loss or at least to prevent its increase."[26]

IV. REIMBURSEMENT OF EXPENSES

Article 7.4.8(2) UNIDROIT Principles expressly provides that an "aggrieved party is entitled to recover any expense reasonably incurred in attempting to reduce the harm." This entitlement is implied from the wording of Art. 77 CISG, which provides an example of loss that might be recouped by the party relying on a breach of contract (i.e., loss of profit). A literal reading of this Article is that this example of loss is non-exhaustive. Any loss is limited to that loss that is reasonable in the circumstances and is foreseeable.[27]

In dealing with recovery of expenses separately from liability for harm suffered, Art. 7.4.8(2) UNIDROIT Principles appears to sever an obligation of the aggrieved party (mitigation of harm) from a right of the aggrieved party (recovery of expenses). Article 77 CISG, however, imposes the obligation to mitigate both loss and loss of profits (thereby including expenses). To this extent, Art. 77 CISG appears to place a broader obligation on the aggrieved party to mitigate than do the UNIDROIT Principles.

V. BURDEN OF PROOF

The non-performing party has to prove that the aggrieved party failed to comply with its obligation to mitigate its loss (including loss of profit) pursuant to Art. 77 CISG.[28] As noted above, there are two elements separately provided for under Art. 7.4.8 UNIDROIT Principles: (1) the obligation to mitigate and (2) the right to be compensated for reasonable expenses. Pursuant to Art. 7.4.8 UNIDROIT Principles, the burden of proof rests on the non-performing party to demonstrate that the aggrieved party has failed to reduce the harm by taking reasonable steps. As it is the aggrieved party who will assert that the expenses incurred as part of its actions to mitigate harm were reasonable in the circumstances, then it has the burden to prove this assertion.[29]

If the above comments on the breadth of the obligation to mitigate under Art. 77CISG are accepted, then the onus would rest with the non-performing party under this Article in relation to both the loss and expenses incurred in mitigating that loss. That is, the burden will not lie with the aggrieved party to prove that measures taken to mitigate expenses were reasonable. There is a rebuttable presumption that lies in favor of the aggrieved party.

[26] *See* Vilus, J., "Provisions Common to the Obligations of the Seller and the Buyer," in Sarcevic, P & Volken P (eds.), *International Sale of Goods: Dubrovnik Lectures*, Oceana (1986) at p. 251; also available at <http://cisgw3.law.pace.edu/cisg/biblio/vilus.html>. Similar comments have been made in relation to Art. 7.4.8(1). The Official Commentary to Art. 7.4.8 of the UNIDROIT Principles, which is available online at <http://cisgw3.law.pace.edu/cisg/principles/uni77.html#official>, Comment 1 states that

> The steps to be taken by the aggrieved party may be directed either to limiting the extent of the harm, above all when there is a risk of it lasting for a long time if such steps are not taken (often they will consist in a replacement transaction: see Art. 7.4.5), or to avoiding any increase in the initial harm.

[27] *See* Art. 74 CISG. It is noted that other provisions in the CISG also place obligations on the party relying on a breach to do certain things to, for example, preserve delivered, non-conforming goods at the cost of the non-performing party (Art. 85 CISG).

[28] Arbitration (ICC) June 1999, Case 9187.

[29] It is generally accepted that the burden of proof rests with the party making the assertion.

VI. CONCLUSION

The above comparative analysis between Art. 77 CISG and Art. 7.4.8 UNIDROIT Principles demonstrates several differences in both the drafting and interpretation of these Articles. Most notably, Article 77 CISG does appear to be drafted in favor of the aggrieved party, whereas Art. 7.4.8 UNIDROIT Principles takes into account the interests of both the non-performing and the aggrieved party. In spite of these differences, Art. 7.4.8 UNIDROIT Principles and its accompanying commentary do facilitate the interpretation of Art. 77 CISG and confirm that an obligation (by whatever name) is placed on an aggrieved party to reduce any damage caused by the non-performing party if it is reasonable to do so in the circumstances.

Interest on sums in arrears: Remarks on the manner in which the UNIDROIT Principles of International Commercial Contracts may be used to interpret or supplement Article 78 of the CISG

Sieg Eiselen

a. The right to claim interest on amounts due and not paid by a contractual party under the CISG is governed by Articles 78 and 84(1).[1] The issue of interest was one of the topics on which no real consensus could be reached in the drafting of the CISG.[2] One commentator has remarked that "Art. 78 is more conspicuous for the questions it fails to answer than the questions it answers."[3] The fact that such a right was included at all represents a compromise reached by the various interests groups that held incompatible views on interest.[4] This compromise was achieved with great difficulty in the final phases of the Conference.[5]

b. Article 78 is formulated in general terms, leaving the following issues open or unresolved: the *rate of interest*, whether interest is payable when the breach of the defaulting party is *excused* under Article 79, whether the amount due needs to be *liquidated* before interest accrues, whether interest is payable on any amount of *damages* due, and whether compound interest may be claimed. The determination of the rate of interest was

[1] Enderlein F. & Maskow D., *International Sales Law – United Nations Convention on Contracts for the International Sale of Goods* (1992 New York) 310–311, also available *online* at <http://cisgw3.law.pace.edu/cisg/biblio/enderlein.html>; Magnus U., in Martinek M. (ed) *J. von Staudingers Kommentar zum Bürgerlichen Gesetzbuch mit Einführungsgesetz und Nebengesetze: Wiener UN-Kaufrecht* (1999 Berlin) Art 78 Rn 2–4; Witz W., Salger H. C. & Lorenz M., *Internationales Einheitliches Kaufrecht* (2000 Heidelberg) Art 78, Rn 1-4; Eberstein H. & Bacher K. in Schlechtriem P. H. & Bacher K. (eds), *Kommentar zum einheitlichen UN Kaufrecht* 3rd ed (2000 Munich) Art 78, Rn 1–4.

[2] Schlechtriem/Eberstein/Bacher Art 78 Rn 2; Ferrari F., "Specific Topics of the CISG in the Light of Judicial Application and Scholarly Writing" 1995 (15) *J. L. & Com.* 1–126 also available *online* at <http://cisgw3.law.pace.edu/cisg/biblio/2ferrari.html>; Liu C., "Recovery of Interest," 2003 *Nordic J. Com. L. Univ. Turku* Issue 1, also available *online at* <http://cisgw3.law.pace.edu/cisg/biblio/chengwei.html>.

[3] Ziegel J. & Samson C., "Report to The Uniform Law Conference of Canada on the Convention on Contracts for the International Sale of Goods" (1981) 149 also available online at <http://cisgw3.law.pace.edu/cisg/wais/db/Articles/english2.html>.

[4] Corterier A., "A New Approach to Solving the Problem of the Interest Rate under Art 78 CISG" 5 (2002) *Int'l. Trade & Bus. L. J. Ann.* 33–42 also available online at <http://cisgw3.law.pace.edu/cisg/biblio/corterier.html>; Ferrari at fn 39–48; Liu at fn 13–15.

[5] Schlechtriem/Eberstein/Bacher Art 78 Rn 2.

intentionally left open in the drafting process of the CISG as no agreement could be reached on the approach to be adopted.[6]

c. Because of the controversies and uncertainties that surround Article 78 the provisions of the UNIDROIT Principles must be considered as one appropriate way of solving these issues. They have been suggested by some commentators[7] and have even been used by arbitral tribunals to justify a certain approach to the awarding of interest.[8] This chapter considers whether the use of the UNIDROIT Principles in these cases was justified.

d. The principle of full compensation is the basic principle underlying the provisions of the CISG where damages have been caused by a breach of contract that is not excused under Article 79. In the interpretation and filling of the gaps left in Article 78, regard should therefore be had to the underlying principle of full compensation.[9] There is a considerable difference of opinion especially among commentators on whether the gap left in Art. 78 regarding the rate of interest is a gap *praeter legem* (i.e., one being governed by, but not expressly settled in the CISG) or whether it is an issue falling outside the scope of application of the CISG (i.e., a gap *intra legem*).[10] The advocates of the former view emphasize the overall objective of the CISG, namely to create a uniform law,[11] whereas the supporters of the latter view refer to the legislative history of Article 78 as the dominant principle in interpreting it.[12]

e. If it is accepted that a uniform approach should be adopted in the filling of the gap in Article 78, then the gap should be filled using the principles contained in Article 7.[13]

[6] Schlechtriem/Eberstein/Bacher Art 78 Rn 2; Corterier at 39. *See* Ferrari at fn 827–847 for a brief history of this Article with reference also to its predecessor in the 1964 Uniform Law on the International Sale of Goods (ULIS).

[7] Corterier 41; Liu at fn 246–250.

[8] ICC Arbitration Case No. 8769 of December 1996 available online at <http://cisgw3.law.pace.edu/cases/968769i1.html>; ICC Arbitration Case No. 8128 of 1995 available online at <http://cisgw3.law.pace.edu/cases/958128i1.html>; Austria 15 June 1994 Vienna Arbitration proceeding SCH-4366 available online at <http://cisgw3.law.pace.edu/cases/940615a3.html>.

[9] Honnold para 417 at 456; Enderlein/Maskow Notes 1 & 4, at pp. 297–298; Witz/Salger/Lorenz Art 74, Rn 12 & 19; Staudinger/Magnus, Art 74, Rn 12, 16 & 19; Bonell 112; Behr V., "The Sales Convention in Europe: From Problems in Drafting to Problems in Practice" (1998 (17) *J.L. & Com.* 281 available online at http://cisgw3.law.pace.edu/cisg/biblio/behr.html; Koneru P., "The International Interpretation of the UN Convention on Contracts for the International Sale of Goods: An Approach Based on General Principles" 1997 (6) *Minn. J. Glob. Trade* 105–152 at fn 90 and 102–120, also available online at <http://cisgw3.law.pace.edu/cisg/biblio/koneru.html>; Ferrari at fn 883; Thiele C., "Interest on Damages and Rate of Interest under Article 78 of the U.N. Convention on Contracts for the International Sale of Goods" 2 *Vindobona J. Int'l. Com. L. & Arbitration* (1998) 3–35, also available online at <http://cisgw3.law.pace.edu/cisg/biblio/thiele.html>, at fn 84.

[10] *See* Ferrari at fn 853–858; Liu at fn 133–136; Behr at 280; Thiele fn 49–58; Austria 15 June 1994 Vienna Arbitration proceeding SCH-4366 available online at <http://cisgw3.law.pace.edu/cases/940615a3.html>; Switzerland 5 November 2002 Commercial Court des Kantons Aargau, available online at <http://cisgw3.law.pace.edu/cases/021105s1.html>; Italy 31 March 2004 District Court Padova, available online at <http://cisgw3.law.pace.edu/cases/040331i3.html>; United States 21 May 2004 Federal District Court (*Chicago Prime Packers, Inc. v. Northam Food Trading Co., et al.*), available online at <http://cisgw3.law.pace.edu/cases/040521u1.html>.

[11] Koneru at fn 89 ff; Thiele at fn 112–119; Liu 134–136; Honnold 525–526; ICC Arbitration Case No. 6653 of 26 March 1993 available online at <http://cisgw3.law.pace.edu/cases/936653i1.html>; Schlechtriem/Eberstein/Bacher Art 78 Rn 21.

[12] Herber/Czerwenka, *Internationales Kaufrechts*, (1991), 347; Germany 13 June 1991 Appellate Court Frankfurt 591, available online at <http://cisgw3.law.pace.edu/cases/910613g1.html>; Austria 15 June 1994 Vienna Arbitration proceeding SCH-4366, available online at <http://cisgw3.law.pace.edu/cases/940615a3.html>; Schlechtriem/Eberstein/Bacher Art 78 Rn 21.

[13] Koneru fn 89 ff; Liu fn 147–153; Austria 15 June 1994 Vienna Arbitration proceeding SCH-4366, available online at <http://cisgw3.law.pace.edu/cases/940615a3.html>; Belgium 19 March 2003 District Court Veurne, available online at <http://cisgw3.law.pace.edu/cases/030319b1.html>; Germany 25 November 2002 District Court Saarbrücken, available online at <http://cisgw3.law.pace.edu/cases/021125g1.html> .

Eberstein and Bacher[14] quite correctly point out that even proponents of the uniform approach do not agree on the method to be adopted. Some authors and cases are of the opinion that the rate should be based on the loss suffered by the non-defaulting party and that the place of business of the *creditor* should therefore be decisive.[15] However, this approach would make Article 78 superfluous as actual loss can be claimed under Article 74 in any event.[16] Other writers conclude that Article 78 is aimed at providing compensation for benefits unjustifiably received and therefore argue that the rate of interest should be based on the *debtor's* place of business.[17] A further approach suggests that a more objective approach should be used, thereby linking the rate of interest to the *currency* in which the debt is to be paid and not to the place of business of either party.[18] However, this approach may be problematic for currencies like the Euro that are linked to more than one country.[19] A fourth approach takes its lead from the Uniform Principles; namely, that the *place of payment* should determine the applicable rate of interest.[20] Despite precedents for each of these approaches, it would seem that the general tendency in the decided cases is to regard the issue as one not regulated by the CISG and therefore that it consists of a gap that should be filled by local law.[21]

f. The conclusion that the rules of private international law should determine the proper law of the contract and that that law should determine the rate of interest applicable seems

[14] Schlechtriem/Eberstein/Bacher Art 78 Rn 23; Honnold para 421; Behr 296; Switzerland 15 January 1998 Appellate Court Lugano, Cantone del Ticino, available online at <http://cisgw3.law.pace.edu/cases/980115s1.html>; ICC Arbitration Case No. 9448 of July 1999, available online at <http://cisgw3.law.pace.edu/cases/999448i1.html>; Italy 29 December 1999 District Court Pavia (*Tessile v. Ixela*), available online at <http://cisgw3.law.pace.edu/cases/991229i3.html>. *See* also the case law discussed by Ferrari at fn 875.

[15] Behr at fn 286; Corterier at 35; Honnold 421; Staudinger/Magnus Art 78 Rn 1; Germany 13 April 2000 Lower Court Duisburg, available online at <http://cisgw3.law.pace.edu/cases/000413g1.html>; Belgium 17 October 2002 Appellate Court Gent, available online at <http://cisgw3.law.pace.edu/cases/021017b1.html>.

[16] Staudinger/Magnus Art 78 Rn 34; Behr 266, 283; Germany 24 April 1990 Lower Court Oldenburg in Holstein, available online at <http://cisgw3.law.pace.edu/cases/900424g1.html>; Germany 18 January 1994 Appellate Court Frankfurt, available online at <http://cisgw3.law.pace.edu/cases/940118g1.html>.

[17] Behr 295–296; Corterier at 35–36; Liu 8.3.2 at fn 184–202; 8.4 at fn 206–215; Belgium 17 February 2000 District Court Hasselt (*J.F. in liquidation v. L.*), available online at <http://cisgw3.law.pace.edu/cases/000217b1.html>. However, this approach has been specifically rejected in case law: *see* Germany 18 January 1994 Appellate Court Frankfurt, available online at <http://cisgw3.law.pace.edu/cases/940118g1.html>.

[18] Belgium 25 April 2001 District Court Veurne (*BV BA G-2 v. AS C.B.*), available online at <http://cisgw3.law.pace.edu/cases/010425b1.html>; Germany 10 October 2001 Appellate Court Rostock, available online at <http://cisgw3.law.pace.edu/cases/011010g1.html>; Belgium 18 February 2002 District Court Ieper (*L. v. SA C.*), available online at <http://cisgw3.law.pace.edu/cases/020218b1.html>.

[19] Liu 8.6 at fn 221; 8.73 at fn 237 ff; Behr 286; Hungary, Arbitration Court attached to the Hungarian Chamber of Commerce and Industry VB./94131, December 5, 1995 CLOUT Case 164; Corterier 37; Hungary 5 December 1995 Budapest Arbitration proceeding Vb 94131, available online at <http://cisgw3.law.pace.edu/cases/951205h1.html>.

[20] Corterier at fn 26; Koneru at fn 140 ff; Zoccolillo "Determination of the Interest Rate under the 1980 United Nations Convention on Contracts for the International Sale of Goods: General Principles vs. National Law," 1 *Vindobona J. Int'l. Com. L. & Arbitration* (1997) 3–43, also available online at <http://cisgw3.law.pace.edu/cisg/biblio/zoccolillo.html>; Liu at fn 138; Netherlands 9 August 1995 District Court Almelo (*Wolfgang Richter Montagebau v. Handelsonderneming Euro-Agra and Te Wierik*), available online at <http://cisgw3.law.pace.edu/cases/950809n1.html>; ICC Arbitration Case No. 7153 of 1992, available online at <http://cisgw3.law.pace.edu/cases/927153i1.html>.

[21] Behr at fn 266 and 296; Ferrari fn 856–868; Magnus U., "*Aktuelle Fragen des UN Kaufrechts*" 1993 *ZEup* 90; Germany 17 September 1993 Appellate Court Koblenz, available online at <http://cisgw3.law.pace.edu/cases/930917g1.html>; Germany 8 February 1995 Appellate Court Hamm, available online at <http://cisgw3.law.pace.edu/cases/950208g3.html>; Belgium 17 October 2002 Appellate Court Gent, available online at <http://cisgw3.law.pace.edu/cases/021017b1.html>; Italy 31 March 2004 District Court Padova, available online at <http://cisgw3.law.pace.edu/cases/040331i3.html>.

inescapable in light of the legislative history of Article 78.[22] The right to claim interest clearly falls within the scope of the CISG; the determination of the rate of interest, however, clearly falls outside its scope and is to be determined by domestic law.[23] This seems to be the dominant view held by commentators and courts, even if it is not the unanimous view as stated by some German courts.[24]

g. The UNIDROIT Principles (UP) have been used in some instances to fill the gap in Article 78.[25] The sole arbitrator in an Austrian case for example referred to Art 7.4.9(2) of the UP to justify his decision to award a commercially reasonable rate of interest.[26] However, these remain isolated cases, and the decisions cannot be justified in light of the principles concerned. As a result of the clear intention of the drafters of the CISG to leave the rate of interest outside the scope of the CISG, the UNIDROIT Principles can play no role in filling this gap and are therefore only of interest for any future development or change of the CISG.[27]

h. Article 7.4.9(2) of the UNIDROIT Principles makes provision for the payment of interest at the average bank short-term lending rate to prime borrowers that prevails for the currency of payment at the place of payment. Where no such rate exists at that place, then the same rate in the State of the currency of payment will apply. In the event that neither such rates are available the impasse is resolved by applying the rate fixed by the law of the State of the currency of payment.[28] The Comments to Art. 7.4.9 indicate that this solution seems to be best suited to the needs of international trade and most appropriate to ensure adequate compensation for the harm sustained. The rate in question is the rate at which the aggrieved party will normally borrow the money that it has not received from the non-performing party. As such it represents a mixture of the first and fourth approaches discussed in paragraph **e.** It links the rate of interest

[22] Italy 31 March 2004 District Court Padova, available online at <http://cisgw3.law.pace.edu/cases/040331i3.html>.

[23] Schlechtriem/Eberstein/Bacher Art 78 Rn 9 and 25; Staudinger/Magnus Art 78 Rn 11. *See* case law cited by Ferrari at fn 874; Thiele 99.

[24] Germany 5 April 1995 District Court Landshut, available online at <http://cisgw3.law.pace.edu/cases/950405g1.html>; Germany 5 November 1997 Appellate Court Hamm, available online at <http://cisgw3.law.pace.edu/cases/971105g1.html>. The aberrant decisions since 2000 have been referred to in footnotes 13 to 19 earlier. Most of the decisions since 2000 however, followed, in our view, the correct approach. The following examples from diverse jurisdictions reflect the trend: Bulgaria 12 March 2001 Arbitration Case 33/98, available online at <http://cisgw3.law.pace.edu/cases/010312bu.html>; France 28 November 2002 Appellate Court Grenoble (*SA AZ I... v. Entreprise Em... de Su... In...*), available online at <http://cisgw3.law.pace.edu/cases/021128f2.html>; Netherlands 28 November 2002 Appellate Court's-Hertogenbosch (*Hagenuk Telecom GmbH v. Analog Devices Nederland B.V.*), available online at <http://cisgw3.law.pace.edu/cases/021128n1.html>; Russia 2 December 2002 Arbitration proceeding 18/2002, available online at <http://cisgw3.law.pace.edu/cases/021202r1.html>; Switzerland 12 December 2002 District Court Zug, available online at <http://cisgw3.law.pace.edu/cases/021212s1.html>; Belgium 25 February 2004 District Court Hasselt (*K BVBA v. BV*), available online at <http://cisgw3.law.pace.edu/cases/040225b1.html>; Italy 31 March 2004 District Court Padova, available online at <http://cisgw3.law.pace.edu/cases/040331i3.html>; Germany 20 July 2004 Appellate Court Karlsruhe, available online at <http://cisgw3.law.pace.edu/cases/040720g1.html>.

[25] ICC Arbitration Case No. 8769 of December 1996, available online at <http://cisgw3.law.pace.edu/cases/968769i1.html>; ICC Arbitration Case No. 8128 of 1995, available online at <http://cisgw3.law.pace.edu/cases/958128i1.html>; Austria 15 June 1994 Vienna Arbitration proceeding SCH-4366, available online at <http://cisgw3.law.pace.edu/cases/940615a3.html>.

[26] ICC Arbitration Case No. 8769 of December 1996, available online at <http://cisgw3.law.pace.edu/cases/968769i1.html>.

[27] *See* abstracts 13, 14, 16, 17, 19, 22, 23, and 25 in Behr at 275 ff; Liu 8.2.1 at fn 156–169; Schlechtriem/Eberstein/Bacher Art 78 Rn 26. For a contrary view, *see* Bonell M.J., *An International Restatement of Contract Law – The UNIDROIT Principles of International Commercial Contracts* (1994 New York).

[28] The provisions of the Principles of European Contract Law are similar, although not quite as detailed and providing no fall-back provision if no rate of interest exists for the currency of payment at the place of payment. Corterier 40 proposes a similar solution. *See* also Liu 7.2 at fn 137–139.

both to the currency of payment and the place of payment. However, it is not directly linked to the place of business of either party as payment will not necessarily always be made at the place of business of the seller.

i. Article 7.4.9(1) of the UNIDROIT Principles determines that interest is payable whenever a party fails to pay that sum when it is due, even if the non-payment is excused.[29] This provision confirms the interpretation of commentators of Article 78 CISG read with Article 79(5); namely, that interest is payable even if the breach of contract is excused in terms of Article 79.[30] Although the primary aim of Article 78 is to provide the non-defaulting party with an easily quantifiable claim in the case of non-payment of money due, it goes further in that it requires no proof of a loss, clearly distinguishing it from the provisions of Art.74.[31] However, it is not clearly stated in the CISG whether interest is payable in the event of a breach that is excusable in terms of Article 79. The clear wording of Article 79(5) ("exercising any right other than to claim damages") seems to suggest that this should be the case.[32] The provisions of Article 7.4.9(1) of the UNIDROIT Principles confirm this interpretation as they clearly provide for the payment of interest, even in cases where the non-payment is excused.

j. The UNIDROIT Principles contain specific provisions dealing with the payment of interest on *damages* that are due. Article 7.4.10 provides that, unless the contract excludes such a right, a party is entitled to claim interest on damages that are due for the non-performance of non-monetary obligations from the time of the non-performance.[33] This provision contains two clear underlying principles: payment of damages is due from the time of non-performance (or by implication from the time the damages are actually suffered[34]), and the damages need not be liquidated at the time of their accrual.[35] This provision and its underlying principles may be helpful in the interpretation of Article 78, which does not address these issues clearly. It confirms the interpretation placed on Article 78 by most commentators on the CISG that interest is due from the date that the liability for damages accrues and that the amount of the damages need not be liquidated.[36] This has also been confirmed in case law.[37]

k. Unlike the Uniform Law on Sales (ULIS) drafts, neither the CISG nor the UNIDROIT Principles contain any provision on whether a party may be entitled to compound interest on any amounts due.[38] There certainly is no right to compound interest in terms of the CISG.[39] However, if a party is entitled to compound interest in terms of the domestic law that governs the rate of interest, a party should probably be entitled to claim compound

[29] *See* also Comment 1 to this Article.

[30] Belgium 4 April 2001 District Court Kortrijk (*H. v. D.*), available online at <http://cisgw3.law.pace.edu/cases/010404b1.html>; Switzerland 12 December 2002 District Court Zug, available online at <http://cisgw3.law.pace.edu/cases/021212s1.html>; Belgium 8 October 2003 Appellate Court Gent, available online at <http://cisgw3.law.pace.edu/cases/031008b1.html>.

[31] Behr at fn 267 and 296; Schlechtriem/Eberstein/Bacher Art 78 Rn 9; Liu 3.2 at fn 31–39; Germany 17 September 1993 Appellate Court Koblenz, available online at <http://cisgw3.law.pace.edu/cases/930917g1.html>.

[32] Schlechtriem/Eberstein/Bacher Art 78 Rn 14; Liu 3.3 at fn 40–46; Enderlein/Maskow 311.

[33] Liu at fn 76.

[34] *See* Comment on the UNIDROIT Principles Art 7.4.10.

[35] Schlechtriem/Eberstein/Bacher Art 78 Rn 14; Liu at fn 76.

[36] Schlechtriem/Eberstein/Bacher Art 78 Rn 12–14 and 15. *See* also Karolus *UN Kaufrecht* (1991 Vienna); Staudinger/Magnus Art 78 Rn 8; Koneru at fn 129 ff; Thiele at fn 38; Liu at fn 66.

[37] Germany 14 June 1994 Lower Court Nordhorn, available online at <http://cisgw3.law.pace.edu/cases/940614g1.html>; Germany 5 April 1995 District Court Landshut, available online at <http://cisgw3.law.pace.edu/cases/950405g1.html>; Switzerland 21 October 1999 District Court Zug, available online at <http://cisgw3.law.pace.edu/cases/991021s1.html>.

[38] *See* Comment on the UNIDROIT Principles Art 7.4.10; Schlechtriem/Eberstein/Bacher Art 78 Rn 35.

[39] Schlechtriem/Eberstein/Bacher Art 78 Rn 35.

interest in cases otherwise governed by the CISG.[40] Although there is a perception that compound interest can generally not be claimed in international transactions, Gotanda shows very convincingly that compound interest may be awarded in many jurisdictions and is even being awarded in some international tribunals.[41]

[40] Schlechtriem/Eberstein/Bacher Art 78 Rn 35.

[41] Gotanda J. Y., "Compound Interest in International Disputes" 2004 (2) *Oxford Univ. Comp. L. Forum* available online <http://ouclf.iuscomp.org/Articles/gotanda/shtml>.

Exemption of liability for damages: Comparison between provisions of the CISG (Art. 79) and the counterpart provisions of the UNIDROIT Principles (Art. 7.1.7)

Alejandro M. Garro

I. TEXT OF CISG ARTICLE 79 AND ITS COUNTERPART PROVISIONS IN ARTICLE 7.1.7 OF THE UNIDROIT PRINCIPLES

UNIDROIT Principles *Article 7.1.7 – Force Majeure*	CISG Article 79
(1) Non-performance by a party is excused if that party proves that the non-performance was due to an impediment beyond its control and that it could not reasonably be expected to have taken the impediment into account at the time of the conclusion of the contract or to have avoided or overcome it or its consequences.	1. A party is not liable for a failure to perform any of his obligations if he proves that the failure was due to an impediment beyond his control and that he could not reasonably be expected to have taken the impediment into account at the time of the conclusion of the contract or to have avoided or overcome it or its consequences.
(2) When the impediment is only temporary, the excuse shall have effect for such period as is reasonable having regard to the effect of the impediment on the performance of the contract.	3. The exemption provided by this article has effect for the period during which the impediment exists.

(3) The party who fails to perform must give notice to the other party of the impediment and its effect on its ability to perform. If the notice is not received by the other party within a reasonable time after the party who fails to perform knew or ought to have known of the impediment, it is liable for damages resulting from such non-receipt.	**4. The party who fails to perform must give notice to the other party of the impediment and its effect on his ability to perform. If the notice is not received by the other party within a reasonable time after the party who fails to perform knew or ought to have known of the impediment, he is liable for damages resulting from such non-receipt.**
(4) Nothing in this article prevents a party from exercising a right to terminate the contract or to withhold performance or request interest on money due.	**5. Nothing in this article prevents either party from exercising any right other than to claim damages under this Convention.**
	2. If the party's failure is due to the failure by a third person whom he has engaged to perform the whole or a part of the contract, that party is exempt from liability only if: (a) he is exempt under the preceding paragraph; and (b) the person whom he has so engaged would be so exempt if the provisions of that paragraph were applied to him.

II. INTRODUCTION

The similarities between the counterpart provisions of the CISG and the UNIDROIT Principles are made obvious in the preceding comparative chart that, although paying no heed to the order of the paragraphs of Article 79 CISG, places in parallel the individual paragraphs of Article 7.1.7 of the UNIDROIT Principles on International Commercial Contracts.

Except for minor differences in syntax, the most noticeable difference is the absence of a counterpart to CISG Art. 79(2) in the UNIDROIT Principles. This omission reflects the gap between the assumed function that this paragraph was to take in the mind of its drafters and the misunderstandings and complexities inherent in the distinction of excuses based on the failure of a third person to perform. One can also notice the difference in phraseology between the last paragraph included in both instruments: CISG Art. 79(5) is expressed in terms of limiting the exemption to liability for damages, whereas UNDROIT Principles Art. 7.1.7(4) refers to the availability of the non-breaching party, in case the other party's non-performance is excused, to terminate, withhold performance, or request interest on money due.

Another less noticeable, yet more significant, difference between both instruments is that the UNIDROIT Principles also contain provisions on hardship (Chapter 6, Section 2, Articles 6.2.1, 6.2.2, and 6.2.3), a subject not specifically addressed in the CISG. This absence affects the interpretation of both texts, even though both seemingly address the same issue.

III. EXEMPTION OF LIABILITY FOR DAMAGES WHEN THE PARTY CLAIMING IMPOSSIBILITY IS A THIRD-PARTY SUPPLIER OF THE SELLER: WHY WAS THIS OMITTED FROM ARTICLE 7.1.7 OF THE UNIDROIT PRINCIPLES?

When the failure to deliver conforming goods results from the failure to perform on the part of "a third person whom (the seller) has engaged to perform the whole or part of the contract," it seems sensible not to exempt the seller from liability because, except in extreme cases,[1] the seller is the party who is in the best position to avoid or minimize non-compliance by someone whom he himself "*has engaged* to perform all or part of the contract" [emphasis added]. Those whom the seller "has engaged" include parties providing the seller with raw materials or semi-manufactured parts; namely, those that may fall under the generic rubric of "ancillary suppliers" of the seller. They are deemed to be within the seller's sphere of influence, and the seller is held responsible for the conformity caused by those employed by him to perform the contract. In other words, the seller cannot be exempted of liability *vis-à-vis* the buyer, even if those ancillary suppliers are in a position to invoke successfully the defense of *force majeure*.

Some delegations, however, pushed for the inclusion of a second paragraph to Article 79 to tighten the prerequisites of the excuse in case the seller engages a subcontractor or a third party who is not deemed to be within his sphere of influence.[2] Thus, CISG Article 79(2) seeks to tighten the conditions under which a seller may claim the defense of impossibility or *force majeure* whenever the defect in performance is attributed to an "independent" third person within the meaning of Article 79(2); that is, a third person genuinely outside the seller's organizational structure and sphere of control who, though not employed by the seller, is nevertheless "engaged" by the seller.

Thus, whereas CISG Article 79(2) is meant to apply whenever the seller claims an exemption of liability for damages due to defects in performance resulting from a failure to perform by a third person (i.e., one who is independently engaged to perform the whole or part of the contract), Article 79(1) addresses a situation where the seller claims an exemption of liability due to the misconduct of a general supplier or some other third person employed by the seller.

The assumed function of CISG Article 79(2) is that the seller's liability stretches to answer for the conduct of an "independent" third person unless the impediment was insuperable for the seller and, additionally, the independent third person would himself qualify for exemption under Article 79(1). Thus, Article 79(2) is meant to increase the seller's liability, because the prerequisites for exemption must be met cumulatively by both the seller and the third person. From the buyer's perspective this means, for all practical purposes, that the seller is in principle responsible for defective performance incurred by independent third persons as if it were the seller's own conduct. It appears then that the failure to perform by a third person, supposing such third person is within the meaning of CISG Art. 79(2), will seldom lead to the exemption of the party to the main contract.

Although it seems more difficult for the defaulting party to be exempted of liability for the acts of an "independent" third person under Article 79(2) than to be exonerated for the delivery of non-conforming goods procured from or manufactured by a supplier whom the seller has engaged to deliver conforming goods, the fact of the matter is that it is not easy to distinguish between both types of third persons. More important, under either the first or second paragraph of CISG Article 79, the third person's failure to perform will seldom lead to the exemption of the party to the main contract.

[1] For instance, if the supplier of the goods is the only available source or when supplies are unavailable due to unforeseeable and extraordinary events that are not related to the typical procurement risks assumed by a seller.

[2] According to UNCITRAL's official records, tightening the conditions under which a seller could claim exemption who sought to avoid a contract includes, among other consequences, "that a party should be exempted from liability because he had chosen an unreliable supplier…" Commentary on the Draft Convention on Contracts for the International Sale of Goods prepared by UNCITRAL's Secretariat, Official Records, United Nations, New York, 1981 [hereinafter Commentary on the 1978 Draft Convention] § 23 at 379 par. 23 (motion by Denmark) and § 35 at 380 (comment by Norwegian delegate).

In those cases where a supplier chosen by the seller had failed to deliver the promised goods, courts and arbitral tribunals have held that the seller was not exempted, even in cases where the failure to deliver was unforeseeable by the seller. Decisions vary, however, as to the method followed by the courts to subsume the seller's exemption of liability under Article 79. Some courts place the analysis of whether the seller qualifies for such an exemption under paragraph (1) of Article 79,[3] other tribunals prefer to examine the seller's exoneration under paragraph (2) of Article 79;[4] and still others opt for deciding the issue on the basis of Article 79 in the abstract.[5] Indeed, the analysis undertaken by the Federal Supreme Court of Germany on March 24, 1999 suggests that those differences are not so great: "From the buyer's point of view, it makes no difference whether the seller produces the goods himself – with the consequence that the non-performance is generally in his actual control so that, as a rule, a dispensation pursuant to CISG Art. 79(1) is generally excluded – or whether the seller obtains the goods from suppliers . . . ".[6]

Therefore, even if a party's excuse due to the failure of an independent third person is likely to be more difficult to be established under the "double *force majeure*" solution provided in CISG Art. 79(2) than if the situation were solely appraised under CISG Art. 79(1), the latter provision should suffice to take care of all possible scenarios of *force majeure* – not only when the defaulting party was to perform himself or with the aid of employees or his staff but also whenever his performance is conditioned upon performance by a third party. Even if that third party's failure to perform may be excused *vis à vis* the defaulting party, the latter is still bound to avoid or overcome such impediment *vis-à-vis* the non-defaulting party to the contract, so that dispensation under Article 79(1) is excluded. This is so because the internal relationship between the third party and the defaulting party is irrelevant to the other contracting party.

It does not make much of a difference, in other words, whether the excuse is sought to be found under the first or second paragraph of Article 79, and even assuming that a distinction between the different types of third parties were warranted, the difficulty in distinguishing between an excuse grounded on the failure to perform by different types of third parties (e.g., employees, agents, suppliers, subcontractors, etc.) is not worth the candle. In essence, the "impediment" to which CISG Article 79(1) refers suffices to cover the situation where the lack of or defective performance is owed to the act or omission of a third party.

It was a wise decision on the part of the drafters of the UNIDROIT Principles Article 7.1.7 not to carry over CISG Article 79(2) into the Principles. In principle, if the seller entrusts the manufacture or delivery of conforming goods to another person or if the buyer entrusts the payment to a bank or an intermediary, both seller and buyer remain responsible with the other party.[7] CISG Article 79(1) suffices to take care of the

[3] Germany 28 February 1997 *Oberlandesgericht* [Appellate Court] Hamburg, case presentation available at <http://cisgw3.law.pace.edu/cases/970228g1.html>; Germany 21 March 1996 *Schiedsgericht der Handelskammer* [Arbitral Tribunal] Hamburg [partial award], case presentation including English translation available at <http://cisgw3.law.pace.edu/cases/960321g1.html>.

[4] ICC Arbitration Case No. 8128 of 1995, International Chamber of Commerce, case presentation including English translation available at <http://cisgw3.law.pace.edu/cases/958128i1.html>.

[5] Russia 16 March 1995 Arbitration proceeding 155/1994, case presentation including English translation available at <http://cisgw3.law.pace.edu/cases/950316r1.html>.

[6] Germany 24 March 1999 *Bundesgerichtshof* [Supreme Court], translation available at <http://cisgw3.law.pace.edu/cases/990324g1.html> with comment by Peter Schechtriem, 15/16 Juristenzeitung (13 Aug. 1999) 794-97.

[7] Compare European Principles of Contract Law (PECL) Article 8:107 ("A party which entrusts performance of the contract to another person remains responsible for performance"). See also Comments and Notes on PECL Art. 8:107, Comment C, available at <http://cisg.law.pace.edu/cisg/text/peclcomp79.html>.

exceptional circumstances in which seller or buyer may be exempted of liability on account of the third person's defaulting performance.

IV. REMEDIES STILL AVAILABLE TO THE AGGRIEVED PARTY WHEN THE OTHER PARTY'S NON-PERFORMANCE IS EXCUSED

When CISG Article 79(1) says that "a party is not liable . . . ," it actually means that the defaulting party to be excused is not liable in damages; all the other remedies of the other party remain unaffected according to CISG Article 79(5). Yet, the other remedies that remain actually available to the other party depend on the particular circumstances of the case and the contractual obligations arising under the contract.

Article 7.1.7(4) of the UNIDROIT Principles does not carry over the restriction found in CISG Article 79(5) to the effect that the party who was to receive performance may be entitled to exercise all his rights under the contract except to claim damages. Instead, the counterpart of the UNIDROIT Principles phrases the potentially available remedies in less restrictive terms, stating that the aggrieved party who was to receive performance from the defaulting party that succeeded in establishing an excuse may nevertheless claim "a right to terminate the contract or to withhold performance or request interest on money due." Indeed, remedies other than damages are not limited to those listed in this provision of the UNIDROIT Principles, because the right to reduce the price (CISG Art. 50) and to compel specific performance (CISG Arts. 46 and 62) may remain as available as the right to avoid or terminate (CISG Arts. 49 and 64) and the right to collect interest on money due (CISG Art. 78).[8]

Indeed, there are good reasons to include price reduction as a possible available remedy in a situation of a qualified exemption for the seller's failure to deliver conforming goods. This is one of those instances where price reduction may well serve its purpose, which is not to compensate the aggrieved buyer in damages, but rather to "preserv[e] the bargain between the parties and [. . .] rebalanc[e] the performance required by both sides . . . ".[9]

The exempting impediment clearly should not preclude the disappointed party from putting an end to the contract, provided that the excused failure to perform amounts to a fundamental breach (CISG Art. 25). If the non-performance were to be total and permanent, termination may be an automatic consequence of the impediment, in which case it may not be necessary to require the aggrieved party (which is the only party entitled to avoid the contract) to serve a termination notice by a unilateral declaration.[10] Once avoidance has been declared, however, the effects of avoidance insofar as "restitution" is concerned apply to both parties (CISG Arts. 81–84).

CISG Article 79(5) exempts the defaulting party of liability for damages in a negative form, without referring expressly to the question whether the aggrieved party may be nevertheless entitled to interest on the money that is owed to him.[11] The nature of

[8] Compare with PECL Art. 8:101, which allows for the aggrieved party's possibility of exercising any other remedy with the exception of damages and performance: "Where a party's non-performance is excused under Article 8:108, the aggrieved party may resort to any of the remedies set out in Chapter 9 except claiming performance and damages."

[9] *See* generally, Erika Sondahl, "Understanding the Remedy of Price Reduction – A Means to Fostering a More Uniform Application of the United Nations Convention on Contracts for the International Sale of Goods," 7 *Vindobona J. Int'l. Com. L. & Arbitration* (2003) 255–276, at fn. 38, also available at <http://cisgw3.law.pace.edu/cisg/biblio/sondahl.html>.

[10] Compare with PECL Art. 9:303(4): "If a party is excused under Article 8:108 through an impediment which is total or permanent, the contract is terminated automatically and without notice at the time the impediment arises."

[11] *See, e.g.*, Dennis Tallon in *Commentary on the International Sales Law: The 1980 Vienna Sales Convention* (ed. by M. Bianca and M. J. Bonnell, Milan, 1987) at 589, also available at <http://cisgw3.law.

the obligation to pay interest, as expressed in the CISG, leads to the conclusion that an Article 79 exemption does not preclude the aggrieved party from claiming and recovering interest. First, the purpose of the obligation to pay interest under CISG Article 78, in addition to the obligation to pay monetary compensation for damages, is to compensate the obligee for the financial cost experienced for not receiving payment at the time it is due. Second, CISG Article 78 seems to distinguish between the obligation to pay damages and the obligation to pay interest when it fixes the commencement of the obligation to pay interest as of the moment there is delay in payment, even if the obligee has not suffered any damage from such delay and the debtor is not liable. It is on the basis of this conceptual understanding that UNIDROIT Principles Article 7.1.7(4) provides, though expressly, that the aggrieved party is entitled to interest. UNIDROIT Principles Article 7.4.9(1) consistently states that "the aggrieved party is entitled to interest . . . whether or not the non-payment is excused."[12]

CISG Article 79(5) seems to warrant the right of the aggrieved party to claim specific performance even if, as a result of an impediment, performance is likely to have become impossible (e.g., the goods are destroyed or the transfer of funds has been prohibited). Of course, there can be no specific performance if the failure to perform turns on the fact that the total goods have perished or payment has been rendered impossible or illegal. Yet, where a temporary impediment results in a partial non-performance or a delayed performance, then in such a case the exemption effect is only for the period during which the impediment exists (CISG Art. 79(3); UNIDROIT Principles Article 7.1.7(2)). In such a case, the right to performance continues to exist and may actually encourage the parties to invest in efforts to overcome the impediments. When the temporary impediment disappears and has no effect any longer, the exemption from specific performance is no longer justified.

Both CISG Article 79(5) and UNIDROIT Principles Article 7.1.7(4) leave open the possibility for the aggrieved party to demand specific performance, a claim that is not necessarily affected by the impediment excusing the non-performance. To this extent, both texts do not rigidly exclude the possibility of specific performance.[13] Whether the temporary impediment merely results in delayed performance or is likely to deprive the performance of most of its value is another question concerning the impact of the temporary impediment in the overall performance; this question is certainly not governed by this provision on *force majeure* and its consequences.

V. IS THERE ANY ROOM FOR AN EXEMPTION OF LIABILITY ON ACCOUNT OF HARDSHIP UNDER CISG ARTICLE 79?

Another issue of significance in the comparison between both instruments is the absence in CISG Article 79 of any reference to a situation, short of physical or legal impossibility, in which performance by one party becomes extremely and totally unpredictably harsh. UNIDROIT Principles Article 6.2.2 expressly provides for a situation of hardship, in addition to the *force majeure* or impossibility scenario contemplated in Article 7.1.7, so that the defaulting party may choose to claim one or the other excuse.[14] Did the

pace.edu/cisg/biblio/tallon-bb79.html>, in favor of exempting the excused defaulting party from the payment of interest on the ground that the payment of interests should be considered as part of an award of damages).

[12] Compare with PECL Arts. 8:101(2) and 9:508 ("Delay in Payment of Money"): "Interest is owed whether or not non-payment is excused under Article 8:108."

[13] Compare with PECL Art. 8:108(1), providing that the aggrieved party may resort to any of the remedies set by PECL Chapter 9, except claiming performance and damages.

[14] See Comment 6 to UNIDROIT Principles Article 6.2.2.

CISG fail to include a provision on hardship because the "impediment" referred to in its Article 79 may conceivably grant relief to a party who finds him- or herself in a dire situation of excessive and unpredictable hardship to perform? Or should the failure to include such a provision be interpreted as a rejection of the doctrine of hardship under the CISG?

Scholarly opinion is divided on this question. Some commentators state that the wording of Article 79 appears sufficiently flexible to include an extreme situation of unexpected hardship within the meaning of "impediment."[15] Others opine that there is no place in the CISG for any relief on account of economic hardship.[16] As to judicial decisions on this subject, they are too few and inconclusive to this date to warrant a stable trend either excluding or including hardship within the purview of CISG Article 79. Moreover, none of the reported decisions has extended the exemption of CISG Article 79 to cases of economic hardship. However, it must be admitted that no real "hard" cases of hardship have been presented so far.

The first issue to tackle is whether it is conceivable to find a situation of hardship calling for a legal response of some kind, be it under a stretched interpretation of CISG Article 79 or the CISG's underlying general principles via Article 7.2 or under some national law that may eventually be rendered applicable. Once we have found a proper hypothetical covering hardship, the next question is to ascertain whether it is at all possible to deal with a genuine hardship situation via CISG Article 79 or whether we should resign ourselves to the application of some national law admitting relief in a situation of hardship (provided, of course, that the applicable rule of private international law would lead to the application of a domestic legal system contemplating relief for hardship, which is not altogether certain).

There are not many real cases dealing with genuine situations of hardship in which courts have found it fair to provide relief and have offered well-grounded reasons explaining why the change in circumstances was actually unpredictable and why one type of relief was more appropriate than others. This notwithstanding, most commentators would not go as far as to deny the possibility that in very rare cases, probably during truly exceptional historical periods (e.g., pre-war Germany during the 1920s) and really unstable economies or countries (e.g., hyperinflation in Argentina during the 1970s), judicial relief from a genuine hardship situation may be fairly justified. Admittedly, there are those who think that "a contract always a contract" and would not admit an inch of an exception to the *pacta sunt servanda*. For those who share this point of view, it makes no sense to explore any further whether CISG Article 79 could be relied upon to tackle a genuine situation of hardship. This chapter goes on to examine the availability of a response on the assumption that *pacta sunt servanda* is a principle rather than a rule, though a principle that ought to be respected at almost all costs. It is at least conceivable that a defaulting party may

[15] *See, e.g.*, Dennis Tallon in *Commentary on the International Sales Law* Article 79 at § 3.2 (1987) ("[T]he judge will have a natural tendency to refer to similar concepts in his own law. Thus, the judge of a socialist country will have a restrictive approach to *force majeure*.... On the contrary a common lawyer will feel inclined to refer to the more flexible notions of frustration and impracticability. In the Roman-German system, the judge will reason in terms of *force majeure* . . ."). *See* also M. J. Bonell, "Force majeure e hardship nel diritto uniforme della vendita internazionale," in *Diritto del commercio internazionale* 590 (1990) (observing that by requiring that the obligor "could not *reasonably* be expected . . . to have avoided or overcome [the impediment] or its consequences" suggests that, at least in principle, the possibility should be entertained that performance has become so onerous that it would be unreasonable to enforce it).

[16] *See, e.g.*, Barry Nicholas, who observed that exemption of liability on account of unexpected and excessive economic hardship was "out of place" in a sales law. Progress Report of the Working Group on the International Sale of Goods on the Work of its Fifth Session (A/CN.9/87, Annex III, reprinted in UNCITRAL Yearbook V: 1974 (1975) at 66). *See* also Fritz Enderlein & Dietrich Maskow, *International Sales Law* (Oceana, 1992) 317, available online at <http://cisgw3.law.pace.edu/cisg/biblio/enderlein.html>.

be justified in obtaining some type of relief, despite the fact that the "impediment" falls short of a strict case of physical or legal impossibility to perform.

Resorting to the type of scenarios designed in the comments accompanying UNIDROIT Principles Article 6.2.2, one may envision a situation where a buyer A, domiciled in State X, concludes a contract of sale with a seller B, domiciled in State Y. Payment is agreed to be made in State Z within three months, upon delivery of the goods, in the currency of State Z. Let us imagine that within a month of the conclusion of the contract a totally unpredictable political and economic crisis, which the parties could not have reasonably taken into account, leads to a massive devaluation of 80 percent of Z's currency. As a result the sale turns out to be extremely burdensome for the buyer A and a gross windfall for the seller B. Admittedly, it is not easy to ascertain whether the change in circumstances could not have been reasonably foreseen. It is not an easier task to distinguish between the risk of loss that every contracting party should be deemed to have assumed and the extraordinary disastrous economic disadvantages amounting to a "limit of sacrifice" (because there is indeed such a limit), beyond which the obligor should not be expected to perform the contract as written. But if there is such a "truly hard hardship problem" (i.e., a deal unexpectedly turned into a nightmare for one party and a steal for the other) well, this is it.[17]

Assuming that the CISG applies to this contract, and also assuming that the foregoing hypothetical falls squarely within a factually justified case of hardship, the most relevant question to explore at this point is whether a case of economic hardship as this one should be settled by the CISG, either by reading the word "impediment" in Article 79 to include economic hardship or by concluding that there is a gap within the CISG to be filled by some underlying general principle via the "governed-but-not-settled" gap-filling technique promoted in CISG Art. 7(2). If the CISG applies, then it naturally preempts other potentially applicable domestic rules dealing with hardship. But if the hardship question cannot be thus settled, then there is no alternative other than resorting to domestic legal rules, hoping that the applicable law would provide for some risk-share allocation of remedies. The alternative of resolving the hardship problem within the four corners of the CISG is more palatable, because leaving the question to the conflict of law rules of the forum leads to a great diversity of potentially applicable legal doctrines (impracticability, frustration, *Wegfall der Geschäftsgrundlage*, *eccesiva onerosità sopravvenuta*, *imprévision*, etc.). Thus, the interpreter who takes seriously the CISG's stated purpose of unifying the law of sales will probably exhaust all technically available means to respond to the hardship problem within the four corners of the Convention.

First, it is necessary to confirm, convincingly, that the hardship situation is not expressly or implicitly excluded from the scope of the CISG. Second, it is important to examine the legislative and drafting history of CISG Article 79 to the extent that it may be considered a legitimate and valuable aid in its interpretation.

To the extent that termination or adjustment of a contract on grounds of hardship may be regarded in some legal systems as a validity-related issue, it may be argued that the hardship issue is excluded from the Sales Convention by CISG Article 4.[18] The argument

[17] *See* Joseph Lookofsky, "Walking the Article 7(2) Tightrope between CISG and Domestic Law," unpublished manuscript submitted to the symposium on "25 Years United Nations Convention on Contracts for the International Sale of Goods (CISG)," Vienna, March 15–16, 2005 (on file with the author).

[18] *See* J. Lookofsky, *Understanding the CISG in the USA* (2d ed., 2004) § 2.6 and J. Lookofsky, "The Limits of Commercial Contract Freedom under the UNIDROIT 'Restatement' and Danish Law," 46 *Am. J. Comp. L.* 485, 496 (1998), also available at <http://cisgw3.law.pace.edu/cisg/biglio/lookofsky6.html>, referring to the hardship provisions in the General Clause of the Danish Contracts Act, authorizing a court to refuse enforcement or to adjust "any unreasonable contract or term, and that includes a term which becomes unreasonable after the contract is made." Professor Lookofsky also refers to Dutch Civil Code Article 6.258(1)

deserves careful consideration, because in some Scandinavian legal systems the issue of hardship appears to be approached as an issue of validity[19] and also because there is something to be said in favor of giving the defaulting party the benefit of choosing among competing domestic doctrines of hardship. But this approach does not sound convincing or persuasive. Unlike a situation of unconscionability (usury, *lésion*, or gross disparity of the performances at the time the contract is concluded), which clearly falls under the rubric of validity, the hardship problem is associated in most legal systems with *force majeure* or impossibility of performance – that is, a situation of exoneration or mitigation of liability due to events subsequent to the conclusion of the contract – more than as a case of nullity or avoidance due to infirmities or flaws affecting the contract from its inception.[20] Moreover, every benefit potentially obtained from allowing national doctrines of hardship to compete for its application is more than offset by the high price in terms of uniformity that is to be paid under this approach.

It is still necessary to trace the legislative and drafting history of the pertinent CISG provisions to ascertain whether they are indicative of a firm intention to exclude hardship from the scope of Article 79. The legislative history clearly indicates that Article 79 was drafted in response to the criticism of Article 74 of the 1964 Uniform Law on International Sales, to the effect that "a party could be too readily excused from performing his contract." The criticism that ULIS Article 74 was insufficiently clear and subjective led to the substitution of the word "impediment" for "circumstances," so that the conditions for exemption are identified more narrowly and objectively under the CISG. But this legislative history is inconclusive to warrant the conclusion that CISG Article 79 cannot exempt a party to perform, in whole or in part, when the impediment is represented by a totally unexpected event that makes performance exceedingly difficult.

The exclusion (*rectius*: rejection) of hardship from the CISG would emerge, according to other authors, from its drafting history.[21] Indeed, at the time of the drafting of the article that later became CISG Article 79, the Working Group of UNCITRAL considered a proposed provision allowing a party to claim avoidance or adjustment of a contract whenever facing unexpected "excessive damages." After setting out the arguments in support of this proposal, the Committee concluded by stating that it was not adopted, and this provision did not reappear in subsequent discussions.[22]

as an illustration of a provision that appears to question the validity" of a contract ("Upon the demand of one of the parties, the court may modify the effects of a contract or it may set it aside; in whole or in part, on the basis of unforeseen circumstances of such a nature that the other party, according to standards of reasonableness and fairness, may not expect the contract to be maintained in unmodified form. The modification or setting aside may be given retroactive effect.").

[19] *See, e.g.*, Tom Southerington, *Impossibility of Performance and Other Excuses in International Trade*, Publication of the Faculty of Law of the University of Turku, Private law publication series B:55, also available at <http://cisgw3.law.pace.edu/cisg/biblio/southerington.html>. Southerington refers to Section 36(1) of the Finnish Contracts Act, which the author considers as a rule of validity akin to unconscionability.

[20] This seems to be the case of Italian law, in which Article 1467 of the *Codice Civile* and the scholarly doctrine surrounding it have been taken as a model in several Latin American legal systems. A much-criticized 1993 decision by the *Tribunale Civile di Monza* entered (unnecessarily for the purposes of the case before the court) to examine the legal nature of hardship under Italian law and its relationship with the CISG. The Italian court stated that "... hardship is not a matter expressly excluded in Article 4 of the CISG. ... Dissolution of the contract for supervening excessive onerousness affects neither the validity of the contract nor ownership over the goods ... "). Italy 14 January 1993 *Tribunale Civile* [District Court] Monza, *Nuova Fucinati v. Fondmetall International*, case presentation including English translation available at <http://cisgw3.law.pace.edu/cases/930114i3.html>.

[21] *See, e.g.*, Barry Nicholas, who observed that exemption of liability on account of unexpected and excessive economic hardship was "out of place" in a sales law. Progress Report of the Working Group on the International Sale of Goods on the Work of its Fifth Session (A/CN.9/87, Annex III, reprinted in UNCITRAL Yearbook V: 1974 (1975) at 66).

[22] Report of Committee of the Whole I Relating to the Draft Convention on the International Sale of Goods (A/32/17, annex I, paras. 458–60), reprinted in UNCITRAL Yearbook VIII: 1977 (1978), 57). *See* also John Honnold, *Documentary History of the Uniform Law for International Sales* 350 (1989).

Others have relied upon another fragment from the drafting history of the Convention – the rejection of a Norwegian proposal linked to CISG Art. 79(3) – to infer a rejection of the possibility of extending the application of Article 79 to a situation of genuine hardship. When the issue of temporary impediment came up for discussion, the delegation from Norway suggested the inclusion of an additional provision to the effect that the temporary exemption from performing may turn into a permanent one if, after the impediment ceases to exist, the circumstances had so changed that performance would become manifestly unreasonable. The proposal gained significant support from other delegations, but it was finally turned down after the French delegate raised concerns that introducing such a provision may be regarded as an acceptance of such doctrines as *imprévision*, frustration of purpose, and the like.[23] Although the recollection of the discussions among the participant delegates, or what should be made out of those discussions, is far from uniform, there is no dispute that the issue of economic hardship was not specifically discussed in connection with those proposals.

Speculation about what the intention of the drafting group might have been with regard to the scope of application of CISG Article 79 is unlikely to be too accurate, especially when we are left to our inferences from fragments in the "*travaux préparatoires.*" Indeed, the dismissal of a proposal that did not even address whether hardship should be given any space within the Convention is no proper foundation upon which to build an argument on the "intention of the legislator." If anything, the drafting history of the Convention is evidence that the discussions were not sufficiently conclusive on this question.

So, if Article 79(1) neither expressly or implicitly excludes the possibility of economic hardship as an impediment that may exempt a party's failure to perform, and if it is accepted that a situation of genuinely unexpected and radically changed circumstances, in truly exceptional cases, deserves some legal response, then we are inclined to favor a broad interpretation of CISG Article 79 that would preempt the application of a domestic rule on hardship, assuming that the applicable domestic law provides for one. Thus, the next and final step is to ascertain the contours of some guidelines on what is to be understood by a genuine situation of hardship and, immediately thereafter, speculate as to what may be the most appropriate remedy or relief after hardship has been found to exist.

I do not think it is possible or even convenient to attempt a definition of hardship, beyond accepting that the impediment may entail a situation of "economic impossibility" (*wirtschaftliche Unmöglichkeit*) that, although short of an absolute bar to perform, imposes what in some legal systems is conceptualized as a "limit of sacrifice" (*äusseerste Opfergrenze*) beyond which the obligor cannot be reasonably expected to perform. It seems clear that in most cases market fluctuations are not to be considered an impediment under CISG Article 79, because such fluctuations are a normal risk of commercial transactions in general. Whether wild and totally unexpected market fluctuations in goods or currency could ever become an impediment is another matter. Indeed, the theoretical possibility of such radical and unexpected changes admits the application of Article 79 in those rare instances as the one exemplified above.

As to the possible remedies following a finding of hardship, the analysis of this problem should start by acknowledging that this is another "governed-but-not-settled" gap that needs to be filled within the Convention. There are no "general principles underlying the Convention" from which to extract the obligation of the parties to renegotiate the terms of the contract, as would be most likely the case if the parties had incorporated a

[23] *See* A/Conf.97/C.1/SR.27 at 10. The Norwegian proposal led to the deletion of the word "only" in Article 79(3), so that even if the initial and temporary impediment vanishes, the resulting change of circumstances, which may well be of an economic nature, may turn into another impediment leading to that party's exemption of liability.

hardship clause. Neither can one find such a widely accepted general principle pointing to the possibility, in case negotiations fail, to adjust or revise the terms of the contract so as to restore the balance of the performances.

For those who are not willing to resort to the principle of good faith buried in CISG Article 7(1) to find a balance of the performances,[24] CISG Article 79(5) may be relied upon to open up the possibility for a court or arbitral tribunal to determine what is owed to each other, thus "adapting" the terms of the contract to the changed circumstances. Other than the payment of damages, a court or arbitral tribunal may order, if justified under the CISG, the termination of the contract as of a certain date. Of course, it is impossible to require specific performance as called for by the contract, but a flexible method for adjusting the terms of the contract may be obtained by resorting to price reduction under CISG Article 50.[25]

[24] A suggestion by Peter Schlechtriem to this effect may be found in "Transcript of a Workshop on the Sales Convention," in 18 *J.L. & Com.* 191–258 (1999), also available at <http://cisgw3.law.pace.edu/cisg/biblio/workshop-79.html>.

[25] *See* Schlechtriem, "Art. 79," in *Kommentar zum Einheitlichen UN-Kaufrecht-CISG* (4th ed., Munich 2004).

Failure of performance caused by other party: Editorial remarks on whether and the extent to which the UNIDROIT Principles may be used to help interpret Article 80 of the CISG

Friederike Schäfer

I. INTRODUCTION

Article 80 CISG is located in Part III of the Convention in the section entitled "Exemptions." It provides an excuse for a party's failure to perform when this failure is caused by an act or omission of the other party. This statement, although seemingly self-evident,[1] is nonetheless an important part of the general principle of good faith. In addition to Article 7(1) CISG, its point of reference is not the interpretation of the Convention but the contractual relationship between the parties. Therefore, Article 80 CISG can be seen as

[1] Honnold, Uniform Law of International Sales Under the 1980 United Nations Convention, Art. 80 para. 436 (3rd ed. 1999 Deventer).

an anchor within the Convention regarding the obligation between the parties to observe good faith in their relationship and forbidding contradictory behavior.[2] However, despite the general character of Article 80 CISG, its scope and meaning have yet to be ascertained. The aim of this comparative editorial is to contribute to ascertaining that scope and mearning and to investigate whether and in which way the counterpart provisions of UNIDROIT Principles can be of help thereby.

II. AN ACT OR OMISSION OF THE PROMISEE CAUSING THE PROMISOR'S FAILURE TO PERFORM

1. Perception under Article 80 CISG

The first issue to be examined is whether the act or omission of the party causing the other party's failure to perform has to be of a certain quality and, if so, of what quality. Generally, any conduct of a party is sufficient to activate Article 80 CISG. It is not a condition that the act or omission was the promisee's fault[3]; in addition, an exemption under Article 79 CISG is irrelevant.[4] Nor is it necessary that the act or omission of the promisee constituted a breach of contract.[5] Nevertheless, in cases in which the contract calls for a certain behavior and the promisee complies with this requirement, the mere causation of a breach of the promisor in terms of *conditio sine qua non* cannot be sufficient to invoke Article 80 CISG; acting in accordance with a contractual requirement to perform a certain action cannot be to the disadvantage of a party. Accordingly, this must be valid for an omission.[6]

Therefore, a typical situation in which Article 80 CISG becomes relevant is one where inadequate or missing cooperation by the promisee is followed by the promisor's failure to properly perform his obligations. Article 80 CISG has been applied in several court decisions. For example, the seller informed the buyer in advance that no further goods would be delivered under the contract, which constituted an anticipatory breach of the contract. Consequently, the buyer was excused for withholding the payment.[7] In another case the buyer was excused for not opening a letter of credit because the seller failed to inform the buyer about the place of loading.[8] The buyer was barred from relying on the

[2] Staudinger/Magnus, Kommentar zum Bürgerlichen Gesetzbuch mit Einführungsgesetz und Nebengesetzen, Wiener UN-Kaufrecht (Cisg), Art. 80 para. 5 (1999). The general principle of the Convention prohibiting contradictory behavior ("*non concedit venire contra factum proprium*") also becomes manifest in the following provisions: Articles 16(2)(b), 29(2) 2nd sentence, 50 2nd sentence Cisg. *See* for material concerning this principle as a "general principle" of transnational law, The Transnational Law Database, available at <http://tldb.uni-koeln.de/php/pub_show_principle.php?pubdocid=907000>.

[3] Germany 31 January 1997 *Oberlandesgericht* [Appelate Court] Koblenz, available online at <http://cisgw3.law.pace.edu/cases/970131g1.html>; Schlechtriem/Stoll, Commentary on the UN Convention on the International Sale of Goods (Cisg), Art. 80 para. 7 (1998).

[4] Schlechtriem/Schwenzer/Stoll/Gruber, Kommentar zum einheitlichen UN-Kaufrecht – Cisg, Art. 80 para. 3 (4th ed. 2004).

[5] Staudinger/Magnus, *supra note* 2, Art. 80 para. 9; Bianca/Bonell/Tallon, Commentary on the International Sales Law, Art. 80 note 2.3 (1987); Herber/Czerwenka, Internationales Kaufrecht, Art. 80 para. 3 (1991). Although it is difficult to find an example of an act or omission causing the failure to perform of the other party that does not amount to a breach of contract itself, it is possible in cases of misunderstandings, etc. between the parties. This is, however, only true if one does not understand Article 80 Cisg as qualifying a certain conduct as breach of contract.

[6] In most cases, the contract will not require that a party should omit a certain action but will rather order the other party to act.

[7] Switzerland 31 May 1996, Zürich Chamber of Commerce, Arbitral Award, available online at <http://cisgw3.law.pace.edu/cases/960531s1.html>; *see* also Albert H. Kritzer, Editorial remarks on this case (available at above URL).

[8] Austria 6 February 1996 *Oberster Gerichtshof* [Supreme Court], available at <http://cisgw3.law.pace.edu/cases/960206a3.html>; *see* for further case law Franco Ferrari/Harry Flechtner/Ronald Brand, ed., The Draft UNCITRAL Digest and Beyond: Cases, Analysis and Unresolved Issues in the UN Sales Convention, pp. 835–840 (2004).

non-conformity of the goods because the buyer refused the seller's offer to cure without justification.[9]

2. Influence of Different Wording in the UNIDROIT Principles

As far as the basic requirements are concerned, the corresponding provision in the UNIDROIT Principles, Article 7.1.2, is equivalent with Article 80 CISG.[10] Art. 7.1.2 UNIDROIT Principles requires an act or omission of the party invoking non-performance that causes this non-performance. Although this is not expressly stated in the text or the Official Comments on the UNIDROIT Principles, the provision, like Article 80 CISG, is based on the premise that if an act or omission becomes a contractual obligation a fulfillment of the latter cannot be a relevant act or omission under Art. 7.1.2 UNIDROIT. But the application of this provision does not depend on the promisee's act or omission being a non-performance or even a non-excused non-performance.[11] The only difference between both provisions results from the additional clause contained in Article 7.1.2 UNIDROIT Principles, which refers to events for which the promisee bears the risk as potential grounds for exemption of the other promisor. Therefore, cases in which the performance of the party is prevented by events not caused by the promisee are expressly included in the scope of Article 7.1.2 UNIDROIT Principles. In the illustration contained in the Official Comments on this Article, the case is even contemplated in which the promisor caused its non-performance but the risk of this very event was contractually allocated to the promisee.[12]

How is one to deal with this regime under Article 80 CISG? What can be deduced from the fact that an additional clause is missing that would clarify that events not caused by the promisee can also lead to an exemption? One possible conclusion is that the scope of Article 80 CISG is indeed narrower than that of Article 7.1.2 UNIDROIT Principles. A second possible conclusion is, however, that the additional clause in Article 7.1.2 UNIDROIT Principles is merely of a declaratory nature. The fact that such clarification does not appear in Article 80 CISG has no impact on the interpretation of this article. The understanding of Article 80 CISG as an expression of the general principle of the observance of good faith[13] demands that a broad interpretation be adopted (i.e., the latter conclusion). This is because it is only appropriate to exempt a party from a non-performance the reason for which lies in the other party's sphere of risk.

Virtually, this is the basic idea underlying Article 80 CISG, as well as Article 7.1.2 UNIDROIT Principles. The causation of the non-performance by the promisee is merely the most evident case in which he bears the risk, simply due to the causation of the problem. As a result, the scope of Article 80 CISG generally corresponds to that of Article 7.1.2 UNIDROIT Principles, despite the different wording with regard to events not caused by the promisee. In this respect one could even understand Article 7.1.2 UNIDROIT Principles as a clarification of the elliptical wording of Article 80 CISG.

[9] Germany 31 January 1997 *Oberlandesgericht* [Appelate Court] Koblenz, available online at <http://cisgw3.law.pace.edu/cases/970131g1.html>.

[10] The different terminology in the UNIDROIT Principles using "non-performance" instead of "failure to perform" does not lead to a different meaning, as can be seen by Article 7.1.1 UNIDROIT Principles defining non-performance as failure by a party to perform any of its obligations under the contract, including defective performance or late performance.

[11] Art. 7.1.2 UNIDROIT Principles Comment 1. [12] Art. 7.1.2 UNIDROIT Principles Comment 2.

[13] HONNOLD, *supra* note 1, Art. 80 para. 436.1; SCHLECHTRIEM/STOLL, *supra* note 4, Art. 80 para. 2.

III. REQUIREMENT OF CAUSATION OF THE PROMISOR'S FAILURE TO PERFORM

1. Limitation of Causation under Article 80 CISG

Article 80 CISG requires that the promisor's failure to perform is caused by the act or omission of the promisee. Article 80 CISG itself does not indicate that the causal link between the act or omission of a party and the failure of the other party to perform has to be of a certain quality. In particular, a mechanism to limit the relevant consequences – like the requirement of foreseeability in Article 74 CISG – is not employed by Article 80 CISG. There is also no restriction to direct causation either; indirect causation is generally sufficient.[14] The only prerequisite that can be taken from the wording is that a causal link of any kind between the act or omission of the promisee and the failure of the promisor to perform any of its obligation does exist. Nevertheless, the mere activation of a chain of causation cannot always be appropiate as the only criterion under Article 80 CISG.[15] In cases in which the failure to perform is not the only logical consequence of the promisee's act or omission (i.e., if the promisor could potentially overcome the consequences of the promisee's conduct), an evaluative contemplation of the causal link between act or omission and failure to perform is necessary. It has to be determined in which cases the promisor can be expected to overcome consequences of the promisee's conduct. Should the seller be expected to inquire if the buyer fails to properly specify the goods?[16] If the seller refuses to deliver the goods because the buyer had not complied with its duty to pay the price arising from an earlier contract, is the non-delivery caused by the buyer's failure to pay?[17]

It is difficult to abstractly determine the line beyond which a causation in the sense of Article 80 CISG should be denied. However, the basic condition is that the promisee's act or omission impairs proper performance by the promisor at all.[18] And if this condition is met, it has to be decided from case to case which effort could reasonably be expected of the promisor to comply with its contractual obligations, despite the consequences of the promisee's act or omission.[19]

[14] SCHLECHTRIEM/SCHWENZER/STOLL/GRUBER, *supra* note 5, Art. 80 para. 4.

[15] Effectively, the narrowing interpretation of the terms act or omission (*cf. supra*) represents already a limitation of causation in the sense of Article 80 CISG because in consequence not every condition set by the promisee is considered relevant as a reason for the failure of the promisor to perform.

[16] *See* SCHLECHTRIEM/SCHWENZER/STOLL/GRUBER, *supra* note 5, Art. 80 para. 5; VINCENT HEUZE, LA VENTE INTERNATIONALE DE MARCHANDISES – DROIT UNIFORME, note 478 (2nd. ed. 2000).

[17] *See* SCHLECHTRIEM/SCHWENZER/STOLL/GRUBER, *supra* note 5, Art. 80 para. 6; Arbitral Award, Zürich Chamber of Commerce, 31 May 1996, *supra* note 8: in this case the seller alleged that the buyer had not paid the price for goods that were already delivered. However, the Tribunal applied Article 80 CISG not in favor of the seller but in favor of the buyer because later the seller informed the buyer that it would not receive any further deliveries. This action "attributable to [seller], caused in the sense of Art. 80 Vienna Convention [buyer] to withhold payments."

Here is a similar case in which the application of Article 80 CISG was denied: Germany 19 April 1996 Aachen *Landgericht* [District Court], available at <http://cisgw3.law.pace.edu/cases/960419g1.html>: the contract calls for the seller to deliver casks. The seller declared it would deliver the goods only if the buyer paid the remaining price for a machine that it had already delivered at an earlier time. The buyer claimed damages for non-delivery, and the seller could not invoke Article 80 CISG. Generally, for a right of retention arising from Article 80 CISG, *see* CHRISTOPH KERN, *Leistungsverweigerungsrechte im UN-Kaufrecht*, available online at <http://cisgw3.law.pace.edu/cisg/biblio/kern2.html>.

[18] SCHLECHTRIEM/SCHWENZER/STOLL/GRUBER, *supra* note 5, Art. 80 para. 6; ENDERLEIN/MASKOW/STROHBACH, INTERNATIONALES KAUFRECHT, Art. 80 note 5.2 (1991); ACHILLES, KOMMENTAR ZUM UN-KAUFRECHTSÜBEREINKOMMEN (CISG), Art. 80 para. 3 (2000).

[19] Although reasonableness seems to be an amorphous standard, it is at least an acknowledged general principle of the Convention and therefore applicable in accordance with Article 7 para. (2) CISG. *Cf.* ULRICH MAGNUS, *Die allgemeinen Grundsätze im UN-Kaufrecht*, RABELSZ 59 (1995), pp. 469–494.

2. Limitation of Causation under Article 7.1.2 UNIDROIT Principles

As well as Article 80 CISG, Article 7.1.2 UNIDROIT Principles requires a party's non-performance to be caused by the other party's act or omission. The wording of Article 7.1.2. UNIDROIT Principles does not go any further than that of Article 80 CISG: it merely affirms the need for a causal link without specifying the nature of this causal connection. Thus, the provision itself cannot be used as a tool to determine causation in the sense of Article 80 CISG. It can be derived from the Official Comments to Article 7.1.2 UNIDROIT Principles that the most important situation that should be covered by this Article is that of performance of a party being made impossible in whole or in part.[20] Although the diction concerning the causation of the non-performance by an event for which the promisee bears the risk is less decisive, using the words "may result from an event,"[21] the underlying concept is that performance becomes impossible due to that very event. This, however, does not mean that the UNIDROIT Principles prohibit an evaluative interpretation of the causal link between the act or omission and non-performance. However, with regard to the issue of causation, Article 7.1.2 UNIDROIT Principles does not provide any information that could contribute new aspects to determining causation in the sense of Article 80 CISG.

IV. FAILURE TO PERFORM CAUSED BY BOTH PARTIES

1. Applicability of Article 80 CISG

Another issue discussed in connection with causation under Article 80 CISG is how to deal with the situation in which both parties contributed to the failure of the promisor to perform its obligations. The provision itself remains silent on this point. The only possible reference is the use of the expression "to the extent."[22] However, relying on this formulation seems rather scholastic. The main argument for applying Article 80 CISG to cases in which the failure to perform was caused by both parties should be a factual one: within a contractual relationship the parties to the contract constantly have to interact with each other. Therefore, applying Article 80 CISG only to cases of exclusive causation by one party would inapproriately narrow the scope of this provision. The decision of which act or omission of the promisee should be considered as the relevant trigger of the chain of causation under Article 80 CISG requires contemplation of the contributions made by both parties to the contract. Thus, Article 80 CISG has to be applied to cases in which both parties caused the promisor's failure to perform as well.[23] When applying Article 80 CISG to such cases the respective contributions of the parties to this result should be evaluated and weighed.[24] Where an adaption of the remedy reflecting the respective contributions of the parties is not practicable,[25] the general rule should be that the promisee cannot

[20] Art. 7.1.2 UNIDROIT Principles Comment 1.
[21] Art. 7.1.2 UNIDROIT Principles Comment 2.
[22] SCHLECHTRIEM/SCHWENZER/STOLL/GRUBER, *supra* note 5, Art. 80 para. 7; PETER RATHJEN, *Haftungsentlastung des Verkäufers oder Käufers nach Art. 79, 80 CISG*, RECHT DER INTERNATIONALEN WIRTSCHAFT 1999, pp. 561–565.
[23] Different view: SCHLECHTRIEM/STOLL, *supra* note 4, Art. 80 para. 5.
[24] STAUDINGER/MAGNUS, *supra* note 2, Article 80 para. 14; BIANCA/BONELL/TALLON, *supra* note 6, Art. 80 note 2.5; HERBER/CZERWENKA, *supra* note 6, Art. 80 para. 7; PETER RATHJEN, *supra* note 23, p. 561; Germany 21 March 1996 *Schiedsgericht der Handelskammer* [Arbitral Tribunal of the Chamber of Commerce] Hamburg Arbitration proceeding, available at <http://cisgw3.law.pace.edu/cases/960321g1.html>. In this case the buyer relies on a breach of a framework agreement between the seller and buyer. The Tribunal was weighing up the respective contributions of the parties to the failure of the framework agreement (i.e., mainly the refusal of both sides to comply with their duties arising from the sales contract).
[25] Namely, in cases in which the subject matter is not a pecuniary claim that could be reduced proportionately.

rely on the promisor's failure to perform if the former's contribution is preponderant to that of the latter.[26]

2. Clarification by Article 7.4.7 UNIDROIT Principles

Article 7.1.2 UNIDROIT Principles also does not expressly address the issue of a failure to perform caused by both parties. The only indication that this case is contemplated is – just as in Article 80 CISG – the formulation. "*to the extent* that such non-performance was caused by the first party's act or omission [. . .]" (emphasis added). However, in contrast to the CISG, the UNIDROIT Principles expressly address a similar situation in Article 7.4.7 dealing with "Harm due in part to aggrieved party." The counterpart provision in the CISG, Article 77, is restricted to mitigation of loss that has already occurred and does not expressly deal with the situation in which the occurrence of the harm is also due to the conduct of the promisor.[27] The basic approach of Article 7.4.7 UNIDROIT Principles is to assess the promisee's contribution to the harm and and to reduce the amount of damages correspondingly. Therefore, the conduct of the parties is also to be taken into account. It seems sensible to apply this approach under Article 7.1.2 UNIDROIT Principles as well. The only difficulty arises from the fact that Article 7.1.2 is not only applicable to damages but, like Article 80 CISG, also to all remedies. Consequently, the relevant adaption cannot always be implemented by reducing a pecuniary claim. However, Article 7.4.7 shows that the UNIDROIT Principles generally allow for an evaluation of the respective contributions of the parties to a non-performance and for a corresponding adaptation of the consequences of this non-performance. The Official Comments to Article 7.4.7 UNIDROIT Principles make clear that Article 7.1.2 is also based on this idea, naturally presuming that the provision comprises cases where the non-performance is in part caused by the promisee.[28] This result matches with the conclusion reached under Article 80 CISG. Therefore, the above analysis of the UNIDROIT Principles offers a plausible argument to interpret Article 80 CISG in that particular manner as well. Considering that the UNIDROIT Principles do provide a guideline in Article 7.4.7 on how to deal with causation of non-performance by both parties whereas the Convention is silent on this point, the UNIDROIT Principles could, concerning this matter, also be consulted in establishing the proper interpretive approach to be taken under Article 80 CISG.

V. EXTENT OF EXEMPTION

Article 80 CISG prohibits a party from relying on a failure of the other party to perform to the extent that such failure was caused by the first party. Two consequences can be deduced for the extent of exemption. First, the promisor is exempted from all legal consequences arising from this failure to perform, meaning the promisee may not resort to any remedy that is based on this failure to perform.[29] Other than Article 79 CISG, Article 80 CISG is not restricted to an exemption from damages, but the promisee is also barred from relying on another remedy[30] (e.g., price reduction, specific performance,

[26] STAUDINGER/MAGNUS, *supra* note 2, Art. 80 para. 14.

[27] Although it is not expressly stated in Article 77 CISG, the provision also requires the aggrieved party to take reasonable measures to avoid the occurrence of loss at all. SCHLECHTRIEM/STOLL, *supra* note 4, Art. 77 para. 6; STAUDINGER/MAGNUS, *supra* note 2, Art. 77 para. 8.

[28] Art. 7.4.7 UNIDROIT Principles Comment 1: "[. . .] the general principle established by Art. 7.1.2 which restricts the exercise of remedies where non-performance is *in part* due to the conduct of the aggrieved party, [. . .]" (emphasis added).

[29] SCHLECHTRIEM/STOLL, *supra* note 4, Art. 80 para. 10; VINCENT HEUZE, *supra* note 17, note 479; ENDERLEIN/MASKOW/STROHBACH, *supra* note 19, Art. 80 note 3.1.

[30] FRANCO FERRARI/HARRY FLECHTNER/RONALD BRAND, *supra* note 9, p. 840.

etc). Second, the promisor is exempted only *to the extent* the failure was caused by the promisee. This means that the promisee is not generally excluded from any remedy, but still can rely on any other failure of the promisor to perform not caused by the promisee. If, for example, the failure of the buyer to provide certain information concerning the shipping causes late delivery, the seller is exempted from damages due to the late delivery. However, this does not prevent the buyer from avoiding the contract if the seller fundamentally breached the contract by delivering non-conforming goods.[31]

The effect of Article 7.1.2 UNIDROIT Principles is similar. The exemption provided by this article is extended to all remedies,[32] but only to the extent the non-performance was due to the interference of the promisee. Article 7.1.2 UNIDROIT Principles is not applicable to cases in which the interference acts only as a partial impediment to performance and concerning a non-performance of any other obligation independently from the promisee's act or omission. Again, Article 80 CISG and its counterpart provision are basically equivalent so that the UNIDROIT Principles cannot introduce new aspects to the interpretation of Article 80 CISG.

VI. CONCLUSION

The comparison of Article 80 CISG and Article 7.1.2 UNIDROIT Principles shows a wide congruency between the two provisions. The relevant requirements and effects are basically the same. The issues to be resolved by interpretation are also similar, and the respective provisions do not indicate a certain direction for interpreting one another. However, where the formulation of Article 7.1.2 UNIDROIT Principles deviates from the one employed by Article 80 CISG and the result of interpretation is nevertheless the same, Article 7.1.2 UNIDROIT Principles can arguably be seen as an important affirmation of the proper interpretation of Article 80 CISG.

[31] *See* STAUDINGER/MAGNUS, *supra* note 2, Art. 80 para. 17.
[32] Art. 7.1.2 UNIDROIT Principles Comment 1: "When the article applies, the relevant conduct does not become excused non-performance but loses the quality of non-performance altogether."

Effects of avoidance and restitution of the goods: Remarks on the manner in which Articles 7.3.5 and 7.3.6 of the UNIDROIT Principles compare with Articles 81 and 82 of the CISG

Florian Mohs

I. INTRODUCTION AND TERMINOLOGY

Although the United Nations Convention on Contracts for the International Sale of Goods (hereinafter CISG) uses the term "avoidance" of contract[1] and the UNIDROIT Principles of International Commercial Contracts (hereinafter UNIDROIT Principles) use the term "termination" of contract,[2] both sets of rules deal with the same situation: one party has lost its interest in the contract due to a fundamental impairment in the performance[3] of the other party and puts an end to the contract. In contrast to this situation, the UNIDROIT Principles use the term "avoidance" of contract only in the context of a remedy available to the aggrieved party in the event of an invalid contract on grounds of mistake, fraud, threat, or gross disparity; see Art. 3 UNIDROIT Principles. According to Art. 29 CISG, "termination" under the Convention means cancellation of the contract by (mere) agreement of the parties. The following primarily provides a comparative overview of Arts. 81 and 82 CISG and Arts. 7.3.5 and 7.3.6 UNIDROIT Principles. On that basis, this chapter addresses whether the UNIDROIT Principles provisions can be used to help interpret or supplement the CISG articles on the issue of the effects of avoidance of contract.[4]

II. GENERAL EFFECTS OF AVOIDANCE UNDER CISG AND TERMINATION UNDER UNIDROIT PRINCIPLES

1. Art. 81 CISG Is Virtually Identical to Arts 7.3.5(1) to (3) and 7.3.6(1) UNIDROIT Principles

The general effects of avoidance under CISG are virtually the same as of termination under UNIDROIT Principles:

- First, both parties are released from their obligations under the contract, Art. 81(1) first sentence CISG/Art. 7.3.5(1) UNIDROIT Principles.[5]

[1] *Cf.* Art. 49 CISG for the buyer's right to avoid the contract, Art. 64 CISG for the seller's right of avoidance, and Arts 81 to 84 CISG for the effects of avoidance.

[2] *Cf.* Arts 7.3.1 to 7.3.6 UNIDROIT Principles. *But cf.* the German translation "Vertragsaufhebung," which equals the German translation of avoidance under CISG; critically to the German language Ernst v. Caemmerer, "Internationale Vereinheitlichung des Kaufrechts," *Schweizerische Juristen-Zeitung*, 257, 264 (1981); Christoph Coen, "Vertragsscheitern und Rückabwicklung – Eine Rechtsvergleichende Untersuchung Zum Englischen und Deutschen Recht, Zum UN-Kaufrecht Sowie Zu Den UNIDROIT Principles und Den Principles of European Contact Law," 210, 211 and at 225, 226 (2003).

[3] "Fundamental breach of contract" in CISG terminology and "fundamental non-performance" in UNIDROIT Principles terminology.

[4] The remainder of this chapter is based on the assumption that in general there are situations in which the UNIDROIT Principles can be used to help interpret the CISG; *see* Albert H. Kritzer, "General Observations," available at <http://cisgw3.law.pace.edu/cisg/text/matchup/general-observations.html>. *But cf.* Schlechtriem/Schwenzer/Ferrari, *Kommentar Zum Einheitlichen UN-Kaufrecht – CISG*, Art. 7 para. 59 *et seq.*, 62 (4 ed. 2004).

[5] On CISG, *see* Schlechtriem/Leser, "Commentary on the UN Convention on the International Sale of Goods (CISG)," Art. 81 paras. 8–10 (1st ed. 1998); Schlechtriem/Schwenzer/Hornung, *supra* note 4, Art. 81 para. 8. On UNIDROIT Principles, *see* Art. 7.3.5 UNIDROIT Principles Comment 1.

- Second, possible damages claims are not precluded, Art. 81(1) first sentence, second part CISG/Art. 7.3.5(2) UNIDROIT Principles.[6]
- Third, dispute settlement clauses are not affected, Art. 81(1) second sentence CISG/Art. 7.3.5(3) UNIDROIT Principles.[7]
- Fourth, even other clauses that operate after avoidance or termination are not affected, Art. 81(1) second sentence, second part CISG/Art. 7.3.5(3) second part UNIDROIT Principles.[8]
- Finally, under both sets of rules either party may claim restitution of what has been performed, Art. 81(2) first sentence CISG/Art. 7.3.6(1) first part of the sentence UNIDROIT Principles. If both parties have received anything under the contract, restitution will take place concurrently, Art. 81(2) second sentence CISG/Art. 7.3.6(1) second part of the sentence UNIDROIT Principles.

Apart from these similarities, there are, however, small differences in the language of these rules. The language of Art. 7.3.5(1) UNIDROIT Principles, which reads "[. . .] obligation *to effect and to receive future performance*" (emphasis added), is more specific than the text of Art. 81(1) CISG, which simply states that the parties are released "from their obligations." This difference in language raises two questions that are analyzed in this chapter.

2. The UNIDROIT Principles Do Not Release from Obligations of Performance Only

The term *performance* might, at a first glance, suggest a restrictive interpretation; that is, the parties are not released from all of their obligations but only from their obligations of *performance*. According to this interpretation, the parties would not be released from ancillary obligations (e.g., the right of sole distribution). However, the structure of the provision shows that the obligations that continue to exist are exhaustively identified by paras. (2) and (3) of Art. 7.3.5 UNIDROIT Principles. Thus, as does the CISG, the UNIDROIT Principles, in general, release the parties from *all* obligations under the contract except with respect to damages, dispute settlement, and other clauses that operate (even) after avoidance. Especially with the provision of para. (3), whether or not a clause qualifies under the prerequisites (e.g., the duty not to divulge confidential information or the duty to restrain from entering into competition) survive termination, is a question of contractual interpretation on a case-by-case basis.[9]

3. Restitution under CISG or UNIDROIT Principles and Domestic Law

The second difference in language is the inclusion of the term "*future* performance" in the UNIDROIT Principles provision, which, practically, points to the crucial question whether the seller, on termination, may claim repossession of goods under his title.[10]

[6] On CISG, *see* SCHLECHTRIEM/LESER, *supra note* 5, Art. 81 para. 10; SCHLECHTRIEM/SCHWENZER/HORNUNG, *supra note* 4, at Vor Artt. 81–84, paras. 7, 7a, 17 and Art. 81 para. 10. On UNIDROIT Principles, *see* Art. 7.3.5 UNIDROIT Principles Comment 2.

[7] On CISG, *see* Schlechtriem/Leser, *supra* note 5, Art. 81 para. 10; Schlechtriem/Schwenzer/Hornung, *supra* note 4, Art. 81 para. 10. On UNIDROIT Principles, *see* Art. 7.3.5 UNIDROIT Principles Comment 3. *Cf. Filanto S.p.A. v. Chilewich International Corp.*, U.S. Dist. Ct. (S.D.N.Y.), 14 April 1992, CISG-online No. 45 (*available at* <http://www.cisg-online.ch>), 789 F. Supp. 1229 where the Court held that Art. 81(1) CISG supports the doctrine of severability.

[8] On CISG, *see* Schlechtriem/Leser, *supra* note 5, Art. 81 para.10; Schlechtriem/Schwenzer/Hornung, *supra* note 4, Art. 81 para. 10. On UNIDROIT Principles, *see* Art. 7.3.5 UNIDROIT Principles Comment 3.

[9] *Cf.* Art. 7.3.5 UNIDROIT Principles Illustration 2. ICC, Case No. 9978/1999, CISG-online No. 708 (*available at* <http://www.cisg-online.ch>): penalty clauses survive contract avoidance under CISG.

[10] For practical relevance, *see* the CISG cases *Usinor Industeel v. Leeco Steel Products, Inc.*, U.S. District Court (N.D. of Illinois, Eastern Division), 28 March 2002, CISG-online No. 696 (*available at*

In other words, the question is whether avoidance causes the contract to cease to exist with the effect that, under certain domestic laws, ownership in the goods will automatically return to the seller. In legal doctrine, this issue is usually addressed by focusing on the concepts of *retroactivity* or *prospectivity*. According to the retroactive approach, the contract is void *ab initio* (*ex tunc*), which means that the parties are placed in the situation they would be in had the contract never been concluded.[11] By contrast, under the prospective approach, the contract remains in existence, with the restitutionary obligations being the reverse of the original obligations of performance.[12] This question of principle should be left open because one can disregard the theoretical questions, but should address the practical consequences.[13]

a. Remedy-Oriented Solution under CISG

It is my opinion that one must distinguish between two issues: on the one hand, the question is whether the seller may under domestic law claim repossession of the goods under his right to title. On the other hand, the question arises as to whether the seller may under domestic law make a claim for compensation or restitution of rights other than that to possess the goods.

<http://www.cisg-online.ch>), *reprinted in Internationales Handelsrecht*, 237–240 (2003) and *Roder Zelt- und Hallenkonstruktionen GmbH v. Rosedown Park Pty Ltd and Reginald R Eustace van Doussa J.*, Fca (Adelaide, SA), 28 April 1995, CISG-online No. 218 (*available at* <http://www.cisg-online.ch>).

[11] Authorities supporting the retroactive approach under CISG: Bianca/Bonell/Tallon, *Commentary on the International Sales Law*, Art. 81 note 2.5; Bernard Audit, *La Vente Internationale De Marchandises*, note 191 (1990); Vincent Heuzé, *La Vente Internationale De Marchandises – Droit Uniforme*, note 426 (2nd. ed. 2000); Claude Samson, *La Convention des Nations Unies sur les contrats de vente internationale de marchandises. Etude comparative des dispositions de la Convention et des règles de droit québécois en la matière*, 23 Les Cahiers de Droit (1982), 919, 962; Maria Angela Bento Soarez/Rui Manuel Moura Ramos, "Les moyens dont dispose l'acheteur en cas de contravention au contrat par le vendeur (autre que le défaut de conformité) dans la Convention de Vienne de 1980 sur les contrats de vente internationale de merchandises", *Revue de droit uniforme*, 67, 87 (1986); Philippe Kahn, "La Convention de Vienne du 11 avril 1980 sur les contrats de vente internationale de marchandises," *Revue internationale de droit comparé*, 951 978 (1981); *cf.* Roy Goode, *Commercial Law*, 933 footnote 35 (2nd. ed. 1995); Mirghasem Jafarzadeh, "Buyer's Right to Withhold Performance and Termination of Contract – A Comparative Study under English Law, Vienna Convention on Contracts for the International Sale of Goods 1980, Iranian and Shi'ah Law," *available at* <http://cisgw3.law.pace.edu/cisg/biblio/jafarzadeh1.html>, at Part Two § 2.5.1.

[12] *Cf.* Oberster Gerichtshof (Austrian Supreme Court), 29 June 1999, CISG-online No. 483 (*available at* <http://www.cisg-online.ch>); LG Düsseldorf (German Regional Court), 11 October 1995, CISG-online No. 180 (*available at* <http://www.cisg-online.ch>); Michael Bridge, *The International Sale of Goods*, para. 3.44 (1999): "As with termination in English Law, avoidance for breach operates with prospective effect"; Schlechtriem/Leser/Hornung, *Kommentar Zum Einheitlichen UN-Kaufrecht – CISG –* , Vor Artt. 81–84, para. 8 and Art. 81 para. 9 (3rd. ed. 2000); Peter Schlechtriem, *Internationales UN-Kaufrecht*, para. 330 (2nd. ed. 2003); Ernst v. Caemmerer, *Internationale Vereinheitlichung des Kaufrechts*, Schweizerische Juristen-Zeitung 257, 265 (1981); Staudinger/Magnus, *Kommentar Zum Bürgerlichen Gesetzbuch Mit Einführungsgesetz und Nebengesetzen, Wiener UN-Kaufrecht (CISG)*, Art. 81 para. 2 (1999); Bamberger/Roth, "Bürgerliches Gesetzbuch," Band 3, Art. 81 para. 4 (2003); Herber/Czerwenka, *Internationales Kaufrecht*, Art. 81 para. 7 (1991); Enderlein/Maskow/Strohbach, *Internationales Kaufrecht*, Art. 81 note 1 (1991); Bertrand Botzenhardt, "Die Auslegung Des Begriffs Der Wesentlichen Vertragsverletzung im UN-Kaufrecht," 61 (1998); Ulrich Ziegler, "Leistungsstörungsrecht Nach dem UN-Kaufrecht," 195 (1995); Botschaft Betreffend Das Wiener Übereinkommen Über Verträge Über Den Internationalen Warenkauf of 11 January 1989, at 235.51; Honsell/Weber, *Kommentar Zum UN-Kaufrecht*, Art. 81 paras. 1, 2 and 4 (1997). *See also* Liu Chengwei, "Remedies for Non-performance: Perspectives from CISG, UNIDROIT Principles & PECL," *available at* <http://cisgw3.law.pace.edu/cisg/biblio/chengwei.html>, at § 10.6.

[13] Schlechtriem/Schwenzer/Hornung, *supra* note 4, at Art. 81 Rn. 9 *et seq.*, 9d: "The language of Art. 81(2) CISG cannot be used to argue the one or the other way." *See also* Rainer Hornung, "Die Rückabwicklung Gescheiterter Verträge Nach Französischem, Deutschem Und Einheitsrecht – Gemeinsamkeiten, Unterschiede, Wechselwirkungen," 109, 110 (1998); Christoph Coen, *supra* note 2, at 216; Markus Krebs, "Die Rückabwicklung Im UN-Kaufrecht," 52, 53 (2000). *Cf.* G. H. Treitel, "Remedies for Breach of Contract, A Comparative Account," 383 (1988).

The first question can be answered in the affirmative, because there is no danger of contradiction with principles of the Convention. Rather, the principle of restitution under the Convention (returning the goods to the seller) is reinforced by domestic law that recognizes a replevin action where foreclosure against the buyer or insolvency of the buyer occurs.[14] The same is true in the situation in which the parties had contractually agreed on a retention of title clause under which the seller retains ownership in the goods until full payment has been made.[15] This solution is in accordance with Art. 4(b) CISG, which provides that the Convention is not concerned with questions as to the effect of avoidance on the property in the goods sold.

Yet, the second question is to be answered in the negative, because the questions concerning compensation for loss of use and compensation for expenses spent on the goods are settled exhaustively by the CISG itself.[16] First, with respect to compensation for loss of use, Art. 84 CISG applies. This Article grants the seller a claim for all benefits that the buyer derived from the goods. Second, although the Convention does not expressly address the issue of compensation for expenditure, general principles of the Convention can be used to fill this internal gap in accordance with Art. 7(2) CISG by way of a damages claim.[17] In the case of a retention of title clause the parties shall not be deemed to have implicitly derogated from the application of the CISG regime regarding restitution.

b. Prospective Approach under UNIDROIT Principles

Termination under UNIDROIT Principles has prospective effect. This becomes apparent when comparing the remedies of termination and avoidance *within* the UNIDROIT Principles. According to Art. 3.17(1) UNIDROIT Principles, "[a]voidance takes effect retroactively," which means that the contract should be regarded as never being concluded.[18] By contrast, in the case of termination of contract, the UNIDROIT Principles do not provide for *retroactive effect*, but rather refer to "*future* performance." This difference shows that termination of contract under UNIDROIT Principles only has *prospective effect*.[19]

[14] *But see* Schlechtriem, *supra* note 14, at para. 330, who argues for the prospective approach and states that, from the viewpoint of the domestic law regarding movable goods, this question, in terms of private international law, qualifies as an "incidental question" (*cf.* Peter M. North and James J. Fawcett, *Cheshire and North's Private International Law*, 46 *et seq.* (13th ed. 1999); another common term is "preliminary question"; *cf.* Martin Wolff, *Private International Law*, 206 (2nd ed. 1950)) and should be answered by recourse to the CISG.

[15] *Cf. Usinor Industeel v. Leeco Steel Products, Inc.*, U.S. District Court (N.D. of Illinois, Eastern Division), 28 March 2002, CISG-online No. 696 (*available at* <http://www.cisg-online.ch>), *reprinted in Internationales Handelsrecht*, 237–240 (2003): third-party creditor prevailed over seller under domestic law; *Roder Zelt- und Hallenkonstruktionen GmbH v. Rosedown Park Pty Ltd and Reginald R Eustace van Doussa J.*, FCA (Adelaide, SA), CISG-online No. 218 (*available at* <http://www.cisg-online.ch>): seller prevailed in buyer's insolvency. *Cf.* also Herbert Bernstein and Joseph Lookofsky, *Understanding the* CISG *in Europe*, §6–25 (2nd. ed. 2003). In Europe, according to Art. 4 of the Directive 2000/35/EC of the European Parliament and of the Council of 29 June 2000 on combating late payment in commercial transactions, each Member State's contract law has to provide for rules that accept and enforce retention in title clauses.

[16] *Cf.* ICC, Case No. 9978/1999, CISG-online No. 708 (*available at* <http://www.cisg-online.ch), where the Tribunal held that "reference to the rules of unjust enrichment of the applicable domestic law is neither necessary nor permissible." *But see* Daniel Friedrich Berg, "Die Rückabwicklung Gescheiterter Verträge Im Spanischen Und Deutschen Recht, Eine Rechtsvergleichende Untersuchung Unter Besonderer Berücksichtigung Des Einheitsrechts," 82 (2002), according to whom the concurrence should be resolved by applying the domestic law solution.

[17] *See* Botschaft Betreffend Das Wiener Übereinkommen Über Verträge Über Den Internationalen Warenkauf of 11 January 1989, at 235.53.

[18] *See* Art. 3.17 UNIDROIT Principles Comment 1; Christoph Coen, *supra* note 2, at 224.

[19] On the drafting process, *see* UNIDROIT Study L – Doc. 35, A&D 1986 II, Sn 8 f; Rainer Hornung, *supra* note 18, at 110, 111; Christoph Coen, *supra* note 2, at 251.

Now, one may argue that the UNIDROIT Principles' prospective approach is an international solution[20] and should thus be applied to the CISG as well. However, as shown previously in the discussion on CISG, it is not necessary to use the UNIDROIT Principles solution to interpret the CISG on this issue, because the question of principle can be left open and the practical consequences are answered by the Convention itself.

III. RESTITUTION OF GOODS AND RISK OF LOSS

1. Parties Bound to Restitution

Both sets of rules provide for restitution of what has been performed under the contract, Art. 81(2) CISG/Art. 7.3.6(1) first sentence UNIDROIT Principles.[21] Under the CISG, partial restitution is allowed expressly, whereas under the UNIDROIT Principles, this possibility must be deduced from the text.[22]

2. Bar of Avoidance or Allowance in Money

The main conceptual difference is that, according to Art. 82(1) CISG, the Convention, in principle, bars the buyer from avoiding the contract if he cannot make restitution of the goods, whereas the UNIDROIT Principles treat this situation as a question of liability, Art. 7.3.6(1) second sentence UNIDROIT Principles.[23] The CISG approach is based on a Roman law principle and was already antiquated at the time the Convention was drafted.[24] The approach of the UNIDROIT Principles is modern and, more importantly, sensible and has thus been incorporated into the Principles of European Contract Law[25] and into various domestic laws of contract by reform statutes (e.g., Netherlands,[26] Germany[27]). However, the CISG provisions must be applied *de lege lata* and thus cannot be overruled by means of interpretation using a totally different concept, such as that of the UNIDROIT Principles. Even in situations governed, but not expressly settled by the CISG, the principles *of the Convention* and not the principles of the UNIDROIT Principles are to be used to fill in any gaps. However, because of the wide range of exceptions to the bar of avoidance under Art. 82(2)(a) to (c) CISG and the objective equalization of benefits according to Art. 84(2) CISG, restitution under the two set of rules will quite often produce the same or, at least, a similar result. Furthermore, one should give broad application to the exceptions of para. (2) and thereby limit the bar of Art. 82(1) CISG.[28]

[20] The same approach shall apply to the Principles on European Contract Law, *see* Francesco G. Mazzotta, "Commentary on CISG Article 81 and PECL Article 9:309," *available at* <http://cisgw3.law.pace.edu/cisg/text/peclcomp81.html>.

[21] On CISG, *see* Schlechtriem/Schwenzer/Hornung, *supra* note 4, Art. 82 para. 11 *et seq.* On UNIDROIT Principles, *see* Art. 7.3.6 UNIDROIT Principles Comment 1.

[22] On CISG, *see* Schlechtriem/Schwenzer/Hornung, *supra* note 4, at Vor Art. 81–84 para. 14 *et seq.* On UNIDROIT Principles, *cf.* Christoph Coen, *supra* note 2, at 246.

[23] On the Principles on European Contract Law, *see* Francesco G. Mazzotta, *supra* note 24, at § 2.

[24] *Cf.* Peter Schlechtriem, "Some Observations on the United Nations Convention on Contracts for the International Sale of Goods," in *The Frontiers of Liability*, Vol. 2 (Peter Birks ed. 1994): "There are good reasons to advocate an entirely different solution for the problem of restitution or inability of the avoiding party to restitute, namely, treating this as a problem of responsibility of the parties for performance of their obligation to restitute and not as one of a bar to avoidance."

[25] *See* Art. 9:309 of the European Contract Principles; *cf.* Francesco G. Mazzotta, *supra* note 24.

[26] *See* Art. 6:265, 269, 271, and 272 of the Nieuw Burgerlijk Wetboek (Civil Code of the Netherlands).

[27] *See* § 346(2), (3) BGB (German Civil Code).

[28] *E.g.*, by holding that Art. 82(2)(b) CISG also covers improvements in the goods as a result of the examination, *see* Bundesgerichtshof (German Federal Supreme Court), 25 June 1997, CISG-online No. 277 (*available at* <http://www.cisg-online.ch>). *E.g.*, by interpreting "lack of conformity" within Art. 82(2)(c) CISG as covering also third-party claims based on intellectual property, *see* Florian Mohs, "The Restitution of Goods on Avoidance of the Contract for Lack of Conformity within the Scope of Art. 82(2)(c) CISG: On the Different Treatment of Defects in Quality, Third-Party Intellectual Property Rights, and Defects in Title as Elements

In the case of an agreement to mutual restitution, Art. 82 is excluded by implication.[29] In the case of a contract including the supply of services, which qualifies under Art. 3(2) CISG as a sales contract, restitution should be made by way of monetary reimbursement of the value of the services based on Art. 84(2) CISG.

IV. CONTRACTS EXTENDING OVER A PERIOD OF TIME

Art. 7.3.6(2) UNIDROIT Principles[30] provides that "if performance of the contract has extended over a period of time and the contract is divisible, [. . .] restitution can only be claimed for the period after termination has taken effect." However, a party can also, contrary to this misleading language, avoid with respect to the (past) defective performance. The counterpart provision of the Convention is Art. 73 CISG,[31] which, however, does not address the question of avoidance of contracts extending over a period of time in general, but does address the most relevant situation in international sales law practice (i.e., the contract for delivery of goods by installments).[32] The first step is to avoid the defective delivery only, Art. 73(1) CISG. If, however, the aggrieved party has good grounds to conclude that a fundamental breach will occur with respect to future installments it can, according to Art. 73(2) CISG, avoid on the grounds of anticipatory breach. Even under CISG, restitution will not take place for deliveries already made if the installments are independent, Art. 73(3) CISG. The CISG and the UNIDROIT Principles provisions will, however, quite often produce the same or, at least, similar results.[33]

The CISG provision has a narrower sphere of application, and for this specific case, the CISG text is more detailed and clearer than the UNIDROIT Principles text. Consequently, the UNIDROIT Principles cannot help in the interpretation of the CISG on the issue of avoidance of contracts extending over a period of time. In the case of a contract extending over a period of time but not qualifying as an installments contract (e.g., a contract calling for delivery of machines and on-site installation by seller's personnel that falls under the Convention according to Art. 3(2) CISG), a general right of avoidance has to be established in accordance with the principles of Art. 73 CISG.

V. CONCLUSION

In a comparison of the rules on restitution of both the CISG and the UNIDROIT Principles, one discovers that both sets of rules agree in the following ways: that restitution takes place on avoidance or termination of the contract, respectively; that partial restitution is possible; on the question of what contractual provisions survive avoidance of the contract;

of the Remedies for the Buyer," *Review of the Convention on Contracts for the International Sale of Goods (CISG) (2002–2003)*; in German: Florian Mohs, "Die Vertragswidrigkeit im Rahmen des Art. 82 Abs. 2 lit. c CISG," *Internationales Handelsrecht*, 59–66 (2002).

[29] *See* Peter Schlechtriem, *supra* note 14, at 323. *Cf.* Oberster Gerichtshof (Austrian Supreme Court), 29 June 1999, CISG-online No. 483 (*available at* <http://www.cisg-online.ch>).

[30] For the operation of Art. 7.3.6(2) UNIDROIT Principles, *see* Comment 3; Rainer Hornung, *supra* note 18, at 176, 177; *critically* Christoph Coen, *supra* note 2, at 246 *et seq.*

[31] For the operation of Art. 73 CISG, *cf.* Schlechtriem/Leser/Hornung, supra note 5, at Art. 73 paras 1–41. *But see* Liu Chengwei, *supra* note 14, at 10.6, according to whom the UNIDROIT Principles do not provide a counterpart to Art. 73 CISG. *Cf.* on the European Contract Principles Christopher Kee, "Remedies for Breach of Contract Where Only Part of the Contract Has Been Performed: Comparison between Provisions of CISG (Articles 51, 73) and Counterpart Provisions of the Principles of European Contract Law," *available at* <http://cisgw3.law.pace.edu/cisg/text/peclcomp51.html>.

[32] *But see* Art. 51 CISG, which addresses the case of partial deliveries although the contract called for performance at once.

[33] *Cf.* Daniel Friedrich Berg, *supra* note 16, at 160.

and that, if both parties had already received performance, restitution must be made concurrently. However, they do not correspond on the legal mechanism to apply in situations where it is impossible for the avoiding party to return what it had received under the contract: the CISG generally bars the aggrieved party from avoiding the contract, whereas the UNIDROIT Principles grants the other party allowance in money.

In conclusion, one cannot successfully argue that the UNIDROIT Principles can be used to help interpret or supplement the CISG on the issue of effects of avoidance of contract.

Freedom of contract: Comparison between provisions of the CISG (Article 6) and the counterpart provisions of the Principles of European Contract Law

Ulrich G. Schroeter

I. INTRODUCTION

CISG Article 6 lays down the general rule that the Convention applies to international contracts of sale of goods, subject to a contrary agreement by the parties. Its counterparts in PECL Articles 1:102 and 1:103 likewise address the principle of freedom of contract and its limitations, but differ from CISG Article 6 in several respects. These differences primarily follow from the different legal nature of the two sets of rules – whereas the CISG in its Contracting States forms part of the substantive law that the courts have to apply (*lex fori*), the applicability of the PECL in general requires an agreement of the parties to submit their contract to the Principles (PECL 1:101). However, these differences also reflect the different approaches adopted by the drafters of the CISG and the PECL to the limitations to the freedom of contract, in particular those limitations arising from so-called mandatory rules of law. As a consequence, the use of PECL Articles 1:102 and 1:103 as an aid to interpret CISG Article 6 is subject to several important caveats discussed below.

II. FREEDOM OF CONTRACT UNDER THE CISG AND THE PECL

The principle of freedom of contract, one of the basic principles underlying the international law of contracts in general, has been recognized by both the drafters of the CISG and of the PECL. The wording of CISG Article 6 and PECL Article 1:102(2) is in fact quite similar, and the prominent position of both provisions among the first articles in the Convention and the PECL illustrates the important role of the parties' autonomy.[1]

[1] *Cf.* Michael Joachim Bonell, Article 6, in *Commentary on International Sales Law*, no. 1.2 (Cesare Massimo Bianca & Michael Joachim Bonell eds., 1987): "the prevailing view in UNCITRAL was in favor of the widest possible recognition of the parties' autonomy"; Kurt Siehr, "Artikel 6," in *Kommentar zum UN-Kaufrecht*, no. 1 (Heinrich Honsell ed., 1997): the drafters of the CISG wanted to grant the parties wide discretion in drafting their contract; *see* also, Germany 12 October 2000 Landgericht [Regional Court] Stendal, *Internationales Handelsrecht* 2001, at 32, where the court stated that CISG Art. 6 affirms the principle of

Articles 1:101(2), (3) and 1:103(1) PECL additionally address a somewhat related issue: the choice of the PECL as the law applicable to the contract. This issue concerns the applicability of the respective set of rules. The question of applicability may also arise under the CISG, albeit in different form: although the PECL are only applicable where the parties have chosen the Principles and the law otherwise applicable allows such a choice, the Convention is applicable as a matter of law whenever the prerequisites of CISG Article 1(1)(a), (b) are fulfilled (and none of the exceptions in CISG Articles 2–5 apply).[2] The parties' choice of the CISG as the law applicable to their contract will therefore lead to the Convention's applicability under CISG Article 1(1)(b) if the rules of private international law of the forum (being situated in a Contracting State) accept the principle of party autonomy,[3] as they will under the private international law rules of most non-Contracting States.[4]

On the contrary, under CISG Article 1(1)(a), which covers cases where both parties have their places of business in different Contracting States (statistically by far the most important group of CISG contracts), any agreement of the parties or any other indication

party autonomy; for English translation of the text of this case, go to <http://cisgw3.law.pace.edu/cases/001012g1.html>.

[2] For agreements to apply the Convention to transactions that fall outside the scope of CISG Articles 1–5, *see* 4, *infra*.

[3] In practice, contractual choice of law clauses usually do not point to the Convention as such, but rather to the law of a certain State. If this State happens to be a Contracting State, the CISG will generally apply, as it forms part of the legal system of each Contracting State: *see* relevant case law, *e.g.*, Germany 23 July 1997 Bundesgerichtshof, [Federal Supreme Court], *Neue Juristische Wochenschrift* (1997) 3309, at 3310; case presentation in English available at <http://cisgw3.law.pace.edu/cases/970723g1.html>;
Austria 22 October 2001 Oberster Gerichtshof, [Supreme Court], 1 Ob 77/01, English translation available at <http://cisgw3.law.pace.edu/cases/011022a3.html>; U.S. Federal District Court [New York], 26 March 2002 (St. Paul Insurance *Company et al. v. Neuromed Medical Systems & Support et al.*), available online at <http://cisgw3.law.pace.edu/cases/020326u1.html>, where the court stated,

> The parties concede that pursuant to German law, the U.N. Convention on Contracts for the International Sale of Goods ("CISG") governs this transaction because (1) both the U.S. and Germany are Contracting States to that Convention, and (2) neither party chose, by express provision in the contract, to opt-out of the application of the CISG. The CISG aims to bring uniformity to international business transactions, using simple, non-nation specific language. To that end, it is comprised of rules applicable to the conclusion of contracts of sale of international goods. In its application regard is to be paid to comity and interpretations grounded in its underlying principles rather than in specific national conventions. See CISG art. 7(1), (2). Germany has been a Contracting State since 1991, and the CISG is an integral part of German law. Where parties, as here, designate a choice of law clause in their contract – selecting the law of a Contracting State without expressly excluding application of the CISG – German courts uphold application of the Convention as the law of the designated Contracting state. To hold otherwise would undermine the objectives of the Convention which Germany has agreed to uphold.

See also Franco Ferrari, "Artikel 6," in *Kommentar zum Einheitlichen UN-Kaufrecht*, no. 22 (Peter Schlechtriem & Ingeborg Schwenzer eds., 4th ed. 2004), with numerous references to international case law.

Whether an "isolated" choice of the CISG as the law applicable to the contract is valid and effective depends on the relevant conflict of law rule. Under the EC Convention of the Law Applicable to Contractual Obligations (Rome, 19 June 1980), this question is heavily disputed; *cf.* Kurt Siehr, "Der internationale Anwendungsbereich des UN-Kaufrechts", 52 Rabels *Zeitschrift für ausländisches und internationales Privatrecht* (1988), at 612. *See* also John O. Honnold, *Uniform Law for International Sales under the 1980 United Nations Convention,* no. 83 (3rd ed. 1999) who argues that full effect should be given to the parties' agreement to apply the Convention; similarly Ulrich G. Schroeter, "Arbitration under the Rules of the Chicago International Dispute Resolution Association (CIDRA)", *J. Int'l. Disp. Resol.* (2005), at 112.

[4] In States that have not ratified the Convention, the courts do not apply CISG Article 1(1)(b) – which, for lack of ratification, does not form part of the *lex fori* – but look to the national private international law rules. *Cf.* C. J. G. Morse, "Conflict of Laws," in *Benjamin's Sale of Goods*, no. 25–026 (Anthony Gordon Guest ed., 6th ed. 2002): "It is therefore possible that a United Kingdom court may have to apply the Vienna Convention on the International Sale of Goods 1980, if the law applicable under the Rome Convention is found to be the law of a country which is a party to that Convention and that country would regard that Convention as applicable." A choice of law clause will thus for all practical purposes yield identical results in Contracting States and non-Contracting States.

that the parties were even aware of the CISG's applicability is unnecessary[5] – the Convention is, unlike the PECL, not merely a model law or Restatement of principles of contract law, but is applicable by law whenever the parties have not excluded its application (so-called opting-out).[6]

III. RESTRICTIONS TO THE PARTIES' FREEDOM OF CONTRACT UNDER THE CISG AND THE PECL

More important differences exist with respect to the restrictions to which the CISG and the PECL submit the parties' freedom to exclude the respective set of rules and modify the effect of their provisions. The Principles list three different categories of restrictions.

1. Good Faith and Fair Dealing

According to PECL Article 1:102(1), the parties may determine the contents of their contract "subject to the requirements of good faith and fair dealing." CISG Article 6 does not contain a similar limitation to the freedom of contract. During the 1980 Vienna Diplomatic Conference, a proposal to add a second sentence to the wording of CISG Article 6 stating that "the obligations of good faith, diligence and reasonable care prescribed by this Convention may not be excluded by agreement" was rejected by a substantial majority.[7]

However, the principles of good faith and fair dealing may under certain circumstances also affect the content of CISG contracts, as may occur in the case where, according to the applicable national law, the validity of the contract or of any of its provisions (CISG Article 4(a)) is subject to these principles. A number of commentators hold that CISG Article 7 similarly requires that the principles of good faith and fair dealing are to be taken into account when determining the parties' rights and obligations under the contract, although this interpretation is subject to dispute.[8]

2. Mandatory Rules Established by the CISG/PECL Themselves

Second, PECL Article 1:102(1) and (2) subjects the freedom of contract to the mandatory rules established by these Principles. Such rules of a mandatory nature are contained in PECL Articles 4:118 (limiting the exclusion or restriction of remedies for fraud, threats, excessive benefit or unfair advantage-taking, mistake, and incorrect information), 6:105 (dealing with the determination of the price and other contractual terms where it is to be determined by one party and that party's determination is grossly unreasonable), and 8:109 (declaring the exclusion or restriction of remedies for non-performance inadmissible when it would be contrary to good faith and fair dealing to invoke that restriction).

[5] Alfonso-Luis Calvo Caravaca, "Articulo 6," in *La Compraventa Internacional de Mercaderias: Comentario de la Convencion de Viena*, at 100 (Luis Díez-Picazo y Ponce de León ed., 1998); Ferrari, *supra* note 3, no. 23; Burghard Piltz, *Internationales Kaufrecht* (1993), § 2 no. 108.

[6] Ferrari, *supra* note 3, no. 6; Ulrich Magnus, "Artikel 6," in Julius von Staudingers *Kommentar zum Bürgerlichen Gesetzbuch mit Einführungsgesetz und Nebengesetzen, Wiener UN-Kaufrecht* (CISG) (2005), no. 2.

[7] The Canadian proposal (A/Conf.97/C.1/L.10) as orally amended aimed at revising the draft of CISG Article 6 to read as follows: "The parties may exclude the application of this Convention or, subject to Article 11 [became CISG Article 12], derogate from or vary the effect of any of its provisions. However, except where the parties have wholly excluded this Convention, the obligations of good faith, diligence and reasonable care prescribed by this Convention may not be excluded by agreement." *See* U.N. Official Records (1981), p. 86.

CISG Art. 6 thus goes beyond the language of the Uniform Commercial Code § 1–102(3), which contains a restriction similar to the one mentioned above, *cf.* E. Allan Farnsworth, "Review of Standard Forms or Terms under the Vienna Convention," 21 *Cornell Int'l. L.J.* (1988) 439, at 441 note 8; also available online at <http://cisgw3.law.pace.edu/cisg/biblio/farns1.html>.

[8] This interpretation of CISG Article 7 seems doubtful to me. In this respect, *see* John Felemegas, "Editorial remarks on CISG Article 7," available online at <http://cisgw3.law.pace.edu/cisg/text/e-text-07.html>.

CISG Article 6, on the contrary, names CISG Article 12 as the one provision in the Convention that the parties may not derogate from, thus making Article 12 the only mandatory rule in the CISG.[9] Although some commentators have suggested that other provisions in the Convention (such as Articles 4,[10] 7,[11] 28,[12] and 89 *et seq.*[13]) are also mandatory despite not being mentioned in CISG Article 6, it is submitted that none of these articles effectively restricts the parties' freedom of contract:

From the outset, derogating from CISG Article 4 would make little sense, as it would lead to the Convention being applicable to questions of contractual validity and transfer of property on which it contains no rules.[14]

An agreement by the parties on principles of interpretation other than those in CISG Article 7 must be allowed under the parties' right to modify the Convention's provisions according to their own preferences.[15] Professor Bonell's argument against allowing parties to do away with CISG Article 7 via the autonomy given to them in CISG Article 6[16] seems, in the last analysis, unconvincing: CISG Article 6 expressly states that the parties may not only accept or exclude the Convention's application in toto but may also derogate from or vary the effect of any provision they consider undesirable, despite the fact that the drafters of the CISG included it. Whenever such a contractual modification of one of the CISG's articles occurs, a court judgment or arbitral award applying the Convention to that particular contract cannot be regarded as a persuasive precedent (which is to be taken into account by other courts under CISG Article 7) as it does not deal with the interpretation of the CISG's original rules, but merely with a modified version of the Convention. A scenario involving a contractual derogation from CISG Article 7 does in this respect not differ from cases where modifications of other provisions are at stake: should the parties – which, it is submitted, will rarely occur in practice – choose to have the CISG "as interpreted by German courts" or "as construed according to the principles of English law" govern their contract, this constitutes an admissible use of their party autonomy according to CISG Article 6, but deprives any judgment or arbitral award dealing with this contract of sale of its future persuasive value under CISG Article 7(1).

Under CISG Article 28, a court is not required to grant specific performance if, under its "own law," it would not do so. If the parties, by explicitly derogating from CISG Article 28 in their contract, have agreed on one or both parties' right to specific performance, it can be assumed that the court would carry out the agreement of the parties.[17]

[9] Rolf Herber, "Article 6," in *Commentary on the UN Convention on the International Sale of Goods*, no. 5 (Peter Schlechtriem ed., 1998); Vincent Heuzé, *La vente internationale de marchandises* (1992), no. 97; Honnold, *supra* note 3, no. 74; Helga Rudolph, *Kaufrecht der Export- und Importverträge* (1996), Art. 6 no. 1; Siehr, *supra* note 1, no. 11.

[10] Bonell, *supra* note 1, no. 3.4.

[11] Bonell, *supra* note 1, Article 7, no. 3.3, who argues that "any legislation has to be interpreted in accordance with the criteria specifically laid down in it or generally adopted within the legal system from which it emanates." This approach accepts that the parties to an international sales contract are free to choose between the application of the CISG and the application of a particular domestic law, but insists that once the contracting parties have accepted that their contract of sale is to be governed by the CISG, the provisions of the Convention must be applied in accordance with CISG Article 7, which provides the Convention's built-in interpretation rules.

[12] Bonell, *supra* note 1, no. 3.4; Ferrari, *supra* note 3, no. 9; Magnus, *supra* note 6, no. 28; Gert Reinhart, "UN-Kaufrecht" (1991), Art. 28 no. 3.

[13] Ferrari, *supra* note 3, no. 9.

[14] Ferrari, *supra* note 3, no. 11; Rudolph, *supra* note 9, no. 1.

[15] Ferrari, *supra* note 3, no. 10; Magnus, *supra* note 6, no. 55.

[16] *See supra* note 11.

[17] Amy H. Kastely, "The Right to Require Performance in International Sales: Towards an International Interpretation of the Vienna Convention," 63 *Wash. L. Rev.* (1988), at 642, also available online at

Although the parties cannot modify the Contracting States' obligations under public international law arising from CISG Articles 89 *et seq.*, they may modify the Final Provisions' effect on their own contract (e.g., by agreeing on the Convention's applicability although the prerequisites of CISG Article 100 are not met). CISG Articles 89 *et seq.* are thus subject to the parties' freedom of contract as far as they deal with the Convention's sphere of application in their particular case.[18]

Thus, the principle of contractual freedom in the Convention goes beyond its counterpart provision in the PECL. The absence of limitations similar to the mandatory PECL rules mentioned above should not come as a surprise as the Convention's scope is restricted to transactions and issues that, within the various domestic laws, are traditionally governed by provisions of a non-mandatory character,[19] whereas the PECL additionally deal, *inter alia,* with questions of contractual validity and are also intended to apply to contracts involving consumers.[20]

3. Mandatory Rules of National, Supranational, and International Law

The third and last category of restrictions to the freedom of contract under the PECL covers the mandatory rules of national, supranational, and international law (PECL Article 1:103(1), (2)).

According to PECL Article 1:103(1), national mandatory rules are applicable if the law otherwise applicable does not allow their exclusion by way of choice by the parties; PECL Article 1:103(2) requires courts and arbitrators to give effect to mandatory rules of national, supranational, and international law that are applicable irrespective of the law governing the contract (mandatory rules carried by a strong public policy, so-called directly applicable rules or *règles d'application immédiate*). The Principles thus demand that, when applying the law, a distinction is drawn between rules of a mandatory and non-mandatory nature; between mandatory rules of national, supranational, and international law; and between "ordinary" mandatory rules and *règles d'application immédiate* – decisions that can be difficult to make and will accordingly be often unforeseeable for the parties.[21]

Under the CISG, the situation is different: As far as matters governed by the Convention – either by way of an express provision or by way of its general principles identified in accordance with CISG Article 7(2) – are concerned, no mandatory rule of national, supranational, and international law may be applied.[22] This follows from the fact that the Contracting States have accepted an obligation under public international law to apply the Convention instead of any other legal rule wherever the Convention provides

<http://cisgw3.law.pace.edu/cisg/biblio/kastely1.html>; Ole Lando, "Article 28," in *Commentary on International Sales Law*, no. 3.1 (Cesare Massimo Bianca & Michael Joachim Bonell eds., 1987).

[18] *See* Siehr, *supra* note 1, no. 11.

[19] Bonell, *supra* note 1, no. 2.1; Calvo Caravaca, *supra* note 5, at 93; Honnold, *supra* note 3, no. 74.

[20] *Cf.* Ole Lando & Hugh Beale, "Introduction," in *Principles of European Contract Law, Parts I and II* (2000), at xxv. Purchases by consumers are excluded from the Convention's scope by virtue of CISG Article 2(a), although the CISG will apply if the seller neither knew nor ought to have known that the goods were bought for personal, family, or household use – a type of situation that may become more common as more consumers purchase goods over the Internet (Ulrich G. Schroeter, *UN-Kaufrecht und Europäisches Gemeinschaftsrecht – Verhältnis und Wechselwirkungen* (2005), § 6 no. 114 *et seq.*). Sales by consumers are, on the contrary, not excluded from the Convention's scope (Magnus, *supra* note 6, Artikel 2 no. 18).

[21] The vagueness of the term "mandatory" was also criticized during the discussions within UNCITRAL; *see* Honnold, *supra* note 3, no. 79.

[22] Fritz Enderlein & Dietrich Maskow, *International Sales Law* (1992), Art. 6 no. 3.1, also available online at <http://cisgw3.law.pace.edu/cisg/biblio/enderlein.html>; Herber, *supra* note 9, no. 24; Manuel Lorenz, "Artikel 6," in *International Einheitliches Kaufrecht: Praktiker-Kommentar und Vertragsgestaltung zum CISG*, no. 20 (Wolfgang Witz, Hanns-Christian Salger & Manuel Lorenz eds., 2000); Magnus, *supra* note 6, no. 55; Schroeter, *supra* note 20, § 15 no. 92.

uniform rules.[23] Thus, provisions outside the CISG are – irrespective of their mandatory or non-mandatory nature – superseded if their subject matter is already covered by the Convention.

As not all matters that are potentially relevant to international sales contracts are governed by the Convention, mandatory rules of national, supranational, and international law are to be given effect whenever a matter is outside the CISG's scope. In this respect, difficult questions may arise under CISG Article 4(a), which stipulates that "except as otherwise expressly provided in this Convention, it is not concerned with [. . .] the validity of the contract or of any of its provisions or of any usage." This provision seems to leave ample room for the application of mandatory rules that deal with questions of validity. However, CISG Article 4(a) sets out an important – and often overlooked – additional condition by requiring courts and arbitrators to establish in advance that the Convention is not itself concerned with the validity question regulated by the otherwise applicable mandatory provision. Accordingly, not all rules of national, supranational, or international law prescribing that a contract or one of its clauses is void or invalid are applicable to CISG contracts by virtue of CISG Article 4(a).[24]

Under CISG Article 4(a), it has thus to be taken into account not only whether the national provision has an effect on the validity of certain clauses in a CISG contract but also why the national law imposes the sanction of invalidity.[25] As a result, for instance, the doctrine on *vices cachés* under French law is inapplicable to CISG contracts, although it addresses the validity of contractual clauses limiting the seller's liability by defining rules on the lack of conformity of the goods on which the Convention itself contains an exhaustive regulation.[26] The same applies to the common law validity doctrine of consideration, which conflicts with the express language of CISG Article 29(1).[27] Both examples are indications of one of the Convention's main contributions to the modern law for international sales, which has been described by Ernst Rabel as "avoiding the awesome relics of the dead past that populate in amazing multitude" the national sales laws.[28]

[23] This has been aptly described by Professor Honnold as "the commitment that Contracting States make to each other: We will apply these uniform rules in place of our own domestic law on the assumption that you will do the same." Honnold, *supra* note 3, no. 103.2; *see* also Calvo Caravaca, *supra* note 5, at 100.

[24] Ferrari, *supra* note 3, Artikel 4 no. 13; Honnold, *supra* note 3, no. 65; Magnus, *supra* note 6, Artikel 4 no. 18; Peter Schlechtriem, "Article 4," in *Commentary on the UN Convention on the International Sale of Goods*, no. 13 (Peter Schlechtriem & Ingeborg Schwenzer eds., 2nd ed. 2005); Schroeter, *supra* note 20, § 6 no. 146. For an interesting discussion on how drafters of standard terms should deal with the interaction between the national rules on validity and the Convention, *see* Farnsworth, *supra* note 7, at 443 *et seq*. *See* also Germany 31 October 2001 Bundesgerichtshof, [Federal Supreme Court], Neue Juristische Wochenschrift (2002) 370, at 371 where the court ruled on the CISG's requirements for the inclusion of standard terms and conditions into contracts of sale; case presentation, including English translation and commentary available at <http://cisgw3.law.pace.edu/cases/011031g1.html>. The court held that CISG Article 8(2) requires the user of standard terms to transmit the respective text to the other party or make it available in another way, and justified its interpretation *inter alia* with the assumption that "a control of the content of standard terms and conditions under national law (CISG Article 4(a)) is not always guaranteed." Although the decision is likely to receive some criticism for imposing excessively strict requirements for the inclusion of standard terms, it indicates a tendency to limit the scope of the validity exception in CISG Article 4(a) in favor of the Convention's own rules.

[25] Schroeter, *supra* note 20, § 6 no. 156.

[26] Bernard Audit, *La vente internationale de marchandises: Convention des Nations-Unies du 11 avril 1980* (1990), at 115 *et seq*.; Heuzé, *supra* note 9, no. 100.

[27] Audit, *supra* note 26, at 32, 74; Heuzé, *supra* note 9, no. 201; Honnold, *supra* note 3, no. 204.1 *et seq*.; *see* also Peter Schlechtriem, "Artikel 29," in *Kommentar zum Einheitlichen UN-Kaufrecht*, no. 3 (Peter Schlechtriem & Ingeborg Schwenzer eds., 4th ed. 2004).

[28] Ernst Rabel, "The Hague Conference on the Unification of Sales Law," 1 *Am. J. Comp. L.* (1952), at 61. *See* also Honnold, *supra* note 3, no. 30: "One may delight in legal antiques and in the patina of ingenious circumlocutions that have had to substitute for fundamental reform but these aesthetics may not be appreciated by a modern merchant and, more especially, by his trading partner from a different legal tradition."

Other national mandatory rules remain applicable under CISG Article 4(a), but only under the condition that the CISG's provisions and fundamental principles are taken into account when they are applied to a CISG contract. If, for example, the national law declares clauses in general business terms invalid if they are incompatible with the essential principles of the rules from which the parties are derogating,[29] the relevant essential principles are those of the Convention.[30]

IV. RESTRICTIONS TO THE PARTIES' FREEDOM OF CONTRACT IN CASES WHERE THE CISG APPLIES SOLELY BECAUSE OF THE PARTIES' CHOICE ("OPTING-IN")

The limited relevance of mandatory rules of national, supranational, or international law for CISG contracts that has been outlined above (see 3c, *supra*), however only extends to international contracts of sale to which the Convention applies by virtue of CISG Articles 1–5. The legal situation is different where the parties have chosen the Convention's rules when the CISG would otherwise not be applicable: nothing in the CISG precludes such a contractual agreement leading to the applicability of the Convention (so-called opting-in).[31] Opting-in can be useful when two parties from non-Contracting States fail to reach agreement on which national law should govern their contract[32]; for example, where "string contracts" or "chain transactions" are at stake that involve parties from CISG Contracting States and from non-Contracting States alike and that may therefore be only partially subject to the Convention if no explicit choice in favor of the CISG is made.[33] Opting-in may be inserted into distribution contracts or other frame contracts applying to sales to international and domestic customers alike.[34]

Thus, whenever the CISG applies solely because of the parties' choice and without the requirements of CISG Articles 1–5 having been met, mandatory rules of national, supranational, or international law remain relevant and need to be applied by courts and arbitrators,[35] as in these cases the CISG resembles the PECL and other Restatements.[36] Accordingly, in such a setting, PECL Article 1:103 may be used as an aid in interpreting or supplementing the CISG.

[29] *See* for example § 307(2) Nr. 1 of the German Civil Code.

[30] Herber, *supra* note 9, no. 28; Robert Koch, "Wieder den formularmäßigen Ausschluss des UN-Kaufrechts," *Neue Juristische Wochenschrift* (2000), at 910; Lorenz, *supra* note 22, no. 14; Magnus, *supra* note 6, Artikel 4 no. 26; Piltz, *supra* note 5, § 2 no. 140); Schroeter, *supra* note 20, § 15 no. 101.

In Austria 7 September 2000 Oberster Gerichtshof [Supreme Court], *Recht der Wirtschaft* (2000), no. 9, the court held that the parties can derogate from CISG Article 49(1) and restrict the buyer's rights under the condition that these clauses are valid under the applicable domestic (here: German) law according to CISG Article 4. However, even if the changes are valid according to the rules of the applicable domestic law, such rules must not contradict the fundamental principles (Grundwertungen) of the CISG. The Court stated that one of the CISG's fundamental principles is the right for the buyer to avoid the contract, which the buyer must have as *ultima ratio* where the seller after an additional period of time still has not delivered the goods or where the goods in spite of the seller's remedies are still essentially useless. This right to avoid the contract can only be validly restricted if the buyer at least retains the right to damages. Case presentation available in English at <http://cisgw3.law.pace.edu/cases/000907a3.html>.

[31] Audit, *supra* note 26, at 41; Enderlein & Maskow, *supra* note 22, Art. 6 no. 3.2; Honnold, *supra* note 3, no. 79 *et seq.*; Lorenz, *supra* note 22, no. 21; Reinhart, *supra* note 12, Art. 6 no. 9; Schlechtriem, *supra* note 24, Article 6 no. 13. For the discussions during the 1980 Vienna Diplomatic Conference, *see* U.N. Official Records (1981), p. 252 *et seq.*

[32] Calvo Caravaca, *supra* note 5, at 100; Reinhart, *supra* note 12, Art. 6 no. 89.

[33] Audit, *supra* note 26, at 41; Honnold, *supra* note 3, no. 82; Lorenz, *supra* note 22, no. 21; Burghard Piltz, "Entscheidungen des BGH zum CISG," *Internationales Handelsrecht – Beilage zu der Zeitschrift Transportrecht* (1999), at 14.

[34] Audit, *supra* note 26, at 40; Heuzé, *supra* note 9, no. 125; Schroeter, *supra* note 20, § 6 no. 252.

[35] Audit, *supra* note 26, at 41; Bonell, *supra* note 1, no. 3.5.1; Calvo Caravaca, *supra* note 5, at 101; Enderlein & Maskow, *supra* note 22, Art. 6 no. 3.2; Heuzé, *supra* note 9, no. 127; Honnold, *supra* note 3, no. 84; Reinhart, *supra* note 12, Art. 6 no. 9; Schlechtriem, *supra* note 31, no. 13; *contra* Lorenz, *supra* note 22, no. 21; Siehr, *supra* note 1, no. 15.

[36] Honnold, *supra* note 3, no. 84; Magnus, *supra* note 6, nos. 62, 65; Rudolph, *supra* note 9, no. 9.

V. CONCLUSIONS

Although the parties' freedom of contract plays a very important role within both the CISG and the PECL, the two instruments are marked by several important differences that concern the legal restrictions to the parties' autonomy. The legal nature of the CISG as an international convention has allowed its drafters to go beyond the limits laid down in PECL Articles 1:102 and 1:103.[37] The specific scope of the freedom of contract under CISG Article 6 therefore makes it difficult to use the PECL as an aid to the interpretation of the said CISG provision.

[37] *See* also Rudolph, *supra* note 9, no. 1: CISG Article 6 grants the parties more freedom than most national laws do; Farnsworth, *supra* note 7, at 441 note 8 (for the U.C.C.).

Comparison between the provisions regarding the concept of good faith in CISG Article 7 and the counterpart provisions of the PECL

John Felemegas

I. GENERAL SCHEME OF INTERPRETATION AND SUPPLEMENTATION IN THE CISG AND PECL

The nature and content of PECL Art. 1:106, as well as its function within the instrument to which it belongs, are very similar to those of CISG Art. 7. In both cases, the respective provisions provide the built-in interpretation and supplementation mechanism that the drafters have embedded in their corresponding instruments. The relevant provisions provide that the interpretation of the law in both instruments must pay regard to the concept of good faith.[1]

The Notes to PECL Art. 1:106(1) confirm that the basic elements found in the structure of Art. 1:106 either are virtually identical or express similar ideas to the ones of the corresponding provision in CISG Art. 7(1).[2]

II. GOOD FAITH AND FAIR DEALING IN THE INTERPRETATION OF THE CONTRACT

The concept of "good faith and fair dealing" does not operate merely as a rule of interpretation of each PECL article. The duty of good faith, as this is embedded in PECL Art. 1:201, is mandatory on the parties.[3]

[1] *See* CISG Art. 7(1); PECL Art. 1:106(1).

[2] *Cf.* PECL Art. 1:106 (1), CISG Art. 7(1). The wording of the two provisions is similar, although PECL Art. 1:106, in addition to the "good faith" and "uniformity of application" that are also prescribed by CISG Art. 7, includes the promotion of "certainty in contractual relationships" as a further relevant factor in the interpretation of the PECL provisions. *See* PECL Art. 1:106(2), which refers to domestic law as an ultimate source of supplementation; *see* also CISG Art. 7(2). The PECL Notes on Art. 1:106, in Ole Lando & Hugh Beale eds., *Principles of European Contract Law: Parts I and II*, Kluwer Law International (2000) 108–121, also available online at <http://cisgw3.law.pace.edu/cisg/text/peclcomp7.html#cnpc>, state that "[t]his is in accordance with CISG art. 7(2)". *See* Note 4.

[3] The PECL Comments make it clear that "good faith" is not confined to specific rules and further elucidate the concept by stating that the concept's purpose is "to enforce community standards of decency, fairness

In contrast to CISG Art. 7(1) (or any other CISG provision), PECL Art. 1:201 imposes upon each party a positive duty of good faith and fair dealing in exercising its rights and performing its duties under the contract. The PECL Comments to Art. 1:201 not only refer to good faith as "a basic principle running through the Principles" but also expressly state that "[g]ood faith and fair dealing are required in the formation, performance and enforcement of the parties' duties under a contract, and equally in the exercise of a party's rights under the contract" (see PECL Comment A).

In contrast, the Vienna Convention does not contain any express provision that the individual contract has to obey the maxim of good faith.[4] The text of CISG Art. 7(1) covers only the application of the Convention, rather than the parties' rights and obligations and their exercise and performance directly. The wording was agreed upon only after lengthy deliberations, and it was meant as a final rejection of more far-reaching proposals to apply the principle of "good faith and fair dealing" to the obligations and the behavior of the parties themselves.

There is, however, a strong body of academic opinion holding that the evaluation of the relations, rights, and remedies of the parties could also be subject to the principle of good faith and fair dealing. In accordance with this view, in addition to its interpretative role on the CISG provisions, good faith has at times been recognized as one of the general principles laid down by the Convention,[5] and further, it has found its way into the operation of CISG Art. 7(2).[6]

The concept's innate definitional difficulties are accentuated by the maxim's suggested dual role in the CISG – its operation in the Convention's interpretation (in the context of CISG Art. 7(1)) and its gap-filling mechanism (in the context of CISG Art. 7(2)).

and reasonableness in commercial transactions [. . .]. It supplements the provisions of the Principles, and it may take precedence over other provisions of these Principles when a strict adherence to them would lead to a manifestly unjust result" (*see* PECL Comment B). Note, however, that PECL Comment G unequivocally states that the courts may limit this duty in particular cases in order to preserve the overriding objectives of "certainty and predictability in contractual relationships." As far as the Convention is concerned, the principle of party autonomy (CISG Art. 6) is the dominant general principle. *See, e.g.*, John O. Honnold, *Uniform Law for International Sales under the United Nations Convention* 47 (2nd ed. 1991); Albert H. Kritzer, *Guide to Practical Applications of the United Nations Convention on Contracts for the International Sale of Goods* 115 (1989).

[4] Such a provision was proposed and rejected at the 1980 Vienna Diplomatic Conference; *see* U.N. *Official Records* (1981), p. 86.

[5] CISG Art. 7(1). *See, e.g.*, Bernard Audit, *La Vente Internationale de Marchandises: Convention des Nations Unies du 11 Avril 1980* [The International Sales of Goods, UN Convention of 11 April 1980] 51 (1990), where the author states that good faith is one of the general principles, even though it must be considered a mere instrument of interpretation. *See also* Enderlein & Maskow, *International Sales Law* (1992) at 59, where the authors list the good faith principle among those principles "which do not necessarily have to be reflected in individual rules"; Rolf Herber & Beate Czerwenka, *Internationales Kaufrecht. Kommentar zu dem Übereinkommen der Vereinten Nationen vom 11 April 1980 über Vertrage über den Internationalen Warenkauf* [International Sales Law, Commentary on the United Nations Convention on Contracts for the International Sale of Goods 49] (1991), where it is stated that the good faith principle is the only general principle expressly provided for by the Convention.

[6] As to the possibility of using the principle of "good faith and fair dealing" on the basis of CISG Art. 7(2) as a rule for the contractual relations between the parties, *see* E. Allen Farnsworth, "Duties of Good Faith and Fair Dealing under the UNIDROIT Principles, Relevant Conventions and National Laws," 3 *Tul. J. Int'l & Comp. L.* (1995), 56. *See also* Michael Joachim Bonell, "General Provisions: Article 7," in *Commentary on International Sales Law*, at 85, stating "[y]et, notwithstanding the language used in article 7(1), the relevance of the principle of good faith is not limited to the interpretation of the Convention . . . if during the negotiating process or in the course of the performance of the contract a question arises for which the Convention does not contain any specific provision and the solution is found in applying, in accordance with article 7(2), the principle of good faith."; Joseph Lookofsky, *Understanding the CISG in the USA* 19, §2–10 (1995), stating "[a]nd since other (very) general CISG principles of loyalty and reliance-protection have also been deduced, the deduction of a general Convention principle requiring the parties to act in good faith seems no great leap, even if it does seem to fly in the face of the *traveaux préparatoires*." *See also* Arthur Rosett, "Critical Reflections on the United Nations Convention on Contracts for the International Sale of Goods," 45 *Ohio St. L.J.* 265 (1984).

III. EXAMPLES OF SPECIFIC MANIFESTATIONS OF GOOD FAITH IN THE CISG AND PECL

The Convention provides that a contract may usually be concluded, modified, or terminated without any formal requirements (see CISG Arts. 11, 29(1); *cf.* CISG Arts. 12, 96). The PECL also have a similar regime (see PECL Art. 2:101(2)).[7]

Both instruments allow for an exception to this regime, based on the principle of good faith. A party may be precluded by his conduct from asserting such a clause to the extent that the other party has reasonably relied on that conduct. One of the general principles upon which the Convention is based relates to the duty of cooperation, according to which the parties must cooperate "in carrying out the interlocking steps of an international sales transaction."[8] This duty is closely related to the principle that a party cannot contradict a representation on which the other party has reasonably relied[9] – that is, the parties must not act *venire contra factum proprium.*[10]

However, unlike the Convention, the PECL also provide stringent rules on pre-contractual negotiations emanating from the concept of good faith: continuing or breaking off pre-contractual negotiations "contrary to good faith"makes the offending party liable for losses caused to the other party (PECL Art. 2:301(2)).[11]

In addition to the negotiation and pre-contractual stage, the concept of good faith in the PECL also manifests itself prominently in the manner in which the PECL deal with issues of material validity[12] that the Convention leaves untouched (see CISG Art. 4(a)). Elements of good faith can be found in the operation of certain Convention provisions.[13] For instance, the parties' express contractual obligations contain elements that can be identified as manifestations of a broader principle of good faith.[14]

[7] However, note that according to PECL Art. 2:106(1), a written modification clause establishes "*only a presumption* that an agreement to modify or terminate the contract is not intended to be legally binding unless it is in writing" (emphasis added). On the other hand, CISG Art. 29(2) states that contracts containing written modification clauses "may not be otherwise modified or terminated by agreement . . . "

[8] Kritzer, *supra* note 3, at 115. *See also* CISG Arts. 32(3), 48(2), 60(a), and 65. *Cf.* PECL Art. 1:202, which expressly imposes on the parties a duty to cooperate with each other in order to give full effect to the contract. It is stated in the Notes to the PECL that the duty to cooperate is derived from the principle of good faith and fair dealing (*see* PECL Note 1).

[9] On contractual formation, both the CISG and the PECL provide that an offer is irrevocable once the offeror has created a situation in which the offeree reasonably relied on the offer as irrevocable and acted in reliance on the offer; *cf.* PECL Art. 2:202(3); CISG Art. 16(2)(b). *Cf. also* PECL Art. 2:106(2) and CISG Art. 29(2), which provide a different illustration of the same point for contractual modification or termination.

[10] For similar affirmations, *see, e.g.*, Gyula Eörsi, "General Provisions," in *International Sales: The United Nations Convention on Contracts for the International Sale of Goods*, ch. 2, at 2–12 (Nina M. Galston & Hans Smit eds., 1984); Rolf Herber, "Article 7," in *Commentary on the UN Convention on the International Sale of Goods* 9, 99 (Peter Schlechtriem ed., 1998); Dietrich Maskow, "The Convention on the International Sale of Goods from the Perspective of the Socialist Countries," in *La Vendita Internazionale, La Convenzione di Vienna dell'* 11 Aprile 1980 (1981) 41, 57.

[11] PECL Art. 2:301(3) states, "It is contrary to good faith and fair dealing, in particular, for a party to enter into or continue negotiations with no real intention of reaching an agreement with the other party." *See also* PECL Art. 2:302, which provides a remedy for breach of confidentiality in the course of negotiations. For comments on pre-contractual liability under the CISG, refer to "Pre-Contract Formation," A. H. Kritzer ed., available at <http://cisgw3.law.pace.edu/cisg/biblio/kritzer1.html>.

[12] *See, e.g.*, PECL Art. 4:109, providing that a party may avoid the contract if the other party takes unfair advantage of the former party's dependence, economic distress, or other weakness.

[13] There are numerous applications of the good faith principle in particular provisions of the Convention; *see* the examples offered in the Secretariat Commentary to the Draft Convention as manifestations of the concept (e.g., CISG Arts. 16(2)(b), 21(2), 29(2), 37, 38, 40, and 85–88); Text of Secretariat Commentary on Article 6 of the 1978 Draft *[draft counterpart of CISG article 7(1)]*, available at: <http://cisgw3.law.pace.edu/cisg/text/secomm/secomm-07.html>. Note also, that the Secretariat Commentary states, "The principle of good faith is, however, broader than these examples and applies to all aspects of the interpretation and application of the provisions of this Convention", *id.* at 4.

[14] *See* CISG Art. 35(3), which provides that the seller is not liable for any lack of conformity of the goods if at the time of the conclusion of the contract the buyer knew or could not have been unaware of the non-conformity.

The PECL are "... intended to be applied as general rules of contract law" (PECL Art. 1:101(1)), and thus they contain no comparable express obligations. Conversely, the PECL expressly state that contractual obligations may be implied under the concept of good faith and fair dealing (PECL Art. 6:102(c)), whereas there is no comparable rule in the Convention's provisions.

The argument in favor of extending the scope of good faith to the behavior of the parties and attributing to it the quality of a "general principle" of the CISG[15] runs the risk of being driven to the conclusion that, as such, the principle of good faith in Art. 7(2) may even impose on the parties "additional obligations of a positive character."[16]

The possibility of imposing on the parties additional obligations is clearly not supported by the legislative history of the Sales Convention.[17] CISG Art. 7(1), as it now stands in the text of the Convention, is the result of a drafting compromise between two diverging views, which reflects the political and diplomatic maneuvering necessary for the creation of an international convention. It cannot now be given the meaning originally suggested by those advocating the imposition of a positive duty of good faith on the parties (i.e., the role of good faith under PECL Art. 1:201), as this runs contrary to the letter of the law and its legislative history.[18]

IV. CONCLUSIONS

Good faith occupies an integral position in the interpretation and supplementation of the CISG and the PECL. The concept of good faith is called upon in the CISG to guide the interpretation of the unified law text itself, whereas in the PECL it prescribes the behavior of the parties in every specific contract.

[15] *See* Isaak I. Dore & James E. De Franco, "A Comparison of the Non-Substantive Provisions of the UNCITRAL Convention on the International Sale of Goods and the Uniform Commercial Code," 23 *Harv. Int'l. L.J.* 49, 61 (1982), where the authors state that the good faith provision does not constitute a mere instrument of interpretation, but rather it "appears to be a pervasive norm analogous to the good faith obligation of the U.C.C." *Id.*

[16] Bonell, *op.cit.*, at 85. According to Bonell, "this will be the case, if during the negotiating process or in the course of performance of the contract a question arises for which the Convention does not contain any specific provision and the solution is found in applying, in accordance with Art. 7(2), the principle of good faith." *Id.*

[17] *Cf.* a case decided in Colombia 10 May 2000 *Corte Constitucional* [Constitutional Court], case presentation including English translation available at <http://cisgw3.law.pace.edu/cases/000510c7.html>. In that case, the Constitutional Court of Colombia established the validity of the CISG in Colombia by declaring valid Colombia Law Number 518 of 1999, which approved the Convention. In regard to good faith, in the course of its opinion the court stated, "[T]he exercise of the commercial activity that the individuals develop with other citizens of different States must fit the principle of good faith, just as the Convention stipulates in paragraph number one of Art. 7. This principle should not only be observed in the contractual relationships or negotiations, but in the relationships between individuals and the State and in the procedural performances"; at *V. Considerations and Foundations, 3. Constitutionality of the Convention, Id.* In other words, the Colombian court, in accordance with the good faith postulate found in Art. 83 of the Constitution of Colombia, appears to have treated the concept of good faith as expansively as it is treated under the PECL.

The provisions in Art. 7 CISG have received extensive treatment in the case law. *See* presentation of more than 270 cases on Art. 7, available online at <http://cisgw3.law.pace.edu/cisg/text/anno-art-07.html> [visited: 2 May 2005].

See also UNCITRAL Digest of Art. 7 case law, available at <http://cisgw3.law.pace.edu/cisg/text/anno-art-07.html#ucd>.

[18] *See also* Disa Sim, "The Scope and Application of Good Faith in the Vienna Convention on Contracts for the International Sale of Goods" (Sept. 2001), at <http://cisgw3.law.pace.edu/cisg/biblio/sim1.html>. The author provides a thorough discussion of the scope and application of the doctrine of good faith in the CISG, concluding that "... good faith can be said to play two roles in the Convention. Firstly, it is a compendious term for the collection of more specific 'good faith' principles that can be used to resolve matters governed by the Convention but not expressly resolved by it. Secondly, these very same principles can be used to resolve questions of textual ambiguity. There does not exist, however, a general doctrine of good faith that can serve as a fount of additional rights and obligations."

The two instruments, apart from a generic textual affinity, have many similarities in origin and substance, as well as a common purpose, which is the unification of international commercial law. Although the PECL could aid the interpretation and application of the CISG where it can be shown that their respective provisions share a common intent, I maintain that the concept of good faith has a different and distinct role in the Convention. As such, good faith in the context of CISG will acquire its own and unique identity with the further development of relevant CISG case law.[19]

Although particular applications of the concept of good faith are present in various settings of the contractual relationship as conceived by the PECL – and to a lesser extent by the CISG as well – the definitional and functional parameters of the concept of good faith in the CISG cannot be provided by a simple synthesis of the relevant provisions in these two instruments.[20]

It is submitted that the concept of good faith in the CISG, as it stands presently, is circumscribed to the interpretation of the law and should not be allowed to impose additional duties of a positive nature to the parties, as it does in the PECL. This limited reading of the role of good faith in the CISG is clearly the one supported by the text and the legislative history of the Convention.

[19] Professor Schlechtriem has commented that the importance of the general principle of "good faith and fair dealing" and the details developed out of it depend on the structure and content of the specific legal system in which they are implemented and on the concrete and specific contract in question. *See* Peter Schlechtriem, "Good Faith in German Law and in International Uniform Laws," *in* Saggi, Conferenze e Seminari No. 24 (Centro di studi e ricerche di diritto comparato e straniero & Michael Joachim Bonell eds., 1997), *available at* <http://soi.cnr.it/~crdcs/crdcs/frames24.htm>.

[20] *Contra* Ulrich Magnus, "Editorial Remarks," in Guide to Article 7 (*available on* the Pace Web site: <http://cisgw3.law.pace.edu/cisg/principles/uni7.html>. Professor Magnus's analysis relates to a comparison between Art. 7 CISG and corresponding Arts. 1.6 and 1.7 of the UNIDROIT Principles. However, the value of that analysis is pertinent to our own comparative study, as both the UNIDROIT Principles of International Commercial Contracts (1994) and the Principles of European Contract Law (PECL) (complete and revised version 1998) are in the form of international Restatements of Contracts, and as such they can be regarded as companions to the CISG. Professor Magnus is of the opinion that the UNIDROIT Principles can aid in the interpretation of the Convention's provisions and states that "the Principles can help to clarify the actual object of the good faith principle contained in the CISG." *Id.*, at para. 10.

Interpretation of the contract: Editorial remarks on the manner in which the PECL may be used to interpret or supplement CISG Article 8

Maja Stanivukovic

I. THE SUBJECT MATTER OF INTERPRETATION

a. Two kinds of interpretation that both the Convention and the Principles of European Contract Law deal with should always be distinguished – first, the interpretation of their own provisions, subject to Art. 7(1) CISG and Art. 1:106 PECL, respectively, and second, the interpretation of the contract, subject to Art. 8 CISG and Art. 5:101 PECL *et seq*., respectively.[1]

b. Nowhere does the Convention mention the interpretation of the contract, however, but rather speaks of interpretation of unilateral statements and conduct of each party (see Art. 8 paras. (1) and (2): "statements made by and other conduct of a party are to be interpreted").[2] In contrast, the Principles expressly state that the contract is the subject matter of interpretation (see Art. 5:101 para. (1): "a contract is to be interpreted"; para. (2): "that one party intended the contract to have a particular meaning," "the contract is to be interpreted"; and para. (3) "the contract is to be intepreted"). It is beyond doubt, however, that Art. 8 CISG is also concerned with interpretation of the contract,[3] no matter whether it is a contract made through an exchange of communications, a single instrument supplied by one party and accepted by the other, a contract drafted and signed by both parties jointly, or a contract concluded in some other way.[4] This difference between the CISG and PECL is in expression and emphasis only. The European Principles are more bilaterally oriented in their formulation, starting from the common intention of the parties[5] and finishing by applying the standard of reasonableness to both parties.[6] In contrast, the Convention concentrates on cases in which one party has had a more active role in the preparing of the contractual instrument. In Art. 8, the Convention puts stress on the intention of each individual party and on the understanding that the other party would have attributed to its statements and conduct.[7] Although the Principles too allow for the possibility of one party's intention to prevail, even when different from the literal meaning of the words, this figures as an exception to the general rule of mutual intention.[8]

The practical importance of this difference may appear in the case of contracts in which both parties fully participated in the drafting of the contractual instrument. Paragraphs (1) and (2) of Art. 8 CISG would seem to be inapplicable to such an instrument, because they differentiate between the one who makes a statement and the one who receives it,[9] whereas Art. 501 PECL would be fully applicable. One reason for the different

[1] The Comment to Art. 5:101 PECL also mentions completive interpretation as a process akin to regular interpretation of a contract, but it is intended for filling the gaps that may arise in the contract. This can be done by resorting to implied obligations in accordance with Art. 6.102(c) PECL. There is no comparable provision in the Convention. The closest CISG equivalent that can be used for completive interpretation is Art. 9 CISG.

[2] Secretariat Commentary on Art. 7 of the 1978 Draft, Official Records, p. 18, paragraph 2.

[3] This is borne out by the emerging case law on the CISG. As of 30 April, the cisgw3 Web site reports 1,500 cases <http://cisgw3.law.pace.edu/cisg/text/casecit.html>, cases that reflect an abundance of express or implicit attention to Art. 8 CISG by judges and arbitrators, including rulings that draw on this provision to assist in the interpretation of the contract as well as the intention of the parties. UNCITRAL cites forty-one cases in its Digest of Art. 8 case law (also available online at <http://cisgw3.law.pace.edu/cisg/text/anno-art-08.html#ucd>). For a presentation of a composite list of Art. 8 cases reporting UNCITRAL Digest cases and other Art. 8 cases go to <http://cisgw3.law.pace.edu/cisg/text/anno-art-08.html>.

[4] Secretariat Commentary on Art. 7 of the 1978 Draft, Official Records, p. 18, paragraph 2; J. Honnold, *Uniform Law for International Sales under the 1980 United Nations Convention*, Second Edition, Kluwer Law and Taxation Publishers, Deventer, Boston 1991, p. 163; J. S. Ziegel, "Report to the Uniform Law Conference of Canada on Convention on Contracts for the International Sale of Goods," Commentary of Art. 8, para. (3), available at <http://cisgw3.law.pace.edu/cisg/text/ziegel8.html>.

[5] PECL Art. 5:101, para. (1).

[6] PECLArt. 5:101, para. (3).

[7] J. Vilus, *Komentar Konvencije UN o meunarodnoj prodaji robe* [Commentary on the United Nations Convention on the International Sale of Goods], Obvezno pravo, Druga knjiga, ed. A. Goldštajn, Informator, Zagreb, 1981, p. 24.

[8] Provided that the other party could not have been unaware of such intention at the time of conclusion of the contract. *See* PECL Art. 5:101 para. 2.

[9] This would mean that a judge or arbitrator would have to interpret such an instrument by reference to Art. 8(3). J. Honnold, *supra* note 4, at 163; Ziegel, *supra* note 4.

approach in formulation probably lies in the history of the Art. 8 provision of CISG. If one keeps in mind the fact that this provision originated from the Commission draft on formation of contracts where it was used for the interpretation of offer and acceptance and became applicable to statements and conduct after formation of the contract only later when the two drafts on formation and sales were merged, its one-party orientation becomes understandable.[10] The second reason for this difference probably lies in the predominance of the theory of mutual intent as the basis of contract in the majority of the laws of European States whose lawyers participated in the drafting of the PECL.[11] Such a unison view of the basis of contract did not exist among the Member States of UNCITRAL.[12]

c. The rules on interpretation of contract (i.e., of the parties' statements and conduct constituting the contract) are necessary when the meaning of certain provisions is ambiguous or when the different clauses of a contract contradict each other.[13] The interpretation of unclear or contradictory provisions may be necessary to determine whether the contract came into existence, what is its content, and what is the effect of certain notices or other acts of the parties upon the performance or existence of the contract.[14] One of the purposes of the rules on interpretation – determining whether a contract has been concluded – has been treated by a separate provision in the PECL, Art. 2:101, thus giving rise to another formal difference between the CISG and PECL. The Principles state in Art. 2:101 that a party's intention to be legally bound, as a condition for concluding a contract under Art. 2:101(1)(a), shall be determined on the basis of that party's statements and conduct (i.e., whether these statements or that conduct gave the other party a reason to believe that the first party wanted to be legally bound). This provision is clearly more inclined to the objective standard of interpretation (see *infra*, **f**). However, in their Notes, the PECL Commentators refer judges and arbitrators to the whole set of rules of interpretation contained in Chapter 5 (with subjective standard inclusive) in determining whether the party to whom a statement or other conduct was addressed had reason to assume that the first party intended to be bound.[15] The CISG does not dedicate a particular provision to this purpose, but instead relies on Art. 8, an all-embracing provision that applies to the interpretation of all statements and conduct of the parties, either during the formation of the contract or during its performance and possible termination. Professor Honnold points out that this article has an even wider scope because it applies also to post-contract communications and actions.[16]

d. There is an obvious difference in the type of contract to which these rules can possibly be applied. Although Art. 8 CISG is to be applied only to the interpretation of contracts for the international sale of goods, this being further limited by the exclusion of certain international sales by the Convention text itself, the purpose of the interpretation rules contained in Chapter 5 of PECL is much wider: they are intended to serve to interpret "any sort of contract,"[17] including contracts for the international sale of goods.

[10] J. Honnold, *supra* note 4, at 162.

[11] *Id.*, at 164. *Principles of European Contract Law, Parts I and II, Combined and Revised*, eds. Ole Lando and Hugh Beale, Kluwer Law International, 2000, Article 5:101, Comment B, p. 288.

[12] Secretariat Commentary on Art. 7 of the 1978 Draft, Official Records, p. 18, paragraph 3.

[13] Principles of European Contract Law, Art. 5:101, Comment A, p. 287.

[14] Secretariat Commentary on Art. 7 of the 1978 Draft, Official Records, p. 18, paragraph 1.

[15] "Even if in his inmost mind a party had no intention to be legally bound, most of the laws will hold that he is bound if the other party to whom the statement or other conduct was addressed had reason to assume that the first party intended to be bound. Whether this is the case is to be decided under the rules of interpretation, *see* Notes to chapter 5." Principles of European Contract Law, Art. 2:102, Notes, p. 145.

[16] J. Honnold, *supra* note 4, at 163.

[17] Principles of European Contract Law, Survey of Chapters 1–9, p. *xxiv*.

II. INTERPRETATION BASED ON SUBJECTIVE STANDARD (ESTABLISHING THE INTENTION)

e. The basic similarity between the CISG and PECL rules on the interpretation of contracts lies in the combination of the subjective and objective methods of interpretation. Both the Convention (Art. 8(1) CISG) and the Principles (Arts. 5:101(1) and 5:101(2) PECL) instruct the judge or arbitrator to start by establishing the intention of the parties. But, as indicated above, the PECL wants judges and arbitrators to primarily look for their common intention (Art. 5:101(1)) and only exceptionally to interpret the contract in the way intended by one party (Art. 5:101(2)), whereas the CISG does not refer to the common intention of the parties at all, but only to the intent of an individual party. There are some further differences in the wording of the respective rules. For example, PECL in Art. 5:101(2) elegantly avoids the repetitive and tautological nature of the formula used in the CISG to describe the awareness that one party had of the other party's particular intent: "where the other party knew or could not have been unaware what that intent was."[18] Instead, the PECL simply states, "[if] the other party could not have been unaware of the first party's intention." Further, the PECL specifies the relevant moment for assessment of the other party's awareness – this is the moment of conclusion of the contract. Such precision is lacking in CISG Art. 8, perhaps naturally, because it refers more broadly to the interpretation of statements and conduct of a party whenever they were given or undertaken.

III. INTERPRETATION BASED ON OBJECTIVE STANDARD (THE CRITERION OF A REASONABLE PERSON)

f. If there are no indicators of the parties' true intentions, both the Convention and PECL instruct the court or arbitrator to apply the objective criterion of an understanding that a reasonable person would attribute to the statements and conduct of the party (i.e., to the contract) in the equivalent circumstances. Again, the PECL is somewhat more precise in defining the situation that triggers the switch from the subjective to objective criterion. This is the case when no intention different from the literal meaning of the words can be established (i.e., when no evidence of the parties' actual intentions is available). The CISG, somewhat laconically, introduces the second paragraph of Art. 8, which calls for an objective interpretation, with the wording, "If the preceding paragraph is not applicable."

IV. AUXILIARY CRITERIA OF INTERPRETATION

g. Both the Convention and the Principles give the judge or arbitrator a non-exhaustive list of matters that may be relevant in determining either the meaning intended by the parties or the reasonable meaning of the contract (see Art. 8(3) CISG and Art. 5:102 PECL).[19] The PECL list is more comprehensive. If we make a close comparison of relevant factors, we notice that the Convention does not mention the following: good faith and fair dealing, the nature and purpose of the contract, the interpretation that has already been given to similar clauses by the parties, the meaning commonly given to terms and expressions in the branch of activity concerned, and the interpretation that similar clauses may have already received. Surely, most of these factors may also be taken into account when applying the auxiliary interpretation rule from CISG Art. 8, para. (3).

[18] This formula was criticized as such by Great Britain during the drafting procedure. *See* J. Vilus, *supra* note 7, at 25.

[19] Principles of European Contract Law, Art. 5:102, Comment, p. 291.

h. Some may question, however, whether good faith and fair dealing could be used as a tool of interpretation of a contract governed by the Convention, because of the well-known fact that the proposals for imposition of this requirement upon parties and their conduct were expressly rejected during the drafting process.[20] In spite of the legislative history of the Convention text, it has become commonplace among commentators of the CISG to mention the observance of good faith by the parties as a general principle on which the Convention is based.[21] If this view is accepted, the principle of good faith and fair dealing could also serve as a potential auxiliary factor in interpretation of the parties' statements, conduct, and contractual provisions in general, even though it is not expressly mentioned in the relevant article of the CISG, as it is in the PECL.

i. Both Art. 8(3) CISG and Art. 5:102 PECL include preliminary negotiations as one of the factors to be taken into account by the judge or arbitrator interpreting the contract. This is generally understood to mean that the parol evidence rule existing in some legal systems is precluded.[22] Even a merger clause possibly inserted into the contract does not automatically bar the judge from considering any evidence of preliminary negotiations for purposes of interpretation under either of these instruments.[23] The parties wishing to exclude such evidence for all purposes, including the purposes of interpretation, can still do so, however, by stating accordingly in the merger clause. This would be a derogation from Art. 8(3) CISG and Art. 5:102 PECL, which is allowed on the basis of party autonomy (see Art. 6 CISG; Art. 1:102(2) PECL).[24]

V. SPECIFIC RULES OF INTERPRETATION

j. The Convention does not frame any rules on interpretation other than the general rule contained in Art. 8 CISG. In contrast, the PECL contain five such specific rules of interpretation: the *contra proferentem* rule (Art. 5:103), the rule on giving preference to negotiated terms (Art. 5:104), the rule on interpreting the individual provisions

[20] For a detailed comparative commentary on the role of good faith in the three instruments – the CISG, the PECL, and the UNIDROIT Principles – see "Guide to Article 7 CISG, Editorial Remarks," by J. Felemegas and U. Magnus, available online at the Pace Institute Web site at <http://cisgw3.law.pace.edu/cisg/text/e-text-07.html>.

[21] *See*, for example: R. Herber, in P. Schlechtriem, ed., *Commentary on the UN Convention on the International Sale of Goods (CISG)*, C. H. Beck, München, 1998, p. 63.

[22] J. Honnold, *supra* note 4, at 171; "Comparative Guide to Art. 8, Editorial Remarks," by J. M. Perillo, item g) <http://cisgw3.law.pace.edu/cisg/principles/uni8.html#edrem>. *See MCC-Marble Ceramic Center, Inc. v. Ceramica Nuova D'Agostino, S.p.A.*, U.S. Court of Appeals (Eleventh Circuit), 29 June 1998, CLOUT Case no. 222, also available at <http://cisgw3.law.pace.edu/cases/980629u1.html>.

See apparently *contra*, *Beijing Metals & Minerals Import/Export Corporation v. American Business Center, Inc.*, U.S. Court of Appeals (Fifth Circuit), 15 June 1993, CLOUT Case no. 24, also available at <http://cisgw3.law.pace.edu/cases/930615u1.html>.

However, in *Mitchell Aircraft Spares v. European Aircraft Service*, U.S. District Court [Illinois], 27 October 1998, CLOUT no. 419, the court confirmed the growing body of U.S. jurisprudence to the effect that, in a case governed by the Convention, Article 8 CISG displaces the U.S. parol evidence rule. *See* <http://cisgw3.law.pace.edu/cases/981027u1.html>.

[*See* also *Calzaturificio Claudia v. Olivieri Footwear*, 6 April 1998 U.S. District Court [New York], CLOUT case no. 413, also at <http://cisgw3.law.pace.edu/cases/980406u1.html>; *Filanto S.p.A. v. Chilewich International Corp.*, 14 April 1992 U.S. Dist. Ct., CLOUT case no. 23, also at <http://cisgw3.law.pace.edu/cases/920414u1.html>.]

The court in *Mitchell Aircraft* also disagreed with the possible holding to the contrary *in Beijing Metals & Minerals*; *see* A. H.Kritzer's editorial comments in the *Mitchell Aircraft* case presentation online, *id.*

[23] J. Honnold, *supra* note 4, at 171. "The search for common intention is compatible with rules which forbid the proof of matters in addition or contrary to a writing, for example if the parties have negotiated a merger clause to the effect that writing contains all the terms of the contract (see Art. 2:105: Merger Clause), as it refers to external elements only to clarify the meaning of a clause, not to contradict it." Principles of European Contract Law, Art. 5:101 Comment, B, p. 288.

[24] Principles of European Contract Law, Art. 5:102, Comment, pp. 291–292.

with reference to the contract as a whole (Art. 5:105), the rule on giving preference to interpretation that renders the terms of contract effective (Art. 5:106), and the rule on interpretation in case of linguistic discrepancies (Art. 5:107). Undoubtedly, these specific rules may be referred to as supplementary rules in aid of interpretation of the CISG, because they are not inconsistent with, and are in accord with the evident intent of, Art. 8 CISG. Indeed, some of these rules are described as the origin of solutions adopted in Art. 8.[25] They are an absolute necessity for interpretation of contracts made in an international and, often, multilingual setting.

[25] *E.g.*, the provision in Art. 8(2) CISG has been described as rooted in the *contra proferentem* rule by J. Honnold, *supra* note 4, at 165.

Usages and practices applicable to the contract: Remarks on the manner in which the PECL may be used to interpret or supplement Article 9 CISG

Anja Carlsen

I. GENERAL SCHEME OF ARTICLE 1:105 PECL AND ARTICLE 9 CISG

The structure and contents of Article 1:105 PECL and Article 9 CISG are similar. The first paragraph of each article deals with the binding effect of usages and practices that are agreed upon by the parties. The second paragraph of Article 9 CISG and Article 1:105 PECL deals with the binding effect of usages not agreed upon by the parties, but that are nevertheless binding due to their general applicability[1] or because the parties implicitly have agreed upon a usage.[2]

Practices and usages will, when applicable to the contract, set aside rules of law of the CISG and provisions of the PECL that would otherwise apply.[3] However, under

[1] *Cf.* Article 1:105(2) PECL.

[2] *Cf.* Article 9(2) CISG.

[3] This precedent is mainly based on the autonomy of the parties pursuant to Article 6 CISG whereby they may opt-out of the CISG or amend it to their individual needs. A contradictory usage can in that sense be seen as an adaptation of the CISG agreed between the parties; *cf.* Patrick X. Bout, "Trade Usages: Article 9 of the Convention on Contracts for the International Sales of Goods" (hereinafter Bout), published at <http://cisgw3.law.pace.edu/cisg/biblio/bout.html>. *See* also Werner Junge, in Peter Schlechtriem ed., *Commentary on UN Convention on the International Sale of Goods (Cisg)*, 2nd edition (translated) (hereinafter Junge), p. 76; M.J. Bonell, in C.M. Bianca and M.J. Bonell eds., *Commentary on the International Sales Law: The* 1980 *Vienna Sales Convention* (hereinafter Bonell), p. 104; F. Enderlein and D. Maskow, *International Sales Law: United Nations Convention on Contracts for the International Sale of Goods*, 1992, pp. 66–67

the PECL, practices and usages are only applicable if they do not violate mandatory rules of the law applicable to the contract; under the CISG, usages can be overridden in accordance with its Article 4(a) validity provision.[4]

II. PRACTICES AND USAGES

Neither Article 9 CISG nor Article 1:105 PECL, defines the terms "usage" and "practice." Therefore, what ultimately constitutes a usage or a practice in CISG and PECL is to be decided by national courts or by arbitral tribunals.[5]

The Secretariat Commentary[6] on Article 8 of the 1978 Draft of the CISG does not include a definition of the terms "usage" and "practice." However, the Commentary to Article 1:105 PECL defines the term "practice" as previous conduct in a particular transaction or a particular kind of transaction between the parties that may be regarded as a common understanding.[7] Furthermore, the Commentary to Article 1:105 PECL defines the term "usage" as a course of dealing or line of conduct that is and for a certain period of time has been generally adopted by those engaged in the trade or in a particular trade.[8]

As the articles of CISG and PECL apply the same terms, the definition of the terms "usages" and "practices" in the Commentary to Article 1:105 PECL may aid in defining the terms "practice" and "usage" in the CISG. The definition of the terms in the Commentary to Article 1:105 PECL is in accord with the definition of the said terms proposed by leading scholars on the CISG.[9]

III. DIFFERENCES IN THE SCOPE OF ARTICLE 9 CISG AND ARTICLE 1:105 PECL

1. Theories of Influence of Trade Usages in Commercial Contracts[10]

Article 9 CISG is based on two theories describing the influence of trade usages in commercial contracts. The first is the subjective theory whereby usages may only be

(hereinafter Enderlein), available online at <http://cisgw3.law.pace.edu/cisg/biblio/enderlein-art09.html>. *See* also Article 9(2) ULIS where it is expressly stated that a usage will set aside the applicable law.

See relevant case law: Austria 21 March 2000, Oberster Gerichtshof [Supreme Court], case presentation available in English, online at <http://cisgw3.law.pace.edu/cases/000321a3.html> (stating that genuine domestic usages for the trade prevailed over the provisions of the CISG because these usages were widely known to and regularly observed by parties in cross-border trade between Austria and Germany).

[4] Article 4(a) CISG states: "... except as otherwise expressly provided in this Convention, it is not concerned with ... the validity of the contract or of any of its provisions or of any *usage*" [emphasis added].

[5] *Cf.* Article 7(2) CISG and 1:106(2) PECL. *See* also Junge, p. 76. Furthermore, the hierarchy between practices and usages is not settled in the CISG or the PECL; however, practices should be considered as having priority in their relationship with agreed usages, as they are generally better geared to the particularities of a concrete relationship because they are of an individual and thus more specific character; *cf.* Enderlein, p. 67. The hierarchy proposed by Enderlein is similar to the UCC, Section 1–204(4), whereby any course of performance shall control both course of dealing and usage of trade.

[6] The Secretariat Commentary on the 1978 Draft of the CISG is the closest counterpart to an official commentary on the CISG. The Secretariat Commentary on Article 8 of the 1978 Draft is available online at <http://cisgw3.law.pace.edu/cisg/text/secomm/secomm-09.html>. The addition of the phrase "or its formation" is the only difference between Article 8 of the 1978 Draft and Article 9 CISG.

[7] *Cf.* Ole Lando and Hugh Beale eds., *Principles of European Contract Law: Parts I and II*, Kluwer Law International (2000) (hereinafter Lando and Beale), p. 104.

[8] *Id.*, at 104.

[9] *Cf.* Bonell, p.106 and 111, Junge, p. 78 and John O. Honnold, *Uniform Law for International Sales under the 1980 United Nations Convention*, 2nd ed., Kluwer Law International (1991) (hereinafter Honnold), p. 146. Furthermore, the definition of the term usage in the Commentary to Article 1:105 PECL is in accord with the definition of said term in CISG's antecedent, Article 13 ULF, where a usage was defined as any practice or method of dealing that reasonable persons in the same situation as the parties usually consider to be applicable to the formation of their contract.

[10] For a helpful overview of the influence of trade usage in commercial contracts, *see* Aleksandar Goldstajn, "Usages of Trade and Other Autonomous Rules of International Trade according to the UN (1980) Sales Convention," in Sarcevic & Volken eds., *International Sale of Goods: Dubrovnik Lectures, Oceana* (1986) Ch. 3, 55–110, available online at <http://cisgw3.law.pace.edu/cisg/biblio/goldstajn.html>.

applicable if the parties have agreed to them. According to the subjective theory, usages unknown to either party are not applicable. In contrast, in the objective theory, usages are applicable if they represent a legal norm. According to the objective theory, usages unknown to both parties may be applicable to an agreement. Both theories agree that the usage must be so widespread and widely recognized that businesspersons knew or ought to have known of it.[11]

Article 9(2) CISG represents a compromise between the subjective and the objective theory.[12] During the preparation of the CISG, delegates from Socialist countries and developing countries were especially opposed to the acceptance of usages based only on their objective normative power because most usages in international trade have their origin in the industrial countries of the Western world.[13]

Because the PECL are intended to be applied as general rules of contract law in the European Union,[14] these concerns were not brought up during the drafting of Article 1:105 PECL. Therefore, the PECL provisions apply the objective theory.

2. Practices and Usages Agreed upon by the Parties

The wording of Article 9(1) CISG and that of Article 1:105(1) PECL are identical. Both provisions deal with the usages and practices that the parties – expressly or tacitly[15] – have established between them. Such practices and usages are binding upon the parties.[16]

3. Practices and Usages Not Explicitly Agreed upon by the Parties

Contrary to Article 9(1) CISG and Article 1:105(1) PECL, there are notable differences in the wording of Article 9(2) CISG and Article 1:105(2) PECL.

According to Article 1:105(2) PECL, the parties will be bound by a usage that would be considered applicable by persons in the same situation as the parties, provided that the usage is not unreasonable and is consistent with the express terms of the agreement.

[11] *Cf.* Junge, p. 76.

[12] *Cf.* Bonell, p. 110.

[13] *Cf.* Junge, p. 76 and Bonell, p. 105.

[14] *Cf.* Article 1:101 PECL.

[15] Although not expressly stated in Article 9(1) CISG and Article 1:105(1) PECL, both expressly agreed usages and practices as well as implicitly agreed usages and practices will be binding upon the parties. This interpretation is in accordance with the antecedent to Article 9(1) CISG, Article 9(1) ULIS, where it is expressly stated that the parties are bound by usages that they expressly or implicitly have made applicable to their contract and any practices established between themselves. *See* also Enderlein, p. 67.

[16] The fact that the parties intend a usage or a practice to apply to their contract entails that there is no need to examine whether the actual sales transactions are covered by the usage or whether the requirements for the existence of a usage as described in Article 9(2) CISG or Article 1:105(2) PECL are satisfied; *cf.* Junge, p. 78 and Lando and Beale, p. 104. *See* the relevant case law:

- Netherlands 6 May 1994, Rb [District Court]'s-Hertogenbosch, case presentation available in English, online at <http://cisgw3.law.pace.edu/cases/940506n1.html> (stating that the previous place of payment was an established practice between the parties). *See* also Germany 24 November 1998, LG [District Court] Bielefeld, English translation available online at <http://cisgw3.law.pace.edu/cases/981124g1.html> (stating that the place of payment shall be established in conformity with the practices between the parties.) However, to the contrary, *see* Italy 7 August 1998, Corte Suprema di Cassazione [Supreme Court], case presentation available in English, online at <http://cisgw3.law.pace.edu/cases/980807i3.html> (stating that a mere practice between the parties, which may well depend on a tolerance on the part of the seller, is not sufficient to justify a derogation from the general rule regarding the place of payment.)
- China, CIETAC Arbitration proceeding, post-1989, English translation available online at <http://cisgw3.law.pace.edu/cases/900000c1.html> (stating that the parties' adoption of a practice of confirming the sample of the goods is binding upon the parties with respect to the quality of the goods.)
- France 21 October 1999, Cour d'appel [Appellate Court] Grenoble, English translation available online at <http://cisgw3.law.pace.edu/cases/991021f1.html> (stating that a contract had been concluded, even in the absence of any express acceptance on the part of the seller, as the seller in previous years had fulfilled the buyer's orders without expressing its acceptance.)
- Germany 13 April 2000, AG [Lower Court] Duisburg, English translation available online at <http://cisgw3.law.pace.edu/cases/000413g1.html> (stating that a party's behavior on two prior occasions does not establish a practice between the parties.)

In contrast, Article 9(2) CISG sets forth two requirements for a usage to be implicitly applicable to a given contract. First, a usage only becomes binding upon the parties if the parties "knew or ought to have known" of the usage. Second, a usage only becomes binding to the parties if the usage "in international trade is widely known to, and regularly observed by, parties to contracts of the type involved in the particular trade concerned."[17]

The requirement of "known or ought to have known" in Article 9(2) CISG entails that there should be an effective link between the application of the usage and the parties' intention.[18] By contrast, pursuant to Article 1:105(2) PECL, a usage may be binding upon the parties even without such a link to the parties' intentions, provided that the usage would be considered applicable by persons in the same situation as the parties.[19]

Although these articles appear to set forth different requirements, the determining factor in Article 9(2) CISG will often be whether the usage is widely known to, and regularly observed by, parties to contracts of the type involved in the particular trade concerned.[20] As the criterion set forth in Article 9(2) CISG is similar to the wording of Article 1:105(2) PECL, Article 9(2) CISG may logically be interpreted in accordance with the criterion set forth in Article 1:105(2) PECL.

According to its wording, Article 9(2) CISG applies to international usages only,[21] whereas Article 1:105 PECL applies to local, national, and international usages.[22] Although Article 9(2) CISG applies to international usages only, regional or national usages may be applicable under the CISG if the usage is regularly observed in international transactions and a large part of the foreign participants in the trade acknowledge the usage.[23] Consequently, both Article 9(2) CISG and Article 1:105 PECL can be applicable

[17] *Cf.* Secretariat Commentary on Article 8 of the 1978 draft (antecedent to Article 9 CISG), section 4. *See* the relevant case law:

- European Court of Justice 20 February 1997, case presentation available in English, online at <http://cisgw3.law.pace.edu/cases/970220eu.html> (stating that it is not enough for a jurisdiction clause to have been concluded in a form that accords with a usage in the particular trade or commerce concerned of which the parties were or ought to have been aware; the usage must have been widely known in international trade or commerce and regularly observed by parties to contracts of the type involved in the particular trade or commerce concerned.)
- ICC Arbitration Case No. 8324 of 1995, case presentation available online at <http://cisgw3.law.pace.edu/cases/958234i1.html> (stating that the parties are bound by usages that are regularly observed by parties to contracts of the type involved in the particular trade concerned.)

[18] *Cf.* Junge, pp. 76–77. *See* the relevant case law:

- Netherlands 24 April 1996, Hof [Appellate Court] 's-Hertogenbosch, case presentation available in English, online at <http://cisgw3.law.pace.edu/cases/960424n1.html> (stating that a party was bound by international practice, as he should have been aware of the fact that general terms and conditions are a common feature in international practice.)
- *See* also Switzerland 21 December 1992, ZG [Civil Court] Basel, English translation available online at <http://cisgw3.law.pace.edu/cases/921221s1.html> (stating that the parties had implicitly made that usage applicable to their contract because they knew or ought to have known the binding nature of a letter of confirmation under both Austrian and Swiss law.)

[19] *Cf.* Lando and Beale, p. 104, Bonell, p. 109, Junge, p. 79 and Honnold, p. 148.

[20] *Cf.* Secretariat Commentary on Article 8 of the 1978 draft (antecedent to Article 9 CISG), section 4. This interpretation of Article 9(2) CISG is also in accordance with CISG's antecedent, Article 9(2) ULIS, stating that the parties are bound by any usages that reasonable persons in the same situation as the parties usually consider to be applicable to their contract.

[21] *Cf.* Junge, pp. 78–79.

[22] *Cf.* Lando and Beale, p. 104.

[23] *Cf.* Junge, p. 79. *See* the relevant case law:

- Austria 9 November 1995 Olg [Appellate Court] Graz, case presentation available in English, online at <http://cisgw3.law.pace.edu/cases/951109a3.html> (stating that Article 9(2) CISG shall not be interpreted as barring the application of national or local usage and that a party, who has been engaging in business in a county for many years and has repeatedly concluded contracts of the type involved in the particular trade concerned, is bound by national usages.)
- Germany 5 July 1995, OLG [Appellate Court] Frankfurt, English translation available online at <http://cisgw3.law.pace.edu/cases/950705g1.html> (stating that regard is to be given only to trade usages that are known to the law in both jurisdictions of the parties)

to local usages as well. Therefore, it is also logical that Article 1:105(2) PECL may be applied as an aid in determining whether a usage falls within the scope of Article 9(2) CISG.

According to Article 1:105(2) PECL, the application of a usage must not be unreasonable. Article 9(2) CISG does not expressly require the usage to be reasonable.[24] However, reasonableness is a general principle of CISG.[25] Therefore, Article 9(2) CISG can well be interpreted to require that the usage is not unreasonable, which is in accordance with the wording of Article 1:105(2) PECL.

4. Newcomers to the Market

Pursuant to both Article 9(1) CISG and Article 1:105(1) PECL, a newcomer to a market may be bound by usages applicable to the market if the parties have agreed upon them.

Pursuant to Article 1:105(2) PECL, a party entering into a new market may be bound by usages generally observed by the parties in that market. This may entail that the newcomer be bound by local usages of the other party if the usages would be considered applicable by persons in the same situation as the parties.[26]

By contrast, as the wording of Article 9(2) CISG relies on the knowledge or the imputed knowledge of the parties in question, it leaves doubt as to whether newcomers in the trade or outsiders are bound by a usage of which they cannot reasonably have any knowledge.[27] If the newcomer indeed knew of the usages applicable in a new market, the parties will be bound by the said usage. However, according to Article 9(2) CISG, the usages applicable in a new market may also apply to the newcomer even if he was not aware of those usages if it can be established that the newcomer should have known them.

Therefore, newcomers to a market are, also under the CISG, probably bound by usages observed in the market they enter.[28] Consequently, both Article 9 CISG and Article 1:105 PECL entail that newcomers may be bound by usages applicable in the market in question. Newcomers should therefore always make an effort to conduct research into the applicable usages applied in a new market.

5. Examples of Other Provisions in the CISG Referring to Usages or Practices

In the CISG, several articles refer to usages and/or practices. For example, Article 8(3) states that due consideration shall be given to practices and usages when determining the intent of a party or the understanding of a reasonable person. Furthermore, Article 18(3) CISG states that an offer can be accepted by the performance of an act, if practices and usages permit that.

An indirect reference to usages and practices can be found in Article 32(2) CISG regarding carriage of goods, according to which carriage shall be made under usual terms.

Finally, another indirect reference can be found in Article 35(2)(a) CISG regarding conformity of the goods to the contract, according to which the goods should be fit for normal use, unless expressly agreed otherwise.[29]

- ICC Arbitration Case No. 5713 of 1989, case presentation available online at <http://cisgw3.law.pace.edu/cases/895713i1.html> (stating that the CISG – reflecting generally accepted trade usages – may prevail over domestic law.)

[24] *Cf.* Lando and Beale, p. 106.

[25] *Cf.* Discussions at the 6th meeting of the First Committee at the Diplomatic *Conference* where a proposal to include the word "reasonable" in Article 9(2) CISG was rejected on the basis that the very existence of a usage implied recognition of its reasonableness; *see* <http://cisgw3.law.pace.edu/cisg/firstcommittee/Meeting6.html>, paras 58–71. *See* also the editorial remarks on the concept of reasonableness as a general principle of the CISG, available online at <http://cisgw3.law.pace.edu/cisg/text/reason.html>.

[26] *Cf.* Lando and Beale, p. 105.

[27] *Id.*, at 105.

[28] *Cf.* Junge, p. 79.

[29] *Cf.* Bout.

IV. CONCLUSIONS

According to the CISG and the PECL, usages and practices are binding upon the parties. Apart from the wording of Article 9(2) CISG and Article 1:105(2) PECL, the two instruments have many similarities in substance as well as a common purpose.

As the wording of Article 9(1) CISG and Article 1:105(1) PECL is identical, Article 1:105(1) PECL and the Commentary to it may aid in the interpretation and application of Article 9(1) CISG.

Furthermore, although the wording of Article 9(2) CISG and Article 1:105(2) PECL are not identical, I maintain that PECL could aid in the interpretation and application of Article 9(2) CISG as the criteria set forth in Article 9(2) CISG may be interpreted in accordance with the criteria set forth in Article 1:105(2) PECL.

Interpretation of "place of business": Comparison between the provisions of CISG Article 10 and counterpart provisions of the Principles of European Contract Law

Allison E. Butler

I. GENERAL INTERPRETATION AND APPLICATION IN THE CISG AND THE PECL

The content and function of Article 7:101(2) and (3) PECL are similar in substance and form to the counterpart provision contained in Article 10 CISG. Both provisions exemplify the drafters' intent to adopt the "closest connection" principle in contract interpretation and supplementation when determining the relevant "place of business" of a party absent an express provision.[1]

The PECL Notes to Article 7:101(2) and (3) confirm that the basic elements are based on Article 10 CISG.[2] However, although the provisions apply the same theory, its application is limited in scope under 7:101(2) PECL as compared to Article 10 CISG.[3]

[1] See Art. 10 CISG and Art. 7:101(2) PECL. The "closest relationship theory" is the place of business having the closest relationship with the contract. In contrast, there is the "theory of the principal place of business," which is the relevant place of business is where the main seat is located. *See* generally, Franco Ferrari, "Specific Topics of the CISG in the Light of Judicial Application and Scholarly Writing," 15 *J.L. & Com* (1995), Section II. 4. "The 'Place of Business' under CISG," available at <http://cisgw3.law.pace.edu/cisg/biblio/2ferrari.html>. The original intent of the drafters of the CISG to adopt the theory of "principal place of business" is evidenced by the proposal reprinted in UNCITRAL Yearbook, vol. II (1971) 52, available at: <http://www.uncitral.org/english/yearbooks/yearbook-index-e.htm>; however, this was later rejected.

[2] Ole Lando and Hugh Beale, eds., *Principles of European Contract Law: Part I and II*, Kluwer Law International (2000) 330–330, 332.

[3] Under 7:101(2) PECL the principle is applied to determine the place of business relevant for the place of performance when the term is absent from a contract and there is more than one place of business. In contrast, however, the theory of "closest connection" is not limited to its content under the CISG. For example, the closest relationship theory as set forth in Article 10 is used to determine the place of business

II. "PLACE OF BUSINESS" IN THE INTERPRETATION OF THE CONTRACT

Subsection (1) of 7:101 PECL prescribes the place of performance in the event where the location for performance of the contract "is not fixed or determinable from the contract."[4] The PECL expressly addresses the situation where a creditor or debtor has two places of business or does not have a place of business. As such, the concept of place of business as set forth in Subsections (2) and (3) operates as a supplementation for determining the location for the performance of a contract, as well as an interpretive guide for defining the location of performance. Thus, the scope of the principle as adapted by the PECL is used to determine the performance of a contract.

In contrast, the issue of determining the relevant place of business of a party frequently arises in several different provisions under the CISG.[5] However, the primary and most common usage of "place of business" as facilitated under Article 10 CISG is its interpretive part in the unilateral conflict rule contained in Article 1(1)(a) CISG. Hence, when both articles are read in conjunction they "form the *lex specialis* of conflicts of laws in contract applicable to contracts of sale of goods between parties whose places of business are in different Contracting States to the Convention."[6]

The concept of "place of business" is not defined under the PECL. In the majority of the cases, however, it refers to a party's permanent and regular place for the transaction of general business and is not a temporary place of sojourn during sales negotiations.[7] Hence, if a corporation conducts business temporarily at a location, the PECL would not consider this location a place of business.

Under Article 10 CISG, there is an overwhelming cognizance that the place of business is where "the center of the business activity directed to the participation is located," which links the contracting party to the State where the business is conducted, provided the party has autonomous power.[8] Notably, a business's "autonomous power" appears to be the key component when courts have scrutinized this term.[9] Consequently, this assumption, as with the PECL, has led many commentators and courts to conclude that a

relevant for the determination of choice of law under an international sales contract when there is more than one place of business, as well as other applications throughout the CISG. *See infra*, note 5. Both 7:101(3) PECL and Article 10 CISG are identical in their treatment of parties without a place of business.

[4] *See* Article 7:101(1) PECL.

[5] There are numerous applications of the place of business in particular provisions of the Convention; *see* the examples offered in the Secretariat Commentary to the Draft Convention as manifestations of the concept (e.g. Arts. 12, 20(2), 24, 31(c), 42(1)(b), 57(1)(a) and 96) CISG; Text of Secretariat Commentary on article 9 of the 1978 Draft [*draft counterpart of Art. 10 CISG*], available at: <http://cisgw3.law.pace.edu/cisg/text/secomm/secomm-10.html>.

[6] Carolina Saf, "A Study of Interplay between the Conventions Governing International Contracts of Sale," available at: <http://cisgw3.law.pace.edu/cisg/biblio/saf.html>. *See* illustrative case, Germany 13 April 2000 Amtsgericht [Lower Court] Duisburg, English translation available online at <http://cisgw3.law.pace.edu/cases/000413g1.html>.

[7] *See* Comments and Notes to Article 7.101(2) PECL, Comment E. Precisely the same approach applies to the CISG. In corroboration, Honnold states, "During the preparation of the Convention, some delegates were concerned lest 'place of business' be construed to extend to a hotel room or other temporary place where a traveling agent might conduct negotiations. Referring to a 'permanent' place of business presented drafting difficulties, and most delegates concluded that temporary sojourns would not establish a 'place of business.' The term that corresponds to 'place of business in the official French text is *établissement* and in the official Spanish text is *establecimiento* – words that seem to be inconsistent with a temporary stopping place." John O. Honnold, *Uniform Law for International Sales*, 3rd ed., Kluwer (1999) 132 [citations omitted].

[8] *See*, Ferrari, *supra* note 1, referencing German Federal Supreme Court's interpretation of "place of business" in ULIS Article 1. Judgment of June 2, 1982, BGH WM 846 = 83 IPRax 212.

[9] *See* the relevant case law:

- Germany 28 February 2000, Oberlandesgericht [Appellate Court] Stuttgart, English translation available at <http://cisgw3.law.pace.edu/cases/000228g1.html> (holding the Spanish representative of a German manufacturer-seller in Spain was not a place of business absent legal authority to bind the German manufacturer to the Spanish buyer)

place of business, such as the location of an agent, representative, or distributor[10]; liaison office[11]; conference center; or exhibition or a rented office(s) at an exhibition, fails to constitute a place of business for the purposes of Article 10 CISG, absent facts to the contrary. Notably, however, one court did find that a corporate branch was the place of business under Article 10 CISG and not the company's headquarters located in a different country. This finding was based on the fact that the branch had the closest relationship to the contract and its performance.[12]

III. SEVERAL PLACES OF BUSINESS UNDER THE CISG AND THE PECL

Article 7.101(2) PECL provides for the determination of place of performance when a party has more than one place of business: it is the place of business that has the closest relationship with the contract and its performance, having regard to the circumstances known to or contemplated by the parties at the conclusion of the contract. Thus, the PECL will look to the knowledge and intent of the parties when determining the place of business.

Article 10(a) CISG also establishes similar criteria to resolve this issue. Notably, when reference is made to the performance of the contract, it is referring to the performance that the parties knew or contemplated when they were entering into the contract. For example, if it was contemplated by a party that performance of the contract would be in State A, a determination that her or his place of business was in State A would not be altered by his or her subsequent decision to perform the contract at his or her place of business in State B.

- Germany 13 November 2000, Landgericht [District Court] Köln, case presentation available online at <http://cisgw3.law.pace.edu/cases/001113g1.html> (holding that the Italian agent in Germany did not have the authority to bind an Italian company in a German-Italian contract dispute)
- United States 27 July 2001, Federal District Court, *Asante Technologies, Inc. v. MC-Sierra, Inc.*, case presentation available online at <http://cisgw3.law.pace.edu/cases/010727u1.html> (holding that a U.S. non-exclusive distributor not acting as an agent did not have authority to bind the U.S. company in contract with a Canadian company)
- France 4 January 1995, Cour de Cassation [Supreme Court], *Fauba France FDIS GC Electronique v. Fujitsu Mikroelectronik GmbH*, English translation available online at <http://cisgw3.law.pace.edu/cases/950104f1.html> (holding that a liaison office of a German company in France was not the principal place of business absent corporate status in action against French buyer)
- ICC Arbitration Case No. 7531 of 1994, case presentation available online at <http://cisgw3.law.pace.edu/cases/947531i1.html> (holding that an Austrian-buyer liaison located in China was not the place of business in a Chinese-Austrian dispute, notwithstanding that the liaison office in China may have been involved in the negotiating process)

[10] *See* case law:
- Germany 28 February 2000, Oberlandesgericht [Appellate Court] Stuttgart, supra note 9; Germany 13 November 2000, District Court Köln, case presentation available online at <http://cisgw3.law.pace.edu/cases/001113g1.html>
- U.S. 27 July 2001, Federal District Court, *Asante Technologies, Inc. v. MC-Sierra, Inc.*, *supra* note 9

[11] *See* case law:
- France 4 January 1995, Cour de Cassation [Supreme Court], *Fauba France FDIS GC Electronique v. Fujitsu Mikroelectronik GmbH*, *supra* note 9
- ICC Arbitration Case No. 7531 of 1994, *supra* note 9

[12] Switzerland 20 February 1997, Zivilgericht [District Court] Saane, case presentation available online at <http://cisgw3.law.pace.edu/cases/970220s1.html>. This is a very interesting case as it illustrates the flexibility and subjectivity in the judicial application of Article 10 CISG. In this case, an Austrian company entered into a contract with the Swiss branch of a company with headquarters in Liechtenstein for the purchase and transport of spirits to Russia. Notably, Liechtenstein is not a Contracting State to the CISG. A contractual dispute arose between the parties and the contract was never performed. The court found that the CISG was applicable because the Swiss branch, not the Liechtenstein headquarters, was the place of business that had the closest relationship to the contract and its performance (Articles 1(1)(a) and 10(a) CISG).

In the judicial application of Article 10 CISG, however, the courts have routinely looked not only to the intent of the parties but also to the "totality of the contract."[13]

This term is used to refer as an examination of the contract as a whole. Hence, the fact that a third party negotiated a contract has had little significance to the courts when determining the place of business. However, certain factors that are not known or contemplated by both parties at the time of entering into the contract may not be taken into consideration. Such factors include, but are not limited to, supervision over the making of the contract by a head office located in another State, the foreign origin of the goods, or the final destination of the goods.[14] As with Article 7:101(2) and (3) PECL, these matters are reviewed subjectively.

IV. HABITUAL RESIDENCE

Article 7:101(3) PECL specifically deals with the case where one of the parties does not have a place of business. In such circumstances, a factual determination is to be made as to the party's habitual residence. Upon such finding, performance is to be effected at the party's habitual residence. "Habitual residence" is where the party actually lives.[15] Notably, it is irrelevant whether he or she has a permit to live in the country or whether the party frequents another country, provided he or she normally returns to the first place.

Article 10(b) CISG provides for a similar situation, so long as the contract is for sale of goods intended for commercial purposes and not simply for "personal, family or household use" within the meaning of Article 2(a) CISG.[16]

V. CONCLUSION

A comparison of the two documents illustrates that both the CISG and the PECL adopt the "closest relationship" theory to determine the relevant place of business. However, in application, it is apparent that Article 10 CISG is broader than Article 7:101(2) and (3) PECL; the latter relies solely on the place of performance of the contract. In contrast, Article 10 CISG, not only extends beyond its jurisdictional application in conjunction with Article 1(1)(a) CISG but also has further application and reference throughout the CISG.

Moreover, judicial review has further refined the definition by expressly excluding those places that do not contribute to the totality of the sale, which the parties had intended. CISG case law has thus provided a valuable insight into the terms and application of the "closest connection" principle.

[13] *See* also Secretariat Commentary on article 9 of the 1978 Draft Convention [*draft counterpart of CISG article 10*], Comment 6, which states: "Subparagraph (a) lays down the criterion for determining the relevant place of business: it is the place of business 'which has the closest relationship to the contract and its performance.' The phrase 'the contract and its performance' refers to the transaction as a whole, including factors relating to the offer and the acceptance as well as the performance of the contract." Secretariat Commentary, *supra* note 5.

[14] *Id.*, Comment 8.

[15] See Comments and Notes to PECL Article 7.101(3), Comment G: "This is a 'factual' not a 'legal' concept."

[16] See Secretariat Commentary, *supra* note 5, Comment 9. *See* also, e.g., Austria 10 November 1994 *Oberster Gerichtshof* [Supreme Court], English translation available online at <http://cisgw3.law.pace.edu/cases/941110a3.html> (finding that an international sale occurred under the CISG in a contract of sale of Chinchilla furs between the breeder and buyer).

Formal requirements: Editorial remarks on the manner in which Article 2:101(2) of the PECL may be used to interpret or supplement Article 11 of the CISG

Allison E. Butler

I. GENERAL INTERPRETATION AND APPLICATION: NO FORMAL REQUIREMENTS

Article 11 CISG and its counterpart PECL Article 2:101(2) are similar in substance and form. Both provisions adopt the principle of "freedom of formalities," which upholds the validity of a contract absent writing or other formalities. Verbal and written evidence is permitted under both provisions to prove the formation of a contract.[1]

[1] *See* CISG article 11and PECL article 2:101(2). Article 11 is one of the many articles whose legislative history illustrates the Convention's broad uniformity provision, CISG Article 7, in which the delegates of the CISG intended to achieve the Convention's uniformity mentioned in Article 7(1) "by removing artificial impediments to commerce caused by differences in national legal systems that govern international sales of goods." Marian Nash (Leich), "Contemporary Practice of the United States Relating to International Law," 88 *Am. J. Int'l L.* (1994) 89, 103; *see* also, Anthony S. Winer, "The CISG Convention and Thomas Franck's Theory of Legitimacy," 19 *Nw. J. Int'l L. & Bus.* (1998) 1, 1–3; *see* also, Carolina Saf [Sweden], excerpt from 1999 thesis available at <http://cisgw3.law.pace.edu/cisg/text/saf96.html>, stating that Article 11 establishes one of the basic rules of the Convention: the theory of consensualism (i.e., that a contract is not subject to any specific formal requirements). For example, the absence of a writing requirement directly conflicts with the common-law Statute of Frauds. This issue is not as obvious under the PECL as most of the countries of the European community are civil law jurisdictions and do not mandate written contracts unless prescribed by law (and even then there are exceptions).

The legislative history of the CISG further reveals that a Canadian Representative proposed to adopt language that would provide "a limitation on admissible evidence in cases where the contracting parties had freely chosen to have a written contract." Several delegates opposed such an amendment as conflicting with principles of civil law where a judge is permitted to review all evidence. Notably, in certain common law jurisdictions the parol evidence rule or similar type of preclusion prohibits certain evidence. One delegation refused to accept such a rigid rule that is difficult to apply and lacked a uniform body of jurisprudence even in common law countries. *See* John O. Honnold, *Documentary History of the Uniform Law for International Sales* (1999) 662, also available online at <http://cisgw3.law.pace.edu/cisg/1stcommittee/summaries11.html> and <http://cisgw3.law.pace.edu/cisg/2dcommittee/summaries96.html>. The Committee rejected the amendment and adopted Article 11 in its current form.

See relevant case law, *e.g.*, Switzerland 5 December 1995, Commercial Court, St. Gallen, available at <http://cisgw3.law.pace.edu/cases/951205s1.html>, holding a sales contract need not be concluded in or evidenced by writing and can be proved by any means including witnesses; an unsigned offer can be valid. *See* also United States 14 April 1992 Federal District Court [New York] *Filanto S.p.A. v. Chilewich* International Corp., available at <http://cisgw3.law.pace.edu/cases/920414u1.html>

- Mexico 4 May 1993 Compromex Arbitration proceeding M/66/92, *Jose Luis Morales v. Nez Marketing*, available at <http://cisgw3.law.pace.edu/cases/930504m1.html>
- United States 29 June 1998 Federal Appellate Court [11th Circuit], *MCC-Marble Ceramic Center v. Ceramica Nuova D'Agostino*, available at <http://cisgw3.law.pace.edu/cases/980629u1.html>
- United States 8 August 2000 Federal District Court [New York], *Fercus v. Mario Palazzo et al.*, available at <http://cisgw3.law.pace.edu/cases/000808u1.html>
- United States 10 May 2002 Federal District Court [New York], *Geneva Pharmaceuticals Tech. Corp. v. Barr Labs. Inc.*, available at <http://cisgw3.law.pace.edu/cases/020510u1.html>

II. "FORMAL REQUIREMENTS" FOR THE VALIDITY OF THE CONTRACT

1. No Formal Requirement for Contracts in General

Although PECL Article 2:101(2) and CISG Article 11 contain the same basic elements, implicit in Article 2:101(2) is its broad application to modification and termination by agreement as well as by unilateral promises.[2] Article 2:101(2) also provides that parties to a contract can stipulate to preclude application of this provision; however, this option is highly unlikely, as this principle is widely accepted among the legal systems within the European community.[3]

In contrast, Article 11 is limited to the formation of a contract; Article 29 explicitly sets forth the applicable principle in the event of modification or termination. Because of the international sphere of application and certain member states' preference for writing, Article 96 permits States that require contracts of sale to be evidenced by writing the option to declare Article 11 inapplicable.[4]

2. Writing Required

In various European member states, laws mandate commercial contracts to be in writing.[5] However, multiple exceptions are noted based in part on the various legal systems' perception of proving contracts. Hence, oral testimony is often permitted even in the absence of a written document.

Similarly, the CISG also provides means for mandating that a contract be in writing. Notably, CISG Article 11 does not apply if a Contracting State has made a Declaration under Article 96.[6] However, this does not mean that the transaction is subject to a writing requirement. The resolution of that issue may depend on a choice of law analysis.[7]

[2] The CISG and the PECL therefore are based on the same principle of freedom of formalities as a starting point. *See* generally, Sieg Eiselen, "Remarks on the manner in which the Principles of European Contract Law may be used to interpret or supplement Article 29 of the CISG," available online at <http://cisgw3.law.pace.edu/cisg/text/peclcomp29.html#er>.

[3] Ole Lando & Hugh Beale eds., *Principles of European Contract Law: Parts I and Part II, Kluwer Law International* (1999\2000) 137, 138, 142–143.

[4] Ten countries – Argentina, Belarus, Chile, China, Estonia, Hungary, Latvia, Lithuania, the Russian Federation, and the Ukraine – have opted for it. The representative of the Soviet Union argued in particular that the preservation of domestic law requiring written documentation in international sales contracts was critical to protect established practices within the Soviet government for the approval and completion of foreign trade agreements. *See* Analysis of Replies and Comments by Government in Hague Conventions of 1964: Report of the Secretary-General, U.N. Doc. A/CN.9/31, reprinted in (1970) 1 Y.B.U.N. *Comm'n on Int'l Trade L.* 159, 170. It has also been reported that the Soviet representatives were more interested in the reservation on the written requirement than the delegates from other Socialist countries.

[5] *See* e.g., Danske Lov art. 5.1.1, SWEDEN, *see* Adlercreutz I 147; FINLAND, *see* Hoppu, 36; GREECE, CC Art. 158; GERMANY, BGB § 125 (impliedly); AUSTRIA, AGBG § 883; PORTUGAL, CC 219 ff.

[6] *See* generally, CISG Articles 12 and 96.

[7] To illustrate, assume a party located in the United States and a party located in Argentina orally agreed to a sales contract. Because Argentina has made the Article 96 reservation, the provisions of Articles 11 and 29 dispensing with any writing requirement are called off by Article 12. That does not, however, mean that the transaction is subject to a writing requirement. The resolution of that issue will depend on a choice of law analysis. If private international law principles lead to the application of Argentinean law, the writing requirements of Argentinean domestic sales law will apply. If the rules of private international law designate U.S. law, then the writing requirements of U.S. domestic sales law will apply. The result in the latter situation is rather ironic. Because one party to the sale is from Argentina and Argentina has made an Article 96 reservation, the transaction becomes subject to the domestic U.S. Statute of Frauds requirements (most likely § 2–201 of the Uniform Commercial Code as enacted in the jurisdiction whose law governs the transaction). And this is the case, even though the United States, by failing to make an Article 96 declaration, in effect declared its willingness to forego its Statute of Frauds rules and accept oral international sales contracts.

As such, the reservation permitted by Article 96 changes the text of the Convention by eliminating those aspects of Articles 11 and 29 (as well as anything in Part II of the CISG) that dispense with writing requirements. The Article 96 reservation has this effect, not just in countries making the reservation, but also in

3. Specific Contracts

The notes to PECL 2:101(2) acknowledge that specific contracts must be in writing or in a notarial document to be valid.

Unlike the PECL, exclusion from the freedom of formalities of specific types of contracts is expressly stated in Article 2 CISG.[8] As such, the CISG only applies to commercial contracts. Although different in subject matter, PECL 2:1010(2) may be of assistance in these circumstances.

III. CONCLUSION

The PECL supports the same principle of freedom of formalities as outlined in the CISG. However, the PECL is apparently more flexible even when a written contract is mandated by law due in part to acceptance by its member states of proving a contract by other means. Although a Contracting State to the CISG can exempt itself from Article 11 via Article 96, a written document may still be mandated under a country's private law. Notably, such a Declaration may not fully exempt one from Article 11's application. Although different in subject matter, PECL 2:101(2) may be of assistance in interpreting Article 11 CISG when the law mandates that specific contracts be evidenced in writing.

non-reserving countries, on a transaction-by-transaction basis. In other words, whether the text of the Convention includes provisions eliminating writing requirements varies, even in a State that has not made the Article 96 reservation, depending on whether one of the parties is located in another State that made the reservation.

See generally, Harry M. Flechtner, "The Several Texts of the CISG in a Decentralized System: Observations on Translations, Reservations and other Challenges to the Uniformity Principle in Article 7(1)," 17 *J. L. & Com.* (1998) 187–217, also available online at <http://cisgw3.law.pace.edu/cisg/biblio/flecht1.html>.

See, e.g., Denmark 23 April 1998 Østre Landsret [Appellate Court], *Elinette Konfektion v. Elodie S.A.* <http://cisgw3.law.pace.edu/cases/980423d1.html>; but *see* Mexico 29 April 1996 Compromex Arbitration proceeding, *Conservas La Costeña v. Lanín*, available at <http://cisgw3.law.pace.edu/cases/960429m1.html>, finding that "the essential terms of the contractual relationship" had been sufficiently established in writing despite Argentina's declaration. The writing requirement does not call for a formal or solemn contract (*contrato formal*) and a different interpretation, in the opinion of Compromex, "would be in conflict with the general principles of the CISG."

[8] In particular, Article 2 of the Convention expressly states that the Convention does not apply to the sale of goods for personal family or household uses unless the seller, at any time before or at the conclusion of the contract, neither knew nor ought to have known that the goods were bought for such use. Also excluded from the Convention is the sale of watercraft, aircraft, natural gas or electricity, letters of credit, auctions, and securities. In the event of a mixed contract, the Convention would apply unless the "preponderant part of the obligations of the party who furnishes the goods consists in the supply of labour or other services." The CISG can apply to the sale of goods aspect of a distributorship; however, it does not apply to exclusivity or other non-sale aspect of distributorship agreements.

Interpretation of "writing": Comparison between provisions of CISG (Article 13) and counterpart provisions of the Principles of European Contract Law

Ulrich G. Schroeter

I. Introduction
II. Requirement of a "Writing" or "Written" Statements in the CISG and PECL
III. Use of Article 1:301(6) PECL in Interpreting Article 13 CISG

I. INTRODUCTION

Article 13 CISG and its counterpart in Article 1:301(6) PECL both provide definitions of similar, albeit not identical terms: Article 13 CISG deals with the term "writing,"whereas Article 1:301(6) PECL addresses "written" statements.

The systematic position of the two provisions in the respective texts makes clear that both are only concerned with formal aspects of the terms "writing" and "written."[1] Article 13 CISG and Article 1:301(6) PECL neither expressly nor implicitly deal with other questions of interpretation of declarations, statements, and communications by the parties[2] (these are subject to Article 8 CISG and Articles 5:101 PECL *et seq.*), nor do they address the question whether a written declaration was or must have been comprehensible to the recipient (which is to be resolved according to Articles 8 and 24 CISG).[3]

II. REQUIREMENT OF A "WRITING" OR "WRITTEN" STATEMENTS IN THE CISG AND THE PECL

Both Article 1:301(6) PECL and Article 13 CISG limit the relevance of their definitions to writing requirements derived from the respective sets of rules ("[i]n these Principles" and "[f]or the purposes of this Convention").[4]

Within the PECL, the provisions containing such requirements can be divided into two groups: the first group consists of provisions that require a written statement to be applicable (Article 1:304(1) defining the moment when a period of time set by a party in a written statement begins to run,[5] Article 2:207(2) addressing late acceptances contained in a writing, Article 2:210 governing professionals' written confirmations,[6] and Article 3:208 regulating the effect of the principal's silence to a third party's written confirmation, including a request to ratify an act of the agent), whereas the provisions of the second group govern cases in which the contracting parties have provided for a writing requirement in their contract (Article 2.105(1) applying to "merger clauses" and Article 2:106(1) dealing with "no oral modifications" clauses in written contracts).

[1] For Article 13 CISG, *see* Peter Schlechtriem, *Internationales UN-Kaufrecht* (3rd ed. 2005), no. 98. For PECL Article 1:301(6), *see* Note 6 to Article 1:301.

[2] Rolf Herber & Beate Czerwenka, "Internationales Kaufrecht: Kommentar zu dem Übereinkommen der Vereinten Nationen vom 11. April 1980 über Verträge über den internationalen Warenkauf" (1980) (1991), Art. 13 no. 4; *contra* Fritz Enderlein & Dietrich Maskow, *International Sales Law* (1992), Art. 13 no. 1 [available online at <http://cisgw3.law.pace.edu/cisg/biblio/enderlein.html>].

[3] *See* Peter Schlechtriem, "Article 24," in *Commentary on the UN Convention on the International Sale of Goods* (Peter Schlechtriem & Ingeborg Schwenzer eds., 2nd. ed. 2005), no. 15 (unintelligible declarations) and no. 16 (foreign languages).

[4] In Austria 2 July 1993 Oberster Gerichtshof [Supreme Court], *Juristische Blätter* (1994) 119, at 121 the court observed that the definition in Article 13 CISG applies only "for the purposes of this Convention" and may therefore not be extended to domestic lease contracts; case presentation also available in English at <http://cisgw3.law.pace.edu/cases/930702a3.html>.

[5] *See* Comment B to Article 1:304 PECL, which refers to the definition in Article 1:301(6) PECL.

[6] *See* Comment B to Article 2:210 PECL, referring to the definition in Article 1:301(6) PECL.

In the CISG, only a few provisions specifically deal with declarations in writing: Article 21(2) CISG, which, being identical to Article 2:207(2) PECL,[7] belongs to the first above-mentioned group of provisions and is subject to Article 13 CISG,[8] and Articles 12, and 96 CISG dealing with form requirements in national laws that may apply due to a declaration of a Contracting State – it is, however, doubtful if Article 13 CISG covers this case as well.[9] Additionally, the definition in Article 13 CISG applies to Article 29(2) CISG:[10] This provision expressly addresses contractual "no oral modifications" clauses and is, according to one author,[11] also applicable to merger clauses.[12]

In practical terms, however, the primary importance of Article 13 CISG lies in the fact that its definition also applies to any other contractual "writing" requirement stipulated by the parties:[13] Apart from the clauses envisaged by Article 29(2) CISG, the parties may also subject other declarations in conjunction with the contract's execution to a form requirement, thereby derogating from the rule in Article 11 CISG. Possible contractual writing requirements, for instance, may concern the notice of non-conformity (Articles 39(1), 43(1) CISG);[14] the notice fixing an additional time for performance (Article 47(1) CISG); the buyer's specification of form, measurement, or other features of the goods (Article 65(1) CISG); the declaration of avoidance (Article 26 CISG); the notice of the intention to declare the contract avoided because of a future fundamental breach of contract by the other party (Article 72(2) CISG); or the notice of the intention to sell the goods (Article 88(1), (2) CISG). In these cases, it is necessary to first look to Article 8 CISG

[7] *See* Note 2 to Article 2:207.

[8] Miguel Coca Payeras, "Articulo 13," in *La Compraventa Internacional de Mercaderias: Comentario de la Convencion de Viena*, at 158 (Luis Díez-Picazo y Ponce de León ed., 1998); John O. Honnold, *Uniform Law for International Sales*, no. 130 (3rd ed. 1999); Ulrich Magnus, "Artikel 13," in Julius von Staudingers *Kommentar zum Bürgerlichen Gesetzbuch mit Einführungsgesetz und Nebengesetzen, Wiener UN-Kaufrecht CISG)* (2005), no. 7; Karl H. Neumayer & Catherine Ming, *Convention de Vienne sur les Contrats de Vente internationale de Marchandises* (1993), Art. 13 no. 2; Wolfgang Witz, "Artikel 13," in *International Einheitliches Kaufrecht: Praktiker-Kommentar und Vertragsgestaltung zum CISG*, no. 1 (Wolfgang Witz, Hanns-Christian Salger & Manuel Lorenz eds., 2000).

[9] It is subject to dispute if the opening phrase of Article 13 CISG ("For the purposes of this Convention") covers cases where the writing requirement itself is rooted in domestic law and CISG Article 96 merely allows its application; *see*, on the one hand, Enderlein & Maskow, *supra* note 2, Art. 13 no. 1; Herber & Czerwenka, *supra* note 2, Art. 13 no. 2; Schlechtriem, *supra* note 3, Article 13, no. 4 (arguing that CISG Article 13 should apply); and, on the other hand, Siegfried Eiselen, "Electronic Commerce and the UN Convention on Contracts for the International Sale of Goods (CISG) 1980," 6 *EDI L. Rev.* (1999), at 36, also available online at <http://cisgw3.law.pace.edu/cisg/biblio/eiselen1.html>; Honnold *supra* note 8, no. 130; Jerzy Rajski, "Article 13," in *Commentary on International Sales Law*, no. 3.1 (Cesare Massimo Bianca & Michael Joachim Bonell eds., 1987) (stating that Article 13 CISG does not apply). As this dispute concerns the scope of Article 13 CISG, the PECL cannot insofar serve as an aid to interpretation.

[10] Bernard Audit, *La vente internationale de marchandises: Convention des Nations-Unies du 11 avril 1980* (1990), at 74; Coca Payeras, *supra* note 8, at 158; Enderlein & Maskow, *supra* note 2, Art. 13 no. 1; Honnold, *supra* note 8 no. 130; Magnus, *supra* note 8, no. 1; Neumayer & Ming, *supra* note 8, Art. 13 no. 2; Rajski, *supra* note 9, no. 1.1; Schlechtriem, *supra* note 9, no. 3.

[11] Schlechtriem, *supra* note 3, Article 29 no. 6. *See* also ICC Arbitral Award, March 1998, No. 9117, where the arbitral tribunal remarked that "[t]he written modification clause [the significance of which was explained referring to Article 29(2) CISG] has the same effects as the merger clause with regard to any future negotiations, promises and any other extrinsic evidence which otherwise might be adduced for supplementing, altering or contradicting the written contract." [Case presentation available at <http://cisgw3.law.pace.edu/cases/989117i1.html>]

[12] The term "writing" is also used in Article 11 CISG. Its exact definition, however, is not necessary for the purposes of this provision as Article 11 CISG also rejects "any other requirement as to form."

[13] Enderlein & Maskow, *supra* note 2, Art. 13 no. 1; Magnus, *supra* note 8, no. 6; Neumayer & Ming, *supra* note 8, Art. 13 no. 2; Rajski, *supra* note 9, no. 3.1; Witz, *supra* note 8, no. 1.

[14] *See* Germany 13 August 1991 Landgericht [District Court] Stuttgart, case presentation also available online at <http://cisgw3.law.pace.edu/cases/910813g1.html>, where the seller's standard terms required the buyer's notice of non-conformity to be given by registered letter (*lettre recommandé*).

to determine the parties' intent when agreeing on the writing requirement.[15] Whenever it is impossible to ascertain a particular intention, Article 13 CISG will apply.[16]

III. USE OF ARTICLE 1:301(6) PECL IN INTERPRETING ARTICLE 13 CISG

Article 13 CISG does not provide an exhaustive definition of the term "writing," but merely states that it "includes" telegram and telex. This provision, which was incorporated only at the 1980 Vienna Diplomatic Conference[17] and has no direct predecessor in the ULF, ULIS, or any of the Convention's previous drafts, thus reflects the technical standards of the year 1980. Since then, a number of other means of communication not explicitly addressed by Article 13 CISG have started to play an important role in international business transactions.[18] This poses the question if, and under which conditions, modern means of communication can be considered to fulfill writing requirements for the purposes of the CISG.

By stating that "writing" includes telegram and telex, the wording of CISG Article 13 makes clear that it does not fix the outer limits of this term.[19] As writing requirements in and arising in connection with contracts of sale are clearly within the scope of the Convention,[20] recourse is thus to be had to the Convention's general principles addressed by Article 7(2) CISG.[21] Unfortunately, the fact that the Convention itself does not impose any form requirements (see Article 11 CISG), that the legislative history of Article 13 CISG is brief and inconclusive, and that the primary role of Article 13 CISG lies in the interpretation of contractual form requirements, makes it difficult to derive a general principle on writing requirements from the Convention.[22] The main purposes of a writing requirement under the CISG identified by some commentators – to establish the content of a declaration[23] and to permit the identification of its author[24] – accordingly seem to have been drawn from national legal systems, not the Convention itself.

In this situation, it is preferable to look to Article 1:301(6) PECL as an aid for interpretation. This provision was drafted fifteen years after its counterpart in Article 13 CISG and therefore specifically takes into account the various modern means of communication that have been developed since 1980. By drawing on a wide range of legal materials

[15] Herber & Czerwenka, *supra* note 2, Art. 13 no. 5; Werner Melis, "Artikel 13," in *Kommentar zum UN-Kaufrecht*, no. 6 (Heinrich Honsell ed., 1997); Neumayer & Ming, *supra* note 8, Art. 13 no. 2; Schlechtriem, *supra* note 1, no. 98.

[16] *See* Schlechtriem, *supra* note 11, no. 7: If one party's use of the term "writing" was intended to impose stricter requirements than in Article 13 CISG (e.g., he intended it to have the sense it has in his own domestic law), that party bears the burden of proving that pursuant to Article 8 CISG his declaration was intended to derogate from Article 13 CISG and that the other party accepted it as such.

[17] *See* U.N. Official Records (1981), at 74.

[18] *Cf.* Eiselen, *supra* note 9, at 36; Franco Ferrari, "Einige kurze Anmerkungen zur Anwendbarkeit des UN-Kaufrechts beim Vertragsschluss über das Internet," *Eur. Legal For.*, (2000/01) 301, at 305.

[19] Wilhelm-Albrecht Achilles, *Kommentar zum UN-Kaufrechtsübereinkommen* (CISG) (2000), Art. 13 no. 1; Enderlein & Maskow, *supra* note 2, Art. 13 no. 1; Honnold, *supra* note 8, no. 130; Magnus, *supra* note 8, no. 5; Neumayer & Ming, *supra* note 8, Art. 13 no.1.

[20] Eiselen, *supra* note 9, at 36. This of course only applies to matters of sales law – as far as writing requirements relating to matters that are often addressed in contracts of sale but are not governed by the CISG are concerned (e.g., arbitration clauses or guarantees of payments and performance), the writing requirement is subject to national law. *See* Schlechtriem, *supra* note 3, Article 11 no. 10; Ulrich G. Schroeter, *UN-Kaufrecht und Europäisches Gemeinschaftsrecht – Verhältnis und Wechselwirkungen* (2005), § 6 no. 31.

[21] Coca Payeras, *supra* note 8, at 159; Eiselen, *supra* note 9, at 29, 36.

[22] Schlechtriem, *supra* note 3, Article 7 no. 30, on the contrary, considers the principle that declarations may be made without observing requirements as to form to be a general principle of the Convention in accordance with CISG Article 7(2).

[23] Rajski, *supra* note 9, no. 2.2; *see* also Peter Schlechtriem, "Artikel 13," in *Kommentar zum Einheitlichen UN-Kaufrecht*, no. 2 (Peter Schlechtriem & Ingeborg Schwenzer eds., 4th ed. 2004).

[24] Coca Payeras, *supra* note 8, at 159; Magnus, *supra* note 8, no. 4; Rajski, supra note 9, no. 2.2.

from within and outside Europe (including the CISG itself),[25] the drafters of Article 1:301(6) PECL have come up with a convincing solution in line with the trend in modern international trade legislation.

IV. MODERN MEANS OF COMMUNICATION UNDER THE CISG AND THE PECL

No differences exist between the two instruments with respect to declarations made by telegram and telex, which are explicitly covered by both Article 13 CISG and Article 1:301(6) PECL. Also, neither of the two provisions deals with form requirements demanding a signature, a document signed by both parties, or an electronic signature:[26] Contractual stipulations of this kind[27] are subject to the general rule on interpretation in Article 8 PECL.

1. Telefax

The first new means of communication introduced to the business community after the Convention's adoption in 1980 was the telefax (telecopy). It is explicitly mentioned in PECL Article 1:301(6) and also in other international instruments containing provisions that have been modeled on CISG Article 13.[28]

Telefaxes are generally considered to be covered by the term "writing" in Article 13 CISG.[29] Some commentators, however, favor a restriction to faxes that have been printed out as opposed to those transferred from computer to computer and only appearing on the recipient's screen or only retrievable.[30] One author wants to apply Article 13 CISG to declarations that have been transmitted "by fax only," but not to those sent "by fax and post."[31] In the light of Article 1:301(6) PECL, it is not necessary that the telefax has been printed out by the recipient, as long as he had the option to obtain a "readable record" of the statement. This condition is certainly fulfilled not only if the fax is stored on the recipient's computer system but also if the fax message merely appears on the recipient's screen and he chooses not to print it out.[32] Accordingly, it is submitted that only telefaxes transferred from computer to computer that merely appear on the recipient's screen without the option of producing a print-out or saving it as an electronic file cannot be

[25] *See* Note 6 to Article 1:301 stating that CISG Article 13 is "narrower."

[26] Schlechtriem, *supra* note 23, no. 2.

[27] The Convention itself does not require a signature in its Articles 21(2) and 29(2); *see* Honnold, *supra* note 8, no. 130. Such requirements can, however, frequently be found in contractual clauses; *see* U.S. District Court S.D.N.Y., 22 September 1994, 92 Civ. 3655 (JFK) – *Graves Import Company Ltd. & Italian Trading Company v. Chilewich International Corp.*, where the contract stipulated that "[n]o amendments and additions to the present Contract shall be valid unless the same are in writing and signed by duly authorized representatives of both parties." [Case presentation available online, at <http://cisgw3.law.pace.edu/cases/940922u1.html>].

[28] *E.g.*, Uniform Act Relating to General Commercial Law of the Organization for the Harmonization of Business Law in Africa (OHADA) Article 209, see Ulrich G. Schroeter, "Das einheitliche Kaufrecht der afrikanischen OHADA-Staaten im Vergleich zum UN-Kaufrecht, Recht in Afrika" (2001) 163, at 167 [available online at <http://cisgw3.law.pace.edu/cisg/biblio/schroeter.html>].

[29] Audit, *supra* note 10, at 73; Eiselen, *supra* note 9, at 29; Herber & Czerwenka, *supra* note 2, Art. 13 no. 4; Vincent Heuzé, *La vente internationale de marchandises* (1992), no. 205; Honnold, *supra* note 8, no. 130; Magnus, *supra* note 8, no. 5; Neumayer & Ming, *supra* note 8, Art. 13 no. 1.

[30] Achilles, *supra* note 19, Art. 13 no. 1; Schlechtriem, *supra* note 23, no. 2; Witz, *supra* note 8, no. 2 (requiring that the fax is "directly" printed out by the recipient).

[31] Melis, *supra* note 15, no. 4. This distinction, it is submitted, is hardly convincing.

[32] The recipient's situation is comparable to that of a person receiving a (paper-based) letter: the declaration contained therein is beyond doubt "in writing," even if the recipient subsequently destroys the letter.

considered to be in "writing" in the sense employed by Article 13 CISG.[33] All other telefaxes constitute a "writing" for the purposes of the Convention.

2. Electronic Data Interchange (EDI)

Where electronic data interchange (EDI), defined as "the electronic interchange of machine processable structured data, which has been formatted according to agreed standards and which can be transmitted directly between different computer systems with the aid of telecommunication interfaces,"[34] is used in connection with a contract of sale, the parties usually have concluded an interchange agreement[35] prior to their first declaration by way of EDI. Such an agreement will often allow courts or arbitrators to determine if the parties had the intent to treat statements made through EDI as a "writing" in the sense employed in their sales contract.[36]

Whenever these indications are insufficient or inconclusive, Article 13 CISG provides the relevant guidelines. A number of commentators have argued that this provision has to be read to include EDI.[37] This interpretation seems to be in line with Article 1:301(6) PECL, which makes no explicit mention of EDI, but covers any "means of communication capable of providing a readable record of the statement on both sides."[38] Accordingly, an EDI message suffices where writing is required for the purposes of the Convention.

3. Electronic Mail (e-mail)

Under Article 1:301(6) PECL, the term "written" statement explicitly includes declarations made by electronic mail. The main difference between e-mail and Electronic Data Interchange lies in the fact that within the latter system a number of different technical standards for data messages are used that, as they are not necessarily compatible with each other, thus usually require a prior agreement between sender and recipient (the interchange agreement); in contrast, e-mail uses "open" data connections and computer networks.[39] In cases where e-mails have been used, it will therefore not be possible to rely on interchange agreements to interpret contractual writing requirements.

As electronic mail is a means of communication capable of providing a readable electronic record of the messages sent (by storing the messages in the mailing systems of the sender and the recipient), it fulfills the standards of Article 13 CISG.[40] This rule applies

[33] This interpretation also conforms to the definition contained in a recent UNCITRAL text: The Convention on the Assignment of Receivables in International Trade (2001), Article 5(c) defines "writing" as "any form of information that is accessible so as to be usable for subsequent reference."

[34] Eiselen, *supra* note 9, at 23.

[35] Eiselen, *supra* note 9, at 37 *et seq.* On standard interchange agreements, *see* Amelia H. Boss, "Electronic Commerce and the Symbiotic Relationship between International and Domestic Law Reform," 72 *Tul. L. Rev.* (1998) 1931, at 1949 *et seq.*

[36] *See* Eiselen, *supra* note 9, at 27: "[i]f an Interchange Agreement specifically prescribes the methods of communications [. . .], that should be heeded." An interchange agreement may also be taken into account if the sales contract incorporating the form requirement was concluded prior to the interchange agreement, as under Article 8(3) CISG due consideration is to be given to "all circumstances of the case including [. . .] any subsequent conduct of the parties" when determining their intent.

[37] Eiselen, *supra* note 9, at 36; Honnold, *supra* note 8, no. 130; Magnus, *supra* note 8, no. 5.

[38] It is my position that a readable record in electronic format suffices for the purposes of CISG Article 13; *see supra*, 4 a) (on telefaxes transmitted from computer to computer); *contra* Witz, *supra* note 8, no. 2.

[39] The most important network system for the transmission of e-mails is the Internet; *see* the text *infra*, at 4d for a brief description.

[40] Eiselen, *supra* note 9, at 36; Magnus, *supra* note 8, no. 5; Willibald Posch, "Article 13," in *Praxiskommentar zum ABGB samt Nebengesetzen*, no. 3 (Michael Schwimann ed., 2nd ed. 1997); *contra* Witz, *supra* note 8, no. 2.

to any e-mail and neither requires the message to be converted into paper-based form[41] nor authenticated by an electronic signature.[42]

4. Internet and World Wide Web

The terms "Internet" and "World Wide Web" are often used interchangeably,[43] although they are not synonymous.

The Internet is a massive networking infrastructure connecting millions of computers globally, forming a network in which any computer can communicate with any other computer as long as they are both connected to the Internet. As far as communications via the Internet are concerned that merely use the Internet as a network of data connections through which electronic messages are transmitted between the mailing systems of the sender and of the recipient, the situation under Article 13 CISG is identical to the one discussed above.

The World Wide Web, on the contrary, is a way of accessing information over the medium of the Internet. It is thus an information-sharing model that is built on top of the Internet and that is often used for purposes of electronic commerce. As the Web is in a number of ways different from e-mail,[44] declarations made over the Web require special attention under Article 13 CISG. Frequently, companies' Web sites are organized in a way that allows statements to be made to the company by using a "form" provided on the site. The Web user types his message into the form and dispatches it by clicking on the relevant "button." As far as contracts of sale are concerned, this means of communication could, for example, be used to give notices of non-conformity according to Article 39(1) CISG to sellers providing the above-mentioned option on their Web site.

A declaration made through a Web site form does, however, not fulfil the writing requirement as defined in Article 1:301(6) PECL, as it does not provide a readable record of the statement on both sides – once the declaration is dispatched, an electronic record remains on the recipient's side only, but not on the side of the sender (contrary to the use of e-mail, the sender's mailing system is not involved). When accepting that the prerequisite of a record existing on both sides serves as a compensation for the lack of a paper-based documentation of the statement,[45] declarations over the World Wide Web of the kind described above cannot be considered to fulfill the requirements of Article 13 CISG.

V. CONCLUSION

As Article 13 CISG does not explicitly deal with the modern means of communication that have been introduced after 1980 and are nowadays frequently used in connection with the conclusion and performance of international sales contracts, the more recently adopted Article 1:301(6) PECL, which has an identical purpose and is based on the same philosophy, provides a useful aid in its interpretation. By looking to its PECL counterpart when applying Article 13 CISG to electronic communications, courts and arbitrators can keep the CISG from becoming a piece of petrified law[46] and, at the same time, allow

[41] Magnus, *supra* note 8, no. 5; *contra* Achilles, *supra* note 19, Art. 13 no. 1; Schlechtriem, *supra* note 1, no. 68.

[42] Magnus, *supra* note 8, no. 5; but *see* Schlechtriem, *supra* note 23, no. 2.

[43] *Cf. e.g.*, Schlechtriem, *supra* note 23, no. 2.

[44] The main technical difference is that the World Wide Web and e-mail rely on different protocols to transmit data over the Internet: The Web uses the HTTP protocol, whereas e-mail uses the SMTP protocol.

[45] It has to be kept in mind that the traditional paper-based form of communication qualifying as a "writing" in the sense employed by Article 13 CISG – the letter – does, once received by the recipient, only provide a record of the statement on one side (the recipient's), but not on the side of the sender.

[46] *See* Eiselen, supra note 9, at 21.

the Convention to take its place as a part of the emerging global legal framework for electronic commerce.[47]

[47] *See* Boss, *supra* note 35, at 1979.

Criteria for an offer: Remarks on the manner in which the PECL may be used to interpret or supplement Article 14 CISG

Predrag Cvetkovik

I. INTRODUCTION

Both the CISG (Art. 14(1)) and the PECL (Art. 2:101) recognize the traditional offer-acceptance model of contracting. The PECL also has a provision (Art. 2:211) on contracts not concluded through the traditional offer and acceptance mode.

Offer-acceptance, the only model explicitly addressed in the CISG, is the principal model in most legal systems of the world. However, it seems to be universally agreed that rules on the traditional model of offer-acceptance can be applied by way of analogy to other models, insofar as this is reasonable and with appropriate adaptations. The Comments on Art. 2:211 PECL may, in this respect, be relevant to the proper interpretation of the CISG.[1]

II. *ANIMUS CONTRAHENDI*

The offeror expresses with his proposal the intention to give an option to the offeree: with the acceptance, the offeree can conclude the contract according to the terms of the offer. This intention has its Latin name: *animus contrahendi*. Both the CISG and the PECL demand *animus contrahendi* in an offer: the offer should show the offeror's "intention to be bound" in the case of acceptance (CISG Art. 14(1)), and an offer must be "intended to result in a contract if the other party accepts it" (PECL Art. 2:201(1)(a)).[2]

[1] Art. 2:211 PECL explicitly extends its formation provisions to contractual situations that do not fit the traditional offer-acceptance model. The Comments to this provision of the PECL <http://cisgw3.law.pace.edu/cisg/text/peclcomp14.html#2211> cite as examples of situations covered by an analogical application of the rules found in PECL provisions on offer and acceptance:

(a) the situation in which it is not easy to tell where in the negotiation process the parties reach an agreement that amounts to a binding contract of sale (*see* the elements required by Article 2:201 PECL, which are sometimes hard to establish)

(b) the situation in which a certain type of contract is made by conduct alone (e.g., car park tickets, etc. [the explanation for this listing of a typical contract transaction with a consumer is that the PECL, which is applicable to consumer as well as commercial contract transactions, has a broader scope than the CISG])

[2] This presumption is also found in Art. 2.2 of the UNIDROIT Principles of International Commercial Contract [UPICC].

In addition, PECL article 2:102 deals with the determination of the parties' intention to be legally bound. Whether a party in fact has such an intention is immaterial if the other party has reason to infer from the first party's statement or other conduct that the first party intends to be bound.

III. THE "SUFFICIENT DEFINITION" OF AN OFFER

An offer is not only the manifestation of the offeror's intention to conclude the contract: as a project of a possible future contractual relationship, the offer must contain all of the elements necessary for the successful conclusion of a valid contract. The completeness of an offer with regard to the contract itself (i.e., considering its terms) should be established *ex ante*: the necessary elements of proposal are those needed for validity of the future contract. More precisely, only an offer containing all of the requisite ingredients – thus making it suitable for acceptance – can lead to the successful formation of a contract. It is not necessary that these fundamental elements be regulated in the contract in a rigid and thorough way; there is a sufficient grade of determination if such elements are definable (e.g., if a contract provides the criteria for such a determination).

The type of a contract determines the requisite elements of the offer. The terms of the contract (using the criteria of their necessity for the formation of the contract) can be divided into three main groups: (1) *essentialia negotii* (terms without which the contract would have no sense); (2) *naturalia negotii* (terms that regulate the parties' obligations logically stemming from the contract itself); and (3) *accidentalia negotii* (terms that are not common for the type of contract in question, but that could be the subject of its terms).

The offer must determine the *essentialia negotii* (the fundamental terms of the contract). The content of other elements of the contract can be derived from the parties' statements and behavior[3] or determined by a court, arbitrator, or third person.

The relevant provisions in the PECL and the CISG demand the "sufficient definition" of a proposal for it to constitute an "offer" for the purposes of formation of the contract. Whereas the PECL establishes this condition only in one laconic sentence (see Art. 2:201(1)(a)), the CISG in Art. 14(1) is more thorough in defining the key conditions for a sale of goods contract. This difference in treatment stems from the different scope of application of the two instruments. The CISG is the uniform code for the international [*commercial*] sale of *goods* with its scope limited to *international* sales contracts, in the sense of Art. 1 CISG, which defines the CISG's concept of internationality, and Art. 2(a) CISG, which excludes consumer sales. The PECL, on the other hand, is designed to "be applied as general rules of contract law in the European Communities."[4] The redactors of the PECL sought to create a frame applicable not only to international commercial contracts for the sale of goods but also to *all* contract transactions – contracts for services as well as goods and domestic as well as international contracts, including contracts with consumers.

2.1. In national codes, the fundamental elements (*essentialia negotii*) of a sales contract and, in accordance with that, of the offer for concluding such contracts are the goods, the quantity, and the price. As the subject of a sales contract, the goods are specified or determined by kind, quantity, and quality.

According to Art. 14(1) CISG, the quantity of the goods can be determined expressly or implicitly.[5] The quality of goods is not expressly regulated by the formation provisions of the CISG. However, Art. 35 CISG can be used for the determination of the goods'

[3] *See* Art. 8 CISG and its PECL counterparts, Arts. 2:101, 5:101, and related PECL provisions <http://cisgw3.law.pace.edu/cisg/text/peclcomp8.html>.

[4] *See* Art. 1:101(1) PECL. *Cf.* the UNIDROIT Contract Principles whose scope is broader than that of the CISG, but not as broad as the PECL. The UNIDROIT Principles "set forth general rules for [all] international commercial contracts" (see the Preamble of UPICC, para. 1): the UNIDROIT Principles thus apply to international commercial contracts for the sale of goods as well as other international commercial contracts.

[5] In a contract of sale for which the PECL is the governing law, the quantity can also be determined not only expressly but implicitly as well. This conclusion can be derived from Art. 6:102 of the PECL, which provides criteria that establish "implied obligations."

quality when it is not determined by the contract itself.[6] As the CISG does not mention the determination of the goods' quality as an element necessary for an offer to be deemed "sufficiently definite," the best solution is for the parties to regulate the importance of fulfilling the obligation concerning the quality of the goods. If one party insists on a certain quality and the offer does not express a clear agreement, there is no valid contract, because there is no valid offer and acceptance.[7]

The PECL has a provision on "average quality" that is more specific than the CISG and that would appear to be consistent with the intent of the CISG legislators. The PECL demands that "if the contract does not specify the quality, a party must tender performance of at least average quality" (Art. 6:108). As the definition of average quality is not incorporated into the PECL, it leaves open the question of how courts and arbitrators will determine the average quality of performance or goods.[8]

2.2. When the content of the contract is in question, there is a disagreement as to the CISG requirements on *specification* of [*ability to determine*] the *price in the offer*.

The CISG rules on price determination are in contradiction. First, Art. 14(1) CISG states that a determined price is a necessary part of an offer.[9] However, Art. 55 CISG provides that if the contract does not expressly or implicitly make provision for the price, "the buyer must pay the price generally charged by the seller at the time of the conclusion of the contract."[10] By prescribing the criteria for the determination of a price that is not defined by the contract, it is presumed that a contract could be valid[11] without a determined price, either by the contract itself or in the offer for its conclusion.

The further requirement of a fixed or determinable price in Art. 14(1) CISG was the subject of intensive debate both in the UNCITRAL deliberations and at the Vienna Diplomatic Conference.[12] Proposals to eliminate the requirement of a fixed or determinable

[6] *See* Art. 35(2) CISG. Through this article, the criteria for the determination of the conformity of goods in the sale contract are established.

[7] In accord, *see* Germany 31 March 1995 *Oberlandesgericht* [Appellate Court] Frankfurt am Main, case presentation including English translation available at <http://cisgw3.law.pace.edu/cases/950331g1.html>. In that case the buyer alleged that, through the course of negotiation, the parties agreed on test tubes of "Duran" quality. The seller delivered tubes of "Fiolax" quality. The buyer refused to pay the price. The Court ruled that there was no valid contract, because the acceptance of the seller's offer was missing as the seller and the buyer had not reached an agreement on quality. Hence, there was no valid offer and acceptance; consequently, no validly concluded contract.

[8] Art 5.6 UPICC (which deals with the determination of a quality of performance that is neither fixed nor determinable by the contract) introduces the criteria of reasonable quality of performance, in addition to "average quality." The PECL have defined the term "reasonableness" (Art. 1:302). The reason why this criterion was not incorporated in the PECL as the supplemental remedy for determination of the quality of performance could not be seen, unless this is to be regarded as an implicit element of the PECL.

[9] Art. 14(1) CISG reads, "A proposal is sufficiently definite if it indicates the goods and expressly or implicitly fixes or makes provisions for determining [. . .] the price."

[10] Art. 55 CISG reads, "Where a contract has been validly concluded but does not expressly or implicitly fix or make provisions for determining the price, the parties are considered, in the absence of any indication to the contrary, to have impliedly made reference to the price generally charged at the time of the conclusion of the contract for such goods sold under comparable circumstances in the trade concerned."

[11] Art. 55 begins, "Where a contract has been *validly* concluded" (emphasis added). Khoo calls attention to the meaning of this reference to validity. He states, "Article 55 deals with cases in which a contract has apparently been concluded but without any agreement on provision as to price. In these instances, Article 55 makes it clear that its provision takes effect subject to the contract having been validly concluded by the criteria of the applicable domestic law." Warren L. H. Khoo, in Bianca-Bonell *Commentary on the International Sales Law*, Guiffrè: Milan (1987), p. 46. The pre-Vienna Diplomatic Conference legislative history of the CISG is in accord. *See* UNCITRALYearbook VIII, A/CN.9/SER.A/1977, pp. 48–49, paras. 323–330, 336–340; *see also* Honnold, *Uniform Law for International Sales under the 1980 United Nations Convention*, 2d ed. (1991), p. 201.

[12] For a clear account of relevant recorded details in these drafting debates, go to

(i) <http://cisgw3.law.pace.edu/cisg/firstcommittee/Meeting8.html>. Here one can access the summary records of the 8th meeting of the First Committee (Monday, 17 March 1980) on CISG Arts. 14 and 55 [A/CONF.97/C.1/L.29, L.36, L.37, L.38, L.46, L.55 and L.69]. One will find in this record some

price failed as a result of the opposition by the Soviet Union, a number of developing countries, France, and other States.[13]

The contradiction between CISG Articles 14(1) and 55 is found in the different approaches adopted in the literature. Professor Honnold's view is that the meaning of Art. 55 CISG is that "a contract may be 'validly concluded' even though it does not expressly or impliedly fix or make provisions for determining the price."[14] On the other hand, Professor Farnsworth is of the opinion that the requirement in Art. 14(1) CISG must be met, so that the offer must contain the price.[15]

This academic debate concerns whether Art. 14(1) CISG should be read alone or in conjunction with Art. 55.[16] Some scholars[17] hold that the most justified approach

very interesting comments and drafting alliances formed between countries irrespective of their level of industrial/economic development. Note especially the position of France, whose representative (Mr. GHESTIN) said that it was "important to retain the sentence as the essential terms of a sale were quality, quantity and price, the main difficulty being the question of the price. The issue was one of balance and fairness. It should be borne in mind that contracts frequently covered raw materials that were to be delivered over a period of years at prices that were difficult to fix (e.g., petroleum products)."

(ii) <http://cisgw3.law.pace.edu/cisg/firstcommittee/Meeting11.html>. Here one can access the Summary Records of the 11th Meeting of the First Committee (Tuesday, 18 March 1980) on CISG Arts. 14 and 55. Report of ad hoc working group on paragraph 1 (A/CONF.97/C.1/L. 103). A report on the significance of the deliberations on Article 14 CISG based on notes taken at the Conference and published shortly thereafter was prepared by Prof. Schlechtriem and is available online at <http://cisgw3.law.pace.edu/cisg/biblio/schlechtriem-14.html>.

[13] *See* Jacob S. Ziegel, "Article 14," in *Report to the Uniform Law Conference of Canada on Convention on Contracts for the International Sale of Goods* (July 1981): "The Francophone countries and delegates from a substantial number of developing states felt that Art. 12(1) [became 14(1) CISG] was doctrinally sound and necessary to prevent buyers from being confronted by sellers with unreasonable prices after the goods had been delivered"; available at <http://cisgw3.law.pace.edu/cisg/text/ziegel14.html>.

"Socialist countries objected to the conclusion of contracts with open-price terms, because the parties are expected to conform their contracts to a predetermined macroeconomic governmental plan. This view makes sense in a planned economy, in which contracts with open-price terms are a nullity from the perspective of the superintending state planning agency. Also, in some civil law systems, contracts of sale with open-price terms are viewed with hostility, particularly when the unilateral fixing of the price works to the disadvantage of the weaker party"; Helen Elizabeth Hartnell, "Rousing the Sleeping Dog: The Validity Exception to the Convention on Contracts for the International Sale Of Goods," 18 *Yale J. Int'l. L*, (1993) 1, 66, also available at <http://cisgw3.law.pace.edu/cisg/biblio/hartnell.html>.

See also Alejandro M. Garro, "Reconciliation of Legal Traditions in the U.N. Convention on Contracts for the International Sale of Goods," 23 *Int'l. Law.* 443, 463 (1989) <http://cisgw3.law.pace.edu/cisg/biblio/garro1.html>.

[14] John O. Honnold, *Uniform Law for International Sale under the 1980 United Nations Convention* (1982) pp. 163. Honnold states, "[T]he added provision, that in such case the parties are considered 'to have impliedly made reference' to the prices generally charged, precludes argument that failure to state the price produces a fatal gap in the contract that contravenes the provisions on definiteness in article 14."

[15] E. Allan Farnsworth, *Formation of Contract* (1984) § 3.04, at. 3–8. In Prof. Farnsworth's opinion, Art. 55 in Part III of the CISG (which deals with the obligations of the parties according to an existing contract) was designed for use only where a Contracting State made a declaration under Art. 92(1) CISG that it will not be bound by Part II of the Convention, and, more precisely, by Art. 14 placed in Part II of the CISG.

[16] "The Honnold position is that the provisions may be read together, while the Farnsworth position is that they cannot." Paul Amato, "U.N. Convention on Contracts for the International Sale of Goods – the Open Price Term and Uniform Application: an Early Interpretation by the Hungarian Courts," 13 *J.L. & Com.* (1993) 1, 10; also available at <http://cisgw3.law.pace.edu/cisg/biblio/amato.html>. *See* also Carlos A. Gabuardi, "Open Price Terms in the CISG, the UCC and Mexican Commercial Law," available at <http://cisgw3.law.pace.edu/cisg/biblio/gabuardi.html>. The author provides an excellent comparative review of the issue of open-price terms. On point, Gabuardi agrees with Honnold that Articles 14 and 55 regulate different issues and are not contradictory. "I think that article 14 only establishes a rule for those cases in which the parties exchange 'offer' and 'acceptance' without making an express commitment to be bound even if the price has not been fixed, while article 55 establishes a rule for those cases in which the parties enter into an agreement in which they commit themselves to be bound by it, even though the price has not been fixed." *Id.*

[17] Amato *supra* note 16, at pp. 1–27; J. E. Murray, Jr., "An Essay on the Formation on Contracts and Related Matters under the United Nations Convention on Contracts for the International Sale of Goods," 8 *J.L. & Com.* (1988), pp. 11–51, also at <http://cisgw3.law.pace.edu/cisg/biblio/murray.html>.

regarding the open-price term is that

> The ultimate criteria for deciding whether a price is the necessary part of an offer or not must be determined by using the rules of the interpretation of the parties' statements.[18] If, even without the price term, the parties consider an offer sufficiently determined and, on the basis of such offer, conclude a sales contract, then there is no reason for the courts and arbitrators not to accept the contractors' will.

Gabuardi has contributed to the substance of the debate by providing an insightful review of the legislative history and doctrine on Arts. 14(1) and 55, as well as the available CISG case law on open-price terms, concluding that

> [W]hile being silent about the discussion within the academic community, the courts have approached the issue of open-price terms in sales contracts acknowledging that articles 14 and 55 of CISG deal with different issues; that is, article 14 deals with the issue of open-price terms at the time of the formation of the contract, while article 55 deals with open-price terms once the parties have already entered into a sales contract.[19]

Should the problem of the open-price term appear in regards to a sale contract governed by the PECL as *lex contractus*, it could be solved by a PECL provision that takes care of the situation in which the price for goods or services is not determined in the contract. By way of contrast with the CISG, when the price for goods or services is not determined by the contract, the PECL presumes that "a reasonable price" is in effect.[20] In commercial practice, the price can be determined as the prevailing price, or as the average price, or in other similar ways.[21] In this sense, the rule of Art. 6:107 PECL becomes quite important. According to this rule, if the price (or any other contractual terms) is to be determined by reference to a non-existent, ceased, or non-accessible factor, the nearest equivalent factor shall be substituted.[22] The provisions of the PECL on "reasonable price" where the price cannot be determined by the contract do not appear relevant to the proper interpretation of the CISG.

The PECL also deals with the possibility that the right to determine the price is given to a third party.[23] If the third party will not or cannot determine the price, "the parties are presumed to have empowered the court to appoint another person to determine it."[24]

In addition, the PECL regulates the situation in which the determination of the price (or any other contractual term) is left to one of the contract parties. When this is the case and the determination is "grossly unreasonable, then notwithstanding any provision to the contrary, a reasonable price or other term shall be substituted."[25]

[18] Those rules are contained in CISG Art. 8, PECL Arts. 1:302 and 5:101, and in UPICC Art. 4.1, Art. 4.2., and Art. 4.3.

[19] Gabuardi, *supra* note 16.

[20] *See* Art. 6:104 PECL.

[21] Some national codes also use terms, such as the "prevailing price"; for example, UCC § 2–724, Italian Codice Civile Art. 1474(2), Yugoslav Code of Obligation (Art. 465(2) (3).

[22] It is necessary to remember that Art. 55 CISG prescribes that, subject to a validly concluded contract that does not expressly or implicitly fixed price or provision for determining the price, "the parties are considered, in the absence of any indication to the contrary, to have impliedly made reference to the price generally charged at the time of the conclusion of the contract for such goods sold under comparable circumstances in the trade concerned."

[23] It should be emphasized that regulation of this question is quite justified and welcome with regard to the practical needs in commercial relations in which the parties can agree that the determination of the price is to be entrusted to commercial agents, trade chambers, stock exchanges, etc.

[24] *See* Art. 6:106(1) PECL. The rule adopted in the PECL trails the "*in favorem contractus*" principle, which is in accord with the needs and nature of international commercial exchange of goods, money, and services. The UPICC also follow this approach in Art. 5.7(3), which presumes the validity of a "reasonable price" in the event the third party did not determine the price.

[25] *See* Art. 6:105 PECL. Art. 57(2) UPICC is to the same effect. In practice, a contract clause that authorizes one party to determine the price is, in most cases, the consequence of a huge economic power inequality

2.3. Non-fundamental elements of an offer are elements whose determination is not necessary for the validity of the offer and, consequently, for a contract to be concluded on the basis of such an offer. Those elements can be turned into fundamental elements if the parties express their will to have them so regarded. In the CISG, it can be concluded from Art. 14(1) that the fundamental elements of an offer are the price, the quantity, and the goods. *A contrario*, other elements are non-fundamental,[26] but can be turned into fundamental elements if that is what the parties want. The redactors of the PECL explicitly sanction this possibility. According to Art. 2:103(2) PECL (sufficient agreement), "if one of the parties refuses to conclude a contract unless the parties have agreed on some specific matter, there is no contract unless agreement on that matter has been reached."[27] However, if parties did not determine the content of the contract's non-fundamental elements, this content should be evaluated according to the rules for the interpretation of the parties' intention[28] or according to Art. 6:102 PECL (implied obligation).[29]

IV. THE DETERMINATION OF OFFER *AD PERSONAM*

In addition to *animus contrahendi* and the element of "sufficient definition," another condition for a proposal to be considered an offer is the determination of the person for whom the offer is intended (determination of offer *ad personam*).

The importance of this condition is especially relevant to offers made using price lists, catalogues, public advertisements, or other similar methods. Some national laws explicitly provide that such proposals are not offers.[30] The PECL, on the other hand, prescribes that an offer "may be made to one or more specific person or to the public."[31] Moreover, even "a proposal to supply goods or services at stated prices made by a professional supplier in a public advertisement or catalogue, or by a display of goods, is presumed to be an offer to sell or supply at the price until the stock of goods, or the supplier's capacity to supply the service, is exhausted."[32]

This provision of the PECL is not relevant to the proper interpretation of the CISG because, conversely, the general rule in the CISG seems not to regard such proposals extended to the public as offers. The CISG deems such a proposal as only an "invitation *ad offerendum*"; CISG Article 14(2) states that a proposal addressed to other than one or more specific persons is to be "considered merely as an invitation to make offers, unless the contrary is clearly indicated by the person making the proposal."

This difference between the PECL and the CISG could be explained again by the different scope of application of the PECL and the CISG. The CISG was brought to life with the intention to be applied only to commercial sales. On the other hand, the PECL is

between the parties. National codes that allow only one party to be empowered to determine the price often restrict this discretion with the principle of good faith (*see*, for example, § 2–305(2) UCC). In that way, arbitrary or fraudulent use of this right is prevented. A similar interpretation is also valid for Art. 6:105 PECL.

[26] Form, measurement, and other features of the goods are examples of elements of offers, and their acceptances that the CISG does not appear to regard as fundamental. *See* Art. 65 CISG.

[27] *See* also Art. 2.13 UPICC.

[28] *See* note 22 *supra* and accompanying text. By way of comparison, it should be mentioned that the UPICC have a particular rule for "supplying an omitted term" (e.g., for the situation in which the parties did not agree with respect to a term that is important for a determination of their rights and duties).

[29] According to Art. 6:102 PECL, along with express terms, a contract may contain implied terms based on the intention of the parties, the nature and purpose of the contract, and good faith and fair dealing. In a wider sense, the content of non-fundamental elements can be derived from this rule. *See* also Arts. 5.1 and 5.2 of the UPICC.

Note that under PECL Arts. 2:101 and 2:103, a contract is only concluded if the parties have agreed on its express terms. This rule must also apply when a party invokes standard terms or other not individually negotiated terms as part of the contract; see the effect of PECL Art. 2:104.

[30] *See*, for example, Art. 7(2) of the Swiss Code of Obligation.

[31] *See* Art. 2:201(2) PECL.

[32] *See* Art. 2:201(3) (offer) PECL.

designed to be applied as general rules of contract law in the European Communities[33]; there is no restriction for PECL application only to commercial contracts.[34] The rule in the PECL, which allows a public advertisement, a catalogue, etc., to be presumed as an offer, is the logical consequence of its scope of application. The PECL rule protects the interest of consumers, who are in most cases the persons to whom such advertisements or similar proposals are intended, an area outside the realm of the CISG.

[33] *See* Art. 1:101(1) PECL.

[34] By way of contrast, the UPICC are strictly intended to be applied to international commercial contracts (*see* Purpose of the UNIDROIT Principles, par. 1.)

Revocability of offer: Editorial remarks on whether and the extent to which the Principles of European Contract Law may be used to help interpret Article 16 of the CISG

Orkun Akseli

I. REVOCATION OF AN OFFER – CISG ARTICLE 16(1)

Article 16 CISG of the U.N. Convention on Contracts for the International Sale of Goods (the Convention) and Article 2:202 of the Principles of European Contract Law (PECL) deal whether an offer is binding and when it is irrevocable.

Both the Convention and the PECL distinguish between the revocation of an offer and the withdrawal of an offer. In the Convention, revocation of an offer that has reached the offeree and is effective is regulated by Article 16; withdrawal of an offer that has not yet reached the offeree is regulated by Article 15(2).[1]

Similarly, under the PECL, an offer becomes effective when it reaches the offeree (Article 1:303(2) and (6)), and a subsequent revocation of the offer is regulated by PECL Article 2:202. However, the offer may be withdrawn before it reaches the offeree. In that situation, it will not become effective (PECL Article 1:303(5)).

There is divergence in the way in which different legal systems deal with the matter of revocation of an offer. In common law systems, the offeror, in the absence of consideration given by the offeree, has been granted the freedom to revoke the offer

[1] CISG Art. 15 reads "(1) An offer becomes effective when it reaches the offeree. (2) An offer, even if it is irrevocable, may be withdrawn if the withdrawal reaches the offeree before or at the same time as the offer." *See also* Schlechtriem, "Uniform Sales Law – The UN-Convention on Contracts for the International Sale of Goods" 52 (1986) [available online at <http://cisgw3.law.pace.edu/cisg/biblio/schlechtriem.html>].

before the contract is concluded (e.g., in the case of written assent, before the offeree dispatches the acceptance), thus weakening the binding force of an offer.

On the other hand, in civil law systems, generally, a firm offer cannot be revoked until its rejection or expiration; therefore, the offeror is bound by the offer for a reasonable time. In the latter regimes, the offeror, with his offer, implicitly grants the offeree a certain reasonable time to consider and respond to the offer. In this context, if the offeror does not indicate otherwise, there is the presumption of irrevocability for a reasonable time, unlike in the common law systems.

Article 16(1) of the Convention provides that an offer is generally revocable[2]; the right of the offeror to revoke his offer terminates at the moment the contract is concluded. However, it must be noted that, in the case in which an offer is accepted by a written indication of assent, CISG Article 16 provides that the right of the offeror to revoke the offer terminates at the moment the offeree has dispatched his acceptance, and not at the moment the acceptance reaches the offeror.[3] That common law "mailbox rule" or dispatch rule is adopted in the Convention, even though CISG Art. 18(2) provides that "acceptance is thus effective when it reaches the offeree."[4] It has been commented that the Convention, in Article 16(1), assumes the common law presumption of revocability.[5]

Here, it is worthwhile to mention briefly how the UNIDROIT Principles deal with this issue. Article 2.4 of the UNIDROIT Principles regulates the revocation of an offer[6] in

[2] *See* Secretariat Commentary on article 14 of the 1978 Draft *[draft counterpart of CISG article 16]*, Comment 1, which makes clear that this provision "states that offers are in general revocable and that the revocation is effective when it reaches [. . .] the offeree." [Hereinafter, *Secretariat Commentary*, also available online at: <http://cisgw3.law.pace.edu/cisg/text/secomm/secomm-16.html>]. *See also* CISG Art. 24, which provides a definition of the term "reaches."

[3] *See* Secretariat Commentary, Comment 4. For comments and comparison with UCC Article 2 *see* Peter Schlechtriem, *Commentary on the UN Convention on the International Sale of Goods* (Peter Schlechtriem ed., 1998) at 119, stating that "[CISG Article 16] restricts [revocability] by providing that not only the conclusion of the contract but even the dispatch of an acceptance rules out the revocation of an offer. The offeror can make his offer binding without the need for 'consideration' or the observance of particular forms and without a time period being prescribed during which the offeror is bound by his offer."

[4] CISG Art. 23 reads, "A contract is concluded at the moment when an acceptance of an offer becomes effective in accordance with the provisions of this Convention." The Secretariat Commentary explains that the basic rule – i.e., the offeror's right to revoke the offer terminates at the moment the contract is concluded – applies only in those cases in which the offeree orally accepts the offer and in those cases in which the offeree accepts the offer in conformity with Article 18(3); *see* Comment 2.

CISG Art. 18(3) provides that "if, by virtue of the offer or as a result of practices which the parties have established between themselves or of usage, the offeree may indicate assent by performing an act, such as one relating to the dispatch of the goods or payment of the price, without giving notice to the offeror, the acceptance is effective at the moment the act is performed." In that context, because the acceptance is effective and the contract is concluded at the moment the act is performed, the right of the offeror to revoke his offer terminates at that same moment; *see* Comment 3.

[5] *See* Alejandro Garro, "Reconciliation of Legal Traditions in the U.N. Convention on Contracts for the International Sale of Goods," 23 *Int'l Law.* (1989) 443 [available online at <http://cisgw3.law.pace.edu/cisg/biblio/garro1.html>; *see also* Honnold, *Uniform Law for International Sales* 167 (2d ed. 1987).

Cf. Secretariat Commentary, Comment 5: "The value of a rule that a revocable offer becomes irrevocable prior to the moment at which the contract is concluded lies in the fact that it contributes to an effective compromise between the theory of general revocability of offers and the theory of general irrevocability of offers. Although all offers except those which fall within the scope of article 14(2) *[draft counterpart of CISG article 16(2)]* are revocable, they become irrevocable once the offeree makes his commitment by dispatching the acceptance."

See also P. Schlechtriem, *Uniform Sale Law – The U.N. Convention on Contracts for the International Sale of Goods* (1986) 52, who states that "the possibility of withdrawing an offer until, or in any case simultaneously with, its arrival coincides with ULF Article 5(1) and § 130(1) sentence 2 of the German Civil Code"; [available at: <http://cisgw3.law.pace.edu/cisg/biblio/schlechtriem-16.html>].

[6] Article 2.4 of the UNIDROIT Principles reads, "(1) Until a contract is concluded an offer may be revoked if the revocation reaches the offeree before it has dispatched an acceptance. (2) However, an offer cannot be revoked (a) if it indicates, whether by stating a fixed time for acceptance or otherwise, that it is irrevocable;

the same manner as CISG Article 16. In this regard, one can argue that the UNIDROIT Principles also assume the common law presumption of revocability.

PECL Article 2:202(1) adopts an approach to the revocation of an offer that is similar to CISG Article 16(1) and Article 2.4 of the UNIDROIT Principles. PECL Article 2:202 provides that, generally, an offer is revocable, but that it may follow from the offer or from the circumstances of the specific case that it is irrevocable.

PECL Art. 2:202(1) states that an offer may be revoked if the revocation reaches the offeree before he has dispatched his acceptance. Also, an offer may be revoked if the contract has not been concluded by an act of performance or conduct by the offeree under Article 2.205(2) or (3).[7] In this type of acceptance, the contract is concluded when the offeror learns of the offeree's conduct, and therefore, the revocation of the offer must reach the offeree before the offeror has learned of the conduct. Furthermore, in the case of acceptance through performance, the revocation should reach the offeree before the performance of the offeree.

II. PUBLIC OFFERS – PECL ARTICLE 2:202(2) AND THE CISG

Although the Convention does not include a provision dealing expressly with the revocation of an offer made to the public,[8] the PECL Article 2:202(2) statement– "An offer made to the public can be revoked by the same means as were used to make the offer"– appears consistent with the intent of the Convention. See, for example, the reference to "due account being taken of the circumstances of the transaction" in CISG Article 18(2), and the concept of "reasonableness" as a general principle of the Convention.[9]

III. IRREVOCABILITY OF AN OFFER – CISG ARTICLE 16(2)

Both the Convention and the PECL indicate that, if the offeror states clearly that the offer is irrevocable, the offeror is bound to the offer until the acceptance.

The most controversial part of Article 16 of the Convention is paragraph 2(a), which reflects a drafting compromise between the civil law and the common law by

or (b) if it was reasonable for the offeree to rely on the offer as being irrevocable and the offeree has acted in reliance on the offer."

[7] PECL Article 2:205 (2) and (3) read, "(2) In case of acceptance by conduct, the contract is concluded when notice of the conduct reaches the offeror. (3) If by virtue of the offer, of practices, which the parties have established between themselves, or of a usage, the offeree may accept the offer by performing an act without notice to the offeror, the contract is concluded when the performance of the act begins."

[8] Schlechtriem, *supra* note 5, at fn. 170, notes, "Unfortunately, a British proposal [. . .] concerning the withdrawal of a public offer found no support because of the misunderstanding that there is no such thing as a real public offer."

See also Jacob Ziegel, who comments on CISG Art. 16 and the question of revocation of an offer made to the public: "This seems inconsistent with art. 14(2) which [. . .] does recognize the validity of offers made to non-specific persons if this was the intention of the person making the proposal. Presumably the meaning of 'reaches' must be relaxed accordingly and, in the case of an offer made to the public, or a part thereof, an offer will be effectively revoked if reasonable steps are taken to bring it to the attention of the offeree." "Report to the Uniform Law Conference of Canada on Convention on Contracts for the International Sale of Goods,"[available online at: <http://cisgw3.law.pace.edu/cisg/text/ziegel16.html>].

On the other hand, PECL Art. 2:202(2) avoids any uncertainty over the matter by making it explicitly clear that "an offer made to the public can be revoked by the same means as were used to make the offer." Accordingly, revocation of offers to the public that are not irrevocable under PECL Article 2:202(2) can be made by the same means as the offer. *See* PECL Comment C, which states that the revocation must be "as conspicuous as the offer." PECL Comments and Notes are also available online at <http://cisgw3.law.pace.edu/cisg/text/peclcomp16.html#cnpc>].

[9] *See* Comments on Reasonableness as a general principle of CISG, available online at <http://cisgw3.law.pace.edu/cisg/text/reason.html>.

accommodating different views; it therefore lacks definitional clarity.[10] On the other hand, Article 2:202 of the PECL provides a more clarified regulation on the problem.

At the Diplomatic Conference on the Convention, the wording of CISG Art. 16(2)(a) had caused disagreements among the delegates representing countries from the civil and common law systems.[11] In Article 16(2) of the Convention there are two restrictions to the concept of revocability.[12] One of the restrictions provides that an offer is irrevocable if it indicates, whether by stating a fixed time for acceptance or otherwise, that it is irrevocable; the second restriction provides that offers on which the offeree has acted in reliance are also irrevocable.[13] Generally, for irrevocability, the offeror should intend to make his offer irrevocable, and his offer should indicate that fact.[14] However, CISG Article 16(2)(a) has not eliminated the controversy as to whether the mere fixing of a time for acceptance makes the offer irrevocable.[15] In the Convention, the question whether merely fixing a time for acceptance makes the offer irrevocable has been left to Article 8, which deals with intent and the interpretation of statements.[16] In the PECL, Article 2:202 provides that an offer is revocable, but also provides three exceptions to that general rule: (1) if the offer indicates that it is irrevocable (Art. 2:202(3)(a))[17]; (2) if it states a fixed time for its acceptance (Art. 2:202(3)(b)); and (3) if it was reasonable for the offeree to rely on the offer as being irrevocable, and the offeree has acted in reliance on the offer (Art. 2:202(3)(c)).

The wording of PECL Article 2:202(3)(b) clears any doubt in CISG Art. 16(2)(a) by stating that a revocation of an offer is ineffective even if it merely states a fixed time for its acceptance. Accordingly, "the offer if accepted becomes binding even though it was purportedly revoked before it was accepted."[18]

In the common law legal system, if an offer indicates a fixed time for acceptance, the offer lapses after expiration of this certain period[19]; the offeror may revoke his offer any time during this fixed period, unless consideration has been paid by the offeree. On the other hand, in most legal systems where civil law is adopted, "every 'open offer' is a 'firm

[10] Schlechtriem, *supra* note 3, at 119.

[11] *See* Summary Records of Meetings of the First Committee (9th Meeting), A/Conf.97/C.1/L.48, L.84 [available online at <http://cisgw3.law.pace.edu/cisg/firstcommittee/Meeting9.html>; *see* also Garro, *supra* note 5, n. 56 and accompanying text.

[12] It must be noted that the Secretariat Commentary explains that this provision "does not require a promise on the part of the offeror not to revoke his offer nor does it require any promise, act, or forbearance on the part of the offeree for the offer to become irrevocable. It reflects the judgment that in commercial relations, and particularly in international commercial relations, the offeree should be able to rely on any statement by the offeror which indicates that the offer will be open for a period of time." Comment 6.

[13] CISG Art. 16(2) provides the instances where an offer cannot be revoked: "(a) if it indicates, whether by stating a fixed time for acceptance or otherwise, that it is irrevocable; or (b) if it was reasonable for the offeree to rely on the offer as being irrevocable and the offeree has acted in reliance on the offer."

See also the Secretariat Commentary, which explains that the offer may indicate that it is irrevocable in different ways: "The most obvious is that the offer may state that it is irrevocable or that it will not be revoked for a particular period of time. The offer may also indicate that it is irrevocable by stating a fixed time for acceptance." Comment 7.

[14] *See* Schlechtriem, *supra* note 3, at 120.

[15] *See Principles of European Contract Law: Parts I and II* (Ole Lando & Hugh Beale eds., 2000) 167.

[16] *See* id., at 167; Schlechtriem, *supra* note 3, at 120 *et seq.*; Summary Records of Meetings of the First Committee (9th Meeting), para. 35, A/Conf.97/C.1/L.48, L.84 [available online, *supra* note 11].

[17] The indication that the offer is irrevocable must be clear; it may be made by declaring that the offer is a "firm offer" or by other similar expressions, and it may also be inferred from the conduct of the offeror; *see* PECL Comment E, available at <http://cisgw3.law.pace.edu/cisg/text/peclcomp16.html#cnpc>.

[18] The PECL Comments explain that if the offeror does not perform the contract he could become liable for non-performance and would have to pay damages under the relevant PECL provisions contained in Chapter 9, Section 5. *See* Principles of European Contract Law, *supra* note 15, at 165; Comment D, also available at: <http://cisgw3.law.pace.edu/cisg/text/peclcomp16.html#cnpc>.

[19] *See* Farnsworth, *Formation of Contract*, §3.04 sub 3–11(2); Feltham, "The United Nations Convention on Contracts for the International Sale of Goods," 24 *J. Bus. L.* (1981) 346, at 352.

offer' simply because it expressly states that it is irrevocable or implicitly indicates so by stating a fixed period for acceptance."[20]

However, in the Convention fixing a time for acceptance is one of the pillars indicating the intention to be bound, and there must be additional grounds for irrevocability. In this regard, there is a real danger that lawyers from different legal systems may interpret Article 16(2)(a) in divergent directions, representing their different jurisprudential heritages. Accordingly, there might be two possible types of interpretations. For a civil law attorney, if an offer states a fixed time for acceptance, as provided under CISG Article 16(2)(a), then the offer is irrevocable until the expiration of the stated fixed time. For a common law attorney, however, a fixed time for acceptance means that the acceptance must be given in that period and also that the offeror can revoke the offer any time until the expiration date; therefore, more precise language or additional grounds are necessary to make the offer irrevocable.[21] PECL Article 2:202(3)(b), on the other hand, explicitly eliminates the doubt as to whether a fixed time for acceptance makes the offer irrevocable. One of the main reasons why PECL regulates this issue explicitly without leaving any doubt might be that the majority of the laws of European states whose lawyers participated in the drafting of the PECL have a civil law origin.[22]

IV. INTERPRETATION OF THE CONTRACT

Interpretation of the contract gains significant importance in the application of CISG Art. 16(2)(a), because "the rules on interpretation of contract are necessary when the meaning of certain provisions is ambiguous."[23] In this context, "under the CISG [whether mere fixing a time for acceptance makes the offer irrevocable] is to be solved by the rules in [its] Article 8 on intent and interpretation of statements."[24] According to CISG Article 8(3), due consideration is to be given to all relevant circumstances of the case, including the negotiations, any practices that the parties have established between themselves, usages, and any subsequent conduct of the parties. In this regard, if the trading parties are both from common law jurisdictions, their understandings and intentions will be interpreted according to common law regulation of the matter; on the other hand, if the parties are both from civil law jurisdictions, it will be interpreted according to civil law regulation of the matter. However, the most important question is, What happens if the parties are from different jurisdictions – one from common law, the other from civil law?

Article 8 of the Convention will be decisive in the interpretation of the intention of the parties; it would supplement Article 16(2)(a). As mentioned elsewhere, the intention

[20] *See* Garro, *supra* note 5.

[21] For different viewpoints *see* Report of the United Nations Commission on International Trade Laws on the Work of its Eleventh Session (New York 30 May–16 June 1973), [1978], 9 UNCITRAL Y.B. 41 U.N. DOC. A/CN.9/SER.A/(1978); *see* also Schlechtriem, *supra* note 1, at 53 & nn. 172–172a stating that "[A] fixed time, which was understood by some delegates to be an irrebuttable presumption of an intent to be bound may be subject to different interpretations depending on the legal system in which the offeror lives."

[22] Under the laws of some European States offers are generally irrevocable, *see* Principles of European Contract Law, *supra* note 15, at 167, e.g., Germany BGB § 145; Austria ABGB § 862; Greece CC art. 185.

[23] *See* Maja Stanivukovic, "Remarks on the manner in which the Principles of European Contract Law may be used to interpret or supplement Article 8 of the CISG," para C., available online at <http://cisgw3.law.pace.edu/cisg/text/peclcomp8.html#er>.

[24] *See* Principles of European Contract Law, *supra* note 15, at 167. *See* also, J. Ziegel, *op. cit.*, commenting on the application of CISG Art. 16, who states, "Since it is often in the interests of the offeror that the offeree should have a reasonable opportunity to determine whether or not to accept the offer, the implication of a firm offer as provided in Art. 16(2)(b) seems to be a fair interpretation of the offeror's intention. Whether the implication should be drawn in a particular case will of course depend on all the circumstances, including the relevant trade practices and usages."

to make the offer irrevocable, and indicating this fact clearly[25] can be sufficient for irrevocability. Also, when the interpretation is made in the light of CISG Article 8(3) the intention of the parties can be found from "circumstances extraneous to the offer."[26] If the parties are from legal systems that regard an offer made subject to a time limit as binding, then according to Article 8(1) of the Convention, it may be presumed that the offeror intended his offer to have such an effect.[27] On the other hand, if the parties are both from common law systems, by virtue of Article 8(2) of the Convention, it may be presumed that unless there are additional grounds to be bound, the offeror does not intend to bind himself with the offer for that period.[28] Article 8(2) requires that the interpretation must be made according to the understanding of the recipient; this is important in an offer made from a country where common law is the legal system to a country where the civil law system governs. Otherwise, an offeror from a common law system may be bound with his offer because the understanding of the recipient governs in the aforementioned case. In Article 5:101(1) of the PECL, the common intention of the parties has been used, and in Article 5:101(2), only in exceptional circumstances may one party's intention be used to interpret. On the other hand, if CISG Article 8 were read literally, the Convention's way of interpreting intention can be based on one party's intention. In issues regarding irrevocability, the common intention of the parties is vital, especially when the parties are from different legal systems.

V. RELIANCE – CISG ARTICLE 16(2)(B)

CISG Article 16(2)(b) and PECL Article 2:203(c) have the same effect. They state that "an offer cannot be revoked" ["a revocation of an offer is ineffective"] "if" ["if…"] "it was reasonable for the offeree to rely on the offer as being irrevocable and the offeree has acted in reliance on the offer."

VI. CONCLUSIONS

Where it is clear that provisions of the PECL and the Convention embody the same intent, concept, or approach, with the PECL text, notes, and illustrations fleshing out the matter to a greater extent, the PECL may be of help in interpreting the Convention. However, this is less likely where counterpart provisions adopt different approaches.

1. PECL Article 2:202(1) and CISG Article 16(1)

PECL Article 2:201(1) and CISG Article 16(1) are similar. PECL explanations may therefore be relevant to the interpretation of this provision of the Convention.

2. PECL Article 2:202(2) and the CISG

PECL Article 2:202(2) appears to dovetail with the intent of the Convention. Here also, PECL explanations may be relevant to interpretation of the CISG.

[25] For unambiguous and clear wording, *see* Schlechtriem, *supra* note 3, at 121 stating that "'firm offer,' 'will be held open' or words which are understood in the particular trade to express an intention to be bound, for example, 'open offer', 'option', 'guarantee'".

[26] *See* Schlechtriem, *supra* note 3, at 121 & n. 25; *see* also Schlechtriem, *supra* note 1, at 53 stating that "[The offeror] does not need to do [the declaration of the offer to be irrevocable] expressly, but rather his intent to be bound can be deduced from the circumstances relevant to the interpretation of the offer and particularly from his setting a fixed period during which the offer is open."

[27] *See* Schlechtriem, *supra* note 3, at 121.

[28] *See* Schlechtriem, *supra* note 3, at 121.

3. PECL Article 2:202(3)(a), (b) and CISG Article 16(2)(a)

This is less apt to be so in the case of PECL 2:202(3)(a), (b) and CISG 16(2)(a) because they take different approaches.

The PECL Notes indicate that it is questionable whether PECL Article 2:202 may be used to help interpret CISG Article 16(a):

> The wording of [CISG] art. 16 para. 2(a) reflects a disagreement among the delegates of the Diplomatic Conference which in 1980 adopted [the Convention]. The common lawyers wished the offeror's fixing of a period for acceptance to be a time limit after which the offer could no longer be accepted but before which it could still be revoked. The civil lawyers saw the fixing of a time limit for acceptance as a promise by the offeror not to revoke the offer within that time limit (see also [ULF] art. 5(2)). The wording of [CISG] art. [16]2(a) was a compromise. The offer can be made irrevocable, but the provision has not cleared the controversy as to whether the mere fixing of a time for acceptance makes the offer irrevocable. Common lawyers believe that it does not per se make the offer irrevocable, there must be additional grounds for assuming that, *see* v. Caemmerer Schlechtriem art. 16 note 10 and Honnold no. 141 ff. [Under the Convention] the question is to be solved by the rules in [CISG] art. 8 on interpretation of statements. Article 2:202 of the [PECL] obviates this doubt. The fixing of a time for acceptance will make the offer irrevocable for that period.[29]

4. PECL Article 2:202(3)(c) and CISG Article 16(2)(b)

As PECL Article 2:202(3)(c) and CISG Article 16(2)(b) are substantively identical, the illustrations and interpretive guidance that accompany PECL 2:202(3)(c) could well be relevant to the interpretation of CISG 16(2)(b).

[29] PECL Notes, para. 2, available at: <http://cisgw3.law.pace.edu/cisg/text/peclcomp16.html>.

Rejection of offer followed by acceptance: Remarks on the manner in which the Principles of European Contract Law may be used to interpret or supplement Article 17 of the CISG

Cecilia Carrara and Joachim Kuckenburg

I. INTRODUCTION

Art. 17 CISG forms part of the set of rules (Arts. 15 to 18 CISG) that provide the grounds upon which the offeror, after having dispatched his offer, may be freed from the binding effects of his offer and therefore reallocate the resources committed. Before the offer has reached the offeree, the offeror may withdraw the offer (Art. 15(2) CISG). Arts. 16 to 18 CISG contemplate actions that can be taken after the offer has reached the offeree: the offeror may revoke the offer unless it is irrevocable (Art. 16). The offeror is also freed from his offer upon the expiration of the time for its acceptance (Art. 18(2), 2nd and 3rd sentences CISG). Art. 17 CISG further foresees, as a cause of termination of the offer, an initiative emanating from the offeree (i.e., the rejection of the offer).

Art. 2:203 PECL, in almost identical terms as Art. 17 CISG, regulates the same issue. There are two minor differences in the wording:(1) Art. 17 CISG contains the clarification that the general rule, whereby the offer terminates when the rejection reaches the offeror, applies also if the offer is irrevocable, and (2) Art. 17 CISG uses the word "terminate" as opposed to the term "lapse" in Art. 2:203 PECL. This second difference is of no significance, because no regulatory difference may be inferred from the use of the words "terminate" or "lapse." With respect to the first difference, it can be observed that the clarification contained in Art. 17 CISG,(i.e., "even if irrevocable") was inserted because this rule was not applicable in all legal systems.[1] However, the Comments and Notes on Art. 2:203 PECL state that the same is true for the PECL, although this wording has not found its way into its text.

II. SCOPE OF APPLICATION

Both Arts. 17 CISG and 2:203 PECL only deal with the issue of termination of the offer through rejection of the same by the offeree. Other causes for termination of the offer, such as death, incapacity, or insolvency of the offeror, are by intent not covered under the CISG.[2] The PECL do not address the issue either. Accordingly, given the absence of a specific rule for these cases, they need to be resolved on the basis of the applicable national law.[3]

III. CONFLICTING DECLARATIONS

Both Arts. 17 CISG and 2:203 PECL make it clear that the rejection must reach the offeror within the meaning of Article 24 CISG: mere dispatch of the rejection is not sufficient. In case of contradicting declarations by the offeree (acceptance sent after rejection or vice versa), the declaration that first reaches the offeror is effective.[4] Where

[1] Secretariat Commentary to Art. 15 of the 1978 Draft Convention [Art. 15 of the 1978 Draft Convention and Art. 17 of the CISG are identical], no. 1, available online at <http://cisgw3.law.pace.edu/cisg/text/secomm/secomm-17.html>. However, it is worth noting that, already in 1964 during the preparatory works for the 1964 Hague Convention on the Uniform Law for the Formation of Contracts (ULF), the UNIDROIT Commission expressly rejected the proposal to include such a proviso considering that it was "so evident that it would seem superfluous" (Honnold, *Uniform Law for International Sales*, 3rd ed., The Hague, 1999, p. 169, fn. 2). The same rule is contained in Art. 15 of the Code Européen des Contrats, which states, under para. 2, "L'offre, même si irrévocable, cesse d'avoir des effets à partir du moment où parvient à l'auteur une déclaration de refus de la part du destinataire, fût -elle jointe à une nouvelle offer" (Code Européen des Contrat, coordinated by Gandolfi, Milano, 2001).

[2] Rapport du Groupe de travail sur la vente internationale des objets mobiliers corporels sur les travaux de sa 9ième session (Genève, 19–30 Septembre 1977, Doc. A/CN.9/142 n. 283).

[3] *Cf.* P. Schlechtriem, in: Schlechtriem, *Commentary on the UN Convention on the International Sales of Goods* (2nd ed., translation by G. Thomas, Oxford 1998) p. 125, Art. 17, note 6: "[. . .] domestic law continues to govern the effects of such events on an existing offer." Schlechtriem goes on to state, "At most where an offer has already become binding owing to the dispatch of an acceptance, could it be argued, in accordance with the prevailing view in may legal systems, that the offer has become 'so depersonalized' that at least the offeror's death or lack of capacity cannot prevent the conclusion of a contract. However, Article 7(2) does not permit recourse to general legal principles derived from a comparative study of the law, but only to the principles upon which the Convention is based. On the other hand, not only does the Convention not contain any principles concerning that problem, but it basically assumes that questions of legal capacity continue to be governed by domestic law. The position must be the same as regards the fate of an offer which has become irrevocable in such cases."

[4] *Cf.* Enderlein/Maskow, *International Sales Law* (New York-London-Rome, 1992) Art. 18, no. 15, p. 91; also available online at <http://cisgw3.law.pace.edu/cisg/biblio/enderlein-art18.html>. "Consequently, if the

the contradicting declarations reach the offeror at the same time, he may only rely on the declaration that has been sent the latest as it corresponds to the real intent of the offeree.[5]

IV. IMPLICIT REJECTION

Both commentaries to the texts specify that the offeree's rejection does not need to be express, but may be implicit, including by conduct. Of course, the determination of whether a certain statement or conduct amounts to a rejection is a question of interpretation (Art. 8 CISG).

1. Rejection by Implied Terms

Art. 19 CISG, by providing that an acceptance in terms that materially alter the offer "is a rejection of the offer" and "constitutes a counter-offer," takes care of most of the situations. According to the clear wording of Art. 19 CISG, an acceptance that must be considered as a counter-offer terminates the initial offer.

By contrast, an acceptance that does not materially alter the terms of the offer only amounts to a rejection if the offeror thereto objects (Art. 19(2) CISG).

Thus, there is in general no room for considering that the initial offer may survive a negotiating process conducted on the basis of such initial offer without the offeree losing the benefit thereof.[6] For example, if A offers to sell *x* quantity for (a) price to B and B answers that he is ready to buy 2x quantity for 2(a) – 10% discount, what happens if A does not react to the answer? According to Arts. 19(1), (2) 1st sentence, (3), and 17 CISG, B has implicitly rejected A's offer and may not rely on it any longer.

If, however, B's statement should be interpreted to the effect that B accepts the initial offer, but would indeed prefer to make the deal on the basis of his proposed terms, it is suggested that a first contract – on the terms of the initial offer – is concluded, but that its effectiveness depends upon whether A accepts B's counter-proposal within the time of acceptance. If A does accept B's counter-proposal within such time, only the second contract is concluded and the first contract never becomes effective.

2. Rejection by Conduct

The CISG, the PECL, and the respective commentaries do not address the issue of whether the offeree's conduct implying rejection of the offer may be directed toward a third person rather than toward the offeror, and yet free the latter. For example, this may arise in a bid situation where the issuer of the bid invites a plurality of irrevocable offers (Art. 14(2) CISG). Offeror A may learn that the issuer of the bid (i.e., the offeree) has accepted the offer of a competitive bidder, offeror B. Does this imply the rejection of A's offer?

The answer depends on whether the issuer of the bid has a legitimate interest in relying on the irrevocable offer of several bidders, having them all bound for the entire duration of the offer.

offeree accepts the offer, for instance by telex, before his letter containing a rejection has reached the offeror, a contract is made."

[5] According to *Heuzé*, in *La vente internationale des marchandises*, Paris, 2000, p. 162: "des articles 15 et 22 il paraît pouvoir être déduit sans témérité que la convention de Vienne a entendu ériger en principe général la règle suivant laquelle l'auteur d'une expression de volonté peut valablement revenir sur celle-ci, dès lors qu'il met son correspondant en mesure de connaître son changement d'intention avant, ou en même temps que sa position initiale."

[6] This rigidity is criticized by *Heuzé*, *id.*, at 163, "cette solution n'est sans doute pas très opportune, dans la mesure où elle décourage la négociation, puisqu'elle expose le destinataire de l'offre à ne plus pouvoir accepter celle-ci, s'il a au préalable vainement tenté d'obtenir une modification de ses conditions."

If the issuer of the bid has accepted B's offer, generally A should be considered freed from his offer. It would in fact not be comprehensible why A, once aware of the fact that he has been ruled out, should still commit his resources to the benefit of the issuer of the bid. This same conclusion should apply even in cases where the issuer of the bid has reserved a right of withdrawal from the first contract (or has reserved a trial period), unless it is clear from the terms of the bid that the purpose of soliciting irrevocable offers was precisely that of granting the issuer of the bid a fall-back solution.

If, however, the issuer of the bid has selected B's offer only for entering into further negotiations, A should not be considered freed from his offer. Indeed, the very purpose of a bid is to keep available the resources of all bidders within the time frame initially fixed in the bid until one offer only is finally accepted.

V. OBLIGATION TO NEGOTIATE IN GOOD FAITH?

The example proposed above under 4a) shows that the CISG system tends to lead to "take it or leave it" situations, whenever there is a reply to an offer that purports to be an acceptance but contains modifications: indeed, if the modifications are substantial, the purported acceptance is a new offer that must, in turn, be accepted to form a contract. However, even if the modifications are not substantial, the offeror may withdraw from the negotiations by simply objecting to the reply of the offeree (Art. 19(2) 1st sentence CISG). It appears that this rule may provide a pretext for the offeror to interrupt the negotiations at any time, even in cases where the proposed modifications to the initial offer are of no material relevance. May the offeror be held liable toward the offeree, who may have relied on the conclusion of the contract?

Although the CISG does not contain any specific rule concerning the parties' liability for breach of an obligation to negotiate in good faith, Art. 2:301 PECL provides that a party negotiating or breaking off negotiations contrary to good faith is liable for the losses caused to the other party.[7]

The CISG does not regulate the issue of pre-contractual liability[8] (including the sub-categories of unjustified interruption of the negotiations, misrepresentation, entering into negotiations without any real intention of coming to the conclusion of the contract, etc.[9]). Indeed, the CISG deals with the negotiations only in order to determine whether a contract has been concluded or not. May pre-contractual liability nevertheless find its way into the system of the CISG by virtue of Art. 7(2) CISG, considering that Art. 2:301 PECL recognizes such liability as a general principle?

It is submitted that Art. 7(2) CISG is not applicable to this situation because pre-contractual liability is a matter that is not governed by the CISG; therefore, the absence of a rule on the issue does not constitute a gap. However, even if one were to consider that a general duty to negotiate in good-faith could be read into the system of the CISG,

[7] *See* also Art. 2.15 UNIDROIT Principles.

[8] Stoll, in Schlechtriem, *Commentary on the UN Convention on the International Sale of Goods* (Oxford, 1998) Art. 74, n° 10; Bonell, Vertragsverhandlungen und culpa in contrahendo nach dem Wiener Kaufrechtsóbereinkommen, RIW 1990, p. 693 *et seq*.

[9] The elaboration and definition of the different subcategories of pre-contractual liability vary in each national legal system. For Anglo-American legal systems *see* Farnsworth, "Pre-contractual Liability and Preliminary Agreements: Fair Dealing and Failed Negotiations," *Col. L. Rev*. (1987), p. 218 *et seq*.; Kessler & Fine, "Culpa in contrahendo, Bargaining in Good Faith and Freedom of Contract: A Comparative Study," *Harv. L. Rev*. (1964) p. 401 *et seq*.; for Italy, Patti, *Responsabilita' contrattuale, Il Codice civile commentato*, Giuffrı 1993; Bianca, *Diritto civile 3, Il Contratto*, Giuffrı 1994, p. 159 *et seq*.; for Germany, new § 311(2) BGB codifying the institute of culpa in contrahendo, *cf*. Koller, in Koller/Roth/Zimmermann, Schuldrechtsmodernisierungs-gesetz (Mónchen, 2002) p. 63–64; Faust, in Huber/Faust, *Schuldrechtsmodernisierung, Einführung in das neue Recht* (Mónchen, 2002) pp. 69–72; Huber, in Huber/Faust, op. cit., pp. 387–390.

the latter does not provide for a specific remedy in case of breach of such a duty: clearly, Art. 74 CISG is not applicable because its plain wording limits it to damages for breach of contract. In addition, the Comments to Art. 2:301 PECL, para. G, expressly state that the party in good faith cannot claim to be put in a situation in which it would have been if the contract had been correctly performed (positive interest), but the damages that it may claim are limited to the costs and expenses incurred (negative interest).[10] This limited protection does not fit in with Art. 74 CISG, which allows for recovery of full damages, as it is always the case for damages out of breach of contract.

However, an additional question may arise; namely whether the absence of any specific provision on pre-contractual liability must be interpreted to exclude any recourse to national applicable laws.[11] The answer, once more, is provided by the fact that pre-contractual liability simply falls outside the scope of the CISG: Art. 2:301 PECL shows that pre-contractual liability is a widely recognized principle, and the party in good faith should be able to have recourse to extra-conventional remedies under national law.

[10] This reflects the general position in the various legal systems recognizing pre-contractual liability.

[11] According to Schlechtriem, op. cit., Introduction to Arts. 14–24, no. 6, fn. 36, going back to national remedies should be possible "only in cases where the parties have not been moving toward a contract through corresponding offer and acceptance," because Arts. 16 and 17 CISG regulate the issue to the exclusion of all other national rules.

Acceptance of an offer: Remarks on the manner in which the Principles of European Contract Law may be used to interpret or supplement Article 18 of the CISG

Cecilia Carrara and Joachim Kuckenburg

I. INTRODUCTION

Whereas Arts. 14 to 17 CISG deal with the offer, Arts. 18 to 23 CISG deal with the acceptance. Art. 18(1) CISG defines the acceptance in general. This provision is in large part supplemented by Art. 19 CISG, which deals with the substantive contents of an acceptance. By contrast, Art. 18(2) and (3) CISG is concerned with the communication of the acceptance and the conditions under which the offeree may be dispensed of such communication. It is thereby supplemented by Art. 20 CISG for the computation of applicable time periods and by Art. 21 CISG with respect to late acceptances. Whereas

Art. 23 CISG may be regarded as the conclusion of Part II of the CISG, defining the moment when a contract is concluded, Art. 24 CISG defines for both offer and acceptance when a certain statement reaches the addressee within the meaning of the CISG.

II. ARTICLE 18(1) CISG – MEANING OF ACCEPTANCE

Article 18(1) CISG substantially corresponds to Art. 2:204 PECL, defining in rather broad terms the meaning of acceptance, which may be express or implied by conduct. Both provisions do, however, clearly deny that silence or inactivity *per se* may constitute an acceptance. Art. 2:204 PECL thereby reconfirms the principle that in commercial dealings silence in itself does not have legal relevance.[1]

III. ARTICLE 18(2) CISG – EFFECTIVENESS OF ACCEPTANCE

1. Reasonable Time

According to Art. 18(2) CISG, an acceptance must reach the offeror within the time open for its acceptance. This provision corresponds to Arts. 2:205(1) and (2) and 2:206(1) and (2) PECL. Both texts thereby reject the mailbox principle as a means of establishing when an acceptance becomes effective.[2] Art. 18(2) CISG provides some guidance as to how to interpret the words "reasonable time" within which an offer must be accepted by referring both to the circumstances of the case and to the means of communication employed.[3] Art. 18(2), last sentence CISG provides in addition a special rule in case of oral offers, which, in general, must be accepted immediately.[4] However, the proviso "unless the circumstances indicate otherwise" shows that immediate acceptance is not a strict rule. On the contrary, the PECL contain neither exemplifications nor special rules for oral offers.[5]

2. Oral Offer

The existence of the specific rule of Art. 18(2), last sentence CISG operates as an inversion of the burden of proof in comparison to Art. 18(2), second sentence CISG. Indeed, if the negotiations have been conducted orally and a dispute arises as to whether the

[1] For silence upon a "commercial letter of confirmation," *cf.* Art. 19 and Editorial Remarks; silence may amount to acceptance as a result of unequivocal practices established among the parties; *see, e.g.*, France 21 October 1999 *Cour d'appel* [Appellate Court] France, *Calzados Magnanni v. Shoes General International*, Grenoble, case presentation including English translation available online at <http://cisgw3.law.pace.edu/cases/991021f1.html>; United States 14 April 1992 Federal District Court [New York] *Filanto v. Chilewich*, 789 Fed. Supp 1229 (1992), also available online at <http://cisgw3.law.pace.edu/cases/920414u1.html>. This is true in particular on the basis of an ongoing relationship based on a framework agreement, such as distributorship, franchise etc. The Notes to Art. 2:204 PECL state that, under various national laws, the offeree will generally be bound by his silence if the offer followed an invitation to deal by the offeree. However, this position is not convincing because it cannot be held that the issuer of the bid intends to waive his right to accept an individual offer, unless the contrary may be inferred from the terms of the bid. Even Restatement (Second) of Contracts, Section 69 "Acceptance by Silence or Exercise of Dominion" (for the full text of Section 69, *see* <http://www.law.unlv.edu/faculty/bam/k2000/r2k.html>, referred to in the Notes to Art. 2:204 PECL, para. 2, as an example does not bear out the position taken in the Notes.

[2] The receipt rule has thus prevailed over the mailbox rule; the latter however keeps a certain importance in the context of Art. 16(1) CISG, because the offeror may not revoke his offer once acceptance has been dispatched. For the special case where acceptance is effective by performing an act, refer below in the text para. 4d).

[3] Regarding the general principle of "reasonableness" under the CISG, *see* <http://cisgw3.law.pace.edu/cisg/text/reason.html>.

[4] The same rule is provided under Art. 2.7 UNIDROIT Principles.

[5] The same exemplifications contained in the text of the CISG are provided, however, by the Comments to Art. 2:206 PECL, para. C.

offeree could only accept the offer immediately or whether he had a period for reflection, Art. 18(2), last sentence CISG places upon the offeree the burden to prove that, in the specific case, he could rely on the offer to stand for an additional period of time.[6]

IV. ARTICLE 18(3) CISG – ACCEPTANCE WITHOUT NOTIFICATION

1. Overview

Art. 18(3) CISG corresponds substantially to Arts. 2:205(3) and 2:206(3) PECL. These provisions constitute an exception to the general rule that an acceptance must reach the offeror to be effective. By merely performing an act, the offeree may render his acceptance effective and thus conclude the contract without the acceptance reaching the offeror. These provisions raise several questions. How is the distinction drawn between the conduct indicating assent of the offeree (Art. 18(1) CISG), which must reach the offeror (Art. 18(2) first sentence CISG), and the act upon the mere performance of which a contract is concluded (*infra* 4b))? What kind of acts qualify to fall within the realm of Art. 18(3) CISG, and when precisely is the contract concluded in such cases (*infra* 4c))? What happens if the offeror revokes his offer or the offeree withdraws his acceptance before the offeror knows about the conclusion of the contract (*infra* 4d))? In case of conclusion of a contract by mere performance of an act, must the offeree notify the offeror thereof in due course (*infra*, 4e))?

2. Conduct versus Performing an Act

One might be tempted to deduce from the difference in terminology used under Art. 18(3) CISG on the one hand ("performance of an act") and Art. 18(1) CISG on the other ("conduct") that the distinction between the two possibilities of acceptance must be made by reference to the specific behavior of the offeree. However, the distinction does not lie in the type of behavior of the offeree. The conclusion of a contract without an acceptance reaching the offeror under Art. 18(3) CISG may occur only if the offeror has, or must be deemed to have, renounced receipt of the acceptance of the offeree, either because his offer so provided or because this results from practices established between the parties or usages that are widely known and observed and of which the offeror could not have been unaware (Art. 9 CISG).

3. Acts Falling under Art. 18(3) CISG

Art. 2:205(3) PECL does not qualify what kind of act is sufficient to determine the conclusion of a contract without the notification of an acceptance. Surprisingly, Art. 2:206(3) PECL speaks of an "act of performance."[7] Such qualification would limit the possible behavior of the offeree to those acts that are at least directly concerned with

[6] It appears that often in case of oral negotiations, specific offers and counter-offers cannot be traced back in the process of the conclusion of the contract. However, the position generally held under the CISG is that its rules on offer-acceptance also apply to cases where the formation of contracts does not occur according to this rigid scheme (*see* Schlechtriem in Schlechtriem, *Commentary on the UN Convention on the International Sale of Goods* (2nd ed., 1998), Introduction to Art. 14–24, para. 2 *et seq.*) Art. 2:211 PECL further supports this position.

[7] In our view this terminology, if it had been used also in Art. 2:205(3) PECL, would better explain the specification provided therein (*i.e.*, that the relevant moment in time for the conclusion of the contract is when the performance of the act "begins"). Furthermore, such a rule would appropriately protect the legitimate interests of the offeror by limiting the kind of acts constituting acceptance, thereby restricting the offeree's possibility of determining in his own discretion whether or not a contract has been concluded. This solution would enhance legal certainty. It is worth noting that the same solution is adopted under Art. 1327(1) Italian Cc whereby the contract is concluded when the performance of the obligation begins (*see* Benedetti, Il diritto commune dei contratti e degli atti unilaterali tra vivi a contenuto patrimoniale (Bracigliano, 1991) p. 119 *et seq.*).

the performance of the contract under consideration.[8] Art. 18(3) CISG, however, gives guidance in this respect in the examples provided: the act may be "one relating to" the dispatch of the goods or the payment of the price. Art. 18(3) CISG would therefore be more restrictive than Art. 2:205(3) PECL, but broader than 2:206(3) PECL: The behavior of the offeree does not need to be directly concerned with the performance as such of the contract, but may include preparatory acts.[9] Given such clarification under Art. 18(3) CISG, no specific inferences may be drawn from the wording used in Art. 2:206(3) PECL, considering as well the fact that Art. 2.6(3) UNIDROIT Principles adopts the wording "performing an act."

Although Art. 2:205(3) PECL makes it clear that the specific moment in time of conclusion of the contract is that of the "beginning" of the act, Art. 18(3) CISG speaks of "the moment the act is performed." It appears that, on this particular point, the PECL provide a more detailed indication, even though it allows for a contract to be concluded upon acts that have only a remote connection to the actual performance of the corresponding contractual obligations. In situations where the acts performed are punctual, the difference in the respective wordings is not significant; however, where the acts are continuing, it is submitted that the stricter rule of Art. 18(3) CISG is preferred.[10]

The act in question must manifest the offeree's will to accept the offer. It is not readily clear whether such an act must leave the sphere of control of the offeree[11] or whether purely internal dispositions (such as instructions given to in-house departments or employees) may constitute the acceptance. One may draw upon Art. 16(1) CISG[12] because, as long as an offer may be revoked, no contract is concluded: the externalization of the accepting party's will, under Art. 18(3) CISG, has the same rationale as the dispatch of the offeree's acceptance referred to in Art. 16(1) CISG (i.e., the alienation of the manifestation of will). Accordingly, before this moment, the offer may be revoked and no contract has been concluded.

Dispatch of non-conforming goods unquestionably amounts to acceptance,[13] unless the goods are of a different kind (*aliud*) than the goods requested. In such case the dispatch will amount to a new offer, except where the offeree was in error in delivering the wrong goods and in fact wanted to accept the offer.[14]

4. Revocation of Offer and Withdrawal of Acceptance

Under Art. 18(3) CISG and Arts. 2:205(3) and 2:206(3) PECL it is therefore clear that the contract is concluded when the performance of the act begins. The consequences are that both the offer cannot be revoked (*arg ex* Art. 16(1) CISG, *cf. supra* 4b) at fn. 11; for Art. 2:205(3) PECL *cf.* Comment para. D: the performance "is one which the

[8] Packing of the goods ordered might fall under such a notion, whereas ordering the goods from a subsupplier or starting production of the goods will hardly qualify as an "act of performance" of the contract; it only relates to the future performance of the contract.

[9] It is, however, generally recognized that the act must be of certain significance, *see* Neumayer/Ming, *Convention de Vienne sur les contrats de vente internationale de merchandises* (Lausanne, 1993) p. 174.

[10] For the reasons, *see* fn. 6 above.

[11] Enderlein/Maskow, *International Sales Law* (New York-London-Rome, 1992) Art. 18, no. 15, p. 96, available online at <http://cisgw3.law.pace.edu/cisg/biblio/enderlein-art18.html>.

[12] Heuzé, *La vente internationale de marchandises* (Paris 2000) p. 171 *et seq.*, fn. 124; Neumayer/Ming, *op. cit.*, no. 8, p. 175.

[13] This holds true also in cases of partial delivery, unless the specific circumstances of the case indicate a different solution (*e.g.*, it can be clearly understood that the seller only wanted to accept the offer partially; thereby the partial delivery constitutes a new offer that, as such, requires the buyer's acceptance for a contract to be concluded); *cf.* for such a solution Germany 23 May 1995 Oberlandesgericht [Appellate Court] Frankfurt/M., case presentation including English translation available at <http://cisgw3.law.pace.edu/cases/950523g1.html>.

[14] Schlechtriem, *op. cit.*, Art. 18, no. 7, pp. 129–130.

offeree cannot revoke"),[15] and the acceptance cannot be withdrawn thereafter (Art. 22 CISG). Therefore, a seller who calls back goods in transit that he shipped in acceptance of a corresponding offer would be in breach of contract.[16]

In addition, neither the text of Art. 18(3) CISG nor Arts. 2:205(3) and 2:206(3) PECL requires the party accepting an offer by performing an act to give notice to the offeror in order to perfect the process of formation of the contract. Absence of such notice, even where it may flow from a general duty of good faith, does not have any effect on the conclusion of the contract.

5. Duty to Inform?

Nevertheless, the further question arises as to whether the accepting party has a "duty to inform" the offeror, and if so, what are the possible consequences in case of breach thereof?[17] Especially in light of the urgency that usually characterizes cases falling under Art. 18(3) CISG, the offeror has a legitimate interest to be informed as soon as possible of the acceptance of the offeree.[18] It could be argued that if the offeror has a special interest in receiving a confirmation of acceptance, it is incumbent on him to request such confirmation from the other party. However, it is submitted that, even if there is no specific request by the offeror, the general duty of good faith and cooperation (Art. 7(1) CISG) imposes on the accepting party the burden of notifying promptly his acceptance to the offeror.[19] This view may find further support in the wording of Art. 1:201(1) PECL[20] and Art. 1.7 of the UNIDROIT Principles.[21] Accordingly, a violation of this duty would entitle the offeror to claim damages suffered as a consequence of failure of prompt notification[22]; the recognition of such a rule would effectively deter all possible attempts by the offeree to "call back" the acts performed at its own volition.

[15] It has been pointed out that the solution adopted by the CISG may lead to unsatisfactory solutions under certain circumstances (among others, *see* Neumayer/Ming, *op. cit.*, p. 176, Enderlein/Maskow, *op. cit.*, p. 96). Indeed, the offeror who is unaware of the beginning of the performance may in good faith believe that he is still entitled to revoke his offer.

[16] In the example proposed in the text, the buyer shall be entitled to damages for breach of contract because the contract was already binding upon the parties as from the beginning of the performance of the act.

[17] Again, Art. 1327(2) Italian Cc explicitly regulates the issue: the accepting party is obliged to notify the offeror promptly that performance has begun, or else the accepting party will be held liable for damages. The damages in question cover the "positive interest" and are those suffered by the offeror as a consequence of having relied on the circumstance that the offeree had not accepted the offer (*see* Bianca, *Il contratto* (Milano, 1987), 244).

[18] Indeed, the offeror has a legitimate interest to know as of when he is precluded from revoking his offer (*e.g.*, for the purpose of entering into a more convenient deal) or as of when the passage of the risk has occurred (*e.g.*, for the purpose of insuring the goods).

[19] This position is shared by the prevailing opinion of the scholars, although the legal basis for such a duty to inform is not always specifically clarified: *cf.* Enderlein/Maskow, *International Sale of Goods* (1992) p. 96; Neumayer/Ming, *op. cit.*, p. 175, consider such a duty only for the case where the offeror has sent a revocation of the offer after acceptance has occurred: upon receipt of the said revocation the offeree has a duty to inform the other party, which derives from a general *"loyauté commerciale"*; *contra*, Schlechtriem, *op. cit.*, no. 23, p. 136, according to whom an ancillary duty to inform on the part of the offeree can only arise on grounds of the practices established between the parties or of usage.

[20] *Cf.*, however, the different view taken by J. Felemegas, "Comparative Editorial Remarks on the Concept of Good Faith in the CISG and the PECL," 13 *Pace Int'l. L. Rev.* (Number II, Fall 2001) 399–406, also available at <http://cisgw3.law.pace.edu/cisg/text/peclcomp7.html#er>.

[21] Supportive U. Magnus, "Comparative Editorial Remarks on the Concept of Good Faith in the CISG and the UNIDROIT-Principles", available at <http://cisgw3.law.pace.edu/cisg/principles/uni7.html#um>.

[22] *E.g.*, the goods in transit perish and no insurance contract has been concluded by the buyer; the delivery is delayed and the offeror, unaware of the conclusion of the contract, concludes a new contract with a third party, etc. In the specific case considered by Neumayer/Ming, *op. cit.*, p. 175, fn. 18, these authors suggest that in case of breach of the duty to notify the offeror of the acceptance, the offeree loses his right to rely upon the validity of the contract.

Acceptance with modifications: Remarks on the manner in which the Principles of European Contract Law may be used to interpret or supplement Art. 19 of the CISG

Pilar Perales Viscasillas

I. THE MIRROR IMAGE RULE AND MODIFIED ACCEPTANCE

An acceptance must coincide with each and every term of an offer in order to conclude a contract (see Articles 19(1) CISG and 2:208(1) PECL). This requirement is known as the "mirror image rule" because the acceptance must be the very reflection of the offer, as in a mirror. An exception is established for the possible introduction of new terms into the acceptance that do not substantially alter the offer. In that case, the acceptance will be valid; the contract will consist of both the terms of the offer and those included in the acceptance that do not substantially alter the offer, so long as the offeror without delay does not object to the new terms (Articles 19(2) CISG and 2:208(3)(b) PECL), or the offer does not expressly limit acceptance to the terms of the offer (Article 2:208(1) PECL),[1] or the offeree does not make his acceptance conditional upon the offeror's assent to the additional or different terms and the assent reaches the offeree within a reasonable time (Article 2:208(3)(c) PECL).[2]

On the other hand, if an element that is included in the acceptance adds new terms, modifies the terms of the offer, or introduces any other type of limitation to the offer that substantially alters it, the contract will not be considered concluded; the response to the offer will be regarded as a counter-offer – that is, if it meets all requirements under the CISG or the PECL to be considered an offer in and of itself (*see* Articles 14 CISG and 2:208(1) PECL).[3]

To determine when an element of an acceptance materially alters the corresponding offer, a list of items is provided by the Vienna Convention. However, the list merely provides examples of such elements, as can be inferred from the expression "among other things" in Article 19(3) CISG. Furthermore, the list has a presumptive nature because it pre-determines that such "[a]dditional or different terms . . . are *considered* to alter the terms of the offer *materially*" (emphasis added).[4]

[1] CISG is silent on this issue.

[2] CISG is silent on this issue.

[3] *See* Germany 4 March 1994 *Oberlandesgericht* [Appellate Court] Frankfurt am Main, case presentation including English translation available at <http://cisgw3.law.pace.edu/cases/940304g1.html>. *See* also the Comments to Article 2:208 PECL indicating that an acceptance by conduct may contain additional or different terms. These terms may be material, for instance, if the offeree dispatches a much smaller quantity of a commodity than that which was ordered by the offeror or immaterial if only a very small quantity is missing.

[4] The list includes, *inter alia*, the following elements:

- price (only those modifications relating to the total amount of the offer price): Spain 28 January 2000 *Tribunal Supremo* [Supreme Court] *Internationale Jute Maatschappij v. Marin Palomares*, online at <http://www.uc3m.es/cisg/sespan7.htm>, case presentation including English translation available at <http://cisgw3.law.pace.edu/cases/000128s4.html>
- clauses that modify the price because of increases in costs: France 4 January 1995 *Cour de Cassation* [Supreme Court], *Fauba v. Fujitsu Mikkroelectronik*, case presentation including English translation available at <http://cisgw3.law.pace.edu/cases/950104f1.html>
- payment method: Germany 22 December 1992 *Landgericht* [District Court] Giessen, <http://cisgw3.law.pace.edu/cases/921222g2.html>

The list provided in the CISG contains only substantive elements that refer to rights and obligations that arise in a sales contract, thereby eliminating certain elements from being considered material alterations (e.g., the initiative of the offeree to negotiate again, any small changes in the wording of the offer that have no effect on the acceptance,[5] and a modification of an offer whose content benefits the offeror).[6]

The European Principles do not provide a similar rule to the one embodied in Article 19(3) CISG. Nevertheless, the PECL Comments to Article 2:208 reach a similar result; the PECL regard a term as material "if the offeree knew or as a reasonable person in the same position as the offeree should have known that the offeror would be influenced in its decision as to whether to contract or as to the terms on which to contract."[7] The PECL Comments state that the list contained in Article 19(3) CISG was not provided with the European Principles because it could only have been illustrative and not exhaustive.

Under both CISG and PECL, the course of dealing, trade practices (see Articles 9 CISG and 1:105 PECL), previous negotiations, and other elements of intent (see Articles 8 CISG and 2:102 and 5:101 PECL) can play an important role in the interpretation of materiality. There are also circumstances in which Article 4(a) CISG may come into play as validity issues can arise in connection with certain of the terms listed in Article 19(3) CISG. For example, where arbitration is the specified method of resolution of disputes, the validity of the arbitration clause can turn on domestic law.[8] In a similar vein, domestic laws on unconscionability can affect the validity of limitation of liability clauses.[9]

- place and time, quality and quantity of merchandise: Germany 31 March 1995 *Oberlandesgericht* [Appellate Court] Frankfurt, case presentation including English translation available at <http://cisgw3.law.pace.edu/cases/950331g1>
- place and time of delivery: Germany 8 February 1995 *Oberlandesgericht* [Appellate Court] München, case presentation including English translation available at <http://cisgw3.law.pace.edu/cases/950208g1.html>
- the extent of one party's liability to the other: Germany 14 August 1991 *Landgericht* [District Court] Baden-Baden, case presentation including English translation available at <http://cisgw3.law.pace.edu/cases/910814g1.html>), or the settlement of disputes

Nevertheless, it is very possible that courts may consider the list in the sense that the aforementioned terms substantially alter an offer in every case. For example, in Germany 22 September 1992 *Oberlandesgericht* [Appellate Court] Hamm, case presentation available at <http://cisgw3.law.pace.edu/cases/920922g1.html>, an indication of a material alteration was the rejection of packaged bacon "in polyethylene bags" by means of a counter-offer in which the packaging was established as "loose."

To arrive at a clear set of rules for interpreting when a modification to an offer is material, the term "material" should be interpreted in a limited way. *See* Fritz Enderlein & Dietrich Maskow, *International Sales Law: United Nations Convention on Contracts for the International Sale of Goods* (New York: Oceana Publications, 1992) p. 100. *See* also Pilar Perales Viscasillas, *La formacion del contrato de compraventa internacional de mercadervas* (Valencia: Tirant lo blanch, 1996) pp. 625–735.

[5] Examples of such non-material alterations are an acceptance in which certain elements are added ("I accept because I urgently need the merchandise," or "I agree but was hoping for a more satisfactory agreement"), where recommendations are made or questions are asked ("I accept. Payment should be in bills of 100 euros," or "I accept. Would it be possible to include an arbitration clause?"), or where requests are made ("keep the acceptance confidential until it is announced publicly by both parties"); *see* Hungary 10 January 1992 Metropolitan Court (*Pratt & Whitney v. Malev*), case presentation including English translation available at <http://cisgw3.law.pace.edu/cases/920110h1.html>.

[6] *See* Austria 20 March 1997 *Oberster Gerichtshof* [Supreme Court], case presentation available at <http://cisgw3.law.pace.edu/cases/970320a3.html>.

[7] *Cf.* Article 1:301(5) PECL, which defines a matter as material "if it is one which a reasonable person in the same situation as one party ought to have known would influence the other party in its decision whether to contract on the proposed terms or to not contract at all."

[8] This was the reasoning of Argentina 14 October 1993 Cámara Nacional en lo Comercial [Appellate Court] *Inta v. Officina Meccanica*, case digest available at <http://cisgw3.law.pace.edu/cases/931014a1.html>. But *see*, United States 14 April 1992 Federal District Court [New York], *Filanto S.p.A. v. Chilewich International Corp.*, case presentation available at <http://cisgw3.law.pace.edu/cases/920414u1.html>.

[9] John O. Honnold, *Uniform Law for International Sales* (3rd ed., Kluwer Law International, 1999) pp. 182 *et seq. See* for example, Sections 2-302 and 2-719 of the United States UCC.

II. RESOLVING THE BATTLE OF FORMS (CONFLICTING GENERAL CONDITIONS)

The battle of the forms is an expression that refers to a situation in which the parties exchange general conditions,[10] usually on pre-printed forms prepared by one of the parties or its trade association that often add one or more terms that materially modify the offer. This is a very controversial issue in the CISG; some scholars believe the *last-shot* rule applies – a rule that has been rejected by Section 2-207(3) UCC, which instead applies the *knock-out* rule. The European Principles (in Article 2:209 PECL, which follows Article 2.22 UNIDROIT Principles) have adopted a variation of the UCC approach. Article 2:209 PECL is an exception to the general rule in Article 2:208 PECL on modified acceptance.

The complexity of this issue is increased by the customary practice of sending offers and acceptances that contain general conditions. Such conditions may reveal contradictions and raise the following two questions: Has a contract been concluded? and, if so, What are the terms of the contract? Practice shows that the answer to the first question is generally affirmative; usually the parties go ahead with the contract although each has referred to its own general conditions, the problem being the determination of the exact content of the contract. Below, some solutions that have been given to the problem under the CISG are examined to show the different approaches to solving this difficult issue of contract formation, with cross-reference to Article 19 CISG.

Under the CISG, the battle of the forms should be considered a gap that must be resolved by applying the general principles upon which the Convention is based. Following this approach, some authors believe that the principle of good faith should apply; they conclude that the clauses contained in the forms that are contradictory would cancel each other out, leaving the issue to be governed by the applicable law, usage, or good faith. That is, they adopt a solution such as that followed in certain legal systems: the "*knock-out* rule" in § 2-207(3) UCC, the "*partiell dissens*" rule in §§ 154 and 155 BGB [German Civil Code], or the similar solution provided in Articles 2:209(1) PECL and 2.22 UNIDROIT Principles.[11] A variation on this theory is that the situation produces an implied exclusion of Article 19 CISG.

The opinion that is followed most, however, leads to the application of what is known as the "*last-shot* rule" – the last person to send his form is considered to control the terms of the contract and therefore the one who wins the battle. An example of the application of this rule is the following: a German buyer ordered doors that had to be manufactured by the seller according to the buyer's specifications. The seller sent the buyer a confirmation letter that contained his general conditions of sale on the back. These conditions included the statement that "the seller must be notified of any defects of the merchandise within eight days of delivery." This provision was at variance with the terms of the buyer's offer. Subsequently, the seller delivered the merchandise and the buyer accepted it. In this case, the seller's confirmation letter was considered to be a counter-offer that was implicitly accepted by the buyer's conduct when he accepted the merchandise. Therefore, the rules of the Convention also apply when forms are used; consequently, any variation in those forms would be a counter-offer. Such a counter-offer could most certainly be accepted through an act of performance.[12]

[10] Article 2:209(3) PECL provides a definition: "General conditions of contract are terms which have been formulated in advance for an indefinite number of contracts of a certain nature, and which have not been individually negotiated between the parties."

[11] *See* generally, Comments to Article 2:209 PECL and illustrations 1 and 2.

[12] Pilar Perales Viscasillas, "Battle of the Forms under the 1980 United Nations Convention on Contracts for the International Sale of Goods: A Comparison with Section 2-207 UCC and the UNIDROIT Principles," *Pace Int'l. L. Rev.* (1998), vol. 10, no. 1, pp. 97–155.

The PECL has decided to follow a more recent approach, applying the "*knock-out* rule" to solve the battle of the forms problem, thus adopting the innovative approach of the UCC. According to Article 2:209(1) PECL, the general conditions form part of the contract to the extent that they are common in substance; therefore, any conflicting terms would be expelled out of the contract. However, following Article 2:209(2) PECL, no contract is formed if one party (a) has indicated in advance, explicitly and not by general conditions, that it does not intend to be bound by a contract on the basis of paragraph (1) (i.e., there is a so-called *clause paramount*) or (b) without delay, informs the other party that it does not intend to be bound by such contract.[13]

III. MODIFICATION OF THE CONTRACT AND COMMERCIAL LETTERS OF CONFIRMATION

Article 29(1) CISG states that a contract may be modified by the mere agreement of the parties. The modification of the contract can be viewed in terms of offer and acceptance. In that sense, an attempt to modify a contract may be deemed to be an offer to modify the contract that must be accepted by the other party.[14]

Sending a confirmation letter following the conclusion of a contract is a very common practice in international commercial transactions. The customary purpose of such a letter is to set in writing that which was previously negotiated, establishing proof of that which was agreed. By setting out the terms by which the contract is governed, confirmation letters are generally designed to eliminate or reduce doubts or errors that might arise. When the terms contained in the confirmation letter coincide with those that were actually agreed upon – they are a summary, an exact repetition, or confirmation of such – no problems exist. However, what can happen is that prior to (or simultaneous with) the execution of the contract, a confirmation letter or invoice is sent out that alters or adds to the terms of the contract that has already been formalized. Such changes can take place by including (i) certain new elements or general conditions, (ii) an entire set of general conditions that had not been previously discussed by the parties or indicated as included in the contract, or (iii) conditions that provide for something different than that which was agreed upon. This issue raises the question of how such confirmation letters should be treated under the law.[15] In the legal systems of Germany, Austria, and Switzerland – when the contractual relationship is between merchants – silence or inactivity on the part of the recipient of a confirmation letter produces an acceptance by silence of the modifications introduced in the commercial letter of confirmation. Even though the modifications may

[13] One also has to take into account the rules of interpretation of Articles 2:104, 5:103, and 5:104 PECL. *See* also France 24 January 1996 *Cour d'appel* [Court of Appeal] Grenoble, *Societe Simri v. Societe Harper Robinson*, Unilex – UNIDROIT Principles, Transnational, June 2000, D.1996-1, citing Article 2.21 UNIDROIT Principles as a principle in international trade whereby the non-standard term prevails over a standard term in case of contradiction. *See* Pilar Perales Viscasillas, "Formation of the contract under the CISG," in *Law and Practice of Export Trade* (Munster: Center for Transnational Law, 2001) vol. 3, pp. 97–114.

[14] *See* for example, Germany 26 September 1990 *Landgericht* [District Court] Hamburg, case presentation including English translation available at <http://cisgw3.law.pace.edu/cases/900926g1.html>; France 29 March 1995 *Cour d'appel* [Court of Appeal] Grenoble (Societe Cámara Agraria v. Andre Margaron), <http://cisgw3.law.pace.edu/cases/950329f1.html>; and Spain 28 January 2000 Supreme Court, *supra* note 4, where the offer of modification of the international sales contract made by a U.S. seller was never accepted by the Spanish buyer; *see* the comment by E. Fernández Masiá, Sentencia de 28 de enero de 2000, Cuadernos Civitas de Jurisprudencia Civil, abril-septiembre 2000, pp .673–689; and F. Oliva Blαzquez, Aceptaciσn, contraoferta y modificaciσn del contrato de compraventa internacional a la luz del articulo 8 del Convenio de Viena. La indemnizaciσn de daρos y perjuicios y el "deber de mitigar" "ex" articulo 77 CISG. Comentario a la STS de 28 enero 2000 (RJ 2000, 454), Revista de Derecho Patrimonial, 2000, I, no. 5, pp. 203–219.

[15] *See* Pilar Perales Viscasillas, Tratamiento jurνdico de las cartas de confirmaciσn en la Convenciσn de Viena de 1980 sobre Compraventa Internacional de Mercaderνas, Revista Jurνdica del Perï (Trujillo), octubre–diciembre 1997, no. 13, pp. 241 *et seq*.

be accepted, this does not mean that the confirmation letters containing them are held in the same light as the offer and acceptance.

In Anglo-American law, confirmation letters are regulated in a manner similar to the battles of the forms (see Section 2-207 UCC), although with certain differences. In particular, jurisprudence has indicated that a confirmation conditional upon the recipient's acceptance of new terms is not acceptable because it would mean imposing new conditions on a contract that has already been concluded.[16]

The CISG is silent on the treatment of commercial letters of confirmation. However, the subject can be analyzed in the familiar context of offer and acceptance; the sending of a writing in confirmation that adds to or modifies the terms previously agreed upon by the parties is treated as an offer to modify the contract that has to be accepted by the addressee for the contract to be concluded on those terms, unless there is an applicable usage or practice to the contrary.[17]

The PECL has an explicit rule that deals with commercial letters of confirmation. The solution offered by the European Principles is to specifically apply the rules of offer and acceptance from Chapter II. With a similar solution to that of Article 2:208 PECL (relating to acceptances with modifications), Article 2:210 PECL provides that additional or different terms that are included in a confirmation letter become part of the contract unless they substantially alter the terms of the contract or the recipient of the letter objects without delay to their inclusion.

IV. CONCLUSIONS

The modification of the offer under both the CISG and the PECL is dealt with in a similar fashion. However, the two instruments differ in their treatment of battles of the forms. In this case, the PECL cannot aid in the interpretation of the CISG because the solutions under the two regimes are completely different.

However, the treatment of the commercial letters of confirmation adopted by the PECL is in accord with the rules of offer and acceptance under the CISG. Therefore, there should be no impediment to use of the PECL to help interpret the CISG in that regard.

[16] James White & Robert S. Summers, *Uniform Commercial Code*. Vol. I. St. Paul, Minn: West Publishing Co, 3rd ed., 1988, §1–3, n. 60, pp. 48 *et seq*. This would mean that the final part of Section 2-207(1) UCC would not be applicable: "[. . .] unless acceptance is expressly made conditional on assent to the additional or different terms."

[17] *See* CISG Article 9. Among the cases applying CISG to commercial letters of confirmation, *see* Switzerland 21 December 1992 Civil Court Basel, case presentation including English translation available at <http://cisgw3.law.pace.edu/cases/921221s1.html>, considering that in a contract of sale between an Austrian buyer and a Swiss seller there is an international trade usage (art. 9(2) CISG) whereby silence in response to a commercial letter of confirmation amounts to an acceptance (note that this is more of a regional usage recognized in Germany, Austria, and Switzerland).

Cf. Germany 9 July 1998 OLG [Appellate Court] Dresden, case presentation including English translation available at <http://cisgw3.law.pace.edu/cases/980709g1.html>; Germany 22 February 1994 OLG [Appellate Court] Köln, case presentation including English translation available at <http://cisgw3.law.pace.edu/cases/940222g1.html>; Germany 5 July 1995 OLG [Appellate Court] Frankfurt, case presentation including English translation available at <http://cisgw3.law.pace.edu/cases/950705g1.html>; reaching a consistent result: denying the value of silence as an acceptance to the usage described when one of the parties does not belong to a country that recognizes that usage of trade.

But *see* Germany 14 February 2001 OLG [Appellate Court] Saarbrücken, case presentation including English translation available at <http://cisgw3.law.pace.edu/cases/010214g1.html>, involving a contract of sale between an Italian seller and a German buyer where the tribunal held that ". . . the contract is binding with the content given to it in the letter of confirmation, unless the sender of the letter has either intentionally given an incorrect account of the negotiations, or the content of the letter deviates so far from the result of the negotiations that the sender could not reasonably assume the recipient's consent. The recipient's silence causes the contract to be modified or supplemented in accordance with the letter of confirmation. . . . "

Interpretation of offeror's time limit for acceptance: Comparison between the provisions of CISG Article 20 and the counterpart provisions of the Principles of European Contract Law

John Felemegas

I. PERIOD FOR ACCEPTANCE FIXED BY THE OFFEROR: CISG ART. 20 AND PECL ART. 1:304

In the situation where the offeror fixes a precise date by which the offeree must accept the offer (e.g., "no later that 31 August"), there are no special problems regarding the period allowed for acceptance of the offer by the offeree. However, in the situation where the offeror merely indicates a period of time for acceptance (e.g., "fifteen days"), problems may arise as to when that period begins because of possible uncertainty in whether the period starts to run from the time the communication was prepared by the offeror, the time it was sent, or the time it was received by the other party.

It is an important element of certainty for parties who contemplate entering into a contract that there is a clear point of time at which the period fixed by the offeror for acceptance of the offer commences.

In Part II of the Convention, entitled "Formation of the Contract," CISG Article 20 provides the rules for calculating when that period begins to run in situations where the commencement of the period of time during which an offer can be accepted by the offeree has not been expressly fixed by the offeror.[1]

PECL Article 1:304, entitled "Computation of Time," seems to have a slightly broader scope than CISG Art. 20: the former provides the rules for computing the commencement of a period of time "set by a party in a written document for the addressee to reply or take other action," whereas the CISG deals specifically with the "time for acceptance fixed by the offeror." Nonetheless, it is arguable that an "acceptance of an offer" is included in the scope of an addressee's "reply or [. . .] other action", in the context of the PECL.

II. COMMENCEMENT OF PERIOD

1. CISG Art. 20(1)

CISG Art. 20 makes a distinction in the rules for calculating the period of time available for acceptance, depending on the means of communication of the offer used by the offeror.

[1] Enderlein and Maskow, *International Sales Law* (Oceana, 1992), also available online at <http://cisgw3.law.pace.edu/cisg/biblio/enderlein.html>, Art. 20, comment 1: "The objective of this rule is for the two parties to find identical bases for the calculation of that period."

a. Non-Instantaneous Means of Communication

CISG Art. 20(1) provides that the period of time for acceptance fixed by the offeror in a telegram "begins to run from the moment the telegram is handed in for dispatch." If the period of time for acceptance is communicated to the offeree by letter, the time runs "from the date shown on the letter, or if no such date is shown, from the date shown on the envelope."[2]

In other words, the CISG adopts the moment of *dispatch* of the communication as being effective.[3]

b. Instantaneous Means of Communication

CISG Art. 20(1) provides that if the period of time for acceptance is communicated by "telephone, telex or other means of instantaneous communication," the period "begins to run from the moment that the offer reaches the offeree."[4]

In such instances in which instantaneous means of communication are used, the moments of dispatch and receipt of the communication are practically identical, as they occur almost simultaneously.

2. PECL Art. 1:304(1)

PECL Art. 1:304 makes no express distinction between non-instantaneous and other means of communication; rather the PECL make an implied distinction between written and oral means of communication.[5]

Similarly to the rule contained in CISG Art. 20(1) regarding non-instantaneous means of communication, PECL Art. 1:304(1) states that the relevant period of time "begins to run from the date stated as the date of the document."[6]

[2] The Secretariat Commentary on Article 18 of the 1978 Draft [*draft counterpart of CISG Article 20*], available at <http://cisgw3.law.pace.edu/cisg/text/secomm/secomm-20.html> explains that "[t]his order of preference was chosen for two reasons: first, the offeree may discard the envelope but he will have the letter available as the basis for calculating the end of the period during which the offer can be accepted and second, the offeror will have a copy of the letter with its date but will generally have no record of the date on the envelope. Therefore, if the date on the envelope had not been checked, the offeror could not know the termination date of the period during which the offer could be accepted." Comment 3.

[3] Enderlein and Maskow, *supra* note 1, Art 20, comment 1, where the authors also note that "the moment of dispatch is generally easier to prove than the moment of receipt."

[4] *Cf.* CISG Art. 24: "For the purpose of this Part of the Convention, an offer, declaration of acceptance or any other indication of intention 'reaches' the addressee when it is made orally to him or delivered by any other means to him personally, to his place of business or mailing address or, if he does not have a place of business or mailing address, to his habitual residence."

[5] PECL Art. 1:304(1) refers to the period of time "set by a party in a written document."

See also Comment and Notes to PECL Article 1:304, Ole Lando & Hugh Beale eds., *Principles of European Contract Law: Parts I and II* (Kluwer Law International, 2000) 131–134, also available at <http://cisgw3.law.pace.edu/cisg/text/peclcomp20.html#cnpc>, Comment B: "If a party sets a period of time in an oral communication, whether face-to-face or by phone, and does not state from when it is to run, the natural assumption is that it runs from the moment of communication. (This would apply even to a message left on a telephone answering machine: the period will start from the moment the message is recorded.) No special rule is needed for this case. Problems arise only with communications in writing (which as defined in Article 1:301 include e-mail and similar electronic forms of communication if they are capable of leaving a written record)."

[6] The Comments to PECL Art. 1:304, *op. cit.*, explain the rationale for the rule adopted in the Principles; *see* Comment D: "In default of a stated method of computation, there might be uncertainty whether the period should start from the time the communication was prepared, the time it was sent or the time it was received. It is well known that delays occur not only in the actual transmission of communications such as telegrams or letters but also in the sending out of all types of communication. For example a fax may be signed on one day but the sender's office may not dispatch it until the next. This will not necessarily be apparent to the sender, who may simply be given back the original; nor to the person in the recipient's office who is charged with responding. Although fax machines record the time the message was received at the top or bottom of the page, this is very easily lost when the document is photocopied again. For this reason the Principles adopt the rule that the date shown as the date of the letter or other document should normally be treated as the starting date by whatever method the document was transmitted."

However, PECL Art. 1:304(1) goes further than the counterpart CISG provision by explicitly clarifying the situation where there is no date shown on the relevant document: "If no date is shown, the period begins to run from the moment the document reaches the addressee."[7]

It is submitted that, despite the broader scope of the provision in PECL Art. 1:394(1), which encompasses the period for an addressee's reply or any other action, and also its lack of a distinction comparable to that contained in CISG Art. 20(1) – regarding instantaneous and other means of communication – the two counterpart provisions share the same rationale (i.e., the creation of certainty for the parties concerned[8]) and they also adopt similar solutions to the problem they address (i.e., by providing rules based first on objective evidence of dispatch, whenever such evidence is available).

III. EFFECT OF HOLIDAYS AND NON-BUSINESS DAYS: CISG ART. 20(2) AND PECL ART. 1:304(2)

The counterpart provisions in CISG Art. 20(2) and in PECL Art. 1:304(2) contain identical rules, phrased in similar wording, providing that official holidays and non-business days occurring during the period fixed for acceptance are included in calculating the period.[9]

Where the notice or acceptance cannot be delivered on the last day of the period fixed for acceptance-reply, because it falls on a holiday or non-business day at the place of delivery (i.e., at the place of the offeror-addressee, as the case may be),[10] both counterpart provisions grant an extension of the period until the first business day that follows.[11]

IV. COMPUTATION OF PERIOD FROM MIDNIGHT TO MIDNIGHT: PECL ART. 1:304(3)

In accordance with the 1972 European Convention on the Calculation of Time-Limits, the PECL provide that time runs from the start of the first day to midnight of the last day of the period.[12]

[7] Note that a similar rule is adopted by the Convention in CISG Art. 20(1) regarding instantaneous means of communication; *see* editorial comments in Section 2 (ii), *supra*.

[8] On the importance of certainty for both parties, *see* PECL Comment A. *See* also Enderlein and Maskow, *supra* note 1; J. Ziegel, *Report to the Uniform Law Conference of Canada on Convention on Contracts for the International Sale of Goods* (July 1981), also available online at <http://cisgw3.law.pace.edu/cisg/text/ziegel20.html>: "[CISG Art. 20] Paragraph (1) provides some sensible rules to determine the commencement of the period of time during which an offer can be accepted and appears to be unobjectionable from a common law point of view."

[9] *See* Enderlein and Maskow, *supra* note 1, comment 5, where the authors state that "[o]nly holidays or non-business days at the place of business of the offeror are being taken into consideration because those may not be known to the offeree."

[10] *See* Enderlein and Maskow, *id.*: "If, however, the last day of the period falls on a holiday at the place of business of the offeree and the offeree is prevented from dispatching an acceptance, he has to take this into account and hand in his acceptance for dispatch earlier." *Id.*

[11] *See* Ziegel *supra* note 8, where the author states that this rule in CISG Art. 20(2) "is a logical corollary to the reception rule for acceptances adopted in art. 18(2). Since the acceptance is not effective until it reaches the offeror some provision is necessary where the last day for acceptance is a non-business day or an official holiday at the offeror's place of business. The practical effect of art. 20(2) appears to be to extend the period for acceptance by at least one day where the notice of acceptance cannot be delivered. It may of course be longer depending on the circumstances."

See also Official Comments to PECL Article 1:304, *op. cit.*, Comment F: "The Principles follow European convention (see the 1972 Convention on the Calculation of Time-Limits, Article 5) in including official non-working days (e.g., Saturday and Sunday) and official holidays in the period, except that if the last day of a period is an official non-working day or official holiday in the relevant place (i.e., where the message is to be delivered or the action performed) the period is extended to include the next working day. If in the relevant trade there is a usage of working on what is officially a holiday, or if there is a local usage of working or not working on the relevant day, the usage will prevail, see Article 1:105." *Cf.* CISG Article 9, on the issue of international trade usages.

[12] *See* PECL Art. 1:304(3), first sentence; *see* also Comments to PECL Art. 1:304, Comment G.

However, the second sentence in Article 1:304(3) states that any reply that has to reach the party who sets the period must arrive "by the normal close of business in the relevant place on the last day of the period."[13]

The Convention does not contain any comparable provision on the calculation of the period fixed for acceptance in terms of hours, but the PECL rule on the "normal close of business in the relevant place on the last day of the period" is not a controversial one and can also be found in other legal systems.[14]

[13] *See* also PECL Comment G: "Moreover, the relevant close of business should be the one where the party is, since the person who has been told to reply within a certain time should not be entitled to assume that this means the period calculated by his own time."

[14] *See* Comments and Notes to PECL Article 1:304, *op. cit.*, Notes 3 and 4.

Late acceptances: Comparison between the provisions of CISG Art. 21 and the counterpart provisions of PECL Art. 2:207

John Felemegas

I. INTRODUCTION

In Part II of the Convention, entitled "Formation of the Contract," Article 21 deals with the issue of *late acceptance*[1] by an offeree, the response to that by the offeror, and the effect that a late acceptance has in the context of contract formation.[2]

Article 2:207, found in the PECL, Chapter 2 "Formation," Section 2 "Offer and Acceptance," regulates the same issues concerning late acceptance in contract formation.[3]

The Convention provides that a late acceptance can nonetheless be effective, and so do the Principles. Both the Convention and the Principles deal with the issue of late acceptance – whether the offeree accepted the offer late or the acceptance was late because of a delay in transmission – in almost identical terms.

[1] *I.e.*, an acceptance that has not reached the offeror in *due time*, *see* CISG Art. 18(2).

[2] CISG Art. 21 is situated among the eleven provisions of the Convention dealing with contract formation; *see* CISG Part II, Arts. 14–24.

[3] PECL Art. 2:207 is situated in the Chapter of the PECL dealing with the rules of contractual formation; *see* PECL Arts. 2:101–2:107 and 2:201–2:211.

II. LATE ACCEPTANCE OF OFFER TO CONCLUDE CONTRACT

Art. 21 of the Convention "deals with acceptances that arrive after the expiration of the time for acceptance."[4] In that sense, Art. 21 must be viewed in the context of the basic rule of the Convention that a late acceptance is ineffective.[5]

Honnold states that CISG Art. 21 "like Article 20, extends and elaborates the basic rule"[6] for late acceptances, by providing the answer to some related, important questions that can arise when an acceptance does not reach the offeror within the time he has fixed for acceptance.[7]

CISG Art. 21 makes a distinction in the rules applicable to a late acceptance, depending on whether the acceptance was sent late by the offeree or the lateness of the acceptance was caused by delays in its transmission. The counterpart provision of the PECL, Article 2:207 makes the same distinction.

III. NOTICE BY OFFEROR GIVING EFFECT TO LATE ACCEPTANCE

1. CISG Art. 21(1)

In the case of a belated dispatch of acceptance by the offeree, a positive subsequent response by the offeror can make the late acceptance nevertheless effective to conclude the contract.[8]

Where the offeree has dispatched belatedly an acceptance – either after the period for acceptance set by the offeror has expired or before the expiration of the fixed period but using a mode of communication that would not ensure that acceptance reaches the offeror in due time – it must be presumed that the offeree is aware that his acceptance is (or is going to be) late for the purposes of contract formation. In that case, it is argued that the offeree "knows that his acceptance is actually a counter-offer and needs to be confirmed through an acceptance. Silence by the offeror cannot be inferred by him to be an acceptance (Article 18, paragraph 1)."[9]

From the basic rule of the Convention that an acceptance of an offer becomes effective at the moment *it reaches the offeror* (pursuant to Art. 18(2)), it follows that the risk of transmission is borne by the offeree.[10] Furthermore, pursuant to Art. 21(1) the offeror has the power to consider a late acceptance as having arrived in due time. If the offeror so elects to be bound by the late acceptance, he must inform *without delay* the offeree "orally or by dispatch of a notice that he considers the acceptance to be effective."[11]

[4] See the Text of the Secretariat Commentary on article 19 of the 1978 Draft [*draft counterpart of* CISG *article 21*], available online at <http://cisgw3.law.pace.edu/cisg/text/secomm/secomm-21.html>: "If the acceptance is late, the offer lapses and no contract is concluded by the arrival of the acceptance." Art. 19 of the 1978 Draft and Art. 21 of the CISG are identical, except for some inconsequential rewording.

[5] CISG Art. 18(2). Available at <http://cisgw3.law.pace.edu/cisg/text/matchup/matchup-d-20.html>.

[6] Honnold J. O., *Uniform Law for International Sales*, Kluwer Law International, 3rd ed. (1999), 195.

[7] For a relevant discussion regarding computation of time for acceptance of offer, *see* Felemegas J., "Comparison between provisions of the CISG (Article 20) and the counterpart provisions of the Principles of European Contract Law," available online, at <http://cisgw3.law.pace.edu/cisg/biblio/felemegas3.html>.

[8] CISG Art. 21(1); *see* also ULF Article 9(1).

[9] Enderlein F. and Maskow D., *International Sales Law*, Oceana Publications (1992) 103; also available at <http://cisgw3.law.pace.edu/cisg/biblio/enderlein-art21.html>. The authors also consider the case where the offeror has not fixed a time for acceptance – the indication of the offeree's assent must reach the offeror within a reasonable time (Art. 18(2)): "In that case, the offeror and the offeree may well consider different periods as being reasonable. Objectively, a reasonable time may have expired already, even though the offeree assumes that the acceptance was made in due time." *Id.*

[10] *See* Enderlein and Maskow, *op. cit.*, 104.

[11] Text of the Secretariat Commentary on article 19 of the 1978 Draft, *op. cit. Cf.* Enderlein and Maskow, *op. cit.*, 104–105, where the authors (a) describe the wording 'without delay' as being "not quite comprehensible" because the offeror probably needs time to reflect on whether to accept the late acceptance, and

It must be stressed that the subsequent – and *without delay* – response by the offeror to a late acceptance acts only as validation of the contractually binding effect of what was a late acceptance by the offeree and it does not constitute a counter-offer.[12]

It follows that the offeror need not respond to the offeree regarding the late acceptance, in which case no contract is concluded.[13]

If the offeror wishes to assent to the contract he may do so by informing the offeree either orally[14] or by dispatching a notice[15] that the late acceptance is effective. The information can also be given to the offeree in an electronic message.[16]

2. PECL Art. 2:207(1)

According to the Principles, a late acceptance is ineffective (i.e., in order for an acceptance to be effective it must reach the offeror within the time fixed for acceptance).[17] That is the same basic rule on late acceptance found in the Convention.

The Principles, like the Convention, make a distinction between an acceptance that was sent late by the offeree[18] and an acceptance that was late because of transmission delays.[19] Like the Convention, the Principles provide a different rule for those two cases.

The wording in Article 2:207(1) is almost completely identical to that used in its counterpart provision of the CISG. In cases of late dispatch of the offeree's acceptance,

(b) state that this rule is "questionable, in particular when the acceptance is declared very late and the circumstances as a whole have changed in the meantime" (further references provided therein are omitted).

[12] Text of the Secretariat Commentary on article 19 of the 1978 Draft, *op. cit.*: "[U]nder this paragraph [CISG 21(1)] it is the late acceptance which becomes the effective acceptance as of the moment of its receipt, even though it requires a subsequent notice to validate it." *See* also Schlechtriem P., *Uniform Sales Law – The UN-Convention on Contracts for the International Sale of Goods*, Manz, Vienna (1986) 55: "This notice [by offeror], however, does not constitute the acceptance of a counter-offer; the date of the contract depends on when the acceptance was received, even though it was received late," also available online at <http://cisgw3.law.pace.edu/cisg/biblio/schlechtriem-21.html>. *See* also Ziegel J., *Report to the Uniform Law Conference of Canada on Convention on Contracts for the International Sale of Goods*, (1981), available at <http://cisgw3.law.pace.edu/cisg/text/ziegel21.html>, who states "the late acceptance takes effect from the date of its receipt and not from the time when the offeror communicates with the offeree." *Cf.* Enderlein and Maskow, *op. cit.*, 105, where the authors state, "It is not clear whether the late acceptance becomes effective at the moment when the offeror informs the offeree or dispatches the relevant communication or whether it becomes effective retroactively from the moment it is received. (Since the offeror needs to inform the offeree without delay, there will only be a slight difference in time [. . .])" (further references provided therein are omitted). For the Convention's rules regarding counter-offers, *see* CISG Art. 19.

[13] *See* Enderlein and Maskow, *op. cit.*, 104: "[I]t *is up to the offeror whether* or not *he considers the acceptance to be valid.* If he wants a contract [. . .] he must inform the offeree accordingly [. . .]. Should the offeror keep silent [. . .] there will be no contract."

The same policy is adopted in PECL Art. 2:206(1). *See* also Lando O. and Beale H. (eds.), *Principles of European Contract Law: Parts I and II*, Kluwer Law International (2000) 176–177, Comment A; also available at <http://cisgw3.law.pace.edu/cisg/text/peclcomp21.html#cnpc>: "Any acceptance which reaches the offeror after that time may be disregarded by the offeror. Normally it does not even have to reject the acceptance."

[14] CISG-AC Opinion no 1, Electronic Communications under CISG, 15 August 2003. Rapporteur: Professor Christina Ramberg, Gothenburg, Sweden. The opinion is available online at <http://cisgw3.law.pace.edu/cisg/CISG-AC-op1.html>. Regarding Electronic Communications in the context of Art. 21(1), the Opinion states, "The term 'oral' includes electronically transmitted sound provided that the offeree expressly or impliedly has consented to receiving electronic communication of that type, in that format, and to that address."

[15] CISG-AC Opinion no 1, *op. cit.* The Opinion states, "The term 'notice' includes electronic communications provided that the offeree expressly or impliedly has consented to receiving electronic messages of that type, in that format, and to that address."

[16] CISG-AC Opinion no 1, *op. cit.* Comment 21.1: "The important factor is that the information be conveyed to the offeree, not in what form it was conveyed."

[17] PECL Art. 2:206(1) and (2). *See* also Lando O. and Beale H. (eds.), *op. cit.*, 176–177, Comment A; also available at <http://cisgw3.law.pace.edu/cisg/text/peclcomp21.html#cnpc>.

[18] PECL Art. 2:207(1).

[19] PECL Art. 2:207(2).

Article 2:207(1) provides that, notwithstanding the rule in Article 2:206, the offeror may validate the effectiveness of the acceptance by treating it as valid.

The offeror may do so if he informs *without delay* the offeree that he assents to the late acceptance. Such response by the offeror has the effect of binding him to the acceptance and concluding the contract, effective from the moment the late acceptance reached him.[20]

The PECL Comment on Article 2:207(1) makes clear that the offeror's notice to the offeree need not be an express statement of acceptance.[21]

Like the Convention, the Principles do not treat the late acceptance as a new offer that the offeror may accept within the time set for acceptance, which is often longer than the time provided for in 2:207(1).[22]

IV. LATE ARRIVAL OF ACCEPTANCE BECAUSE OF TRANSMISSION DELAYS

1. Cause of Delay Evident to Offeror: Duty to Inform Offeree

According to the Convention, if the late arrival of the acceptance was evidently caused by a delay in transmission, the acceptance is effective unless the offeror informs the offeree that the offer has indeed lapsed.[23]

a. CISG Art. 21(2)

Art. 21(2) provides that, if "a letter or other writing[24] containing the late acceptance shows that it was sent in such circumstances that if its transmission had been normal it would have reached the offeror in due time" the offeror has an obligation to notify – either orally or by dispatching[25] a relevant notice[26] – without delay, the offeree in order to prevent a contract from being concluded.[27]

[20] Lando and Beale, *op. cit.*, Comment B. [21] *Id.*

[22] *Id.*, Comment D.

[23] PECL Art. 21(2); *see* also ULF Art. 9(2). *See* also the Text of the Secretariat Commentary on article 19 of the 1978 Draft [*draft counterpart of CISG article 21*], available online at <http://cisgw3.law.pace.edu/cisg/text/secomm/secomm-21.html>: "[I]f the letter or document which contains the late acceptance shows that it was sent in such circumstances that if its transmission had been normal, it would have been communicated in due time [. . .] the late acceptance is considered to have arrived in due time, and the contract is concluded as of the moment the acceptance reaches the offeror, unless the offeror without delay notifies the offeree that he considers the offer as having lapsed."

[24] CISG-AC Opinion no 1, Electronic Communications under CISG, 15 August 2003. Rapporteur: Professor Christina Ramberg, Gothenburg, Sweden. The opinion is available online at <http://cisgw3.law.pace.edu/cisg/CISG-AC-op1.html>. Regarding electronic communications in the context of Art. 21(2), the Opinion states, "The term 'writing' covers any type of electronic communication that is retrievable in perceivable form. A late acceptance in electronic form may thus be effective according to this article."

[25] CISG-AC Opinion no 1, *op. cit.* The Opinion states, "The term 'dispatch' corresponds to the point in time when the notice has left the offeree's server. A prerequisite is that the offeree has consented expressly or impliedly to receiving electronic messages of that type, in that format, and to that address."

Comment 21.5, *id.*: "It is enough that the notice has been dispatched; it does not have to reach the addressee. However, it must have been dispatched correctly. This means that the address must be correctly stated and that the sender uses a computer program that the addressee has indicated he is willing to accept."

[26] CISG-AC Opinion no 1, *op. cit.* Comment 21.6: "The offeror should inform the offeree about a late acceptance by dispatching a notice. Dispatch occurs when the notice leaves the offeror's server. If, however, the offeree does not use the kind of electronic communication that the notice is sent in, the offeror is not considered to have dispatched the notice. The offeree must have indicated that he is willing to receive electronic acceptances of the type and format used by the offeror. CISG Arts. 8 and 9 may be of assistance in determining whether the offeree has impliedly indicated his willingness to receive such messages."

[27] CISG-AC Opinion no 1, *op. cit.* Comment 21.4: "When the offeror provides a quick notice that that the acceptance has arrived too late, the acceptance is not effective. Information to the offeree about the late acceptance can be given in an electronic message. The important factor is that the information be conveyed to the offeree, not in what form it is conveyed. According to this Article such notice shall be communicated orally or by a [written] notice. The offeror may provide the information by electronically conveyed sound or

It is said that the provision in Art. 21(2) mitigates the rigor of the Convention's rule that an acceptance must *reach the offeror* to be effective (Art. 18(2)), and thus it "protects the offeree's reasonable reliance interests where he has no reason to anticipate that his acceptance will not reach the offeror on time."[28]

It must be noted, however, that the offeror is not obliged to be bound by the late acceptance.[29] Furthermore, if it is shown that the relevant communication of acceptance was sent late and the offeror does not want to conclude a contract, he should be under no duty to do anything and can simply disregard the late acceptance. Conversely, if the offeror nonetheless wishes to conclude the contract, he must notify, *without delay*,[30] the offeree that he considers the late acceptance to be effective pursuant to Art. 21(1).[31]

b. PECL Art. 2:207(2)

The wording in Article 2:207(2) is almost completely identical to that used in its counterpart provision of the Convention.

The PECL Comment on Art. 2:207(2) explains that where the offeree sent his acceptance in a timely fashion but a delay in its transmission caused its late arrival at the offeror, the offeror has a duty to notify the offeree if he does not assent to the contract.[32]

2. Failure So to Inform Offeree: Acceptance Is Effective

a. CISG Art. 21(2)

It follows from what was said earlier that if the offeror does not inform the offeree – either orally or by dispatching a relevant notice – that he considers his offer as having lapsed, the acceptance is effective and concludes the contract pursuant to Art. 21(2).[33] In

by an electronic message under the precondition that the sender of the late acceptance has indicated that he is willing to receive such electronic messages."

[28] Ziegel J., *Report to the Uniform Law Conference of Canada on Convention on Contracts for the International Sale of Goods* (1981), available at <http://cisgw3.law.pace.edu/cisg/text/ziegel21.html>.

[29] Enderlein and Maskow, *op. cit.* 105, where the authors point out that "[t]he offeror could not foresee that an acceptance would arrive even after the period for acceptance had expired" and he "may have made other arrangements or have lost his interest in the transaction."

For a similar approach in the PECL, *see* Lando and Beale, note 32, *infra*.

[30] Kritzer A. H., *Guide to Practical Applications of the United Nations Convention on Contracts for the International Sale of Goods*, Kluwer, (1988) 190, stresses that "if the offeror wants to treat such an acceptance as invalid, he may if he proceeds *without delay*. A concern is that where an acceptance is late under these circumstances, Article 21 may give the offeror an opportunity to speculate and decide whether to honor the late acceptance on the basis of a rise or fall of prices in the interim period."

Regarding the potential for opportunistic speculation by the offeror at the expense of the offeree, in the application of Art. 21, Honnold, *op. cit.*, at 197, opines that "[t]his opportunity will be avoided [...] by construing Article 21(1) in relation to the basic rule in Article 18(1) that a statement is an acceptance only if it indicates 'assent' to the offer in the light of the objective facts available to both parties when (Art. 18(2)) the reply 'reaches the offeror.' This result would also respond to the rule of Article 7(1) that 'in the interpretation of this Convention, regard is to be had ... to the need to promote ... the observance of good faith in international trade'."

[31] *See* the Text of the Secretariat Commentary on article 19 of the 1978 Draft [*draft counterpart of CISG article 21*], available online at <http://cisgw3.law.pace.edu/cisg/text/secomm/secomm-21.html>.

[32] Lando and Beale, *op. cit.*, Comment C. "The offeror, however, only has this duty if the acceptance shows that it was sent in time and that it arrived late due to an unexpected delay in transmission." *Id.*

[33] CISG-AC Opinion no 1, *op. cit.* 21.3: "The purpose of this Article is to make a delayed acceptance effective when the offeror does not inform the other party that the acceptance has been delayed and the acceptance has reached the offeror too late. A typical situation is when an electronic acceptance is delayed and does not reach the offeror within the normal time-span. The article is only applicable if the acceptance is sent in a letter or other writing. The article applies also when the acceptance is sent by an electronic message as long as this electronic message fulfills the two functions of writing, i.e. that it can be understood and saved."

that case, the late acceptance is considered to have arrived in due time, and the contract is concluded as of the moment the acceptance reaches the offeror.[34]

b. PECL Art. 2:207(2)

It is clear also in the PECL provision that where the offeree sent his acceptance in a timely manner but its arrival was late because of transmission delays, the acceptance should be considered effective unless the offeror without delay informs the offeree that it considers its offer as having lapsed or gives notice to that effect.[35]

V. CONCLUSION

The wording used in the counterpart provisions of the CISG and the PECL is almost completely identical. Furthermore, based on the striking similarity in policy and structure of the approach adopted in the CISG and the PECL to deal with the issue of late acceptance, it can be concluded that the counterpart provisions are substantively identical.[36]

[34] Schlechtriem, *op. cit.*, states "the acceptance becomes effective on arrival and thus concludes the contract, unless the offeror protests orally or in writing." *See* also *supra*, note 14.

[35] Lando and Beale, *op. cit.*, Comment C.

[36] *See* also Lando and Beale, *op. cit.*, Note 1: "Article 2:207(1) is in accordance with CISG, art. 21(1)"; Note 2: "Article 2:207(2) is identical to CISG art. 21(2)."

Time of conclusion of the contract: Remarks on the manner in which the Principles of European Contract Law may be used to interpret or supplement Art. 23 of the CISG

Pilar Perales Viscasillas

I. Introduction to Contract Formation in the CISG and the PECL
II. Specific Rules Concerning Contract Formation in the CISG and the PECL
III. Contract Formation outside the Traditional Model of Offer and Acceptance
IV. Exact Time and Place of Contract Formation
V. Conclusions

I. INTRODUCTION TO CONTRACT FORMATION IN THE CISG AND THE PECL

Section II of the PECL and Part II of the CISG follow the classic pattern of two *declarations of will* (offer and acceptance) in deeming a contract concluded. The adoption of this process, which is designed in almost the same terms under both texts, is justified for two reasons: (1) it is adopted by the great majority of legal systems and (2) it makes analyzing the formation of the contract easy for the parties and judges or arbitrators. Nevertheless, at times it is difficult to determine what exactly is an offer or an acceptance, such as when negotiations are long and complicated. That, however, does not prevent the conclusion of a contract.

Article 23 CISG fixes the time of the conclusion of the contract by connecting it with the moment at which the acceptance takes effect *in accordance with the provisions of the Convention*. It seems clear that, although Article 23 is a central piece in Part II of the Convention, it must be viewed in conjunction with the rest of the dispositions of Part II that establish a precise moment at which the indication of assent takes effect, depending on the manner chosen by the offeree to accept the offer. In Part II of the PECL there is no provision similar to Article 23 CISG, although Article 2:205 PECL (Time of conclusion of the contract) tries to embody in a single disposition the precise time of the conclusion of the contract depending on the way in which acceptance of the offer takes place. However, Article 2:205 PECL alone is not enough to fix the time of the conclusion of the contract; to have a complete picture of the exact moment at which a contract is concluded, one must turn to other rules of the PECL. The significance of finding the exact moment of the conclusion of the contract is that the parties are bound to the contract (i.e., they are obliged to fulfill the obligations derived from a contract that is born to the law at that exact moment).

II. SPECIFIC RULES CONCERNING CONTACT FORMATION IN THE CISG AND PECL [ART. 23 CISG AND ART. 2:205 PECL]

Article 23 CISG is directed to the rest of the norms of Part II of the Convention that point out when the indication of assent is effective. It, in turn, must be referenced to the relevant provision in Article 18(2) CISG, which must be analyzed in accordance with Article 24 CISG. Article 18(1)–(3) and Articles 19 and 21 CISG are also relevant to this matter. Similarly, Article 2:205 PECL has to be analyzed considering other rules of the European Principles – mainly, Articles 1:303 (similar to Article 24 CISG); 2:204(2) (counterpart of Article 18(1) CISG, in relation to acceptance by silence or inaction); 2:207 (for late acceptances, ruled on in Article 21 CISG); Article 2:208 (modified acceptance, similar to Article 19 CISG); and, finally, Article 2:209 (which refers to conflicting general conditions).

Articles 18(2) CISG and 2:205(2) PECL state that the acceptance becomes effective and therefore the contract is concluded when the indication of assent reaches the offeror. These provisions fix the general rule on the moment at which the acceptance takes effect. In this regard, the Convention, the PECL, and also the UNIDROIT Principles for International Commercial Contracts follow the same rule to determine the conclusion of the contract, as do some national legal systems. However, other systems adopt the dispatch principle to deem the contract concluded (see Notes to Article 2:205 PECL).

Both the CISG and the PECL have adopted for their relevant provisions the term "reaches," which is defined in Articles 24 CISG and 1:303(3) PECL in a comprehensive way. One consideration in regard to the comparison between the CISG and PECL provisions is the location of Article 1:303(3) PECL. Located in Chapter I (General Provisions) of the European Principles, it entails that, in contrast to the Convention (*cf.* Articles 23 and 27 CISG), the receipt rule is applied as a general principle to fix the effectiveness of *any* notice (i.e., the communication of a promise, statement, offer, acceptance, demand, request, or other declaration – Article 1:303(6) PECL) and not only to establish the time of conclusion of the contract, as does Article 23 CISG.

Article 24 CISG indicates when a Part II (Formation) communication, including the acceptance, "reaches" the addressee. A Part II (Formation) communication reaches the addressee "when it is made orally to him or delivered by any other means to him personally, to his place of business or mailing address or, if he does not have a place of business or mailing address, to his habitual residence." By the flexible and broad definition given in Article 24 CISG, the Convention seems to adopt as a general rule for written statements the *receipt theory*; and, for oral communications, the *information theory*.[1] The solution

[1] There are only a few scholars – a great many are silent about this point – who hold that when the offeror knows the acceptance, the contract orally made is concluded. *See*, for example, Pilar Perales Viscasillas, *La*

adopted by the PECL is slightly different: Article 1:303 adopts the *receipt theory* as a general rule for both oral and written notices.

The "*reaching principle*" as a general rule in both the CISG and PECL is applied to the following ways of indicating assent:

1) *Indication of assent made by written statements* [Article 18(1) CISG and Articles 2:205(1) and 1:303(2) PECL]. A written declaration represents the most usual way in which the offeree shows his conformity with the offer.[2] In such a case, the contract is concluded when the communication "reaches" the offeror at his place of business or mailing address or, if none exists, at his habitual residence. This means that the contract is concluded, for example, by the delivery of the communication by a messenger, the printing of a fax transmission, leaving the letter in the mailbox, the delivery of the notification informing of the arrival of a letter or telegram at the Post Office,[3] when an EDI or e-mail message enters into the offeror's computer system of information, or when the message is deposited in the electronic or informatic mailbox.
2) *Indication of assent made by oral statements* [Article 18(1) CISG, and Articles 1:303(1)(3) and 2:205(1) PECL]. Oral statements are made not only when the parties negotiate face to face but also when they use other means of communication, such as phone, radio, video-conference, etc. In such cases, under the CISG the contract is concluded when the offeror has knowledge of the acceptance,[4] whereas under the PECL the oral communication need merely be received.
3) *Indication of assent made by conduct* [Article 18(1) CISG and Article 2:205(2) PECL]. There are two types of acceptances by conduct that need to be considered:
   a) Some kind of behavior or conduct (e.g., raising a hand and nodding one's head). Under the CISG, this is deemed effective when the offeror understands the meaning of the conduct. Consequently, this system of information should be adopted by an extensive interpretation of Article 24 CISG. The PECL has a specific rule dealing with this matter that follows the general receipt theory: in case of acceptance by conduct, the contract is concluded when notice of the conduct reaches the offeror (Article 2:205(2) PECL).[5]

formación del contrato de compraventa internacional de mercadervas, (Tirant lo blanch, 1996), 232–237. *See* note 5 *infra* for an illustration of the information theory.

[2] As *written statements* we can consider those made by letter, telegram, telex, fax, electronic mail (e-mail, using Internet), electronic data interchange (EDI), and any other that could be included in the concept of "writing," For this solution, *see* Rafael Illescas Ortiz, "La Convencion de Viena de 1980 sobre compraventa internacional de mercadervas: ámbito de aplicación y perfección del contrato," 16 *Derecho de los Negocios*, 7 (1992).

[3] Against, Peter Schlechtriem, "Begriff des Zugangs," in Schlechtriem, *Kommentar zum Einheithlichen UN-Kaufrecht Das Übereinkommen der Vereinten Nationen über Verträge über den internationalen Warenkauf-Cisg. Kommentar-*, 3rd ed. (C. H. Beck: Munchen, 2000), no. 12.

[4] Information communicated orally by a third person could be also considered as an oral statement. It is doubtful when the reply to an offer recorded in an answering machine is effective: for Schlechtriem, it is effective when the offeror knows it (i.e., when he hears it) (Peter Schlechtriem, "Begriff des Zugangs," in Ernst von Caemmerer & Peter Schlechtriem, *Kommentar zum Einheitlichen UN-Kaufrecht. Das Übereinkommen der Vereinten Nationen óber Verträge über den internationalen Warenkauf - Cisg.- Kommentar*, 1st. ed. (C. H. Beck: Mónchen, 1990) no. 8. However, this author seems to follow another orientation in the second and third edition of his commentary (*see* Schlechtriem, *supra* note 3, at no. 8); for some authors, the moment that fixes the conclusion of the contract is the moment determined by the recording of the message: Karl Neumayer & Catherine Ming, *Convention de Vienne sur les contrats de vente internationale de marchandises* (Cededac: Lausanne, 1993) 202; and Perales Viscasillas, *supra* note 1, at 233.

[5] However, the PECL Comments to Article 2:205(2) state that the contract is concluded when the offeror learns of the conduct; thus, the information theory applies as shown by PECL illustration 1: "Having learned from a colleague that B may be interested in buying and reselling A's goods, A sends unsolicited goods to B.

b) Acts of performance (e.g., dispatch of the goods and payment of the price) that, contrary to the situation regulated in Articles 18(3) CISG and 2:205(3) PECL, must reach the offeror in order to conclude the contract: (1) by the goods reaching the offeror's place of business; 2) by the communication, which informs of the making of the act indicating assent, reaching the other party; or (3) by the payment of the price.[6]

4) *Late acceptance due to some irregularity during the transmission process* [Article 21(2) CISG and Article 2:207(2) PECL]. Such acceptances are deemed effective when they reach the offeror.[7]

In addition to the general rule established by the aforementioned Articles of the CISG and the PECL, there are some other dispositions relevant to the formation of the contract that state exceptions to the receipt rule:

1) *Silence or inaction* [Articles 18(1) CISG and 2:204(2) PECL]. The recognition of silence and inaction as acceptances implies the irrelevance of the communication. Strictly speaking, silence and inaction are not exceptions to the general rule because they cannot be submitted in any of the other classic theories devised to fix the moment of the conclusion of the contract – Declaration and Expedition (the latter known for the contract *inter absentes* in the common law systems as the dispatch, mailbox, or post rule). Silence and inaction, by definition, mean the concession of legal effects to an abstainer attitude of the offeree. The moment of the conclusion of the contract by silence or inaction is diverse and hangs on the factors that contribute to give them legal effect:
   a) When silence or inaction is considered as an acceptance by the dispositions of the Convention, their effectiveness is determined by the interpretation of the expression "without delay." The offeror is given an option to confirm (by his silence or inaction) in the situations contemplated by Articles 19(2) and 21(2) CISG and 2:207(2) PECL) or to negate (also by his silence or inaction) in the hypothesis, regulated by Articles 21(1) CISG and 2:207(1) PECL, the conclusion of the contract. Thus, the termination of the period of time to confirm or negate the conclusion of the contract determines the failure or, on the contrary, the effectiveness of the acceptance.
   b) When usages or the practices that the parties have established between themselves and the agreement of the parties give the effect of an acceptance to silence or inaction, the time given to the offeree to accept is determined (expressly or

B accepts by advertising the goods for sale in a trade paper which A reads. A learns of the acceptance when she reads the advertisement."

[6] Germany 24 November 1992 LG [District Court] Krefeld, case presentation available at <http://cisgw3.law.pace.edu/cases/921124g1.html> made clear that an offer, made by an Italian seller, was accepted conclusively when the German buyer received the goods without objecting to them. The Vienna scholars have not made any special effort to clarify the structural differences between an indication of assent made by acts of performance under Article 18(1) and indicia of assent under Article 18(3). When the acts of performance are protected by the factors enumerated in Article 18(3) (offer, practices, and usages), the offeree can accept without communicating his acceptance, the contract being concluded when he makes the relevant act of performance. On the contrary, if the offeree accepts by an act of performance without the factors contemplated in Article 18(3), his indication of assent must reach the offeror in order to conclude the contract – Article 18(1) and (2). In these cases the moment when the contract is concluded is different, as well as the limit to revoke the offer under Article 16(1) CISG. The decision of Germany 27 November 1979 OLG [Appellate Court] Frankfurt, established clearly the difference in the predecessor to Article 18 CISG, which is Article 6 of the 1964 Uniform Law on the Formation of Contracts (ULF).

[7] There is a general accord among the scholars about the moment when the acceptance takes effect in this hypothesis. *See*, among others, Katharina S. Ludwig, "Der Vertragsschluss nach UN-Kaufrecht im Spannungsverhältnis von Common Law und Civil Law: dargestellt auf der Grundlage der Rechtsordnungen Englands und Deutschlands, Studien zum vergleichenden und internationalen Recht," *Comp. & Int'l. L. Stud.*, Band 24 (Peter Lang: Frankfurt am Main, 1994), at 344 *et seq.*

implicitly) by the agreement (practices) of the parties previously established or the agreement considered by applicable trade usages. Thus, the effectiveness of the agreement will be established by the expiration of the period of time previously agreed on.[8]

c) When silence and inaction are deemed as acceptances due to any other circumstances – such as the existence of a "duty to speak" derived from the good faith principle – the expiration of the time in which the negative reply should have reached the offeror leads to the concession of positive effects to the offeree's silence at that moment.[9]

2) *Acts of performance* [Articles 18(3) CISG and 2:205(2) PECL]. These provisions deal with situations in which the offer, the practices already established between the parties, or usages authorize the offeree to accept by performing an act without the need to communicate it to the offeror. In this case, the contract is deemed concluded when the performance of the act begins (i.e., following the CISG, when the dispatch of the goods and the payment of the price are made).[10] Notwithstanding the clear meaning of these provisions, some CISG scholars believe that the acceptance by act of performance under Article 18(3) needs to be communicated to deem the contract concluded.[11]

   Usually the Battle of the Forms involves situations in which a contract is concluded by acts of performance.[12]

3) *Late acceptance* [Article 21(1) CISG]. The last exception to the "reaching principle" in the Vienna text is the one contemplated by Article 21(1). This Article states that the contract is concluded when the offeror dispatches a notice (dispatch principle) informing the offeree of the effectiveness of his declaration or when the offeror orally so informs the offeree (information theory). Thus, the CISG adopts the dispatch principle to regulate the conclusion of the contract when the offeror sends a written notice.[13] However, some scholars (following the Secretariat Commentary on Article 19 of the 1978 Draft Convention)[14] believe that the moment of the

[8] *See* the Secretariat Commentary on Article 16(1) of the 1978 Draft of the CISG. Official Records, note 1, p. 23.

[9] This solution is supported by Pilar Perales Viscasillas, "La perfección por silencio de la compraventa internacional en la Convención de Viena de 1980," 52 *Derecho de los Negocios* 9–14 (enero 1995), commenting on the first decision on the value of the silence or inaction of the offeree under the Vienna Convention. *See* United States 14 April 1992 Federal District Court [New York], *Filanto S.p.A. v. Chilewich International Corp.*, case presentation available at <http://cisgw3.law.pace.edu/cases/920414u1.html>. *See* also supporting the same solution but extending it to every case in which silence or inaction plays the role of acceptance: Ludwig, *supra* note 7, at 348.

[10] *See*, among the authors who do not demand a communication in such cases: Gyula Eorsi, "Formation of Contract," in *The 1980 Vienna Convention on the International Sale of Goods*. Lausanne Colloquium of November 19–20, 1984. Institut Suisse de Droit Comparı (3) (Schulthess Polygraphischer: Zórich, 1985) 50.

[11] The vast majority of the scholars follow the thesis supported by Professor Honnold, who thinks that there is a general principle applicable to Article 18: the need to communicate the acceptance. This principle is also applicable to paragraph (3) of Article 18 unless in a given case a quick reaching of the goods could substitute for the notice informing of the act of acceptance. *See* John O. Honnold, *Uniform Law for International Sales* (3rd ed., Kluwer Law International, 1999) no. 164, pp. 178–181.

See, against this thesis, the legislative history: during the Diplomatic Conference held in 1980 in Vienna a proposal made by Professor Farnsworth to introduce the obligation to notify of the performance of the act was withdrawn due to lack of support (Official Records, pp. 280 *et seq.*).

[12] *See* Pilar Perales Viscasillas, "Acceptance with modifications: Remarks on the manner in which the Principles of European Contract Law may be used to interpret or supplement Art. 19 of the CISG" (editorial remarks: comparative commentary on Article 19 CISG and its PECL counterparts) available at <http://www.cisg.law.pace.edu/cisg/text/peclcomp19.html#er>.

[13] Perales Viscasillas, *supra* note 1, at 606–610. Honnold, *supra* note 11, at 196, no. 175, footnote 2, so indicates when he comments on the time limit to withdraw the acceptance.

[14] The Secretariat Commentary on Article 19 of the 1978 Draft [*antecedent to CISG Article 21*] states that "under this paragraph it is the late acceptance which becomes the effective acceptance as of the moment of

conclusion of the contract in the circumstances contemplated by Article 21(1) CISG is the reception of the late acceptance. Precisely the same result is derived from Article 2:207(1) PECL (and the corresponding PECL Comments), because the PECL do not adopt the dispatch theory. Therefore, under the PECL, the conclusion of the contract in case of a late acceptance is governed by the receipt rule – when the late acceptance reaches the offeror.

III. CONTRACT FORMATION OUTSIDE THE TRADITIONAL MODEL OF OFFER AND ACCEPTANCE

Two relevant questions arise concerning the existence of contracts that have not followed the traditional offer and acceptance pattern:

(a) Can a contract be concluded under the rules of the CISG when there is no offer and acceptance?
(b) If the answer to the first question is positive, when is the contract concluded?

Both questions receive an affirmative answer under the PECL.[15]

Under the Vienna Convention, the first answer could also be considered affirmative. There is a general accord among many scholars on this issue.[16] The fact that a contract during its formation process did not follow the traditional scheme and was subsequently (or consequently) concluded without isolating an offer and a corresponding acceptance does not reduce the value of the dispositions in Part II of the Convention.[17] In such cases, the contract regulation is derived from the general principles to be found in Part II of the Convention, always taking into account the need for a uniform interpretation and application of the Convention (as per Article 7 CISG). Although finding the precise moment in which the contract is concluded could be very difficult absent any other conclusive proof, in many cases the contract shall be deemed concluded either when there is a sufficient agreement between the parties or when there is performance of the contract by both parties.

its receipt, even though it requires a subsequent notice to validate it," Official Records, para. 3, p. 25. *See* supporting this view, Ludwig, *supra* note 7, at 341–342 and 405–406. *See* also comment 2 of Article 2.9 of the *UNIDROIT Principles of International Commercial Contracts*, International Institute for the Unification of Private Law (Rome, 1994) 39.

[15] Article 2:211 PECL [Contracts not concluded through offer and acceptance] states that the rules of formation of the contract through offer and acceptance apply with appropriate adaptations to the aforementioned situations.

[16] *See*, supporting this view: Eorsi, *supra* note 10, at 44; Michael Joachim Bonell, "Formation of Contracts and Pre-Contractual Liability under the Vienna Convention on International Sale of Goods," in *Formation of Contracts and Precontractual Liability* (ICC: Paris, 1990, publication no. 440/9), 161 *et seq*.; Honnold, *supra* note 11, at no. 132.1, 144 *et seq*.; and Perales Viscasillas, *supra* note 1, at 117–124. Against: Ulrich von Huber, "Der UNCITRAL-Entwurf eines übereinkommens über Internationale Warenkaufverträge," 43 *Rabels Zeitschrift*, No. 3, 445 *et seq*. (1979).

[17] *See* in this sense: John Honnold, "International Sales Law and the Open-Price Contract", in *Homenaje a Jorge Barrera Graf, tomo II* (Universidad Nacional Autónoma de México: México, 1989) 917; and Perales Viscasillas, *supra* note 1, at 117–124. They adopt the doctrine stated in Section 2–204(2) UCC and in Section 22(1) *Restatement (Second) of Contracts*.

Chapter 2 of the UNIDROIT Principles dedicated to the formation of the contract analyzes the formation process in the context of two declarations of will: offer and acceptance. Nevertheless, the UNIDROIT Principles also recognize the possibility that the contract could be deemed concluded by the conduct of the parties. *See* Article 2.1 (Manner of Formation) of the UNIDROIT Principles. In this regard, the *Ad Hoc Arbitral Award*, Rome (Italy) of 4 December 1996, Unilex – UNIDROIT Principles, Transnational, June 2000, D-1996-9, cited Articles 1.2, 2.1, 2.6, and 2.12 to demonstrate the possibility of the valid conclusion of the contract for the sale of fuel oil between an English and Italian company. *See* Pilar Perales Viscasillas, "Formation of the contract under the CISG," in *Law and Practice of Export Trade*. Munster: Center for Transnational Law, 2001, vol. 3, pp. 97–114.

IV. THE EXACT PLACE AND TIME OF CONTACT FORMATION

Contracts concluded between parties located in the same place do not raise problems in relation to the place where the contract is deemed to be concluded. However, when the parties negotiate from a distance – even when they use means of instantaneous communication – the exact place where the contract was concluded may require further investigation.

Neither the CISG nor the PECL say anything on this point. The Secretariat Commentary states that the fact that draft Article 21 [Article 23 CISG], in conjunction with draft Article 16 [Article 18 CISG], fixes the moment at which the contract is concluded may be interpreted in some legal systems to be determinative of the place at which the contract is concluded.[18] In any case, it seems clear that this is a question that must be solved in accordance with the applicable national law (as per Article 7(2) CISG), because there is neither a provision nor a general principle that could point out where the contract is concluded.[19]

Lastly, whether the time of the conclusion of the sales contract may be important to determine the application of some specific matters, like domestic fiscal or regulatory laws, should also be decided by the applicable domestic law.[20]

V. CONCLUSIONS

The PECL and the CISG have adopted the receipt theory as a general rule to deem the contract concluded, following the most modern approach in comparative law.

As an exception, both instruments adopt the dispatch principle or even the information theory in certain circumstances.

Although both texts regulate the contract conclusion in a comprehensive way, the PECL can help interpret the CISG in some situations (such as late acceptances) or may even be used to supplement the CISG (for instance, in cases in which the contract has not been concluded via the traditional exchange of the two declarations of will – offer and acceptance).

[18] Secretariat Commentary on Article 21 of the 1978 Draft, Official Records, para. 2, p. 26.

[19] During the Diplomatic Conference, a proposal made by the Italian delegation was rejected; the proposal suggested the extension of its field of application to the place of performance (Official Records, pp. 291 *et seq.*).

[20] As stated by Honnold, *supra* note 10, at no. 178, 200.

Fundamental breach of contract: Remarks on the manner in which the Principles of European Contract Law may be used to interpret or supplement Article 25 of the CISG

Hossam El-Saghir

III. Comparison of PECL Article 8:103 with CISG Article 25
IV. Conclusion

I. SIGNIFICANCE OF A BREACH BEING FUNDAMENTAL

The CISG uses the term "fundamental breach" in various settings. This concept is a milestone in its remedial provisions. Its most important role is that it constitutes the usual precondition for the contract to be avoided (CISG Art. 49(1)(a), Art. 51, Art. 64(1)(a), Art. 72(1), and Art. 73).

In addition, where the goods do not conform to the contract, a fundamental breach can give rise to a requirement to deliver substitute goods. (CISG Art. 46(2)). Furthermore, a fundamental breach of contract by the seller leaves the buyer with all of his remedies intact, despite the risk having passed to him[1] (CISG Art. 70).

II. DEFINING FUNDAMENTAL BREACH

Article 25 attempts to define fundamental breach in terms of (foreseeable) "substantial detriment."[2] This chapter focuses on the meaning of substantial detriment and foreseeabilty, as understood by Article 25.

1. Substantial Detriment

Under the CISG, the basic criterion for a breach to be fundamental is that "it results in substantial detriment to the injured party."[3] The substantial detriment test is one of the innovations of the Convention as compared with the ULIS.[4] However, the CISG does not define the term "detriment." Van der Velden argues that

> A paraphrase of detriment, acceptable for international use could . . . be the one given by the *Corpus Juris Secundum*, namely: . . . in its technical use it has been said that the detriment need not be real and need not involve actual loss, [n]or does it necessarily refer to material disadvantage to the party suffering it, but means a legal detriment as distinguished from a detriment in fact and has been defined as giving up something which one had the right to keep, or doing something which he had the right not to do [C.J.S., Volume 26a, p. 984].[5]

However, the international origin of the CISG, the fact that the "international legislator" attempted to find autonomous, original terms without using a single system of laws or legal terminology,[6] and the need to promote uniformity in its application[7] make an autonomous method of interpretation necessary. Above all, one should not interpret the CISG from national juridical constructions and terms.[8]

[1] Peter SCHLECHTRIEM, *Commentary on the UN Convention on the International Sale of Goods* (*CISG*), (Clarendon Press, Oxford, 1998) at 176.

[2] Joseph LOOKOFSKY, *Understanding the CISG in the USA* (Kluwer Law International, 1995) at 70.

[3] Commentary on the Draft Convention on Contracts for the International Sale of Goods, prepared by the UNCITRAL Secretariat (Doc. A/CONF. 97/5), Official Records, 26.

[4] Michael WILL, in Bianca-Bonell, *Commentary on the International Sales Law* (Giuffrè:Milan, 1987) at 210.

[5] "The Law of International Sales: The Hague Conventions 1964 and UNCITRAL Uniform Sales Code 1980 – Some Main Items Compared," *Hague-Zagreb Essays 4 on the Law of International Trade*, Voskuil & Wades eds. (Nijoff: The Hague, 1983, pp. 64–65), as quoted by Albert KRITZER, in *Guide to Practical Applications of the United Nations Convention on Contracts for the International Sale of Goods*, Vol. I (Kluwer, 1989) 211.

[6] Frank DEIDRICH, "Maintaining Uniformity in International Uniform Law via Autonomous Interpretation: Software Contracts and the CISG," 8 *Pace Int'l. L. Rev.* (1996) 303–308, also available at <http://cisgw3.law.pace.edu/cisg/biblio/Diedrich.html>.

[7] *See* CISG Art. 7(1).

[8] Fritz ENDERLEIN & Dietrich MASKOW, *International Sales Law, United Nations Convention on Contracts for the International Sale of Goods* (Oceana, 1992) at 55.

Therefore, the term "detriment" should be interpreted autonomously in light of the Convention's legislative history, as well as its intended purpose.[9] The Secretariat Commentary to Article 23 (former draft of Article 25) might shed light on the meaning of "substantial detriment." It states that "the determination whether the injury is substantial must be made in the light of the circumstances of each case, e.g., the monetary value of the contract, the monetary harm caused by the breach, or the extent to which the breach interferes with other activities of the injured party."[10] From this Comment it is possible to conclude that the drafters simply and naturally intended the word "detriment" to be synonymous with monetary injury or harm, or with a consequential harm, and that the determination of a fundamental breach was to be made on a case-by-case basis.[11]

One must consider that the Secretariat Commentary was written prior to the introduction of the refined expectation interest of Article 25. For the breach to be fundamental under Article 25, the aggrieved party must suffer a detriment that must "substantially to deprive him of what he is entitled to expect under the contract." From the history of Article 25 it is clear that – unlike the drafts – it does not refer to the extent of the damage, but instead to the importance of the interests that the contract and its individual obligations actually create for the promisee.[12]

To determine the degree of a given detriment, thereby drawing the line between substantial and insubstantial, is no longer left to the judges' sole and sovereign discretion, but is tied to the expectation of the injured party. In turn, those expectations are not left to the party's inner feelings but instead tied to the terms of the existing contract.[13] This means that there is a fundamental breach of contract if the injured party has no further interest in the performance of the contract after the particular breach.[14] This definition suggests not merely a substantial or material breach of contract, or one that substantially impairs the value of the contract to the injured party, but rather a breach that goes "to the root" of the contract.[15]

In a judgment of a German appellate court regarding a contract concluded for the sale of a stock of womens shoes, the court applied the CISG and stated that the lack of conformity entitles the buyer to declare the contract avoided only when it amounts to a fundamental breach of the contract (Art. 49(1)(a) CISG). In the opinion of the court this requirement is not met, for instance, when the defects do not prevent the buyer from making reasonable use of the goods. In the case at hand, the buyer had only alleged that the shoes had "defects" and that they had been made with a material different from the material agreed upon by the parties; the buyer, however, had not proved that the shoes could not be reasonably used otherwise because of their defects. Therefore, the court decided that the buyer is not entitled to avoid the contract, and it granted the seller the right to payment of the balance of the price as well as interest.[16]

In 1995 a Swiss court, ruling on the sale and installation of a fitness device (an isolation tank containing water with a high salt concentration), applied the same strict standard

[9] Will, *supra* note 4 at 211.

[10] Official Records, *supra* note 3, 26.

[11] Andrew BABIAK, "Defining 'Fundamental Breach' under the United Nations Convention on Contracts for the International Sale of Goods," 6 *Temple Int'l. & Comp. L.J.*, 120 (1992).

[12] Schlechtriem, *supra* note 1, at 177.

[13] Will, *supra* note 4, at 215.

[14] Peter SCHLECHTRIEM, *Uniform Sales Law: The UN-Convention on Contracts for the International Sale of Goods*, 59 (1986).

[15] Jacob S. ZIEGEL, "The Remedial Provisions in the Vienna Convention: Some Common Law Perspectives," in Galson/Smit (ed.), *International Sales: The United Nations Convention on Contracts for the International Sale of Goods* (1984) ch. 9, at 9–14.

[16] Germany 18 January 1994 *Oberlandesgericht* [Appellate Court] Frankfurt, case presentation including English translation available at <http://cisgw3.law.pace.edu/cases/940118g1.html>.

for avoidance; it held that the leak of water did not amount to a fundamental breach as it could easily be repaired.[17]

2. Foreseeability

According to the second part of Article 25, a breach of contract causing material prejudice is not fundamental if the party in breach "did not foresee and a reasonable person of the same kind in the same circumstances would not have foreseen such a result." This means that the party in breach, as well as a reasonable person of the same kind in the same circumstances, must have foreseen the injury. Therefore, the fundamentality of a breach is dependent not only on its consequences but also on its foreseeability by the breaching party.[18]

It is the responsibility of the aggrieved party to prove that he suffered a detriment that substantially deprived him of what he is entitled to expect under the contract. Where such detriment and substantial deprivation are established, the burden of proof is said to shift to the party in breach.[19] To successfully invoke unforeseeability, the party in breach should prove two points: first, that he himself in no way anticipated the substantial detriment caused by the breach, and second, that a reasonable person in his place would not have done so.[20] If the party in breach can prove that he did not foresee the substantial loss of expectation interest that the breach caused the non-breaching party and can prove that a reasonable person similarly situated, facing the same market conditions, would not have foreseen that the breach would cause a substantial loss of expectation interests, there is no fundamental breach.[21]

III. COMPARISON OF PECL ARTICLE 8:103 WITH CISG ARTICLE 25

Unlike the CISG, which is a uniform sales law adopted by countries that account for over two-thirds of all world trade in goods, the PECL are a set of principles whose objective is to provide general rules of contract law in the European Union. They will only apply when the parties have agreed to incorporate them into their contract or have agreed that their contract is to be governed by them.[22]

"Non-performance" is the PECL term analogous to "breach" as used in the CISG. Both the PECL and the CISG distinguish between fundamental non-performance of the contract and non-performance that is not of a serious nature. The concept of fundamental non-performance referred to in PECL Article 8:103 corresponds generally to the concept of fundamental breach referred to in CISG Article 25. The main significance of the fundamental non-performance, in both systems, is to empower the aggrieved party to terminate the contract.

PECL Article 8:103(a), (b), and (c) identifies three situations in which non-performance of an obligation is fundamental to the contract.

Although CISG Article 25 has no express provision like PECL Article 8:103(a), the expectation interests in both Articles are tied entirely to the terms of the contract. Therefore, if a contract governed by the CISG requires strict compliance with an obligation of the buyer or seller – for example, where the contract contains a clause providing that

[17] Switzerland 26 April 1995 Handelsgericht [Commercial Court] Zürich, case presentation available at <http://cisgw3.law.pace.edu/cases/950426s1.html>.

The provisions in Art. 25 CISG have received extensive treatment in the case law. *See* presentation of more than 155 cases on Art. 25, available online at <http://cisgw3.law.pace.edu/cisg/text/anno-art-25.html> [visited: 2 May 2005]. *See* also UNCITRAL Digest of Art. 25 case law, available at <http://cisgw3.law.pace.edu/cisg/text/anno-art-25.html#ucd>.

[18] Enderlein & Maskow, *supra* note 8, at 115.

[19] Krtizer, *supra* note 5, at 210.

[20] Will, *supra* note 4, at 216–217.

[21] Babiak, *supra* note 11, at 123.

[22] PECL Art. 1:101(1) and (2).

"time is of the essence"– a minor deviation from the defined standard of performance would amount to a fundamental breach of contract.

The similarity between PECL Article 8:103(b) and CISG Article 25 is obvious. However, they have subtle differences. Under PECL Article 8:103(b) the basic criterion for a fundamental non-performance is that it substantially deprives the aggrieved party of what he is entitled to expect under the contract. The main difference between the language of this provision and CISG Article 25 is that on the part of the aggrieved party, under the CISG, there must be substantial detriment; whereas under PECL Article 8:103(b), a detriment is not a pre-condition of a fundamental non-performance of the contract. However, in both systems the fundamentality of a non-performance is dependent on its consequences (substantial deprivation), as well as its foreseeability by the breaching party.

The CISG has no provision similar to PECL Article 8:103(c), which is confined to intentional non-performance. Under this provision even if the non-performance in itself is minor and its consequences do not substantially deprive the aggrieved party of what he is entitled to expect under the contract, it might be treated as fundamental if there is indication of intentionality that gives the aggrieved party reason to believe that he cannot rely on the other party's future performance. Unlike the PECL, the CISG does not interfere with special rights and remedies that domestic law gives to persons who have been induced to enter into contract by fraud.[23]

IV. CONCLUSION

PECL Article 8:103 generally follows CISG Article 25, though the terms and content sometimes differ. Both distinguish between fundamental breach/non-performance and breach/non-performance that is not of a serious nature. The distinction is of great importance, because the concept of fundamental breach/non-performance plays a central role in both systems with regard to remedial provisions. It can primarily determine the life or death of the contract.[24]

The need for uniformity and harmony in international trade can be expected to lead to growth in the number of international transactions subject to the CISG, UNIDROIT Principles, and PECL. As a consequence, it is important that the Bar and bench are aware of their content, similarities, and differences. It is hoped that this chapter will provide guidance to improve understanding between persons of different countries and cultures in this respect.

[23] John HONNOLD, *Uniform Law for International Sales under the 1980 United Nations Convention*, (3rd edition, 1999) at 67.
[24] Will, *supra* note 4, at 205.

Right to require specific performance: Remarks on whether the Principles of European Contract Law may be used to interpret or supplement Articles 28 or 62 of the CISG

Jarno Vanto

a. Article 28 of the CISG does not have a counterpart as such in the Principles of European Contract Law. Article 28 became a part of the Convention because of the need to acknowledge the difference in the application of the concept of specific performance in different legal systems.

b. The remedy of specific performance has extensive application in civil law countries, and its function is primarily to uphold the *pacta sunt servanda* principle.[1] In common law countries the scope of the remedy of specific performance is more limited, and damages are seen as the primary remedy upon a breach of contract.[2] This difference in doctrine led to the adoption of CISG Art. 28, when it was acknowledged that, for the Convention to enter into force and for it to become adopted widely, some of the signatory States could not be expected to relinquish the fundamental principles of their judicial procedure.[3]

c. Articles 46 and 62 of the CISG give the buyer and the seller, respectively, the right to require the party in breach to perform its duties under the contract or the Convention. CISG Art. 28 provides, however, that if the law of the forum does not require specific performance in similar domestic cases of contract law, the court is not bound to enter a judgment of specific performance.[4]

d. PECL Art. 9:101 provides that, even in cases where it is clear that the buyer does not want the goods, the seller may deliver the goods and demand the price unless the seller could have made a reasonable substitute transaction without significant effort or expense or the circumstances indicate that it would be unreasonable for the seller to perform.

e. PECL Art. 9:102 (2) (a) states that specific performance cannot be obtained where performance would be impossible or unlawful. The Official Comment on PECL Art. 9:102[5] provides that there is no right to require performance if the performance is prohibited by law, even if this prohibition, or illegality, does not nullify the contract itself. Furthermore, PECL 9:102 (2)(b) provides that performance cannot be obtained when it would cause the debtor unreasonable effort or expense; or (c) the performance

[1] Huber, Ulrich in Schlechtriem Peter ed., *Commentary on the UN Convention on the International Sale of Goods* (Clarendon Press, Oxford, 1998), p. 199.

[2] *Id.*

[3] *See* the Secretariat Commentary and Subsequent Comments by Prof. Eric E. Bergsten on Art. 28 of the CISG (and its draft counterpart, article 26 of the 1978 Draft Convention), available online at <http://cisgw3.law.pace.edu/cisg/text/secomm/secomm-28.html>.

[4] Bernstein, H., Lookofsky, J., *Understanding the CISG in Europe* (Kluwer, 2003) p. 120. For relevant case law *see*

- United States 7 December 1999 Federal District Court [Illinois] (Magellan International v. Salzgitter Handel), presentation available online at <http://cisgw3.law.pace.edu/cases/991207u1.html>, where the Court stated that the remedy of specific performance is generally available under the Convention (Art. 46(1) CISG), with the exception that a Court is not bound to enter judgment for specific performance unless it would do so under its own law of contracts
- Switzerland 31 May 1996 Zürich Arbitration proceeding, presentation available online at <http://cisgw3.law.pace.edu/cases/960531s1.html>, where the Arbitral Tribunal, dealing with the *remedies* claimed by the buyers, stated

  348. The Arbitral Tribunal believes that this is primarily a question of the applicable law. It sees no basis for claims for *specific performance* under Russian law. The Vienna Convention does not provide for this. If the law applicable to the procedure (Swiss law? – again the Vienna Convention) applied, the Arbitral Tribunal sees no basis for specific performance either.

  349. Apart from that the Arbitral Tribunal fails to see how specific performance could be an appropriate remedy for [buyers] in this case. They can hardly expect to be able, under the New York Convention or otherwise, to have an award enforced in Russia providing that [seller] must specifically perform its obligations under the various contracts for the next eight or ten years, producing the aluminum and delivering it to [buyers]. The Arbitral Tribunal will accordingly grant [buyers'] "alternative" request for relief in the form of damages.

[5] The Official Comment to Article 9:102 is available online at <http://cisgw3.law.pace.edu/cisg/text/peclcomp28.html#9102>.

consists in the provision of services or work of a personal character or depends upon a personal relationship; or (d) the aggrieved party may reasonably obtain performance from another source.[6]

f. The language of PECL Art. 9:102 and the commentary to it hint at a different scope of application from that of Art. 28 CISG. The nature of the performance itself is of relevance in the PECL, whereas Art. 28 serves as a guideline for the court to uphold the law of the forum with regard to that law allowing, or not allowing, specific performance as a remedy in a domestic sales contract dispute. Article 28 is devoid of a qualitative analysis of the performance as such and serves to exclude specific performance in some jurisdictions as a remedy for a breach of contract governed by the CISG. It does so not because of the circumstances surrounding the claim, but because a jurisdiction does not grant the right to specific performance in similar contracts of sale in the first place. It is a general right under the CISG that the aggrieved party is entitled to specific performance, unless the party has resorted to a remedy that is inconsistent with it. CISG Art. 28 is based on the premise that the party is entitled to specific performance if he fulfills the requirements under the Convention. This right is limited, however, by the rules of the jurisdiction with regard to the remedies available to the aggrieved party. There is no similarity between the approaches of CISG Art. 28 and PECL Art. 9:102 because the Articles do not serve the same purpose in determining a party's right to specific performance.

g. Articles 9:101 and 9:102 of the PECL lead to largely the same results as other intertwined CISG articles do, but differ in their effects from Art. 28 of the CISG. Consequently the Principles of European Contract Law cannot be used to interpret Art. 28 of the Convention.

h. Art. 62 CISG provides that the seller may require the buyer to pay the price, take delivery, or perform his other obligations, unless the seller has resorted to a remedy that is *inconsistent* with this requirement.[7]

i. PECL Art. 9:101[8] may give a hint to the interpreter as to what kind of remedy is *inconsistent* with the requirement to pay the price. If a seller has entered into a substitute transaction that is reasonable in nature, no right to demand the payment of the price would exist in the meaning of Art. 62. The seller has the right to deliver and demand the payment of the price, albeit limited by the aggrieved party's duty to mitigate her damages. However, the intervening circumstances between the buyer's non-performance and the seller's insistence on the buyer's performance may warrant the exclusion of the seller's right to demand the buyer's performance. Article 62 CISG is one-sided in its approach in that it leaves the application of the remedy of specific performance dependent only on the seller's choice of a remedy and not on extraneous circumstances that might otherwise render the use of that remedy useless. Consequently, Art. 9:102 (2) of the PECL does not provide an interpretive platform to Art. 62 of the Convention.

[6] For an analysis of the manner in which Art. 9:102 PECL may be used to interpret or supplement Art. 46 of the CISG, *see* Jarno Vanto, "Editorial Remarks," available online at <http://cisgw3.law.pace.edu/cisg/text/peclcomp46.html#er>.

[7] *See* the Secretariat Commentary on Article 58 of the 1978 Draft Convention (predecessor to Article 58 of the CISG) [Art. 58 of the 1978 Draft and Art. 62 of the CISG are substantively the same], available online at <http://cisgw3.law.pace.edu/cisg/text/secomm/secomm-62.html>, which provides that for the seller to exercise the right to require performance of the contract he must not have acted inconsistently with that right (e.g., by avoiding the contract under Art. 64 CISG).

[8] *See* the Official Commentary on PECL Art. 9:101, available online at <http://cisgw3.law.pace.edu/cisg/text/peclcomp62.html#9:101>.

Modification or termination of contract and formalities: Remarks on the manner in which the Principles of European Contract Law may be used to interpret or supplement Article 29 of the CISG

Sieg Eiselen

a. Article 29 of the CISG deals with the requirements for the modification and termination of contracts. It further entrenches the principles of party autonomy, freedom of contract, and freedom from formalities contained in Article 11 of the CISG.[1] These principles also form the foundation of the Principles of European Contract Law (PECL) as expressed in Articles 1:102, 2:101(2), and 2:106 and should therefore form the governing principles in the interpretation of any contract, as well as its modification or termination.[2] Art 1:102 PECL, however, pertinently subjects the principle of freedom of contract to the principle of good faith and fair dealing, which may not be excluded.[3]

b. The first object of Article 29 CISG is to reinforce the principle that any agreed modification or termination will be valid in whatever form it is made or contained.[4] Its second object is to eliminate an important difference in approach between civil

[1] Ferrari F., in Schlechtriem P. H. & Bacher K., *Kommentar zum einheitlichen UN Kaufrecht* 3rd ed. (2000 München) Art 7 Rn 48; Magnus U., in Martinek M. (ed) *J. von Staudingers Kommentar zum Bürgerlichen Gesetzbuch mit Einführungsgesetz und Nebengesetze: Wiener UN-Kaufrecht* (1999 Berlin) Art 7 Rn 42, Art 29 Rn 1, 2 & 9; Karollus M., in Honsell H., *Kommentar zum UN Kaufrecht* (1997 Berlin) Art 29 Rn 9; Witz W., Salger in Salger H. C. & Lorenz M., *Internationales Einheitliches Kaufrecht* (2000 Heidelberg) Art 29 Rn 8; Kritzer A. H., *Guide to the Practical Applications of the United Nations Convention on Contracts for the International Sale of Goods* (1989 Deventer) 115.

[2] *See* Lando O. & Beale H., *Principles of European Contract Law Parts I and II – Combined and Revised* (2000 The Hague) Comments to Article 1:102; 2:101 and 2:106; Bonell M. J., 1995 *Tul. L. Rev.* 1134–1135. See art 1:201.

[3] As to the role of good faith in the CISG, *see* Schlechtriem/Ferrari Art 7 Rn 26. For a thorough and up-to-date discussion of the good faith principle in the CISG, *see* the Editorial Remarks to Article 7 by Magnus U., at <http://cisgw3.law.pace.edu/cisg/principles/uni7.html#um>. For a contrary view on how the application of good faith in the CISG should be limited as a result of the drafting history of the CISG and the clear text of the CISG, *see* the "Editorial Remarks on the Concept of Good Faith in the CISG and the PECL," by Felemegas J., at <http://cisgw3.law.pace.edu/cisg/text/peclcomp7.html#er>. *See* also Schlechtriem Art 29 Rn 10; Honnold Rn 204 footnote 8; Salger Art 29 Rn 16; Kritzer 235; Honsell/Karollus Art 29 Rn 18 & 19; Enderlein F. & Maskow D, *International Sales Law – United Nations Convention on Contracts for the International Sale of Goods* (1992 New York) <http://cisgw3.law.pace.edu/cisg/biblio/enderlein.html>, Art 7 par 5 at p. 56 and Art 29 para 5.1 at p 125. *See* also Austria 15 June 1994 Vienna Arbitration proceeding SCH-4318 <http://cisgw3.law.pace.edu/cases/940615a4.html> para 5.4. These principles are underpinned by the principle of bona fides contained in Art 7 CISG. In this regard, *see* the comments in Mexico 30 November 1998 Compromex Arbitration (*Dulces Luisi v. Seoul International*) <http://cisgw3.law.pace.edu/cases/981130m1.html> and Austria 15 June 1994 Vienna Arbitration proceeding SCH-4318 <http://cisgw3.law.pace.edu/cases/940615a4.html>.

[4] Enderlein & Maskow par 1.1 at p. 123; Salger Art 29 Rn 13; Honsell/Karollus Art 29 Rn 1 & 8; Schlechtriem Art 29 Rn 3; Magnus Art Rn 7 & 9; and United States 22 September 1994 Federal District Court [New York] (*Graves v. Chilewich*) <http://cisgw3.law.pace.edu/cases/940922u1.html>. In the case Germany 22 February 1994 *Oberlandesgericht* [Appellate Court] Köln <http://cisgw3.law.pace.edu/cases/940222g1.html>, the court held that although a termination could not be construed from silence or inaction in itself, silence or inaction in conjunction with other factors may provide sufficient evidence of an acceptance of an offer of termination. It is suggested that this also holds true for modifications. *See* Switzerland 5 October 1999 *Obergericht* [Appellate Court] Basel <http://cisgw3.law.pace.edu/cases/991005s1.html> where the principle was discussed but the court found that on the facts an amendment had not been proven; and Belgium 17 May 2002 *Hof van Beroep* [Appellate Court] Gent <http://cisgw3.law.pace.edu/cases/020517b1.html> where the failure of the one party to respond to the letter of another was interpreted as constituting an acceptance of the amendment offered by the other party. On this issue, *see* also Enderlein & Maskow para 6.1 at p. 125.

and common law, namely clearly establishing that no consideration is necessary for any amendment to be valid.[5] However, it also entrenches the time-honored principle that, where parties have by agreement voluntarily restricted their ability to modify or terminate a contract by requiring formalities for such actions, that agreement will be valid and enforceable.[6]

c. Article 2:106 PECL, which deals with written modification clauses, differs somewhat from Article 29 CISG in that it merely creates a presumption of invalidity where there is a clause requiring formalities for modification or termination.[7] There is, therefore, an evidentiary onus on the party who wants to rely on an oral modification or termination to prove that the parties nevertheless intended such modification or termination, despite not complying with the agreed formalities. This approach, which is less strict than that found in the CISG, is based on the principle of good faith.[8]

d. The application of the principle of good faith may as a consequence be useful in interpreting Article 29 CISG, especially in respect of the abuse exception in Article 29(2). Where the reliance of a party on the written modification or termination clause would be against the dictates of good faith under the circumstances, such reliance ought not to be countenanced.[9]

e. Although the PECL do not specifically state that contracts may be informally modified or terminated, it is clear from the provisions of Article 2:101(2), which entrenches the freedom of form, and from Article 2:106(1) that freedom of form is the actual point of departure in these principles. The CISG and the PECL therefore are based on the same principle of freedom of formalities as a starting point.

f. The PECL, however, do not accord the same strong effect to oral modification clauses as does the CISG, as outlined in paragraph **b.** It may therefore well result in the PECL following a more lenient approach than the CISG. An informal agreement to modify or terminate a contract may therefore be interpreted as "an implied abrogation" of the clause itself in terms of the PECL, whereas this is not the case with the CISG.[10]

g. Both Article 29 CISG and Article 2:106 PECL seem to apply only where the modification or restriction clause is contained in a "written agreement."[11] In interpreting

[5] Commentary of the UNCITRAL Secretariat on Article 27 of the 1978 Draft, Document A/CONF.97/5 p. 27–28 as reprinted in Honnold J., *Documentary History of the Uniform Law for International Sales* (1989 Deventer) and at <http://cisgw3.law.pace.edu/cisg/text/secomm/secomm-29.html>. *See* also John E. Murray, Jr., excerpt from 8 *J.L & Com.* (1988) 11–51 "An Essay on the Formation of Contracts and Related Matters under the United Nations Convention on Contracts for the International Sale of Goods" <http://cisgw3.law.pace.edu/cisg/text/murray29.html>). This has been confirmed in the following decisions: United States 17 December 2001 Federal District Court [Michigan] (*Shuttle Packaging Systems v. Tsonakis* et al.) <http://cisgw3.law.pace.edu/cases/011217u1.html>; ICC Arbitration Case No. 7331 of 1994 <http://cisgw3.law.pace.edu/cases/947331i1.html>.

[6] Honsell/Karollus Art 29 Rn 1, 9, & 11; Salger Art 29 Rn 13 & 14; Magnus Art 29 Rn 7 & 9.

[7] Lando & Beale 154–155.

[8] *See* Comment A to PECL Article 2:106, Lando & Beale 155.

[9] In this regard, *see* the comments in Mexico 30 November 1998 Compromex Arbitration (*Dulces Luisi v. Seoul International*) <http://cisgw3.law.pace.edu/cases/981130m1.html> and Austria 15 June 1994 Vienna Arbitration proceeding SCH-4318 <http://cisgw3.law.pace.edu/cases/940615a4.html>. For an evaluation of some case law on good faith, *see* Powers Paul J., "Defining the Undefinable: Good Faith and the United Nations Convention on Contracts for the International Sale of Goods," 18 *J.L. & Com.* (1999) 346–348 at <http://cisgw3.law.pace.edu/cisg/biblio/powers.html#inter>. In respect of the PECL on this issue, *see* Lando & Beale 155.

[10] *See* Schlechtriem Art 29 Rn 5.

[11] Schlechtriem Art 29 Rn 9; Honsell/Karollus Art 29 Rn 12.

what constitutes a "written agreement" the PECL may be helpful as Article 13 CISG only extends the concept of writing to telegrams and telexes. Article 1:301 PECL defines "written statements" as "[including] communications made by telegram, telex, telefax, and electronic mail and other means of communications capable of providing a readable record of the statement on both sides." Therefore, a readable record produced by a telephone receiver that is capable of converting sound into writing is not a written statement under Article 1:301(6).[12] It is generally recognized that Article 13 CISG contains a gap in that it only refers to older forms of technology and does not provide for more modern forms of electronic communications, such as e-mail, fax, or Internet communications.[13] It is suggested that the meaning of "written" should be extended to include these forms of communications in accordance with the definition in Article 1:301 PECL.[14] That definition has the advantage of being clear, practical, and technologically neutral without losing sight of the object of the written formality, namely preserving an objective reproducible record of the communication between the parties.

h. The issue of merger clauses is not dealt with in this chapter as they are more appropriately covered under Article 8 CISG, which deals with the interpretation and proof of agreements.[15]

i. The exception created in Article 29(2) CISG is one area where the application of Article 29 may lead to interpretational difficulties.[16] The rule is based on principles contained in the so-called *Mißbrauchseinwan* of German law or the "*nemo suum venire contra factum proprium*" principle of Roman law or the doctrine of waiver and estoppel of Anglo-American law.[17]

j. Under Article 2:106 PECL, it is required that the reliance by the party acting upon the informal modification or termination must have been reasonable. It would seem that this requirement is justifiable also under the CISG when viewed in the light of the

[12] Lando & Beale Comment to Article 1:301(6).

[13] Eiselen S., "Electronic Commerce and the UN CISG," 1996 *EDI L. Rev.* 21 <http://cisgw3.law.pace.edu/cisg/biblio/eiselen1.html>; Schlechtriem Art 13 Rn 2; Magnus Art 29 Rn 13.

[14] *See* also Honnold J. O., *Uniform Law for International Sales under the 1980 United Nations Convention* 3rd ed. (1999 Deventer) Rn 130; Eiselen 21. For a contrary view on electronic communications, *see* Schlechtriem Art 13 Rn 2.

For a further relevant discussion of CISG Art. 13, *see* Schroeter Ulrich G., "Editorial remarks on the manner in which the PECL may be used to interpret or supplement CISG Article 13," at <http://cisgw3.law.pace.edu/cisg/text/peclcomp13.html#er>.

[15] *See* the Editorial Remarks by Stanivukovic M. on Article 8 CISG and its PECL counterpart provisions, at <http://cisgw3.law.pace.edu/cisg/text/peclcomp8.html#er>.

[16] *See* the discussion in Honsell/Karollus Rn 17–23; Hillman Robert A., "Article 29(2) of the United Nations Convention on Contracts for the International Sale of Goods: A New Effort at Clarifying the Legal Effect of 'No Oral Modification' Clauses," 21 *Cornell Int'l. L.J.* (1988) 449–466 at <http://cisgw3.law.pace.edu/cisg/biblio/hillman2.html> p. 458, 460, and 465. In the case law the exception has been mentioned but denied in cases where there was a lack of any evidence showing reliance. *See* Belgium 2 May 1995 District Court Hasselt (*Vital Berry Marketing v. Dira-Frost*) <http://cisgw3.law.pace.edu/cases/950502b1.html>. However in Austria 15 June 1994 Vienna Arbitration proceeding SCH-4318 <http://cisgw3.law.pace.edu/cases/940615a4.html> the arbitrator did apply the exception relying on the principle of estoppel.

[17] Schlechtriem Art 29 Rn 10; Honnold Rn 204 footnote 8; Salger Art 29 Rn 16; Kritzer 235; Honsell/Karollus Art 29 Rn 18 & 19; Enderlein & Maskow para 5.1 at p. 125. *See* also Austria 15 June 1994 Vienna Arbitration proceeding SCH-4318 <http://cisgw3.law.pace.edu/cases/940615a4.html> para 5.4 These principles are also underpinned by the principle of *bona fides* contained in Art 7 CISG. In this regard *see* the comments in Mexico 30 November 1998 Compromex Arbitration (*Dulces Luisi v. Seoul International*) <http://cisgw3.law.pace.edu/cases/981130m1.html> and Austria 15 June 1994 Vienna Arbitration proceeding SCH-4318 <http://cisgw3.law.pace.edu/cases/940615a4.html>.

principle of good faith.[18] Where reliance was not reasonable under the circumstances, a party ought not to be allowed to use the defense contained in Article 29(2) CISG.[19] The requirement of reasonableness under the PECL is further refined in Article 1:302 of the PECL.[20] In considering what is reasonable, it should be asked what persons under the same circumstances and acting in good faith would have considered to be reasonable. In deciding what is reasonable, all relevant factors should be taken into consideration, including the nature and purpose of the contract, the circumstances of the case, and the usages and practices of the trade or profession.[21] These factors generally reflect the behavior of reasonable parties. This test could equally well be utilized in respect of the CISG.[22]

k. Another issue that crops up is whether the provisions of the exception in Article 29(2) can be upheld in circumstances where writing is obligatory because a country made a reservation in terms of Article 96 of the CISG to Article 12.[23] It is suggested that even in those instances oral modifications or terminations should be upheld where Article 29(2) circumstances are found.[24] The decision in Belgium 2 May 1995 District Court Hasselt,[25] however, seems to indicate that courts would be willing to apply the exception even in those instances.

l. Neither the CISG nor the PECL make provision for the case where the parties have agreed to further formalities, such as signatures or witnesses for an amendment or termination.[26] In this respect there may be a divergence between the approach of the CISG and the PECL. It is submitted that it would be in accordance with the provisions of Article 29 CISG that the parties are held bound to such formalities and that non-complying modifications or terminations would be void, unless the abuse exception contained in Article 29(2) CISG should apply.[27] In filling the gap under Article 2:106(1) it is submitted that in accordance with the basic premises of that Article, such requirements will only constitute a presumption and will not be valid and binding *per se* as under the CISG. This divergence is a result of the more lenient approached followed in terms of the PECL outlined in paragraphs **b.** and **f.** above.

[18] This would seem to be the scope of the decision in Germany 22 May 1992 *Landgericht* [District Court] Mönchengladbach <http://cisgw3.law.pace.edu/cases/920522g1.html> where the court says that when someone receives a document, such as an expert's opinion rendered on behalf of the other party, he should be held bound to that document as a declaration of will if the party receiving it should have understood it as such and in fact understood it as such looking at it objectively.

[19] Magnus Art 29 Rn 17; Honsell/Karolus Art 29 Rn 20. *See* also the discussion of the necessity to apply this exception with *flexibility* in Salger Art 29 Rn 17.

[20] For a discussion of the concepts of "reasonableness" and "unreasonableness" in the PECL, *see* Lando & Beale 126–128.

[21] Lando & Beale 126.

[22] In respect of the concept of reasonableness as a general principle of the CISG, *see* <http://cisgw3.law.pace.edu/cisg/text/reason.html>.

[23] *See* for instance the decision in Russia 1997 High Arbitration Court [Ruling No. 4, case 2] <http://cisgw3.law.pace.edu/cases/970325r1.html>.

[24] The decision in Russia 16 February 1998 High Arbitration Court: Information Letter 29, available at <http://cisgw3.law.pace.edu/cases/980216r1.html> deals with the general requirement without referring to the exception in Art 29(2).

[25] Belgium 2 May 1995 District Court Hasselt (*Vital Berry Marketing v. Dira-Frost*) <http://cisgw3.law.pace.edu/cases/950502b1.html>.

[26] Honsell/Karollus Art 29 Rn 14.

[27] Enderlein & Maskow para 3.2 at p. 124; Honnold Rn 202. Note the contrary view of Honsell/Karollus Art 29 Rn 14 who argue that unless there is a clear indication that the parties indeed insisted on stricter formalities, there should be no presumption that the parties required such strict compliance.

Place of performance: Comparative analysis of Articles 31 and 57 of the CISG and counterpart provisions in Article 7:101 of the PECL

Chengwei Liu

I. GENERAL: PLACE OF PERFORMANCE

a. The place where a party must perform a contractual obligation is important in a variety of contexts.[1] In the Convention, of particular relevance are Articles 31 and 57, which, respectively, specify the place where goods are to be delivered and the place where payment is to be made. In particular, CISG Art. 31

> covers three cases, numbered (a) to (c), or rather four cases, if we include the introduction to the article. The first case is that the seller is bound to deliver the goods at a particular place (the introduction). The three other cases (a, b, and c) presuppose that he is not so bound. Under rule (a), if the contract of sale involves carriage of the goods, delivery consists in handing the goods over to the first carrier for transmission to the buyer. The other two cases [. . .] refer to two different situations in which the contract does not involve carriage of goods. The gist of rules (b) and (c) is that the goods are delivered at the seller's place of business.[2]

Under CISG Art. 57(1),

> [i]n the absence of agreement, payment must be made at the seller's place of business (Article 57(1)(a)). Where there is an agreement for immediate payment – 'cash against documents' – payment is to be made at the place where the goods or the documents are transferred (Article 57(1)(b)). In a sale involving carriage, if immediate payment has not been agreed upon, the seller's place of business remains the place of payment.[3]

Furthermore, CISG Art. 57(2) anticipates the possibility that the seller might change its place of business after the conclusion of the contract, in which case any increase in the expenses incidental to payment caused by the change in the place of business is to be borne by the seller.[4]

[1] *See* Comment A on PECL Art. 7:101 at <http://cisgw3.law.pace.edu/cisg/text/peclcomp31.html#cnpc>, where the following is made clear:

> The place of performance is significant in several respects. A party who is to perform services will have to bear the inconvenience and the costs of presenting himself at the place and tendering performance there. For a debtor to tender or offer performance at a wrong place will often constitute a non-performance. In a contract for the delivery of goods the party who is to perform will in general have to bear the costs and carry the risk of the goods until they have been put at the disposal of the creditor at the place of performance. A creditor who is unable to receive performance in due time because it mistook the place of performance may also fail to perform the contract or bear the risk of a non-performance by the other party [. . .].

[2] *See* Jan Hellner, "The Vienna Convention and Standard Form Contracts," in Petar Sarcevic & Paul Volken eds, *International Sale of Goods: Dubrovnik Lectures*, Oceana (1986), Ch. 10, pp. 343–344. Also available online at <http://cisgw3.law.pace.edu/cisg/biblio/hellner.html>.

[3] *See* Peter Schlechtriem, *Uniform Sales Law – The UN-Convention on Contracts for the International Sale of Goods*, Manz, Vienna (1986), pp. 81–82. Also available online at <http://cisgw3.law.pace.edu/cisg/biblio/schlechtriem-57.html>.

[4] *See* Digest 2 on CISG Art. 57 in "The UNCITRAL Digest of Case Law on the United Nations Convention on the International Sale of Goods" (June 2004). Available online at <http://cisgw3.law.pace.edu/cisg/text/anno-art-57.html>.

b. Resembling to a substantial extent the CISG approach, the counterpart PECL provisions in Art. 7:101 also contemplate that, above all, where the place of performance is fixed in the agreement or determinable from the agreement, such an agreement prevails (introduction of para. (1)). Rules are, however, needed to cover cases where the contract is silent on the matter and circumstances do not indicate where performance should take place. PECL Art. 7:101(1) provides two solutions. The general rule is that a party is to perform its obligations at its own place of business (Art. 7:101(1)(b)). The second rule is specific to monetary obligations where the converse solution applies; namely, that the obligor is to perform its obligations at the obligee's place of business (Art. 7:101(1)(a)). These solutions may not be the most satisfactory in all cases, but they do reflect the need for rules where the parties have not made any other arrangement or where the circumstances do not indicate otherwise.[5] In applying such solutions, on the other hand, if the party at whose place of business performance is to be made has more than one place of business, the place of performance is that which has the closest connection with the contract and its performance, having regard to the circumstances known to or contemplated by the parties at the conclusion of the contract.[6] This is a clear rule in PECL Art. 7:101(2). Although no counterpart rule is found under CISG Arts. 31 and 57, a general rule to that effect has already been introduced in CISG Art. 10(a).[7] However, it remains difficult to give an exact definition of the term "place of business." In most cases it is a party's permanent and regular place for the transaction of general business and not a temporary place of sojourn during sales negotiations.[8] In any event, if a party has no place of business, performance is to be effected at his habitual residence. This is a "factual," not a "legal" concept. A person has his habitual residence at the place where he actually lives, regardless of whether he has a permit to live in the country and whether he sometimes goes to another place to stay for some time, provided that he normally returns to the first place.[9] This is the rule contemplated by PECL Art. 7:101(3). Although no counterpart rule is found in the Convention, it again follows from the general rule of CISG Art. 10(b)[10] that the place of business referred to in CISG Arts. 31 and 57 includes a party's habitual residence where that party has no place of business.[11]

c. Hence, in general, there is no difference in substance between the CISG and the PECL as regards the place of performance. In addition, it is to be noted from the outset that many of the court decisions concerning CISG Arts. 31 and 57 have referred to these rules for the determination of the jurisdiction (particularly that under Art. 5(1) of the 1968 Brussels and 1988 Lugano Conventions).[12] Most national courts interpret the place of delivery under Art. 31 as the place of performance of delivery for purposes of determining jurisdiction where the CISG governs the place of delivery.[13] However,

[5] *Cf.* Art. 6.1.6 (*Place of performance*) of the UNIDROIT Principles and its Comment (specifically Comment 2).

[6] *Supra* n. 1, Comment F.

[7] CISG Art. 10(a) reads, "For the purposes of this Convention: (a) if a party has more than one place of business, the place of business is that which has the closest relationship to the contract and its performance, having regard to the circumstances known to or contemplated by the parties at any time before or at the conclusion of the contract."

[8] *Supra* n. 1, Comment E.

[9] *Supra* n. 1, Comment G.

[10] CISG Art. 10(a) reads, "For the purposes of this Convention: (b) if a party does not have a place of business, reference is to be made to his habitual residence."

[11] *See* Jacob S. Ziegel, "Report to the Uniform Law Conference of Canada on Convention on Contracts for the International Sale of Goods," Comment 2 (c). Available online at <http://cisgw3.law.pace.edu/cisg/text/ziegel31.html>.

[12] For relevant decisions, *see* Digest 2 on CISG Art. 31 (*infra* n. 36); Digests 4, 5 on CISG Art. 57 (*supra* n. 4).

[13] *See* Larry A. DiMatteo, Lucien Dhooge, Stephanie Greene, Virginia Maurer, and Marisa Pagnattaro, "The Interpretive Turn in International Sales Law: An Analysis of Fifteen Years of CISG Jurisprudence,"

it has been appropriately noted (see Austria 10 September 1998 *Oberster Gerichtshof* [Supreme Court]) that when the parties agreed on a certain place for delivery, they would envisage such aspects as the costs of the carriage of goods, the modalities of delivery, and the bearing of risk. It would be inappropriate to combine these issues with matters of jurisdiction, especially if the place for delivery is neither the place of business of the seller nor that of the buyer.[14] In this case, the Supreme Court of Austria has added, however, that it is a matter of interpretation whether a contractual term fixing the place for delivery is, at the same time, intended to determine special jurisdiction under Art. 5 No. 1 of the Lugano Convention.[15] It has been noted, on the other hand, that the issue remains unresolved whether Art. 57 grants jurisdiction to national courts with respect to disputes concerning payment of the purchase price independent of national laws. Regardless of the ultimate resolution of this issue, "parties to sales transactions subject to the CISG are well-advised to utilize choice of forum provisions. Unlike some other provisions, there is broad consensus among national courts with respect to the enforceability of forum selection agreements."[16]

d. To supplant the operation of CISG Arts. 31 and 57, however,

> the forum selection agreement must comply with stringent requirements established by national courts. The forum selection provision should be express. Past practices between the parties in prior transactions are usually not sufficient to overcome this requirement. In addition, the mention of bank accounts and other commercial relationships in states other than where the delivery of the goods occurs is insufficient to constitute a forum selection agreement in the absence of an express intent by the parties. Finally, usage of the trade in question also fails to constitute a forum selection agreement in most circumstances. Such usages would only serve to select the forum if it was widely known in the trade that certain actions undertaken by the parties to the transaction had the indelible effect of selecting an exclusive forum for the resolution of disputes between the parties.[17]

II. PLACE DETERMINABLE FROM THE CONTRACT, USAGE, OR ESTABLISHED PRACTICE

e. Very often the place of performance is fixed in the agreement or determinable from the agreement.[18] Neither CISG Arts. 31 and 57 nor PECL Art. 7:101 denies the fact that the place where an obligation is to be performed is often determined by an express term of the contract or is determinable from it. It is obvious, for instance, that an obligation to build must be performed on the construction site and that an obligation to transport goods must be performed in accordance with the agreed route.[19] In this respect, it is the principle of contract freedom (party autonomy) that underlies both the Convention and the PECL; therefore, where parties have agreed on a particular place of performance, such an agreement prevails over the provisions of either the Convention or the PECL.

f. Many CISG decisions dealing with Art. 31 refer to the parties' autonomy. For instance, a German Appellate Court (8 January 1997 *Oberlandesgericht* Köln) held that "the legal consequences of Art. 31 CISG only come into play if the seller is 'not bound to deliver

34 *Nw. J. Int'l. L. & Bus.* (Winter 2004), p. 387; also available online at <http://cisgw3.law.pace.edu/cisg/biblio/dimatteo3.html>.

[14] Citing Willibald Posch & Thomas Petz in "Austrian Cases on the UN Convention on Contracts for the International Sale of Goods," 6 *Vindobona J. Int'l. Com. L. & Arbitration* (2002) 1–24, at 14–15. Available online also at <http://cisgw3.law.pace.edu/cases/980910a4.html>.

[15] Citing Willibald Posch & Thomas Petz, *id.*

[16] *See* Larry A. DiMatteo etc., *supra*. n. 13; pp. 373–374.

[17] *Id.*, pp. 374–375.

[18] *Supra* n. 1, Comment B.

[19] *Supra* n. 5, Comment 1.

the goods at any other particular place.' "[20] Similarly, another German Appellate Court (3 December 1999 *Oberlandesgericht* München) held that according to CISG Art. 31 "the contractual agreement prevails"[21]; the Supreme Court of Italy (10 March 2000 *Suprema Corte di Cassazione*) has held that "the parties' contractual autonomy prevails over that provision [CISG Art. 31]."[22] Of particular frequency and significant relevance, the parties' agreement will normally spell out the seller's shipping obligations quite precisely by adopting a recognized trade term, such as FOB, CIF, etc.,[23] as defined in the ICC INCOTERMS. Rather often the parties refer to customary delivery clauses, in particular to INCOTERMS.[24] INCOTERMS, when invoked properly, can be very useful in defining precisely some of the central steps that the parties should take.[25] It has been noted that if a contract contains an explicit reference to INCOTERMS, no problem arises. The INCOTERMS are so complete that there is likely no need to supplement them with the rules of the Convention: they have been "derogated" by the contract. If a trade term is used but there is no explicit reference to INCOTERMS, and if it is not indicated by any other fact (such as the "previous course of dealing" of the parties) that INCOTERMS or some other set of provisions are to apply, it is, however, more uncertain whether Art. 31 of the Convention has any significance.[26]

g. The position is the same under Art. 57 CISG.[27] Because of the importance of the question at hand, the contract will usually contain specific provisions on the mode and place of payment. Accordingly, the rule in CISG Art. 57 is expressly stated to apply only if "*the buyer is not bound to pay the price at any other particular place.*"[28] This result is also reached through the operation of CISG Art. 6,[29] which can be regarded as an *orientation of the parties* toward an agreement of the place of payment.[30] However, the express reiteration of the principle (in CISG Art. 57) emphasizes the importance that the contract will usually attach to the place of payment of the price.[31] Enderlein and Maskow state in this respect,

> The parties, in general, attach great attention to the terms of payment which include the place of payment. Where an express agreement of the place of payment is lacking, an implicit

[20] *See* Germany 8 January 1997 Oberlandesgericht [Appellate Court] Köln; case presentation including English translation is available online at <http://cisgw3.law.pace.edu/cases/970108g1.html>.

[21] *See* Germany 3 December 1999 Provincial Court of Appeal München; case presentation including English translation is available online at <http://cisgw3.law.pace.edu/cases/991203g1.html>.

[22] *See* Italy 10 March 2000 Supreme Court; case presentation including English translation is available online at <http://cisgw3.law.pace.edu/cases/000310i3.html>.

[23] *See* Ziegel, *supra* n. 11.

[24] *See* Fritz Enderlein and Dietrich Maskow, *International Sales Law: United Nations Convention on Contracts for the International Sale of Goods*, Oceana Publication (1992), p. 129. Also available online at <http://cisgw3.law.pace.edu/cisg/biblio/enderlein.html>.

[25] *See* John O. Honnold, "Uniform Law and Uniform Trade Terms – Two Approaches to a Common Goal" in Horn & Schmitthoff eds, *Transnational Law of International Commercial Transactions* (Kluwer 1982), p. 170.

[26] *See* Hellner, *supra* n. 2.

[27] *See* Ulrich G. Schroeter, "Vienna Sales Convention: Applicability to 'Mixed Contracts' and Interaction with the 1968 Brussels Convention," 5 *Vindobona J. Int'l. Com. L. & Arbitration* (2001), p. 81. Available online at <http:// cisgw3.law.pace.edu/cisg/biblio/schroeter1.html>. Schroeter, however, submits that contracting parties "only rarely seem to include a clause on the place of payment in their contract." *Id.*

[28] *See* Secretariat Commentary on Art. 53 of the 1978 Draft [*draft counterpart of CISG Art.* 57]; Comment 1. Available online at <http://cisgw3.law.pace.edu/cisg/text/secomm/secomm-57.html>.

[29] CISG Art. 6 reads, "The parties may exclude the application of this Convention or, subject to article 12, derogate from or vary the effect of any of its provisions." Under the PECL, the counterpart rule is Art. 1:102, which reads under the title "Freedom of Contract": "(1) Parties are free to enter into a contract and to determine its contents, subject to the requirements of good faith and fair dealing, and the mandatory rules established by these Principles. (2) The parties may exclude the application of any of the Principles or derogate from or vary their effects, except as otherwise provided by these Principles."

[30] *See* Enderlein and Maskow, *supra* n. 24, at p. 216.

[31] *Supra* n. 28, at fn. 1.

> agreement may be inferred from the way in which the payment is made. This may be done considering non-governmental codifications for specific categories of payment (Uniform Customs and Practices for Documentary Credits – Article 9 fol; Uniform Rules for Collections – Articles 11 and 12) which become binding through the agreements between the parties, business conditions of the banks engaged or directly as an established practice.[32]

Thus, a German court (24 November 1998 *Landgericht* [District Court] Bielefeld) held,

> According to Art. 57 CISG, which governs the contract between the parties, the place of performance is the [seller]'s place of business – however, only if the [buyer] is not bound to pay the purchase price at any other particular place. *The place of performance is primarily to be determined by the agreement between the parties (Art. 6 CISG), respectively by any usage to which they have agreed to and any practices, which they have established between themselves* (emphasis added).[33]

h. Indeed, it is also the case for CISG Art. 31 (and PECL Art. 7:101(1) too) that the place of performance may be determined according to the applicable usage and practice established between them. Generally speaking, from either CISG Art. 9 or its counterpart PECL Art. 1:105, it follows, "Usages and practices may fix a different place of performance, [. . .]. It is probably a universal usage that a customer of a bank who wishes to draw his money will have to come to the bank. However, if the bank agrees to send the money to a customer the money will travel at the bank's risk."[34] On the other hand, the ruling is also of significance in an Italian case (Italy 7 August 1998 *Corte di Cassazione*), where the Italian Supreme Court ruled that the derogation contemplated under CISG Art. 57(1) "cannot consist of a mere practice; the practice may simply be the consequence of a mere tolerance by the seller and, as such, incapable of establishing a place of performance different from the legal one."[35] The rationale that is particularly relevant is that, under either CISG Art. 31 or Art. 57, the alleging party is under an obligation to prove its claims agreement on the place of performance; namely, to establish the existence of a relevant agreement, usage, or practice. That is to say, the party asserting that a particular

[32] *Supra* n. 30.

[33] The court held, "According to the payment procedure established between the parties during many years, the place of performance for the payment of the price is the [buyer]'s place of business. From the start of their business relations, it was the [seller] who bore the cost of the money transfer. Under the CISG, the issue of which party bears the cost of the money transfer is determined by the place of performance for the payment obligation (citations omitted). It follows vice versa that the place of performance is the [buyer]'s place of business if the parties established the practice that the [seller] was to bear the cost of the money transfer." (*See* Germany 24 November 1998 Landgericht [District Court] Bielefeld; case presentation including English translation available online at <http://cisgw3.law.pace.edu/cases/981124g1.html>.) *Cf.* Germany 7 December 2000 District Court Trier, where the court, similarly taking into account the parties' ordinary course of business, holds that the parties implicitly agreed on a specific manner of payment, in which the seller directly debits the buyer's bank account in the Netherlands. By this agreement the court held that the parties have established a practice between them under which the place of payment was at the buyer's bank in the Netherlands. (*See* the UNILEX abstract at <http://www.unilex.info/case.cfm?pid=1&do=case&id=800&step=Abstract>.)

[34] Official Comment on PECL Art. 7:101, Comment H, *supra* note 1. CISG Art. 9 reads, "(1) The parties are bound by any usage to which they have agreed and by any practices which they have established between themselves. (2) The parties are considered, unless otherwise agreed, to have impliedly made applicable to their contract or its formation a usage of which the parties knew or ought to have known and which in international trade is widely known to, and regularly observed by, parties to contracts of the type involved in the particular trade concerned." PECL Art. 1:105 reads, "(1) The parties are bound by any usage to which they have agreed and by any practice they have established between themselves. (2) The parties are bound by a usage which would be considered generally applicable by persons in the same situation as the parties, except where the application of such usage would be unreasonable."

[35] *See* Italy 7 August 1998 Supreme Court; case presentation including English translation available online at <http://cisgw3.law.pace.edu/cases/980807i3.html>.

place of performance – other than the place provided for in Arts. 31 and 57 – had been agreed upon (or established by a usage or practice) must prove such agreement.[36]

i. Thus, regarding the application of CISG Art. 57, the Italian Supreme Court (7 August 1998 *Corte di Cassazione*) ruled that the wording of CISG Art. 57(1) "clearly indicates that the buyer must be 'bound' to pay at a different place, which is to say, obliged (the word is repeated in the subsequent Article 58 CISG), by virtue of a title that may be legal or contractual"; therefore, "in the absence of undisputed facts capable of justifying a derogation from the legal rule regarding the place of performance, such place ([. . .]) must be determined on the ground of the general rule set out in Article 57(1) CISG."[37] Along a similar line, a German Appellate Court (16 July 2001 *Oberlandesgericht* Köln) dealing with CISG Art. 31 stated,

> The contract between [seller] and [buyer] was concluded orally and does not explicitly determine the place of performance. The parties undisputedly agreed on a delivery "free farm," but this simply means that the [seller] was to bear the costs of transport. Under Art. 8(1) and (2) CISG, a contractual clause is to be interpreted according to the parties' hypothetical intent or, in case that intent cannot be determined, according to the understanding that a reasonable person of the same kind would have had in the circumstances. As there are insufficient grounds to determine the hypothetical intentions of the parties, the clause "free farm" needs to be interpreted under objective criteria. Following the prevailing opinion, the similar clause "free house" does not possess an unambiguous meaning in trade; rather, the clause is to be interpreted following the circumstances of each individual case (citations omitted). However, there are no objective criteria which could decide the place of delivery in the present case. Thus, the Court falls back on the general principles of Art. 31 CISG.[38]

j. Regarding the burden of proof, the ruling of a German court (13 April 2000 *Amtsgericht* [Lower Court] Duisburg), which deals with the proof under CISG Art. 31 but seems to apply *mutatis mutandis* to that under CISG Art. 57, provides some guidance: The *onus of proof* is on "the party who contends that the parties derogated from the Convention by agreeing on a different place of performance." The wording of Art. 31 "does not lead to a shift in the burden of proof"; the stipulation that "*if the seller is not bound to deliver the goods at any particular place, his obligation to deliver consists*" in the acts referred to in paras. (a)–(c) is "simply a clarification." This interpretation "finds its first footing in the wording of the provision itself. The use of the word 'particular' shows that the [contending buyer] bears the onus of submission and proof that a place for the handing over of the goods was agreed on." This is "further supported by the structure of Art. 31 CISG. The paragraphs (a) and (b) provide the rules for special instances, followed by the general rule in paragraph (c). It would be inconsistent with this structure to apply paragraph (c) only if the [challenged] seller proves that a particular place of performance has not been defined." Finally the interpretation

> corresponds to the systematic position of Art. 31 CISG and its corresponding purpose. The provision applies to cases in which the parties failed to form a contractual agreement (citation omitted). Keeping this in mind, it would be unreasonable if the provision at the same time put the burden of proof on the seller. If that was the case, Art. 31 CISG would deviate from *the general rule that each party bears the onus of proof for the provisions which are favorable to him and which he therefore relies upon* (emphasis added). In the case of an agreement

[36] *See* Digest 13 on CISG Art. 31 in "The UNCITRAL Digest of Case Law on the United Nations Convention on the International Sale of Goods" (June 2004). Available online at <http://cisgw3.law.pace.edu/cisg/text/anno-art-31.html>.

[37] *Supra* n. 35.

[38] *See* Germany 16 July 2001 Provincial Court of Appeal Köln; case presentation including English translation is available online at <http://cisgw3.law.pace.edu/cases/010716g1.html>.

stipulating the [buyer's] place of business as the place of performance, the favored party is the buyer. Were Art. 31 CISG to be interpreted as putting the burden of proof on the seller, the provision would effectively restrict its own sphere of application. That is not the purpose of Art. 31 CISG.[39]

k. In any event, if "there is no basis for letting the [performing party] bear the risk of any disagreement between the parties"[40]– namely, where the contending party has not proved that it derogated from Arts. 31 and 57 CISG by agreeing with the other party on a particular place and where it neither submits, nor is it evident that a trade usage or business practice in the meaning of Art. 9 CISG existed between the parties to that effect – the general rule set out in CISG Arts. 31 and 57 applies. Indeed, the Convention gives general but useful answers to questions that the parties have not answered by contract provisions, by invoking relevant usages, or by incorporating established practice or trade terms, such as the ICC INCOTERMS. In addition, the Convention provides a way to avoid or resolve disputes in a wide range of situations, not mentioned in, for example, INCOTERMS, when a party fails to perform his duties under the contract.[41]

III. CREDITOR'S PLACE FOR MONEY OBLIGATIONS

l. In many systems the place of performance for money obligations, if it has not been agreed expressly, is the creditor's residence or place of business.[42] It is held that in commercial transactions "the general rule would seem to be that payment is to be made at the place where the creditor resided or carried on business at the time of the contract."[43] This is also the approach adopted under CISG Art. 57 and PECL Art. 7:101(1)(a), which both confirm, "If the place of performance is not fixed or determinable from the contract the place of performance of a money obligation is the creditor's place of business. 'The debtor must seek the creditor.' This rule will leave the debtor with a free choice of how it will send or transfer the money to the creditor, which, when the debtor carries the risk of transmission, will have no right to interfere with the mode of transportation or transfer used."[44]

m. It is stated that the determination of the place of payment, as it is made in CISG Art. 57(1),

> entails generally *four essential consequences for the buyer*: First, he must initiate the payment so early that it arrives on the settlement date (Article 58) at the place of payment. He thus bears the risk of a delay insofar as he is not exempted from liability under Articles 79 and 80. Second, he must take all measures and go through all the formalities at a commercial level and vis-à-vis the authorities so that the payment can be made at the place of payment, i.e. exceptionally also the fulfillment of formalities in the seller's country (Article 54). Third, he must bear the cost of the payment procedure up to this place. Fourth, he also bears the risks

[39] *See* Germany 13 April 2000 Amtsgericht [Lower Court] Duisburg; case presentation including English translation is available online at <http://cisgw3.law.pace.edu/cases/000413g1.html>.

[40] *See* Denmark 15 February 2001 Højesteret [Supreme Court] (*Damstahl A/S v. A.T.I. S.r.l*), case presentation including English translation is available online at <http://cisgw3.law.pace.edu/cases/010215d1.html>.

[41] *See* Honnold, *supra* n. 25, at p. 171.

[42] *Supra* n. 1, Note 1. It is also noted, "In some of the laws the debtor's residence or place of business is the place of performance of a money obligation, see SPANISH CC art. 1171(3); FRENCH, BELGIAN and LUXEMBOURG Civil Codes art. 1247(3), except that if the price for goods is payable on delivery it is payable at the place of delivery, arts. 1609 and 1651. The debtor who sends money to the creditor bears the risk of loss or delay, *see* for Belgian law Cass. 6 Jan. 1972, Arr. Cass., 441; Cass. 23 Sept. 1982, Pas. I, 118; similarly Luxembourg District Court 31 Jan. 1874, 1, 128." *Id.*

[43] *See Benjamin's Sale of Goods*, Guest ed. (1975); p. 705.

[44] *Supra* n. 1, Comment C.

> up to this place, i.e. when the initiated payment procedure is not successful because of the bankruptcy of a bank engaged it has to be repeated.[45]

It is thus "a question of considerable importance in international trade because of the widespread existence of exchange controls and other restrictions on the transfer of funds."[46] As it is stated in the Secretariat Commentary, "It is important that the place of payment be clearly established when the contract is for the international sale of goods. The existence of exchange controls may make it particularly desirable for the buyer to pay the price in his country whereas it may be of equal interest to the seller to be paid in his own country or in a third country where he can freely use the proceeds of the sale."[47] Thus, the principle on which the CISG is based "characterizes the obligation of payment as an *obligation to be performed at the creditor's place of business* in order to ensure that the seller can indeed dispose of the proceeds of the transaction without having to confront the foreign exchange rules of other countries."[48]

n. Furthermore, CISG Art. 57(1)(b) (no counterpart rule is found under PECL Art. 7:101) specifically deals with the place of payment when payment is to be made against the handing over of the goods or of documents. It

> provides that payment must be made at the place where the handing over takes place. This rule will be applied most often in the case of a contract stipulation for payment against documents. The documents may be handed over directly to the buyer, but they are often handed over to a bank which represents the buyer in the transaction. The "handing over" may take place in either the buyer's or the seller's country or even in a third country.[49]

The Austrian Supreme Court (10 November 1994 *Oberster Gerichtshof*) has held that CISG Art. 57(1)(b) *"ties up to the principle of mutual simultaneous performance laid down in Article 58 CISG* (emphasis added); it is only reasonably applied where intermediaries (e.g., a warehouse-keeper or carrier) are used and payment is to be made to these intermediaries. Otherwise payment must be made to the seller. In this case, after delivery of the goods, the buyer has to pay the purchase price at the seller's place of business (citation omitted)."[50] Thus, the German Supreme Court (4 December 1996 *Bundesgerichtshof*) has ruled that "the regulation of CISG Art. 57(1)(b), according to which, under certain circumstances, the payment must take place at the location of the handover of the goods, does not apply because the conditions of payment agreed upon [...] *do not contain a reciprocal and simultaneous [performance] provision in the sense of the mentioned rule* (emphasis added)."[51] According to Enderlein and Maskow, if the *payment is bound only to the handing over of the goods*, the place of payment under the CISG is the place where the goods are handed over to the first carrier, the place

[45] *See* Enderlein and Maskow, *supra* n. 24, at pp. 214–215.

[46] *See* Ziegel, *supra*. n. 11.

[47] *Supra* n. 28, Comment 2. It is also noted, on the other hand, that "[t]his Convention does not govern the extent to which exchange control regulations or other rules of economic public order may modify the obligations of the buyer to pay the seller at a particular time or place or by a particular means. The buyer's obligations to take the steps which are necessary to enable the price to be paid are set forth in article 50 [draft counterpart of CISG article 54]. The extent to which the buyer may be relieved of liability for damages for his failure to pay as agreed because of exchange control regulations or the like is governed by article 65 [draft counterpart of CISG article 79] [For the extent to which the seller may be relieved of the duty to deliver the goods if the buyer does not pay as agreed, see articles 54(1), 60, 62, 63, and 64 [*draft counterpart of CISG articles 58(1), 64, 71, 72, and 73*].]." (*Supra* n. 28, Comment 3.)

[48] *Supra* n. 30.

[49] *Supra* n. 28, Comment 5.

[50] *See* Austria 10 November 1994 Supreme Court, case presentation including English translation is available online at <http://cisgw3.law.pace.edu/cases/941110a3.html>.

[51] *See* Germany 4 December 1996 Bundesgerichtshof [Federal Supreme Court], case presentation including English translation is available online at <http://cisgw3.law.pace.edu/cases/961204g1.html>.

where the goods are made available, or the place of business of the seller (Art. 31)[52]; where payment is to be made *against the handing over . . . of documents*, the documents mentioned here are obviously the same as under Art. 58 (i.e., the *documents that entitle to dispose of the goods.*)[53] Payment is to be made *only against the handing over of the documents* if the seller has determined it pursuant to Art. 58 or if the terms of payment "cash against documents" or "payment according to letter of credit" have been agreed. *Where the documents are to be handed over* is made dependent in the Convention on the agreement between the parties (Art. 34). However, regularly established practices and/or rules referred to by the parties in one form or another intervene here.[54]

o. CISG Art. 57(1) has attracted a vast amount of comment in case law.[55] For instance, the Italian Supreme Court (7 August 1998 *Corte di Cassazione*) has held,

> The meaning of this provision [CISG Art. 57(1)] is clear enough: it sets out a general rule whereby the buyer has to pay the seller at the place of business of the latter; the buyer, however, may be obliged to pay the price 'at any other particular place', but the existence of such an obligation must obviously descend from a certain source; if, finally, payment is to be made against the handing over of the goods or the documents, the place of payment coincides with the place where the handing over takes place.[56]

This Article provides, according to the Italian Supreme Court (14 December 1999 *Corte di Cassazione*), "a general rule, which does not approve the payment in any place other

[52] *See* Enderlein and Maskow, *supra*. n. 24, at p. 218.

[53] Schlechtriem wants to interpret the documents referred to in Art. 58 in the meaning of Arts. 30 and 34 because the right of the seller to refuse performance is at stake; see Schlechtriem, *supra* n. 3. In the opinion of Enderlein and Maskow, Arts. 30 and 34, however, refer to documents that relate to the goods. An extended version of the term "documents" is used there, which may include certificates relating to quality and analysis, operating manuals, technical descriptions, and drawings. Enderlein and Maskow are also in favor of a functional interpretation and not of a limitation of the relevant documents to mere documents of title without wanting to consider the two groups of documents as identical. Reference is made here in the first place to shipping documents, such as bills of lading, warehouse certificates, combined transport documents, international forwarding notes, etc. (i.e., the so-called *documents of title*). Depending on the basis for delivery agreed, the *documents* can also be such *that* only *certify the taking over of the goods* (quay receipt, mate's receipt, forwarding agent's receipt) and/or such that *prove the conclusion of a freight or storage contract* that serve to substantiate an obligation to deliver (sender copies of the waybill in transportation by way of railroad, motor traffic, airship, and inland navigation). The requirements for those documents are determined according to the rules applicable to the respective category of performance. The category of transportation documents that will have to be presented can usually be inferred from the INCOTERMS referred to in them. Where the buyer has to pay customs duties to obtain the goods, the seller has to provide the necessary documents, such as invoices (if agreed, having account of specific form requirements – consular invoices) and certificates of origin. Depending on what is agreed in the contract *other documents* are added, such as insurance documents, certificates of quality, etc. The Uniform Customs and Practices for Documentary Credits contain the requirements that most of these documents will have to meet. (*See* Enderlein and Maskow, *supra* n. 24, at pp. 219–220.)

[54] *See* Enderlein and Maskow, *supra* n. 24, at p. 220. According to the authors, the places determined according to the handing over of the documents are different in the case of specific terms of payment. In the event of the term "cash against documents," the documents have to be submitted as a rule at the buyer's (Article 8, Uniform Rules for Collections). However, the buyer has to be considered as obligated to satisfy all formalities that are necessary to allow transfer of the payment to the seller's country. But he is obliged only insofar as that one depends on him and, in particular, only to the extent to which he is legally entitled and actually in a position to do so. Where a *letter of credit* is agreed, all banks engaged act on behalf of the buyer; this includes the issuing bank and also other banks engaged by it, including the bank in the seller's country that notifies the seller of the opening of the letter of credit. Its place of business is also the place of payment, which again entails the consequences described under note 1.2. This is also in line with the Uniform Customs and Practices for Documentary Credits according to which the bank sending the notification is under certain circumstances entitled to make the payment pursuant to the conditions prescribed (Article 2, (ii); Article 11, subpara. (d). Where a payment made under a reservation is reclaimed later, because the bank where the letter of credit is issued does not pay, the payment is considered as not having been made. (*See* Enderlein and Maskow, *supra* n. 24, at pp. 220–221.)

[55] *Supra* n. 4, Digest 3.

[56] *Supra* n. 35.

than seller's place of business, unless defined otherwise by the parties, law or convention regulation."[57] That is to say, as a Belgian Appellate Court (15 May 2002 *Hof van Beroep Gent*) explained, "According to article 57(1) CISG, without any contrary stipulation the payment of the price – which undoubtedly is the principal obligation of the buyer – has to be made at the place of business of the seller."[58]

p. Regarding the respective application of the variants indicated in CISG Art. 57(1), a German court (19 January 2001 *Landgericht* [District Court] Flensburg) has held, "According to Art. 57(1)(a) CISG, the obligation to pay the purchase price under a sales contract is generally an obligation to be performed at the creditor, i.e., the [seller], place of business, provided that (i) a seller performed in advance his delivery duties under the relevant sales contract; and (ii) the obligations of the parties are not to be performed concurrently pursuant to Art. 57(1)(b) CISG."[59] And the Austrian Supreme Court (22 October 2001 *Oberster Gerichtshof*) has held,

> Failing an agreement to the contrary, the interpretative rule of Art. 57(1)(a) CISG determines that the [buyer] was bound to pay the price at the [seller's] place of business in Hungary (the [seller's] place of business needs to be established under Art. 10 CISG). The purchase price is a debt payable at the creditor's place of business (annotation omitted). That the prerequisites of Art. 57(1)(b) are met (place where the handing over of the goods takes place), was neither submitted nor has it been established.[60]

It is similarly analyzed by a German court (20 September 2002 *Landgericht* [District Court] Göttingen): "According to Art. 57(1)(a) CISG, the buyer is obliged to pay the purchase price at the seller's place of business, unless the parties provided otherwise. The parties have not provided for a specific provision on the place of performing [buyer]'s payment obligation under their sales contract. Further, payment of the purchase price was not to be effected concurrently with provision of the goods (Art. 57(1)(b) CISG)."[61] A German Court of Appeal (10 December 2003 *Oberlandesgericht* Karlsruhe) has also held that according to CISG Art. 57(1)(a), "the buyer has to pay the purchase price at the seller's place of business if – as is the case here – nothing else has been agreed and the payment is also not to be made against the handing over of the goods or of documents."[62]

q. Moreover, Enderlein and Maskow note,

> The rule only mentions the "price," but is to be applied, as we believe, also to *other payments under the contract*, like the payment of damages, liquidated damages, interests and reimbursement of expenses. Since there is not regularly a direct dependence between performance and counter-performance, and in particular no contemporaneous performance, this refers above all to subpara. (a) with the "seller" having to be read as the "obligee" and the "buyer" as "obligor."[63]

[57] *See* Italy 14 December 1999 Supreme Court, case presentation including English translation is available online at <http://cisgw3.law.pace.edu/cases/991214i3.html>.

[58] *See* Belgium 15 May 2002 Hof van Beroep [Appellate Court] Gent, case presentation including English translation is available online at <http://cisgw3.law.pace.edu/cases/020515b1.html>.

[59] *See* Germany 19 January 2001 District Court Flensburg, case presentation including English translation is available online at <http://cisgw3.law.pace.edu/cases/010119g1.html>.

[60] *See* Austria 22 October 2001 Supreme Court, case presentation including English translation is available online at <http://cisgw3.law.pace.edu/cases/011022a3.html>.

[61] *See* Germany 20 September 2002 District Court Göttingen, case presentation including English translation is available online at <http://cisgw3.law.pace.edu/cases/020920g1.html>.

[62] *See* Germany 10 December 2003 Appellate Court Karlsruhe, case presentation including English translation is available online at <http://cisgw3.law.pace.edu/cases/031210g1.html>.

[63] *See* Enderlein and Maskow, *supra*. n. 24, at p. 215.

Thus, the decision of a German court (17 December 2002 *Landgericht* [District Court] Giessen) "joins the opinion commonly adapted nowadays that for *place of performance of an obligation to repay the purchase price* (emphasis added), an obligation not specifically regulated in the CISG, one may look to Art. 57(1)(a) CISG by way of analogy."[64] A German Appellate Court (10 December 2003 *Oberlandesgericht* Karlsruhe) ruled, "Even if *the freight costs* (emphasis added) are shown separately, they form a part of the purchase price in the sense of the CISG (Art. 31 CISG; annotation omitted), which thus, also pursuant to Art. 57(1)(a) CISG, has to be paid at the [buyer]'s place of business."[65] Another German Appellate Court (2 July 1993 *Oberlandesgericht* Düsseldorf) has held that the basic solution with regard to the sales price in CISG Art. 57(1)(a) is used as "a gap filler under Art. 7(2) of the CISG"[66] in determining *the place of performance for the obligation to pay damages*. The court stated,

> The place of performance for the indemnification claim pursuant to Arts. 45, 74 of the CISG, however, is not set forth by the CISG. It is determined from the Convention's general principles which are derived from Art. 7(2) of the CISG. Art. 57(1)(a) of the CISG provides [. . .] that the duty to tender payment of the purchase is an obligation to be performed at the seller's place of business. Accordingly, the place of performance is where the seller maintains its principle place of business (citation omitted). Therefore, *if the place where payment is to be tendered [. . .] is the seller's place of business, it then seems to be appropriate to recognize this as a general rule governing the place of performance for all claims for payment under the CISG. The reasoning behind a rule governing the place of performance for claims for the purchase price are just as applicable to other claims for payment* (emphasis added). The claim that seller should be required to take over buyer's liability to buyer's sub-purchaser pursuant to Arts. 45, 74 is keyed to payment of money (citation omitted). Consequently, performance is to be tendered at the seller's principal place of business.[67]

r. The case law on the question at issue[68] also indicates, albeit not uniformly, that the rule established by CISG Art. 57(1) (referring above all to subpara. (a)), establishing payment of the price at the seller's place of business as a general principle, can be applied also to other monetary obligations emerging from the contract of sale. These obligations include compensation due from a party who has been in breach of contract or return of the sale price by the seller after avoidance of the contract. A German Appellate Court (28 October 1999 *Oberlandesgericht* Braunschweig) has generally held, "Under Art. 57(1) CISG, the place of performance for the [buyer's] obligation to pay the purchase price is the seller's place of business. The secondary obligations under Art. 61 CISG – including the above-mentioned claim for damages – follow the primary obligation of payment of the purchase price. Consequently, the place of performance for a remedy [of monetary nature] for breach of contract is also determined by Art. 57(1)(a) CISG" (citation omitted).[69]

s. In addition, it is to be noted that payment is usually made only after the seller has received an invoice. The relevant provision in CISG Art. 57(1) only speaks of the situation where the buyer is bound to pay at a particular place. This would seem to have a bearing

[64] *See* Germany 17 December 2002 District Court Giessen, case presentation including English translation is available online at <http://cisgw3.law.pace.edu/cases/021217g1.html>.

[65] *Supra* n. 62.

[66] *See* Peter Schlechtriem, "Commentary on Oberlandesgericht Düsseldorf 2 July 1993," in *International Contract Manual: Guide to UN Convention, Suppl.* 9 (Kluwer: April 1994), case presentation also available online at <http://cisgw3.law.pace.edu/cases/930702g1.html>.

[67] *See* Germany 2 July 1993 Provincial Court of Appeal Düsseldorf, case presentation available online at <http://cisgw3.law.pace.edu/cases/930702g1.html>.

[68] In this respect, *see* Digests 6 to 8; *supra* n. 4.

[69] *See* Germany 28 October 1999 Provincial Court of Appeal Braunschweig, case presentation including English translation is available online at <http://cisgw3.law.pace.edu/cases/991028g1.html>.

on a clause in the seller's invoice stating that payment is to be made to the seller's account in a certain bank. The invoice may indicate which place of business the seller considers to be relevant, and such a statement may be interpreted as acceptance of payment being made at that place. On the other hand, the buyer is not bound by such an indication. It may well be that the seller, for his own convenience, wishes payment to be made at a particular place. If such a clause is not based on the contract it may be interpreted as a statement by the seller that he will accept payment to have been adequately made if made in time to that account. It is clear that the seller cannot unilaterally impose on the buyer an obligation to make payment in such a manner. Article 57 of the Convention is thus applicable irrespective of such a clause in the invoice.[70]

t. The above comments and decisions focusing on CISG Art. 57(1) to a large part apply *mutatis mutandis* to the consequences under PECL Art. 7:101(1)(a). A slight difference (except for the absence of a rule similar to CISG Art. 57(1)(b)) is that the place referred to in PECL Art. 7:101(1)(a) is expressly limited to *"at the time of the conclusion of the contract."* In contrast, under the Convention, this reference must be deduced from the text of Art. 57(2), the idea underlying which is to be deduced *vice versa* from the PECL wording *"at the time of the conclusion of the contract."* If one accepts the soundness of the proposition that the debtor must "follow" the creditor's place of business, "then it seems reasonable to allow the [debtor] to claim reimbursement for any additional expenses incurred by him because of a change in the [creditor]'s place of business."[71] This is made clear in CISG Art. 57(2).[72] In providing that the seller must bear any increase in the expenses incidental to payment that is caused by a change in its place of business subsequent to the conclusion of the contract, Art. 57(2) seems to impose on the buyer the obligation to pay the price at the seller's new address (*cf. infra.* para. u). This being so, it is necessary that the seller should have informed the buyer of the change in a timely manner. Under Art. 80 of the Convention the seller has no right to rely on any delay in payment of the price caused by late notification of the change of address.[73]

u. Although no counterpart is found under the PECL expressly resembling CISG Art. 57(2), it is submitted that a similar result may be reached with the emphasis on the wording in PECL Art. 7:101(1)(a) of *"at the time of the conclusion of the contract."* This is particularly so on the basis of the PECL Comment, where it is clearly stated,

> The place of performance is the party's place of business (or his habitual residence) at the time of the conclusion of the contract. If after that time the party moves to another place, the first place remains the place of performance. However, if the party chooses to move the place of performance to its new place, good faith requires that it should be permitted to do so unless it will cause an unreasonable inconvenience for the other party or where the party which moves does not notify the other party in due time, see Article 1:201. If as a result of a change of the place of performance, there is any increase in the expense of performance, this increase must be borne by the party which has changed the place of performance. If as a result of the change of the place of performance, the risk of transportation is perceptibly increased, the party whose change of place of performance increases the risk of transportation will have to carry that risk.[74]

[70] *See* Leif Sevón, "Obligations of the Buyer under the UN Convention on Contracts for the International Sale of Goods" in Petar Sarcevic & Paul Voken eds. *International Sale of Goods: Dubrovnik Lectures*, Oceana (1986), p. 213, also available online at <http://cisgw3.law.pace.edu/cisg/biblio/sevon1.html>; *see also* Leif Sevón. "Obligations of the Buyer under the Vienna Convention on the International Sale of Goods," in *Suomalainen Lakimiesten Yhdistys: – Tidskrift utgiven av Juridiska Föreningen i Finland* [Finnish Law Society] 126 (1990), p. 333, also available online at <http://cisgw3.law.pace.edu/cisg/text/sevon57.html>.

[71] *See* Ziegel, *supra* n. 11.

[72] *Supra* n. 28, Comment 6.

[73] *Supra* n. 4, Digest 9.

[74] *Supra* n. 1, Comment I.

Indeed, it has been codified in Art. 6.1.6(2) of the UNIDROIT Principles, which establishes a general rule that each party must bear any increase of expenses occasioned by a change in its place of business.[75]

IV. DEBTOR'S PLACE FOR OTHER OBLIGATIONS

v. It seems to be generally accepted that for obligations other than monetary ones the place of performance is, unless otherwise agreed, the debtor's residence or place of business.[76] This is clearly stipulated in PECL Art. 7:101(1)(b) and also explained in the Official Comment on that provision: "As far as obligations other than money obligations are concerned the place of performance is the debtor's place of business. This is in conformity with the general principle that in cases of doubt the debtor is implied to have undertaken the least burdensome obligation."[77]

w. Under the Convention, Art. 31, which states the obligation to deliver "in a dispositive rule"[78] due to its being pre-conditioned by the parties' particular agreement, specifies the place of performance of the seller's duty of delivery. The provision fixes where the seller has to deliver the goods and what the seller has to do for that purpose. Art. 31 addresses three different cases for which different rules apply. The general rule, however, appears to be that the seller's place of business is preferred as the regular place of performance.[79] This is supported by the ruling of a German Appellate Court (16 July 2001 *Oberlandesgericht* Köln), which held that "Art. 31(b) and (c) regulate the buyer's duty to collect the goods, whereas Art. 31(a) specifies the seller's obligation to deliver, if the contract involves the carriage of the goods, as complied with when handing the goods over to the first carrier for transmission. Thus, the provisions of the CISG set the general principle that the place of performance for the obligation to deliver is the seller's place of business (citations omitted)."[80] Unlike the general distinction between money obligations and other obligations, however,

> Art. 31 CISG, which deals with the content of the seller's delivery obligation, *distinguishes between contracts that involve the carriage of goods and such contracts where carriage is not necessary* (emphasis added). Art. 31 CISG does not include a situation where the seller himself has to deliver the goods to one of the buyer's places of business. Such a form of delivery of the goods owed is not provided for in Art. 31. In doubtful cases, such an obligation cannot be assumed: If the contract requires carriage of the goods at all, it is an obligation to dispatch the goods; in other cases the goods are to be placed at the buyer's disposal at the seller's place of business (citation omitted).[81]

x. Among the three paragraphs of CISG Art. 31, para. (a) refers to *the contract of sales involving carriage*. According to Enderlein and Maskow, this type of contract is found

[75] This Article reads:], "A party must bear any increase in the expenses incidental to performance which is caused by a change in its place of business subsequent to the conclusions of the contract." According to its Comment (specifically Comment 3),

> [i]n view of the importance of the parties' respective places of business for the application of para. (1), it is necessary to cater for the situation where a party changes its location after the conclusion of the contract, a move which may involve additional expense for the performing party. The rule established in para. (2) is that each party must bear any such increase of expenses occasioned by a change in its place of business. . . . It is moreover possible that a party's move may entail other inconvenience for the other party. The obligation to act in good faith (Art. 1.7) and the duty to cooperate (Art. 5.3) will often impose on the moving party an obligation to inform the other party in due time so as to enable the latter to make such arrangements as may be necessary.

[76] *Supra* n. 1, Note 2.

[77] *Supra* n. 1, Comment D.

[78] *See* Russia 24 January 2002 Arbitration proceeding 27/2001, case presentation including English translation is available online at <http://cisgw3.law.pace.edu/cases/020124r1.html>.

[79] *Supra* n. 36, Digest 1.

[80] *Supra* n. 38.

[81] *See* Switzerland 10 February 1999 Handelsgericht [Commercial Court] Zürich, case presentation including English translation is available online at <http://cisgw3.law.pace.edu/cases/990210s1.html>.

regularly in the international sale of goods, unless the goods are already in the possession of the buyer (e.g., in the event of a sale of an object that had originally been leased or goods that were available for inspection) or the buyer himself collects the goods from the seller (e.g., in the event of the clause Ex Works). International sales contracts usually involve several carriers. A carrier is the collective term used for the different means of transportation (see, for instance, multimodal carrier). Here, *carriage* is always *transport* by one or several independent carriers. Insofar as the parties have their own vehicles and therewith transport the goods, this does not fall under carriage. The goods may, however, also be handed over to a carrier that was hired by the buyer, if the clause FOB was agreed, in which case the buyer will have to provide a means of transportation. To what extent a forwarding agent can be considered as the carrier depends on whether he himself undertakes to transport the goods.[82] In any event, if the seller has not undertaken to perform any part of the transportation, his duties should not depend on where it is possible to find an independent carrier.[83] The principal function of Art. 31(a) is to provide a rule for the cases in which it is clear that the seller has a duty of transportation, but no further indication of the extent of his duties can be found. The rule that handing over the goods to the first carrier, rather than shipping the goods in a ship, constitutes delivery makes the Convention rule coincide with the trade terms already defined in the ICC INCOTERMS.[84]

y. In cases *not within* para. (a) of Art. 31, which "means that there is neither an arrangement under the contract as to the place of delivery nor is carriage an obligation of the seller,"[85] Art. 31(b) applies, which covers future goods – goods to be manufactured or produced at a particular place – and goods to be drawn from a specific stock as well as specific goods.[86] The second alternative of Art. 31 requires, first, that no carriage of the goods in the sense of Art. 31(a) is involved so that it is the buyer's task to get possession of the goods. Second, specific goods or goods of a specific stock or goods to be manufactured or produced are required. The third requirement is that both parties knew when the contract was concluded that the goods were (or were to be manufactured or produced) at a particular place. If those conditions are met, the seller has to place the goods at the buyer's disposal at that place.[87] In other cases not covered by subparagraphs (a) and (b) of Art. 31,[88] Art. 31(c) "reduces the seller's liability to place the goods at the buyer's disposal at the place where the seller had his place of business at the time of the conclusion of the contract."[89] Although subparagraph (c) is "a residuary rule" to cover those situations not discussed in subparagraphs (a) and (b), it does not state a rule for "all other cases." In particular, the contract may provide for delivery to be made at the buyer's place of business or at some other particular place not mentioned in this Article. The opening phrase of Art. 31 recognizes that in all such cases delivery would be made by handing over the goods or by placing them at the buyer's disposal, whichever is appropriate, at the particular place provided in the contract.[90]

z. The gist of the rules in subparagraphs (b) and (c) (of CISG Art. 31) is that the goods are delivered at the seller's place of business.[91] However, both rules require the goods to be placed *at the buyer's disposal*, which means that "the seller has done that which is

[82] *See* Enderlein and Maskow, *supra* n. 24, at pp. 131–132.

[83] *See* Hellner, *supra*. n. 2, at p. 345.

[84] *See* Hellner, *supra*. n. 2, at p. 346.

[85] *Supra*. n. 82.

[86] *See* Ziegel, *supra*. n. 11.

[87] *Supra* n. 36, Digest 8.

[88] *See* Secretariat Commentary on Art. 29 of the 1978 Draft [*draft counterpart of CISG Art. 31*]; Comment 14. Available online at <http://cisgw3.law.pace.edu/cisg/text/secomm/secomm-31.html>.

[89] *See* Germany 19 December 2002 Appellate Court Karlsruhe, case presentation including English translation is available online at <http://cisgw3.law.pace.edu/cases/021219g1.html>.

[90] *Supra* n. 88, Comment 15.

[91] *See* Hellner, *supra* n. 2.

necessary for the buyer to be able to take possession. Normally, this would include the identification of the goods to be delivered; the completion of any pre-delivery preparation, such as packing, to be done by the seller; and the giving of such notification to the buyer as would be necessary to enable him to take possession."[92] In general, "the obligation to deliver in such circumstances consists of taking all steps necessary under the contract"[93] so that the buyer has nothing else to do other than to take the goods at the place of delivery.[94] In addition, if the goods are in the possession of a bailee, such as a warehouseman or a carrier, they might be placed at the disposal of the buyer by such means as the seller's instructions to the bailee to hold the foods for the buyer or by the seller handing over to the buyer in appropriate form the documents that control the goods.[95]

[92] *Supra*. n. 88; Comment 16.
[93] *See* Germany 23 June 1998 Provincial Court of Appeal Hamm, case presentation including English translation is available online at <http://cisgw3.law.pace.edu/cases/980623g1.html>.
[94] *Supra* n. 36, Digest 9.
[95] *Supra* n. 88, Comment 17.

Time for delivery and early delivery: Comparison between the provisions of CISG Articles 33 and 52(1) and the counterpart provisions of the PECL (Articles 7:102 and 7:103)

Colin Ying

I. INTRODUCTION

According to Article 30 CISG, the seller has three obligations that should be performed as required by the contract and the Convention: (i) an obligation to deliver the goods, (ii) an obligation to hand over any documents relating to the goods, and (iii) an obligation to transfer the property in the goods. Article 33 CISG deals with one aspect of the seller's first-mentioned obligation to deliver the goods,[1] ascertaining the time for delivery, whereas Article 52(1) CISG sets out the legal consequences of an early delivery of the goods by the seller.

[1] The Convention does not generally deal with the third obligation, *see* Article 4: "[. . .] except as otherwise expressly provided in this Convention, it is not concerned with: [. . .] (b) the effect which the contract may have on the property in the goods sold."

In this context, Article 33 provides for three situations: (i) where the contract fixes a date or permits a date to be fixed; (ii) where the contract fixes a period of time or permits a period of time to be fixed; and (iii) any other situation (e.g., where the contract is silent as to the date or time for delivery). In the first situation, the seller must deliver the goods on the date so fixed. In the second situation, the seller must deliver the goods on any date within the period so fixed, unless circumstances indicate that the buyer is to choose a date within that period. In the third situation, the seller must deliver the goods within a reasonable time after the conclusion of the contract.

Delivery by the seller on the due date obliges the buyer to take delivery of the goods, as well as to pay the price for them as required by the contract and the Convention (Article 53 CISG). On the other hand, if the seller delivers the goods before the due date, the buyer is not obliged to take delivery at that time, but has the option of taking or refusing to take delivery (Article 52(1) CISG). If the seller delivers the goods after the due date, he will be in breach of contract, although the buyer may still be obliged to accept delivery then while being entitled to appropriate remedies (damages being the norm) in accordance with Article 45 CISG. This chapter focuses on early rather than late delivery.

Article 7:102 PECL is virtually identical to Article 33 CISG in all material respects, if one treats the CISG seller as the PECL party required to perform and the CISG buyer as the PECL "other party." The same three situations in the CISG are dealt with in the PECL using the same terminology.

Like Article 52(1) CISG, Article 7:103(1) PECL gives a party in the position of the buyer the same option to decline a tender of early performance by the other party, but goes on to qualify the exercise of the option. The party in question loses the option where acceptance of the tender of early performance "would not unreasonably prejudice its interests." In addition, Article 7:103(2) PECL states that "[a] party's acceptance of early performance does not affect the time fixed for the performance of its own obligation," but the Convention has no comparable Article.

There thus appear to be two differences between Article 52(1) CISG and Article 7:103 PECL, and these differences are analyzed after a comparison is made between Article 33 CISG and Article 7:102 PECL.

II. ASCERTAINING THE TIME FOR DELIVERY (ARTICLE 33 CISG AND ARTICLE 7:102 PECL)

Delivery of the goods consists of placing the goods at the buyer's disposal at the appropriate place, doing such act as may constitute delivery under the terms of the contract, or, where the contract of sale involves the carriage of goods, handing the goods over to the first carrier for transmission to the buyer.[2]

It should not be problematic to determine the time for delivery in the first two situations covered by paragraphs (a) and (b) of Article 33 CISG or paragraphs (1) and (2) of Article 7:102 PECL. A specific date or period of time can be stated in or determinable from the contract,[3] and where the contract fixes the period of time or allows it to be fixed from objective criteria, any date within that period can be the date of delivery, unless circumstances indicate that the buyer is to choose a date within that

[2] *See* Article 31 CISG, which deals with the place of delivery. Article 33 CISG deals with the time for delivery; *see* also the Secretariat Commentary on Article 31 of the 1978 Draft [*draft counterpart of CISG article 33*], § 2, available online at <http://cisgw3.law.pace.edu/cisg/text/secomm/secomm-33.html>. Article 31 of the 1978 Draft is identical to Article 33 CISG, except for the omission of "or" between paragraphs (a) and (b) of Article 33.

[3] A date determinable from a usage that is applicable to the contract under Article 9 CISG or Article 1:105 PECL comes within the first situation.

period. One such circumstance may be where the buyer is to arrange for the transport of the goods and the contract is FOB or where the intention is to permit the buyer to schedule the exact arrival time of the goods so as not to overtax his storage and handling capacity.[4]

The date in the third situation (paragraph (c) of Article 33 or paragraph (3) of Article 7:102 PECL) is more flexible and indeterminate. Where no date or period of time for delivery is fixed or capable of being fixed from the contract, the time for delivery is within "a reasonable time after the conclusion of the contract." A reasonable time after the conclusion of the contract will vary from case to case and will depend on all the circumstances, such as the nature of the goods, the distance covered, and the parties' statements during negotiations.[5] According to Honnold, "[w]hat is 'reasonable' can appropriately be determined by ascertaining what is normal and acceptable in the relevant trade."[6] Schlechtriem has suggested that the rule in paragraph (c) should take precedence over a hypothetical inconsistent national law that might provide that where an indeterminate delivery date has been agreed upon, the seller is liable to deliver immediately.[7] On the other hand, one might suppose that if a seller did deliver immediately, even if not obliged to do so, the seller would have delivered "within" a reasonable time after the contract was concluded.

As was previously mentioned, under both the Convention and PECL, in the first situation where the delivery date is fixed by or determinable from the contract, the seller must deliver the goods on the date so fixed or determined. In the second situation where a period of time for delivery is fixed by or determinable from the contract, the seller must deliver the goods on any date within that period, unless circumstances indicate that the buyer is to choose a date within that period. In any other case, the seller must deliver the goods within a reasonable time after the conclusion of the contract.

Delivery after the relevant due date amounts to a breach of contract, which entitles the buyer to the remedies described in Article 45 CISG and in particular the remedy of damages. Late delivery in itself does not automatically allow the buyer to avoid the contract. Under Article 49 CISG the buyer can avoid the contract for late delivery only if (i) the seller's failure to deliver on time amounts to a "fundamental breach of contract," as defined in Article 25 to mean in essence a breach that results in such detriment to the buyer as substantially to deprive him of what he is entitled to expect under the contract, or (ii) the seller fails to, or declares that he will not, deliver within a reasonable additional

[4] Secretariat Commentary on Article 31 of the 1978 Draft [*draft counterpart of CISG article 33*], *supra* note 2, §§ 6 and 7; Peter Schlechtriem, *Uniform Sales Law – the UN Convention on Contracts for the International Sale of Goods*, Manz (1986), p. 66, fn 244; Fritz Enderlein and Dietrich Maskow, *International Sales Law: United Nations Convention on Contracts for the International Sale of Goods; Convention on the Limitation Period in the International Sale of Goods*, Oceana (1992), p. 136; Ole Lando and Hugh Beale (eds), *Principles of European Contract Law*, Kluwer (2000), pp. 332–333.

[5] Germany 27 April 1999 *Oberlandesgericht* [Appellate Court] Naumburg, case presentation including English translation available online at <http://cisgw3.law.pace.edu/cases/990427g1.html> (the court took into account the buyer's statement nominating 15 January 1997 as the latest delivery date in ruling that delivery after that date would not be within a reasonable time under Article 33(c) CISG).

[6] John Honnold, *Uniform Law for International Sales under the 1980 United National Convention*, 3rd ed., Kluwer (1999) p. 101. Frans van der Velden argues that reasonableness must be regarded as a general principle of the Convention: *see* "The Law of International Sales: The Hague Conventions 1964 and the UNCITRAL Uniform Sales Code 1980 – Some Main Items Compared" in CCA Voskuil and JA Wade (eds.), *Hague-Zagreb Essays 4 on the Law of International Trade*, Martinus Nijhoff (1983) p. 59. *Cf.* Article 1:302 PECL, which states how reasonableness is to be judged.

[7] Peter Schlechtriem, "The Seller's Obligations under the United National Convention on Contracts for the International Sale of Goods" in NM Galston and H Smit (eds), *International Sales: The United Nations Conventions on Contracts for the International Sale of Goods*, Matthew Bender (1984), pp. 6-1-6-4 and 6-15.

time fixed by the buyer under Article 47 CISG.[8] The position is essentially the same under Articles 8:106, 9:103, and 9:301 PECL.[9]

III. CONSEQUENCES OF EARLY DELIVERY BY THE SELLER (ARTICLE 52(1) CISG AND ARTICLE 7:103 PECL)

Both Article 52(1) CISG and Article 7:103 PECL deal with performance of its obligations by a contracting party (the seller in the Convention) before the due date, as well as the consequential position of the other party (the buyer in the Convention). It is thought that neither Article can apply to the situation where the date or period of time for delivery is not fixed by or determinable from the contract and where the seller's obligation is only to deliver before a reasonable time has elapsed after the contract is concluded (i.e., where Article 33(c) CISG or Article 7:102(3) PECL sets the delivery time). Delivery at any time within that period cannot amount to early delivery under Article 52(1) CISG or early performance under Article 7:103 PECL.

Article 52(1) CISG is placed in Part III (Sale of Goods), Chapter II (Obligations of the Seller), Section III (Remedies for Breach of Contract by the Seller) of the Convention. It therefore appears to treat delivery by the seller before the due date determined in accordance with Article 33 CISG as ordinarily a breach of contract. Early delivery is at least non-performance by the seller of its obligation to deliver, and in those circumstances, the buyer has the option of taking or refusing to take delivery of the goods, because having to accept early unanticipated delivery by the seller may cause the buyer additional expense or inconvenience. Article 52(1) CISG does not purport to qualify the buyer's right to exercise that option.[10]

Article 7:103(1) PECL gives a party in the position of the buyer the same option, but qualifies the exercise of the option. The party in question loses the option where acceptance of the tender of early performance "would not unreasonably prejudice its interests." In addition, Article 7:103(2) goes on to provide that "[a] party's acceptance of early performance does not affect the time fixed for the performance of its own obligation." Consequently, the fact that the buyer accepts early delivery may not mean that the buyer in turn has to pay the purchase price (the buyer's only relevant obligation for our purposes[11]) before the contractual date for payment. The Convention has no express provision that parallels Article 7:103(2).

Whether the apparent silence of the Convention on these two PECL points means that the buyer's position under the CISG is different from that under the PECL is now examined.

1. Qualification of the Buyer's Option to Refuse to Take Delivery

The buyer's general obligation to take delivery set out in Article 60 CISG includes an obligation to do "all the acts which could *reasonably* [emphasis added] be expected of him in order to enable the seller to make delivery" and to take over the goods. Although Article 52(1) CISG appears to give the buyer an absolute option to refuse to take early

[8] Article 47 CISG gives the buyer the right to extend the seller's time for performance while preserving the former's right to claim damages for the delay. The seller's failure to, or declaration that he will not, deliver within the extended period allows the buyer to avoid the contract.

[9] *See* Bruno Zeller, *Editorial Remarks: Guide to Articles 47 and 49(1)(b) CISG, and Comparison with Principles of European Contract Law*, available online at <http://cisgw3.law.pace.edu/cisg/text/peclcomp47.html>.

[10] However, Article 86 CISG may compel the buyer in some circumstances to take possession of the goods on the seller's behalf although the buyer has rejected the goods.

[11] The buyer has two obligations under the CISG: to pay the price for the goods and to take delivery of the goods. The former obligation is more relevant for present purposes, where the hypothesis is that the buyer has taken early delivery.

delivery, the exercise of such an option may arguably be constrained by Article 60 CISG and in any event must be governed by the general principle of reasonableness applicable under the CISG.[12] In addition, there is a separate view that, when considering whether to refuse to take early delivery, the buyer must act in good faith under Article 7(1) CISG.

On the issue of good faith generally in the Convention, Felemegas has argued forcefully that the CISG imposes no substantive duty of good faith on parties to a contract of sale and that Article 7(1) only requires the observance of good faith in interpreting the Convention.[13] Magnus adopts a contrary stance,[14] and his approach finds support in the Secretariat Commentary on Article 48 of the 1978 Draft [*draft counterpart of CISG Article* 52].[15] The Secretariat's opinion on the point was that, although the buyer's right to refuse to take delivery does not depend on whether early delivery causes the buyer extra expense or inconvenience, "the buyer must have a reasonable commercial need to refuse to take delivery since article 6 [the draft counterpart of Article 7(1) CISG] requires the observance of good faith in international trade."[16]

Given therefore an obligation under the CISG on the buyer's part to conduct himself reasonably or to observe good faith when exercising the option under Article 52(1), the buyer's right to refuse early delivery cannot be unqualified, and the counterpart provision in Article 7:103 PECL contains an appropriate qualification consistent with the principles of the Convention. Thus, if the ship carrying the goods arrives a week before the contractual delivery date, the buyer who has storage room available will not be entitled to refuse to take early delivery, where the seller is prepared to cover the buyer's expenses and carry the risk during storage of the goods until the contractual delivery date.

2. Effect of Acceptance of Early Delivery on the Time for the Buyer's Performance of His Obligations

Two situations should be distinguished: where the contract specifies the time for payment and where it does not.

a. Time for Payment Specified

One of the buyer's two obligations under Article 53 CISG is to pay the contract price for the goods "as required by the contract and [the] Convention."[17] Article 59 CISG governs the time for payment by the buyer, which is "the date fixed by or determinable from the contract and [the] Convention." Therefore, if the contract fixes a particular date for payment, the buyer is not obliged to pay the seller before that date arrives, even if the

[12] Peter Schlechtriem writes that "the rule that the parties must conduct themselves according to the standard of the 'reasonable person' . . . must be regarded as a general principle of the Convention": *supra* note 4, p. 22 fn 41, and p. 39. Frans van der Velden, *supra* note 6, p. 59, also argues that reasonableness must be regarded as a general principle of the Convention. *See* also Albert Kritzer, "Overview Comments on reasonableness as a general principle of the CISG," available online at <http://cisgw3.law.pace.edu/cisg/text/reason.html>.

[13] John Felemegas in his editorial remarks on Article 7 CISG, comparing it with Article 1:106 PECL, available online at <http://cisgw3.law.pace.edu/cisg/text/peclcomp7.html>.

[14] Ulrich Magnus in his editorial remarks on Article 7 CISG, comparing it with Article 1.6 UNIDROIT Principles, available online at <http://cisgw3.law.pace.edu/cisg/principles/uni7.html>.

[15] Article 48 of the 1978 draft corresponds and is identical in wording to Article 52 CISG.

[16] Secretariat Commentary on Article 48 of the 1978 Draft [*draft counterpart of CISG article* 52], § 3 and fn 1, available online at <http://cisgw3.law.pace.edu/cisg/text/secomm/secomm-52.html>. Although accepting that the buyer's freedom to refuse early delivery is necessarily restricted by the obligation in Article 7(1) CISG to observe good faith, Michael Will has criticized the restriction of "reasonable commercial need" placed on the buyer by the Secretariat Commentary as placing an unwarranted burden on the buyer: in CM Bianca and MJ Bonell (eds.), *Commentary on the International Sales Law*, Giuffrè (1987), p. 380.

[17] The buyer's other obligation under Article 53 CISG is to take delivery of the goods, but that obligation is largely academic for our purposes, because the hypothesis here is that the buyer has accepted the seller's early delivery.

seller chooses to deliver the goods to the buyer early and the buyer chooses to accept that early delivery. This is likewise the position under Article 7:103(2) PECL.

However, Enderlein and Maskow suggest in relation to Article 52(1) CISG that where the buyer accepts early delivery, in some circumstances that "may" constitute a contractual modification in regard to the period of performance under Article 29 CISG; if so, the buyer will have to perform his obligations at an earlier date.[18] It is difficult to appreciate why, if a given contract is modified under Article 29 as to the delivery date by the buyer's acceptance of the seller's early delivery (thereby negating any claim for damages by the buyer for the early delivery), the buyer's obligation to pay the price must necessarily be brought forward. A possible justification for that conclusion may lie in the reasoning that the contractual date for payment must be taken to have been displaced in the modified contract, with the result that, because there is no longer a fixed payment date, Article 58(1) CISG requires the buyer to pay on actual delivery. This reasoning is not entirely convincing.

The Secretariat Commentary on Article 48 of the 1978 Draft (identical to Article 52 CISG) also recognizes that the buyer's acceptance of early delivery may in some circumstances amount to an agreed modification of the contract pursuant to Article 27 of the 1978 Draft (now Article 29 CISG).[19] It is unclear what Enderlein and Maskow and the Secretariat envisage as the circumstances accompanying early delivery by the seller that will point to the contract being modified. To avoid any inference under the CISG that the contract has been modified simply by the buyer's acceptance of the seller's early delivery, a prudent buyer should declare a relevant reservation when taking delivery. Under the PECL, although a contract and any obligations under it can be likewise modified by agreement,[20] any implication along the lines suggested by Enderlein and Maskow advancing the date of the buyer's obligation to pay should arise less readily because of the express provision in Article 7:103(2) PECL, even if theoretically possible.

3. Time for Payment Unspecified

If the contract specifies no date for payment, the Convention provides in Article 58(1) that the buyer must pay the price when the seller places the goods or the documents controlling their disposition at the buyer's disposal in accordance with the contract and the Convention.[21] In such a case, early delivery by the seller accepted by the buyer requires the latter to pay earlier than he would otherwise have done. This will have a bearing on whether the buyer will or should exercise the option under Article 52(1) CISG to refuse to take delivery. The result is the same if the contract expressly links the day when payment is to be made to the day of delivery, whenever that may be, without a particular date being specified: the earlier the delivery by the seller, the earlier the payment by the buyer who accepts the early delivery.

Whether the contract gives no specific time for payment or whether the contract links the time for payment to the time of delivery, the position under the PECL is similar to that outlined above under the CISG. If the contract "fixed" no specific date for the buyer to pay the seller, on one view Article 7:103(2) is inapplicable, and the time for the buyer's

[18] Enderlein and Maskow, *supra* note 4, p. 200.

[19] Secretariat Commentary on Article 48 of the 1978 Draft, § 6, *supra* note 16.

[20] *See* Articles 2:105, 2:106 and 2:107 PECL.

[21] However, even so, the buyer may not be bound to pay until he has had an opportunity to examine the goods: Article 58(3) CISG. *See* further Leif Sevón, "Obligations of the Buyer under the UN Convention on Contracts for the International Sale of Goods" in Petar Sarcevic and Paul Volken (eds.), *International Sale of Goods: Dubrovnik Lectures*, Oceana (1986), Chap 6, p. 217, § 2.4.2; Secretariat Commentary on Article 54 of the 1978 Draft [*draft counterpart of CISG article 58*], §§ 5–9, available online at <http://cisgw3.law.pace.edu/cisg/text/secomm/secomm-58.html>.

payment is determined solely by Article 7:104 PECL, which is effectively the time of actual delivery. If one takes the broader view that Article 7:103(2) does not require the contract to specify a particular date for the performance of the buyer's obligation to pay before it can apply, the time "fixed" for the buyer to pay the seller must be first identified. Article 7:104 PECL fixes that time as effectively the time when the seller delivers the goods in the proper performance of his contractual obligations. On that basis, according to Article 7:103(2) PECL, the buyer's acceptance of the seller's early delivery does not affect the time fixed by Article 7:104 PECL for the performance by the buyer of his obligation to pay, because that time remains the time of delivery by the seller, whenever that occurs.

IV. CONCLUSION

Article 33 CISG and Article 7:102 PECL set out the applicable rules for ascertaining the time for delivery by the seller and require the seller to deliver on time. As was earlier observed, both Articles are virtually identical in all material respects, with the same three situations in the CISG being dealt with in the PECL using the same terminology. Article 33 CISG is thus substantively on all fours with Article 7:102 PECL, and both should have the same legal effect.

In relation to early delivery by the seller, there are two differences between Article 52(1) CISG and Article 7:103 PECL. First, the former appears not to qualify the buyer's right to accept or reject the seller's early delivery, whereas the latter does so. Second, the former is silent on the effect of early delivery by the seller on the time for payment by the buyer, whereas the latter provides that a party's acceptance of early performance does not affect the time for the performance of its own obligations. However, in my opinion, these two differences are largely immaterial, as the latter merely makes more explicit what is implicit in the former. Consequently, both Articles would likely have the same effect.

Remedies available: Comparison between the provisions of CISG Articles 45 and 61 and the counterpart provisions of the PECL Articles 8:101 and 8:102

Chengwei Liu

a. Remedies available to a party are a key consideration for that party, particularly if the contract is breached. However, issues relating to the remedial provisions are difficult and have been the focus of a large part of the discussion and deliberation surrounding the application of commercial law.[1] At the same time, no aspect of a system of contract law

[1] "Among the provisions in the Draft Convention on Contracts for the International Sale of Goods which were the most difficult to formulate and are among the most likely to generate controversy are those dealing with the remedies of buyer and seller for breach of contract by the other party. Many aspects of the law of sales reflect merchant practice, and to the extent that this practice is standardized in international sales transactions, the problems in formulating the text of the Draft Convention were reduced. However the provisions in respect of breach of contract do not reflect merchant practice. They reflect the efforts of lawyers from many legal systems to reconcile their views on the appropriate actions to be taken by the parties and by a tribunal in case of breach. The result has been a series of provisions which . . . are in general harmony with one another but which will often be unfamiliar to lawyers from any given legal system." *See* Eric

is more revealing of its underlying assumptions than is the law that prescribes the relief available for breach of contract.[2] It is where a system's solutions to a large proportion of real-world disputes in commercial transactions are to be found. In practical terms, it may be said that the remedial scheme is the substantive heart of a particular system of contract law, which will be a powerful support for the harmonization of actual outcomes and will improve the reliability of the often unpredictable results of disputes.[3]

b. Generally speaking, the remedies available to an aggrieved party for a breach of contract can in all significant legal systems be classified into three basic categories.

- First, an aggrieved party may be able to claim specific performance. As such, specific performance hardly gives the aggrieved party exactly the performance to which he was entitled to, unless it is supplemented with some kind of an additional remedy, such as monetary relief.
- Second, the aggrieved party may have the right to require substitutionary relief. A relevant relief here is compensation, and almost always a monetary compensation, for the loss that the party has suffered for performance not received.
- Third, the aggrieved party may have the right to put an end to the contractual relationship. In such a case, the third remedy can also be seen in that the aggrieved party is put into a position where he would have been had the contract never been made.

The three categories are not exclusive in that monetary compensation will very often be available together with a claim for specific performance and an act to put an end to the contract. Furthermore, the above-mentioned basic categories of remedies also appear in different variations, such as a right to price reduction and suspension of performance.[4]

c. The CISG follows the above-mentioned three-category system. The remedies available for a breach of contract are summarized under the Convention in Arts. 45 and 61. These Articles set forth reciprocal remedies for the buyer and seller for breach of contract. According to Art. 45(1), which specifies remedies for breach of contract by the seller, in case of a seller's non-compliance with a contract or CISG obligation, in principal the following five legal remedies (defects rights) are at the buyer's disposal:

- Right to performance (Art. 46(1));
- Right to cure (Art. 48);

E. Bergsten & Anthony J. Miller. "The Remedy of Reduction of Price," 27 *Am. J. Comp. L.* (1979) 255–277 at 255. Available online at <http://cisgw3.law.pace.edu/cisg/biblio/bergsten.html>. This is a commentary on the remedy of reduction of price under Art. 46 of the 1978 Draft Convention, from which the basic concept of price reduction under CISG Art. 50 remains unchanged but nevertheless differs from the latter in several respects. For comparison of Art. 46 of the 1978 Draft with CISG Art. 50, see the match-up, available online at <http://cisgw3.law.pace.edu/cisg/text/matchup/matchup-d-50.html>.

[2] *See* E. Allan Farnsworth, "Damages and Specific Relief," 27 *Am. J. Comp. L.* (1979) 247–253. Available online at <http://cisgw3.law.pace.edu/cisg/biblio/farns.html>.

[3] For example, when commenting on Chapter 7 of the UNIDROIT Principles, Arthur Rosett states,

> In practical terms, it is the substantive heart of the whole Principles. It is where the Principles' solutions to a large proportion of real world disputes in commercial transactions are to be found. It is here that the remedial consequences of serious failures of performance are defined: orders of performance, damages, contract termination by rescission, and restitution. These are difficult and central substantive issues. Indeed, Chapter 7 is probably the most imaginative synthesis to emerge in this generation of some of the most difficult practical questions of contract law. It will be a powerful support for the harmonization of actual outcomes and improve the reliability of the often unpredictable results of disputes. The substantive content of Chapter 7 is important as an illustration of the creative power of the UNIDROIT Principles.

See Arthur Rosett, "UNIDROIT Principles and Harmonization of International Commercial Law: Focus on Chapter Seven." Available online at <http://www.unidroit.org/english/publications /review/articles/1997-3.htm>.

[4] *See* Jussi Koskinen, "CISG, Specific Performance and Finnish Law," *Publication of the Faculty of Law of the University of Turku, Private law publication series B:47* (1999). Available online at <http://cisgw3.law.pace.edu/cisg/biblio/koskinen1.html>.

- Right to avoid the contract because of a fundamental breach of contract (Art. 49(1)(a));
- Right of price reduction (Art. 50, sentence 1);
- Right to damages (Art. 45(1)(b) in connection with Arts. 74–77).[5]

Thus, Art. 45 offers an overview of the remedies available to the buyer in the event of a breach – specific performance, avoidance, compensatory damages, and price reduction. In a parallel manner, the seller's remedies are enumerated at Art. 61(1) when the buyer is in default. Although the remedies available to the seller under Art. 61(1) are comparable to those available to the buyer under Art. 45(1), they are less complicated. This is so because the buyer has only two principal obligations, to pay the price and to take delivery of the goods, whereas the seller's obligations are more complex. Therefore, the seller has no remedies comparable to the following ones that are available to the buyer: reduction of the price because of non-conformity of the goods (Art. 50), right to partially exercise his remedies in the case of partial delivery of the goods (Art. 51), and right to refuse to take delivery in case of delivery before the date fixed or of an excess quantity of goods (Art. 52).[6]

d. Under the Convention the notion "breach of contract" covers all failures of a party to perform any of his obligations,[7] comprising *any non-fulfillment of contractual obligations*. Those obligations may have their origin not only in the contract between parties but also in the Convention, established practices, and usages (Art. 9). The notion of breach of contract refers to non-fulfillment of obligations by the seller and to non-performance of obligations by the buyer. The rights of the other party are provided for in parallel: compare Art. 45 *et seq*. with Art. 61 *et seq*. There is no distinction between breaches of main obligations or breaches of auxiliary obligations; rather, a *distinction is made between fundamental breaches of contract and other breaches of contract* (Art. 25). A breach of contract constitutes an objective fact; no matter whether the party who commits the breach is at fault or not.[8] In other words, by contrast with the ULIS approach where each individual type of breach was followed by the proper remedy, the CISG uses the uniform term of breach of contract, which under the CISG comprises any non-fulfillment of contractual obligations whether the party who commits the breach is at fault or not.

e. The PECL also use the unitary concept of non-performance (for the sake of simplicity, the term *non-performance* is used here synonymously with the CISG *breach*) both for the excused and the non-excused non-performance. It is noted that non-performance as used in the PECL covers the failure to perform an obligation under the contract in any way, whether by a complete failure to do anything, late performance, or defective performance. Furthermore, it covers both excused and non-excused non-performance.[9] On the other hand, according to PECL Art. 8:101, the remedies available for non-performance depend upon whether the non-performance is not excused, is excused due to an impediment under Art. 8:108, or results from the behavior of the other party. A non-performance that

[5] *See* the decision by the Swiss Commercial Court *(Handelsgericht)* Aargau [OR.2001.00029], 5 November 2002, translated by Martin F. Koehler. Available online at <http://cisgw3.law.pace.edu/cases/021105s1.html>.

[6] *See* Secretariat Commentary on Art. 57 of the 1978 Draft *[draft counterpart of CISG Art. 61]*, Comment 2. Available online at <http://cisgw3.law.pace.edu/cisg/text/secomm/secomm-61.html>.

[7] *See* Fritz Enderlein, "Rights and Obligations of the Seller under the UN Convention on Contracts for the International Sale of Goods" in Petar Sarcevic & Paul Volken eds., *International Sale of Goods: Dubrovnik Lectures*, Oceana (1996), p. 188. Available online at <http://cisgw3.law.pace.edu/cisg/biblio/enderlein1.html>.

[8] *See* Fritz Enderlein and Dietrich Maskow, *International Sales Law: United Nations Convention on Contracts for the International Sale of Goods*, Oceana Publication (1992), p. 174. Available online at <http://cisgw3.law.pace.edu/cisg/biblio/enderlein.html>.

[9] *See* Comment and Notes to the PECL Art. 8:101. Note 1. Available online at <http://cisgw3.law.pace.edu/cisg/text/peclcomp45.html>.

is not excused may give the aggrieved party the right to claim performance – recovery of money due (Art. 9:101) or specific performance (Art. 9:102) – to claim damages and interest (Arts. 9:501 through 9:510), to withhold its own performance (Art. 9:201), to terminate the contract (Arts. 9:301 through 9:309) and to reduce its own performance (Art. 9:401). If a party violates a duty to receive or accept performance the other party may also make use of the remedies just mentioned.[10] Thus, the PECL generally correspond with the major legal systems in granting the three-category remedial system.

f. However, under certain conditions the breaching or non-performing party may be exempted from certain consequences of a failure to perform his obligations while the other remedies remain unaffected and are still available to the aggrieved party. Textually, the excuse granted in Art. 79 CISG exempts *only* the breaching party from liability for damages. All the other remedies of the other parties are not affected by this excuse (i.e., demand for performance, reduction of the price, or avoidance of the contract).[11] The Secretariat Commentary clearly states, "Even if the impediment is of such a nature as to render impossible any further performance, the other party retains the right to require that performance under article 42 or 58 *[draft counterpart of CISG article 46 or 62]*."[12] In other words, even in case of impossibility, the other party could ask for specific performance – a result that is hardly convincing.[13] By contrast, PECL Art. 8:101(2) specifies that where there is an impediment that fulfils the conditions set by PECL Art. 8:108, the aggrieved party may resort to any of the remedies set out in PECL Chapter 9 *except claiming performance* and damages. Any form of specific performance (Arts. 9:101 and 9:102) is by definition impossible.[14] However, this rigid solution might lead to some unreasonable situations, particularly in the case of temporary impediments. Although it seems to amount to an obvious contradiction because it is supposed that performance is not possible, it has become clear at least that the right to performance continues to exist in the event of temporary grounds for exemption and that auxiliary claims that are related to it, such as interest, continue to accumulate.[15]

g. Despite the exempted remedies difference the CISG and the PECL agree that the fact that the non-performance is caused by the creditor's act or omission has an effect to that extent on the remedies open to the obligee. This is expressed by either CISG Art. 80 or PECL Art. 8:101(3). It would be contrary to good faith and fairness for the creditor to have a remedy when it is responsible for the non-performance. In such a case, the most

[10] *Id.*, Comment B.

[11] *See* Secretariat Commentary on Art. 65 of the 1978 Draft *[draft counterpart of CISG Art. 79]*, Comment 8. Available online at <http://cisgw3.law.pace.edu/cisg/text/secomm/secomm-79.html>.

[12] *Id.*, Comment 9.

[13] It could be argued that paragraph (5) of CISG Art. 79 yields unrealistic results. It would allow an action for specific performance in a case where the goods are destroyed and thus, the performance is physically impossible. *See* Denis Tallon, in *Commentary on the International Sales Law – The 1980 Vienna Sales Convention, C. M. Bianca & M. J. Bonnell* eds., Giuffrè: Milan (1987), p. 588.

[14] *See* Comment and Notes to the PECL Art. 8:108. Comment D. Available online at <http://cisgw3.law.pace.edu/cisg/text/peclcomp79.html>.

[15] In this respect, the UNIDROIT Principles have found a flexible answer to the question of what is to become of the right to performance. Unlike either the CISG or the PECL that specifies the remedies, though differing from each other slightly, which the aggrieved party cannot resort to in case of exemption, the UNIDROIT Principles adhere to the principle that the excuse is general. However, in Art. 7.1.7(4) they make important exceptions in determining certain claims that are not affected by *force majeure*, namely the right to terminate the contract, withhold delivery, or request interest on money due. The Official Comment makes some of its deliberations clear: "In some cases the impediment will prevent any performance at all but in many others it will simply delay performance and the effect of the article will be to give extra time for performance. It should be noted that in this event the extra time may be greater (or less) than the length of the interruption because the crucial question will be what is the effect of the interruption on the progress of the contract." *See* Comment 2 on Art. 7.1.7 UNIDROIT Principles of International Commercial Contracts.

obvious situation is the so-called *mora creditoris,* where the creditor directly prevents performance (e.g., access refused to a building site). But there are other cases where the creditor's behavior has an influence on the breach and its consequences. In other cases where there is also a non-performance by the debtor, the creditor may exercise the remedies for non-performance to a limited extent. When the loss is caused both by the debtor – which has not performed – and the creditor – which has partially caused the breach by its own behavior – the creditor should not have the whole range of remedies. The creditor's contribution to the non-performance has an effect on the remedy *"to the extent that (the other party's) failure to perform (is) caused by its own act or omission."* In other words, this effect may be total; that is to say that the creditor cannot exercise any remedy, or partial. The exact consequence of the creditor's behavior will be examined with each remedy.[16] In any event, a non-performance that is due solely to the other party's wrongful prevention does not give the latter any remedy. In most of the systems, the party who has prevented performance will himself be the non-performing party against whom the remedies may be exercised.[17]

h. Among other things, CISG Art. 45(2)/61(2) provides that a party who resorts to any remedy available to him under the contract or this Convention is not thereby deprived of the right to claim any damages that he may have incurred. Thus, the cumulation of damage claims with other remedies is explicitly contemplated. In other words, either Art. 45(2) or Art. 61(2) rejects the notion that the buyer/seller is forced to elect between claiming damages and exercising the other remedies conferred on him under the Convention; that is, specific performance and avoidance. The common law position is the same, and in particular, it is basic law that a buyer who rejects non-conforming goods or cancels the contract on some other ground is not thereby deprived of his entitlement to damages.[18] Thus, the right to claim damages exists either as an exclusive right or as a supplementary right in addition to the right to require performance or payment, to reduce the price, or to avoid the contract. The rule in CISG Art. 45(2)/61(2) is followed and furthered in a separate Art. 8:102 under the PECL, which states, "Remedies which are not incompatible may be cumulated." A party that is entitled to withhold its performance and to terminate the contract may first withhold and then terminate. A party that pursues a remedy other than damages is not precluded from claiming damages. A party that terminates the contract may, for instance, also claim damages.[19]

i. It is a truism that a party cannot at the same time pursue two or more remedies that are incompatible with each other. Thus a party cannot at the same time claim specific performance of the contract and terminate it. If a party has received a non-conforming tender, it cannot exercise its right to reduce its own performance and at the same time terminate the contract. A non-performance that causes the aggrieved party to suffer a loss may give it a right to be compensated for that loss, but it cannot be awarded more than the *"réparation intégrale."* Thus, if it has accepted a non-conforming tender, the value of which is less than that of a conforming tender, and if it has claimed or obtained a reduction of the price corresponding to the decrease in value, it cannot also claim compensation for that same decrease in value as damages. When two remedies are incompatible with each other, the aggrieved party will often have to choose between them. However, PECL Art. 8:102 does not preclude an aggrieved party that has elected one remedy from shifting to another later, even though the later remedy is incompatible

[16] *Supra.* fn. 10.

[17] *Supra.* fn. 9, Note 3.

[18] *See* Jacob S. Ziegel, "Report to the Uniform Law Conference of Canada on Convention on Contracts for the International Sale of Goods": Comment 2. Available online at <http://cisgw3.law.pace.edu/cisg/text/ziegel45.html>.

[19] *See* Comment and Notes to the PECL Art. 8:102. Comment A. Available online at <http://cisgw3.law.pace.edu/cisg/text/peclcomp45.html>.

with the first remedy elected. If, after having claimed specific performance, it learns that the defaulting party has not performed or is not likely to do so within a reasonable time, the aggrieved party may terminate the contract. On the other hand, an election of a remedy is often definite and will preclude later elections of incompatible remedies. A party that has terminated the contract cannot later claim specific performance, because by giving notice of termination the aggrieved party may have caused the other party to act in reliance of the termination. If a defaulting party has adapted itself to a claim for specific performance and taken measures to perform within a reasonable time, the aggrieved party cannot change its position and terminate the contract. This applies when the defaulting party has received a notice fixing an additional time for performance. The rule is in accordance with the widely accepted principle that when a party has made a declaration of intention that has caused the other party to act in reliance of the declaration, the party making it will not be permitted to act inconsistently with it. This follows from the general principle of fair dealing.[20]

j. However, it should be mentioned here that not only the obligations of the parties but also the remedies may be changed by them in their contract. The provisions in either CISG Art. 45/61 or PECL Arts. 8:101 and 8:102 are based on the assumption that the parties have not chosen some other remedy or remedies within their contractual relationship. Any such remedies chosen by the parties would always prevail. Contractual freedom is thus the rule, also reflecting the starting point for various legal systems in general. Moreover, it is important to note that the remedies available for a breach of contract will be subject not only to the express agreement made between the parties but also to any practice or usage that can be regarded as an implied part of the agreement. In case of a breach of contract it is, therefore, necessary to first look into the contract executed between the parties or any practice or usage of relevance.[21] Only if the agreement and any relevant practice or usage is silent may the provisions concerning remedies of the applicable rules – CISG, UNIDROIT Principles, or PECL or any other laws – be at hand. However, it should also be noted that, in cases of such remedies chosen by the parties or implied by relevant practice or usage, potential uncertainty may arise depending on the types of remedies chosen by the parties. This becomes a clearer problem in the context of the CISG Art. 4,which sets forth the scope of its application and expressly excludes "the validity of the contract or of any of its provisions or of any usage." Moreover, although the CISG does give the parties the freedom to choose their own remedies, it is not necessarily clear that these remedies will be enforced the same way in every country, if at all.[22]

k. Finally, it is to be noted that, under the Convention, Arts. 45(3)/61(3) both provide that if the entitled party resorts to a remedy for breach of contract, no court or arbitral tribunal may delay the exercise of that remedy by granting a period of grace either before,

[20] *Id.*, Comments B, C.

[21] *Supra.* fn. 4.

[22] One such example would be if the parties operating under the CISG specifically agreed that the only available remedy was specific performance. Under English law, specific performance is a discretionary remedy. Although it is unlikely that the parties would agree to such a remedy, there would be no conflict between the agreement for specific performance and Art. 46 of the CISG. On the other hand, an English court applying general legal principles would be unlikely to grant specific performance where the court did not consider that the situation merited the exercise of discretion in favor of specific performance. A more likely issue is the question of the amount of damages agreed by the parties. Under the CISG, there is no limit on the amount of compensation that may be agreed to be paid upon breach of a contract. In contrast, English common law draws a distinction between genuine pre-estimates of damage (referred to as "liquidated damages") versus clauses viewed as punitive or penal. Penalty clauses are considered invalid and will not be enforced by an English court. So although the parties are generally free to choose their own remedies, English law will not enforce all of the remedies, at least not to the same degree. (*See* Peter A. Piliounis, "The Remedies of Specific Performance, Price Reduction and Additional Time (*Nachfrist*) under the CISG: Are These Worthwhile Changes or Additions to English Sales Law?" (1999). Available online at <http://cisgw3.law.pace.edu/cisg/biblio/piliounis.html>.)

at the same time as, or after the buyer has resorted to the remedy. Such provision seems desirable in international trade.[23] Thus, domestic laws that permit the courts or arbitral tribunals to grant a seller in breach extra time to perform are expressly excluded. This is mainly because the Convention specifically rejects the idea that in a commercial contract for the international sale of goods the party may, as a general rule, avoid the contract merely because the contract date for performance has passed and the obligated party has not as yet performed its obligations. In these circumstances, as a general rule, the other party may do so if, and only if, the failure to perform on the contract date causes him substantial detriment *[results in such detriment to the other party as substantially to deprive him of what he is entitled to expect under the contract]* and the party in default foresaw or had reason to foresee such a result. As a result of this rule in the Convention there was no reason to allow the buyer/seller to apply to a court for a delay of grace, as is permitted in some legal systems. Moreover, the procedure of applying to a court for a delay of grace is particularly inappropriate in the context of international commerce, especially because doing so would expose the parties to the broad discretion of a judge who would usually be of the same nationality as one of the parties.[24] Nonetheless, if the parties have expressly referred to an arbitral procedure that allows such a feature, the arbitration rule should prevail over Art. 45 or 61, following the principle of Art. 6. But the mere fact that the parties are litigating before a court whose procedure allows some "*délai de grace*" should not be regarded as an agreement to have such a rule apply.[25]

[23] *See* Secretariat Commentary on Art. 41 of the 1978 Draft [*draft counterpart of* CISG *Art. 45*], Comment 6. Available online at <http://cisgw3.law.pace.edu/cisg/text/secomm/secomm-45.html>; *See* also Secretariat Commentary on Art. 57 of the 1978 Draft [*draft counterpart of* CISG *Art. 61*], Comment 6. Available online at <http://cisgw3.law.pace.edu/cisg/text/secomm/secomm-61.html>.

[24] *See* Secretariat Commentary on Art. 43 of the 1978 Draft [*draft counterpart of* CISG *Art. 47*], Comments 4, 5. Available online at <http://cisgw3.law.pace.edu/cisg/text/secomm/secomm-47.html>; *See* also Secretariat Commentary on Art. 59 of the 1978 Draft [*draft counterpart of* CISG *Art. 63*], Comments 4, 5. Available online at <http://cisgw3.law.pace.edu/cisg/text/secomm/secomm-63.html>.

[25] *See* Bernard Audit, "The Vienna Sales Convention and the *Lex Mercatoria*" in *Lex Mercatoria and Arbitration*, rev. ed., T. Carboneau ed.; Juris Publishing (1998) p. 285 n. 47.

Buyer's right to compel performance: Remarks on the manner in which the Principles of European Contract Law may be used to interpret or supplement Article 46 of the CISG

Jarno Vanto

a. Article 46 of the Convention gives the buyer the right to specific performance unless the buyer resorts to a remedy that is inconsistent with it. As is evident throughout the provisions of the CISG, the rights of the buyer and the seller are balanced in the Convention, and the seller is also entitled to demand specific performance as stated in CISG Article 62. Resorting to the remedy of specific performance does not deprive the buyer of his right to claim damages, as stated in CISG Article 45(2)[1]. Another aspect of this balance between

[1] The PECL contain an equivalent provision: PECL Article 9:103 [Right to Performance: Damages Not Precluded]: "The fact that a right to performance is excluded under this Section does not preclude a claim for damages."

the rights of the buyer and the seller is that according to CISG Article 48(1) the seller may, even after the date for delivery, remedy at his own expense any failure to perform his obligations, if he can do so without unreasonable inconvenience or uncertainty of reimbursement by the seller of expenses advanced by the buyer. If the seller makes use of this right, the buyer need not make use of his right to require performance under CISG Article 46. In fact, if the seller requests an opportunity to remedy in accordance with CISG Article 48(1) and the buyer does not comply with the request within a reasonable time, the seller may remedy within the time indicated in his request and the buyer may not resort to any remedy that is inconsistent with performance by the seller during that time (see CISG Art. 48(2)).

b. Specific performance often assumes the nature of an extra-judicial remedy, because it is in the buyer's interest to receive the goods under the contract while the seller retains the opportunity to obtain the agreed price.[2] It is a logical reaction on the buyer's part to request performance. Specific performance is reflective of the contract law principle *pacta sunt servanda* – i.e., contracts are to be obeyed. CISG Article 46 gives the parties an opportunity to honor the contract. [3] It gives the buyer the right to obtain the contracted, conforming goods and the seller the right to obtain the full purchase price. It also aims to prevent the seller's efforts to buy himself out of the contract.[4]

c. CISG Article 46 is a remedy for breach of the sales contract, but it may also be regarded as an enforcement mechanism of CISG Article 30. Article 30 provides,

> The seller must deliver the goods, hand over any documents relating to them and transfer the property in the goods, as required by the contract and this Convention.

This provision defines one of the main duties of the seller, and CISG Article 46 enforces that duty in giving the buyer the right to demand performance from the seller.

d. CISG Article 46 sets as a prerequisite for its application that the buyer does not resort to a remedy that is inconsistent with the remedy of specific performance. Remedies that are inconsistent with specific performance are (i) avoidance of the contract, defined in CISG Article 49, and (ii) reduction of price if the buyer could have demanded repair of

[2] See Honnold J., *Documentary History of the Uniform Law for International Sales. The Studies, Deliberations and Decisions That Led to the 1980 United Nations Convention with Introductions and Explanations*, Deventer, Kluwer Law International 1989, p. 428: "... the buyer's principal concern is often that the seller perform the contract as he originally promised. Legal actions for damages cost money and may take a considerable period of time. Moreover, if the buyer needs the goods in quantities and with the qualities ordered, he may not be able to make substitute purchases in the time necessary."
See also
- the Secretariat Commentary on the 1978 Draft of the CISG Article 46, available online at <http://cisgw3.law.pace.edu/cisg/text/secomm/secomm46.html>;
- the comparison of CISG Article 46 with PECL Article 9:102, including the following comment on PECL Article 9:102: "If the non-performing party performs, but its performance does not conform to the contract, the aggrieved party may choose to insist upon a conforming performance. This may be advantageous for both parties. The aggrieved party obtains what it has originally contracted for and the non-performing party eventually obtains the full price." The commentary is available online at <http://cisgw3.law.pace.edu/cisg/text/peclcomp46.html#cnpc>.

[3] On efforts in maintaining the contractual relationship, specific performance, and subsequent avoidance of the contract, *see* France 29 January 1998 Appellate Court Versailles, *Giustina International v. Perfect Circle Europe* 56; R.G. n:o 1222/95, available online at <http://cisgw3.law.pace.edu/cases/980129f1.html>.

[4] Huber in Schlechtriem P., *Commentary on UN Convention on the International Sale of Goods (CISG)*, Clarendon Press, Oxford, 1998 p. 376.

the non-conforming goods or additional deliveries.[5] Avoidance of the contract exempts the seller from the obligation of specific performance by virtue of CISG Article 81(1).[6]

An instance where specific performance is also excluded is when the buyer claims damages for the seller's failure to perform some other of his obligations, such as assembly of the goods.[7] An additional requirement for making use of the remedy is that the buyer first examines the goods in accordance with CISG Article 38[8] and subsequently gives notice of the nature of the non-conformity of the goods within a reasonable time after he has discovered it or ought to have discovered it, as stated in CISG Article 39[9,10]. The Principles of European Contract Law also impose such a requirement, which is stated in Article 9:102(3).[11] The PECL are of assistance in interpreting CISG Article 46 and adding clarity to the meaning of that provision; that meaning must be derived from many interconnected Articles of the Convention.

e. The PECL make a clear distinction between performance of monetary obligations and of non-monetary obligations – i.e., the buyer's and seller's right to compel performance. PECL Article 9:102 gives the buyer the right to demand specific performance from the seller. The Article goes further than CISG Article 46 in characterizing situations where specific performance may not be obtained, and it is of assistance in interpreting CISG Article 46. PECL Article 9:102(2) states that specific performance may not be obtained when (a) performance would be unlawful or impossible, (b) performance would cause the debtor unreasonable effort or expense, (c) the performance consists of the provision of services or work of a personal character or depends upon a personal relationship, or (d) the aggrieved party may reasonably obtain performance from another source.

f. In the CISG realm, Article 79 limits the extent to which specific performance may be requested.[12] Even though CISG Article 79 mentions only damages as excluded because of an impediment beyond the seller's control, it would be unreasonable to require the seller to overcome an impediment to perform that is of such nature that it would exclude liability for damages altogether.[13] This approach is also adopted in the

[5] Schlechtriem P., "Uniform Sales Law: The UN Convention on Contracts for the International Sale of Goods, Claims for Performance (Articles 46 and 47)," available at <http://cisgw3.law.pace.edu/cisg/biblio/schlechtriem-46.html>.

[6] Article 81 (1) first sentence states, "Avoidance of the contract releases both parties from their obligations under it, subject to any damages which may be due." *See* Huber, *op. cit.*, p. 378.

[7] *Id.*, p. 378.

[8] *See* relevant case law: Germany 10 February Appellate Court Düsseldorf 6 U 32/93, available online at <http://cisgw3.law.pace.edu/cases/940210g1.html>.

[9] *See* relevant case law:

- Germany 9 November 1994 District Court Oldenburg, available online at <http://cisgw3.law.pace.edu/cisg/wais/db/cases2/941109g1.html>
- France 24 October Appellate Court, Colmar, Pelliculest v. Morton International, available online at <http://cisgw3.law.pace.edu/cases/001024f1.html>
- Icc Arbitration case No. 9083 of August 1999, available online at <http://cisgw3.law.pace.edu/cases/999083i1.html>

[10] On the requirement for such notification in connection with remedying the lack of conformity by repair under CISG Article 46(3), *see* Germany 20 September 1995 OLG Nürnberg, 12 U 2919/94, available online at <http://www.jura.uni-freiburg.de/ipr1/cisg/urteile/text/267.htm>.

[11] PECL Art. 9:102(3): "The aggrieved party will lose the right to specific performance if it fails to seek it within a reasonable time after it has or ought to have become aware of the non-performance."

[12] Huber, *op. cit.*, p. 379.

[13] On CISG Article 79 not *per se* precluding the right to compel performance, *see* the Cross-references and Editorial analysis on CISG Article 46, by Vivian Grosswald Curran, available at <http://cisgw3.law.pace.edu/cisg/text/cross/cross-46.html>.

regime of the PECL. As noted above, PECL Article 9:102(2)(a) provides that impossibility of performance operates to exclude the remedy of specific performance. The same PECL provision also takes into account the possible unlawfulness of performance. Such a situation might emerge, for example, when the government of the seller's country imposes an export ban on the contracted goods. This would make performance on the seller's part both impossible and unlawful. In these instances one has to consider the nature of the impediment to perform. If the impediment is only of a temporary nature, the buyer retains his right to demand performance after the impediment has been overcome.[14]

g. Another prerequisite for the application of specific performance is the lack of conformity of the goods to the contract. Article 35(1) of the Convention states that the goods do conform to the contract if they are of the quantity, quality, and description required by the contract. The goods also need to be contained or packaged in the manner required by the contract. Additionally, CISG Article 35(2) states that the goods do not conform with the contract unless they (a) are fit for the purposes for which goods of the same description would ordinarily be used; (b) are fit for any particular purpose expressly or implicitly made known to the seller at the time of the conclusion of the contract, except where the circumstances show that the buyer did not rely, or that it was unreasonable for him to rely, on the seller's skill and judgment; (c) possess the qualities of goods that the seller has held out to the buyer as a sample or model; and (d) are contained or packaged in the manner usual for such goods or, where there is no such manner, in a manner adequate to preserve and protect the goods.[15]

Furthermore, CISG Article 41 provides that the seller must deliver goods that are free from any right or claim of a third party, unless the buyer agreed to take the goods subject to that right or claim.

Concerning third-party claims to the goods, CISG Article 42 provides that the seller must deliver goods that are free from any right or claim of a third party based on industrial property or other intellectual property, of which at the time of the conclusion of the contract the seller knew or could not have been unaware; this is provided that the right or claim is based on industrial property or other intellectual property under the law of the state where the goods will be resold or otherwise used, if it was contemplated by the parties at the time of the conclusion of the contract that the goods would be resold or otherwise used in that state or in any other case, under the law of the state where the buyer has his place of business. Third-party claims have been often classified as falling within the ambit of CISG Article 46 and thus entitling the buyer to demand specific performance[16] in cases of defects in title.[17] This entitlement seems plausible not only because a defect in title is a failure to perform on the seller's part as stated in CISG Article 46(1) but also because CISG Article 30 states that the seller must transfer the property in the goods.

[14] CISG Article 79 (3): "The exemption provided by this Article has effect for the period during which the impediment exists."

[15] *See* Handelsgericht ded Kantons Aargau, 5 November 2002, OR.2001.00029, available online at <http://www.cisg-online.ch/cisg/urteile/715.htm>.

[16] Lookofsky, Joseph, *Understanding the CISG in Europe*, 2003, Kluwer International, p. 121.

[17] *See* Huber, *op. cit.*, p. 383, stating that defects in title are not subject to the fundamental breach requirement of Article 46(2) but that the buyer is entitled to compel performance solely on the basis of Article 46(1). Huber also states that because 46(2) is not applicable, the right to demand substitute goods is out of the question and the seller's duty to perform is to remove the defect in title in any suitable manner.

h. Article 46(2) of the Convention states that the buyer may require delivery of substitute goods only if the lack of conformity constitutes a fundamental breach of contract.[18,19] CISG Article 25 provides,

> A breach of contract committed by one of the parties is fundamental if it results in such detriment to the other party as substantially deprive him of what he is entitled to expect under the contract, unless the party in breach did not foresee and a reasonable person of the same kind in the same circumstances would not have foreseen such a result.

A fundamental breach entitles the party, as an alternative to demanding delivery of substitute goods, to declare the contract avoided in accordance with CISG Article 49(1)(a).[20] The choice between avoidance of the contract and specific performance is reflective of the *pacta sunt servanda* principle, but is limited by the factors stated in PECL Article 9:102(2). Those factors enumerated in the PECL may provide some guidance in the application of the counterpart provision in the CISG. For instance, specific performance may not be required when performance is impossible. The impossibility must be of such nature that it is objective and permanent.[21] Determining whether it is impossible comes down to evaluating the seller's ability to perform and the buyer's right to require specific performance. In this context, the emphasis must be placed on criteria that are independent from the subjective views and circumstances of the seller or the buyer.

Therefore, even if a seller's breach of contract is fundamental, the buyer may not require specific performance if performance is impossible, and consequently the buyer has to avoid the contract and claim damages. This is self-evident[22] because specific performance in such cases would be an exercise in futility. In this instance, one also has to differentiate between specific goods and generic goods. If the specific goods delivered are non-conforming, it is impossible for the seller to make a substitute delivery of conforming goods for such goods do not exist.

Exclusion of specific performance in situations of impossibility also reflects the general principle of good faith.[23] PECL Article 9:102(2) provides that specific performance cannot be obtained if it would cause seller unreasonable effort or expense. This is reflective of the principle of good faith, the promotion and observance of which comprise an interpretative standard laid down in Article 7(1) of the Convention.[24] Similarly, if

[18] For more comments on fundamental breach, *see* Lorenz, B. "Fundamental Breach under the CISG," available online at <http://cisgw3.law.pace.edu/cisg/biblio/lorenz.html>; *see also* Schlechtriem, P., "Uniform Sales Law, The Experience with Uniform Sales Law in the Federal Republic of Germany," available online at <http://cisgw3.law.pace.edu/cisg/text/schlechtriem25.html>.
See also the following case law:
- Germany 10 February 1994 OLG Düsseldorf, 6 U 32/93, available online at <http://www.jura.uni-freiburg.de/ipr1/cisg/urteile/text/192.htm>;
- Germany, 31 January 1997, Appellate Court Koblenz, available online at <http://cisgw3.law.pace.edu/cases/970131g1.html>

[19] The Secretariat Commentary on CISG Article 46(2) provides the following:

> If the goods which have been delivered do not conform to the contract, the buyer may want the seller to deliver substitute goods which do conform. However, it could be expected that the costs to the seller of shipping a second lot of goods to the buyer and disposing of the non-conforming goods already delivered might be considerably greater than the buyer's loss from having non-conforming goods; available online at <http://cisgw3.law.pace.edu/cisg/text/secomm/secomm-46.html>.

[20] *See* Enderlein F. and Maskow D., "Commentary on CISG Article 46, at para 5," available online at <http://cisgw3.law.pace.edu/cisg/text/peclcomp46.html#cnpc>.

[21] Huber, *op. cit.*, p. 380.

[22] *Id.*, p. 380.

[23] Lookofsky, *op. cit.*, p. 119.

[24] For editorial comments on the proper interpretation and application of the concept of good faith in the CISG, *see* the opposing views offered by John Felemegas and Professor Ulrich Magnus: Felemegas J., "Comparative Editorial Remarks on the Concept of Good Faith in the CISG and the PECL," 13 *Int'l. L. Rev.* (Number II, Fall 2001) 399–406, *also* available online, at <http://cisgw3.law.pace.edu/cisg/biblio/felemegas2.html>;

the performance consists of the provision of services or work of a personal character or depends upon a personal relationship, as contemplated in PECL Article 9:102(2)(c), enforced performance in such circumstances may be regarded as abuse of the buyer's rights[25]; it could also be seen as an extension of operation of the principle of good faith.

i. Another prerequisite for the exercise of the buyer's right to demand specific performance is that the buyer is able to return the goods substantially in the condition in which he received them (see CISG Article 82(1)). Article 82 states that the buyer does not lose his right to specific performance:

(a) if the impossibility of making restitution of the goods or of making restitution of the goods substantially in the condition in which the buyer received them is not due to his act or omission;
(b) if the goods or part of the goods have perished or deteriorated as a result of the examination provided for in Article 38; or
(c) if the goods or part of the goods have been sold in the normal course of business or have been consumed or transformed by the buyer in the course of normal use before he discovered or ought to have discovered the lack of conformity.

j. If the seller's failure to perform is less than fundamental (i.e., it does not substantially deprive the buyer of what he was entitled to expect under the contract), the buyer may require the seller to remedy the lack of conformity by repair, unless this is unreasonable having regard to all the circumstances. The buyer may alternatively claim price reduction under CISG Article 50, and in any event he is entitled to claim damages as provided in Articles 74–77 of the Convention.

k. In the context of CISG Article 46(3), where the buyer requires the seller to remedy the lack of conformity by repair, that right is limited by reasonableness considerations as stated in that provision and also in PECL Article 9:102(2)(b).[26] The "reasonableness" is on the part of the seller, for if it would be unreasonable on the buyer's part to demand repair of defects he would not make such a demand. If efforts to repair would result in unreasonable expenses in relation to the value of the goods, for example because of travel expenses associated with international commercial relations, imposing a duty of repair on a seller would be unreasonable and against good faith in international trade.

l. If the repair of goods requires work of a highly personal nature as described in PECL Article 9:102(2)(c), such as creative work, it would be highly unlikely that the seller would perform if such a duty was imposed on him if he did not perform in the first place. In these instances the buyer may resort to other remedies at his disposal.

m. Upholding of good faith can also be seen in the exclusion of specific performance when the aggrieved party may reasonably obtain performance from another source (PECL Art. 9:102(2)(c)). The interests of the buyer and the seller must be weighed in relation to one another when determining whether it would be more reasonable for the buyer to obtain performance elsewhere than to impose a duty to perform on the seller. This is applicable

Magnus U., "Editorial Remarks on Good Faith," available online at <http://cisgw3.law.pace.edu/cisg/principles/uni7.html#um>.

[25] Huber, op. cit., p. 381.

[26] "Reasonableness" is a general principle of the CISG. For further comments on the definition and operation of the concept of "reasonableness" in the CISG, *see* <http://cisgw3.law.pace.edu/cisg/text/reason.html>. For the definition of "reasonableness in the PECL, *see* PECL Article 1:302.

both when delivery of substitute goods and remedying the lack of conformity by repair are concerned.[27]

n. The buyer has the burden of proof to the effect that the seller's performance is defective.[28] The seller has the burden of proof insofar as he claims that performance would be impossible, unlawful, or unreasonable. Furthermore, if the seller claims that the buyer could reasonably obtain performance from another source, the buyer has to prove the seller wrong.

o. In conclusion, it is submitted that the provisions of the PECL add clarity to the slightly narrower terminology employed by CISG Article 46 and, together with the comments to the PECL, illuminate the meaning of the said Article. Thus, the PECL provide an important tool for interpreting CISG Article 46 by combining some of the criteria that one would otherwise have to draw from other Articles of the Convention. It is arguable that a wise contract drafter may want to incorporate the PECL into a contract for the international sale of goods as an interpretative tool of the Convention insofar as the contract concerns European contracting parties. In common law jurisdictions specific performance assumes a narrower scope of application.[29]

[27] On the inability of obtaining performance elsewhere under the U.S. Uniform Commercial Code and on CISG Article 46(1) and Article 28 (exception to Article 46), *see* United States Federal District Court 7 December 1999 *Magellan International v. Salzgitter Handel* 99 C 5153, available online at <http://cisgw3.law.pace.edu/cases/991207u1.html>.

[28] Ferrari F., in *Review of the Convention on Contracts for the International Sale of Goods, 2000–2001*, Kluwer Law International, p. 6: "...the following three general principles (1) any party which wants to derive beneficial legal consequences from a legal provision has to prove the existence of the factual prerequisites of that provision (2) any party claiming an exception has to prove the existence of the factual prerequisites of that exception; and (3) those facts are exclusively in a party's sphere of responsibility and which therefore are, at least theoretically, better known to that party have to be proven by that party, since it is that party who exercises the control over that sphere."

[29] *See, e.g.*, the United Kingdom: Sale of Goods Act 1893, sect. 52 (in part): "In any action for breach of contract to deliver specific or ascertained goods the court may, if it thinks fit, on the application of the plaintiff, by its judgment or decree direct that the contract shall be performed specifically, without giving the defendant the option of retaining the goods on payment of damages."

See also, the U.S. Uniform Commercial (Code, sec. 2–716(1)): "Specific performance may be decreed where the goods are unique or in other proper circumstances."

Buyer's notice fixing additional final period for performance: Remarks on the manner in which the Principles of European Contract Law may be used to interpret or supplement Articles 47 and 49(1)(b) of the CISG

Bruno Zeller

I. SCHEME OF CISG ARTICLES 47 AND 49(1)(B)

CISG Articles 47 and 49(1)(b) are part of the regime of remedies of breach of contract within the CISG, which in general can be divided into two categories: remedies where the contract can be terminated or avoided, such as fundamental breach, and remedies where the contract is still in force, such as damages.

Articles 47 and 49(1)(b) are provisions that span both remedies through the principle of the *Nachfrist*, which is the granting of additional time for the delivery of goods. The principle has been mainly borrowed from German domestic law, as well as from the French procedure of *mise en demeure*. However, there are significant differences between the German and French treatment of *Nachfrist* and the one accorded to in the CISG. This is a good time to remind ourselves of the mandate of Article 7(1) where uniformity of application demands the autonomous interpretation of the CISG; that is, without relying on principles founded in domestic law. In other words, German and French treatment of *Nachfrist* and *mise en demeure* must be ignored and cannot be used to explain the principle within the CISG, despite significant similarities in doctrine and jurisprudence.

Common law attorneys may find the concept of *Nachfrist* foreign as this term has no direct common law counterpart. In brief, the various Sale of Goods Acts do not rely on the principle of "fundamental breach"; they rather approach avoidance of contract through the breach of contractual terms; that is, breach of a major term or a condition. Breach of warranties (minor terms) only gives rise to a claim of damages. Common law in general holds parties strictly to their time commitments. A breach of a condition automatically allows the aggrieved party to repudiate the contract. There is no need to determine whether such a delay constitutes a fundamental breach or not; the question is one of breach of warranty or condition. The matter is clear, perhaps not flexible, but certain. This does not mean that the buyer cannot give the seller additional time to perform its obligation. A waiver of the time obligation followed by a new notice making time of the essence would achieve in two steps what *Nachfrist* achieves in one.

The purpose behind the flexible remedy of *Nachfrist* is that the CISG, as one of its principles, attempts to keep the contract afoot as long as there is a possibility to perform contractual obligations. This is in line with the attempt to overcome some of the problems of distance, expense, and time involved in terminating an international contract where, operating under another general principle of the CISG, namely good faith, remedial action could have been possible, resulting in a win-win situation.

II. MEANING AND PURPOSE OF *NACHFRIST*

The idea behind *Nachfrist* is that the buyer should not be able to avoid the contract merely because the goods are not delivered on time. A contract can be avoided under the principle of fundamental breach pursuant to CISG Article 25. Under certain circumstances, such as when time is of the essence, late delivery may become a fundamental breach. Article 47 in itself is not a remedy, but rather clarifies a situation that otherwise would be unclear. If the buyer is in a situation where there is uncertainty as to the existence of a reason to avoid the contract, he can overcome this by fixing a *Nachfrist*. As far as the seller is concerned the additional period is a final period; however, the buyer is not barred from fixing additional periods if he so wishes or if he wants to respond to the seller's request for additional time.

The importance the CISG places in reading provisions within the context of the Convention is clearly demonstrated in this instance. Article 47 is closely linked to Article 49(1). In Article 49(1)(a), the buyer is entitled to avoid the contract if the failure of the seller amounts to a fundamental breach. Late delivery, unless time is of the essence, does not amount to a fundamental breach. A buyer may not be certain whether late delivery may be construed as a fundamental breach; however, by fixing a *Nachfrist*, this problem is overcome as the buyer now can rely on Article 49(1)(b), which takes away the uncertainty.

The only uncertainty is the question of "reasonable length" of the additional period of time fixed by the buyer. Article 9 (customary practices), Article 6 (additional time is a clause in the contract), and Article 8 (previous conduct or statements made by parties) provide assistance to the buyer in defining what is a reasonable length of time. Most important, the buyer will rely on the general principles of reasonableness and of good faith, as contained in Article 7. While the additional period is in existence the buyer can only rely on damages for late delivery, but most important, the seller is protected while he is making efforts, perhaps at considerable expense, to deliver the goods as requested.

III. COMPARISON OF PECL ARTICLE 8:106 WITH CISG ARTICLES 47 AND 49(1)(B)

At first glance the two systems have a remarkable similarity, but are also subtly different. The first point to note is that the PECL also introduce *Nachfrist* as an important concept in contractual relations. The mere inclusion indicates that the CISG was correct in its assessment that the concept of *Nachfrist* is important in an international contractual relationship. The second point is a confirmation of the foresight of the CISG because PECL did not introduce major changes, but rather only subtle differences. From this we can deduce that the concept of *Nachfrist* as introduced by the CISG was correct and is of importance in international sales.

The CISG and the PECL recognize the difference between non-performance that amounts to a fundamental breach and non-performance that is not serious enough to constitute a fundamental breach. Both allow the buyer who is not sure whether the non-performance amounts to a fundamental breach the ability to avoid the contract by allowing him to set an additional period of time to perform the contract. Both the CISG and PECL recognize that two conditions must be met. First, the period must be fixed. A telephone call by the buyer to demand prompt delivery does not amount to a fixing of time pursuant to CISG Article 47(1). Second, the period so fixed must be reasonable. The question of what is a reasonable time is a question of fact and is left to the courts to decide.[1] Good faith, which is a principle in both the CISG and PECL, will influence the court in its decision. However, the PECL in its Comment make it clear that, if less than reasonable time was fixed, the aggrieved party "need not serve a second notice; it may terminate after a reasonable time has elapsed from the date of the notice." As far as the CISG is concerned, no jurisprudence has solved this issue; however, it can be argued that a court would invoke good faith and could set a date that fulfills the requirements of the principle of reasonableness.

The CISG in its jurisprudence indicates that *Nachfrist* is not restricted to non-delivery but also extends to faulty delivery.[2] The question as to what is a fixing of an additional period has been interpreted by courts in a liberal sense; that is, with the principle of good faith in mind. A Spanish appellate court[3] held that the buyer's tolerance of late deliveries was equivalent to the granting of a *Nachfrist*. However, a fixing of a period is not necessary if the seller manifests a clear intention not to deliver the goods, and therefore the contract can be avoided pursuant to Article 49.

[1] *See* presentation of more than sixty cases on Art. 47 CISG, available online at <http://cisgw3.law.pace.edu/cisg/text/anno-art-47.html> [visited: 2 May 2005]. *See* also UNCITRAL Digest of Art. 47 case law, available at <http://cisgw3.law.pace.edu/cisg/text/anno-art-47.html#ucd>.

[2] *See* presentation of more than 200 cases on Art. 49, available online at <http://cisgw3.law.pace.edu/cisg/text/anno-art-49.html> [visited: 2 May 2005]. *See* also UNCITRAL Digest of Art. 47 case law, available at <http://cisgw3.law.pace.edu/cisg/text/anno-art-49.html#ucd>.

[3] Spain 3 November 1997 *Audiencia Provincial* [Appellate Court] Barcelona, CLOUT No. 246, case presentation available at <http://cisgw3.law.pace.edu/cases/971103s4.html>.

One area of uncertainty within the CISG has been removed by clearly stating that the buyer may withhold his own performance while an additional period of time is fixed. Another point well worth noting is the different terms used. In the CISG under Article 47 it is the buyer who may fix a time, whereas in PECL it is the aggrieved party, which can be the buyer or seller, depending on the circumstances. Such a variance makes sense as unlike the CISG, the PECL also cover contracts of service. Furthermore, the PECL have managed to cover substance in one Article that in the CISG is contained in Articles 47, 49(1)(b), 63, and 64(1)(b). In the CISG, the latter Articles cover the remedies open to the seller and are reviewed in this database in the discussions on that subject.

IV. CONCLUSION

The principle of *Nachfrist* must be viewed in two ways: as a mandate within the CISG and as another example of the "sea change in the landscape of international trade." The "additional period of time" is contained in basically the same form in both the PECL and the UNIDROIT Principles. It is the domestic systems of law and specifically the common law that are out of step with international developments. The reality is that there is a drastic change in the marketplace for legal services. The PECL in a subtle way will be shaping English common law practices, and it will not be too far in the future when English courts need to deal with such concepts as *Nachfrist*. The fact that the concept of *Nachfrist* has been included in various international laws indicates that certainty now has a brother, namely flexibility.

Globalization requires that legal rules must be flexible in order to be applicable to changing circumstances and avoid costly disputes in circumstances that could have been solved by an instrument like the *Nachfrist*. Common law attorneys must become aware of the existence and basic content of different concepts contained in uniform international law, the CISG, and in international "Restatements" of the law – the PECL and the UNIDROIT Principles – because they will be shaping the rules for contractual dealings in the future.

Cure after date for delivery: Comparison between provisions of the CISG (seller's right to remedy failure to perform: Article 48) and the counterpart provisions of the PECL (Articles 8:104 and 9:303)

Jonathan Yovel

I. GENERAL

A contractual party's right to cure a non-performance under the condition that such cure does not create any – or at least any excessive – hardship for the aggrieved party has emerged from common law traditions to become almost a staple of modern contract law, and of modern sales law in particular.[1]

Different justifications for the principle may be cited, whether in terms of risk allocation, good faith obligations, or the relational approach to contract as a framework of relations between parties that shifts the analytic emphasis from overt rules (whether set contractually or by statute) to the actual framework of relations and interests involved. Whatever the theoretical overview, the principle of cure is perhaps the most important deviation from strict doctrines of liability for breach, and as such it maintains an important relation to the doctrine of contract avoidance ("termination" in the context of the PECL), as discussed next.

Curing a non-performance may be relevant in various contexts: payment, defective or missing documents, non-conforming or non-delivered goods, etc. In the PECL – which apply to any and all contractual transactions, not only sales or international sales – Art. 8:104 recognizes a non-performing party's general right to cure, limited by parameters that are discussed presently. In the CISG – divided as it is into seller's and buyer's rights and obligations – the right to cure non-performance depends upon the nature of the non-performance and the time of cure; it is divided into different typical situations, covered by several Articles. Some grant parties the right to cure defective performance prior to the time of the projected performance as contracted: in those cases, cure limits the aggrieved parties' power to declare contracts avoided in situations of anticipatory breach. Thus, Art. 34 relates to curing defective or non-conforming documents, and Art. 37 deals with breach in respect to goods. Other articles, such as Art. 46(2) and (3), refer to the aggrieved party's power to require curative performance. These are relatively non-controversial issues, and one may argue that refusal to allow cure prior to the time set for performance is *ad definitio* a breach of good faith obligations. Indeed, the true meaning of cure pertains to a defaulting party's right to cure a defective performance or non-performance *after* the time of the projected performance has passed. Thus, this commentary deals with the seller's right to cure under CISG Art. 48 and PECL Art 8:104, which extend the right to cure once the fact of breach has been established.

[1] For a survey of national systems *see* Ole Lando & Hugh Beale eds., *Principles of European Contract Law: Parts I and II*, Kluwer Law International (2000) 368–370; *also* Treitel, *Remedies*, §276. Such is the general case in common law, expressed already in *Borrowman, Phillips & Co. v. Free & Hollis* (1878) 4 Q.B.D. 500. *See* Jacob S. Ziegel, "The Remedial Provisions in the Vienna Sales Convention: Some Common Law Perspectives" in Galston & Smit (ed.), *International Sales: The United Nations Convention on Contracts for the International Sale of Goods* (Matthew Bender, 1984) pp. 9–1 to 9–43, available online at <http://cisgw3.law.pace.edu/cisg/biblio/ziegel6.html>. The English Sales of Goods Act does not include a seller's general right to cure, whereas the UCC §2–508 famously does. For elaboration on the position of English law *see* Goode, "Commercial Law" 298–301; Rex J. Ahdar, "Seller Cure in the Sale of Goods", *1990 Lloyd's Mar. Com. L. Q.* 364. Other commentators are more skeptical concerning the availability of post-breach cure under English law; *see* Anette Gärtner, "Britain and the CISG: The Case for Ratification – A Comparative Analysis with Special Reference to German Law" *in Review of the Convention on Contracts for the International Sale of Goods (CISG)*, Kluwer Law International (2000–2001) 59–81, available online at <http://cisgw3.law.pace.edu/cisg/biblio/gartner.html>; *see also* "Sale and Supply of Goods," 85, *Scot. Law Com.* 58 (1983) para 2.38 according to which "There is great uncertainty, at least in English law, as to the existence and extent of the seller's right to repair or replace defective goods."

Although both the PECL and CISG recognize a right to cure under certain conditions, they differ both in general approach and in the specific rights granted. This may not be surprising, as the PECL apply to any and all contractual transactions, not only sales or international sales; however, the seller's right to cure is closely related to the buyer's right to avoid the contract, an issue on which the CISG and PECL share similar approaches.[2] Indeed, the relation between cure and avoidance must be a central topic for analysis once the nature of the right to cure has been clarified.

II. THE JURISPRUDENTIAL NATURE OF THE RIGHT TO CURE

One must distinguish between a breaching party's *general* (or *unqualified*) right to cure and a *qualified* right. A general right means that within certain time frame and other objective constraints, the breaching party may exercise the right unilaterally, independent of anything the aggrieved party may do in respect to the breach. A qualified right means that the breaching party's right to cure a non-performance depends upon the aggrieved party's failure to use some power or exercise some right that renders cure unavailable.[3]

The primary right that aggrieved parties may hold and whose exercise would frustrate any subsequent attempt to cure is the right to declare the contract avoided.[4] Once the contract is legally avoided there can be no cure.[5] Thus a contractual regime may subject the power to avoid the contract to the right to cure.[6] In such cases, the breaching party is immune – at least temporarily, until the curative period is over and cure fails – from the aggrieved party's power to declare the contract avoided. In all other cases, any post-avoidance communication or indeed curative performance by the breaching party would fail *qua* cure, amounting to an offer of a new or modified contract that may or may not excuse past breaches.[7]

The following discussion analyzes the relations between cure and avoidance of the contract in the PECL and CISG along these theoretical lines. Both the CISG and PECL allow for post-breach cure, and both restrict the right to circumstances discussed in

[2] *See* Jonathan Yovel, "Comparison between provisions of the CISG (Buyer's right to avoid the contract: Article 49) and the counterpart provisions of the PECL (Articles 9:301, 9:303 and 8:106)," available online at <http://cisgw3.law.pace.edu/cisg/biblio/yovel49.html>.

[3] Commentators frequently use "right" and "power" interchangeably. Hohfeld's analytic language would be useful here (Hohfeld supplied a Saussurian-style analytic syntax whereby legal concepts are defined through their relation to other concepts): to claim that A holds a *right* – properly defined – correlates with B's *duty*; A's *liberty* correlates with B's *lack of right* to object, and A's *power* correlates with B being *subject* to that power in the sense that using the power would change the normative array of rights, duties, liberties, powers, subjections, immunities etc. between the parties. Thus the "right to declare the contract avoided" is, properly speaking, a legal *power* (it changes the parties' legal relations), as is the buyer's *power* to set a *Nachfrist* period; but as the seller's "right to cure" does not in itself change the relational framework yet does require the buyer to accept the curative tender it is, properly speaking, a *right*. Had it required no compliance from the buyer – had it been performed, say, by the seller and a third party – cure would be, properly speaking, a *liberty*. *See* Welsley Hohfeld, *Fundamental Legal Conceptions as Applied in Juridical Reasoning* (New Haven: Yale University Press, 1964 [1919]). For an application of the Hohfeldian matrix to the analysis of contractual relations *see* Jonathan Yovel, "What is Contract Law 'About'? Speech Act Theory and a Critique of 'Skeletal Promises,'" 94 *Nw. U. L. Rev.* (2000) 937–962.

[4] *See* PECL Art. 9:305.

[5] *See* Ziegel, *supra* note at 9–21.

[6] *See*, e.g., UNIDROIT Principles Art. 7.1.4(2); BGB [German Civil Code] §323(1); *see also infra* note 32 and keyed text.

[7] Cure may, of course, be reached at in this way as well. Such may be the case even when declarations of avoidance were deemed ineffective (e.g., because the alleged breach was not fundamental). In such cases, following a new agreement the question of the scope of the seller's obligation, although in essence being curative in nature and in relation to the prior contractual relations between the parties, is a matter of general contractual interpretation. Courts would take into consideration the curative context, but allow that parties have since undertaken a new allocation of performances and risks. Such was the case in France 26 April 1995 *Cour d'appel* [Appellate Court] Grenoble (*Marques Roque Joachim v. Manin Rivière*), available online at <http://cisgw3.law.pace.edu/cases/950426f2.html>.

detail below; however, whereas the CISG allows for cure subject to avoidance of the contract, the PECL make no such overt, general qualification. As argued below, contextual considerations both rationalize this discrepancy and mitigate it.

III. CURE FOR WHAT?

When analyzing cure mechanisms, two initial questions emerge: What failures of performance may be cured? Under what restrictions? Although the second question is dealt with in detail below, the former requires special initial attention. Under CISG Art. 48(1) the seller is allowed to cure "*any* failure" to perform his obligations. As scholars comment,[8] this is a general provision that covers fundamental and non-fundamental breaches alike. Likewise, PECL Art. 8:104 covers all "tenders of performance" that do not "conform to the contract," whether the non-conformance is fundamental or not, as long as the delay in performance itself does not constitute a fundamental non-performance. The breaching party's right to cure, then, initially operates independently of the distinction between fundamental and non-fundamental breaches on which its inverse right – the aggrieved party's right to avoid the contract – hinges.

However, unlike the CISG, PECL Art. 8:104 restricts the right to cure to those cases in which the very delay in performance does not constitute a fundamental non-performance. In cases where "time is of the essence" as the Comment to PECL 8:104 puts it,[9] the only way to achieve cure is through the aggrieved party setting a *Nachfrist* period; otherwise, the non-performing party has no right to cure. Indeed, this point requires some clarification: PECL Art. 8:104 sets apart a category of curative tenders that, although indeed remedying the initial non-performance at the time of the projected contractual performance – whether fundamental or not (e.g., a non-conformity of goods) – would, if allowed, constitute a fundamental non-performance at the time of cure. In transactions in which the time of performance is of the essence, the delay inherently associated with any curative performance may be such as to constitute a fundamental non-performance, even if the initial failure of performance was not fundamental and is indeed cured. In such cases, the non-performing party has no right to cure, and, accordingly, the aggrieved party has no obligation to accept cure. In granting the right to cure, Art. 8:104 is indifferent to the question of the fundamentality of the initial non-performance, but would not allow the curative tender itself to amount to a fundamental non-performance. Otherwise, the right to cure under Art. 8:104 exists in all (and only in all) cases where the delay itself – although *ad definitio* amounting to a non-performance in relation to the contract – does not constitute a fundamental non-performance.

In both the CISG and PECL, the crucial question of the relation between the seller's right to cure and the buyer's right to avoid the contract arises; ultimately, that question will determine in what cases the right to cure may actually take effect as a right, rather than a newly arrived agreement between the parties. This topic must be analyzed in detail as follows.

IV. THE RELATION BETWEEN CURE AND AVOIDANCE (TERMINATION) OF THE CONTRACT

Both the CISG and PECL must regulate the relations between the seller's right to cure "any" failure to perform and the buyer's power to declare the contract avoided in certain cases (namely, fundamental and tantamount breaches). That is because cure and avoidance cannot both occur in the context of the same contract – it is an absurdity to have a contract both avoided and cured. Cure and avoidance compete for positions of relative

[8] *See* Chengwei Liu, "Cure by Non-Conforming Party: Perspectives from the CISG, UNIDROIT Principles and PECL," available online at <http://cisgw3.law.pace.edu/cisg/biblio/chengwei1.html>.
[9] Ole Lando & Hugh Beale, *supra* note 1, at 368–372.

preeminence in the same normative space while each is operated by a different party.[10] Granted, a successful curative performance by the seller – one that adheres to the relevant rules, etc. – cures her breach, *ex post*; it, however, does not entail that the seller's *ex-ante right* to cure pre-empts the aggrieved buyer's power to avoid the contract. Accordingly, one can identify three theoretical models for relations between the right to cure and the power to avoid the contract:

1) The pre-emptive model, according to which the right to cure pre-empts the power to declare the contract avoided, with the logical corollary that no avoidance can become effective unless proper opportunity for cure has been allowed;[11]
2) The unconditional model, according to which avoidance of the contract is allowed irrespective of the availability of cure, and once the contract has been avoided no cure – even when otherwise available – could take place;
3) The independent or "race" model according to which whether the right to cure or a declaration of avoidance is invoked earlier in time determines which becomes effective, rendering the other unavailable; but no *a priori* normative hierarchy is established.

In the remainder of this section, the three models are invoked in the contexts of the Convention and the European Principles while remarking on the differences between their approaches, as well as that of the UNIDROIT Principles. As we shall see, both PECL and CISG take the unconditional model (2) as their general framework while weaving in elements of the independent model (3) as well.

1. Cure for Non-Fundamental Breaches under the CISG

The relation between cure and avoidance of the contract in the CISG has been subject to considerable controversy within the drafting committee[12] and remains an academic controversy today.

Obviously, whether the right to cure is contingent upon the contract not having been avoided is a major relational characteristic of the contractual framework. However, both PECL and to an even greater degree the CISG apply a stringent approach to the buyer's right to avoid the contract following breach by the seller.[13] To wit, declaring the contract avoided is generally reserved – with one significant exception – to *fundamental* breaches. This means that the right to cure is unqualified in the sense defined above in both PECL and CISG for any non-fundamental breach.

Does that last statement indeed hold? It might be argued that under both PECL and CISG avoidance of the contract may precede and thus frustrate the seller's attempt to cure even in the cases of some non-fundamental breaches. The issue here is, of course, that dealt with by CISG Art. 49(1)(b), whose proper interpretation has resulted in several scholarly disputes, and by its counterpart PECL 8:106(3). Those provisions allow for avoidance of the contract even for non-fundamental breaches, as long as three conditions are satisfied:

1) That the breach in question is one of non-delivery (according to CISG) or delay in performance (according to PECL);

[10] Although avoidance and enforcement of the contract also negate each other in the same normative space – they maintain opposite obligations for the parties – it is only the aggrieved party that chooses between them.
[11] *See infra* note 32 and keyed text.
[12] *Official Records of the United Nations Conference on Contracts for the International Sale of Goods*, Vienna 10 March–11 April 1980, A/CONF. 97/19, at 40 *et seq.*, available online at <http://cisgw3.law.pace.edu/cisg/text/link48.html>.
[13] *See* Yovel, *supra* note 2.

2) That the non-performing party was allowed a reasonable time extension to perform – the so-called *Nachfrist* period; and
3) That he has failed to do so. The non-fundamental breach is then "upgraded" and avoidance of the contract becomes available.

On the face of it, this seems to belie the cure doctrine of CISG Art. 48. In fact, however, the two doctrines sit very well together because of the curative nature of the *Nachfrist* mechanism. In fact, whether the buyer allows a curative period on a *Nachfrist* mechanism, such as provided by CISG Art. 47 or PECL Art. 8:106, or whether the seller invokes cure based on the provisions discussed here, are two sides of the same coin and probably of little practical importance. Because the requirements of reasonableness direct both doctrines,[14] the curative period in both cases is of the same nature.

2. Cure for Non-Fundamental Breaches under the PECL

The first clause of PECL Art. 8:104 simply states the right to cure a non-conforming tender at any time prior to the designated time for performance; it is therefore the counterpart of CISG Art. 37 rather than Art. 49 and is relatively non-controversial. The second clause of Art. 8:104 grants a non-performing party the right to cure *after* the designated time to perform has passed (of course, following the sphere of application of the PECL, in any contractual context and not limited to sellers). However, unlike the CISG, this right under the PECL is limited to cases where the delay would not amount to a fundamental non-performance. The nature of this limitation is discussed below in the section devoted to cure; it does not affect the clear rule that, in all cases of non-fundamental non-performance, the non-performing party maintains a general right to cure.

What is being cured under Art. 8:104? The language here is somewhat peculiar: it is a "tender of performance" that "does not conform" to the contract. The term "tender performance" appears elsewhere in the Principles, though infrequently[15]; in most cases, to "tender performance" seems to mean "to perform," whether the performance conforms to the contract or not. To emphasize this meaning, the examples given in the PECL Comment on cure include both cases of sales and of services.[16] Art. 8:104 also indicates that cure occurs in cases where the other party refused "acceptance" of the performance, although parties under the PECL generally have no right to reject non-conforming tender and the so-called perfect tender of the UCC § 2–601 is unknown to it.[17] The defining words are, therefore, "tender conforming to the contract," similar to that used in Art. 9:401 (Right to Reduce Price).

[14] For reasonableness being a general principle of the CISG (and in this somewhat mitigating the absence thereof of a general obligation to act in good faith) *see* Albert H. Kritzer, "Overview Comments on Reasonableness," available online at <http://cisgw3.law.pace.edu/cisg/text/reason.html>: "Reasonableness is specifically mentioned in thirty-seven provisions of the CISG and clearly alluded to elsewhere in the Uniform Sales Law. Reasonableness is a general principle of the CISG." *See* also comments by Jelena Vilus, available online at <http://cisgw3.law.pace.edu/cisg/text/reason.html#vilus>; rpr. in *Homenaje a Jorge Barrera Graf*, vol. 2, Mexico: Universidad Nacional Autónoma de Mexico (1989) 1440–1441. For the definition of reasonableness recited in the Principles of European Contract Law and references to reasonableness in continental and common law domestic rules, doctrine, and jurisprudence, go to <http://cisgw3.law.pace.edu/cisg/text/reason.html#def>. For further discussion regarding the correlation between the PECL's definition of reasonableness and the meaning of this term to CISG legislators when they used the concept in drafting the Convention's provisions, *see* <http://cisgw3.law.pace.edu/cisg/text/reason.html#over>.

[15] *See* especially PECL Arts. 6:108 (Quality of Performance), 7:103 (Early Performance), 9:201 (Right to Withhold Performance), and 9:303 (Notice of Termination).

[16] *See supra* note 9.

[17] *See* Peter Schlechtriem, "Interpretation, gap-filling and further development of the UN Sales Convention," available online at <http://cisgw3.law.pace.edu/cisg/biblio/schlechtriem6.html>.

What does "non-conformity" of tender to the contract (as opposed of non-conformity of goods) mean?

- Specifically, is the language of "non-conforming tender" different in any material sense from the simpler "non-performance," which is more prevalent in the PECL?
- Is the right to cure under Art. 8:104 reserved to cases where some performance was tendered, as opposed to total failure to perform?

There is nothing in the short PECL Comment on cure to indicate such a construction. Although legal regimes sometimes distinguish between complete failure to perform and partial failure,[18] and although one can admit to the logic of allowing for cure in cases of debtors who at least tried and managed to complete a portion of their obligations, such a distinction is generally reserved to specific areas of law and is justified by specific contexts. It does not seem correct to make it a core precept of the general principle of cure.

Thus, for the time being and until tribunals and cases offer casuistic constructions of Art. 8:104, the conclusion should be that there is no essential difference between "tender non-conforming to the contract" and "any failure to perform," the more overt language of the CISG Art. 48(1).

3. Cure for Fundamental Breaches under the CISG

The CISG's treatment of the relation between cure and avoidance of the contract changes drastically in respect to fundamental breaches. Under CISG Art. 48(1) the seller is allowed to cure "*any* failure" to perform his obligations. On the other hand, under Art. 49(1) the buyer may avoid the contract where the seller's failure amounts to a fundamental breach, whether the seller offers to cure or not.

The relation between the two competing rights is set up in Art. 49(1) where the operative language makes the seller's right to cure "subject to Art. 49." Art. 49 regulates avoidance of the contract following either fundamental breach or "constructed fundamentality" following the failure to perform throughout a *Nachfrist* period. As the second case in fact allows for cure – initiated by the aggrieved buyer – the remainder of this section discusses cure in cases of fundamental breaches. What does "subject to Art. 49" mean?

- Does it mean that under CISG the seller's right to cure is qualified, so that in case of fundamental breach it can be cut off through the buyer's exercise of his power to declare the contract avoided?
- Or does it even indicate that cure is not designated for cases of fundamental breaches at all?

If either of these is the proper construction of the relation between Arts. 48 and 49, then the right to cure in cases of fundamental breach under CISG seems limited indeed; it would then also stand in contrast to the PECL's much more liberal approach to cure. In the following, I argue that the proper construction of the relation between cure and avoidance of the contract under the PECL in fact allows for cure even in cases of fundamental breach. However, in those cases they are indeed subject to being cut off by the buyer's exercise of the right to avoid the contract; hence a qualified right to cure in the terms specified above.

[18] Such is the case with the construction of "non-delivery" in CISG Art. 49(1)(b) that authorities agree is different from "partial delivery"; *see* Yovel, *supra* note 2. In other contexts, some legal systems allow defenses against enforcement of negotiable instruments in cases of complete failure of consideration tendered but not in cases of partial failure, etc.

It is worthwhile to note that under the UNIDROIT Principles the breaching party's right to cure is unequivocally stronger than the aggrieved party's power to terminate the contract. UNIDROIT Principles Art. 7.1.4(2) states, "The right to cure is not precluded by notice of termination"; the Comment adds, "If the aggrieved party has rightfully terminated the contract . . . the effects of termination . . . are also suspended by an effective notice of cure. If the non-performance is cured, the notice of termination is inoperative." This is not the place for a comprehensive critique of this approach; this approach seems unattractive in the extreme in the sense that rightful terminations of contracts may posthumously be rendered inoperative, thus introducing serious uncertainty into the calculations of the aggrieved part who has terminated the contract rightfully and wishes to move on; it also plays havoc with the conceptual integrity of termination of contract.[19] Nor does the PECL contain a similar provision, as discussed below.

According to Professor Honnold, the seller's right to cure under Art. 48, being more specific than the general right to avoid the contract, prevails over the buyer's right to avoid the contract.[20] With respect, such a construction might hold absent the operative words "subject to Art. 49." As the clause stands,[21] following a long and tortured legislative history in the drafting committee,[22] it clearly regulates the relationship between cure and avoidance by creating a hierarchy between them: cure is available only inasmuch as the power to avoid the contract under Art. 49 has not been rightfully exercised.[23]

[19] For a similar criticism *see* Christopher Kee, "Commentary on the Manner in which the UNIDROIT Principles May Be Used to Interpret or Supplement Article 48 of the CISG," July 2004, available online at <http://cisgw3.law.pace.edu/cisg/principles/uni48.html>.

[20] *See* John Honnold, *Uniform Law for International Sales under the 1980 United Nations Convention, Kluwer Law International*, 3d ed. (1999); pp. 320–21, available online at <http://cisgw3.law.pace.edu/cisg/biblio/ho48.html>. With respect, I dispute this jurisprudential point on the following grounds. Cure is certainly more specific than breach in general, in the sense that the set of all the cases of cure is a subset of all the cases of breach (it is complemented by the set of non-cured breaches). Had avoidance been available for any breach, the set of all available avoidances would then be identical with the set of all breaches and Honnold's argument would hold. However, under both the CISG and the PECL, avoidance of the contract is generally limited to cases of fundamental breach (and even then not to all such cases, as reasonable time limitations render avoidance unavailable in some cases). There are cases where cure is available but avoidance is not, namely the set of non-fundamental breaches. Hence both the set of all instances of cure and the set of all rightful avoidances are both independent subsets of the general set of breaches – they maintain a certain zone of convergence, namely, the set of fundamental breaches that where the contract has not been avoided – yet none is more or less specific than the other. Indeed, to claim that the set of instances of cure is in some sense a subset of the set of available avoidances is simply assuming that which is to be determined.

[21] I use the term "clause" here according to the American usage of normative rather than textual structure to designate a complete and separate norm, even if within the formal structure of the text holding it, it does not occupy a separate position.

[22] *See UNCITRAL Digest of Case Law on the United Nations Convention on the International Sale of Goods* (8 June 2004), A/CN.9/SER.C/DIGEST/CISG/48; Digest 2. Available at: <http://www.uncitral.org/english/clout/digest_cisg_e.htm>. *See also* John O. Honnold, *Uniform Law for International Sales under the 1980 United Nations Convention* (Kluwer 1980) 296 (hereafter cited as "Honnold"); Michael Will, "Article 48" *in Bianca-Bonell Commentary on the International Sales Law*, Giuffrè: Milan (1987) 347–358 available online at <http://cisgw3.law.pace.edu/cisg/biblio/will-bb48.html>; and Mirghasem Jafarzadeh, "Buyer's Right to Withhold Performance and Termination of Contract: A Comparative Study under English Law, Vienna Convention on Contracts for the International Sale of Goods 1980, Iranian and *Shi'ah* Law" (2001) available online at <http://cisgw3.law.pace.edu/cisg/biblio/jafarzadeh1.html>.

[23] Some courts appear to have in fact established a different hierarchy. In one German case, the court held that the right to avoid the contract under Art. 49(b)(2) was not available to a buyer who did not allow the seller the proper opportunity to cure; hence, the declaration of avoidance in that case was deemed unlawful. However, in that case the court also ruled that no fundamental breach was committed as the goods that were delivered – fabrics for the manufacture of goods – passed the relevant tests of conformity. As this was not a case of non-delivery, Art. 49(b) could not apply, and if avoidance of the contract was unavailable, that must have been the cause, not the relations between avoidance of the contract and cure. Furthermore, this case should be read in the context of CISG Arts. 47 and 48(2); as the seller has communicated to the

As Professor Ziegel puts it, "no right to cure survived avoidance of the contract by the buyer."[24] Thus, under terms of CISG Art. 48(1), the buyer's right to avoid under Art. 49 is an independent right unaffected by the seller's intentions to cure. This conclusion is strengthened by Art. 48(2) that deals with suspension of the buyer's power to declare the contract avoided during a curative period requested by the seller: the aggrieved buyer's communicative act (including failure to communicate) is necessary for such a suspension. Had the seller's right to cure been pre-emptive in relation to the buyer's power to avoid the contract, no such communicative act on behalf of the buyer would be necessary: the buyer would then have been automatically enjoined from exercising the power to avoid the contract during the period specified in the seller's notice (which would not then be a "request" at all) (for discussion see below). Case law generally supports this conclusion,[25] although cases exist in which courts remark, at least in *obiter dicta*, and *contra* the analysis presented here,[26] that the buyer's right to avoid the contract is in some manner contingent upon giving the seller a proper opportunity to cure the defect.[27]

buyer his intention to cure; the unavailability of avoidance during the ensuing period follows Art. 48(2), not necessarily an inverse relation between Arts. 48 and 49 to the one argued for above. Additionally, the court held that by sending samples of fabric instead of curing goods themselves the seller has performed lawfully, as there was no certainty that the buyer would accept the substitute goods. To me, it seems that the court deemed that the seller has performed reasonably and in good faith in attempting to cure the alleged breach. In itself, however, that cannot change the normative hierarchy between avoidance of the contract (which under the CISG as under PECL is not a matter of fault but one of objective performance) and cure under CISG. Indeed, the fact that the power to avoid is normally suspended following Art. 48(2) is a logical corollary of that hierarchy; it would be redundant otherwise. Germany, 24 September 1998 *Landgericht* [District Court] Regensburg; case presentation including English translation available online at <http://cisgw3.law.pace.edu/cases/980924g1.html>.

[24] Ziegel, *supra* note 1, at 9–21. Such is also Professor Schlechtriem's opinion, *see* Peter Schlechtriem, *Uniform Sales Law – The UN-Convention on Contracts for the International Sale of Goods* (Manz, Vienna: 1986) pp. 76–77, available online at <http://cisgw3.law.pace.edu/cisg/biblio/schlechtriem.html>. Professor Schlechtriem adds that this construction was objected to at the committee by the German delegation that wished to strengthen the right to cure so that it did not become cut off by avoidance of the contract, but that this approach was not ultimately accepted. For case law where the court had – among other determinations – accepted the buyer's effective declaration of avoidance of the contract as putting an end to the availability of cure by the breaching seller, *see* Italy 24 November 1989 Court of First Instance Parma (*Foliopack v. Daniplast*), presentation including English translation available online at <http://cisgw3.law.pace.edu/cases/891124i3.html>.

[25] This conclusion is supported by case law. *See*

- Italy 24 November 1989 Court of First Instance Parma (*Foliopack v. Daniplast*), CLOUT case No. 90, case presentation including English translation available at <http://cisgw3.law.pace.edu/cases/891124i3.html>;
- Germany 17 September 1991 *Oberlandesgericht* [Appellate Court] Frankfurt, CLOUT case No. 2, case presentation including English translation available at <http://cisgw3.law.pace.edu/cisg/cases/910917g1.html>;
- Germany 1 February 1995 *Oberlandesgericht* [Appellate Court] Oldenburg, CLOUT case No. 165, case presentation including English translation available at <http://cisgw3.law.pace.edu/cisg/cases/950201g1.html>;
- Germany 25 June 1997 *Bundesgerichtshof* [Supreme Court], CLOUT case No. 235, case presentation including English translation available at <http://cisgw3.law.pace.edu/cisg/cases/970625g2.html>;
- ICC Arbitration Case No. 7531 of 1994, CLOUT case No. 304, case presentation available at <http://cisgw3.law.pace.edu/cisg/cases/947531i1.html>.

See also Official Records of the United Nations Conference on Contracts for the International Sale of Goods, Vienna, 10 March–11 April 1980 (United Nations publication, Sales No. E.81.IV.3), p. 41.

[26] As well as *contra* the proper construction of CISG Art. 49 that requires no grace period for performance as a condition for declaring the contract avoided.

[27] *See supra* note 23; other courts casually argue that "[seller] offered to repair the defect: [buyer] should have accepted this proposal, instead of seeking avoidance of her contract with the [seller]", even in cases of alleged fundamental breach; Switzerland 27 April 1992 District Court Locarno Campagna, case presentation including English translation available at <http://cisgw3.law.pace.edu/cases/920427s1.html>. Such dicta, in consideration of the above argument, seem to reflect preferred rather than the applicable law.

4. Cure and Termination under the PECL

As noted above, unlike the CISG, PECL Art. 8:104 restricts the right to cure to those cases in which the very delay in performance does not constitute a fundamental non-performance. This is not a matter of competition between the non-performing party's right to cure and the aggrieved party's power to terminate the contract (under PECL Art. 9:301), which would obviously kick in in such cases. Whether the aggrieved party intends to terminate or not, in cases where "time is of the essence" as the PECL Comment on Art. 8:104 puts it,[28] the only way to achieve cure is through the aggrieved party setting a *Nachfrist* period (i.e., suspending its power to terminate the contract for the duration of the curative period).

Although the CISG, in the opening words of Art. 48(1), sets the relations between cure and avoidance of the contract, the PECL does not overtly make the right to cure subject to the buyer's power to terminate the contract. In the terms discussed above, the right to cure in Art. 8:104, although limited to the classes of cases discussed above, is general, rather than qualified.

This would seem to indicate a stronger right to cure in the PECL than in the CISG that would extend to the relation between cure and termination. However, as noted above, Art. 8:104 limits the right to cure to cases where the *delay* in performance would not amount to a fundamental non-performance. Under PECL 9:301, only fundamental non-performances allow the buyer to terminate the contract.[29] It thus follows that the seller has no right to cure in any case where due to the delay the buyer holds the power to terminate the contract, even if the buyer eventually does not exercise that power.

Under PECL Art. 8:104, the question of whether the seller's right to cure is or is not subject to the buyer's power to terminate the contract simply cannot occur in cases where the power to terminate stems from the very delay associated with the curative tender. What about cases of fundamental non-performance that may be cured without the delay amounting to fundamental non-performance? Such cases potentially involve two competing norms: ostensibly, they allow for the non-performing party's right to cure under Art. 8:104, as well as for the aggrieved party's power to terminate the contract under Art. 9:301. What is the relation between these two norms?

Had there been no overt solution to this question we would have to move toward jurisprudential considerations, such as offered by Honnold (e.g., examining whether there is some established solution to a clash of the two norms (such as the application of the more specific over the more general one) or employing some general framework of risk allocation). In the context of the PECL, however, interior analysis shows that the power to terminate the contract is generally independent and effectively not contingent upon the right to cure, as follows.

The general way in which termination of contract in the PECL is executed is through appropriate notices (see Art. 9:301). It is typical of the PECL that it regulates substantive rights through a regulation of the corresponding notices.[30] Art. 9:303(3)(a), allows the aggrieved party to give a notice of termination either before or after a late tender – such as

[28] *See supra* note 9.

[29] Termination for non-fundamental delays in performance is also available following a *Nachfrist* period set by the buyer (*see* PECL Art. 8:106(3)); however, in such cases it is pointless to ask if cure is available as the essence of the *Nachfrist* mechanism is the granting of a curative period, although set by the buyer rather than by the seller.

[30] This is of course not particular to the PECL: as the German *Bundesgerichtshof* [Federal Court] spells it, "provisions of the law ... like para. 323 BGB [provision of the Civil Code of Germany that deals with termination], are only applicable if the notice of termination ... was validly declared." Case VIII ZR 140/75, Date 3 November 1976, English translation available online at <http://www.ucl.ac.uk/laws/global_law/german-cases/print_bundes.shtml?03nov1976>

cure – has been made; the only restriction is that for a post-cure notice of termination to be effective it must be given in reasonable time. This is therefore not merely a procedural rule regarding the proper way to exchange notices, but a regulation of the relations between termination and cure in the PECL. Under PECL Art. 9:305(1), which governs the effects of termination of contract, "Termination of the contract releases both parties from their obligation to effect and to receive future performance." Cure is obviously a future performance (the language of Art. 8:104 is "tender of performance," but the semantic difference is meaningless), and so termination of the contract under PECL releases the aggrieved party from any obligation to receive cure, exactly as its effect is to relinquish her right to enforce the contract through specific performance.

PECL Art. 9:303(3)(b) mitigates the harshness – for the non-performing party – created by the strict hierarchy in favor of termination over cure in Art. 9:303(3)(a). It determines that in cases in which the aggrieved party "knows or has reason to know" of forthcoming cure in reasonable time, it must notify the curing party of its refusal to accept cure in order to maintain its power to terminate the contract. Failure to notify the curing party accordingly will render termination of the contract unavailable and the road to cure open; however, a notice of refusal to accept cure would keep the power to terminate the contract alive. Even then – unless the refusal to accept cure includes or is constructed to include a notice of termination of the contract – the right to cure under Art. 8:104 would still hold. Only a termination of the contract would relieve the aggrieved party from her obligation to accept cure. The conclusion then must be that the right to curative performance depends on the contract not having been previously terminated.

Art. 9:303(3)(b) is a relational protection of the non-performing party's reliance interests in the context of curative performance, but it obviously recognizes the aggrieved party's power to terminate the contract, which can be rendered ineffective only under the specified circumstances indicated. Note, that the onus-creating language in PECL Art. 9:303(3)(b) relating to the aggrieved party "knows or has reason to know" is wider than under the corresponding CISG Art. 48(2) and (3), according to which the information relating to the forthcoming cure must be communicated by the breaching party itself. The PECL recognizes that there are instances in which the aggrieved party should assume that cure is forthcoming, even absent direct communication from the breaching party to that effect.

Of course, the aggrieved party's notification to the non-performing, cure-aspiring party under 9:303(3)(b) may be that it refuses cure and hereby terminates the contract; like under the CISG, the PECL do not offer non-performing parties a pre-emptive right to cure in cases of fundamental and tantamount non-performances (there are no other relevant cases in fact), unless the aggrieved party assents to accept cure or unreasonably fails to notify the curing party that it would not accept it.

The analytic conclusion then must be that the power to terminate the contract under PECL – which exists only in cases of fundamental and tantamount breaches – is independent of any allowance for cure, except where the aggrieved party's power becomes suspended under Art. 9:303(3)(b). This differs from the approach of several national legal systems. As Professor Zimmermann explains it, in German sales law the right to "supplementary performance" is the aggrieved buyer's "primary right."[31] Although not spelt out as such,[32] termination of the contract under German law generally becomes

[31] Reinhard Zimmermann, "Liability for Non-Conformity: The New System of Remedies in German Sales Law and Its Historical Context," 10th John Maurice Kelly Memorial Lecture, Dublin 2004, at pp. 38–9.

[32] *See* BGB §§ 437 *et seq*.

available to the aggrieved party following the breaching party's failure to cure.[33] That is not the approach of either the CISG or the PECL.

Under the PECL, termination of the contract releases the aggrieved party from the obligation to accept cure and thus nullifies the non-performing party's right to cure, which otherwise exists in relation to both fundamental and non-fundamental non-performances alike (with the exception of the fundamentality of the delay itself, as discussed above). The aggrieved party is allowed to terminate the contract even after a curative tender, as long as it does so in reasonable time. Of course, a successful cure may frustrate the availability of post-cure termination if the cure – as a successful cure should – renders the non-performance at the time of cure non-fundamental.

5. No Pre-Emptive Cure as Unqualified Right under the CISG and PECL

Both the CISG and PECL allow for some measure of pre-emptive cure (i.e., cure that renders avoidance of the contract unavailable, whether temporarily or irrevocably). This does not mean, however, that pre-emptive cure is given the normative status of *right* that unilaterally tramps rights and powers held by the aggrieved party. Under CISG Art. 48(2), if the aggrieved buyer allows the seller to cure during the time indicated in his request (whether by assenting or failing to reply), she is barred from avoiding the contract during that period. Note, however, that the decision whether to suspend the power to avoid the contract or not remains with the aggrieved buyer: she may always answer in the negative to a seller's request. As the seller's right to cure operates whether the buyer consents to accept cure or not, the buyer's refusal to accept cure in itself has no legal effect other than keeping her power to avoid the contract effective. However – as concluded above – nor is the buyer's power to avoid the contract effected merely by the seller's intention or efforts to cure. That power becomes available only in cases of fundamental and tantamount breaches, and we conclude that those are the cases in which Art. 48(2) really matters.

The question of pre-emptive cure becomes relevant in cases of fundamental breach, because otherwise the seller has no right to avoid the contract. Yet the only way in which cure can be pre-emptive in those cases is when the buyer agrees in advance to withhold exercising her power to avoid the contract for an indicated duration; and under both the PECL and CISG the buyer's silence operates as such an assent to cure.

6. Conclusion

Under the risk-allocating terms of CISG Art. 48(1) (no unreasonable delay, no inconvenience to buyer, and assumption of costs by seller), the seller holds an unqualified right to cure in all cases of non-fundamental breach.[34] However, the seller's right to cure in cases of fundamental breach is qualified in that it may be cut off and become unavailable if the seller rightfully avoids the contract under Art. 49(1), unless the buyer has assented to accept cure or failed to object to it, which would result in suspension of her power to avoid the contract under Art. 48(2).[35]

[33] BGB § 323(1). That is the general case; there are specific clauses, such as § 635 (for contractor's option to cure). BGB § 323(2) lists several categories of exemptions and scattered clauses add to those categories (e.g., § 440 and the obvious § 325(5)).

[34] Cure obviously becomes available also in cases of non-fundamental non-delivery if the buyer has set a *Nachfrist* period. Failure to cure throughout that period makes avoidance of the contract available to the buyer under CISG Art. 49(1)(b).

[35] Honnold's proposal to internalize the offer to cure into the construction of the fundamentality of the breach would have been a brilliant resolution to the relation between cure and avoidance; unfortunately it was not accepted. *See* Ziegel, *supra* note 1, at 9–21. *See also* Michida, "Cancellation of Contract," 27 *Am. J. Comp. L.* 286–288 (1979), available online at <http://cisgw3.law.pace.edu/cisg/biblio/michida.html> Occasionally courts would determine that willingness to cure may reduce the severity of the breach from fundamental to not-fundamental; *see* Germany 31 January 1997 *Oberlandesgericht* [Appellate Court] Koblenz, CLOUT

Under PECL Art. 1:804, the right to cure is not qualified for either fundamental or non-fundamental non-performances, although it is limited in cases where time is of the essence, as discussed above. However, under Art. 9:303(3)(a) the aggrieved party's power to terminate the contract is unaffected by later cure as long as the notice of termination is given in reasonable time after cure was performed. This provides a strong incentive to non-performing parties to communicate their intention to cure so as to bring about the suspension of the aggrieved party's power to terminate the contract under Art. 9:303(3)(b), as otherwise their cure will not operate pre-emptively.

V. EXPENSES OF CURE AND ASSOCIATED RISKS

Cure may accrue costs and internalize risks that are not allocated between the parties in the contract. If any exist, the CISG Art. 48(1) allocates them to the seller.[36] As far as the buyer is concerned, the curative performance is to be as close as possible to the projected contractual performance. Obviously, any associated costs that would effectively serve to remove or reduce the seller's susceptibility to a lawsuit for breach of contract must be borne by the seller. The PECL are silent on this point, but as this rule seems germane to the logic of cure they must hold under them as well. Also, as cure is a substitute performance, PECL Art. 7:112, according to which each party must bear "the costs of performance of its obligations," will apply here, by analogy if not directly.[37]

VI. "WITHOUT UNREASONABLE DELAY"

There must be a limit to the period during which the aggrieved seller must accept cure. CISG Art. 48(1) limits cure only to cases where it can be achieved without unreasonable delay.[38] This language, similar to the "*unverzüglich*" of the BGB [German Civil Code][39] or the "*interpellation suffisante*" prevalent in the French Code Civil,[40] indicates a relatively shorter period than the "reasonable time" under which a declaration of avoidance must be given according to CISG Art. 49.[41] It is therefore a further application of the general

case No. 282, case presentation available online at <http://cisgw3.law.pace.edu/cisg/cases/970131g1.html>. This is an attractive relational notion, consistent with the PECL's general obligations of good faith and fair dealing; however, I doubt whether it may hold under the CISG's approach to avoidance of contract; *see* Yovel, *supra* note 2.

[36] Germany 9 June 1995 *Oberlandesgericht* [Appellate Court] Hamm, CLOUT case No. 125, case presentation available including English translation available online at <http://cisgw3.law.pace.edu/cases/950609g1.html> (costs for replacing defective windows).

[37] By analogy because in curing, the seller is not performing an obligation but exercising a right. The purported gap in Art. 8:104 – the allocation of costs and risks associated with cure – calls for completion by analogy from within the PECL before we proceed to external sources of construction.

[38] ICC Arbitration Case No. 7754 of January 1995, *ICC International Court of Arbitration Bulletin* 2000, 46, case presentation available at <http://cisgw3.law.pace.edu/cases/957754i1.html> (the conditions are satisfied when, for example, defective motors can easily be adjusted in due time and at minimal costs).

[39] *See* BGB § 121. German courts acknowledged a possible discrepancy between "reasonable time" and "without unreasonable delay," even when the facts happened to satisfy both; *see* Germany 17 September 1991 *Oberlandesgericht* [Appellate Court] Frankfurt, case presentation including English translation available at <http://cisgw3.law.pace.edu/cases/910917g1.html> (in this case a one-day delay in sending an avoidance telex after the breach was discovered at a trade fair was judged both reasonable and *unverzüglich*). In another case, an Italian buyer of a used car was allowed to avoid the contract three months after she discovered the car was previously stolen and title cannot be transferred; the court accepted the time as pertinent to the various inspections required. Had the seller attempted to cure, however, it might have been determined that the condition of "without reasonable delay" could not be met: Germany 22 August 2002 *Landgericht* [District Court] Freiburg, case presentation including English translation available at <http://cisgw3.law.pace.edu/cases/020822g1.html>.

[40] *E.g.* Arts. 1139, 1146.

[41] *See* ICC Arbitration Case No. 9083 of August 1999, case presentation including English translation available online at <http://cisgw3.law.pace.edu/cases/999083i1.html>.

principle of reasonableness that, as Professor Kritzer has argued, is a general principle of the CISG.[42]

In cases where the seller has indicated to the buyer the length of the intended cure period – as must be the case when the breach is fundamental (under CISG Art. 49(2)) and is prudent also when it is non-fundamental – that indication, subject to the requirement of reasonableness, will determine the period for cure. In no case other than when he has explicitly accepted is the buyer obligated to accept cure later than that.[43]

The PECL's generally stringent approach to delay bears an interesting relation to the parallel requirement in CISG Art 49(1). PECL Art. 8:104 in fact uses language that appeared in early drafts of the CISG and was later scrapped for the "*unverzüglich*" principle.[44] In the context of the PECL, the general obligation to act in good faith and fair dealing (Art. 1:201) governs the substantial right to cure. It should be added that in similar contexts the PECL treat delayed performance more severely than the CISG. For instance, whereas avoidance of contract for non-fundamental breaches is available under CISG in cases of non-delivery only (following a *Nachfrist* period, see CISG Art. 49(1)(b)), the PECL allow avoidance following *Nachfrist* in the wider category of cases of non-fundamental delays in performance (see PECL Art. 8:106(3)).

May there be cure in a time that is longer than "reasonable"? Honnold[45] emphasizes that the seller's request according to Art. 48(2) should not necessarily be restricted to the conditions of cure of Art. 48(1); the seller may therefore request to perform cure under different conditions, to which the buyer may agree or not, but will be held to if she fails to respond to the said request.

What if the seller's request under Art. 48(2) and (3) does not indicate a time frame for cure? According to some sources, such an indication is a *sine qua non* of the request, and without it, it can have no effect.[46] This seems too harsh to me; if the seller does not indicate a time for cure, the default time indicated in Art. 48(1) – namely, "without reasonable delay" – would kick in and govern the undertaking to cure. Art 48(2) allows the seller to attempt to divert from the minimal time requirement, but does not oblige him to do so.

VII. RETAINING THE RIGHT TO DAMAGES

The performance of cure does not obliterate the fact that a breach was in fact performed. Thus, although the performance of appropriate cure virtually substitutes for that of the original contractual obligation (hence making both avoidance of the contract and any order for specific performance inappropriate), it does not preclude an additional order for damages.[47] Under CISG Art. 48(1) these are damages "as provided for in this Convention"

[42] *See supra* note 14.

[43] *See Official Records of the United Nations Conference on Contracts for the International Sale of Goods, Vienna 10 March–11 April 1980*, A/CONF. 97/19, at 40 *et seq.*, available online at <http://cisgw3.law.pace.edu/cisg/text/link48.html>.

[44] Namely, the seller may cure "if he can do so without such delay as will amount to a fundamental breach of contract."] Art. 44 (later became Art. 48) of the 1978 Draft. *See Official Records*, *supra* note 42.

[45] *See Honnold*, 298.

[46] *See Official Records of the United Nations Conference on Contracts for the International Sale of Goods, Vienna, 10 March–11 April 1980* (United Nations publication, Sales No. E.81.IV.3), 41, para. 14.

[47] In one French case, reliance damages were awarded the aggrieved buyer for expenses incurred in the process of cooperating with the performance of cure by the seller (applying extra transportation, etc.) In that case, however, the damages were assessed as 10% of the full sale price. To me, this seems a dubious approach: determining damages must be an empirical, verifiable matter. Damages added to cure – the "whether" covering expectation or reliance interests – should be determined according to evidence pertaining to actual losses suffered (including loss of expected gain), as opposed to a lump sum or a neat

(i.e., including those damages covered by Art. 74).[48] (A dictum by an Austrian court suggests that although the CISG generally provides for reliance as well as expectation damages for breach of contract, cure generally revokes the availability of the latter).[49] However, although in cases of successful cure expectation damages will not be awarded on the merits (that, after all, is what cure is aimed to achieve), it does not follow that this is the proper construction of the damages clause in Art. 48. Even cure that is identical to the projected contractual performance in all save the time of performance may fail to compensate for loss of some of the projected (and foreseeable, etc.) added value to the buyer expected from the contract. There is no reason to indemnify the seller from liability in such cases. From this perspective, what cure affords breaching sellers (and to what it subjects aggrieved buyers) is, in fact, the possibility of mitigating any damages to which the seller would otherwise be liable through substitute performance. There is no guarantee that the substitute performance will cover the entire loss to the buyer generated by the breach.

PECL Art. 8:104 says nothing about damages; however, it does not preclude further damages in cases of cure and the same logic should apply here. Thus the general PECL clauses that make damages available to aggrieved buyers would operate here. Cure would not preclude damages, although it would contribute toward their mitigation, and a perfect performance of cure would mitigate those damages completely.

VIII. SYSTEM OF NOTICES

Although avoidance is *declared*, cure is *performed*. However, declaring the *intention* to cure (or otherwise making it known to the aggrieved party, *cf.* PECL Art. 9:303(3)(b)) may carry with it a legal effect in the sense of shifting a certain communicative onus to the aggrieved party who wishes to retain the power to avoid the contract. This is true for both the PECL (as discussed cursorily above) and the CISG, as follows.

Although PECL Art. 8:104 does not indicate any special mode for notices of cure exchanged by the parties – and is thus subject to the regular rules governing communication set in Art. 1:303 and indirectly those governing notices of termination in Art 9:303 – the CISG designates an entire communicative system to govern the establishment of cure: Art. 48(2), (3), and (4). This system governs, however, more than merely the ways in which notices in the context of cure are to be exchanged between the parties, as it

proportion of the total sale price. *See* France 26 April 1995 *Cour d'appel* [Appellate Court] Grenoble (*Marques Roque Joachim v. Manin Rivière*), case presentation including English translation available online at <http://cisgw3.law.pace.edu/cases/950426f2.html>.

[48] It may be argued that the damages clause in CISG Art. 48 is redundant because such cases as would fall under it would fall under the more general Art. 45(2) according to which "The buyer is not deprived of any right he may have to claim damages by exercising his right to other remedies." That would be a jurisprudential mistake, as under CISG (and PECL) cure is not a right of the aggrieved buyer but of the breaching seller. So although both clauses are consistent they do not cover the same cases. *Contra* Oberlandesgericht Hamm, *supra* note 35.

[49] *See* Austria 14 January 2002 *Oberster Gerichtshof* [Supreme Court], case presentation including English translation available online at <http://cisgw3.law.pace.edu/cases/020114a3.html>. The court also curiously refers to cure as a "right" of the aggrieved buyer although under CISG (and PECL) the seller does not generally have an obligation to cure; she has a right to cure, as analyzed above. Had there been a buyer's right to impose cure and a seller's obligation to make one, and the seller would default on that, that would have to become an issue separate from her breach of the contractual obligation itself. Obviously, nowhere in the CISG is a party obligated to perform more than the contract stipulates. Of course, under certain conditions the buyer has a right to specific performance that needs to be enforced in court (*see* CISG Arts. 28 and 46) but that is a different matter entirely, not to be mixed with that of cure. Switzerland 5 November 2002 *Handelsgericht* [Commercial Court] des Kantons Aargau, case presentation including English translation available at <http://cisgw3.law.pace.edu/cases/021105s1.html>.

regulates some of the *substantive* rights of the parties contingent on their communicative behavior.

Under both the CISG and PECL (but not under the UNIDROIT Principles), cure may be exercised without notice to the aggrieved buyer.[50] CISG Art. 48(2), however, discusses the case in which the seller "requests" the buyer's approval of the seller's intended cure.[51] (Literally, the relevant language is "accept[ing] performance," by the buyer, a slightly awkward wording within the context of the CISG that does not operate under the perfect tender rule, and thus buyers have no right to reject performance other than by avoiding the contract).[52]

There are two separate operations involved here. In the case of non-fundamental breach, the seller is not so much "requesting" anything as much as giving notice of cure; it is not a request because the buyer has no right to refuse. The operation of the request is much more significant under conditions of fundamental breach. As under such conditions the buyer retains the right to avoid the contract, the seller in fact offers to cure the breach on the condition that the buyer forebears from exercising her right to declare the contract avoided. The buyer may, of course, refuse the offer to cure and exercise her power to avoid the contract (or not avoid it, as the case might be and resort instead to other remedies, such as damages). But if she agrees to "accept" cure, or simply fails to respond to the request within a reasonable time, she will become estopped from exercising her right to avoid the contract or reducing the price for the duration indicated in the request. Note that this is an exception to the general rule of CISG Art. 18(1), according to which "Silence or inactivity does not in itself amount to acceptance."

The harshness of this rule is mitigated by Art. 48(4), according to which a request according to Art. 48(2) becomes effective upon *receipt* by the buyer (itself an exception to the general rule in Art. 27 where it suffices to dispatch the notice).[53] Of course, whether a breach is fundamental or not may be controversial; the buyer herself may be unsure of the availability of avoidance and the seller unsure whether she holds a right to cure. Art. 48(2) provides a strong incentive to the cautious seller to communicate with the buyer and sort this out. There is no prejudice to the seller for if the breach is non-fundamental than she retains to right to cure, whatever the buyer's response may be. Yet it would prevent the situation of a seller engaging in costly cure while buyer intends to declare the contract avoided. The "race" between cure and avoidance is thus best resolved through application of CISG Art. 49(2).

[50] *Contra* Liu, *supra* note 8 at 5.

[51] In terms of speech acts, the matter of request is not determined literally but as a matter of contextually constructing a communicative performance: under Art. 48(3) a "notice" by the seller that she intends to cure within a specified time is assumed to amount to such a request. This is an "indirect" speech act; *see* Jerrold Fodor, *Semantics* (New York: Crowell, 1977), at p. 57 *et seq*.

[52] *See* Jonathan Yovel, "Comparison between provisions of the CISG (Buyer's right to avoid the contract: Article 49) and the counterpart provisions of the PECL (Articles 9:301, 9:303 and 8:106)," available online at <http://cisgw3.law.pace.edu/cisg/biblio/yovel49.html>.

[53] Seller must then allow "reasonable time" for the buyer to answer. *See* Finland 12 November 1997 Turku Court of Appeal, case presentation including English translation available at <http://cisgw3.law.pace.edu/cases/971112f5.html>. See *also* when a communication "reaches" an addressee, CISG Art. 24.

Buyer's right to avoid the contract: Comparison between provisions of the CISG (Article 49) and the counterpart provisions of the PECL (Articles 9:301, 9:303, and 8:106)

Jonathan Yovel

I. GENERAL

Avoidance ("termination" in the context of the PECL) of the contract is normally the most extreme measure a party may take in response to a breach ("non-performance" in the context of the PECL) of contract.[1] Avoidance puts a stop to any future performance, except for contractual performances designated to take effect upon avoidance, such as dispute resolution clauses or liquidated damages.[2] (Any restitution following avoidance is not, properly speaking, a contractual performance, but a statutory or common law requirement, as the case may be).[3] Both the CISG and the PECL offer aggrieved parties

[1] Ole Lando, "Salient Features of the Principles of European Contract Law: A Comparison with the UCC," 13 *Pace International Law Review* (Fall 2001) 339, at p. 361.

[2] *See* CISG Art. 81(1) and PECL Art. 9:305(2). Nor does avoidance preclude recourse to any remedy consistent with it, such as damages (*see* CISG Art. 81(1) and PECL Art. 8:102) The Secretariat Commentary (referring to the 1978 Draft) notes, "Such a provision was important because in many legal systems avoidance of the contract eliminates all rights and obligations which arose out of the existence of the contract. In such a view once a contract has been avoided, there can be no claim for damages for its breach and contract clauses relating to the settlement of disputes, including provisions for arbitration and clauses specifying 'penalties' or 'liquidated damages' for breach, terminate with the rest of the contract" (Official Records pp. 41–42).

[3] *See* CISG Art. 81 and PECL. Arts. 9:307 (concerning money) and 9:308 (concerning property). In variations, this seems to be a universal feature of contract avoidance. The effect of CISG Art. 81 on avoidance was even described as "chang[ing] the contractual relationship into a restitutional relationship." *See* Germany 11 October 1995 *Landgericht* [District Court] Düsseldorf, case presentation including English translation available at <http://cisgw3.law.pace.edu/cases/951011g1.html>. *See* also Harry M. Flechtner, "Remedies under the New International Sales Convention: The Perspective from Article 2 of the Ucc," 8 *J.L. & Com.* 53 (1988), at 80; Francesco G. Mazzotta, "Commentary on CISG Article 81 and its PECL Counterparts," available online at <http://cisgw3.law.pace.edu/cisg/text/peclcomp81.html>; Günter H. Treitel, "Remedies for Breach of Contract" in *International Encyclopedia of Comparative Law* (Tübingen, Mouton, The Hague, Paris: J.C.B. Mohr, 1976). Courts acknowledge the CISG restitution as a matter of course; *see* Switzerland 5 February 1997 *Handelsgericht* [Commercial Court] Zürich, case presentation available at <http://cisgw3.law.pace.edu/cases/970205s1.html>; Switzerland 20 February 1997 *Bezirksgericht (Zivilgericht)* [District Court] Saane, case presentation including English translation available at <http://cisgw3.law.pace.edu/cases/970220s1.html>.

less extreme measures to deal with breach or with anticipatory breach, such as suspension of performance and requirement of assurances,[4] requirement of performance,[5] or unilateral price reduction.[6] They likewise contain various cure measures that – when applied or applicable – allow for delayed or remedial performance and thus either delay recourse to avoidance or render it unnecessary. In this, both the CISG and PECL manifest a "relational" bias[7]; namely, they attempt to salvage fractured contractual relations by providing an escalation of remedial measures, whose eventual failure ultimately leads to breaking up of the contractual framework through avoidance. In this, the CISG and PECL differ from several national systems that either allow for avoidance in cases of lesser breaches or simply fail to offer such sliding scales.[8]

II. FUNDAMENTAL BREACH

Due to its extreme nature, both the CISG and the PECL reserve avoidance to special cases, namely to fundamental breaches (non-performances) of the contract.[9] This restriction, however, can be bypassed (or extended) by use of a special mechanism in the case of non-delivery of the goods even without establishing that the failure constitutes a fundamental breach.. In the case of the CISG, although fundamental breaches make avoidance available immediately, non-fundamental non-delivery allows for avoidance if the aggrieved party has fixed a curative period for performance – a so-called *Nachfrist* period – and the breach has continued throughout that period.[10] In the case of the PECL, "delay in performance" followed by further failure to perform throughout a *Nachfrist* period may allow for avoidance. Thus the CISG allows for an "upgrade" of post-*Nachfrist* non-fundamental non-delivery to allow for avoidance, whereas the PECL provide for avoidance under similar circumstances for "delay" in performance, whether that of delivery or another.[11] These types of cases are discussed in detail next.

In making avoidance of the contract available only in cases of fundamental breach, both the CISG and PECL seem to deviate from commercial practices that allow parties to reject goods – and, more importantly, documents – that fail to strictly conform with the contractual specifications, even if that discrepancy is of little practical significance.[12] Such

[4] *See* CISG Art. 71 and PECL Art. 8:105.

[5] *See* CISG Arts. 46 and 62 (but *see* Art. 28) and PECL Arts. 9:101 and 9:102.

[6] *See* CISG Art. 50 and PECL Art. 9:401.

[7] For the general aspects of relational contract theory as applied both to sales and other kinds of contractual transactions, and especially its emphasis on ongoing, long-term contractual relations that are heavily based in commercial practices, *see* Ian Macneil, *The New Social Contract: An Inquiry into Modern Contractual Relations* (1980); *id.*, "Contracts: Adjustment of Long-Term Economic Relations under Classical, Neoclassical, and Relational Contract Law," 72 *Nw. L. Rev.* 854 (1978); Stewart Macaulay, "Non-Contractual Relations in Business: A Preliminary Study," 28 *Am. Soc. Rev.* 55 (1963); Robert W. Gordon, "Macaulay, Macneil and the Discovery of Solidarity and Power in Contract Law," 1985 *Wis. L. Rev.* 565; Jonathan Yovel, "What is Contract Law 'About'? Speech Act Theory and a Critique of 'Skeletal Promises,'" 94 *Nw. U. L. Rev.* 937–962 (2000).

[8] Some authors remark that in international sales, the effects of avoidance on the breaching party may prove especially onerous; hence the stringent application in the Cisg (*see, e.g.*, Joseph Lookofsky and Herbert Bernstein, *Understanding the CISG in Europe,* Deventer, 1997, 87). The PECL, of course, apply to domestic as well as international sales.

[9] For what constitutes a fundamental breach (non-performance) *see* CISG Art. 25 and PECL Art. 8:103, respectively; according to Lando, the latter was modeled on the former, *see* Lando, *supra* note 2 p. 362. For a discussion of fundamental breach in CISG law and related UNIDROIT Principles as well as the related topic of non-conformity of goods, *see* Robert Koch, "Commentary on Whether the UNIDROIT Principles of International Commercial Contracts May Be Used to Interpret or Supplement Articles 47 and 49 of the CISG," available online at <http://cisgw3.law.pace.edu/cisg/biblio/koch2.html> and references noted there.

[10] *See* CISG Art. 49(1)(b), discussed below.

[11] *See* PECL Art. 8:106(3), discussed below.

[12] Such discrepancies indeed generated several criticisms regarding the CISG's application to documentary transactions in general. *See* Alastair Mullis, "Avoidance for Breach under the Vienna Convention:

practices are prevalent in documentary transactions[13] such as CIF,[14] and in particular in those that involve documentary credit, such as an L/C or "unclean" documents such as bills of lading.[15] Under the fundamental breach rule it would seem that such rejection would not amount in itself to avoidance but instead to a demand for cure (see CISG Arts. 30, 34, and 47) that, if unmet, may then constitute a breach allowing avoidance, as discussed below.[16] However, two considerations mitigate the apparent difference between the fundamental breach and strict compliance approaches to avoidance of contract. The first is contractual, namely the parties' general freedom to stipulate what breaches would count as fundamental; in documentary transactions, strict documentary compliance may simply be agreed upon. The second has to do with the function of custom, usage, and commercial practices. Under CISG Art. 9(2), parties are generally bound by prevalent usages; this general principle would certainly apply to the construction of fundamental breach under CISG Arts. 25 and 49. Perhaps even more significantly, PECL 1:105 makes a similar provision for contracts in general, beyond *lex mercatoria*. Strict compliance with documentary requirements may fall under both categories: contractual stipulation and prevalent usage.[17]

III. NO FAULT, NO GRACE, NO REGARD FOR TITLE, NO "PERFECT TENDER"

Both the PECL and CISG share a no-fault approach to breach of contract that allows for avoidance. In this, the general common law rather than general civil law approach is followed (see, however, PECL Art. 8:103(c)).

Neither the CISG nor the PECL set a default "grace period" for performance, during which the aggrieved party is enjoined from avoiding the contract. However, both treat the matter of a cure or remedial period set or allowed by the aggrieved party as a special

A Critical Analysis of some of the Early Cases," *in* Andreas & Jarborg (eds.), *Anglo-Swedish Studies in Law* (Uppsala: Iustus Forlag 1998), p. 326 *et seq.*; *also* Peter Schlechtriem, "Interpretation, gap-filling and further development of the UN Sales Convention" available online at <http://cisgw3.law.pace.edu/cisg/biblio/schlechtriem6.html>. Prof. Schlechtriem's critique is also germane to the commercial realities of the commodification of contracts, where practitioners regard themselves as dealing not in goods but in "contracts"; in so doing, they move away from the language of the assignment of *in-personam* (contractual) obligations to the *in-rem*, "propertized" language of goods or of commodities. The general question of the adjusted application of commercial law originally designed for transactions in goods (such as the CISG) to transactions in contracts is of course broader than can be dealt with here. Possibly, however, relational approaches to functional conformity of goods – the CISG's approach in the context of avoidance and its limitation to fundamental breach for lack of conformity (CISG Art. 35) – can be extended at least to *some* documentary transactions, the exception continuing to be financial (payment and credit) as well as investment instruments. This cautious approach is partially expressed by CISG Art 2(d).

[13] According to the Secretariat Commentary, Art. 2(d) CISG does not exclude documentary sales of goods from the scope of application of the Convention. The Commentary warns, however, that in some legal systems such sales may be characterized as sales of commercial paper, excluded by Art. 2(d). *See* Secretariat Commentary on Art. 2, available online at <http://cisgw3.law.pace.edu/cisg/text/secomm/secomm-02.html>. As prevalent kinds of commercial paper tend to be "negotiated" rather than sold, paper falling under UCC Article 3 ("Negotiable Instruments") – ostensibly given to strict or "formalist" construction based on flaws discernible "on the face of the instrument" – would not fall under the scope of application of the CISG to begin with.

[14] *See* Secretariat Commentary, para 7.

[15] *See*, e.g., INCOTERMS 2000, CIF, provisions A8, B8.

[16] *See* paragraph 8 below, and especially Prof. Schlechtriem's view that extends the right to declare the contract avoided for non-delivery of goods following a *Nachfrist* period to non-delivery of documents of title, *infra* note 51. One way to solve the apparent discrepancy between Art. 49 and prevalent commercial practices is through Art. 9 CISG and its counterpart, Art. 1:105 PECL. These important provisions subject parties to regularly observed usages and practices (*see* Art. 9(2) ULIS for the strongest formulation of the binding force of *lex mercatoria*). The strict compliance practices widely associated with documentary transactions would then take contractual effect between the parties.

[17] *E.g.* under various INCOTERMS 2000 (for instance, A8 in all but Ex-Works).

case during which the power to avoid the contract is suspended, as discussed below. Similarly, curative performance intended and indicated by the party in breach may limit the aggrieved seller's power to avoid the contract for a certain duration. Under PECL 9:303(3)(b) when the aggrieved party knows of the intention of the non-performing party to tender curative performance and fails to notify it that it will not accept cure, it forfeits the power to terminate the contract if the non-performing party in fact performs. Likewise, according to CISG Art. 48(2) an aggrieved buyer who failed to object to the breaching seller's indication that it intends to cure is estopped from avoiding the contract for an indicated period.[18]

Additionally, the fundamental breach requirement itself may sometimes operate as setting a grace period in relation to avoidance, in the sense that the buyer's failure to pay – or to carry out any other of her allocated or derivative[19] performances – may become fundamental only some time after the breach itself has come to pass. For example, a very short delay – in respect to the contractual stipulation – in opening a letter of credit will normally not constitute a fundamental breach, but a longer delay may.[20]

As the CISG deals exclusively with obligatory questions,[21] the aggrieved buyer's power to declare the contract avoided is wholly independent from questions of title to the goods. If questions of title need to be resolved, domestic law would apply and determine entitlements.[22] The PECL, wider in scope and application than the CISG, are also limited to contractual (and related obligation) context.[23] Discharging rights granted by the CISG and PECL – such as the right to restitution following avoidance of the contract – may be found subject to third-party interests and property rights, as regulated by domestic law.

Neither the CISG nor the PECL contain a so-called perfect tender rule that allows for rejecting[24] non-conforming goods after tender was performed (such as the UCC §2–601).[25] Instead, the buyer must accept the non-conforming goods, returning them to the

[18] *See* Jonathan Yovel, "Seller's Right to Remedy Failure to Perform: Comparison between provisions of the CISG (Article 48) and the counterpart provisions of the PECL (Articles 8:104 and 9:303)," available online at <http://cisgw3.law.pace.edu/cisg/biblio/yovel48.html>.

[19] *See* CISG Art. 54 according to which "The buyer's obligation to pay the price includes taking such steps . . . to enable payment to be made."

[20] *See* Honnold at p. 354, Lookofsky at p. 114.

[21] *See* CISG Art. 4(b).

[22] *See* the Australian case *Roder v. Rosedown*, Federal District Court Adelaide, 28 April 1995, available online at <http://cisgw3.law.pace.edu/cases/950428a2.html> (the contract of sales contained a retention of title clause whereby title to the goods did not pass to the purchaser until the purchase price had been paid in full, which was not the case). *See* Robert Koch, "Commentary on Whether the UNIDROIT Principles of International Commercial Contracts may be Used to Interpret or Supplement Article 25 Cisg," *Pace Review of the Convention on Contracts for the International Sale of Goods* (1998) 246, available online at <http://cisgw3.law.pace.edu/cisg/biblio/koch1.html>.

[23] Whether obligations stemming from PECL Arts. 2:301–3 should be properly classified as strictly contractual or belonging to the periphery of contract (quasi-contract, collateral (or "implied" contract), even tort) is a question that cannot be dealt with here; all these legal constructs are, however, obligatory in nature.

[24] CISG Art. 86(2) indeed uses the language of buyer's "right to reject" non-conforming goods. As there is no such general right in the CISG, this clause should be read in the context of prospective avoidance of the contract (i.e., the case covered by Art. 42(2), in which the buyer, prior to the avoidance of the contract, must – on the seller's behalf and at his expense – preserve the goods during the interim period or in the context of either premature delivery or delivery in excess (CISG Art. 52(1) and (2), respectively).

[25] Prof. Schlechtriem considers this a major deviation from common law doctrines, to the extent that the buyer's duty to take over defective goods "must be repugnant to the Anglo-Saxon legal convictions" (Peter Schlechtriem, "Interpretation, gap-filling and further development of the UN Sales Convention" available online at <http://cisgw3.law.pace.edu/cisg/biblio/schlechtriem6.html>). However, White and Summers suggest that, at least in the context of sales transactions governed by the Uniform Commercial Code, various courts' rulings have so eroded the perfect tender rule that "the law would be little changed if §2–601 gave the right to reject only upon 'substantial' non-conformity [instead of the UCC language that grants a right to reject for failure of the goods "in any respect to conform to the contract" – JY]." James J. White & Robert S. Summers, *Uniform Commercial Code* (4th ed., 1995) p. 441.

seller only upon avoidance.[26] Such taking of the goods does not constitute "acceptance" in the common law sense of the contract having been discharged and the power to avoid the contract having been lost.[27]

IV. SELF-HELP

Contract avoidance is sometimes referred to as a "self-help" remedy although, properly speaking, it is not a remedy in the strict contractual sense: rather than remedial, its effects are to excuse parties from further performances and to restore pre-performance conditions by either requiring reciprocal restitution of all exchanges or making such restitution or its substitute available to parties.[28] The basic feature of avoidance in the CISG is its autonomous, unilateral character: it requires no court action and may be executed entirely through appropriate declarations. The PECL share the CISG's approach to contract avoidance as a unilateral act requiring merely a declaration (notice) to the other party.[29] In this, the PECL are "markedly different" from several continental systems, where the general principle is that avoidance requires court proceedings.[30] Note that this unilateral approach is consistent with the rule, shared by CISG and PECL, under which the aggrieved party need not serve the non-performing party with notice to put the latter into breach (such as a *mise en demeure* or *Mahnung*).[31] Parties must, of course,

[26] Prof. Schlechtriem suggests a construction according to which the buyer, although not permitted to reject non-conforming goods outright, may nevertheless postpone taking them over for a reasonable duration necessary for determining whether under the circumstances avoidance is available or forthcoming (*see* Schlechtriem, *supra* note 25). Although any such conduct will still be subject to Art. 86 obligations – namely the buyer's duty to care for the goods taken – such physical taking would not carry any legal effect in the sense of "taking over" the goods according to Art. 69; thus the risk would remain with the seller and would not pass to the buyer who acts, in essence, as the seller's agent in respect to preserving the goods. Note that this construction sits well with Art. 86 that carefully distinguishes between the act of "taking over" (Art. 69), which carries the effect of passage of risk, and "receiving" (Art. 86(1)) or "taking possession" (Art. 86(2)), which does not.

[27] *See* Schlechtriem, *supra* note 25.

[28] With significant exceptions, under the CISG a buyer's inability to make restitution forfeits his right to avoid the contract (CISG Art. 82), which has no exact PECL counterpart (*see* PECL Art. 9:309, which states a right to monetary recovery of value that cannot be restituted, but does not restrict the power to terminate as such).

[29] In one case, the PECL allows for termination even without a termination notice; *see* PECL Art. 8:106(3), discussed above.

[30] In Israel's "hybrid" legal system in which contract law combines common law, civil law, and original elements, all terminations of contract must be either in reasonable time or in reasonable time after the expiration of a *Nachfrist* period. This is the prevalent common law rule, which holds also in "hybrid" legal systems such as in Israel, *see* Contract Law (Remedies for Breach of Contract) 1970, Art. 8. It conforms to several continental rules such as the Danish Sale of Goods Act Arts. 27, 32, and 52; Finnish and Swedish Sale of Goods Acts Arts. 29, 39, and 59; Portuguese Civil Code Art. 436(1); and the Dutch BW 6:267, but differs from other legal systems that require court intervention, such as French, Belgian and Luxembourg Civil Code Art. 1184(2), Italian Civil Code Art. 1453, and Spanish Civil Code Art.1124 (though in Spain a notice of termination may be effective if it is accepted by the defaulting party: *Diez-Picazo*, II, 722; *Lacruz-Delgado* II, 1, 26, 204; and *Ministerio de Justicia*, art. 1124). *See also* Ole Lando and Hugh Beale (eds.), *Principles of European Contract Law: Parts I and II* (Kluwer Law International (2000) (hereinafter "Lando and Beale"), 415 n1.

[31] *See* commentary to PECL Art. 8:101. Strangely enough, litigants in countries where the rule for avoidance of domestic contracts is different still approach courts for declarations of avoidance even when they themselves claim that the CISG governs the case. *See, e.g.*, France 4 June 2004 *Cour d'appel* [Appellate Court] Paris, SARL NE...v. SAS AMI...et SA Les Comptoirs M..., case presentation including English translation available at <http://cisgw3.law.pace.edu/cases/040604f1.html> where plaintiffs sued for a declaration of avoidance and for damages. Presumably, a court may refuse to hear the first part of the suit (in a common law country it probably would), referring the plaintiff instead to CISG Art. 49(1)(a). The risk for making an unlawful declaration of avoidance then sits with the aggrieved party; continuing to refer the matters to courts (which are accustomed to such procedures in domestic issues) may be a clever way to avoid that risk, tantamount to a declaratory verdict concerning the fundamentality of the breach that could, conceivably, be sought in a common law system.

be cognizant of the fact that in subsequent litigation courts may disagree with a claim that avoidance was either available or executed properly. Such risk is associated with all self-help measures. In the case of CISG or PECL avoidance, however, this risk is especially pronounced because of the insistence that only fundamental and tantamount breaches may allow the aggrieved party to declare the contract avoided. A prudent buyer unsure of the fundamentality of the seller's breach may then attempt to "upgrade" the severity of the breach through the usage of a *Nachfrist* mechanism (discussed next), available under both the CISG and PECL. Although it suspends her power to avoid the contract for the length of the curative period (unless an anticipatory breach becomes apparent during that period), the two-tier mechanism significantly reduces her exposure to counter-claims regarding the unlawfulness of declaring the contract avoided.

V. AVOIDANCE (*TERMINATION*) IN REASONABLE TIME

The CISG distinguishes between two categories of cases for the purpose of contract avoidance: whether the goods were in fact delivered or were not delivered. In each case, the CISG fixes a different point of balance between the seller's risk and the buyer's risk. Quite obviously, avoidance – as it results in mutual restitution – typically creates hardship for the seller in the former case, when goods may be stranded.[32] Sellers must internalize such risks into the contractual price, and the drafters of the CISG sought to reduce such risks (such *ex-post* expenditures may also provide buyers with overly strong bargaining positions in negotiations for mutual contract adjustment). The seller may incur substantial loss from retrieving the goods, finding a substitute transaction under unfavorable conditions, and even – in extreme cases where the latter is not forthcoming and the cost of the former onerous – be compelled to relinquish the goods altogether. Furthermore, a breaching party has a distinct interest in knowing as soon as possible whether the aggrieved party intends to avoid the contract or not. Although the aggrieved party has an interest in extending a period of time for deliberation and calculation, both the CISG and the PECL contain some time limitations on exercising the power of avoidance (termination).

Herein, however, lays a distinct difference of approaches. PECL Art. 9:303(2) restricts the power to terminate to a "reasonable time" after the party has become aware of non-performance or after it ought to have been aware. This applies to all cases of non-performance and is a general limitation on the power to terminate.[33] The CISG contains no such general limitation; instead, CISG Art. 49(2) enumerates cases in which the power to avoid is limited to a reasonable time after a certain occurrence has come to pass.[34] Such limitations apply only in cases in which the seller has delivered the goods and are divided into breaches of late delivery and other breaches. The following section examines these limitations in the CISG, followed by their PECL counterparts.

VI. BUYER'S RIGHT TO AVOID CONTRACT AFTER THE GOODS HAVE BEEN DELIVERED

In cases in which the goods have been delivered, CISG Art. 49(2) restricts the buyer's right to avoid even under the relatively tight conditions – i.e., fundamental breach – of

[32] *See* Peter Schlechtriem, "Uniform Sales Law in the Decisions of the Bundesgerichtshof," in *50 Years of the Bundesgerichtshof, A Celebration Anthology from the Academic Community* (2001), at III.1, available online at <http://cisgw3.law.pace.edu/cisg/biblio/schlechtriem3.html>. Professor Schlechtriem emphasizes the risks associated with retrieving stranded goods. *See* also John Honnold, *Documentary History of the Uniform Law for International Sales* (Deventer: Kluwer, 1989) 575–577; Lando, *supra* note 1, p. 361.

[33] However, *see* above for termination in case of anticipatory breach.

[34] Another issue pertinent to avoidance in reasonable time is that a buyer loses his right to rely on a lack of conformity of the goods – including the right to avoid the contract – if he does not give the seller notice thereof within a reasonable time after he has discovered the lack of conformity or ought to have discovered it; *see* CISG Art. 39.

CISG Art. 49(1). The restriction is one of a time limit on the exercise of the power to avoid. In cases of late delivery, CISG Art. 49(2)(a) restricts the power to avoid to a "reasonable time" after the buyer has become aware that delivery has been made. Circumstances obviously play an important role in how long "reasonable" is.[35] With any breach other than late delivery –such as non-conformity – the power to avoid will expire within a reasonable time after she knew or ought to have known of the breach (CISG Art. 49(2)(b)(i)).[36] Likewise, a *Nachfrist* period fixed in accordance with CISG Art. 47(1) (see below) limits the power of avoidance to a reasonable time, unless the seller has declared continuing default (see CISG Art. 49(2)(b)(ii) governing a case tantamount to anticipatory breach, where additional delay would serve no purpose.) This is also the case if the curative period was initiated by the defaulting seller according to Art. 48(2) (see Art. 49(2)(b)(iii)).[37]

VII. REASONABLE TIME

As noted, the PECL require notice in a reasonable time for all terminations. In this, they express a comprehensive commitment to the good faith principle (PECL Art. 1:201). The provision corresponds with those of several European and other legal systems,[38] although some require briefer delays, such as "*unverzüglich*," "without undue delay"[39]

7.1 In fact, the PECL show special concern for cases of late tender (e.g., when goods were delivered by the seller). Art. 9:303 makes further provisions in this vein dealing with late tender. Art. 9:303 (3)(a) mitigates the effects of Art. 9:303 to the effect that, in cases of late tender, a notice of termination need not be given before the late tender is made. It must, however, be given within a reasonable time after the party has become, or ought to have become, aware of the late tender. In this, the provision is similar to that of CISG Art. 49(2)(a).

[35] *See, e.g.*, ruling by a Dutch court of appeal according to which a period of almost eight weeks was considered reasonable for purpose of a declaration of avoidance of a flour sale contract between Dutch and Mozambique parties: Netherlands 23 April 2003 *Gerechtshof's-Gravenhage* [Appellate Court], *Rynpoort Trading & Transport NV et al. v. Meneba Meel Wormerveer B.V. et al.*, case presentation including English translation available at <http://cisgw3.law.pace.edu/cases/030423n1.html>.

[36] For the time in which the buyer ought to know of the breach, *see* CISG Art. 38, which governs the time in which the buyer must examine the goods. One might expect avoidance following *Nachfrist* to be rather swift; however, disagreements might occur over the question of whether additional periods were granted or not. In one German case involving the sale of printing machines to an Egyptian buyer, an additional period of two weeks was set by the buyer, who subsequently avoided the contract seven weeks after the expiration of the period. The court found this to be a reasonable time: Germany 24 May 1995 *Oberlandesgericht* [Appellate Court] Celle, case presentation including English translation available at <http://cisgw3.law.pace.edu/cases/950524g1.html>.

[37] Some commentators deem Arts. 49(2)(b)(ii) and (iii) redundant as they spell out the obvious. *See* John Honnold, *Uniform Law for International Sales* (Kluwer, 1999), at 308, available at <http://cisgw3.law.pace.edu/cisg/biblio/honnold.html>. This is not necessarily the case: the use of additional cure periods according to Arts. 47 or 48 does not in itself limit any subsequent termination period to a "reasonable time" after the cured failed. Indeed, Art. 49 itself makes the distinction between cases in which the goods have been delivered and those in which they were not, reserving any "reasonable time" provisions to the former cases.

[38] In Israel, in which contract law combines common law, civil law, and original elements, all terminations of contract must be made either in a reasonable time after knowledge of the breach, or in a reasonable time after the expiration of a *Nachfrist* period. *See* Contract Law (Remedies for Breach of Contract) 1970, Art. 8.

[39] *See* BGB §121 (controlling all acts of rescission, including HGB §377). German courts acknowledged a discrepancy between the two criteria, even when the facts satisfied both; *see* Germany 17 September 1991 *Oberlandesgericht* [Appellate Court] Frankfurt, case presentation including English translation available at <http://cisgw3.law.pace.edu/cases/910917g1.html> (in this case a one-day delay in sending an avoidance telex after the breach was discovered at a trade fair was judged both reasonable and *unverzüglich*). In another case, an Italian buyer of a used car was allowed to avoid the contract three months after she discovered the car was previously stolen and the title could not be transferred; the court accepted the time as pertinent to the various inspections required: Germany 22 August 2002 *Landgericht* [District Court] Freiburg, case presentation including English translation available at <http://cisgw3.law.pace.edu/cases/020822g1.html>.

7.2 PECL Art. 9:303(3)(b) deals with an especially tricky situation that exists when tender is late, yet the non-performing party still intends to – and, in fact, does – cure by effecting tender in a reasonable time. Although the aggrieved party has no general obligation to accept late tender,[40] it loses its power to terminate the contract altogether if it knew, or has reason to know, that the other party in fact intended to cure by tender in a reasonable time, yet it failed to notify the non-performing party in a reasonable time that it will refuse tender. This too may be termed a "relational" clause: it protects the non-performing party's reliance on the aggrieved party's cooperation and encourages the parties to exchange information about their respective actions and intentions even when a breach situation occurs.[41]

7.3 Although used frequently, the expression "reasonable time" is not defined in the CISG or in the PECL. Courts and commentators offer contextual criteria, noting that what may constitute reasonable in any given case may be affected by the nature of the goods, the transaction, the payment arrangements, third-party claims, and whether legal advice or expert opinions were actually necessary to determine concrete rights (e.g., in cases of non-conformity merely sorting the matter out may, for practical reasons, take longer than under no tender at all).[42] Courts have ruled on the reasonable length of time taking all such circumstances into account; and, in the absence of clear indicators, the question of when does the period begin to run is invariably left to judicial discretion.[43]

7.4 PECL Art. 1:302 supplies some guidelines about "reasonableness" in general, but those are somewhat circular – "reasonable" is what reasonable persons, acting in good faith, would "consider reasonable." More helpful is the notion that reasonableness is contextual and takes into consideration "the nature and purposes of the contract, the circumstances of the case" etc. Prof. Kritzer has persuasively suggested that reasonableness is a "general principle of the CISG."[44]

[40] *See* PECL Art. 8:104; compare with CISG Art. 48.

[41] For CISG-PECL comparative match-up, *see* commentary to CISG Art. 48, available at <http://cisgw3.law.pace.edu/cisg/text/peclcomp48.html>.

[42] *See* e.g. Germany 31 January 1997 *Oberlandesgericht* [Appellate Court] Koblenz, case presentation available at <http://cisgw3.law.pace.edu/cases/970131g1.html>; *see* also Plate, "The Buyer's Remedy of Avoidance under the CISG: Acceptable from a Common Law Perspective?," 6 *Vindobona J. Int'l. Com. L. & Arbitration* (2002) 57, at 67. For a historical and analytic review of German law *see* Reinhard Zimmermann, "Liability for Non-Conformity: The New System of Remedies in German Sales Law and its Historical Context," 10th John Maurice Kelly Memorial Lecture, Dublin 2004.

[43] *See* France 14 June 2001 *Cour d'appel* [Appellate Court] Paris, *Aluminum and Light Industries Company v. Saint Bernard Miroiterie Vitrerie*, case presentation including English translation available at <http://cisgw3.law.pace.edu/cases/010614f1.html>, where the court applied CISG Art. 49(2) to a transaction of faulty fancy glass panels, determining that the eight months that lapsed from the determination of the breach to the notice of avoidance was an unreasonably long period. The court took into account the various expert inspections of the panels sought in this case and began counting the period from the last one. In different circumstances, the German Supreme Court ruled that the five months that elapsed between the buyer's being informed of the seller's breach (a delivery stop) made for too long a period and could not be considered as a reasonable time under article 49(1)(b): *see* Germany 15 February 1995 *Bundesgerichtshof* [Supreme Court], case presentation including English translation available at <http://cisgw3.law.pace.edu/cases/950215g1.html>.

[44] *See* Prof. Albert H. Kritzer, "Overview Comments on Reasonableness," available online at <http://cisgw3.law.pace.edu/cisg/text/reason.html>: "Reasonableness is specifically mentioned in thirty-seven provisions of the CISG and clearly alluded to elsewhere in the Uniform Sales Law. Reasonableness is a general principle of the CISG." *See* also comments by Jelena Vilus, available online at <http://cisgw3.law.pace.edu/cisg/text/reason.html#vilus>; rpr. in *Homenaje a Jorge Barrera Graf*, vol. 2, Mexico: *Universidad Nacional Autónoma de Mexico* (1989) 1440–1441. For the definition of reasonableness in the PECL and references to reasonableness in continental and common law domestic rules, doctrine, and jurisprudence, *see* Lando & Hugh Beale, pp. 126–128 available online at <http://cisgw3.law.pace.edu/cisg/text/reason.html#def>. For further discussion regarding the correlation between the PECL's definition of reasonableness and the meaning of this term for CISG drafters *see* <http://cisgw3.law.pace.edu/cisg/text/reason.html#over>.

7.5 Another approach would be to consider reasonableness in the definition and execution of contractual obligations as an articulation of the principle of good faith,[45] which in the context of CISG Art. 49 would seem to mean that buyers have a duty to avoid in good faith only in cases where the goods have been delivered.[46] A different construction – one that would apply a general obligation of good faith to CISG obligations – would undermine the distinction between CISG Art. 49(1) and (2): under a general obligation of good faith, surely any declaration of avoidance by the buyer must be made in reasonable time so as not to create undue hardship for the seller. The limitation of the power of avoidance to a "reasonable time" under CISG Art. 49(2) would then become, in fact, tautological. For further considerations, see commentaries to CISG Arts. 7, 8, and 9 and their PECL counterparts.[47]

VIII. AVOIDANCE (*TERMINATION*) FOLLOWING A *NACHFRIST* PERIOD

Consistent with the relational approach, CISG Art. 49(1)(b) and PECL Art. 8:106(3) allow for avoidance of the contract even for some non-fundamental breaches (or, under a different construction, for what may be termed "constructed fundamentality"). The mechanism in such cases has two tiers. First, the aggrieved buyer sets an additional, curative period of reasonable length for the seller to perform, a "*Nachfrist*" period so called after similar provisions in German, Swiss, and other legal systems.[48] Upon the seller's failure to tender curative performance throughout a *Nachfrist* period (or, under conditions tantamount to anticipatory breach, even during it) the aggrieved buyer may avoid the contract (the *Nachfrist* mechanism of PECL Art. 8:106(3) also allows automatic

[45] Peter Schlechtriem, *Uniform Sales Law* (tr. From German: Einliches UN Kaufrecht, Manzsche, Vienna, 1986) 39. *See also id.* (ed.), *Commentary on the UN Convention on the International Sale of Goods (CISG)*, Oxford 1998; Klein, J, "Good Faith in International Trade," 15 *Liverpool L. Rev.* 114–141 (1993).

[46] A scholarly controversy exists regarding whether or not good faith is a general principle of the CISG, as it clearly is of the PECL (Art. 1:106). Professor Magnus, drawing on comparisons between CISG Art. 7 and the UNIDROIT Principles (Art. 1.6.) claims that it is (*see* Ulrich Magnus, "Remarks on good faith," available online at <http://cisgw3.law.pace.edu/cisg/principles/uni7.html>. Dr Felemegas reads Art. 7 differently, as applying to the interpretation of the CISG only and not to performances in general, *see* John Felemegas, "Remarks on Good Faith and Fair Dealing," available online at <http://cisgw3.law.pace.edu/cisg/text/peclcomp7.html>.This is certainly not the proper place to attempt to resolve this important issue or even to determine whether it is, properly stated, merely an interpretative question – albeit a pre-eminent one – as Magnus and Felemegas approach it, or whether its determination transcends mere interpretative approaches. One may doubt, however, whether courts in legal systems that regard good faith obligations (in either the negotiation or performance stage) as immutable tenets of private law – metaphorically speaking, a part of the "constitution" of private law – might not impose derivative obligations also when dealing with contractual obligations governed by the CISG. Such may be inferred from dicta of the Israel Supreme Court, where good faith is a general principle of private law, (*see e.g.*, *Klemer v. Guy* (1993), 50(1) PD 184) following the Contracts (General Part) Law, 1973, §§12, 39, 61(b) and expressed in the anticipated Civil Code, §§2, 163.

[47] Regarding CISG Art. 7, *see* Felemegas, *op. cit.*; regarding CISG Art. 8, *see* Maja Stanivukovic, "Remarks on the Manner in which the PECL may be Used to Interpret or Supplement CISG Article 8," available online at <http://cisgw3.law.pace.edu/cisg/text/peclcomp8.html#er>. Regarding CISG Art. 9, *see* Anja Carlsen, "Remarks on the Manner in which the PECL may be Used to Interpret or Supplement CISG Article 9", available at <http://cisgw3.law.pace.edu/cisg/text/peclcomp9.html#er>.

[48] *See* Lando and Beale, *op. cit.*, at 377. BGB § 326 practically makes *Nachfrist* periods compulsory in most cases, whereas the CISG and PECL merely make it available to the non-breaching party. For the Swiss "Nachfristmodell," *see* Art. 107, 108 Obligationenrecht (Swiss Law of Obligations). Professor Treitel makes the point that other legal systems contain similar mechanisms. *See* Günter H. Treitel, "Remedies for Breach of Contract," in *International Encyclopedia of Comparative Law* (Tübingen, Mouton, The Hague, Paris: J.C.B. Mohr, 1976) Ch. 16, §§ 149–151. Such is Art. 7(b) of the Israeli Contract Law (Remedies for Breach of Contract), 1970, which combines the optional version of a *Nachfrist* with the exception that avoidance under a *Nachfrist* for non-fundamental breaches may be objected to on grounds of injustice, with courts retaining appropriate discretion.

expiration of the contract once the additional period has expired to no avail). Thus these non-fundamental breaches are "upgraded" through the use of the *Nachfrist* mechanism to the status of avoidance-justifying breach.[49]

Curative periods are set by the aggrieved buyer under CISG Art. 47 and PECL Art. 8:106, respectively. They share the same basic structure: under both, the aggrieved buyer may resort to remedies during the curative period (such as damages), but not avoid the contract, unless the party in breach declares that no curative performance is forthcoming. The main constraint applying to *Nachfrist* periods is that, to allow for eventual avoidance of the contract, the period must be of contextually reasonable length to allow the party in breach to cure its non-performance. Under CISG Art. 47(1), curative periods must be of "reasonable length." Under PECL Art. 8:106(3) if the additional period is "too short," the aggrieved party may terminate only after an overall reasonable time has passed, even if the additional period had already expired.

The *Nachfrist* mechanism may also be used in cases of uncertainty as to the fundamentality of the seller's breach. Although avoiding the contract post-*Nachfrist* delays the avoidance, the seller's continuing breach becomes "upgraded." As a consequence a buyer who is apprehensive about assuming the risk involved in unlawful avoidance may significantly reduce her exposure if she follows the *Nachfrist* venue.

The several types of situations where post-*Nachfrist* avoidance under CISG and PECL is available are explored next.

IX. NON-PERFORMANCE DURING THE *NACHFRIST* PERIOD

A buyer who suffers a non-fundamental non-delivery (or "delay" in the case of the PECL), may, on CISG 49(1)(b) (PECL Art. 8:106(3)), go the two-tier way: first, fix an additional period for performance according to CISG Art. 47 (PECL Art 8:106(1)), and then, if the seller fails to perform accordingly, avoid the contract. However, under the CISG such a strategy is limited to cases of non-delivery only (i.e., situations that, in sale of goods contracts, would often constitute fundamental breach anyway). Prof. Schlechtriem considers the non-delivery in CISG Art.49(1)(b) to extend by analogy to the failure to transfer documents of title, the argument being that in typical contexts goods without appropriate documentation cannot be legally possessed: they have been delivered physically perhaps, but not legally, which is tantamount to non-delivery.[50] Under PECL Art. 8:106(3), the post-avoidance *Nachfrist* is limited to non-performances of "delay in performance." That may include performances other than delivery of goods, such as delivery of documents, clearing essential formalities, assisting in training personnel, setting a promotion scheme, etc. This interpretative matter requires further elaboration. Scholarly controversy emerged from the fact that the language of CISG Art. 49(1)(b) – "in

[49] In one French case, the seller sent the buyer a notice of avoidance following the buyer's refusal to take delivery on a certain early date (amended from the original contractual stipulation). The court judged the breach non-fundamental and determined that the only way for the seller to avoid the contract was to first fix a *Nachfrist* period, which was not done: France 4 February 1999 Cour d'appel [Appellate Court] Grenoble (*Ego Fruits v. La Verja Begastri*), case presentation including English translation available online at <http://cisgw3.law.pace.edu/cases/990204f1.html>. In ICC Court of Arbitration case 7585/1992, the tribunal deemed the buyer's failure to open a letter of credit according to the contract a breach, but not a fundamental breach; nevertheless, the seller's declaration of avoidance was effective as it took place several months after the breach, and that time was constructed to operate as a valid *Nachfrist* period. Published (in English) in the *ICC International Court of Arbitration Bulletin* Vol. 6/N.2 – November 1995, 60–64; available online at <http://cisgw3.law.pace.edu/cases/927585i1.html>.

[50] *See* Peter Schlechtriem, *Uniform Sales Law: The UN Convention on Contracts for the International Sale of Goods* (Vienna: Manz 1986), 77 also available online at <http://cisgw3.law.pace.edu/cisg/biblio/schlechtriem.html> Koch and others support this construction, *see* Koch, *op. cit.* note 6.

case of non-delivery" – does not seem to clearly require that the non-delivery *itself* be the breach for which the additional time is fixed, so that the breach may conceivably be another non-performance (e.g., non-conformity of goods or of documents).[51] Thus, the question is whether Art. 49(1)(b) covers breaches other than non-delivery, committed under *circumstances* of non-delivery. For instance, assume that the breach in question is the seller's failure to deliver a certificate of origin as required by the buyer and specified in the contract. The buyer then may proceed to set a curative period according to CISG Art. 47(1), namely extending the time frame for obtaining the certificate. Let us assume that the certificate is required well ahead of the delivery of the goods and that, although the goods were not yet delivered within the *Nachfrist* period, that in itself is no breach. May the buyer declare the contract avoided according to Art. 49(1)(b), assuming Art. 49(1)(a) does not apply? Although some legal systems extend *Nachfrist*-based avoidance of contract to non-fundamental breaches in general,[52] commentators warn that, despite the allowance by the CISG's *Nachfrist* mechanism of an aggrieved buyer to exert pressure upon a defaulting seller, "the Nachfrist avoidance procedure was not to be extended any further than the essential obligation of delivery."[53] Art. 49(1)(b) is therefore not designed to allow aggrieved parties to bypass the fundamentality requirement of Art. 49(1)(a) for any reason other than non-delivery of goods[54] or, as suggested above, also of documents of title. Any other conclusion would erode considerably the dependence of avoidance on the fundamentality of breach, as it would suffice to set a *Nachfrist* period for any breach and then declare the contract avoided upon the continuing failure to perform.[55] Professors Schlechtriem and Koch add that drawing analogies from non-delivery to other kinds of non-performance is jurisprudentially dubious, for where no lacuna exists there is no justification for expanding the scope of the clause by analogy – there is here no gap to be filled, but rather a positive apparatus privileging non-delivery over all other breaches.[56] Commentators likewise note that the non-delivery must be complete non-delivery in order to allow application of Art. 49(1)(b); partial performance is not non-performance.[57]

The case is slightly different with PECL Art. 8:106(3), which does not limit failure to perform following a *Nachfrist* period to non-delivery only but to the more general category of "delay in performance which is not fundamental." This still will not include non-performances in terms of non-conforming goods, yet certainly will include – as was

[51] This is not to say that all commentators even acknowledge the existence of an interpretative ambiguity: for instance, Lookofsky and Bernstein take for granted that Art. 49(1)(b) applies only to breaches of non-delivery. *See* Joseph Lookofsky and Herbert Bernstein, *Understanding the* CISG *in Europe* Deventer, 1997, 91–2. For a scholarly debate on this and other issues *see* "Transcript of a Workshop on the Sales Convention: Leading CISG Scholars Discuss Contract Formation, Validity, Excuse for Hardship, Avoidance, *Nachfrist*, Contract Interpretation, Parol Evidence, Analogical Application, and Much More," 18 *J. L. & Com.* (1999) 191, at 201 *et seq.*; available online at <http://cisgw3.law.pace.edu/cisg/biblio/workshop.html>.

[52] *See e.g.* the Israeli Contract Law (Remedies for Breach of Contract), 1970 Art. 7(b) (Failure to perform following a *Nachfrist* period may generate a right to declare the contract avoided even for non-fundamental breaches, subject to judicial discretion (the latter does not apply in case of a fundamental breach).

[53] Michael R. Will, *Bianca-Bonell Commentary on the International Sales Law* (Giuffrè: Milan 1987), p. 363, available at <http://cisgw3.law.pace.edu/cisg/biblio/will-bb49.html>.

[54] Although not an overriding interpretative consideration in my view, this interpretation sits well with the legislative history of Art. 49. *See* "Legislative History; 1980 Vienna Diplomatic Conference Summary Records of Meetings of the First Committee," 22nd meeting, 25 March 1980, available online at <http://cisgw3.law.pace.edu/cisg/firstcommittee/Meeting22.html>, paras. 61–96.

[55] Or in Prof. Schlechtriem's words, "you cannot reach avoidance of the contract in the case of non-conforming goods where the non-conformity itself does not constitute a fundamental breach, by blowing up minor non-conformities through the process of setting an additional period of time to have them repaired. Because then you could avoid all contracts." *Transcript, supra* note 52, at p. 201.

[56] *See* Koch, *op. cit.*, II.I.b.

[57] Or in Prof. Honnold's words, "non-delivery of the whole package", *see Transcript, supra* note 51, p. 211.

the conclusion concerning CISG Art. 49(1)(b) – delay in tendering documents of title. However, the language of the PECL is wider and more liberal – from the aggrieved party's point of view – than the stringent criterion of the CISG. For non-delivery is a case of "delay," but not the only case. It may be argued that in the example rendered above, failure ("delay") to deliver a certificate of origin throughout a *Nachfrist* period may allow for avoidance under PECL 8:106(3) although – the document in question not pertaining to title and thus not "essential" to the goods – that would not be the case under CISG 49(1)(b). Three comments mitigate this discrepancy. The first is that any interpretation of the "delay of performance" language of PECL 8:106(3) must be conducted within the general framework of PECL Art. 9:301, namely the fundamental breach principle. Thus, exceptions to the principle under PECL Art. 8:106(3) should be construed narrowly and contextually. This relates to the second comment, which is that such exceptions must pass the good faith test – no trivial delays in performance should be allowed to result in contract avoidance through a *Nachfrist* mechanism. This mechanism allows for "upgrade" of some non-fundamental delays, but certainly not any and all of them. Third, in the context of international sales, tribunals may look to CISG Art. 49(1)(b) as an interpretative guideline in construing what non-performances would be allowed to result in avoidance of the contract. Certainly, such rulings may still allow for more extensive sets of cases than would the CISG. The drafters of the PECL were cognizant of the parallel rule in the CISG, and the choice to apply *Nachfrist* to non-performances other than delivery is meaningful.

Because of the "crossing of the Rubicon" status that delivery has in sales of goods transactions – and in international sales, where risks to the seller pursuant post-delivery avoidance are especially acute – non-delivery is a prerequisite for CISG Art. 49(1)(b) to kick in. Thus, the delivery of non-conforming goods ("*peius*") and that of "wrong goods" ("*aliud*") is to be treated under CISG Art. 49(1)(b) and Art. 49(2) in the same category; namely, they both put the parties in the category of "goods delivered."[58] Recent case law tends to regard these traditional categories as points on a single continuum, which the CISG as well as the PECL in fact endorse. Recent German[59] and Austrian[60] case law confirms this view. According to the German Supreme Court, non-delivery could only be assumed in very blatant and obvious cases of divergence between the goods agreed upon and the goods actually delivered.[61] Once the goods are delivered, the conditions for declaring the contract avoided for non-fundamental breach – on Art. 49(2) – become stricter. The contextual interpretation of general PECL clauses such as Art. 8:106(3) should attempt to follow an identical logic.

X. ANTICIPATORY BREACH DURING THE *NACHFRIST* PERIOD UNDER THE CISG

Under CISG Arts. 49(1)(b) and 49(2)(b)(ii) the buyer may avoid the contract even before the additional fixed period has elapsed, in cases where the seller himself declares that he will not perform within that period (this is also the rule set in CISG Art. 49(1)(b)(iii),

[58] Likewise, both would put the buyer under Art. 69 obligations, namely to preserve the goods on the seller's behalf. For in-depth discussion *see* Koch, *op. cit.* II.I.c.

[59] For relevant case law, *see* Germany 3 April 1996 *Bundesgerichtshof* [Supreme Court], case presentation including English translation available at <http://cisgw3.law.pace.edu/cases/960403g1.html>; Germany 12 March 2001 *Oberlandesgericht* [Appellate Court Stuttgart], case presentation including English translation available at <http://cisgw3.law.pace.edu/cases/010312g1.html> (stating that the delivery of an *aliud* does not constitute a non-delivery for the purposes of Art. 49(1)(b) CISG). For further case law, *see* Koch, *op. cit.*

[60] *See* Austria 29 June 1999 *Oberster Gerichtshof* [Supreme Court], presentation including English translation available at <http://cisgw3.law.pace.edu/cases/990629a3.html>.

[61] *See* VIII ZR 51/95 *Bundesgerichtshof* (Germany) 3 April 1996, *supra* note 60 (as a rule, *aliud* delivery does not amount to non-delivery, leaving the question open for the case of an especially blatant deviation of the goods from the contractual specifications).

governing avoidance of the contract during a curative allowance initiated by the breaching seller under Art. 48(2)). These clauses are tantamount to avoidance for anticipatory breach, with the double distinction that they apply only within CISG Art. 47 periods and that the information pertaining to future non-performance must originate from the seller himself and not come by the buyer's way from incidental sources.[62] In this it differs from the provisions of CISG Art. 72 that allow avoidance of the contract if "it is clear" that a fundamental breach is to occur: for example, a careful buyer may discover non-conformity through proper inspection prior to delivery. "Clear" appears to be a mid-level degree of certainty between the lower level "it becomes apparent" of CISG Art. 71 (which allows for suspension of performance in cases of anticipatory breach) and the highest level of CISG Art. 49(1)(b), (2)(b)(ii) and (iii) that requires a declaration by the seller himself. Note however, that even the stricter provisions in CISG Art. 49 do not require that the said declaration be a specific one directed at the seller to the effect that buyer will continue defaulting on this specific transaction. Although under CISG Art. 26 a declaration of avoidance – a legal act – must be made by notice *to* the party in breach, this is not necessarily the case with declarations of continuing default made *by* the party in breach. A general declaration of insolvency, for instance, should fulfill the "declaration" requirement of CISG Art. 49(1)(b), (2)(b)(ii), and (iii), unless accompanied by a specific communication to the contrary (even an insolvent seller may go ahead with a transaction that will eventually generate value for distribution in eventual bankruptcy). Yet in the communicative framework of *Nachfrist* general third-party information is not basis enough to declare the contract avoided prior to the expiry of the duration.[63]

XI. NON-PERFORMANCE FOLLOWING THE *NACHFRIST* PERIOD UNDER THE PECL

As noted above, PECL Art. 8:106(3) allows an aggrieved party to terminate a contract following a delay in performance that does not amount to fundamental breach, if it had fixed a *Nachfrist* period during which curative performance did not occur. However, the *Nachfrist* mechanism cannot be used to bypass the reasonable time requirement set in PECL Art. 9:303(2). PECL Art. 8:106(3) requires that the additional period be of "reasonable length." If that additional period is "too short," the aggrieved party may terminate only after an overall reasonable time has passed, even if the additional period has expired. For purposes of termination, this imposes a de-facto "reasonable length" on the *Nachfrist* period, although such is not generally required in PECL Art. 8:106(1). Art. 8:106(3) includes a useful mechanism, in that the *Nachfrist* notice may include a conditional termination notice, which will apply automatically if the non-performing party fails to remedy during the additional period.[64] In this case a contract may be terminated without a designated notice: the *Nachfrist* notice then doubles as a conditional notice of termination.[65] In case the additional period is not deemed to be reasonably long, such automatic termination will take effect after a reasonable time only, in accordance with the principle examined above.

[62] Note the specific language of CISG Art. 49(2)(b)(ii): "[A]fter the seller has declared that he will not perform his obligations within such an additional period."

[63] *See also* the language of the UCC §2–609, "reasonable grounds for insecurity" with respect to either party's performance. For further comparative and cultural insights, *see* Mirghasem Jafarzadeh, "Buyer's Right to Withhold Performance and Termination of Contract: A Comparative Study under English Law, Vienna Convention on Contracts for the International Sale of Goods 1980, Iranian and Shi'ah Law," Part II § 2.2.2.2, available online at <http://cisgw3.law.pace.edu/cisg/biblio/jafarzadeh.html>.

[64] Whether the *Nachfrist* notice in fact makes this provision or not would become an interpretative question. *See*, in a similar context, such an approach to a *Nachfrist* notice by the Austrian Supreme Court: Austria 28 April 2000 *Oberster Gerichtshof* [Supreme Court], case presentation including English translation available at <http://cisgw3.law.pace.edu/cases/000428a3.html>.

[65] *See* Lando and Beale, *op. cit.*, at 415.

XII. TERMINATION FOR ANTICIPATORY BREACH DURING THE *NACHFRIST* PERIOD UNDER THE PECL

Similar to CISG Arts. 49(1)(b) and (2)(b)(ii), PECL Art. 8:106(2) maintains a device whereby the aggrieved party who has set a *Nachfrist* period is allowed to terminate the contract *during* that period if she "receives notice from the other party" to the effect that no curative performance is forthcoming. This requirement is likewise narrower than the general one governing anticipatory breach under the PECL, according to which it must be "clear" that default would persist (PECL Art. 9:304).[66] In this the PECL apply to *Nachfrist*-situations the general rule governing anticipatory breach, with the exception, which is indeed adequate in the special communicative context of *Nachfrist*, that the notice of continuing default must originate from the defaulting party itself.

This balance follows also from good faith obligations: *ceteris paribus*, it would be in bad faith for a party to object to termination during a *Nachfrist* period when it knows that no performance is forthcoming, thus merely delaying termination to the period's conclusion. Yet it would be in bad faith for the aggrieved party to merely assume default based on third-party information, once the special communicative framework of *Nachfrist* has been established.

There are two remaining questions. The first is whether termination during a *Nachfrist* period due to anticipatory non-performance is limited to a reasonable time after the anticipatory non-performance becomes clear. There is no obvious reason here to deviate from the rules of PECL Arts. 9:303 and 8:106(3), and so the answer must be in the affirmative. The second question is whether such notice of termination on anticipatory breach should be allowed to shorten the overall *Nachfrist* period to less than what would otherwise be deemed "reasonable." Here the answer should also be in the affirmative, which does not violate the general rule: if the period is shortened on reasonable grounds, what is left is not an unreasonable time. Once the occurrence of an anticipatory non-performance is declared by the defaulting party, there should be no further limitations on the power to avoid by a buyer who has already fixed a valid additional period. A further delay would serve no purpose and could no longer be justified on the grounds of reasonableness. This answer is consistent with the lack of any mandatory "grace period" for termination in the PECL both in general and in anticipatory breach under Art. 9:304.

NOTES

1. PECL Art. 9:303(4), dealing with automatic avoidance upon impediment, was omitted from this comparative analysis.
2. For avoidance\termination of an installment contract, *see* also CISG Art. 73 and PECL Art. 9:302.

[66] It may be argued that the main effect of the "notice" clause of PECL Art. 8:106(2) is to limit the buyer's power to avoid during *Nachfrist* rather than to empower her to do so in the first place. The reason is that the PECL's general doctrine of anticipatory non-performance, expressed in PECL Art. 9:304, may otherwise apply in *Nachfrist* situations. This provision makes termination available whenever a fundamental non-performance becomes "clear" even before the performance's designated time. This may well cover performances expected throughout *Nachfrist* periods. The apparent problem here would be the limitation in PECL Art. 8:106(2) on the aggrieved party's power to terminate during the *Nachfrist*. However, the doctrine of anticipatory breach stipulated in PECL Art. 9:304 is specific to such cases and could conceivably hold also under *Nachfrist* conditions. Superimposing the two articles on each other would allow for termination, under *Nachfrist*, even of non-fundamental anticipatory non-performance. Of course, the termination due to notice of continuing default included in PECL Art. 8:106(2) is narrower and more specific than the said superimposition, and thus the argument is purely speculative.

Remedy of reduction of price: Remarks on the manner in which the Principles of European Contract Law may be used to interpret or supplement Article 50 of the CISG

Jarno Vanto

(a) Article 50 of the Convention is a part of the remedial scheme of the CISG. This provision is reflective of the general CISG approach of trying to balance the rights of the buyer and the seller, in the sense that it gives the buyer the right to reduce the price, but the seller may remedy the non-conformity and subsequently obtain the original price agreed on in the contract. PECL Article 9:401 gives the buyer the same right of reducing the price, even though the Principles do not use the term "buyer" but instead use a "party who accepts the tender of performance." It must be noted that the Principles apply not only to contracts for the sale of goods but also to other types of contracts.[1] In the CISG's realm, the buyer has at his disposal,[2] in addition to price reduction, the remedies of specific performance (CISG Article 46), request for remedying of the non-conforming performance (CISG Article 48), avoidance of the contract in cases of fundamental breach of contract (CISG Article 49(1)), and damages (CISG Articles 45(1) and 74–77).

(b) The objective of CISG Article 50 is to give the buyer an opportunity to keep the received goods that, even though not entirely conforming to what had been agreed on in the contract, he may still make use of, but he may take the non-conformity into account when paying the purchase price. This means that price reduction is a remedy that is available to the buyer only if the goods are not in conformity with what the parties had agreed on in the contract and not, for example, in cases where the price of the contracted goods has gone down in the world market after the conclusion of the contract and the buyer feels trapped in a bad contract. This is the case also with PECL Article 9:401.

(c) Both CISG Article 50 and PECL Article 9:401 set as a prerequisite for their application that the goods do not conform with the contract.[3] Article 35(1) of the Convention states that the goods conform with the contract if they are of the quantity, quality, and description required by the contract. The goods also need to be contained or packaged in the manner required by the contract. Additionally, CISG Article 35(2) states that the goods do not conform with the contract unless they (a) are fit for the purposes for which goods of the same description would ordinarily be used; (b) are fit for any particular purpose expressly or implicitly made known to the seller at the time of the conclusion of the contract, except where the circumstances show that the buyer did not rely, or that it was unreasonable for him to rely, on the seller's skill and judgment; (c) possess the qualities of goods that the seller has held out to the buyer as a sample or model; and (d) are contained or packaged in the manner usual for such goods or, where there is no such manner, in a manner adequate to preserve and protect the goods.

[1] Wilhelmsson, Thomas, Ole Landon kyydissä kohti Eurooppalaista Sopimusoikeutta, available online at <http://www.cbs.dk/departments/law/staff/ol/commission_on_ecl/literature/wilhelmsson/ole-landon-kyydissa-korjattu.rtf>.

[2] Handelsgericht des Kantons Aargau, 5. November 2002, available online at <http://www.cisg-online.ch/cisg/urteile/715.htm>.

[3] Germany 12 October 2000, District Court Stendal, case presentation available online at <http://cisgw3.law.pace.edu/cases/001012g1.html>.

(d) The Official Comment[4] on PECL Article 9:401 brings forth that the remedy of price reduction is available to the aggrieved party where the other party's performance is incomplete or otherwise fails to conform to the contract and is available whether the non-conformity relates to the goods' quantity, quality, time of delivery, or other characteristic. In connection with this remedy, CISG Articles 41 and 42 state that the seller has an obligation to deliver the goods free from any third-party right or claim or a third-party right or claim based on industrial property or other intellectual property. Opinions have been raised that price reduction could be used as a remedy also in relation to third-party claims. Unless the third-party claim would amount to a fundamental breach of contract (e.g., the consignment is owned entirely by a third party), use of this remedy would seem plausible in light of the Comment to PECL Article 9:401.[5]

(e) The buyer bears the burden of proof with regard to the nature and extent of the non-conformity of the goods.[6]

(f) In addition to the non-conformity of the goods, a prerequisite for the buyer's right to reduce the price is that the buyer give notice to the seller and specify the nature of the lack of non-conformity within a reasonable time after he has discovered it or ought to have discovered it, as defined in CISG Article 39, unless the seller knew or could not have been unaware of the lack of conformity (CISG Article 40).[7]

[4] Like the commentary to the UNIDROIT Principles and the U.S. Restatements, the Comments to the PECL help explain the text. The PECL Notes identify civil law and common law antecedents and related domestic provisions. With the permission of the Commission on European Contract Law, the Comments and Notes to PECL Article 9:401 are available online at <http://cisgw3.law.pace.edu/cisg/text/comparison50.html>. The source of that material is Ole Lando & Hugh Beale eds., *Principles of European Contract Law: Parts I and II* (Kluwer Law International, 2000) 430–433.

[5] Third-party claims are problematic in terms of price reduction because it is difficult to calculate the price reduction in these instances. *See, e.g.*, Schlechtriem P. *Uniform Law – The UN Convention on Contracts for the International Sale of Goods* d) Reduction of the Price (Article 50): "The general similarity of the prejudice caused by these defects with that caused by other defects justifies the availability of price reduction in these cases as well. But the formula for calculating the decrease in value due to such defects surely would have required thorough deliberations for which no time remained at the Conference," available at <http://cisgw3.law.pace.edu/cisg/biblio/schlechtriem-50.html>.

However, the structure of Section II, namely the "Conformity of the goods *AND* third party claims," points to another direction. The Section title presents these as separate items of the section. Article 50 talks about the conformity of the goods. If one were to adhere to the structuring of Section II in the way that its wording seems to hint, one would possibly not apply price reduction to third-party claims. However, Article 44 specifically states that price reduction is applicable to third-party claims and gives leverage to the argument that third-party claims are subject to price reduction despite the difficulties in calculation.

[6] *See* the relevant case law:

- Switzerland 9 September 1993 Commercial Court Zürich, available online at <http://cisgw3.law.pace.edu/cases/930909s1.html>;
- Netherlands 15 October 2002 Netherlands Arbitration Institute, Case No. 2319, available at <http://cisgw3.law.pace.edu/cases/021015n1.html>;
- Switzerland 30 November 1998 Commercial Court Zürich, available at <http://cisgw3.law.pace.edu/cases/981130s1.html>;
- Italy 12 July 2000 District Court Vigevano (*Rheinland Versicherungen v. Atlarex*), available at <http://cisgw3.law.pace.edu/cases/000712i3.html>;
- ICC Arbitration Case No. 6653 of 1993, available at <http://cisgw3.law.pace.edu/cases/936653i1.html>.

See also Ferrari F., in *Review of the Convention on Contracts for the International Sale of Goods* (Kluwer Law International 2000–2001), at p. 6: ". . . the following three general principles (1) any party which wants to derive beneficial legal consequences from a legal provision has to prove the existence of the factual prerequisites of that provision (2) any party claiming an exception has to prove the existence of the factual prerequisites of that exception; and (3) those facts are exclusively in a party's sphere of responsibility and which therefore are, at least theoretically, better known to that party have to be proven by that party, since it is that party who exercises the control over that sphere."

[7] Netherlands 19 December 1991, District Court, *Roermond Fallini Stefano v. Foodik*, case presentation available online at <http:/cisgw3.law.pace.edu/cisg/cases/911219n1.html>, where it was held that, for the

(g) PECL Article 9:401(3) states that "a party who reduces the price cannot also recover damages for reduction in the value of the performance but remains entitled to damages for any further loss it has suffered so far as these are recoverable under Section 5 of this Chapter."

On the other hand, CISG Article 50 does not explicitly state that when the buyer reduces the price he may not recover damages for reduction in the value of the performance. However, it is stated in CISG Article 45(2) that the buyer is not deprived of any right he may have to claim damages by exercising his right to other remedies. It is reasonable to presume that the reduction in value may not be claimed both as price reduction and as damages and that in this sense the effect of CISG Article 50 and PECL Article 9:401 is similar, even though both the PECL and the CISG give the buyer the right to claim any further losses as damages.[8,9,10]

The Comment on PECL Article 9:401 states that the two remedies are incompatible, so there is no right to cumulate them. As is clear, the two remedies are incompatible only to the extent that they overlap.[11] Furthermore, both CISG Article 50 and PECL Article 9:401 give the buyer an opportunity to demand price reduction even if damages are not, or cannot be, claimed; for instance, when CISG Article 79 is applicable.[12]

(h) Price reduction as a remedy for contractual breach can in many cases be regarded as a pre-procedural remedy in the sense that the buyer presumably often demands a reduction in price from the seller in case retaining the goods delivered serves his interests, even though they do not conform entirely with what the parties had agreed on in the contract. If the requested price reduction is not met with acceptance on the seller's side, the dispute in all likelihood will be dealt with in court. It has been argued that when price reduction is claimed in court it often assumes the nature of a defense, rather than a claim. This is

seller not to be able to rely on CISG Articles 38 and 39, the buyer had to prove its allegation that the seller knew or could not have been unaware of the lack of conformity of the goods. The court observed that, if the buyer were able to meet that burden of proof, it would be entitled to a reduction of the purchase price pursuant to Article 50 CISG.

[8] Kritzer A. H., *International Contract Manual, Guide to Practical Applications of the United Nations Convention on Contracts for the International Sale of Goods* (Kluwer Law, 1989), p. 441: "Article 45 (2) makes it clear that the buyer can claim damages in addition to declaring the reduction of the price in those cases where reducing the price does not give as much monetary relief as would an action for damages. A buyer might wish to combine the two remedies in a case if there was some possibility that damages could not be recovered, either because there was a question as to whether the seller was exempted from damages (but not from a reduction of price under Article 79) or because there was a question as to whether the damages had been foreseeable under Article 74. A declaration of reduction of the price would give the buyer some immediate relief while the rest of the claim for damages was subject to negotiation or litigation OFFICIAL RECORDS: p. 43, para. 13."

[9] *See* UNCITRAL Yearbook VIII A/CN. (/SER.S/1977, p. 42, para. 231). *See* also Honnold J., *Documentary History of the CISG*, p. 355: "Even in cases where the buyer had declared the price reduced he might have suffered additional damages, for instance because of delay. It was considered that the remedy scheme of the Convention should not preclude the buyer from obtaining such damages from the seller."

[10] Will, Michael R. in Bianca/Bonell Commentary, at p. 373: "It is up to the buyer to decide which is more advantageous for him: price reduction, or damages or price reduction and damages."

[11] "Der Schadensersatzanspruch konkurriert mit anderen Rechtsbehelfen, insbesondere auch der Minderung des Kaufpreises. Der Gläubiger kann allerdings keinen Schadensersatz verlangen, so weit er einen anderen Rechtsbehelf erfolgreich ausgeübt und dadurch erreicht hat, dass der Schaden ganz oder teilweise beseitigt wird (von Caemmerer/Schlechtriem, *Kommentar zum einheitlichen UN-Kaufrecht*, 2. Aufl., Rn. 5 zu Article 74" (Damages claim exists in concurrence with other remedies including price reduction. The claimant may not claim damages if he has pursued another remedy which already covers the extent of the loss suffered . . .) in Oberlandsgericht Schleswig 08/22/2002 11 U 40/01, available online at <http://www.cisg-online.ch/cisg/urteile/710.htm>.

[12] On differences between price reduction and damages, *see* Eric E. Bergsten & Anthony J. Miller, "The Remedy of Reduction of Price," 27 *Am. J. Comp. L.* (1979) 255–277, also available online at <http://cisgw3.law.pace.edu/cisg/biblio/bergsten.html>.

so when the seller claims the purchase price for delivered goods and the buyer brings forth a claim for price reduction on the basis of non-conforming goods.[13] Even though in practice price reduction has assumed the character of a defense rather than a claim, it must be emphasized that it is still a unilateral right of the buyer.

(i) Both PECL Article 9:401 and CISG Article 50 apply the same manner of calculating the reduction in price. The price reduction is proportionate to the reduction in value caused by the non-conforming performance.[14] Thus, the contract price is the value without defect, and the reduced price is the value with the defect. The defining moment for determining the price is the time of delivery of the goods.[15,16] This means that if the price of the goods has fallen when the buyer demands price reduction he may still calculate the price reduction based on the original, higher price, which results in the price reduction being beneficial to him. Then again, if the price of the goods has risen after the non-conforming goods were delivered, the buyer may only demand that the price be reduced in proportion to the contracted lower price. In these situations it may be more beneficial for the buyer to claim damages as an alternative to price reduction.

(j) It has been acknowledged that the remedy of price reduction is traditionally a civil law remedy that has its origins in the Roman law remedy of *actio quanti minoris.*[17,18] *Actio quanti minoris* has been brought forward in the Comment on PECL Article 9:401.[19] The original meaning of the *actio* was that the buyer could bring an action against the seller to reduce the price when there was a hidden or latent defect in the goods.[20] Both CISG Article 50 and PECL Article 9:401, sharing similar rationale and modus operandi, are somewhat qualified expressions of *actio quanti minoris.*[21]

(k) The terminology employed by both CISG Article 50 and PECL Article 9:401 appears similar and would presumably produce largely similar results in resolving a contractual dispute. PECL Article 9:401 lays out many of the criteria for the application of the remedy of price reduction that in the CISG have to be drawn from many intertwined

[13] Sondahl E., "Understanding the Remedy of Price Reduction – A Means to Fostering a More Uniform Application of the United Nations Convention on Contracts for the International Sale of Goods," available online at <http://cisgw3.law.pace.edu/cisg/biblio/sondahl.html>.

[14] Lookofsky, J, *Understanding the CISG in Europe* (2nd ed., Kluwer Law International) 135.

[15] Landgericht Aachen, 3 April 1990, 41 0 198/89, available online at <http://www.jura.uni-freiburg.de/ipr1/cisg/urteile/text/12.htm>.

[16] Switzerland 27 April 1992 District Court Locarno Campagna, available online at <http://cisgw3.law.pace.edu/cases/920427s1.html>: in that case, an Italian seller of furniture claimed the purchase price that the Swiss buyer refused to pay, alleging lack of conformity of the goods. It was held that as the buyer had resold some of the defective furniture without notifying the seller in time about the resale, the buyer had lost its right to rely on non-conformity of the goods. With regard to other goods, the buyer was granted a reduction of price, because he had promptly notified the seller about the defects and the seller had refused to remedy the defects. The court rejected an offer made by the seller during the proceedings to pay the repair cost, holding that Article 50 CISG was not intended to provide for restitution of the repair cost, but rather a reduction of the purchase price in the same proportion as the value that the goods actually delivered had at the time of delivery bore to the value that conforming goods would have had at that time.

[17] Piliounis, Peter A., "The Remedies of Specific Performance, Price Reduction and Additional Time (*Nachfrist*) under the CISG: Are these Worthwhile Changes or Additions to English Sales Law," *Pace Int'l. L. Rev.* (Spring 2000), 1–46, Zimmerman, R., *The Law of Obligations: Roman Foundations of the Civilian Tradition* (Oxford, Clarendon Press, 1996), 318.

[18] Ole Lando & Hugh Beale eds., *Principles of European Contract Law: Parts I and II* (Kluwer Law International, 2000), 430–433.

[19] The Official Comments and Notes on PECL Article 9:401 are available online at <http://cisgw3.law.pace.edu/cisg/text/comparison50.html>.

[20] *See* Lando & Beale, op. cit.]

[21] On *actio quanti minoris* in civil law systems and on common law understanding of price reduction, *see* the Official Comment on PECL Article 9:410 containing notes on the match-up between continental and common law rules, available online at <http://cisgw3.law.pace.edu/cisg/text/comparison50.html>.

Articles of the Convention. The utility of the PECL to interpret CISG Article 50 is more extensive in civil law jurisdictions where the concept underlying PECL Article 9:401 (i.e., *actio quanti minoris*) as a conceptual tool for understanding price reduction has more weight. Common law systems do recognize the remedy of price reduction, but it assumes a narrower scope than it does in civil law systems. PECL Article 9:401, however, is of use even for a common law lawyer wanting to understand the remedy of price reduction in a CISG-related dispute.

Remedies for breach of contract where only part of the contract has been performed: Comparison between provisions of the CISG (Articles 51 and 73) and counterpart provisions of the Principles of European Contract Law

Christopher Kee

I. INTRODUCTION

CISG Articles 51 and 73 are often considered concurrently as they both deal with the scenario in which only part of a contract has been performed. However, by doing so, some very important distinctions between the two articles may be overlooked. As one would expect, Article 51, which appears under the heading, "Remedies for Breach of Contract by the Seller," does provide rights that are only exercisable by the buyer. The first two sub-articles of Article 73, on the other hand, are provisions common to both the seller and the buyer.[1]

A further crucial distinction within the subject matter of the two articles is the type of contract considered by each. Article 51 applies where there has been a failure to deliver part of a contract intended to be delivered as a whole. Article 73 applies to installment contracts and the failure to perform an obligation in respect to an installment.[2] Further,

[1] Both CISG Articles 51 and 73 belong to the Convention's Part III: *Sale of Goods*. Article 51 is listed in Chapter II: *Obligations of the Seller*, Section III: *Remedies for Breach of Contract by the Seller*. Article 73 is listed in Chapter V: *Provisions Common to the Obligations of the Seller and of the Buyer*, Section I: *Anticipatory Breach and Installment Contracts*.

Schlechtriem, commenting on the operation of CISG Art. 73, states that "this provision is concerned with successive deliveries, not installment payments. By analogy, however, Article 73(2) can also apply to missed payments if they coincide with installment deliveries. Otherwise, the entire contract may be avoided under Article 72. Article 73(2) is also applicable to other breaches by the buyer, such as not taking delivery of an installment." P. Schlechtriem, *Uniform Sales Law – The U.N. Convention on Contracts for the International Sale of Goods*, (1986) at p. 96, relevant excerpt also available online at <http://cisgw3.law.pace.edu/cisg/biblio/schlechtriem-73.html>.

[2] *Cf.* Karollus, Martin., "Judicial Interpretation and Application of the CISG in Germany 1988–1994," *Cornell Review of the Convention on Contracts for the International Sale of Goods* (1995) 51–94, also available at <http://cisgw3.law.pace.edu/cisg/biblio/karollus.html>. Karollus provides a critique of the Germany 14 August 1991 Landgericht [District Court] Baden-Baden, case presentation including English translation

although in both scenarios the buyer may ultimately obtain the same remedy, the two Articles follow different paths to that result.[3]

The PECL do not draw a distinction between rights of the seller and buyer in the same manner as the CISG. Nor is the PECL intended to relate solely to contracts for the sale of goods. As a consequence of the latter difference the term "delivery" makes way for "performance." At first glance, PECL Article 9:302 is most comparable to CISG Article 73 as it considers a failure of performance in the situation where "... the contract is to be performed in separate parts and in relation to a part to which counter performance can be apportioned..." However, as discussed in this chapter, this language does not exclude those circumstances contemplated by CISG Article 51. Further, despite wording that may initially indicate the contrary, and arguably unlike CISG Article 73(3),[4] PECL Article 9:302 does not release an aggrieved party of any obligations that may have accrued at the time of the failure.

II. SCHEME OF CISG ARTICLES 51 AND 73 AND PECL ARTICLE 9:302

Leser describes CISG Article 51 as creating a "de facto division" in the contract.[5] This artificial dichotomy was created to promote one of the fundamental tenets of the CISG – to keep contracts "on foot." An unintended consequence has been competition with CISG Article 73. From a buyer's perspective, Article 51 offers a considerably more certain method of avoiding the offending part of the contract.

By providing recourse to the *Nachfrist* provisions in CISG Articles 47 and 49(1)(b),[6] Article 51 allows circumstances in which the buyer does not need to show the fundamental breach required by CISG Article 73.[7] CISG Article 51(2) also offers the buyer the ability to avoid the entire contract in instances where failure relating to a part amounts to a fundamental breach of the whole contract.[8] CISG Article 73(3) would instead appear to

available at: <http://cisgw3.law.pace.edu/cases/910814g1.html>. This was a case where the German buyer placed an order for two tile sets A and B with an Italian seller. Both sets contained basic and decorative tiles. The basic tiles belonging to set A were non-conforming, and the buyer sought to avoid the contract in respect of the entirety of set A. In a step that appears to be inconsistent with Article 51, the German Court accepted avoidance of that set, based on the rationale that without the appropriate basic tiles, the decorative tiles in set A were useless. Had Article 51 been followed strictly the only two remedies available would have been either avoidance of the whole contract (i.e., set A and B) or avoidance of the basic tiles of set A only. Karollus supports the court's decision as such a remedy is contemplated by Article 73, and he argues there is no reason why it should not apply to non-installment contracts as well.

[3] *Cf.* CISG Article 64 for seller's rights and remedies for a breach of contract by the buyer.

[4] *See* note 9 *infra*.

[5] Leser, Hans G., in: Schlechtriem, P. (ed.) *Commentary on the UN Convention on the International Sale of Goods (CISG)*, 2nd edition. Clarendon Press, Oxford, 1998 at p. 545.

[6] *See* Zeller, B., "Comparison between CISG Articles 47 and 49(1)(b) and counterpart provisions in the PECL," available at <http://cisgw3.law.pace.edu/cisg/text/peclcomp47.html#er>.

[7] *See* further Honnold, J., *Uniform Law for International Sales under the 1980 United Nations Convention* (2nd ed. 1991) Kluwer Law and Taxation Publishers, Deventer, Boston, at 501, where he notes that the idea of a *Nachfrist* notice cannot be compatible with CISG Articles 73(2) and 73(3). Honnold does, however, suggest that in certain circumstances – for example delivery of an installment or the failure to establish a letter of credit – it is not repugnant to all scenarios contemplated by CISG Article 73(1).

[8] "The approach in CISG Art. 51 follows logically from its linkage of the right of avoidance to the gravity of the breach." Jacob S. Ziegel, "Report to the Uniform Law Conference of Canada on Convention on Contracts for the International Sale of Goods" (July 1981) [available online at <http://cisgw3.law.pace.edu/cisg/text/ziegel51.html>]. That approach has been widely recognized in the case law; *see, e.g.*, Germany 24 May 1995 *Oberlandesgericht* [Appellate Court] Celle, English translation available at <http://cisgw3.law.pace.edu/cases/950524g1.html>, where the court reiterated that regarding a delivery or conformity of only part of the goods, the rules of CISG Articles 46 to 50 apply to the part that is missing or non-conforming under Art. 51(1), and further, that if the seller's offer to deliver conformed with

take the curious position of forcing the buyer to elect between avoiding future or previous deliveries, although this distinction has been dismissed.[9]

As is the case with all of buyer's remedies under the CISG, Articles 51 and 73 are both subject to the examination and notice regimes of Articles 38 and 39 (examination of the goods "within as short a period as is practicable under the circumstances" and "notice to the seller specifying the nature of [any] lack of conformity within a reasonable time after [the buyer] has discovered it or ought to have discovered it"). If the buyer elects the remedy of avoidance where the goods have been delivered, Article 49(2) also requires the buyer to declare the contract avoided "within a reasonable time." Article 51 states that "articles 46 to 50 apply" to it; hence this further reasonable time requirement is an element of an avoidance proceeding pursuant to Article 51. There is no reference to that in Article 73(1).[10] Even so, the general consensus of scholarly opinion tends to favor the

the contract, the buyer would not have the right to avoid the contract unless he could show that a partial delivery was a fundamental breach and therefore the missing part [a used printing press] entitled him to avoid the entire contract under CISG Art. 51(2). *See* also Germany 3 July 1992 Landgericht [District Court] Heidelberg, English translation available online at <http://cisgw3.law.pace.edu/cases/920703g1.html>. In that case, a German buyer concluded a contract for the sale of computer components with a U.S. seller, but after delivery of five parts had been carried out, the buyer refused payment and declared the contract avoided on the grounds that the delivery of eleven parts had been agreed. The German court held that even if delivery of eleven parts had been agreed the dispatch of only five parts would not entitle the buyer to declare the contract in its entirety avoided according to CISG Art. 51(2). *See* further, R. Koch, "The Concept of Fundamental Breach of Contract under the U.N. Convention on Contracts for the International Sale of Goods," *Review of the Convention on Contracts for the International Sale of Goods (CISG)* 1998, Kluwer Law International (1999) 177–354, also available online at <http://cisgw3.law.pace.edu/cisg/biblio/koch.html>.

See also ICC Arbitration Case No. 7660 of 1994, available at <http://cisgw3.law.pace.edu/cases/947660i1.html>, where the arbitral tribunal noted that Article 51(1) CISG provided for a partial avoidance of the contract as declared by the buyer and that under Article 51(2) CISG such partial avoidance was the rule rather than the exception in cases of partial non-performance amounting to a non-fundamental breach of the contract (Article 49(1)(a) CISG). In that case, the arbitral tribunal determined that a partial avoidance under Article 51(1) CISG was permissible where the defective piece of machinery formed an independent part of the contracted goods as it was in the case at issue. However, the arbitral tribunal further determined that the buyer's partial avoidance was barred by the 18-month time limit contained in the contract.

[9] *See* further Leser, *supra* note 5 at p. 551. He states that often in these situations as it will be not possible to achieve the purpose of the contract as a whole, there must be a fundamental breach allowing avoidance of the entire contract despite this wording. It is, however, interesting to note that ULIS Article 75 on which CISG Article 73 is modeled did specifically refer to deliveries already made or future deliveries or both. *Cf.* Schlechtriem, commenting on the operation of Art. 73(3). He states, "If, due to the interdependence of the installments, the defective or failed performance makes past or future installments worthless, those installments can be avoided as well. However, this is true only if the purpose of the entire contract was clear to both parties at the conclusion of the contract (Article 73(3)). The buyer's interest in receiving complete performance must, therefore, have been recognizable to the seller." P. Schlechtriem, *Uniform Sales Law – The U.N. Convention on Contracts for the International Sale of Goods* (1986), relevant excerpt also available online at <http://cisgw3.law.pace.edu/cisg/biblio/schlechtriem-73.html>.

See, e.g., Switzerland 30 November 1998, [Commercial Court] Zürich, CLOUT abstract no. 251, also available at <http://cisgw3.law.pace.edu/cases/981130s1.html>, where that court stated that regarding avoidance in installment contracts under CISG Art. 73, installment deliveries do not have to be of the same type of goods.

[10] Though CISG Article 73(2) provides that, in respect of refusal of future installments, a buyer may declare the contract avoided for the future, provided he does so within a reasonable time. *See, e.g.*, Switzerland 5 February 1997, *Handelsgericht* [Commercial Court] Zürich, CLOUT no. 214, also available at <http://cisgw3.law.pace.edu/cases/970205s1.html>. In that case, a German buyer had entered into a contract with a French seller for the delivery to Romania of 2 to 4 million liters of sunflower oil per month at a specified price. Although the buyer had paid a timely installment for the first delivery, the seller did not ship the goods to Romania. The buyer declared the contract avoided and sued the seller for restitution of the first installment and for damages. The Swiss court held that the buyer had a right to declare the contract avoided as the seller did not deliver the goods and this failure to perform its obligation gave reason to believe

buyer applying the CISG Article 51 approach in the absence of a very clearly defined installment contract.[11]

The drafters of the PECL have avoided the competition between CISG Articles 51 and 73 by not including a specific provision that explicitly directs the parties to act in the same manner as CISG Article 51. Although using the same language of CISG Article 51 (i.e., "parts") a plain reading of PECL Article 9:302 does only allow termination[12] as to the part where there has been fundamental non-performance.[13] Therefore, with the exclusion of this linguistic argument, PECL Article 9:302 does represent a shorter restatement of CISG Article 73. However, it is important not to immediately assume that the PECL promote the rights and remedies afforded by CISG Article 73 and by its silence condemn the approach of CISG Article 51.

III. ADVANTAGES AND DISADVANTAGES OF THE DIFFERENT PHRASES

When considering these particular articles, several opposing conclusions may be drawn from using the PECL to help interpret the CISG. Those familiar with arguing around the common law doctrine of precedent will appreciate that in this instance the omission of the PECL to explicitly address a CISG Article 51 scenario does not in and of itself suggest a criticism of the approach. Although that view could be taken, it is suggested that the better view is that the combined PECL articles promote the CISG Article 51 position in two ways – by providing a restrictive definition of termination and by requiring fundamental non-performance.

As was foreshadowed in the introduction to this chapter, PECL Article 9:302 allows termination of the "contract as a whole" where non-performance is fundamental to the contract as a whole. However, "contract as a whole" does not, as it might initially appear, mean the entire contract. PECL Article 9:305 describes the effect of termination as it applies to all references to this word within the PECL. With two exceptions, termination of a contract as a whole will only relieve the parties of their future obligations. The Article specifically leaves intact the rights and liabilities that have accrued at the date of termination. The two exceptions are where the value of property already delivered has been fundamentally reduced (PECL Article 9:306) and where recovery of property already delivered can be made (PECL Article 9:308).

It must also be remembered that PECL Article 9:302 only allows termination in instances where there has been fundamental non-performance or, to use the CISG terminology, a fundamental breach. In doing so, the PECL is similarly promoting the notion of keeping contracts "on foot." Where the failure to perform, or non-performance, is not fundamental, there are a variety of other remedies available to the innocent party. One such remedy is PECL Article 8:106, a *Nachfrist*-type notice. Although this remedy is consistent with the CISG, its applicability in this instance may not be. It is important to be mindful of the rationale that guides PECL Article 9:302 and CISG Articles 51 and 73 – where the failure to perform or deliver a part of the contract does not compromise

that a fundamental breach of contract was to be expected for further installments (Articles 49(1)(b) and 73(1) and (2) CISG).

[11] Leser, *supra* note 5 at p. 551 and authorities cited at his n. 24.

[12] "Termination" is the PECL's counterpart to the CISG's term "avoidance."

[13] About the terminology adopted, the PECL Comments to Article 9:302 state, "'Termination in relation to a part' of the contract is a slightly awkward phrase, as the contract is not terminated, but it has the advantage that the general rules on termination (such as the need to give notice under Article 9:303) applies. CISG Article 73 takes the same approach." Comment B, also available online at <http://cisgw3.law.pace.edu/cisg/text/peclcomp51.html#9:302>.

the purpose of the entire contract, it would be unreasonable to allow the entire contract to be ended.[14] If one cannot find a similar theme to CISG Article 51 in the PECL generally, then this rationale may be circumvented by PECL Article 8:106. Frequently, an extremely unfortunate consequence when apportioning counter-performance is the relatively simple matter of identifying a monetary value.[15]

Therefore, when considering PECL Articles 9:302, 9:305, and 9:306 together and in context, it is possible to see that the same philosophy that drives CISG Article 51 emerges. Recourse is first given to what might be described as "non-drastic" remedies. If the failure to perform a part of the contract amounts to fundamental non-performance of the entire contract, then with the assistance of PECL Article 9:306, all obligations including those previously accrued can be avoided.

IV. CONCLUSION

The PECL endorse and promote many of the principles outlined in the CISG. Although, in this instance, the Articles are not drafted in an identical or substantially similar manner, it is nonetheless possible to identify support for the notion of restricting a party's ability to unreasonably end an entire contract.

[14] *See* further PECL Comments to Article 9:302, Comment A, available online at <http://cisgw3.law.pace.edu/cisg/text/peclcomp51.html#cnpc>.

[15] The PECL Comments to Article 9:302 make it clear that where one party's obligations consists of distinct parts and the non-performance affects only one of those parts, PECL Article 9:302 is still applicable even though payment is not made separately. Comment C.

Cf. Ziegel who, commenting on the operation of CISG Art. 51, points out, "Read literally, Art. 51(1) suggest that the non-conforming goods may be subject to the remedy of avoidance regardless of the commercial viability of the rejected goods. UCC 2-601, by way of contrast, provides that only a 'commercial unit' may be accepted or rejected by the buyer. Presumably the Convention did not intend a different result." Jacob S. Ziegel, "Report to the Uniform Law Conference of Canada on Convention on Contracts for the International Sale of Goods" (July 1981), available online at <http://cisgw3.law.pace.edu/cisg/text/ziegel51.html>.

Open-price contracts: Editorial Remarks on whether and the extent to which the Principles of European Contract Law (PECL) may be used to help interpret Article 55 of the CISG

Andrea Vincze

I. INTRODUCTION TO THE OPEN-PRICE CONTRACT PROVISION IN THE CISG

a. Article 55 CISG,[1] which addresses the issue of open-price terms, is a highly debated provision in light of Article 14(1) CISG,[2] which describes the requirements of an offer. Yet, a close link between these two provisions is evident. The main controversy concerning the interaction between these provisions and their proper application derives from the fact that, at first sight, Articles 14(1) and 55 contradict each other, and therefore the application of Article 55 seemingly makes no sense. A theoretical debate between a broad (e.g., Honnold) and narrow (e.g., Farnsworth) interpretation has been going on for some time, but the controversy remains. It is, therefore, necessary to examine whether Articles 6:104, 6:105, 6:106, and 6:107 of the PECL may be used to help interpret the provision of open-price terms in the CISG.

II. BROAD AND NARROW INTERPRETATION OF ART. 55

b. Before comparing the relevant provisions of the CISG and the PECL, this chapter discusses the problem with interpreting Article 55 CISG. The question whether or not Articles 14(1) and 55 CISG should be read together arose because these two articles deal with very similar issues. Article 14(1) implies that for an offer to be sufficiently definite, which is a pre-condition for concluding a valid contract, among others, the price shall be expressly or implicitly fixed or a provision shall be made to determine the price. Article 55, however, seems to contradict the latter by providing that a contract may be validly concluded even without expressly or implicitly fixing or making provision for determining the price. It is important to note at this point that sales without prior fixing of a price are common in international trade.[3]

The two leading theories on interpretation are Professor Farnsworth's narrow interpretation, inferring that Articles 14(1) and 55 cannot be read together, and Professor Honnold's broad interpretation, which allows for parallel application of the two provisions.

Professor Farnsworth's position is that, by Article 55 expressly providing for its applicability to validly concluded contracts, the contract must have already been concluded for the price term to be supplied. Yet, under Article 14(1) a contract cannot be validly concluded without a sufficiently definite price term.[4] Therefore, following that interpretation, a "vicious circle" is present in the text of the CISG. Professor Farnsworth further contends that in spite of that vicious circle, Article 55 has some use because it can be applied by countries that made a reservation under Art. 92(1) CISG excluding the

[1] Article 55 CISG reads, "Where a contract has been validly concluded but does not expressly or implicitly fix or make provision for determining the price, the parties are considered, in the absence of any indication to the contrary, to have impliedly made reference to the price generally charged at the time of the conclusion of the contract for such goods sold under comparable circumstances in the trade concerned." It shall be noted that the Secretariat Commentary is on 1978 Draft Article 51, which was later amended, and therefore it cannot be applied to today's Article 55.

[2] Article 14 (1) CISG reads, "A proposal for concluding a contract addressed to one or more specific persons constitutes an offer if it is sufficiently definite and indicates the intention of the offeror to be bound in case of acceptance. A proposal is sufficiently definite if it indicates the goods and expressly or implicitly fixes or makes provision for determining the quantity and the price."

[3] As stated by the ICC Tribunal in ICC Arbitration 9819 of September 1999, *see* case presentation at <http://cisgw3.law.pace.edu/cases/999819i1.html>.

[4] E. Allan *Farnsworth*, "Formation of Contract," in *International Sales: The United Nations Convention on the Contracts for the International Sale of Goods* § 3.04 [1], at 3–8 (Nina M. Galston & Hans Smit eds., 1984), also cited by Paul *Amato*, "U.N. Convention on Contracts for the International Sale of Goods – The Open Price Term and Uniform Application: An Early Interpretation by the Hungarian Courts," available online at <http://cisgw3.law.pace.edu/cisg/biblio/amato.html>.

application of Part II of the Convention, including the controversial Article 14(1). In such cases, and also because the CISG is not concerned with the validity of a contract,[5] if the contract is found valid under the domestic law of that country, a legal dispute concerning the price terms of that contract can be resolved by Article 55 of the Convention.[6] Yet, such an interpretation is disputed by several authors because "in a codified set of rules . . . every effort should be made to construe seemingly incompatible provisions in order to make sense out of them,"[7] and they state that Article 55 must be read in conjunction with Article 14.[8] The balance of academic opinion seems to be in favor of Professor Honnold's approach to the issue.

Professor Honnold had initially opined[9] that a contract may be validly concluded even if the price is not settled because "the term 'validity' in Article 55 relates only to requirements of validity other than the determination of price" upon which an offer indefinite with respect to the price can be interpreted in the light of Article 55. However Professor Sclechtriem,[10] in referring to that approach, contended that most commentators disagree on this point. Professor Honnold also moved away from this interpretation and expressed his disagreement with it in the later edition of his book, stating that "[t]he legislative history shows that [the addition of the reference to 'validity' to the opening phrase of Article 55] was designed . . . to restrict the scope of the article 'to agreements that were valid by the applicable law' – i.e., domestic law applicable under rules of private international law."

Honnold further contends that Article 14(1) deals only with the question whether a communication not stating the price, and also without making express commitment to be bound, should be regarded as an offer – and not with the validity of an agreement not indicating the price. In contrast, Article 55 applies to validly concluded contracts to which the parties committed themselves to be bound but that did not expressly or implicitly fix the price or failed to make any provisions on determination of the price,[11]

[5] Art. 4 reads, "This Convention governs only the formation of the contract of sale and the rights and obligations of the seller and the buyer arising from such a contract. In particular, except as otherwise expressly provided in this Convention, it is not concerned with: (a) the validity of the contract or of any of its provisions or of any usage; (b) the effect which the contract may have on the property in the goods sold."

[6] *Farnsworth*, *supra* note 4; John E. *Murray*, Jr., "An Essay on the Formation of Contracts and Related Matters Under the United Nations Convention on Contracts for the International Sale of Goods," 8 *J.L. & Com.* 11 (1988), available online at <http://cisgw3.law.pace.edu/cisg/biblio/murray.html>, cited by Paul Amato, *supra* note 4; Phanesh *Koneru*, "The International Interpretation of the UN Convention on Contracts for the International Sale of Goods: An Approach Based on General Principles," available at <http://cisgw3.law.pace.edu/cisg/biblio/koneru.html>; Official Records of the United Nations Conference on Contracts for the International Sale of Goods (O.R.) 45.

[7] Alejandro M. *Garro*, "Reconciliation of Legal Traditions in the U.N. Convention on Contracts for the International Sale of Goods," available at <http://cisgw3.law.pace.edu/cisg/text/garro14.55.html>; Carlos A. *Gabuardi*, "Open Price Terms in the CISG, the UCC and Mexican Commercial Law, at <http://cisgw3.law.pace.edu/cisg/biblio/gabuardi.html#23>. *See* also Fritz *Enderlein* & Dietrich *Maskow*, "International Sales Law," at <http://cisgw3.law.pace.edu/cisg/biblio/enderlein-art55.html>.

[8] Jacob S. *Ziegel*, "Report to the Uniform Law Conference of Canada on Convention on Contracts for the International Sale of Goods," at <http://cisgw3.law.pace.edu/cisg/text/ziegel55.html>; Leif *Sevón*, "Obligations of the Buyer under the UN Convention on Contracts for the International Sale of Goods," at <http://cisgw3.law.pace.edu/cisg/biblio/sevon1.html>. *See* also Peter *Schlechtriem*, "Uniform Sales Law – The UN Convention on Contracts for the International Sale of Goods," available online at <http://cisgw3.law.pace.edu/cisg/biblio/schlechtriem-55.html>; and *Koneru*, *supra* note 6.

[9] John *Honnold*, *Uniform Law for International Sales* § 87 (1987), cf. § 325.3 of the 1999 3d ed. of that text.

[10] Peter *Schlechtriem*, "Uniform Sales Law," *supra* note 8.

[11] See Carlos A. *Gabuardi*, *supra* note 7; also supported by Martin *Karollus*, "Judicial Interpretation and Application of the CISG in Germany 1988–1994," at http://cisgw3.law.pace.edu/cisg/text/karollus14,55.html. *See* also *Koneru supra* note 6, commenting on *Entreprise Veyon v. Societé Ambrosio*, Court of Appeals Grenoble, 26 April 1995, available at <http://cisgw3.law.pace.edu/cases/950426f1.html>, where the court did not even address the question whether the missing price affects the validity of the contract.

Other authors have different views based on the mainstream opinions by Professor Farnsworth and Professor Honnold. Yet, for the purposes of this chapter, emphasis is placed only on the views of the latter two commentators.[12]

c. When examining the narrow and the broad interpretation of the interaction between the two relevant provisions, regard should be had to their legislative history as well. First, the text of Article 55 (i.e., originally Article 51 of the 1978 Draft) was adopted before adopting Part II of the Convention, which includes Article 14(1); thus a contradiction with Article 14(1) was apparent.[13] This seems to emphasize further that saving a contract with open-price terms should prevail over the narrow interpretation, which would stop the process of contracting at the very beginning if the proposal did not fix the price or did not provide a mechanism for determining the price.

Also, it is apparently true that "[t]he adoption of Art. 55 eventually responded to the desire of the Scandinavian countries to accept Part I of the Convention without Part II, and to have a provision in Part III in case the price has not been determined."[14] On the other hand, it is hard to believe that such a contradictory set of rules would have been created in favor of only four of the then-59 Contracting States, while the rest of the parties would have agreed to adopt a contradiction.[15]

d. In conclusion, the application of Professor Honnold's broad approach seems to be more pertinent when dealing with the CISG itself. However, when comparing Article 55 CISG with the similar set of rules of the PECL, the applicability and contractual validity requirements of the latter should be taken into account based on the particular context of the PECL.

e. In the PECL there is no such contradiction as the one between Articles 14 and 55 CISG. Article 2:201(1) provides that a "proposal amounts to an offer if: (a) it is intended to result in a contract if the other party accepts it, and (b) it contains sufficiently definite terms to form a contract." Consequently, if the *essentialia negotii* are present then subparagraph (a) indicates that a proposal can become an offer if the parties consider to be bound by that. Thus, the contract is concluded if the offer is accepted,[16] and Articles 6:104 to 6:107 apply only to validly concluded contracts to which the parties undoubtedly intended to be bound but where the price was not agreed upon for some reason. The approach of the PECL aims at eliminating the difficulties in some legal systems where the absence or insufficiency of determination of the price causes the contract to be void; the PECL regime supports saving such contracts. Therefore, it seems appropriate to follow the approach advocated by Honnold when comparing Article 55 CISG with the relevant articles of the PECL because under that view Article 55 CISG applies to validly concluded contracts, just as do Articles 6:104–107 PECL. Likewise, Article 14 is applied to determine whether a communication can be regarded as an offer without the parties' intent to be bound

[12] Some authors state that without a fixed price there is no offer under Article 14; therefore no delivery can be taken and there is no contract, resulting that provisions dealing with the substance of the contract (i.e., neither Article 55) cannot be applied. Others claim that the validity of the contract in this case shall be determined solely under national law (*see Enderlein & Maskow, supra* note 7, at para 2). Further commentators assume that once a contract is concluded, the offer becomes irrelevant and the conclusion of the contract itself proves that the offer was sufficiently definite, irrespective of whether a provision was made for determining the price (*see Garro, supra* note 7, at 95).

[13] Comment by Mr. *Loewe* (Austria), Official Records of the United Nations Conference on Contracts for the International Sale of Goods (O.R.), Vienna 10 March–11 April 1980, A/CONF. 97/19.

[14] *See* Alejandro M. *Garro, supra* note 7 at 18.

[15] *See Gabuardi, supra* note 7. The four countries opting out of Part II were Denmark, Finland, Sweden and Norway.

[16] Articles 2:204–2011 PECL.

by that, similarly to Article 2:201 PECL. The following analysis is based on Honnold's approach while not denying that other interpretations are also present in practice.

III. APPLICABILITY OF ARTICLE 6:104 PECL TO ARTICLE 55 CISG: DETERMINATION OF PRICE

f. Regarding Article 6:104 PECL, the wording of the relevant provisions of the PECL,[17] as stated above, and the Comments on the PECL[18] assume that the parties intended to conclude a contract (i.e., there is no doubt that they intended to be bound, but they did not agree on the price). The same is substantiated with regard to Article 55 CISG; a further proof, in addition to the above argument, is that "UNCITRAL in 1977 changed the opening clause . . . to read 'If a contract has been validly concluded . . . ' [in order to] introduce an express statement into the article to make it clear that it only applied to agreements which were considered valid by the applicable law."[19]

g. The basic condition of having failed to fix the price itself or the method for determining the price is provided for in the same way in the CISG and PECL provisions. Therefore, the condition is met if the price is not fixed either directly or indirectly, explicitly or implicitly. Concerning implicit determination in the PECL, usages and practices established between the parties must be taken into account, which is also applicable with regard to Article 55 CISG.[20] Similarly, references to list prices, stock market or market prices, commercial most-favored-party clauses, or the determination of the price by an expert is sufficient[21]; furthermore, the price is implicitly fixed not only when, for example, the buyer knows that the seller sells the goods according to price lists but also when the buyer should know about that.[22]

h. When not even an implicit provision on the price can be found, the PECL clarifies the meaning of Article 6:104 by suggesting that it seems better to save a contract not specifying the price in several exceptional cases; for example, when (a) the goods were

[17] Articles 2:201 and 6:104–107 PECL.

[18] Ole *Lando* & Hugh *Beale* eds., *Principles of European Contract Law: Parts I and II*, Kluwer Law International (2000) 307–314; also available online at <http://cisgw3.law.pace.edu/cisg/text/peclcomp55.html>.

[19] John O. *Honnold*, *Uniform Law for International Sales under the 1980 United Nations Convention*, 2nd ed., Kluwer 1991, p. 201.

[20] *See* Article 9 CISG. *See* also *Enderlein & Maskow*, *supra* note 7 at para 2; *Sevón*, *supra* note 8. In *Adamfi Video Production v. Alkotók Stúdiósa Kisszövetkezet*, Metropolitan Court Budapest, 24 March 1992, case presentation available at <http://cisgw3.law.pace.edu/cases/920324h1.html>, the court held that quality, quantity, and price were all fixed by practices between the parties. *See* also *Koneru supra* note 6.

[21] *Schlechtriem*, "Uniform Sales Law – The Experience with Uniform Sales Laws in the Federal Republic of Germany," at <http://cisgw3.law.pace.edu/cisg/text/schlechtriem14,55.html>; *Enderlein & Maskow supra* note 7 at para 4. Leif *Sevón* even suggests that an invoice sent in advance that is not objected to by the buyer could mean his agreement with the price indicated therein (*see Sevón*, *supra* note 8).

[22] *Enderlein & Maskow*, *supra* note 7. An interesting interpretation of the Austrian courts can be found in the "chinchilla pelts case" where the buyer ordered pelts of middle or better quality at a price between 35 and 65 German Marks per piece. The Court of Appeal found that such an "agreement as to the price range did not preclude the valid conclusion of a contract since under Article 55 of the Convention, if the price is not explicit or implicit in the contract, the parties are considered to have agreed on the usual market price." Later the Supreme Court confirmed this decision but by applying Article 14 instead of 55 CISG. It was held that the order was sufficiently definite to constitute an offer under Article 14 CISG because it could be perceived as such by a reasonable person in the same circumstances as the seller (Article 8(2) and (3) CISG). Also, the Supreme Court took into consideration the behavior of the Austrian buyer who accepted the delivered goods and sold them further without questioning their price, quality, or quantity. In particular, the price was found to be sufficiently definite, so as to make the application of Article 55 CISG unnecessary. *See* the online presentation of the case at <http://cisgw3.law.pace.edu/cases/941110a3.html> and comments on it in Willibald *Posch* & Thomas *Petz*, "Austrian Cases on the UN Convention on Contracts for the International Sale of Goods," 6 *Vindobona J. Int'l. Com. L. & Arbitration*, 2002, p. 1–24, available online at <http://cisgw3.law.pace.edu/cisg/biblio/posch-petz.html>.

needed urgently and there was no opportunity to agree on the price,[23] (b) it is not the custom to ask the price in advance, or (c) the obligor leaves it to the obligee to fix the price (e.g., when an opinion is sought from a professional person)[24]. This seems to be helpful in interpreting Article 55 CISG as well, supporting the principle of saving open-price contracts.

i. In the absence of any indication of the price, the PECL and the CISG provide for the application of different substitutes, the former for "reasonable price"[25] and the latter for "the price generally charged at the time of the conclusion of the contract for such goods sold under comparable circumstances in the trade concerned."[26] The wording in the CISG also refers to some kind of reasonable price that should also be "general" at the time of the conclusion of the contract (i.e., the seller will not enjoy later price increases and the buyer will not enjoy later reductions[27]), for "goods sold under comparable circumstances" (i.e., taking into account commercial terms, territorial criteria, quantity, periods of order, special needs, terms of payment etc.[28]) and in "the trade concerned."

j. Yet, determining the price under Article 55 CISG may involve uncertainties (e.g., special items or a certain product that is only made by one company, etc.)[29]. We can contend that it is appropriate to apply the "reasonableness" standard of the PECL to interpret the similar and, at first glance, more detailed definition of the CISG. Although the reasonableness standard is not expressly dealt with by the CISG, the definition in the PECL

[23] The situation described in para (a) is commonly mentioned with regard to the CISG. It is a very unique situation where the parties, pursuant to Article 6 CISG, derogate from Article 14 and intend to conclude a binding contract without providing for the price.

[24] Excerpt from Ole *Lando* & Hugh *Beale* eds., *Principles of European Contract Law: Parts I and II*, Kluwer Law International (2000) 307–314, available at <http://cisgw3.law.pace.edu/cisg/text/peclcomp55.html>; *see* also Peter *Schlechtriem*, "Uniform Sales Law – The Experience with Uniform Sales Laws in the Federal Republic of Germany," at <http://cisgw3.law.pace.edu/cisg/text/schlechtriem14.55.html>.

[25] Article 6:104 PECL.

[26] Article 55 CISG.

[27] *Enderlein & Maskow, supra* note 7, at para 7. See also *Veyron v. Ambrosio, supra* note 11, where the commercial agent asserted that his successor benefited from lower prices than those charged to him and requested the court to reduce accordingly the debt claimed by the seller, referring to Article 55 providing for the price generally charged in the relevant circumstances. The court found this argument inadmissible because it is overridden by a contrary agreement between the parties governing the totality of the provisions of the CISG.

[28] *Enderlein & Maskow, supra* note 7, at para 10. *See Russian Federation arbitration proceeding* 99/1994 of 22 November 1995, available online at <http://cisgw3.law.pace.edu/cases/951122r1.html>.

[29] *See* also Peter *Schlechtriem* (ed.), *English Commentary on the UN Convention on the International Sale of Goods (CISG)*, Comment on Art. 55 by Günter Hager, Oxford 1998, p. 462; CENTRAL List of Lex Mercatoria Principles, Rules and Standards, No. IV.5.1., available at <http://tldb.uni-koeln.de/TLDB.html> under 'List of Lex Mercatoria Principles,' Chapter IV 'Contract,' Section 5 'Contractual Obligations,' No. IV.5.1. That link leads to the Transnational Law Database of the Centre for Transnational Law (CENTRAL), which is maintained by the University of Cologne, Germany, and provides the "world's first online code for transnational law, the new lex mercatoria." The CENTRAL list of *lex mercatoria* principles includes in Chapter IV, Contract, Section 5, Contractual Obligations, No. IV.5.1. "Subsequent fixing of contract price," the following principle: "If the contract does not contain a provision fixing the price or a method for determining it, the parties are to be treated as having agreed to the price generally charged at the time of the conclusion of the contract for such performance in comparable circumstances in the trade concerned, or, if no such price is available, to a reasonable price."

Hager and *Enderlein & Maskow* are in favor of objectivization of the price determination. Although *Hager* explains that using the term "average price" would be more appropriate, *Enderlein & Maskow*, without wishing to change the wording of the CISG, interpret the "general price" term as meaning (a) a uniform price level if there is such in the relevant trade or (b) an average price if the prices in the trade differ but such a price can be calculated on the basis of prices used by representative sellers. *Eörsi* even suggests that, in case of doubt, the world market price shall prevail. *Cf. Enderlein & Maskow*, who instead of the latter, opine that a price typically agreed upon between partners from the countries where the parties have their place of business should be agreed upon.

fits the manner in which this concept is used in the CISG. Therefore, reasonableness requirements of the PECL can be applied to the interpretation of Article 55 CISG.[30]

If we look only to the CISG, Article 8 provides for a reasonable person standard in determining how to understand statements made by and other conduct of a party, in which due consideration is to be given to all relevant circumstances of the case including the negotiations, any practices that the parties have established between themselves, usages, and any subsequent conduct of the parties. The CISG lists only three of the "*all* relevant circumstances"; therefore, and also because the PECL concept of reasonableness fits to that of the CISG, other relevant circumstances included in the PECL can be taken into consideration in a case governed by the CISG. Therefore, some other factors to be taken into account when determining the price under Article 55 CISG are the following: the nature and purpose of the contract, comparable contracts made in analogous situations,

See also the much debated decision in *United Technologies International, Pratt & Whitney v. MALÉV Hungarian Airlines*, Legfelsőbb Bíróság, Gf. I. 31, 349/1992/9, also available online at <http://cisgw3.law.pace.edu/cases/920925h1.html>. The Hungarian Supreme Court reversed the decision of the Metropolitan Court Budapest by stating that the price of an additional Boeing engine, which was added to the contract later, was not fixed and that the price of the Airbus engine, which Malév did not choose, did not cover additional accessory equipment, meaning that the proposal did not include a sufficiently definite price; therefore, it did not qualify as an offer and there was no contract. The Supreme Court further held that Article 55 CISG was not applicable because "jet engines have no market price." The term "sufficiently definite price" was obviously misinterpreted, which has been confirmed by several authors and several national laws would find the decision strange too. First, Article 8 was completely disregarded by the court and instead, domestic law was applied; second, here was enough information in the communications that would have allowed for finding an implicitly fixed price. On the other hand, the court's reasoning concerning a non-existent market price is also questionable with regard to the possible methods of determining the price detailed above. The Hungarian Court made a mistake with regard to the interpretation of Article 55 CISG by viewing it as a method for determining the price and created a questionable link between the possibility to cure the lack of price term in the offer, an existing market price, and acceptance. Yet, the Court failed to clarify the relationship between the elements of Articles 14 and 55. Because of all the criticism concerning the decision of the Supreme Court, its applicability to further legal disputes is questionable. It would have the result of dismissing the requirements of Article 7 CISG concerning uniform interpretation. However, it should not be forgotten that the Malév decision was a very early interpretation of the CISG by Hungarian courts.

For further comments on the Malév decision, *see Amato, supra* note 4; *see* also *Koneru, supra* note 6; *see* also Harry M. *Flechtner*, The Several Texts of the CISG in a Decentralized System: Observations on Translations, Reservations and Other Challenges to the Uniformity Principle in Article 7 (1)," available at <http://cisgw3.law.pace.edu/cisg/wais/db/editorial/flechtner920925h1.html>; Claude *Witz*, "The Interpretive Challenge to Uniformity," at <http://cisgw3.law.pace.edu/cisg/wais/db/editorial/witz920925h1.html>.

See also the following decisions: Oberlandesgericht Frankfurt am Main, 4 March 1994 (Germany) where the Court found that an offer is not an offer unless it contains all essential elements of Article 14 and that Article 55 is only applicable in cases where there is performance of the contract; Bezirksgericht St. Gallen, 3 July 1997 (Switzerland) where the court mistakenly considered that the invoice price was to be interpreted as the price generally charged under comparable circumstances in the trade concerned; Tribunal of International Commercial Arbitration at the Russian Federation Chamber of Commerce and Industry, 3 March 1995 (Russia) where the tribunal ruled that the agreement of the parties to agree on the price in the future was not a valid method for determining the price; it therefore found Article 55 inapplicable. For deeper analysis *see* comments by Pilar *Perales Viscasillas* in *The Draft UNCITRAL Digest and Beyond: Cases, Analysis and Unresolved Issues in the U.N. Sales Convention – Papers of the Pittsburgh Conference Organized by the Center for International Legal Education (CILE)*, Franco Ferrari, Harry Flechtner & Ronald A. Brand eds., Sweet & Maxwell, Thomson, Sellier, 2004, p. 271–281.

[30] The universality of the reasonableness standard is evidenced by the fact that even though reasonableness is a common law institution, it is also an attribute of civil law systems where "*bonus pater familias*" or "good businessman" standards are used. *See* "Overview Comments on Reasonableness," Albert *Kritzer*, available online at <http://cisgw3.law.pace.edu/cisg/text/reason.html>: "Reasonableness is specifically mentioned in thirty-seven provisions of the CISG and clearly alluded to elsewhere in the Uniform Sales Law. Reasonableness is a general principle of the CISG." *See* also comments by Jelena *Vilus*, available online at <http://cisgw3.law.pace.edu/cisg/text/reason.html#vilus>; Ziegel, *supra* note 8.

the status of the parties, and any usages and practices established not only between the exact parties but also those within the trade or profession concerned.[31]

k. There is one further significant proviso concerning the applicability of Article 55 CISG, which is that it is inapplicable if there is any indication to the contrary (i.e., to the fact that, for example, the contract is to be formed only where there is agreement on the price or if there is no generally calculable price for the goods concerned).[32] Such a situation is not covered by Article 6:104 PECL either. Although there is no express provision for that in the PECL, the Comments on the PECL deal with the question as follows: Article 6:104 PECL is not applicable if the parties failed to agree on the price – for instance, because the parties could not reach an agreement on it during the negotiations, or they left the question open for future negotiation that was also unsuccessful. Yet, even in such cases, Article 6:104 can be applied if the subsequent behavior of the parties indicates that they did intend to enter into contractual relations.[33]

The latter approach might help interpret Article 55 CISG, especially with regard to the fact that Article 8 CISG provides for the determination of the parties' intent. Consequently, it is evident that if the parties failed to agree on the price for any of the reasons above, in all likelihood, a specific price would have been intended. Therefore, if the parties failed to agree upon it, there was no contract either, except when the subsequent behavior of the parties indicates that they did intend to enter into a contractual relationship (e.g., when the buyer placed a further offer with the seller). Of course, this approach adds nothing new to Article 55 CISG if we were to follow Professor Honnold's view, according to which that provision is only applicable to validly concluded contracts.

IV. APPLICABILITY OF ARTICLE 6:105 PECL TO ARTICLE 55 CISG: UNILATERAL DETERMINATION

l. Article 6:105 PECL deals with the situation where a unilateral determination of the price (or other contractual terms) by one of the parties has been made, but it is grossly unreasonable.[34] Applicability of this PECL provision to the CISG depends on whether Article 55 CISG allows for unilateral determination of the price by one of the parties. Professor Schlechtriem contends that "one-sided privilege to determine the price can neither be developed from general principles of the Convention, nor arrived at by recourse to internal law via the rules of private international law in order to apply the domestic right to determine the price . . . [t]his, however, is bound with the risk . . . that the courts will use the unavoidable degree of leeway in the consideration of evidence to the benefit of the home party."[35]

In theory, at least, the scope of the method of determining the price would not be restricted in such a way. Also in some civil law systems contracts of sale with open-price terms are viewed with hostility, particularly when the unilateral fixing of the price works to the disadvantage of the weaker party.[36]

[31] *See Kritzer, supra* note 30, citing Ole *Lando* & Hugh *Beale, supra* note 18 at 126–128.

[32] *Enderlein & Maskow, supra* note 6 at para 5.

[33] Ole *Lando* & Hugh *Beale, supra* note 17.

[34] Article 6:105 PECL: "Where the price or any other contractual term is to be determined by one party and that party's determination is grossly unreasonable, then notwithstanding any provision to the contrary, a reasonable price or other term shall be substituted."

[35] Peter *Schlechtriem*, "50 Years of the Bundesgerichtshof [Federal Supreme Court of Germany] – A Celebration Anthology from the Academic Community – Uniform Sales Law in the Decisions of the Bundesgerichtshof at II," at <http://cisgw3.law.pace.edu/cisg/biblio/schlechtriem3.html>. *See* also the Malév decision, *supra* note 29.

[36] *Garro, supra* note 7.

To the contrary, Enderlein and Maskow opine that it should "be admissible that reference be made to a price which a party, in practice particularly the seller, has to fix individually, i.e. not on the base of generally applicable lists. [. . .] Even when no reservation is made in this context, e.g., that the price is reasonable, that it is the usual price on the market, etc., and that there has to be a reasonable proportion between the price and the seller's prime costs, the fixing of an unjust price would nevertheless not be binding. This can be inferred from Articles 7, 8 or 9."[37]

m. Perhaps it is precisely Article 6:105 PECL that helps resolve this controversy by limiting the prospective "home-field advantage" and also the automatic lack of binding force of unilaterally fixed prices only to the case when those prices are "*grossly* unreasonable." Finding a unilaterally fixed price *grossly unreasonable* (e.g., a result of a clear mistake of arithmetic or a grossly wrong evaluation) instead of simply *unreasonable* requires a higher level of unfairness whereby one should refer again to the applicability of the reasonableness standard of the PECL that is discussed above. Those circumstances relevant in determining reasonableness or unreasonableness should be applied in this case as well.

All in all, Article 6:105 seems to help interpret Article 55 CISG, even though unilateral determination of the price is not expressly provided for in the CISG.

V. APPLICABILITY OF ARTICLE 6:106 PECL TO ARTICLE 55 CISG: DETERMINATION BY THIRD PERSON

n. Article 6:106 PECL addresses two issues concerning determination of the price (or other contractual terms) by third persons: first, the situation where the third person cannot or will not do so and, second, if its determination is grossly unreasonable.[38] Applicability of this provision to Article 55 CISG, again, depends on the admissibility of determination of the price by third parties in the CISG. It is acknowledged that in determining the method of fixing the price it is sufficient to refer to determination by an expert[39] and also that the relationship between Articles 14 and 55 CISG would not seem to pose any problems "when the parties have agreed, explicitly or implicitly, that the price may be fixed by a third party."[40]

o. Applicability of Article 6:106(2) raises no problems in that it provides for the substitution of a reasonable price if the third party determined a grossly unreasonable price.[41] The same applies to this situation, as stated earlier when examining Article 6:105.

[37] *Enderlein & Maskow, supra* note 7, at para 4. Unilateral determination is allowed, for example in the German BGB, the Greek CC, the Portuguese CC, the Danish, the Swedish, and the Finnish Sale of Goods Act, or in England. Limited unilateral determination is allowed in the Austrian ABGB. The Spanish CC, the Italian CC and French, Belgian, and Luxembourg law do not permit unilateral determination of the price for sale of goods contracts.

[38] Article 6:106 PECL provides, "(1) Where the price or any other contractual term is to be determined by a third person, and it cannot or will not do so, the parties are presumed to have empowered the court to appoint another person to determine it. (2) If a price or other term fixed by a third person is grossly unreasonable, a reasonable price or term shall be substituted."

[39] *See supra* note 21 and accompanying text.

[40] *Sevón, supra* note 8; *see* also *Enderlein & Maskow, supra* note 7, para 4.

[41] The reasonable price can be fixed by the court in Germany (under BGB § 317 (1)), Greece (under CC Art. 371), Italy (CC Art. 1349 (1)), and Portugal (under CC Art. 400). Even judicial revision of the price determined by the third person is also available in Italy and Germany. Fixing of a reasonable price by the court is not permitted in France and Luxembourg, for example (*see, e.g.*, French Cour de Cassation, Civ. 2, 6 June 1950, Bull. II no. 205, p. 141). All references to sources of law are taken from Ole *Lando* & Hugh *Beale, supra* note 18.

p. However, it is not certain that Article 6:106(1) would be also applicable. Although this provision of the PECL was designed to save the contract,[42] it cannot be inferred from the wording in the CISG that failure or inability of the third person to determine the price would entitle a court or arbitral tribunal to appoint another person to determine it.[43]

It seems more appropriate to conclude that, in that case, the general provision of Article 55 CISG is applicable, whereby the court or arbitral tribunal would determine the price generally charged in the relevant circumstances, which are also specific upon the special nature of originally having appointed an expert third person.[44]

VI. APPLICABILITY OF ARTICLE 6:107 PECL TO ARTICLE 55 CISG: REFERENCE TO A NON-EXISTENT FACTOR

q. Article 6:107 PECL provides that "[w]here the price [or any other contractual term] is to be determined by reference to a factor which does not exist or has ceased to exist or to be accessible, the nearest equivalent factor shall be substituted." This is a unique provision because national laws vary on this point, either opting for modification of the contract by substituting an existing factor[45] or termination of the contract, depending on the interpretation of the parties' intent.[46]

A similar provision cannot be found in the CISG; however, as the CISG is also aimed at saving the contract, it is arguably appropriate and useful to apply the PECL rule in connection with Article 55. If we contend that Article 6:107 might help interpret Article 55 CISG, regard is to be had of to Articles 8 and 9 CISG (i.e., intent, usages, practices, negotiations and subsequent conduct of the parties) so that a non-existent factor be replaced by another one that fits into the particular contractual relationship.

r. Yet, one should not forget two things. First, "[i]n the interpretation of this Convention, regard is to be had to its international character."[47] Second, the PECL were designed to "be applied as general rules of contract law in the European Communities which is applicable not only to international commercial contracts for the sale of goods, but to *all* contract transactions – contracts for services as well as goods and domestic as well as international contracts, including contracts with consumers."[48]

[42] For example, Art. 1592 (1) of the French CC and Section 9 of the UK Sale of Goods Act 1979 provide that the contract disappears in such cases. All references to sources of law are taken from Ole *Lando* & Hugh *Beale*, *supra* note 18.

[43] Yet, this is the case in Dutch (BW arts. 6:2 and 6:248) and Belgian law (see M.L. and M.E. Storme TPR 1985, 732 Nos 15 and 16). All references to sources of law are taken from Ole *Lando* & Hugh *Beale*, *supra* note 18.

[44] The German BGB and the Greek, the Italian, and the Portugal CC provide that if the third person fails to act, the court will act for him. (For references *see supra* note 41.) However, in some legal systems, the contract is void if the third person fails to determine the price (e.g., in the French and Luxembourg CC arts. 1592, the Austrian ABGB (Arts. 1056 and 1057), in the Spanish CC (Art. 1447 (2)) for sale of goods, in England and Scotland under the Sale of Goods Act 1979 (s. 9(1)). All references to sources of law are taken from Ole *Lando* & Hugh *Beale*, *supra* note 18.

[45] For example, Denmark, Germany (BGB § 242), or The Netherlands (BW Art. 6:258). All references to sources of law are taken from Ole *Lando* & Hugh *Beale*, *supra* note 18.

[46] In French and Luxembourg law the contract is terminated in such cases. But nowadays French law is more in favor of interpreting the intents of the parties (*see* Cass.Civ.2, 18 July 1985, Bull II no. 113 p. 84)). The same applies to Belgium (*see* Cour de Bruxelles 29 Oct. 1962, JT 1963 102), Portugal (CC Art. 239), Greece (CC Art. 200), Spain (CC Art. 1158), and Austria (ABGB § 194). All references to sources of law are taken from Ole *Lando* & Hugh *Beale*, *supra* note 18.

[47] Article 7 (1) CISG.

[48] *See Predrag Cvetkovik*, "Remarks on the manner in which the PECL may be used to interpret or supplement Article 14 CISG," available online at <http://cisgw3.law.pace.edu/cisg/text/peclcomp14.html#er>.

Concerning the international character of the CISG, the issues of choice of law and the applicable law come into question and may limit the applicability of Article 6:107 to Article 55 CISG. Therefore, a substituting factor should be adjusted to the requirements of the Convention, should have a very close connection to the law applicable to the contract, and should be a factor that is applicable to *international* sales.

On the other hand, we should not forget that Article 6:107 PECL applies to all contracts, not only to sale of goods contracts. Therefore, its applicability is limited again – it is not clear whether such a provision would have been incorporated into a similar legal instrument dealing exclusively with the principles of the law of sale of goods.

VII. CONCLUSIONS

On the various approaches concerning the relationship between Articles 14 and 55 CISG, it is not always evident that even similar provisions of the PECL would be applicable to interpret Article 55 CISG. The present analysis is based mainly on Professor Honnold's theory of broad interpretation,[49] which allows for parallel application of the two provisions of the Convention and by which the following consequences could be drawn.

Applicability of 6:104 PECL to Article 55 CISG

Article 6:104 PECL provides good interpretative guidance to Article 55 CISG in terms of the exact and practical meaning of the provision, carefully taking into account the conditions of applying the PECL.

Applicability of 6:105 PECL to Article 55 CISG

Although there is no express provision in the CISG regarding unilateral determination of the price, applying Article 6:105 PECL to interpret Article 55 CISG in that manner seems to be helpful in balancing the controversial views concerning the admissibility of unilateral determination of the price under the CISG.

Applicability of 6:106 PECL to Article 55 CISG

Article 6:106(1) PECL seems to be inapplicable to Article 55 CISG because it cannot be inferred from the wording in the CISG that failure or inability of the third person to determine the price would entitle a court or arbitral tribunal to appoint another person to determine it. However, Article 6:106(2) PECL, similarly to what is stated with regard to the applicability of Article 6:105, can help interpret Article 55 CISG.

Applicability of 6:107 PECL to Article 55 CISG

As no similar provision exists in the CISG, the applicability of Article 6:107 PECL seems to be disputed. Applicability of the PECL provision would serve the aim of saving the contract, but its practical execution could cause uncertainty and probably also resistance by the contracting parties.

[49] For the reasons, *see* paras. [a]–[d], *infra*.

Time for payment: Comparison between the provisions of CISG Art. 58 and the counterpart provisions of PECL Arts. 7:102 and 7:104

John Felemegas

I. INTRODUCTION

CISG Article 58 is located in the Convention's Part III "Sale of Goods," Chapter III "Obligations of the Buyer," Section I "Payment of the Price"; the stated provision governs the time for the buyer's payment of the purchase price in relation to performance by the seller.[1]

In essence, CISG Art. 58 regulates the important matter of when must the buyer pay the price for the purchased goods. There are, however, several related questions concerning payment that are answered in Art. 58: is the seller obliged to hand over the goods before he is paid, how does a contract that calls for carriage of the goods affect the payment of the price against the handing over of the goods, and whether the seller may require the buyer to pay the purchase price before the latter has an opportunity to examine the goods.[2]

The counterpart provisions of the PECL dealing with similar matters are located in the Principles Chapter 7 "Performance," Articles 7:102 "Time of Performance" and 7:104 "Order of Performance."

II. EXCHANGE OF GOODS FOR PRICE: THE PRINCIPLE OF SIMULTANEOUS PAYMENT OF THE PRICE AND HANDING OVER OF THE GOODS (CISG ART. 58(1))

The general rule stated in CISG Art. 58(1), first sentence, is that, subject to a contrary arrangement agreed by the parties to the contract, the buyer is obliged to pay the price

[1] CISG Art. 33 and PECL Art. 7:102 set out rules for ascertaining the time for delivery by the seller and require the seller to deliver on time. CISG Art. 52(1) and PECL Art. 7:103 provide rules regarding early delivery by the seller.

For a comparative analysis of the two instruments, *see* Ying C., "Comparison between provisions of the CISG (Articles 33 and 52(1)) and the counterpart provisions of the PECL (Articles 7:102 and 7:103)", available online at <http://cisgw3.law.pace.edu/cisg/biblio/ying.html>. Ying concludes in his analysis that

(a) the counterpart provisions of the first match-up (time for delivery) are virtually identical in all material respects and both should have the same legal effect; and

(b) regarding early delivery by the seller, (i) the Convention appears not to qualify the buyer's right to accept or reject the seller's early delivery, while the PECL does so, and (ii) The Convention is silent on the effect of early delivery by the seller on the time for payment by the buyer, while the PECL provides that a party's acceptance of early performance does not affect the time for the performance of its own obligations.

[2] *See* Honnold J. O., *Uniform Law for International Sales*, (Kluwer Law International, 3rd ed., 1999), at 363: Procedures for payment are of concern to the parties and usually are dealt with in the contract; Article 58 provides answers only when the contract is silent (Art. 6). [. . .] Article 58 is designed to minimize risks for both parties – risk to the seller from the delivery before payment and risk to the buyer from payment for defective goods.

at the time the seller makes the goods available to the buyer, by placing either the goods or documents controlling their disposition at the buyer's disposal.[3]

Furthermore, it is stated in Art. 58(1), second sentence, that the seller "may make such payment a condition for handing over the goods." From this follows that if the buyer does not pay at that time, the seller may refuse to hand over the goods (or *documents controlling their disposition*[4]).

[3] *See* the Text of the Secretariat Commentary on Art. 54 of the 1978 Draft *[draft counterpart of CISG Art. 58]*, available online at <http://cisgw3.law.pace.edu/cisg/text/secomm/secomm-58.html>.

> Comment 2. [Article 58(1)] recognizes that, in the absence of an agreement, the seller is not required to extend credit to the buyer.

CISG Art. 58 is substantially the same as Art. 54 of the Draft Convention; therefore, the Secretariat Commentary on 1978 Draft Art. 54 should be relevant to the interpretation of CISG Art. 58. *See* corresponding match-up, available at <http://cisgw3.law.pace.edu/cisg/text/matchup/matchup-d-58.html>. For case law confirming that pursuant to CISG Art. 58(1), in the absence of specific provisions within the contract establishing the time for the buyer's payment of the price, payment is due upon delivery (i.e., that payment was to be effected when the seller placed the goods at the buyer's disposal), *see*

- Switzerland 20 December 1994 *Tribunal Cantonal* [Appellate Court] Valais (*Marmipedretti Graniti S.r.l. v. Nichini S.A. Pierres naturelles et artificielles*), CLOUT abstract no. 197, case presentation including English translation available at <http://cisgw3.law.pace.edu/cases/941220s1.html>;
- Switzerland 30 June 1995 St. Gallen *Gerichtskommission* Oberrheintal, CLOUT abstract no. 262, case presentation available at <http://cisgw3.law.pace.edu/cases/950630s1.html>.

[4] The expression "documents controlling [the] disposition [of the goods]" was not clarified at the Vienna Diplomatic Conference. There is still uncertainty among commentators regarding the precise *meaning* of the expression, as well as the *type* of documents that satisfy that meaning for the purposes of CISG Art. 58. *See* Sevón L., "Obligations of the Buyer under the Vienna Convention on the International Sale of Goods," 106 *Juridisk Tidskrift* (Suomen Lainopillinen Yhdistys) (1990) 335, available online at <http://cisgw3.law.pace.edu/cisg/biblio/sevon.html>:

> The expression "documents controlling their disposition" clearly covers the situation where the goods are to be delivered only against surrender of the documents. This would be the case with a bill of lading where the carrier may only deliver the goods to the person presenting the bill of lading. The expression would also seem to cover a warehouse receipt entitling the holder to claim the goods. It is uncertain whether the expression covers international way bills issued under the CMR and CIM Conventions governing carriage by road and rail respectively. Under these documents the carrier is required to deliver the goods to the consignee named in the document. The sender may appoint another consignee. However, he may do so only if he can produce the relevant copy of the way bill. Having acquired the way bill, the consignee/buyer is thus protected against dispositions by the sender/seller. As the handing over of the relevant copy of the way bill has the effect that the consignor can no longer alter the consignee to whom the goods are to be handed over, the holder of that copy controls the disposition of the goods in a manner which would seem sufficient for the purposes of Article 58(1).

See also Schlechtriem P., – *Uniform Sales Law – The UN-Convention on Contracts for the International Sale of Goods*, Manz, Vienna (1986), at 82, fn 327; also available online at <http://cisgw3.law.pace.edu/cisg/biblio/schlechtriem-art58.html>:

> The expression concerns chiefly negotiable documents of title and is therefore unsuitable for its function in Article 58. [...] It is not just a matter of delivery of the goods (and the documents controlling them), but rather of performance of the seller's principal obligations. Insurance policies, certificates of origin, etc. relate to the goods and, when in doubt, their delivery must be part of the seller's performance even when they are not always necessary for the further disposition of the goods. The fact that Article 58 is designed to regulate the time of payment and to give the seller the right to withhold the goods until they are paid for justifies the view that "controlling" documents should be interpreted in the sense of Articles 30 and 34. Therefore, even if an insurance policy, for example, is not required for the disposition of the goods, nevertheless, the seller has not placed the goods at the buyer's disposal, according to Article 58(1) sentence 1, until he tenders the policy together with the goods. Moreover, under Article 58(2), the seller has the right to withhold the insurance policy until the buyer pays. For the application of Article 58(1) and (2) to the insurance policy, one need only imagine the case in which the purchased goods are destroyed after the contract has been concluded and the risk of loss has passed to the buyer. For unimportant documents that nevertheless relate to the goods, Article 58(1) and (2), interpreted in the light of Article 7(1), would permit Article 71(1) – concerning the suspension of performance where one party has failed to perform 'a substantial part of his obligations' – to be used as a yardstick: If unimportant documents are missing or withheld, the buyer must pay, but he can sue for damages or specific performance.

See also relevant case law on what constitute "documents controlling the disposition of the goods" within the meaning of CISG Art. 58(1):

- Switzerland 12 August 1997 *Kantonsgericht* [District Court] St. Gallen, CLOUT abstract no. 216, case presentation also available at <http://cisgw3.law.pace.edu/cases/970812s1.html>. In short, the court found that the handing over of documents controlling the disposition of the goods to the buyer caused the price to become due, as provided in CISG Art. 58(1). Note, however, that customs documents necessary to clear the importation of the goods into the buyer's country were held not to constitute "documents

The converse of the general rule – that, unless otherwise agreed, the buyer is not obliged to pay the price until the seller places either the goods (or documents controlling their disposition) at the buyer's disposal – also follows as a logical corollary of the stated general rule.[5]

It must be noted, however, that, in addition to the effect of contrary contractual terms, international usages and practices established between the parties may also derogate from the principle of simultaneous performance in handing over the goods and paying the price.[6]

It must further be noted that the buyer is not obliged to pay the price until he has had an opportunity to examine the goods (see CISG Art. 58(3), discussed *infra*: IV. The Buyer's Right to Examine the Goods in Advance).

The Convention's principle of simultaneous performance of the parties' obligations is also entrenched in the counterpart provisions of PECL Art. 7:102[7] and Art. 7:104.[8]

Pursuant to PECL Art. 7:102,[9] a party (the buyer, in the context of CISG Art. 58) has to perform its obligations:

1. if a time is fixed by or determinable from the contract, at that time
2. if a period of time is fixed by or determinable from the contract, at any time within that period, unless the circumstances of the case indicate that the other party (the seller in the Convention) is to choose the time

controlling the disposition of the goods." Furthermore, the court held that the procurement of customs documents is incumbent upon the seller, only if so provided in the contract between the parties;

- Germany 3 April 1996 *Bundesgerichtshof* [Federal Supreme Court], CLOUT abstract no. 171, case presentation including English translation available at <http://cisgw3.law.pace.edu/cases/960403g1.html>. In short, the court held that certificates of origin and quality do not constitute "documents controlling the disposition of the goods." Furthermore, the delivery of wrong certificates of origin and of quality did not amount to a fundamental breach of contract because the buyer could obtain correct documents from other sources. Accordingly, the court held that the buyer could not justifiably refuse payment under CISG Art. 58.

[5] See Text of Secretariat Commentary, *op. cit.*, Comment 3. *See* also Honnold, *op. cit.*, at 364: "In short, goods are to be exchanged for the price."

[6] *See* Switzerland 18 January 1996 *Bundesgericht* [Federal Supreme Court], CLOUT abstract no. 194, case presentation available at <http://cisgw3.law.pace.edu/cases/960118s1.html>. In short, the court held that in the absence of a contrary agreement between the parties, payment of the price was to be made at the seller's place of business (CISG Art. 57(1)(a)), and not at the place of delivery of the goods (CISG Art. 57(1)(b)). The latter rule applies only when payment is to be made against the handing over of the goods or documents. The court held that this happens only when the respective obligations of the buyer and the seller have to be simultaneously fulfilled (CISG Art. 58(1)) and not when, as in the case at hand, the buyer is entitled to pay part of the price after performance by the seller (delivery and installation). The court thus held that the parties had derogated from the principle of simultaneous performance.

[7] *See* Lando O. & Beale H., eds., *Principles of European Contract Law: Parts I and II*, Kluwer Law International (2000) 332, Comments on PECL Art. 7:102. Comment B, also available online at <http://cisgw3.law.pace.edu/cisg/text/peclcomp58.html#7:102>: "B. Concurrent performance of the parties' obligations: It is the general rule that the two performances have to be rendered simultaneously, so that each party can withhold its performance until the other performs."

[8] PECL Art. 7:104 [Order of Performance] reads,

> To the extent that the performances of the parties can be rendered simultaneously, the parties are bound to render them simultaneously unless the circumstances indicate otherwise.

See Lando & Beale, *op. cit.*, at 335–336:

> Article 7:104 provides that in general performances should be rendered simultaneously. This is because, if one party is to perform first, it will necessarily have to extend credit (in one form or another) to the other party, thereby incurring a risk that the other will default when the time for its performance comes. This additional risk is avoided if the performances are made simultaneously. Thus it is the general rule in sales contracts that, unless otherwise agreed, delivery and payment are to be simultaneous.

[9] PECL Art. 7:102 mirrors, in terms of structure as well as substance, another provision of the Convention (Art. 33), which deals with the time for performance of the seller's obligation to deliver the goods. *See* Ying, *op. cit.*:

> Article 7:102 PECL is virtually identical to Article 33 CISG in all material respects, if one treats the CISG seller as the PECL party required to perform, and the CISG buyer as the PECL "other party." The same three situations in the CISG are dealt with in the PECL using the same terminology.

3. if no time of performance is agreed, within a reasonable time after the conclusion of the contract

First, the rule in PECL Art. 7:201(1) follows from the parties' freedom of contract. Thus, both under the Principles and the Convention (CISG Art. 6, Art. 33(a), and Art 58(1), first sentence), the terms of the contract control the time of performance in the first instance, and only when the contract is silent do the corresponding provisions of the counterpart instruments become applicable.

Second, the rule in PECL Art. 7:201(2) permits the possibility that, in an appropriate case, the creditor (the seller, in the context of CISG Art. 58) may choose the time for performance by the debtor (the buyer, in the context of CISG Art. 58).[10]

Pursuant to CISG Art. 58(1), second sentence, and Art. 58(2), the seller may refuse to hand over the goods or documents controlling their disposition to the buyer if the latter does not pay the price at that time.[11] In effect, the seller enjoys the right to retain the goods or documents controlling their disposition in these circumstances, and thus, the seller (the "other party" in the context of PECL Art. 7:201(2)) *may* require payment for the goods (i.e., performance by the debtor) upon dispatch of the goods (or documents controlling their disposition) to the carrier.

Last, the default rule in PECL Art. 7:201(3), when no time of performance has been agreed between the parties, is based on the application of the concept of *reasonableness*, which is also one of the general principles upon which the Convention is based.[12]

III. CONTRACTS INVOLVING CARRIAGE OF GOODS (CISG ART. 58(2))

The general rule stated in CISG Art. 58(1), which is based on the principle of simultaneous payment of the price and handing over of the goods, is also applicable to contracts involving *carriage* of goods – such an arrangement is common in international sales.

Where a contract involves carriage of goods, CISG Art. 58(2) provides that a seller may dispatch the goods on terms whereby the goods will not be handed over to the buyer except against payment of the price. In effect, the seller may deliver the goods to the carrier in exchange for documents controlling the disposition of the goods[13] – "usually a

[10] *See* Lando & Beale, *op. cit.*, at 333:

> If the contract or the circumstances do not indicate that the receiving party is to choose the time of performance, it is for the party which has to make the performance to choose the time. [. . .] It may follow from the circumstances of the case that the period of the time fixed for the performance begins as soon as the contract is made and as soon as the creditor – or in an appropriate case the debtor – requires performance.

[11] *See* Schlechtriem, *op. cit.*, at 82:

> In principle, the seller may demand immediate payment upon delivery. Thus, as long as the contract does not obligate the seller to perform first, the seller can make payment a condition precedent to a transfer of the goods or documents controlling their disposition (Article 58(1) sentence 2 and 58(2)).

[12] *See* Lando & Beale, *op. cit.*, at 333:

> What is reasonable time is a question of fact depending upon the nature of the goods or services to be performed and the circumstances, see Article 1:302.

PECL Art. 1:302 provides the definition of "reasonableness" in the Principles:

> Under these Principles reasonableness is to be judged by what persons acting in good faith and in the same situation as the parties would consider to be reasonable. In particular, in assessing what is reasonable the nature and purpose of the contract, the circumstances of the case and the usages and practices of the trades or professions involved should be taken into account.

"Reasonableness" is also regarded as a general principle of the CISG. *See* Kritzer A. H., "Overview Comments on Reasonableness," available online at <http://cisgw3.law.pace.edu/cisg/text/reason.html>.

[13] *See* the Text of Secretariat Commentary, *op. cit.*, Comment 4:

> [CISG Art. 58(2)] states a specific rule in implementation of [CISG Art. 58(1)]. [. . .] The goods may be so dispatched unless there is a clause in the contract providing otherwise, in particular by providing for credit.

See also Sevón, *op. cit*, at 336:

> Article 58(2) deals with the situation where the contract involves carriage of the goods. This expression covers cases where the seller is required or authorized to ship the goods. The contract does not involve carriage if the buyer takes delivery at the seller's place of business and is to make arrangements for the goods to be shipped. Where the contract involves carriage, the seller must dispatch the goods but he may do so on terms according to

bill of lading providing that the goods will only be delivered in exchange for the surrender of the document."[14] It follows that, in the absence of contractual terms to that effect, the seller cannot act on the above assumption; accordingly, in the absence of particular terms, the buyer is not obliged to make payment until the moment when the goods or documents controlling their disposition are handed over to him by the carrier.

Because of the importance of these particular questions, the contract will usually contain specific provisions on the mode[15] and place of payment. In the absence of an express provision in the contract between the parties, the relevant questions must be answered via an interpretation of the Convention's provisions.

Exchanging the goods for the price also brings into operation CISG Art. 57(1), which provides a rule regarding the *place* at which payment of the price is to be made.[16]

CISG Art. 57(1)(a) states the general rule that *if* the buyer is not obliged to pay the price at any other particular place (i.e., in the absence of specific contractual provisions on the mode and place of payment) he must pay the price at the seller's place of business.

Regarding cases in which payment is to be made against the handing over of the goods or of documents, CISG Art. 57(1)(b) provides that payment must be made at the place where the handing over takes place.[17]

IV. THE BUYER'S RIGHT TO EXAMINE THE GOODS IN ADVANCE (CISG ART. 58(3))

CISG Art. 58(3) provides that as a general rule the buyer is not obliged to pay the price unless he has had an opportunity to examine the goods.[18]

which the goods or documents controlling their disposition will not be handed over to the buyer except against payment of the price. The impact of the provision with reference to the time of payment seems to be that the seller may not, unless agreed upon in the contract, make dispatch dependant on previous receipt of payment. On the other hand, the provision states that an arrangement whereby the seller dispatches the goods but does so on terms enabling him to retain control over them until payment is made, does not amount to a breach of contract.

[14] Honnold, *op. cit.*, at 364, with further references therein to

- INCOTERMS (1990), in which C.I.F., C.P.T. & C.I.P. terms call for the seller to provide the "usual transport document" that may be a "negotiable bill of lading"; and
- (U.S.A.) U.C.C. 2–310(b), which provides that seller may ship the goods "under reservation."

[15] In the Information Age, electronic processes are speeding the transmission of funds and documents (e.g., payment might be made by letter of credit issued and dispatched electronically). The Convention does not refer to the use of letters of credit.

[16] The interplay between CISG Art. 57 and Art. 58 has practical consequences for documentary exchanges. Sevón has commented on that interplay:

> In conjunction with Article 58, Article 57 states that if there is a delay in the transfer of the amount to the place where payment is to be made, e.g. due to lack of the authorization of transfer by the appropriate authorities or to a mistake by the buyer's bank, having the effect that the amount is not available at the place of payment in time, there is a breach of contract on part of the buyer.

See also Honnold, *op. cit.*, at 364–367, where the author informatively discusses the interplay between those two provisions of the Convention, before concluding at 367:

> In short, it is possible to satisfy the standards of Article 58 for a mutually safe exchange of the goods and the price in a manner that is consistent with the rule of Article 57(1)(a) on the place of payment.

For an illustration of step-by-step performance implementing the principle of concurrent exchange of the goods for the price, in the setting of a typical international contract of sale involving payment by letter of credit, *see* Honnold, *op. cit.*, at 368–369.

[17] *See* the Text of the Secretariat Commentary on Art. 53 of the 1978 Draft *[draft counterpart of CISG Art. 57]*, available online at <http://cisgw3.law.pace.edu/cisg/text/secomm/secomm-57.html>.

The Commentary states that the rule in CISG Art. 57(1)(b)

> will be applied most often in the case of a contract stipulation for payment against documents. The documents may be handed over directly to the buyer, but they are often handed over to a bank which represents the buyer in the transaction. The "handing over" may take place in either the buyer's or the seller's country or even in a third country.

CISG Art. 57 is virtually identical to Art. 53 of the Draft Convention; therefore, the Secretariat Commentary on 1978 Draft Art. 53 should be relevant to the interpretation of CISG Art. 57. *See* corresponding match-up, available at <http://cisgw3.law.pace.edu/cisg/text/matchup/matchup-d-57.html>.

[18] *See* Enderlein F. & Maskow D., *International Sales Law*, Oceana (1992), p. 226; also available online at <http://cisgw3.law.pace.edu/cisg/biblio/enderlein-art58.html>:

In implementing this rule, it is commented that it is the seller's obligation "to provide a means for the buyer's examination prior to payment and handing over."[19]

The buyer, however, loses the right to examine the goods prior to payment where the procedures for delivery or payment agreed upon by the parties are *inconsistent*[20] with the buyer having such an opportunity.[21] It must be stressed, however, that, even in such cases, the buyer does not lose his right to examine the goods prior to payment where *the contract provides* that he must pay the price against the handing over of the documents *after the arrival* of the goods.[22] In other words, prior examination of the goods by the buyer may be excluded by a contractual stipulation to that effect or by modalities of delivery or payment that are incompatible with such examination (e.g., clauses involving payment against handing over of documents or payment against handing over of the delivery slip).[23]

V. CONCLUSION

The Convention's provisions regarding the time when the buyer must pay for the goods are based upon the principle of simultaneous performance of the parties' obligations. The same principle is also entrenched in the counterpart provisions of the PECL.

The primary rule in both sets of counterpart provisions follows from the parties' freedom of contract. Thus, both under the Principles and the Convention the terms of the contract concluded between the parties control the time of performance in the first

> This right to examine the goods in substance is not identical to the obligation of examination under Article 38. Even when the buyer pays the price after having examined the goods for the first time, he does not lose the possibility to examine the goods more carefully under Article 38 and to possibly claim a lack of conformity.

[19] Text of Secretariat Commentary, *op. cit.*, Comment 5. *See* also Comment 6 of the Secretariat Commentary:

> Where the contract of sale involves carriage of the goods and the seller wishes to exercise his right under [CISG Art. 58(2)] to ship the goods on terms whereby neither the goods nor the documents will be handed over to the buyer prior to payment, the seller must preserve the buyer's right to examine the goods. Since the buyer normally examines the goods at the place of destination [CISG Art. 38(2)] the seller may be required to make special arrangements with the carrier to allow the buyer access to the goods at the destination prior to the time the goods or documents are handed over in order to allow for the buyer's examination.

[20] *See* the Text of Secretariat Commentary, *op. cit.*, Comment 7, which explains,

> [The] Convention does not set forth which procedures for delivery or payment are inconsistent with the buyer's right to examine the goods prior to payment. However, the most common example is the agreement that payment of the price is due against the handing over of the documents controlling the disposition of the goods whether or not the goods have arrived. The quotation of the price on CIF terms contains such an agreement.

See also Sevón, *op. cit.*, at 336, where the author explains,

> Normally, goods which have arrived at their destination cannot be sold there to another buyer at a price corresponding to the contract price. Some buyers may use this fact as a means to force the seller to accept a reduction of the price by refraining from taking delivery of the goods on the alleged ground of non-conformity. The seller may protect himself against such claims by a provision in the contract specifying a procedure for delivery according to which the buyer may not inspect the goods until payment has been made.

[21] *See* Enderlein & Maskow, *op. cit.*, at 227:

> Where the terms of payment already preclude the possibility for examination, it is irrelevant to search the *terms of delivery* for such an opportunity. Hence, this is only of importance when the terms of payment offer such an opportunity.

[22] *See* the Text of Secretariat Commentary, *op. cit.*, Comment 8:

> Since payment is to take place *after* the arrival of the goods, the procedure for payment and delivery are consistent with the right of examination *prior to payment*. Similarly, the buyer does *not* lose his right to examine the goods prior to payment where the seller exercises his right under [CISG Art. 58(2)] to dispatch the goods on terms whereby the documents controlling the disposition of the goods will be handed over to the buyer only upon the payment of the price [emphasis added].

See also Honnold, op. cit., at 368:

> Article 38 establishes a *duty* to inspect: "(1) The buyer *must* examine the goods . . . within as short a period as is practicable . . . " – a preface to Article 39 whereby a buyer may lose the right to rely on lack of conformity of the goods by failure to notify the seller within "a reasonable time." In sharp contract, Article 58(3) gives the buyer a *privilege* to inspect before payment – a privilege that the buyer may forego without violating any obligation to the seller.

[23] *See* the *UNCITRAL Digest of case law on the United Nations Convention on the International Sale of Goods*, para 8, available online at <http://cisgw3.law.pace.edu/cisg/text/anno-art-58.html#art583>.

instance and only when the contract is silent do the corresponding provisions of the counterpart instruments become applicable.

The default rule in the Principles, when no time of performance has been agreed between the parties, is based on the application of the concept of *reasonableness*, which is also one of the general principles upon which the Convention is based.

Seller's notice fixing additional final period for performance: Remarks on the manner in which the Principles of European Contract Law may be used to interpret or supplement Articles 63 and 64(1)(b) of the CISG

Bruno Zeller

I. SCHEME OF CISG ARTICLES 63 AND 64(1)(B)

CISG Articles 63 and 64(1)(b) are part of the regime of remedies of breach of contract within the CISG, which in general can be divided into two categories: remedies where the contract can be terminated or avoided such as fundamental breach and remedies where the contract is still in force such as damages.

Articles 63 and 64(1)(b) are provisions that span both remedies through the principle of *Nachfrist*, which is the granting of additional time by the seller to the buyer to perform his obligation to pay the price or take delivery of the goods. The principle has been mainly borrowed from German domestic law as well as from the French procedure of *mise en demeure*. However there are significant differences between the German and French treatment of *Nachfrist* and the one in the CISG. This is a good point to remind ourselves of the mandate of Article 7(1) where uniformity of application demands the autonomous interpretation of the CISG; that is, without relying on principles founded in domestic law. In other words, German and French treatment of *Nachfrist* and *mise en demeure* must be ignored and cannot be used to explain the principle within the CISG despite significant similarities in doctrine and jurisprudence.

Common law attorneys may find the concept of *Nachfrist* foreign as it has no direct commonlaw counterpart. In brief, the various Sale of Goods Acts do not rely on the principle of "fundamental breach." They rather approach avoidance of contract through the breach of contractual terms; that is, breach of a major term or a condition. For remedies of breach of contract by the seller, see the editorial remarks on Article 47 and 49(1)(b). However, under the Sale of Goods Acts the remedies available for a breach of contract are not the same when the buyer is in breach. The seller cannot treat the breach as a cause to repudiate the contract. He can only recover the price of the goods as an ordinary debt. Where ownership has not passed and the buyer refuses to accept the goods, the buyer again can only sue for damages. The seller additionally has also a right against the goods; namely, lien and stoppage in *transitu*.

It is therefore important that common law attorneys have a good grasp of the concept of *Nachfrist* as in the CISG both buyer and seller can terminate the contract under the principle of fundamental breach. *Nachfrist* gives the buyer additional time to perform his part of the bargain. If he fails to do so the seller can avoid the contract in accordance with Article 64(1)(b).

The purpose behind the flexible remedy of *Nachfrist* is that the CISG, as one of its principles, attempts to keep the contract afoot as long as there is a possibility to perform contractual obligations. This is in line with the attempt to overcome some of the problems of distance, expense, and time in having an international contract terminated where, operating under another general principle of the CISG – namely good faith – remedial action could have been possible, resulting in a win–win situation.

II. MEANING AND PURPOSE OF *NACHFRIST*

The idea behind *Nachfrist* is that the seller should not be able to avoid the contract merely because the goods are not accepted or payment is not made on time. A contract can be avoided under the principle of fundamental breach as defined in CISG Article 25. Under certain circumstances, such as when time is of the essence, late payment or refusal to accept goods may become a fundamental breach. Article 63 in itself is not a remedy; rather it clarifies a situation that otherwise would be unclear. If the seller is in a situation where there is uncertainty as to the existence of a reason to avoid the contract, he can overcome this by fixing a *Nachfrist*. As far as the buyer is concerned the additional period is a final period; however, the seller is not barred from fixing additional periods if he so wishes or if he wants to respond to the buyer's request for additional time.[1]

The importance the CISG places in reading provisions within the context of the Convention is clearly demonstrated in this instance. Article 63 is closely linked to Article 64(1). In Article 64(1)(a) the seller is entitled to avoid the contract if the failure of the buyer amounts to a fundamental breach. Late payment or refusal to accept delivery unless time is of the essence does not amount to a fundamental breach. A seller may not be certain whether late payment may be construed as a fundamental breach, but by fixing a *Nachfrist* this problem is overcome as the seller now can rely on Article 64(1)(b), which takes away the uncertainty. The only uncertainty is the question of "reasonable length" of the additional period of time fixed by the seller. The seller will have assistance in such a definition through Article 9 (customary practices) or Article 6 (definition of additional time is a clause in the contract), as well as Article 8 (previous conduct or statements made by parties). Most important, the seller will rely on the general principle of reasonableness, as well as on the principle of good faith, which is contained in Article 7.

An Austrian case can be used to illustrate the above. The seller declared the contract avoided after the buyer failed to pay the price without fixing a *Nachfrist*. The court found that there was no need to fix such a period as the buyer implicitly agreed to the avoidance of the contract.[2]

While the additional period is in existence the seller can only rely on damages for late payment or refusal to accept delivery, but most important, the buyer is protected while he is making efforts to remedy the situation.

[1] Regarding Art. 63 case law, *see* presentation of more than thirty cases on Art. 63 CISG, available online at <http://cisgw3.law.pace.edu/cisg/text/anno-art-63.html> [visited: 2 May 2005].
See also UNCITRAL Digest of Art. 63 case law, available at <http://cisgw3.law.pace.edu/cisg/text/anno-art-63.html#ucd>.

[2] Regarding Art. 64 case law, *see* presentation of more than forty-five cases on Art. 64, available online at <http://cisgw3.law.pace.edu/cisg/text/anno-art-64.html> [visited: 2 May 2005].
See also UNCITRAL Digest of Art. 64 case law, available at <http://cisgw3.law.pace.edu/cisg/text/anno-art-64.html#ucd>.

III. COMPARISON OF PECL ARTICLE 8:106 WITH CISG ARTICLES 63 AND 64(1)(B)

At first glance the two systems have a remarkable similarity, but are also subtly different. The first point to note is that PECL also introduced *Nachfrist* as an important concept in contractual relations. The mere inclusion indicates that the CISG was correct in its assessment that the concept of *Nachfrist* is important in an international contractual relationship. The second point is a confirmation of the foresight of the CISG because PECL did not introduce major changes but as indicated above only subtle differences. From this we can deduce that the concept of *Nachfrist* as introduced by the CISG was correct and is of importance in international sales.

The CISG and the PECL recognize the difference between non-performance that amounts to a fundamental breach and non-performance that is not serious enough to constitute a fundamental breach. The PECL, like the CISG, give the seller who is not sure whether non-performance amounts to a fundamental breach the ability to avoid the contract by allowing him to set an additional period of time to perform the contract. In a contract concluded between a Spanish seller and a French buyer for the sale of pure orange juice to be delivered by installments, a French Appellate court[3] held that the buyer would not have understood that a delay of a few days in taking delivery would amount to a fundamental breach. As the seller did not allow for a *Nachfrist*, his unilateral avoidance was a wrongful termination of the contract.

Both the CISG and PECL recognize that two conditions must be met. First, the period must be fixed. Second, the period so fixed must be reasonable. What amounts to a reasonable time is a question of fact and is left to the courts to decide. An ICC Arbitration award[4] provides an interesting example of how a period can be fixed. A. H. Kritzer in his commentary[5] to the case pointed out that commentators have conflicting views about

[3] France 4 February 1999 *Cour d'appel* [Appellate Court] Grenoble, *Ego Fruits v. La Verja Begastri*, CLOUT No. 243, case presentation including English translation available at <http://cisgw3.law.pace.edu/cases/990204f1.html>. In that case the Appellate court held that the seller was not entitled to avoid (terminate) the contract on the ground of Art. 64(1)(a) CISG, as the buyer's breach in taking delivery of the goods by the end of August did not amount to a fundamental breach of contract under Art. 25 CISG.

[4] ICC Arbitration Case No. 7585 of 1992, CLOUT No. 301, case presentation available at <http://cisgw3.law.pace.edu/cases/927585i1.html>, including Editorial commentary by A. H. Kritzer, at <http://cisgw3.law.pace.edu/cases/927585i1.html#ce>. In that case, an Italian seller and a Finnish buyer entered into a contract for the sale of a production line of foam boards. The parties agreed that after the inspection of the machine the buyer would open a letter of credit in favor of the seller. The buyer failed to open the documentary credit at the agreed time; three and a half months later the seller declared the contract avoided and the seller commenced action against the buyer seeking damages and interest. The Arbitral tribunal ruled that, although a delay in opening the documentary credit in itself does not necessarily amount to a fundamental breach, in the case at hand the seller was entitled to avoid the contract: the fact that the seller waited several months before declaring the contract avoided was considered as equivalent to the fixing of an "additional period of time" for performance pursuant to Art. 63 CISG, with the result that the failure by the buyer to perform within that period of time entitled the seller to avoid the contract pursuant to Art. 64(1)(b) CISG. *See* also Italy 11 December 1998 Appellate Court Milan (*Bielloni Castello v. EGO*), case presentation including English translation available at <http://cisgw3.law.pace.edu/cases/981211i3.html>. In that case an Italian seller and a French buyer concluded a contract for the sale of a printing press. The buyer made a partial payment, but it failed to pay the balance and to take delivery of the press at the agreed date. The Appellate Court held that the total time from the original delivery date to the expiration of the additional period fixed by the seller (totaling two and a half months) was altogether considered to be of reasonable length (Art. 63(2) CISG); therefore, the seller was entitled to declare the contract avoided as the buyer had failed to perform within the additional period of time that the seller had fixed (Art. 64(1)(b) CISG). The Court considered the contract avoided upon expiration of the additional period of time.

[5] A. H. Kritzer, *Editorial comments* on ICC Arbitration Case No. 7585 of 1992, online at <http://cisgw3.law.pace.edu/cases/927585i1.html#ce>.

the fixing of an additional time period. The debate is whether it must be done "in such a way as to make it clear to the buyer that the additional period sets a fixed and final limit on the date for performance or whether no such unequivocal warning is necessary." The ICC tribunal declared that the period between the buyer's default and the declaration of avoidance after several months by the seller was "an additional period" pursuant to Article 63. In effect, an implied *Nachfrist* can be construed in some circumstances as being sufficient to satisfy the requirements of Article 63.

In any event, good faith, which is a principle in both the CISG and PECL, will also influence the court in its decision. However, the PECL in its commentary make it clear that if less than reasonable time was fixed, the aggrieved party "need not serve a second notice; it may terminate after a reasonable time has elapsed from the date of the notice." As far as the CISG is concerned, no jurisprudence has solved this issue; however, it can be argued that a court would invoke good faith and could set a date that fulfills the requirements of the principle of reasonableness.

One area of uncertainty within the CISG has been removed in the PECL, which state clearly that the buyer may withhold his own performance while an additional period of time is fixed. Another point well worth noting is the different terms used. In the CISG it is the seller who may fix a time, whereas in the PECL it is the aggrieved party, which can be buyer or seller depending on the circumstances. Such a variance makes sense as unlike the CISG, the PECL also cover contracts of service. Furthermore the PECL have managed to cover in one Article substance that in the CISG is contained in Articles 47, 49(1)(b), 63, and 64(1)(b). CISG Articles 47 and 49(1)(b) cover the corresponding remedies open to the buyer for breaches by seller and are reviewed in other chapters in this book.

IV. CONCLUSION

The principle of *Nachfrist* must be viewed in two ways: as a mandate within the CISG but also as another example of the "sea change in the landscape of international trade." Is the principle of "additional period of time" is stated in basically the same form in the PECL and also in the UNIDROIT principles. It is the domestic systems of law and specifically the common law, which is out of step with international developments. The reality is that there is a drastic change in the marketplace for legal services. The PECL in a subtle way will be shaping English common law practices, and it will not be too far in the future when English courts will need to deal with such concepts as *Nachfrist*. The fact that the concept of *Nachfrist* has been included in various international laws indicates that certainty now has a brother, namely flexibility.

Globalization requires that legal rules must be flexible to be applicable to changing circumstances and avoid costly disputes in circumstances, which could have been solved by an instrument like *Nachfrist*. Common law attorneys must become aware of the existence and basic content of different concepts contained in uniform international law, the CISG, international "Restatements" of the law, the PECL, and the UNIDROIT Principles because these concepts will be shaping the rules for contractual dealings in the future.

Seller's right to avoid the contract in international transactions: Comparative analysis of the respective provisions in the CISG and the PECL

Jonathan Yovel

I. GENERAL

Avoidance of the contract ("termination," in the language of the PECL) by an aggrieved seller is the most extreme measure offered by both the CISG and PECL in response to breach by the buyer ("non-performance," in the language of the PECL).[1] Avoidance severs the contractual relations and nullifies obligations pertaining to any future performance, except for contractual performances designated to take effect upon avoidance, such as dispute resolution clauses or liquidated damages.[2] (Any restitution following avoidance is not, properly speaking, a contractual performance, but a statutory or common-law requirement designed to reinstate as much as possible the respective parties' pre-contractual positions, as opposed to post-avoidance measures designed to protect the expectation interest, such as damages).[3] Both the CISG and the PECL offer

[1] Ole Lando, "Salient Features of the Principles of European Contract Law: A Comparison with the Ucc," 13 *Pace In'l. L. Rev.* (Fall 2001) 339, at 361, available online at <http://cisgw3.law.pace.edu/cisg/biblio/lando.html>.

[2] *See* Cisg Art. 81(1) and PECL Art. 9:305(2). Nor does avoidance preclude recourse to any other remedy consistent with it, such as damages (*see* Cisg Art. 81(1) and PECL Art. 8:102) The UNCITRAL Secretariat Commentary (referring to the 1978 Draft) notes, "Such a provision was important because in many legal systems avoidance of the contract eliminates all rights and obligations which arose out of the existence of the contract. In such a view once a contract has been avoided, there can be no claim for damages for its breach and contract clauses relating to the settlement of disputes, including provisions for arbitration and clauses specifying 'penalties' or 'liquidated damages' for breach, terminate with the rest of the contract" (Official Records pp. 41–42, available online at <http://cisgw3.law.pace.edu/cisg/text/secomm/secomm-45.html>.

[3] *See* Cisg 81–84 and PECL Arts. 9:307 (concerning money) and 9:308 (concerning property). Money refunded accrues interest (Cisg Art. 84 and PECL Art. 9:508) at a rate determined by non-Cisg law otherwise applicable to the contract (*see* Switzerland 20 February 1997 Bezirksgericht [District Court] Saane, case presentation including English translation available at <http://cisgw3.law.pace.edu/cases/970220s1.html>. In

aggrieved parties less extreme measures to deal with breach or with anticipatory breach,[4] and both contain various cure measures that – when applied or applicable – allow for delayed or remedial performance and thus either delay recourse to avoidance or render it unnecessary or unavailable.[5] In this, both the CISG and PECL manifest a "relational" bias; namely, attempting to salvage fractured contractual relations by providing an escalation of remedial measures, whose eventual failure ultimately leads to breaking up of the contractual framework through avoidance.[6] Therefore both the CISG and PECL generally reserve avoidance of the contract to instances of so-called fundamental breach,[7] although both allow for some non-fundamental breaches to be "upgraded" to the status of "avoidable" breaches through the use of curative (*Nachfrist*) periods set by the aggrieved seller.[8]

The general analytical structure of the clauses analyzed in this chapter is as follows: Power of avoidance is granted to seller only in cases of fundamental breach (CISG 64(1)(a), PECL 9:301(1)), but in certain cases is expanded to non-fundamental breaches that follow a *Nachfrist* notice ("constructive fundamentalism") (CISG 64(1)(b), PECL 8:106(3)). Under the PECL, all notices of termination must be given in reasonable time (PECL Art. 9:303(2). The CISG reserves this restriction to instances in which the buyer has already paid the price (CISG Art. 64(2)). This complex approach to the power of avoidance is intended to respond to respective risk allocations borne by the parties. This chapter analyzes those risks, their treatment by the respective CISG and PECL Articles, and points out the major interpretative questions raised by any application of these provisions. It begins by examining the general framework and analyzing the main

variations, mutual restitution seems to be a universal feature of contract avoidance. The effect of CISG Art. 81 on avoidance was even described as "chang[ing] the contractual relationship into a restitutional relationship." *See* Germany 11 October 1995 Landgericht [District Court] Düsseldorf, case presentation including English translation available at <http://cisgw3.law.pace.edu/cases/951011g1.html>. *See* also Harry M. Flechtner, "Remedies under the New International Sales Convention: The Perspective from Article 2 of the U.C.C.," 8 *J.L. & Com.* 53 (1988), at 80, available online at <http://cisgw3.law.pace.edu/cisg/biblio/flecht.html>; Francesco G. Mazzotta, "Commentary on CISG Article 81 and its PECL Counterparts," available online at <http://cisgw3.law.pace.edu/cisg/text/peclcomp81.html#er>; Günter H. Treitel, "Remedies for Breach of Contract," in *International Encyclopedia of Comparative Law* (Tübingen, Mouton, The Hague, Paris: J.C.B. Mohr, 1976). Courts acknowledge the CISG restitution as a matter of course; *see* Switzerland 5 February 1997 Handelsgericht [Commercial Court] Zürich, case presentation available at <http://cisgw3.law.pace.edu/cases/970205s1.html>; Switzerland 20 February 1997 Bezirksgericht (Zivilgericht) [District Court] Saane, case presentation including English translation available at <http://cisgw3.law.pace.edu/cases/970220s1.html>.

[4] Such as suspension of performance and requirement of assurances (*see* CISG Art. 71 and PECL Art. 8:105), requirement of performance (*see* CISG Arts. 46 and 62 (but *see* Art. 28) and PECL Arts. 9:101and 9:102).

[5] *See* CISG Arts. 37, 47, 48, 49(2)(b), 63, 64(2)(b), etc. and PECL Arts. 8:104, 8:106, etc.

[6] *See* Ian Macneil, *The New Social Contract: An Inquiry into Modern Contractual Relations* (1980); Robert W. Gordon, "Macaulay, Macneil and the Discovery of Solidarity and Power in Contract Law," 1985 *Wis. L. Rev.* 565.

[7] For what constitutes a fundamental breach (non-performance) *see* CISG Art. 25 and PECL Art. 8:103, respectively; according to Lando, the latter was modeled on the former, *see* Lando, *supra* note p. 362. For a discussion of fundamental breach in CISG law and related UNIDROIT Principles as well as the related topic of non-conformity of goods, *see* Robert Koch, "Commentary on Whether the UNIDROIT Principles of International Commercial Contracts May Be Used to Interpret or Supplement Articles 47 and 49 of the CISG," available online at <http://cisgw3.law.pace.edu/cisg/biblio/koch2.html> and references noted there.

[8] *See, e.g.*, cases discussed in note *infra*. In the case of the CISG, although fundamental breaches make avoidance available immediately, non-fundamental non-delivery allows for avoidance if the aggrieved party has fixed a curative period for performance – a so-called *Nachfrist* period – and the breach has continued throughout that period. This is available in cases of non-payment or failure to take the goods, even without establishing that the failure constitutes a fundamental breach, under CISG Art. 64(1)(b). Under the PECL, "delay in performance" followed by further failure to perform throughout a *Nachfrist* period may allow for termination (PECL Art. 8:106(3)). This matter is discussed in detail next.

concepts and then proceeds to more detailed aspects of avoidance of the contract by the seller under the two documents.

II. BREACH AND FUNDAMENTAL BREACH

Although the buyer's primary obligation in most transactions is to tender the contractual price,[9] contracts that govern both domestic and international transactions frequently allocate to the buyer substantial other performances – such as taking delivery – whose breach may allow the aggrieved seller to declare the contract avoided ("terminate," in the context of the PECL). Some failures to perform may create considerable costs for the seller or place her at risk in relation to third-party contractors such as carriers, etc. (consider, for example, the numerous performances allocated to the buyer under all the standard contract types stretching from Ex-Works to FOB). The seller's power to declare the contract avoided therefore mirrors the respective risks associated with the buyer's similar power when the seller breaches the contract, as regulated by CISG Art. 49. The PECL, ranging as it does over contracts in general rather than merely sales contracts,[10] do not reflect the CISG's distinction between avoidance by the buyer and the seller; both are covered by PECL Art. 9:301 (Right to Terminate the Contract), Art. 9:303 (Notice of Termination), and Art. 8:106 (Termination after Additional Period for Performance).[11]

As stated above, the main feature of avoidance of the contract shared by both CISG and PECL is that it is generally restricted to cases of fundamental breach. Furthermore, the seller's power to avoid is further restricted in cases where the buyer has already paid the price. Payment typically puts the buyer in the least favorable position should the contract be avoided; in some senses it is parallel to the seller having delivered the goods, although the special character of payment is peculiar among all objects of exchange. On the one hand, it is the least costly object for restitution in terms of transaction costs (although restitution of funds may be subject to third-party rights, preferences in bankruptcy, and other impediments to the collection of debt). On the other hand, payment is almost costless to keep, necessitating the kind of legal action for the collection of debt that modern payment systems seek to avoid.[12] Indeed, it is impossible to analyze the kinds of risks parties are exposed to in such situations without a proper understanding of payment systems and their role as risk-allocating mechanisms in contractual relations in general, and in international commerce in particular. Even the interpretation of what it means to have "paid the price" may depend on the finality of the financial tender that typically complements sales transaction, and different types of payment systems are governed by varying rules concerning that.[13]

"Paying" the contractual price – typically, the buyer's chief obligation – may sound straightforward enough, but that, of course, is far from true whenever a payment system or other complexities of a financial transaction are involved. Many payment modes involve

[9] *See* CISG Art. 53 and any of the several INCOTERMS 2000.

[10] At the risk of sounding pedantic one might caution, that at least for the time being it would not be quite correct to talk of the PECL as "applying" to any legal relations; having no legally binding force of any kind they do not legally "apply" to the cases that fall under them.

[11] For avoidance\termination of an installment contract *see* also CISG Art. 73 and PECL Art. 9:302.

[12] There are two such types of risks: enforcement risks, whereby the seller's right to restitution is subject to defenses or other impediments, and credit risks whereby the buyer becomes insolvent. As restitution in the form of payment becomes debt, it is exposed to bankruptcy and similar defenses even when other legal rights are effective. *See* Robert L. Jordan, William D. Warren, and Steven D. Walt, *Negotiable Instruments, Payments and Credits* (5th ed. 2000) at pp. 3–4.

[13] Consider, for example, the finality of payment via credit cards to that of fund transfers in the United States, as well as negotiable instruments – checks in particular. In barter or other transactions where "payment" is in kind, the same risks are associated with both sides.

necessary preparatory steps, such as procuring or at least applying for credit, a letter of credit, or bank guarantees; obtaining adequate foreign currency[14]; complying with required formalities where applicable, etc.,[15] without which eventual payment would become infeasible, delayed, or at any count contrary to the contractual stipulation. Such performances are normally considered inherent to the buyer's "obligation to pay the price."[16] Some tribunals may consider such failures under the doctrine of anticipatory breach of the buyer's obligation to pay the price, whereas others may consider them actual breaches.[17] Defaulting in this respect may even constitute a fundamental breach if fulfilling the respective conditions of CISG Art. 25 and PECL Art. 8:103. Yet even when not considered fundamental, failure to properly arrange for payment may allow the seller to avoid the contract if the failure is not remedied throughout an additional curative period (*Nachfrist*) set by the seller for this purpose.[18] This important mechanism, allowing for bypassing the fundamental breach requirement in some cases, is discussed in detail in Section 5.

In making avoidance of the contract available only in cases of fundamental breach, both the CISG and PECL seem to deviate from commercial practices that allow parties to reject goods – and more importantly, documents – that fail to strictly conform with the contractual specifications, even if that discrepancy is of little practical significance.[19] Such practices are prevalent in documentary transactions[20] such as CIF,[21] and

[14] For default rules applying to currency *see* PECL Art. 7:108.

[15] However, note that under PECL Art. 7:107(1) the debtor is entitled to pay "in any form used in the ordinary course of business." A clear contractual stipulation to the contrary (e.g., such that requires a buyer to open a letter of credit) would of course trump this default rule. The interesting question, however, is that of an implied obligation to pay by L/C absent a contractual stipulation, yet where such is the prevalent custom, as in CIF contracts. CISG Art. 9 may then make such an imposition binding on the buyer.

[16] CISG Art. 54.

[17] *See* CISG Art. 72 and PECL Art. 9:304. For failure to open a letter of credit as being presumably both a (fundamental) breach and an anticipatory breach under CISG, *see* Australia 17 November 2000 Supreme Court of Queensland (*Downs Investments v. Perwaja Steel*), case presentation available at <http://cisgw3.law.pace.edu/cases/001117a2.html>, also available at UNILEX (all cases recorded by UNILEX are available online at <http://www.unilex.info>, affirmed on appeal [2001] QCA 433. For discussion in the context of avoidance of the contract *see* section 6, below.

[18] *See* CISG Art. 64(1)(b) and PECL Art. 8:106(3).

[19] Such discrepancies indeed generated several criticisms regarding the CISG's application to documentary transactions in general. *See* Alastair Mullis, "Avoidance for Breach under the Vienna Convention: A Critical Analysis of Some of the Early Cases," in Andreas and Jarborg (eds.), *Anglo-Swedish Studies in Law* (Upsala: Iustus Forlag 1998), p. 326 et seq., available online at <http://cisgw3.law.pace.edu/cisg/biblio/mullis1.html>; *also* Peter Schlechtriem, "Interpretation, Gap-Filling and Further Development of the UN Sales Convention," available online at <http://cisgw3.law.pace.edu/cisg/biblio/schlechtriem6.html>. Prof. Schlechtriem's critique is also germane to the commercial realities of the commodification of contracts, where practitioners regard themselves as dealing not in goods but in "contracts," moving away from the language of the assignment of *in-personam* (contractual) obligations to the *in-rem*, "propertized" language of goods or of commodities. The general question of the adjusted application of commercial law originally designed for transactions in goods (such as the CISG) to transactions in contracts is of course broader than can be dealt with here. Possibly, however, relational approaches to functional conformity of goods – the CISG's approach in the context of avoidance and its limitation to fundamental breach for lack of conformity (CISG Art. 35) – can be extended at least to some documentary transactions, the exception continuing to be financial (payment and credit) as well as investment instruments. This cautious approach is partially expressed by CISG Art 2(d).

[20] According to the Secretariat Commentary, Art. 2(d) CISG does not exclude documentary sales of goods from the scope of application of the Convention. The Commentary warns, however, that in some legal systems such sales may be characterized as sales of commercial paper, excluded by Art. 2(d). *See* Secretariat Commentary on Art. 2, available online at <http://cisgw3.law.pace.edu/cisg/text/secomm/secomm-02.html>. As prevalent kinds of commercial paper tend to be "negotiated" rather than sold, paper falling under UCC Article 3 ("Negotiable Instruments") – ostensibly given to strict or "formalist" construction based on flaws discernible "on the face of the instrument" – would not fall under the scope of application of the CISG to begin with.

[21] *See* Secretariat Commentary, para 7.

in particular those that involve documentary credit such as an L/C or "unclean" documents such as bills of lading.[22] Under the fundamental breach rule it would seem that such rejection would not amount in itself to avoidance, but instead to a demand for cure (see CISG Arts. 30, 34, and 47) that, if unmet, may then constitute a breach allowing avoidance, as discussed below.[23] However, two considerations mitigate the apparent difference between the fundamental breach and strict compliance approaches to avoidance of contract. The first is contractual; namely, the parties' general freedom to stipulate what breaches would count as fundamental; in documentary transactions, strict documentary compliance may simply be agreed upon. The second has to do with the function of custom, usage, and commercial practices. Under CISG Art. 9(2), parties are generally bound by prevalent usages; this general principle would certainly apply to the construction of fundamental breach under CISG Arts. 25 and 64. Perhaps even more significantly, PECL 1:105 makes a similar provision for contracts in general, beyond *lex mercatoria*. Strict compliance with documentary requirements may fall under both categories: contractual stipulation as well as prevalent usage.[24]

III. SELF-HELP

Contract avoidance is sometimes referred to as a "self-help" remedy although, properly speaking, it is not a remedy in the strict contractual sense: rather than remedial, its effects are to excuse parties from further performances and to restore pre-performance conditions by either requiring reciprocal restitution of all exchanges or making such restitution or its substitute available to parties.[25] The basic feature of avoidance in the CISG is its autonomous, unilateral character: it requires no court action and is executed entirely through appropriate declarations.[26] A declaration of avoidance of the contract is made by notice to the party in breach (CISG Art. 26); the declaration is performative in that, once lawfully made, the contract is avoided. The PECL share the CISG's approach to contract avoidance as a unilateral act requiring merely a notice to the party in breach.[27] In this, the PECL are "markedly different" from several continental systems,[28] where the general principle is that avoidance requires court proceedings.[29] Note that

[22] *See*, e.g., INCOTERMS 2000, CIF, provisions A8, B8.

[23] According to Prof. Schlechtriem's view, the right to declare the contract avoided for non-delivery of goods following a *Nachfrist* period should be construed as extending to non-delivery of documents of title as well. Peter Schlechtriem, *Uniform Sales Law: the UN Convention on Contracts for the International Sale of Goods* (Vienna: Manz 1986), 77 also available online at <http://cisgw3.law.pace.edu/cisg/biblio/schlechtriem.html>.

[24] *E.g.* under various INCOTERMS 2000 (for instance, B8 in all but Ex-Works).

[25] With significant exceptions, under the CISG a buyer's inability to make restitution forfeits his right to avoid the contract (CISG Art. 82), which has no exact PECL counterpart (*see* PECL Art. 9:309, which states a right to monetary recovery of value that cannot be restituted, but does not restrict the power to terminate as such).

[26] For provisions governing declarations of notice of avoidance by notice, *see* CISG 26 and PECL 9:303; *see also* UNIDROIT Art. 7.3.2.

[27] There are two exceptions to the rule that notice of termination is required. Under PECL Art. 8:106(3), a notice setting a *Nachfrist* period during which the defaulting party may yet perform may provide that at the end of the period the contract will terminate automatically upon failure to cure; and according to PECL Art. 9:304(4), the contract terminates automatically upon total and permanent impediment.

[28] For a comparison between CISG's approach to avoidance of the contract by notice as opposed to domestic law requiring otherwise, *see* Belgium 1 March 1995 Rechtbank [District Court] van koophandel Hasselt (*J.P.S. v. Kabri Mode*), available at <http://cisgw3.law.pace.edu/cases/950301b1.html>.

[29] This is the prevalent common law rule, which holds also in "hybrid" legal systems such as in Israel; *see* Contract Law (Remedies for Breach of Contract) 1970, Art. 8. It conforms to several continental rules, such as the Danish Sale of Goods Act Arts. 27, 32, and 52; Finnish and Swedish Sale of Goods Acts Arts. 29, 39, and 59; Portuguese Civil Code Art. 436(1); and the Dutch BW 6:267, but differs from other legal systems that require a resolution by judicial pronouncement, whereby the court must decide whether the non-performance was sufficiently significant to justify termination of the contract, such as French, Belgian, and

this is consistent with the rule, shared by CISG and PECL, under which the aggrieved party need not serve the non-performing party with notice to put the latter into breach (such as a *mise en demeure* or *Mahnung*).[30] Parties must, of course, be cognizant of the fact that in subsequent litigation, tribunals may disagree with a claim that a given breach justified avoidance of the contract (or that pertinent declarations were properly executed). The risk then is that an unlawful declaration of avoidance is construed itself as a breach or anticipatory breach of the contract, rendering the presumably aggrieved party liable to remedies (including avoidance of the contract) generated by such breach. Such risk is associated with all self-help measures and is typically born by aggrieved parties employing them. In avoidance of the contract under the CISG or PECL, this risk is especially pronounced by the insistence that only fundamental breaches allow the aggrieved party to declare the contract avoided. A prudent seller unsure of the fundamentality of the buyer's breach may then attempt to "upgrade" the severity of the breach through the usage of a *Nachfrist* mechanism, available under both the CISG and PECL. While suspending her power to avoid the contract for the length of the curative period (unless an anticipatory breach becomes apparent during that period), the two-tier mechanism significantly reduces her exposure to counter-claims regarding the unlawfulness of declaring the contract avoided. This useful mechanism is examined in detail below.

IV. NO FAULT, NO GRACE, NO REGARD TO TITLE

Both the PECL and CISG share a no-fault approach to breach of contract that allows for avoidance. In this, the general common law rather than general civil law approach is followed (see, however, PECL Art. 8:103(c)).

Neither the CISG nor the PECL set a default "grace period" for performance, during which the aggrieved party is enjoined from avoiding the contract.[31] However, both treat the matter of a cure or remedial period set or allowed by the aggrieved party as a special case during which the power to avoid the contract is suspended, as discussed next. Similarly, curative performance intended and indicated by the party in breach may limit the aggrieved seller's power to avoid the contract for a certain duration. Under PECL 9:303(3)(b) when the aggrieved party knows of the intention of the non-performing party to tender curative performance and fails to notify it that it will not accept cure, it forfeits the power to terminate the contract if the non-performing party in fact performs. Likewise, according to CISG Art. 48(2) an aggrieved buyer who failed to object to the

Luxembourg Civil Code Art. 1184(2) (although clauses allowing automatic termination – *clauses résolutoire de plein droit* – are also available); Italian Civil Code Art. 1453; and Spanish Civil Code Art. 1124 (though in Spain a notice of termination may be effective if it is accepted by the defaulting party). *See also* Lando and Beale at pp. 410, 415 n1.

[30] *See* commentary to PECL Art. 8:101. Strangely enough, litigants in countries where the rule for avoidance of domestic contracts is different still approach courts for declarations of avoidance even when they themselves claim that the CISG governs the case. *See, e.g.*, France 4 June 2004 Cour d'appel [Appellate Court] Paris (SARL NE . . . v. SAS AMI . . . et SA Les Comptoirs M . . .), case presentation including English translation available at <http://cisgw3.law.pace.edu/cases/040604f1.html>, where plaintiffs sued for a declaration of avoidance and for damages. Presumably, a court may refuse to hear the first part of the suit (in a common law country it probably would), referring the plaintiff instead to CISG Art. 64(1)(a) (in that case it was a matter of avoidance by the buyer, but the principle is the same). The risk of making an unlawful declaration of avoidance then sits with the aggrieved party; continuing to refer the matters to courts (who are accustomed to such procedures in domestic issues) may be a clever way to avoid that risk, tantamount to a declaratory verdict concerning the fundamentality of the breach that could, conceivably, be sought in a common law system.

[31] By contrast, compare the French and Belgian *délai de grâce* (Code Civil Art.1184; similarly, Spanish Code Civil Art. 1124 (3)).

breaching seller's indication that it intends to cure, is estopped from avoiding the contract for an indicated period.[32]

Additionally, the fundamental breach requirement itself may operate as setting a grace period in relation to avoidance, in the sense that the buyer's failure to pay – or to carry out any other of her allocated or derivative[33] performances – may become fundamental only some time after the breach itself has come to pass. For example, a very short delay – in respect to the contractual stipulation – in opening a letter of credit will normally not constitute a fundamental breach, but a longer delay may.[34]

As the CISG deals exclusively with obligatory questions,[35] the aggrieved seller's power to declare the contract avoided is wholly independent from questions of title to the goods. The power to avoid is likewise indifferent to the question who is in possession of the goods, if the buyer has either taken delivery or accepted them, or who is in possession of documents of title.[36] If questions of title need to be resolved, domestic law would apply and determine entitlements.[37] The PECL, wider in scope and application than the CISG, are nevertheless limited to the contractual (and related obligation) context too.[38] As noted above, discharging rights granted by the CISG and PECL – such as the right to restitution following avoidance of the contract – may be found subject to third-party interests and property rights, regulated by domestic law.[39]

V. AVOIDANCE BY SELLER IN CASES OF NON-FUNDAMENTAL BREACH: SELLER'S *NACHFRIST* MECHANISM IN CISG AND PECL

The general principle according to which both the CISG and the PECL reserve avoidance of the contract to cases of fundamental breach can be, in some cases, bypassed. In cases of some non-fundamental breaches, both the CISG and PECL allow the aggrieved seller to avoid the contract if she first sets an additional period of time of reasonable length for the buyer to perform, and the buyer has failed to perform throughout that curative period, which is called a *Nachfrist* period after similar provisions in German, Swiss, and other legal systems.[40] Using a *Nachfrist*, aggrieved sellers may "upgrade" certain

[32] *See* Jonathan Yovel, "Seller's Right to Remedy Failure to Perform: Comparison between Respective Provisions of the CISG and the PECL," available online at <http://cisgw3.law.pace.edu/cisg/biblio/yovel48.html>.

[33] *See* CISG Art. 54 according to which "The buyer's obligation to pay the price includes taking such steps . . . to enable payment to be made."

[34] *See* Honnold at 354; *also* Joseph Lookofsky and Herbert Bernstein, *Understanding the CISG in Europe* (Deventer, 1997) 114.

[35] *See* CISG Art. 4(b).

[36] Except, of course, for determining the existence of breach or fundamental breach, in which case failure to effect a change of title may be the breach that makes avoidance of the title available. *See, e.g.*, discussion that follows, *infra* note 43.

[37] *See* the Australian case *Roder v. Rosedown*, Federal District Court Adelaide, 28 April 1995, available online at <http://cisgw3.law.pace.edu/cases/950428a2.html> (the contract of sales contained a retention of title clause whereby title to the goods did not pass to the purchaser until the purchase price had been paid in full, which was not the case). *See* Robert Koch, "Commentary on Whether the UNIDROIT Principles of International Commercial Contracts may be Used to Interpret or Supplement Article 25 CISG," *Pace Review of the Convention on Contracts for the International Sale of Goods* (1998) 246, available online at <http://cisgw3.law.pace.edu/cisg/biblio/koch1.html>.

[38] Whether obligations stemming from PECL Arts. 2:301–3 should be properly classified as contractual or other in nature (tort, quasi-contract, collateral, or "implied" contract) is a question that cannot be dealt with here; all these legal constructs are, however, obligatory in nature.

[39] *See infra* note 64.

[40] *See* Lando and Beale, op. cit., at 377. BGB § 326 practically makes *Nachfrist* periods compulsory in most cases, whereas the CISG and PECL merely make it available to the non-breaching party. For the Swiss "Nachfristmodell," *see* Art. 107, 108 Obligationenrecht (Swiss Law of Obligations). Professor Treitel makes the point that other legal systems contain similar mechanisms; *see* Günter H. Treitel, "Remedies for Breach of Contract," in *International Encyclopedia of Comparative Law* (Tübingen, Mouton, The Hague, Paris:

non-fundamental breaches to the status of avoidance-justifying breach.[41] Moreover, the CISG seems more generous in allowing aggrieved sellers to avoid the contract following a *Nachfrist* period than it is toward aggrieved buyers (the PECL, of course, make no such distinction to begin with).[42] This and the following sections examine the conditions under which avoidance of the contract becomes available to aggrieved sellers following a *Nachfrist* period.

Curative periods set by the aggrieved seller fall under CISG Art. 63 and PECL Art. 8:106, respectively. They share the same basic structure: under both the aggrieved seller is empowered to fix an additional period for the buyer to come through on her obligations. During that period the aggrieved seller may resort to remedies (such as damages), but not avoid the contract, unless the party in breach declares that no curative performance will be forthcoming. The main constraint applying to *Nachfrist* periods is that, to allow for eventual avoidance of the contract, the period must be of contextually reasonable length to allow the party in breach to cure its non-performance. When this condition is met and the party in breach fails to perform throughout the *Nachfrist* period, the aggrieved party is empowered to avoid the contract (the *Nachfrist* mechanism of PECL Art. 8:106(3) also allows automatic expiration of the contract once the additional period has expired to no avail). However, post-*Nachfrist* avoidance under CISG and PECL is available only for certain types of breach. Those are explored next.

VI. WHAT BREACHES ALLOW FOR AVOIDANCE OF THE CONTRACT FOLLOWING NACHFRIST?

Although the *Nachfrist* mechanism shared by the CISG and PECL relaxes the principle that only fundamental breaches allow for avoidance of the contract, it does so in a limited way. For not all breaches (non-performances) allow for post-*Nachfrist* avoidance of the contract. The CISG allows the aggrieved seller to avoid the contract post-*Nachfrist* in two categories of the buyer's non-fundamental failures to perform: (1) if the buyer has

J.C.B. Mohr, 1976) Ch. 16, §§ 149–151. Such is Art. 7(b) of the Israeli Contract Law (Remedies for Breach of Contract), 1970, which combines the optional version of *Nachfrist* with the exception that avoidance under *Nachfrist* for non-fundamental breaches may be objected to on grounds of injustice, with courts retaining appropriate discretion.

[41] In one French case, the seller sent the buyer a notice of avoidance following the buyer's refusal to take *delivery* on a certain early date (amended from the original contractual stipulation). The court judged the breach non-fundamental and determined that the only way for the seller to avoid the contract was to first fix a *Nachfrist* period, which was not done: France 4 February 1999 Cour d'appel [Appellate Court] Grenoble (*Ego Fruits v. La Verja Begastri*), case presentation including English translation available online at <http://cisgw3.law.pace.edu/cases/990204f1.html>. In ICC Court of Arbitration case 7585/1992, the tribunal deemed the buyer's failure to open a letter of credit according to the contract a breach, but not a fundamental breach; nevertheless, the seller's declaration of avoidance was effective as it took place several months after the breach, and that time was constructed to operate as a valid *Nachfrist* period. Published (in English) in the *ICC International Court of Arbitration Bulletin* Vol. 6/N.2 – November 1995, 60–64; available online at <http://cisgw3.law.pace.edu/cases/927585i1.html>.

[42] Under CISG Art. 49, an aggrieved buyer may declare the contract avoided following a *Nachfrist* period only in cases of non-delivery of goods, whereas Art. 64 permits avoidance following *Nachfrist* for either the buyer's failure to pay or to take delivery of the goods. Regarding Art. 49, scholarly exegesis has broadened the avoidance-sanctioning defect to non-delivery of documents of title as well; Prof. Schlechtriem's argument is that in typical contexts, goods without appropriate documents are not the contracted goods at all: they have been delivered physically perhaps, but not legally. By analogy, the failure to take delivery of goods under Art. 64(1)(b) should also extend to failure to accept documents of title. *See* Peter Schlechtriem, *Uniform Sales Law: The UN Convention on Contracts for the International Sale of Goods* (Vienna: Manz 1986), available online at <http://cisgw3.law.pace.edu/cisg/biblio/schlechtriem.html>, 77; Jonathan Yovel, "Buyer's Right to Avoid the Contract: Comparative Analysis of Respective Provisions of the CISG and PECL," *Nord. J. Com. L.* (forthcoming 2005), available online at <http://cisgw3.law.pace.edu/cisg/biblio/yovel49.html>. Prof. Koch and others support this construction; *see* Robert Koch, "Commentary on Whether the UNIDROIT Principles of International Commercial Contracts May Be Used to Interpret or Supplement Articles 47 and 49 of the CISG," available online at <http://cisgw3.law.pace.edu/cisg/biblio/koch2.html>.

failed to pay the price; and (2) if the buyer has failed to take delivery of the goods (CISG Art. 64(1)(b)).[43] These failures may occur in conjunction with each other or independently.

1. Non-Payment and Nachfrist under CISG

As noted above, "payment" in the CISG may entail several performances, such as complying with legal formalities and taking preparatory steps to ensure that the eventual payment will come through. Examples are obtaining or at least applying for credit, for a letter of credit, or for bank guarantees[44]; procuring adequate foreign currency; complying with required formalities where applicable, etc.[45] Such performances that "enable payment to be made" are normally considered inherent to the buyer's "obligation to pay the price,"[46] and thus failing on them throughout a *Nachfrist* period would normally allow the aggrieved seller to avoid the contract. However, a seller who has actually received the price – even in a manner inconsistent with the contract – should be considered as having forfeited the power to avoid the contract on those grounds, although he is still entitled to damages if applicable.[47]

2. Not Taking Delivery and Nachfrist under CISG

CISG Art. 64(1)(b) allows the seller to avoid the contract post-*Nachfrist* also where the buyer has failed to take delivery of the goods. In some circumstances, a simple delay in the buyer's performance in taking the goods may do no more than accrue storage and associated costs (insurance, etc.) that are imposed on the seller and refundable from the buyer according to CISG Art. 85. However, in other situations the seller may be seriously burdened with the responsibility of caring for perishable goods[48] or goods stranded in

[43] Note that the corresponding provision regarding the buyer's power to avoid the contract post-*Nachfrist* is limited to cases of non-delivery only (CISG Art. 49(1)(b)). Prof. Honnold refers to Art. 64 as maintaining a "problem of consistency": presumably, the seller's non-delivery is parallel to the buyer's non-payment, and the buyer's failure to take delivery of the goods has no direct counterpart in Art. 49. Prof. Honnold worries that this may allow sellers to avoid contracts prematurely on the basis of short *Nachfrist* periods so they can, for example, benefit from a sharp increase in market value of the goods. Yet as he notes, CISG Art. 63(1) requires that the additional curative period be of "reasonable length," and although this requirement is not mirrored in PECL Art. 8:106(1), only a reasonably long period would allow for avoidance under PECL Art. 8:106(3). *See* Honnold, at 387–8.

[44] *See* ICC Court of Arbitration case 7197/1992, where the tribunal ruled that the Bulgarian buyer's failure to open a letter of credit according to the contract was a fundamental breach of its obligation to pay and that legal impediments to the payment of debt in foreign currency did not constitute *force majeure*. Published (in French) *Journal du Droit International*, 1993, 1028–1037; and UNILEX, also available at <http://cisgw3.law.pace.edu/cases/927197i1.html>. In an Australian case, the court also deemed the buyer's failure to open a letter of credit as agreed a fundamental breach, especially as the buyer was expected during this time to continue performance (charter a ship for the sale of scrap metal, etc.), *Downs Investments Pty Ltd v Perjawa Steel SDN BHD*, *supra* note 18. For the matter of letter of credit, *see also* Honnold at 387, 510; as well as United States 21 July 1997 Federal District Court [New York] (*Helen Kaminski v. Marketing Australian Products*) CLOUT abstract no. 413, case also available online at <http://cisgw3.law.pace.edu/cases/970721u1.html>.

[45] The Secretariat Commentary to Article 64, para 7, stipulates, "The buyer's obligation to pay the price includes taking such steps and complying with such formalities which may be required by the contract . . . to enable payment to be made, such as registering the contract with a government office or with a bank, procuring the necessary foreign exchange, as well as applying for a letter of credit or a bank guarantee to facilitate the payment of the price." Available online at <http://cisgw3.law.pace.edu/cisg/text/secomm/secomm-64.html>.

[46] *See* CISG Art. 54.

[47] *See* UK Sales of Goods act §10, according to which contractual stipulations as to time of payment are not "of the essence" absent contrary intent and thus would not normally provide grounds for avoidance of the contract.

[48] In a Vietnamese case, the buyer failed to take delivery of a quantity of monosodium glutamate; the court justified the seller's immediate avoidance of the contract on grounds of fundamental breach due to the goods being "a very delicate substance" that could have deteriorated in prolonged storage; an immediate avoidance of the contract was therefore in reasonable time. The court seems not to assign ample weight to the fact

faraway places, ports, or places of transit.[49] Even if not a fundamental breach, the untimely taking of delivery may create hardships that for the seller would warrant post-*Nachfrist* avoidance of the contract, especially if the price had not yet been paid (commentators note that even in such situations it would be an extraordinary case in which a seller would avoid the contract having been paid).[50]

3. Delay in Performance and Nachfrist under PECL

The approach of the PECL to post-*Nachfrist* termination by the seller is different from the approach of the CISG. It does not limit the availability of post-*Nachfrist* termination to cases of the buyers' failure to pay or take delivery, but instead focuses on the matter of *delay* in performance – any performance. In case of delay in performance, PECL Art. 9:301(2) refers to and authorizes termination of the contract *also* according to PECL 8:106(3),[51] which governs all post-*Nachfrist* terminations. Thus, in the context of termination of the contract by the buyer, also governed by Art. 8:106(3), non-fundamental non-conformity cannot be grounds for termination of the contract even when a *Nachfrist* period has been set according to PECL Art. 8:106(1) and passed to no avail, because the crux of the matter is not one of delay.[52] The reflection of this in the case of the seller would be non-conformity of payment – either in method, currency, etc., which although it may be subject to a *Nachfrist* period under PECL Art. 8:106(1), would not allow for termination on the contract under PECL Art. 8:106(3) as the matter is not one of delay in performance.

Making post-*Nachfrist* avoidance of the contract available to delays in performance, as PECL Art. 8:106(3) does, may prove tricky to those comfortable with the CISG's tighter approach. For whether the buyer's non-performances – e.g., to pay and/or take delivery – are definite or merely delays in performance would typically be unknown at the time of non-performance. The seller would then have an option to treat them as definite failures (either as fundamental non-performances or not) or as non-fundamental delays of performance, for which she might fix a *Nachfrist* period according to PECL Art. 8:106(1) and terminate the contract upon the buyer's continued failure to perform on PECL Art. 8:106(3). The PECL's allowance for post-*Nachfrist* termination may thus encompass non-performances by the buyer that would not allow for post-*Nachfrist* avoidance under CISG. A buyer who is slack in her contracted obligations to set up a service system, or a promotion campaign, or to conform with some formality in which the seller has an interest may risk being held as delaying performance and may be subject to post-*Nachfrist* termination. In the absence of a material criterion that distinguishes between the several kinds of performances (to pay, to take delivery, to promote, to care for reputation or rights, etc.), tribunals must come up with clear yet contextual criteria to distinguish between any non-performance and a delay in performance, lest the former be masked as the latter

that the buyer has opened (and prolonged) a letter of credit and has already paid 50% of the price, on top of expressing intention – as well as eventually attempting to perform – to take the goods after a few day's delay. Vietnam 5 April 1996 Appellate Court (*Ng Nam Bee Pte Ltd. v. Tay Ninh Trade Co.*), case presentation including English translation available at <http://cisgw3.law.pace.edu/cases/960405v1.html>.

[49] *See*, e.g., the circumstances of the case: United States 14 April 1992 Federal District Court [New York] (*Filanto v. Chilewich*), available at <http://cisgw3.law.pace.edu/cases/920414u1.html>, in which quantities of footwear were delivered DAF ("Delivered at Frontier") in several installments by the Italian manufacturer to be received by agents of the UK/USA buyer at the Yugoslav border.

[50] *See* Honnold, p. 389.

[51] Somewhat redundantly perhaps: it seems that PECL Art. 8:106(3) would be effective also absent the reference by Art. 9:301(2). The term "also" in PECL Art. 9:301(2) retains the availability of termination according to PECL Art. 9:301(1) in cases of fundamental non-performances. It has the same effect as the words "which is not fundamental" in PECL Art. 8:106(3).

[52] Compare with the clause regarding the buyer's setting a *Nachfrist* period in cases of non-delivery under CISG Art. 49(1)(b).

and the *Nachfrist* mechanism abused in the sense of wrongly applying to breaches where delay in performance is not the essential factor. Tribunals may take into consideration the following points.

1) Any interpretation of the "delay of performance" language of PECL 8:106(3) must be conducted within the general framework of PECL Art. 9:301, namely the fundamental breach principle. Thus, exceptions to the principle under PECL Art. 8:106(3) should be construed narrowly and contextually.
2) All such exceptions must pass the good faith test – no trivial delays in performance or masking definite non-fundamental non-performances as "delays" should be allowed to result in contract termination. The *Nachfrist* mechanism allows for "upgrade" of some non-fundamental delays, but certainly not any and all of them.
3) In the context of international sales, tribunals may look to CISG Art. 64(1)(b) as an interpretative guideline in construing what non-performances should be allowed to result in avoidance of the contract.

Certainly, such rulings may still allow for more extensive sets of cases where contracts would be terminated under PECL than under CISG; these may cover, for instance, the buyer's failure to supply certain documents other than documents of title. No *Nachfrist* period would allow for avoiding the contract under CISG 49(1)(b) for such a failure, but the case can turn differently under PECL 8:106(3). In conclusion, although the aforementioned constraints must not allow for the erosion of the fundamental breach principle of the PECL, it is also a mistake to obscure the differences between the two post-*Nachfrist* avoidance rules. The drafting of the PECL was done with full cognizance of the approach taken by the CISG, and the differences, even if not great, are material nonetheless.

VII. *NACHFRIST* AND REASONABLE TIME

The *Nachfrist* mechanism cannot be used to bypass the reasonable time requirement governing all notices of termination set in PECL Art. 9:303(2). PECL Art. 8:106(3) requires that the additional curative period be of "reasonable length." If it is "too short," the aggrieved party may terminate only after an overall reasonable time has passed, even if the additional period has already expired. For purposes of termination, this imposes a de-facto "reasonable length" on the *Nachfrist* period, although such is not generally required (see PECL Art. 8:106(1)).[53]

It is not always clear, however, as of when should the period in question be counted. In some cases, courts looked not to the *Nachfrist* period indicated by the seller, but instead to the entire period available for the buyer's cure – from breach to termination – although the actual *Nachfrist* period involved was much shorter.[54]

PECL Art. 8:106(3) includes a useful mechanism, in that the *Nachfrist* notice may include a conditional termination notice, which will apply automatically if the non-performing party fails to remedy during the additional period.[55] In this case, a contract

[53] The CISG contains such a time limitation only in cases where delivery was made (CISG Art. 49(2)(b)(ii)), a limitation that applies also to the cure period under Art. 48 (CISG Art. 49(2)(b)(iii)).

[54] *See* Italy 11 December 1998 Corte di Appello [Appellate Court] Milan (*Bielloni Castello v. EGO*), case presentation including English translation available at <http://cisgw3.law.pace.edu/cases/981211i3.html>; seller set two consecutive *Nachfrist* periods of fifteen days each, but the overall period made de facto available for the buyer's performance after breach totaled two and a half months, which the court judged to be a reasonable time. *See* also ICC Court of Arbitration case 7585/1992, *infra* note 59.

[55] Whether the *Nachfrist* notice in fact makes this provision or not would become an interpretative question. *See*, in a similar context, such an approach to a *Nachfrist* notice by the Austrian Supreme Court where the seller – mistakenly considering German domestic law to be applicable – gave a notice according to BGB § 326; the court judged this to satisfy the conditions of a *Nachfrist* notice under CISG Art. 63 and therefore

may be terminated without a designated notice: the *Nachfrist* notice then doubles as a conditional notice of termination.[56] This means that the seller must make the *Nachfrist* nature of the notice obvious to the defaulting buyer, less the latter consider it merely a "grace" period bereft of legal effect in terms of ensuing avoidance of the contract.[57] In case the additional period is not deemed to be of reasonable length, such automatic termination will take effect after a reasonable time only, in accordance with the principle examined above. However, there is one case in which there is no sense in insisting on a reasonably long curative hiatus prior to the termination of the contract taking effect. That is the case of anticipatory breach during *Nachfrist*, when clearly no curative performance is forthcoming. This case is examined next.

VIII. ANTICIPATORY BREACH DURING *NACHFRIST* PERIOD

Both the CISG and PECL operate on the general principle that anticipatory breach may provide grounds for remedies – including avoidance of the contract in case of anticipatory fundamental breach – even before the time of performance has arrived.[58] This principle is carried into the respective provisions governing avoidance of the contract following a *Nachfrist* period.

CISG Art. 64(b) stipulates that avoidance of the contract during a *Nachfrist* period becomes available upon the buyer's "declaration" that she will not perform within the set curative period. That is a more limited criterion than that of CISG Art. 72, which allows for avoidance of the contract if "it is clear" that a fundamental breach is to take place. Under Art. 64(b), that information must originate from the defaulting buyer. However, there is no requirement that the said declaration be a specific one directed at the seller to the effect that buyer will continue defaulting on this specific transaction. A general declaration of insolvency, for instance, should fulfill the "declaration" requirement of CISG Art. 64(1)(b), unless accompanied by a specific communication to the contrary (even an insolvent buyer may go ahead with a transaction that will eventually generate value for distribution in eventual bankruptcy).[59] In the communicative framework of *Nachfrist*, unlike the general rule governing anticipatory breach, general third-party information is not basis enough to declare the contract avoided prior to the expiration of the duration of the curative period.

under Art. 64(1)(b) as well. Austria 28 April 2000 Oberster Gerichtshof [Supreme Court], case presentation including English translation available at <http://cisgw3.law.pace.edu/cases/000428a3.html>.

[56] *See* Lando and Beale, *op. cit*., at 415.

[57] Thus in ICC Court of Arbitration case 7197/1992, *supra* note 45, the tribunal held (*in obiter*) that although the buyer had failed to perform its obligation within the additional period of time fixed by the seller, the seller would have been entitled to avoid the contract under Art. 64(1)(b) CISG only if it had declared its intention to do so and had given notice to the buyer pursuant to Art. 26 CISG. As things stood, the extra period set by the seller did not qualify as a *Nachfrist* period for the purpose of avoidance of the contract because the seller did not communicate it as such. This seems a certain deviation from CISG Art. 64(1)(b) as the provision applies to "additional period of time fixed by the seller in accordance with paragraph (1) of article 63," which does not require any mention of the seller's intention to avoid the contract upon the buyer's continued default.

[58] *See* CISG Art. 72 and PECL Art. 9:304.

[59] Thus, to the tribunal's approval in ICC Court of Arbitration case 7585/1992, the aggrieved seller postponed a notice of avoidance for a little over three months – operating as a *Nachfrist* period – although "it was absolutely clear that Defendant [defaulting buyer] did not have financial resources" to pay the contractual price (but did not communicate this to the aggrieved seller). *See supra* note. However, in the Australian case *Roder v. Rosedown*, *supra* note, the buyer's going "into administration" was judged grounds enough for the seller to avoid the contract under CISG Art. 64(1) as no possible performance could be expected. The seller in a Swiss case was cautious too, providing consecutive *Nachfrist* periods to no avail after the buyer, who has paid a portion of the price, has gone into bankruptcy (and eventual liquidation); presumably, the seller was very anxious to go through with the deal as the goods involved were specially produced and required costly disassembly for an alternative transaction. Switzerland 3 December 2002 Handelsgericht [Commercial Court] St. Gallen, case presentation including English translation available online at <http://cisgw3.law.pace.edu/cases/021203s1.html>.

PECL Art. 8:106(2) maintains a similar device, whereby the aggrieved party who has set a *Nachfrist* period is allowed to terminate the contract during that period if she "receives notice from the other party" to the effect that no performance is forthcoming. This requirement is likewise narrower than the general one governing anticipatory breach under the PECL, according to which it must be "clear" that default would persist (PECL Art. 9:304). The reasons for diverging from the general rule in the context of a curative *Nachfrist* period are the same as discussed above in the context of the CISG.

IX. TIME RESTRICTIONS ON THE SELLER'S POWER TO AVOID THE CONTRACT

1. General

Under CISG Art. 64(1), the seller's power to avoid the contract is unrestricted, time-wise.[60] An aggrieved seller is thus allowed to either set a curative period under CISG Art. 63(1) or simply wait and refrain from avoiding the contract in hope that the buyer comes through, knowing that her power to avoid the contract at a later time will not expire by this delay alone.[61] The tables are turned, however, once the price – the total price[62] – has been paid. CISG Art. 64(2) then restricts the seller's power to avoid the contract in terms of the time in which a declaration of avoidance may be considered effective. These restrictions are examined in detail below.[63] Before examining them, however, one should note the meaning of the payment of the price as the "crossing of the Rubicon" in the CISG.

Professor Honnold notes that, as avoidance of the contract normally involves mutual restitution, sellers will generally be reluctant to avoid contracts after the price has been paid.[64] However, one can conceive of serious risks to the seller generated by the buyer's other breaches, such as failure to take possession of the goods (which may create problems

[60] Prof. Honnold admits this "may seem anomalous" but justifies the rule on grounds of the position of the aggrieved seller neither wishing to jump the gun and avoid the contract too early, on the grounds that avoidance on fundamental breach is not yet available, nor avoid too late and risk unreasonable delay. *See* Honnold, at 389.

[61] However, *see* Prof. Kritzer's important argument that even when not spelled out, "reasonableness is a general principle of the CISG." Performing reasonably does not always mean that performance must be "made in reasonable time," as in contexts of provisions that make specific distinctions between cases in which powers (such as power to avoid the contract) must be exercised in reasonable time or not. Otherwise, the overt distinctions between cases in which avoidance must be declared in reasonable time and those in which it is not would be meaningless. Kritzer's point is well taken in that even these provisions must be interpreted against the general principle of reasonable performance. Albert H. Kritzer, "Overview Comments on Reasonableness,' available online at <http://cisgw3.law.pace.edu/cisg/text/reason.html>. *See* also comments by Jelena Vilus, available online at <http://cisgw3.law.pace.edu/cisg/text/reason.html#vilus>; rpr. in *Homenaje a Jorge Barrera Graf*, vol. 2, Mexico: Universidad Nacional Autonoma de Mexico (1989) 1440–1441. For the definition of reasonableness expressed in the PECL and references to reasonableness in continental and common law domestic rules, doctrine, and jurisprudence, go to <http://cisgw3.law.pace.edu/cisg/text/reason.html#def>. For further discussion regarding the correlation between the PECL's definition of reasonableness and the meaning of this term to CISG legislators when they used the concept in drafting the Convention's provisions, *see* Kritzer, *id.*

[62] *See* Secretariat Commentary on CISG Article 64, paras 8, 12, available online at <http://cisgw3.law.pace.edu/cisg/text/secomm_64.html>.

[63] It is typical of the architecture of the CISG and PECL that, although the former regulates substantive rights of termination mostly in discrete clauses (such as Art. 64), the latter regulates several substantive rights through its general treatment of notices of termination, common to both sides. *See* PECL Art. 9:303.

[64] Honnold § 356 (p. 388). Of course, the practical availability of retrieving either funds or goods from a defaulting party rests on more than contract or sales law, especially as rights against third-party creditors and bankruptcy preferences are regulated by domestic law; the CISG itself does not govern property rights; *see* CISG Art. 4(b). *See* Jacob S. Ziegel, "Report to the Uniform Law Conference of Canada on Convention on Contracts for the International Sale of Goods" (July 1981), at 130, available at <http://cisgw3.law.pace.edu/cisg/text/ziegel81.html>. Commercial debts will typically be inferior in preference to those held by secured creditors, and the restitution according to Art. 81(2) would become that weakest of types of debt in bankruptcy – an unsecured commercial debt (unless under contractual or statutory lien).

with carriers, port authorities, etc.) or arranging for formal conformities; the seller may find herself not only in breach of contract with other parties but also in possible legal trouble (e.g., for holding imported goods without import license, veterinary or other clearances, or required certificates, etc. that were supposed to be generated by the buyer). As Honnold notes, the seller may also be invested in long-term interests that require the buyer's performance, such as setting up a distributorship or a promotion program.[65] Nevertheless, a buyer who has paid the price yet defaulted otherwise is in a precarious position herself. This is the mirror-image of the situation of the seller who has delivered the goods, and the CISG treats both situations similarly in restricting the aggrieved party's power to avoid the contract to a reasonable time.

The PECL differs in its general approach. First, there is no "crossing of the Rubicon" – the PECL do not distinguish between cases in which the price had been paid and those in which it was not. Second, PECL Art. 9:303(2) requires that in *all* cases notice of termination be given in reasonable time after awareness of the non-performance became effective.[66] This approach looks rather to the interest of the non-performing party in duly knowing whether its breach will cause termination or not. However, in one important case the PECL actually grant the aggrieved seller a wider power to terminate the contract than the CISG: that of a buyer's late performance. The next section examines the CISG and PECL provisions governing these types of cases.

2. Late Performance by the Buyer after the Price Was Paid

Under the CISG, when the price was paid yet the buyer is still in breach in that her performance is *late*,[67] the aggrieved seller's declaration of avoidance must be given before she becomes aware that the performance has been tendered (CISG Art. 64(2)(a)). This restriction protects the reliance interest of the aggrieved buyer during her cure efforts and is an incentive both to the aggrieved seller not to postpone a declaration of avoidance unnecessarily and to the curing buyer to notify the seller of the curative performance as soon as possible, in order to cut off the latter's power to avoid the contract.[68]

By contrast, under PECL Art. 9:303(3)(a) the aggrieved party retains the power to terminate the contract until a reasonable time *after* it has or ought to have become aware of the late tender. In fact, PECL Art. 9:303(3)(a) goes out if its way to emphasize that the

[65] *Id.*

[66] Lando and Beale note that this rule corresponds to those in several legal systems, notably civil law regimes, but these in fact feature a certain variation that may very well decide cases differently: from "without delay" to "shortly" to "reasonable time." *See* Danish Sale of Goods Act §§ 27, 32 ("promptly" or "within a short time"); Finnish and Swedish Sale of Goods Acts, §§ 29, 32, 39, 59 ("reasonable time"); Dutch BW Art. 6:89 ("promptly"); French, Belgian, and Luxembourg Code Civil Art. 1648 for *garantie des vices cachés ("dans un bref délai")* and, in Belgium, in some other cases on the basis of good faith, *see* Cass. 18 May 1987, Arr. Cass. 546 and Cass. 8 Apr. 1988, Arr. Cass., no. 482; UK Sale of Goods Act 1979, §§ 34 and 35 (and *see* Treitel, *op. cit.* at 711); Portuguese Civil Code Art. 436(2). *See* Lando and Beale, *at p.* 415. Austrian and German law maintain a shorter time limit, "*unverzüglich*" ("without undue delay.") *See* BGB § 121 (controlling all acts of rescission, including HGB § 377), ABGB §§ 932, 933. German courts acknowledged a discrepancy between the two criteria, even when the facts satisfied both; *see* Germany 17 September 1991 Oberlandesgericht [Appellate Court] Frankfurt, case presentation including English translation available at <http://cisgw3.law.pace.edu/cases/910917g1.html> (in this case a one-day delay in sending an avoidance telex after the breach was discovered at a trade fair was judged both reasonable and *unverzüglich*). In another case, an Italian buyer of a used car was allowed to avoid the contract three months after she discovered the car was previously stolen and the title could not be transferred; the court accepted the time as pertinent to the various inspections required: Germany 22 August 2002 Landgericht [District Court] Freiburg, case presentation including English translation available at <http://cisgw3.law.pace.edu/cases/020822g1.html>.

[67] Said non-performance may be the non-payment or another non-performance. The Secretariat Commentary envisions that "in most cases" the late performance would indeed be the payment of the price, but the performance in question may of course be a different one. *See* Secretariat Commentary, *supra* note 63 at para. 9.

[68] For a discussion of the relationship between the power to avoid the contract and the right to cure *see* above, text related to note.

aggrieved party need not terminate before the late tender has been made. The exception to this rule is that the aggrieved party loses its power to terminate the contract if it fails to notify the party in breach that it will refuse to accept a curative performance, as long as it has reason to know that the party in breach intends such cure (PECL Art. 9:303(3)(b), which completes the general cure provision of Art. 8:104).[69] Although no legal system studied has a mechanism identical to that of PECL Art. 9:303(3)(b),[70] the CISG maintains a similar provision regarding limitation of an aggrieved buyer's power to avoid the contract (CISG Art. 48(2)), with the difference that the intention to cure must be communicated by the seller-in-breach to the buyer. CISG has no direct counterpart to Art. 48 regarding cure by buyer.[71] Note that the PECL do not make a special provision for cases in which the price was paid, and Art. 9:303(2) applies whether it was or was not paid.

3. Buyer's Breach other than Late Performance

The seller's power to avoid the contract when the price had been paid for breaches other than late performance is limited by the CISG Art. 64(2)(b) to a "reasonable time" after one of the following occurrences has come to pass: either the aggrieved seller knew or ought to have known of the breach (CISG Art. 64(2)(b)(i)), or a *Nachfrist* period (set according to Art. 63(1), as discussed above) has passed to no avail (CISG Art. 64(2)(b)(ii)).[72] The former obviously correlates with PECL Art. 9:303(2) (general duty to terminate in reasonable time). The correlation is less perfect in the case of the latter, which is in fact a limitation on the power of avoidance following a *Nachfrist* period – as set out in Art 64(1)(b) – to the effect that once the price had been paid and the *Nachfrist* on the persisting breach *other* than late performance had passed to no avail, the seller's power to avoid the contract must be executed in reasonable time or else expire. This provision seems not to have a direct counterpart in the PECL. PECL Art. 8:106(3) limits termination following failed *Nachfrist* periods to cases of "delay in performance" only, which correlates to what CISG 64(2)(b) in fact excludes ("in respect to any breach other than late performance, etc."). The non-correlation, however, is merely a slight technical problem, as PECL Art. 9:303(2) would govern cases falling under CISG Art. 64(2)(b)(ii), as well.

4. Reasonable Time

Although used frequently, the expression "reasonable time" is not defined in the CISG nor in the PECL. Courts and commentators offer contextual criteria,[73] noting that what may

[69] *See* Jonathan Yovel, "Seller's Right to Remedy Failure to Perform: Comparison between Respective Provisions of the CISG and the PECL," available online at <http://cisgw3.law.pace.edu/cisg/biblio/yovel48.html>.

[70] *See* Lando and Beale, p. 415. The authors surmise that such forbearance may be implied by the duty of good faith or, in common law systems, promissory estoppel. Indeed, to my mind, neither source of obligation may create such a forbearance as under the circumstances indicated in PECL Art. 9:303, which include communicative passivity on the part of the debtor. Certainly no promissory estoppel may come into effect where not a modicum of promise was given, as Lando and Beale note (for a communicative alternative, *see* CISG Art. 48(2)–(4)). The duty to perform in good faith would probably cut the other way: it would require the party in breach – who intends to cure and wishes the aggrieved party to forebear from termination – to at least take pains to communicate this intention. Requiring the aggrieved party to forebear on mere hearsay without a substantive basis for knowing that cure is forthcoming seems itself an act in bad faith.

[71] *See* Yovel, *supra* note 69.

[72] In this aspect CISG Art. 64 resembles CISG Art. 49, except that the latter adds a similar provision limiting the power of avoidance when cure has been effected according to CISG Art. 48(2); namely, on the defaulting seller's initiative rather than the buyer's. As the CISG does not contain a buyer equivalent to the seller's right to cure after the time for performance has passed (Art. 48), Art. 64(2)(b) contains only two subclauses to the three of Art. 49(2)(b).

[73] Lando and Beale remark, "What is a reasonable time will depend upon the circumstances. For instance the aggrieved party must be allowed long enough for it to know whether or not the performance will still be useable by it. If delay in making a decision is likely to prejudice the defaulting party, for instance because it

constitute "reasonable" in any given case may be affected by the nature of the goods,[74] the transaction, the payment arrangements, third-party claims, and whether legal advice or expert opinions were actually necessary to determine concrete rights (e.g., in cases of non-conformity merely sorting the matter out may take, for practical reasons, longer than under no tender at all).[75] Courts have ruled on the reasonable length of time taking all such circumstances into account, and in the absence of clear indicators, the question of when does the period begin to run is invariably left to judicial discretion.[76]

PECL Art. 1:302 supplies some guidelines to "reasonableness" in general, but those are somewhat circular – "reasonable" is what reasonable persons, acting in good faith, would "consider reasonable." More helpful is the notion that reasonableness is contextual and takes into consideration "the nature and purposes of the contract, the circumstances of the case," etc. Another approach would be to consider reasonableness in the definition and execution of contractual obligations as an articulation of the principle of good faith.[77] In the context of CISG Art. 64, this seems to mean that as far as delaying the declaration of avoidance, the seller has a duty to avoid in good faith only in cases where the goods have been delivered.[78] Under the comprehensive commitment to good faith expressed in PECL Art. 1:201, however, this duty applies to all terminations. A different

may lose the chance to prevent a total waste of its efforts by entering another contract, the reasonable time will be shorter than if this is not the case." *Op. cit.* at p. 413.

[74] *See Cong ty Ng Nam Bee v. Cong ty Thuong mai Tay Ninh*, *supra* note 48, discussing perishable goods.

[75] *See, e.g.*, Germany 31 January 1997 Oberlandesgericht [Appellate Court] Koblenz, case presentation available at <http://cisgw3.law.pace.edu/cases/970131g1.html>; *see also* Plate, "The Buyer's Remedy of Avoidance under the CISG: Acceptable from a Common Law Perspective?," 6 *Vindobona J. Int'l. Com. L. & Arbitration* (2002) 57, at 67, available online at <http://cisgw3.law.pace.edu/cisg/biblio/plate.html>.

[76] As "reasonable time" operates in cases of the seller's breach (under CISG Art. 49) as well as the buyer's breach, decisions pertaining to the former are useful in constructing the latter. Thus *see* France 14 June 2001 Cour d'appel [Appellate Court] Paris, *Aluminium and Light Industries Company v. Saint Bernard Miroiterie Vitrerie*, case presentation including English translation available at <http://cisgw3.law.pace.edu/cases/010614f1.html>, where the court applied CISG Art. 49(2) to a transaction of faulty fancy glass panels, determining that the eight months that lapsed from the determination of the breach to the notice of avoidance was an unreasonably long period. The court took into account the various expert inspections of the panels sought in this case and began counting the period from the last one. In different circumstances, the German Supreme Court ruled that the five months that had elapsed between the buyer's being informed of the seller's breach (a delivery stop) made for too long a period and could not be considered as a reasonable time under Article 49(1)(b): *see* Germany 15 February 1995 Bundesgerichtshof [Supreme Court], case presentation including English translation available at <http://cisgw3.law.pace.edu/cases/950215g1.html>.

[77] Peter Schlechtriem, *Uniform Sales Law* (trans. from German: Einliches UN Kaufrecht, Manzsche, Vienna, 1986) 39. *See also* Schlechtriem (ed.), *Commentary on the UN Convention on the International Sale of Goods (CISG)*, Oxford 1998; Klein, J, "Good Faith in International Trade," 15 *Liverpool L. Rev.* 114–141 (1993), available online at <http://cisgw3.law.pace.edu/cisg/biblio/Klein.html>.

[78] A scholarly controversy exists regarding whether or not good faith is a general principle of the CISG, as it clearly is of the PECL(Art. 1:106). Professor Magnus, drawing on comparisons between CISG Art. 7 and the UNIDROIT Principles (Art. 1.6.), claims that it is (*see* Ulrich Magnus, "Remarks on Good Faith," available online at <http://cisgw3.law.pace.edu/cisg/principles/uni7.html>. Dr. Felemegas reads Art. 7 differently, as applying to the interpretation of the CISG only and not to performances in general; *see* John Felemegas, "Remarks on Good Faith and Fair Dealing," available online at <http://cisgw3.law.pace.edu/cisg/text/peclcomp7.html>. This is certainly not the proper place to attempt to resolve this important issue or even to determine whether it is, properly stated, merely an interpretative question – albeit a pre-eminent one – as Magnus and Felemegas approach it, or whether its determination transcends mere interpretative approaches. One may doubt, however, whether courts in legal systems that regard good faith obligations (in either the negotiation or performance stage) as immutable tenets of private law – metaphorically speaking, a part of the "constitution" of private law – might not impose derivative obligations also when dealing with contractual obligations governed by the CISG. Such may be inferred from dicta of the Israel Supreme Court, where good faith is a general principle of private law; *see, e.g.*, *Klemer v. Guy* (1993), 50(1) PD 184) following the Contracts (General Part) Law, 1973, §§ 12, 39, 61(b) and expressed in the anticipated Civil Code, §§ 2, 163 of the 2004 draft, available online at <http://www.justice.gov.il/MOJHeb/Codex/>.

construction – one that would apply a general obligation of good faith to CISG obligations – would undermine the distinction between CISG Art. 64(1) and (2): under a general obligation of good faith, any declaration of avoidance by the seller would have to be made in reasonable time so as not to create undue hardship for the buyer. The limitation of the power of avoidance to a "reasonable time" under CISG Art. 64(2) would then become, in fact, tautological.[79]

[79] Regarding CISG Art. 7, *see* Felemegas, *op. cit.*; regarding CISG Art. 8, *see* Maja Stanivukovic, "Remarks on the Manner in which the PECL may be Used to Interpret or Supplement CISG Article 8," available online at <http://cisgw3.law.pace.edu/cisg/text/peclcomp8.html#er>. Regarding CISG Art. 9, *see* Anja Carlsen, "Remarks on the Manner in which the PECL may be Used to Interpret or Supplement CISG Article 9," available at <http://cisgw3.law.pace.edu/cisg/text/peclcomp9.html#er.>

Specifications and the contractual relationship: Article 65 of the CISG in light of PECL Article 7:105

Andrea L. Charters

I. INTRODUCTION

Article 65 of the Convention on Contracts for the International Sale of Goods (CISG),[1] which sets forth an opportunity for the seller to impose certain specifications in light of the buyer's failure to do so, raises particular questions of interpretation given the Principles of European Contract Law (PECL).[2] CISG Article 65 sets forth a mechanism for the seller to supply specifications for a sale of goods transaction where the buyer has failed to do so. The PECL, on the other hand, state a similar right of parties in a generalized fashion, not merely applying to a narrow context. These provisions are set forth next,

[1] United Nations Convention, adopted 1980, available at <http://cisgw3.law.pace.edu/cisg/text/treaty.html>. [hereinafter referenced in the text by article].

[2] Principles of European Contract Law, complete and revised version 1998, available at <http://cisgw3.law.pace.edu/cisg/text/textef.html>. [hereinafter referenced in the text by article].

in comparison, with emphasis added to heighten the contrast and the key provisions of each section:

CISG Article 65	PECL Article 7:105
(1) If under the contract the buyer is to specify the *form, measurement or other features of the goods* and he fails to make such specification either on the date agreed upon or within a reasonable time after receipt of a request from the seller, the seller may, without prejudice to any other rights he may have, *make the specification himself* in accordance with the requirements of the buyer that *may be known* to him.	**(1) Where an obligation may be discharged by one of alternative performances, the choice belongs to the party which is to perform, unless the circumstances indicate otherwise.**
(2) If the seller makes the specification himself, he must inform the buyer of the details thereof and *must fix a reasonable time within which the buyer may make a different specification*. If, after receipt of such a communication, the buyer fails to do so within the time so fixed, the specification made by the seller is binding.	**(2) *If the party which is to make the choice fails to do so by the time required in the contract*, then: (a) if the delay in choosing is fundamental, the right to choose passes to the other party; (b) if the delay is *not fundamental*, the other party may give a *notice fixing an additional period of reasonable length* in which the party to choose must do so. If the latter fails to do so, the right to choose passes to the other party.**

Thus, the CISG provision is limited to certain basic information about the goods, such as the "form, measurement or other features of the goods," which have not been specified by the buyer where the contract calls for the buyer to do so by a certain date. The portion of the PECL that is more directly applicable is the second paragraph of Article 7:105, which applies "[i]f the party which is to make the choice fails to do so by the time required in the contract . . ." Thus, the PECL do not limit the remedy to the basic choice of specifications pertaining to the goods.

This approach of the PECL thus generalizes through the substantive provision of Article 7:105, rather than through offer and acceptance provisions, as in the CISG, which was drafted a decade and a half earlier.[3] There is thus movement over time toward a more relationship-based principle and away from the technical features of offer and acceptance. This legal history observation may be eclipsed, however, by recent developments, discussed in Section IV, which may have greater practical effect.

II. CONTEXT FOR INTERPRETING CISG ARTICLE 65 IN LIGHT OF PRINCIPLES OF EUROPEAN CONTRACT LAW ARTICLE 7:105

1. Canonical Interpretations Show That the Practical Needs Of Traders Require an Article 65 Provision

Practical needs of traders require an Article 65 provision. Article 65 of the CISG is clearly necessary to show that the contract is not voided for vagueness and to prevent a "hold up" by the buyer, who might force the seller to seek adjudication, rather than negotiation in the face of declining demand or increasing supply for the product.[4]

[3] *Compare supra* CISG, note 1, *with supra* PECL, note 2 (citing adoption dates).

[4] See Albert H. Kritzer, "International Contract Manual: International Sales Law Reporter, Guide to Practical Applications of the United Nations Convention on Contracts for the International Sale of Goods," at 519–522 (1994) (as supplemented) (analyzing provisions of Article 65, reviewing other commentaries, and comparing with the Uniform International Sales Law and Uniform Commercial Code Section 2–311(3)); John O. Honnold, *Uniform Law for International Sales*, 3d ed. (1999) 357–58, at 358 (arguing that wasteful production and failure to mitigate damages would be subject to "commercial and legal hazards that are so

Certain features of the goods may be left to future choice by the buyer, such as color or style, and even automobile option[5] specifications. This provision should not, of course, extend to having the seller supply complex, scientific, or technical specifications of custom goods for which a design supplied by the buyer is essential. The language of the CISG and past commentary agree on these issues.[6]

Three factors would point away from application of Article 65 in the context of custom-engineered goods. First, a long series of exchanges about the goods would be likely. Thus, the failure of the buyer to respond to a deadline for a specification would not be an abrupt failure to call for the goods. Second, the custom nature of the contract could involve a service component to the contract, which might be supplied by another party. Third, the countervailing feature of the risk of quality claims by an already dissatisfied or lackadaisical buyer would increase the risk of suit over quality.

2. Legislative History Is Sparse

The legislative history of Article 65 is sparse. During the drafting of the CISG, significant disagreement about including the provision was raised, but it had an antecedent in the Uniform Law of International Sales, the predecessor of the CISG, and the consensus of opinion was in favor of keeping a provision of this type.[7]

3. Sparse Case Law Does Not Obviate Need for the Provision

The sparse case law does not obviate the need for this provision, although only two cases reported or digested in English, or in any language in a major international source of cases, address Article 65.[8] The cases reaffirm what would be concluded based on the text of Article 65. One 1996 German case, not available in translation into English, is cited in the Draft UNCITRAL Digest as stating that, where the seller has failed to make a specification, "the buyer retains the right to make its own specification."[9] A 1995 German case, available in English, pertaining to options on standard BMW Series 3 automobiles, involved no objection by the buyer to the specifications and objection only to the dates of delivery.[10]

serious that extreme cases are unlikely to arise"); Gunter Hager, "Article 65," in Peter Schlechtriem, ed., *Commentary on the International Sale of Goods (CISG)* (1998) (Geoffrey Thomas, trans.) 497–499, at 498 (arguing that in cases of extreme refusal to supply specifications when asked, production of goods according to the seller's own specifications is warranted, without a duty to mitigate loss) (citations omitted); and Annotated Text of CISG Article 60 (collecting sources on the meaning of Article 60 buyer's obligation to take delivery, referred to in Article 65, primarily as a duty of cooperation, not specific performance), available at <http://cisgw3.law.pace.edu/cisg/text/e-text-60.html>. *But see* Jacob S. Ziegel, "Report to the Uniform Law Conference of Canada on Convention on Contracts for the International Sale of Goods" (1981) ("it is difficult to become excited over art. 65 one way or the other") referring to the debate over specific performance vs. damages, available at <http://cisgw3.law.pace.edu/cisg/text/ziegel165/html>.

[5] *See infra* note 10 and accompanying text.

[6] CISG, *supra,* note 1 at Article 65 ("form, measurement, or other features of the goods"); Kritzer, *supra* note 4 at 520 (analyzing example of 1,000 pairs of shoes).

[7] *See* Victor Knapp, "Article 65," in C. M. Bianca and M. J. Bonell, eds., *Commentary on the International Sales Law: The 1980 Vienna Sales Convention* (1987) 475–482, at 476.

[8] *See infra* notes 9 and 10 and sources cited therein. The Pace CISG W3 database and the Draft Digest are the two major sources of collected cases and digests in English. *See also* Ralph Amissah, "Cross-References and Editorial Analysis, Article 65," available at <http://cisgw3.law.pace.edu/cisg/text/cross/cross-65.html>.

[9] Franco Ferrari, Harry Flechtner, and Ronald A. Brand, eds., *The Draft UNCITRAL Digest and Beyond: Cases, Analysis and Unresolved Issues in the U.N. Sales Convention*, (2004) at 749, note 1, citing Landgericht Aachen, Germany, 19 April 1996, available online at <http://www.jura.uni-freiburg.de/iprl/cisg/urteile/text/165.htm>.

[10] Oberlandesgericht [Provincial Court of Appeal] Munchen, 7 U 1720/94, 8 February 1995, available at <http://cisgw3.law.pace.edu/cases/950208g1.html>. (holding that notice of avoidance of the contract after $2^1/_2$ years violated the principle of good faith, where the seller had been ready to deliver the automobiles a few months hence and that, in fact, there was not breach at all).

The lack of case law may reflect the operation of Article 65 as law that allows parties to operate "in the shadow of the law" without adjudication. This is particularly likely, because where a seller believes that a buyer is not likely to adhere to the contract, the seller will probably avail itself of other remedies that may be more swift, with fewer responsibilities on the seller. Where there is a good relationship between the parties, however, the seller might avail itself of Article 65 procedures without any ensuing litigation.

We return to this emphasis on the contractual relationship after a discussion of how four comparative issues may be resolved.

III. PECL ARTICLE 7:105 SUPPORTS AN INTERPRETATION IN LIGHT OF THE CONTRACTUAL RELATIONSHIP

1. Reading in Light of the PECL: Resolving Four Comparative Issues

Four technical issues are raised by PECL Article 7:105 in relation to CISG Article 65: (1) whether the buyer retains the right to choose if the seller does not do so, (2) whether the PECL concept of fundamental delay influences the CISG provision, (3) whether PECL provisions regarding (a) currency matters and (b) a number of issues related to each other affect the CISG provision, and (4) whether usages may influence CISG rights and obligations.

The PECL specifies, "If the [seller] fails to do so, the right to choose passes to the [buyer]."[11] It is implicit in the language of the CISG, however, that the right to choose remains with the buyer if the seller does not avail itself of its Article 65 rights, and it was reportedly so held, as digested in the Draft UNCITRAL Digest regarding the 1996 German case.[12]

The PECL provide that failures to choose shall be divided into failures that are fundamental and those that are not, with those that are not fundamental requiring notice, as in the CISG.[13] Given the apparent reticence of parties to avail themselves of CISG Article 65 in contentious situations, as evidenced by the sparse case law,[14] it is difficult to imagine parties concluding that they could rely on the "fundamental" delay provision of PECL Article 7:105(2)(a), however. The "fundamental" delay provisions of the PECL thus do not appear to influence CISG Article 65.

The PECL further provide that currency of payment matters shall be governed by Article 7:108, and matters of performance of a number of obligations related to each other will be governed by Article 7:109.[15] Neither of these specialized provisions addresses the general issue of specifications of goods, provided for in CISG Article 65.

Although the major English commentary to the PECL also suggests that usages may determine who shall make a choice,[16] this suggestion is not relevant where the issue of the specifications of the characteristics of goods clearly dictates that the seller take over this responsibility from the buyer, in Article 65 of the CISG. The implementation of Article 65, on the contrary, might be seen to benefit greatly from the insights of CISG Article 8(3) regarding circumstances and Article 9 regarding usages under the CISG. Expert testimony or prior case experience might address these issues.

[11] *See* PECL Article 7:105, *supra* note 2 at paragraph (2)(b).

[12] *See supra* note 9 and accompanying text.

[13] *Compare* PECL Article 7:105, *supra* note 2 at paragraph (2)(a) and CISG Article 65, supra note 1 at paragraph (1).

[14] *See supra* notes 8–10 and accompanying text.

[15] Ole Lando and Hugh Beale, eds. *Principles of European Contract Law, Parts I and II*, Combined and Revised (2000), at Article 7:105 Commentary.

[16] *Id.*

2. Reading in Light of the PECL: Relationship between Offer and Acceptance and Knowledge

The 1995 German case pertaining to delivery of BMW automobiles addressed the delivery date through CISG Articles 18 and 29, pertaining to contract formation and offer and acceptance.[17] There was apparently less recourse for the seller under Article 65, the language of which points to "features of the goods." In contrast, the PECL language, which is not so limited to specifications, could have included the delivery date of the goods under its Article 7:105. This contrast in approach shows an important development in the law, creating a more relationship-based provision, rather than an offer and acceptance provision.

In the PECL, the substitution of choice provision is much broader than in the CISG. Rather than leaving other matters, such as delivery of the goods,[18] to the offer and acceptance provisions, the PECL adopts a more modern approach of handling substitution of choice through a relationship-oriented provision, the broad Article 7:105. Although litigants could consider a PECL-inspired approach to CISG Article 65 if, in some cases, the offer and acceptance provisions were inadequate, the major observation here is that the PECL, drafted a decade and a half after the CISG, takes a more relationship-based approach, rather than an offer and acceptance approach.

In addition, CISG Article 65 explicitly requires that the seller act on preferences of the buyer *"which may be known to him."* The PECL do not directly include such a provision, although the "fundamental" delay requirement adverts to some knowledge requirements.[19] Although the more flexible language of the PECL again indicates a more modern drafting, the usefulness of this provision as a guide to interpretation of the CISG leaves the litigant with little to rely on. The knowledge requirements of the CISG are complex, subtle, and varied,[20] and one such requirement is clearly included in Article 65.

IV. COMMUNICATIONS TECHNOLOGY AND CISG-AC OPINION NO. 1 HOLD THE PROMISE FOR MORE USE OF ARTICLE 65

Any reticence of sellers to avail themselves of the Article 65 provisions, which require a *"reasonable time within which the buyer may make a different specification"* after notice, may be reduced by the recent scholarship of CISG-Advisory Council Opinion no. 1 on Electronic Communication under CISG.[21] It clarifies the provisions required

[17] *Supra* note 10 at 15(bb); *see generally* Peter Schlechtriem, "Effectiveness and Binding Nature of Declarations (Notices, Requests or Other Communications) under Part II and Part III of the CISG," *Cornell Review of the Convention on Contracts for the International Sale of Goods* (1995) 95–114 (discussing offer and acceptance, the "receipt" rule, and related subjects), reproduced and available at <http://cisgw3.law.pace.edu/cisg/biblio/schlecht.html>.

[18] *See* Kritzer, *supra* note 4 at 521–22 (discussing Article 77 provisions relating to the selection of the vessel for shipment).

[19] For a discussion of the "fundamental" requirement in the context of a breach, rather than a delay, *see* the sources identified in the "Guide to Article 65," available at <http://cisgw3.law.pace.edu/cisg/text/peclcomp65.html>, including PECL Article 8:103, defining "fundamental non-performance" as including a foreseeability requirement in one paragraph and "intentional" non-performance in another. *See also* "Principles of European Contract Law: Knowledge and behavior of person for whom a party is responsible" (discussing PECL Article 1:305 on imputed knowledge and intentions), available at <http://cisgw3.law.pace.edu/cisg/text/knowbeh.html> (including reproducing Lando & Beale, *supra* note 15 at 134–136).

[20] *See* Article 8(3) of the CISG for a discussion of general guidance on the knowledge requirements; Amissah, *supra* note 8 at definition of "may be known to" (citations omitted); and Annotated Text of CISG: Article 65 words and phrases – Degrees of knowledge (cross-referencing numerous knowledge requirements).

[21] 15 August 2003. Rapporteur: Professor Christina Ramberg, Gothenburg, Sweden, available at <http://cisgw3.law.pace.edu/cisg/CISG-AC-op1.html>.

for a writing and thus, for written notice, [22] which may be required by many contractual provisions.

V. CONCLUSION

Interpretation of CISG Article 65 in light of PECL Article 7:105 thus shows an historical progression in the drafting, but does not leave a litigant with much recourse to obtain strategic advantage, either in terms of flexibility or tightening of the provisions. The Articles seem to pass each other without contact. A bigger benefit for interpretation of Article 65 seems to stem not from interpretation in light of the PECL, but from the practical advance of CISG-AC Opinion no. 1, which I have recently argued is a great benefit to clarity in defining "writing," [23] and thus to notice-related provisions generally.

[22] *Id.*
[23] *See* Andrea L. Charters, "Growth of the CISG with Changing Contract Technology: 'Writing' in Light of the UNIDROIT Principles and CISG-Advisory Council Opinion no. 1," available at <http://cisgw3.law.pace.edu/cisg/biblio/charters.html>.

Anticipatory breach: Remarks on the manner in which the Principles of European Contract Law may be used to interpret or supplement Articles 71 and 72 of the CISG

Sieg Eiselen

a. Articles 71, 72, and 73 of the CISG deal with the situation where it becomes apparent or clear that one of the parties to an agreement will or may not perform a substantial part of its obligations in terms of the agreement.[1] The object of Article 72 is to provide the innocent party with a remedy in cases where it is clear that the other party will not perform at all or will commit another fundamental breach.[2] This remedy based on the Anglo-American doctrine of anticipatory breach allows the innocent party to avoid the contract when the breach occurs without having to wait until performance becomes due.[3] Whereas Article 72 is aimed at the phenomenon of anticipatory breach of contract (i.e., a breach of contract that takes place before the performance is due by the party in

[1] Leser H. G. & Hornung R., in Schlechtriem P. H. & Bacher K., *Kommentar zum Einheitlichen UN Kaufrecht* 3rd ed (2000 München) Art 71 Rn 1; Art 72 Rn 1, Art 73 Rn 1; Magnus U., in Martinek M. (ed) *J von Staudingers Kommentar zum Bürgerlichen Gesetzbuch mit Einführungsgesetz und Nebengesetze: Wiener UN-Kaufrecht* (1999 Berlin) Art 71 Rn 1, Art 72 Rn 1, Art 73 Rn 1; Burkhart F., *Interpretatives Zusammenwirken von CISG und UNIDROIT Principles* (2000 Baden-Baden) 194; Schnyder A. K. and Straub R. M., in Honsell H., *Kommentar zum UN Kaufrecht* (1997 Berlin) Art 71 Rn 1, Art 72 Rn 1, Art 73 Rn 1; Witz W., Salger H. C. & Lorenz M., *Internationales Einheitliches Kaufrecht* (2000 Heidelberg) Art 71 Rn 1, Art 72 Rn 1 & 2, Art 73 Rn 1; Kritzer A. H., *Guide to the Practical Applications of the United Nations Convention on Contracts for the International Sale of Goods* (1989 Deventer) 465–467; Honnold J. O., *Uniform Law for International Sales* 3rd ed (1999 The Hague) also available online at <http://cisgw3.law.pace.edu/cisg/biblio/honnold.html>, para 395 at p. 437.
[2] Enderlein F. & Maskow D., *International Sales Law – United Nations Convention on Contracts for the International Sale of Goods* (1992 New York), also available at <http://cisgw3.law.pace.edu/cisg/biblio/enderlein.html> para 1 at p. 291.
[3] Witz/Salger/Lorenz Art 72 Rn 2.

breach), Article 71 has a wider scope in that it deals with both anticipatory breach and incomplete performance.[4] The remedies in Article 71 are aimed at keeping the contract intact, whereas the remedies in Article 72 are aimed at avoiding the contract.[5] Article 73 provides for anticipatory breach in installment contracts. It is for that reason that these Articles contain different requirements for exercising their respective remedies.[6]

b. The PECL is similarly structured in Articles 9:304 and 8:105. Article 9:304 makes provision for a party to terminate the agreement where it is clear that there will be a fundamental non-performance by the other party. There is no requirement to give notice, as is the case with Article 72 of the CISG. If a party is uncertain as to whether there will be a fundamental breach or not, but has a reasonable belief that it may occur, that party is, in terms of Article 8:105, entitled to demand an adequate assurance from the other party that the latter will perform and it may withhold its own performance as long as such reasonable belief continues. Failure to provide an adequate assurance is a ground in terms of Article 8:105 to terminate the agreement. There is, therefore, quite a close connection between the provisions of Articles 9:304 and 8:105. As is shown below, this is not necessarily the case with the very similar Article 72 and Article 71 of the CISG.

c. There are several interpretational issues regarding Article 72 on which there is a divergence of opinion. Commentators differ on the exact interpretation and meaning of the meaning of the words, "it is clear" (Article 72(1)) and "it becomes apparent" (Article 71(1)),[7] and whether there is any difference in the meaning or the standards to be applied.[8] They also differ on whether the giving of notice of termination is an essential requirement to become entitled to the remedy or whether it is only necessary in circumstances where objectively speaking the other party would have been able to give an adequate assurance.[9] Lastly there is also a difference of opinion on whether a failure to give an adequate assurance on demand under Article 71(1) automatically entitles a party to avoid the contract under Article 72.[10] The construction and provisions of Articles 9:304 and 8:105 of the PECL may be helpful in solving these issues.

d. In certain circumstances, a party may be entitled to rely on either Article 71 or 72.[11] If an anticipatory breach occurs, the innocent party may want to enforce specific performance, in which case it would make use of its right to suspend performance under Article 71, rather than to avoid the contract under Article 72, even if it is entitled to do so. However, in the case of part performance a party may apparently only rely on Article 51 in conjunction with Article 45 where Article 51 applies, or on Article 71 (if it wants to enforce full performance), or on Article 49 (if it wants to avoid the contract), but not on Article 72. Article 72 is therefore a remedy that is only to be used in true circumstances of

[4] Staudinger/Magnus Art 71 Rn 34.

[5] Staudinger/Magnus Art 71 Rn 1; Art 72 Rn 1.

[6] *See* Schlechtriem P., *Uniform Sales Law – The UN-Convention on Contracts for the International Sale of Goods* (Vienna 1986) 389 *et seq.* <http://cisgw3.law.pace.edu/cisg/biblio/schlechtriem-72.html>; Staudinger/Magnus Art 72 Rn 8 & 9; Flechtner H. M., 8 *J. L. & Com.* (1988) 53–108, also at <http://cisgw3.law.pace.edu/cisg/text/flecht71,72.html>. Initial efforts to combine the articles during the drafting process were intentionally rejected. *See* Enderlein/Maskow p. 284 Note 1 & 2, p. 291 N 1; Honsell/Schnyder/Straub Art 72 Rn 10.

[7] Enderlein/Maskow p. 286 Note 2; Honsell/Schnyder/Straub Art. 71 Rn 24-26, Art 72 Rn 25; Staudinger/Magnus Art 71 Rn 18. Honnold p. 429 para 388 remarks that these provisions were consciously so drafted and that this difference in terminology is also found in the French and Spanish versions of the CISG. *See* also Kee C., "Comparative Editorial Remarks to Articles 51 & 73," available online at <http://cisgw3.law.pace.edu/cisg/text/peclcomp51.html>.

[8] Enderlein p. 286 Note 2; Honnold para 388 at p. 429.

[9] Enderlein p. 293 Note 6; Honsell/Schnyder/Straub Art 72 Rn 35 & 36.

[10] Enderlein/Maskow p. 290 Note 1.

[11] Enderlein/Maskow p. 286 Note 3; Schlechtriem Art 72 Rn 9.

anticipatory breach and not where an actual breach has already taken place.[12] However where the contract consists of a series of performances (installments, for instance, delivery of a certain number of goods on a monthly basis), a serious deficiency in quality of the first consignment entitles the innocent party to exercise its rights under Article 73 and avoid the contract.[13]

e. The most difficult aspect of interpreting Article 72 (and Article 71 for that matter), is to establish what measure of certainty is required that a fundamental breach will occur.[14] Article 9:304 of the PECL is, unfortunately, of no assistance in this regard as it uses exactly the same terminology as Article 72. The court in the 1992 German case *Landgericht* [District Court] Berlin[15] has given the best judicial exposition of the standards required under Article 72. It defined the words, "it is clear" ("*offensichtlich*"), in terms of the probabilities that a fundamental breach will be committed. It stated that a very high degree of probability is required,[16] but that this did not mean a probability almost reaching certainty.[17]

f. Both the CISG and the PECL require a clear indication of a fundamental non-performance (i.e., that it must be clear that there will be a fundamental non-performance).[18] The terminology used is very similar, and the PECL therefore shed little light on what measure should be used to determine whether "it is clear." Commentators have a difference of opinion on whether "it is clear" (in Article 72) has the same meaning as "it becomes apparent" (in Article 71).[19] The majority opinion seems to be that Article 72 requires a higher standard of prospective certainty than Article 71 mainly because of the more drastic nature of the remedy under Article 72, namely avoidance.[20] Suspension as provided for in Article 71 is less drastic in that it is only a temporary remedy, especially if the contract is to be avoided without giving notice to the other party.[21]

[12] Honsell/Schnyder/Straub Art 72 Rn 15; Germany 18 November 1993 *Oberlandesgericht* [Appellate Court] Düsseldorf <http://cisgw3.law.pace.edu/cases/931118g1.html>; Germany 15 February 1995 *Bundesgerichtshof* [Federal Supreme Court] <http://cisgw3.law.pace.edu/cases/950215g1.html]>.

[13] This is to be distinguished from the situation where only 1,000 pairs of shoes have been delivered instead of 2,000 on the date of performance. In this instance the correct remedies are either Article 51 and Article 45 or Article 71 and not Article 72. *See* Witz/Salger/Lorenz Art 71 Rn 1; Art 73 Rn 1; Honsell/Schnyder/Straub Art 72 Rn 15; Austria 10 December 1997 Vienna Arbitration proceeding S 2/97 <http://cisgw3.law.pace.edu/cases/971210a3.html>; Germany 18 November 1993 *Oberlandesgericht* [Appellate Court] Düsseldorf. <http://cisgw3.law.pace.edu/cases/931118g1.html>; Germany 15 February 1995 *Bundesgerichtshof* [Federal Supreme Court] <http://cisgw3.law.pace.edu/cases/950215g1.html]>.

[14] Staudinger/Magnus Art 72 Rn 7; Honnold p. 439 para 397; Honsell/Schnyder/Straub Art 72 Rn 26–28; Australia 17 November 2000 Supreme Court of Queensland (*Downs Investments v. Perwaja Steel*) <http://cisgw3.law.pace.edu/cases/001117a2.html>.

[15] Germany 30 September 1992 *Landgericht* [District Court] Berlin <http://cisgw3.law.pace.edu/cases/920930g1.html>.

[16] In the words of the court, "*einer sehr hohen naheliegender Wahrscheinlichkeit.*"

[17] In the words of the court, "*eine an Sicherheit grenzende Wahrscheinlichkeit.*" *See* also Germany 18 November 1993 *Oberlandesgericht* [Appellate Court] Düsseldorf <http://cisgw3.law.pace.edu/cases/931118g1.html>; Germany 28 April 1993 *Landgericht* [District Court] Krefeld <http://cisgw3.law.pace.edu/cases/930428g1.html>; Australia 17 November 2000 Supreme Court of Queensland (*Downs Investments v. Perwaja Steel*) <http://cisgw3.law.pace.edu/cases/001117a2.html>.

[18] *See* Schlechtriem P., *Uniform Sales Law – The UN-Convention on Contracts for the International Sale of Goods* (Vienna 1986) 389 *et seq.* <http://cisgw3.law.pace.edu/cisg/biblio/schlechtriem-72.html>; Staudinger/Magnus Art 72 Rn 8, 9 & 18; Flechtner H.M., 8 *J. L. & Com.* (1988) 53–108, also at <http://cisgw3.law.pace.edu/cisg/text/flecht71,72.html>.

[19] Enderlein/Maskow p. 291 Note 1; Honsell/Schnyder/Straub Art 72 Rn 20–24; Witz/Salger/Lorenz Art 72 Rn 7; Staudinger/Magnus Art 72 Rn 8 & 9.

[20] Honsell/Schnyder/Straub Art 72 Rn 23–25 indicates that this is the proper interpretation when due regard is had to the history and drafting of these articles. *See* also Staudinger/Magnus Art 72 Rn 9; Salger/Lorenz Art 72 Rn 8.

[21] Staudinger/Magnus Art 72 Rn 9–11.

g. This approach also seems to be supported by the case law.[22] It is also supported by the provisions of Article 9:304 and 8:105 of the PECL, where there is a clearly formulated difference in the requirements. Article 9:304 requires that it must be clear that there will be a fundamental non-performance, whereas in Article 8:105 there need only be a reasonable belief on the part of the innocent party that there will be a fundamental non-performance.

h. If there is any doubt on whether, because of the conduct of the other party or the prevailing circumstances, there is an anticipatory breach objectively speaking, a party should rather exercise the right to suspend performance under Article 71 CISG and require an adequate assurance from the other party than issue a notice of avoidance under Article 72(2).[23] It is the safer option because the giving of a notice of avoidance in terms of Article 72(2) under circumstances where it is not warranted may in itself constitute an anticipatory breach that entitles the other party to avoid the contract.[24]

i. There is a difference of opinion among commentators on whether a failure or a refusal to produce adequate security where it has been demanded is in itself a fundamental breach or whether it may only be a clear indication that the other party will commit a fundamental breach.[25] Article 8:105 PECL may be of assistance in interpreting the interplay between Article 72 and 71, as it makes express provision for the innocent party to demand an adequate assurance where it reasonably suspects that there will be a fundamental non-performance. Article 8:105 clearly stipulates that a failure to provide this assurance within a reasonable period of time entitles the other party to terminate (avoid) the agreement. Whether this is possible in light of the drafting history of the CISG is debatable.[26]

j. The CISG takes a more lenient approach to anticipatory breach than the PECL in that it obliges the innocent party, when time allows, to notify the other party if it intends avoiding the contract, except where the other party has clearly declared its intention not to perform.[27] The object of the notification is to enable the other party to provide adequate assurance that it will perform. There are different opinions on whether the obligation to give notice is a condition precedent for the valid exercising of the right to avoid.[28] It is submitted that in interpreting the duty to inform, a court should follow a stricter approach toward the necessity to inform if regard is had to the approach followed

[22] The clearest example where this has been applied has been ICC Arbitration Case No. 8786 of January 1997 <http://cisgw3.law.pace.edu/cases/978786i1.html> where one party declared that it would not perform by the date agreed due to a delay. Under the circumstances the delay was a fundamental breach, and it was held that it was not necessary to give notice to the other party. *See* also Austria 10 December 1997 Vienna Arbitration proceeding S 2/97 <http://cisgw3.law.pace.edu/cases/971210a3.html>. In Switzerland 20 February 1997 *Zivilgericht* [District Court] Saane <http://cisgw3.law.pace.edu/cases/970220s1.html> and Switzerland 31 May 1996 Zürich Arbitration proceeding http://cisgw3.law.pace.edu/cases/960531s1.html reliance on Article 72 was rejected due to a lack of evidence that there was an intention to repudiate; it was not clear.

[23] Enderlein/Maskow p. 292 Note 3.

[24] Commentary of the Secretariat, Comment 2, Document A/CONF.975 p. 53 as reported in Honnold *Documentary History of the Uniform Law for International Sales* (Deventer 1989) and at <http://cisgw3.law.pace.edu/cisg/text/secomm/secomm-72.html>; Enderlein/Maskow p. 291 Note 1; Germany 21 September 1995 *Landgericht* [District Court] Kassel <http://cisgw3.law.pace.edu/cases/950921g1.html>.

[25] Secretariat Commentary 2 p. 53; Enderlein/Maskow p. 290 Note 10; Honsell/Schnyder/Straub Art 71 Rn 51; Staudinger/Magnus Art 71 Rn 52; Honnold Art 71 Rn 394.

[26] *See* Secretariat Commentary 2 p. 53.

[27] Honsell/Schnyder/Straub Art 72 Rn 34 & 35.

[28] Honsell/Schnyder/Straub Art 72 Rn 35 & 36. Witz/Salger/Lorenz is of the opinion that the failure to give notice does not affect the effectiveness of the avoidance. However, *see* the decision to the contrary in ICC Arbitration Case No. 8574 of September 1996 <http://cisgw3.law.pace.edu/cases/968574i1.html>.

under the PECL.[29] If there is doubt on whether the innocent party should have been informed or not, the court ought to rule in favor of the innocent party (i.e., that there was no duty to inform). In terms of Article 9:304 of the PECL a party is not obliged to inform the other party, but may as a precaution require an adequate assurance of due performance, failing which that party is entitled to terminate the agreement.

k. Where it is apparent that notice will be totally ineffective in that it is impossible for the obligor to prevent the eventual breach, is there still a formal obligation to notify? It is submitted that this is a situation where the innocent party is not required to notify the other party.[30] The object of the notice requirement is to enable the other party to provide adequate assurance of his performance. If that has become impossible, then the necessity to give notice must surely fall away. There is, however, also a strong contrary view on this issue.[31]

l. In the literature there is a controversy on whether the requirement of "reasonableness" only refers to the notice or whether it also has a reference to the duty to give notice.[32] The controversy, however, is mainly among German writers due to an inaccurate translation into the (unofficial) German text.

[29] For a contrary opinion, *see* Honsell/Schnyder/Straub Art 72 Rn 41 & 42.

[30] Enderlein/Maskow p. 293 Note 6; Witz/Salger/Lorenz Art 72 Rn 15; Staudinger/Magnus Art 72 Rn 22; Schlechtriem Art 72 Rn 16 & 17; Honsell/Schnyder/Straub Art 72 Rn 45; ICC Arbitration Case No. 8574 of September 1996 <http://cisgw3.law.pace.edu/cases/968574i1.html>.

[31] *See* Honsell/Schnyder/Straub Art 72 Rn 36; Schlechtriem /Leser/Hornung Art 72 Rn 13 *et seq*; Germany 9 July 1992 *Landgericht* [District Court] Düsseldorf <http://cisgw3.law.pace.edu/cases/920709g1.html>.

[32] The controversy is mainly among German writers due to an inaccurate translation into the (unofficial) German text. *See* Honsell/Schnyder/Straub Art 72 Rn 45; Staudinger/Magnus Art 72 Rn 21.

Remarks on the damages provisions in the CISG (Article 74), Principles of European Contract Law (PECL), and UNIDROIT Principles of International Commercial Contracts (UPICC)*

Friedrich Blase and Philipp Höttler

I. Damages in International Sales Law: CISG, PECL, and UPICC

II. Matters Governed by CISG Art. 74 and Expressly Settled in It

1. Breach of Contract: Right to Damages
2. Measure of Damages: Full Compensation
3. Foreseeability of Loss

III. Matters Governed by the Convention, But Not Expressly Settled in It

1. Offsetting Losses with Gains
2. Loss Partly Attributable to Aggrieved Party
3. Proof of Non-Pecuniary Loss
4. Currency of Damages

*Adapted version of a research paper on the use of the UNIDROIT Principles on International Commercial Contracts (UPICC) and the Principles of European Contract Law (PECL) to help interpret regulations of the Convention on Contracts for the International Sale of Goods (CISG): "Claiming Damages in Export Trade."

I. DAMAGES IN INTERNATIONAL SALES LAW: CISG, PECL, AND UPICC

Contract law, whether national or international, is – almost universally and entirely – at the disposition of the parties when they are modeling their individual contractual situation; very few of its provisions are usually considered mandatory.[1] Mandatory rules are confined to questions of validity because of a party's immorality, illegality, or incapacity, as well as the rudimentary protection of the balance of the duties owed between the parties. Even in situations where the contract partners actively negotiate the terms of their contract, and especially in the manifold situations in which they do not discuss the conditions, the commercial parties of cross-border transactions often do not consider the substantive law applicable to their contract. This holds true not only for the contract drafting stage but also for the fulfillment stage of performing the duties owed under the contract. Somewhat prematurely, the parties (and their legal counsel) might even believe that their elaborate contract deals with all the issues of fulfillment and no reference to the underlying law must be made.[2] Whatever the scenario, this view dramatically changes when the relationship deteriorates and one or both of the parties deliberate about damages. In practice virtually all less extensively negotiated, elaborated, and documented contracts – and thus the vast majority of them[3] – do not provide any rules of either accounting or awarding damages.[4] The pursuit of compensation almost invariably leads the parties to turn to the applicable law. In more and more cases, such a search will lead to the U.N. Convention on Contracts for the International Sale of Goods (CISG).[5]

The success of the CISG since its creation at a diplomatic conference in Vienna in 1980 has fueled the hopes of uniform law supporters around the world that more global

[1] *Cf.* for these fundamental principles the regulations in the sets of rules discussed here: CISG Art. 6; UPICC Arts. 1.1, 1.4, and 1.5; and PECL Arts. 1.102 and 1.103.

[2] *See* the reference by the arbitral tribunal in ICC Award No. 7375 of 5 June 1996, reprinted in Mealeys Publications, Document # 05-961223-101, at 85: "In many international disputes, the question of the law which is applicable to a contract is of rather peripheral importance only, as the dispute will be decided on the basis of the relevant contract and, as far as necessary an interpretation thereof, such that in most cases it will not be necessary to resort to an underlying applicable law for obtaining 'legal guidance'"; *see* also Berger, "The Relationship Between the UNIDROIT Principles of International Commercial Contracts and the New *Lex Mercatoria*," 5 *Unif. L. Rev.* (2000), at 153, 164: "The contract becomes the 'substitute law' for the parties by virtue of its self-sufficient character"; Lundmark, "Die detaillierte Natur anglo-amerikanischer Kaufverträge," in *Festschrift Otto Sandrock*, at 623, 625; *cf.* also Merkt, "Grundsatz- und Praxisprobleme der Angloamerikanisierungstendenzen im Recht des Unternehmenskauf," in *Festschrift Otto Sandrock*, at 657, 659.

[3] For an interesting observation on the detailed nature of investment contracts, *see* Berger, "Renegotiation and Adaptation of International Investment Contracts: The Role of Contract Drafters and Arbitrators," 36 *Vand. J. Transnat'l. L.* (2003), at 153 *et seq*.

[4] Two issues are more frequently dealt with in respect of damages: (1) the inclusion of liquidated penalty clauses and similar concepts of penalties and abstractly calculated damages, on this *see* also Berger, "Vertragsstrafen und Schadenspauschalierungen im Internationalen Wirtschaftsvertragsrecht," *Recht der internationalen Wirtschaft* (1999), at 401 *et seq*.; (2) clauses on the method of determining the amount of damages (often through arbitral tribunals or expert reports).

[5] For thoughts on a uniform abbreviation *see* Flessner/Kadner, "CISG? – Zur Suche nach einer Abkürzung für das Wiener Übereinkommen über Verträge über den internationalen Warenkauf vom 11," April 1980, 3 *ZEuP* (1995), at 347 *et seq*.

standardization of private law aspects would be possible. Even before the CISG came to see the light of day, various groups had been formed to measure the scope of international harmonization beyond the realm of sales transactions by focusing on nothing less than the general rules applied to all business transactions (i.e., the law of international commercial contracts). Albeit not anticipated, the political changes in Central and Eastern Europe and the former Soviet Union at the beginning of the last decade of the twentieth century provided additional stamina for the hard-working groups[6] and made a possible formulation of such general contract law that much more likely – especially now that the world was to seemingly unite behind the principles of democracy, market forces, and capitalism.[7]

The 1990s therefore saw the presentation of the results of two such projects: the UNIDROIT Principles of International Commercial Contracts[8] (UPICC[9]) and the Principles of European Contract Law[10] (PECL[11]). The UPICC were released by the Institute for the Unification of Private Law (UNIDROIT)[12] in 1993[13] and were received with considerable *laudatio* and an unusually high level of promotion.[14] Their first version of 1994 still stands ten years later and was due to be updated by an extended version in 2004.[15] The European-focused PECL were released in 1994,[16] thus losing the first race against their global counterpart.[17] However, the PECL were updated in 1999 and

[6] However, it should not be forgotten at this point that the political changes also brought a similar project started by representatives of socialist and communist countries to a premature end: the Project of the Former Council for Mutual Economic Assistance for a General Law on International Commercial Contracts, *cf.* Berger, *Creeping Codification of the Lex Mercatoria*, at 123 *et seq.*

[7] The fall of communism in Europe and the Soviet Union also meant that a number of legal systems and laws, namely those of a socialist/communist nature, would no longer be significantly taken into consideration. The Chinese, as the only remaining considerable economic power under communist rule, has recently changed its contract law, drawing substantially on the CISG and further international sources; for a brief overview *see* Will (ed.), *CISG and China – An Intercontinental Exchange*, passim; *see* also for a review of this book Blase, "PECL and China – An Intercontinental Exchange," 4 *Vindobona J.* (2000), at 95 *et seq.*

[8] UNIDROIT (ed.), *Principles of International Commercial Contracts*, Rome 1994. For various language versions *see* <http://www.unidroit.org>.

[9] The abbreviation for the Principles is not universally applied. However, it conforms to the typical method of abbreviation for many laws and Conventions and is based on the English version of the Principles' name.

[10] Lando/Beale (eds.), *Principles of European Contract Law – Parts I and II* – Combined and Revised – Prepared by The Commission on European Contract Law (2000). Other language versions are now available.

[11] *Supra* note 9.

[12] For more information on the work of the Institute *see* <http://www.unidroit.org>.

[13] For an extensive description of the UPICC see Bonell, *An International Restatement of Contract Law – The UNIDROIT Principles of International Commercial Contracts* (2nd ed. 1997).

[14] For some observations on support for and activity around the UPICC, *see* Blase, "Leaving the Shadow for the Test of Practice – On the Future of the Principles of European Contract Law," 3 *Vindobona J.* (1999), at 3 *et seq.*

[15] *UNIDROIT Principles* 2004 contains five new chapters (Authority of Agents; Third Party Rights; Set-off; Assignment of Rights, Transfer of Obligations, and Assignment of Contracts; Limitation Periods) as well as an expanded Preamble and new provisions on Inconsistent Behavior and on Release by Agreement. Moreover wherever appropriate the 1994 edition of the Principles was adapted to meet the needs of electronic contracting.

[16] For an extensive description of the PECL *see* Blase, *Die Grundregeln des Europäischen Vertragsrechts als Recht grenzüberschreitender Verträge* (2000).

[17] Experts involved in the drafting of both UPICC and PECL stress the common elements of both sets of rules and the mutual benefit that the drafters received from the work of the other group. *See* particularly the publications by the two respective chairmen, Ole Lando and Michael Joachim Bonell. *Cf.* Bonell, "The UNIDROIT Principles of International Commercial Contracts and the Principles of European Contract Law: Similar Rules for the Same Purposes?," 1 *Unif. L. Rev.* (1996), at 229, 233. For a detailed comparison of the two sets of rules *see* Bonell, *An International Restatement of Contract Law – The UNIDROIT Principles of International Commercial Contracts*, at 88 *et seq.*; Blase, *Die Grundregeln des Europäischen Vertragsrechts* (2000), at 125. On the existence of such a race *see* Blase, "Leaving the Shadow for the Test of Practice," 3 *Vindobona J.* (1999), at 3 *et seq.*

now cover more ground than their rival UPICC.[18] Most recently, the PECL have been called on by the European institutions[19] as the centerpiece of a possible European-wide unification of contract law.[20]

Should the CISG apply to a contract, a search for a claim for damages brings to light its Art. 74 and a few further provisions on damages. The result of a first scan, however, can hardly be satisfying, as more questions seem to be raised than answered. Unfamiliar and broad terminology is found in a surprisingly brief description of the legal mechanisms. By comparison, the provisions of the PECL[21] and UPICC[22] both display a higher degree of regulation on the matter of damages. As those two instruments deal with contractual agreements in general, not just contracts for the sale of goods, and because it is said that they have often been inspired by the CISG, it has been asserted that the UPICC and PECL could help interpret certain provisions of the Sales Convention.[23] This may also hold true for the provisions on damages, in particular its central provision contained in Art. 74 CISG. The following remarks attempt to shed further light on the interpretative use of the UPICC and PECL.

In line with the interpretive canon required by Art. 7(1) and (2) CISG, we first examine matters that are expressly settled in the Convention (*infra* at 2). Then we deal with those matters that are governed by the Convention, but are not expressly settled in it (*infra* at 3). Finally, we provide an outlook on those matters that are not governed by the CISG, but may call for an application of the PECL or UPICC (*infra* at 4).

II. MATTERS GOVERNED BY CISG ART. 74 AND EXPRESSLY SETTLED IN IT

A number of matters that are governed by Art. 74 and expressly settled in the Convention can be reaffirmed by turning to the UPICC and PECL as persuasive authority:

1. Breach of Contract: Right to Damages

Although Art. 74 CISG does not define the term "breach of contract," it can be interpreted as any non-performance of a contractual obligation as reflected in Art. 9:501(1) PECL and Art. 7.4.1 UPICC, each of which provide that damages can be claimed for by the other party's "non-performance." Also, neither PECL nor UPICC demand that the aggrieved party is only entitled to damages if the non-performing party was at fault.

2. Measure of Damages: Full Compensation

The general principle of full compensation, which is generally held to be an underlying principle of the CISG,[24] is expressly laid down and defined in Art. 9:502 PECL and Art.

[18] The PECL also contain rules on direct as well as indirect agency in the formation of contracts, whereas the UPICC have not addressed this issue.

[19] *See* the note on European contract law by the European Commission, KOM (2000), at 398 (final), *passim*, the working paper on the approximation of civil and trade law of the member states by the committee on law and internal markets of the European Parliament, DT\424755EN.doc, *passim*.

[20] For substantive work on this, *see* the results and ambitions of the Study Group on a European Civil Code (SGEEC) at <http://www.sgeec.net>, which in many ways has inherited the role of the Commission on European Contract Law, drafters of the PECL.

[21] The PECL deal with damages and interest in Arts. 9:501–9:510.

[22] The UPICC deal with damages and interest in Arts. 7.4.1–7.4.13.

[23] For detailed research on this interaction see Burkart, *Interpretatives Zusammenwirken von CISG und UNIDROIT Principles* (2000), *passim*.

[24] *See* relevant case law:

- Austria 14 January 2002 Oberster Gerichtshof [Supreme Court], case presentation including English translation available at <http://cisgw3.law.pace.edu/cases/020114a3.html>;
- Austria 28 April 2000 Oberster Gerichtshof [Supreme Court], case presentation including English translation available at <http://cisgw3.law.pace.edu/cases/000428a3.html>;

7.4.2(1) UPICC. Hence, both the latter instruments follow the same principle that is useful when addressing some issues not expressly settled in the CISG.

3. Foreseeability of Loss

A foreseeability test as contained in Art. 74 CISG is also applied in both Art. 9:503 PECL and Art. 7.4.4 UPICC. Like Art. 74 CISG, both other instruments do provide for a subjective and objective test of foreseeability.[25] Art. 9:503 PECL and Art. 7.4.4 UPICC require, however, that the loss suffered is a "likely result" of the non-performance. The CISG seems to apply a wider standard by providing that the loss must have been foreseen as a "possible consequence" of the breach.[26] There is a distinct difference in the wording that results in a different standard to be applied by the CISG, on the one hand, and the UPICC and PECL, on the other. Hence, the UPICC and the PECL cannot serve as a persuasive authority to clarify a real question concerning a matter that, despite being expressly settled in the Convention, arguably remains ambiguous.[27]

- Germany 26 November 1999 Oberlandesgericht [Appellate Court] Hamburg, case presentation including English translation available at <http://cisgw3.law.pace.edu/cases/991126g1.html>;
- Austria 15 June 1994 Vienna Arbitration proceeding SCH-4318, case presentation including English translation available at <http://cisgw3.law.pace.edu/cases/940615a4.html>; and
- Austria 15 June 1994 Vienna Arbitration proceeding SCH-4366, case presentation including English translation available at <http://cisgw3.law.pace.edu/cases/940615a3.html>;

See also Stoll/Gruber, in Schlechtriem/Schwenzer (ed.), *UN-Kaufrecht* (2004), Art. 74 para 2; Knapp, in Bianca/Bonell (ed.), *The 1980 Vienna Sales Convention* (1987), Art. 74, note 3.2; Enderlein/Maskow (ed.), *International Sales Law* (1992), Art. 74, note 4, also available online at <http://cisgw3.law.pace.edu/cisg/biblio/enderlein-art74.html>;

[25] *See*, for instance, Austria 14 January 2002 Oberster Gerichtshof [Supreme Court], case presentation including English translation available at <http://cisgw3.law.pace.edu/cases/020114a3.html>, *see* relevant excerpt:

> Generally an objective standard is applied for foreseeability here. The obligor must reckon with the consequences that a reasonable person in his situation (Art. 8(2) CISG) would have foreseen considering the particular circumstances of the case. Whether he actually did foresee this is as insignificant as whether there was fault [. . .]. Yet, subjective risk evaluation cannot be completely ignored: if the obligor knows that a breach of contract would produce unusual or unusually high losses, then these consequences are imputable to him.

See also Enderlein/Maskow (ed.), *International Sales Law* (1992), Art. 74, note 8 and 10, also available at <http://cisgw3.law.pace.edu/cisg/biblio/enderlein-art74.html>.

[26] Stoll/Gruber, in Schlechtriem (ed.), *UN-Kaufrecht* (2004), Art. 74, para 35; Ferrari, "Comparative Ruminations on the Foreseeability of Damages in Contract Law," 53 *La. L. Rev.* (1993), at 1257, 1268; *see* also Faust, Die Vorhersehbarkeit des Schadens gemäß Art. 74 Satz 2 *UN-Kaufrecht* (*CISG*) (1996), at 50 *et seq.* and 71, 72, who proves that not only the wording but also historical considerations speak in favor of a wider interpretation.

[27] The opposite view – i.e., that the foreseeability test should be interpreted narrowly as in the case of PECL and UPICC – is held by Prof. Sieg Eiselen; *see* Eiselen, "Remarks on the Manner in which the UNIDROIT Principles of International Commercial Contracts May Be Used to Interpret or Supplement Article 74 of the CISG," para h., available at <http://cisgw3.law.pace.edu/cisg/principles/uni74.html#editorial>.

For further points of view on both sides of this issue, *see* Jacob S. Ziegel, "Report to the Uniform Law Conference of Canada on Convention on Contracts for the International Sale of Goods" (July 1981), available at <http://cisgw3.law.pace.edu/cisg/text/ziegel74.html>: "The test of foreseeability in art. 74 is substantially broader than the test in *Hadley v. Baxendale*, as refined by the House of Lords in *The Heron II* (1969 1 A.C. 350. In the latter case Lord Reid expressly rejected the test of 'possible' damages adopted in Art. 74. Its retention in Art. 74 could lead to the admissibility of damage claims that have hither-to been rejected and enlarge the seller's already very substantial exposure to liability'" And E. Allan Farnsworth, "Damages and Specific Relief," 27 *Am. J. Comp. L.* (1979) 247–253, available at <http://cisgw3.law.pace.edu/cisg/biblio/farns.html>: "The requirement of foreseeability, known throughout the common law world as 'the rule of *Hadley v. Baxendale*, appears as the second sentence of Art. [74]... Any such formula is inevitably imprecise. It comes close to blending the [U.S.] Restatement of Contracts § 330, which allows recovery for 'injuries that the defendant had reason to foresee as a possible result of his breach when the contract was made and UCC 2–715(2)(a), which allows the buyer recovery for 'any loss resulting from general or particular requirements and needs of which the seller at the time of contracting had reason to know." Although the use in Art.[74] of "*possible* consequences" may seem at first to cast a wider net than the Restatements "*probable* result," the preceding clause ('in the light of the facts... ') cuts this back at least to the scope of the Code language."

III. MATTERS GOVERNED BY THE CONVENTION, BUT NOT EXPRESSLY SETTLED IN IT

Turning to other matters that are governed by the Convention, but are not expressly settled in it, one could find a number of ways in which both PECL and UPICC might aid in the interpretation of CISG Art. 74.

1. Offsetting Losses with Gains

The Convention does not expressly stipulate whether the amount of damages should be reduced by any advantages that the breach brings for the promisee.[28] However, by applying the principle of full compensation, which is a general principle underlying the Convention, this question is generally answered in the affirmative. Whereas the UPICC address this issue in Art. 7.4.2(1), second sentence, in the same manner, the PECL do not provide for an express rule on the issue. However, the Official Commentary on Art. 9:502 PECL highlights the same principles by stating that "[t]he aggrieved party must bring into account in reduction of damages any compensating gains which offset its loss."[29] Hence the mechanics of both PECL and UPICC can be used as persuasive authority in confirming the solution predominantly favored under the regime of the CISG.

2. Loss Partly Attributable to Aggrieved Party

Another matter not expressly settled in the CISG is that of joint responsibility for losses. Most legal scholars agree that it falls into the scope of the Convention.[30] The correct legal approach is to turn to the underlying principles of the CISG.[31] The amount of damages is thus to be apportioned between the parties in accordance with the degree of causation by the respective parties. This result is also found expressly in both PECL (Art. 9:504) and UPICC (Art. 7.4.7). Both regimes require an apportionment of damages that reflects the parties' contribution to causation. PECL and UPICC are therefore again a persuasive authority for resolving this issue.

3. Proof of Non-Pecuniary Loss

Courts and arbitral tribunals face immense difficulties with awarding claims for non-pecuniary losses. The proof of harm and the extent of it seem to cause special problems for judges and arbitrators, in particular when loss of reputation or goodwill is at stake

[28] *Cf.* Witz, in Witz/Salger/Lorenz (ed.), *International Einheitliches Kaufrecht: Praktiker-Kommentar und Vertragsgestaltung zum CISG* (2000), Art. 74, para 14; Magnus, in Staudinger, *Wiener UN-Kaufrecht* (*CISG*)(1999), Art. 74, para 22; Neumayer/Ming, *Convention de Vienne sur les contrats de vente internationales de marchandises* (1993), Art. 74, note 2.

[29] *Cf.* Lando/Beale (ed.), *Principles of European Contract Law – Parts I and II*, at 439. Official Comment on Art. 9:502 PECL, Comment C, also available online at <http://cisgw3.law.pace.edu/cisg/text/peclcomp74.html#cnpc>, reads,

> The aggrieved party must bring into account in reduction of damages any compensating gains which offset its loss; only the balance, the net loss, is recoverable. Similarly, in computing gains of which the aggrieved party has been deprived, the cost it would have incurred in making those gains is a compensating saving which must be deducted to produce a net gain [. . .].

[30] *See* Tallon, in Bianca/Bonell (ed.), *The 1980 Vienna Sales Convention* (1987), Art. 80, note 2.5; Herber/Czerwenka, *Internationales Kaufrecht* (1991), Art. 80, paras 7 and 8; Stoll/Gruber, in Schlechtriem/Schwenzer (ed.), *UN-Kaufrecht* (2004), Art. 80, para 7; Enderlein/Maskow (ed.), *International Sales Law* (1992), Art. 80, note 6, available at available at <http://cisgw3.law.pace.edu/cisg/biblio/enderlein-art74.html>; Neumayer/Ming, *Convention de Vienne sur les contrats de vente internationales de merchandises* (1993), Art. 80, note 3; Magnus, in Staudinger, *Wiener UN*-Kaufrecht (*CISG*)(1999), Art. 80, para 14, 15; Magnus, in Honsell (ed.), *UN-Kaufrecht* (1997), Art. 80, para 12; Rathjen, *Haftungsentlastung des Verkäufers und Käufers* nach Art. 79, 80 CISG, *Recht der Internationalen Wirtschaft* (1999), at 561, 565; *cf.* Lüderitz/Dettmeier, in Soergel, *CISG* (2000), Art. 80, para 4, Art. 77, para 3.

[31] Stoll, in Schlechtriem (ed.), *UN-Kaufrecht* (2000), Art. 80, para 6; for an overview of the different approaches taken to tackle this problem *see* Stoll/Gruber, in Schlechtriem/Schwenzer (ed.), *UN-Kaufrecht* (2004), Art. 80, para 7.

and the economic disadvantages are not quantifiable.[32] The different approaches taken by legal scholars do not really clear up the problem, but rather contribute to more confusion.[33]

To deny such claims altogether seems to be the wrong approach here. Both PECL (Art. 9:501(2)(a)) and UPICC (Art. 7.4.2(2)) acknowledge the recoverability of such losses, including the loss of goodwill and reputation. The same should apply to cases governed by the CISG, especially because the principle of full compensation underlies the Convention.[34]

As far as the proof of the existence and the extent of the harm is concerned, the foreseeability test contained in Art. 74 CISG could be made more compatible when supplemented with the rules of Art. 7.4.3 UPICC. According to that provision, compensation for harm is only to be granted for such harm that is established with a reasonable degree of certainty. The PECL do not explicitly address the question of proof for harm; Art. 9:501(2) PECL only specifies the foreseeability test for future loss. The test contained in Art. 7.4.3(1) UPICC, however, applies to both the existence and the extent of the harm. It is thus also helpful in cases where the harm is difficult to quantify (e.g., when non-material harm is at stake). Where the amount of damages cannot be established with a sufficient degree of certainty, the assessment is at the discretion of the court (or arbitral tribunal), pursuant to Art. 7.4.3(3) UPICC. The application of Art. 7.4.3 UPICC would thus allow for compensation of commercial damages even in cases where the degree of damages is difficult to quantify and the applicable procedural law does not provide for an abstract sum to be granted.[35] As a consequence, however, domestic procedural rules on proof and certainty of loss would find no application – a result that is in line with the position taken by most legal scholars. This result is justified if one does not qualify questions of certainty of loss and other similar questions as procedural, but as substantive matters that are to be settled by substantive rather than procedural law.[36] The application of the UPICC then helps further the ultimate goal of fostering uniformity in the application of the CISG.

4. Currency of Damages

Art. 74 CISG does not provide for the currency in which the damages are to be paid. The predominant view is that damages are payable in the currency in which the loss was

[32] Courts have rejected claims for loss of good will as no actual loss was proven. *See*, for instance,

- Germany 9 May 2000 Landgericht [District Court] Darmstadt, case presentation including English translation available at <http://cisgw3.law.pace.edu/cases/000509g1.html>

A similar approach is to be found in the following cases:

- France 21 October 1999 Cour d'appel [Appellate Court] Grenoble(*Calzados Magnanni v. Shoes General International*), case presentation including English translation available at <http://cisgw3.law.pace.edu/cases/991021f1.html>; and
- Switzerland 10 February 1999 Handelsgericht [Commercial Court] Zürich, case presentation including English translation available at <http://cisgw3.law.pace.edu/cases/990210s1.html>.

[33] *See*, for instance, the different approaches of Faust, Die Vorhersehbarkeit des Schadens gemäß Art. 74 Satz 2 *UN-Kaufrecht* (*CISG*) (1996), at 19 *et seq.*; Schönle, in Honsell (ed.), *UN-Kaufrecht* (1997), Art. 74 para 7; Karollus, *UN-Kaufrecht, Eine systematische Darstellung für Studium und Praxis* (1991), at 218; Honsell, Die Vertragsverletzung des Verkäufers nach dem Wiener Kaufrecht, 88 *Schweizerische Juristen-Zeitung* (1992), at 361, 364.

[34] *Cf.* Eiselen, "Remarks on the Manner in which the UNIDROIT Principles of International Commercial Contracts May Be Used to Interpret or Supplement Article 74 of the CISG," paras d. and e., available online at <http://cisgw3.law.pace.edu/cisg/principles/uni74.html#editorial>.

[35] Such use of the UPICC has also been proposed by Eiselen, *op. cit.*, note k.; Garro, "The Gap-Filling Role of the UNIDROIT Principles in International Sales Law: Some Comments on the Interplay between the Principles and the CISG," *Tul. L. Rev.* (1995), p. 1188.

[36] Saidov, "Methods of Limiting Damages under the Vienna Convention on Contracts for the International Sale of Goods," available at <http://cisgw3.law.pace.edu/cisg/biblio/saidov.html>.

suffered or in which a particular profit would have been made.[37] Art. 9:510 PECL points to the same direction as it provides that damages are to be measured by the currency that most appropriately reflects the aggrieved party's loss. A similar, yet more specific solution is offered by Art. 7.4.12 UPICC, which provides that damages are to be assessed either in the currency in which the monetary obligation was expressed or in which the harm was suffered, whichever is more appropriate. This suggests that under the Convention damages should generally be measured in the currency that most appropriately reflects the aggrieved party's loss. This may in single cases be the currency in which the monetary obligation was expressed.

5. Loss of Profit

The CISG does not provide for specific rules as to the degree of probability to be applied when assessing whether a certain profit would have been made and what the amount of that profit would be.[38] As a consequence thereof courts and arbitral tribunals take recourse to the general law of evidence of the *lex fori*[39] or reject damages for future loss, including the loss of a chance altogether. Here similar problems are faced as in the case of non-pecuniary losses and losses of good will. Again, the approaches taken in both PECL and UPICC suggest that such recourse to domestic law is not necessary. Art. 9:501(2)(b) PECL provides that recoverable loss comprises future loss that is reasonably likely to occur. This means that the judge or arbitrator would have to evaluate both the likelihood that the future loss will occur and its likely amount. Such future loss may also take the form of the loss of a chance.[40] The UPICC apply a similar test in their Art. 7.4.3(1), which was mentioned earlier in the context of proof of existence and extent of harm that had already accrued. The provision applies the same rule to future harm by demanding that it is recoverable only when established with a reasonable degree of certainty. If there is no sufficient degree of certainty, the assessment is at the discretion of the court or tribunal, Art. 7.4.3(3). Moreover, compensation may be due for the loss of a chance in proportion to the probability of its occurrence, Art. 7.4.3(2). As has been shown before, when asked to assess the existence and the extent of loss, including future loss, the user of the CISG is called upon to apply either the UPICC or the PECL to avoid recourse to domestic law for promoting uniformity in the application of the CISG.

6. Incidental Losses

It is widely assumed that incidental losses[41] are only recoverable if they prove to be reasonable.[42] Such a restriction, however, is not to be found in the wording of Art. 74 CISG. It is submitted that the artificial bar imposed by the reasonableness test serves no

[37] *See*, for instance, Remien, Die Währung von Schaden und Schadensersatz, 53 *Rabels Zeitschrift* (1989), at 245, 260 *et seq*.; Stoll/Gruber, in Schlechtriem/Schwenzer (ed.), *UN-Kaufrecht* (2004), Art. 74, para 30; Magnus, in Staudinger, *Wiener UN-Kaufrecht (CISG)* (1999), Art. 74 para 56.

[38] Stoll, in Schlechtriem (ed.) *UN-Kaufrecht* (2000), Art. 74, para 24.

[39] *See*, for instance, United States 6 December 1995 Federal Appellate Court [2nd Circuit] (*Delchi Carrier v. Rotorex*), case presentation available at <http://cisgw3.law.pace.edu/cases/951206u1.html>, affirming United States 9 September 1994 Federal District Court [New York], case presentation available at <http://cisgw3.law.pace.edu/cases/940909u1.html>.

[40] *Cf*. Lando/Beale, *Principles of European Contract Law, Parts I and II*, at 436.

[41] These are qualified as expenditures suffered by the aggrieved party that have occurred as a consequence of the breach of contract.

[42] *See* relevant case law:

- Germany 25 June 1997 Bundesgerichtshof [Supreme Court], case presentation including English translation available at <http://cisgw3.law.pace.edu/cases/970625g2.html>;
- Germany 8 January 1997 Oberlandesgericht [Appellate Court] Köln, case presentation including English translation available at <http://cisgw3.law.pace.edu/cases/970108g1.html>;

purpose and should be abandoned. This position is supported by looking at the PECL and UPICC counterpart regimes, both of which do not apply a reasonableness test. It is a false concern that without the reasonableness requirement doors would open for the compensation of losses that would otherwise not be recoverable. The foreseeability test, which is entrenched in the CISG, enables the user to achieve the same results as with such a reasonableness test. The inclusion of the reasonableness test stems primarily from the writings of American scholars. However, in American law incidental losses need to pass only the test of reasonableness, but are not subject to a foreseeability test.[43] The requirement of reasonableness makes the foreseeability test redundant as reasonable expenses are always foreseeable.[44] The same, however, can also be said to be true of the reverse situation. Unreasonable expenses must generally be considered as not foreseeable according to Art. 74 CISG. Such analysis of the CISG receives persuasive backing from the PECL and the UPICC. Both instruments only provide for the foreseeability test in Art. 9:503 PECL and Art. 7.4.4 UPICC. Both sets of Principles get by without the additional requirement of a reasonableness test. The same arguably could be held for the CISG.

- Russia 9 September 1994 Arbitration proceeding, Award No. 375/93, CISG online case No. 450 cited in Peter Winship, in Ferrari/Flechtner/Brand (ed.), *The Draft UNCITRAL Digest and Beyond* (2004), at 784 (Fn. 29); case presentation also available at <http://cisgw3.law.pace.edu/cases/940909r1.html>. *See* case Abstract available on UNILEX database at <http://www.unilex.info/case.cfm?pid=1&do=case&id=249&step=Abstract>: The seller performed the contract in accordance with its terms and conditions and delivered the goods to the buyer. The buyer did not present any claims with regard to the goods nor did it pay the price of these goods. The seller requested the buyer to pay for the goods, as well as compensation for the loss sustained as a result of the buyer's breach of contract. This loss included the cost of storage of the goods at the port of loading on account of the delay of the ship, which was to be provided by the buyer. The seller presented to the tribunal the bills it had paid for storage. The amount indicated on these bills corresponded to the charges usually made for this kind of operation. The Tribunal decided in favor of the seller and ordered the buyer to pay the price of the goods as well as damages as provided in Art. 74 CISG. The Tribunal also awarded, on the basis of Art. 78 CISG, interest on all the sums the seller owed at the rate provided for by the law of the seller's country.

For concrete examples of such expenditures, *see* Winship, at 784; *see* also Magnus, in Staudinger, *Wiener UN-Kaufrecht* (CISG) (1999), Art. 74, para 53; Stoll/Gruber, in Schlechtriem/Schwenzer (ed.), *UN-Kaufrecht* (2000), Art. 74, para 18. *See* also Austria 14 January 2002 Oberster Gerichtshof [Supreme Court], case presentation including English translation available at <http://cisgw3.law.pace.edu/cases/020114a3.html>. *See* excerpt from case Abstract available on UNILEX database at <http://www.unilex.info/case.cfm?pid=1&do=case&id=858&step=Abstract>:

> As to the amount of damages claimed by the buyer, the Court held that, according to Art. 74 CISG, the aggrieved party is entitled to full compensation of the losses suffered as a result of the other party's non-performance, including loss of profit, provided that the losses were foreseeable at the time of the conclusion of the contract. However, in the case at hand the seller's standard terms expressly excluded the compensability of the so-called consequential damages. As a consequence the buyer was entitled to recover the expenses it had incurred in repairing the goods, but not the other losses it had suffered in its relationship with its costumer as a consequence of the seller's non-performance.

For the role of *reasonableness* as a general principle of the Convention, *see* Kritzer, "Editorial Remarks," which include further citations and references, at <http://cisgw3.law.pace.edu/cisg/text/reason.html>: "Reasonableness is specifically mentioned in thirty-seven provisions of the CISG and clearly alluded to elsewhere in the Uniform Sales Law. Reasonableness is a general principle of the CISG. [. . .] Although not specifically defined in the CISG, reasonableness is so defined in the Principles of European Contract Law. Moreover, the PECL definition of reasonableness [Art. 1:302] also fits the manner in which this concept is used in the CISG. This definition can help researchers apply reasonableness to the CISG provisions in which it is specifically mentioned and as a general principle of the CISG. [. . .] regarding reasonableness as a fundamental principle of the CISG and reading reasonableness into every article of the CISG, whether specifically mentioned in the article or not . . . is required by virtue of the good-faith and uniform-law mandate recited in Article 7(1) of the CISG."

[43] *Cf.* Anderson, "Incidental and Consequential Damages," 7 *J. L. & Com.* (1987), at 327, 338 *et seq.* and 343; Faust, Die Vorhersehbarkeit des Schadens gemäß Art. 74 Satz 2 *UN-Kaufrecht (CISG)* (1996) at 100.

[44] Anderson, *op. cit.*

IV. MATTERS NOT GOVERNED BY THE CONVENTION

Finally, we turn to matters that are not governed by the CISG, but need to be dealt with in the complete assessment of damage claims. Turning to the PECL and UPICC is possible in these cases, when the general conflicts of laws provision allows for the application of "rules of law" to the contract. Conversely, if the application of "law" is required, the courts and tribunals may be barred from applying either set of Principles.

1. Civil Liability for Personal Injury

The compensation covered by Art. 74 CISG comprises both expectation interest and indemnity interest.[45] However, Art. 5 CISG states that the CISG does not deal with any liability issues for death or personal injury caused by the goods. Damages claims in these circumstances are beyond the scope of the CISG, because the Convention was not intended to intervene with the rules and regulations that signatory states had in place for such situations. In particular, the European Union (EU) Member States had incorporated an EU directive on defective goods into national law. The PECL and UPICC also do not seem to deal with this matter. Although they govern certain damage claims that some jurisdictions may qualify as tort claims, such as damages for negotiations contrary to good faith, for incorrect information, or for fraud and threat during the formation of the contract, neither framework deals with damages for death or personal injury caused by the goods. Neither the wording of the provisions nor the commentaries by either group of authors lead to the assumption that such damage claims should be addressed through the general damages provisions. On the contrary, although the UPICC authors do not even discuss this question in their commentary, the PECL authors state, "The Principles may be applied to claims which arise out of the contract, even if under some national systems the claim might be qualified as delictual rather than contractual."[46] They list the issues that they deem to cover, but that list does not include the situation of a damage claim for personal injury or death from defective goods.[47] Hence, the arbitral tribunal or court will not find grounds in the PECL or UPICC to decide such a claim, but will have to rely on applicable national laws.

2. Reliance Interest

The intensely debated matter of reliance interest[48] may fall outside the scope of the Convention and may thus be addressed by the PECL and UPICC. The two private codifications themselves suggest that damages to compensate for the reliance interest must be seen as different and separate from the damages awarded with respect to a contractual non-performance. Both Art. 4:117 PECL and Art. 3.18 UPICC explicitly deal with damage claims that put the aggrieved party in the same position in which it would have been, if it had not concluded the contract. The authors of both works emphasize the need to differentiate between this claim and those concerning non-performance[49] that

[45] *See* Magnus, in Staudinger, *Wiener UN-Kaufrecht* (*CISG*) (1999), Art. 74 para 20; Lüderitz/Dettmeier, in Soergel, *CISG* (2000), Art. 74, para 8; Stoll/Gruber, in Schlechtriem/Schwenzer (ed.), *UN-Kaufrecht* (2004), Art. 74 para 2.

[46] Lando/Beale (ed.), *Principles of European Contract Law, Parts I and II*, at 97.

[47] *Id.*, at xxv.

[48] Reliance interest does generally call for placing the party in the position in which it would have been if it had not relied on the due performance of the contract. But the recoverability of reliance interest under the CISG is not the only fairly unresolved issue; it also seems to be unclear which losses fall under it and what pre-conditions need to be met for such claims to be successful; *see* e.g., Stoll, in Schlechtriem (ed.), *UN-Kaufrecht* (2000), Art. 74, para 3.

[49] UNIDROIT (ed.), *Principles of International Commercial Contracts*, at 87. Lando/Beale (ed.), Principles of *European Contract Law, Parts I and II*, at 281.

are dealt with in very different parts of the codifications. Hence, the PECL and UPICC may – first – serve as persuasive authority to suggest that a damage claim based on the reliance interest is not covered by the CISG. Following that, both sets of rules will – second – apply with their respective provisions to cover those claims.

3. Punitive Damages and Penalty Clauses

It is generally assumed that punitive damages and penalty clauses can be agreed upon by the parties, whereas the admissibility and validity of such clauses are not governed by the CISG.[50] In contrast, both PECL, in Art. 9:509, and the UPICC, in Art. 7.4.13, deal with this matter, and both frameworks are coherent as to the way they deal with it. Where the contract provides for a specified sum of damages for non-performance, this sum is to be awarded irrespective of the actual sum that the aggrieved party has suffered. Despite any agreement to the contrary, the specified sum may be reduced to a reasonable amount where it is grossly excessive in relation to the loss or harm resulting from the non-performance and the other circumstances. As both the PECL and the UPICC provide a complete set of regulations on the issue of penalty clauses and liquidated damages, both may be applied by the courts and tribunals, rather than turning to any domestic law when dealing with agreed arrangements for non-performance.[51]

V. CONCLUSIONS

The furtherance of international trade law is no easy business. Despite intense debate and increasing practical use of the CISG, many questions remain unresolved. In fact, it is most likely that more debate and more practice will increase the number of questions in doubt by shedding light on previously unconsidered situations requiring judgment. The PECL and the UPICC are both very able legal instruments that can be used to fill or to assist in filling some of the gaps of the Convention. With respect to damage claims under the Convention there are several questions toward the resolution of which the Principles could provide practical assistance.

[50] *See* relevant case law:

- ICC Arbitration Case No. 7197 of 1992, case presentation available at <http://cisgw3.law.pace.edu/cases/927197i1.html>; *see* excerpt from case Abstract available on UNILEX database at <http://www.unilex.info/case.cfm?pid=1&do=case&id=37&step=Abstract>: In the court's opinion, as the CISG does not contain any provision concerning penalty clauses, Austrian law had to be applied pursuant to Art. 7(2) CISG. Applying Austrian law, the court held that the seller had the right to recover all damages suffered notwithstanding the limit fixed by the penalty clause.
- Germany 8 February 1995 Oberlandesgericht [Appellate Court] München, case presentation including English translation available at <http://cisgw3.law.pace.edu/cases/950208g1.html>.

[51] The opposing view is held by Prof. Eiselen, *see* Eiselen, "Remarks on the Manner in which the UNIDROIT Principles of International Commercial Contracts May Be Used to Interpret or Supplement Article 74 of the CISG," para o., available online at <http://cisgw3.law.pace.edu/cisg/principles/uni74.html#editorial>.

Measurement of damages when contract is avoided: Remarks on the manner in which the Principles of European Contract Law may be used to interpret or supplement Article 75 of the CISG

Bojidara Borisova

I. INTRODUCTION

Article 75 of the Convention is part of the set of rules and principles that provide the law of damages in the CISG.[1] CISG Article 75 regulates the operation of a substitute transaction, which is adopted in most legal systems as well as in basic multilateral instruments, such as the CISG and the PECL.[2] Pursuant to CISG Art. 75, as a result of a breach of contract the aggrieved party may carry out a substitute transaction in a reasonable manner and within a reasonable time after avoidance and may recover the difference between the contract price and the price of the substitute transaction.

The same issue is regulated in substantively identical terms in PECL Art. 9:506. However, the drafters of the PECL go further and in other provisions of the European Principles define terms that may help the interpretation and application of PECL Art. 9:506 and its counterpart CISG provision.

CISG Article 75 provides a method for measuring damages when a party avoids a contract, usually because of a fundamental breach by the other party. This provision represents a specific application of CISG Art. 74, which states the general rule for the measurement of damages.[3]

Both CISG Art. 75 and PECL Art. 9:506 stipulate the same basic premises that have to exist before the substitute transaction takes place.

- First, one of the contracting parties must breach the contract, and in consequence the innocent party must undertake action to terminate the contract. As far as concerns this premise, a problem may arise in determining the moment when the contract is declared avoided.

[1] *See* also the text of CISG Articles 74, 76, 77, and 78.

[2] *See* Vilus, "Provisions Common to the Obligations of the Seller and the Buyer," Petar Sarcevic & Paul Volken eds., *International Sale of Goods: Dubrovnik Lectures*, Oceana (1986), also available online at <http://cisgw3.law.pace.edu/cisg/biblio/vilus.html>.

[3] *See* Sutton, "Measuring Damages under the United Nation Convention on the International Sale of Goods," 50 *Ohio St. L.J.* (1989), 737–752, also available online at <http://cisgw3.law.pace.edu/cisg/biblio/sutton.html>. *See* also the following case decisions [All decisions cited in this note and the subsequent notes are available in original language and English translation at the citations indicated]:
- Austria 6 February 1996 Supreme Court, <http://cisgw3.law.pace.edu/cases/960206a3.html>;
- Austria 9 March 2000 Supreme Court <http://cisgw3.law.pace.edu/cases/000309a3.html>;
- Russia 22 October 1998 Arbitration 196/1997 <http://cisgw3.law.pace.edu/cases/981022r1.html>;
- Austria 28 April 2000 Supreme Court <http://cisgw3.law.pace.edu/cases000428a3.html>,

where it is stated that CISG Art. 75 is a specific provision about the calculation of damages in the case of avoidance of a contract following a breach.

- Second, there must be a substitute transaction effected by the aggrieved party. Here the issues that have to be discussed are in respect of the substitute transaction's characteristics and aspects.
- Third, the substitute transaction must be performed in a reasonable manner and within a reasonable time after avoidance. Specific attention must be drawn to the concept of "reasonableness."
- Fourth, the amount of the damages claimed by the aggrieved party must be assessed. The method for measuring damages stipulated in CISG Art.75 is seemingly clear, but still needs elucidation.
- Finally, CISG Art. 75, like PECL Art. 9:506, provides for the possibility of recovery of further damages.

II. SCOPE OF APPLICATION

CISG Article 75 and PECL Art. 9:506 deal with the issues of substitute transaction and the amount recoverable. The basic contractual obligation imposed on both the buyer and the seller is the obligation that each contracting party must perform all of its obligations required by the contract.[4] Logically, the remedy stipulated in CISG Art. 75 is applicable to both contracting parties – the buyer and the seller depending on which party breaches the contractual agreement.[5]

III. WHEN IS THE CONTRACT DEEMED AVOIDED

In the interpretation of CISG Art. 75, the issue of determining the time of avoidance is important because it substantiates the moment from which the "reasonable" time period starts to run. The other provisions that regulate the law of damages in the CISG and the PECL cannot contribute to the clarification of this issue because no clear determination of that issue can be found either explicitly or implicitly. However, Article 72(1) of the 1978 Draft Convention, corresponding to Art. 76 of the CISG, refers to the time of avoidance as the time when the injured party first could have declared avoidance.[6] The purpose of creating such a rule had been to prevent the injured party from speculating at the other's expense. However, the drafters of the final text of the Convention did not elect to include that rule in this text because of its controversial nature and uncertainty.[7]

In the interpretation of CISG Art. 75, it must be emphasized that the problem in determining the time of avoidance appears especially in the event of delayed or non-conforming performance. In this situation, the aggrieved buyer cannot undertake a substitute transaction until the moment of avoidance is defined. Some scholars[8] propose that the provision of CISG Art. 49(2) be used for identifying the time of avoidance. But especially in the case of Art. 49(2)(b)(i), the identification of the exact time of avoidance is difficult and a matter of subjective judgment, because the initial moment from which the reasonable time period starts to run precedes the moment when the buyer could avoid the contract since at that moment the buyer is still not aware of the breach. To draw a general conclusion, the substitute transaction can be made within a reasonable time limit, which begins

[4] *See* CISG Arts. 30 and 53, stating the principal obligations of the parties.

[5] *See* Sutton, *op. cit.*

[6] The legislative history of CISG Art. 76 and its match-up in the 1978 Draft are available online at <http://cisgw3.law.pace.edu/cisg/text/matchup/matchup-d-76.html>.

[7] *See* Schlechtriem, "Extent and Measure of Damages (CISG Arts. 74–76)," in *Uniform Sales Law – The UN Convention for the International Sale of Goods*, Vienna: Manz (1986), also available online at <http://cisgw3.law.pace.edu/cisg/biblio/schlechtriem-76.html>.

[8] *Id.*

to run not until the aggrieved party had in fact declared the contract avoided, which must be proved undeniably by the party's conduct.[9]

IV. SUBSTITUTE TRANSACTION

Although using slightly different wording, CISG Art. 75 and its counterpart PECL provision are substantively similar. It might be said that CISG Art. 75 uses a more descriptive method, whereas the corresponding PECL Art. 9:506 applies more general terminology that emphasizes the essence of the substitute transaction.

According to the text of the Convention, the remedy provided in CISG Art. 75 applies to cases where the initial contract has been avoided and replacement goods have in fact been purchased or the seller has in fact resold the goods. The basic characteristic of the purchase and the resale is their substitute, replacement function. All the other elements of the transaction must be subordinated to this primary function and to the reasonableness criterion. To this effect, the substitute transaction may occur in a different location or have different terms than the original transaction, but should not be so different from it in value or nature as not to be a reasonable substitute.[10] Such lack of complete correspondence to the initial transaction may not influence the right to receive the remedy provided in CISG Art. 75 if the substitute transaction corresponds to the other premises outlined in it, but may lead to the adjustment of the exact amount of the damages, so that any increase in costs or expenses saved could be taken into consideration.[11] Neither CISG Art. 75 nor PECL Art. 9:506 provides any other details or specifications concerning the substitute transaction beyond requiring that it should be made in a reasonable manner and within a reasonable time after avoidance.[12]

V. REASONABLENESS

Although "reasonableness" is considered to be a general principle of the CISG and is mentioned in thirty-seven provisions of the Convention,[13] there can be found no legal

[9] *See* the texts of the following decisions stating that the substitute transaction may be performed only after the contract has been properly avoided:

- Germany 14 January 1994 Appellate Court Düsseldorf, case presentation available at <http://cisgw3.law.pace.edu/cases/940114g1.html>;
- Icc Arbitration Case No. 8574 of September 1996, case presentation available at <http://cisgw3.law.pace.edu/cases/968574.html>;
- Russia 24 January 2000 Arbitration 54/1999, case presentation available at <http://cisgw3.law.pace.edu/cases/000124r1.html>;
- Germany 6 April 2000 District Court München, case presentation available at <http://cisgw3.law.pace.edu/cases/000406g1.html>;
- Germany 13 January 1999 Appellate Court Bamberg, case presentation available at <http://cisgw3.law.pace.edu/cases/990113g1.html>.

See also the text of Austria 6 February 1996 Supreme Court decision, *supra* note 3, according to which "the intention of the buyer not to adhere to the contract anymore has to be obvious beyond any doubt."

[10] *See* Sutton, *op. cit. See* also the legislative history of Cisg Art. 75 and its match-up in the 1978 Draft Convention, which is available online at <http://cisgw3.law.pace.edu/cisg/text/matchup/matchup-d-75.html>; the Secretariat Commentary on the 1978 Draft provision of Cisg Art. 75 is available online at <http://cisgw3.law.pace.edu/cisg/text/secomm/secomm-75.html>.

[11] See Text of Secretariat Commentary on Article 71 of the 1978 Draft Convention, available online at <http://cisgw3.law.pace.edu/cisg/text/secomm/secomm-75.html>.

[12] *See* Flechtner, "Remedies under the New International Sales Convention: The Perspective from Article 2 of the U.C.C.," 8 *J. L. & Com.* (1988) 53–108, also available online at <http://cisgw3.law.pace.edu/cisg/biblio/flecht.html>.

[13] For a discussion of the concept of "reasonableness" in the Cisg, see the editorial comments available online at <http://cisgw3.law.pace.edu/cisg/text/reason.html> and also the following case decisions:

- Germany 14 January 1994 Appellate Court Düsseldorf, *supra* note 9;

definition of the concept in the text of the Convention. Such a definition exists in the PECL, Article 1:302, where it is said that "reasonableness" is to be judged by what persons acting in good faith and in the same situation as the parties would consider to be reasonable. All relevant factors should be taken into consideration when deciding what is reasonable.[14]

The concept of "reasonableness" outlined in Art. 1:302 PECL can be applied to the definition of this issue as regards CISG Art. 75. In relation to the interpretation and application of that Article of the Convention, it should first be determined what is a reasonable period for waiting before concluding the substitute transaction (i.e., what is meant by the expression "within a reasonable time"). Next, the nature and the purpose of the avoided contract and the characteristics of the substitute transaction should be examined (i.e., what is meant by the expression "in a reasonable manner").

In general, both aspects of the required "reasonableness" – the reasonable *time* and the reasonable *manner* – must be examined within the concept of the "reasonable person,"[15] because the manner and the time of acting are manifestations of a personal and, consequently, subjective choice. To make the determination of the issue more impartial, it should be emphasized that the criterion of a "reasonable person" should be assessed in conformity with the conduct of a person "of the same kind" engaged in the same kind of business or in the same trade, etc.[16]

Examining the "reasonable manner," it must be said that the reasonable person's behavior should be to perform the substitute transaction at the most favorable conditions (i.e., the resale to be made at the highest price reasonably possible in the circumstances or the cover purchase to be made at the lowest price reasonably possible).[17] The same criteria should be applied for the determination of the fairness of the substitute transaction terms and conditions.

As far as the "reasonable time" is concerned, the concept of the reasonable person must also be applied. In the first place, account should be taken of the nature and the purpose of the avoided contract and of the substitute transaction; second, the circumstances of the particular case should be examined; and third, the behavior of the reasonable person is reflected by the usages and the practices of the trade or profession in which he is engaged.

VI. DAMAGES

The damages recoverable under CISG Art. 75 amount to the difference between the contract price and the price in a reasonable substitute transaction.[18] PECL Article 9:506 defines the remedy provided for a substitute transaction in a similar fashion.

- Italy 11 December 1998 Appellate Court Milan, case presentation available at <http://cisgw3.law.pace.edu/cases/981211i3.html>;
- Netherlands 15 October 2002 Netherlands Arbitration Institute Case No. 2319, case presentation available at <http://cisgw3.law.pace.edu/cases/021015n1.html>.

[14] PECL Art. 1:302 provides the following definition of "reasonableness": "Under these Principles reasonableness is to be judged by what persons acting in good faith and in the same situation as the parties would consider to be reasonable. In particular, in assessing what is reasonable the nature and purpose of the contract, the circumstances of the case and the usages and practices of the trades or professions involved should be taken into account."

[15] *See* Schlechtriem, *op. cit.*

[16] *See* Honnold, *Uniform Law for International Sales under the 1980 United Nations Convention*, 3d ed., Kluwer Law International (1999).

[17] See Text of Secretariat Commentary on Article 71 of the 1978 Draft Convention, *op. cit.*

[18] National courts and arbitral tribunals apply very consistently the method for measuring damages provided in CISG Art. 75, which leads to the conclusion that this part of CISG Art. 75 generates no controversy. In confirmation of this statement, *see* the following case decisions:

Both counterpart Articles use the so-called concrete method[19] of establishing damages, which accomplishes the common law goal of having contract remedies lead to the "relief of the promisee" instead of the "compulsion of the promisor."[20] This method of establishing damages eliminates the burden of having to prove the market price of the goods and instead applies a more pragmatic criterion.

Under this basic formula for measuring damages, the aggrieved party often may not be able to recover all the damages that it suffered by the breach of the contract – such as additional expenses caused by receipt of non-conforming goods, the necessity to search for substitute goods, advertisement expenses for the resale of the goods under the original contract, losses caused by the later delivery of the substitute transaction goods compared to the original contract date, etc.

Considering the possibility that such additional expenses may occur, plus the desire to restore the aggrieved party into the position that it should have been if the original contract had not been breached, both CISG Art. 75 and PECL Art. 9:506 stipulate that the injured party may seek further damages under the basic rule for recovery of full compensation. The calculation of these additional damages is based on the principle of foreseeability.[21] This regulation confirms the statement that CISG Art. 75 represents a specific application of Art. 74 CISG, although a detailed analysis of the latter provision is not a subject of this study.

- Switzerland 20 February 1997 District Court Saane, case presentation available at <http://cisgw3.law.pace.edu/cases/970220s1.html>;
- Spain 28 January 2000 Supreme Court, case presentation available at <http://cisgw3.law.pace.edu/cases/000128s4.html>;
- Germany 6 April 2000 District Court München, *supra* note 9;
- Germany 30 July 2001 District Court Braunschweig, case presentation available at <http://cisgw3.law.pace.edu/cases/01730g1.html>;
- Austria 28 April 2000 Supreme Court, *supra* note 3.

[19] *See*, Sutton, *op. cit.; see* also Saidov, "Methods of Limiting Damages under the Vienna Convention on Contracts for the International Sale of Goods," 2001, available online at <http://cisgw3.law.pace.edu/cisg/biblio/saidov.html>. In a similar manner, the Switzerland 15 September 2000 Supreme Court decision, case presentation available at <http://cisgw3.law.pace.edu/cases/000915s2.html>, describes as "concrete" the method of establishing damages used in CISG Art. 75.

[20] *See* Farnsworth, "Damages and Specific Relief," 27 *Am. J. Comp. L.* 247 (1979), also available at <http://cisgw3.law.pace.edu/cisg/biblio/farns.html>.

[21] In confirmation of the aggrieved party's right to obtain full compensation including the additional costs, *see* Germany 13 January 1999 Appellate Court Bamberg decision, *supra* note 9.

Measurement of damages when contract avoided: Comparison between the provisions of CISG Article 76 and the counterpart provisions of PECL Article 9:507

Jonathan Yovel

I. GENERAL: CURRENT PRICE DAMAGES UNDER THE CISG AND PECL

Both the CISG and the PECL distinguish between two mutually exclusive types of situations following breach ("non-performance" in the context of the PECL) of contract and avoidance ("termination" in the context of the PECL) by either party.

1.1 In one type of situation, the aggrieved party engages in an alternative transaction that substitutes for the performance expected from the original, now avoided (terminated) contract; this is a so-called cover transaction. Such transactions fall under CISG Art. 75 and PECL Art. 9:506. In the other type of situation, the aggrieved party does not resort to a substitute transaction. In such cases, market-price-based damages may become available to the aggrieved party under so-called current price clauses, CISG Art. 76 and PECL Art. 9:507. Note that under perfect market conditions, the two types of situations converge.[1] This chapter begins by exploring the general logic of current price damages shared by the CISG and PECL and subsequently identifies and analyzes the differences in approach between the two instruments.

1.2 Monetarily speaking, current price damages are a compensation for a devaluation or increase of price in terms of a *theoretical* substitute transaction. They represent the difference between the contractual price of goods (or, in the case of the PECL, also services, etc.) and their price at a certain later time, whether higher or lower (how this later time is determined is discussed below). Thus, an aggrieved seller may demand such damages if, in consequence of the buyer's breach, the goods left at her disposal have a lower market value than the contractual price.[2]

1.3 An aggrieved buyer is entitled to such compensation if the available current price is higher than the contractual price, even without proof of intentions to resell or otherwise engage in a transaction with the goods under such conditions.[3] Had the contract been performed, the aggrieved buyer would have been in a position to capitalize on the price increase; therefore, this premium – held by the breaching seller – should be transferred to the buyer. Seen from this perspective, current price damages are a measure of restitution following unjust enrichment, rather than a kind of expectation damages; they share a distinct family relation with recovery of gains made in breach from a substitute transaction. Thus, current price damages require no proof of expectation, foreseeability, or any actual loss, beyond the change in actual current price.[4] Consequently, current price damages

[1] In one case at least, the court calculated damages according to Art. 76, although a substitute transaction did in fact take place. However, as the actual price collected by the aggrieved seller on the substitute transaction was only about 25% of the contract price, the court deemed the transaction not "in a reasonable manner" as required by Art. 75 CISG and instead invoked the formula of Art. 76. Note that the goods in question (lots of bacon) were perishable and that the seller acted according to his general duty to mitigate the loss (CISG Art. 77). Germany 22 September 1992 *Oberlandesgericht* [Appellate Court] Hamm, 19 U 97/91, CLOUT abstract no. 227, available online at <http://cisgw3.law.pace.edu/cases/920922g1.html>.

[2] For usage of the formula calculating the price differential between the contractual price and a generally verifiable standard such as market price *see* Switzerland 21 October 1999 *Kantonsgericht* [District Court] Zug, A3 1997 61, available online at <http://cisgw3.law.pace.edu/cases/991021s1.html>.

[3] Current price clauses are subject to the parties' general power to derogate under CISG Art. 6. Post-breach agreements such as settlement agreements may be construed to include a waiver of current price damages (as well as other remedies available according to the governing law). *See* China 1 April 1993 CIETAC Arbitration proceeding, available online at <http://cisgw3.law.pace.edu/cases/930401c1.html>.

[4] Consequently, Lando and Beale refer to the assessment of current price damages as "abstract"; *see* Ole Lando and Hugh Beale (eds.), *Principles of European Contract Law: Parts I and II* (Kluwer Law International (2000) (hereinafter "Lando and Beale") p. 211. *See also* Joseph Lookofsky and Herbert Bernstein, *Understanding the* CISG *in Europe*, Deventer, Kluwer 1997 (henceforth "Lookofsky and Bernstein") p. 102. Yet other authors term current price damages as "virtual," although to both those who pay them and those who

do not exclude, either in the CISG or in the PECL, other kinds of damages for breach of contract, in particular expectation or consequential damages, such as under CISG Art. 74 or PECL Art. 9:501.[5]

1.4 Although not universal,[6] current price clauses exist in many national systems, and especially so in the case of sales.[7] Note that a condition for a claim of current price damages is that the contract had been avoided (terminated) (i.e., no forthcoming performance is expected).[8] In that condition it differs from both expectation and reliance damages, claims to which are indifferent to the theoretical possibility of further performance. Likewise, current price damages can obviously not be claimed together with enforcement of performance ("specific performance"), which would result in double compensation.

II. CURRENT PRICE AND RISK

The current price against which the contractual price is measured must be general and reliably verifiable, given to "fair determination."[9] Because current price damages do not apply in cases of alternative transactions, they are not measured against an actual, idiosyncratic price paid. Although the terminology is that of "damages," the issue can be seen as a matter of the *exposure to risk* borne by the breaching party. The breaching party is not exposed to the risk that an idiosyncratic transaction might become available to the aggrieved party, but only to a risk determined by a generally verifiable standard. Therefore, although "current price" and "market price" are not identical, and although in principle current price damages are available not only under market conditions, market prices obviously provide a good indication for determining both the availability of current price damages and their amount.[10] Courts have occasionally recognized standards other than market price to determine current price damages.[11] Conceivably, however, aggrieved parties will fail to prove the existence of either market-based or other verifiable ways of determining prevailing current prices, resulting in the disallowance of current price damages altogether.[12]

collect them they must seem real indeed (the transaction they represent is virtual, or rather imaginary), *see* D. Busch, E. H. Hondius, H. J. Van Kooten, H. N. Schelhaas, and W. M. Schrama, eds., *The Principles of European Contract Law and Dutch Law: A Commentary* (Kluwer 2002) (Henceforth "Busch et al."), p. 420. Some courts seem to have caught up with the terminology, *see* Germany 2 September 1998 *Oberlandesgericht* [Appellate Court] Celle, 3 U 246/97, available online at <http://cisgw3.law.pace.edu/cases/980902g1.html>.

[5] *See* Grant R. Ackerman (ed.) *U.N. Convention on Contracts for the International Sale of Goods, Annotated,* Boston, 1993, Commentary on Article 76, p. 76–2, 76–3.

[6] Busch et al., p. 420–1.

[7] Lando and Beale, Notes to Article 4.506, p. 211. Provisions may be found in Danish, Dutch, German, and Italian codes, as well as the UK Sale of Goods Act 1979 law and Israel's Contract Law (Remedies for Breach of Contract) 1970, Art. 11. Judicial allowance for current price damages exists in France, Belgium, and the Netherlands (*see* Lando and Beale), as well as in Spain and Greece with respect to commercial transactions. For further comparative information *see* Hugo Treitel, "Remedies for Breach of Contract," in *International Encyclopedia of Comparative Law* (Tübingen, Mouton, The Hague, Paris: J. C. B. Mohr, 1976) §§ 102 ff, and John O. Honnold, *Uniform Law for International Sales under the 1980 United Nations Convention*, 3rd ed. (The Hague: Kluwer, 1999) (henceforth "Honnold") §§ 409–15, available online at <http://cisgw3.law.pace.edu/cisg/biblio/honnold.html>.

[8] This condition has been stressed by courts; *see* Germany 6 April 2000 *Landgericht* [District Court] München 12 HKO 4174/99; case presentation including English translation available online at <http://cisgw3.law.pace.edu/cases/000406g1.html>.

[9] *See* Busch et al. 420.

[10] For case law *see supra* note 2, *infra* note 19.

[11] *See* Germany 28 October 1999 *Oberlandesgericht* [Appellate Court] Braunschweig, 2 U 27/99, available online at <http://cisgw3.law.pace.edu/cases/991028g1.html>, where the court calculated Art. 76 damages based on the seller's relevant margin of profit – at the time, the lowest available standard (set at 10%).

[12] *See* Germany 2 September 1998 *Oberlandesgericht* [Appellate Court] Celle, 3 U 246/97, available online at <http://cisgw3.law.pace.edu/cases/980902g1.html>, where the plaintiff failed to prove the current price for

III. NO SUBSTITUTE TRANSACTION

A problem arising from the functional "division of labor" between the substitute transaction and current price provisions is the determination, necessary for the application of the latter, whether a substitute transaction did in fact take place. The problem is especially acute in cases of large turns of business: it would not be obvious whether unspecified goods later sold (or any equivalent non-sales transaction) should be dealt with as a substitute transaction or an independent one.[13] The structure of CISG Art. 75 may assist in making this determination, as it requires substitute transactions to stand in some relation of reasonableness to the original transaction; namely, they are required to be performed "in a reasonable manner and within a reasonable time after avoidance" of the contract. As Art. 76 grants the price differential between the contractual price and that prevailing at the time of avoidance (or of tender, in cases of delivery – see below), it leaves little room to manipulation of time: if an alternative transaction was not performed within a reasonable time, Art. 75 damages would no longer be available, but Art. 76 damages would be. For example, such would be the case of a seller who attempts a substitute transaction but eventually fails; current price damages will still be available as a fall-back option.[14]

Because of obvious considerations, courts prefer to grant "actual" rather than "abstract" price differentials – namely, those resulting from a substitute transaction, rather than market price.[15] The choice, however, is in the hands of the aggrieved party, but so is the burden of proof to show that no substitute transaction has in fact taken place.[16] Professor Schlechtriem argues that this burden is easily met in cases of "constant dealing" because it is "difficult or impossible" to determine which particular transaction should be considered the cover for the breached contract.[17] However, this may cut the other way: in such situations, there is a high probability that a cover transaction in fact occurred, even

generic, "no-name vacuum cleaners." An instance of an important, more general case was expressed in ICC award No. 8740, of 1996, UNILEX, available online at <http://cisgw3.law.pace.edu/cases/968740i1.html>. The question was whether current price may be established for quantities of coal, with the seller arguing that the determinative factors were too volatile for any accurate estimate and the buyer claiming that "an experienced trader would be capable of establishing a price for a particular quality of coal to be delivered at a certain time to a certain place." Analyzing the various factors, the tribunal ruled that "the value of coal is primarily subjective in nature and dependent on the specific needs of the consumer and, therefore, there is no market value on which to award damages." The aggrieved buyer was unable to establish current price and thus not entitled to recover under Art. 76. This raises the general question whether volatile commodity markets are ever appropriate standards for Art. 76 damages, and furthermore the broader question of the applicability of the CISG – designed chiefly for international transactions in goods as its prototype – to transactions in commodities. For discussions *see* Michael Bridge, *The International Sale of Goods: Law and Practice* (Oxford University Press 1999) note 2.41; *also* Peter Schlechtriem, "Interpretation, gap-filling and further development of the UN Sales Convention," available online at <http://cisgw3.law.pace.edu/cisg/biblio/schlechtriem6.html>.

[13] The Secretariat Commentary acknowledges this difficulty, commenting, "If the seller has a finite supply of the goods in question or the buyer has a finite need for such goods, it may be clear that the seller has resold or that the buyer has made a cover purchase, as the case may be. However, if the injured party is constantly in the market for goods of the type in question, it may be difficult or impossible to determine which of the many contracts of purchase or sale was the one in replacement of the contract which was breached." Secretariat Commentary to CISG Art. 76, available online at <http://cisgw3.law.pace.edu/cisg/text/secomm/secomm-76.html#3>.

[14] *See* Honnold, pp. 452–3.

[15] Every rational system would assume preference for a substitute transaction over one in which goods are "lost," transaction-wise. *See* Germany 22 September 1992 *Oberlandesgericht* [Appellate Court] Hamm, 19 U 97/91, available online at <http://cisgw3.law.pace.edu/cases/920922g1.html>. *See also* Germany 26 November 1999 *Hanseatisches Oberlandesgericht* [Appellate Court] Hamburg, 1 U 31/99, CLOUT Abstract No. 348, available online at <http://cisgw3.law.pace.edu/cases/991126g1.html> where the court ruled for a preference of Art. 75 over Art. 76 damages in cases where either could conceivably be claimed.

[16] Parties will fail to meet this requirement if courts deem a pursuant transaction to be a substitute one; *see* Germany 26 November 1999 *Hanseatisches Oberlandesgericht* [Appellate Court] Hamburg, available online at <http://cisgw3.law.pace.edu/cases/991126g1.html>.

[17] *See* Peter Schlechtriem, *Uniform Sales Law: The UN Convention on Contracts for the International Sale of Goods* (Vienna: Manz 1986) pp. 97–8, available online at <http://cisgw3.law.pace.edu/cisg/biblio/schlechtriem.html>.

if it were difficult to identify a single, specific substitute. The fact that any of a number of transactions may have been the substitute transaction does not allow one to conclude that there was no substitute transaction. The breaching party opposing the allowance of current price damages need not point to a distinct cover transaction if he can point to a number of them, of which one (or more) function as the cover transaction, even if it is impossible to differentiate it from the commercial aggregate. Thus, as current price provisions state the lack of a substitute transaction as a condition for recovering current price damages, the burden of proof – carried by the aggrieved party seeking current price damages[18] – may, in many instances, determine this point.

IV. RELEVANT PLACE

CISG Art. 76(2) determines that current price is the price prevailing at the place where delivery should have taken place (see CISG Art. 31 for determination of the place of delivery), but allows for a "reasonable substitute" in case there is no current price at the designated place of delivery. Prices for goods may vary considerably among some markets, and evidence regarding a prevalent price in one market may be rejected as not amounting to a "reasonable substitute" for the originally intended market.[19] The reasonable substitute structure does not allow the plaintiff to engage in "current price shopping." Such behavior fails to constitute a "*reasonable* substitute," as well as runs counter to standards of good faith.[20] The PECL are silent on the question of place according to which the current price is to be determined. One may reasonably apply the CISG's criterion there, unless there were good reasons to diverge from it. Performances that are easily transferable from one place to another may attempt to command the current price of an emerging or other market that is more lucrative than the original contract entailed, and thus jumble the *ex-ante* assessment of risk involved with current price damages. Such a manipulation may or may not be considered legitimate under the "reasonable substitute" principle as applied to various types of transactions, but the burden of proof that the substitute market is indeed a "reasonable" substitution lies with the aggrieved party requiring it. The measure in which the original performance was in any significant way geographically entrenched may serve as a criterion for the "reasonableness" of different current price determinations.

Art. 76(2) adds a clause that is seemingly out of synch with the general logic of current price damages and is furthermore not expressed in PECL 9:507: namely, that when calculating current price differentials according to a price prevalent in a place other than the designated place of delivery, the cost of transporting the goods is to be taken into account. One may reasonably object that when no actual transaction is involved current price is based on a "virtual" or "abstract" or "imagined" transaction, and it is irrelevant to internalize transportation costs into the price differential. However, the existence of this clause expresses the strong ties of current price damages to those resulting from an actual substitute transaction (such as under CISG Art. 75). The clause assumes that commerce,

[18] Plaintiff carries the onus of proof as to all the constituents of the claim for damages. In the context of Art. 76, *see* Germany 2 September 1998 *Oberlandesgericht* [Appellate Court] Celle, 3 U 246/97, available online at <http://cisgw3.law.pace.edu/cases/980902g1.html>.

[19] *See* China 18 April 1991 CIETAC-Shenzhen Arbitration, available online at <http://cisgw3.law.pace.edu/cases/910418c1.html>. The tribunal rejected steel prices published in a trade journal as a basis for Art. 76 damages, even though the aggrieved buyer had them adjusted from U.S. prices to Chinese prices; the tribunal ruled that no dependable formula for adjusting the price from a foreign market was available, and that under an POB (Chinese port) contract, a local price could and should be used. The current price damages were thus determined according to a price negotiated in the context of a substitute transaction that was not ultimately concluded whose details were similar to the original contract and were presented to the court without a specific claim of representing a "market price."

[20] *See* CISG Art. 7 and PECL Art. 1:201.

production, and other activities go on and that current price damages need be such as to in fact allow the aggrieved party to engage in some future transaction, even when that will no longer fall under the "reasonable time" requirement of Art. 75.[21] Hence the two mutually exclusive mechanisms truly attempt to approach identical concerns, making current price damages appear less "abstract" than the authors cited above take them to be.

V. RELEVANT TIME

As current price damages are determined *ex-post*, the question of the time of their determination is significant. The CISG and PECL differ somewhat on this point. The PECL determine that the current price against which the contractual price is determined is the current price at the time of the contract's termination. This gives the aggrieved party – who terminates the contract – an *ex-ante* measure of control in determining the current price damages. One could theoretically consider – and indeed national courts have at times recognized – other standards: the time of breach, the time when the breach became known or should have become known to the aggrieved party, the time when avoidance (termination) first became available, or the time of any number of notices exchanged between the parties.

VI. CURRENT PRICE DAMAGES AFTER GOODS WERE DELIVERED

Regarding the time according to which current price damages are calculated, there is an apparent difference between the PECL and CISG with respect to one special category of cases in which such damages may become available. Dealing as it does with the special risks associated with international sales of goods, the CISG is consistently sensitive to situations in which contracts are avoided pursuant to delivery.[22] As current price damages become available only following avoidance of the contract, Art. 76(1) makes a special provision for such damages in cases where the aggrieved party has avoided the contract after taking over the goods (e.g., for failure of conformity or any other fundamental breach, or following a *Nachfrist* period). In such cases, the current price is determined according to the time of the taking of the goods, instead of the time of avoidance of the contract. Thus, aggrieved parties who have taken the goods may not benefit from deferring avoidance tactically or speculatively, until such time as a more favorable current price emerges.[23] The PECL, dealing with all contractual situations, include no such provision. This apparent shortcoming is mitigated by two factors. One is the PECL's more overt imposition of good faith obligations, which would presumably disallow such tactical behavior. The other, more specific factor considers that, under both the CISG and PECL, avoidance (termination) of the contract pursuant to delivery is restricted to a "reasonable time,"[24] a determination germane to both the availability and the amount of

[21] For the close relation between an actual substitute transaction and an "imagined" one in the context of internalizing shipment to/from other regions as well as other factors that require adjusting the imagined transaction to a real one, *see* CIETAC-Shenzhen Arbitration case, *supra* note 19.

[22] *See* CISG Arts. 49 and 64.

[23] *See* Lookofsky and Bernstein, p. 102 f141; *also* B. Audit, *La vente internationale de marchandises*, Paris: LGDJ, 1990, p. 178; *also* Burghard Piltz, *Internationales Kaufrecht*, München 1993, § 5 Rd.Nr. 439.

[24] *See* CISG Art. 49(2) and PECL Arts. 9:303(2) and (3)(a). *See* commentaries on CISG Arts. 46 and 64. Some legal systems insist on shorter times for declarations of avoidance or rescission, such as the German "*unverzüglich*," "without undue delay," BGB §121 (controlling all acts of rescission, including HGB §377) or the French "*interpellation suffisante*" prevalent in the Code Civil. German courts acknowledged a discrepancy between the two criteria, even when the facts satisfied both; *see* 17 September 1991 *Oberlandesgericht* Frankfurt, 5 U 164/90, available online at <http://cisgw3.law.pace.edu/cases/910917g1.html> (in which a one-day delay in sending an avoidance telex was judged both reasonable and *unverzüglich*); 22 August 2002 *Landgericht* Freiburg, 8 O 75/02, available online at <http://cisgw3.law.pace.edu/cases/020822g1.html> (in

current price damages. As also under the PECL current price damages become available only upon avoidance of the contract, the "reasonable time" restricting the latter – in cases in which tender was assumed – also limits the time frame of the former. This does not make for an absolute congruence between the two systems, as aggrieved parties under the PECL are allowed to defer termination of the contract – and thus to an extent determine the amount of current price damages – under the reasonable time restriction. Under CISG, the aggrieved party has no such power, and current price damages under conditions of tender will be determined according to the time of tender.

Mitigation of damages: Comparison between the provisions of the CISG (Art. 77) and the counterpart provisions of the Principles of European Contract Law (Art. 9:505)

Bruno Zeller

I. GENERAL COMMENTS

Mitigation is a principle that is an obligation in the common law, but is not clearly defined in civil law. In arbitration practices mitigation has become a general principle of international trade, and Mustill refers to the principle as "[to] constitute the *lex mercatoria* in its present form."[1] He went further by noting that mitigation is merely treated as obvious.[2]

The CISG has incorporated the doctrine of mitigation specifically into Article 77, but the rule is also reflected in Articles 85 and 86, which are concerned with the preservation of the goods after a breach. The idea behind Article 77 is that the plaintiff cannot recover damages or losses that he should have avoided. This principle is also accepted in the Principles of European Contract Law (PECL) in Article 9:505.[3]

The first obvious difference between the PECL and the CISG is that Article 77 clearly states that losses include loss of profit, whereas the PECL are silent on this aspect. It can be assumed that the loss of profit is included in the PECL, as the official commentary to Article 9:501, specifically illustration 4, explains that loss of profit is included.[4] Furthermore, Article 9:502 PECL stipulates that a party has the right to recover losses and "the gain of which it has been deprived."[5] In addition, the CISG can be used as an analogical tool that would confirm that losses, as explained in the PECL, include the loss of profits and therefore are identical to the CISG; hence, mitigation follows the same pattern of losses in the counterpart provisions.

which an Italian buyer of a used car was allowed to avoid the contract as late as three months after she discovered the car was previously stolen and title cannot be transferred; the court accepted the time as pertinent to the various inspections required).

[1] Mustill M., "The New Lex Mercatoria: The First Twenty-Five Years," 4 *Arb. Int'l (1988)* 86–119, at 113 [available on the Internet courtesy of CENTRAL Transnational Law Database (TLDB)].

[2] *Id.* at 100.

[3] Lando, O., and Beale, H., *Principles of European Contract Law*, Kluwer Law (2000), 445.

[4] *Id.* at 435.

[5] *Id.* at 438.

Another point worth noting is that the PECL in its language only refer to losses, whereas the CISG introduces the word "damages" in addition to losses. The question is, Should the term "damages" be understood as expanding on losses? Stoll is correct in arguing that mitigation includes the conclusion of cover transactions – or even avoidance must be contemplated – if it will reduce damages.[6] The PECL arguably cover the same ground by referring to a reduction of losses "by taking reasonable steps." Such language is broader than in Article 77 as it will allow a court or tribunal wider discretion as to what is included in "reasonable steps." Whether avoidance or cover transactions are included in "reasonable steps" is not certain; however, those transactions are not specifically excluded either.

A real problem seems to be the choice of words in the CISG and PECL. The CISG text provides that a party who relies on a breach of contract "must" take measures to mitigate the loss. Arguably in its language Article 77 imposes a duty on the plaintiff to mitigate the "loss," whereas the PECL only suggest that the non-performing party is not liable for damages that the aggrieved party "could" have reduced. The wording is not as strong as in the CISG, as the PECL appear to rely on a subjective appraisal of the situation by the non-breaching party and to that effect by the court or tribunal.

The question that has been posed is whether, because of its choice of wording, Article 77 imposes a legal obligation[7] and hence allows the original breaching party to claim a set-off. The Secretariat Commentary to Article 73 of the 1978 Draft (draft counterpart of CISG Article 77) suggests that it is "a duty owed by the injured party to the party in breach."[8] Another view is that the injured party "is under an obligation to herself to mitigate the loss."[9] This latter view can be supported because the second sentence of Article 77 makes it clear that, should the aggrieved party not follow the advice given in the first sentence, he will bear some of the costs associated with the breach. It could not have been clearer that "must" is linked to the second sentence, which means that inactivity or the failure to take reasonable steps to mitigate is no excuse.[10]

This position could be contrasted with the English view, which can be formulated as follows:

> A plaintiff is under no duty to mitigate his loss, despite the habitual use by the lawyers of the phrase 'duty to mitigate'. He is completely free to act as he judges to be in his best interests.[11]

Arguably the English view is mirrored by the PECL but not by the CISG, where the reading suggests that the non-breaching party has a legal duty to mitigate the loss.

The PECL simplified the whole process by starting with the premise that the non-performing party simply is not liable for any losses that the aggrieved party could have avoided. However, the PECL do require a positive step by the aggrieved party to mitigate any possible losses.

II. QUESTION OF *REASONABLENESS*

Both the CISG and PECL suggest that reasonable steps must be taken to mitigate the loss. In both instruments this is not a question of law, but rather a question of fact. Every case

[6] Stoll H. in Schlechtriem P., *Kommentar zum Einheitlichen UN-Kaufrecht*, (2000), 587.

[7] Saidov D., "Methods of Limiting Damages under the Vienna Convention on Contracts for the International Sale of Goods," available online at <http://cisgw3.law.pace.edu/cisg/biblio/saidov.html>.

[8] Secretariat Commentary to Article 73 of the 1978 Draft, para 3, available online at <http://cisgw3.law.pace.edu/cisg/text/secomm/secomm-77.html>.

[9] Bernstein H. and Lookofsky J., *Understanding the* CISG *in Europe,* Kluwer, 2nd ed. (2003), 103.

[10] Zeller B., *Damages under the Convention on Contracts for the International Sale of Goods*, Oceana Press (2005), 112.

[11] Sir John Donaldson, in *The Solholt* [1983] 1 *Lloyd's Rep*. 605.

will have different circumstances; hence, if a person takes steps that are in good faith – which is a principle found in both instruments – he has acted reasonably, particularly if the measures adequately prevent losses. However, it will be within the court's discretion to evaluate measures of mitigation. Obviously, if no measures have been taken, then a party will be in breach of CISG Article 77 or PECL Article 9:505. It is never suggested that the efforts to mitigate must be exceptional.

The argument is, however, how far, or how much action is required to satisfy the reasonable standard test. The Supreme Court of Austria considered that

> a possible measure to reduce damages is reasonable, if it could have been expected as bona fide conduct from a reasonable person in the position of the claimant under the same circumstances.[12]

It appears that, given the facts of the case, the court chose to look at the objective measure of a situation. As such, excessive measures, or those that entail unreasonable high expenses and risks, are not necessary.[13] This has been confirmed by the Austrian Supreme Court, which noted that

> the buyer may not undertake any unreasonable expenditures (Art. 77 CISG): if the costs to effect a cure stand in no reasonable proportion to the benefit of the cure for the buyer, then they are not recoverable.[14]

This conclusion was confirmed by a Swiss court, which pointed also to the fact that mitigation not only obliges the aggrieved party to take positive steps but also that these positive steps cannot be undertaken when they result in unnecessary costs. In essence the court stated,

> Seller's counterclaim may be reduced to the extent he took measures to mitigate the losses or ought to have taken such measures. Such measures entail namely the re-sale or respectively the re-utilization of the sold machine, if there was not any market place for such a kind of production machine, because it was unique. Furthermore, these measures also entail the avoidance of any unnecessary expenditures and costs.[15]

A reading of PECL counterpart provisions leads to the same result. However, Article 9:505(2) turns the obligation around by allowing the aggrieved party only to recover costs that are "reasonably incurred." The interpretation of the CISG as pointed out above

[12] Austria 6 February 1996 *Oberster Gerichtshof* [Supreme Court], case presentation including English translation available at <http://cisgw3.law.pace.edu/cases/960206a3.html>.

The plaintiff, a German buyer, and the defendant, an Austrian seller, entered into an agreement for the FOB delivery of a certain quantity of propane gas. *See* analysis of Austrian case law by Willibald Posch & Thomas Petz, "Austrian Cases on the UN Convention on Contracts for the International Sale of Goods," 6 *Vindobona J. Int'l. Com. L. & Arbitration* (2002) 1–24, at 23:

> When dealing with the Convention's provision on mitigation of damages (Article 77 CISG), the Court held that the loss, including lost profits, suffered from a breach of contract may only be claimed to the extent to which the loss should not have been mitigated by measures that would have been reasonable in the circumstances. Examples of such reasonable measures to mitigate the loss would be those which under the circumstances of the individual case could have been expected in good faith. In the Court's view, the answer to the question of which measures would be reasonable and ought to be taken depends on how a reasonable creditor would have acted in the same situation. [Because of the absence of any substantial argument on this point during the proceedings, this question was not answered by the Austrian Supreme Court in greater detail.]

[13] Saidov, *supra* note 7.

[14] Austria 14 January 2002 *Oberster Gerichtshof* [Supreme Court], case presentation including English translation available at <http://cisgw3.law.pace.edu/cases/020114a3.html> (a German seller and an Austrian buyer concluded a contract for the sale of a cooling system to be specifically manufactured by the seller).

[15] Switzerland 3 December 2002 *Handelsgericht* [Commercial Court] St. Gallen, case presentation including English translation available at <http://cisgw3.law.pace.edu/cases/021203s1.html> (the plaintiff, a buyer incorporated in Tel Aviv, Israel, ordered from the defendant, a seller, of Switzerland, a sizing machine for the production of textiles).

suggests that the non-breaching party can incur expenses until the costs to mitigate become unreasonable. In sum, though, the practical effect is the same.

Not surprisingly, courts have been relatively strict in their interpretation of CISG Article 77. A Swiss Court dismissed the claim of the plaintiff that it had to pay damages to a third party as it neglected to involve the defendant in the negotiations with the third party. In such a case, the defendant could have contributed to the costs or even indemnified the plaintiff.[16]

Not all cases are controversial or difficult, as seen in a Russian arbitration proceeding. The tribunal paid attention to the fact that the buyer did not take any measures whatsoever to mitigate the loss:

> He did not cancel the contract with a third party, nor conclude substitute transactions and did not resort to Article 76 when calculating the damages.[17]

The same approach was taken by the Intermediate People's Court of Shandong Province. The court apportioned the main responsibility to the buyer, who "did not take reasonable measures and just let the losses grow until the value of the PTO shrimp was nearly extinguished."[18] Arguably, though, the courts would have come to the same conclusion if they had applied the PECL to the case.

Mitigation is not necessarily restricted to minimizing actual costs. Courts have viewed the circumstances of the contract in very broad terms and merely ask the question, "could the situation have been changed but for the buyer's behavior." In an interesting case the buyer did not produce evidence asked for by the arbitral panel to determine whether he took measures to eliminate a negative impression of the seller's products. The arbitral panel found it inexcusable that the buyer in effect agreed with the unsubstantiated allegations of his consumers.[19] Whether the same result would have been achieved under the PECL is debatable and would depend on the definition of "loss." Under the CISG this debate is avoided as "damages" are also included in Article 77, and a negative impression will cause damages but not necessarily a loss.

III. CONCLUSION

In summary, the above cases illustrate that courts and tribunals simply ask whether the prudent business person has taken all reasonable steps and done all he can to keep costs to the breaching party to a minimum. Merely ignoring the situation is in breach of CISG Article 77, as is willful adherence to contractual terms. In effect, it is of little value to try to give a definition of what is "reasonable," as each court has demonstrated that in a practical sense the word "reasonable" is well understood. One point noted by Saidov

[16] Switzerland 1 March 2002 *Zivielgesetz* [Civil Court] Basel, P 1997/482, para 3.7; case presentation including English translation available at <http://cisgw3.law.pace.edu/cases/020301s1.html> (a Belgian seller and a Swiss buyer concluded a contract for the sale of soy protein products).

[17] Russia 6 June 2000, Arbitration proceeding 406/1998; case presentation including English translation available at <http://cisgw3.law.pace.edu/cases/000606r1.html> (an English buyer and a Russian seller concluded a contract for the sale of goods to be shipped to a certain port on CIF terms. When the seller notified the buyer that it would not perform the contract due to an increase in tax rates that, in its view, amounted to *force majeure*, the buyer filed a motion for arbitral proceeding claiming damages).

[18] China 17 December 1999 Rizho Intermediate People's Court, Shandong Province (Hang Tat v. Rizhao), case presentation including English translation available at <http://cisgw3.law.pace.edu/cases/991217c1.html> (a U.S. buyer concluded a contract with sellers, of China, for the sale of a quantity of frozen shrimp).

[19] Russia 24 January 2000 Arbitration proceeding 54/1999, case presentation including English translation available at <http://cisgw3.law.pace.edu/cases/000124r1.html> (a U.S. firm, the buyer, commenced proceedings against a Russian company, the seller, in connection with a contract concluded between the parties, which involved the delivery of two consignments on an FCA (free carrier) basis, in accordance with INCOTERMS under the contract).

is that mitigation can bring about certain forms of costs as well. Arguably, Article 77 is broad enough here to cover the situation where the mitigating party incurred costs, which could be offset.[20] However, costs to mitigate will be subject to the same rules as the mitigation process itself. If costs are not necessary, the mitigating party cannot claim any recompense. It is argued that the PECL in most circumstances would deliver the same results as those achieved by the CISG. The only question that possibly is unanswered is whether PECL Article 9:505 could be as broadly interpreted as the CISG (i.e., as set-off and mitigation of abstract damages, such as negative impressions or loss of reputation).

[20] Saidov, *supra* note 7.

Right to interest: Comparison between the provisions of CISG Articles 78 and 84(1) and counterpart provisions of the PECL

Francesco G. Mazzotta

I. INTRODUCTION

The main goal of this chapter is to establish whether the Principles of European Contract Law (PECL) may be of assistance in construing the meaning of Article 78 of the United Convention on Contracts for the International Sale of Goods (CISG). I believe that the method for calculating interest rate as determined by the PECL may not be used under the CISG.

II. CISG ARTICLE 78

1. Background

It is well known that Article 78 is "more conspicuous for the questions it fails to answer than the questions it answers."[1] Because it was impossible to reach an agreement among

[1] *See* Jacob S. Ziegel, "Report to the Uniform Law Conference of Canada on the Convention on Contracts for the International Sale of Goods" 149 (1981).

the delegations at the Vienna Convention,[2] the present version of Article 78 does not fix any rate of interest. It should be noted, however, that although considered as a "headless corpse," Article 78 introduces a far-reaching principle of a general entitlement to interest,[3] which is still rather important because it makes clear that a fixed interest rate (however, one not set by the Convention) must be applied to sums paid with delay (*normativity* feature)[4] and that the entitlement to interest is not limited by grounds for release as provided for by CISG Article 79 (*absoluteness* feature).[5]

2. Operation of CISG Article 78

Failure to pay the price or any other sum that is in arrears is the condition to be satisfied under Article 78.[6] Failure refers to a failure to comply with the obligation to pay the price by a specific time, whether the time is set by contract or by the CISG (Article 58).[7] Interest is due regardless of proof of any losses,[8] and it is independent of any claim for damages.[9] Although there should not be too many problems in determining the time when the buyer is bound to pay the price (as explained, it will be either governed by the agreement between the parties or, as a default rule, by CISG Article 58),[10] there are no default rules regarding the time of performance with respect to "other sums." In the latter case, in the absence of any other indication, it must be assumed that interest is to be paid immediately when the claim for other sums arises.[11] No other additional requirements must be satisfied under domestic law (e.g., the issue of a formal prior warning).[12]

[2] For an historical account on the issue of the rate of interest raised during the drafting period of the Vienna Sales Convention, *see* Pace University School of Law, Institute of International Commercial Law, Guide to CISG Article 78, visit <http://cisgw3.law.pace.edu/cisg/text/e-text-78.html>. For literature specifically relevant to the provisions of CISG Article 78 visit <http://cisgw3.law.pace.edu/cisg/text/mono78.html>.

[3] *See* Fritz Enderlein & Dietrich Maskow, International Sales Law, United Nations Convention on Contracts for the International Sale of Goods – Convention on the Limitation Period in the International Sale of Goods 310, 311 (1992). *See, e.g.*, Italy 31 March 2004 District Court [Tribunale] Padova, *available at* <http://cisgw3.law.pace.edu/cases/040331i3.html>.

[4] *See* Enderlein & Maskow, *supra* note 4.

[5] *Id.*

[6] *See, e.g.*, Switzerland 12 December 2002 District Court [Kantonsgericht] Zug, *available at* <http://cisgw3.law.pace.edu/cases/021212s1.html>.

[7] *See* Germany 18 January 1994 Provincial Court of Appeal [Oberlandesgericht] Frankfurt am Main, *available at* <http://cisgw3.law.pace.edu/cases/940118g1.html>; Germany 13 June 1991 Provincial Court of Appeal [Oberlandesgericht] Frankfurt am Main, *available at* <http://cisgw3.law.pace.edu/cases/910613g1.html>.

[8] *See* Germany 26 September 1990 District Court [Landgericht] Hamburg, *available at* <http://cisgw3.law.pace.edu/cases/900926g1.html>; Germany 24 April 1990 Petty District Court [Amtsgericht] Oldenburg in Holstein, *available at* <http://cisgw3.law.pace.edu/cases/900424g1.html>.

[9] *See, e.g.*, Germany 14 January 1994 Provincial Court of Appeal [Oberlandesgericht] Düsseldorf, *available at* <http://cisgw3.law.pace.edu/cases/940114g1.html>; Germany 17 September 1993 Provincial Court of Appeal [Oberlandesgericht] Koblenz, *available at* <http://cisgw3.law.pace.edu/cases/930917g1.html>; ICC International Court of Arbitration, 1992, award No. 7197, *available at* <http://cisgw3.law.pace.edu/cases/927197i1.html>. *See also*, *e.g.*, Enderlein & Maskow, *supra* note 4, at 311; Rolf Herber and Beate Czerwenka, Internationales Kuafrecht 348 (1991); Hans Stoll, "Internationalprivatrechtliche Fragen bei der landesrechtlichen Ergänzung des einheitlichen Kaufrechts," in *Festschrift für Murad Ferid* 495, 509–10 (Andreas Heldrich ed., 1988). *But see* F.J.A. van der Velden, *Het Weense Koopverdrag 1980 en zijn Rechtsmiddelen* 405 (1988) who argues that interest is part of damages. According to this view, payment of interest could be exempted on the grounds of impediments.

[10] *See*, Hans H. Eberstein & Klaus Bacher, "Annotations 1–36 on Article 78," *in* Commentary on the UN Convention on the International Sale of Goods 591 (Peter Schlechtriem, ed., 1998); Enderlein & Maskow, *supra* note 4, at 313. *See, e.g.*, Germany 12 October 2000 District Court [Landgericht] Stendal, available at <http://cisgw3.law.pace.edu/cases/001012g1.html>.

[11] *See* Eberstein & Bacher, *supra* note 11, at 593. *See also* Herber & Czerwenka, *supra* note 10.

[12] *See, e.g.*, Switzerland 12 December 2002 District Court [Kantonsgericht] Zug, available at <http://cisgw3.law.pace.edu/cases/021212s1.html>. *But see* Finland 12 April 2002 Court of Appeal [Hovioikeus] Turku, *available at* <http://cisgw3.law.pace.edu/cases/020412f5.html>; Germany 19 March 1999 District Court [Landgericht] Zwickau, *available at* <http://cisgw3.law.pace.edu/cases/990319g1.html>.

As mentioned, Article 78 does not fix any specific interest rate. As suggested by many authors and courts, the issue is not within the CISG, and therefore, interest should be determined by the domestic law of the forum state or, more frequently, by the law that would otherwise govern the contract, absent the CISG, which usually is the law of the country resulting from the application of the rules of private international law of the forum state.[13] If the contract is between European Community nationals, absent a choice of law, the law of the country in which the seller has his principal place of business will be applied, according to Article 4(2) of the EEC Convention on the Law Applicable to Contractual Obligations.[14] There are many cases where the law of the country of the creditor was applied without making any reference to the rules of private international law.[15] The law of the country of the debtor has also been applied by the courts[16] or suggested by commentators.[17] There are also cases in which the law of the country of the legal tender to be used was applied[18] as well, as cases in which the law of the country where the price must be paid was applied.[19] Finally, some courts have also applied the rate of interest as determined by the UNIDROIT Principles of International Commercial Contracts (Art. 7.4.9).[20] In cases where the applicable law prohibits the payment of interest, domestic public policy (very likely) makes CISG Article 78 unenforceable notwithstanding the language of CISG Article 4.[21] I believe, however, that interest should be awarded also

[13] *See, e.g.*, Barry Nicholas, COMMENTARY ON THE INTERNATIONAL SALES LAW 570 (Massimo C. Bianca & Michael Joachim Bonell eds., 1987); Peter Schlechtriem, UNIFORM SALES LAW – THE UN CONVENTION ON CONTRACTS FOR THE INTERNATIONAL SALE OF GOODS [hereinafter *Uniform Sales Law*] 100 (1986); Leif Sevón, INTERNATIONAL SALES OF GOODS: DUBROVNIK LECTURES 230 (Petar Sarcevic & Paul Volken eds., 1986); Enderlein & Maskow, *supra* note 4, at 312; Herber & Czerwenka, *supra* note 10, at 349; Martin Karollus, "Judicial Interpretation and Application of the CISG in Germany 1988–1994," *Cornell Review of the Convention on Contracts for the International Sale of Goods* 51–94, (1995); Leif Sevón, "Obligations of the Buyer under the Vienna Convention on the International Sale of Goods," 106 *Jurisdisk Tidskrift* 341 (1990). As to case law, *see, e.g.*, Germany 28 February 2000 Provincial Court of Appeal [Oberalandesgericht] Stuttgart, *available at* <http://cisgw3.law.pace.edu/cases/000228g1.html>.

[14] See EEC Convention on the Law Applicable to Contractual Obligations of June 19, 1980, 1980 O.J. (L 266). See Schlechtriem, *Uniform Sales Law*, *supra* note 14, at 99; Volker Behr, "The Sales Convention in Europe: From Problems in Drafting to Problems in Practice," 17 *J. L. & Com.* 296, 263–299 (1998). Note, however, that the Hague Convention of June 15, 1955, on the law applicable to the international sales of goods, may come into play when the forum is located within a contracting state of the Hague Convention. *See* Carolina Saf, "A Study of the Interplay between the Conventions Governing International Contracts of Sale," *available at* <http://cisgw3.law.pace.edu/cisg/biblio/saf.html>; Franco Ferrari, "Uniform Application and Interest Rates Under the 1980 Vienna Sales Convention," 24 *Ga. J. Int'l. & Comp. L.* 467 (1995).

[15] *See, e.g.*, Germany 13 April 2000 Petty District Court [Amtsgericht] Duisburg, *available at* <http://cisgw3.law.pace.edu/cases/000413g1.html>; Switzerland 9 December 1994 District Court [Bezirksgericht] Arbon, *available at* <http://cisgw3.law.pace.edu/cases/941209s1.html>.

[16] *See* Switzerland 11 March 1996 Canton Appellate Court [Tribunal Cantonal] Vaud, 163/96/BA and 164/96/BA, *available at* <http://cisgw3.law.pace.edu/cases/960311s1.html>.

[17] *See* Stoll, *supra* note 10.

[18] *See, e.g.*, Switzerland 5 November 2002 Commercial Court [Handelsgericht] Aargau, *available at* <http://cisgw3.law.pace.edu/cases/021105s1.html>.

[19] *See, e.g.*, Switzerland 5 February 1997 Commercial Court [Handelsgericht] Zürich, *available at* <http://cisgw3.law.pace.edu/cases/970205s1.html>; Netherlands 9 August 1995 District Court [Arrondissementsrechtbank] Almelo, *available at* <http://cisgw3.law.pace.edu/cases/950809n1.html>.

[20] *See, e.g.*, ICC International Court of Arbitration, 1988, award No. 9333, *available at* <http://cisgw3.law.pace.edu/cases/989333i1.html>; France 6 April 1995 Appeal Court [Cour d'appel] Paris, *available at* <http://cisgw3.law.pace.edu/cases/950406f1.html>. *See also* Austria 15 June 1994 Arbitral Tribunal [Internationales Schiedsgericht der Bundeskammmer der gewerblichen Wirtschaft] Vienna, SCH-4366, *available at* <http://cisgw3.law.pace.edu/cases/940615a3.html>; Austria 15 June 1994 Arbitral Tribunal [Internationales Schiedsgericht der Bundeskammmer der gewerblichen Wirtschaft] Vienna, SCH-4318, *available at* <http://cisgw3.law.pace.edu/cases/940615a4.html>, which expressly mentions the UNIDROIT Principles.

[21] *See* Schlechtriem, *Uniform Sales Law*, *supra* note 14 at 100. *See also* Joseph M. Lookofsky, "The 1980 United Nations Convention on Contracts for the International Sale of Goods," in *International Encyclopedia of Laws* 1, 128 (Blanpain gen. ed., 1993). *Contra, see e.g.*, Enderlein & Maskow, *supra* note 4, at 312.

in those countries where domestic applicable law forbids payment of it.[22] Indeed, the express language of the Convention provides for a general entitlement to interest, and not enforcing it would be against the express text and purpose of Article 78.[23]

Other relevant topics to be considered include compound interest and the meaning of "sums" under Article 78. CISG Article 78 does not expressly deal with the compound interest issue. Although there is controversy also on this issue, it seems, however, that compound interest cannot be claimed.[24] As to the meaning of the word "sums" under Article 78, it seems that the applicable law should define it.[25]

3. Nature of Interest under CISG Article 78

Some authors argue that interest under CISG Article 78 is aimed at fully compensating the aggrieved party for the benefit of the bargain. Accordingly, this view applies Article 74 of the Convention to determine the interest rate. This view, however, results from a misunderstanding of the nature of the interest as defined by Article 78, the express wording of Article 78, and its legislative history. Article 78 draws a clear, distinct line between damages as defined under Article 74 and interest as defined under Article 78.[26] Under Article 78, interest is not meant to fully compensate the creditor for the benefit of the bargain.[27] Therefore, provisions that normally are to be used to calculate damages (full compensation) cannot be used to calculate the interest rate under Article 78.[28] Article 78 expressly excludes that interest at any rate is linked to damages because interest is due even when damages are excluded (a party is entitled to interest "without prejudice to any claim for damages recoverable under article 74").[29] It should also be considered that the interest rate provision belongs to Section III (Interest) and thus is completely separated

[22] Enderlein & Maskow, *supra* note 4, at 312; Franco Ferrari, "Specific Topics of the CISG in the light of Judicial and Scholarly Writing," 15 *J. L. & Com.* 1, 125 (1995); Jelena Vilus, International Sales of Goods: Dubrovnik Lectures 252 (Petar Sarcevic & Paul Volken eds., 1986). As to case law mentioning the issue *see* Austria 15 June 1994 Arbitral Tribunal [Internationales Schiedsgericht der Bundeskammmer der gewerblichen Wirtschaft] Vienna, SCH-4366, *available at* <http://cisgw3.law.pace.edu/cases/940615a3.html>; Austria 15 June 1994 Arbitral Tribunal [Internationales Schiedsgericht der Bundeskammmer der gewerblichen Wirtschaft] Vienna, SCH-4318, *available at* <http://cisgw3.law.pace.edu/cases/940615a4.html>.

[23] For example, there is no language on the interest issue that recognizes and/or tries to reach a compromise among the different legal systems similar to the provisions set forth by Cisg Article 28, according to which, where under domestic law in a similar case specific performance would not be granted, a court is allowed not to grant specific performance.

[24] *See* Eberstein & Bacher, *supra* note 11, at 599; Enderlein & Maskow, *supra* note 4, at 315. *But see* John O. Honnold, Uniform Law for International Sales Under the 1980 International Sale Law 469 (1999). *See also* Icc International Court of Arbitration, 1997, award No. 8864, *available at* <http://cisgw3.law.pace.edu/cases/978644i1.html>: "Compound interest is not awarded. Art. 78 Cisg does not provide a sufficient basis for such a claim, at least not under the circumstances of the present case. Compound interest is not customary in international trade and thus a claim for compound interest could only be derived from Art. 78 Cisg if this Article clearly provided for it. This is not the case." Similarly, *see* Icc International Court of Arbitration 1988, award No. 8908, *available at* <http://cisgw3.law.pace.edu/cases/988908i1.html>. On the compound interest issue, *see also* John Yukio Gotanda, "Compound Interest in International Disputes," *Oxford Univ. Comp. L. Forum* 2 *available at* <http://ouclf.iuscomp.org/articles/gotanda.shtml>.

[25] *See* Nicholas, *supra* note 14, at 571.

[26] *See* Icc International Court of Arbitration, 1992, award No. 7585, *available at* <http://cisgw3.law.pace.edu/cases/927585i1.html> where the Court states, "Article 78 . . . provides that the creditor is entitled to interest 'without prejudice to any claim for damages.' The purpose of this provision is to make a distinction between interest and damages and to give compensation for the financial loss due to the mere fact that delay in payment has a financial cost"; *see also* Italy 29 December 1999 District Court [Tribunale] Pavia, *available at* <http://cisgw3.law.pace.edu/cases/991229i3.html>.

[27] Id. *But see* Icc International Court of Arbitration, 1997, award No. 8864, *available at* <http://cisgw3.law.pace.edu/cases/978644i1.html>.

[28] Behr, *supra* note 15, at 296.

[29] *Id.*

from the section dealing with damages (Section II,. Damages).[30] Finally, the legislative history of Article 78 tells us that the choice of keeping the two concepts (interest as opposed to damages) distinct and separate was an informed decision.

Failure to consider the difference between the two concepts stems from a failure to understand the core function of interest as defined by Article 78. Interest under Article 78 is based on the general principle that the party who benefited from property belonging to another must remunerate the latter. This remuneration is based on the assumption that money naturally produces interest. It should also be noted that interest as described under Article 78 is different from interest under Article 84(1). Interest under Article 84(1) is provided to compensate the creditor for the fruits (interest) of not having benefited from money owed by the debtor due to the avoidance of the contract. In other words, interest under Article 78 is due because money naturally produces interest and therefore is owed automatically. Interest under Article 84(1) is based on the same principle (money produces fruits), but is owed only when, as a result of the avoidance of the contract, the price must be refunded.

Moreover, it must be emphasized that, although the scope and requirements of Articles 78 and 74 are different, as expressly stated by the courts,[31] a party may be able to recover under both provisions. Pursuant to Article 78, entitlement to interest is without prejudice to any claim for damages recoverable under Article 74. Entitlement to interest is an automatic consequence of a failure to pay a sum at the due date. Entitlement to damages under Article 74, on the other hand, requires a party to meet and prove all of the requirements set forth by Article 74.[32]

III. WHETHER PECL ARTICLE 9:508(1) MAY BE OF ASSISTANCE IN THE INTERPRETATION OF CISG ARTICLE 78

1. PECL Article 9:508(1)

PECL Article 9:508(1) simply states that "[i]f a payment of a sum is delayed, the aggrieved party is entitled to interest on that sum."[33] Interest is owed from the date payment is due.[34] Moreover, interest is owed regardless of whether or not payment may be excused under Article 8:108.[35] The aggrieved party is entitled to it regardless of whether it has taken reasonable steps to mitigate its loss. The rate of interest is fixed by making reference to the average commercial bank short-term lending rate applicable to prime borrowers prevailing for the contractual currency of payment[36] at the place of payment.[37] It should be noted that a right to interest arises only on primary contractual obligations to pay; the provision does not cover interest on secondary monetary obligations, such as damages or

[30] *See* Nicholas, *supra* note 14 at 570; Schlechtriem, *Uniform Sales Law, supra* note 14, at 100.

[31] *See, e.g.*, Germany 14 January 1994 Provincial Court of Appeal [Oberlandesgericht] Düsseldorf, Germany, *available at* <http://cisgw3.law.pace.edu/cases/940114g1.html>; ICC International Court of Arbitration, 1997, award No. 8962, *available at* <http://cisgw3.law.pace.edu/cases/978962i1.html>; Belgium 17 June 1998 District Court [Rechtbank van Koophandel] Hasselt, *available at* <http://cisgw3.law.pace.edu/cases/980617b1.html>; Switzerland 28 October 1998 Supreme Court [Schweizerisches Bundesgericht], *available at* <http://cisgw3.law.pace.edu/cases/981028s1.html>.

[32] *See, e.g.*, Germany 9 May 2000 District Court [Landgericht] Darmstadt, *available at* <http://cisgw3.law.pace.edu/cases/000509g1.html>.

[33] *See* PECL Article 9:508 *available at* <http://www.cisg.law.pace.edu/cisg/text/textef.html#a9508>.

[34] *See* PECL Article 7:102 *available at* <http://www.cisg.law.pace.edu/cisg/text/textef.html#a7102>.

[35] *See* PECL Article 8:108 *available at* <http://www.cisg.law.pace.edu/cisg/text/textef.html#a8108>.

[36] *See* PECL Article 7:108 *available at* <http://www.cisg.law.pace.edu/cisg/text/textef.html#a7108> for the definition of "Currency of Payment" under the PECL.

[37] *See* PECL Article 7:101 *available at* <http://www.cisg.law.pace.edu/cisg/text/textef.html#a7101> for the definition of "Place of Performance" under the PECL.

interest. Finally, interest is not a species of ordinary damages. Thus, the general rules on damages do not apply.

2. PECL Article 9:508 and its Relevance in Determining the Operation of CISG Article 78

PECL Article 9:508 has limited relevance as a tool for construing the meaning of CISG Article 78, at least with regard to the method of calculating the interest rate. However, PECL 9:508 is very useful in understanding the nature of the interest and its relationship to damage provisions.

The main difference between the two Articles relates to the method of computing interest. Whereas CISG Article 78 expressly does not deal with this issue, PECL Article 9:508, on the other hand, sets forth a precise method for computing interest. Although a method like the one set by PECL may be useful and may encourage uniformity, it still cannot be used under the CISG. The CISG does not establish a method because state delegations could not reach any agreement on the issue. This means that there was not a uniform and commonly accepted rate of interest, even in terms of general principles, that could be applied in all transactions falling within the scope of the Convention. This is still true today as there is no agreement among commentators either, even though the majority of the courts clearly prefer the private international law solution. Allowing courts to use the PECL method, as well as any other method,[38] will be against the spirit of the Convention and the will of the majority of the Member States.[39] It must be acknowledged that proposals to include express reference to the domestic rules of private international law (within Article 78) and to delete any provision making reference to interest were both rejected by the CISG drafters.[40] Some commentators have drawn the conclusion that the "drafters saw the question at issue not outside the scope of the Convention but rather wanted it to be governed by Article 7(2)."[41] I believe that, had the drafters wanted to have the issue (the actual rate, not the entitlement to interest) dealt with in the Convention, there was no better place to do it (*Ubi lex voluit. Dixit. Ubi noluit. Tacuit.*). Thus, lacking any CISG general principle as well as any indication by the very same CISG, one can only conclude that the matter must be deferred to the domestic

[38] *See* ICC International Court of Arbitration, 1993, award No. 6653, *available at* <http://cisgw3.law.pace.edu/cases/936653i1.html>.

[39] *See Official Records of the United Nations Conference on Contracts for the International Sale of Goods*, Vienna, March 10 – April 11, 1980 (United Nations publications, Sales No. E.81.IV.3), pp. 137–138. *See* Eberstein & Bacher, *supra* note 11, at 596, stating "[i]f the Conference was unable to solve that task [determining an uniform interest rate], *any solutions proposed by legal writers and courts will need to be treated with particular caution* [emphasis added]." *See* Eberstein & Bacher, *supra* note 11 at 596; Behr, *supra* note 15, at 290.

[40] The delegations rejected the proposal seeking to exclude any rule on interest because they believed that it would leave the question totally governed by the applicable domestic law, including the question whether damages include interest, which was one of the major differences among the delegations. The drafters, therefore, not being able to reach any agreement, were perfectly aware that the matter would be regulated under the applicable domestic law, with one limitation to its application: interest is not a type of damages and may be awarded in addition to any damages due under Article 78.

[41] *See* Christian Thiele, "Interest on Damages and Rate of Interest under Article 78 of the U.N. Convention on Contracts for the International Sale of Goods," 2 *Vindobona J. Int'l. Com. L. & Arbitration* 3–35 (1998). "The goal of the delegations that believed that a special interest provision was necessary was precisely to prevent interest from being considered as damages and thereby to maintain the obligation to pay interest in the case of exemptions under Article 79." Schlechtriem, *Uniform Sales Law*, *supra* note 14, at 99. By no means, therefore, should one draw the further conclusion that the drafters wanted to have the Convention also governing the matter of the method of calculating the interest rate. Again, through the limited wording of Article 78, the delegations, being aware that no agreement, even on the general principles, was reachable, merely wanted to make clear that the aggrieved party does have a right to interest, which is owed regardless of any damage claim. *See* Summary Records of the Plenary Meetings, 11th Plenary Meeting, April 10, 1980, *available at* <http://cisgw3.law.pace.edu/cisg/firstcommittee/Meeting37.html>.

rule of private international law. Actually, resorting to private international law is not only admissible, but expressly required by Article 7(2).[42] Moreover, those courts and authors who believe that the matter is outside the CISG also prefer the private international law solution. In fact, as worldwide case law indicates, courts do not apply outright their own interest rates, but very likely, will rely on their own rules of private international law to determine the rate. Therefore, whether the matter is within the CISG or not, once a court concludes that the general principles of the Convention do not give an answer on the interest issue (which is what normally happens),[43] the matter would be in any event governed by the domestic rule of private international law. Thus, rules of private international law, although not expressly indicated as the applicable method under Article 78, nonetheless will be applied ex Article 7(2), if a court concludes that the interest issue is within the scope of the CISG.[44] Moreover, courts have shown that they would very likely reach the very same conclusion (i.e., private international law solution) even when they believe that the interest issue is not within the CISG.[45]

In light of the relevant case law, it seems correct to conclude that the interest rate is not determined by the Convention and that courts normally determine it according to their own rules of private international law.[46] Given that (i) the drafters deliberately omitted any indication on how the interest rate should be determined, (ii) there are not general principles that can be of guidance in determining the applicable rate, and (iii) whether the matter is governed or not by the CISG, courts have applied Article 78 almost uniformly as though it requires reliance on the domestic rules of private international law,[47] it is clear that any other method is not appropriate.

Allowing courts to apply any *ad hoc* and *ex post* method is a clear violation of the Convention. Thus, the PECL formula and any other formula, although they state clear methods for calculating the interest rate in a way that may be acceptable in many countries, are not of any support in the construction of the current text of Article 78 of the CISG. The PECL formula may, however, be a very good starting point in a *de jure condendum* analysis when a new Article 78 is drafted, if an interest rate method will ever be embodied in the text of an international convention. On the other hand, PECL Article 9:509, as construed, gives a definition of the nature of interest similar to the definition herein contended. The commentary to PECL Article 9:509 clearly states that interest is *not* a type of damage *and that it cannot be determined by resorting to the rules for calculating damage*.[48] Therefore, under both CISG and PECL, interest is meant to remunerate one party for having conferred a benefit to another; it does not have a compensative goal (in other words, it is not a species of ordinary damages), and general rules on damages do not apply. In fact, the aggrieved party is entitled to it regardless of whether it has taken reasonable steps to mitigate its loss.

[42] Michael Joachim Bonell, COMMENTARY ON THE INTERNATIONAL SALES LAW 74 (Massimo C. Bianca & Michael Joachim Bonell eds., 1987).

[43] *See, e.g.*, Italy 31 March 2004 District Court [Tribunale] Padova, *available at* <http://cisgw3.law.pace.edu/cases/040331i3.html>.

[44] Franco Ferrari, "Tasso degli interessi ed applicazione uniforme della Convenzione di Vienna sui contratti di vendita internazionale," *Rivista di Diritto Civile* II 277 (1995). *See also* Germany 12 May 1995 Petty District Court [Amtsgericht] Alsfeld, *available at* <http://cisgw3.law.pace.edu/cases/950512g1.html>.

[45] *See* Italy 31 March 2004 District Court [Tribunale] Padova, *available at* <http://cisgw3.law.pace.edu/cases/040331i3.html> citing other several cases holding the same.

[46] *Id.*

[47] Switzerland September 9 1993 Commercial Court [Handelsgericht] Zürich, HG 930138, *available at* <http://cisgw3.law.pace.edu/cases/930909s1.html>.

[48] *See* Pace Law School Institute of International Commercial Law, "Guide to CISG Article 78 & 84(1), Comment and Notes on PECL 9:508," *available at* <http://cisgw3.law.pace.edu/cisg/text/peclcomp78.html>.

Similar to CISG Article 78, PECL Article 9:508 (2), provides that "[t]he aggrieved party may in addition recover damages for any further loss so far as these are recoverable under this Section." Therefore, both CISG Article 78 and PECL Article 9:508 allow the damaged party to recover additional damages as long as the requirements for the recovery of damages (CISG Article 74) are met.

IV. CISG ARTICLE 84[49]

The last provision of Section V (Effects of Avoidance) of Article 84 introduces complementary obligations with respect to the obligations of each party to return what they received under a contract once the contract has been avoided. Paragraph (1) of Article 84 introduces the principle that a party who is required to refund the price or the part received as a result of the avoidance of the contract must pay interest on the sum received from the date of its payment.[50] Article 84 applies independently of the applicable rules on damages.[51] However, recovery of interest can be barred if it is claimed cumulatively with damages.[52] It should be noted that Article 84(1) applies only to restitution and cannot be used in any other case.[53] The obligation to pay interest is automatic[54] because it is assumed that the seller has benefited from being in possession of the price during this period. Which party gave rise to the avoidance of the contract is irrelevant.[55] Interest is due from the date the seller received payment[56] and runs until the request for restitution for the price lapses.[57] No mention is made as to how to calculate interest. The Secretariat Commentary states that "[s]ince the obligation to pay interest partakes of the seller's obligation to make restitution and not of the buyer's right to claim damages, the right

[49] *See* Pace Law School Institute of International Commercial Law, "Guide to CISG Article 84," for a record of the legislative history of CISG Article 84, *available at* <http://cisgw3.law.pace.edu/cisg/text/e-text-84.html-leg>.

[50] *See* Hans G. Leser, "Annotations 1–28 on Article 84," *in* COMMENTARY ON THE UN CONVENTION ON THE INTERNATIONAL SALE OF GOODS 654, 659 (Peter Schlechtriem ed., 1998); Enderlein & Maskow, *supra* note 4, at 314, according to whom "[t]he same rule should apply to the refunding of reduced price under Article 50." *See* ICC International Court of Arbitration, 1999, award No. 9978, *available at* <http://cisgw3.law.pace.edu/cases/999978i1.html>; Germany 29 December 1998 Arbitral Tribunal [Schiedsgericht Hamburger Freundschaftliche Arbitrage] Hamburg, December 29, 1998, *available at* <http://cisgw3.law.pace.edu/cases/981229g1.html>.

[51] *See* Leser, *supra* note 51, at 657 stating "[t]he inclusion of interest within the scope of restitution . . . emphasizes the independent nature of restitution when compared with damages [footnote omitted]. Interest due under Article 84(1) should not be regarded as damages but as equalization of benefits, as the legislative history makes clear. [footnote omitted]." Further Leser adds "[i]t follows from the independent nature of the right to interest under Article 84(1) that the seller cannot claim exemption under Article 79 in respect of that interest [footnote omitted] as may also be inferred from Article 79(5) and the fact that entitlement to interest under article 78 is stated to be without prejudice to claims for damages. [footnote omitted]." *Id.* at 658.

[52] *Id.* at 655–656. *See also* Enderlein & Maskow, *supra* note 4, at 348, note 1; Schlechtriem, *Uniform Sales Law*, *supra* note 14, at 100.

[53] *See* Leser, *supra* note 51, at 656.

[54] ICC International Court of Arbitration, 1993, award No. 6653, *available at* <http://cisgw3.law.pace.edu/cases/936653i1.html>: Interest is due regardless of any formal request.

[55] *See* Commentary on the Draft Convention on Contracts for the International Sale of Goods, prepared by the Secretariat, U.N. Document A/CONF.97/5, Article 69 (*draft counterpart of* CISG *Article 84*), *available at* Pace Law School Institute of International Commercial Law, "Guide to CISG Article 84" <http://cisgw3.law.pace.edu/cisg/text/secomm/secomm-84.html> [hereinafter *Secretariat Commentary*]. *See also* Leser, *supra* note 51; Enderlein & Maskow, *supra* note 4 at 349.

[56] *See* Enderlein & Maskow, *supra* note 4, at 349. *See also* ICC International Court of Arbitration, 1993, award No. 6653, *available at* <http://cisgw3.law.pace.edu/cases/936653i1.html> *But see* Italy 24 November 1989 Court of First Instance [Pretura] Parma, sez. di Fidenza, *available at* <http://cisgw3.law.pace.edu/cases/891124i3.html>. In this case the court, contrary to what is provided by article 84(1), held that interest was payable from the date of avoidance of the contract.

[57] *See* Enderlein & Maskow, *supra* note 4, at 349.

of interest payable would be based on that current at the seller's place of business."[58] However, similarly to what happens with regard to CISG Article 78, there are different views on the issue. Although several methods have been applied,[59] courts and arbitral tribunals clearly agree that "[t]he rate of the interest is not governed by the Convention, and must therefore be determined by internal law resulting from the application of the pertinent rules of conflict of laws."[60] The same comments made under Article 78 may be repeated herein,[61] which means that interest is due as of the date of payment of the sum and must be determined by the domestic law applicable pursuant to the rules of private international law. Any other method, including the PECL method, may not be used as the drafters expressly excluded the embodiment of any method in the Convention except for the one determined in "conformity with the law applicable by virtue of the rules of private international law" (CISG Art. 7(2)).[62]

[58] *See also* Leser, *supra* note 51, at 659 note 45a; Enderlein & Maskow, *supra* note 4, at 349. *See* Switzerland 5 February 1997 Commercial Court [Handelsgericht des Kantons] Zürich, *available at* <http://cisgw3.law.pace.edu/cases/970205s1.html>. However, this approach is considered to be "debatable", *see* Denis Tallon, COMMENTARY ON THE INTERNATIONAL SALES LAW 612 (Massimo C. Bianca & Michael Joachim Bonell eds., 1987), stating "[t]he determination of the applicable rate is, in effect, much more complex"; Honnold, *supra* note 25.

[59] Among them, *see*, *e.g.*, ICC International Court of Arbitration, 1993, award No. 6653, *available at* <http://cisgw3.law.pace.edu/cases/936653i1.html>: "[I]t appears logical to retain a percentage currently applied between merchants and that conforms with the currency in which the settlement was made and in which the payment must be made. This solution, which is in the eyes of the Arbitral Tribunal the most logical one from the economic point of view, leads to retaining the percentage that operators of international commerce apply to settlements made in Eurodollar, i.e., the one-year percentage of LIBOR (London Inter-Bank Offered Rate), published every day in the Wall Street Journal". *But see* France 6 April 1995 Appeal Court [Cour d'appel] Paris, *available at* <http://cisgw3.law.pace.edu/cases/950406f1.html>: The French appellate court reversed that part of that arbitral award "requiring the seller to pay interest at the LIBOR rate, on the grounds that the Convention is silent on the way in which the rate of interest is be determined, and that the decision to apply the LIBOR rate had been taken by the arbitrators without the parties being given the possibility to make their defense on that point, whereas the international trade usage invoked by the buyer does not provide rules to determine the applicable rate"; Germany 22 August 2002 District Court [Landgericht] Freiburg, *available at* <http://cisgw3.law.pace.edu/cases/020822g1.html>: "The claim for interest on the purchase price is justified under Art. 84(1) CISG; the claim for interest on damages is justified under Art. 78 CISG. As the CISG does not provide for an interest rate, it is appropriate to rely on § 288 I 2 BGB because this is the rule more favorable to the seller in comparison to corresponding regulations in Italian law, which grant higher interest rates"; ICC International Court of Arbitration, 1992, award No. 7585, *available at* <http://cisgw3.law.pace.edu/cases/927585i1.html>: Pursuant to the law of the currency to be used.

[60] *See* Switzerland 15 January 1998 Appeal Court [Tribunale d'Appello] Lugano, *available at* <http://cisgw3.law.pace.edu/cases/980115s1.html>. *See, e.g.*, Spain 12 February 2002 Appeal Court [Audiencia Provincial] Barcelona, *available at* <http://cisgw3.law.pace.edu/cases/020212s4.html>; ICC International Court of Arbitration, 1999, award No. 9978, *available at* <http://cisgw3.law.pace.edu/cases/999978i1.html>; Germany 24 May 1995 Provincial Court of Appeal [Oberlandesgericht] Celle, *available at* <http://cisgw3.law.pace.edu/cases/950524g1.html>. Germany 18 January 1994 Provincial Court of Appeal [Oberlandesgericht] Frankfurt am Main, *available at* <http://cisgw3.law.pace.edu/cases/940118g1.html>.

[61] *See* Germany 5 April 1995 District Court [Landgericht] Landshut, *available at* <http://cisgw3.law.pace.edu/cases/950405g1>: "The rate of interest is not regulated by Art. 84 CISG. Also, in Art. 78 CISG no mention is made of the rate of interest. According to the prevailing opinion, the rate of interest within the scope of Art. 78 CISG is governed by the applicable national law, which is determined by the rules of private international law. This notion is also applicable to Art. 84 CISG."

[62] *See* Germany 18 January 1994 Provincial Court of Appeal [Oberlandesgericht] Frankfurt am Main, *available at* <http://cisgw3.law.pace.edu/cases/940118g1.html>: "In this case . . . the court has to decide according to the prevailing legal opinion. Since the amount of interest intentionally is not prescribed in the Convention, the answer can only be taken from the rules of international private law. Absent any point of reference, no principle can be derived from the Convention such as saying that the domicile of the debtor would be decisive"; France 6 April 1995 Appeal Court [Cour d'appel] Paris, *available at* <http://cisgw3.law.pace.edu/cases/950406f1.html>; ICC International Court of Arbitration, 1994, award No. 7660, *available at* <http://cisgw3.law.pace.edu/cases/947660i1.html>.

V. CONCLUSIONS

The PECL cannot be used in construing CISG Article 78 to determine the proper rate of interest. The PECL counterpart provisions, however, are quite useful in clarifying the nature of interest ant its relationship to the damage provisions. Under both CISG and PECL, interest cannot be calculated based on damage provisions. Pursuant to both PECL Article 9:508(2) and CISG Article 78, the recovery of interest does not preclude a recovery for damages. The recovery of damages is subject to the requirements set forth by the damage provisions, respectively, Section V of Chapter 9 of the PECL and Article 74 of the CISG.

Exemption and hardship: Remarks on the manner in which the Principles of European Contract Law (Articles 6:111 and 8:108) may be used to interpret or supplement CISG Article 79

Dionysios Flambouras

I. INTRODUCTION TO THE CONCEPT OF "EXEMPTION" IN ARTICLE 79 CISG

Different legal concepts exist in all legal systems dealing with the problem of changed circumstances and excusing a party from performance of its obligations when a contract has become unexpectedly onerous or impossible to perform. Some systems only accept a narrow range of excuses; others are more generous (e.g., the concepts of *imprévision* or hardship, *force majeure*, or *Wegfall der Geschäftsgrundlage*).[1]

The rules dealing with situations of changed or supervening contractual circumstances are based on the two basic concepts of hardship and *force majeure* – they constitute exceptions to the cardinal canon of *pacta sunt servanda* and ameliorate its strictness.

[1] See Albert H. Kritzer, "International Contract Manual – Guide to Practical Applications of the United Nations Convention on Contracts for the International Sale of Goods – Detailed Analysis" (1994) 623. For an excellent discussion of the two competing attitudes on whether courts should intervene to provide relief or require an adjustment in the obligation of performance of a contract when an unforeseen frustrating event occurs, *see* Sarah Howard Jenkins, "Exemption for Nonperformance: UCC, CISG, UNIDROIT Principles – A Comparative Assessment," 72 *Tul. L. Rev.* (1998) 2015–2030; also available at <http://cisgw3.law.pace.edu/cisg/biblio/jenkins.html>.

For an interesting comparison *see* also Dionysios Flambouras, "The Doctrine of Impossibility of Performance and *Clausula Rebus Sic Standibus* in the 1980 Convention on Contracts for the International Sale of Goods and the Principles of European Contract Law – A Comparative Analysis," 13 *Pace Int'l. L. Rev.* (Fall 2001) 261–293.

Hardship refers to the performance of the disadvantaged party having become much more burdensome, but not impossible, whereas *force majeure* refers to the performance of one party's obligations that has become impossible, even on a temporary basis.[2]

II. IS *HARDSHIP* COVERED UNDER ARTICLE 79 CISG?

The CISG deals with the issue of changed circumstances on an international level by avoiding any reference to existing domestic concepts.

The most difficult question concerning the application of Article 79 CISG is whether situations of hardship (i.e., where the performance by one of the parties has become much more onerous and difficult – but not impossible – usually in financial terms) are covered in the embedded exemption.[3]

The solution to this issue cannot come by direct reference to domestic legal systems[4] that differ greatly from each other in regard to rules of hardship or *imprévision*,[5] as this would produce divergent results in the interpretation and application of the Convention. This would contravene the uniformity mandate of Article 7(1) CISG.

In addition, no reference to domestic laws can be attempted under the gap-filling operation of Article 7(2), as the legislative history of Article 79 excludes the possibility of the existence of a relevant gap.[6]

As the term *impediment* is not defined, an interesting question is whether the *hardship* provisions in Articles 6:111 (Change of Circumstances) and 8:108 (Excuse due to an impediment) of the Principles of European Contract Law can be invoked to expand the meaning of *impediment* found in the CISG to include cases of economic or commercial hardship.[7]

III. THE LEGISLATIVE HISTORY OF ARTICLE 79 CISG

Article 79 CISG uses the term "impediment" to describe the types of event beyond the contracting party's control that will be acceptable as an excuse for non-performance of its obligations under the contract.

[2] For a discussion of these two concepts and a comparative analysis of their function in the CISG and the UNIDROIT Principles, *see* J. Rimke, "Force Majeure and Hardship: Application in International Trade Practice with Specific Regard to the CISG and the UNIDROIT Principles of International Commercial Contracts," *Pace Review of the Convention on Contracts for the International Sale of Goods*, Kluwer (1999–2000) 197–243; also available at <http://cisgw3.law.pace.edu/cisg/biblio/rimke.html>.

[3] In other words, the difficulty arises in the cases where it is hard to distinguish between "absolute impossibility" and "economic impossibility" ("rendering performance extremely onerous"; *see* Tallon in C. M. Bianca & M. J. Bonell (eds), *Commentary on the International Sales Law – The 1980 Vienna Convention* (1987) § 2.6.4 p. 581–582.

[4] "The Convention's autonomy, illustrated by the lack of reference to accepted wording and concepts of domestic laws (*force majeure*, frustration, impracticability, *Wegfall der Geschäftsgrundlage*), renders the interpretation of Article 79 extremely difficult because one cannot resort to these laws as a guide." *See* Fritz Enderlin & Dietrich Maskow, *United Nations Convention on Contracts for the International Sale of Goods*, (1992), at 320.

[5] *See* Stoll, in *Commentary on the UN Convention on the International Sale of Goods* (Peter Schlechtriem ed., 1998), at 618.

[6] The legislative history of the Convention reveals that the problem of hardship was considered during the drafting process of Article 79, but a provision specifically dealing with it has been deliberately omitted from the CISG (i.e., no gap *praeter legem* exists). *See* Rimke, *op. cit.*, at 220; *see* also John O. Honnold, *Documentary History of the Uniform Law for International Sales* (1989), at 349–350.

[7] Cf. J. Ziegel, "Comparative Editorial Remarks on Article 79 CISG and its UNIDROIT Principles Counterparts", available at <http://cisgw3.law.pace.edu/cisg/principles/uni79.html>, where the author discusses the same question in terms of Article 79 CISG and the comparable provisions in the UNIDROIT Principles of International Commercial Contracts.

The drafting history of the Convention is a legitimate and valuable aid in the interpretation of the Convention's provisions. It reveals that Article 79 CISG is indeed a stricter version of its predecessor, Article 74 ULIS, which had been criticized for excusing non-performance too readily, such as where performance merely became more difficult.[8]

The legislative history of Article 79 also indicates that a party cannot rely on the exemption merely on the ground that performance has become unforeseeably more difficult or unprofitable.[9]

The UNCITRAL debates show that the CISG drafters were opposed to allowing commercial or economic hardship as an excuse for non-performance and that this was the reason for adopting the requirement of an *impediment* as a pre-condition for relief in place of the more liberal ULIS test of a change of circumstances.[10]

It is clear in the *travaux préparatoires* that the purpose of Article 79 CISG is to set definite limits on the promisor's liability for breach of contract and that the word "impediment" represents a unitary conception of exemption from liability in contracts governed by the Convention, as opposed to other theories of *imprévision* or *hardship* that are based on "changed circumstances."[11]

IV. THE LEGAL EFFECT OF THE EXEMPTION IN CISG AND ISSUES OF SPECIFIC PERFORMANCE

The legal effect of the exemption in the Convention is stated in Art. 79(5) CISG.[12] Although the wording of Article 79(5) would allow a claim for performance in situations where obligations are physically impossible to fulfill, it is thought that the general belief expressed at the Vienna Conference that judgment for a physically impossible performance would neither be sought nor obtained should lead to a reasonable limitation of Article 79(5) CISG.[13]

The term "impediment" was used in the drafting of the Convention to denote an external force that objectively interferes with performance of the contract and renders

[8] For instance, the term "circumstances" in Article 74 ULIS was replaced by the term "impediment" in Article 79 CISG, thus narrowing the exemption and providing an objective criterion. See John Honnold, *Uniform Law for the International Sales under the 1980 United Nations Convention* (3rd ed., 1999) §§426–427. *See* also, generally, Rimke, *op. cit.*, at 222.

Cf. Stoll, *op. cit.*, at 603, where it is noted that the deletion of the word "only" from the draft Article 79(3) – previously limiting the exemption "only" for the period during which the impediment existed – indicates that when the impediment ceases to exist, an exemption for the non-performing party on account of a change in circumstances cannot be ruled out entirely.

[9] *See* also Rimke, *op. cit.*, at 223. However, note that under a literal interpretation of the text, a very serious change in circumstances could arguably qualify as an "impediment" for the purposes of Article 79 CISG. *See* generally Honnold (1999); Enderlein & Maskow, *United Nations Convention on Contracts for the International Sale of Goods* (1992), at 325.

"The borderline between impracticability and a reasonably insurmountable impediment is [...] uncertain." *See* Denis Tallon, in *Commentary on the International Sales Law – The 1980 Vienna Sales Convention*, C. M. Bianca & M. J. Bonnell eds. (1987), at 576, where the author concludes that the standard demanded in Article 79 CISG is more flexible than that of traditional *force majeure*, but stricter than *frustration* or *hardship*.

[10] *See* Honnold (1999), §§ 432.1–432.2.

[11] *See* J. Honnold, *Documentary History of the Uniform Law for International Sales* (1989)185, 252.

[12] "Paragraph (5) restrains the effects of the exemption to one remedy alone and reserves to the party who did not receive the agreed performance all of its remedies except damages. These remedies include the right to reduce price (Article 50), the right to compel performance (Articles 46 and 62), the right to avoid the contract (Articles 49 and 64) and the right to collect interest as separate from damages (Article 78)"; *see* Rimke, *op. cit.*, at 217. *See* also text contained in footnote 22, *infra*, that refers to the Secretariat Commentary to the Draft Convention 1978.

[13] *See* Albert H. Kritzer, "International Contract Manual – Guide to Practical Applications of the United Nations Convention on Contracts for the International Sale of Goods – Detailed Analysis" (1994) 642. *Cf.* Article 28 CISG (limiting orders of specific performance) and Article 8.109 PECL (clause limiting or excluding remedies for non-performance).

performance impossible.[14] The creditor of the obligation in question may still require specific performance of the obligation under Article 79(5) CISG. This solution, however, may not appear satisfactory in the situations where performance has been rendered impossible; for example, the subject matter of the performance no longer exists (the goods have perished) or the performance would be excessively onerous or expensive (e.g., the need for an expensive salvage operation or subsequent illegality).[15]

One suggested approach to the problem in such extreme situations is to admit a "limit of sacrifice" beyond which the promisor of the obligation could not reasonably be expected to perform his obligation.[16]

In a leading case on Article 79 CISG, the German Supreme Court identified the existing debate among scholars as to whether "CISG Art. 79 encompasses all conceivable cases and forms of non-performance of contractual obligations creating a liability and is not limited to certain types of contractual violations and, therefore, includes the delivery of goods not in conformity with the contract because of their defectiveness" or "whether a seller who has delivered defective goods cannot rely on Art. 79 CISG at all."[17]

[14] *See* Honnold (1999), at § 427. The impediment must actually prevent performance, *see id.* § 432.1. *Cf.* Some other commentators have noted that Article 79 embodies the CISG's provisions for frustration of purpose and impossibility; *see, e.g.*, Henry D. Gabriel, "A Primer on the United Nations Convention on the International Sale of Goods: From the Perspective of the Uniform Commercial Code," 7 *Ind. Int'l. & Comp. L. Rev.* 279, 280 (1997).

See also, e.g., Italy 14 January 1993, District Court Monza, *Nuova Fucinati v. Fondmetall International*, CLOUT case no. 54, also available at <http://cisgw3.law.pace.edu/cases/930114i3.html>. In that case, an Italian court held that although the Convention did not apply to the contract, even if Art. 79 CISG had applied, nonetheless the court would have rejected the seller's request for dissolution on the basis of supervening excessive onerousness (caused by a market price increase by 30%) by reading "impediment" to mean "impossible," as per the domestic law (Article 1463 of the Italian Civil Code). In the court's opinion, the seller could not rely on hardship as a ground for avoidance, because the Convention did not contemplate such a remedy in Article 79 or elsewhere in the CISG.

It seems that the Italian court would have dealt with the matter as one that was governed but not expressly settled by the Convention, and it would have resolved the issue by turning to the conflict of law rules of the forum, under Art. 7(2) CISG.

It is arguable that this approach to the interpretation of impediment does not promote uniformity. Similarly, divergent results would be produced by the possible introduction of "hardship" as a general principle of the Convention under Art. 7(2); a possibility that would be contrary to the intention of the drafters and the legislative history of the Convention.

[15] Honnold, *Uniform Law for International Sales* (1999) pp. 493–495 § 435.5. Note that, even though not precluded by Article 79(5) CISG, there can be domestic law restrictions on one's ability to require specific performance under such circumstances by virtue of the statement in Article 28 CISG that "a court is not bound to enter a judgment for specific performance unless the court would do so under its own law in respect of similar contracts of sale not governed by this Convention." *See* related reference to Article 28 in paragraph 9 of note 22 *infra*.

[16] *See* Stoll in Schlechtriem ed., *Commentary*, (1998) §§ 55, 57 p. 622. This approach is advocated mainly by German commentators, who refer to cases of *imprévision* or great difficulty to perform as "economic impossibility" (*wirtschaftliche Unmöglichkeit*) – and suggest that a "limit of sacrifice" (*Opfergrenze*) should be allowed, in the event of an unforeseeable impediment to performance as a result of a material change in economic conditions.

That approach to the problem of change in circumstances bases the exemption on the principle of good faith, as stated in Article 7(1) CISG. Note, however, that this approach has been criticized as hindering uniformity/harmony in the Convention's application; *see* Rimke, *op. cit.*, at 224.

[17] The court did not deem it necessary to resolve this conflict, stating that the specific defect in the goods was not outside the seller's control, and thus, the seller was responsible for the consequences of a delivery of goods not in conformity with the contract. *See* Germany 24 March 1999 *Bundesgerichtshof* [Federal Supreme Court], CLOUT case no. 271, case presentation including English translation available at <http://cisgw3.law.pace.edu/cases/990324g1.html>. Thus, the court left open the question of whether or not Art. 79 CISG can be invoked by a party to excuse the failure to perform "any of its obligations" under the contract, including the delivery of defective goods.

It is arguable that an interpretation based on the plain meaning of the language in Article 79 CISG would suggest that a seller's obligation to deliver goods in conformity with the contract under Art. 35 may also be conceivably excused due to an impediment under Art. 79(1).

V. ARTICLE 8:108 PECL (EXCUSE DUE TO AN IMPEDIMENT)

There is an apparent similarity in the wording of the corresponding PECL provisions to Article 79 CISG.[18] However, the differences in the scope of the two regimes become clear when we consult the PECL commentary. The Comments to the PECL help explain its provisions. The scope of application of Article 8:108 is defined by Comment A to the PECL, which states that "unlike the equivalent Article of CISG [. . .] Article 8:108 has to apply only in cases where an impediment prevents performance."

Comment C expressly states that the circumstances of the impediment are like those "traditionally required for *force majeure*."[19]

VI. ARTICLE 6:111 PECL (CHANGE OF CIRCUMSTANCES)

Although the question whether financial difficulties constitute a ground for exemption was a controversial point of discussion in UNCITRAL during the drafting of the CISG, "in the end, the general view was probably that both physical and economic impossibility could exempt an obligor. [. . .] As a rule, however [. . .] increased procurement and production costs do not constitute exempting impediments."[20]

According to Professor Schlechtriem, "under very narrow conditions – impediment also includes 'unaffordability.' " Schlechtriem explains that "[i]t is imperative, in [his] opinion to treat radically changed circumstances as 'impediments' under Article 79 in exceptional cases in order to avoid the danger that courts will find a gap in the Convention and invoke domestic laws and their widely divergent solutions."[21]

The court also spoke on many other CISG-related issues in the case (issues of validity, international character of the Convention, conformity of the goods, damages, mitigation; *see* A. H. Kritzer, "Editorial Comments" in the online presentation of the court judgment, at <http://cisgw3.law.pace.edu/cases/990324g1.html#ce>).

Regarding Art. 79 case law: *See* presentation of nearly eighty cases on Art. 79, available online at <http://cisgw3.law.pace.edu/cisg/text/anno-art-79.html> [visited: 2 May 2005].

See also UNCITRAL Digest of Art. 79 case law, available at <http://cisgw3.law.pace.edu/cisg/text/anno-art-79.html#ucd>.

For another analysis of Article 79 case law – also Art. 79 doctrine and legislative history – *see* Sonja A. Kruisinga, "(Non-)conformity in the 1980 UN Convention on Contracts for the International Sale of Goods: A Uniform Concept?," *Intersentia* (2004), 123–154.

[18] Compare the wording in CISG Articles 79(1)–(5) with the corresponding provisions in PECL Articles 8.107, 8.108(1)–(3), and 8.109.

[19] See Comment and Notes to PECL Article 8:108, available online at <http://cisgw3.law.pace.edu/cisg/text/peclcomp79.html>.

[20] Peter Schlechtriem, *Uniform Sales Law – The UN-Convention on Contracts for the International Sale of Goods* (Manz, Vienna: 1986), at 102. Also available at <http://cisgw3.law.pace.edu/cisg/biblio/schlechtriem-79.html>.

Also note that a proposal aimed at incorporating an Article in the Convention that allowed a party to "claim an adequate amendment of the contract or its termination" on account of "excessive difficulties" was expressly rejected by UNCITRAL'S Working Group; *see* J. Honnold, *Documentary History of the Uniform Law for International Sales* (1989), at 350.

[21] Schlechtriem (1986), at footnote 422a; *see* also that author's text in footnote 423, *id.*

In contrast to the single paragraph found in the Convention (see Art. 79(1) CISG),[22] the Principles deal with the issue of change of circumstances in a quite thorough way, providing not only a basic statement of principle (see Article 6:111(1) PECL) and the operational parameters of the concept (see Article 6:111 (2) PECL) but also the mechanism for the adaptation or termination of the contract by the court (see Article 6:111(3) PECL).

It is also clear that the PECL provisions follow a different scheme, because they entitle the party whose performance has become "excessively onerous because of a change of circumstances" to request re-negotiation of the contract, with the support of the court and even its intervention if the parties fail to reach agreement. The adaptation of the contract by the judge, however, is not expressly allowed by the CISG and must therefore be regarded as impossible in that context.[23]

VII. CONCLUSIONS

Both the CISG and the PECL contain provisions for exemption for the non-performance of contractual obligations. Article 79 CISG only governs impossibility of performance, and the majority of academic opinion supports that a disturbance that does not fully exclude performance, but makes it considerably more difficult or onerous (e.g., change of circumstances, hardship, economic impossibility, commercial impracticability, etc.) cannot be considered as an impediment (doctrine of *clausula rebus sic standibus*).[24] In contrast to the Convention, which in Article 79 CISG only includes *impediments* that must be equated with actual impossibility, the PECL provide for special rules concerning hardship (Article 6:111 PECL). Although there is some generic similarity in language

[22] Note that the text of the Secretariat Commentary on Article 65 of the 1978 Draft [*draft counterpart of CISG Article 79*], available at <http://cisgw3.law.pace.edu/cisg/text/secomm/secomm-79.html>, provides additional important guidance:

> Comment 8: The effect of Article 65 [draft counterpart of CISG Article 79(1)] in conjunction with Article 65(5) [draft counterpart of CISG Article 79(5)] is to exempt the non-performing party only from liability for damages. All of the other remedies are available to the other party, i.e. demand for performance, reduction of the price or avoidance of the contract. However, if the party who is required to overcome an impediment does so by furnishing a substitute performance, the other party could avoid the contract and thereby reject the substitute performance only if that substitute performance was so deficient in comparison with the performance stipulated in the contract that it constituted a fundamental breach of contract.
>
> Comment 9: Even if the impediment is of such a nature as to render impossible any further performance, the other party retains the right to require that performance under Article 42 or 58 [draft counterpart of CISG Article 46 or 62]. It is a matter of domestic law not governed by this Convention as to whether the failure to perform exempts the non-performing party from paying a sum stipulated in the contract for liquidated damages or as a penalty for non-performance or as to whether a court will order a party to perform in these circumstances and subject him to the sanctions provided in its procedural law for continued non-performance. [Cf. Article 26 [draft counterpart of CISG Article 28] which provides that if, in accordance with the provisions of this Convention, one party is entitled to require performance of an obligation by the other party, a court is not bound to enter any judgment for specific performance unless the court [would] do so under its own law in respect of similar contracts of sale not governed by this Convention].

[23] *See* Denis Tallon, in *Commentary on the International Sales Law – The 1980 Vienna Sales Convention* (C. M. Bianca & M. J. Bonnell eds., 1987), at 592. *See* also Todd Weitzmann, "Validity and Excuse in the U.N. Sales Convention," 16 *J. L. & Com.* (1997) 265–290, also available at <http://cisgw3.law.pace.edu/cisg/biblio/1weitzm.html>. Weitzmann examines some theoretical issues of contract law that flow from the similarities between the effects of excuse and validity provisions (including the academic debate between Honnold and Tallon), as well as the pitfalls created in the application of Article 79 CISG that undercut the development of a uniform excuse principle. The author has captured the essence of the problem when he states, "Two theoretical difficulties with Article 79 emerged [. . .] both of which could undercut the development of a uniform excuse principle. First, Article 79 could be supplanted directly by a country's domestic law of excuse by virtue of a court concluding that excuse is a validity issue, to be decided under domestic law according to Article 4(a). Second, the principle of justice represented by Article 79 could be averted indirectly when a court reads the language of the Convention in light of presuppositions derived from domestic traditions."

[24] *See e.g.*, Tallon, *op .cit.*, at § 3.1, p. 592.

and in the substantive requirements between the Convention and the PECL, both the scope and the rationale, as well as the application of the respective provisions, vary substantially.[25]

[25] For a similar conclusion (in the context of the UNIDROIT Principles this time and their potential to supplement Art. 79 CISG), *cf.* J. Ziegel, "Editorial Remarks on Article 79 CISG and the UNIDROIT Principles," in *The UNIDROIT Principles, CISG and National Law*, Presentation at a seminar on the UNIDROIT Principles at Valencia, Venezuela (6–9 November 1996), reproduced with permission from the author at <http://cisgw3.law.pace.edu/cisg/biblio/ziegel2.html>. *See* also Anja Carlsen, "Can the Hardship Provisions in the UNIDROIT Principles be Applied When the CISG is the Governing Law?" (Pace Essay 1998), available at <http://cisgw3.law.pace.edu/cisg/biblio/carlsen.html> where the author, in a more expansive and thorough discussion of the issues, also concludes that the "hardship" provisions in the UNIDROIT Principles should not be applied in a gap-filling manner when the CISG is the governing law of a contract.

Cf. Tom Southerington, "Impossibility of Performance and Other Excuses in International Trade", available online at <http://cisgw3.law.pace.edu/cisg/biblio/southerington.html>. In the Southerington article, the author points out that under Section 36(1) of the Contracts Act (Finland), which contains rules on validity of contracts, a term of a contract governed by Finnish law (the Sale of Goods Act and the CISG, because Finland is a Contracting State) may be adjusted or set aside if that term "is unconscionable or its application would lead to unconscionability." Under Finnish internal law, a term of the contract or even the entire contract may be adjusted or declared discharged if it is considered to be unconscionable.

There is a concern that the rationale for excluding issues of validity from the realm of the CISG is linked to differences in approach to the issue by the divergent legal traditions. It is the Southerington thesis that, in a contract governed by the CISG, it is possible that a domestic doctrine of hardship may coexist with the UN Sales Convention via Article 4(a) of the CISG (i.e., in circumstances in which there is a domestic validity rule on unconscionability such as the Section 36(1) of the Contracts Act (Finland)). This is arguably an indirect way of removing issues from the sphere of the Convention and resorting to national laws, and as such it undercuts uniformity in the application of the international sales law.

See also footnote text reference to Todd Weitzmann's article, *supra* note 23.

Cf. P. Schlechtriem suggests a possible basis for arguing that the problem of hardship and adjustment of the sales contract is a matter governed by the Convention; see "Transcript of a Workshop on the Sales Convention," 18 *J. L. & Com.* (1999) 191–258, excerpt available at <http://cisgw3.law.pace.edu/cisg/biblio/workshop-79.html>. The Schlechtriem argument refers to the remedy of price reduction under CISG Art. 50 as "a kind of adjustment of the contract to reflect a disturbed balance between performance on one side and obligation on the other side. The defects in the goods, or the non-conformities of the goods, constitute a disturbance of the equilibrium or balance of the exchanged performances." *Id.*, at 237. Schlechtriem's argument for the use of the principle underlying Art. 50 "as a springboard to develop a general rule of adjustment in hardship cases" would entail that the solution comes from within CISG, thus eliminating divergent results in the interpretation and application of the Convention's provisions.

Limitation of remedies due to failure of performance caused by other party: Comparison between the provisions of CISG Article 80 and counterpart provisions of the Principles of European Contract Law

Allison E. Butler

I. General Interpretation and Application in the CISG and PECL: Limitation of Remedies Available
II. "Acts" Constituting Failure of Performance
III. Failure of Performance Wholly or Partially Attributable to the Creditor or Aggrieved Party
IV. Imputed Knowledge and Intention, Negligence, and Bad Faith
V. Conclusion

I. GENERAL INTERPRETATION AND APPLICATION IN THE CISG AND THE PECL: LIMITATION OF REMEDIES AVAILABLE

The content and function of Article 8:101(3) PECL[1] are similar in substance and form to its counterpart provision contained in Article 80 CISG.[2] Both provisions exemplify the prohibition against contradicting one's own behavior – "*venire contra factum proprium*" – thereby incorporating an expression of general principles of good faith and fairness.[3] Both Articles, however, prevent entitlement to remedies if the reason for the non-performance was the result of the act(s) or omission(s) of the party seeking relief. However, Article 8:101(3) PECL provides valuable insight as to the terms, definitions, and applications therein via cross-reference to other PECL Articles,[4] thereby providing a supplemental source for interpreting Article 80 CISG.

II. "ACTS" CONSTITUTING FAILURE OF PERFORMANCE

Under Article 8:101(3) PECL, a cross-reference to Article 1:301 PECL provides that the definition of "act" includes omission. Such acts would include failure to provide information to the other party or giving wrong or incomplete information. This understanding of the term is commonly held true in all European legal systems[5]; however, in Germany, the statutory provision that has been drafted for acts is not automatically applicable to omissions.[6] In contrast, the CISG explicitly provides for acts and omissions. Hence, both provisions provide that a party seeking relief cannot seek relief if the failure to perform was due to the first party's act or omission.[7]

III. FAILURE OF PERFORMANCE WHOLLY OR PARTIALLY ATTRIBUTABLE TO THE CREDITOR OR AGGRIEVED PARTY

There are two applicable Articles in the PECL that address the issue of non-performance – Articles 1:301 and 9:504 PECL. As to the former, a creditor who directly prevents performance or the so-called *mora creditoris* is prevented from seeking a remedy. An illustrative example would provide that if Party A failed to perform due to its failure to give instruction

[1] PECL Article 8:101(3) states, "A party may not resort to any of the remedies set out in Chapter 9 to the extent that its own act caused the other party's non-performance."

[2] CISG Article 80 states, "A party may not rely on a failure of the other party to perform, to the extent that such failure was caused by the first party's act or omission." Notably, this article was based on a proposal by the German Democratic Republic and was unanimously adopted and included in the Convention (O.R., 386 fol, 135, fol) "out of an abundance of caution." *See* Jacob S. Ziegel and Claude Samson, "Report to the Uniform Law Conference of Canada on Convention on Contracts for the International Sale of Goods" (July 1981), available at <http://cisgw3.law.pace.edu/cisg/wais/db/articles/english2.html>.

[3] *See, e.g.*, Germany 25 November 1998 Supreme Court, translation and link to original text available at <http://cisgw3.law.pace.edu/cases/981125g1.html> (acknowledging the principles of good faith apply to Article. 80 CISG), *but see*, Commentary by Fritz Enderlein & Dietrich Maskow, excerpt from *International Sales Law: United Nations Convention on Contracts for the International Sale of Goods*, Convention on the Limitation Period in the International Sale of Goods, Oceana Publications, 1992, also available at <http://cisgw3.law.pace.edu/cisg/biblio/enderlein-art80.html>, stating that "Article 42, paragraph 2; subpara. (b) provides for a concrete manifestation of the principle of Article 80. This special norm existed before Article 80 was drafted and continues in existence, although it is consumed by the latter."

[4] *See* generally, PECL Article 1:301(1) Meaning of Terms; PECL 1:305 Imputed Knowledge and Intentions; and PECL Article 9:504 Loss Attributable to Aggrieved Party.

[5] *See, e.g.*, Austria, ABGB § 861 sent. 1; Greece, Simantiras No. 555.

[6] *See, e.g.*, BHG § 241, *but see* RB 31 March 1909, RGZ 70, 234 (241).

[7] Germany 1 July 2002 Appellate Court München, translation and link to original text available at <http://cisgw3.law.pace.edu/cases/020701gl.html>; Germany, 9 July 1992, District Court Düsseldorf, available at <http://cisg3.law.pace.edu/cases/920709g1.html>; Ukraine 21 June 2002 Tribunal of International Commercial Arbitration, Ukrainian Chamber of Commerce & Trade, translation available at <http://cisgw3.law.pace.edu/cases/020621u5.html>.

within a stipulated time to Party B, which prevented Party B from performing, then Party B would have a remedy against Party A. However, Party A would have no remedy against Party B. If the facts revealed that A's non-performance was due to a *force majeure* or unforeseen event, then A is not liable for damages for its failure to instruct and B has no remedies in damages against A. In other cases, where there is also a non-performance by the debtor, the creditor may exercise the remedies for non-performance to a limited extent. However, when the loss is caused by both parties, a limitation in the whole range of remedies is warranted as to the creditor.

In most of the European systems, the rules apply where the party who has prevented performance is the non-performing party against whom the remedies may be exercised.[8] This is set forth in Article 9:504 PECL, which embodies the principle that an aggrieved party should not recover damages to the extent that its loss is caused by its own unreasonable behavior. This concept embraces three distinct situations[9] due in part to the common law system's legal concept of "contributory negligence" and "failure to mitigate." Most continental European legal systems do not distinguish between the concepts; however, a similar result is achieved by using concepts such as causation.

Under the CISG, causation is not explicitly set forth. However, the opinions of commentators have been consistent with the reasoning set forth in both PECL Articles, although no distinction is readily apparent.[10] In the majority of the case law, courts have applied this concept in the event one party fails to secure financial arrangements,[11] make payment,[12] or makes payment to a third party,[13] thereby precluding the remedy of avoidance or damages. At least one opinion found no causation when a seller failed to perform due to the buyer's failure to pay a previous debt, finding that the terms of agreement made it irrelevant "as far as the question of the cause of the buyer's failure to perform according to Article 80 CISG is concerned."[14] Similarly, case law exists that illustrates the application of degrees of negligence, thereby allocating a loss between both parties.[15]

IV. IMPUTED KNOWLEDGE AND INTENTION, NEGLIGENCE, AND BAD FAITH

To neutralize the risks, imputation of actual or constructive knowledge or a legally relevant state of mind is relevant in performance of the contract pursuant to PECL Article 1:305.[16]

[8] Note, however, that in Belgian, Dutch, German, Greek, and Nordic law it is not generally considered to a *tekortkoming*, *Vertragsverletzung*, or *Kontraktsbrott* to prevent performance by the other party. It will depend upon whether the acceptance of the performance is a main obligation (*Hauptpflicht*) of the creditor.

[9] It embraces three distinct situations. The first is where the aggrieved party's conduct was a partial cause of the non-performance; the second, where the aggrieved party, though not in any way responsible for the non-performance itself, exacerbated its loss-producing effects by its behavior. A third situation, where the loss resulting from the non-performance could have been reduced or extinguished by appropriate steps in mitigation, is covered by PECL Article 9:505.

[10] *See* Ziegel, *supra* at note 2.

[11] *See* Austria 6 February 1996 Supreme Court [10 Ob 518/95], 6 *Vindobona J. Int'l. L. & Arbitration* 153–168 (2002), also available at <http://cisgw3.law.pace.edu/cases/960206a3.html>.

[12] *See* Germany 1 July 2002 Appellate Court München, translation and link to original text available at <http://cisgw3.law.pace.edu/cases/020701gl.html>.

[13] *See* Germany 9 July 1992 District Court Düsseldorf, available at <http://cisg3.law.pace.edu/cases/920709g1.html>.

[14] Germany 21 March 1996 Hamburg Arbitration proceeding, translation and link to original text available at <http://cisgw3.law.pace.edu/cases/960321g1.html>; *see also* Germany 23 June 1995 Lower Court München, translation and link to original text available at <http://cisgw3.law.pace.edu/cases/950623g1.html>.

[15] Russian Federation arbitration proceeding 55/1998 of 10 June 1999, translation available at <http://cisgw3.law.pace.edu/cases/990610r1.html> (arbitrators acknowledge degree of negligence on the part of the seller); *see also* Israel 22 August 1993 Supreme Court (*Eximin v. Textile and Footwear*), available at <http://cisgw3.law.pace.edu/cases/930822i5.html> (ruling under the Hague Sales Convention (ULIS) which refers to the CISG as well "by way of analogy").

[16] Several provisions use the criteria of knowledge, awareness, foreseeability, and contemplation (*see* PECL Articles 1:301(5), 2:104, 3:102(2) 3:204(2), 3:205(1) and (3), 3:208, 3:209(1), 3:301(1), 4:103(1), 4:109(1),

A party that should have known or foreseen a fact is usually treated as if it had the knowledge or foresight. As such, the law of agency becomes relevant. This is due in part to the fact that performance of a contract rarely is performed by the contracting party, but by its agents, employees, subcontractors, and other third persons.

When a contract is being made, a party is normally only fixed with the knowledge imputed to his employees or agents involved in making the contract. For the purposes of Article 1:305 PECL, knowledge or intention even of any subcontractor or other person to whom it has entrusted performance may be imputed to the party with exception.[17] Under several rules, intentional or grossly negligent behavior or bad faith by a party creates or increases his liability.[18] Even if the contracting party has not entrusted performance to a third person, a third person may nevertheless under certain conditions be entitled to perform the contract.[19] The intentional or grossly negligent behavior of a party or of a person whose state of mind is imputed to a party only refers to the act or omission that constitutes the non-performance. It is not necessary that the intention or gross negligence also extend to the consequences that may follow from the non-performance.

These issues are not clearly established in the national law of the countries of Europe.[20] In some national laws, there is the imputation of intention, negligence, and bad faith.[21] According to several provisions, a non-performing party is responsible for the culpable behavior of persons whom he has charged with performing his obligations. This also appears to have been the intent of the drafters of Article 80 CISG.[22]

4:111(2), 4:113(1), 4:114, 4:117(1), 6:101(2) and (3), 6:110(3), 6:111(2), 7:101(2), 8:103 subparagraph (b), 8:108(3), 9:102(3), 9:303(2), and (3), 9:503).

[17] The employee or other person must have been someone who was, or who appeared to be, involved in the negotiation or performance of the contract. If a person not so related to the contract knows a relevant fact he may not be able to appreciate its relevance to the contract and thus might not report it. The burden of proving that the person for whom the contracting party is held responsible was not and did not reasonably appear to the other party to be involved in the making or performance of the contract rests on the first party.

[18] *See* PECL Articles 2:301(2), 4:107(2), 5:101(1) and (2), 6:102, 8:103 subparagraph (c), and 9:503; *cf.* also PECL Article 1:201(1).

[19] *See* PECL Article 7:106. If the third person acted with the contracting party's assent (PECL Article 7:106(1)(a)) that is equivalent to an entrustment and therefore falls under PECL Article 1:305.

[20] Imputation of knowledge (Article 1:305 (a)) is dealt with in rules on agency in Belgium (*De Page & Dekkers* I no. 52), Germany (BGB § 166), Italy (Cc art. 1391) and Portugal (CC art. 259(1)). In Germany, it is held that the rule of BGB § 166 on agency expresses a general principle: a person who entrusts another with executing certain affairs on his own responsibility will have imputed to him knowledge that the other has acquired in that context. Although there is no explicit rule in the Austrian Code, the OGH reaches the same result by reference to ABGB § 1017. Austrian ABGB § 1313a; Belgium: Cass. 24 January 1974, Pas. I 553 and Cass. 21 June 1979, Pas. I 1226; Denmark: Danske Lov 1683 art. 3-19-2; Germany: BGB § 278 sent. 1; Greece: CC arts. 330 and 334; Italy: Cc art. 1228; Netherlands: BW art. 6:76; Portugal: CC art. 800(1)). French law reaches the same result for exclusion clauses (*Malaurie & Aynès*, Obligations no. 861). Under Spanish law, there is no corresponding general rule for contractual liability, but legal writers and case law acknowledge contractual liability for acts of persons for whom the non-performing party is responsible (*Diez-Picaso* I paras. 724–726; *Jordano Frago* 561 ff.; STS 22 June 1989 (Ar. 4776); STS 1 March 1990 (Ar. 1656)), although intention probably cannot be imputed. In English law, the question does not arise because the fact that a breach is deliberate usually does not affect a party's liability.

[21] Some of the aforementioned modern codes in civil law countries also deal with good and bad faith. Italy and Portugal start out from the general principle set out *supra* (sub 1). If, however, the principal is in bad faith, he cannot invoke the agent's ignorance or good faith (Italian CC art. 1391(2) and Portuguese CC art. 259(2)).

[22] The following excerpt from the Summary Records of Committee Meetings of the Diplomatic Conference at which the CISG was promulgated indicates that the reference in CISG Article 80 to a party's act or omission is intended to include the act or omission of the party's employees.

> Mr. ROGNLIEN (Norway) asked whether the expression 'by his own act or omission' covered the acts and omissions not only of the party concerned but also of persons whom the party might employee in the performance of the contract. After an exchange of views in which Mr. MASKOW (German Democratic Republic), Mr. MICHIDA (Japan), Rapporteur of the Committee, Mr. KHOO (Singapore), Chairman of the Drafting Committee, and Mr. SHAFIK (Egypt) took part, the CHAIRMAN [Mr. LOEWE (Austria)] proposed that the Committee should keep the current working of article 65 *bis* [became article 80 CISG] on the understanding

The CISG fails to address culpability of agents[23]; however, Article 8 of the CISG addresses the intent of the parties.[24] Undoubtedly, PECL rules may be referred to as a supplementary reference to aid in the interpretation of the CISG. They are particularly useful for the interpretation of contracts made in an international and, often, multilingual settings.[25]

V. CONCLUSION

A comparison of the two documents illustrates that both the CISG and the PECL adopt the prohibition against obtaining remedies if the damages were the result of one's own unreasonable behavior. However, it is apparent that the collective application of several articles in the PECL and illustrative examples are broader in scope and therefore provide a supplemental resource for interpreting Article 80 CISG.

that the expression 'by his own act or omission' was unanimously recognized as covering not only the acts or omissions of the party concerned but also those of persons who might be employed by him for the purposes of the performance of the contract. *It was so decided*. (Official Records, p. 430).

[23] Germany 24 January 1994 Appellate Court Berlin, No. 2U7418/92, UNILEX, available at <http://www.unilex.info/case.cfm?pid=case&id=46&step=Sources> (finding that the CISG does not address agency law referencing CISG Article 4, thereby applying Italian law); *see also* Convention on Agency in the International Sale of Goods (Geneva 17 February 1983); Albert H. Kritzer, "Guide to Practical Applications of the United Nations Convention on Contracts for the International Sale of Goods," p. 86 (1989).

[24] *See* generally, Maja Stanivukovic, "Editorial remarks on the manner in which the PECL may be used to interpret or supplement CISG Article 8," available at <http://cisgw3.law.pace.edu/cisg/text/peclcomp8.html#er>.

[25] CISG Article 7(1).

Effects of avoidance: Comparison between the provisions of CISG Article 81 and its PECL counterparts

Francesco G. Mazzotta

I. SIMILARITIES BETWEEN THE COUNTERPART PROVISIONS ON THE EFFECT OF CONTRACTUAL AVOIDANCE IN THE CISG AND THE PECL

1. The Operation of CISG Article 81

In Section IV of the Convention, entitled *Effects of Avoidance*, Article 81 provides that an avoidance of the contract allows parties to terminate their respective obligations arising out of the contract[1]: "Avoidance is a process through which an aggrieved party, by notice

[1] Note, however, that is "subject to any damages that may be due" [Article 81(1)]. Section IV of the Convention also includes the provisions of Article 82 (which deals with issues and effects of impossibility of restitution by buyer), Article 83 (preserving "all other remedies under the contract and the [CISG]" for a buyer who lost

to the other side, terminates the contractual obligations of the parties. If the contract is not avoided, the Convention contemplates that the basic exchange of goods and price will be completed despite a breach, with damages or other remedies to compensate for defects in the exchange."[2]

"The primary effect of the avoidance of the contract by one party is that both parties are released from their obligations to carry out the contract. The seller need not deliver the goods, and the buyer need not take delivery or pay for them."[3] However, avoidance of a contract does not affect[4] any provision of the contract that governs the rights and obligations of the parties subsequent to the avoidance of the contract, nor does it eliminate the right to seek damages for breach of the contract.[5] Furthermore, the enumeration in Article 81(1) of two typical contract clauses that are not terminated by the avoidance of the contract is not exhaustive.[6] Some continuing obligations are set forth in other CISG provisions,[7] whereas others may be found in the contract itself[8] or may arise out of fairness considerations.[9]

As a result of the avoidance, both parties are released from their obligations (CISG Art. 81(1)). However, it is likely that either party might be left with property that has been transferred or payment that has been made by the other. In this case, each party that has performed its own obligation can claim restitution of whatever was paid (price) or supplied (goods or something ancillary to them) under the contract, and if both parties have to make restitution, it must be done concurrently[10] (see CISG Art. 81(2)). Although

the right to avoid the contract), and Article 84 (obligating the seller to pay interest on the refund of price and the buyer to account for any benefits derived from the goods).

[2] *See* Harry M. Flechtner, "Remedies under the New International Sales Convention: The Perspective from Article 2 of the U.C.C.", 8 *J.L. & Com.* 53, 56 (1988), also available at <http://cisgw3.law.pace.edu/cisg/biblio/flecht.html>. For literature specifically relevant to the provisions of CISG Article 81 visit <http://cisgw3.law.pace.edu/cisg/text/mono81.html>.

[3] See Commentary on the Draft Convention on Contracts for the International Sale of Goods, prepared by the Secretariat, U.N. Document A/CONF.97/5, Article 66 (*draft counterpart of CISG Article 81*), available online at <http://cisgw3.law.pace.edu/cisg/text/secomm/secomm-81.html> [hereinafter *Secretariat Commentary*]. According to CISG Articles 51 and 73, partial avoidance is also possible: "Partial avoidance of the contract under Article 47 or 64 [draft counterpart of CISG Article 51 or 73] releases both parties from their obligations as to the part of the contract which has been avoided and give rises to restitution under paragraph (2) [CISG Article 81(2)] as to that part." *Id.*

[4] The Convention only provides that these provisions will survive the avoidance of the contract, but it does not say that such clauses are valid. In fact, the validity of such provisions must be assessed according to the applicable law. *See* Denis Tallon, COMMENTARY ON THE INTERNATIONAL SALES LAW 601, 603 (Massimo C. Bianca & Michael Joachim Bonell eds.) 603 (1987); Jelena Vilus, INTERNATIONAL SALES OF GOODS: DUBROVNIK LECTURES 255, 256 (Petar Sarcevic & Paul Volken eds.) 1986, also available at <http://cisgw3.law.pace.edu/cisg/biblio/vilus.html>.

[5] See Peter Schlechtriem, UNIFORM SALES LAW – THE UN CONVENTION ON CONTRACTS FOR THE INTERNATIONAL SALE OF GOODS 107 (1986), also available at <http://cisgw3.law.pace.edu/cisg/biblio/schlechtriem.html>, who states "[a]n avoidance only 'redirects' the main obligations of the contract; it does not void the contract *ab initio*. Under Article 81, damage claims for breach, dispute-settlement mechanisms (arbitration clauses), liquidated damages and penalty clauses, etc., are not affected by an avoidance (Article 81 sentence 2)." *See* also United States 14 April 1992 Federal District Court [New York], *Filanto S.p.A. v. Chilewich International Corp.*, available at <http://cisgw3.law.pace.edu/cases/920414u1.html>.

[6] The clauses mentioned regard provisions for settlement of disputes or governing the rights and obligations of the parties consequent upon the avoidance of the contract. *See Secretariat Commentary, supra* note 3. *See* also Hans G. Leser, "Annotations 1–20 on Article 82," in COMMENTARY ON THE UN CONVENTION ON THE INTERNATIONAL SALE OF GOODS 638, 640 (Peter Schlechtriem ed.) (1998).

[7] *See, e.g., CISG* Articles 81(2), 84, and 86(1).

[8] *See Secretariat Commentary, supra* note 3.

[9] *Id.*

[10] As to the mechanism of a "concurrent restitution" in Article 81(2), *see* Flechtner, *supra* note 2, at 80. *See* also Denis Tallon, *supra* note 4, at 605 who states, "[t]he rules governing the suspension of the performance (Article 71) are applicable by analogy. The buyer can refuse to restore the goods if the seller does not offer to restitute the price and vice-versa by virtue of the principle that a party may suspend the performance of his obligation if . . . it becomes apparent that the other party will not perform a substantial part of his

the Convention provides that both parties may declare the contract avoided, it has been argued by commentators that the general structure of the Convention concerning the buyer's obligation to return the goods may create some problems.[11]

It should be noted that the right of either party to require restitution as recognized by CISG Article 81(2) may be limited by other rules that fall outside the scope of the Convention, such as bankruptcy or other insolvency procedures. In addition, exchange control laws or other restrictions on the transfer of goods or funds may prevent the transfer of the goods or money to the demanding party in a foreign country. Such limitations, however, may reduce the value of the claim for restitution, but do not affect the validity of the rights between the parties.[12]

2. The Operation of PECL Article 9:305

The PECL provisions that are relevant to this comparative analysis are to be found in Chapter 9, entitled "Particular Remedies for Non-Performance," in Section 3, entitled *Termination of the Contract*.[13]

The principal provisions are to be found in PECL Article 9:305, entitled *Effects of Termination in General*, which basically provides, much like CISG Article 81, that termination[14] releases both parties to the contract from their obligation to effectuate and receive future performance (PECL Art. 9:305(1)).[15] However, that does not affect any provision of the contract for the settlement of disputes or any other provision that is to operate even after termination (PECL Art. 9:305(2)).

However, except for these basic textual similarities, the two sets of rules differ distinctly in their application.

II. DIFFERENCES BETWEEN THE COUNTERPART PROVISIONS ON THE EFFECT OF CONTRACTUAL AVOIDANCE IN THE CISG AND PECL

The ability to return the goods received in substantially the condition in which one received them is "a prerequisite for avoiding a contract or demanding substitute goods. If, because he cannot return the goods, the buyer is barred from avoiding the contract or demanding substitute goods, his other remedies under the contract or the Convention (damages, reduction of price) remain unaffected."[16] CISG Article 81(2) "incorporates the idea that, as regards restitution, the avoidance of the contract undermines the basis on which either party can retain that which he has received from the other party."[17] In other words, the Convention clearly requires that whatever is exchanged between the

obligations"; Leser, *supra* note 6, at 641. As to the restitution/refund duty, *see, e.g.*, Switzerland 5 February 1997 *Handelsgericht* [Commercial Court] Zürich, available at <http://cisgw3.law.pace.edu/cases/970205s1.html>; Switzerland 20 February 1997 *Bezirksgericht* [District Court] Saane, case presentation including English translation available at <http://cisgw3.law.pace.edu/cases/970220s1.html>.

[11] *See* Leser, *supra* note 6, at 642.

[12] *See Secretariat Commentary*, *supra* note 3. *See* also Harry M. Flechtner, *supra* note 2, at 67 and 81; Micheal A. Tessitore, "The U.N. Convention on International Sales and Seller's Ineffective Right of Reclamation under the U.S. Bankruptcy Code", 35 *Willamette L. Rev*. 367 (1999); David Frisch, "Commercial Common Law, the United Nations Convention on the International Sale of Goods, and the Inertia of Habit," 74 *Tul. L. Rev*. 495; Denis Tallon, *supra* note 4, at 606; Jelena Vilus, *supra* note 4, at 256.

[13] The relevant PECL provisions are to be found in Articles 9:305, 9:306, 9:307, 9:308, and 9:309.

[14] "Termination" is the PECL's counterpart to the CISG term "Avoidance". *See* Comments and Notes to the PECL Articles, [hereinafter *PECL Comments*] also available at <http://cisgw3.law.pace.edu/cisg/text/peclcomp81.html>.

[15] "[B]ut, subject to Articles 9:306 to 9:308, does not affect the rights and liabilities that have accrued up to the time of termination". PECL Article 9:305(1).

[16] *See* Schlechtriem, *supra* note 5, at 106.

[17] *See Secretariat Commentary*, *supra* note 3. *See* M. C. Capponi, *infra* note 23, who states, "L'adozione del principio per cui la possibilità di operare la restituzione della prestazione ricevuta costituisce presupposto

parties because of the contract must be returned, and if this is not possible, subject to the exceptions considered by CISG Article 82, avoidance of the contract is no longer an option.[18]

PECL Articles 9:305, 9:307, and 9:308 do not adopt the above approach of the Convention. First, the PECL also take into consideration contracts for services, which are beyond the scope of the CISG. Second, the PECL introduce the idea that there are circumstances in which it might be inappropriate to make the restitution.[19] Such an idea is not shared with the CISG. The general approach adopted by the PECL is that, upon termination of a contract, both parties are released from their duties to effect and to receive performance (PECL Art. 9:305). A restitution duty, which does not affect the right to terminate the contract, may arise only where one party has conferred a benefit on the other party without receiving the promised counter-performance in exchange.[20]

To understand how the two approaches differ, it is important to study the PECL Comment on Article 9:305, which states,

> It would be also inconvenient to treat a contract which as being retrospectively cancelled in the sense that performances received must be returned or restitution made of their value. This is not appropriate where the contract was to be performed over the period of time when there can be termination for the future without undoing what has been achieved already [. . .] Even though termination is forward looking in the way just explained, there are situations in which it is appropriate to "undo" what has taken place before termination. Thus the aggrieved party may need the right to reject a performance already received if termination means that it is of no value to it; either party may need to recover money already paid to the other party if nothing has been received in return; and either may need to be able to recover other property which has been transferred.[21]

PECL Article 9:306 provides for cases where the aggrieved party received from the other party some property whose value has been fundamentally reduced because of the other party's non-performance or because, as a result of the termination, it cannot secure the remaining performance. Restitution of the property will occur where it is useless for the party that received it. This rule clearly is not compatible with the CISG set of rules.

Also inconsistent with the CISG principles is the rule set forth in PECL Article 9:307, which deals with the recovery of money paid. PECL Article 9:307 states, "On termination of the contract a party may recover money paid for a performance which it did not receive or which it properly rejected." Article 9:308 introduces the same principle, although it deals with property other than money. Both PECL Articles 9:307 and 9:308 restrict the restitution to the instance where one party has conferred a benefit, but has not received the promised counter-performance. Moreover, it should be noted that PECL Articles 9:307 and 9:308 also apply to situations, such as service contracts, where the CISG cannot be applied.

necessario della risolubilità del contratto è sembrata ispirarsi alla Saldotheorie tedesca." (The adoption of the rule that requires restitution as a necessary requirement for avoidance of a contract seems to be drawn from the German *Saldotheorie*). *See* also Giardina, in *Nuove Leggi Civili Commentate* 322 (1989).

[18] *See, e.g.*, Germany 27 September 1991 OLG [Appellate Court] Koblenz, case presentation available at <http://cisgw3.law.pace.edu/cases/910927g1.html>; Germany 17 September 1991 OLG [Appellate Court] Frankfurt, case presentation including English translation available at <http://cisgw3.law.pace.edu/cases/910917g1.html>; Germany 10 February 1994 OLG [Appellate Court] Düsseldorf, case presentation including English translation available at <http://cisgw3.law.pace.edu/cases/940210g2.html>.

[19] PECL Article 9:306 reads, "A party which terminates the contract may reject property previously received from the other party if its value to the first party has been fundamentally reduced as a result of the other party's non-performance." *See PECL Comments, supra* note 14.

[20] *See* PECL Articles 9:307 (recovery of money paid); 9:308 (recovery of property that can be returned), and 9:309 (recovery of reasonable amount for the value of performance that cannot be returned).

[21] *See PECL Comments, supra* note 14.

In addition, the PECL refer to "termination," whereas the CISG refers to "avoidance." In the comparison between CISG Article 81 and the PECL Articles 9:305, 9:307, and 9:308, the two words do have the same meaning. However, it has to be noted that the PECL also use the term "avoidance," but in a different context. In fact, the relevant PECL provision that deals with validity issues provides that "[i]f a ground of avoidance affects only particular terms of a contract, the effect of an avoidance is limited to those terms unless, giving due consideration to all the circumstances of the case, it is unreasonable to uphold the remaining contract."[22]

Finally, it should be also mentioned that neither the Convention nor the PECL have any specific provisions dealing with the following:

(i) the expenses incurred in making restitution[23]
(ii) the rights acquired by third parties[24]
(iii) the location where the restitution must be made[25]
(iv) the buyer's responsibility when the goods that must be returned are destroyed after the effective date of a declaration of avoidance[26]

III. CONCLUSIONS

The PECL rules do not add any tool that is useful for the interpretation of CISG Article 81. Instead, the PECL introduce a set of rules – the PECL rule according to which the restitution of the goods is available only if the goods do not have any value for the party who received them (9:306); the principle that restitution of the money paid is subject to the circumstance that the party who paid for a performance did not receive it or it was properly rejected (9:307); and the rule according to which the party who performed will be entitled to restitution, where possible, only in the absence of payment or counter-performance by the other party – which are incompatible with the CISG.

As stated by the Commentary on PECL Article 9:307, "The Principles only give a compensatory remedy after termination, where one party has conferred a benefit on the other party but has not received the promised counter-performance in exchange. The benefit may consist of money paid (Article 9:307), other property which can be returned

[22] *See* PECL Article 4:116.

[23] It is understood that the breaching party is liable not only for his own expenses in carrying out the restitution of the goods or money but also for the expenses of the other party. Such expenses would constitute damages for which the party in breach is liable. However, it should be noted that Article 77 provides that the "party who relies on a breach must take such measures as are reasonable in the circumstances to mitigate the loss." If this party fails to take such measures, the breaching party may claim a reduction of the damages that may be recovered. *See* Schlechtriem, *supra* note 5, at 106. *See* also M. C. Capponi, "Comment on Article 81," in COMMENTARIO BREVE AL CODICE CIVILE 1443, 1531 (Guido Alpa & Paolo Zatti eds., 1999); Tallon, *supra* note 4 at 605; Leser, *supra* note 6.

[24] The Convention, as well as the PECL, does not provide for rights acquired by third parties. *See* CISG Article 4. *See* M. C. Capponi, *id.*, who explains that CISG "*non tratta dei diritti acquistati dai terzi, tale disciplina* [Article 81] *ha riguardo soltanto ai rapporti istituiti tra le parti, e alle conseguenze della loro cancellazione*" (The CISG is not concerned with rights acquired by third parties as it only concerns the rights and obligations arising between the parties and the results of the avoidance of the contract). *See* also Alpa & Bessone, Foro It. 1980, V, 252. Comment on PECL Article 9:308 expressly states that it "deals exclusively with the relationship between the parties and not with the effect which the contract may have on the property in goods sold or bartered. Whether a creditor of the buyer, the buyer's receivers in bankruptcy, or bona fide purchaser may oppose the restitution of goods sold is to be determined by the applicable national law." *See PECL Comments*, *supra* note 14.

[25] *See* Schlechtriem, *supra* note 5, at 108, who states that the "place of performance for transactions following avoidance of the contract should be determined according to the provisions governing the performance of contract obligation" (footnote omitted). *See* also Leser, *supra* note 6.

[26] Schlechtriem, *id.*, where the author proposes the following solution: "the gap-filling rules of Article 7(2) should be preferred to a hasty retreat domestic law. Articles 82 and 84(2)(b) make it clear that the impossibility or inability to make restitution are matters governed by the Uniform Law for International Sales."

(Article 9:308) or some benefit which cannot be returned, e.g., services or property which has been used up (Article 9:309)."[27]

On the other hand, the CISG clearly requires restitution of whatever is received as a condition to avoid the contract.[28] Such differences arise out of the different understanding regarding the retroactivity concept. Although both the Sales Convention and the Principles of European Contract Law provide that avoidance of a contract does not have retroactive effect, because both expressly exclude that a terminated contract should be treated as never made, the CISG and the PECL differ on what survives after avoidance and on the regime to be applied to the performances made under the contract. These are major differences that must to be taken into consideration when comparing the CISG and PECL. It is beyond the scope of this chapter to explore which of the sets of rules might work better, although the difference between them is clear: whereas the CISG tends to eliminate the consequences of an already partially performed contract, the PECL tend to maintain the exchange when it is satisfactory for both parties.

[27] *See PECL Comments, supra* note 14.

[28] *See* Commentary on the Draft Convention on Contracts for the International Sale of Goods, prepared by the Secretariat, Article 67 [*draft counterpart of CISG Article 82*] also available at Pace Law School Institute on International Commercial Law, at <http://cisgw3.law.pace.edu/cisg/text/secomm/secomm-82.html>. The Comment clarifies that "[t]he rule in paragraph (1) [82(1)] recognizes that the natural consequence of the avoidance of the contract or the delivery of substitute goods is the restitution of that which has been already delivered under the contract. Therefore, if the buyer cannot return the goods, or cannot return them substantially in the condition in which he received them, he loses his right to declare the contract avoided under Article 45 [draft counterpart of CISG Article 49] or to require the delivery of substitute goods under Article 42 [draft counterpart of CISG Article 46]."

Restitution of the goods: Comparison between the provisions of CISG Article 82 and the counterpart provisions of PECL Article 9:309

Francesco G. Mazzotta

I. THE OPERATION OF CISG ARTICLE 82

Article 82 of the Convention belongs to Section IV of the Convention, entitled *Effects of Avoidance*.[1] According to the provisions contained in CISG Article 82,[2] the buyer

[1] In that Section of the CISG, the basic rule on contractual avoidance is contained in CISG Article 81, which provides that an avoidance of the contract allows parties to terminate their respective obligations arising out of the contract. Note, however, that is "subject to any damages that may be due" [Article 81(1)]. Section IV of the Convention also includes the provisions of Article 82 (which deals with issues and effects of impossibility of restitution by buyer), Article 83 (preserving "all other remedies under the contract and the [CISG]" for a buyer who lost the right to avoid the contract), and Article 84 (obligating the seller to pay interest on the refund of the price and the buyer to account for any benefits derived from the goods).

[2] In general, for monographs and anthologies that should be considered in construing the meaning and operation of CISG Article 82, visit <http://cisgw3.law.pace.edu/cisg/text/mono82.html>.

loses the right to avoid the contract or to demand substitute goods when it is impossible[3] for him to make restitution of the goods in a condition substantially[4] similar to that in which he received them.[5] However, the buyer retains the right to avoid the contract if the following conditions are met: the damages to the goods are not due to the buyer's act or omission [Article 82(2)(a)]; the deterioration or consumption of the goods results from the examination as required by CISG Article 38 [see Article 82(2)(b)]; or the goods are sold in the normal course of business or consumed or transformed by him in the normal course of use before he discovered, or should have discovered, their lack of conformity [(Article 82(2)(c)].

The general rule of the Convention– i.e., that the contract may be avoided *only if* the goods can be returned substantially in the condition in which the buyer received them–is stated in Article 82(1).[6] However, Article 82(2), provides three considerable exceptions to that rule. Paragraph 2 in Article 82, therefore, deals with the allocation of the risk of loss of the goods before avoidance.[7]

In particular, according to Article 82(2)(a), the seller, whose breach determined the exercise of the buyer's right to avoid the contract, is responsible for any circumstances that lead to the loss of the goods, unless these circumstances are due to the buyer's act or omission.[8]

[3] It has been suggested that "[t]he possibility for the buyer of making restitution must be apprised objectively, according to the understanding of the reasonable person referred to in Article 8(2)" (footnote omitted); *see* Hans G. Leser, "Annotations 1–29 on Article 82," in *COMMENTARY ON THE UN CONVENTION ON THE INTERNATIONAL SALE OF GOODS* 632, 645 (Peter Schlechtriem, ed.) (1998).

[4] See Commentary on the Draft Convention on Contracts for the International Sale of Goods, prepared by the Secretariat, Article 67 [*draft counterpart of CISG article 82*], available at <http://cisgw3.law.pace.edu/cisg/text/secomm/secomm-82.html>: "It is not necessary that the goods be in the identical condition in which they were received; they need be only in 'substantially' the same condition. Although the term is not defined, it indicates that the change in condition of the goods must be of sufficient importance that it would no longer be proper to require the seller to retake the goods as the equivalent of that which he had delivered to the buyer even though the seller had been in fundamental breach of the contract." *See* also Denis Tallon, *COMMENTARY ON THE INTERNATIONAL SALES LAW* 601, 608 (Massimo C. Bianca & Michael Joachim Bonell eds.) (1987); Hans G. Leser, *supra* note 3, at 646.

[5] *See* M. C. Capponi, "Comment on Article 81," in *COMMENTARIO BREVE AL CODICE CIVILE* 1443, 1531(Guido Alpa & Paolo Zatti eds., 1999), who states as follows: *"L'adozione del principio per cui la possibilità di operare la restituzione della prestazione ricevuta costituisce presupposto necessario della risolubilità del contratto è sembrata ispirarsi alla Saldotheorie tedesca."* (The adoption of the rule that requires restitution as a necessary requirement for avoidance of a contract seems to be drawn from the German *Saldotheorie*). *See* also Giardina, *in Nuove Leggi Civili Commentate* 322 (1989). For relevant jurisprudence *see, e.g.*, Germany 21 August 1995 LG [District Court] Ellwangen, *infra* note 10; Germany 25 June 1997 BGH [Supreme Court], *infra* note 9.

[6] *See, e.g.*, Germany 10 February 1994 OLG [Appellate Court] Düsseldorf, CLOUT Case No. 82, English translation available at <http://cisgw3.law.pace.edu/cases/940210g2.html>, where it was held that the buyer had lost the right to declare the contract avoided on the ground that he had sold further the goods bought, thus having made restitution of the goods impossible (Article 82(1) CISG).

[7] Leser, *supra* note 3, at 644.

[8] *See, e.g.*, Germany 27 September 1991 OLG [Appellate Court] Koblenz, CLOUT Case No. 316, also available at <http://cisgw3.law.pace.edu/cases/910927g1.html>. In this case, the change in the condition of the goods (marble slabs) had been caused by the buyer's own act and had not been the result of the examination of the goods under Article 38 CISG; rather it had arisen after the discovery of the lack of conformity (the buyer had started to work on and with the marble plates after discovery of lack of conformity of the goods). Thus, the Court held that the buyer had lost its right to declare the contract avoided (Article 49 CISG) pursuant to Article 82(1) CISG. Furthermore, the buyer had not met the requirements of Article 82(2) CISG in order to exclude the application of Article 82(1).

For a mention of this case in the context of an excellent discussion of the right of avoidance under the CISG, *see* Anna Kazimierska, "The Remedy of Avoidance under the Vienna Convention on the International Sale of Goods," *Pace Review of the Convention on Contracts for the International Sale of Goods*, Kluwer (1999–2000) 79–192, also at <http://cisgw3.law.pace.edu/cisg/biblio/kazimierska.html>.

Under Article 82(2)(b), if the contract is avoided due to the seller's breach, the seller bears the risk and consequences of the examination made according to the relevant provisions contained in CISG Article 38.[9]

Under Article 82(2)(c), the seller bears the risk of the resale, consumption, or transformation of defective goods.[10] However, in this case, the seller bears the risk only until the time the buyer discovered or should have discovered the defect. In this case, the provisions of Article 84(2) also apply. There are no express rules as to the loss and impairment of the goods after the avoidance. However, it is understood that once the buyer is aware or should be aware of the lack of conformity he is also responsible for the goods that he received.[11]

Although the construction of Article 82(2)(b)[12] and 82(2)(c)[13] is rather straightforward, some explanation is required for Article 82(2)(a). It is generally understood that under Article 82(2)(a), the buyer is responsible for damages caused by acts or omissions by his personnel and by third persons if he made it possible, by means of acts or omissions, for them to damage the goods.[14] In particular, as to damages provoked by third persons, it is deemed that "that the buyer must not merely have provided the opportunity for third persons or *force majeure* to affect the goods, but also have increased this chance by his act or omission."[15]

Finally, it must be noted that the buyer will retain other remedies even after he loses his right to avoid the contract.[16]

II. THE OPERATION OF PECL ARTICLE 9:309

PECL Article 9:309, entitled *Recovery for Performance That Cannot Be Returned*, belongs to the Principles of European Contract Law, in Chapter 9, entitled "Particular

[9] *See, e.g.*, Germany 25 June 1997 BGH [Supreme Court], CLOUT Case No. 235, also available at <http://cisgw3.law.pace.edu/cases/970625g2.html>, where the impossibility of restoring the goods to their original condition did not disqualify the buyer from avoiding the contract under Article 82(1) CISG. Both parties were aware that the goods had to be processed before any non-conformity could be discovered. Moreover, the buyer was entitled to declare the contract avoided if upon examination it was discovered that the goods had perished or deteriorated (CISG Article 82(2)(b)).

[10] *See, e.g.*, Germany 21 August 1995 District Court Ellwangen, case presentation including English translation available at <http://cisgw3.law.pace.edu/cases/950821g2.html>, where the court discussed the operation of the rule in Article 82:

> According to Art. 82(1) CISG, the buyer loses the right to declare the contract avoided if it is impossible for her to make restitution of the goods substantially in the condition in which she received them. This rule does not apply if the goods or part of the goods have perished or deteriorated as a result of the examination provided in Article 38 – or if the goods or part of the goods have been sold in the normal course of business or transformed by the buyer in the course of normal use before she discovered or ought to have discovered the lack of conformity (Art. 82(2)(b) and (c) CISG). These requirements are met in the present case. [. . .] In the period between the delivery and the point in time when [buyer] obtained knowledge of the maintained non-conformity, the [buyer] packed the delivered goods in small amounts and delivered them to various warehouses (cf. [buyer's] notice to [seller's representative] in the letter of 16 January 1995). This conduct represents a normal course of business in the meaning of Art. 82(2) CISG.

[11] Leser, *supra* note 3, at 647.

[12] *See, e.g.*, Germany 21 August 1995 LG Ellwangen, *supra* note 10.

[13] It has been noted that such an exception sounds surprising: in fact, the buyer retains the right to declare the contract avoided and to claim for compensation even though the goods cannot be returned. In these cases the reason why the buyer elects to avoid a contract rather than to recover damages should lie in the fact that, through Article 81, the buyer is enabled to obtain damages without proving them. *See* also Denis Tallon, *supra* note 4, at 609; John O. Honnold, *UNIFORM LAW FOR INTERNATIONAL SALES UNDER THE 1980 INTERNATIONAL SALES LAW* 502, 512 (3rd ed. 1999).

[14] See Peter Schlechtriem, *UNIFORM SALES LAW – THE UN CONVENTION ON CONTRACTS FOR THE INTERNATIONAL SALE OF GOODS* 106 (1986) also available at <http://cisgw3.law.pace.edu/cisg/biblio/schlechtriem.html>.

[15] Schlechtriem, *id. See* also Tallon, *supra* note 4; Leser, *supra* note 3, at 648. It has been suggested that the standard to be used to establish whether an act or omission is wrongful should be based on the Convention, rather than domestic tort law; *see* Honnold, *supra* note 13, at 511.

[16] *See* CISG Article 83, paragraph 2. *See* also Leser, *supra* note 3, at 646.

Remedies for Non-Performance," under Section 3, entitled *Termination of the Contract*.[17]

According to PECL Article 9:309, recovery for performance that cannot be returned is subject to the following three requirements: (i) that there is a termination of the contract, (ii) that a party has rendered performance and has not received payment or counter-performance for it, and (iii) that performance cannot be returned by the other party.

If those requirements are met, the entitled party may recover a reasonable amount for the value of the performance rendered to the other party. In calculating this amount, the PECL Comment on Article 9:309 provides that, upon termination of a contract, the party that received the benefit, which cannot be returned and was not paid for, "should not be required to pay the cost to the other of having provided it, if the net to it is less, since it is only enriched by the latter amount,"[18] whereas if the net benefit to the recipient is greater than the cost of providing it, the recipient "should not be liable under this article for more than an appropriate part of the contract price."[19]

III. DIFFERENCES BETWEEN THE TWO COUNTERPART REGIMES

The two sets of rules contained in the respective regimes of the Sales Convention and the Principles of European Contract Law are quite different. CISG Article 82 deals exclusively with whether avoidance is still possible even when goods cannot be returned. As a general rule in the Convention, avoidance of the contract is not possible, unless one of the exceptions listed in CISG Article 82(2) occurs. As already mentioned earlier, avoidance of a contract is available regardless of whether the party that rendered the goods received the performance or other counter-performance.

On the other hand, as a general rule the PECL "only give a restitutionary remedy after termination, where one party has conferred a benefit on the other party, but has not received the promised counter-performance in exchange. The benefit may consist of money paid (Article 9:307), other property which can be returned (Article 9:308) or some benefit which cannot be returned, e.g., services or property which has been used up (9:309)."[20] In particular, PECL Article 9:309 provides that, when restitution cannot be made, the party who delivered the goods may recover a reasonable amount for the value of the goods to the other party if it has not received payment for them or counter-performance. Therefore, PECL Article 9:309 addresses the issue of restitution, but only to set the rules on how to calculate the amount of recovery.

IV. CONCLUSIONS

Pursuant to CISG, if the buyer cannot make restitution for what he received, the contract cannot be avoided unless one of the exceptions set by CISG Article 82(2) is met. The PECL do not require any restitution as a condition for avoidance. Therefore, whereas under the CISG restitution is an obligatory step toward the avoidance of a contract, under the PECL restitution is only a possible consequence of the avoidance of a contract. In fact, a restitution remedy arises only where there was a performance for which payment was not made. Thus, PECL Article 9:309 cannot be used as an aid to construe CISG

[17] The relevant provisions in the PECL that deal with the effects of termination are to be found in Articles 9:305 (effects of termination in general), 9:306 (property reduced in value), 9:307 (recovery of money paid), 9:308 (recovery of property), and 9:309 (recovery of performance that cannot be returned).

[18] *See* Comment on PECL Article 9:309, available at <http://cisgw3.law.pace.edu/cisg/text/peclcomp82.html#cnpc>.

[19] *Id.*

[20] *See* Comment on PECL Article 9:307, available at <http://cisgw3.law.pace.edu/cisg/text/peclcomp81.html#9:307>.

Article 82 because the two sets of rules adopt different approaches to the issue of avoidance. However, although PECL Article 9:309 cannot be useful for that purpose, it is arguable that limiting the recovery where the party did not get what it bargained for may be a good way to reduce possible disputes between parties over issues related to restitution and/or the reasonable amount of the value of performance.[21]

[21] *See* PECL Article 9:309. For the definition of the term "reasonableness" recited in the Principles of European Contract Law and further references to the concept of reasonableness in continental and common law domestic rules, doctrine, and jurisprudence, go to PECL Article 1:302 and the Comment and Notes prepared for this provision, available at <http://cisgw3.law.pace.edu/cisg/text/reason.html#def>. PECL Article 1:302, states, "Under these Principles reasonableness is to be judged by what persons acting in good faith and in the same situation as the parties would consider to be reasonable. In particular, in assessing what is reasonable the nature and purpose of the contract, the circumstances of the case and the usages and practices of the trades or professions involved should be taken into account."

Reasonableness is one of the Convention's most recognized general principles; it is specifically mentioned in numerous provisions of the CISG and clearly alluded to elsewhere in the Uniform Sales Law. As a general principle of the Convention reasonableness is to be read into each Article of the CISG whether or not specifically mentioned in the CISG. For overview comments on reasonableness as a general principle of the CISG and further references and confirming citations (establishing an arguable correlation between the PECL's definition of *reasonableness* and the evident same meaning of this term in specific CISG provisions and as a general principle of the CISG), *see* Albert H. Kritzer, "Editorial Remarks," available at <http://cisgw3.law.pace.edu/cisg/text/reason.html#over>.

Preservation of the goods: Comparison between the provisions of CISG Articles 85–88 and counterpart provisions of the Principles of European Contract Law

Francesco G. Mazzotta

I. Preservation of the Goods under the CISG
1. Seller's Duty to Preserve the Goods (Art. 85)
2. Buyer's Duty to Preserve the Goods (Art. 86)
3. Provisions Common to Both Parties: Deposit tn Warehouse (Art. 87) and Sale of Goods (Art. 88)

II. Preservation of the Goods under PECL (Arts. 7:110–7:112)
1. Situations Where PECL Article 7:110 Is Useful in Construing the Meaning of the Counterpart Provisions of the CISG

III. Conclusion

I. PRESERVATION OF THE GOODS UNDER THE CISG

As a general rule, Section VI of Chapter 5 of the CISG requires that the party left in possession of, or, otherwise in control of the disposition of, the goods has the duty to protect and preserve the goods. This duty, which applies to any party to the transaction, "is an expression of the general obligation to cooperate, as it can be deduced from this provision [CISG Article 85] or that provision of the CISG as one of the Convention's underlying principles."[1]

[1] *See* Fritz Enderlein & Dietrich Maskow, International Sales Law, United Nations Convention on Contracts for the International Sale of Goods – Convention on the Limitation

1. Seller's Duty to Preserve the Goods (Article 85)[2]

The scope of the provision comprises two situations: first, where the buyer is in delay in taking the goods,[3] and, second, where the buyer fails to pay the price when payment is to be made concurrently with delivery.[4] In these cases, the seller is obligated to take measures to preserve the goods.

The standard to be applied is that the seller is required to take any reasonable step under the circumstances to preserve the goods, which will often be decided based on usage.[5] Failure to fulfill this duty may give rise to stringent consequences, especially in those cases where the risk of loss has already passed to the buyer although the seller still has control over the disposition of the goods.[6] In fact, a seller's failure to preserve the goods releases the buyer from liability arising from loss even though the risk has already passed to the buyer,[7] "regardless of whether or not the property in the goods has passed"[8] to the buyer. This is the "substance" of the obligation to preserve the goods.[9] If, however, the risk of loss has not passed to the buyer, even though found liable for preservation costs, the seller is not entitled to damages to the good for prolonged storage.[10]

Moreover, it must be noted that "reasonable circumstances and reasonable expenses are common law notions which provide standards according to which a judge or arbitrator can evaluate the necessary steps and expenses."[11]

PERIOD IN THE INTERNATIONAL SALE OF GOODS, Oceana Publications 351 (1992). *Available at* <http://cisgw3.law.pace.edu/cisg/biblio/enderlein.html>.

[2] For literature specifically relevant to the provisions of Article 85, *see* <http://cisgw3.law.pace.edu/cisg/text/mono85.html>. *See* also Harry Flechtner, in THE DRAFT UNCITRAL DIGEST AND BEYOND: CASES, ANALYSIS AND UNRESOLVED ISSUES IN THE U.N. SALES CONVENTION, 861 (Franco Ferrari, Harry Flechtner, Ronald A. Brand eds. 2004) [hereinafter *UNCITRAL Digest*].

[3] *See* Hans E. Eberstein, Annotations 1–18 on Article 85, *in* COMMENTARY ON THE UN CONVENTION ON THE INTERNATIONAL SALE OF GOODS (CISG) 663, 667 (Peter Schlechtriem, ed. 1998) [hereinafter *Annotations 85*]; Herbert Bernstein & Joseph Lookofky, UNDERSTANDING THE CISG IN EUROPE 103 (2003) [hereinafter *CISG in Europe*]; Flechtner, *UNCITRAL DIGEST*, *supra* note 3. *But see* ICC Arbitration Case No. 7197 of 1992 *available at* <http://cisgw3.law.pace.edu/cases/927197i1.html> [the preservation costs were awarded as result of failure to open a letter of credit].

[4] This language is also explained in a colloquy at the 1980 Vienna Diplomatic Conference available at <http://cisgw3.law.pace.edu/cisg/text/link85.html>. Official Records of United Nations Conference on Contracts for the International Sale of Goods, Vienna, March 10–April 11, 1980, A/CONF. 97/19 (hereinafter *Official Records*). *See also* Jorge Barrera Graf, *in* COMMENTARY ON THE INTERNATIONAL SALES LAW 614, 613–619 (Massimo C. Bianca and M. Joachim Bonell eds., 1987); Eberstein, *Annotations 85*, *supra* note 4, at 667; Bernstein & Lookofky, *CISG in Europe*, *supra* note 4 at 103; Flechtner, *UNCITRAL DIGEST*, *supra* note 4. *See also* Hamburg Arbitration proceeding, Germany, December 29, 1998, *available at* <http://cisgw3.law.pace.edu/cases/981229g1.html>.

[5] Eberstein, *Annotations 85*, *supra* note 4, at 664 and 668.

[6] *See* Peter Schlechtriem, UNIFORM SALES LAW – THE UN CONVENTION ON CONTRACTS FOR THE INTERNATIONAL SALE OF GOODS, Manz: Vienna 108 (1986). *Available at* <http://cisgw3.law.pace.edu/cisg/biblio/schlechtriem.html>.

[7] *See* the Secretariat Commentary on Article 74 of the 1978 Draft [*draft counterpart of CISG Article 85*] reprinted in Official Records, *supra* note 5, at 62, available at <cisgw3.law.pace.edu/cisg/text/seccomm-85.html>; *see* Schlechtriem, *supra* note 7; John O. Honnold, UNIFORM LAW FOR INTERNATIONAL SALES UNDER THE 1980 UNITED NATIONS CONVENTION, 519 (1999); Harry M. Flechtner, "Remedies under the New International Sales Convention: The Perspective from Article 2 of the U.C.C.," 8 *J. L. & Com.* 53, 104 (1988) [*available at* <http://cisgw3.law.pace.edu/cisg/biblio/flecht.html>] [hereinafter "*Remedies*"]; and Jelena Vilus, "Provisions Common to the Obligations of the Seller and the Buyer," in INTERNATIONAL SALES OF GOODS: DUBROVNIK LECTURES, Oceana Publications 259, 237–264 (Petar Sarcevic & Paul Volken eds., 1986) [available at <http://cisgw3.law.pace.edu/cisg/biblio/vilus.html>].

[8] Eberstein, *Annotations 85*, *supra* note 4, at 665.

[9] *See* Enderlein & Maskow, *supra* note 2, at 352.

[10] ICC Arbitration case, No. 7197 of 1992, available at <http://cisgw3.law.pace.edu/cases/927197i1.html>.

[11] *See* Vilus, *supra* note 8; *see also* Enderlein & Maskow, *supra* note 2, at 352, "[w]hat is to be considered as steps that are reasonable in the circumstances will have to be determined using the measure which the CISG applies to flesh out such vague descriptions. It amounts to taking such steps that they would be taken by a reasonable person in the same circumstances;" Carlo Scognamiglio, NUOVE LEGGI CIVILI COMMENTATE 326, 325–342 (Massimo C. Bianca ed., 1989). For the definition of reasonableness under the CISG and

The CISG does not state the length of the obligation to preserve the goods. However, "[i]t follows from Article 88(1) that the seller is quite entitled to limit the period of preservation and that upon certain conditions [Article 88], he may at any time proceed to sell the goods, provided that he has previously informed the buyer of that intention."[12] The seller may also be freed from the obligation to preserve the goods when he avoids the contract under Article 64.[13] In addition, it must be noted that the seller's obligation to preserve the goods does not end if the seller brings an action to require the buyer to pay the price.[14]

The seller is responsible for the costs arising from reasonable measures to be taken to preserve the goods.[15] However, the seller can sell the goods and retain from the proceeds an amount equal to the reasonable expenses incurred in preserving the goods, and the seller also has the right to retain the goods until those expenses are paid.[16] However, according to many authors,[17] "the buyer will have to be allowed a right to satisfy the right of retention by providing reasonable security."[18]

The Article 85–88 provisions on the preservation of the goods may be easily overcome by means of interim relief procedural tools, which are governed by domestic law.[19]

Courts often regard damages arising from preserving the goods pursuant to Article 85 as damages recoverable under CISG Article 74.[20]

2. Buyer's Duty to Preserve the Goods (Article 86)[21]

The buyer, similar to the seller, is bound to preserve the goods when (i) after receiving them, (ii) he intends to exercise the right to reject them. If both requirements are met, the buyer must take such reasonable[22] measures as the case may be. The buyer is, however, entitled to retain the goods until the seller reimburses the buyer for the reasonable

PECL and references to reasonableness in continental and common law domestic rules, doctrine and case law, visit <http://cisgw3.law.pace.edu/cisg/text/reason.html#overv>. As to case law, *see* Oberlandesgericht Braunschweig, Germany, October 28, 1999, available at <http://cisgw3.law.pace.edu/cases/991028g1.html>; Tribunal of International Commercial Arbitration at the Russian Federation Chamber of Commerce and Industry, April 25, 1995, case 142/1994, available at <http://cisgw3.law.pace.edu/cases/950425r2.html>.

[12] Eberstein, *Annotations 85, supra* note 4, at 668.

[13] *Id.*, at 669. If a contract has been avoided, the seller may not claim reimbursement of expenses incurred in preserving the goods: Hamburg Arbitration proceeding, Germany, December 29, 1998, available at <http://cisgw3.law.pace.edu/cases/981229g1.html>.

[14] Honnold, *supra* note 8, at 520.

[15] Eberstein, *Annotations 85, supra* note 4, at 669.

[16] *See* Oberlandesgericht Braunschweig, Germany, October 28, 1999, available at <http://cisgw3.law.pace.edu/cases/991028g1.html>; Tribunal Cantonal Vaud, Switzerland, 17 May 1994, available at <http://cisgw3.law.pace.edu/cases/940517s1.html>.

[17] Eberstein, *Annotations 85, supra* note 4, at 669; Enderlein & Maskow, *supra* note 2, at 353.

[18] Eberstein, *Annotations 85, supra* note 4, at 669.

[19] *See* Tribunal Cantonal Vaud, Switzerland, May 17, 1994, available at <http://cisgw3.law.pace.edu/cases/940517s1.html> where the court states, "[t]he Vienna Convention . . . rules only on substantive issues. Therefore it does not exclude that a different solution may be given in the frame of provisional measures."

[20] *See, e.g.*, Oberlandesgericht Braunschweig, Germany, October 28, 1999, available at <http://cisgw3.law.pace.edu/cases/991028g1.html>, where the court also stated "[w]hen applying the CISG, the duty to pay damages is based on Article 74, in part also on Article 85"; Federal Appellate Court 2nd Circuit, USA, December 6, 1995, available at <http://cisgw3.law.pace.edu/cases/951206u1.html> Federal District Court, New York, USA, September 9, 1994, available at <http://cisgw3.law.pace.edu/cases/940909u1.html>; ICC Arbitration case, No. 7531 of 1994, available at <http://cisgw3.law.pace.edu/cases/947531i1.html>; ICC Arbitration Case No. 7197 of 1992 available at <http://cisgw3.law.pace.edu/cases/927197i1.html>.

[21] For selected texts specifically relevant to the provisions of Article 86, visit <http://cisgw3.law.pace.edu/cisg/text/mono86.html>. *See also* Bernstein & Lookofsky, *CISG in Europe, supra* note 4; Flechtner, *UNCITRAL DIGEST, supra* note 3, at 864.

[22] *See supra* note 12.

expenses incurred in preserving the goods.[23] Failure to take reasonable measures regarding the goods may result in denial of a claim for warehouse expenses (Article 86(1)).[24]

The rejection may be exercised from the time the right to reject[25] arises until it expires.[26] While the period to decide whether to reject the goods is running, the buyer still has a duty to preserve the goods,[27] which continues until the duty has been discharged pursuant to Articles 87 and 88.[28]

If the goods have been dispatched to the buyer and placed at his disposal without his having physical possession of them, the buyer, in order to be able to reject the goods, must take them into custody on behalf of the seller as long as it can be done without the payment of the price and without unreasonable inconveniences or unreasonable expenses (Article 86(2)). Of course, this rule does not apply if the seller or a person authorized by the seller to take charge of the goods is present at the place of destination of the goods.

Articles 85 and 86 establish the duty to preserve the goods. As already mentioned, a party may discharge his duty by (i) depositing the goods in a warehouse and/or (ii) selling the goods.

3. Deposit in Warehouse (Article 87)

The deposit of the goods in a warehouse[29] (of a third person, if necessary) will be at the expense of the other party. However, unless otherwise provided, the party who deposits the goods is primarily liable to the warehouse, although he may seek reimbursement from the other party to the sale contract.[30] To be recoverable, depositing expenses must be reasonable.[31] It should be noted that unreasonable expenses only affect the depositing party's right to obtain full reimbursement. The right of reimbursement exists only in

[23] *See* Cour de Cassation, France, January 4, 1995, case 92-16.993, available at <http://cisgw3.law.pace.edu/cases/950104f1.html>; ICC Arbitration Case No. 7531 of 1994 available at <http://cisgw3.law.pace.edu/cases/947531i1.html>.

[24] *China International Economic and Trade Arbitration Commission [CIETAC] – Shenzhen Commission*, (June 6, 1991, arbitration proceeding 164/1996, available at <http://cisgw3.law.pace.edu/cases/910606c1.html>): the court stated that warehouse expenses, which almost amounted to the price of the contract, were unreasonable. The court also noted that the extend deposit caused the goods to decompose.

[25] *See, e.g.*, Articles 46(1), 46(2), 49(1)(a), and 49(1)(b), and perhaps a right to reject exists under Articles 52 and 71. *See* Hans E. Eberstein, "Annotations 1–26 on Article 86," in COMMENTARY ON THE UN CONVENTION ON THE INTERNATIONAL SALE OF GOODS (CISG) 671 (Peter Schlechtriem, ed., 1998) [hereinafter *Annotations 86*].

[26] It can be exercised even at a later time after receiving the goods – e.g., non-conforming goods must be rejected within a reasonable time after the buyer discovers or should have discovered the defects.

[27] *See* Honnold, *supra* note 8, at 524; *See also* Eberstein, *Annotations 86, supra* note 26, at 671; Fritz Enderlein, Dietrich Maskow and Heinz Strohbach, INTERNATIONALES KAUFRECHT, Article 86, note 3.2 (1991).

[28] It has been suggested that the buyer has no duty to take the goods in possession when he rejected them at earlier stage (*see* Secretariat Commentary on Article 75 of the 1978 Draft [*draft counterpart of CISG Article 86*] reprinted in Official Records, *supra* note 5, at 62, available at <cisgw3.law.pace.edu/cisg/text/seccomm-86.html>; Rolf Herber and Beate Czerwenka, INTERNATIONALES KAUFRECHT, Article 86, paragraph 6 (1991). However, the provisions do not support such views, as once the goods are at the buyer's disposal whether he rejects them or only intends to reject them, he is still bound to preserve the goods pursuant to Articles 87 and 88. *See also* Eberstein, *Annotations 86, supra* note 26, at 675; Enderlein/Maskow/Strohbach, *supra* note 28, at Art. 8, note 7.

[29] The term "warehouse" means "any place appropriate for the storage of goods of the type in question." Secretariat Commentary on Article 76 of the 1978 Draft [*draft counterpart of Cisg article 87*], reprinted in Official Records, *supra* note 5, *available at* <cisgw3.law.pace.edu/cisg/text/seccomm-87.html>.

[30] Honnold, *supra* note 8, at 525. As to case law, *see* ICC Arbitration Case No. 7531 of 1994, *available at* <http://cisgw3.law.pace.edu/cases/947531i1.html>; *cf.* Tribunal Cantonal Vaud, Switzerland, May 17, 1994, available at <http://cisgw3.law.pace.edu/cases/940517s1.html> [in the context of interim relief].

[31] Tribunal of International Commercial Arbitration at the Russian Federation Chamber of Commerce and Industry, April 25, 1995, case 142/1994, available at http://cisgw3.law.pace.edu/cases/950425r2.html>.

regards to those expenses that are proportionate.[32] Moreover, "[t]he incurring of unreasonable expense does not lead to the risk of storage in a warehouse being transferred to the other party."[33]

Two issues may give rise to some uncertainty as they are not regulated by the CISG: (i) the relationship between the parties to the storage contract and the parties to the sale of goods contract, which, as has been suggested, should be "governed by the domestic law applicable in each particular case"[34] and (ii) the legal consequences to the sale contract of the deposit of the goods in a warehouse: whether the deposit in a third person's warehouse is to be qualified as a substitute for the original obligation. It should not be deemed to constitute an exemption from the original obligation[35] unless the property involved is money.

4. Sale of the Goods (Article 88)

Article 88(1) allows the party who is bound to preserve the goods to sell them if the other party fails to take action in a reasonable time (also known as self-help sale). It is an option (not an obligation).[36] There are only two requirements the selling party must comply with to exercise such an option: (i) unreasonable delay by the other party in taking the property[37] and (ii) reasonable notice to the other party of the intention to sell the goods.[38] This notice does not need to be in a specific form: it needs only to be appropriate under the circumstances.

Article 88(2) requires the party who is bound to preserve the goods to sell them when the "goods are perishable or their preservation would involve unreasonable expenses" (also known as emergency sale). In this case, selling the goods is a duty. Failure to sell the goods in an emergency situation may give the other party the right to seek damages.[39]

Two issues arise in connection with Article 88(1) and 88(2) that are not dealt with by the CISG: (i) the legal consequences of the failure to give notice and (ii) whether the other party may object. As to the first issue, it has been suggested that "a party who performs a self-help sale, without giving notice of his intention to do so, breaches an ancillary contractual obligation and will be under an obligation to compensate the other party for any resultant damage."[40] On the other hand, in an emergency sale situation, a claim for lack of notice may be difficult to bring successfully. As to the second issue, some authors believe that the sale can be made regardless of any objection made by the other party,[41] although the other party may bring an action for breach of an obligation to proceed based on the reasonableness standard.

[32] *Id.*

[33] *See* Hans E. Eberstein, "Annotations 1–12 on Article 87," in COMMENTARY ON THE UN CONVENTION ON THE INTERNATIONAL SALE OF GOODS (CISG) 677 (Peter Schlechtriem, ed., 1998) [hereinafter *Annotations 87*] [footnote omitted].

[34] *Id.* at 678. *See also* Enderlein & Maskow, *supra* note 2, at 357.

[35] *See* Herber/Czerwenka, *supra* note 29, at Art. 87, paragraph 5; Eberstein, *Annotations 87*, *supra* note 34, at 678. *But see* Enderlein/Maskow/Strohbach, *see supra* note 28, at Art. 87, note 1.2.

[36] *See* Honnold, *supra* note 8, at 526.

[37] *See* Tribunal of International Commercial Arbitration at the Russian Federation Chamber of Commerce and Industry, April 25, 1995, case 142/1994, available at http://www.cisgw3.law.pace.edu/cases/950425r2.html>; ICC Arbitration Case No. 7531 of 1994, available at <http://cisgw3.law.pace.edu/cases/947531i1.html>.

[38] Oberlandesgericht Braunschweig, Germany, October 28, 1999, available at <http://www.cisg.law.pace.edu/cases2/991028g1.html>.

[39] *See* Hans E. Eberstein, "Annotations 1–32 on Article 88," in COMMENTARY ON THE UN CONVENTION ON THE INTERNATIONAL SALE OF GOODS (CISG) 683 (Peter Schlechtriem, ed., 1998) [hereinafter *Annotations 88*].

[40] *Id.* at 682 [footnote omitted]; Scognamiglio, *supra note* 12, at 340.

[41] *Id.*

5. Article 88(3)

Whether it has been a self-help or emergency sale, the party may retain from the proceeds of the sale the reasonable expenses incurred in preserving and selling the goods and require the other party to pay the balance. There is no reference in the CISG regarding (i) how any objections in connection with the reasonable expenses standard may be raised; (ii) whether the party who sold the goods may retain damages from the proceeds, as some authors have suggested; and (iii) how the balance should be returned to the other party. However, based on the general principles behind the rules on the preservation of goods, as well as the other principles on which the CISG is based, it may be possible to assume the following: (i) claims regarding the proper application of the reasonableness standard may be brought as damages for breach of a secondary obligation, and (ii) as the provision clearly states that the party may retain the costs to preserve the goods and the costs to sell the same, there should not be any doubt that the balance must be accounted for by the other party.[42] This does not mean, however, that the party may not bring an action for damages setting-off his claim from the proceeds,[43] and (iii) the balance should be paid at the other's party place of business. If the party still refuses to take the money back, it may be useful to resort to a solution similar to PECL Article 7:111 (depositing the money to the order of the other party in accordance with the law where the payment is due).

II. PRESERVATION OF THE GOODS UNDER PECL (ARTICLES 7:110–7:112)[44]

PECL Article 7:110 considers mainly three cases: (i) the buyer refuses to take delivery of goods, (ii) the buyer rejects the goods and the seller refuses to take them back, and (iii) the contract has been terminated and the goods must be returned to the other party who refuses to take them back. Article 7:110 may be helpful, as the issue is not dealt with by the CISG.

The substance of PECL Article 7:110[45] is, therefore, very similar to CISG Articles 85–88. Thus, what has been said about the CISG also applies under the PECL with the following distinctions. First, the main difference between the two sets of rules concerns the structure: PECL Article 7:110 comprises both the seller's and buyer's duty to preserve the goods in only one provision, whereas the CISG considers both parties' duties separately. The other difference concerns the wording: PECL Article 7:110 outlines more simply than the CISG how the party left in possession of the goods may discharge its duty.

1. Situations where PECL Article 7:110 is Useful in Construing the Meaning of the Counterpart Provisions of the CISG

(1) *Preservation of money*. PECL specifically deals with the case where the property to be protected and preserved is money (Article 7:111), a case not specifically dealt with by the CISG; therefore, the PECL may be of help when applying the CISG in such instances. Specifically, the provision applies where the debtor attempts to perform a primary (e.g.,

[42] *See* Ebersten, *Annotations 88*, *supra* note 40, at 684; Flechtner, *Remedies*, *supra* note 8, at 80; *but see* Scognamiglio, *supra note* 12, at 341; (as to ULIS) H. J. Mertens and E. Rehbinder, INTERNATIONALES KAUFRECHT, Articles 94 and 95, note 8 (1975).

[43] *See* Secretariat Commentary on Article 77 of the 1978 [*draft counterpart of CISG Article 88]*, reprinted in Official Records, supra note 5, at 63, available at <cisgw3.law.pace.edu/cisg/text/seccomm-88.html>. *See also* Flechtner, *Remedies*, *supra* note 8, at 81; Eberstеn, *Annotations 88*, *supra* note 40, at 684 citing *also* Herber/Czerwenka, *supra* note 29, Art. 88, paragraph 8; Enderlein/Maskow/Strohbach, *supra* note 28, Art. 88, note 9.

[44] For the full text of the Principles of European Contract Law, visit <http://cisgw3.law.pace.edu/cisg/text/textef.html>.

[45] For the text of PECL Article 7:110, visit <http://cisgw3.law.pace.edu/cisg/text/textef.html–a7110>.

payment of the goods) or secondary (e.g., repayment of money received or payment of damages under Chapter 9, Section 5) duty to pay.[46] Pursuant to Article 7:111, the debtor discharges its duty to pay by "depositing the money to the order to the first party [creditor] in accordance with the law of the place where payment is due,"[47] after giving the creditor a reasonable notice. By dong so, the debtor may also prevent claims by the creditor concerning interest on the sum to be held on behalf of the creditor.

(2) *Avoidance and preservation of goods*. Reading Articles 81 and 86 CISG, with the guidance of the PECL, one should draw the conclusion that, where the contract has been avoided, the buyer must arrange the restitution of the goods to the seller, as the former cannot keep those goods nor can he destroy or let them be destroyed. While the party is in possession of goods to be taken by the other party, the very same party must also arrange a way to preserve them pursuant to Articles 87–88.[48]

As to the seller, if (i) the seller still has possession of, or control of, the goods, and (ii) the contract has been avoided, he cannot claim expenses from the buyer for preserving the goods.

The PECL, contrary to CISG, do clearly deal with the case just mentioned, which makes Article 7:110 useful when dealing with restitution and preservation of the goods when the contract has been avoided.

III. CONCLUSIONS

The PECL's language is very similar to that of the CISG. However, one feature makes PECL Articles 7:110 and 7:111 very useful when dealing with preservation of money and preservation of goods as result of the avoidance of the contract, as these situations are not directly dealt with by the CISG.

As a general rule, for all of the other general legal issues herein mentioned that are not directly solved by the CISG, it may be appropriate to first resort to the general principles of the CISG, unless the matter is clearly outside the scope of the CISG (e.g., storage agreement). The otherwise applicable domestic law, however, should control all of the more technical and detailed questions of substantive and, of course, procedural law.

[46] *See* "Comment and Notes on Article 7:111" in PRINCIPLES OF EUROPEAN CONTRACT LAW: PARTS I AND II 352–357 (Ole Lando & Hugh Beale eds., 2000) *available at* <http://cisgw3.law.pace.edu/cisg/text/peclcomp85.html>.

[47] *See* Oberster Gerichtsof, Austria, June 29, 1999, available at <http://cisgw3.law.pace.edu/cases/990629a3.html>, where the court dealing with the issues of determining the place of restitution as a result of the avoidance of the sale contract (CISG Article 81), found that "[t]he CISG does not contain any provisions pertaining to the place of performance for restitution. Nevertheless, the gaps arising from the absence of relevant agreements within the framework of Art 7(2) CISG can be bridged without recourse to national provisions (*Leser, op. cit.*, Art. 81 Annotation 17; *Weber, op. cit.*, Art. 81 Annotation 21). The place of performance for the obligations concerning restitution should mirror the place of performance for the primary contractual obligations (*Posch*, in Schwimann, 2d ed., CISG Art. 81, Annotation 9)." I expect, however, that other courts may refer this issue to the law otherwise applicable to the contract.

[48] ICC Arbitration Case No. 7531 of 1994, available at <http://cisgw3.law.pace.edu/cases/947531i1.html>.

Index